The Psychology
of Interpersonal Relationships

Ellen Berscheid
Department of Psychology
University of Minnesota

Pamela Regan
Department of Psychology
California State University, Los Angeles

PEARSON
Prentice
Hall

Pearson Education
Upper Saddle River, NJ 07458

Library of Congress Cataloging-in-Publication Data
Berscheid, Ellen.
    The psychology of interpersonal relationships / Ellen Berscheid, Pamela Regan.
      p. cm.
    Includes bibliographical references and index.
    ISBN 0-13-183612-9 (alk. paper)
    1. Interpersonal relations.   I. Regan, Pamela C. II. Title

HM1106.B47   2005
302—dc22   2003060180

Senior Acquisitions Editor: Jayme Heffler
Editor-in-Chief: Leah Jewell
Editorial Assistant: Jennifer M. Conklin
Marketing Manager: Sheryl Adams
Assistant Managing Editor: Maureen Richardson
Production Liaison: Fran Russello
Permissions Specialist: Michael Framer
Manufacturing Buyer: Tricia Kenny
Cover Design: Bruce Kenselaar
Photo Researcher: Melinda Alexander
Image Permission Coordinator: Charles Morris
Composition/Full-Service Project Management: Fran Daniele/Preparé Inc.
Printer/Binder: R.R. Donnelly & Sons
Cover Printer: Phoenix Color Corp.

Credits and acknowledgments borrowed from other sources and reproduced, with permission, in this textbook appear on page 531.

Pearson Prentice Hall™ is a trademark of Pearson Education, Inc.
Pearson® is a registered trademark of Pearson plc
Prentice Hall® is a registered trademark of Pearson Education, Inc.

Pearson Education LTD., London
Pearson Education Singapore, Pte. Ltd
Pearson Education, Canada, Ltd
Pearson Education–Japan
Pearson Education Australia PTY, Limited

Pearson Education North Asia Ltd
Pearson Educación de Mexico, S.A. de C.V.
Pearson Education Malaysia, Pte. Ltd
Pearson Education, Upper Saddle River, New Jersey

10 9 8 7 6 5 4 3 2 1

ISBN 0-13-183612-9

Brief Contents

Table of Contents

Preface

Just a little over two decades ago, at a conference addressed to interpersonal relationship phenomena, our host related to some of us that he had submitted a course proposal to the dean of his college suggesting that the psychology department offer a relationships course. His proposal was summarily rejected. At that time, his dean was not the only one who viewed the study of interpersonal relationships as fragmented empirically, immature conceptually, uncohesive theoretically, and lacking in the methodological rigor that characterized established lines of inquiry. Many, both inside and outside of psychology, believed the relationship field to have the potential to yield only an inchoate collection of "interesting" findings and "how to" advice to college students about their romantic relationships. Even within social psychology, the study of interpersonal relationships was regarded as teetering dangerously on the brink of the outer edge of "soft psychology."

Today, no major research university can afford not to have a relationship course in its psychology curriculum. Scholars in virtually all of the traditional areas of psychological inquiry have come to recognize that human behavior and development take place in the context of relationships with other people, and thus, in order to accomplish psychology's aim of understanding and predicting human behavior, it is necessary to incorporate the relationship context into psychological theory and research. "Contextualism" is in ascendance in psychology, and no context is more omnipresent and omnipotent than the relationships in which people are embedded from the time they are born to the time they die. The growing recognition of the critical role that relationships play in human behavior and development is partly due to the fact that the relationship field has confronted and successfully overcome many of its conceptual and methodological obstacles and currently is drawing on and contributing to virtually all areas of psychology—including clinical, counseling, educational, industrial and organizational, developmental, and social and personality psychology, as well as behavior genetics, cognitive and affective neuroscience, and psychoimmunology, to name just a few.

As a consequence, increasing numbers of upper-division undergraduate and graduate students in psychology and many of the other social, behavioral, biological, and health sciences are seeking a brief but comprehensive introduction to the field that will inform their own specialized pursuits within psychology and other disciplines. This textbook is intended to provide an integrated and organized foundation for such students. It emphasizes the relationship field's intellectual themes, roots, and milestones; discusses its key constructs and their conceptualizations; describes its methodologies and classic studies; and, most important, presents the theories that have guided relationship scholars and produced the field's major research themes. This text is intended to reflect the fact that relationship science has proved to be an intellectually cohesive and cumulative endeavor, one with vast potential to advance progress in most areas of psychological inquiry as well as many other disciplines.

Although relationship science is multidisciplinary, this text is titled *The Psychology of Interpersonal Relationships* for a number of reasons: Psychology has been and continues to be a major contributor to the field; psychology is likely to be the major beneficiary of the advancement of relationship science; the authors are psychologists; and, finally, most relationship courses at present are taught within academic departments of psychology. It is not difficult to foresee that there will someday be departments of relationship science that will bring together scholars from all the contributing disciplines, but such developments must await a loosening of the financial constraints that currently afflict higher education. As a multidisciplinary field, relationship science covers vast terrain and presents a challenge to instructors who generally are themselves interested in only certain subsets of relationship phenomena. By providing the student with a broad and comprehensive foundation in relationship science in the course text, we hoped to free instructors (including ourselves) from the necessity of presenting this foundation in lecture or through supplementary readings, thereby affording them the opportunity to emphasize their own disciplines.

Finally, we should note that although this text assumes that the reader has had an introductory course in psychology, it does not assume a strong background. Many students currently earning degrees in other disciplines have taken only an introductory psychology course (sometimes in the distant past). Students in relationship courses are, we have discovered, nothing if not eclectic. It is not unusual to have students from psychology and sociology alongside those from business, nursing, pharmacy, mortuary science, theater, family practice, social work, and anthropology. We have tried to make relationship science accessible to interested and motivated students in these disciplines as well as to upper-division undergraduates and graduate students in psychology.

ACKNOWLEDGMENTS

A number of people contributed to this endeavor. In particular, we thank Melissa Waltman (University of Minnesota) for her time and careful attention to detail. We also thank our reviewers, who generously contributed their expertise:

Daniel J. Canary, Ph.D.
Professor
Arizona State University

Margie Geasler, Ph.D.
Professor Emerita
Western Michigan University

Jenny Gutbezahl, Ph.D.
Professor
Harvard University Extension School

Benjamin R. Karney, Ph.D.
Associate Professor
University of Florida

Edgar C. O'Neal, Ph.D.
Professor
Tulane University

Phillip R. Shaver, Ph.D.
Professor, Department Chair
University of California at Davis

Jeff Simpson, Ph.D.
Professor
Texas A & M University

Ann L. Weber, Ph.D.
Professor of Psychology
University of North Carolina at Asheville

PART 1
RELATIONSHIPS: THE WEB OF LIFE

Chapter *1*

First Relationships

INTRODUCTION

In the afterword to his play *Angels in America*, Tony Kushner (1993) wrote: "The smallest indivisible human unit is two people, not one. . . . From such nets of souls societies, the social world, human life springs" (p. 307). Quite literally, human life springs from human relationships. Modern reproductive technology not withstanding, most of us were conceived the old-fashioned way. Thus, all of us owe our very existence to a relationship that once existed between a man and a woman. The sexual mating relationship has been written and sung about more than any other because it often is accompanied by love, frequently of the "romantic" variety, which has captivated philosophers, poets, novelists, and other artists for centuries—perhaps even throughout human history, some anthropologists (Jankowiak & Fischer, 1992) and psychologists now maintain (Hatfield & Rapson, 1987). This topic is discussed in Chapter 11, "Love."

From the perspective of relationship science, each of us represents a specific manifestation of the laws of mate selection. The color of our hair and the shape of our eyes, our mental capabilities and our physical infirmities, as well as a host of other attributes known to be strongly genetically determined, reflect the mate selection principles discussed in Chapter 12, "Mate Selection and Sex." Charles Darwin (Figure 1.1) was the first to urge scientists to identify the laws that

FIGURE 1.1   Charles Darwin.

1

govern mate selection. In *The Origin of Species by Means of Natural Selection: The Descent of Man, and Selection in Relation to Sex* (1871/1952) he argued:

> No excuse is needed for treating this subject in some detail; for, as the German philosopher Schopenhauer remarks, "The final aim of all love intrigues, be they comic or tragic, is really of more importance than all other ends in human life. What it all turns upon is nothing less than the composition of the next generation. . . . It is not the weal or woe of any one individual, but that of the human race to come, which is here at stake." (p. 578)

From the moment of our conception, we become dependent on others for our continued existence. Most directly, we become dependent on our mothers. Because a mother, in turn, is dependent on others for support during her pregnancy, we, too, are indirectly dependent on those others. For example, low birth weight is a primary cause of infant death, and birth weight has been shown to be a function of the support our mother receives—or fails to receive—from her family, her mate, and others during our gestation period (Feldman, Dunkel-Schetter, Sandman, & Wadhwa, 2000).

The human's gestation period is one of the longest of all species. If a woman dies during pregnancy—by disease, accident, domestic violence, suicide, or other means—it is likely that the baby, too, will die. If she suffers from malnutrition, the infant may be born with a host of physical infirmities. If she drinks alcohol, especially during the months of gestation when the brain is rapidly developing, we may be afflicted with fetal alcohol syndrome—the cerebral hemispheres will be smaller than normal and the cortex covered with an abnormal layer of tangled cells and fibers (Blakemore, 1998). If a pregnant woman contracts AIDS, the baby may be born afflicted with that disease, and if she ingests cocaine or heroin, the baby may be born chemically addicted and suffer the pain of withdrawal at birth or die. If she ingests nicotine, the baby may arrive prematurely and may be especially vulnerable to ear infections and a host of other diseases. If she takes the acne drug Accutane, the baby may be born with a number of even more

serious birth defects. Researchers now suspect that these immediate consequences of life in the mother's womb may be just the tip of the iceberg. Evidence is accumulating that the effects of gestational life may not reveal themselves until years later. Conditions in the womb may program how the brain, liver, heart, and other organs function in midlife (Nathanielsz, 1999). As a consequence, some developmental psychologists have concluded that the prenatal period may be the most consequential period of a person's life (Thompson & Nelson, 2001).

During the gestational period our **dependency** on another person—the degree to which we are affected by another's behavior—is as great as we ever will experience. This is one reason the mother–child relationship is viewed by many as the prototype, the very best example, of a close relationship, as discussed in Chapter 5, "Varieties of Relationship," and why most people view maternal love as the prototype of what love really is (Fehr & Russell, 1991). The extreme dependency of humans on the mother during gestation is perhaps most vividly reflected in the fact that if the mother decides to terminate a pregnancy, the fetus almost surely will die. She may do so to save her own life or for other reasons, some of which vary from culture to culture and country to country. For example, females face a relatively high risk of dying before birth if their mother is a citizen of China or India or one of the many other countries where females are less culturally valued than males. Population experts at the Chinese Academy of Social Sciences estimate that almost one-third of girls are missing because of gender-based abortions (Beech, 2002).

A newspaper article, "China's 'Dying Rooms': Cries Finally Heard 'Round the World," illustrates the plight of many female infants (Hilditch, 1995):

> Mei-ming has lain this way for 10 days now; tied up in urine-soaked blankets, scabs of dried mucus growing across her eyes, her face shrinking to a skull, malnutrition slowly shriveling her 2-year-old body. The orphanage staff call her room the 'dying room,' and they have abandoned her for the very same reason her parents abandoned her shortly after she was born. She is a girl.

When Mei-ming dies four days later, it will be of sheer neglect. Afterward, the orphanage will deny she ever existed. She will be just another invisible victim of the collision between China's one-child policy and its traditional preference for male heirs. She is one of perhaps 15 million female babies who have disappeared from China's demographics since the one-child policy was introduced in 1979.

Unlike many other animals that are born relatively mature and independent, without a mother to care for it, or a father, or someone—anyone!—to care whether it lives or dies, the human infant will not survive. Fortunately, most human infants are born into a ready-made web of interpersonal relationships that provide them with the essentials of life.

THE HUMAN INFANT'S SOCIAL INHERITANCE

Our first life-sustaining relationship web is our social inheritance or, as the early psychological theorist and evolutionist James Mark Baldwin (e.g., 1897) called it, our "social heredity." As with other kinds of inheritances, some infants are born richer than others. Some of us are born into a large network of socially, economically, and psychologically secure people for whom our birth was an occasion for celebration and joy. Many of them arranged to be in close proximity when we drew our first breath. Roused from sleep in the middle of the night or called from work or play, they abandoned their activities to be present at our birth, and many celebrate that day with us each year. Even before we were born, some had already showered us with gifts and contributed to our welfare through donations of time, energy, money, and other resources to furnish our nest, to clothe us, to provide toys to amuse us, or even to fund our later education. Before they ever laid eyes on us, they helped ensure not only that would we survive, but we would survive as happily and healthily as possible.

In contrast to those infants born with a silver relationship spoon in their mouths, others are not so fortunate, as the short, painful life of Mei-ming and the thousands, perhaps millions, like her all over the world illustrate. Some infants inherit a relationship web that involves few people and is impoverished in quality. For an increasing number of infants in the United States and other countries, their social inheritance does not include their fathers. As a result, it also does not include their paternal grandparents, aunts, uncles, and cousins. Moreover, their mother, more than most mothers, is likely to be poverty-stricken. According to the U.S. census (1999), families with a female head of household in the richest country in the world had a poverty rate of 30% and comprised the majority of poor families. Poverty is associated with substandard housing, homelessness, inadequate childcare, unsafe neighborhoods, and poor schools. Impoverished children are at risk for a wide range of problems, including detrimental effects on brain development and intelligence, low academic achievement, deficient socioemotional functioning, developmental delays, behavioral problems, and physical illnesses (e.g., McLoyd, 1998). Two-thirds of poor mothers report that they suffered severe violence at the hands of their childhood caretaker, and almost half report that they were sexually molested in childhood; in turn, their children are more likely to be sexually abused than other children are (Browne & Bassuk, 1997). Thus, whereas some infants inherit a rich relationship web, many others inherit one that is indifferent or actively hostile to them.

THE EVOLUTIONARY PERSPECTIVE

In contrast to the infant's social inheritance, which ranges from very rich to very poor, almost all humans are born with an exceedingly rich biological inheritance that helps them make the most of their social inheritance. Interest in the evolutionary development of the human's innate predispositions to respond to specific features of the social environment has increased in recent years. Evolutionary psychologists and developmental psychologists are in agreement that human infants are born with sufficient biological equipment to almost immediately interact with the people they find around them and to do their part in developing and sustaining the relationships they need in order to survive. Often referred to as "the social animal," the human is one of the most social creatures in the animal kingdom.

Most psychologists believe that the human's social nature was programmed into our biological makeup over evolutionary time. For any species to survive, its members need, at minimum, to find food, avoid injury, reproduce, and, at least for the higher animals whose young tend to be born immature, rear the young. Although the exact date is subject to perennial debate, the emergence of *Homo sapiens* is evident in the fossil record beginning at least 250,000 years ago, which coincides with the time certain primates left the forests of Africa, which were shrinking in size, for the plains, where food was scarce and they were easily visible to predators. The brains of these humanlike primates increased dramatically in size in a relatively short period of time, presumably as a result of the strong selection pressures produced by their extremely harsh environment (see Plutchik, 1980). Not only were those primates with larger and more powerful brains more likely to survive, so too were those who banded together with others to improve their food-finding chances and to defend against predators. Those early humans who could not form relationships with their companions for food and defense purposes and to mate and rear their young probably didn't survive to contribute to the genetic heritage of present-day humans. As a consequence, it seems likely that the human's social nature is "wired" into our biological makeup in ways we are only beginning to understand.

Consideration of early humans' survival challenges has led many theorists to propose that evolutionary psychology should be based on the premise that the most important feature of human evolutionary history was—and still is—selection for small group living; that is, humans who possessed features that facilitated their interactions with others survived, repro-duced, and contributed to the biological make-up of present-day humans, whereas those who could not form relationships with others died. Such theorists argue that our dependence on other people has been a fundamental fact of the human condition since the evolution of *Homo sapiens* began. Brewer and Caporael (1990) are among those who argue that the small cooperative group has been the primary survival strategy characteristic of the species from the beginning of human time to the present day. According to these theorists, social organization "provided a buffer between early hominids and the natural physical environment, including protection from predators, access to food supplies, and insulation from the elements" (p. 240). If the social group constituted the selection environment for human evolution at the individual level, then

the species characteristics that we would expect to be biologically built in would be those associated with human sociality—propensities toward cooperativeness, group loyalty, adherence to socially learned norms, and fear of social exclusion. (pp. 240–241)

Caporael's (1997) analysis of the probable role in human evolution of such group configurations as **dyads** (two-person groups), work/family groups, and larger groups concludes that "dyads are the most ancient core configuration" (p. 284). In addition to such functions as mating and ensuring infant survival, the dyad is important to the infant's development of skills fundamental to all social interactions (Burgoon, Steen, & Dillman, 1995). For example, within their early dyadic relationships infants mirror their partner's actions and learn to synchronize their behavior with their partner's (e.g., taking turns). Mimicry of our interaction partner's postures, facial expressions, and other behaviors—unconsciously performed—appears to continue into adulthood, and it has been shown to facilitate the smoothness of interactions and to increase the partners' liking for each other (Chartrand & Bargh, 1999).

The Need to Belong

Social psychologists Baumeister and Leary (1995) posit that over evolutionary time, the human developed a fundamental motivation for interpersonal attachments—a need to belong. They theorize that the human's **need to belong** is manifested in a drive to form and maintain at least a minimum number of lasting, positive, and significant interpersonal relationships. These theorists believe that in order to fulfill our need to belong, we must satisfy two criteria: First, we must engage in frequent and affectively pleasant interactions with at least a few other people; and second, those interactions must take place in the context of a temporally stable and enduring framework of each partner's concern for the other partner's welfare. Baumeister and Leary maintain, "Interactions with a constantly changing sequence of partners will be less satisfactory than repeated interactions with the same person(s), and relatedness without frequent contact will also be unsatisfactory" (p. 497). In sum, these theorists believe that the need to belong can be satisfied only by frequent interaction combined with persistent caring.

A great deal of evidence supports Baumeister and Leary's thesis. Many studies show that we humans form social relationships easily. People in virtually every society typically belong to small, primary groups that involve face-to-face interactions. Moreover, social psychologists have found that people prefer to like rather than to dislike others even when disliking them may satisfy other intrapsychic needs (Newcomb, 1968). In addition, many studies demonstrate that changes in an individual's belongingness status reliably produce emotional responses. Increases in belongingness—such as entry into a desirable group, the beginning of a new friendship, or the promise of a new romantic relationship—are often associated with positive affective states such as joy and happiness. Conversely, decreases in belongingness usually are associated with negative affect; for example, rejection by a group or by one's friend or lover often produces feelings of sadness, depression, anger, or fear. Moreover, people universally appear to respond with distress and protest to the end of a relationship, sometimes even to the end of an unsatisfying relationship, as discussed in Chapter 9, "Affective Processes," and Chapter 14, "Intervention and Dissolution."

Evidence that interpersonal concerns strongly influence how our minds store and process information also supports the thesis that people have a need to belong. For example, Gardner, Pickett, and Brewer (2000) experimentally demonstrated that people who were subjected to brief rejection experiences in a simulated computer chat room, as contrasted to those who received acceptance, subsequently showed selective memory for social events over individualist events in a diary they read. Thus, "social hunger" appears to influence the mind in the same ways as other biological drive states such as those for food, water, and sex —by increasing attention and retention in memory of drive-relevant information, as discussed further in Chapter 8, "Cognitive Processes." Some psychologists have argued that during evolutionary development, the human mind was shaped to deal with the recurring social problems our ancestors faced. One recurring social problem, according to Cosmides and Tooby (e.g., 1989), is that some people fail to fulfill their agreements ("I'll gather firewood tomorrow if you get it today"). Cosmides (1989) hypothesized that the human brain evolved in such a way that we are able to quickly and accurately detect social cheaters. As a consequence, it seems that we do much better solving a problem in logic when the solution leads to the identification of a social cheater than we do when the identical logical problem is framed in a nonsocial way, for example, as a mathematical puzzle.

In sum, many evolutionary models emphasize the significance of the human's social environment over evolutionary time in forming the biological features of present-day humans. In their review of the evolutionary psychology literature, Buss and Kenrick (1998) assert that

evolutionary psychology places social interaction and social relationships squarely within the center of the action. In particular, social interactions and relationships surrounding mating, kinship, reciprocal alliances, coalitions, and hierarchies are especially critical, because all appear to have strong consequences for successful survival and reproduction. From an evolutionary perspective, the functions served by social relationships have been central to the design of the human mind. (p. 994)

THE HUMAN INFANT'S BIOLOGICAL INHERITANCES FACILITATIVE OF SOCIAL INTERACTION

Several of the biological features human infants inherit from their evolutionary ancestors facilitate social interaction. We might expect this because forming relationships with others was critical to the survival of the species. It is difficult to identify uniquely social innate response systems because virtually all of the infant's innate biological properties facilitate social interactions in some way (see Siegel, 1999). However, some innate response systems appear to be particularly facilitative of social interaction and relationship formation.

Psychologists have been interested in identifying the human's **innate behavioral response systems** (present at birth and thus unlearned) at least since William James (1893) addressed the subject. Even psychology's premier environmentalist and the father of behaviorism, John B. Watson (1914), gave full treatment to **instincts**, which he described as complicated, concatenated behaviors unfolding serially to appropriate stimulation. Donald Hebb (1958) later defined instinctive behavior as "complex species-predictable behavior: at a higher level than reflex behavior, not requiring special conditions of learning for its appearance, but predictable simply from knowing that we are dealing with a particular species in its ordinary habitat" (p. 110). "In its ordinary habitat" is an important phrase because in order for instinctive behavior to be expressed, the animal usually must be observed in the environment in which the species evolved,

for it is presumably in response to the demands of that environment that the instinctive behavior developed. This is one reason why ethologists, who study animal behavior, usually study animals in the wild, not in the laboratory.

With a few exceptions (e.g., Elman et al., 1999), most psychologists adopt Hebb's definition of instinctive behavior. Further, most agree with Harlow and Mears (1983) that unlearned responses (1) typically follow developmental maturation stages in orderly fashion; (2) tend to be extremely persistent over time, sometimes throughout life; and (3) are influenced by many different variables and thus tend to be complex in nature.

The first studies to reveal the existence of innate response systems to certain social stimuli were conducted with nonhuman primates, our closest relatives in the animal kingdom. Hebb (1946) demonstrated that nonhuman primates possess a spontaneous and unlearned fear response system; that is, they exhibit agitated fight and flight behaviors to certain stimuli they have never seen before. One social stimulus that reliably activates their fear response system is the sight of an anesthetized, and thus unresponsive and seemingly lifeless, **conspecific** (a member of the same species). The adaptive value of fear responses to a seemingly dead fellow primate seems obvious: Whatever was responsible for its death may be lurking in wait for another victim, so preparation to fight or flee has survival value.

The Attachment Behavioral System

Perhaps the most important and clearly social of the innate response systems is the attachment behavioral system. The first experimental report of such a system appeared in 1958 when Harry Harlow (Figure 1.2) published a seminal article in *American Psychologist* titled "The Nature of Love."

Harlow's Love System

Harlow observed that although the word "love" has the highest reference frequency of any word cited in Bartlett's *Familiar Quotations*—reflecting its importance in the lives of humans—

FIGURE 1.2 Harry Harlow.

psychologists had almost completely ignored the subject. At that time, psychologists concentrated on physical needs:

> The basic motives are, for the most part, the primary drives—particularly hunger, thirst, elimination, pain, and sex—and all other motives, including love or affection, are derived or secondary drives. The mother is associated with the reduction of the primary drives—particularly hunger, thirst, and pain—and through learning, affection or love is derived. (Harlow, 1958, p. 673)

Despite the fact that love is important to humans of all ages in all kinds of relationships, most of the quotations in Bartlett referred to romantic love between a man and a woman, leading Harlow to protest, "These authors and authorities have stolen love from the child and the infant and made it the exclusive property of the adolescent and adult" (p. 673).

Harlow's studies of the love of an infant for its caretaker, usually its mother, came about by accident. The University of Wisconsin's Primate Laboratory, where Harlow worked, was desperate because its monkeys were dying of tuberculosis, a disease that had been imported from India along with some of the monkeys. Not only were monkeys dying, but laboratory personnel were in constant danger of contracting this contagious disease as well. To reduce their dependence on imported monkeys, the lab directors decided to establish a breeding colony. A small number of disease-free infant monkeys were selected to be bred later; to keep them free of disease, the researchers isolated them from their mothers and from each other. The procedure of raising the infant monkeys alone in hygienic wire cages was successful in keeping them physically healthy. However, the researchers subsequently discovered that not only had they eliminated disease from their infant monkeys, but they also had eliminated their ability to mate! When introduced to their prospective mates, the monkeys responded with trembling and fear. The monkeys' solitary rearing had produced healthy bodies but unhealthy minds. Harlow and his colleagues tried to repair the damage they had done but discovered they could not easily remedy the deficits in these monkeys' social behavior.

To learn more about this unanticipated and unfortunate effect of the monkeys' solitary childhood, Harlow again separated neonatal monkeys from their mothers 6 to 12 hours after birth, suckled them on tiny bottles, and housed them once again in solitary cages. (Infant mortality using this procedure was only a fraction of what it would have been had the infants been raised by their monkey mothers.) Harlow subsequently noticed that when the folded gauze diapers used to carpet the floor of the infants' cages were replaced periodically for sanitary purposes, the monkey infants violently protested. To Harlow, the monkeys' attachments to their gauze diapers seemed reminiscent of the human infant's attachment to a favorite blanket or cuddly toy. This gave Harlow the idea of constructing two kinds of surrogate mothers for the infants, one made of soft cloth and the other of wire (Figure 1.3). Half of the surrogate mothers of each type lactated milk and half did not. Harlow found that the infant monkeys disdained their wire mothers, even when they

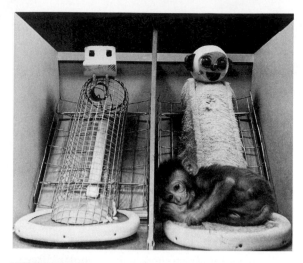

FIGURE 1.3 Wire and cloth "mothers."

fear and danger. The frightened or ailing child clings to its mother, not its father; and this selective responsiveness in times of distress, disturbance, or danger may be used as a measure of the strength of affectional bonds. (p. 678).

To experimentally test his "safe haven" hypothesis, Harlow exposed his infant monkeys to fear stimuli and found that those with cloth mothers ran to her for comfort, but those with wire mothers tended to ignore her even when they were fearful.

Harlow (1958) demonstrated that infant monkeys possess, quite literally, an "attachment" system—an innate predisposition to physically attach themselves to a soft, warm, and furry body. Importantly, Harlow showed that the "reward" of food was *not* responsible for the monkeys' preference. In his original article, Harlow illustrated his findings with poems and photos of various animals and their infants. For example, beneath the photo of a crocodile baby and its mother (Figure 1.4), he said:

> Here is the skin they love to touch
> It isn't soft and there isn't much
> But its contact comfort will beguile
> Love from the infant crocodile. (p. 678)

About the snake, he said:

> To baby vipers, scaly skin
> Engenders love 'twixt kith and kin.
> Each animal by God is blessed
> With [the] kind of skin it loves the best. (p. 677)

And of the rhinoceros, Harlow wrote:

> The rhino's skin is thick and tough,
> And yet this skin is soft enough
> That baby rhinos always sense
> A love enormous and intense. (p. 677)

were a source of milk, but loved their cloth mothers—even when their cloth mothers didn't supply food. How did Harlow know the infants loved their cloth mothers? They approached and clung to "her"; they rubbed their faces against her face and their bodies against her body; and they showed great distress when they were separated from their upholstered "mom."

Harlow concluded that infant monkeys possess an innate predisposition to prefer soft mothers. He speculated that *contact comfort* has long served the animal kingdom as a motivating agent for affectional responses. For obvious ethical reasons, Harlow's studies were conducted with macaque monkeys rather than with human infants. Although the macaque is more mature than the human infant at birth and grows more rapidly, Harlow asserted that its basic affectional responses, such as nursing, contact, clinging, and visual and auditory exploration, are not fundamentally different from those of the human infant.

As a result of his experiments, Harlow (1958) claimed that an important, perhaps primary, function of nursing is to ensure frequent and intimate body contact of the infant with the mother. Moreover, Harlow hypothesized:

> One function of the real mother, human or subhuman, and presumably of a mother surrogate, is to provide a haven of safety for the infant in times of

In sum, Harlow asserted, all infants need contact comfort. He may have been more right than he could have known at the time. Neurophysiologist Olausson and his associates (2002) have discovered that among the different kinds of nerve cells in the skin that register different tactile sensations such as temperature and pain, there are a few that register only gentle touches and caresses. Moreover, these nerve cells appear to be "wired" to regions of the brain associated

FIGURE 1.4 Mother and baby animals.

evacuated children from London and other highly populated cities to the country to protect them from German bombings. In these mass evacuations, children of all ages and backgrounds were torn from their caretakers and families (Figure 1.6). Bowlby noticed that many of the children who had been separated from their loved ones subsequently exhibited a variety of psychological disorders, and he became interested in the effects of disrupted child–mother bonds on psychopathology and on human development in general (see Bowlby, 1973a).

with the experience of pleasant emotion. These twenty-first-century neuroscientists comment, "The profound importance of such a system for human well-being has long been suggested, at least since the classical study of baby monkeys who show affection for a surrogate mother in response to tactile comfort" (p. 3).

Bowlby's Attachment Theory

At about the same time Harlow was conducting his experiments, British psychoanalyst and ethologist John Bowlby (1953, 1958; see Figure 1.5) reported his initial observations of the human infant's "bond" with its mother—a bond that he, too, said was evidenced by the child's seeking to achieve and maintain proximity to its mother and by feelings of distress when separated from her. As for Harlow, it was Bowlby's keen powers of observation that led to his interest in the infant–mother relationship. During World War II, the British government

FIGURE 1.5 John Bowlby.

FIGURE 1.6 During World War II, the British government evacuated many children from London and other highly populated cities to the country to protect them from bombings. In these mass evacuations, children were often separated from their caretakers and families and subsequently exhibited extreme stress and a variety of psychological disorders.

Bowlby (1979) observed that at each phase of our lives, we humans tend to form strong attachments to a few other special individuals. "The core of what I term an 'affectional bond,'" he said, "is the attraction that one *individual* has for another *individual*" (p. 67). Affectional bonds are personal and specific (e.g., another individual will not substitute). As long as our affectional bonds remain intact, we feel secure, but when they are broken—by the death of the attachment figure or by involuntary separation—we become anxious and distressed. "The essential feature of affectional bonding," Bowlby said, "is that bonded partners tend to remain in proximity to one another" (1973a, p. 39). Bowlby believed that affectional bonding is built deep into our biologi-

cal inheritance because attachment behaviors provided survival advantage.

Like Harlow, Bowlby (1973a) observed that his theory that human infants are born with an innate predisposition to quickly form an attachment to another human was in opposition to conventional psychological wisdom at the time:

> Until the mid-1950s only one view of the nature and origin of affectional bonds was prevalent, and on this matter, if on few others, psychoanalysts and learning theorists were at one. Bonds between individuals develop, it was held, because an individual discovers that, in order to reduce certain drives, e.g., for food in infancy and for sex in adult life, another human being is necessary. . . . As Anna Freud puts it, it is a cupboard love theory of human relations. (pp. 40–41)

Thanks to Harlow's and Bowlby's efforts and those of their students, by the mid-1970s Bowlby (1973a) was able to declare that the evidence was clearly pointing to a different way of looking at human bonding:

> First, it is now well attested that strong bonds can develop between individuals without any reward being given of the sort hitherto supposed to be essential. Secondly, it is now known that young creatures show fear and take avoiding action without pain having played any part whatsoever. Thirdly, a study of animals in the wild shows that, if any species is to survive, its members have to be equipped to deal with much else besides nutrition and reproduction or avoiding parts of the environment that have already been experienced as painful: a protection from predators is a top priority. (p. 41)

Bowlby's **attachment theory** also helped account for evidence that an infant can develop a strong bond to a caregiver, and attempt to remain in close proximity to that person, even in instances in which the caregiver has been punishing. The proximity-seeking behavior of a battered child toward an abusive adult caregiver is a poignant example that attachments can develop and persevere despite repeated punishments from the attachment figure. Eibl-Eibesfeldt (1989) notes that "it is known that abused children generally have a very powerful bond with their parents and protest, to the amazement of the authorities, when they are removed from their care and placed in a foster home" (p. 78). He also notes, however, that child abuse is relatively uncommon and that, overall, bonding to a caregiver has had survival value.

Findings of a strong bond between a child and an abusive caregiver or an adult and an abusive partner were troublesome for psychological learning theorists, whose reward–punishment frameworks predict that people approach, or are "attracted," only to others who provide them with rewards and that they avoid those who are punishing. Some learning theorists attempted to incorporate the new findings into their theories, but most such accounts were excruciatingly convoluted and frequently accomplished little more than to label an individual's approach to an unrewarding person as "masochistic," a term that describes the behavior but does not explain it. In contrast, attachment theory *did* provide an explanation: specifically, that humans are born with an innate predisposition to stay in close physical proximity to other members of the species who can act to protect them from survival threats (even if, in unusual instances, the caregiver–child relationship is marked by punishment).

Bowlby reasoned that it is particularly important for infants, who lack the benefit of learning experiences to inform them what or who is likely to be a threat to their survival, to be born with an instinctive proximity-promoting mechanism that leads them to stay physically close to persons who can supply food, shelter, and protection from disease and injury. Many animals who are born immature do possess such a mechanism, as ethologist Konrad Lorenz (e.g., 1952) demonstrated in his famous object-imprinting experiments with ducklings and goslings, who have an innate following response to the object they are near when they hatch (Figure 1.7). That object is usually their mother, but the public was amused by many experimental demonstrations that ducklings also would follow a ball, a person, or even a pig if that was the first object they set eyes on. If the duckling follows the object for a period of time during its "sensitive period," the bond that is formed is irreversible—the duckling becomes "imprinted" on the object. Ethologists subsequently found that the duckling is confident and self-assured when its "mother" (whether a duck, a ball, or a human) is present but becomes fearful when the mother is absent (see Eibl-Eibesfeldt, 1989). Human infants, too, quickly develop a strong preference to stay in close proximity to a person with whom they are familiar and who meets certain minimum visual, auditory, or tactile requirements that are typically satisfied by another human.

Bowlby classifies any behavior as an **attachment behavior** if it results in the achievement or maintenance of proximity between one

FIGURE 1.7 Many infant animals, including ducklings and goslings, possess an innate proximity-promoting mechanism that leads them to stay physically close to the first object they see when they hatch.

FIGURE 1.8 Stressful situations tend to elicit attachment behavior. Here, people reach out for comfort after the shootings at Columbine High School on April 20, 1999 (left) and the attacks on the World Trade Center on September 11, 2001 (right).

individual and another: "Whether the behavior is crying, calling, following, clinging, or any other, if it results in proximity it counts as attachment behavior" (1973a, pp. 42–43). Thanks to modern-day technology, to the list of proximity-achieving behaviors can be added telephone calls, email, and fax communications that maintain interactional proximity to the attachment figure. In addition, Bowlby states that attachment behavior is usually exhibited by a younger, or subordinate, or weaker animal toward an older, or more dominant, or stronger one.

Although attachment behavior is especially evident between the child's first and third years, Bowlby argues that attachment behavior characterizes humans at all ages. He states, "So far from its being regressive, as is sometimes suggested, attachment behavior is a normal and healthy part of human nature from the cradle to the grave" (1973a, p. 46). He reached this conclusion on evidence that attachment behavior tends to be elicited at high intensity in situations of alarm (Figure 1.8). Such events may occur at any age. Thus, attachment behavior in adults is likely to be evident when the individual is distressed, ill, or frightened. It is not

unusual, for example, for mortally wounded soldiers on the battlefield to cry out for their mothers.

Bowlby's (1969; 1973a, b; 1980; 1988) many theoretical works spurred systematic empirical studies of childhood attachment as well as countless theoretical elaborations and refinements, activities that continue to the present day. Much of this research was facilitated by the development of a standardized procedure for classifying individual differences in the quality of a child's attachment to a caretaker by Bowlby's student Mary Ainsworth (Figure 1.9) and her colleagues (e.g., Ainsworth, Blehar, Waters, & Wall, 1978). The **strange situation procedure** was constructed to be somewhat stressful for the infant (thereby activating the infant's attachment behavioral system) because it exposes the infant to persons and settings that are "strange" to him or her. It is usually administered to children around 12 to 18 months of age. The child's behavior is observed in a laboratory situation that involves a series of separation and reunion episodes with the caregiver (Figure 1.10). The episodes begin with the caregiver (usually the mother) and the infant entering an unfamiliar room where the infant plays

FIGURE 1.9 Mary Ainsworth.

FIGURE 1.10 The strange situation is designed to activate the infant's attachment behavioral system by exposing the infant to a stranger. The infant's response to the situation allows researchers to assess the quality of his or her attachment to the caregiver.

with toys with the caregiver present. After a brief period, a stranger enters the room and the caregiver exits, leaving the infant alone in the room with the stranger. A short time later, the caregiver returns and the stranger leaves. Next, the caregiver leaves and the infant is left alone in the room. Finally, the stranger returns, followed a short time later by the return of the caregiver.

The strange situation assesses the *quality*—not the existence or strength—of the infant's attachment to his or her caretaker. Although Bowlby originally suggested that attachments might vary in strength, by the late 1970s he declared, "To think of attachment as varying according to its strength . . . has proved extremely misleading and has been abandoned by informed workers" (1979, p. 66). The quality of the behavior pattern the infant exhibits during the episodes generally is one of three kinds (see Weinfield, Sroufe, Egeland, & Carlson, 1999): secure, insecure/resistant, or insecure/avoidant.

Children who display the *secure* attachment pattern are able to use the mother as a secure base for exploration in the novel room and, when distressed, actively seek contact with her and are readily comforted. When the mother is absent, secure children show confident expectations of her return. The hypothesis that children are more likely to explore the environment when they feel protected by their caregiver's presence has been called attachment theory's **secure base hypothesis**, and it has received much support.

The secure pattern of behavior appears to be rooted in reliable care and, especially, sensitivity and responsiveness to the child's expressions of need. There is a great deal of empirical support for what has been termed attachment theory's **sensitivity hypothesis**—that sensitive care results in secure attachment (see van IJzendoorn & Sagi, 1999). For example, Bakermans-Kranenburg, van IJzendoorn, and Juffer 2003 meta-analyzed over 70 parental intervention studies that were aimed at enhancing parents' positive behaviors, including sensitivity and responsiveness to the child, and that also used observational (rather than self-report) measures of actual changes in parenting behavior. These reviewers concluded that the interventions that were effective in enhancing parental sensitivity were also the interventions most effective in enhancing the child's attachment security. About two-thirds of infants in American middle-class families exhibit the secure behavior pattern.

In the *insecure/resistant* (sometimes called anxious-ambivalent) pattern, which characterizes about 10% of infants tested, the child is unable to use the caregiver as a secure base for exploration. This behavior pattern is characterized by little exploration even in the mother's presence, by low thresholds for threat, by extreme separation distress, and, upon reunion, by being resistant to being comforted by the caretaker. These infants are preoccupied with the caregiver but may angrily reject her soothing overtures. Such behavior appears to be rooted in inconsistent, hit-or-miss, or chaotic care; the child's expectations seem to be that the mother will be available only with vigilance and the self will be ineffective in eliciting care (Sroufe & Fleeson, 1988).

Insecure/avoidant children treat the caregiver much as they do the stranger and are unlikely to be distressed when the mother leaves or to seek contact with her after experiencing the distress of separation. Sroufe and Fleeson (1988) state, "Underlying such a paradoxical response to brief separation is a history of [the caregiver's] chronic emotional unavailability and/or rejection" (p. 32). About 20% to 25% of children are classified as avoidant. Thus, about two-thirds of children tested are classified as secure and about one-third as insecure, with the insecure group composed of two subgroups: resistant and avoidant.

Bowlby theorized that the quality of the child's early attachment relationship influences later interpersonal relationships because from this first relationship, the child develops a view of what other people are like (e.g., trustworthy, available) and of him- or herself as worthy or unworthy (e.g., of care). People's views of themselves as worthy or unworthy have implications for their future relationships. For example, Murray, Holmes, Griffin, Bellavia, and Rose (2001) found that dating and marital partners who were troubled by self-doubt (partly measured by the individual's self-report of attachment orienta-

tion) underestimated the actual strength of their partner's love; such underestimation, in turn, was associated with less satisfaction with the relationship and less optimism for its future than the partner's actual feelings warranted. Bowlby characterized the child's developing view of relationships as a *mental working model of relationships*—"working," not final, because Bowlby believed that people's view of relationships could change in response to the quality of subsequent relationships.

Bowlby's emphasis on the importance of early relationships in the development of psychopathology was consistent with his psychoanalytic training and Freud's belief that many mental disorders could be traced back to the individual's earliest relationships. A central tenet of attachment theory, then, is that different patterns of early attachment have different consequences for the individual's subsequent relationships. For example, the theory predicts that securely attached children become more socially and emotionally competent than do those who are insecurely attached. The **competence hypothesis** of attachment theory has received a great deal of support. In their longitudinal study of children whose attachment classifications were assessed at an early age, Sroufe, Egeland, and Kreutzer (1990) report that relative to their insecure counterparts, those children who were classified as securely attached to their caregivers in their first year of life subsequently coped better with developmental transitions, developed superior social skills, were more popular with their peers, were better liked by their teachers, and had fewer behavior problems.

In assessing social competence, developmental psychologists are sensitive to the fact that the nature of a social interaction depends on the characteristics of *both* partners, not simply one. This fundamental fact—that the nature of social interaction is a function of the properties of both partners—underlies all relationships. For example, when Sroufe and his colleagues (see Sroufe & Fleeson, 1986) paired preschool-age children with different attachment histories for play, they found that children with secure histories neither victimized other children nor were the victims of other children regardless of whom they were paired with, but those with ambivalent (i.e., resistant) histories were vulnerable to victimization by other children and those with avoidant histories were prone to victimize unless paired with a more powerful partner. The pairing of an avoidant child with another avoidant child or with an ambivalent child quickly led to abusive interactions. Other researchers also have found that children's interactions are a function of both partners' attachment classifications. Pastor (1981), for example, found that the interactions of securely attached toddlers, rated as higher in sociability and positive orientation toward their peers, are more harmonious when they interact with each other than with an insecurely attached child.

Most attachment theorists and researchers have viewed attachment theory's sensitivity, secure base, and social competence hypotheses to be *universal*—applicable to all persons in all cultures. Indeed, from their review of the relatively few cross-cultural studies available, van IJzendoorn and Sagi (1999) conclude that attachment theory possesses cross-cultural validity. However, Rothbaum, Weisz, Pott, Miyake, and Morelli (2000) have argued persuasively that attachment theory measures are saturated with Western values. They observe, for example, that behaviors regarded as manifestations of social competence in Western culture, such as self-reliance and autonomy, are viewed as less desirable in many Asian cultures, which stress community and interdependence with others. Rothbaum and colleagues advocate a more context-conscious approach to attachment phenomena and the use of measures sensitive to the ways in which attachment processes reflect the cultural values of the society in which the individual is embedded.

In addition to investigating the effects of childhood attachment on later relationships, much recent research has focused on the attachment orientations adults display toward their close relationships—especially their romantic relationships. This work was stimulated by Hazan and Shaver's (1987) construction of an **adult attachment style** self-classification scheme intended to roughly parallel the three child attachment classifications derived from the strange situation. A great number of studies have used this classification method, or one of its variants, to examine the correlates and social consequences of adult attachment style (e.g., Cassidy & Shaver, 1999; Simpson & Rholes, 1998), as discussed in Chapter 10, "Dispositional Influences." The association between the classification an individual receives using the adult attachment style self-report method and the classification the individual would have received had he or she been observed as a child in the strange situation is not yet clear. (This general method subsumes many specific tests and scales.) Another issue concerns the fact that although most attachment researchers have regarded individuals as possessing a single "global" attachment orientation toward all relationships, recent evidence suggests that individuals may develop many different attachment orientations, each tied to a particular type of relationship or even a specific relationship within a type (e.g., Cook, 2000; La Guardia, Ryan, Couchman, & Deci, 2000).

Although most current attachment research, whether conducted with children or with adults, currently focuses on differences among individuals in attachment orientation, both Bowlby and Harlow believed that *all* humans are innately predisposed to form strong attachments to at least some other people. Attachment, as Harlow explicitly stated, is one variety of human love. It appears in at least some contemporary taxonomies of varieties of love (e.g., Berscheid, 1985b), and, as previously noted, some theorists view attachment processes as especially important in understanding the dynamics of an individual's romantic relationships because they believe that for most adults, a romantic partner becomes an attachment figure (e.g., Shaver, Hazan, & Bradshaw, 1988), as discussed further in Chapter 11, "Love." In addition to romantic partners, adults also frequently name close friends as attachment figures (see Mikulincer, Gillath, & Shaver, 2002). Adult attachment figures share the same characteristics as child attachment figures: (1) They are a target of *proximity maintenance* (e.g., separation is resisted); (2) they provide a *safe haven* in times of need (e.g., they provide support); and (3) they provide a *secure base* (e.g., facilitating exploration and personal development) (see Hazan & Shaver, 1994; Mikulincer et al., 2002).

Other Innate Social Response Systems

Investigations of innate social response systems have focused almost exclusively on attachment. Its only rival is temperament, also believed to be innately determined. As for attachment, individual differences in temperament have many implications for social interaction and relationship dynamics.

Temperament

The concept of **temperament**, according to developmental psychologist Jerome Kagan (1994), "refers to any moderately stable, differentiating emotional or behavioral quality whose appearance in childhood is influenced by an inherited biology, including differences in brain neurochemistry" (p. xvii). This definition allows for the possibility of many different temperaments. Kagan (1989) has suggested that the number of possible temperament traits may be larger than 6 but less than 60, and one of the early studies of temperament in infants and children identified 9 different temperament dimensions (Thomas & Chess, 1977). Nevertheless, researchers have focused on only one dimension. The dimension that has captured researchers' attention was first identified by a fourth-century physician, Galen of Perganon, who speculated that some people inherit a tendency toward "melancholia," whereas others have a constitutional bias toward "sanguine," or cheerful, behavior.

Today, Galen's distinction is frequently called the **extraversion–introversion** dimension (or sometimes the inhibited–uninhibited dimension), and it has been identified as one of the "big five" factors that underlie individuals' personality differences (the others being agreeableness, conscientiousness, emotional stability, and intellect/imagination; see Goldberg, 1993).

As this suggests, the line between temperament and personality traits is blurred, although, as McCrae and colleagues (2000) discuss, psychologists have a long tradition of distinguishing the two. Temperament usually is viewed as a constitutionally determined predisposition, as we have noted, whereas personality traits generally are believed to be acquired patterns of thought and behavior that, developmentally, build on temperament (see Rothbart, Ahadi, & Evans, 2000).

In *Galen's Prophecy* (1994), Kagan states that the extraversion–introversion dimension describes people who are

> excessively restrained when they meet a stranger, wary when they confront an unexpected event, or cautious when they must act with a risk of possible failure. Fiction is full of examples that contrast this personality with its complement—the sociable, fearless, bold agent who is unaffected by these everyday events. Walter Matthau and Jack Lemmon in *The Odd Couple* are a well-known movie example. (p. xv)

Like Galen, most psychologists believe that differences along this dimension are largely innate—that "inhibited and uninhibited children inherit unique neurochemistries that affect their thresholds of reactivity to novelty, leading them to react in opposite ways to experiences that are transformations of the familiar and require a brief period of adjustment" (Kagan, 1994, p. xviii). Rothbart and Bates (1998), who review temperament theory and research, observe that the temperament response system is usually "activated under conditions of novelty, sudden or intense stimuli, reactions to danger . . . , social interactions with unfamiliar conspecifics, and conditioned responses to punishment" (p. 109). People differ not only in their thresholds of response to these conditions (with introverts showing lower thresholds than extraverts) but also in the intensity and duration of their responses.

An individual's temperament has many implications for his or her social interactions and close relationships. For example, there is a great deal of evidence that extraverts more frequently and intensely experience positive affect (positive moods, emotions, and feelings) than introverts do (e.g., Costa & McCrae, 1980; Diener & Lucas, 1999). Assembling the many studies that have examined the association between the experience of positive affect and an individual's standing on the extraversion–introversion dimension, Lucas and Fujita (2000) performed a **meta-analysis**—a quantitative procedure whereby the findings of many studies testing the same hypothesis are synthesized in order to reach a more reliable conclusion about the truth of the hypothesis than is afforded by any one study (see Rosenthal, 1991; Rosenthal & DiMatteo, 2001). Lucas and Fujita concluded that extraverts may have a susceptibility to experience pleasant affect and that, in fact, pleasant affect may form the very core of extraversion. Like others (e.g., Lucas, Diener, Grob, Suh, & Shao, 2000; Lucas & Diener, 2001), they conclude that the mere preference for social interaction—independent of the degree to which the social interaction is rewarding—is *not* the central feature of extraversion. Rather, the pleasantness of the situation, not whether it is social or nonsocial, seems to predict whether extraverts will enjoy the situation more than introverts will. Extraverts and introverts thus seem to differ in their sensitivity to reward.

Ashton, Lee, and Paunonen (2002) subsequently presented evidence that although extraverts and introverts do indeed differ in reward sensitivity, the essential feature that distinguishes extraverts from introverts is that extraverts enjoy being the *object of social attention*. Because reward-sensitive people tend to show enthusiasm, energy, and excitement, these qualities often make extraverts the center of attention in social situations, and it is their engagement and enjoyment of attention—not reward sensitivity in itself—that distinguishes extraverts from introverts.

Although most agree that temperament is innate, ambiguity about the nature and number of dimensions encompassed by the term "temperament," as well as the diversity of meanings associated with the terms "extraversion," "introversion," "inhibited," and "uninhibited," have made it difficult to come to clear conclusions about the biological bases of temperament (see Strelau, 1994). In addition, although most re-

searchers agree that experience can modify temperament, much needs to be learned about how it does so. For example, a difficult, cranky baby is likely to elicit different care from a parent than a placid, happy baby, and that care may increase or decrease the baby's distress (van den Boom, 1994). Whether the infant's temperament leans toward negative or positive affectivity also may interact with its mother's standing on the extraversion–introversion dimension to affect the pattern of interaction between the mother and her child. Clark, Kochanska, and Ready (2000) found that highly extraverted mothers exhibited more "power-assertive" parenting behavior with infants high in negative affectivity (associated with introversion and with "difficult" infant behavior), whereas mothers low in extraversion were not power-assertive with either easy *or* difficult children. Thus, just as children paired with others of different attachment histories exhibit different interaction patterns, the interaction pattern that develops in parent–infant relationships is a function of the characteristics of *both* partners to the interaction—not the parent alone.

The extraversion–introversion temperament classifications and the attachment classifications share several features: (1) Each has been treated as an *individual difference variable*; that is, differentially classified individuals exhibit different behaviors. (2) Each is believed to be *heavily genetically determined*, although modifiable by experience. (3) Each is believed to be most clearly *displayed under conditions of stress and threat*. (4) Each has *implications for the individual's social interactions*. Thus, it has been natural to ask whether—and how—attachment and temperament are associated with each other. Some researchers argue that because an infant's temperament influences his or her behavior, it also influences measurements of attachment security (e.g., Kagan, 1982). Others maintain that temperament is largely independent of attachment security because most caregivers are sensitive to the needs of infants regardless of the child's temperament (e.g., Sroufe, 1985). So far, few linkages between measures of temperament and attachment security classifications have been found (Rothbart & Bates, 1998).

The Caregiving System

Both Bowlby and Harlow proposed that humans are born with several other innate social response systems. For example, Bowlby theorized that humans innately possess the complement to the attachment behavioral system—a **caregiving system**, which was loosely comparable to the "maternal love" system proposed by Harlow. Although most evolutionary approaches to human behavior emphasize reproduction, Scott (1967) notes that "reproduction is not solely a matter of fertilization" (p. 138) because the offspring must be nurtured to survive. It seems doubtful that an attachment system could have evolved without its complement of adult response to the infant's attachment behavior of calling, crying, and otherwise attempting to remain in proximity to the caregiver.

That primates not only possess a caregiving system but that it sometimes extends to caring for members of other species was illustrated some years ago when a child visiting a zoo leaned too far over a fence and fell into the gorilla pit. One of the gorillas, Binti Jua (Swahili for "Daughter of Sunshine") observed the boy's fall and his seemingly lifeless body lying at the bottom of the concrete trench that separated the visitors from the gorillas. Onlookers held their breath as the gorilla quickly scrambled down the concrete wall to examine what had fallen into her territory. They needn't have worried, for when Binti reached the boy she gently lifted his injured body into her arms and carefully carried him up to her home, where she laid him on the grass and watched over him until human rescuers arrived. Media worldwide publicized Binti's "heroic" actions (Figure 1.11), but animal behaviorists interviewed by *USA Today* said Binti was just following her motherly caregiving instincts (Buckley, 1996). Animal experts also pointed out that long-lived socialized animals, including such companion animals as dogs and cats, form attachment bonds with their human caregivers such that species barriers become blurred and they look upon us humans as "family" (which, of course, we are in the evolutionary sense); they often exhibit separation distress and reunion reactions with their human caregivers similar to those observed between human infants and their caregivers.

The caregiving system, at least as it was described by Bowlby, has been neglected by attachment researchers (Bell & Richard, 2000; Berscheid & Collins, 2000), as is illustrated by the fact that the *Handbook of Attachment* (Cassidy & Shaver, 1999) contains only one chapter directly

FIGURE 1.11 Binta Jua gently cradles a three-year-old boy who fell into the gorilla pit at the Brookfield Zoo in Illinois.

addressed to caregiving (George & Solomon, 1999). One reason for the neglect may be that most attachment researchers are developmental psychologists and developmental psychologists typically study children, whereas caregiving behavior is mostly performed by adults. However, social psychologists, who typically study adult behavior, have extensively investigated the conditions under which people are likely to help others in distress under theoretical umbrellas other than attachment, including the theories of social support discussed in Chapter 2, "Relationships and Health."

Like Bowlby, some adult attachment style theorists view the caregiving system as an integral part of the attachment system (e.g., Kunce & Shaver, 1994). Researchers have found significant associations between adult attachment style classification and caregiving to marital and dating partners (e.g., Simpson, Rholes, & Nelligan, 1992; Feeney & Hohaus, 2001). Again, the attachment classifications of *both* the prospective caregiver and the recipient influence whether caregiving or rejection will occur in interaction. For example, Westmaas and Silver (2001) measured their experimental participants' adult attachment style and then paired each participant in interaction with a person who, in her answers to interview questions overheard by the participant, conveyed characteristics of a specific attachment style and also revealed she had recently been diagnosed with cancer. Both the participant's own attachment style and the perceived attachment style of the cancer victim predicted whether the participant rejected or supported the victim in their subsequent interaction.

In addition to a caregiving system, Bowlby posited a "reproductive behavioral system" that appears in adolescence when sexual mating and reproduction become possible. The reproductive system received little attention from Bowlby and even less from subsequent theorists, although Ainsworth (1989) attempted to elaborate and integrate such a system with the other systems proposed by Bowlby, as have Shaver and his associates (e.g., Shaver, Hazan, & Bradshaw, 1988). Harlow's proposal of a "peer love" system also has been almost wholly neglected. The

relative neglect of these systems theorized to be manifested later in life may stem from the same reason Harlow studied monkey infants rather than human babies: "The human neonate," Harlow (1958) explained, "is a limited experimental subject because . . . by the time the human infant's motor responses can be precisely measured (e.g., approach behavior), the antecedent determining conditions cannot be defined, having been lost in a jumble and jungle of confounded variables" (p. 674). The "jumble and jungle of confounded variables" increases exponentially with age; as the human grows older, it becomes increasingly difficult to identify which behaviors are innate and which have been learned.

The Face Perceptual System

Harlow's monkeys exhibited what may be yet another innate response system especially targeted toward other members of the species. Harlow noticed that his infant monkeys were especially attentive to their cloth mothers' faces. The researchers had made heads for the mother surrogates out of round wooden balls on which they had painted eyes, nose, and a mouth (Harlow & Suomi, 1970). On one occasion, however, an infant monkey was born before her surrogate mother was finished, and, pressed for time, the researchers gave its mother an unpainted wooden ball for a face. By the time the researchers got around to giving the mother a painted face, the baby was 3 months old. "Better late than never," the researchers must have been thinking, but they were shocked to see what happened when they finally mounted the ball with a face on the body of the infant's surrogate mother:

The baby took one look and screamed. She fled to the back of the cage and cringed in autistic-type posturing. After some days of terror the infant solved the medusa-mother problem in a most ingenious manner. She revolved the face 180° so that she always faced a bare round ball! Furthermore, we could rotate the maternal face dozens of times and within an hour or so the infant would turn it around 180°. Within a week the baby resolved her unfaceable problem once and for all. She lifted the maternal head from the body, rolled it into the corner, and abandoned it. No one can blame the baby. She had lived with and loved a faceless mother, but she could not love a two-faced mother. (p. 164)

Attentiveness to faces is characteristic of human infants as well as monkey infants. One of the most important tasks of the human perceptual system is recognition of the faces of other humans. Not only do a person's facial features provide the maximum number of cues that allow us to differentiate one human from another, but the face is the richest source of cues to another's feelings and behavioral intentions toward us. As a consequence, when we interact with people, we look at their faces—not their arms or feet— and what we see in their faces influences our interpretation of what they say (Hassin & Trope, 2000). The belief that "the face is the window to the soul" and the art of "face-reading" date back to classical antiquity (Fridlund, 1994). Interest in people's attempts to read what is written in the faces of others continues to the present day (e.g., see Russell & Fernández-Dols, 1997; Zebrowitz, 1997).

Because face perception is of great importance to humans, some cognitive neuroscientists have hypothesized that our biological inheritance includes a specialized face-processing module in the brain (e.g., Farah, 2000). Their investigations of whether human face perception employs a different neurological processing system than that involved in the perception of other objects have addressed three questions: (1) Do face perception and object perception depend on different regions of the brain? (2) Are the systems functionally independent? That is, can each operate without the other? (3) Do the two systems process information differently? Each of these questions has been tentatively answered in the affirmative (see Gazzaniga, Ivry, & Mangun, 1998).

Although most psychologists believe face perception is "special," the ways in which it is similar to or different from the perception of other objects remains under investigation (Marsolek, 1999). One way in which face perception seems to differ from the perception of other objects is that we tend to perceive faces "holistically"; that

is, the overall configuration of the face, rather than its individual features, is perceived and remembered. In perceptually processing a house, for example, it appears that we mentally break the house down into at least some of its constituent parts—its windows, doors, and roof, for example—which we can recognize later even when we see those parts in isolation from the remainder of the house. In contrast, we have difficulty recognizing a person's eyes, nose, or any other facial feature when it is not attached to his or her face (Farah, Wilson, Drain, & Tanaka, 1998; Tanaka & Farah, 1993).

Psychologists do not know why face perception tends to be more holistic than the perception of other kinds of objects. Unlike most other objects, faces always have the same number of components and the same overall arrangement of those components but, as neuroscientist Antonio Damasio (1994) observes, faces nonetheless are "infinitely diverse and individually distinguishable because of small anatomical differences in size, contour, and position of these invariant parts and configuration" (p. 23). Perhaps holistic perception most efficiently allows us to distinguish these small differences. Another hypothesis, for which there is mounting support, is that all humans are "face experts" and anyone expert in anything may gradually come to perceive initially differentiated stimuli holistically. Diamond and Carey (1986), for example, showed some similarities between the perception of faces and the perception of dogs by dog experts but not by nonexperts, and Gauthier, Skudlarski, Gore, and Anderson (2000) have found that the same area of the brain involved in face perception is utilized by car and bird experts.

It seems likely that at least some aspects of face perception ability may be innate because the recognition and differentiation of faces seems to occur rapidly. Infants only 30 minutes old will visually track a slowly moving schematic face stimulus with their head and eyes farther than they will follow other moving patterns of comparable complexity, such as scrambled faces, although such differential tracking appears to decline during the second month of life (e.g., Johnson, Dziurawiec, Ellis, & Morton, 1991). To account for this decline, Morton and Johnson (1991; and see Johnson, 1999) have proposed a "two-process theory" of infant face perception. These theorists noted that although laboratory studies of imprinting in baby chicks show that the chicks recognize and develop an attachment for the first conspicuous object presented to them after hatching, chicks in the wild invariably imprint on the mother rather than on other objects that happen to be present, such as a mouse. Experimentation revealed that chicks possess a neural system present at birth that supports a predisposition to turn toward and approach objects resembling conspecifics. Like chicks, Morton and Johnson above suspect, human infants are born with some information about the structure of faces and a neural system that supports attention to conspecifics. They theorize that a second neural system, which appears to begin to operate in the human infant's second month of life, subsequently supports the acquisition of information about the objects to which the infant attends. Thus, the first system ensures that the second system acquires information about the particular individual mother in close proximity. Because the two systems have different developmental time courses, they differentially influence behavior at different ages (e.g., a decline in differential tracking).

Pascalis, deHaan, and Nelson (2002) have shown that as infants gain experience in viewing faces, their brains begin to focus on the kinds of faces they see most often in the environment and they tune out other types. Infants at ages 6 and 9 months as well as adults were able to distinguish among human faces, but the 6-month-old infants outperformed the two older groups in distinguishing among the faces of monkeys. Because primates are most familiar with the faces of their own species, they come to distinguish those types of faces better than other types. For example, adult monkeys are better able to distinguish among monkey faces than among human faces. Thus, humans are born with the innate potential to recognize faces, but with experience their ability to recognize faces narrows and becomes specialized in recognizing the kinds of faces the environment provides (usually the faces of conspecifics), and they lose the ability to easily recognize types infrequently encountered (although, with effort, that ability may be recaptured). In sum, the innate face perception capabilities of the human appear to interact with **nurture** (i.e., an individual's experience with the environment) just as it does in many other aspects of brain development.

An early appearing preference for the familiar over the strange has been shown in virtually all primates (see Harlow & Mears, 1983). Thus, it seems possible that present at birth are not only neural sensitivities to the probable social environment, including the faces of conspecifics, but certain evaluative preferences with respect to those frequently encountered stimuli as well. Infants only 2 or 3 months old display a preference for physically attractive over unattractive faces (e.g., Langlois et al., 1987). Even infants between 14 and 151 hours old have been found to prefer (to look longer at) female faces that are attractive as opposed to unattractive, as judged by adults (Slater et al., 1998). Some evolutionary psychologists believe the ability to distinguish between attractive and unattractive faces had, and may still have, survival value. In addition, attractive faces have been shown to be more representative of the average of faces in the species (e.g., Langlois & Roggman, 1990), as further discussed in Chapter 6, "Birth of a Relationship." In adults, the perception of facially attractive people may be tied into the fundamental "reward circuitry" of the brain (Aharon et al., 2001); whether such a connection is innate or learned is not known.

Empathic Accuracy

Because the face is the richest source of cues of a person's thoughts and emotional state (Ekman & Davidson, 1994a), attention to another's face is vital to **empathic accuracy**, usually defined as the ability to decode the meaning of another's behavior (Ickes, 1997). Empathic accuracy is different from *sympathy*, which refers to the experience of feeling another's emotional state (see Berscheid & Reis, 1998). Empathic accuracy—knowing another's thoughts, feelings, and intentions—is, of course, vital to survival.

Developmental psychologists have long been interested in the development of a person's ability to perceive and understand another's thoughts and emotions. The age at which the infant can recognize and discriminate among different facial expressions, including those that express emotional states, is a matter of current investigation and controversy (see Eisenberg, Murphy, & Shepard, 1997). Some investigators have shown that even 10-week-old infants differentially respond to their mothers' sad, happy, and angry expressions (see Eisenberg et al., p. 79). Others have shown that at 4 months of age, infants smile more at smiling faces than nonsmiling faces (Oster, Daily, & Goldenthal, 1989). By 10 months of age, infants' tendency to smile appears to be at least partially dependent on whether a human audience is present to observe the smile (Scanlon-Jones, Collins, & Hong, 1991). By the end of their first year of life, infants can decode emotional information and adjust their behavior in accord with an adult's facial expression (e.g., Klinnert, 1984). In sum, the evidence suggests that even very young children possess some degree of empathic accuracy.

Females, however, may be more skilled in empathic accuracy than males. McClure (2000) concludes from a meta-analysis of studies examining sex differences in facial expression processing that there is a female advantage from infancy through adolescence, with maturational neurological factors playing an important early role and socialization factors subsequently maintaining and even amplifying the initial sex difference. With respect to socialization factors, there is a large body of evidence suggesting that boys and girls receive different types and amounts of information from adults about emotions and emotional expression. Klein and Hodges (2001), however, conclude that sex differences in empathic accuracy may be the result of motivational differences rather than ability. They found the usual female advantage when their participants had no special incentive to

perform the empathic accuracy task, but this difference evaporated when participants were offered payments in exchange for accuracy. The authors conclude that men and women may have similar empathic accuracy ability, but women generally are more motivated to use it. Additional research on sex differences in empathic accuracy is discussed in Chapter 10, "Dispositional Influences."

The predisposition to be attentive to faces of conspecifics and to accurately interpret the cues seen therein is facilitative of smooth, coordinated social interaction, which is associated with relationship satisfaction, as discussed in Chapter 13, "Satisfaction and Stability." We spend much time in social interaction seeking and decoding cues to our partner's thoughts, beliefs, feelings, and intentions, and we usually perform this feat easily and quickly, often unconsciously. The critical role that empathic understanding of others' emotions and thoughts plays in interaction can be appreciated when we consider the social interactions of children who manifest the neurological disorder of autism. Autistic children do not possess the empathic skills most of us take for granted. As Simon Baron-Cohen (1995) put it in his book *Mindblindness*, autistic children are oblivious to the minds of other people. They cannot "read" another person's nonverbal behaviors—a tone of voice, for example, or a raised eyebrow that signal the other's sentiments and emotional state—and so they often cannot distinguish another person's joke from a threat and are prey to many other misunderstandings in social interaction. Needless to say, the frustration experienced by the parents of these infants is enormous. Autism usually is diagnosed by the age of 2 or 3 when parents despair over their child's failure to be responsive to them and to others. Autism is an extreme case of a lack of empathic accuracy.

Ickes and his colleagues regard empathic accuracy as the basis of an evolved general affiliative phenomenon that is characteristic of all creatures (e.g., Ickes, 1997; Ickes, Buysse et al., 2000). Buck and Ginsberg (1997), in fact, believe that empathy involves "a biologically based, spontaneous communication process that is fundamental to all living things" (p. 17). Thus, some theorists believe that spontaneous communication between individuals, especially emotional communication, is innately determined and fundamental to life, for it allows people to coordinate their activities for their mutual benefit and facilitates bonding with others.

Many studies have shown that people differ from each other in their degree of empathic accuracy, and a single individual may show different levels of empathic accuracy at different times over the life span. An example of the latter, and its consequences for social interaction, is provided by a biographical account of novelist F. Scott Fitzgerald, author of *The Great Gatsby*, and his interactions with his longtime friends Sara Murphy and Ernest Hemingway, both of whom felt that Fitzgerald had become so wrapped up in himself that he could no longer understand even those closest to him. Frustrated with Fitzgerald's behavior, Sara tried to warn Fitzgerald of the damaging effects of his lack of empathic accuracy: "I feel obliged in the honesty of a friend to write you: that the ability to know what another person feels in a given situation will make—or ruin—lives" (Tomkins, 1971/1998, p. 129). She was correct.

The study of empathic accuracy has had a tortured history in psychology (see Ickes, 1997; Kenny, 1994a), but newly developed techniques are helping to surmount methodological obstacles. One such technique is the **dyadic interaction procedure**, developed by Ickes and his associates (e.g., Ickes, Bissonnette, Garcia, & Stinson, 1990). First, participants view a videotape of their spontaneous interaction with another person and stop the tape when they recall having had a specific thought or feeling. Then the videotape is replayed for their interaction partner and stopped at each point at which the individual reported having had a specific thought or feeling, and the partner reports what he or she believes the individual was thinking or feeling at that point in their interaction.

Although the identification of the characteristics of people who possess empathic accuracy has been the aim of much empathic accuracy research, researchers have come up mostly empty-handed. Davis and Kraus (1997) performed a meta-analysis of the many studies that have examined the associations between myriad individual difference variables and empathic accuracy but found only intelligence and a few other related characteristics to be associated with this important skill. To explore why replicable individual-difference correlates of empathic accuracy are so hard to identify, Ickes and his colleagues (2000) used a research design they believed to be optimal for uncovering such differences but found only one "best candidate" for a predictor of empathic accuracy: verbal intelligence. These investigators warn that it remains to be seen whether even this finding will survive tests of replicability.

Language

Another innate and uniquely social predisposition may be the human's ability to use language to communicate to others. Use of language long has been regarded as the feature that most distinguishes the human from other animals, including our close primate relatives. It also is regarded as especially social—we speak to communicate to other humans, not to inanimate objects. The noted linguist Noam Chomsky (e.g., 1965) proposed that humans are born with an innate language-acquisition device. Although Chomsky's theory that the infant is born with a wealth of innate knowledge that facilitates the acquisition of language remains controversial, his views continue to frame debate and research in the field of language acquisition (see Ritchie & Bhatia, 1999). At present, a great deal of evidence favors his assertion that the human brain is prewired to acquire language, at least within an early sensitive period (see Pinker, 1994). For example, Elbert, Heim, and Rockstroh (2001) conclude from their review of the literature, "There is compelling evidence that neonates, and even fetuses, are endowed with a remarkable sensitivity to phonetic units used in human speech" (p. 196); and DeCasper and Spence (1986) demonstrated that newborns are able to differentiate prose passages they heard in the womb during their last 6 prenatal weeks from novel passages. Some language researchers have speculated that there is an early "sensitive period" during which phoneme discrimination is learned easily; at 6 months infants can discriminate sounds of nearly all languages, but, as is true of face perception, they seem to become specialized in discriminating the sounds of their native language—the sounds their environment most frequently provides them to hear—and lose the ability to easily discriminate other sounds. As a consequence, another language usually can be acquired in later life only with considerable effort.

SOCIAL INTERACTION AND BRAIN DEVELOPMENT

Interest in identifying the human's innate response systems has intensified in recent years as a result of the emergence in the 1990s of the field of **developmental neuroscience** (see Nelson & Luciana, 2001), which examines the neurobiological structures and processes underlying behavioral development by using techniques such as functional magnetic resonance imaging (fMRI) to study human brain activity in response to controlled stimuli. Developmental neuroscientists already have shattered two long-held beliefs. First, it was believed that brain development was wholly a function of genetically determined rules and programs invulnerable to environmental influence. Second, it was believed that the human brain is fully developed at birth. The evidence now indicates that human infants are born with almost all the brain neurons they will ever have; the brain grows larger because the neurons increase in size and the connections, or synapses, between them increase in number. However, the way these neurons are structurally organized is not set out in a biological blueprint. Moreover, research findings suggest that neural connections in the brain elaborate themselves after birth from a rudimentary pattern of wiring that only slightly approximates the adult pattern (Shatz, 1992) and that **neural plasticity**, the ability of the brain to alter its functional organization, is very high after birth

and thus responsive to the infant's social and emotional experiences (see Elbert et al., 2001).

Early in its development the brain appears to overproduce neural connections that are subsequently reduced in number through disuse. Which connections are retained and which eliminated appears to depend on early stimulation from the infant's social and physical environment, leading to the cultivation of some neural synapses and the "pruning" of others (see Thompson & Nelson, 2001). Greenough and his colleagues (e.g., Black, Jones, Nelson, & Greenough, 1998; Greenough & Black, 1992) have found suggestive evidence that the overproduction of synapses is "in expectation of experiences that will determine their selective survival" (Greenough, Black, & Wallace, 1987, p. 552). An "expected experience" is one that is typical for the species—certain patterns of visual stimulation, for example, such as the faces of conspecifics. If those expected experiences with the physical and social environment do not occur within a relatively restricted early period, the unused synapses will not participate in the developing organization of the brain and will disappear.

The nature and timing of early experiences that are influential in shaping the brain's neural architecture are only now being identified, but it is presumed that among the most important are those associated with sensitive, nurturant, and responsive care from people in the infant's social environment and that these key experiences must occur during early periods of sensitivity to stimulation (see M. H. Bornstein, 1989). Gunnar (2001) has reviewed studies of the developmental effects of an impoverished early social environment on human infants, such as that experienced by many children in orphanages. Even in settings in which the child's nutrition and other physical health needs are met, and even when the environment provides adequate social and physical stimulation, it appears that the absence of stable relationships with consistent caregivers has profound effects on human development. One such effect may be shallowness of later relationships.

Further evidence of the importance of early relationships comes from studies of "resilient" children who are born and raised in poor environments yet, despite being exposed to such adversities as war, poverty, natural disasters, and family violence, seem to develop normally and become competent adults nonetheless. Masten and Coatsworth (1998), who review this literature, report that the most widely documented predictors of a child's resilience to adversity are early relationships with caring, prosocial adults and good intellectual functioning—for example, good problem-solving skills. They conclude, "Resilient children do not appear to possess mysterious or unique qualities; rather they have retained or secured important resources representing basic protective systems in human development" (p. 212). In other words, the same basic protective systems found to be important to children living in ordinary circumstances also are important to children who are not so fortunate and help them overcome their adverse environments. For example, proximity to the caregiver is a powerful predictor of a child's response to its exposure to the trauma of war or a natural disaster (Garmezy & Masten, 1994).

In sum, there is growing evidence that the development of the brain and other biological systems is a function of an interaction between the infant's biological inheritance and his or her social inheritance at birth. In interpreting this evidence, most psychologists and neuroscientists take an evolutionary point of view. For example, British neuroscientist Colin Blakemore (1998) describes how, before birth, the genes "rough out" the architecture of the brain, and how, after birth, the infant's experience with his or her social and physical environment "fine tunes" that circuitry. Blakemore comments, "The appearance, during evolution, of mechanisms by which the strengths of synaptic connections could be changed as a result of stimulation, so as to capture information about the outside world and about individual experiences, was surely one of the most important and portentous steps in organic evolution" (p. 55). That the brain an individual develops is the brain the individual needs to survive in the environment he or she encounters was indeed a "portentous" step in human evolution.

Nature vs. Nurture: A False Dichotomy

It can be seen, as Blakemore and many others emphasize, that the classical controversy of nature versus nurture was wrongly framed and now is in the process of being buried. Findings in developmental neuroscience underscore that the role of experience is neither opposed to, nor separate from, innate influences on the nature of the developing brain and mind. Nature and nurture interact with each other to influence brain development and other outcomes; this position is now taken by almost all developmental psychologists (see Collins, Maccoby, Steinberg, Hetherington, & Bornstein, 2000).

An illustration of how nature and nurture may interact to influence a developmental outcome is provided by experiments conducted by Mineka (e.g., 1987). Rhesus monkeys reared in the wild are always afraid of snakes, but those reared in the laboratory rarely are. When Mineka showed lab-reared monkeys a videotape of a wild-reared monkey exhibiting a fear response to a snake, the lab monkeys developed an enduring fear of snakes, but when Mineka showed the lab-reared monkeys a videotape of a wild-reared monkey exhibiting a fear response to a flower, the lab-reared monkeys did *not* develop a fear response to flowers. Reviewing similar studies conducted both with nonhuman primates and humans, British ethologist and relationship scholar Robert Hinde (1998) concludes that "in both humans and rhesus monkeys the fear response to snakes appears to depend both on a relatively stable biological predisposition and on learning from experience" (p. 19). The operative word is "both." Why did the lab-reared monkeys who observed another monkey exhibiting a fear response to a snake (a social experience) subsequently develop a snake phobia themselves? It couldn't have been their biological predisposition alone, because they had never shown such fear before. It couldn't have been their social experience alone, because they did not develop a fear of flowers when their fellow monkey responded with fear to a flower. Their snake phobia was the result of an *interaction* between their biological heritage and their experience with their social environment. The human's fear of snakes, spiders, and certain other stimuli is often explained by an evolutionary "preparedness theory of phobias" (Seligman, 1971). Because such stimuli were dangerous to our ancestors, it is believed that natural selection favored those persons who possessed an innate predisposition that prepared them to learn very quickly to fear these stimuli, sometimes after just a single learning trial.

The manner in which early social experiences may modulate gene expression to influence future social interactions also is illustrated by a series of experiments conducted by Suomi (1987, 1999). Rhesus monkeys were selectively bred for differences in temperamental reactivity (either *highly reactive* or *normally reactive*) and after birth were placed with foster mothers who varied in the degree of nurturance they had exhibited with their past offspring (either *highly nurturant* or *normally nurturant*). During the period of crossfostering, the normally reactive infants displayed normal patterns of development regardless of whether their foster mother was highly *or* normally nurturant. In contrast, the mother's degree of nurturance clearly influenced the development of highly reactive infants. Highly reactive infants raised by normally nurturant foster mothers showed deficits in early exploration and strong responses to minor environmental disruptions. Those raised by highly nurturant mothers, however, not only explored their environment more and displayed fewer behavioral disturbances than their normally nurtured counterparts but also displayed more exploration and fewer behavioral disturbances than did the normally reactive infants. Moreover, when the highly reactive monkeys reared by highly nurturant mothers were moved into larger social groups at age 6 months, they tended to rise to the top of their groups' dominance hierarchies, whereas their biologically highly reactive counterparts who had been raised by less (that is, normally) nurturant mothers tended to drop to the bottom of their groups' social hierarchies. Thus, the infants' biological inheritance of differential temperament interacted with their social inheritance of a normally or highly nurturant foster mother to influence the infants' behavior not only during the period they were with their mother but also in their later social interactions.

The biologically highly reactive monkeys who were placed with highly nurturant mothers were gifted with a rich social inheritance. Their counterparts were not so fortunate, nor are many human infants, as we have noted. Although maltreatment of a child is known to greatly increase that individual's risk of later criminality (by about 50%), most maltreated children do not become criminals. Caspi and colleagues (2002) wondered why some maltreated children later become violent but others do not. They hypothesized that a deficiency in the action of a gene that helps govern brain neurotransmitter systems interacts with maltreatment to influence later tendencies toward violence. The longitudinal records of men who had been followed from birth to adulthood were examined, and those who had been beaten, molested, or otherwise maltreated in childhood and those who had not were identified and their genotypes obtained. As other studies have found, men who were abused as children were significantly more violent than those who had not been abused. However, those who had been maltreated as children and who *also* possessed the deficiency genotype were, as adolescents, twice as likely to have been diagnosed with conduct disorder and convicted of violent crimes, and to exhibit other symptoms of antisocial personality, than those who also had been maltreated but who did not have the deficiency. Moreover, those who possessed the deficiency genotype but had *not* been maltreated were no more likely to be violent than those who did not have it, thus providing evidence of a gene–environment interaction. Along with the many studies that have identified gene–environment interactions with nonhuman animals (see Rutter & Silberg, 2002), Caspi and associates' findings suggest that there may be many genetically influenced individual differences among humans in sensitivity to specific features of the social environment, such as abuse.

Some psychologists currently are attempting to construct theoretical frameworks within which to view the impact of early social relationships on brain development. Siegel (1999), for example, reviews a great deal of neurobiological and psychological evidence in support of his thesis that the human "mind" (which he views as emerging from the activity of brain neurons) develops at the interface of neurophysiological processes and interpersonal relationships. In accord with Hebb's (1949) maxim that "neurons that fire together wire together," Siegel, like Blakemore and others, argues, "Experience—the activation of specific neural pathways . . . directly shapes gene expression and leads to the maintenance, creation, and strengthening of the connections that form the neural substrate of the mind" (p. 14). The primary source of the infant's early experience is its interpersonal relationships, especially those with its caregivers. Evidence is accumulating that the infant's experiences in early relationships interact with gene expression in shaping neurological circuits within the major structures of the brain (see Suomi, 1999).

Other information about the ways in which early relationships affect developmental outcomes has come from investigations of the association between early relationships and later reactions to stressful events. These studies were generated by findings that infant rat pups who were handled early by humans subsequently showed less reactivity to stressful situations than did pups who were not handled (e.g., Meaney et al., 1985). Subsequent studies showed that rat pups who received highly nurturant and sensitive care by their mothers (e.g., much licking and grooming) later exhibited less severe stress reactions than those raised by less nurturant mothers (e.g., Liu et al., 1997). Moreover, contact with a responsive mother has been found to reduce stress reactivity in nonhuman primate infants as well (e.g., Levine & Wiener, 1988). Strong neurohormonal reactions to stress, partially evidenced in humans by the release of high levels of cortisol, are believed to adversely affect brain development and function.

Gunnar (e.g., 2000) and her associates, who have examined the association between cortisol reactivity to stress and the infant's security of attachment, find that infants in secure attachment relationships show less evidence of a neurohormonal stress response when exposed to stressful situations than do insecurely attached infants. For example, a study of infants whose temperaments were such that they displayed high wariness and fear of strange events revealed that those who were securely attached to the parent who was present during exposure to a stressful event (e.g., a clown asking them to play) did not exhibit cortisol elevation, but those who were insecurely attached did show significant cortisol increases (Nachmias, Gunnar, Mangelsdorf, Parritz, & Buss, 1996). In sum, evidence is accumulating that early treatment by caregivers may "program" neurological systems associated with emotional experience and regulation.

The Infant's Contributions to Relationship Initiation and Maintenance

Relationships are not one-way streets. Both partners must participate in interaction for a relationship to be established and maintained, as discussed in Chapter 6, "Birth of a Relationship," and Chapter 7, "Relationship Growth and Maintenance." Although the caregiver or other adult usually is responsible for initiating and maintaining a relationship with a child, even very young infants are prepared to play an active role in relationship initiation and maintenance.

Tronick, Als, Adamson, Wise, and Brazelton (1978) systematically examined infants' contributions to their interactions with their mothers in a standardized situation. They describe a normal interaction between a 2-month-old infant and his mother:

> Baby [seated in a highchair in the laboratory] is looking off to side where mother will come in. He sits completely quiet, back in his baby seat, face serious, cheeks droopy, mouth half open, corners down, but there is an expectant look in his eyes as if he were waiting. His face and hands reach out in the same direction. As his mother comes in, saying "Hello" . . . he follows her with his head and eyes as she approaches him. His body builds up with tension, his face and eyes open up with a real greeting which

ends with a smile. His mouth opens wide and his whole body orients toward her. He subsides, mouths his tongue twice, his smile dies, and he looks down briefly, while she continues to talk in an increasingly eliciting voice. . . . He looks up again, smiles widely, narrows his eyes, brings one hand up to his mouth, grunting, vocalizing, and begins to cycle his arms and legs out toward her. (p. 5)

After a period of play and reciprocal responsivity, the mother

> loses her broad smile, gets up to leave, letting his legs [which she had been holding] go. At this he looks beseechingly up into her face, his mouth turns down, his eyebrows arch, his legs and arms quiet, and he follows her with his eyes and head as she moves away. (p. 7)

This normal pattern of interaction is in contrast to what is observed when the mother has been instructed to enter the room and maintain an impassive and unresponsive face:

> The infant is looking contemplatively down at his hands, fingering the fingers of one hand with the other. As the mother enters, his hand movements stop. He looks up at her, makes eye-to-eye contact and smiles. Her masklike face does not change. He looks away quickly to one side and remains quiet, his facial expression serious. He remains this way for 20 seconds. Then he looks back at her face, his eyebrows and lids raised, his hands and arms startling slightly out toward her. He quickly looks down at his hand, stills for 8 seconds, and then checks her face once more. This look is cut short by a yawn, with his eyes and face turning upward. His fingers pull at the fingers of his other hand, the rest of his body is motionless. The yawn and neck stretches last 5 seconds. He throws out one arm in a slight startle and looks briefly at her face. Arm movements are jerky, his mouth curves downward, his eyes narrow and partially lid. He turns his face to the side, but he keeps his mother in peripheral vision. He fingers his hand again, his legs stretch toward her and rapidly jerk back again. He arches forward, slumps over, tucks his chin down on one shoulder, but he looks up at her face from under his lowered eyebrows. This position last for over a minute, with brief checking looks at the mother occurring almost every 10 seconds. He grimaces briefly and his facial expression becomes more serious, his eyebrows furrowing. Finally, he

completely withdraws, his body curled over, his head down. He does not look again at his mother. . . . He looks wary, helpless, and withdrawn. As the mother exits at the end of the 3 minutes, he looks halfway up in her direction, but his sober facial expression and his curled body position do not change. (pp. 7–8)[1]

This infant tried to engage his mother in interaction but failed. He failed, in this case, because the mother was following the experimenter's instruction. In naturalistic situations, the baby may fail because the mother is tired, busy, distracted, ill, absent, or otherwise unable to respond to—or perhaps even notice—her baby's invitation to interact. Social interaction, it is becoming evident, is necessary to the optimal development of the baby's brain.

IMPLICATIONS FOR SOCIETY

An improved understanding of the developmental significance of the child's social relationships, both with adults and peers, is considered by many to be one of the most significant advances psychology has made over the past quarter century (Hartup, 1989; see Hartup & Laursen, 1999). Findings pointing to the importance of early relationships, and of providing infants with adequate experience and stimulation and a safe, secure, and supportive environment as the brain and other structures develop after birth, have many implications for society. In his review of the many relevant findings, Rosenzweig (1996) quotes an early report issued by the Carnegie Task Force on Meeting the Needs of Young Children:

> Beginning in the 1960s, scientists began to demonstrate that the quality and variety of the environment have direct impact on brain development. Today, researchers around the world are amassing evidence that the role of the environment is even more important than earlier studies had suggested. . . . Studies of children raised in poor environments—both in this country and elsewhere—show that they have cognitive deficits of substantial magnitude by eighteen months of age and that full reversal of these deficits may not be possible. (p. 22)

Researchers have continued to investigate the effects of a poor social inheritance, including the ways in which it interacts with the child's biological inheritance. Repetti, Taylor, and Seeman (2002) review the wealth of evidence that "risky families"—families characterized by conflict, anger, and aggression and by cold and unsupportive relationships that are neglectful of a child's needs—are associated with children's poor mental and physical health. These theorists present a model that outlines how risky families may create early vulnerabilities and deficits in the child's control and expression of emotions and in social competence (Figure 1.12). The model outlines how the effects of these early deficits may cascade through early childhood to produce and exacerbate other of the child's deficits and vulnerabilities, such that the risk for adverse health outcomes

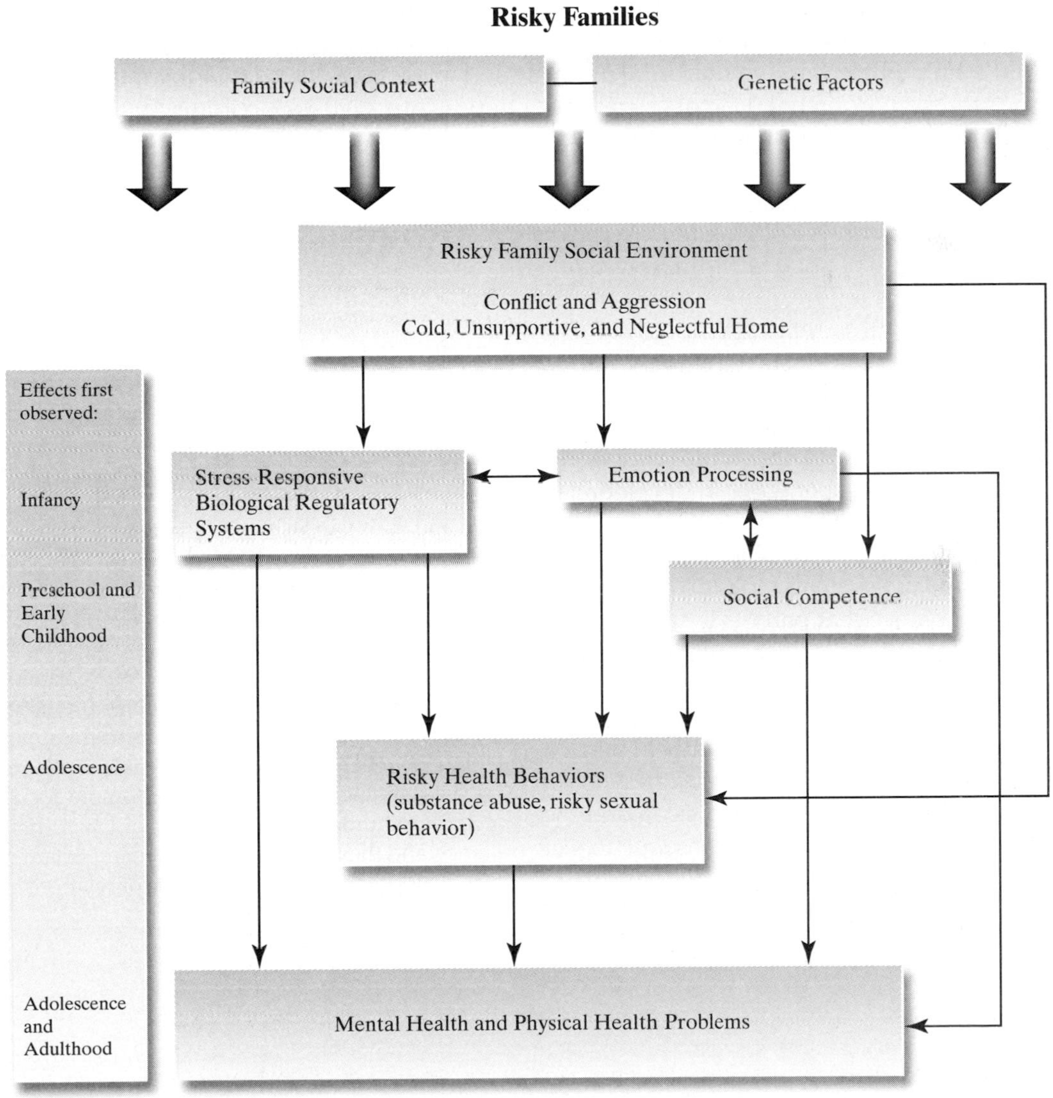

Risky Families

FIGURE 1.12 The risky families model. *Reprinted from Repetti, Taylor, & Seeman, "Risky Families" (2000), Fig. 1, p. 331.*

accumulates through adolescence and adulthood. In accord with mounting evidence, the model highlights the role of early disturbances in biological systems involved in reactions to stress. It also includes the influence of the poor physical and social environments (poverty, high-crime neighborhoods, inadequate medical care) in which risky families are often embedded and that contribute to the chronically high stress levels family members often experience. It includes, too, the influence of genetic factors, which themselves may be associated with a variety of the child's deficits but which may subsequently interact with the child's immediate family environment and with the larger environmental factors surrounding the child and the family to increase the child's vulnerability to adverse outcomes.

Apart from the individual tragedy that each child who fails to receive adequate care represents, all members of society ultimately pay a high price for each failure. This is why governments in virtually all societies attempt to regulate behavior in close relationships, usually family relationships (but with varying success, as discussed in Chapter 5, "Varieties of Relationship").

Findings documenting the importance of the human's early social experiences in development have implications not only for society but for every man and woman who is, or plans to be, a parent. Prospective and new parents today do not have the luxury of ignorance that parents in the past had about the consequences of their parenting practices for the welfare of their children. Knowledge about the importance of early relationships to a child's development has become available only in the past few decades. As a result, educated persons who become parents now bear both the burden and the blessing of knowing the possible consequences of their failure to provide the conditions necessary to their child's optimal development.

Finally, the evidence that the human is truly a social animal—that our biological systems, including our brain, are wired in such a way as to facilitate the formation and maintenance of relationships with others of the species—has implications for the discipline of psychology. A body of knowledge about the behavior of fish would be incomplete at best without reference to the water in which fish evolved, are born, live, and die. Likewise, a science devoted to understanding and predicting the behavior of an animal that evolved, is conceived and born, develops, lives, and dies within relationships with others must recognize and incorporate the influence of the human's relationship web (see Kelley, 1983/2002a; Reis, Collins, & Berscheid, 2000).

SUMMARY

From the time of our entry into the world at birth, we live our lives enmeshed in a complex web of interpersonal relationships. Not only are human infants born into an existing interpersonal reality (their social inheritance), but they also come bearing an extraordinary array of biological gifts that allow them to develop and sustain relationships with others in the social world. The innate need to belong impels each of us to form and maintain lasting interpersonal relationships; the face perceptual system enables us to attend and respond to the human face; empathic accuracy allows us to accurately decipher emotional and behavioral cues from other social objects; language allows us to communicate with our species and our partners; and the attachment and caregiving systems predispose us to quickly form strong bonds to important others and to engage in behaviors which promote close proximity. These biological propensities promote social connectedness and enhance health and well-being in infancy, and they continue to play an important role in the development and maintenance of relationships as they unfold across the life span.

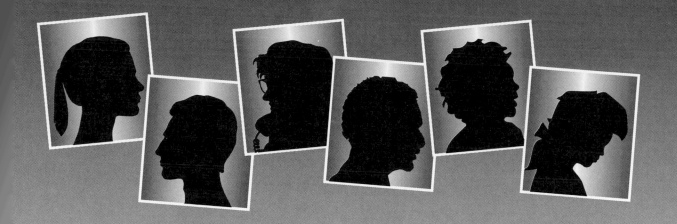

Chapter *2*

Relationships and Health

INTRODUCTION

The ways in which an individual's relationships influence his or her physical and mental health across the life span have become of great interest to biological scientists and social and behavioral scientists, who are beginning to recognize their need for each other (see Krantz & McCeney, 2002). Biological scientists originally believed that the human's internal biological systems mostly operated independently of the brain and, thus, of the mind. As a consequence, they assumed that the mechanisms underlying physical health could be understood by using a biological approach alone. In the mid-1970s, however, that assumption was challenged as a result of experimental demonstrations by biomedical researchers that the operation of the immune system in rats was significantly influenced by the rat's memory of previous experiences—in other words, by the rat's mind (e.g., see Straub, 2001, p. 156). Evidence soon followed that the brain and the endocrine system act together in a coordinated way to influence the immune system. For example, the release of hormones is not the exclusive province of the endocrine system—the brain, too, synthesizes and releases hormones into the bloodstream. These events generated the field of **psychoneuroimmunology** and shattered the belief that bodily processes operate independent of the mind.

Once the influence of the mind on bodily processes was acknowledged, it became recognized that the human mind acts as a conduit through which the individual's relationships, along with other aspects of the individual's sociocultural environment, influence the human's biological systems. The social and physical environment powerfully affects an individual's *central nervous system* (the brain and the spinal cord) and *peripheral nervous system* (the autonomic nervous system and the somatic nervous system) (see Figure 2.1). These operate in concert to influence the *cardiovascular system* (e.g., heart rate and blood pressure), *endocrine system* (which regulates release of hormones from such organs as the adrenal glands), and *immune system* (which governs resistance to disease). Because the biological and social approaches to human health developed independent of each other, an

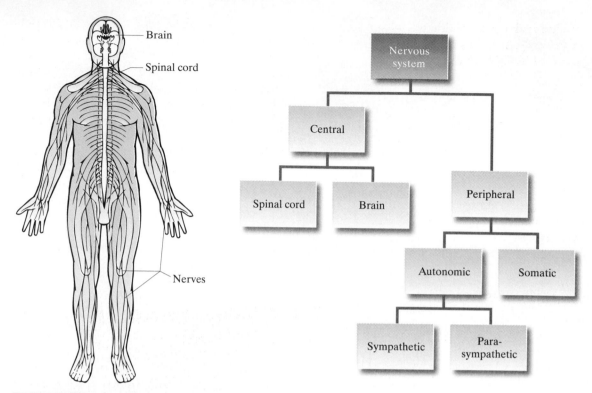

FIGURE 2.1 Divisions of the nervous system.

understanding of the ways in which people fall prey to premature death and disease requires an integration of these two approaches. The biological sciences have typically used *molecular* constructs (e.g., constructs addressed to the neural substrates of human behavior, such as "neuron") to describe the phenomena of interest. The social and behavioral sciences, in contrast, developed *molar* constructs addressed to the complex systems that an understanding of human behavior requires (e.g., constructs addressed to relationship formation, such as "interpersonal attraction"). Both the molecular and molar levels of analysis are necessary for an understanding of human physical and mental health (see Cacioppo & Berntson, 1992).

The field of **social neuroscience** emerged in response to the need to integrate the biological and social approaches to human health and behavior (Cacioppo, Berntson, Sheridan, & McClintock, 2000), as have analytic methods that promise to further that integration (e.g., Kosslyn

et al., 2002). The subfield of *social cognitive neuroscience* attempts to understand psychological phenomena, including health phenomena, in terms of interactions between (1) the social level of analysis, which is concerned with the influence that others exert on an individual's behavior; (2) the cognitive level of analysis, which is concerned with the information-processing mechanisms through which perceptions and thoughts about others influence the individual's behavior; and (3) the neural level of analysis, which is concerned with the brain mechanisms that underlie cognitive-level processes (see Ochsner & Lieberman, 2001). Similarly, the subfield of *social affective neuroscience* attempts to develop theories of emotion and feeling that draw on all three levels of analysis to understand human emotional experience (e.g., Davidson, Jackson, & Kalin, 2000).

Relationships with others have been revealed to be a potent influence on the operation of the biological systems that affect an individual's physical and mental health, but the precise mechanisms by which they do so have only begun to be traced (see Ryff & Singer, 2001).

RELATIONSHIPS AND MORTALITY

The general association between a person's relationships and his or her risk of **mortality**, or likelihood of death, was documented very early in the social and behavioral sciences. Sociologist Emile Durkheim, whose classic book *Suicide* was published in 1897, systematically examined the association between people's social ties and their likelihood of dying by their own hand. His examination of archival data contained in church and other records revealed that the highest rates of suicide were among people who had few social ties to family, community, and church. Durkheim theorized that weak social ties led to an absence of clear social norms and roles and to a psychological state he called "anomie"— detachment from others—and thence to suicide.

Almost a century later, epidemiologists, who study the incidence of mortality and **morbidity** (disease) in different populations, examined the association between an individual's relationships and his or her mortality and morbidity risks (Figure 2.2). In 1978, Bloom, Asher, and White presented data from which they concluded that there is "an unequivocal association between marital disruption and physical and emotional disorder" (p. 886). Divorced adults were found to be at severely greater risk for mental and physical illness, automobile accidents, alcoholism, and suicide. At about this time, too, trumpeted by the headline "Get Married," *Parade* magazine (September 24, 1978) reported a study conducted by the American Council of Life Insurance said to reveal that the mortality rate for divorced American men under 65, as opposed to their married counterparts, was double for strokes and lung cancer, 10 times as high for tuberculosis, 7 times as high for cirrhosis of the liver, double for both stomach cancer and heart disease, and 5 times as high for suicide. The council's statistics for divorced women were reported to be similar.

A year later, Berkman and Syme (1979) published the results of a study that examined age-adjusted mortality rates for a stratified random sample of residents in Alameda County, California. For both males and females, in every age group, mortality rates were significantly higher for those low in social integration. **Social integration** in the classic Alameda study, as in many studies thereafter, was measured by combining assessments of marital status, degree of contact with friends and relatives, participation in formal and informal organizations, and church membership. Persons who lacked ties to others were found to be between 2 and 3 times more likely to have died 9 years later than those who possessed more relationships.

FIGURE 2.2 A lack of social integration has been linked to both morbidity and mortality.

At the same time, other health researchers had begun to examine the association between social relationships and cardiovascular disease, the leading cause of death in the United States. In *The Broken Heart: The Medical Consequences of Loneliness*, James Lynch (1977) presented data revealing that premature death from heart disease was significantly more frequent among those he termed the "loneliness prone"—people who were divorced, widowed, and single, whether old or young. Lynch put a human face on the statistics he published with his personal observations of hospital patients who, quite literally, were dying of loneliness:

> The full impact of the awesome destructiveness of loneliness, human isolation, and bereavement does not strike home until you look at heartbroken patients "being saved" by medical technology, lying all alone in coronary care units. While there are many patients whose lives have been filled with love, it is difficult to describe the emptiness and pain that fill some of these patients' lives, and it is clear that no antiarrhythmic drug by itself will prolong their lives much longer. These patients are not abstract statistics at all—they are old men and women, sometimes even young men and women, whose children have gone far away, or whose loved ones have recently died, or who don't know the names of even one person in their neighborhood, or who don't know who you should notify in case they die, and who lie in hospital beds for weeks without visitors. They are literally brokenhearted—there really is no other term to describe it—and something beyond drugs, heart transplants, coronary bypass operations, or artificial pacemakers is needed to save them. (pp. 154–155)

Lynch and his colleagues also found that the mere touch of another human—as when medical personnel took the patient's pulse—was followed by a significant reduction in the irregularity of the patient's heartbeat (Lynch, Thomas, Paskewitz, Katcher, & Weir, 1977).

Many investigations have since corroborated the link between heart disease and social isolation and other psychosocial factors (see Krantz & McCeney, 2002, for a review). For example, a longitudinal study of more than 1,000 heart attack survivors found that those who lived alone were almost twice as likely to suffer another heart attack—or die of one—within 6 months as contrasted to those who lived with companions (Case, Moss, Case, McDermot, & Eberly, 1992). None of the known risk factors for second heart attacks—including advanced age, low socioeconomic status, and severity of heart damage—accounted for the ill health of those who lived alone. Other investigators have reported that unmarried heart patients who did not have a close personal confidant were significantly less likely to survive for 5 years (Williams et al., 1992). From their review of studies of the role of social relationships in cardiovascular disease, Atkins, Kaplan, and Toshima (1991) concluded that the strength of the association between social isolation and heart disease is at least as strong as it is for all other known risk factors. For example, even when other risk factors are statistically controlled, the risk for cardiovascular disease among the socially isolated is as high as it is for the well-publicized smoking risk factor.

Berkman's (1995) review of eight major large-scale epidemiological studies that examined the association between social integration and mortality from any cause concluded that despite the fact that each of the eight studies used different measures of social integration and that some of these measures were relatively crude, each found that mortality rates were significantly lower among persons who were more socially integrated. House, Landis, and Umberson (1988) earlier had reached the same conclusion but thought they detected suggestive evidence that social integration may be less strongly associated with women's mortality than men's. Hints that relationships may have a stronger protective effect against death for men than for women continue to be found.

Social integration measures range from the rudimentary (e.g., marital status) to the complex, and they do not always produce the same results. Examining resistance to the common cold, Cohen, Doyle, Skoner, Rabin, and Gwaltney (1997) asked volunteers to report the people they spoke with, in person or on the telephone, at least once every 2 weeks and to report the *type* of relationship they had with each, such as friend, parent, spouse, or co-worker. The volunteers, all of whom had been deemed to be in excellent health, then were given nasal drops that contained a low dose of one of two infectious rhinoviruses and quarantined for 5 days. From analyses of nasal secretion samples collected each day, Cohen and colleagues found that people who participated in many different types of social relationship were less susceptible to the common cold, produced less mucus, were more effective in clearing their nasal passages, and shed less virus than those with fewer types of social relationship. People who reported having only one to three types of relationship suffered more than 4 times the risk of falling ill than those who reported having six or more types of relationship. The association between relationship diversity and susceptibility to disease held even when each individual's initial antibody resistance to each of the two rhinoviruses, measured when they entered the study, was taken into account. Moreover, the association between diversity of relationship type and susceptibility held even after controlling for the number of an individual's relationships. Since most studies find an association between number of relationships and morbidity, it is not clear why diversity of relationship type was associated with disease susceptibility, nor is it clear why the number of the individual's relationships was not.

Large-scale epidemiological studies and smaller-scale laboratory studies, such as that conducted by Cohen and his associates, are not the only sources of evidence of an association between an individual's social ties and his or her mortality and morbidity. Researchers in other disciplines contributing to relationship science have found the same association using the methodologies typical of their discipline. For example, anthropologist Donald Grayson (1990) examined diaries and other records to determine the fate of each member of a group of 87 pioneers who formed a wagon train in Illinois in the summer of 1846 to travel to California's Sacramento Valley (Figure 2.3). When the Donner party decided to take a new and untried route recommended to them as a "shortcut," their fate was sealed. Not only was the shortcut not a shortcut, but it took substantially more time to traverse than the usual route. As a consequence,

the Donner party's progress to the Sierra Nevada was delayed; they did not reach the mountains that divide Nevada and California until fall instead of late summer as they had hoped. Then, what could go wrong, did go wrong. It snowed early and heavily that year and the pioneers were trapped high on the mountain for the duration of the winter. Only 47 members of the original group were still alive when a rescue party reached them in the spring. Many people remember the Donner party because its members engaged in cannibalism in order to survive. After slaughtering their draft animals for food, they killed their pets to eat, and when those were gone, they ate the bodies of those members of their party who had died.

Grayson's analyses of which of the original 87 pioneers outlived the ordeal revealed that age, sex, and what he calls "degree of social connectedness" had a striking effect on a person's chances of survival. Not surprisingly, mortality rates were highest among the youngest and oldest members of the party. In addition to age, an individual's sex was associated with survival: The men died at almost twice the rate women did—30% of the males died but only 10% of the females. Moreover, the men died early, whereas the women held out longer; those women who died tended to do so just before the rescue in the spring. (Women's lower basal metabolism and higher amount of subcutaneous fat may have been protective factors, and men undoubtedly performed more strenuous tasks and were more exposed to the elements.) In addition, Grayson's analysis revealed that those with larger family groups were most

FIGURE 2.3 Two members of the Donner party.

likely to survive: 9 of the 11 single men who were traveling alone died, whereas all 9 members of one family, including a 1-year-old infant, lived. The group with the highest survival rate was composed of people between the ages of 20 and 39. Within this age group, survivors had an average family size of 6.8 persons, whereas those who died were members of families whose size averaged only 2.3 persons.

Grayson concluded that those who had more "social connectedness" not only enjoyed more material assistance, but their relationships provided them emotional support and a reason to struggle to continue living. A similar conclusion was reached by McCullough and Barton (1991), who examined kin relatedness and survival among those who arrived in Plymouth in 1620 on the *Mayflower*. Relatedness was the major determinant of survival of these people—the more relatives an individual had in the group, the greater his or her chance of survival.

Social Networks

Findings of a strong association between social relationships and mortality and morbidity stimulated interest in learning more about people's social networks. An individual's **social network** is composed of his or her close associates, usually friends and kin, with whom the individual regularly interacts (see Milardo, 1988; Milardo & Helms-Erikson, 2000). Social network theory and analysis typically does not focus on any one individual, however; it usually assesses the degree of social integration within relatively large social units—a sorority, a community, or even a nation. Thus, social network researchers usually examine patterns of relationships within groups.

Sociometry

Sociologist Jacob Moreno is widely regarded as the father of social network analysis because he was the first to develop a technique, which he called **sociometry**, to examine relational patterns within a group by systematically asking each of its members such questions as "Whom do you like most in the group?" and "Whom would you like least to work with?" The answers portray the group's affectional system, or the pattern of the interpersonal attraction and repulsion within the group. Popular group members are called sociometric "stars" and disliked persons social "isolates." Moreno presented the sociometric method in his book *Who Shall Survive?* (1934/1953). Although his title may have seemed overly dramatic at the time, it was prophetic of later research findings that would document that in order to survive, humans need the good will of others, which the sociometric method assesses.

Structural Network Measures

The sociometric method continues to be used today to assess patterns of attraction within groups, particularly within groups in which successful task performance requires positive feelings among their members, such as military combat units. Since Moreno's time, however, social network measurement and analysis have become highly sophisticated. The features of an individual's social network most frequently assessed are such structural characteristics as (1) *size*, or the number of persons in the network; (2) *density*, or the extent to which the members of a person's network associate directly with each other; (3) *homogeneity*, the similarity of network members; and (4) *frequency of contact* with network members.

Significant associations between some of the structural characteristics of the individual's network and his or her likelihood of illness and death have been found (House & Kahn, 1985). For example, persons with larger social networks are generally healthier and live longer. Shye, Mullooly, Freeborn, and Pope (1995) tallied the number of people with whom subjects aged 65 or older reported having had "informal social contact" and found that of those who earlier had small networks, 21% were still alive 15 years later; of those who had medium-sized networks, 30% were still alive; and the greatest percentage of survivors, 37%, was found for the group who earlier had the largest social networks. The finding that the larger a network was, the greater an individual's chance of survival, is consistent with the results of many epidemiological studies.

Moreover, the more frequently people engage in social interaction with others in their network, the better their health and the lower their mortality risk (Berkman & Syme, 1979).

It is both practically and ethically difficult to experimentally manipulate the number and nature of an individual's social relationships. As a consequence, studies demonstrating the association between social integration and mortality and morbidity are correlational. **Correlational studies** can provide evidence that the two variables, social integration and morbidity, *covary*; for example, when one is present, the other tends also to be present, and when one is absent, the other also tends to be absent. Unfortunately, correlational studies cannot determine whether (1) poor health causes weaker social ties; (2) weaker social ties cause poor health; (3) a third variable, such as poverty, is responsible for both poor health and weaker social ties; or (4) whether all, or some combination, of these causal links operate in concert to produce the observed correlation between social integration and health. Nevertheless, more is known about causality after knowledge of correlation is obtained than was known before (see Jussim, 2002); specifically, it is known that at least one and perhaps more of the four causal possibilities exist—in this case, that social integration lies somewhere in the causal nexus surrounding health.

There is some evidence that poor health may cause weaker social ties. Booth and Johnson (1994) examined the effects of health changes on marital quality over a 3-year period in a large national sample of married persons and found that decrements in health had an adverse effect on the quality of the marriage. Much of the decrease in marital quality associated with illness was accounted for by changes in financial circumstances, shifts in the division of household labor, declines in marital activities, and problematic be-

havior on the part of the ill spouse. Although people in poor health appear to be less able than healthy people to maintain satisfying social relationships, and although many third variables, such as psychological maladjustment (e.g., Martin et al., 1995), produce both poor social integration and poor health and thus are at least partially responsible for the well-established association between social integration and health, researchers have focused their attention on a single hypothesis—that social support is the variable actually responsible for the association.

SOCIAL SUPPORT

Fine-grained analyses of correlational epidemiological data (e.g., Atkins et al., 1991) and other evidence quickly suggested to many researchers that social integration does not in itself lower mortality and morbidity risk; rather, they reasoned, social integration usually is associated with social support and it is the receipt or absence of social support that affects health. Social support thus is believed to be the **mediating variable** (i.e., the causal variable) actually responsible for the social integration–health association (see Figure 2.4).

It is not surprising that researchers quickly adopted the hypothesis that social support—not social integration itself—is the generative, causal mechanism that reduces risk of mortality and morbidity. Personal testimonials to the efficacy of social support in combating illness abound. In 1999, for example, the world was amazed when Lance Armstrong won the grueling 2,290-mile Tour de France bicycle race because just 2 years earlier, Armstrong had been diagnosed with testicular cancer that had spread to his brain, lungs, and abdomen. Analyses of his astounding comeback from death's door to athletic triumph

FIGURE 2.4 Research suggests that the association between social integration and health (mortality, morbidity) is mediated by social support. People who possess a high degree of social integration generally have access to high levels of social support; this social support, in turn, lowers mortality and morbidity risk.

FIGURE 2.5 Lance Armstrong.

pointed to the strong social support he enjoyed, as well as his determination and fine medical care. Armstrong himself gave much credit to his support network: "In the end, Armstrong says the unstinting support of his friends, family, and doctors 'helped me stay positive, helped me stay brave'" (Schultz & Kulman, 1999). Armstrong has continued to race professionally and in 2003 tied the record for winning the Tour de France five times in a row.

The Concept of Social Support

Despite the prevalence of personal testimonials to the efficacy of social support in promoting and restoring health, investigation of its role in health has been plagued with difficulties. The greatest of these difficulties has been defining just exactly what social support is. Although Cobb (1976)

early defined social support as information that led a person to believe that he or she is "cared for and loved, esteemed, and a member of a network of mutual obligations" (p. 300), many researchers initially assumed that the terms "social network" and "social support network" were synonymous (see Vaux, 1988). As a consequence, it was assumed that the strength of an individual's support system could be assessed by measuring the size of his or her social network.

To understand why social support researchers now recognize that it is a mistake to regard an individual's social support system as identical to his or her social network, one need only consider people in the midst of divorce. Divorce is a stressor of high magnitude for most people. Holmes and Rahe (1967), who attempted to quantify the effect of many common life events on health, found that death of a spouse, divorce, and marital separation were at the top of the list of events associated with subsequent illness. Given that divorce usually is a highly distressing event, one might suppose that divorcing spouses receive social support from their close friends and relatives during this difficult period. However, Spanier and Thompson (1984) conducted extensive interviews with recently divorced men and women and found that approximately one-third experienced disapproval of the separation by their own biological parents and more than two-thirds reported disapproval by their parents-in-law. The disapproval of these important members of the social network often was manifested in direct interference and withholding previously given support, especially when child custody was an issue (see Milardo, 1987). One's own parents and the children's maternal and paternal grandparents are likely to remain in the individual's social network both during and after separation and divorce. Thus, these social network members frequently not only do *not* provide support but they often *add* to the divorced individual's distress.

Researchers came to realize they could not identify an individual's social support network until they answered the question "What is social support?" After exhaustively reviewing the massive and confusing social support literature, Vaux (1988) gave his personal opinion:

Social support has to do with everyday things—sharing tasks and feelings, exchanging information and affection—as well as dramatic but common human experiences—the joy of love, the pain of isolation, family ties, and bonds of friendship. The idea underlying social support is both commonplace and immensely rich. Therein lie both the appeal and promise of the construct and the obstacles to its systematic study. (p. 1)

The richness of ideas about social support resulted in a plethora of definitions and conceptual confusion about social support, which is partly responsible for many inconclusive and contradictory findings in the social support literature (see Stroebe & Stroebe, 1996).

The Transactive View of Support

Vaux (1988) concluded that social support is too complex an idea to be encapsulated within a single theoretical concept and advocated that social support instead be viewed as a "metaconstruct" comprised of several conceptual components. He also suggested that as opposed to viewing social support as a property of a person's social network, social support be thought of as a process that involves *transactions* between the person and the support network:

The individual must develop and maintain supportive relationships, mobilize such resources through help seeking, manage the incidents during which assistance is proffered, and perform evaluative and integrative appraisals of both numerous incidents and his or her resources more generally. (p. 297)

Many social support researchers and theorists now endorse the **transactional perspective of social support**, which requires attention not only to the interaction between the person and his or her social environment but also to the different kinds of relationships that may or may not compose the individual's support network (e.g., Lakey & Lutz, 2000; Sarason, Sarason, & Pierce, 1990a).

The need to differentiate the different kinds of relationships in an individual's social network was highlighted by Surra and Milardo (1991),

who distinguished between *interactive social networks*, consisting of people with whom the individual engages in frequent face-to-face interaction, and *psychological networks*, composed of people with whom the individual feels close or whom he or she believes to be important. There may be little overlap between these two networks. Surra and Milardo reported in one study that 75% of the people identified by the respondents were members of only one of these networks. Moreover, there was no significant correlation between the sizes of the two networks, nor was there an association between the size of the psychological network and frequency of daily interaction with persons in the network. This suggests that people with larger psychological networks aren't necessarily more socially active and those with smaller psychological networks aren't necessarily socially isolated. Surra and Milardo's distinction is particularly relevant to the kinds of support (e.g., emotional, informational) that are likely to be available to ameliorate different kinds of distress. Different kinds of distress require different kinds of support, according to several social support theories (e.g., Hobfoll, 1988; Cutrona, 1990). For example, the recipient's satisfaction with another's supportive action has been shown to depend on whether it matches the recipient's need—for example, for advice as opposed to sympathy (Horowitz et al., 2001).

Measures of Support

Considerable progress has been made in refining the social support construct (see Lakey & Cohen, 2000) and these efforts continue (e.g., Trobst, 2000). Among the first steps toward conceptual clarity was a distinction made by Cohen and Wills (1985) between structural and functional measures of social support. **Structural social support** measures refer to the relatively objective features of social ties and activities, such as those social network analysts typically examine. **Functional social support** measures pertain to the fulfillment of people's psychological needs and goals within the relationships that compose the social network. Berscheid and Reis (1998) observe that most functional measures of social support emphasize three basic themes: (1) *emotional support*, such as expressions of esteem and reassurance of worth; (2) *appraisal support*, including advice, guidance, and information; and (3) *instrumental support* involving material assistance, such as money. These three elements of functional support tend to covary; that is, if one is present in a relationship, the other two also tend to be present, and if one is absent, the others tend to be absent also. Of the three, emotional support may be particularly health protective (Uchino, Cacioppo, & Kiecolt-Glaser, 1996).

Social support researchers initially believed that they would be able to observe the giving and receiving of social support in social interaction, but correlations between **enacted support** (support a person believes he or she has given or support outside observers believe the supporter has given) and **perceived support** (support the recipient believes he or she has received) proved to be discouragingly low (e.g., Coriell & Cohen, 1995; Wethington & Kessler, 1986). For example, Cutrona (1990) asked one person in pairs of students to play the role of "helper" while the other student disclosed a stressful event experienced within the previous 6 months. No type of supportive behavior significantly affected the recipients' perception of support despite the fact that two observers of the interaction corroborated the helpers' perceptions that they had indeed been supportive. Using a similar observational paradigm, Cutrona and Suhr (1994) found that the number of supportive behaviors wives actually received from their husbands in an interaction (as determined by outside observers) was associated with the wives' perceptions of the supportiveness of the interaction, but husbands' perceptions of their wives' supportiveness were influenced primarily by the husband's mood and by his degree of marital satisfaction.

Fincham and Bradbury (1990) argue that husbands' and wives' perceptions of whether their spouse's behavior is voluntary and selflessly motivated is an important determinant of whether the spouse's behavior is seen as supportive. Mood, too, they note, is a factor because someone in a good mood is more likely to recall and perceive positive actions by others, whereas someone in a bad mood may be less likely to see others as supportive. In addition, when people feel strongly positive or negative toward a support provider, judgments of the person's supportiveness are not likely to be based solely on the resources provided—*who* is providing the support and *why* also are likely to be factors (see Hobfoll & Stokes, 1988).

The "who" is likely to be someone with whom the recipient has an ongoing relationship. Badr, Acitelli, Duck, and Carl (2001) note that because social support is usually given and received in the "mundane" context of daily interactions in ongoing relationships, an understanding of social support requires examination of the meaning of supportive actions within the context of the relationship between the support provider and the recipient. Sarason, Sarason, and Gurung (2001), too, emphasize that "an adequate understanding of social support processes must specify the role of personal relationships in the provision, receipt, and appraisal of social support" (p. 41). Conceptualizing support generally as acts that reflect responsivity to another's needs, and more particularly as "acts that communicate caring; that validate the other's worth, feelings, or actions; or that facilitate adaptive coping with problems through the provision of information, assistance, or tangible resources" (p. 10), has allowed Cutrona (1996) to draw theoretical connections between support as it is given or received in close relationships and such traditional relationship constructs as trust, love, and commitment. Cutrona has emphasized the role that responsivity to a partner's minor needs on a daily basis plays in relationship quality. To better understand the determinants and consequences of partners' support in ongoing relationships, including marital relationships, Cutrona and her associates have developed a measure of the frequency and type of social support partners give each other during a brief laboratory interaction (see Cutrona & Suhr, 1994).

Unfortunately, most previous social support theory and research have failed to recognize the influence of the specific context in which support may be given and received. For example, measures of perceived support have generally assessed the individual's overall, or "global," perception of support regardless of source. Global perceptions of support availability may differ from relationship-specific perceptions, which may vary from one relationship to another. Both types of measures—global and relationship-specific—have been found useful in accounting for health outcomes (Pierce, Sarason, & Sarason, 1991).

The poor correspondence between enacted support and perceived support, and the fact that perceived support seems to be more closely associated with health outcomes, has led social support researchers to almost exclusively adopt measures of perceived support and to neglect measures of enacted support. As a consequence, McCaskill and Lakey (2000) note that a major question in social support research is the extent to which perceived support represents the actual supportiveness of the social environment as opposed to the perceptions of the perceiver. Indeed, some have argued that the tendency to perceive social support is so stable it may constitute a personality characteristic (e.g., Pierce, Sarason, & Sarason, 1992). To complicate matters further, there may be a positive feedback loop between perceived support and actual support; Salovey, Rothman, Detweiler, and Steward (2000) speculate that the perception that support is available may elevate mood, which increases the likelihood of positive interactions with others, which increases the likelihood of actual support, which then further increases the perceived availability of support.

Most studies find the perceived social support–health association, but some do not (e.g., Bolger, Foster, Vinokur, & Ng, 1996). Perceived support sometimes fails to be beneficial, Bolger, Zuckerman, and Kessler (2000) hypothesized, because the individual's awareness of receiving support has emotional costs. For example, it often increases the recipient's awareness that he or she is having difficulty coping and thus lowers the recipient's self-esteem. Support sometimes also produces uncomfortable feelings of indebtedness and obligation to the provider. In such instances, the psychological costs of support may negate its health benefits. As a consequence, Bolger and his colleagues hypothesized that **invisible social support**—support that occurs outside of the recipient's awareness, such as supportive advice given in an indirect way to preclude the recipient from coding it as support—may be the most effective form of support.

To test their hypothesis, Bolger and colleagues (2000) asked both members of cohabiting romantic couples to record in a daily diary the help they gave and received during a period before one of the partners was to face a highly stressful event—taking the New York State bar examination—and then correlated these reports with daily measures of the prospective test-taker's anxiety and depression. As the investigators suspected, many of the support transactions recorded by the examinee's partner were not reported by the examinee and, overall, these invisible support transactions were more effective in reducing the examinee's anxiety and depression than were visible support transactions in which both the examinee and the partner agreed that support had been given and received. Moreover, the worst situation for the examinees, in terms of an increase in depression, was one in which their partners said they did not give support but examinees reported they had received support; in such cases, the examinees experienced the costs of support receipt but failed to experience its benefits.

Investigators generally differentiate between two kinds of perceived support: (1) support the individual believes he or she is *currently receiving or has received in the past* and (2) support the individual believes is *available in the future* should it be needed. Of these two measures, **perceived support availability** appears to be most closely associated with good health and adjustment to stressful events (see Sarason, Sarason, & Gurung, 2001). Not surprisingly, the expectation that support will be available from a relationship partner is associated with the degree of intimacy (e.g., Reis & Franks, 1994) and affection in the relationship (Burleson, 1994).

Although some researchers now believe that perceived support should be conceptualized as a general expectation about a partner's likely future behavior (Sarason, Sarason, & Pierce, 1990b), a recent autobiographical report suggests that perceived past support also may be valuable.

Barry Collins (2001), a social psychologist who twice suffered a heart attack followed by coronary bypass surgery, characterizes his two surgeries as a single-subject (Collins himself) repeated-measures (Collins's feelings of well-being on the two occasions) quasi-experiment (the same trauma was experienced, first with low support and then with high support). On the first occasion, Collins had been recently divorced and was estranged from his children and thus endured the trauma in social isolation; on the second, his second wife and his children were present and supportive. Collins's personal chronicle is yet another testimonial to the efficacy of social support, but more important, it provides insight into difficulties of studying support:

> I am no longer surprised that what social supporters do in real time is uncorrelated with perceived social support. The most important gifts my supporters gave me were a *history* of nourishing social interactions. . . . Loving exchanges in the past were gifts from my supporters that kept on giving [as they were remembered during the ordeal]. (p. 352)

Collins also highlights the importance of emotional support, but he comments that it would have been difficult for an outside observer to accurately differentiate emotional from instrumental support. For example, without being asked, his son handed him a glass of water he needed. An outside observer probably would have coded the act as instrumental support, but Collins himself coded it as emotional support because it indicated to him that his son was aware of his pain, immediately perceived his need for the water, and recognized his inability to reach the glass. Again, the specific relationship context in which support is given and received makes a difference not only in whether an action is perceived to be supportive but also in the kind of support it is perceived to be.

Support Perceivers and Providers

Personal characteristics associated with developing a large and active social network have been found to be associated with perceived support availabil-ity. For example, people who are more socially competent tend to believe that they have more support available to them than do people of lesser social competence (e.g., Sarason, Sarason, Hacker, & Basham, 1985). Social competence, of course, facilitates access to relationships, and it also increases the likelihood that the emotional tenor of those relationships will be positive. Indeed, people who perceive that social support is available seem to be less neurotic than those who don't (Watson & Pennebaker, 1989); neuroticism and associated characteristics (e.g., negative mood and expectations) may hinder recognition of supportive behavior even if it occurs (Lakey & Cassady, 1990). In addition, people with a secure adult attachment style orientation toward relationships have been found to be more willing than others to seek support when needed (e.g., Florian, Mikulincer, & Bucholtz, 1995), whereas an avoidant attachment style is associated with ineffective support seeking and an anxious-ambivalent attachment style with poor support provision (Collins & Feeney, 2000). Overall, however, perceived support availability is associated with well-being for everyone (e.g., Cohen, Sherrod, & Clark, 1986).

Few social support investigators have investigated which persons in the individual's social network will attempt to provide support and when they will do so, but from their review of such evidence as is available, Stroebe and Stroebe (1996) concluded that the probability of help is greatest when the potential helper perceives the other to be in need of support, the other is seen as not personally responsible for his or her plight, and the other is believed to be making an effort to cope with the problem. These three determinants of helping by familiar others also have been identified by prosocial behavior researchers as determinants of helping by strangers. There are other parallels. People who are in a bad mood, busy, or otherwise self-absorbed are less likely to help strangers (e.g., Darley & Batson, 1973). These factors also influence a relationship partner's likelihood of giving support. In a series of studies, Barbee and her associates found that people in an experimentally induced positive mood were much more likely to notice a friend's distress and to provide effective supportive and problem-solving strategies than were people in neutral or negative moods—in fact, sad and depressed partners often were so self-focused they failed to notice that their friends needed support (see Cunningham & Barbee, 2000).

The identity of people perceived to provide support changes with age. Furman and Buhrmester (1992) found that fourth graders reported that their mothers and fathers were their most frequent providers of support; seventh graders named both parents and same-sex friends; tenth graders said their same-sex friends most frequently gave them support, but romantic partners had moved up in rank; finally, college students reported that their romantic partners, along with friends and mothers, gave them the most support. Girls generally perceived same-sex friendships to be more supportive than boys did.

Sex Differences in Support

Women tend to give more support than men do. For example, men's same-sex friendships, including their best-friend relationships, have been consistently found to be perceived as less supportive than women's friendships (see Fehr, 1996). Bank and Hansford (2000) asked men and women to describe their best friendships and found that men, as expected, scored lower than women on measures of relationship intimacy and supportiveness (although there was no sex difference in the degree to which men and women reported enjoying intimacy and supportiveness in their friendships when it was present). Of the several possible explanations examined for this sex difference, the two that seemed most likely responsible for the lesser supportiveness of men's friendships were men's emotional restraint and homophobia.

Other factors also contribute to the differences between men and women in the support they give and receive in their relationships. Helgeson (e.g., 1994; Fritz & Helgeson, 1998) and her associates have assembled a great deal of evidence that women score higher than men on two personality traits associated with support giving: communion and unmitigated communion. **Communion**, generally defined as a focus on connection with others, usually is assessed with

instruments that were originally regarded as measures of psychological femininity (e.g., Spence, Helmreich, & Stapp, 1974) but are now believed to reflect an orientation toward relationships that involves emotional expressivity and concern with the other's needs (Spence, 1984). **Unmitigated communion**, in contrast, is viewed as "a focus on others to the exclusion of the self, resulting in the neglect of one's own needs" (Helgeson & Fritz, 1998, p. 174). Unmitigated communion is currently measured by a scale that includes such items as "I always place the needs of others above my own," "I worry about how other people get along without me when I am not there," and "I often worry about others' problems."

Unmitigated communion is positively but modestly correlated with communion, but unlike communion, it also is strongly associated with distress, which appears to stem from low self-esteem, fear of negative evaluation by others, the perception of others as disapproving, and an overinvolvement with others that leads to greater exposure to others' problems. Both communion and unmitigated communion are strongly associated with the provision of support (e.g., Helgeson & Fritz, 1998) but people who score high on unmitigated communion carry their support behavior to the extreme. Most people distance themselves when support provision threatens their own physical and psychological health; for example, Bolger et al. (1996) found that the close relationship partners of breast cancer patients tended to withdraw when the patients' emotional distress was severe and unrelenting. Those who score high on unmitigated communion regard another's adversity as their own and are unlikely to withdraw, sometimes leading to self-neglect, health problems, and distress.

People high in unmitigated communion also may have different motivations for giving support than do those high in communion; they are more distressed by their friend turning to someone else for help than they are by their friend going without any support at all, whereas those high in communion are more distressed by their friend not receiving help than they are by the friend turning to others for aid (see Helgeson & Fritz, 1998). Thus, helping others appears to be central to the self-concept of people high in unmitigated communion and may temporarily elevate their self-esteem; whether another actually receives aid may be of lesser concern.

Social Support Intervention

Support providers usually are family members and close friends, but the increasing prevalence of support intervention groups composed of strangers and acquaintances has raised questions about their efficacy. People initially were encouraged by a well-publicized study conducted by Spiegel, Bloom, Kraemer, and Gotthel (1989), who assigned women with terminal breast cancer either to a no-treatment control group or to an intervention group in which problems associated with their illness and ways to improve their personal relationships were discussed at weekly 90-minute meetings for a year. After 10 years it was found that the women in the intervention group had survived an average of 18 months longer than women in the control group. Unfortunately, meta-analyses of cancer support group studies indicate that although participation is associated with better psychological adjustment and fewer self-reported symptoms and treatment side effects, it does not seem to result in actual physical improvement (Helgeson & Cohen, 1996; Meyer & Mark, 1995). Although groups like Alcoholics Anonymous are generally regarded as efficacious for alcoholism and drug abuse, the usefulness of peer support groups for other physical and mental illnesses remains at issue.

Lakey and Lutz (2000) conclude from their review of experimental social support intervention studies that the results have been "disappointing" (p. 461). Several factors may be responsible, among them the fact that interventions rarely are able to change an individual's naturally occurring level of social support. Not often considered is that some peer support groups (and possibly family and friends as well) do more harm than good. For example, people coping with grief or a severe physical problem often experience intense negative emotion. Because social support therapy usually involves arranging for the individual to interact with others also experiencing the problem and thus negative emotion, the process of "emotional contagion" may reverberate throughout the group to increase, rather than decrease, members' distress (see Hatfield, Cacioppo, & Rapson, 1994).

Some studies have shown that people who are experiencing strong emotion prefer to avoid interaction with others, especially when they fear interaction will increase, not decrease, their distress (see Wheeler, 1974). Their fear may be justified. Hobfoll and London (1986) found that among Israeli women whose husbands and other family members were serving in the military, those who had more intimates to talk to and who received more social support experienced more—not less—distress. Because this correlational finding may have been caused by highly distressed women seeking interaction more frequently than less distressed women (and thus distress led to greater social interaction rather than the reverse), Winstead and Derlega (1991) explored the finding experimentally. Their participants, each of whom brought a friend with them to the laboratory, were led to expect to guide a tarantula though a maze. In the interaction period before the task was to be performed, the friend was instructed to either (1) talk only about personal feelings concerning the task (the *disclosure-of-feelings* condition), (2) talk only about the task itself (the *task-problem-solving* condition), or (3) limit conversation to topics unrelated to the task (the *unrelated-talk* condition). Depression and anxiety scores were higher—not lower—in the disclosure-of-feelings condition than in the task-problem-solving and unrelated-talk conditions.

Disclosure of negative feelings has been viewed as health enhancing by many psychologists, including Freud and his followers, who theorized that "bottled-up" negative emotion is responsible for many psychosomatic disorders and that full expression of a negative emotion has a cathartic—or "purging"—effect of the poison it represents. An experiment by Bushman (2002), however, casts doubt on the catharsis hypothesis. Bushman's participants first were made angry by another's harsh criticism of an essay they had written. One-third of the participants were then instructed to think about the person who had angered them while hitting a punching bag (the *rumination* group), another third were instructed to think about becoming physically fit while punching the bag (the *distraction* group), and the remaining third simply sat quietly for a comparable period (the *control* group). Subsequent measurement of participants' anger revealed that, in direct opposition to the theorized effect of catharsis, those in the rumination group were angrier than those in the distraction and control groups and more aggressive on a later task.

Social Support and Stress

Investigations of the causal pathways between social support and health have been heavily influenced by Cohen and Wills's (1985) conjecture that social support may benefit health in two ways. First, there may be a direct relationship between support and well-being such that the more the support, the higher the well-being. The **direct effects hypothesis of social support** would predict, for example, that people who enjoy social support may take better care of their health for a variety of reasons, including others' encouragement of such health-enhancing behaviors as exercise, adequate nutrition, and optimal weight maintenance. Second, social support may promote health by "buffering" the effects of stress, which long has been known to be destructive of health (see, e.g., Salovey et al., 2000). The **stress-buffering effect hypothesis** posits that perceived social support protects and enhances well-being *only* if stress is experienced and has no effect when stress is absent. However, few people manage to live through a day, much less a life, without experiencing stress, so it is likely that most people who enjoy social support receive this health benefit if the hypothesis is true.

Of the two pathways through which social support may promote health, it is the stress-buffering hypothesis that has attracted the most interest, perhaps because stress long has been known to be harmful to health and anything that significantly reduces stress or its effects is of great potential importance.

Stress and Health

The renowned physiologist Walter B. Cannon (1929, 1932) was among the first to use the term "stress" and study its physiological effects. He found that when people are confronted with an environmental change such as lack of oxygen or extreme heat that threatens their welfare and survival, they exhibit a syndrome of physiological responses that Cannon named the **fight-or-flight reaction**. This emergency reaction includes changes in the cardiovascular system (e.g., increased blood pressure and heart rate), the endocrine system (e.g., increased release of such hormones as epinephrine [or adrenaline] and cortisol), and the immune system (e.g., a decrease in the production of cells that support the lymph nodes and rid the body of such foreign materials as bacteria, viruses, parasites, and fungi) that lower immunocompetence. These physiological changes work together in concert to mobilize the body's energy resources to help the individual defend against the threat by attacking it or running away. Subjectively, people experiencing the fight-or-flight reaction may feel their heart pound, their face flush, their hands become sweaty, and their stomach full of "butterflies."

Theory and research have delved into the precise patterns of reaction of each of the principal systems involved in the fight-or-flight reaction and their permutations, interactions, and interfaces with each other and with yet other bodily systems. Many psychologists simply refer to the greater or lesser increase in activity—or "activation"—of the physiological systems involved in the fight-or-flight reaction as **physiological arousal**. Physiological arousal usually is assessed by instruments measuring galvanic skin response, heart rate, and blood pressure; where possible, blood samples are sometimes taken and assayed, often for hormone levels.

Today, the term **stress** usually is used to refer to the *process* by which people perceive and respond to events that threaten their welfare, whereas the term **stressor** is used to refer to the *event* that triggers the process of coping and adjusting to the threat. The stressor may be physical,

FIGURE 2.6 Walter Cannon.

such as fire, or psychological, such as a spouse's threat of divorce. **Psychological stress** is often defined as "a negative emotional experience accompanied by predictable biochemical, physiological, and behavioral changes that are directed toward adaptation either by manipulating the situation to alter the stressor or by accommodating its effects" (Baum, 1990).

Different people find different events stressful—what is perceived as threatening by one individual may not be seen as threatening by another. The **transactional model of stress** proposed by Richard Lazarus (e.g., Lazarus, 1993) and his colleagues posits that it is the *interaction* between the properties of an event and the properties of the person that determines whether an event will be perceived as threatening and will subsequently invoke coping responses. How an individual will respond to an event is theorized to depend on the individual's *cognitive appraisal* of the event as benign or threatening and, if threatening, whether the individual believes he or she can cope successfully with the demand. The process of stress thus is believed to be triggered by an event the individual perceives to be harmful *and* by an estimate that the personal re-

sources necessary to eliminate or reduce the stressor are not available.

Cannon (1929, 1932) believed that the persistence of a threatening stimulus—one that the individual could neither escape nor destroy—would result in "the persistent derangement of bodily functions" (p. 261), which eventually would cause illness. The physiological effects of prolonged or **chronic stressors** were detailed a few years later by Hans Selye (1936; 1956/1976/1978), generally regarded as the founder of **psychosomatic medicine**—the study of how the mind ("psycho") and body ("soma") interact to affect health. Selye's interest in chronic stressors came about by accident. As a young endocrinologist hoping to discover a new sex hormone, Selye was elated to see that the rats he injected with his concoctions of ovarian and placental extracts showed a distinct syndrome of physiological reactions. He assumed the rats were reacting to the new hormone, but to make sure, he injected them with other organ extracts. When Selye saw the rats display the same syndrome of physiological responses they had previously, the horrific thought occurred to him that perhaps he had not distilled his extracts properly—perhaps the rats were simply responding to impurities in his extracts. To check whether the syndrome of response he had observed could have been produced by any impure substance, he injected the rats with a poisonous fluid used to fix tissue samples for microscopic examination. The rats' physiological responses to the fixative were the same as those they had displayed to the organ extracts! Selye (1978) recalls, "I do not think I had ever been more profoundly disappointed! Suddenly all my dreams of discovering a new hormone were shattered. All the time and all the materials that went into this long study were wasted" (p. 27).

The rats Selye injected with the toxic substance, like the rats injected with organ extracts, exhibited a syndrome of physiological reactions that suggested their bodies were mobilizing to try to adapt to the noxious agent. Trained as a physician, Selye recalled the general "cures" physicians have used for centuries—immersion in ice water, bloodlet-

FIGURE 2.7 Hans Selye.

by Diverse Nocuous Agents." The editors insisted he call his syndrome the **general adaptation syndrome**; Selye had named it the stress syndrome, but the biologically oriented editors thought that phrase implied "nervous strain" and was too psychological. The syndrome progressed through three stages: first, an *alarm* reaction, in which the organism mobilizes its forces to cope with the stressor (this is the fight-or-flight emergency reaction Cannon had identified); second, a stage of *adaptation*, or resistance, in which physiological arousal drops somewhat but remains at a relatively high level as the body continues to try to defend against the stressor; and third, a stage of *exhaustion*, in which the prolonged exposure to the stressor has depleted the body's energy resources, often in turn leading to disease and, sometimes, to bodily collapse and death (Figure 2.8).

Selye's general adaptation syndrome is still producing "miraculous" cures. For example, a Harvard Medical School oncologist thought he had been given the wrong file because the x-rays of his patient's lungs, which had been riddled with tumors just months before, appeared to be completely clear ("Priming the Body's Natural Defenses," 2000). The physician, Dr. Frank Haluska, subsequently learned that his patient had been operated on for a brain tumor since his last visit and his surgical incision had become severely infected. The patient's feverish response to the infection apparently eradicated not only the infection but also the lung tumors.

ting by applying leeches or cutting veins, prescribing goat urine elixirs, inducing fever by injecting germs of every variety, and, for the mentally ill, flogging or applying severe electric shock. These treatments often worked. No one knew *why*, but they worked often enough that physicians continued to use them. Selye wondered if such treatments sometimes worked because a sudden stressful event of *any* kind, such as injection of a toxic substance, generated a syndrome of strong physiological reactions that sometimes, as an incidental by-product, caused patients to "snap out" of a lingering disease or cured whatever had been ailing them.

After conducting numerous experiments in which he demonstrated that many different types of persistent physical stressors, including extreme heat and cold as well as injections of foreign materials, produced the same general pattern of physiological reactions, Selye (1936) published in the British journal *Nature* an article of only 74 lines titled "A Syndrome Produced

Allostatic Load

Cannon (1932) coined the word **homeostasis** (meaning "similar position" in Greek) to refer to the maintenance of equilibrium in bodily processes:

FIGURE 2.8 The general adaptation syndrome.
Selye identified a three-phase response to stressors in which the organism mobilizes its resources to cope with the stressor (the alarm phase), continues to defend against the stressor (the adaptation phase), and finally becomes exhausted and ill and/or dies as the body's energy resources are depleted (the exhaustion phase).

for example, when blood pressure rises, counterbalancing processes bring it down to its basal level. Useful as the concept of homeostasis has proved to be, Sterling and Eyer (1988) questioned how adequately it describes the operation of bodily processes in people actually going about their daily lives. These theorists were seeking answers to such puzzles as "Why does blood pressure increase with age in modern societies?" "Why does this rise seem to start at the age children enter school?" "Why is it that a large cohort of youth entering the labor market during an economic contraction has a higher death rate from all causes than a small cohort entering the labor market during an economic expansion?" and "Why is social disruption, such as mass immigration or war, associated with higher mortality rates?" No explanations were available in physiology textbooks, perhaps because, Sterling and Eyer muse, "the dominant conceptual model in physiology for a century has viewed the body as operating almost independently of the brain" (p. 631).

Most of the evidence in support of Cannon's homeostasis thesis was gathered from observations of organs and tissues surgically removed from the individual—and thus studied in isolation from other organs, including the brain. Sterling and Eyer (1988) dryly comment, "It turns out that most organs function remarkably well when they are disconnected from the rest of the body and brain and placed in a dish" (p. 631). However, the operation of physiological systems in an intact, unanesthetized person functioning in his or her natural habitat does not remain constant—normally functioning bodily systems *fluctuate* across an operating range in their levels of activity as the individual responds and adapts to environmental demands. For example, blood pressure is rarely stable over a day or even part of a day. There often are periods of elevation, such as while the individual is working in a stressful job or heatedly arguing with a roommate, and periods in which blood pressure is much lower, such as while listening to music, doing a crossword puzzle, or snuggling with a pet. Sterling and Eyer coined the word **allostasis** (meaning "stability through change") to refer to the body's ability to increase or decrease the rate of bodily functions to a new steady state in response to environmental challenges.

By inducing bodily systems to move to a new steady state of operation, environmental challenges not only increase the activity level of those systems; they increase, too, the activity of counterbalancing systems. McEwen and Stellar (1993) reason that dramatic changes in the operating range of physiological systems wreak "wear and tear" on those systems. They use the analogy of a seesaw with two heavy weights on either end compared to one with two lighter weights. Although the seesaw is balanced in both cases, it is subjected to more strain with the heavy weights than with the light weights. Moreover, even when the environmental demand is removed, the body may take some time to return to a lower level of activation; in fact, some systems may become "stuck" at the higher level of activity. For example, blood pressure may remain at a high level through classical conditioning and other processes. McEwen and Stellar define **allostatic load** as the strain on the body produced by repeated ups and downs of physiological response, as well as the elevated activity of these systems as they respond to prolonged environmental demand. Allostatic load thus represents the *cumulative* price the body has paid over time to cope with environmental demands. Indicators of high allostatic load include departures from normal blood pressure, cholesterol ratio, and urinary cortisol levels and other measures (Ryff, Singer, Wing, & Love, 2001, p. 160). High allostatic load is predictive of lowered immunocompetence (Herbert & Cohen, 1993; A. O'Leary, 1990) as well as cardiovascular disease, decline in physical function, memory loss, and elevated mortality risk (see Seeman, 2001; Seeman, Singer, Rowe, Horwitz, & McEwen, 1997).

Relationships and Stress

Among the first studies to suggest that social relationships could reduce stress were those conducted by social psychologist Bibb Latané and his colleagues (e.g., Latané & Glass, 1968), who demonstrated that rats placed in a fear-arousing situation when accompanied by a fellow rat responded with less fear than rats who confronted the stressful situation alone or rats who had only a toy car for companionship. The effect held even when the companion rat was anesthetized and immobile.

A similar effect was also found by psychoneuroimmunologist Coe and his associates (see Coe & Lubach, 2001), who measured immune response in monkeys who had been weaned and removed from their mothers at 6 months and housed either with other monkeys or alone. Although all exhibited immune alteration, those housed with other monkeys showed less alteration than those housed alone. The investigators also found that infants who were removed from their mother at 6 months showed more immune alteration than monkeys housed continuously with their mothers, and that the most dramatic deviation from normal immune response occurred when the monkey was raised from birth by humans (as Harlow's monkey infants were, suggesting that although they had been protected against tuberculosis, they had become more vulnerable to disease in general). These investigators conclude that the mother is critical for establishing normal immunity in the infant. In addition, because deviant immune response was still present when the monkeys were examined at 2.5 years of age, they speculate that early relationship disruption may establish a lifelong bias for disease.

In sum, it appears that some degree of social support is provided by the mere passive presence of a familiar conspecific (not necessarily the caregiver or attachment figure). The operative word is "familiar," however, because the introduction of a stranger is a highly stressful event for most animals, including humans. Familiar surroundings also may be important; Coe and his associates found that if the monkey's companions are removed, immune alteration is reduced if the individual remains in his or her home environment rather than being relocated.

Social support also has been shown to reduce stress in human adults. Gerin, Pieper, Levy, and Pickering's (1992) experimental participants were subjected to verbal attack during a group discussion of a controversial issue. The discussion group was composed of the participant and three other persons who, unknown to the participant, were confederates of the experimenters. During the discussion, two of the confederates were instructed by the experimenters to disagree and argue with the participant (thereby inducing stress). In half of the groups, the third confederate was instructed to defend the participant's position (the *social support* condition), whereas in the other half, the third confederate was instructed to simply sit quietly while the participant was under attack (the *no support* condition). Continuous blood pressure and heart rate measures revealed that participants in the social support condition showed significantly smaller increases in these cardiovascular measures than did those in the no support condition, thus providing evidence that social support did seem to reduce stress.

The concept of allostatic load, as noted, highlights the *cumulative* effects of stress over an individual's lifetime. Several studies have now documented that chronically stressful relationships are associated with poorer physical health (Seeman, 1996); for example, enduring interpersonal difficulties with family or friends are associated with susceptibility to the common cold (Cohen et al., 1998). The association is also evident in preliminary findings from the Wisconsin Longitudinal Study (see Ryff et al., 2001), a long-term survey of a random sample of over 10,000 men and women who graduated from Wisconsin high schools in 1957. This study examines associations between current measures of allostatic load (e.g., blood pressure) and adult participants' recollections of the positive and negative aspects of their early relationship with their parents and the positive and negative aspects of their current relationship with a significant other (usually the spouse). Overall, people with more negative (relative to positive) relationship experiences exhibit high allostatic load, presumably reflecting the excessive wear and tear their physiological systems have borne in adjusting to the challenges of negative relationship experiences. Although a higher ratio of cumulative negative to positive relationship experiences is associated with high allostatic load for *both* men and women, the association is more pronounced for men than for women.

Many studies now have examined the associations between stress, social support, and cardiovascular, endocrine, and immune system functioning in humans (e.g., Kiecolt-Glaser et al., 1984; see Kiecolt-Glaser, McGuire, Robles, & Glaser, 2002). From their meta-analyses of these studies, Uchino and colleagues (1996) conclude that social support is reliably associated with beneficial effects on aspects of these systems. This appears to be especially true for men (Stroebe & Stroebe, 1996, p. 608). Moreover, social support has been shown to improve adjustment to specific illnesses (e.g., cancer, Helgeson & Cohen, 1996). Some investigators find direct effects (e.g., Jemmott & Magloire, 1988), others show stress-buffering (or allostatic load–reducing) effects (e.g., Gerin et al., 1992), and still others, like Rook (1987), have found both direct and stress-buffering effects in a single study, each associated with a different measure of social integration.

Although the available evidence indicates that social support is beneficial to immune functioning, Cohen and Herbert (1996) conclude from their review of the relevant studies that it has not yet been established that the size of the effects (low to moderate) are of sufficient magnitude and reliability to prevent illness. Along with many other health psychologists, however, they believe that in addition to protecting immune function to some degree, the direct effects of social support may include the fostering of such health-enhancing behaviors as lower rates of smoking and alcohol consumption, higher rates of exercise, good nutrition, and other health-promoting behaviors (see Salovey et al., 2000).

Family Relationships and Stress

Uchino and associates' (1996) meta-analyses of social support and immune function suggest that familial ties are an especially important source of social support. That hypothesis is currently receiving much attention not only from social support researchers (Cutrona, 1996; Pierce, Sarason, & Sarason, 1996) but also from psychoneuroimmunologists, as the Wisconsin Longitudinal Study reflects. One outgrowth of such research

has been the realization that even happy family relationships are not invariably supportive; hence, investigators need to examine social support within the context of relationships and to examine both the positive and negative aspects of those relationships. One researcher studying the effects of social support in couples in which one or both had fallen ill comments:

> Not all support is positive, even if well intended. The line between support, smothering, and controlling is not clear. Not all people need or want the same type of support, and not every healthy partner knows what type of support is desired or is capable of providing that type of support. (Turk, 2000, p. xiii)

The health effects of the marital relationship have received the most attention. Marital status is almost always a central component (and sometimes the only component, as noted earlier) of measures of social integration. Morbidity and mortality risk remains significantly lower for the married than the unmarried (e.g., Gordon & Rosenthal, 1995; Seeman, 2001). However, the marriage–mortality association is considerably stronger for husbands than for wives. Relative to their married counterparts, single women have 50% greater mortality than their married counterparts, whereas single men have a 250% greater mortality than married men do (Ross, Mirowsky, & Goldsteen, 1990).

Researchers continue to try to identify the causal pathways responsible for the marriage–health association. An early review suggested that the effects of marital status and other specific relationship variables on health outcomes would not be easily identified because they seemed to be indirect and diffuse (Burman & Margolin, 1992). However, Kiecolt-Glaser and Newton (2001) conclude from their review of further evidence that when the *quality* of the marital relationship is considered, health effects are apparent. For example, as contrasted to happy marriages, unhappy marriages are associated with a 2.5-fold increase in risk for major depressive disorder (Weissman, 1987); depression itself, from any cause, is associated with adverse immunological alterations (Herbert &

Cohen, 1993; Weisse, 1992). In an especially valuable longitudinal study in which physical illness and marital quality were tracked for each of 364 wives and husbands over 3 years, Wickrama, Lorenz, Conger, and Elder, Jr. (1997) found that, even after controlling for work stress, education, and income, there was a strong negative association between an individual's marital quality and his or her likelihood of becoming physically ill; no difference in the size of this correlation was observed for husbands and wives. Although marital quality and physical illness are probably causally reciprocal, the investigators found suggestive evidence that marital quality may be more likely to affect the probability of illness than the reverse.

Conflict is often the source of negative emotional experiences and poor relationship quality in married couples. Kiecolt-Glaser, Malarkey, Cacioppo, and Glaser (1994) examined 90 newlywed couples, selected to be in excellent health, who were admitted to a hospital research unit for purposes of study. Each couple was asked to discuss areas of disagreement for 30 minutes. Measurements of neuroendocrine activity collected immediately before, during, and 15 minutes after the conflict discussion showed that negative and hostile behavior exhibited in the interaction produced changes associated with immunological downregulation. The differences between the high and low hostility groups were relatively larger for women than for men. The finding that wives were more affected by hostile interactions with their spouses than husbands is consistent with other findings (see Groth, Fehm-Wolfsdorf, & Hahlweg, 2000).

Blood samples drawn by Kiecolt-Glaser and her colleagues (1994) for immunological analyses on entry and exit from the hospital also revealed that spouses who engaged in *highly negative* behavior showed greater decrements in measures of immunological function and larger and more persistent increases in blood pressure than those who were less negative, a finding also consistent with those of other investigators. Noting that the couples in their study were young and exceptionally healthy, the investigators speculate that these findings may have special import for older,

conflict-ridden couples because immune function typically declines with age and infectious illness is the fourth leading cause of mortality among older adults.

In contrast to negative behaviors, the positive discussion behaviors of Kiecolt-Glaser and colleagues' (1994) couples were not associated with immunological or blood pressure changes. This finding also is consistent with those of other investigators. For example, Ewart, Taylor, Kraemer, and Agras (1991), who examined the association between blood pressure and marital discord, telegraphed their results in the title of their report: "Not Being Nasty Matters More Than Being Nice." Their findings may be yet another instance of a general principle that the impact of bad events tends to outweigh the impact of good events over a wide range of psychological phenomena (see Taylor, 1991; Baumeister, Bratslavsky, Finkenauer, & Vohs, 2001).

As these studies illustrate, researchers now recognize that in order to adequately measure the association between relationship quality and health, it is necessary to assess the positive and negative aspects of a relationship separately, for their effects may be independent (as discussed further in Chapter 9, "Affective Processes"). For example, using the Rochester Interaction Record, Gable, Reis, and Elliot (2000) found that, not surprisingly, positive social events that had occurred during the day were associated with higher positive mood ratings at the end of the day, whereas negative social events were associated with higher negative mood ratings. However, the functional independence of positive and negative social events was revealed by the fact that positive events were not associated with negative mood (that is, the occurrence of positive events did not make negative mood more or less likely), and similarly, negative events were not associated with positive mood (did not make positive mood more or less likely).

Conflict is not the only common source of stress in marital relationships; caregiving is another, especially for older couples (see Schmaling & Sher, 2000). Kiecolt-Glaser and her colleagues (1994) examined changes in depression, immunity, and health in a group of spousal caregivers who had been providing care for an average of 5 years to their partners who were suffering from Alzheimer's disease. Relative to noncaregiving controls, caregivers showed decrements on three immunological measures and showed substantially greater incidence of depressive disorders during the 13-month interval between the initial measures and the follow-up measures. Caregivers who reported lower levels of social support initially and who were most distressed by the dementia-related behaviors of their spouse showed the greatest negative changes in immune function at follow-up.

ADVERSE EFFECTS OF RELATIONSHIPS ON HEALTH

Many researchers, not just those investigating the relationship–health association, have come to recognize that many, perhaps most, close relationships have a dark side (see Spitzberg & Cupach, 1998). For example, Harter (1999) asked adolescents to "think back to the most depressing thing that has happened to you in the past year" (p. 217) and to describe the event. Of the eight categories of events these teenagers described, seven dealt with relationship problems such as rejection, conflict, separation, and loneliness. Similarly, when a representative sample of more than 2,000 American adults were interviewed and asked to describe "the last bad thing that happened to you," half recounted an interpersonal event, primarily disruption of a significant relationship or relationship conflict (Veroff, Douvan, & Kulka, 1981); moreover, of those people who had sought professional help, nearly two-thirds said it was for a relationship problem. Troubled relationships are indeed the most common presenting problem of psychotherapy seekers (e.g., Pinsker, Nepps, Redfield, & Winston, 1985), again testifying to the fact that although relationships are a source of social support for many people, not all relationships enhance health (Coyne & Downey, 1991; Rook & Pietromonaco, 1987).

Physical Aggression and Violence

Some relationships are not merely somewhat negative but highly toxic—even lethal. The U.S. Department of Justice reports that about half of victims of violent crime are attacked by an intimate partner, with another third attacked by other family members; only 20% of such crimes are committed by strangers ("Just 20%," 2001). Nevertheless, physical aggression and violence in romantic, marital, and family relationships received little attention from health professionals until the 1980s, a neglect that has been attributed by some observers to societal norms that have supported men's domination of women and the use of physical aggression against wives and children (O'Leary & Cascardi, 1998).

Neglect of violence in close relationships came to a screeching halt in 1980 when mental health professionals and the general public alike were shocked by data reported in a book by family sociologists Straus, Gelles, and Steinmetz, *Behind Closed Doors: Violence in the American Family*. In a nationally representative sample of husbands and wives, approximately 12% of the husbands and 12% of the wives had engaged in physical aggression against their partners during the past year. Moreover, 3.8% of the wives had been beaten by their husbands the previous year, and—surprising to the investigators and the public as well—4.6% of the husbands had been beaten by their wives. These data suggested to some that the family may be the most violent institution in America. The National Family Violence Survey now puts the yearly percentage of marital violence at 16% (Christopher & Lloyd, 2000).

After Straus and associates (1980) opened the closed door on marital violence, research on aggression and violence in close relationships increased dramatically (see Christopher & Lloyd, 2000). Nevertheless, theory and research on relationship violence remain uncohesive, partly because many findings and interpretations engage important public policy issues and incite controversy. Even the word "violence" is politically sensitive. As Muehlenhard and Kimes (1999) discuss, what counts as an act of violence is socially constructed and varies over time: "Whose behavior gets defined as violent and under what circumstances, and who gets to decide this, reflects the interests of those in power" (p. 234).

Straus and colleagues' (1980) report of an unexpectedly high rate of physically aggressive acts performed by wives almost instantly became controversial. The finding startled many people because men, overall, are more physically aggressive than women (e.g., Baron & Richardson, 1994). There are at least two opposing views of partner violence in heterosexual relationships (see Archer, 2000a). Some researchers who study family conflict, such as Straus and his colleagues (1980), believe there is a high degree of aggression by *both* men and women, and thus they emphasize causal influences that are common to both sexes, such as alcohol and conflict-aroused anger. Other researchers believe that violence in heterosexual relationships involves mostly male perpetrators and female victims and that the measures used by family conflict researchers do not consider the context and the consequences of physically aggressive acts.

Confounding these two opposing views of violence in heterosexual relationships is the fact that, as Johnson (1995; Johnson & Ferraro, 2000) observes, family conflict researchers typically study representative samples of the population as opposed to clinical samples. Moreover, they principally study what Johnson calls *common couple violence*, which mostly involves lapses of control by the partners which result in pushing, shoving, slapping, and kicking—behaviors usually not associated with injury and fear of the partner and which, some contend, have become almost normative behaviors in some segments of the population. Johnson maintains that common couple violence is to be contrasted to three other types of relationship violence: *intimate terrorism*, in which violence is only one tactic in a general pattern of control and is less likely to be mutual and more likely to escalate over time and result in serious injury; *violent resistance*, which is more likely to be perpetrated by women in response to partner violence and often in self-defense; and *mutual violent control*, which, Johnson notes, can be viewed as two intimate terrorists battling for control.

Whereas family conflict researchers tend to study representative samples from the general population, and thus common couple violence, those who believe men usually are the perpetrators and women their victims tend to study violence in small clinical populations, such as women in refuge shelters and men in wife-battering treatment programs. Such violence, Johnson (1995) believes, often represents *patriarchal terrorism* because its roots lie in cultural norms and beliefs that support husbands' control of their wives. Thus, the two opposing viewpoints of relationship violence are believed to stem from the two groups of researchers using (1) different samples of people (representative vs. clinical samples), (2) different measures of violence (e.g., kicking and shoving vs. murder), and (3) different theoretical approaches (lapses of self-control vs. patriarchal terrorism).

To reconcile the opposing viewpoints and conflicting data, Archer (2000a) performed a meta-analytic review of studies examining sex differences in physical aggression and its consequences within heterosexual relationships. It should be borne in mind that what one gets out of a meta-analysis depends on the nature of the studies available to be included in the analysis. Most of the available studies of physical aggression in relationships have used Straus's (1980) Conflict Tactics Scale to measure aggression, and most also have studied community and representative samples (with about half of these composed of high school or college students) as opposed to clinical samples. Archer concludes from his analyses that, at least in heterosexual relationships, women are slightly *more* likely than men to use one or more acts of physical aggression—and to use such acts more frequently. Men, however, are more likely to inflict an injury; overall, 62% of those injured are women.

Data from sources outside the United States, though limited, suggest that the pattern of more women than men using physical aggression is not restricted to this country. According to Archer, the pattern of women being more likely to physically aggress was even stronger for three other Western nations. The United States does differ from other countries, however, in one respect: Wilson and Daly (1992) found that in dramatic contrast to Canada, Australia, and Great Britain, wives in the United States kill their husbands almost as often as U.S. husbands kill their wives. They also concluded that the greater frequency with which U.S. wives kill their husbands cannot be attributed to greater gun use in the United States, and none of the other data they examined could sufficiently account for the observed difference between the victim sex ratios in these countries.

Archer found suggestive evidence that the occurrence of violence in intimate relationships may be influenced by two conflicting social norms that act as moderator variables. (A **moderator variable** increases or decreases the rate at which a behavior is performed—in this case, the rate at which men engage in aggressive behavior; see Baron & Kenny, 1986.) The first of these norms, often cited by feminist commentators, is associated with patriarchal values in the United States and elsewhere that accept and even encourage wife-beating. In contemporary Western societies, however, there is a second norm that prescribes that men should restrain themselves from physically aggressing toward women. Archer presents evidence suggesting that men's physical aggression toward their partners is greater in societies where patriarchal values are strong and norms inhibiting men from hitting women are absent. In the United States, the two opposing norms exist side by side; differential salience and acceptance of each norm may moderate the degree of violence observed by different individuals and within different American subcultures.

K. D. O'Leary (2000), a leading researcher of violence in dating and marital relationships, accepts Archer's findings for representative samples of the population but believes he may not have emphasized enough that few samples of battered women were available to be included in his analyses. Men in clinical samples engage in aggression against their partners more frequently than the women do. Moreover, O'Leary points out, the answer to the question of whether there are sex differences in violence depends on what behaviors are termed "violent." Most studies investigate common forms of physical aggression;

they often do not examine murder and acts of sexual aggression, such as rape or stalking. For example, Archer could not include studies of sexual aggression in his analyses because he could find too few studies that included reports of such behavior by both men and women. O'Leary contends that when murder and sexual aggression are considered, the data consistently show that men are more aggressive than women. Nevertheless, when injuries of *any* kind and severity are considered, Archer's analyses reveal that although women suffer more injuries than men, the difference is small. Thus, it is *not* the case that women's violence toward men does not cause injury or that the incidence of women's violence toward men is negligible.

O'Leary also emphasizes that men and women who engage in the milder forms of aggression must be distinguished from those who engage in severely aggressive behaviors (who typically appear in clinical samples). Moreover, physical aggression in teenagers and in young engaged or married couples, he argues, has different meaning and consequences than partner aggression in midlife; the latter may have become habitual and is usually associated with chronic marital discord. The association between physical aggression against intimate partners and age is represented by an inverted U-shaped curve: Low rates are observed in the young, but physical aggression increases dramatically between ages 15–25; after age 25 it starts to decrease and continues to diminish across the life span (O'Leary & Cascardi, 1998).

Psychological Aggression

When we think of lethal relationships, we usually think of physical violence, but psychological violence also kills. Seligman (1975) relates a case history recorded in the *Journal of Psychosomatic Medicine* (Mathis, 1964) that illustrates how subtle, but at the same time how powerful, the effects of a toxic relationship can be:

A healthy, middle-aged man had spent most of his life in the shadow of his mother. Fatherless, he described her as "a wonderful lady who made all the family decisions correctly and who never met a situation she could not control." At 31, financed by his mother, he bought a nightclub and she helped him run it. At 38 he married, and his wife, not surprisingly, began to resent his dependence on his mother. When he received a profitable offer to sell the nightclub, he told his mother he was considering it, and she became distraught. Finally, he decided to sell. His mother told him, "Do this, and something dire will happen to you."

Two days later he had his first asthma attack. He had no previous history of respiratory illness and had not even had a cold in ten years. The day after he closed the sale, his asthma attacks became much worse when his mother told him angrily that "Something will strike you." He now became depressed and frequently protested that he was helpless. With psychiatric help, he began to see the connection between the asthma attacks and his mother's "curse"; he improved greatly. His psychiatrist saw him for a 30-minute session at 5:00 p.m. on August 23 and found him in excellent physical and mental shape. At 5:30 he called his mother to tell her that he planned to reinvest in a new business without her help. She reminded him of her curse and told him to prepare for "dire results." At 6:35 he was found gasping for breath, cyanotic and in coma. He died at 6:55. (pp. 175–176)

"Heart failure"—not "homicide"—was no doubt written on this man's death certificate. Some, however, will recognize his collapse as an instance of "voodoo death," a phenomenon also called "sudden death syndrome," first studied by the physiologist Walter Cannon (1942) and subsequently elucidated by research on the exhaustion phase of the general adaptation syndrome (Hughes & Lynch, 1978; Richter, 1955). Close relationships are, by definition, influential, and the influence one partner exerts on the other can be deadly.

Some relationships, although not causing sudden death, are a chronic source of stress. Rook's contention (1984, 1998) that bad relationships diminish well-being more than good relationships enhance it was instrumental in spurring examination of debilitating relationships. To investigate the effects of both positive and negative social ties on the well-being of elderly widowed women, Rook assessed the extent to which they possessed *supportive* social relationships with people from whom they said they received emotional support and also the extent to which they had *problematic* relationships. The number of supportive people reported was unassociated with the number of problematic others; thus, at least in this sample, positive and negative interpersonal experiences on a daily basis were relatively independent. When Rook examined the association between each of the two measures and the women's psychological well-being, she found that the number of problematic relationships was more strongly related to well-being than the number of supportive relationships; that is, although both positive and negative social ties were associated with well-being, negative ties seemed to have the greater impact—again, bad seemed to have more impact than good.

Almost all relationships are associated with at least some stress on a day-to-day basis and with both positive and negative interaction experiences. Even highly sought after and positively valued relationship experiences may be stressful, for they demand adaptation to new environmental conditions. Marriage and the birth of a child are examples (Holmes & Rahe, 1967). Moreover, the same partner who provides support on most occasions may undermine the individual on other occasions by reducing the individual's confidence and feelings of self-worth. **Social undermining** is defined as behaviors toward another that display (1) negative affect, such as anger; (2) negative evaluation or criticism of the person in terms of his or her attributes, actions, and efforts; and (3) behaviors that interfere with the attainment of the individual's goals (Vinokur & van Ryn, 1993).

Abbey, Abramis, and Caplan (1985) found that social support and social undermining had opposite effects of about the same magnitude on the health and well-being of college students. Although there was, not surprisingly, a negative correlation between support and undermining in close relationships, there is some evidence that support and undermining are not the opposite poles of the same factor (e.g., McCaskill & Lakey, 2000). For example, Vinokur and van Ryn (1993) examined over a 4-month period the perceived supportive and undermining behaviors of "significant others" in a sample of individuals who had lost their jobs and thus were experiencing a high level of stress. These investigators concluded that the effects of a close relationship partner's behavior on the individual's mental health could not be adequately accounted for by the partner's supportive behaviors alone and that the partner's undermining behavior may have had an even stronger impact on the individual's mental health than supportive behaviors did.

Bereavement

Those who love another living creature, whether human or animal, give a hostage to fortune. A price will be paid for the joys and benefits of a happy and satisfying close relationship when the relationship ends—and relationships always end, through rejection, involuntary separation, or death. Part of the price the individual will pay for the loss of a beloved partner is an increased risk of morbidity and mortality. Dissolution of a close relationship is a major life event, believed to be among the most stressful people experience (Holmes & Rahe, 1967).

The belief that people can die of a broken heart following the death of a loved person appears early in human history and in most cultures. For example, as early as 1657 the cause of 10 deaths in London was officially recorded as "griefe," according to Stroebe and Stroebe (1987, p. 2), and the earliest systematic study of the effects of bereavement on mortality was conducted in 1858 in France (the investigator concluded that the formerly married were most likely to die). Subsequently, Durkheim (1897/1963) found not only that weak social ties were associated with suicide but that the suicide risk of the widowed was much higher than that of comparable married people, a finding that continues to be corroborated and elaborated today. For example, one contemporary study found a peak in suicide rates of the widowed for the first week after their spouse's death as well as a highly significant sex difference—the excess in the suicide rate of wid-owed men over their married counterparts was 66-fold as contrasted to 9.6-fold for widowed women (see Stroebe & Stroebe, 1987).

Examinations of the causes of death among widowed persons find that, for many, their hearts—quite literally—broke. Stroebe and Stroebe (1987) examined the results of several studies that have looked at differences in the cause of death of widowed and married people and found that although coronary heart disease is the leading killer of all humans (followed by stroke and then cancer), cardiovascular diseases are to a large extent responsible for the *excess* in the mortality of the widowed compared to their married counterparts. Most studies find that the excess mortality risk of the widowed (over that expected of their married counterparts) is highest during the first 6 months after the loss of the spouse.

In addition to higher mortality rates, the bereaved also suffer higher morbidity rates. For example, recent bereavement is associated with depression, and again, men are more vulnerable than women; in turn, and as previously noted, depression from any cause has been shown to be associated with lowered immunocompetence (Weisse, 1992). Higher incidence of other psychiatric disorders also is associated with spousal bereavement, as are higher rates of disability, hospitalization, and drug and medication use. Stroebe and Stroebe (1987) conclude from their rigorous review, "We can say that the evidence from longitudinal and cross-sectional studies across all major areas in which normal and pathological grief reactions have been manifested all support the conclusion that the experience of partner loss is associated with health deterioration" (p. 167). They characterize the convergence of the findings as impressive, regardless of the method used or the health outcome variable chosen.

Loss of a Companion Animal

Although the bereavement literature has focused almost exclusively on the loss of a spouse, the loss of any close relationship should pose a threat to the bereaved person's health. Often overlooked is the grief experienced by those who have lost a beloved companion animal. Some studies have found that the grief associated with the loss of a pet is rivaled only by the loss of a person in the individual's immediate family (Figure 2.9). In their survey of over 1,500 families, Gage and Holcombe (1991) found that the death of a pet often causes more stress than many other life-changing events. Death of a pet was rated as less stressful than the death of a member of the immediate family or a close friend but more stressful than the death of another relative, the loss of a close friendship, the marriage of a family member, or a child leaving home.

People who lose a close relationship with a pet experience **disenfranchised grief**—grief that is not commonly recognized by society. As a result, no institutionalized rituals are available to these bereaved men, women, and children, who also typically receive little sympathy and social support following their loss. Loss of a pet is a common bereavement event for at least two reasons. First, many people have pets; some surveys suggest that more households in the United States now have pets than have children (see Gage & Holcombe, 1991; Melson, 1998). Second, unless the pet is an elephant or a tortoise, it is likely to die before its human companion. During Gage and Holcombe's study, more families reported experiencing pet loss than reported any other kind of stressful family event in the past year.

Bereavement upon the loss of a pet may be why "Dear Abby" replied the way she did to a 56-year-old woman who said her fiancé, described as perfect in every way except that he hated dogs, would not allow her to keep her beloved German shepherd after they married. Abby replied that if the woman wanted to enjoy life, she should keep the dog and get rid of her fiancé ("Fiance Hates Dogs," 2000). Perhaps the woman should have told her fiancé what Saint Bernard is alleged to have said about his dog, Barry, who found many winter travelers lost in the Swiss Alps and saved their lives by lying down beside them to keep them warm until human help arrived: "*Qui me amat, amat et canem meum*—Love me, love my dog" (Coren, 1998, p. 18).

FIGURE 2.9 Pet gravestone.

Although the loss of a pet is stressful, evidence is mounting that a relationship with a companion animal may confer health benefits similar to those provided by human companions (e.g., Serpell, 1991; Wilson & Turner, 1998). Heart researchers Friedmann and Thomas (1995) examined the effects of pet ownership, social support and other psychosocial factors, and disease severity on one-year survival after acute myocardial infarction and found that although the individual's physiological factors were the best independent predictors of survival (the physiological profile of dog owners did not differ from that of nonowners), dog ownership also made a significant, independent, and positive contribution. Social support also independently contributed to survival. The results for cat ownership were more complex and difficult to interpret—a finding that no doubt pleased many cats.

Pets also seem to have a stress-buffering effect. For example, Allen, Blascovich, Tomaka, and Kelsey (1991) measured women's autonomic responses during a standard experimental stress task in the laboratory with only the experimenter present and contrasted those responses to autonomic responses exhibited when the women performed the same task at home 2 weeks later in the presence of a female friend (*friend* condition), their dog (*pet* condition), or neither (*control* condition). Women in the pet condition showed less physiological reactivity during stressful tasks than women in the other two conditions. Women in the friend condition exhibited the highest physiological reactivity and the poorest performance. Evidence of the stress-buffering effect of pets was also provided by Allen, Blascovich, and Mendes (2002). Freud kept his dog in his treatment room because he believed that the animal's presence calmed and relaxed his patients. His belief seems to have been justified.

RELATIONSHIPS AND HAPPINESS

Despite the fact that relationships can be troubling, stressful, and even deadly, most of us are aware that we need relationships with others and that the quality of our lives depends on those relationships. From his review of studies that have examined the things people believe to be essential to their happiness, Argyle concludes that "social relationships are a major source of happiness, relief from distress, and health" (1986, p. 31), a conclusion reached by many others (e.g., Diener, 1984; Myers, 1993, 1999, 2000; Myers & Diener, 1995). A national survey of over 2,000 Americans found that people named marriage and family life as the major sources of their overall life satisfaction; less importance was given to work, housing, religious faith, and financial security (Campbell, Converse, & Rodgers, 1976). Summarizing the results of two early large-scale surveys of happiness, Freedman states, "There is no simple recipe for producing happiness, but all of the research indicates that for almost everyone one necessary ingredient is some kind of satisfying, intimate relationship" (1978, p. 48). Although individual differences in personality also are associated with happiness—for example, introverted and emotionally unstable people tend to be less happy than extraverts and emotionally stable individuals (see Russell & Wells, 1994)—close personal relationships seem to be important to most everyone's welfare.

Investigators of people's reports of **subjective well-being**, a combination of happiness and life satisfaction, obtain similar findings. For example, Ryan and Deci (2001) conclude from their review of the evidence that high well-being is associated with high-quality close relationships. Researchers of the determinants of subjective well-being initially focused on the role of the marital relationship, not only because this type of relationship is of importance to society and to the individual but also because marital status can easily be ascertained in surveys. Wood, Rhodes, and Whelan's (1989) meta-analysis of almost 100 studies relating marital status and reports of life satisfaction, happiness, and general well-being found that people who are married are, on average, happier than those who aren't.

The difference in happiness between married and single people is worldwide. Diener, Gohm, Suh, and Oishi (2000) examined a sample of more than 50,000 people in 42 nations and found that that the association between marital status and people's feelings of well-being held throughout the world. An association between marital status and happiness also was found in 16 of the 17 industrialized nations examined by Stack and Eshleman (1998), who determined that the link between marriage and happiness was 3.4 times stronger than the link between cohabitation and happiness. Unlike marriage, cohabitation was negatively associated with financial satisfaction and health, which were even more strongly associated with happiness than marital status by itself was.

Many studies have found that women are happier in general than men are (e.g., Wood, Rhodes, & Whelan, 1989). Married women also seem to be happier than married men, but the differences generally are not large (see Russell & Wells, 1994), and some investigators find married men and women about equally satisfied with their marriages (Feeney, Peterson, & Noller, 1994). Nevertheless, women tend to report experiencing more negative feelings and emotions within their marriages than men do, and they also tend to have more complaints about the marriage. Some investigators have suggested that whereas simply being married accounts for most of the increase in men's well-being, the *quality* of the marriage may be more important to women's subjective well-being (Gove, Hughes, & Style, 1983). Examining a number of correlates of happiness in a large sample of married couples, Russell and Wells (1994) found that for *both* men and women, happiness was most strongly associated with the individual's report of the quality of the marriage. Although such variables as extraversion had some impact on happiness, these investigators conclude that "compared to quality of marriage, other potential predictors pale into insignificance" (p. 318). There is suggestive evidence, however, that the size of the difference in happiness between married and single persons may be shrinking somewhat (Glenn & Weaver, 1988).

Because most studies of happiness and relationships are correlational, the nature of the causal link between the two is not clear. Happiness may be a causal factor in producing satisfying relationships; satisfying relationships may be a cause of happiness; and both happiness and satisfying relationships may be caused by other factor(s), such as health or certain personality trait constellations (Myers & Diener, 1995). With respect to factors that may influence both happiness and relationship satisfaction, Lykken and Tellegen (1996) claim that about half of the variance in subjective well-being is associated with genetic factors. They speculate that genetically based predispositions to positive or negative affectivity are causally responsible for behaviors that promote or disturb interpersonal relationships.

Over and above genetic factors that may predispose an individual to be happy or unhappy (see Lykken, 1999), there is evidence that for almost everyone most of the time, relationships enhance subjective feelings of happiness beyond what they would otherwise be (see Reis, 2001). For example, people's affective states are generally more positive when they are in a social setting than when they are alone, and their mood changes accordingly when they leave or enter the presence of others (Delespaul, Reis, & deVries, 1996; Diener, Larsen, & Emmons, 1984; Larson & Csikszentmihalyi, 1983). Reis, Sheldon, Gable, Roscoe, and Ryan (2000) examined people's reports of the activities they had engaged in each day and found that self-reports of vitality and positive affect were associated with the extent to which the individual had been en-gaged that day in social interactions that were fun, involved meaningful conversation, and left the individual feeling understood.

Loneliness

Because satisfying close relationships are associated with happiness, it is not surprising that their absence is associated with unhappiness and the unpleasant psychological state of loneliness. In addition to being psychologically aversive, loneliness has been associated with impaired physical and mental health and suicide, as Durkheim (1897/1963) was the first to document.

Research on loneliness grew rapidly in the late 1970s and the 1980s (see reviews by Ernst & Cacioppo, 1999; Marangoni & Ickes, 1989; Rook, 1988). An important stimulant was Robert S. Weiss's publication of *Loneliness: The Experience of Emotional and Social Isolation* (1973), in which he asserted, "Loneliness is caused not by being alone but by being without some definite needed relationship or set of relationships" (p. 17). Each type of relational deficit, Weiss maintained, requires a different remedy:

> We have repeatedly found in our studies that a form of loneliness that appears in the absence of a close emotional attachment, which we characterize as "the loneliness of emotional isolation," can be only remedied by the integration of another emotional attachment or the reintegration of the one that had been lost.
>
> Conversely, we have found that the form of loneliness associated with the absence of an engaging social network—the "loneliness of social isolation"—can be remedied only by access to such a network. (pp. 18–19)

Although Weiss's distinction between emotional and social loneliness was neglected for many years, its usefulness now has been supported by several investigators (e.g., Vincenzi & Grabosky, 1989). DiTommaso and Spinner (1997) found that, at least in college students, emotional loneliness appears to be composed of two elements: *romantic* emotional loneliness and *family* emotional loneliness. Although emotional and social loneliness appear to be moderately correlated for both young and older adults, Green, Richardson, Lago, and Schatten-Jones (2001) found that people in both age groups reported less emotional loneliness when a romantic partner was in their network, but social loneliness was most strongly related to the size of the network for college students and to feelings of closeness to members of the network for older adults.

The growth of loneliness research was greatly facilitated by the development of the UCLA Loneliness Scale (Russell, Peplau, & Cutrona, 1980), a unidimensional scale that does not differentiate between emotional and social loneliness. Researchers quickly found that reported loneliness does not covary directly with amount of social contact (Rook, 1984). People can and do feel lonely in a crowd. Most researchers now believe that the experience of loneliness occurs when a person's existing social relationships are discrepant from the person's expected or desired relationships. Peplau and Perlman (1982), for example, define **loneliness** as a perceived discrepancy between the desired and the achieved pattern of social relationships. Because both loneliness and its presumed causes are typically assessed via the individual's self-reports, it is not clear whether the differences found between people who are lonely and people who are not reflect differences in their behavior or in their perceptions. Moreover, because most loneliness research is correlational and research on the causal processes involved in loneliness is sparse, it often is unclear whether a specific factor is a cause or an effect of loneliness (Ernst & Cacioppo, 1999).

Shaver, Furman, and Buhrmester (1985) distinguished between trait loneliness and state loneliness. **Trait loneliness** is viewed as enduring and cross-situational and linked to personality function and mental health. Among the dispositional factors associated with the experience of loneliness are shyness, depression, introversion, self-consciousness, low self-esteem, external locus of control, and insecure attachment style (Marangoni & Ickes, 1989). Loneliness also appears to be associated with such social skill deficiencies as a lack of assertiveness, situationally inappropriate self-disclosure, and greater self-focus and lesser responsiveness to partners (Jones, 1982; Rook, 1988). In addition, lonely people appear to make harsher judgments of others than do the nonlonely (Wittenberg & Reis, 1986), especially when they are personally involved with the other (Duck, Pond, & Leatham, 1994), and they also expect others to evaluate them negatively (Jones, Sansone, & Helm, 1983).

In contrast to trait loneliness, **state loneliness** is viewed as time-limited and strongly associated with individuals' social situations, such as those in which the individual feels rejected, misunderstood, and estranged from others or those in which desired activities must be forgone for lack of a partner. Another important situational factor associated with loneliness was identified by Wheeler, Reis, and Nezlek (1983). Using the **Rochester Interaction Record**, a diary method in which participants note, describe, and evaluate each of their daily social interactions that last 10 minutes or longer, Wheeler and colleagues found that an individual's subjectively felt loneliness is negatively associated with the amount of time the individual (whether male or female) spends interacting with women. Loneliness also is negatively associated with the degree of intimacy and disclosure in the individual's social interactions with persons of either sex.

State loneliness frequently is associated with transitional events, such as changing residence or terminating a close relationship—events that often change an individual's social network. Rands (1988) examined people's retrospective perceptions of the network changes they had experienced as a consequence of divorce, a major transitional event. Respondents described their social networks at each 3-month interval between Time 1 (defined as the most recent time before separation in which they felt reasonably confident that they would stay married) through Time 2 (defined as the point after separation when the respondent began to "feel like a single person again," which for most people was about 8 months after separation) and Time 3 (the present, which was about 2 years after separation for participants in this study). The network was defined as those persons with whom there had been actual exchanges during each interval.

Rands found that approximately 40% of an individual's Time 1 predivorce network had been dropped by Time 2, following separation. New additions to the network following divorce did not compensate for the decrease. Networks not only tended to be smaller after separation but network members were less apt to know one another. By Time 3, when respondents participated in the study, on average 51% of their initial associates remained. Network turnover thus appears to be highest immediately following divorce and then tapers off. These findings, as well as others (e.g., Milardo, 1987), underscore that often people who divorce lose many relationships, not just their relationship with their spouse. It is not surprising that the divorced may be lonely, especially immediately following the divorce.

Estimates of loneliness in national surveys range from 11% to 26% (Peplau, Russell, & Heim, 1979). Loneliness appears to be most prevalent during adolescence, declining gradually over the life span (Rubenstein & Shaver, 1982). As for sex differences, Borys and Perlman (1985) conclude from their review of the evidence that women tend to receive higher loneliness scores than men do on scales that explicitly use the words "lonely" or "loneliness"; scales that omit this word tend to find either no difference or higher loneliness among men. These findings are often attributed to men's relative unwillingness to admit to feeling lonely.

One important study that found sex differences in features of men and women's social networks was conducted by Fischer and Phillips (1982), who studied more than 1,000 randomly selected adults living in 50 Northern California communities. Defining social isolation as "knowing relatively few people who are probable sources of rewarding exchanges" (p. 22), these investigators asked their respondents to name (1) persons with whom they would discuss their worries, (2) persons whom they might ask to care for their homes if they went out of town, (3) persons from whom they might be able to borrow a large sum of money, and (4) those persons over 15 years old who lived in their own household. Fischer and Phillips included in the individual's

social network only those persons who were "readily available" (defined as living within a 1-hour drive) to provide the respondent with a rewarding interaction. By this criterion, the average person's network consisted of 10.6 names. From their data, Fischer and Phillips concluded that, all else being equal,

(1) for both genders, high social status, especially more education, leads to less chance of moderate isolation from nonkin, but more chance of moderate isolation from kin; (2) for men, aging is strongly associated with isolation of all kinds (but being married protects them from kin isolation); (3) for women, a marriage, even if terminated, increases the risk of isolation from nonkin. (p. 30)

Fischer and Phillips also investigated whether the individual had a "confidant"—someone with whom he or she could discuss personal matters and whose opinion was considered in making important decisions. Spouses were most commonly named as confidants, especially by men, and other close relatives also were overrepresented. But 30% of the respondents had not one person in whom they could confide, and an additional 18% named only one confidant (who tended to be their spouse). Poorly educated people named fewer confidants, and older people, especially men, tended not to have any confidant at all. Overall, in fact, men were more likely than women to have no, or only one, confidant; 20% of the men named no confidants outside of their own households, as contrasted to 9% of the women.

Underscoring the importance of considering people's psychological reactions to objectively assessed social isolation, however, Fischer and Phillips found that having a small network did not greatly influence the individual's assessment of the adequacy of that network. Moreover, very few of their respondents said that they wished they knew more people. Nevertheless, isolated people were significantly less likely than others to say they were happy. Thus, although people with small networks may not necessarily desire more relationships, they may be adversely affected by their isolation (and unaware of its cause). On the other hand, it may be that people who are unhappy for other reasons do not desire to interact with others and, in fact, may actively avoid social interaction.

Although most loneliness and social network studies have been conducted in the United States, an exception is Sumbadze's (1999) study of a sample of residents of Georgia, a country recently separated from the Soviet Union, that used Moreno's (1947) little-known Social Atom Test (the "social atom" being defined as the smallest social unit containing a person's emotional relationships). The test permits the respondent to report not only actual relationships but also relationships with deceased and inaccessible persons, animals, and objects that are emotionally important to him or her, somewhat similar to Surra and Milardo's (1991) concept of "psychological network." Sumbadze's respondents named an average of 11.3 emotionally significant relationships, the number decreasing significantly with age, particularly for men. Among these people, 71% named friendships, 66% named relationships with deceased or inaccessible persons, 65% named immediate kin, and 65% named animals or objects. For Georgian men, the proportion of nonactual relationships (e.g., with objects or deceased persons) increased sharply with age. When the respondents' positive or negative evaluations of each relationships were examined, it was found that whereas the percentage of negatively evaluated relationships increased with age for both men and women, the increase was particularly dramatic for men. Disliked relationships, in fact, represented one-fifth of the men's emotionally important relationships (although it is not clear whether these were actual or nonactual relationships).

Sumbadze's finding of a decrease in the number of emotionally important relationships with age is in accord with Carstensen's (1991) socioemotional selectivity theory, which attempts to account for age-related reductions in social contact. The theory posits that social contact is motivated by a variety of goals, such as physical protection or the experience of pleasant emotions and feelings, whose importance fluctuates depending on the individual's place in the life cycle. Regulation of emotion—for example, by avoidance of troubling and negative emotion-arousing contacts—is theorized to become increasingly salient with age, whereas

such goals as the acquisition of information is posited to decrease in importance. Lang and Carstensen (1994) find that the social networks of very old people in the United States are nearly half as large as those of younger (but still old) people, but the number of very close relationships does not differentiate these age groups. The evidence thus suggests that as people age, they appear to become increasingly selective in their choice of relationships, presumably in an effort to optimize emotional enhancement and social functioning (Fredrickson & Carstensen, 1990). Green and colleagues' (2001) finding that social loneliness was more associated with the size of the network for young people but closeness to network members for older adults also supports Carstensen's theory.

SUMMARY

Researchers have assembled extensive evidence that interpersonal relationships influence physical and mental health and longevity. Persons who possess strong ties to the community and social institutions, and who have a supportive network of family, friends, and other close associates, tend to exhibit better health and a lower risk of mortality than less integrated individuals. Although the precise manner in which social integration influences health is not yet clear, many researchers believe that social support is the critical mediating factor. People who are socially integrated are believed to have greater access to actual social support, which leads to greater perceived social support, which in turn appears to have health benefits. Currently, social support researchers are turning their attention to support as it is given and received on a daily basis between partners in close relationships.

Although most close relationships are supportive, some may be a potent source of stress. Physical aggression, violence, emotional abuse, bereavement and grief, and other unpleasant interpersonal events occur with some frequency in many, if not most, close relationships and are associated with a multitude of adverse outcomes for the individual. However, most people recognize that relationships are essential for personal happiness. Research corroborates the belief that loneliness is alleviated and subjective well-being is enhanced by involvement in satisfying close relationships. In sum, relationships—both their presence and their absence in our lives—have important physical and psychological health consequences.

PART 2

RELATIONSHIP SCIENCE

Chapter 3

The Development of Relationship Science

INTRODUCTION

Historically, people have looked to philosophers, theologians, novelists, poets, biographers, composers, and other artists to gain a better understanding of their relationships. Treatises on various aspects of relationships date back thousands of years to Aristotle (Figure 3.1), who provided a lengthy analysis of friendship and romantic relationships in his *Ethica Nichomachea*. For example, he says that

> in the friendship of lovers sometimes the lover complains that his excess of love is not met by love in return (though perhaps there is nothing lovable about him), while often the beloved complains that the lover who formerly promised everything now performs nothing. Such incidents happen when the lover loves the beloved for the sake of pleasure while the beloved loves the lover for the sake of utility, and they do not both possess the qualities expected of them. If these be the objects of the friendship it is dissolved when they do not get the things that formed the motives of their love. (quoted in Ross, 1915/1966, p. 1163)

Given the important and pervasive role that relationships play in human life, and the interest people have shown in understanding their relationships throughout human history, it may seem surprising that a field of inquiry directly addressed to developing a systematic body of knowledge about interpersonal relationships was slow to develop. Its late emergence was partially due to the inherently multidisciplinary nature of relationship science and the fact that its development was dependent on progress in many disciplines in the social, behavioral, biological, and health sciences. In addition, the relationship field faced numerous challenges—societal, ethical, and methodological—some of which are still being confronted. In this chapter, we discuss the obstacles that hindered the study of interpersonal relationships and briefly describe the nature of the contributions many disciplines currently are making to the development of relationship knowledge.

The study of relationships did not secure a toehold in the scientific arena until the latter half of the nineteenth century when Darwin (1871/1952) became interested in relationship

Towards Understanding Relationships, Hinde focused attention on the many conceptual problems that needed to be solved before such an integration was possible, as did Kelley and his colleagues (1983/2002) in *Close Relationships*. Thus, by the early 1980s, the winds of the zeitgeist were blowing toward the development of a formal science of relationships, and, as discussed more fully in Chapter 4, "The Concept of Relationship," work on conceptual problems was proceeding in earnest. A potent force in furthering recognition of the need for a science of relationships was the dramatic increase in divorce that began in the late 1950s and early 1960s and, with it, the public's growing demand for understanding and help with their close relationships (see Berscheid & Peplau, 1983/2002).

OBSTACLES TO THE STUDY OF RELATIONSHIPS

Ironically, one of the greatest obstacles to the development of relationship science was societal prohibition against the study of relationships. The public's growing insistence in the 1970s that the social and behavioral sciences were obligated to provide information about the dynamics of close relationships represented a sea change in attitude.

Societal Taboos

Widespread belief that relationships, especially close relationships, were not an appropriate subject for scientific study was evident far into the twentieth century. Burgess and Wallin (1953), pioneering sociologists of marriage and the family, observed that this attitude held as recently as the 1950s:

> Love and marriage were regarded as belonging to the field of romance, not of science. The theory of romantic love held full sway. The predominant view was that in some mysterious, mystic and even providential way a person was attracted to his or

phenomena, most notably the roles that mate selection and the communication of emotion have played in the survival of the human species. Durkheim's (1897/1963) documentation of an association between suicide and social ties was another important milestone, as was Sigmund Freud's contention that psychopathology often had its roots in the individual's earliest relationships. Despite these and other forays into the study of relationships, and despite the fact that all of the social and behavioral sciences are addressed in some way to the processes and products of people's associations with one another, relationships failed to receive systematic attention until well into the twentieth century.

In the late 1970s, British relationship scholar Robert Hinde observed that the study of relationships "lies within the domain of a variety of disciplines from the social, medical, and natural sciences" (1979, p. v) but that it remained at the periphery of each of these fields. Not only did the subject of relationships not occupy a central position in any discipline, but few attempts had been made to integrate the scattered findings. In her predestinate. The general assumption was that young people fell in love, married and lived happily ever afterwards, as a result of some mystic attraction. Even when marriages turned out unhappily, the disillusioned partners explained the failures as being due to their having mistaken infatuation for love. Or else they placed the blame on bad luck or fate. (p. 11)

In addition, many people believed that even if relationship phenomena were studied, nothing useful could be learned because relationships were too complex and mysterious to yield to scientific analysis. This view was shared by many scientists, including psychologists, who believed that relationships were conceptually and methodologically inaccessible for scientific observation, description, and analysis and that, therefore, it was only misguided adventurers who tried to study such ephemeral phenomena (see Berscheid, 1986).

Those investigators who defied the societal taboo against the study of relationships were punished. In the 1920s, a professor of psychology at the University of Minnesota, Harlow Gale, was fired for administering a questionnaire to his students that asked such questions as "Have you ever blown in the ear of a person of the opposite sex in order to arouse their passion?" It is not surprising that when Burgess (1926) surveyed the available literature in the 1920s, he concluded that there existed not a single work that had systematically studied family behavior.

The taboo against the study of relationships continued well into the latter half of the century. Harry Harlow (e.g., 1958), whose seminal work on attachment and bonding was discussed in Chapter 1, was called before a congressional investigating committee and subjected to ridicule for his federally funded studies of what the media called "monkey love." In 1976, a U.S. senator attacked an investigator of interpersonal attraction and romantic love funded by the National Science Foundation, declaring that such matters should be left to Elizabeth Barrett Browning and Irving Berlin (Berscheid, 2002b). The sys-

tematic study of sexuality also remained taboo well into the twentieth century. For example, Kinsey and his colleagues (e.g., Kinsey, Pomeroy, & Martin, 1948) were subjected to professional and public harassment for their pioneering work.

In addition to the beliefs that relationship phenomena were not amenable to systematic study and that even if they were studied nothing useful could be learned, some scholars believed that certain relationship phenomena couldn't be studied because they simply did not exist. In the 1930s, for example, Linton (1936) expressed the views of many social scientists about romantic love:

All societies recognize that there are occasional violent emotional attachments between persons of opposite sex, but our present American culture is practically the only one which has attempted to capitalize on these, and make them the basis for marriage. . . . The hero of the modern American movie is always a romantic lover, just as the hero of the old Arab epic is always an epileptic. A cynic may suspect that in any ordinary population the percentage of individuals with a capacity for romantic love of the Hollywood type is about as large as that of person able to throw genuine epileptic fits. (p. 175)

Still others, including the senator who thought love should be left to poets and songwriters, believed that love existed but that examination of this and other relationship phenomena would reduce their value and enjoyment—a view incomprehensible to many scientists, for, as Hinde (1979) put it, "Newton did not destroy the beauty of the rainbow" (p. 5). In addition, some people maintained that they already knew everything worth knowing about relationships and, thus, the social and behavioral sciences should focus on things people didn't already know—the behavior of primitive peoples in faraway places, for example.

In sum, for many years the study of relationships was hindered by the beliefs that relationships were too complex and mystical to yield to systematic examination; that if such examination proved to be successful, the value and enjoyment of close relationships would be diminished; and, finally, that everyone already knew everything there was to know about relationships.

Recruitment of Research Participants

If these societal beliefs were not enough to discourage the study of relationships, there was yet another: People believed that relationships were too sacred to be subjected to scientific scrutiny. Burgess and Wallin (1953) noted that until the latter half of the twentieth century, many people would have refused to answer questions on the subjects of marriage and love, considering these areas of their lives to be too personal and sacred to be discussed with strangers. This refusal had very practical consequences because, like other social and behavioral scientists, relationship researchers are dependent on people's willingness to participate in their research.

Fortunately, this obstacle to relationship research has evaporated. Today most people are eager to talk about their relationships—even in such public venues as television and even when the recipients of their revelations express profound disinterest. Although the recruitment of people willing to participate in relationship studies is no longer difficult, there are systematic biases in people's willingness to volunteer for relationship research. These biases mandate that relationship researchers, and the consumers of their results, be vigilant for unrepresentative sampling of participants from the population to which the results are generalized.

One recruiting bias, observed among college students—the most accessible, and thus the most frequent, population studied by relationship researchers—is that women are more likely than men to volunteer for participation in relationship studies. This is particularly unfortunate because men's relationship behavior is often different from women's (e.g., Winstead, Derlega, & Rose, 1997), although some have argued that these differences are not as great as sometimes represented (e.g., Canary & Emmers-Sommer, 1997). As a consequence, it is important that relation-

ship studies include both men and women, but unless the investigator exerts special effort to recruit sufficient male participants to perform analyses to determine whether the phenomenon of interest differs by sex, the results likely will be generalizable only to females.

There are a number of other systematic biases in the kinds of people who volunteer for relationship studies. For example, the manner in which participants are recruited makes a difference. Karney, Davila, Cohan, Sullivan, Johnson, and Bradbury (1995) compared the effects of two recruitment techniques often used by marital researchers: newspaper advertisements and mail solicitation of married couples whose names are obtained from marriage license records. The characteristics of couples recruited through newspaper advertisements offering $50 to "newlywed couples interested in participating in a study of marriage" were contrasted to couples identified from marriage license data and invited through a mail solicitation to earn $75 for participating in a longitudinal study of marriage. Couples in both groups were first screened to meet a number of eligibility criteria, including the requirements that the marriage be the first for both spouses, neither partner be a parent, both partners be over 18, and wives be age 35 or younger. Despite meeting identical eligibility criteria, the couples recruited through newspaper advertisements were found to be at substantially greater risk for marital discord than couples recruited through marriage licenses. Not only did those who responded to the advertisement report lower marital satisfaction, but they also were more likely to have cohabited before marriage, less likely to have received premarital counseling, and more likely to report depressive symptoms and exhibit neuroticism.

Karney and colleagues also investigated whether those who responded to their mail solicitation differed from those who did not respond. Licensing record information revealed that responding couples were of higher socioeconomic status than those who did not respond. Responders also were less traditional than nonresponders—they were more likely to have cohabited premaritally (as indicated by similarity of address), the husbands were more likely to be students, and the wives were older and less likely to be housewives. Karney and associates note that the couples most likely to respond to their invitation to participate in longitudinal marital research were similar to those most likely to volunteer for psychological research in general (e.g., higher socioeconomic status; Rosenthal & Rosnow, 1975).

Ethical Considerations

In addition to societal taboos that slowed the development of relationship science, ethical problems involved in studying close relationships were, and continue to be, problematical. For example, ethical considerations usually preclude experimentation with people's ongoing relationships. In addition, even studies in which people simply are interviewed or asked to respond to questionnaires do not always escape ethical problems because asking people to think systematically about their relationships may have unintended and negative effects. Furthermore, the particular response categories included on a structured questionnaire may have an adverse effect on participants because they may suggest to the participant what the researcher believes to be the "normal" range of that behavior. In a study of emotion, Schachter and Singer (1962) used that fact to arouse anger in men in the early 1960s; the question was "With how many men other than your father has your mother had sexual relations?" and the lowest response category provided was "7 or less" (a response option tailor-made to produce anger and consternation in even the most placid individual). Researchers must ask themselves whether they are justified in asking people to think about a particular relationship and confronting them with questions about it even if, as is always the case, participants are advised they can leave the study any time or refuse to respond.

Participation in a relationship study, particularly over an extended period of time, is likely to affect the relationship. For example, Rubin and Mitchell (1976) report that most of the participants in the Boston Couples Study (e.g., Hill, Rubin, & Peplau, 1976), one of the first longitudinal studies of courtship, later said that their research participation did have an impact on their relationship. Fortunately, most said the impact was beneficial. Some noted, however, that although participating in the study was helpful in the long run, it was painful in the short because they learned things from taking part in the study they would rather not have known. One woman said, "At the time I cursed the study for destroying a lot of my fantasies about my boyfriend" (p. 22). The general finding that most people believe that their participation in relationship studies has positive effects has been corroborated by other investigators. For example, Bradbury (1994) reports that most of the newlywed couples who have participated in his studies later state that their participation not only heightened their awareness of their relationship with their spouse but also enhanced their appreciation of their marriage.

Participants in relationship studies often view the investigator not just as a researcher but also as a counselor and therapist. As Rubin and Mitchell (1976) recount, participants in the Boston Couples Study were eager to learn what the researchers thought of their relationships and to receive advice on how to improve them. The researchers, of course, could not give such advice during the course of their longitudinal study without affecting its results and, moreover, they were not trained as relationship therapists. Nevertheless, and whether they want to be or not, relationship researchers are often placed in a dual role by their participants and may have to provide counseling resources in the course of their investigation.

Informed Consent

Relationship researchers must obtain the **informed consent** of their participants *before* their participation. "Informed" means that potential participants must be told the nature of their participation and its possible negative consequences. Sometimes those negative consequences cannot be foreseen. An example is provided by experiments conducted in the 1970s in Seattle and Denver to determine whether a program of income maintenance would prove to be less expensive and more beneficial to low-income families in the long run than the usual welfare assistance programs (Hannan, Tuma, & Groeneveld, 1977). More than 5,000 low-income families were randomly assigned either to a control condition (in which they continued to receive the usual assistance) or to one of several *income-maintenance* conditions (in which each participant was guaranteed a specified level of income). All were interviewed 3 times a year during the 3- to 5-year experiment and for a 2-year period after the experiment. Unexpectedly, and as contrasted to the control group, the income-maintenance conditions displayed a significant increase in their rate of marital dissolution.

The experiment by Hannan and colleagues probably was ethical before it was performed because the researchers had no reason to believe that the income-maintenance treatment would cause marital dissolution. It would not be ethical to perform such an experiment today, however, even if prospective participants gave their fully informed consent to participate. It also is unlikely that researchers could obtain a representative sample, because some prospective participants would refuse to participate when told that by random assignment they might be placed in a condition in which their risk of marital dissolution would be significantly elevated. Moreover, even those who agreed to participate but whose marriage later dissolved might later challenge the validity of their consent, saying that they never really believed they were taking a risk because they were confident their *own* marriage was invulnerable to dissolution.

Another type of experiment that now would be viewed as unethical as a result of previous experimentation is one that involves the manipulation of an individual's self-esteem. Jacobs, Berscheid, and Walster (1971) found that such manipulations are difficult to erase. Like many other psychologists in the 1960s, these investigators randomly assigned participants to conditions in which the individual's self-esteem was either raised or lowered (via false test results). After the experiment had concluded, the investigators followed the usual protocol to erase the effect of the self-esteem manipulation by conducting an extensive (30- to 60-minute) debriefing of participants during which the participants were provided with incontrovertible evidence that they had been randomly selected to receive negative (or positive) test result feedback. Ordinarily, that would have been the end of the story because all participants convincingly said during debriefing that they understood that the feedback they received was false. As it happened, however, Jacobs and associates conducted a second experiment shortly after the first with the same participants. When they looked at the results of the second study, the investigators were both surprised and dismayed to see that significant traces of the self-esteem manipulation in the first experiment remained even after the participants' assurance that they understood that the feedback they had received was false.

Lepper, Ross, and Lau (1986) further examined this earlier finding in a carefully controlled experiment and verified that self-esteem manipulations are extraordinarily difficult to erase. They termed the effect the **self-esteem perseverance phenomenon**. The perseverance phenomenon has an obvious and important implication for close relationships. If it is difficult, if not impossible, to erase the effect of remarks that lower the self-esteem of an educated adult in the isolated context of a laboratory experiment, where random assignment to negative feedback can be later demonstrated and intellectually accepted by the recipient, imagine how hard it is to erase the self-esteem–damaging remarks romantic partners sometimes hurl at each other in anger—or worse, that parents or other adults sometimes unthinkingly make to a child who not only has formed an attachment to them but regards them as possessing the utmost credibility.

Methodological and Analytical Challenges

In addition to ethical problems, relationship research presents special methodological and analytical problems, many of which are unfamiliar to those psychologists who study a single individual's behavior rather than the relationship between two people (e.g., see Huston & Robins, 1982; Thompson & Walker, 1982). One persistent question is the proper **unit of analysis** for relationship research. Although researchers frequently study the responses of only one member of a couple—for example, asking about one individual's attitude toward the relationship—some maintain that research focused on a single individual does not qualify as true relationship research because, although useful, it is no different from research focused on the individual's attitudes toward anything else—say, a political candidate or capital punishment. Often omitted is the necessary next step—observation of how that characteristic of the individual, such as his or her attitude toward the relationship, is expressed in interaction with the partner and influences the couple's relationship. Thus, some relationship researchers define relationship research as that in which the couple, not the individual, is the unit of analysis.

When the dyad is the unit of analysis, however, and when data are obtained from both relationship partners, relationship researchers face special problems in analyzing their data. The problems arise because most psychological statistics assume that the each observation to be analyzed is *independent* of all other observations. Violation of the independence assumption is likely to produce biased results (e.g., for analysis of variance, see Kenny & Judd, 1986). When both partners' behaviors are observed, the assumption of independence of within-pair observations rarely is justified. In a study of marital satisfaction, for example, it would be necessary to assume that the husband's report of the degree to which he is satisfied with his marriage has *not* been influenced by his wife's degree of marital satisfaction and, conversely, that her satisfaction is independent of his. That assumption is patently false. Thus, as Gonzalez and Griffin (1997) explain, the question confronted by relationship researchers has been "How do we capture the psychology of *inter*dependence with the statistics of *in*dependence?" (p. 271, emphasis added).

Relationship researchers have proposed several answers to this question. For example, to avoid the problem of violating the independence assumption required by most psychological statistics, some researchers obtain data from only one member of the couple, thus assuring that each observation analyzed is independent of every other observation. Or, if data from both partners are available, some researchers engage in awkward strategies to deal with the interdependence of their within-couple (e.g., husband-and-wife pairs) observations. One such strategy has been to simply discard the responses of one member of the couple. Of course, discarding important information in order to obtain a data set that meets the independence assumption is wasteful and precludes asking questions about within-relationship phenomena. Another strategy has been to average the observations (e.g., scores) of both partners within each couple to create a set of "couple" observations; although each couple's score is independent of the other couples' scores, this strategy also does not take advantage of the information available to investigate important questions such as the degree of attitude similarity of partners within couples. Yet another strategy used to analyze data obtained from heterosexual relationships has been to average the responses of all the women in a group and then compare that average to the averaged response of all the males. This practice has led to specious interpretations. For example,

> A researcher may find that, *as a group*, wives report more consultation with their spouses during decision-making than do their husbands. To conclude that this reflects the decision-making process occurring *within pairs* [emphasis added] is an ecological fallacy. . . . Put simply, the analysis is at the aggregate level, whereas the conclusion is at the relationship level. (Thompson & Walker, 1982, p. 892)

Relationship researchers, of course, seek conclusions at the relationship level—not simply at the aggregate level (e.g., a group of wives) or at the individual level of analysis.

Fortunately, the unsatisfactory and cumbersome stratagems that marked much early relationship research have become less necessary as a result of recent developments in dyadic data analysis (e.g., see Gonzalez & Griffin, 1997; Griffin & Gonzalez, 1995; Griffin, Murray, & Gonzalez, 1999; Kenny, 1990; Kenny, Kashy, & Bolger, 1998). Nevertheless, researchers must be sensitive to the facts that (1) observations of each partner within a couple are interdependent—not independent, (2) most psychological statistics assume independence of observations, (3) violation of this assumption is likely to produce specious results, and (4) analytical techniques are available to deal with interdependence of observations.

Despite progress in the development of analytic techniques for relationship data, ethical and practical obstacles to conducting experiments with ongoing relationships continue to preclude tests of many relationship hypotheses. Without experimental data—the most powerful tool scientists have to determine causation—it is hard secure the knowledge necessary to understand and predict relationship phenomena.

The Prediction of Relationship Phenomena

Most people want to avoid negative relationship outcomes. In order to do so, it is necessary to (1) estimate the probability that the relationship is heading toward a negative outcome, (2) identify the causal conditions currently in force that are likely to produce the undesired outcome, and (3) change those causal conditions. The first step, forecasting a relationship outcome, may be accomplished through statistical prediction or through causal prediction.

Statistical (Actuarial) Prediction

Statistical, or actuarial, prediction is what insurance companies do when they decide how much an individual should pay for insurance. They keep records of the outcomes experienced by people who possess certain characteristics. As a consequence, a teenage boy with a red sports car will be charged more for auto insurance than an elderly woman who drives her white sedan to church on Sundays, and a person with a poor credit history will be charged more than a person with a good credit history. Why is credit history

a good indicator that the policyholder will file an auto insurance claim? "'We're not sure,' says a spokesman for Allstate. 'But we know it's a fact'" (AuWerter, 2001). Not only does the insurance company not know why it's a fact, but the company doesn't care. Understanding the causal dynamics underlying the associations they observe is not the job of insurance actuaries, who simply make outcome probability statements based on outcomes experienced by persons who are similar to the person requesting insurance.

All scientific prediction, both statistical and causal, rests on the assumption that what happened in the past is likely to happen again in the future. Statistical prediction is an important tool used by almost all researchers, including relationship researchers. For example, the relationship counselor who is asked to predict the chances of a stable marriage for a couple in which neither partner has been married before is likely to say that the couple's chance of success is about 50% and that their chance of failure is about the same (e.g., Karney & Bradbury, 1995b). Few couples will be satisfied with that answer. What people really want to know is whether they personally—Joe and Mary—fall in the 50% whose marriage is likely to fail or the 50% likely to succeed. People want behavioral scientists to refine their actuarial predictions to the extent that they can make reliable *point predictions*—predictions custom-tailored to each individual case and its unique circumstances. This, it should be noted, is a difficult, almost impossible, task. Other scientists are not expected to make point predictions about natural phenomena outside of the laboratory. For example, no one ever expected Isaac Newton to predict exactly *which* apple would fall off the tree and hit him on the head and *when* it would do so. Physical scientists know that such predictions usually are too difficult to make outside the laboratory because they depend on too many unknown, interacting, and hard-to-measure events. Moreover, such predictions require the application of laws from several domains (e.g., gravity, wind pressure) but there is no known law—in the material sciences or in the behavioral sciences—that can describe the sequence in which several causally connected events are likely to occur (Lieberson, 1997; Popper, 1964).

Nevertheless, in response to popular demand, researchers have been attempting to use premarital data to refine their actuarial predictions about marital success at least since the 1940s (Adams, 1946; see Hill & Peplau, 1998; Holman & Linford, 2001). In one of the first such attempts, Burgess and Wallin (1953) followed a sample of couples engaged in the 1930s for a few years after their marriage and found that, at least for that sample, such factors as happily married parents, self-confidence, and longer courtships were significantly associated with an individual's later marital stability. Some researchers now claim very high levels of predictive accuracy for marital stability. For example, Olson and his colleagues (e.g., Fowers & Olson, 1986) claim 80% accuracy with their PREPARE questionnaire, frequently administered to engaged couples undergoing church-mandated premarital counseling. They state that such factors as realistic relationship expectations and similarity of religious values seem to be associated with marital stability. Gottman and his colleagues also claim to predict divorce with high accuracy (e.g., Buehlman, Gottman, & Katz, 1992). For example, Gottman, Coan, Carrere, and Swanson (1998) observed newlywed couples interact in a laboratory session and coded the negativity and positivity of their behavior in interaction with each other as well as other variables previously shown to be correlated with marital satisfaction. The marital status and satisfaction of the couples were assessed once a year for 6 years. Using features of their interaction as newlyweds—such as the husband's rejections of his wife's influence attempts—the investigators claim to be able to predict a couple's likelihood of divorce with 83% accuracy and their later marital satisfaction with 80% accuracy.

Unfortunately, there is less than meets the eye to such claims of high predictive accuracy for divorce, certainly much less than the media have represented. The predictive formula an investigator develops to predict whether a couple will divorce is custom-tailored to the sample used to arrive at the formula; that is, the investigator works backward from knowledge of who in that sample ultimately divorced to identify the characteristics that initially differentiated those people from the people in the sample whose marriages remained intact. In commenting on such studies, Heyman and Slep (2001) have reminded researchers that the usefulness of any predictive scheme developed from one sample is determined by how well it predicts for a different sample because the predictive equation will capitalize on the idiosyncrasies of the couples in the sample used to derive the equation. For example, if it should happen by chance that in the sample used to construct the predictive formula, all of the people who divorced had blue eyes, then blue eyes might appear in the predictive equation for divorce. Chance associations are particularly likely in the relatively small samples that have been used in divorce prediction studies. (Insurance companies, it might be noted, have access to extraordinarily high volumes of data relevant to the outcomes on which they are making monetary bets.)

As a consequence, the true usefulness of any predictive formula is revealed by seeing how well it predicts across other samples of people—in other words, by **cross-validation** of the formula. When Heyman and Slep performed the illustrative exercise of developing a divorce prediction equation with one sample of couples, they found they were able to predict divorce for that particular sample in the high ranges reported by some researchers (correctly classifying 90% of the couples). However, when they attempted to cross-validate that same predictive formula with another sample, drawn from the same population at the same time, the predictive value of the equation dropped precipitously, improving little on chance. Heyman and Slep note that no published study predicting divorce for couples in the general population has cross-validated its predictive scheme. Nevertheless, as discussed in Chapter 13, "Satisfaction and Stability," certain relationship properties repeatedly appear as diagnostic of later outcomes across the many studies that have attempted to predict marital satisfaction from characteristics of the premarital relationship.

At base, using actuarial prediction to forecast the future of a relationship is a lot like forecasting the weather: If the sky is cloudy and threatening in the relationship now, storms are likely later. If the sun is shining in the relationship now, there is a better chance it will be sunny later. Marital researchers have been able to refine the latter prediction by their discovery that although the presence of certain types of clouds may not be occluding the sun presently, they are likely to do so shortly after marriage and dampen the couple's happiness; in other words, several factors associated with later marital unhappiness appear to have little effect on the couple's premarital happiness (again, as discussed in Chapter 13).

Causal Prediction

The problem with actuarial prediction—and the reason scientists try so hard to move beyond it to causal prediction—is that events that happened in the past are likely to happen in the future only if the unknown conditions that caused those past events stay the same. To the extent that the unknown causal conditions producing today's outcomes change, actuarial predictions about tomorrow are likely to be wrong. If teenage boys suddenly develop a craze for white sedans and elderly women develop an affinity for red sports cars, past predictions about future outcomes are likely to become inaccurate.

With respect to marital relationships, many societal changes have occurred in the United States and other countries throughout the world in the past few decades, and as a consequence, the causal conditions influencing relationships today are different from those in force just a few decades ago. For example, many organized religions have liberalized their views of divorce; thus, religiosity may not be as good a predictor of marital stability as it once was. Similarly, the conditions that influence relationships decades from now are likely to be different from those affecting relationships today. It is therefore important to identify the causal conditions that are producing the statistical associations observed today in order to make accurate predictions about tomorrow.

Identifying the causal conditions producing a relationship outcome is important not only for prediction but also for control. People want to control their destiny, and the behavioral scientist is dedicated to helping them do just that. Couples who see storm clouds brewing over their relationship often ask the relationship expert to help make the clouds go away (actually, and unfortunately, it usually is raining cats and dogs before couples get to the therapist, as discussed further in Chapter 14, "Intervention and Dissolution"). Identification and understanding of the causal conditions responsible for generating an effect is a *necessary condition* for control—a future event cannot be prevented if the causes of the event are not known. However, knowledge of the causal conditions responsible for an effect is not a *sufficient condition* for control because people do not always have the power to change those conditions; for example, they do not have the financial resources to move away from meddling in-laws or to quit the stressful job that is destroying their family life.

The Relationship System and Other Systems

The task of making causal predictions for relationships is especially difficult because each relationship is a **system**, as evidenced by the fact that a change in one part of the system (such as the wife in the marital relationship) is likely to produce a change in another part of the system (the husband). Relationships are not static entities—they are dynamic and ever-changing systems. Moreover, the relationship system is nested in larger systems. As physicist Fritjof Capra observes: "An outstanding property of all life is the tendency to form multileveled structures of systems within systems. . . . Throughout the living world we find living systems nesting within other living systems" (1996, p. 28). Each succeeding level of organization within a hierarchy of systems tends to be more complex than the levels subordinate to it, and each produces emergent properties that do not exist at the lower levels.

Making causal predictions for relationships is especially difficult because relationships are not only systems but **open systems**. In contrast to closed systems, where events external to the system do not affect the system's operation, open systems exchange information, energy, and material with the other systems in which they are nested and also with the systems they encapsulate (see Reis, Collins, & Berscheid, 2000). For example, relationships are nested in larger social and cultural systems that influence relationships through laws and customs regulating marriage and divorce, and in turn, relationships influence the nature of social and cultural systems (e.g., making divorce easier to obtain by instituting "no-fault" divorce laws). Relationships also influence the systems they encapsulate. For example, as discussed in Chapter 2, "Relationships and Health," hostile interactions between partners influence the many biological systems nested within each partner, including the cardiovascular system. In addition, the operation of those systems influences relationship dynamics. For example, interaction with a partner who is frequently ill as a result of poor immunocompetence is different from interaction with a healthy partner.

Because changes both in the systems in which a relationship is embedded and in those it encompasses are likely to have an impact on the relationship, causal prediction of relationship phenomena requires knowledge of these other systems and the ways in which they influence the relationship. For an understanding of the biological systems nested within each individual partner, relationship researchers rely on findings in psychology and several of the biological and health sciences. For an understanding of the social and cultural systems in which relationships are embedded, relationship scholars typically rely on sociology, anthropology, and economics. All of these disciplines currently are contributing to the development of relationship science.

In sum, causal prediction for relationships requires a vast amount of knowledge, some of which is not yet available in the disciplines on which relationship science depends. As a consequence, both relationship prediction and relationship intervention are hazardous endeavors. In this, relationship science does not differ from

other, longer established sciences. For example, George Meany, the twentieth-century labor leader, is alleged to have exclaimed in frustration, "Economics is the only discipline where one can be considered an expert and never be right!" Similarly, an often heard joke about meteorology is that it is the only occupation in which one can always be wrong and still keep one's job. Economic systems and weather systems are large, complex open systems in which prediction and intervention are difficult. The same is true of relationship systems.

Experimental Studies

Obtaining the knowledge necessary for the accurate prediction of relationship phenomena is difficult because, as noted previously, the most powerful method of determining causation—the experimental method—is often not available to relationship researchers for both ethical and practical reasons. Normal scientific investigation consists of formulating questions about *why* a specific event occurs. The basic question asked by all scientists takes the form "Is X a cause of Y?" The question usually is stated in the form of a hypothesis—X is a cause of Y—which then may be confirmed or disconfirmed by experimental test. Hypotheses are usually derived from theories, which are conjectures about the nature of the world; that is, theories propose that a certain effect is produced by certain causal conditions. Thus, a **theory** is simply a network of constructs connected by causal statements. A theory of interpersonal attraction, for example, may propose that similarity between two persons will produce attraction. As shown in Figure 3.2, both X (similarity) and Y (attraction) are constructs, joined together in the theory by a causal statement (X is a cause of Y).

Theories about relationships are plentiful—virtually everyone has theories about relationship phenomena. To be useful, however, a theory must be *testable*; there has to be some way to determine whether the assertions the theory makes about the causal connections between events accurately reflect the world in which we live. Theories about human behavior *must* make contact

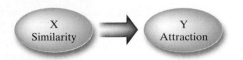

FIGURE 3.2 A theory specifies the causal relation between constructs.

with observable behavior. Behavior is the **observational base** for all behavioral scientists, including psychologists. If a theory defines its constructs with reference to the empirical base of observation—for example, specifying how similarity and attraction can be observed and measured—then the theory can be tested.

John Stuart Mill (1872/1965), the nineteenth-century British philosopher of science who was an early advocate of the experimental method in psychology (see Boring, 1950), called the **classic experimental design** the "method of difference." It rests on the assumption that *causes always precede their effects*. Thus, the experimental method hinges on knowing the *temporal occurrence of X and of Y*. Knowing the time at which X appears and the time at which Y appears is the defining characteristic of an experiment: If X is a cause of Y, then the appearance of X at Time 1 should produce the appearance of Y at a later point in time, Time 2. Moreover, if X is the only cause of Y, then if X does not appear at Time 1, Y should not appear at Time 2.

It is the experimenter who makes X appear at Time 1 in the experimental condition and makes X not appear at Time 1 in a control condition. Thus the experimenter is the puppet-master who "manipulates" X—makes X appear in one condition and makes sure it does not appear in another. For this reason, X is sometimes called the *manipulated variable* or, more usually, the **independent variable**. The independent variable is the presumed *causal variable* that appears at Time 1 in the experimental, or "treatment," group, but it does not appear at Time 1 in the control group. The experimenter then watches to see if the presence of X makes a difference in how people in the experimental group behave (i.e., does Y follow X?). If Y does follow the appearance of X in the experimental group but does not appear in the control group where X was absent, then some evidence in support of the hypothesis that X is a cause of Y has been found; that is, the experimenter has found evidence that X and Y covary in the appropriate temporal way—when X appears, Y follows. Y is called the **dependent variable** because its appearance is presumed to be dependent on the appearance of its cause, X. Figure 3.3 illustrates an experimental design.

Random Assignment

Unfortunately, effects in the natural world rarely have only one cause—they often have many. Thus, the independent variable X, which is sus-

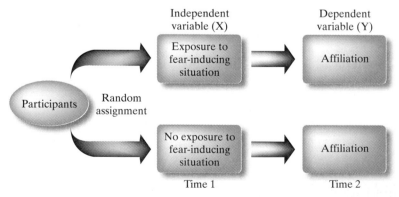

FIGURE 3.3 A basic experimental design. To test the hypothesis that fear produces a desire to affiliate, researchers randomly assign participants to an experimental (exposure) or control (no exposure) group, and measure subsequent behavior. If affiliative behavior occurs (or is higher) in the experimental group and does not occur (or is lower) in the control group, then support has been found for the hypothesis that fear causes affiliation.

pected to be a cause of Y, may be only one of several causes of Y, some of which may be known but usually are unknown. Despite the fact that Mill (1872/1965) stated that his method of difference was applicable only to effects that have a single cause, the same experimental logic has been applied to instances in which it is suspected that Y may have causes other than X. As a consequence, problems arise in the interpretation of results if the experimental group differs from the control group in any way other than in the appearance of X because that difference may represent an unknown cause of Y; if so, the conclusion that it was X that produced Y in the experimental group will be in error.

Random assignment of participants to the experimental and control groups helps "control" for causes of Y other than X. Randomization, it is assumed, will ensure that the unknown causes of Y are equally represented in both the experimental and control groups and thus are not more likely to produce Y in the experimental group than in the control group. Unfortunately, the prophylactic effect of randomization tends to break down when there are small numbers of participants in the study, as is often the case in relationship research. In a personal letter to one of the authors, Ladd Wheeler, a well-known relationship researcher, expressed his frustration with such an experience:

> I've just discovered that the second straight experiment I've done was a washout because of pre-manipulation differences between conditions. There is no accounting for it other than chance (at $p < .008$). If I hadn't had the personality measures on which these differences appeared, I would have reported a set of spurious results without knowing it (because the personality measures were strongly related to the dependent variables). I wonder how many of our journal articles this is true of; perhaps we have too much faith in random assignment. (February 23, 1993)[1]

Wheeler was aware that random assignment had failed because he administered a number of personality measures he suspected might be possible causes of Y and then took care to check whether participants of one personality type were more represented in his experimental group than in his control group (they were) and whether that difference was associated with the dependent variable (it was). Unfortunately, most experimenters usually do not know that random assignment has failed because they cannot fathom what other possible causes of Y might be. However, *all* researchers are aware (or should be aware) that random assignment sometimes fails. This is one reason scientists insist that the results of an experiment be *replicated* by other researchers working in different laboratories, with different experimental participants, using different measures and operationalizations of the constructs X and Y, before they will put much confidence in a particular finding.

Sometimes researchers will know what some of the other causes of Y are. If so, the investigator will not simply passively control for those known causal variables by randomization of research participants to the experimental and control groups but, rather, will attempt to *actively control* these other causes in various ways. For example, if it is known that Y covaries with a person's biological sex, the experimenter will make certain that both men and women are equally represented in the experimental and control groups and will analyze the results to determine whether and how biological sex interacts with X to affect Y.

In relationship research, as in other areas of investigation, some investigators carelessly omit the proper control group. This practice is always dangerous in both experimental and nonexperimental studies. For example, several popular beliefs about the characteristics of children of drug-dependent parents and their need for special therapeutic treatment stemmed from surveys indicating that adult children of drug-dependent parents often endorse such questionnaire items as "I feel I am different from other people," "I don't enjoy life as much as I'd like," and "I try to control others and events too much." Many concluded that these personal problems were the *effect* of being raised by a drug-dependent parent. However, these surveys had omitted the appropriate control group. When the responses of children of drug-dependent parents were compared to those of a control group composed of children of non–drug-dependent parents, two-thirds of the respondents within each of the two groups endorsed items previously believed to be special characteristics of the adult children of drug-dependent parents (see Sher, 1991). Apparently, almost everyone feels different from other people, tries to control things, and doesn't enjoy life as much as he or she would like. This fact is often used by fortune-tellers whose seeming accuracy then amazes customers—even though such predictions are likely to be accurate for most people. This is an example of what researchers call the *P. T. Barnum effect* (Barnum allegedly claimed, "There's a sucker born every minute!"). Control groups are vital to interpretation of both experimental and nonexperimental findings.

Natural Experiments

Although ethical considerations often preclude researchers from experimenting with ongoing relationships, Mother Nature—not noted for her fairness and ethicality—sometimes does so. In a **natural experiment** some naturally occurring event, which randomly affects some people (the experimental group) and not others (the control group), acts as the independent variable. The researcher then observes whether the hypothesized effect later appears in the experimental group but not in the control group. For example, a researcher may hypothesize that the spouse who contributes the most money to the relationship makes the major decisions in the relationship. To experimentally test that hypothesis it would be necessary to manipulate the partners' ratio of monetary contributions and then observe how patterns of dominance in decision-making vary with changes in the ratio. No researcher would want to have (or has) the power to conduct such an experiment. Sometimes, however, fate randomly lays off workers and the result is a change in the partners' ratio of economic contributions to the relationship. If the prospect of layoffs is known in advance, the researcher can assess relationship decision-making both before and after the partners' financial contribution ratio is changed for some couples but not for others.

Attridge (1995; see Berscheid & Ammazzalorso, 2001) used the natural experiment method to study long-distance romantic relationships, which have become increasingly prevalent in recent years because of couples' educational and occupational exigencies. Specifically, Attridge wanted to test hypotheses about couples' emotional reactions to separation. Researchers have neither the power nor the ethical right to impose a physical separation on some couples (the experimental group) while leaving others (a control group) together. However, many colleges offer international learning programs in which students spend anywhere from a month to a year abroad; because there are more applicants than openings, students often are randomly selected for participation. With the cooperation of several colleges, Attridge was able to assess the emotions experienced by a group of students before, during, and after they became separated from their romantic partners as well as the emotions experienced by a similar group of students who were not separated from their partners. Thus, Attridge could be fairly confident that the effects he observed in the experimental group (e.g., an increase in intense emotional experiences associated with the partner and the relationship), as contrasted to those observed in the control group, were caused by the separation.

Nonexperimental (Correlational) Studies

Because natural manipulations of independent variables of interest are rare, and because both ethical and practical considerations often preclude experimentation with ongoing relationships, **nonexperimental studies**, in which levels of variables are not manipulated and are not randomly assigned or controlled in other ways, are frequently used in relationship research. Examples of nonexperimental studies are (1) large-scale surveys that assess people's attitudes toward subjects such as infidelity; (2) time-series designs in which measurements of a variable are made at successive times, as in **longitudinal studies** where the same people are measured at successive times on a variable such as marital satisfaction; and (3) **cross-sectional studies**, in which variables are measured at a single point in time in groups of people who differ in some way, such as age. Variables assessed in nonexperimental studies are uncontrolled, and the data usually include measurements of variables considered to be "effects" or "outcomes" (e.g., married vs. divorced) and of variables suspected to be causes of those effects and outcomes (e.g., age, attractiveness, feelings of love).

Nonexperimental data are frequently called correlational data because the answers to the questions typically asked of these data—"Does the appearance of Y covary with the appearance of X?" or "Can the level of Y be predicted from the level of X?"—usually are expressed in some kind of correlation coefficient that ranges from +1.00 to −1.00. A *positive correlation* such as $r_{xy} = .90$ indicates that the two variables positively covary; if they are discrete events then they tend to appear together, and if they are continuous variables then high (or low) levels of Y can be predicted from high (or low) levels of X. If the researcher is using the degree of covariation between two variables to predict future events, the prediction must be accompanied by the assumption that nothing in the causal system in which X and Y are embedded (which is unknown) has changed. A *negative correlation* such as $r_{xy} = .90$ also indicates that X and Y covary; if X appears then Y does not and vice versa, or if the level of X is high then the level of Y is low and vice versa. If the correlation between two variables is 0, then the appearance of X provides no information about the likely appearance of Y and the level of Y cannot be predicted from the level of X. Figure 3.4 illustrates these concepts.

As discussed in Chapter 2, "Relationships and Health," correlational studies can establish covariation but usually not causation. Even if it is found that X and Y covary, (1) X may be a cause of Y, (2) Y may be a cause of X, or (3) both may be effects of a third variable Z, in which case neither X nor Y is a cause of the other. There is yet another causal possibility, which is often true in

relationship research. Many relationship variables have been shown experimentally to be **causally reciprocal**—that is, X and Y are both causes and effects of each other in the natural world. For example, as discussed in Chapter 6, "Birth of a Relationship," it has been experimentally demonstrated that the perception that another person is similar to oneself causes attraction to that person. It also has been experimentally shown that attraction to another (on grounds other than similarity) causes people to perceive the liked person as similar to themselves. Thus, attraction and similarity are causally reciprocal variables.

Correlational studies usually cannot establish causation because the temporal order in which X and Y occurred rarely is known. In some correlational studies, however, it is clear that one variable preceded the other or for other reasons cannot be an effect of the other variable. Age is an example. It is not reasonable to conclude from the frequently found positive correlation between youth and divorce that divorce causes people to be young; thus, that causal path is eliminated and it seems likely that youth (or, more likely, one or more of the characteristics associated with youth) is a causal factor in divorce.

Ex Post Facto Correlational Studies

A common correlational design has been called the ex post facto correlational design. The Latin phrase *ex post facto* means "after the deed has been done." In such studies, the responses of two or more groups of people who differ in some way—for example, married vs. divorced persons—are examined. The fact that the person is married or divorced is a fact that was established before the researcher entered the research participants' lives by asking them to fill out a questionnaire; that is, the difference between the groups was created not by the experimenter but by events whose causes are unknown.

The most common ex post facto design in relationship research is one in which the investigator classifies the respondents into a "distressed" or "nondistressed" couples group on

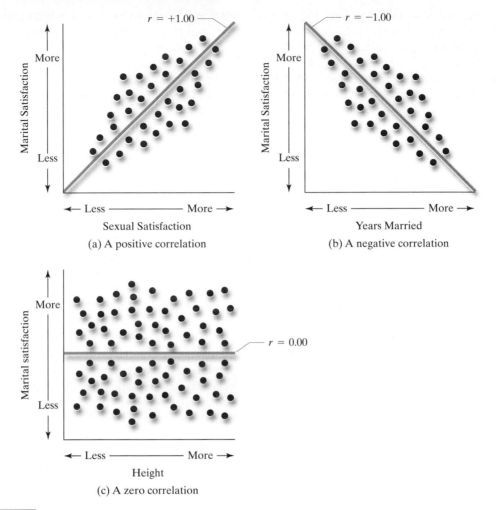

FIGURE 3.4 Correlations. Scatter diagrams provide a graphic representation of the relationship between two variables. The graphs here illustrate a positive correlation (a), a negative correlation (b), and a zero correlation (c). Each point locates the position of a single participant's scores on the two measured variables. The solid straight lines depict what the correlations would look like if they were "perfect".

the basis of their responses to a relationship satisfaction questionnaire. The distressed couples often are recruited from those who have appeared at a clinic for relationship therapy and the nondistressed couples usually are selected by the experimenter to be as similar as possible to the distressed couples on dimensions believed to be associated with the variable of interest. For example, if the hypothesis under test is that communication quality is positively correlated with

relationship satisfaction, the investigator may first try to match the two groups on length of relationship, socioeconomic status, or any of the several other variables believed to be associated with relationship satisfaction. If the partners in the distressed group display poorer communication quality than couples in the nondistressed group, it is tempting to conclude that poor communication is a cause of their marital distress. However, it may be the case that marital distress produces poor communication or that both were caused by a third factor, such as the necessity of holding two jobs due to financial difficulties, which led to both marital distress and a lack of time for spousal communication. From these non-experimental data, it can be concluded only that marital distress and poor communication covary.

Longitudinal (Prospective) Studies

Many correlational studies simply examine whether two or more responses a person has made on a questionnaire at a single point in time are correlated. That is, the research participant's Response A at Time 1 is correlated with his or her Response B, also made at Time 1. In the longitudinal (or prospective) design the investigator correlates the response a participant makes at one point in time (Response A, Time 1) with the response he or she makes at a later point in time (Response B, Time 2) (see Bradbury, 1998; Holmes & Poole, 1991). For example, the investigator's hypothesis may be that marital stability at Time 2 is a function of marital satisfaction at Time 1. If so, the person's Time 1 response to a marital satisfaction questionnaire is correlated with his or her Time 2 response to a marital status question such as "Are you still married?"

Many longitudinal relationship studies are **two-wave studies** in which the respondents are measured at only two points in time and, usually, the time interval between measurements is relatively short (months rather than years). However, **multiple-wave studies**, in which measurements are made at several points in time over a period of years, are becoming more frequent, as is the development of statistical techniques to analyze such data (e.g., growth curve analyses; see Chapter 13, "Satisfaction and Stability"). Longitudinal studies are valuable, not the least because many of the questions relationship scholars ask concern the developmental course relationships take through time. Moreover, although longitudinal studies usually cannot establish causation, they often provide stronger clues to causal relationships between variables than other kinds of nonexperimental studies because even though they do not manipulate or control variables, they do provide information about the temporal order in which events occur.

The Regression Method of Causal Inference

All scientists want to move beyond knowledge of covariation to knowledge of causation, as we've discussed. Relationship researchers, as well as scholars in many of the social and behavioral sciences, have been frustrated by their frequent inability to use the experimental method to test their causal hypotheses about relationship phenomena and by the limitations of the nonexperimental methods to which they are so often restricted. In recent years, some statisticians have attempted to help them find a way out of their predicament. Just as medieval alchemists tried to develop methods that would transform common base metals into precious gold, some statisticians have tried to develop methods to transform common correlational data into yielding information not just about the degree of covariation between variables but about their causal relations as well. Highly sophisticated and complex statistical methods such as path analysis and structural equation modeling (see Maruyama, 1998) are intended to extract causal information from nonexperimental data and are based on **multiple regression analysis (MRA)**. The r in the frequently used Pearson correlation coefficient (e.g., $r_{xy} = .90$), which expresses the degree of covariation between two measured variables, originally stood for the word "regression," referring to the statistical method used to determine the degree to which two variables covary.

MRA refers to any one of several related statistical methods for evaluating the effects of more than one—or "multiple"—"independent" variables on one or more "dependent" variables. When an MRA technique is used to analyze *experimental* data, levels of more than one independent variable $(X_1, X_2, \ldots, X_n)$ are manipulated, the effects of each of these variables on the dependent variable(s) $(Y_1, Y_2, \ldots, Y_n)$ are observed and measured, and the effects of other known or suspected causes of Y $(Z_1, Z_2, \ldots, Z_n)$ are controlled either directly or through randomization. For example, if Y is test performance, the experimenter is likely to *directly control* test preparation time, assuring that it is equal for participants in all experimental conditions, but differences in participants' learning aptitudes are likely to be *controlled through randomization* of participants to conditions. It is the manipulation of the independent variables and the control of other known or possible causes of Y that allow the data to satisfy the conditions necessary for causal inference using MRA and other statistical techniques.

When MRA is used to analyze *nonexperimental* data, however, it is necessary to make a number of logical and statistical assumptions about the nature of the data before proceeding to causal inference because (1) no variable has been manipulated; (2) no variable has been controlled, either directly or through randomization; (3) all variables simply have been measured, often at a single point in time on a questionnaire; and (4) the temporal order in which the variables appear in the natural world usually is not known. When a type of MRA is used with nonexperimental data, at least one of the measured variables—the variable with cause(s) of special interest—is designated the *dependent* variable, the *criterion* variable, or often the *outcome* variable. For example, Y may be "marital happiness." The other measured variables, suspected to be causes of the dependent or outcome variable, are usually called the *independent* or *predictor* variables. In this case, X_1 may be sex or gender, X_2 may be "love," and X_3 may be number of years married.

It can be seen that the terminology used to describe MRA analyses, even when used with nonexperimental data, has been borrowed from the classic experimental design. For example, many investigators present their nonexperimental data in tables in which the rows are labeled "dependent variables" and the columns represent "levels of the independent variable" even though no variable was manipulated; no variables were controlled; all often were measured at a single point in time, usually by questionnaire or interview; and their temporal order in the natural world to which the research findings are to be generalized is not known. Mar-

golin and White (1987, p. 25) illustrate one example of this regrettably confusing practice. Thus, it is easy for the research consumer to become confused about the kind of data that an investigator has collected—experimental or nonexperimental—and, as a consequence, confused about how easily the data can meet the assumptions and conditions for using the regression method of causal inference.

The basic tenet of **regression methods of causal inference** is that when all causes of Y have been measured, the effect on Y of each individual independent/predictor variable (e.g., X_1) can be estimated while holding *statistically constant* the effects on Y of each of the other independent/predictor variables $(X_2, \ldots, X_n)$. In other words, the assumption is that *statistical control can replace experimental manipulation of an independent variable and actual control of other possible causes*. However, that assumption is valid for nonexperimental data only if the data satisfy several critical mathematical conditions and assumptions (see Clogg & Haritou, 1997). It is the failure to provide evidence that the nonexperimental data in a specific instance *do* satisfy those conditions and assumptions—as well as severe doubt that those conditions and assumptions can *ever* be met by nonexperimental social-behavioral data—that has created enormous controversy and judgments of "causal farce" by some eminent statisticians and logicians (see McKim & Turner, 1997). Freedman (1997), for example, notes that although most treatments of regression assume that the investigator has identified the relevant variables associated with an effect, knows their causal order and the form of the relationships between them, and is able to measure each of those variables without significant error (as many of the physical sciences are able to do), this is rarely the case.

> In the social sciences, the situation seems quite different. Regression is used to discover relationships or to disentangle cause and effect. However, investigators have only vague ideas as to the relevant variables and their causal order; functional forms are chosen on the basis of convenience or familiarity; serious problems of measurement are often encountered. (pp. 113–114)

Although some psychologists have been willing to make the leaps of faith that the regression method of causal inference from nonexperimental data requires, others have been skeptical from the beginning. Over two decades ago, Diana Baumrind (1983) observed that the psychological research literature was exploding with studies in which causal inferences were being made from correlational data. Discussing several specious causal attributions frequently made from longitudinal studies, Baumrind attempted to "discourage the fantasy that *any* statistical system can justify drawing causal inferences from correlational data" (p. 1289). She was unsuccessful. Such methods—for good or for ill—have become entrenched, partly because most investigators blindly accept without examination that their nonexperimental data satisfy the assumptions that permit use of the regression method of causal inference and partly because most research consumers are not expert statisticians and are unable to evaluate the appropriateness of the analytical technique that is presumed to support the investigator's conclusions.

Baumrind's observations about causation remain instructive, however. All social interventions, such as therapeutic interventions into distressed relationships, require **generative theories of causation** that try to identify the precise *mechanism* by which a cause produces its effect (Shultz, 1982). The generative mechanism is sometimes called a *mediating variable* because it is the "causal engine" that produces the correlation between two variables. For example, as discussed in Chapter 2, "Relationships and Health," social support is hypothesized to mediate the association between social integration and health. In contrast to generative theories of causation, **regularity theories of causation** simply focus on *covariation* (which can be determined by correlational studies in which both responses are made at a single point in time) and on *regularity of succession* (which can be determined by longitudinal studies showing that Y consistently follows X). To illustrate why knowledge of generative transmission is vital to intervention, Baumrind (1983) cites an example that appears in many elementary statistics textbooks:

The number of never-married persons in certain British villages is highly inversely correlated with the number of field mice in the surrounding meadows. Marital status of humans was considered an established cause of field mice by the village elders until the mechanisms of transmission were finally surmised: Never-married persons bring with them a disproportionate number of cats relative to the rest of the village population *and* cats consume field mice. With the generative mechanisms understood, village elders could concentrate their attention on increasing the population of cats rather than [increasing] the proportion of never-married persons. (p. 1297)

Nonexperimental data and correlational studies are useful because they often provide clues that guide the search for the generative cause of an effect. Longitudinal studies are especially valuable for identifying variables that show regularity of succession and thus suggest the causal generative mechanism that might be responsible for an observed covariation between two variables. That possibility may then be investigated in a more controlled, usually experimental, investigation. Consider, for example, a frequently cited longitudinal study of marital stability conducted by Filsinger and Thoma (1988), who hypothesized that "the stability and adjustment of intimate relationships depends upon the nature of the couple's interaction" (p. 785). (Phrases such as "depends upon" and words such as "affects" or "influences" assert a causal connection.) Features of premarital partners' interaction were observed at Time 1, the beginning of the study, and then correlated with the couple's marital stability 5 years later (Time 2). The results indicated that the extent to which the partners reciprocated negative and positive affect in their premarital interaction was correlated with marital instability at Time 2, as was the frequency with which the wife-to-be interrupted her prospective spouse in their interaction at Time 1. Filsinger and Thoma concluded that their findings supported the notion that behavioral patterns of interaction predate later relationship distress.

The couples' interactions patterns did indeed "predate" their later stability or instability, but were they the *cause?* Although it is known that the women's interruptions occurred before the instability observed at Time 2, one cannot conclude that this interruptive behavior played a causal role in relationship dissolution. However, the significant correlation between women's frequency of interruption and the later stability of the relationship suggests an experimentally testable hypothesis. To determine whether wives' interruptive behavior is a cause of marital instability, the investigator might identify couples in which the wife frequently interrupts the husband and then randomly select half of these wives to receive instruction in conversational courtesy (the experimental group) while leaving the other wives to continue their interruptive ways (thus serving as a control group). If a wife's interruptive behavior is a causal factor in marital stability, the couples in which the wife stops interrupting her husband should prove to be more stable than the control couples.

To arrive at experimentally testable hypotheses about cause from correlational data, however, researchers typically draw on everything they know about the phenomenon of interest—in this case, marital stability. For example, some researchers might guess that an unmeasured third variable was causing *both* the wife's interruptive behavior at Time 1 and marital instability at Time 2. They might recall that Tzeng's (1992) analysis of National Longitudinal Survey data found that marital instability is highest among couples who have different levels of education and who do not follow a traditional working arrangement (the "traditional" arrangement being one in which only the husband is employed full time). They might put that finding together with previous findings indicating that higher-power partners, whether male or female, tend to interrupt their lower-power partners more than the reverse (see Geis, 1993). This might cause them to conjecture that, in contrast to the noninterrupting women, Filsinger and Thoma's (1988) interruptive wives enjoyed more power in their relationship because they were employed. That might lead the researchers to think about the evidence that women who are economically independent and have larger social networks usually are less dependent on, and more willing to dis-

solve, a relationship than women who are socially and financially dependent on the relationship. They might conclude, then, that it was the interruptive wives' greater access to economic and social resources and lesser dependency on the relationship—*not* their propensity to interrupt—that was the *causally generative* factor associated with later relationship instability. Such a conclusion would lead to abandonment of the social skills intervention experiment and dictate a different future research direction.

Sometimes the evidence needed to shed additional light on a finding such as Filsinger and Thoma's interruption–instability association is not available at the time the results are obtained. A decade after Filsinger and Thoma published their study, Daigen and Holmes (2000) hypothesized that although conversational interruptions usually are rude, sometimes they are expressions of agreement and clarification rather than disagreement and "tangentialization" (changing the subject). Coding couples' interactions for these different types of interruption revealed that agreement interruptions were positively—not negatively—correlated with relationship satisfaction, whereas disagreement interruptions were associated with dissatisfaction. Filsinger and Thoma did not code the type of interruptions their wives-to-be made in interaction with their partners, but looking back at their results in the light of Daigen and Holmes's findings, one suspects that the women were interrupting because they disagreed with their partners. If so, it was not their interruptive behavior per se that caused later maladjustment and instability but rather the disagreements themselves and the conflict they represented.

In sum, the determination of cause is always an extraordinarily difficult endeavor because cause can never be directly observed—it is always inferred. Causal inference always requires many logical, statistical, and mathematical assumptions about the data and auxiliary evidentiary knowledge. Mackie (1965) discusses the complex logical problems involved in determining causation; Shadish, Cook, and Campbell (2001) discuss the problems involved in making causal inferences from various experimental and quasi-experimental data collection designs; and McKim and Turner (1997) discuss the great difficulties behavioral scientists face in making causal inferences about social phenomena from nonexperimental data. As a consequence, it is important for consumers of relationship research to (1) identify the nature—experimental or nonexperimental—of the data from which causal conclusions are drawn; (2) understand that the assumptions necessary for causal inference are more easily satisfied with experimental than with nonexperimental data; (3) be aware that, in the absence of evidence that nonexperimental data satisfy the several mathematical conditions they must meet before causal inference is valid, the acceptance of causal interpretations from such data may require a leap of faith; and (4) heed sociologist Stanley Lieberson's (1997) caution: "Above all we should resist seeking a precision that is inappropriate for either our subject matter or the nonexperimental tools with which we must work" (p. 384). In other words, it is as important to know what we do *not* know about relationship phenomena as to know what we do know.

Qualitative Studies

Experimental and correlational studies use quantitative methods—numbers and mathematically based models to analyze those numbers—to describe the data collected and to make inferences from them. In contrast, qualitative studies primarily describe data in words rather than numbers, although some qualitative researchers also use statistical analyses to describe and draw inferences from their data (see Denzin & Lincoln, 2000). Qualitative research differs from quantitative research in a number of other ways. Discussing its use in relationship science, Allen and Walker (2000) note that qualitative research tends to be *naturalistic*; that is, the investigator observes people behaving in their natural habitat rather than in the laboratory. Qualitative researchers may examine people's conversations and interactions in naturalistic settings or in such human artifacts as journals, letters, diaries, and autobiographies. They also may obtain life histories or narrative stories from people or videotape their

behavior. In sum, the data collected in qualitative research need not be limited to those amenable to quantification and statistical analysis.

Qualitative research requires sustained observation and reflective interpretation. The researcher describes what he or she sees and uses his or her intellect and experience to reach conclusions from what was observed. The reliability, validity, and usefulness of the conclusions the qualitative researcher reaches depend heavily on the talent and credibility of the researcher. For example, one would not trust the qualitative research of a Mr. Magoo, the myopic cartoon character who cheerfully goes about his business oblivious to the perils around him. However, many researchers have valued the qualitative reports of Erving Goffman, the sociologist who presented his observations and conclusions about social interaction in such classic works as *The Presentation of the Self in Everyday Life* (1959). The focus of qualitative research usually is on generating causal hypotheses rather than on testing them, and many researchers have devoted considerable time and effort to experimentally investigate Goffman's impressions.

Researchers who use qualitative means to understand behavioral phenomena tend to be especially sensitive to people's perspectives on their lives and the meanings and interpretations they place on events. As a consequence, another defining feature of qualitative research is that the investigator often develops a close relationship with his or her research participants because involvement in the participants' lives makes it easier for the researcher to view the world through their eyes. Qualitative researchers generally continue their study until they reach a personally satisfying understanding of the phenomena they are studying.

Yet another characteristic of qualitative research is that it frequently is conducted with a point of view. For example, the researcher may be trying to further a sociopolitical cause such as fathers' custody rights or domestic violence laws. Because qualitative researchers often collect and view their data through a partisan lens, some researchers view qualitative research methodology with skepticism (see Cizek, 1995).

THE MULTIDISCIPLINARY NATURE OF RELATIONSHIP SCIENCE

As we have discussed, because relationships are open systems they are influenced by the systems in which they are nested and they influence the systems nested in them. As a consequence, the study of relationships involves many levels of social and biological complexity (see Figure 3.5; see also Hinde, 1997, p. xv) and requires the contributions of many disciplines in the social, behavioral, biological, and health sciences.

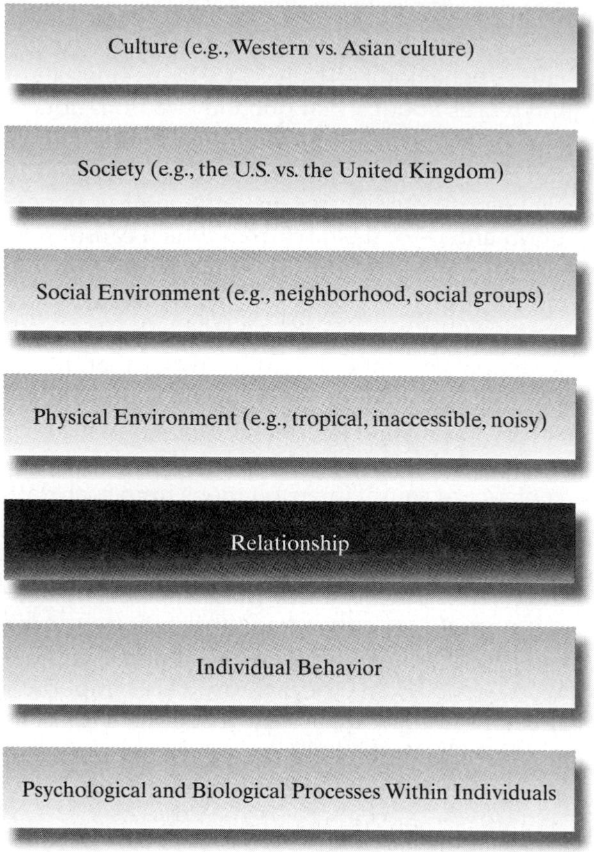

That relationship science is a multidisciplinary enterprise, dependent on progress in many different disciplines to even answer a single and seemingly simple question, is illustrated by the effort needed to answer a question posed by Edward Westermarck in the last decade of the nineteenth century: "Does early childhood association between a girl and a boy cause a lack of sexual attraction between them in adulthood?" Westermarck speculated:

> Generally speaking, there is a remarkable absence of erotic feelings between persons living closely together from childhood. Nay more, in this, as in many other cases, sexual indifference is combined with the positive feeling of aversion when the act is thought of. . . . Persons who have been living closely together from childhood are as a rule near relatives. Hence their aversion to sexual relations with one another displays itself in custom and law as a prohibition of intercourse between near kin. (cited in Wolf, 1995, p. 1)

The **Westermarck hypothesis**, that there is a natural human aversion to sexual relations with familiar persons, became highly controversial for several reasons. One was its obvious implications for societal legislation against incest. Another was that Westermarck's assertion was, in effect, a slap in the face to Sigmund Freud.

Freud quickly recognized that if Westermarck was right, he was wrong. As anthropologist Arthur Wolf (1995), who was to devote his entire professional life to answering Westermarck's

| Culture (e.g., Western vs. Asian culture) |
| Society (e.g., the U.S. vs. the United Kingdom) |
| Social Environment (e.g., neighborhood, social groups) |
| Physical Environment (e.g., tropical, inaccessible, noisy) |
| Relationship |
| Individual Behavior |
| Psychological and Biological Processes Within Individuals |

FIGURE 3.5 A simplified view of the systems in which relationships are embedded and which relationships encapsulate. Each system may directly or indirectly influence or be influenced by any other system, including the Relationship system.

question, explains: "The possibility that early childhood association suppressed sexual attraction had to be denied lest the basis of the Oedipus complex crumble and with it his conception of personality dynamics, his explanation of neuroses, and his grand view of the origins of law, art, and civilization" (p. 19). Freud had no choice but to pick up Westermarck's gauntlet and engage in the duel:

> [Some] have asserted that propinquity from early childhood has deflected sexual desire from the persons concerned. . . . Psychoanalytic investigations have shown beyond the possibility of doubt that *an*

incestuous love-choice [emphasis in the original] is in fact the first and the regular one, and that it is only later that any opposition is manifested towards it, the causes of which are not to be sought in the psychology of the individual. (cited in Wolf, 1995, p. 1)

Although words flew, neither side could claim victory because no one could ethically and practically conduct an experiment to settle the controversy. The only nonpartisan finding bearing on the issue did not appear until the 1960s when Talmon (1964) reported that marriage rarely, if ever, took place between male and female children raised together from infancy in Israeli kibbutzim.

The matter remained in limbo until Wolf (1995), a graduate student in anthropology doing field research in China as part of his doctoral training, stumbled across records revealing that Mother Nature, in one of her most remarkable feats, had constructed a natural experiment that satisfied the conditions a test of the Westermarck hypothesis requires: (1) A particular society that permitted two forms of marriage, one involving early and intimate association between the prospective bride and groom and the other prohibiting all contact between the two prior to marriage, thus providing a manipulation of the independent variable (early childhood association between spouses). (2) The only difference between the two marriage forms was that the spouses had early and intimate association in one and no contact before marriage in the other, thus controlling for other variables that might be confounded with the independent variable and that might themselves affect sexual attraction. (3) The process by which people were selected for the two forms of marriage was random, also controlling for confounding variables. (4) The women in the two groups differed in their premarital experience only with respect to early association with their husbands or the absence of such association, again controlling for potentially confounding variables. (5) The general socioeconomic conditions after marriage were the same for the two groups, eliminating another potentially confounding variable. (6) There was an objective means for measuring the dependent variable—sexual attraction between the spouses.

For a time in South China and parts of the Korean peninsula, Wolf discovered, there were two forms of marriage. In the first (now defunct) form, the future groom's parents ensured that their son would have a wife by making a marriage contract with the wife's parents, who then transferred the girl at a young age (often as a nursing infant) to her future husband's home, where she was raised with him and his siblings. The bride was called a *sim-pua*, meaning "little daughter-in-law." In the second form of marriage, the parents also made the marital contract, but the bride and groom met each other only hours before marriage. Assignment to each form of marriage was essentially random, and both forms were structurally similar in that they were enacted in the same three stages: First, the future wife left her father's home and custody; second, she entered her father-in-law's home and custody; and third, she and the groom together worshiped his ancestors and were thereby united as husband and wife. The principal difference between the two marriage forms was that whereas in the second form the bride moved through the three stages in a period of 4 or 5 hours, a *sim-pua* and her husband experienced a delay of 10 to 15 years between the second and third stages.

Wolf conceived his project when he was 25 and published his results when he was 63. Over those many years, he exhaustively examined and rigorously analyzed the archival records of the two forms of marriage and searched for and analyzed data from appropriate comparison and control groups. His final conclusion is reflected in the subtitle of his report: *Sexual Attraction and Childhood Association: A Chinese Brief for Edward Westermarck*. In other words, Westermarck was right: Early familiarity *does* diminish later sexual attraction, as evidenced by significant differences in the fertility and divorce records of couples brought together in the two forms of marriage.

Wolf's lifetime of research has not only resolved the Westermarck–Freud debate but has raised another question that may surpass the original in importance. Wolf noticed something curious in his data: The success of a *sim-pua* marriage depended on the wife's age at adoption—not the husband's age at her arrival—and the absence of sexual attraction was most dramatically evident among couples brought together in the wife's first or second year. These are the years during which children form their most intense attachments. Wolf speculates that Westermarck's aversion and Bowlby's attachment might be closely related phenomena—even two sides of the same coin. Because a child forms strong attachments during his or her first and second years, and because the wife is usually younger than the husband, Wolf hypothesizes that *she* is the one who develops an attachment to him and an accompanying aversion to sexual relations with him. Wolf also speculates, however, that those husbands who became caregivers to the female infant also may have experienced an accompanying contrasexual disposition. As noted in Chapter 1, the caregiving system has been relatively ignored by attachment researchers. Only future research on what surely will become known as the Wolf hypothesis will determine whether the attachment and caregiving systems are in fact contrasexual systems. At present, the only evidence relevant to the hypothesis is anecdotal (e.g., a letter to "Ann Landers" ["Her illness," 2001] from a husband who, despite his invalid wife's pleas, was disinterested in sex with her because, he said, he felt like her caregiver, not her lover).

It is necessary for relationship scholars to be familiar with many disciplines other than the one in which they were formally trained, as Wolf's (1995) study illustrates. To answer the relationship question he posed, Wolf found it necessary to draw on sinology, which gave him access to the data and an understanding of the context in which they were produced; social anthropology, which enabled him to conceptualize the different forms of marriage in China; demography, which contributed quantitative techniques he used to analyze the archival data involved in testing his hypotheses; sociology, which suggested a number of alternative hypotheses and ways of evaluating them; biology, which inspired a critical revision of the central hypothesis along the way

and provided an evolutionary perspective that illuminated its power; philosophy of science, which prepared him to formulate the many questions involved in answering the central question in ways they could be answered; and psychology, which contributed theory and findings on attachment.

Wolf (1995) observes that his study "repudiates the view that the boundaries partitioning scholarly activity into 'fields' are anything other than arbitrary and artificial" (p. viii). The view that such boundaries, and the increasing compartmentalization and specialization within fields, hinder the advancement of knowledge has been persuasively articulated and elaborated by E. O. Wilson, the noted biologist. In *Consilience: The Unity of Knowledge* (1998), Wilson argues that in the future, major discoveries in science are most likely to emerge through viewing the natural world as an integrated whole and integrating concepts and methodological and analytical tools across many disciplines. The word "consilience" comes from two Latin words that mean "leaping together" and refers to advancing knowledge by linking theory and facts across many disciplines to create a common groundwork of explanation. Relationship science is a consilient science.

DISCIPLINES CONTRIBUTING TO RELATIONSHIP SCIENCE

The many disciplines currently contributing to relationship science can be ranged along a continuum extending from society to the individual (see Figure 3.6). Although many of the biological and health sciences also are contributing vital knowledge to relationship science, the social and behavioral sciences are the major contributors. Each discipline tends to examine different kinds of relationships, different variables, and different questions and uses different theories and methodologies to identify the causal conditions that influence relationship interaction patterns.

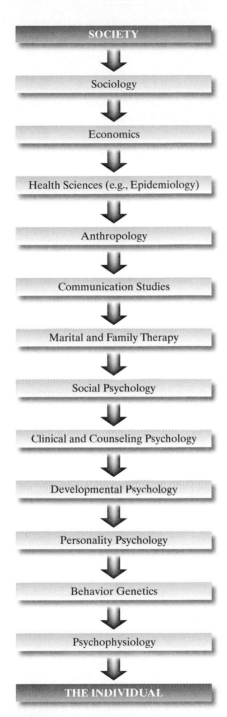

FIGURE 3.6 The many disciplines currently contributing to the development of relationship science can be ranged along a continuum extending from society to the individual.

Psychology

Most of psychology's contributions to relationship science are indirect because psychology principally focuses on discovering general laws, many of which derive from the human's biological properties, that apply to all individuals within the species. Such knowledge is essential to understanding relationships because many of the regularities in interaction are a product of the mental and physical characteristics of humans (Hinde, 1979; Kelley, 1983/2002a).

In addition to discovering general laws of behavior, psychologists identify behavioral laws that pertain to differences among individuals, such as differences in personality, attitudes, and genetic background; that is, many psychologists take an *individualistic–psychometric* approach to human behavior. This approach has predominated in psychology (Reis et al., 2000) and is another Darwinian legacy. The sources of the individual differences that are associated with differential behavior have received less attention than identification of the differences. One important source of these differences, as discussed in Part 1, is people's relationships.

Because psychologists have been major contributors to relationship science, and because most bring with them the individualistic perspective characteristic of the field, much relationship theory and research is individualistic in nature (Sarason, Sarason, & Pierce, 1995). Such individualistic research focuses on identifying associations between the properties of the individual, such as neuroticism or adult attachment style, and the individual's relationship experiences and outcomes, such as marital stability. One of psychology's first contributions to relationship science, a longitudinal study conducted by Terman (1938) on marital satisfaction, is illustrative. Typical of the individualistic approach, Terman measured his participants on a great number of characteristics and then later assessed their satisfaction with their marriages. A similar longitudinal study was reported by Kelly and Conley (1987) who, between 1935 and 1938, measured a number of characteristics of persons engaged to be married and then conducted

THE DEVELOPMENT OF RELATIONSHIP SCIENCE   **87**

follow-ups on these individuals' marital fate (finding that, for example, the personality trait of neuroticism was associated with marital dissatisfaction).

Developmental Psychology

Within psychology, developmental psychology is currently one of the most important contributors to relationship science. It is likely to retain that status as the influence of early relationships on human development continues to expand. An exemplar of the close relationship—the parent–child relationship—long has been of interest to developmental psychologists. Like other psychologists, however, developmentalists traditionally approached questions of socialization and development from an individualistic point of view. With respect to socialization, for example, the direction of influence in the parent–child relationship was believed to be almost exclusively from the parent (or other adult) to the child.

The traditional "one-way direction of influence" view of socialization began to change at midcentury when Robert Sears delivered an intellectually challenging presidential address to the American Psychological Association. Sears observed that psychology was almost exclusively "monadic"—focusing solely on the individual and his or her behavior—and it sought only monadic laws, universal laws of behavior that related only to a single individual. Sears (1951) urged psychologists to expand their horizon and study dyadic phenomena:

> A diadic [sic] unit is one that describes the combined actions of two or more persons. A diadic unit is essential if there is to be any conceptualization of the *relationships* between people, as in the parent–child, teacher–pupil, husband–wife, or leader–follower instances. To have a science of interactive events, one must have variables and units of action that refer to such events. While it is possible to systematize some observations about individuals by using monadic unit, the fact is that a large proportion of the properties of a person that compose his [or her] personality are originally formed in diadic situations

and are measurable only by reference to diadic situations or symbolic representations of them. (p. 479)

Sears pointed the direction, but little changed until Richard Bell published a powerful essay in 1968 titled "A Reinterpretation of the Direction of Effects in Studies of Socialization." At that time, the socialization literature was composed almost entirely of correlations between the parent's and the child's behaviors. After reviewing that literature, Bell concluded that the traditional model of socialization, which focused only on the parent's influence on the child, was too limited to accommodate data that had been emerging from studies of humans and infrahuman animals. Because correlation cannot specify the direction of an effect, Bell contended that the influence of children on their parents could no longer be dismissed as an implausible explanation of many of the associations obtained. Developmental psychologists often directly examine interaction patterns, as the work of Tronick and associates (1978), discussed in Chapter 1, illustrates.

Social Psychology

Social psychologists focus on the processes underlying social behavior. Prominent among those processes are those associated with interpersonal attraction, as discussed in Chapter 6, "Birth of a Relationship." Although initially most attraction research was conducted with strangers who met and interacted in the laboratory (Berscheid & Walster, 1969), by the early 1980s attraction researchers had grown frustrated with the limitations of such research. As a consequence, they became more willing to confront the many conceptual, methodological, and ethical difficulties associated with research on ongoing relationships (see Berscheid, 1985b).

Social psychology's focus on the processes underlying social behavior and a special interest in interpersonal attraction were the legacies of Kurt Lewin (Figure 3.7), the founder of experimental social psychology and the first formal systems theorist in psychology (Deutsch, 1954). Lewin rebelled against psychology's individualistic

FIGURE 3.7 Kurt Lewin. *Archives of the History of American Psychology-The University of Akron*

approach, which concentrated the search for the causes of behavior solely in the properties of individuals. At that time, psychologists maintained that only the individual was "real" and a proper subject for psychological study—relationships were said to exist only in the mind of individuals (e.g., Allport, 1924; see Berscheid, 2002a).

Lewin's field theory (1936/1951), the core of which is expressed in his well-known formula $B = f(P, E)$, stated that behavior B is a function of an interaction between the properties of the person P and the properties of the environment E, which is the "field" in which the individual is located. In addition to the individual's physical environment, Lewin viewed the field as including the person's social environment; thus, an individual's relationships were theorized to have an important influence on his or her behavior. Lewin (1948) himself was interested in close relationships, as the title of one of his early articles, "The Background of Conflict in Marriage," reflects.

Many of Lewin's disciples began to theorize about and study relationships in the late 1940s and the 1950s. Two of his students, John Thibaut and Harold Kelley, formulated interdependence theory, which they initially presented in *The Social Psychology of Groups* (1959). Although the

book's title suggested their theory was addressed to the behavior of persons within larger groups, interdependence theory was in fact addressed to the dyad and to phenomena that occur within close relationships, particularly romantic and marital relationships, as discussed in Chapter 4, "The Concept of Relationship."

Social psychology began to retreat from its interest in relationships, however, as the learning theories, all highly individualistic, became dominant in psychology (see Steiner, 1974). Social psychology's movement toward an individualistic approach was further propelled by the subsequent advent of the "cognitive revolution" in psychology. Social cognition, the study of how an individual structures and processes information about other people, continues to be the major focus of social psychology, but researchers now recognize that social cognition is primarily in the service of people's relationships with others (S. T. Fiske, 1992; Berscheid, 1994; Berscheid & Reis, 1998), and they are incorporating the implications of this fact into social cognition theory and research (see Reis & Downey, 1999).

Clinical and Counseling Psychology

The contributions of clinical and counseling psychology to relationship science tend to focus on effective interventions into distressed relationships. Like most psychologists, clinical and counseling psychologists traditionally took an individualistic approach to the treatment of distress, psychoanalysis being a prime example. Some training programs in counseling and clinical psychology remain heavily individualistic, but others are recognizing that people's presenting problems usually concern their relationships with others (as noted in Chapter 2, "Relationships and Health"). As a consequence, relationship therapy training is increasingly featured in clinical and counseling training.

Marital and Family Therapy

The discipline of marital and family therapy, a hybrid field that itself was initially multidisciplinary, was developed and is maintained outside the mainstream of psychology. For example, graduate training programs in marital and family therapy and training programs in clinical psychology do not share the same accreditation procedures. The emergence of marital and family therapy as a distinct field was partly a response to the public's growing demand for help with their close relationships and partly a reaction to the limitations of psychology's individualistic view of psychological distress and dysfunction. In the mid-1950s, several influential therapists began to formulate "conjoint" therapeutic approaches that involved *both* members of a distressed marital relationship and often all members of a family system (e.g., Jackson & Weakland, 1961; see Chapter 14, "Intervention and Dissolution").

Many formative constructs and concepts in the marital and family therapy field were borrowed from an array of other fields, including mathematics, social work, communication studies, cybernetics, sociology, social psychiatry, and general systems theory (see Alexander, Sexton, & Robbins, 2001). Today, there is agreement in the field that the family is best conceived as a social system, that relationship variables are critical to understanding the family, that observation of actual family interaction is often essential to successful intervention, and that in many cases, if an individual distressed person or a distressed relationship is to change, the entire relationship system must be treated. This is in contrast to the traditional view (sometimes called the medical view or the identified patient view) that the problem lies solely within the distressed individual or the person whose behavior is problematic.

In response to concern that the practice of relationship therapy long ago outstripped its knowledge base, a distinct subspecialty within family psychology, family psychology intervention science, has emerged over the past two decades (see Liddle, Santisteban, Levant, & Bray, 2001). This empirically based field takes a systems view and thus awards special attention to multiple systems and levels of social influence, such as peers and communities, in the treatment of relationship dysfunction.

Communication Studies

The field of communication studies is closely associated with the field of marital and family therapy. Many original contributors to the family therapy field were communication scholars (e.g., Watzlawick & Jackson, 1977) who viewed interpersonal behavior as attempts to influence the partner and define the relationship (see Christensen, 1983/2002). Today, many communication scholars are studying the role that dysfunctional communication patterns play in distressed relationships (e.g., Noller & Feeney, 1998; Noller & Ruzzene, 1991). Indeed, as discussed in Chapter 14, "Intervention and Dissolution," many marital and family intervention programs have found that communication skills training is efficacious in treating distressed relationships.

Sociology

Sociology long has been an important contributor to the development of relationship knowledge. Durkheim's (1897/1963) study of the importance of social ties is an early example. Today, sociology also encompasses the field of social network theory and analysis discussed in Chapter 2, "Relationships and Health." Perhaps the greatest contribution sociologists have made to relationship science has been their sustained study of the institution of marriage and the family. Sociological marriage and family research typically investigates a very broad range of topics whose underlying theme is the causal linkages between the family and larger society.

In recent years, several sociologists have argued that continued focus on the family as a coherent entity is no longer fruitful and that broader and more abstract constructs addressed to relationships are needed (see Scanzoni, Polonko, Teachman, & Thompson, 1989). Classical microsociology, which focuses on interaction in social situations, provides an avenue for such an approach. Sociological theories of symbolic interactionism, for example, address how people define social situations, give meaning to their own and others' actions, and create and negotiate their roles in social interaction (e.g., Mead, 1934; Stryker, 1980). Goffman's (1959) qualitative research on impression management, which he believes occurs in all social interactions, was inspired by these theories. Contemporary microsociology overlaps considerably with contemporary psychological approaches to relationships (e.g., Kelley et al., 1983/2002).

Anthropology

The study of mortality and social ties among the Donner party conducted by Grayson (1990, discussed in Chapter 2) and Wolf's (1995) investigation of the Westermarck hypothesis (discussed in this chapter) illustrate the kinds of contributions anthropologists make to relationship science. These studies also illustrate that although anthropologists generally look at constellations of relationships within larger groupings of people, they historically have investigated all aspects of close relationship behavior. Not only are anthropologists sensitive to the influence of culture on behavior (an influence psychologists are only belatedly recognizing) but the investigation of cultural differences in relationship behavior is central to that field.

Economics

Economic theorists often invoke the "rational man [and woman]" model to explain and predict behavior; that is, they view people as rational beings who systematically research and weigh the economic utility of their behavioral options and act accordingly. Relationship phenomena are increasingly addressed by economic theories. For example, economist Gary Becker received the 1992 Nobel Prize in Economic Sciences for his extension of microeconomic analysis to a wide range of personal relationship behavior, including the distribution of work and decisions regarding marriage, divorce, and children.

Many societal economic problems have their roots in relationship phenomena. For example, Becker and Murphy (2000) finger assortative mating as the prime causal culprit in income in-

equality (the gap between rich and poor), which has increased dramatically in the United States over the past several decades. Assortative mating—like marrying like—results in the rich, healthy, and educated marrying the rich, healthy, and educated and, of course, the poor marrying the poor. The harmful effect of resource inequality is the reason, Becker and Murphy note, that Plato, in his *Republic*, urged the rich not to marry the rich but rather to form relationships with their "inferiors."

National and state governments long have been aware of the potent economic implications relationship behavior has for the larger society. As a consequence, they often try to tinker with relationship dynamics through legislation. For example, the U.S. tax code penalizes marriage but benefits parents; the establishment of "covenant" marriages in such states as Louisiana makes some marriages difficult to dissolve; and in 2002 the Bush administration was developing programs to encourage welfare recipients to marry.

China, too, has launched a number of efforts to legislate relationship behavior for the economic benefit and welfare of the larger society. China's "one couple, one child" law, instituted in the early 1980s to solve the country's overpopulation problem, is perhaps the most ambitious relationship intervention any nation has ever attempted. Although the intervention has been a success, it has created other problems: "When we started our family-planning policy 20 years ago, we had no idea of the social problems that would follow," says the director-general of China's family planning commission (Beech, 2001). Many of these problems stem from the fact that the one-child law interacted with the high value Asian cultures place on males, with the result that sex-based abortions and female infanticide and abandonment dramatically increased (as noted in Chapter 1, "First Relationships"). Although the true figures are not available ([officials] refused to release the sex ratio from the 1991 census, according to the *New York Times* ["China's Crackdown," 1993]), China now has a highly skewed **sex ratio**, defined as the number of males per 100 females (Guttentag & Secord,

1983; Secord, 1983). In China today, 117 boys are born for every 100 girls, which suggests that the current difficulties young Chinese men are having in finding a wife are not likely to ease in a culture that reveres family (Beech, 2001). India, which also prizes males over females, is heading toward the same problem; it is estimated that if present trends continue, India soon could have about 70 million males without female partners (Doll, 1998). It should be noted that China and India are not alone in preferring sons over daughters; the preference is shared worldwide (see Belsky, 1990). In the United States, the preference may be reflected in the fact that for couples with only one child, risk of marital dissolution is 9% higher for those with a daughter than with a son; for those with two children, couples with two daughters have an 18% higher dissolution risk than those with two sons (Morgan, Lye, & Condran, 1988).

We have said that accurate relationship prediction is hazardous because it requires a great deal of knowledge at many system levels. If the effect of a governmental intervention into relationship behavior is not accurately predicted, it is likely that subsequent actions will need to be taken to try to correct the unanticipated ill effects of the first action, and those subsequent actions often create their own problems. An example is China's attempt to control the female abortion and infanticide consequences of the one child law by proclaiming that women are as valuable as men, as reported in the headline "China Drafts Measure Declaring Women Are Equal to Men" (1992). Because no enforcement mechanisms were attached to the declaration, it seems unlikely that it erased cultural values ingrained over centuries. Subsequently, to prevent the abortion of females, the Chinese government outlawed sex screening via ultrasound. But that law now is interacting with another of China's laws, passed in 1995, decreeing that "inferior births" (defined as infants with congenital infirmities) should be prevented because of the high cost of health care for such children ("Quality Not Quantity," 1994). To further complicate matters, the incidence of children born with birth defects is likely to increase as

Chinese men, faced with a scarcity of females, increasingly marry first cousins within their families, thereby almost doubling their risk of having children with birth defects (Beech, 2002).

CULTURAL DIFFERENCES IN RELATIONSHIPS

Relationship theory and research have been produced mostly within Western cultures in the United States, Canada, and western Europe. For example, most family research has been conducted with white, middle-class heterosexual families in the United States (see Engel, 1982; Parke, 2000). Western cultures are different from East Asian, Middle Eastern, Central and South American, Eastern European, and other cultures in many ways, but particularly in sociality and the role that relationships play in people's lives (Markus & Kitayama, 1991; Triandis, 1995).

For example, whereas Western cultures have been characterized as **individualistic** in nature, many Eastern cultures have been viewed as **collectivist**, or socially interdependent. East Asians, for instance, tend to view themselves as (1) connected and bound to others; (2) constrained, guided, and enabled in their actions by their relationships, roles, groups, and institutions; (3) oriented toward the harmonious functioning of the social entities of which they are a part, subordinating their personal beliefs and needs to societal norms and relationships; (4) sensitive to the needs of the collective, evaluating their lives with reference to their contributions to satisfying those needs; and (5) mutually responsible for those with whom they interact and for the consequences of their own and their partners' joint behavior (see Fiske, Kitayama, Markus, & Nisbett, 1998). In contrast to East Asians, persons in many Western cultures (1) view themselves as autonomous and "free"; (2) are enabled and guided in their actions by their preferences, motives, goals, attitudes, beliefs, and abilities; (3) are oriented primarily toward independent success and achievement; (4) evaluate their lives with reference to their achievement of personal goals; and

(5) regard relationships as competing with their personal needs and group pressures as interfering with the achievement of personal goals.

Within each geographical region, cultural ideas "are regularly embodied in most of the major prevailing practices, institutions, and public symbols and meanings of most of the dominant cultures" (Fiske et al., 1998, p. 920). Socialization practices, which instill in children the beliefs and behaviors appropriate for a particular culture or subculture, are particularly important in maintaining cultural ideas and values. Illustrative is the tale told by the former chief medical consultant to Project Head Start, Robert Mendelsohn (1975), of how one American couple proposed to develop their son's self-reliance and independence from others: The father of a 3-year-old boy remarked to Mendelsohn that because he had lost his job, his wife had taken a job at the same day-care center his child attended. Mendelsohn replied that this was fortuitous, for it would be reassuring to the child to have his mother close by. Mendelsohn's response horrified the father. He and his wife did not want their son to be reassured, he exclaimed, they wanted him to be independent! In fact, to encourage the tot's self-reliance, they had already arranged for him and his mother to take separate buses to the day-care center.

Meta-analyses of studies examining relational differences between individualism and collectivism conducted by Oyserman and her colleagues (2002) confirm that European Americans are both more individualistic than other groups—for example, they value personal independence—and less collectivistic in feelings of duty to the groups to which they belong. Americans interact with more groups, feel freer to choose those groups, and are more at ease with strangers, whereas collectivist cultural groups tend to favor the in-group, accommodate in-group members, and distribute resources equally rather than equitably. Like people in collectivist cultures, Americans feel obligated to family, but they view these obligations as a voluntary personal choice. However, although there are reliable cultural differences between groups, Oyersman and associates conclude that these differences are not as systematic or as large as sometimes represented. For example, European Americans are individualistic, but not more so than African Americans or Latinos, and they are not less collectivistic than Japanese or Koreans. Among Asians, however, the Chinese show large effects; they are less individualistic and more collectivistic than others.

Within a geographical region, people within certain subcultures may hold very different beliefs than those promulgated by the dominant culture. Even within the United States, there are many subcultures that more resemble East Asian culture than they do Western culture. For example, when a Lakota Native American says "Hau Metakuyeayasi"—meaning "Hello, my relatives"—the word "relatives" refers not only to family members, such as brothers and sisters, parents and grandparents, but also to future generations and all of humankind, to the earth and sky, to sunlight, to insects, birds, animals, and fish, and, in fact, to virtually everything in our human world. According to Churchill (1996), "What is conveyed in this Lakota concept is the notion of the universe as a relational whole, a single interactive organism in which all things, all beings are active and essential parts; the whole can never be understood without a knowledge of the function and meaning of each of the parts, while the parts cannot be understood other than in the context of the whole" (p. 462). Churchill claims that, like the Lakotas, indigenous cultures throughout the world view the world as composed of interdependent systems.

Concentration on relationships in Western cultures has influenced relationship knowledge in two ways: First, and perhaps most obviously, available knowledge is most clearly generalizable to persons in Western cultures. Second, and not so obvious, is that the theoretical and methodological approaches taken to obtaining relationship knowledge are permeated with the assumptions that underlie Western worldviews and the Western philosophy of science; for example, in contrast to the systems worldview that all living things are interconnected and that human well-being depends upon coexisting in harmony with nature, Western culture and Western science focus on manipulating, controlling, and subduing nature (see Capra, 1982). **Reductionism**—breaking apart the whole of a functioning system to examine its individual parts, as by observing the operation of a human organ in a laboratory dish rather than in its natural context of the rest of the body—has long been the methodological mainstay of Western science.

In contrast to the shift toward system views that has taken place in many of the biological and material sciences, psychology remains mostly individualistic in orientation, studying the properties of the individual and their associations with behavior, often outside the context in which people usually behave. The slowness with which a science devoted to understanding human relationships has developed is at least partly a consequence of the fact that it has been dependent on advances in the social and behavioral sciences, which are products of Western culture and individualistic in nature.

Oyserman and her colleagues (2001) and many others have concluded that psychologists need to better understand the social, interactive, and context-dependent nature of psychological functioning. Relationship science promises to advance that understanding. In the meantime, however, it is important to recognize that relationship knowledge has mostly been produced by, and is most applicable to, persons in Western cultures. It also is necessary to be aware that the assumption that psychological processes are pan-human and, thus, universally applicable is increasingly questioned.

SUMMARY

Because relationships play such an important and pervasive role in human life, it may surprise students and scholars alike to find that relationship science has been relatively slow to develop. Its late emergence was due in part to the multidisciplinary nature of the field and the fact that its progression was dependent on advancements in many other sciences. In addition, relationship science has faced (and continues to face) a number of obstacles to its development, including societal taboos that deemed relationship events and experiences inappropriate for, or unamenable to, scientific investigation, and recruiting biases that make it difficult to properly interpret data collected from participants. A variety of ethical considerations also plague relationship research. For example, it is generally inappropriate to experimentally manipulate ongoing relationships, and it is often difficult to foresee the negative consequences of research participation and obtain truly informed consent from participants. Furthermore, relationship research poses special methodological and analytical problems to investigators, ranging from identifying the proper unit of analysis to accurately identifying the causal conditions that produce various relationship phenomena. In an effort to overcome these obstacles, relationship scientists have mined theory, research, and methodology from a number of disciplines, including psychology, marital and family therapy, communication studies, sociology, anthropology, and economics (among others). Consequently, relationship science is one of the most multidisciplinary endeavors. This, too, however, poses a problem for relationship scholars; for example, research conducted by many social and behavioral scientists (and by relationship scientists themselves) has been produced within Western cultures and therefore is most applicable to persons living in those cultures.

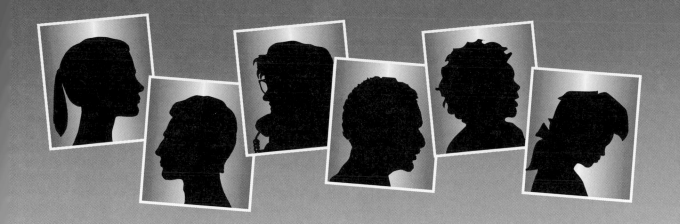

Chapter 4

The Concept of Relationship

INTRODUCTION

One of the greatest obstacles to the development of a systematic body of knowledge about relationships was relationship scholars' lack of common understanding of what a relationship is. As we have discussed, advancement of knowledge about human relationships is dependent on contributions from many different disciplines in the social, behavioral, biological, and health sciences. Multidisciplinary fields are often slow to take coherent shape because each contributing discipline tends to be interested only in certain phenomena—and, in the case of relationships, only in certain phenomena within certain types of relationships. Moreover, each discipline attacks those phenomena from the perspective of its traditional theories and concepts, using its own terminology and methods. As a consequence, new multidisciplinary fields often experience communication problems. Relationship science was no different. Relationship scholars soon recognized that the term "relationship" meant different things to different people, both across and within disciplines,

and that little progress could be made until they reached agreement on the meaning of the term.

Most people, most of the time, think they know what the word "relationship" means. The word is part of our everyday language, as are the many descriptive adjectives we use to differentiate one kind of relationship from another ("close," "committed," "dysfunctional," and so on). In the beginning, relationship researchers, too, believed that the meaning of the word "relationship" and its common descriptors were so obvious that they need not waste time clarifying them. As the relationship field grew, however, it became apparent that one scholar's "relationship" often was another scholar's "something else," but it was seldom clear what that something was (Berscheid & Peplau, 1983/2002). By the late 1970s, relationship scholar Robert Hinde characterized the relationship field as a "conceptual jungle that chokes the unwary" (1979, p. 6).

The communication problem initially experienced by relationship scholars is often experienced by many of us in our daily lives: We ourselves know what the word "relationship" means, and we assume not only that everyone else (including our relationship partner) knows what we mean by the term but also that the word means the same to all of us. That assumption is frequently incorrect. Ann Weber (1998), who discusses the difficulties of studying how men and women cope with the breakup of their romantic relationships, observes that some people deny that their relationship with another broke up because, they protest, "There was no relationship to break up!" (p. 272). Similarly, more than one public figure charged with infidelity has asserted in all sincerity to inquiring reporters, "I did not have a relationship with that person!" One politician who was asked how his denial squared with the detailed description of their interactions by the woman in question responded, "It would probably be her definition of a relationship versus mine" (Isikoff & Thomas, 2001).

The fog that surrounds the common usage of the word "relationship" sometimes becomes painfully apparent when events cause people to begin to wonder if they have a relationship with another. Unable to reach a conclusion themselves, they resort to asking their partner, "Do we still have a relationship?" How their partner answers that question will depend on what he or she means by the word "relationship." The meaning of that word, and the meanings of other relational terms, vary across sex (Peplau & Gordon, 1985), age (Dickens & Perlman, 1981), and culture (Markus & Kitayama, 1991).

INTERACTION: THE ESSENCE OF A RELATIONSHIP

There is now substantial agreement among relationship scholars about what a relationship is (Berscheid & Reis, 1998). Most believe that the essence of a relationship between two people lies in their interaction with each other; in other words, the partners' interactions are the living tissue of their relationship. By **interaction**, relationship scholars mean that the partners *influence* each other; that is, how one partner behaves affects how the other partner subsequently behaves and vice versa. In relationships, there is a ping-

pong of influence back and forth such that one partner's behavioral activities at a given point in time influence the other partner's activities at a later point in time and vice versa. Because this oscillating rhythm of influence occurs over time, relationships are inherently *temporal* in nature—they are composed of a series of events that take place over time. As Hinde (1979) observes, "There is a degree of arbitrariness in the distinction between an 'interaction' and a 'relationship'" (p. 15), but in general, an **interaction episode** involves a limited span of time, whereas a relationship involves a longer duration of time.

Thus, at base, the term "relationship" in the interpersonal realm means the same as it does in the material realm and in the sciences that study matter, such as physics. Two entities, whether two people or two objects, are in a relationship if a change in the state of one produces a change in the state of the other. In other words, two entities are in a relationship if the behavior of each is *dependent* on the behavior of the other. Thus, a relationship is a **system**. Systems, as we have discussed, are identified by determining whether a change in one entity (posited to be one part of the system) will cause a change in another entity (posited to be a second part). If a change in one part does *not* produce a change in the other, then the two entities are not in a system. If two persons do not influence each other's activities, they are not in a relationship. This is why growing indifference to the behavior of another—not anger, as popularly believed—is symptomatic of a dying relationship. In sum, two people are in a relationship with each other to the extent that they are **interdependent** (Kelley et al., 1983/2002).

Amount and Kind of Interaction

Although most relationship scholars agree that interaction is the substance of a relationship, they differ on how *much* interaction between two people, and what *kind* of interaction, must take place before they are willing to say that two people are in a relationship. This is an important issue for many reasons. For example, in order to trace the development of a relationship, its beginning point must be identified. Some relationship development theorists place the beginning of a relationship at the point at which one individual becomes *aware* of another, whether or not the other person is aware of the first individual (e.g., Berscheid & Graziano, 1979; Levinger, 1974). Such theorists require only that there be unilateral—not necessarily mutual—awareness. A relationship may not develop beyond the point at which one person captures another's attention, however. If it does not, no relationship scholar would be willing to call that single event of awareness a relationship. If, however, the individual and the other person subsequently maintain interaction, many scholars would, in retrospect, identify the point of initial awareness as the relationship's beginning. Thus, some relationship scholars agree with songwriters Rogers and Hammerstein that a relationship may begin on some enchanted evening when a stranger is first seen across a crowded room.

Other theorists maintain that even a single extended interaction episode in which both persons strongly influence each other's behavior does not constitute a relationship. Sociologist George Homans (1979), for example, maintains, "Not until a person enters into repeated exchanges [interactions] with the same other may we even begin to speak of a relationship existing between them" (p. xviii). Hinde (1979) goes further. He asserts that even repeated "strings" of interactions do not necessarily constitute a relationship. Hinde and others take this position because the interaction may be role-based. In **role-based interactions** each person's behavior is influenced not by the partner's behavior but by societal norms and prescriptions that govern the behavior of all people who assume that particular role.

Many social interactions are role-based. The interaction between a customer and a sales clerk, for example, is largely dictated by their respective roles, and as a consequence, each person's behavior tends to be the same regardless of who the customer is, who the sales clerk is, where the interaction takes place, or what the object being purchased is. Hinde (1979) emphasizes that a series of interactions between two people whose behaviors are independent of each other—as is the case when people enact their respective roles in interaction—does not constitute a relationship: "An essential character of a relationship is that each interaction is influenced by other interactions in that relationship" (p. 16). In other words, a relationship is influenced by what occurred in *past* interactions. Because the customer and the sales clerk's present interactions are not much different from the interactions between countless other customers and clerks or from the past interactions of that particular customer and that particular clerk, most relationship scholars would not consider their interactions to constitute a relationship even if these two people have repeated the same interaction pattern many times over the years. At the least, it is not the kind of relationship that psychological relationship scholars typically study, although investigators in other disciplines, such as sociologists and anthropologists, do study role-based interactions.

Interactions, then, are a *necessary condition* for a relationship to exist—*all* relationships involve interactions. However, interactions are not a *sufficient condition* for the existence of a relationship because not all interactions constitute a relationship, as noted for role-based interactions. As this implies, relationship researchers tend to examine relationships in which the partners' interaction pattern is different from the interaction patterns each partner has with other persons and different from the interaction patterns characteristic of other sets of partners (Berscheid & Reis, 1998). In addition, most relationship scholars would not view two people as being in a relationship with each other unless both have cognitively represented and organized their past interactions and hold them in memory. It is the memory of past interactions, of course, that is responsible for the influence of past interactions on the present interaction. These mental representations of the relationship, developed over past interactions, thus constitute an important contextual feature of the partners' current interactions (e.g., Bradbury & Fincham, 1988, 1989), as discussed in Chapter 8, "Cognitive Processes."

In sum, most relationship scholars believe that in order for two people to be in a **relationship**, three conditions must be met:

- The two people must interact—they must *influence* each other's behaviors.
- Each person's interactions with the other must be different from his or her interactions with other people and, also, different from other people's interactions with each other.
- As a result of their interaction(s), the partners must have formed a mental representation of their relationship (usually termed a relationship schema), which influences their future interactions.

A relationship, then, does not reside within a single individual; rather, the locus of a relationship is in the interaction that takes place between two people. As John Gottman (1999), a leading researcher of marital therapy, explains with respect to marriage:

> I think marriage is like the music a jazz quartet makes when the musicians come together. The marital interaction is the music. As they interact, the two people create a third element, just like the music of the jazz quartet is a new entity, the fifth element produced by the four musicians. It is the *music* we must study. The temporal forms that spouses create and the way they feel about what they create when they are together are the essence of marriage. The "temporal forms" are like music; they are the repeated sequential patterns or themes of the marriage. . . . To understand the music of the quartet, it helps very little to describe the personalities of the players. Even the solo work of the musicians will often not predict how much a particular quartet is, or is not, "in the groove"—that is, making beautiful music together. (p. 20)

Lack of Interaction

Sometimes it is difficult to determine whether people currently are in a relationship with another even if they say are. Some sincerely deluded people will say they have a relationship with another despite the fact that there is not now, and never has been, any interaction with the person they claim is their relationship partner. Weber (1998) cites the strange case of John Hinckley, Jr.

(Figure 4.1), the man who attempted to assassinate President Ronald Reagan in 1981 in order to impress Jodie Foster, the actress he believed to be his romantic relationship partner:

> Foster took the stand at Hinckley's trial, and responded to the attorney's request that she describe her relationship with the defendant by insisting that she had no relationship with John Hinckley. Hinckley was observed weeping at this irrefutable denial of his love—the only emotional reaction he had been seen to display through the long legal proceedings that culminated in his commitment to a psychiatric hospital. Hinckley had no relationship with Foster, he merely had a fantasy about her. . . . Yet, his dream had nothing to do with either the real John Hinckley or the real Jodie Foster—or reality itself, for that matter. (p. 273)

People who fail to stay in contact with reality—the reality of their relationships or reality in any other realm of their lives—often meet with bad ends, commitment to a psychiatric hospital being only one of them. Although it is not unusual for people to fantasize about having a relationship with another person, often a celebrity or another person they find attractive, most do not mistake their fantasy for the reality of a relationship.

FIGURE 4.1 John Hinckley, Jr.

If two people seldom interact, there is not likely to be much of a relationship between them. Such associations are usually characterized as casual acquaintanceships or superficial relationships. Sometimes, however, people will report that they currently are in a relationship with another, and even that the relationship is a close one, despite the fact that they are not presently interacting with the other and have not interacted with him or her for many years.

There are a number of reasons people will report a moribund relationship as being alive and well. When people report a relationship with a person with whom they have had no ongoing interaction for many years, in most instances they interacted frequently with that person in the past. For example, brothers and sisters may have interacted frequently as children, but now an annual obligatory holiday visit to their parents' home may be the only occasion on which they interact. If the siblings are asked whether they currently are in a relationship with each other, they probably will unhesitatingly respond "Yes." Many relationships, especially relationships with **kin** (persons joined by blood or legal contract), have no sharply discernible ending point, and the individual often is unaware that a kin relationship is dead or dying. Relationships often wither and die as a result of the failure of the partners to interact, and not infrequently both the withering process and the fact that the relationship finally succumbed to neglect have escaped the individual's attention. Moreover, because biological associations continue in family relationships—one's parents continue to be one's parents and one's siblings continue to be one's brothers and sisters even if our relationships with them are in name only—it is particularly likely that long absences of interaction will not preclude kin from being named as current relationship partners. In addition, many people believe they are in a relationship with family members simply by definition. Some would even report that their relationship with a sibling or parent they have not seen or interacted with in decades is a "close" relationship because they believe that all family relationships are close relationships—again, simply by definition.

Similarly, most people will report that they have a relationship with their spouse even if they seldom interact with him or her (as in a long-distance relationship where the partners do not cohabit) and even if their spouse's behavior has no discernible effect on their own behavior and vice versa. From observation of the spouses' interaction pattern, the relationship researcher and other outside observers may conclude that these marital partners have an "empty shell" relationship or "parallel" marriage. Such spouses may live in close proximity to each other in time and space, but their behavioral tracks rarely cross; the partners go their separate and independent ways. But because their names are on the same marriage certificate, both spouses are likely to report that they have a relationship. Saying otherwise—that theirs is a marriage in name only—is likely to invite social disapproval and curiosity. Admitting that one does not have a current relationship with one's spouse, children, or other family members risks social disapproval because societal norms, some of which are codified into law, encourage people to maintain their family relationships.

In contrast to relationships with kin and current spouses, most romantic relationships do have a clear dissolution point. People generally are aware of the death of such relationships for several reasons. First, their ending is often contentious and unpleasant and therefore memorable. In addition, interaction in romantic relationships usually is frequent and, as a consequence, when interactions decline in number or cease altogether, it is likely to be noticeable to the partners and to others as well. Moreover, romantic relationships are often characterized by many specific agreements and understandings, which, when violated, clearly signal that at least one partner considers the relationship to be dying or dead. Finally, many people in our society endorse the ideal of monogamy (at least serial monogamy) for romantic relationships; believing that a current romantic relationship must be clearly dissolved before beginning another, they are likely to obtain a mental death certificate for the current relationship before moving on to another.

Apart from kin and spousal relationships, where biological associations and social desirability lead people to report such relationships as intact, there are yet other reasons why people will report they presently have a relationship with another despite the fact that they have no current interaction with that other and have not had any for a long time. For example, they may have developed a mental representation of the relationship from previous interactions and have frequently retrieved the relationship from memory, which may result in feelings that the relationship is still alive.

In yet other cases, the person may be hanging on to the corpse of a relationship as a way of honoring it—the dead relationship lies in state in the individual's mind and is never buried (e.g., see Hansson, Berry, & Berry, 1999). August Comte, for example, the nineteenth-century French philosopher who foresaw the development of relationship science and believed it would be the pinnacle of all the sciences, suffered enormous grief when the woman he loved died prematurely. To try to keep his relationship with his beloved alive, Comte resolved to think of her three times each day (Pickering, 1993). Others do the same, constructing shrines of photos and artifacts of the absent partner to help them remember. In such cases, what transpired in the past relationship sometimes continues to influence the individual's current behavior, but the partners are no longer interdependent because the influence is not mutual.

Feelings of guilt that more effort wasn't devoted to keeping a relationship alive sometimes make it difficult for a person to recognize that the relationship died a long time ago. Neglect is probably the most frequent cause of relationship deaths. Relationships consume time, energy, and other resources, which impose a limit on the number of relationships an individual can maintain, particularly close relationships. For example, in addition to the published findings from his study of persons engaged in extramarital sexual affairs, sociologist and sex researcher Gerhard Neubeck (e.g., Neubeck & Schletzer, 1962) observed that most of the participants in his study quickly became physically exhausted from trying to maintain two such demanding relationships and soon terminated one or the other (personal communication to Berscheid).

In sum, people may be entirely sincere when they report that they have a relationship with another despite the fact that they haven't interacted with that person in years and their current activities show little or no residual influence of that relationship. Given a robust and still accessible mental representation of the relationship, the individual may believe that the relationship could be resumed at any time—that he or she and the partner could simply "pick up where they left off" should they choose to do so or should fate bring them together. However, the fact that a relationship is dead often becomes uncomfortably apparent at family get-togethers, high school reunions, or chance meetings with former partners. After a brief period of "catch-up" conversation, there often is little for formerly close relationship partners to say or do. The interaction becomes strained and uncomfortable because the partners are no longer the people they once were. Having grown and developed into different people, the former partners are now "estranged"—strangers to one another.

Discomfort and awkwardness in interactions between formerly close relationship partners sometimes result in their regressing back to the interaction pattern characteristic of their relationship when it was alive and well. But if their previous relationship was a childhood relationship, the interaction may strike outside observers, and even the partners themselves, as peculiar. For example, the holiday get-together at their parents' home may find the now distinguished banker throwing pillows at his brother and heckling him in other ways, just as he used to do, and their sister, the eminent judge, cheating again at checkers, just as she used to do. People can pick up where they left off in a relationship only if they and their partners are the same persons they once were—an unlikely circumstance if many years have passed since their last interaction. After such reunions, people often shake their heads and think of Thomas Wolfe's assertion

"You can't go home again." We can't go home again because we no longer are the people we once were, and neither are the people who were our partners.

Multiple Views of a Current Relationship

Not only may an individual's listing of his or her current relationships differ from an outside observer's listing of that person's relationships, but even when there is agreement that a specific relationship is alive and active, there may be disagreement on the *nature* of the relationship (see Surra & Ridley, 1991). People often arrive at different views of events even when they have witnessed precisely the same events, as illustrated in Akira Kurosawa's classic film *Roshomon*.

To understand the dynamics of a relationship, at least three views of the relationship must be considered: the view of each of the relationship partners and the view of an outside observer(s), often the relationship researcher or therapist, who is likely to focus on the pattern of the partners' interdependence. Olson (1977) was among the first to emphasize that the views of the partners themselves—the "insiders" to the relationship—are essential to understanding the relationship's dynamics, if only because the insiders usually have far more information about the history of the relationship than an "outsider" does. They also may be better able than outside observers to decode the meaning of their partner's interaction behavior. From past experience, for example, spouses may know that the expression on their partner's face, which the outside observer takes to be a friendly smile, actually is a hostile smirk. Discrepancies between the partners' and outsiders' views provide valuable information about the relationship.

Symmetry of Influence

Many discrepancies between the two insiders' views of the relationship stem from differences in the degree to which each partner's behavior is influenced by the other. Although two people would not be said to be in a relationship if each person's interaction behaviors were not dependent on the partner's behavior to some extent, it probably is rarely the case that the partners exert equal influence on each other and thus are equally dependent. As a consequence, an important property of the partners' interaction pattern is the degree to which the partners' influence on each other's behavior is equal, or **symmetrical**. Asymmetrical relationships are those in which the individual has more power to influence the partner's outcomes and well-being than the partner has to affect the individual's outcomes. A relationship between a parent and a young child is an example; the parent usually has more influence on the child's behavior than the child has on the parent's behavior. Even in that asymmetrical relationship, however, the child has some influence, as parents of a colicky or hungry baby will readily testify, and thus the partners are interdependent.

In rapidly developing romantic relationships, people often attempt to ascertain their partner's dependence to ensure that their own does not exceed their partner's. Rather than directly questioning the partner about his or her level of dependence, however, individuals often create and administer "secret" dependence tests, including "endurance tests" (e.g., how much bad behavior the partner will tolerate or his or her reaction to separation) and "triangle tests" to gauge the partner's reaction to a potential competitor (Baxter & Wilmot, 1984). People are wary of their own dependence outstripping that of their partner for good reason: Asymmetrical relationships invite exploitation. In accord with a French epigram to the effect that in every love affair there is always one who loves and one who permits himself [or herself] to be loved (Waller & Hill, 1951), sociologist Willard Waller (1937), a pioneer in the field of marriage and the family, very early observed the operation in dating relationships of what he called the **principle of least interest**: "That person controls who is less interested in the continuation of the affair" (p. 733). The partner who is less dependent on the relationship is able to dictate the conditions for its continuance, and should these not be met to his or her satisfaction, it is this partner who is most likely to end the relationship. Thus, as far as the stability of the relationship is concerned, the less dependent partner is the relationship's "weak link"—the partner who is most likely to dissolve the relationship (Attridge, Berscheid, & Simpson, 1995; Drigotas & Rusbult, 1992; Hill, Rubin, & Peplau, 1976).

The asymmetry of many traditional marital relationships was highlighted by sociologist Jesse Bernard in her best-selling book *The Future of Marriage* (1972). The book jacket illustrated her thesis that the wife's marriage is often very different from the husband's marriage:

> **His:** Traditionally, men consider marriage a trap for themselves and a prize for their wives. Statistically, marriage is good for men—physically, socially, and psychologically.
> **Hers:** Traditionally, all women want to marry, and most want to become mothers. Statistically, childless marriages are happier; and marriage, literally, makes thousands of women sick.

Bernard's observation that "his" and "hers" marriages are different is particularly true for the traditional form of marriage prevalent at the time she published her book. In **traditional marriage**, roles and responsibilities are allocated on the basis of sex (e.g., Luepnitz, 1988; Rubin, 1976; Turner, 1970). The husband's role includes responsibility for the economic welfare of the family; stereotypically "male" activities such as garbage, snow, and pest removal and car maintenance; and decision-making for the entire family, especially economic decisions (e.g., Blood & Wolfe, 1960). The wife's role includes domestic tasks, such as management of the house and children. Traditional marital relationships often involve little direct emotional expressiveness, and both partners tend to draw on relatives and same-sex friends for companionship and affection (Peplau, 1983/2002). In contrast, in an **egalitarian marriage** (also called peer or equal-status marriage), the spouses share roles and responsibility in all spheres of married life, including emotional caregiving and expression and the economic welfare of the family. Although there are other patterns of married life (e.g., see Johnson,

Huston, Gaines, & Levinger, 1992), virtually all contemporary typologies of marriage include these two types of marriage.

Many of Bernard's (1972) contentions remain true today. Although married people, on average, enjoy better physical and mental health than those who are not married, the protective effects for morbidity and mortality appear to be significantly stronger for men than they are for women (see Kiecolt-Glaser & Newton, 2001). Moreover, most studies continue to show that childless marriages are happier than marriages with children (Feeney, Noller, & Ward, 1997), although spouses with children are somewhat less likely to divorce, particularly when the children are young (see Belsky, 1990).

However, many changes have taken place in marriage in the past 30 years, as discussed in Chapter 5, "Varieties of Relationship." For example, egalitarian marriages have become increasingly common, and the number of married women employed outside the home has increased dramatically (see Gilbert, 1993; Scanzoni, Polonko, Teachman, & Thompson, 1989; Schwartz, 1994). Bernard (1972) observed that those women in her sample who were employed outside the home did not seem to show the deleterious effects of marriage typical of those whose activities were largely confined to the home. That outside employment makes a difference has been confirmed by the results of a large-scale mental health survey conducted in Australia, which indicates that marriage no longer "makes thousands of women [mentally] sick" (de Vaus, 2002). Married people, male *or* female, were found to be the least likely to suffer from any type of mental disorder, and working outside the home was associated with a reduction in the risk of mental disorder for both men and women, whether they were married or single or parents or nonparents. A job appears to be especially important to the well-being of married men. Moreover, no sex differences in mental disorder risk were found between husbands and wives or between single men and women, but the *type* of disorder to which men and women were prone differed (women were more likely than men to suffer from mood and anxiety disorders and men were more prone to drug abuse).

Despite the increasing prevalence of egalitarian marriage and wives' participation in the labor force, one element of traditional marriage seems to have changed little: Most marriages maintain the traditional division of household labor (e.g., Blair & Lichter, 1991). Although both sexes have a tendency to overestimate the amount of time they spend engaged in housework (Press & Townsley, 1998), and although remarried men demonstrate greater involvement in parenting and household tasks than do men in first marriages (Ishii-Kuntz & Coltrane, 1992), there is abundant evidence that married women spend more time on domestic tasks than married men do (e.g., Brines, 1994; Grote & Clark, 2001; Steil, 2000; South & Spitze, 1994). As a consequence, wives have less "free time" than husbands do (Robinson, Yerby, Fieweger, & Somerick, 1977). Even in dual-income families, women average approximately twice as many hours per week as men on housework (Blair & Johnson, 1992). As a consequence of their different degrees and kinds of participation in household tasks, the husband's and the wife's views of their marriage are likely to differ for this reason alone.

Sociologists Orbuch and Timmer (2001) believe marriage remains a "gendered" institution for several reasons. Like others, they observe that newlyweds typically confront issues that require negotiation in at least three domains: work and family, including division of household labor; kin and relationship ties (with whom does one spend holidays?); and parental responsibilities. Orbuch and Timmer maintain that these issues not only tend to have different importance but also different meanings to husbands and wives as a result of three factors: (1) *different socialization* (e.g., boys are taught to be competitive and aggressive, characteristics that present obstacles to intimacy, whereas girls are socialized to be nurturing and caring; see Gilligan, 1982); (2) the *social structure*, which is associated with different resources, opportunities, and constraints for men and women and which has generally favored men; and (3) the *immediate social and cultural context* in which the marriage is embedded (e.g., black couples have more egalitarian attitudes regarding household labor and other tasks than

white couples do, and as a consequence, husbands' participation in home labor has been found to be beneficial to the happiness of black wives but not white wives; Orbuch & Eyster, 1997). In sum, her marriage still is likely to be different from his.

Perhaps it is not surprising, then, that spouses are likely to view their own and their partners' behaviors differently. Even studies that simply ask husbands and wives to report their own and their spouse's daily behaviors find poor correspondence between the two reports (e.g., Christensen & Nies, 1980; Jacobson & Moore, 1981). In addition to differences between the two insiders' views of their relationship, each one of the partner's views may differ from that of an outside observer. Robinson and Price (1980) found, for example, that observers of spouses' interactions recorded about the same hourly rates of positive (or "pleasurable") behaviors for happy couples as for unhappy couples. However, examination of the reports of the spouses themselves revealed that unhappy spouses reported about 50% fewer positive behaviors than the outside observers did.

THE OBSERVATIONAL BASE OF RELATIONSHIP SCIENCE

All sciences must have an intersubjectively accessible observational base; that is, one researcher's observations must be accessible and verifiable by other researchers. Because the essence of a relationship lies in the partners' interaction, the focus of relationship research, either directly or indirectly, is the partners' interaction with each other. Thus, the **observational base of relationship science** consists of the behaviors of two persons (usually denoted by "Person" and "Other," or simply "P" and "O") observed over the same real timeline (see Kelley et al., 1983/2002).

At any given point in time, an individual usually is simultaneously engaged in several kinds of behavior. He or she may be engaged in an overt action, such as walking toward the door (a motor behavior), thinking "I never want to see you again!" (a cognitive behavior), and feeling anger (an affective behavior). Motor activities usually are easily observable. It is not difficult to see one partner throw a frying pan and observe the other partner duck. But observing what the partners were thinking and feeling during the interaction is not as easy. To find out what they were thinking and feeling, their friends and associates often simply ask them, as do researchers (e.g., the dyadic interaction procedure discussed in Chapter 1). However, people also sometimes deduce that another is experiencing emotion from observation of a flushed face, sweaty forehead, and other physiological symptoms of emotional experience. Researchers, too, often are interested in the physiological indicants of emotional state. To obtain reliable observations of these indicants of emotional experience, researchers sometimes bring the partners into the laboratory where they can monitor such variables as heart rate and skin conductance and where blood, saliva, and urine samples can be obtained and analyzed to assess changes in physiological state associated with emotional experience. Ideally, the relationship researcher would like to have an observational record of both partners' motor, cognitive, and affective behaviors over the same real timeline, as illustrated in Figure 4.2.

Understanding and predicting relationship phenomena directly or indirectly involves examination of the invisible causal interconnections, or **causal linkages**, between two persons' behaviors. Although these linkages are invisible, we can deduce their existence from observing the *effects* of one partner's behavior on the other partner's behavior. For example, he smiles at Time 1; she blushes at Time 2; he moves closer to her at Time 3; she leans toward him at Time 4; he kisses her at Time 5. Each behavior in this particular interaction sequence is both a response to the partner's previous behavior and a stimulus for the partner's next behavior. Thus, although we cannot see, touch, or feel influence itself, we can observe and measure its effects. Although the study of interpersonal influence sometimes strikes people as mysterious, many sciences involve the systematic study of invisible interconnections between entities. Subatomic physics is

an example; as physicist Fritof Capra (1982) describes, "Subatomic particles . . . are not 'things' but are interconnections between 'things' and these 'things,' in turn, are interconnections between other 'things,' and so on" (p. 80).

The pattern of causal linkages between the partners' behaviors is sometimes referred to as the **relationship infrastructure**—"infra" because the causal linkages lie below the visible surface of the relationship and "structure" because the causal linkages between the partners' behaviors represent their pattern of interdependence. The infrastructure of the interaction depicted in Figure 4.2 is illustrated in Figure 4.3.

Establishing Interdependence

Interdependence is the hallmark of a relationship. In practice, to determine whether two people are interdependent, investigators often simply ask the people if they are in a relationship with another. However, self-reports of relationship are not always accurate, as we've discussed. Moreover, investigators sometimes want to determine the partners' degree of interdependence. The most reliable way to establish whether two persons are interdependent is to observe them interact and determine whether there are causal linkages between the partners' behaviors.

Correlation Between the Partners' Behaviors

If the partners behave similarly—for example, engaging in positive behaviors in each other's presence or both behaving negatively—it is tempting to conclude that they are influencing each other and thus are interdependent. However, the fact that two people's behaviors are correlated is not infallible evidence that they are interdependent because the partners may be responding not to each other but to other, extradyadic stimuli. For example, both the husband and the wife may exhibit a great deal of negativity, such as sarcasm and complaints, when conversing with each other, and thus their degree of negative behavior may be correlated. However, the cause of the husband's negative behavior may lie in his neurotic personality; if so, he is likely to

P–O Interaction

Person P

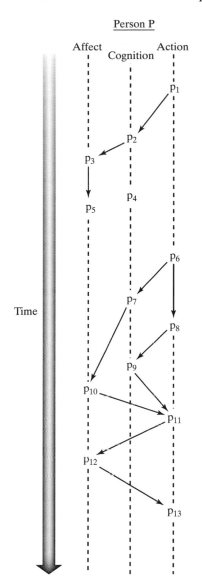

Person O

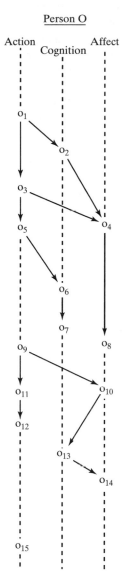

FIGURE 4.2 The causal connections between an individual's behavior at one point in time and his or her behavior at later points in time. Every individual is simultaneously engaging in three types of behavior over time (affect, cognition, and action). Some of these behaviors are part of a sequence of organized, causally connected events. In the example above, p_1 (P's action of turning off the alarm clock) is followed by p_2 (P's cognition "I can't be late for the exam today!") and p_3 (P's affective response of anxiety); these specific actions are causally connected and form part of the sequence of events of "getting ready for school in the morning." *After Kelley et al., "Analyzing Close Relationships" (1983/2002), Fig. 2.1, p. 28.*

behave negatively toward everyone, not just his wife. His wife's behavior, then, is not the cause of his negative behavior. Similarly, the cause of the wife's high rate of negative behavior in conversation with her husband may be her physical discomfort and poor health; if so, she, too, would behave negatively in conversation with anyone and, thus, her husband's behavior is not the cause of her negative behavior. In situations in which the partners respond similarly to stimuli other

than each other, the partners' **behavior base rates** (the rate at which behaviors occur over a specified unit of time) will be correlated even though the partners are not interdependent.

In sum, if the partners *are* interdependent, their behavior base rates *will* be correlated; thus, evidence of a correlation between the partners' behaviors is a necessary condition for interdependence. It is not a sufficient condition, however, because two persons' behavior base rates

P–O Interaction

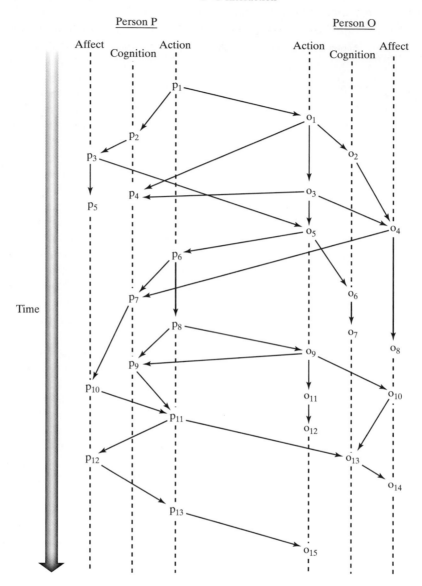

FIGURE 4.3 This figure depicts the portion of each individual's behavior that is caused by his or her partner's behavior. As can be seen, not only are the affect, cognition, and action events within each person's chain of events causally connected (as in Figure 4.2), but the two chains are causally interconnected (shown by arrows from a p to an o or from an o to a p). For example, p_1 (P's action of turning off the alarm clock) causes o_1 (O enters the bedroom and hands P a cup of coffee), which causes p_4 (P's cognition "Actually, I've got plenty of time. What am I worried about?"). These causal interconnections between P's and O's behaviors constitute the infrastructure of their relationship, and it is the pattern of these interconnections that relationship researchers hope to identify and understand. *Kelley et al., "Analyzing Close Relationships" (1983/2002), Fig. 2.1, p. 28.*

may be correlated even if they are not interdependent (they are not responding to each other). A correlation between the partners' behaviors is not an infallible indicant of interdependence.

The Social Relations Model

Behavioral interdependence between two people can be established by other means, however. One method that permits determination of interdependence is the social relations model (SRM) technique developed by David Kenny and his associates (e.g., Kenny, 1994b; Kenny & La Voie, 1984; Kenny, Mohr, & Levesque, 2001). This method requires observation of the extent to which two people display a particular behavior, such as smiling, in each other's presence. Both the husband and wife may exhibit a high base rate of smiling when interacting with each other, but to determine whether he is smiling in response to her behavior and she to his, we also must observe the husband and wife interacting with other people and calculate each spouse's smiling base rate in each of those other interactions. Thus, the SRM technique requires that the partners not only interact with each other but also that each interact with several other persons—and precisely the same other persons. Kenny calls this a *round-robin design*; everyone in the group converses at least once with every other person in the group.

Chances are that in his conversations with his wife and the other members of the group the husband will display different smiling base rates. His variance in smiling behavior across conversations with other people may have a number of sources: First, everyone in the group may be smiling because it is payday Friday. If so, at least some of the husband's smiles in his conversation with his wife are not "personal" toward his wife because he is not responding to her; he, like everyone else in the group, just feels good and at least part of his smiling behavior in conversation with his wife can be traced to the time and setting in which they are conversing. Examining the amount of smiling behavior, on average, everyone in the group displays in conversations with everyone else provides an estimate of the portion of the husband's smiling behavior in his conversation with his wife that should be attributed to a source common to everyone in the group. This is called the *constant effect*.

A second possible source of the husband's smiling behavior in his conversation with his wife may be that he learned just hours ago that he got a raise in salary. Although he smiles often in his conversation with his wife, the round-robin design may reveal that he also smiles often in his conversations with everyone. Again, the husband is not uniquely responding to his wife; he is displaying a high rate of smiling behavior regardless of who he is conversing with, and at least a portion of his smiles in his interaction with his wife should be attributed not to his relationship with her but rather to something unique about him—in this case, to the prospect of an increased salary. This source of the husband's smiling behavior is called the *actor effect*.

A third possible source of the husband's smiling behavior in his conversation with his wife may lie in the properties of the wife. For example, she may be pleasant to everyone, not just her husband, and consequently everyone tends to smile in her presence. This is called the *partner effect*. It also represents a portion of the husband's smiling behavior in conversation with his wife that is not unique to their relationship.

The actor and partner effects are called *individual-level effects*. If the analysis finds only significant individual effects, we would conclude that there is something about these particular individuals, this man and this woman—not their relationship with each other—that is responsible for the husband's high base rate of smiling in his conversation with his wife. That portion of the husband's smiling in interaction with his wife that remains after the constant and individual-level effects are removed represents the *relationship effect*. The relationship effect is an estimate of the degree to which the husband is responding to his wife differently from how he responds to other people and differently from how other people respond to her.

To determine **dyadic reciprocity**, or that the two partners *both* are responding to each other in unique ways, a similar analysis must be conducted on the wife's smiling behavior in her conversations with her husband and with every other person in the group. If the husband's relationship effect is correlated with the wife's relationship effect, then the two spouses are mutually dependent, or interdependent. In other words, there is evidence that each partner's smiling behavior is influenced by the other partner's smiling behavior. Dyadic reciprocity on any behavioral dimension is always evidence of a relationship. In this particular case, we would conclude that *positive behavior reciprocity* is a feature of this couple's interaction pattern.

In sum, and as illustrated in Figure 4.4, the SRM technique assumes that an individual's behavior in the presence of another is a function of

- a *constant*, representing how frequently, on average, all people behave that way at that time in that setting
- an *actor effect*, representing how frequently the individual tends to exhibit that behavior regardless of who is present
- a *partner effect*, representing how frequently the other person with whom the individual may or may not be in a relationship tends to be the target of the behavior when in the presence of others
- a *relationship effect*, which represents the extent to which there is something unique about the relationship between the individual

and the other person that is responsible for the individual's behavior in the presence of that other

The SRM technique is labor-intensive both for the investigator and for research participants, and some of the method's mathematical underpinnings remain controversial. Nevertheless, in addition to the empirical findings associated with the model, it has made a conceptual contribution to an understanding of relationships. The logic of the model illustrates the meaning of the terms "relationship" and "interdependence." Perhaps most important, the SRM model highlights that it is difficult, if not impossible, to determine whether two people are interdependent simply from observing those persons interact only with each other.

Sequential Analysis

Another technique for establishing interdependence, sequential analysis, is as labor-intensive as the SRM technique. In sequential analysis, the investigator records the precise *time* at which the behaviors of interest are exhibited by the interaction partners. This observational record of both partners' behaviors over the same real timeline then is examined to determine whether a particular behavior performed by one partner (e.g., a complaint) significantly changes the probability that the other partner will exhibit a specific

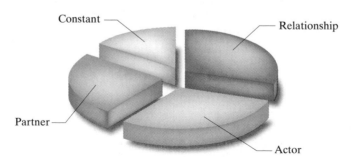

FIGURE 4.4 The SRM technique assumes that an individual's behavior in the presence of another person is a function of a constant effect, an actor effect, a partner effect, and a relationship effect. To determine how much variability in the person's behavior is due to the unique relationship between the person and his or her partner, the SRM technique estimates the variance due to the constant and the individual-level effects (the actor and partner effects). The portion of "unexplained" variance left over is assumed to be due to the relationship effect.

behavior (e.g., a sarcastic comment) from what it would otherwise be (that partner's base rate for the behavior). For example, is the probability that the husband will experience an asthma attack following his wife's criticism higher than the base rate at which he experiences asthma attacks? Is the wife's likelihood of going on a shopping spree higher than usual when her husband spends the weekend golfing? Two persons' interdependence is established if sequential analysis reveals that their behaviors are causally linked—that P's behavior at Time 1 and O's behavior at a later point in time can be viewed as a single cause-and-effect unit (see Bradbury & Fincham, 1991; Castellan, 1979).

John Gottman has been a leader in the development and use of sequential analysis in relationship research (e.g., Gottman, 1979; Gottman & Roy, 1990). In one of the first studies to use sequential analysis, Levenson and Gottman (1983) hypothesized there would be an association between the pattern of emotional behavior that spouses display in their interactions and the couple's satisfaction with their marriage. When couples in both distressed and nondistressed marriages came to the investigators' laboratory

at the end of their workday, the partners were seated across from each other at a table and monitored with devices that recorded their cardiovascular activity, sweat gland activity (or skin conductance), and general somatic activity such as "wiggling" (see Figure 4.5). These physiological measures are indicants of emotion.

The spouses first sat quietly, not speaking while the researchers obtained a baseline for each spouse on the physiological measures, and then they talked for 20 minutes about the events of their day just as they would do at home (the *neutral events* conversation). After resting again, they discussed a problem in their marriage (the *conflict* conversation). Finally, each spouse returned to the laboratory 3 to 5 days later to view a videotape of the interaction while turning an "affect rating dial" to indicate the positivity or negativity of the emotions and feelings he or she recalled having experienced at each point in the interaction. The investigators thus obtained a continuous record of the partners' motor and verbal behaviors in interaction with each other, their concurrent physiological activities, and their recollected affect over the same real timeline.

FIGURE 4.5   In Gottman's research, couples are seated across from each other and each partner is attached to devices that record various physiological measurements.

Levenson and Gottman then attempted to identify the causal linkages between the spouses' behaviors. The central question addressed by sequential analysis is "Can the behavior of an individual at a future point in time (Time 2) be better predicted from the *partner's* previous behavior (Time 1) than it can from the individual's *own* previous behavior?" Sequential analysis thus recognizes that the behavior of an individual at Time 2 is often influenced by that person's own Time 1 behavior—*not* the partner's Time 1 behavior. For example, if the husband blows his nose at Time 1, his cessation of sniffling at Time 2 may be a consequence of his nose-blowing behavior at Time 1—not his wife's Time 1 command, "Stop sniffling!" The correlation between the individual's own behavior at Time 1 and that same individual's behavior at Time 2 is called the *autocorrelation* (see Dumas, 1986). Evidence that the husband's behavior at Time 2 has been influenced by his wife's Time 1 behavior requires that the correlation between the husband's behavior at Time 2 and his wife's behavior at Time 1 be significantly *higher* than the husband's Time 1–Time 2 autocorrelation. If it is, then evidence that his behavior is dependent on his wife's behavior has been obtained. If the wife's behavior also can be better predicted from her husband's previous behavior than from her own previous behavior, the spouses are interdependent—they are influencing each other's behavior.

Levenson and Gottman (1983) found evidence of significant linkage in the physiological behaviors of the maritally distressed spouses during the conflict discussion; that is, an individual's physiological behavior at an earlier point in time predicted his or her spouse's later physiological behavior. Moreover, the more causally linked the partners' physiological measures were, the less satisfied they were with their marriage (as assessed by a marital satisfaction questionnaire). Because the physiological measures represented negative emotionality during discussion of relationship conflicts, another way of viewing Gottman and Levenson's results is that the more the partners displayed high reciprocity of negative emotion in interaction, as evidenced by their linkage on the physiological measures, the more

likely they were to be dissatisfied with their marriage. The degree of negative affect the couples recalled having experienced during the conflict discussion also helped account for degree of marital satisfaction over and above their degree of physiological linkage.

The investigators reported that the interaction pattern displayed by the unhappily married couples was characterized by a poverty of positive affect (e.g., an absence of laughter), an abundance of negative affect (e.g., many complaints), and also, as reflected in the physiological data, **negative affect reciprocity**. Again, dyadic reciprocity on any behavioral dimension is evidence of interdependence. After looking at the results of their study, Levenson and Gottman had some advice for marital and other relationship therapists: Instead of focusing on increasing positive affect and positive affect reciprocity in distressed marriages, as has been frequently the focus of therapeutic efforts, they believe therapists should devote more effort to reducing the negative affect reciprocity pattern that is a reliable marker of unhappy relationships.

Three years later, Levenson and Gottman (1985) contacted 19 of the original 30 couples and examined their current level of marital satisfaction. They found that degree of physiological linkage three years earlier was *not* associated with their present marital satisfaction, but that the more physiologically aroused the couple had been 3 years earlier during their interactions, the more their marital satisfaction had declined. (Again, another way of describing this result is to say that the more negative emotion the couple displayed earlier, the more their satisfaction with the marriage continued to decrease over the following 3 years.) For example, husbands' heart rate during the conflict discussion by itself accounted for 85% of the later deterioration in satisfaction. The investigators also found that marital satisfaction declined most when husbands did *not* reciprocate their wives' negative affect but rather were unresponsive and when wives *did* reciprocate their husbands' negative affect. Thus, according to Levenson and Gottman (1983), a loose metaphorical description of the dyadic pattern of distressed marriages would be that of an underaroused, unreactive husband and an emotionally reactive wife: "A picture emerges of the husband being the nonresponsive partner in dissatisfied marriages. Compared to satisfied marriages, he was less likely to reciprocate the wife's positive affect" (p. 595).

The difficulty and expense of collecting data that permit sequential analysis, like the difficulty and expense of obtaining the data necessary for SRM analysis, preclude their routine use in relationship studies. Again, however, in addition to the empirical findings associated with sequential analysis, the logic underlying this methodological technique illustrates the meaning of the terms "relationship" and "interdependence."

Interaction Patterns

Recurring patterns of causal linkages are likely to be observed in partners' interactions over time. Some of these patterns are especially important for understanding a variety of relationship phenomena and for describing the nature of the partners' interdependence.

Facilitative and Interfering Interaction Sequences

Every person has habits or sequences of actions emitted as a single unit—when the first action in the sequence occurs, the remainder almost always follow because each action in the sequence is both a response to the previous action and the stimulus for the next action. Most people, for example, have habitual morning routines that are triggered when the alarm clock goes off. Each action in the sequence—for example, taking a shower—is both a response to the previous action (getting out of bed) and a stimulus for the next action (getting dressed). **Organized action sequences** have a number of characteristics: (1) they invariably occur when the triggering stimulus appears (e.g., the alarm rings); (2) once the first action occurs, the action sequence tends to "run off" to completion; and (3) the sequence has been repeated so many times that it is performed easily, smoothly, and automatically, without conscious awareness. Because they are performed automatically when the triggering stimulus appears, habits are hard to break.

Organized action sequences usually develop in the service of fulfilling personal plans and goals. Getting up in the morning and going to school may be in the service of getting a degree, which is in the service of getting a job, which is in the service of having a roof over one's head, getting married, and having children. In other words, some organized action sequences are nested in other, higher-order action sequences, which are nested in yet other, even higher-order action sequences—all usually developed to promote personal welfare and survival.

People enter relationships carrying their habits, plans, and goals with them. A new relationship partner may **facilitate** the execution of the individual's established action sequences and the achievement of his or her goals. For example, the partner may facilitate execution of the individual's plan to obtain a college degree by paying the individual's tuition, thereby removing the need for the individual to work, which allows more courses to be taken and the goal to be reached earlier than originally planned. It is the facilitation of each other's hopes, plans, and goals that relationship partners usually believe their relationship will accomplish.

However, partners also sometimes **interfere** with the performance of each other's habits, the execution of personal plans, and the achievement of important goals. For example, the partner may preempt the bathroom in the morning, disrupting the individual's usual routine and causing the individual to be late for school or work. Or the partner may turn out to be a feckless spendthrift, which requires the individual to get a second job, in turn endangering the achievement of the goal of earning a college degree. Causal linkages that interfere with the partner's execution of habits, plans, and goals are associated with conflict, as discussed in Chapter 13, "Satisfaction and Stability." The point at present is that whereas the existence of causal linkages between the partners is evidence of their interdependence, an important feature of their pattern of interdependence is the extent to which those linkages are facilitating or interfering.

Meshed Interaction Sequences

Just as individuals have habits, relationships—particularly long-term relationships—also develop habits (Ouellette & Wood, 1998). Studies of family routines and rituals, such as celebration of birthdays or preparation of Thanksgiving dinner, have found that these organized behaviors are associated with marital satisfaction, parenting competence, and child adjustment and that their disruption is symptomatic of family crisis (see a review by Fiese et al., 2002). They also have found that family routines frequently revolve around meals. Most family mealtime routines constitute **meshed interaction sequences** in which both partners (and often the children as well) are simultaneously performing organized action sequences; each individual's action is both a *response to the partner's action* and a *stimulus* not only for the individual's own next action but also for the partner's next action (see Figure 4.6). When one partner brings the groceries home, the other can start food preparation, which may be the cue for the first to set the table and call

the children in to clean up, and so forth. If one partner fails to perform the appropriate action at the appropriate time in a meshed interaction sequence, it is likely that one or both partners will experience disruption and, often, anger and frustration ("You forgot to light the coals, so now I can't barbecue the meat, and the Smiths will be arriving for dinner in 10 minutes"). Smooth and effortless performance of many tasks and pleasures (including sexual interactions) requires that *both partners perform the appropriate action at the appropriate time in a meshed interaction sequence.* When one partner fails to do so, that failure is *interfering* with the other's successful completion of the sequence.

Like an individual's habits, meshed interaction sequences, which represent the partners' joint interaction habits, can be observed in the partners' interaction pattern by noting (1) their frequent repetition; (2) the lack of variability in the shape and form of each partner's behavior in the sequence; (3) the speed and efficiency with which the behavior sequence is performed; and (4) the tendency for such behavior sequences to run off to completion once started. Meshed interaction sequences are an important class of relationship habits because, with frequent repetition, they gradually recede from the partners' conscious awareness just as other habits do.

The coordination that meshed interaction sequences represent facilitates the efficient achievement of goals that benefit both partners. Moreover, because such sequences are performed automatically, other behaviors—those requiring conscious deliberation and guidance—often can be performed simultaneously with these organized behavior sequences. For example, the partners can try to solve a problem or make vacation plans while they get dinner on the table. Moreover, the performance of habitual behaviors such as meshed interaction sequences is less stressful than interaction behaviors that must be consciously guided (Wood, Quinn, & Kashy, 2002). The downside of meshed interaction sequences is that because they tend to be performed automatically, without conscious thought and deliberation, people often lose awareness of the extent to which the daily fabric of their life is dependent on the facilitative behavior

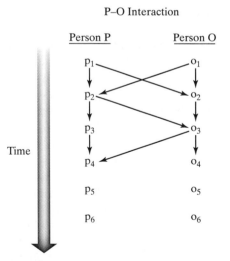

P–O Interaction

FIGURE 4.6 A meshed interaction sequence. Both partners are simultaneously performing action sequences in which each person's action is both a response to the partner's action and a stimulus for the subsequent actions of both partners. *Berscheid, "Emotion" (1983/2002), Fig. 4.3, p. 141.*

of their partner. Instances in which the partner fails to do what he or she is expected to do and has done many times in the past—perhaps because of illness or because the relationship has been terminated voluntarily or by death—interfere with completion of the sequence, which, in turn, is frequently associated with the experience of negative emotion (Berscheid, 1983/2002).

Not all relationship habits are positive and facilitative of the partner's goals. Some destructive arguments have the characteristics of meshed interaction sequences. Relationship therapist George Bach called these arguments "round-robin, merry-go-round" fights that occur over and over again, with little variation and no resolution (see Bach & Wyden, 1969). Destructive meshed interaction sequences are hard to change because, like other habits, they are automatically performed without conscious thought once they are triggered. People often not only are unaware of the trigger but are unaware that the sequence, once triggered, tends to ineluctably be performed as a single stimulus–response unit. Because such arguments are hard to stop midstream, most therapists recommend identifying the stimulus trigger and, if possible, removing it. For example, Bach and Wyden give the example of a couple whose merry-go-round fight was triggered each month when the bank statement arrived; the husband complained about how much the wife had spent, her rejoinder was that he never told her how much was appropriate, he said he had told her, and so forth. The therapists asked the couple to introduce a change that would ensure that the *exact situation* that preceded their repetitive money fight (the triggering stimulus) could not occur again. They did—they opened a separate checking account for the wife.

THE AIM OF RELATIONSHIP SCIENCE: IDENTIFYING CAUSAL CONDITIONS

It is the recurring patterns of causal linkages observed in partners' interactions over time that relationship scientists wish to understand and that partners sometimes seek help from relationship therapists to change. The aim of relationship science is to identify the causal conditions responsible for the regularities in the relationship's interaction patterns, as well as the correlates and consequences of those patterns. Control of events is possible only when the causes responsible for the regularities and changes in the phenomenon of interest are understood. To help a distressed couple change their relationship, for example, the relationship therapist must first identify the distressed couple's interaction regularities. Second, the causal forces producing that interaction pattern must be located. Third, and finally, the therapist must help the couple modify those causal conditions that are producing distressing interaction patterns. Thus, identification of the causal conditions responsible for interaction regularities is a necessary condition for changing a relationship. Unfortunately, it is not sufficient because it sometimes is not within the power of the couple to change the conditions adversely influencing their relationship: for example, they cannot put an aging parent in a nursing home, or they cannot quit their stressful jobs.

A relationship **causal condition** is a relatively stable force that influences the relationship **interaction pattern** (the repeated occurrence of interaction sequences). The causal conditions that influence interaction patterns can be divided into three major classes: personal, relational, and environmental (Kelley et al., 1983/2002).

Personal causal conditions are the stable factors associated primarily with an individual partner (P or O) that affect the interaction pattern. Personal causal conditions affecting a couple's interaction pattern may include a partner's physical characteristics, attitudes, education, personality, and other dispositions that the individual brings to his or her interactions with others. Kenny, Mohr, and Levesque (2000), using the SRM technique, found evidence for "moderate" behavioral consistency in a person's behavior across different interaction partners. Caspi, Bem, and Elder (1989), examining longitudinal data, find evidence of two processes that appear to sustain an individual's characteristic behavior patterns over the life course. (1) *Cumulative continuity* arises when the individual's interactional style channels him or her into situations that themselves reinforce that style; for example, a highly competitive person might engage in competitive sports whereas a cooperative person would opt for individualistic sports. (2) *Interactional continuity* arises when an individual's style elicits from the partner behaviors that sustain the individual's interactional style; for example, a competitive person evokes competitive responses from others.

Relational (P × O) causal conditions are located in neither partner but instead result from the joint configuration of the characteristics each partner brings to the interaction, or they emerge from the partners' previous interactions (Berscheid, Lopes, Ammazzalorso, & Langenfeld, 2001). For example, the degree to which the partners share similar values, attitudes, and interests is likely to be responsible for some regularities in their interaction pattern. The "similarity" causal condition is located neither in P nor in O but rather represents the joint configuration of P and O's characteristics. Another relational causal condition that usually produces regularities in the couple's interaction pattern is physical proximity, which results not from the location of P alone or O alone but rather the partners' relative spatial locations. Some relational causal conditions, such as similarity, may be present at the start of the relationship. Other relational conditions may emerge from the partners' interaction. As their interactions continue, the partners often develop norms, rules, agreements, and shared understandings. These agreements and understandings—for example, that the partners' will reserve every Saturday night for each other—will be responsible for some interaction regularities.

Environmental causal conditions include factors in the physical and social environment in which every relationship is embedded. Together, the relationship's physical and social environment constitutes the relationship's *ecological niche*. Certain properties of the relationship's ecological niche have been shown to influence interaction patterns. With respect to the physical environment, for example, many studies have shown that people who interact under adverse physical circumstances—such as a hot and stuffy

room—generally come not to like each other as much as people who interact under pleasant circumstances, such as the deck of a Caribbean cruise liner. The social environment, too, has an important influence on the relationship. For example, the extent to which the social environment contains attractive alternative partners to a romantic relationship is associated with the relationship's stability, as discussed in Chapter 7, "Relationship Growth and Maintenance." Because a relationship's ecological niche influences the relationship's interaction pattern, that pattern can be expected to change when the relationship's social or physical environment changes (the couple moves to a different city, her parents move to town, or they move into cramped quarters).

All of these types of relationship causal conditions—personal, relational, and environmental—may interact with each other, often in a **continuous causal feedback loop** (see Figure 4.7). For example, two people who become attracted to each other may decide to move within closer physical proximity, thereby changing the relationship's physical environment, which also is likely to change the relationship's social environment, which may contain more attractive alternatives to the relationship, which then may diminish the partners' attraction to each other, which may cause them to move farther apart from each other. For this reason, the identification of the causal conditions responsible for a couple's interaction pattern is not an easy task.

SOURCES OF INTERACTION DATA

Interaction data may be obtained from at least three sources: (1) people's *self-reports* of the nature of their relationship interactions or their reports of the relationship's properties and features, such as their satisfaction with the relationship, which is assumed to have emerged from their interactions; (2) direct *observation* of the relationship partners' interactions by outside observers (e.g., as in Levenson and Gottman, 1983); and (3) examination of records and traces of the individual's interaction behavior, such as *archival information and personal diaries* (e.g., as in Grayson,

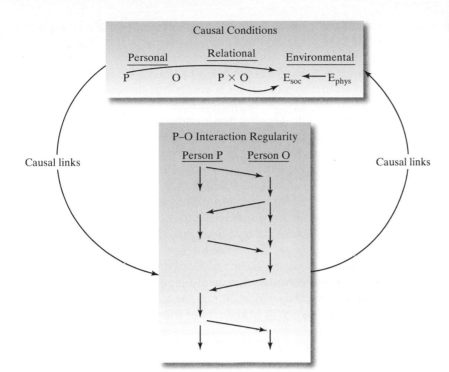

Causal Conditions

Personal | Relational | Environmental

P   O   P × O E_{soc} ← E_{phys}

Causal links

P–O Interaction Regularity

Person P   Person O

Causal links

FIGURE 4.7 The causal context of dyadic interaction. The arrows within the interaction represent interevent causal connections within and between P's and O's chains. Causal conditions affect the interaction (through the downward causal links), and the interaction affects the causal conditions (through the upward causal links). Causal conditions are also often linked directly to each other, as in the upper part of the diagram. *Adapted from Kelley et al., "Analyzing Close Relationships" (1983/2002), Fig. 2.5, p. 57.*

1990). The advantages and disadvantages of each method have been extensively examined and discussed by relationship scholars (e.g., Harvey, Christensen, & McClintock, 1983/2002; Montgomery & Duck, 1991).

Self-Reports

Relative to the other two major methods of collecting relationship data, self-reports are easy and inexpensive to collect. Moreover, they often access emotions, feelings, and perceptions not readily observable to outsiders to the relationship, as we have noted. Although these are important advantages, there are dangers in relying exclusively on an individual's reports of relationship events (see Metts, Sprecher, & Cupach, 1991). There also are problems in relying exclusively on the individual's reports of his or her own thoughts and feelings, not only because of social desirability and self-enhancement biases but because people can report only what they are conscious of and what they can verbalize; they cannot report unconscious thoughts or feelings or those they cannot readily put into words (see

Wilson, 1994). When people are asked to report retrospectively on events that happened in the (sometimes distant) past, there almost always is a discrepancy between what they remember about an *autobiographical event* (which relationship events always are) and what an objective outside observer would have reported had he or she observed the event. As we have noted, even the reports of the two partners (the "insiders") may not agree on whether a mundane relationship event did or did not occur (e.g., Christensen, Sullaway, & King, 1983).

Most of the discrepancies between the self-reports of the two partners and between the reports of a partner and an outside observer are the result of faulty memory rather than deliberate prevarication. Many of the ways in which people's memories of an event are likely to be biased have been identified, both in the general case (e.g., Smith, 1998) and in the relationship realm (e.g., Berscheid, 1994; Karney & Coombs, 2000). As discussed in Chapter 8, "Cognitive Processes," relationship memory is always an active, constructive process that may be influenced by the individual's general views of relationships, current mood, personal theories concerning the event of interest, and other factors, including the individual's current motivational concerns. For example, McDonald and Hirt (1997) demonstrated that an individual's current motivation not only influences memory *search* but also the *reconstruction* of existing memory traces upon retrieval. In another study, Karney and Coombs (2000) examined 20 years of retrospective data from a longitudinal sample of wives and found that at least one memory bias, the perception that the relationship is improving and becoming more satisfying than it once was, may be a mechanism whereby people maintain satisfaction in long-term close relationships.

Among the several factors shown to exert a significant influence on recollections of the relationship's past is the present state of the relationship (e.g., Holmberg & Veroff, 1996; Miell, 1987). McFarland and Ross (1987) compared evaluations of dating partners obtained 2 months earlier with people's recall of their earlier impressions and found that those persons whose impressions had become more favorable over the period recalled that their initial impressions had been more favorable than was actually the case, whereas those whose impressions had become more negative recalled that their initial impressions had been more negative than they actually were.

Because we all tend to be revisionist historians of our relationships, researchers have developed techniques to overcome the vicissitudes of memory for past relationship events. For example, people are often asked to report on the occurrence of events almost immediately after the event occurs, using structured questionnaires (Reis, 1994; Reis & Gable, 2000). One frequently used questionnaire is the Spouse Observation Checklist (SOC; e.g., see Weiss & Margolin, 1977) on which marital partners are asked to check off daily the behaviors that occur in their relationship. Another is the Rochester Interaction Record (RIR), developed by Ladd Wheeler and Harry Reis (see Reis & Wheeler, 1991), which is an *event-contingent sampling* method: respondents are asked to report when an event satisfying a specified definition has occurred. The RIR specifies that a social interaction lasting 10 minutes or longer is the event to be recorded in a diary and evaluated on a number of dimensions, such as degree of pleasantness and degree of intimacy.

Another frequently used daily experience sampling method is *signal-contingent sampling*, developed by Csikszentmihalyi, Larson, and Prescott (1977), wherein respondents are periodically signaled by the researcher, usually via beepers, pagers, or telephone calls, and instructed to complete a brief questionnaire describing their current activities, thoughts, and impressions. The signal intervals may be fixed, random, a combination of fixed and random, or interval-contingent, where respondents report on their experiences at regular, predetermined intervals such as at the end of the day or after each meal.

In addition to minimizing the problems of retrospection and response biases, studies of daily experience enhance *ecological validity*; that is, artifacts associated with laboratory settings are reduced and the validity of the findings increased because the relationship behaviors of interest are examined in the partners' natural interaction settings (see Reis & Gable, 2000). Although daily experience sampling methods are not a substitute for questionnaires and interviews, they provide information about people's thoughts, feelings, and activities in their everyday lives, and this information often generates hypotheses that may be investigated in more controlled contexts.

Observation

Because researchers recognize that self-report measures are sometimes unreliable, many investigators bring the couple into the laboratory to observe their interaction (see Weiss & Heyman, 1990). Observation of interaction is labor-intensive and expensive. Moreover, to be useful the observations must be coded in some way for descriptive and analytical purposes (see McClintock, 1983/2002). Many different interaction coding schemes are available (e.g., see Kerig

& Lindahl, 2001). One of the oldest is the Marital Interaction Coding System (MICS; Hops, Wills, Patterson, & Weiss, 1972). What coding scheme is adopted will influence what the investigator sees in the interaction. What the investigator sees in the interaction also is dependent on what the partners happen to be doing at the time they are observed. For example, Melby, Ge, Conger, and Warner (1995) found inconsistencies between spouses' warmth/support behaviors when they were performing a discussion task and when they were engaged in a problem-solving task. Investigators who observe couples as they try to resolve a conflict tend to see many negative behaviors, especially in distressed couples, as discussed in Chapter 14, "Intervention and Dissolution." However, investigators who observe spouses disclose a current source of personal distress in their lives (not caused by the partner or the relationship) see partners exhibiting many more supportive, positive behaviors than negative behaviors (e.g., Cutrona, 1996; Cutrona & Suhr, 1994). Thus, observation of partners' interaction is not without its own reliability, validity, and interpretive problems (see Baucom & Sayers, 1989; Sillars, 1991).

Perhaps the most persistent and troubling problem associated with direct observation of interaction is **observation reactivity**—people often behave differently when they know they are being observed than when they believe they are not. Thus, partners' behavior in the laboratory (where they almost always know they are being observed) may be different from their behavior in their usual habitats. Some researchers initially believed that reactivity could be reduced and validity increased if, instead of bringing the relationship partners into the laboratory, they visited the partners' home and observed them behave in their natural setting. Pessimism about the validity of "in-home" observations developed after Patterson (e.g., 1979) and his associates published their studies of children with severe behavior problems and reported that placing an observer in the home affected both the frequency and type of behavior displayed by family members. Subsequent experimental studies revealed that mothers were able to influence the observed rate of deviant behavior in their children when the mothers were instructed to "look good" or "look bad" to the observer (Vincent, Friedman, Nugent, & Messerly, 1979).

In an attempt to reduce the intrusiveness of the observer, some researchers subsequently placed electronic devices in the home to gather interaction data. For example, Christensen and Hazzard (1983) placed an audio recording device in three homes; the first week each family was aware the device was recording their behavior, the second week they were told the device had broken down (although it hadn't), and the third week they were told the device was again working. Two of the three families showed no difference in behavior between conditions, whereas the third family did show differences.

That in-home observation via electronic recording devices may produce reliable data was demonstrated by Jacob, Tennenbaum, Seilhamer, Bargiel, and Sharon (1994) in an experiment involving more than 80 families. In a third of the families, the father had been diagnosed as alcoholic; in another third, the father had been diagnosed as depressed; in the remaining third, neither parent exhibited a psychiatric disorder. For one week, dinnertime recordings were obtained by the family themselves by activating a recording apparatus (the *fixed recording* condition). For the second week, the investigators placed three suitcases in the home and the family was told that each contained random-interval recording devices. Thus, the families had no control over the equipment and did not know when they would be observed (the *random recording* condition), but in actuality, during the second week only one device recorded, and it did so during the family's dinnertime. The investigators believed that these two conditions represented a marked difference in obtrusiveness of observation and, thus, if observation reactivity effects were present, there would be significant differences in the rate and nature of the family's behavior between the conditions. The family's interactions subsequently were coded for several behaviors, including negative exchanges, positive exchanges, and commands.

Jacob and associates found few reactivity effects. Although the fixed recording condition produced more positive exchanges than the random recording condition, the expected differential behaviors of the three family groups was apparent in both conditions; that is, the nondistressed families, for example, exhibited higher rates of positivity than did either of the two groups of distressed families. The investigators offer three possible reasons for the lack of reactivity in their study: First, family units, compared with groupings of strangers, share a long interactional history, and it is difficult for people to overcome the force of interaction habits (as we've discussed) even if they are motivated to change their interactional pattern in order to look good to outside observers. Second, families are busy environments in which there are tasks more important than impressing researchers; one wife said, "Taking care of our children takes up much of our time; we were just too busy to be affected by your study." Third, most persons have little motivation to alter their routine behaviors for researchers when the researchers have no control over the person's outcomes.

Jacob and colleagues (1994) conclude that "reactivity effects are relatively few in number and relatively limited as to their impact on the interpretability of other study variables" (p. 361). Supporting this conclusion, Lindahl, Clements, and Markman (1998) report that although couples communicated more positively when they were aware they were being videotaped than when they believed they were not, and although overall levels of positivity and negativity may change from setting to setting as a result of reactivity, the actual sequencing and patterning of a couple's interactions tend to be similar across interaction settings and similar whether or not the partners believe they are being observed.

Archives and Other Public Records

Relationship scholars frequently obtain important information about relationships from public archives. Marriage licenses, divorces, births and deaths, and other information is a matter of public record in most countries. Newspapers and diaries are also a source of information about close relationships. The Donner party's diaries (discussed in Chapter 2, "Relationships and Health") are just one example of the information that can be gleaned from such sources.

Archival research is often labor-intensive, time-consuming, and sometimes frustrating for the investigator. The experiences of Paul Rosenblatt, an anthropologist and social psychologist, are illustrative. Believing that diaries could be a valuable source of information about close relationships, he tracked down nineteenth-century diaries in libraries across the United States. Many of the published diaries seemed to have been edited, however, and it was difficult to determine what had been removed. Moreover, he found that the phenomena he was especially interested in were not well represented in the diaries; only "a few diaries dealt with marital disenchantment, a few with courtship, a few with problems of childrearing" (1983, p. vii). What *was* well represented in the diaries of these nineteenth-century men and women (Figure 4.8) however, was the experience of loss and separation from loved ones, perhaps reflecting the hardships of life in the nineteenth century. As a consequence, Rosenblatt changed his research focus, and the result was *Bitter, Bitter Tears: Nineteenth-Century Diarists and Twentieth-Century Grief Theories* (1983). The title was taken from passages in two diaries:

> "[We] came to steamer. All the folks came down. It was killing work for me to say farewell. This done & I must not look mournfully into the past. We are not out of sight of land. . . . I only cried as the steamer sailed away—bitter, bitter tears."
> —*Diary of Nellie Wetherbee, unpublished manuscript, Bancroft Library, University of California, Berkeley, entry of March 5, 1860*

> My darling only brother is dead. . . . I cannot wish the dear one back. His body lies beside dear Susan's now. I hope his soul is with hers in heaven. . . . The bitter tears will come. I cannot keep them back.
> —*Diary of Mrs. Charles C. Carpenter (Feronica Nancy Rice Carpenter), unpublished manuscript on microfilm*

FIGURE 4.8 The cover of Paul Rosenblatt's (1983) book.

at Public Archives of Canada, Ottawa, entry of June 12, 1863 (Rosenblatt, 1983, frontispiece)

Archival research not only is laborious and time-consuming; it sometimes is hazardous to the researcher's physical and mental health. Rosenblatt (1983) relates:

> Work in the archives was demanding. It was physically exhausting to spend long hours reading difficult handwriting, breathing the inevitable dust of stored and deteriorating paper. In addition, the diaries that gripped me strongly, that gave me a strong sense of the personality and concerns of the diarist, were often painful to read. The most self-disclosing diaries, diaries by people I came to feel that I knew relatively well, gave poignant and often painfully detailed accounts of personal and family tragedies. On my early visits to archives, I would return to my motel or hotel room after an archive closed for the evening emotionally and physically exhausted, too drained to do anything but sleep. (pp. vii–viii)

Rosenblatt's comments illustrate that archival relationship research sometimes is no less demanding and labor-intensive than other methods are. Archival research often combines qualitative description with quantitative analysis. For example, Rosenblatt provides statistical analyses of the diarists' reactions to separations from those they loved, either through death or other events, in his examination of the predictions made by several contemporary grief theories.

GENERAL THEORIES OF SOCIAL INTERACTION

Many relationship theories have been formulated, but most address a particular variety of relationship (parent–child, husband–wife) or a specific facet of relationships (sexual behavior, conflict). Almost all of these limited-focus theories have been influenced by, or are elaborations and extensions of, the general theories of social interaction. General social interaction theories address a wide range of behaviors and usually are applicable to all types of relationships and all settings in which interaction takes place.

Social Learning Theory

Early in the twentieth century, Edward Thorndike proposed a number of general principles of learning that he called "connectionism." One of the most important of these principles was the law of effect—behaviors followed by reward are more likely to be repeated than behaviors that are not. Elaborating and expanding on the law of effect and other of Thorndike's principles, psychologists developed several "grand theories" of learning in the 1930s and 1940s. One of these theories, constructed by experimental psychologist Clark

Hull, generated voluminous research on learning in rats and other nonhuman animals (see Hilgard, 1948). One of Hull's graduate seminars at Yale was addressed to the possible applications of his learning theory to humans. Two students in that seminar, John Dollard and Neal Miller, and their colleagues later applied Hullian learning theory's "four fundamentals of learning"—drive, cue, response, and reward—to an analysis of human aggression in *Frustration and Aggression* (Dollard, Doob, Miller, Mowrer, & Sears, 1939). Shortly thereafter, Miller and Dollard (1941) published a second classic book, *Social Learning and Imitation*, which argued that "imitative behavior follows the laws of learning and arises under the *social conditions* which reward it" (p. 12, emphasis added). Albert Bandura (e.g., 1973, 1997) extended Miller and Dollard's analysis and demonstrated in a series of classic experiments that children could acquire new behaviors simply by observing another person get rewarded for performing them (e.g., Bandura, Ross, & Ross, 1961). Currently, the degree to which a child imitates a parent has been viewed as a measure of the child's responsiveness to the parent, an indicant of relationship quality, and a factor that likely influences the child's socialization (Forman & Kochanska, 2001).

As it is now applied to relationships, the social learning theoretical approach represents an eclectic collection of principles borrowed from several learning theories (see Berscheid, 1998), all of which are based on the general principle that behavior that is rewarded is more likely to be repeated than behavior that is not rewarded. This approach assumes that when choosing between alternative courses of action, the behavior chosen is a result of the individual's estimate (conscious or unconscious) of the extent to which each behavioral alternative will result in rewarding, as opposed to costly or punishing, outcomes. The "social" in the social learning theory approach comes from its contention that people in an individual's social environment are the major source of that individual's rewards and punishments (either directly or indirectly through imitation). As Andrew Christensen (1983/2002), a marital and family therapist and researcher, explains: "According to this [social learning] approach, the important causal conditions for human behavior are not to be found by a search of the individual's traits, personality structure, or unconscious, but rather by a detailed examination of the environmental stimuli that impinge on the individual" (p. 418).

The social learning approach to social interaction posits that the individual's partner sets the individual's *reinforcement contingencies* (events commonly called "rewards" or "punishments" and "costs" that follow behavior and influence the probability that the individual will repeat the interaction behavior). Thus, researchers who take this approach tend to focus on the rewards and costs partners experience in their interactions. In addition, because the receipt of rewards and costs is often associated with emotional and other affective responses, these researchers often examine people's affective responses in interaction (as illustrated by the study conducted by Levenson & Gottman, 1983). Moreover, reflecting the roots of the social learning approach in experimental psychology, researchers who take this approach highly value direct observation of the partners' interaction and are uncomfortable with reliance on self-report (as also illustrated by Levenson & Gottman, 1983).

The social learning approach to understanding relationship satisfaction and constructing interventions into distressed relationships was taken by Robert L. Weiss, Gerald Patterson, and many of their associates and students. Affiliated with the University of Oregon and the Oregon Research Institute, these seminal researchers of marital interaction, their many colleagues, and influential students became known as the Oregon School of marital and family research (see Chapter 14, "Intervention and Dissolution"). One of their first—and classic—studies illustrates the social learning approach to relationships and to marital interaction. Questioning the validity of using spouses' retrospective reports about aspects of their marriages and also doubting the validity of popular marital satisfaction scales,

Wills, Weiss, and Patterson (1974) asked each spouse in seven happily married couples to complete, once a day for 14 days, the Spouse Observation Checklist (SOC). The SOC asked the individual to report the number of times that day their spouse had performed one of the listed *instrumental* behaviors ("took out the garbage," "shopped for groceries") and, also, how *pleasing or displeasing* that behavior was to the individual. In addition, the researchers asked participants to record the occurrence of their spouse's *affectional* behaviors, both pleasurable and displeasurable, on portable event counters. Finally, each spouse's marital satisfaction was recorded for each morning, afternoon, and evening during which a significant interaction with the spouse had occurred.

Not surprisingly, Wills and colleagues found that an individual's marital satisfaction was negatively associated with the spouse's displeasurable behaviors and positively correlated with the spouse's performance of pleasurable behaviors (which occurred 3 times more frequently than displeasurable behaviors, according to the reports of the happily married partners). However, the spouse's displeasurable instrumental and affectional behaviors accounted for far more of the individual's variance in satisfaction than did the spouse's pleasurable behaviors (65% vs. 25%), an early indication of the relative independence of positive and negative affective dimensions in relationships and the relatively greater impact of negative affective behavior on relationship satisfaction, as discussed further in Chapter 9, "Affective Processes." In addition, negative behaviors were more likely to be reciprocated than positive behaviors. Negative reciprocity subsequently would be found by many researchers to be the hallmark of distressed marriages (see Weiss & Heyman, 1990), although, as this study of happy couples suggests, it appears to be somewhat characteristic of nondistressed marriages as well.

Wills and colleagues (1974) also found that for both husbands and wives, both instrumental and affectional behaviors that were displeasurable were related to satisfaction, but the association between satisfaction and instrumental and af-

fectional pleasurable behaviors was more complicated. Wives' satisfaction was not much influenced by the husband's performance of pleasurable instrumental behaviors, but it was influenced by his pleasurable affectional behaviors; husbands' satisfaction was only marginally influenced by the wife's pleasurable affectional behaviors, but it clearly was influenced by the wife's pleasurable instrumental behaviors. When asked by the researchers to increase their pleasurable affectional behaviors, some men responded by increasing their pleasurable instrumental behaviors such as washing their wife's car—in other words, they performed the kind of behaviors they themselves found especially pleasing. The researchers comment:

> Studies of the role expectations of marriage partners . . . have shown that husbands are expected to fulfill a primarily instrumental role in the marriage relationship, whereas wives are expected to enact a role dealing with the affectional aspects of the relationship. The present results suggest that the actual sources of satisfaction are the opposite of these role prescriptions, and that in order to provide satisfaction for the spouse, a person must provide behaviors that (a) he or she perceives as counter to the appropriate role and (b) he or she does not perceive as pleasurable for the self. (p. 810)

In other words, to please their spouse, a partner has to "go against the grain" and *not* do unto the other the things they would have the other do unto them. We further discuss the social learning theory approach to marital interaction in Chapter 13, "Satisfaction and Stability," and Chapter 14, "Intervention and Dissolution."

Homans's Social Exchange Theory

To predict people's choice of interaction partners and their subsequent interaction behavior, sociologist George Homans (1961, 1974) also drew on the psychological learning theories, but he added principles from elementary economics. In his social exchange theory, Homans assumes that people are sensitive to rewards and costs and try to maximize their **profits** (rewards minus costs) in their interactions with others. Thus, he predicts that people will attempt to interact with those persons with whom they expect interaction to be profitable. Like the social learning theorists, Homans assumes that the individual will repeat interaction behaviors that were rewarded in the past and avoid those that proved costly; the more valuable the reward and the more frequently a past behavior has led to reward, the more probable it is that the individual will perform that behavior.

A major problem with theories of reward and punishment is *not* that the principle is invalid—it is that it is difficult to specify in advance what is likely to be a reward or a punishment for whom and when. It is easy to predict that a starved rat will find food a reward, but correctly predicting what an individual will find rewarding is more difficult. In his social exchange theory, Homans tried to specify some of the factors that would affect the value of a reward. For example, he incorporated the economists' **principle of scarcity**: The scarcer the reward the partner provides, the higher the price the partner can demand for it and the more costs the individual is likely to have to endure to obtain it. For example, male octogenarians can command many considerations from their same-age female romantic partners because older women have a smaller pool of available partners than older men do.

Homans also incorporated the learning **principle of satiation**, which is similar to the economists' principle of diminishing marginal utility: The more of a specific rewarding activity a person has recently received from an interaction partner, the less valuable to the individual are further units of that activity. This is why the partner's first expression of esteem is more valuable than his or her hundredth expression of affection and the first kiss is a greater reward than the thousandth kiss. Similarly, Homans adopted the learning **principle of fatigue**, analogous to the economists' principle of increasing marginal costs: The more often the individual recently has performed a costly activity, the more costly it is for him or her to perform additional units of that activity. Thus, giving a co-worker a ride home for the tenth time is more costly than performing the favor the first time. Together, the principles of satiation and fatigue predict that in long-term relationships, the value of repeated rewards will decrease and the value of repeated costs will increase. Some marital and family therapists refer to this effect as **relationship reinforcement erosion**, which is associated with increasing relationship dissatisfaction (Christensen & Walczynski, 1997; Jacobson & Margolin, 1979).

Another's expression of approval or disapproval of the individual, **sentiment**, plays a central role in Homans's theory. Homans believed that another person's expression of esteem is so valuable that it comes close to being a *generalized reinforcer* for humans, likely in any context to increase the probability that the behavior that preceded the expression of positive sentiment will be repeated (and, conversely, expressions of disapproval will lower the probability that the behavior will be performed in the future). The prominent role Homans gave expressions of positive and negative sentiment in his theory of social interaction is recognition of the fact that people need the good will of others for their well-being and survival.

In sum, the fundamental assumption of social exchange theory is that people interact with each other in order to obtain rewards but, in the process, costs must be incurred. For example, one cost that accompanies every interaction is the rewards from other activities and interactions that must be forgone in order to engage in the present interaction. The theory assumes that people try to gain as many rewards as possible while incurring the fewest costs in their social interactions, and it predicts that people will attempt to interact with those from whom they expect to receive high profits and will avoid interacting with those from whom they expect low rewards and high costs. This last assumption—that satisfying interactions should increase the frequency with which the partners interact—has received empirical support from White (1983), who examined factors associated with frequency of marital interaction and found that marital happiness is a significant determinant of spousal interaction frequency. Although the reverse effect also holds—interaction increases marital satisfaction—White found evidence that this effect is not as strong as the effect of satisfaction on interaction. It should be noted that the reciprocal causal relationship between relationship satisfaction and frequency of interaction is not unusual among relationship variables and makes assuming causation from correlational data particularly hazardous.

Equity Theories

The equity theories were inspired by Homans's (1961) **principle of distributive justice**:

> A [person] in an exchange relation with another will expect that the rewards of each [person] be proportional to his [or her] costs—the greater the rewards, the greater the costs—and that the net rewards, or profits, of each [person] be proportional to his [or her] investments—the greater the investments, the greater the profit. (p. 75)

Investments are defined by Homans as the individual's positively or negatively valued past activities such as education plus such positively or negatively valued personal characteristics as social status, physical appearance, age, and sex. (In some societies, for example, being male is viewed as an investment for which extra profit is expected in interactions with females.) Homans hypothesizes that people perceive distributive justice—fair and equitable exchange—if their profits from the interaction are equal to the profits of those whose investments are similar to their own. Homans predicts that when the rule of distributive justice is violated—that is, when another receives more profits for the same investments—people will be angry and will try to redress the inequity.

Equity theorists (e.g., Adams, 1965; Walster, Walster, & Berscheid, 1978) subsequently elaborated and extended the rule of distributive justice by incorporating the basic proposition of the cognitive consistency theories—that holding logically inconsistent beliefs such as "I am an ethical person" and "I have behaved in an inequitable manner" produces an uncomfortable state the individual is motivated to reduce. Walster and colleagues define an **equitable relationship** as one in which the ratio of P's *outcomes* (rewards or benefits) to *inputs* (costs and investments) is equal to O's outcome/input ratio. The theory assumes that human societies (and smaller groups within the larger society) maximize their collective reward by evolving systems for equitably apportioning resources among their members. By rewarding those who treat others equitably and punishing those who do not, a group induces its members to adhere to its resource allocation system. Because most people internalize the societal norm that people should be fair and equitable in their dealings with others, these researchers predict that when people find themselves in an inequitable relationship, they will become distressed—whether the inequity underbenefits or overbenefits them—and the greater the inequity, the greater the distress. Distress induced by inequities that unjustly benefit the individual may be of two types: (1) *retaliation distress*, which has its source in anticipation that the partner, other people, or even God, will retaliate and restore equity to the relationship; and (2) *self-concept distress*, stemming from the violation of the internalized societal norm that people should be equitable and fair in their dealings with others.

Walster and colleagues predict that people who discover they are in an inequitable relationship will try to reduce their distress by restoring equity to the relationship in one of two ways: First, they may attempt to restore *actual equity* to the relationship by altering their own or their partner's profits by providing more (or less) rewards to the partner, for example, or lowering (or raising) the partner's costs. Second, they may attempt to restore *psychological equity* by distorting reality in such a way as to convince themselves that the inequitable relationship is, in fact, equitable. For example, they may cognitively minimize or exaggerate the amount and value of their own or their partner's input to the relationship or minimize or exaggerate the value of their own or their partner's relationship outcomes. When overbenefited, restoring psychological equity to the relationship usually is less costly than restoring actual equity, but even this equity restoration route involves some cost because it requires a distortion of reality, which is always dangerous to well-being and survival.

Walster and colleagues emphasize that a relationship is equitable or inequitable depending on the subjective view of the person viewing the relationship. Equity, in other words, is in the eye of the beholder. As a consequence, one partner may view the relationship as equitable while the other partner believes it to be inequitable. Discrepancies in the partners' judgments of the equity of their relationship are not unusual for a variety of reasons, including the fact that most people are more aware of their own costs in the relationship than they are of their partner's (e.g., Ross & Sicoly, 1979).

Although most hypotheses derived from the principle of distributive justice and equity theory formulations were initially tested in employer–employee or co-worker relationships (e.g., Adams, 1965), Walster and her colleagues (1978) theorized that equity principles should apply to close romantic and friendship relationships as well. Some investigators have found that people's perception of inequity in a close relationship is associated with dissatisfaction and poor relationship quality (e.g., Buunk & Van Yperen, 1989; Hatfield, Traupmann, Sprecher, Utne, & Hay, 1985). As a whole, however, the now large equity literature is inconsistent at best and contradictory at worst (see Clark & Chrisman, 1994; Sprecher & Schwartz, 1994; Van Yperen & Buunk, 1994). Buunk and Van Yperen (1991) have found that equity principles are not equally important to everyone. These investigators found that marital satisfaction was associated with perceptions of equity only among spouses who had a strong "exchange orientation," defined as an individual's predisposition to seek immediate reciprocity from the partner for benefits given (see Murstein, Cerreto, & MacDonald, 1977).

Not only may equity principles not be important to everyone, but even if they are important, people in close relationships may not think about them all the time. Grote and Clark (2001) suspect that people do not regularly track the benefits they and their partner are giving and receiving and do not regularly think about issues of fairness and equity. They hypothesized, however, that relationship distress, generated on other grounds, may initiate a search for evidence of unfairness in a relationship (which, once sought, usually is easily found in most relationships). In other words, although equity theory originally hypothesized that perceptions of inequity would produce distress, Grote and Clark proposed that sometimes the reverse is true—people's dissatisfaction with their relationship causes them to closely scrutinize the benefits they are giving and receiving in the relationship, which then leads to perceptions of unfairness, which may further increase the initial relationship distress.

Supporting their hypothesis, Grote and Clark found evidence, in a longitudinal study that tracked married couples across their transition to parenthood, of a cycle: distress → perception of unfairness → heightened distress. Marital dissatisfaction at Time 1 was associated with heightened perception of unfairness in the allocation of household tasks at Time 2, and perception of unfairness at Time 2 was associated with heightened dissatisfaction at Time 3. Thus, like many other relationship variables, perceptions of inequity and poor relationship quality appear to be causally reciprocal in nature: Perceptions of unfairness may lead to dissatisfaction with the relationship, relationship dissatisfaction may lead to perceptions of unfairness, and both may operate in a cyclic causal loop.

Interdependence Theory

The most influential general theory of relationship interaction has been the interdependence theory of John Thibaut and Harold Kelley (Figure 4.9), published in 1959 (see Rusbult & Van Lange, 1996, 2003). Like social learning theory and social exchange theory, in-

FIGURE 4.9 John Thibaut and Harold Kelley.

terdependence theory assumes that people will not repeat an interaction behavior unless it is rewarded in some way. Unlike those theories, which are addressed to the prediction of a single *individual's* behavior in interaction, interdependence theory is a relational theory addressed to how the structure of the situations in which two people interact influences the interaction patterns the partners are likely to develop over time. The theory highlights the fact that different situations present the partners with different problems and different opportunities. Different situations also allow or preclude the expression of different dispositions, such as a disposition to compete or to cooperate. An atlas of the types of situations partners frequently encounter has been presented by Kelley and his colleagues (2003).

Interdependence theory assumes that when choosing a behavior to perform in interaction

from the options available, an individual must also consider the behavioral options open to the partner in that time frame and the likely effect that the partner's behavioral choice will have on the individual's own **goodness of outcomes** (rewards minus costs). For example, the behavioral option of watching *Monday Night Football* on television may be, in absolute terms, a highly rewarding activity to the husband. He may be aware, however, that his wife wants to watch *Masterpiece Theatre*, which would be highly rewarding to her, also in absolute terms. As a consequence, he may anticipate that if he turns to the football channel, she may elect her behavioral option of revving up the vacuum cleaner to do some overdue cleaning in the vicinity of the television set. The partners may compromise by performing the *set* of behavioral options that provides *both* partners with relatively good outcomes; for example, they may watch an adventure movie.

Interdependence theory thus assumes that the interaction patterns or recurring regularities likely to develop in a relationship are a function of the relationship's **outcome matrix**, a concept borrowed from game theory. The concept of relationship outcome matrix is intended to represent, at least metaphorically, the behavioral options available to each partner at a given point in time and the goodness of outcomes likely to result for each person should the partners *jointly perform* a particular combination of behaviors in that time frame. The theory predicts that as the partners become familiar with each other's behavioral options and the goodness of joint outcomes associated with each, over time they will locate the most mutually advantageous sets of behavioral combinations and coordinate their interaction behaviors in order to achieve mutually satisfying outcomes. Thus, an important property of the situations couples encounter is the extent to which the goodness of the outcomes associated with the partners' possible behaviors covary, that is, whether certain sets of acts produce equally beneficial outcomes for both partners (as opposed to, for example, zero-sum situations in which one partner's gain is the other partner's loss—the perfect setup for conflict).

Kelley (1979) provides an empirically derived example of a relationship outcome matrix associated with that portion of a couple's life having to do with cleaning their apartment. The data were obtained from cohabiting heterosexual couples from the undergraduate community at the University of California, Los Angeles, who were asked to assume that cleaning their shared apartment was a disagreeable job but that it had reached the point that something had to be done. On a 21-point scale, ranging from -10 (very dissatisfied) to $+10$ (very satisfied), they were asked to rate the satisfaction they would feel for each of four possible events: (1) Both of you clean. (2) You clean and your partner does other things. (3) You do other things and your partner cleans. (4) You both do other things (and the apartment stays dirty). Kelley's results are displayed in Figure 4.10. Both partners indicated that they would be most satisfied if both participated in cleaning the apartment. Also evident in the outcome matrix Kelley obtained, however, are traditional sex-role attitudes: Both reported they would be less satisfied if the man did the cleaning alone than if the woman cleaned alone.

Because the goodness of an individual's outcomes for electing to perform a specific behavior is affected by the behavioral option the partner chooses within that same time frame, people often can influence their partner's behavioral choices by varying their response to it. Interdependence theory calls this kind of power in a relationship **behavior control**: An individual has behavior control over the other if, by varying his or her own behavior, he or she can make it desirable for the partner to elect to perform one behavior rather than another (Figure 4.11). The exercise of behavior control is always costly because it requires careful attention to what the partner is doing (or about to do) and then shifting one's own behavioral choices accordingly.

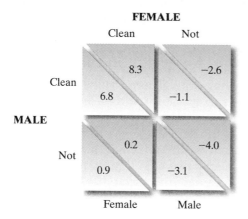

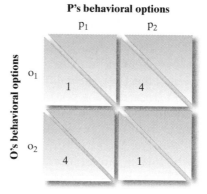

FIGURE 4.10 Behavioral outcome matrix. On a scale ranging from -10 to $+10$, participants indicated how satisfied they would be at obtaining four possible outcomes for cleaning the apartment (man and woman both clean, man cleans but woman does not, woman cleans but man does not, both do not clean). Female satisfaction outcomes are above the diagonal within each quadrant; male outcomes are below the diagonal within each quadrant. *Kelley, Personal Relationships: Their Structures and Processes (1979), Fig. 2, p. 25.*

FIGURE 4.11 Illustration of P's behavior control over O. An individual has behavior control over the other if, by varying his or her own behavior, he or she can make it desirable for the partner to elect to perform one behavior rather than another. Here, only O's outcomes are shown (below the diagonal within each quadrant). As can be seen, by changing his or her behavior from p_1 to p_2, P can motivate O to make a corresponding change in behavior from o_2 to o_1. *Thibaut and Kelley, The Social Psychology of Groups (1959), Table 7.2, p. 103.*

Given a situation of **mutual behavior control**, where *both* partners can influence each other's outcomes, interdependence theory predicts that the partners will eventually find the most mutually advantageous cell in their relationship outcome matrix and begin to repeat that particular combination of behaviors, forming a regularity in their interaction pattern.

Some individuals can influence the partner's outcomes regardless of what the partner does. Such people have **fate control** over their partners. An example of such a matrix is depicted in Figure 4.12, where it can be seen that whether O performs Behavior o_1 or o_2, P can decide O's outcomes; that is, by deciding to perform Behavior p_1, P can give O a poor outcome and by performing Behavior p_2, P can give O a good outcome. People who have fate control over their partner obviously have a great deal of power in the relationship. However, an individual's fate control over the partner rests on the individual's

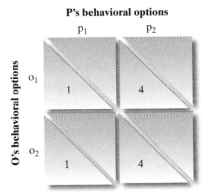

P's behavioral options

FIGURE 4.12 Illustration of P's fate control over O. An individual has fate control over the other if, by varying his or her own behavior, he or she can affect the partner's outcomes regardless of what the partner does. Only O's outcomes are shown (below the diagonal within each quadrant). By changing his or her behavior from p_1 to p_2, P can increase O's outcomes from 1 to 4 (and can also, of course, reduce O's outcomes later by changing back to p_1—and in neither case does O have the power to do anything about the situation). *Thibaut and Kelley, The Social Psychology of Groups (1959), Table 7.1, p. 102.*

ability to deliver high rewards (or punishments) to the partner at very low cost to him- or herself; that is, it should be no more costly for P to elect to perform p_1 than to perform p_2. Moreover, the degree of fate control the individual can exert over the partner is limited by the partner's dependence on the relationship because an important behavioral option almost always available to the partner is to leave the relationship. If in exercising fate control over the partner in order to obtain good outcomes for him- or herself, the individual reduces the partner's outcomes below that which could be obtained elsewhere, interdependence theory predicts that the partner will dissolve the relationship. Mutual behavior control is more usual than fate control in relationships; that is, each partner's outcomes usually vary not as the sole function of the individual's behavioral choices or the partner's behavioral choices alone but rather as a function of the interaction between them.

As in social learning theory and social exchange theory, in interdependence theory an individual's power to reward or punish, and thus influence, his or her partner plays a central role. Some people have regarded such theories of relationship behavior as crass, believing that power considerations may be useful for understanding business and superficial relationships but are not applicable to understanding the dynamics of close relationships. However, many marital and family researchers and therapists have found that power—especially asymmetry of power—is an important dimension underlying relationship interaction (Christensen & Jacobson, 2000; Gottman, 1994). The same conclusion has been reached experimentally in the laboratory. For example, Georgesen and Harris (2000) examined the effects of perceived power on dyadic problem-solving interactions and concluded that its effects were pervasive.

Within close relationships, however, raw power differentials may be—and often are—layered over with the partners' adoption of rules that override their power disparities. For example, the partners may adopt a rule that they will always maximize joint outcomes even though one of the partners could get better outcomes if the rule were not adopted. Kelley and Thibaut (1978) and Kelley (1979), who analyzed a variety of patterns of interdependence that characterize close relationships, revised interdependence theory to distinguish between two types of outcome matrices: The **given outcome matrix** is defined as "a set of outcomes [associated with different behavioral options] provided to the person by external reward and incentive systems" (Kelley, 1979, p. 69), or, as Rusbult, Wieselquist, Foster, and Witcher (1999) put it, "the given situation describes each individual's 'gut level,' self-centered behavioral preferences based on the immediate, personal outcomes he or she might obtain in that situation" (p. 429). The given outcome matrix is distinguished from the **effective outcome matrix**, which results from the partners' *transformation* of the given matrix—for example, by adoption of a rule that the partners' outcomes shall be equal—and guides the partners' *actual* behavior in the relationship.

Unfortunately, not a great deal is known about the processes associated with when, how, or why people transform the given matrix. Presumably, some transformations may be motivated by individuals' philosophical or religious considerations like "Do unto others as you would have others do unto you" and others by the prospect of societal sanctions that punish selfish behavior and the misuse of power. Still other transformations may be motivated by concern for the continuance of the relationship. Several studies, many of them conducted by Caryl Rusbult and her associates (e.g., Rusbult, Yovetich, & Verette, 1996), find that close relationship partners do frequently overlook their own immediate self-interest and adhere to transformation rules in order to promote the health and continuance of the relationship, as discussed further in Chapter 13, "Satisfaction and Stability."

Not only is little known about outcome matrix transformation processes, it also is not known how divergent the transformed matrix typically is from the relationship's given matrix or under what conditions (e.g., increases in the partners' disparity of power) the partners will revert back to the given matrix. This is an important issue for several reasons, including the fact that most romantic relationship partners, including newlyweds, usually start out with approximately equal resources and power. In such circumstances, if the partners transform the given matrix by adopting an **equality rule of exchange** (where both partners' goodness of outcomes are to be equal) or a **communal rule of exchange** (which prescribes that each partner's goodness of outcomes will be proportionate to his or her needs even if this means that one partner's goodness of outcomes exceeds that of the other partner's), outcomes derived from the transformed matrix are not likely to diverge greatly from those from the given matrix. Over time, however, one partner may become more powerful than the other and demand that the allocation rule reflected in the transformed matrix be renegotiated in favor of the now more powerful partner.

The development of a power imbalance in an initially equal-power relationship is illustrated by a traditional marriage in which (1) two college students of equal education and resources meet and marry; (2) the husband goes on to obtain additional education while his wife works at a menial job to support his further education; (3) his advanced education allows him to obtain a well-paying job and career, which he pursues while she performs household tasks and raises their children. Over this time period, he is developing far more social and economic resources than she and is likely to have many more alternatives to the present relationship than she.

Partners often foresee that their relative circumstances may change over time and promise each other that this will not change their behavior in the relationship. They vow, for example, to love and care for each other "in sickness and health" and "for richer or poorer." They promise, in other words, that even if the given matrix changes, they will not abandon the relationship for a better alternative, nor will they use their greater power to exploit the other. In previous times, spouses did not have to worry unduly about a growing power differential because they could be confident that if the partner became more powerful and broke the marriage vows, society, through courts of law and social sanctions, would demand compensation for the betrayed partner. With the advent of "no-fault" divorce and other recent societal changes that have reduced the costs of divorce (Attridge & Berscheid, 1994), marital partners may have become more concerned about resource disparities and growing power imbalances.

Kelley and Thibaut (1978) believe that over time in some relationships, both partners may undergo changes in their personal motivations, which changes the value of their own outcomes in ways that change the given matrix. Such **transformation of motivation** processes may change the given outcome matrix in ways that increase the correspondence of the partners' outcomes and reduce the likelihood of conflict. For example, an interviewer asked film actor Tom Cruise if he was jealous of the success of his then wife, Nicole Kidman. He replied, "You have to understand: Her dreams are now my dreams" (Roach, 1996, p. 5). In other words, he now was as motivated to fulfill her goals as his own and would be happy if she succeeded in her career as an actress.

Levinger and his associates (Borden & Levinger, 1991; Holmes & Levinger, 1994) propose that in addition to transformation of motivation, a **transformation of disposition** process also may occur. For example, over time the wife may come to enjoy *Monday Night Football* as much as her husband does or he may develop an enthusiasm for *Masterpiece Theatre's* dramatizations of classic works. If so, the partners' correspondence of outcomes is increased and presumably occasions for conflict are decreased. Both transformation of motivation and transformation of disposition appear to be processes by which partners move from a selfish "me" orientation with respect to the rewarding outcomes they receive from the relationship to a communal "we" orientation. It should be recognized, however, that individuals may experience transformations of motivation and of disposition that result in *less* correspondence of outcomes with their partner and lead to increased conflict. For example, both may have been avid mountain climbers when they first met, but one partner may come to see the sport as dangerous and expensive.

In sum, interdependence theory is about the *situations* within which people interact. These situations are defined by the partners' relationship outcome matrix. As Holmes (2000) explains, interdependence theory is about

> the particular interpersonal problems individuals face, including the degree to which their interests correspond or conflict, the amount and type of power and influence each has over the other. . . . These features combine to form a limited set of prototypical situations, each of which "pushes" for or affords certain types of interactions. (p. 450)

Although interdependence theory primarily is concerned with interaction situations, it also presented two concepts, comparison level and comparison level for alternatives, that have proved highly useful in predicting an individual's satisfaction with the relationship and his or her likelihood of terminating the relationship. These two interdependence theory concepts are discussed in Chapter 7, "Relationship Growth and Maintenance."

Finally, it should be noted that although all the general theories of social interaction are often referred to collectively as social exchange theories, perhaps because their common denominator is that they all posit that social interaction involves an exchange of rewards and costs, only Homans explicitly uses the term "social exchange." The label glosses over differences between the theories, including the relational character of interdependence theory.

Summary

Despite the conceptual confusion that initially surrounded the term "relationship," most scholars now agree that the essence of a relationship lies in two persons' interaction. For two individuals to be in a relationship, three conditions must be met: (1) The two individuals must interact, each influencing the other's behavior; (2) each individual's interactions must be different from his or her interactions with other people; and (3) as a result of interaction, each individual must have formed a mental representation of the relationship, which then influences future interactions with the partner. In other words, two people are in a relationship with each other if they are interdependent—if the behaviors of one are influenced by the behaviors of the other.

Relationship researchers have developed at least two methods to reliably assess interdependence and thereby establish that two people are in a relationship: the social relations model technique and sequential analysis. Each of these requires an outsider's observation of interaction. In addition to observation by objective outside observers of the two individuals' interaction, interaction data are often obtained from two other sources: individuals' self-report and archives and other records that reflect interaction.

The principal aim of relationship science is to understand and predict the regularities that occur in the partners' interaction pattern. Those regularities are a product of three classes of causal conditions that affect the interaction patterns that develop: personal, relational, and environmental. At least four general theories of social interaction—social learning theory, social exchange theory, equity theory, and interdependence theory—have been developed to investigate the dynamics and outcomes of social interaction in general and within ongoing relationships in particular.

Chapter 5

Varieties of Relationship

INTRODUCTION

All science begins with observation and then proceeds to a description of what was observed. Description of a couple's pattern of interaction is not easy because relationships differ from one another along many dimensions. They differ in terms of the characteristics of the partners, the social norms and laws that govern behavior in the relationship, the activities in which the partners engage, and countless other details. Relationship partners themselves are sometimes puzzled about how best to describe their relationship to others—and to themselves. They wonder if their relationship is "healthy" or "dysfunctional," "superficial" or "close," "platonic" or "romantic," "significant" or "meaningless." The array of adjectives people commonly use to describe their relationships is vast. Choosing the right adjectives to accurately and succinctly describe a relationship is difficult not only because relationships differ from one another on so many dimensions but also because the meanings of many descriptors are unclear.

Relationship scholars have found certain descriptors especially useful in differentiating one relationship from another. Most of these descriptors refer to properties of the partners' interaction pattern. An exception to this rule is the descriptor "family." Family relationships take a variety of forms and are characterized by many different interaction patterns.

FAMILY RELATIONSHIPS

Of the many varieties of relationship, family relationships historically have captured the most attention and systematic study—and for good reason. This type of relationship has especially important consequences for the individual and for society. The concept of family is central to American life and values, just as it is in virtually all societies. American politicians express their concern about the well-being of the institution of the family with the frequency with which they praise apple pie and promise to protect the Social Security program. However, politicians often disagree on just what it is about the family that should be valued and preserved. They also disagree about what a family is (Figure 5.1).

FIGURE 5.1 Definitions of what groupings of people constitute a "family" have changed over time.

For the past several decades, sociological scholars of marriage and the family also have had trouble defining exactly what a family is. In 1979, for example, the problem of defining a family bedeviled the debate in a special issue of the *Journal of Marriage and the Family* on the question of whether the United States should have a national family policy (Nye & McDonald, 1979). A major obstacle to the development of a national policy to benefit the American family is that there now are many family types and none is dominant (Moroney, 1979). The question of what a family is continues to haunt scholars of marriage and the family (e.g., Gubrium & Holstein, 1990). Although the U.S. Bureau of the Census defines a family as a group of two or more persons related by blood, marriage, or adoption (see Ross, Mirowsky, & Goldsteen, 1990), this definition leaves out many groupings others would consider a family, such as people who have long lived together and are committed to continuing their relationship but are unrelated by blood or legal contract.

Lack of consensus about what social groupings constitute a family is not just a problem for relationship scholars. It is a problem for society, as illustrated by the number of court cases that now engage this issue. For example, the Supreme Court agreed to consider the case of *Troxel vs. Granville* and decide whether grandparents, other relatives, and certain nonrelatives should be able to gain court-ordered visitation rights with children despite the parents' objection (Greenhouse, 2000). Dozens of organizations filed opinions with the court, including one by the 30-million-member American Association of Retired

Persons, which noted that today grandparents are the functional parents of almost 1.5 million American children. Scholars, too, have weighed in on this complex issue, finding, for example, that children's closeness to their grandparents is associated with fewer adjustment problems for the child in many but not all family forms (Lussier, Deater-Deckard, Dunn, & Davies, 2002).

Changes in the American Family

Rapid changes in the shape of the family, society's nuclear unit, are, of course, responsible for the current confusion about what a family is. Societal concern about the health of the American family grew when divorce and serial marriage began to increase dramatically in the early 1960s and when many domestic problems in the United States began to be attributed to the "disintegration" of the traditional American family.

The Traditional Family

The word "family" often brings to mind the so-called traditional type of family epitomized in the 1950s and 1960s by the Nelsons (*The Adventures of Ozzie and Harriet*), the 1970s by the Cunninghams (*Happy Days*), and the 1980s by the Keatons (*Family Ties*)—a husband and father who is the breadwinner and works outside the home and a wife and mother who works inside the home caring for their biological children. This family form is rare today. Even apart from the question of who works outside or inside the home, and apart from the question of whether the children are his, hers, or theirs, the 2000 census revealed that fewer than one-fourth of American households were "married with children" ("Married-Couple Families," 2001). In the early 1970s, this figure was 46%, dropping to 36% in 1995 and then 26% in 1998 ("A Mere 26%," 1999). This trajectory far outstripped a 1997 Census Bureau prediction that the percentage of married-couple households would decrease to a figure as low as 30% only by 2010 ("Downsized Families," 1997).

Not only has the percentage of households of married couples with children decreased, but several features of those households have changed. The 2000 census revealed that among women age 40 to 44, 19% were childless in 1998 compared to 10% in 1976; both spouses were employed at least part time in 51% of the married couples with children compared to 33% in 1976. Moreover, the proportion of married couples who identify the wife rather than the husband as the householder tripled—from 7.4% in 1990 to 22.9% in 1998 ("Most Families," 2000). Consistent with an increase in wife householders, a 1999 survey by Yankelovich Partners found that 79% of the female respondents believed they had as much responsibility as men to support a family. In sum, there has been a significant decrease in the proportion of households composed of married couples, and within such households, there has been a decrease in those with children and an increase in those in which the wife and mother is employed outside the home. The traditional family form is hard to find today. Perhaps it always was.

The so-called traditional family may never have been the prevalent family form we assume. In *The Way We Never Were: American Families and the Nostalgia Trap*, sociologist Stephanie Coontz (1992) argues that many of our beliefs about the family are myths. For example, it is popularly believed that pregnancy out of wedlock is a modern phenomenon, a consequence of the breakdown of the family. However, Coontz found that one-third of the brides in rural New England during the 1780s and 1790s were pregnant despite the strong religious values held at that time and despite strictly enforced community rules that governed all aspects of family life. Moreover, although many think of marriages in the past as enduring, in colonial times the average marriage lasted only 12 years, mostly because life expectancies were short.

Marriage in colonial times was primarily an economic institution. Gadlin (1977) describes the colonial household as a business, a school, a vocational institute, a church, a house of correction, and a welfare institution. Because it played such an important role, the household fell under the authority of the community. Although domestic violence is often viewed as a relatively recent societal problem (and yet another symptom of the breakdown of the family and the weakening of "family values"), in colonial times there was an almost obsessive societal concern with curbing domestic violence:

> The writings of church leaders abound with proscriptions against physical and verbal abuse between husband and wife. The court records of colonial villages are replete with instances of complaints like the following, of which John Dunham was convicted in Plymouth, "abusive carriage toward his wife in continual tiranising over her, and in pticulare for his late and abusive and uncivill carryage in endeavoring to beate her in a deboist manner". . . or that of Joan Miller charged for "beating and reviling her husband, and egging her children to healp her, bidding them knock him in the head, and wishing his victuals might coak him." (Gadlin, 1977, p. 37)

Increase in Divorce

Perhaps the most dramatic change in the institution of marriage has been the increase in divorce. Since colonial times, in fact, the divorce rate in the United States has increased 700 percent. The proportion of all marriages in a given year that eventually end in divorce has increased at an accelerated rate since the 1850s (Cherlin, 1992). From 1876 to 1915 alone, divorce increased 15-fold, giving the United States the world's highest divorce rate at that time (Simon & Cannon, 2001). From the early 1960s to the early 1980s, the U.S. divorce rate increased dramatically and continuously, dropping slightly in the late 1980s and early 1990s but remaining among the highest rates ever recorded (see Brody, Neubaum, & Forehand, 1988; Coontz, 1997). Projections that the percentage of recent marriages will end in divorce or permanent separation range from 44% to as high as 64% (e.g., Castro-Martin & Bumpass, 1989). About half of all divorces occur by the seventh year of marriage (Cherlin, 1992).

Despite little better than chance odds of success in one of life's most consequential enterprises, many single men and women express a desire to marry (Frazier, Arikian, Benson, Losoff, & Maurer, 1996) and 9 out of every 10 people are estimated to marry at least once (Tucker &

Mitchell-Kernan, 1995). Moreover, those who fail in marriage seldom give up. Two-thirds of divorced women and three-fourths of divorced men eventually remarry; the rate of divorce for remarriages is higher than for first marriages for the first several years but then becomes similar to first marriages (Clarke & Wilson, 1994; Cherlin, 1992; Kirn, 2000). African Americans, however, are less likely to marry or to remarry following divorce than other groups (Bennett, Bloom, & Craig, 1989; Strube & Davis, 1998) even though interracial unions have increased in recent years (Schwartz & Rutter, 1998). The imbalanced male-to-female sex ratio within the African-American subpopulation may be at least partially responsible (e.g., Dickson, 1993; Secord, 1983).

The prevalence of remarriage is reflected in the fact that in the late 1980s, half of all marriages involved at least one previously married partner (Bumpass, Sweet, & Castro-Martin, 1990). **Serial marriage**, defined as a remarriage pattern in which the individual has experienced at least three marriages, has emerged as a new family form (Brody et al., 1988).

Increase in Singlehood and Delay of Marriage

Although people highly value marriage, they may not value it quite as highly as they did in the past. International surveys indicate that marriage rates have declined around the world (Lester, 1996). The United States, in particular, has experienced a sharp decrease (e.g., see Witwer, 1993). According to 1998 census data, only 5% of U.S. adult women and men over age 75 had never been married, but given that fewer people are marrying, the Census Bureau has doubled its estimate (to 10%) of people who will never marry in their lifetime. Indeed, the 2000 census found that in the past decade the number of people currently living alone increased 21% ("Married-Couple," 2001).

People are waiting longer to marry. The median age at first marriage has steadily risen, with more men and women delaying marriage until their mid- to late twenties ("Americans Marrying Later," 2000; Witwer, 1993). The median age at first marriage for men rose from 22.6 in 1955 to 23.2 in

1970 and then to 26.8 in March 2000. The increase was even greater for women: The median age at first marriage rose from 20.2 in 1955 to 20.8 in 1970 to 25.1 in 2000. In 2000, 73% of women age 20 to 24 had never married, an increase of 36% from 1970; 84% of men in the same age group had never married, an increase of 55% since 1970. Men and women in the United States now have the highest mean age at marriage in this century, and the proportion of adults who are married at a given time continues to decline, as we have noted (Witwer, 1993). These changes are unlikely to reverse. A nationwide poll of teenagers conducted by the *New York Times* and *CBS News* ("More Boys," 1994) found that the girls surveyed were more likely than the boys to say they could have a happy life even if they did not marry and that they would consider becoming a single parent; moreover, 86% of the girls said they expected to be employed after marriage but only 58% of the boys said they expected their wives to be.

Increase in Cohabitation

In 2003, the North Dakota Senate voted to retain an 1890 law that makes it a crime for unmarried couples to live together "openly and notoriously" as if they were married; the impotence of the law against the ever-increasing prevalence of this social living arrangement is reflected in recent census data showing that this sparsely populated state alone has more than 11,000 unmarried couples living together ("Cohabitation Remains Illegal," 2003). The popularity of this living arrangement in the United States also is documented in the 2000 census data showing that since 1990, the number of cohabiting couples soared 71%, a 3% increase over the decade, and represented 5% of all households ("Medianwise," 2001). Although cohabitation has increased dramatically in this country, the percentage is still small as contrasted to Sweden, where cohabitors represent 30% of households (Tolson, 2000). Today, over 50% of newlyweds in the United States have lived together before marrying, compared to about 10% in 1965. In the 1970s, two-thirds of cohabiting couples married within three years, but now only about half marry, and

one-fourth of the women say they don't expect to ever marry their partners (Smock, 2000). Cohabitation, of course, is the only alternative for same-sex couples who reside in U.S. states and in other countries that do not permit same-sex marriage (Halvorsen, 1998), although many say they would marry if possible (Lever, 1994, 1995).

Heterosexual cohabitors report more egalitarian attitudes toward division of household labor (Clarkberg, Stolzenberg, & Waite, 1995), a less sex-stereotyped division of chores (Cunningham & Antill, 1994), and a more equitable allocation of time spent on household tasks (Shelton & John, 1993) than do married couples who did not cohabit (although cohabiting women continue to spend more time on housework than their mates; South & Spitze, 1994). Homosexual cohabitors exhibit the same pattern. Both gay and lesbian cohabitors divide tasks more equitably than do married couples (Kurdek, 1993a; see Peplau & Spalding, 2000).

Heterosexual couples who cohabit have higher rates of marital separation and divorce (estimates range from 50% to 100% higher) than do those who do not cohabit (e.g., Bennett, Blanc, & Bloom, 1988; DeMaris & Rao, 1992). Although some have interpreted the higher rate of divorce among cohabitors as indicating that cohabitation itself is detrimental to marital satisfaction and stability, that has not been established. The effect of prior cohabitation on marital stability has been difficult to determine for several reasons. Among them is the fact that people who cohabit have a higher risk of divorce even before cohabiting than do people who do not cohabit. For example, cohabitors are more likely than noncohabitors to have experienced parental divorce, to have been divorced themselves, to be less religious and more accepting of divorce, to consume more alcohol, to be younger and less educated, and to have lower income—all characteristics shown to increase divorce risk (Bennett et al., 1988; Bumpass & Sweet, 1989; Cohan & Kleinbaum, 2002; Teachman & Polonko, 1990). In addition, Cohan and Kleinbaum (2002), who examined marital communication in newlyweds who had or had not cohabited with each other or with others, found that cohabitors exhibited more negative and less positive problem-solving in interaction with their spouse; prior cohabitors also were found to be less effective in soliciting support from their spouse and in providing support. Thus, it has not been established that cohabitation itself is detrimental to marital stability. The kinds of people who cohabit carry a higher divorce risk whether or not they cohabit prior to marriage.

Another factor clouding determination of the effect of cohabitation on later marital stability has been the failure of many investigators to take into consideration the fact that newlyweds who cohabited have been living together longer than newlyweds who did not cohabit. Because relationship satisfaction tends to steadily decline from the point of marriage (e.g., Karney & Bradbury, 1995b), which is when cohabitation usually begins for couples who were not cohabiting before marriage, it is possible that cohabiting couples, who have lived together longer than married couples who did not cohabit, may be further along on the satisfaction-decline gradient. The evidence pertinent to this point is mixed. When Teachman and Polonko (1990) considered the length of time couples had been together (regardless of the couples' marital status), cohabitation prior to marriage was not associated with marital stability, nor were variables associated with cohabitation, such as lesser commitment to the relationship. DeMaris and Rao (1992), however, found that even after counting time spent in cohabitation as part of marital duration, cohabitation in the United States was associated with greater dissolution risk. It is possible that the experience of cohabitation changes people in ways that contribute to later marital instability. Axinn and Thornton (1992) found that as compared to their views before cohabitation, cohabitors later showed increased acceptance of divorce and decreased participation in religious activities. In sum, several factors may contribute to the observed association between prior cohabitation and divorce.

Worldwide Changes in Marriage

Changes in marital and family relationships are not confined to the United States. The divorce rate in China, for example, rose 70% from 1980 to 1985

(Gander & Lin, 1985). The percentage of all marriages ending in divorce in the United States (49%) is exceeded by the figures for Russia (65%), Sweden (64%), Finland (56%), and Britain (53%) (Kirn, 2000). Thus, the structure of family life is changing rapidly around the world—in rich and poor countries alike. An author of a report released by the Population Council in 1995 states, "The idea that the family is a stable and cohesive unit in which father serves as economic provider and mother serves as emotional caregiver is a myth" (Lewin, 1995). Among the Population Council's findings:

- Marriages are dissolving with increasing frequency around the world, whether because of abandonment, separation, divorce, or death of the spouse. Divorce rates doubled between 1970 and 1990 in many developed countries; in less developed countries, about 25% of first marriages end before the wife turns 50.
- Parents are facing increasing burdens as their children need to be supported through more years of education and their own parents are living into old age.
- Unwed motherhood is increasingly common in all countries, accounting for as many as one-third of all births in northern Europe.
- Children in single-parent households—typically with only the mother present—are more likely to be poor than children living with two parents, principally because of the lack of support from absent fathers.
- Even when the father is present, mothers are carrying increasing economic responsibility for the children.

The Changing Socioeconomic Status of Women

An important contributor to these national and international trends, many observers believe, is the changing economic status of women worldwide and associated changes in sex-based divisions of labor. The percentage of women in "prime working ages" (i.e., 25–54) in the paid U.S. labor force increased from 43% in 1960 to 50% in 1970 to over 75% in the mid-1990s (Cohen & Bianchi, 1999), and the number of dual earner couples more than doubled from 20% to 43% between 1950 and 1996 (Barnett & Gareis, 2000). The Population Council reports that women worldwide continue to work longer hours than men, both on the job and at home—about 20% longer in industrialized societies and 30% longer in less developed countries. A 1995 Harris poll conducted in the United States found that almost half of employed married women contribute half or more of their family's income (Ingrassia & Wingert, 1995).

Nevertheless, women in the United States still earn a fraction of the amount that men earn. In the mid-1960s, when women began to demand "equal pay for equal work," a woman was paid 69 cents for every dollar a man made. Syndicated columnist Molly Ivins (1999) wrote:

> After 30 years of struggle and hard work, we now make 74 cents for every dollar a man makes, according to the National Committee on Pay Equity. At the rate of 5 cents every 30 years, we can expect to achieve equal pay sometime in the 22nd century.

Two years later, women continued to earn only 74 cents on the male dollar ("Vital Statistics," 2001). There are many reasons for the sex differential in pay, discrimination being only one of them (e.g., Will, 1999). But the basic fact of men's and women's economic inequality, even in the United States, where the disparity is not as large as it is in many other countries, looms large in understanding the dynamics of heterosexual relationships. For example, many of the "sex" differences observed in relationships actually are power differences based on unequal access to resources and would be observed in any relationship in which the partners' power is imbalanced.

Increase in Binuclear and Single-Parent Families

From the 1940s through the 1960s, about 70% of American children lived in a **nuclear family**, into which the child was born after his or her parents married and both biological parents were present. Since then there has been a steady decline in the two-parent family. In 1991, only about half of American children under age 18 lived in nuclear families ("Census Bureau Says," 1994). Thus, many children are now physically separated from one of their biological parents.

The array of social groupings that have come to represent American families include multigenerational homes in which the grandparents help raise the children and groupings of stepparents and half-siblings. This last configuration, most often composed of the remnants of previous nuclear families, is usually called a **binuclear family**, or sometimes a *reconstituted family, stepfamily*, or *blended family*. The diversity of names for this family form reflects its newness. According to 1991 census data, about 1 in 4 children were living in a binuclear family. These figures sum over large differences in race and ethnicity, however; whereas 56% of white children lived in a nuclear family, only 26% of African-American and 38% of Hispanic children did.

In addition to binuclear families, single-parent families also have increased greatly. The number of women raising children on their own surged in the United States between 1990 and 2000, increasing 25% over the decade ("Married-Couple," 2001). The number of single-father families increased 242% from 1973 to 1989 (Zaldivar, 1992) and went up another 62% during the 1990s ("Married-Couple," 2001; Simon & Cannon, 2001). Although most single-father families are headed by divorced men, the number of children living with never-married fathers also has increased. Families headed by never-married fathers, in fact, have shown the fastest growth of all family structures, although the total number of such families is still small. Despite the increase in single-father households, some investigators believe that demographic and social changes have resulted in fathers overall being less involved with children than perhaps at any time in the history of the United States (Amato & Booth, 1997). It is projected that over half of all children born in the 1990s will spend at least some of their formative years living in a single-parent family (Bianchi, 1995).

The origins of single parenthood also have changed. Whereas in the early 1900s most single-parent families resulted from the death of a spouse, in the 1950s and 1960s an increasing proportion of single-parent families were the result of parental divorce (Fine, 2000). Different origins of single parenthood may be associated with different consequences for the children involved.

Kiernan (1992) found few differences between adults who grew up in a first-marriage family and those whose parent died, but several differences between these children and children of single parents who had been divorced or who had never married; for example, the latter were more likely to cohabit before age 21 and to have a birth outside of marriage.

Effects of Changes on Children

Interest in identifying the effects of parental divorce on children increased over the past several decades (e.g., Wallerstein, 1991). Amato and Keith (1991) concluded from their meta-analysis of 92 studies conducted in the 1950s through the 1980s that children suffer a variety of negative short- and long-term effects of parental divorce. In contrast to children with continuously married parents, children with divorced parents score lower on measures of subjective well-being and have more psychological adjustment and behavior problems as well as lower self-esteem. Amato (2001) found little change in an update that included 67 studies published in the 1990s, except that the gap between children with divorced parents and those with married parents seemed to decrease during the 1980s and increase during the 1990s.

Amato and Booth (1997) reported a 15-year longitudinal study of the associations between parents' reports of family characteristics in 1980 and their offspring's reports of well-being in 1992–1995:

■ The proportion of families and children experiencing economic hardship has continued to rise, partly because of the rise in income inequality and also because of an increase in single-parent households. Financial stress is associated with long-term negative consequences for the children's socioeconomic achievement and later marital quality, although it is little associated with the degree of social integration and psychological well-being of offspring when they leave home and reach adulthood.

■ A general increase in parental education has had beneficial effects for children; young adult offspring of well-educated parents experience a higher level of general well-being than do those whose parents are poorly educated.

■ When parents have nontraditional gender relations—for example, the mother works and the father is highly involved in child care—their offspring experience few negative consequences and are more unconventional. For example, the children are more likely to cohabit as adults.

■ The long-term consequences of "interparental discord," whether or not the discord is followed by divorce, are pervasive and consistently detrimental for children. These consequences include (1) lower marital quality, (2) greater probability of dissolution of cohabiting and marital relationships, (3) lower social integration, (4) less education, and (5) poorer psychological well-being (e.g., lower self-esteem, less happiness, and lower life satisfaction). Because some data suggest that marital quality is declining in general (Glenn, 1991; Rogers & Amato, 1997), these results do not bode well for children.

■ In addition to marital conflict, parental divorce also has negative consequences for offspring, such as increased probability of divorce or lower socioeconomic attainment, although these effects were not found to be as pervasive as the effects of the parents' marital quality. The investigators conclude that poor parental marital quality lowers offspring well-being and parental divorce lowers it further.

Perhaps the most consequential finding of Amato and Booth's (1997) study is that some of the consequences of divorce depend on the *level* of marital conflict that precedes it. Parental divorce appears to benefit children in some ways when it removes them from a highly discordant parental household. However, these investigators estimate that less than one-third of parental divorces involve highly conflicted marriages. They comment:

> If divorce were limited only to high-conflict marriages, then divorce would generally be in children's best interest. But the fact that one-half of all

marriages today end in divorce suggests that this is not the case. Instead, with marital dissolution becoming increasingly socially acceptable, it is likely that people are leaving marriages at lower thresholds of unhappiness now than in the past. Unfortunately, these are the very divorces that are most likely to be stressful to children. Furthermore, if the threshold of marital unhappiness required to trigger a divorce continues to decline, then outcomes for children of divorced parents may become more problematic in the future. (p. 220)

In sum, the worst situations for a child ensue when parents in a high-conflict marriage do not divorce and when parents in a low-conflict marriage do divorce. Wallerstein, Lewis, and Blakeslee (2000), who reached a similar conclusion, also found that divorce produces adverse *sleeper effects*—effects that do not reveal themselves until years later, when the children reach adulthood and begin to form romantic relationships and marry. These investigators maintain that marriages of less than ideal quality do not necessarily produce unhappy children. "Good enough" marriages—those without high conflict, violence, and serious psychological disorder—will "do" for children.

The conclusions of these and other reports attracted a great deal of public attention and reaction—most of it negative. Many people would prefer to believe that when the marriage is an unhappy one, it is best to divorce "for the sake of the children." A poll taken in 2000 by Yankelovich Partners (see Kirn, 2000) found that 62% of their respondents *disagreed* with the statement that "for the children's sake, parents should stay together and not get a divorce, even if the marriage isn't working." It appears, however, that most divorces occur for the sake of the spouses and may not be in the best interests of the children.

"Family" Today

Changes in the shape of the nuclear social unit will continue to present problems to American society until consensus is reached about the appropriate answer to the question "What is a family?" That answer will affect most people's personal lives, as illustrated in the case of grandparents turning to the Supreme Court to help them maintain their relationships with their grandchildren, and it will affect everyone's financial well-being. The monetary implications of different definitions of the word "family" are illustrated in a 1995 case in which the Court again had to decide what a family was. A grandmother living in her Los Angeles home with her granddaughter and her two grandnieces had been receiving two separate welfare checks, one for the granddaughter and one for the two grandnieces (Epstein, 1995). The grandmother sued when the state of California reduced the two checks to one. The Supreme Court ultimately decided that states can cut their welfare payments by counting all youngsters living together as one "family," even if the children are not brothers and sisters. Thus, the Supreme Court's answer to the question "What is a family?" was "One household equals one family"—at least so far as welfare monies are concerned.

Most scholars now agree that the family is more a matter of social definition than it is a concrete institution (Surra, 1991). That social definition is in flux. A national telephone survey conducted by the Massachusetts Mutual Life Insurance Company ("Family Values," 1989) found, as usual, that when people were asked to list their close family members, it was clear that most (75%) now think of the family in emotional rather than legalistic terms. For example, 10% of those surveyed included their friends when listing close family members, and half of the respondents who had stepchildren did *not* consider them to be family members. Thus, many Americans no longer think of the family in structural terms, as a group of people related by blood, marriage, or adoption. Rather, as syndicated columnist Ellen Goodman (1993) writes, social consensus is growing that "people earn their family stripes through sweat equity, through caring, and taking care"; that is, a family is increasingly defined in emotional terms, as a group of people who love and care for each other.

Notions of what constitutes a family are still evolving. Respondents to a 1992 Roper survey were presented with a number of family constellations and asked whether they regarded each as a "family." Ninety-eight percent agreed that "a married couple living with their [own] children" was a family, even though only about 30% of U.S. families fit that definition at the time the survey was conducted. A married childless couple was regarded as a family by slightly fewer respondents (87%), and a divorced mother living with her children and a divorced father living with his children were regarded as a family by 84% and 80%, respectively. A never-married mother living with her children was regarded as a family by 81%, but only 73% were confident that a never-married father living with his children constituted a family. A man and woman who had lived together for a long time but who were not married were viewed as a family by 53% of the sample. Two lesbian women raising children were believed to be a family by 27%, and two gay men committed to each other and living together were regarded as a family by only 20% of the respondents. It is likely that the views expressed in the Roper survey have already changed and will change again as society's basic organizational unit itself continues to change.

One consequence of the change from a structural to a social definition of family is that it can no longer be assumed that the term "family" necessarily refers to blood **kin**, or genetic relatedness. Kinship traditionally long has been a central construct in many fields, such as anthropology, and it remains a central construct in evolutionary analyses of social phenomena (see Daly, Salmon, & Wilson, 1997). The increasing divergence between a family relationship and a kin relationship adds complexity to the study of these types of relationship.

CLOSE RELATIONSHIPS

A relationship descriptor of great interest to relationship scholars has been the adjective "close" because the relationship property of closeness is believed to be associated with many important interpersonal phenomena (e.g., Clark & Reis, 1988). Nevertheless, and like the construct of relationship itself, the construct of closeness remained conceptually vague for some time. Again, it was simply assumed that everyone understood what was meant by the term "close" relationship.

Even those who recognized that the construct needed explication often defined closeness with reference to other poorly defined constructs: "Such words as *love, trust, commitment, caring, stability, attachment, one-ness, meaningful,* and *significant*, along with a host of others flicker in and out of the numerous conceptions of what a 'close relationship' is" (Berscheid & Peplau, 1983/2002, p. 12).

The ambiguity surrounding conceptions of closeness was not immediately recognized as an obstacle to understanding relationships because a close relationship was identified by commonly accepted conventions whose underlying assumptions were rarely questioned. The most frequent assumption was that if the relationship was a family relationship, it also was a close relationship. The converse, that most people's close relationships were family relationships, also was assumed to be true. These assumptions began to be questioned in the late 1960s when it became increasingly difficult to identify a family relationship and when other kinds of relationships became many people's closest and most significant.

Conceptualizations of Closeness

When scholars lost confidence that the descriptors "family" and "close" were synonymous, they turned their attention to finding other means to identify a close relationship. This required that they first clarify the meaning of the descriptor "close."

Subjective Feelings of Closeness

To identify individuals' close relationships, many investigators ask people to simply name those others with whom they have a close relationship. The disadvantage of this approach is that the investigator does not know what criteria the respondent is using to classify a relationship as close or nonclose. Like the word "relationship" itself, the meaning of closeness varies across sex, age, and culture (Milardo, 1988). Not only are there systematic differences between groups of people, but there are idiosyncratic differences between individuals within these groups in the criteria used for regarding a relationship as close.

Nevertheless, self-reports are frequently used to identify an individual's close relationships. For example, Berscheid, Snyder, and Omoto (1989a, 1989b) constructed a Subjective Closeness Index (SCI) that asked respondents to indicate on a scale ranging from "extremely close" to "not close at all" their answers to two questions: "Relative to *all* your other relationships (both same- and opposite-sex), how would you characterize your relationship with this person?" and "Relative to what you know about other people's relationships, how would you characterize your relationship with this person?"

The most rigorously developed subjective closeness scale is Aron, Aron, and Smollan's (1992) Inclusion of Other in the Self Scale (IOS). The IOS is a single-item pictorial measure intended to measure people's subjective sense of personal interconnectedness with another person. The respondent is asked to choose from 7 pairs of two circles (labeled "self" and "other" and overlapping in varying degrees) the pair that best describes his or her relationship (Figure 5.2). The IOS is derived from a theoretical view of closeness as an overlapping of selves and a sense of "oneness" with the other. A feeling of unity is an element in many theoretical views of closeness, including Aron and Aron's (e.g., 1996) theory of love as an "expansion of self." Expansion of self theory posits that in a close relationship the individual thinks and acts as if some or all aspects of the partner are partly the individual's own; that is, the self is "expanded" by incorporating attributes of the other into the self-concept (see Aron, Aron, Tudor, & Nelson, 1991). The IOS is reliable and valid; for example, IOS scores were found to be significantly associated with romantic relationship stability over a 3-month period. The scale's pictorial nature may make it useful for children and also for adults not fluent in English.

Closeness and Positive Sentiment

Some people believe the positivity of their feelings for their partner is a good barometer of the closeness of their relationship. They would not describe their relationship with another as close if they did not like, love, or otherwise feel positive sentiment for their partner. An investigator who took this view would want to examine the partners' interaction record for instances in which the two individuals experienced a positive emotion or feeling as a result of the partner's behavior, as Wills, Weiss, and Patterson (1974) did by asking spouses to rate whether their partner's behavior was "pleasing" or "displeasing." Alternatively, the partners might simply be asked to report the frequency and intensity with which they experience positive and negative emotions such as joy and anger in the relationship.

Although all investigators of close relationships are interested in the affective properties of

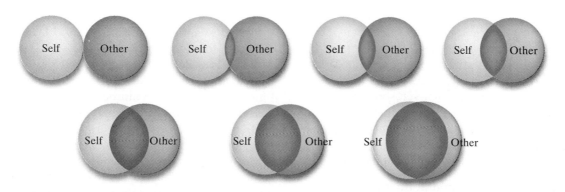

FIGURE 5.2 The Inclusion of Other in the Self Scale. *From Aron, Aron, & Smollan, "Inclusion of Other in the Self Scale and the structure of interpersonal closeness" (1992), Fig. 1, p. 597.*

the relationship, some have argued that using the partners' positivity of affect as a criterion of closeness is problematical because many close relationships ("close" using other criteria) are characterized not only by positive affect but also by intense experiences of negative affect (Berscheid, 1983/2002; Kelley et al., 1983/2002). Close relationships are the most frequent setting for the experience of strong emotion—negative as well as positive, as discussed further in Chapter 9, "Affective Processes." For example, Fitz and Gerstenzang (1978) found that the anger people experience in their daily lives is most often directed toward a blood relative or a romantic partner, including a spouse. Similarly, Attridge, Berscheid, and Sprecher (1998) found that one of the items on their Dependency Scale endorsed by romantic partners who loved each other but not by partners who only liked each other was "My partner has been the cause of my worst depressions." And, as discussed in Chapter 2, "Relationships and Health," intensely negative arguments and sometimes even physical violence occur in relationships between couples who say they love each other and whose relationships appear to be close. An affective criterion of closeness also excludes many long-term relationships in which the partners rarely experience *any* strong emotion and feeling, either positive or negative. These relationships, though seemingly emotionally dead, may be highly interdependent. The closeness of their relationship is often revealed when the partners are separated through death or other factors; the same partners who experienced little emotion when the relationship was alive may experience intense grief when it ends.

Most relationship scholars today agree that at any given time the emotional tenor of a close relationship may be positive, negative, or neutral. In their daily lives, however, some people use positive affective experience as their personal criterion of closeness and would not regard an affectively negative relationship as close even if both partners were interdependent.

Closeness and Behavioral Interdependence

Because the essence of a relationship lies in the partners' interaction pattern, and descriptors of a relationship ultimately must refer to that pattern, Kelley and colleagues (1983/2002) reason that closeness should be conceptualized as a property, or set of properties, of the partners' interaction pattern. These investigators maintain that a close relationship is one in which the partners exhibit *high* interdependence in their interaction pattern. Although relationship scholars differ as to which properties of the interaction pattern are the best indicants of interdependence, and thus which best differentiate a close relationship from those less close, most would require that an examination of the interaction pattern reveal four properties:

- First, the partners *frequently* influence each other's behavior—not just at the annual company picnic.
- Second, each partner influences many different kinds—a *diversity*—of the other partner's activities. For example, examination of the interaction pattern might reveal that the partners' influence on each other is limited to sexual activities; they do not influence the books the other reads, the movies the other watches, the other's political attitudes, the neighborhood the other lives in, and so forth. Such a relationship may be more accurately described as a sexual relationship than as a close one.
- Third, the partners' influence on each other is *strong*. Strength of influence is often indicated by the speed with which the partners respond to each other's behavior. For example, if the individual complains that the television is too loud and the partner immediately turns down the volume, the individual could be said to have strong influence on the partner. A long *latency of response*—15 minutes later, after the football game ends, the partner turns down the volume—suggests the individual has less influence on the partner. Strength of influence also is sometimes indicated by high *amplitude of response*. For example, if the individual's statement that the television is too loud results in the partner turning down the volume an infinitesimal amount, the individual's influence on the partner might be considered weaker than that

of an individual whose partner turns the television off. Additionally, strength of influence may be exhibited when *many behaviors over a long period of time* are influenced by a single act of the partner. And strength of influence is sometimes revealed by the fact that the individual is able to influence *important behaviors*; for example, cult leaders who persuade their followers to relinquish their possessions or to commit suicide are exhibiting very strong influence.

■ Finally, Kelley and colleagues maintain that in addition to frequency, diversity, and strength of influence, in order to be confident that the partners are highly interdependent and thus that the relationship is a close one, these three properties should characterize the interaction pattern for a relatively long *time duration*. Thus, two persons assigned to the same tent at a two-week summer camp might temporarily satisfy the frequency, diversity, and strength criteria during those two weeks, but because they do not satisfy the duration criterion, some researchers would not be confident that the relationship is a close one. Some romantic relationships, too, seemingly satisfy the first three criteria very quickly, but again, many researchers would not be comfortable classifying such relationships as close until they meet the duration criterion.

In accord with the view of closeness as high behavioral interdependence, Berscheid, Snyder, and Omoto (1989a, 1989b) constructed the Relationship Closeness Inventory (RCI), composed of three self-report subscales equally weighted and summed to obtain a total closeness score. The Frequency subscale assesses the amount of time the partners spend together alone (without other people present). The researchers reasoned that the more time the partners spend together, the more opportunity they have to influence each other's activities; moreover, the more time the partners are together without other people present, the less likely each partner's influence is diluted by others' influence. The Diversity subscale of the RCI presents respondents with a list of activities intended to be exhaustive of the activities typically engaged in by persons in the population from which the sample is drawn. For example, an elderly population might include a "went to the doctor" item, whereas a teenage or young adult population might have an "engaged in an athletic activity" item. Respondents are asked to indicate those activities they and their partner did together alone the previous week. On the Strength subscale of the RCI, the respondent is asked to indicate the degree of influence the partner has on the respondent's activities, plans, and goals ("how I spend my free time," "my occupational plans"). Relationship duration is measured but not included in the RCI score.

Comparisons of Closeness Measures

Berscheid and her associates (1989b) asked college students to name the person with whom they currently had their "*closest*, deepest, most involved, and most intimate relationship" and also to indicate the type of relationship it was (for example, romantic, family, friend). Most respondents, men and women alike, named a romantic partner as the person with whom they had their closest relationship (see Figure 5.3). Respondents then completed the SCI to assess their feelings about the closeness of this relationship; an Emotional Tone Index to assess the frequency of different positive and negative emotions experienced in the relationship, allowing calculation of the emotional tenor of the relationship; and finally, the RCI measure of behavioral interdependence.

When the distributions of scores on the three measures were compared, Berscheid and her colleagues found that closeness as measured by the RCI—that is, behavioral interdependence—was not highly associated with closeness as measured by the SCI, the individual's subjective feeling of the closeness of his or her closest relationship; nor was it highly associated with the positivity of the relationship's emotional tone (see Figure 5.4).

Given the popular belief that a close relationship is characterized by positive sentiment, the investigators predicted that an individual's subjective evaluation of the closeness of his or her closest relationship *would* be associated with the extent to which the individual experienced positive emotions and feelings in interaction with the partner.

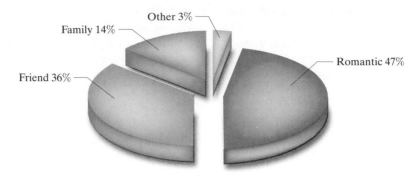

Other 3%

Family 14%

Friend 36%

Romantic 47%

FIGURE 5.3 Berscheid and her colleagues (1989b) asked college students to indicate the person with whom they had their closest relationship and what type of relationship it was. There was no difference between men and women in the type of relationship nominated as the closest. Most respondents named a romantic partner as the person with whom they had their closest relationship. *From Berscheid, Snyder, & Omoto, "Issues in Studying Relationships: Conceptualizing and Measuring Closeness" (1989), Fig. 3.1, p. 74.*

Indeed, scores on the SCI were positively correlated with scores on the Emotional Tone Index. Thus, liking of the partner is likely to affect an individual's feelings of closeness. As predicted, SCI scores were *not* correlated with RCI scores. However, comparison of the SCI and RCI closeness measures revealed a systematic sex bias. Scores on the SCI indicated that women believed their closest relationship was closer than men believed their closest relationship was, but as measured by the RCI, women's closest relationships were no closer than men's in their degree of interdependence.

All three indices of closeness—the partners' subjective feelings of closeness, the relationship's emotional tone, the partners' degree of behavioral interdependence—reflect equally "correct" definitions of closeness in the sense that what is meant by the word "close" is clearly delineated by each scale. A more important question concerns the usefulness of each scale in enhancing an understanding of relationships. One means of evaluating the usefulness of any instrument is to examine its **predictive validity**—whether it reliably predicts important behaviors that a closeness scale ought to be able to predict.

Because so many respondents in this study named a romantic relationship as their closest, and because this type of relationship not only tends to be unstable but also has a clear dissolution point, the investigators could track their

respondents' romantic relationships (which were also the respondents' closest relationships) at 3 months and again at 9 months to see which closeness measure best forecast later breakup. Only closeness as assessed by the RCI—behavioral interdependence—reliably predicted relationship stability. The closer the relationship was at Time 1 as measured by the RCI, the more likely it was to remain intact over 9 months. Moreover, among those relationships that eventually dissolved, those with lower RCI scores at Time 1 dissolved sooner (terminated by 3 months) than those with higher RCI scores (terminated by 9 months). An individual's score on the SCI—his or her feeling of the closeness of the relationship—did not predict its later stability, nor did the positivity of the relationship's emotional tone forecast later breakup. In addition, the individual's own forecast of the likelihood that the relationship would last did not predict its stability. The RCI has been translated into Japanese and German and has proved to be reliable and valid in these populations (see Berscheid, Snyder, & Omoto, 2004).

Aron and colleagues (1992) compared their IOS scale with the RCI and the SCI. Again, an individual's RCI score was not significantly correlated with his or her subjective feelings of the relationship's closeness, but SCI scores were positively correlated with IOS scores. Factor analyses of responses on all three scales yielded two factors

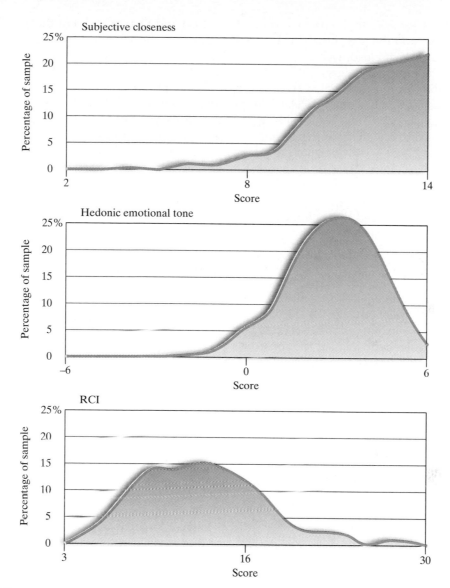

FIGURE 5.4 Distribution of three putative indices of closeness. *From Berscheid, Snyder, & Omoto, "Issues in Studying Relationships: Conceptualizing and Measuring Closeness" (1989), Fig. 3.2, p. 77.*

or underlying dimensions, which Aron and associates labeled "feeling close" and "behaving close." The SCI appears to measure the "feeling close" factor, the RCI primarily measures the "behaving close" factor, and the IOS seems to measure both but mostly the "feeling close" factor.

Closeness scales allow researchers to measure this important dimension of naturalistically formed relationships. Experimental manipulation of the closeness of an individual's ongoing relationship with another is not possible—ethically or practically. However, Aron, Melinat, Aron, Vallone, and Bator (1997) have developed a procedure that may at least temporarily manipulate feelings of closeness among strangers. Some participants were instructed to perform a series of self-disclosure and other "relationship-building" tasks, whereas others were instructed to simply engage in small talk for 45 minutes. Closeness to the partner as measured on the SCI and the IOS showed that those who engaged in self-disclosure *felt* closer to their partners than did those who engaged in small talk. Because self-disclosure is associated with liking another (as discussed in Chapter 7, "Relationship Growth and Maintenance") and because liking another is also associated with subjective feelings of closeness to another, it is possible that other factors known to be determinants of attraction to strangers also may be effective in increasing subjective feelings of closeness.

It should be emphasized that anyone can define a "close" relationship in any manner he or she desires. Indeed, people approach the assessment of closeness in different ways (see Mashek & Aron, 2004). Only two rules govern the conceptualization of psychological constructs: (1) The conceptualization must be clear. (2) The conceptualization must be grounded in observable behavior. If these rules are violated, the construct cannot further an understanding of behavior—in this case, relationship behavior.

INTIMATE RELATIONSHIPS

The descriptor "intimate," as used to describe a relationship, has rivaled the adjective "close" in its variety of meanings and confusing usage, and in fact the two terms are often used as synonyms. Intimacy not only has been used interchangeably with closeness, but it has also been used to refer to positive feelings such as affection between relationship partners, to their mutual disclosure of innermost thoughts and feelings, and to engagement in relatively intense forms of nonverbal interaction such as touch, eye contact, physical proximity, and sexual activity (see Berscheid & Reis, 1998). In addition, the phrase "intimate relationship" has been used to refer to a particular relationship form, such as marriage, or to a specific stage of relationship development. The many uses of the term "intimacy" led Acitelli and Duck (1987) to liken relationship scholars studying intimacy to the blind men probing different parts of an elephant and subsequently developing entirely different views of the nature of elephants.

Reis and Shaver's (1988) theory of intimacy (subsequently elaborated by Reis & Patrick, 1997) has clarified the construct of intimacy. They propose that intimacy be viewed as a special case of closeness; that is, they maintain that not all close relationships are intimate, but all intimate relationships are close relationships. In Reis and Shaver's theory, **intimacy** refers to an interactive process in which the individual, as a result of the partner's response to the individual's behavior, comes to feel understood, validated in terms of personal worth, and cared for by the partner. The transactive process they sketch involves a number of steps people typically take on their way to intimacy (Figure 5.5):

■ The process begins with the individual's *self-disclosure of self-relevant material*—perhaps a thought or a feeling ("I was just fired from my job for showing up late to work").

■ *The partner's response might be supportive and encouraging* ("Someone as talented as you will quickly find another job"). Or the partner might be unresponsive to the disclosure and may change the subject or make another type of distancing response ("What did you think of the concert last night?").

■ If the partner's response increases the individual's feelings that the partner *understands* him or her and believes the individual is a *worthy and valuable* person, and that the partner is *caring*, then intimacy is increased. If, however, the individual believes that the partner's response was unresponsive, disinterested, or otherwise inappropriate, then the relationship is unlikely to develop into an intimate one.

■ The individual's subsequent response will be influenced by the partner's reaction to the individual's previous revelation of self-relevant material. If intimacy has increased, the individual may discuss his or her thoughts and feelings further; if intimacy has not increased, however, the individual may simply terminate the interaction and, sometimes, the relationship.

Reis and Shaver emphasize that the process of intimacy is recursive—the partners' thoughts, feelings, and behaviors are continually modified

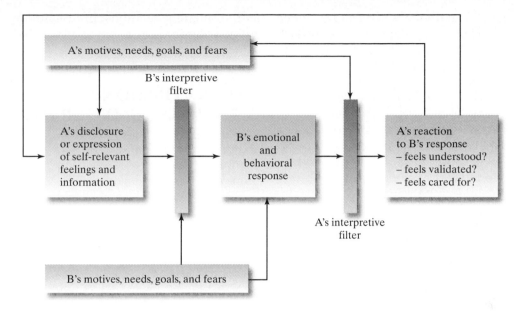

FIGURE 5.5 According to Reis and Shaver (1988), intimacy is an interactive process that typically involves a number of steps. *From Reis & Shaver, "Intimacy as an Interpersonal Process" (1988), Fig. 1, p. 375.*

and revised over time depending on the nature of the events that previously occurred in the interaction. As discussed in Chapter 1, "First Relationships," most partners decode each other's feedback rapidly, effortlessly, and often unconsciously, and thus they cycle and recycle through the stages of the intimacy process quickly.

Prager's (1995) view of intimacy, similar to Reis and Shaver's, identifies self-disclosure, attentive listening and understanding, and positive affect as essential ingredients in fostering the partners' feelings of intimacy in their interactions. Lippert and Prager (2001) asked cohabiting couples to keep diaries of their interactions for one week and to rate those interactions on a number of dimensions. Interaction pleasantness, disclosure of private information, expression of positive feelings, the perception of being understood, and disclosure of emotions were associated with the partners' feelings of intimacy.

Rather than viewing intimacy as a property of a relationship, and examining the process by which some relationships become intimate whereas others do not, some relationship theorists have viewed intimacy as a property of the person and have addressed individual differences in people's dispositions to prefer (or to avoid) intimate relationships (e.g., McAdams, 1989), as discussed in Chapter 10, "Dispositional Influences."

Responsivity

Reis and Shaver's (1988) intimacy model underscores that an intimate relationship—or any kind of relationship at all, for that matter—is not likely to develop with an unresponsive partner. Interdependence is displayed in the partners' mutual responsivity, and thus responsivity is at the heart of what is meant by the term "relationship."

It seems likely that all creatures prefer responsive partners—even rats, who are generally regarded as unsociable. Latané and Glass (1968) placed rats in an open field, either with (1) an anesthetized and therefore unresponsive rat, (2) a stationary toy car (also unresponsive to the rat's behavior), (3) a moving toy car that was preprogrammed (and thus, though active, unresponsive to the rat's behavior), or (4) a normal rat. As measured by approach and distance-maintaining behavior, the rats overwhelming preferred to interact with the normal rat. Subsequent studies revealed that rats placed together in a large enclosure spent 50% to 70% of their time chasing, sniffing, and climbing over each other. Werner and Latané (1974) suspected that what accounted for the interaction preference was each rat's responsiveness to the other's behavior, and they hypothesized that even a human hand projecting into the open field would be attractive to the rats. It was— but only when the hand was active and responsive to the rat.

Human children, too, prefer responsive interactions. For example, Dunham, Dunham, Tran, and Akhtar (1991) found that when 2-year-olds interacted with robots, they were more likely to engage in a verbal dialogue with a responsive robot than a nonresponsive one. The role of the caregiver's responsivity to the child in attachment processes, and Tronick's studies of mothers who were impassive in interaction with their infants (both discussed in Chapter 1 "First Relationships"), also illustrate this interaction principle.

Davis (1982) theorizes that interpersonal responsiveness is a function of three sequential response contingencies: (1) the probability with which each partner responds to the communicative behaviors of the other, (2) the proportion of responses that are related in content to the preceding behaviors of the other (an "I'm hungry" response to the individual's expression of sadness probably would be unrelated), and (3) the proportion of responses of the appropriate degree of elaboration, such as a monosyllabic response versus an extended one.

People prefer responsive partners for many reasons, but one of the most important of these is that the partner's responsiveness in interaction increases the predictability of his or her behavior. Predictability of the partner's behavior is, in turn, necessary for the individual's control of the interaction and the achievement of the individual's interaction goals. Moreover, unresponsive partners communicate to the individual that they value neither the individual nor the relationship (Davis & Perkowitz, 1979). A partner's repeated failure to respond appropriately and in timely fashion is likely to result in frustration

and, ultimately, relationship dissolution. Empathic accuracy is essential to responsive interaction, as discussed in Chapter 1.

OTHER COMMON RELATIONSHIP DESCRIPTORS

Along with "close" and "intimate," people often use three other sets of relationship descriptors: "compatible versus incompatible," "functional versus dysfunctional," and "healthy versus unhealthy." All three refer to many of the same elements of the relationship's interaction pattern. They also are sometimes used synonymously. It is frequently assumed that compatible relationships are functional and healthy relationships, whereas incompatible relationships are dysfunctional and unhealthy relationships.

Compatible Relationships

Ickes (1985) illustrates the distinction between relationship compatibility and incompatibility:

> Consider the relationships within two sets of gears: In the first set, the two gears are precisely matched to each other; in the second set, the two gears are badly mismated. When the two gears are compatible (i.e., precisely matched), their relationship "works," and they operate together in a smooth, synchronized manner. On the other hand, when the two gears are incompatible (i.e., badly mismated), their relationship does not "work," and instead of meshing together and integrating their respective movements without unnecessary friction, they grind and grate against each other, producing heat, discordant noise, mutual wear and tear, and—in some cases—complete mutual inhibition of movement. (p. 3)

Ickes's analogy highlights the two elements most people associate with incompatible relationships: (1) The partners *interfere* with each other as each performs his or her daily activities and attempts to satisfy needs and achieve personal goals, and (2) the partner's interference not only sometimes results in blocking achievement of the individual's aims and objectives but also often results in negative emotion. As Ickes puts it, the relationship doesn't "work"—it is "dysfunctional." In compatible relationships, on the other hand, the partners *facilitate* the satisfaction of each other's needs and help them achieve each other's goals. In that sense, compatible relationships are functional relationships. Thus, **relationship compatibility** refers to the *ratio of facilitating to interfering and conflictful events* in the partners' interaction (Berscheid, 1985a; Levinger & Rands, 1985). Facilitation usually is associated with positive feelings and relationship satisfaction, whereas interference is associated with dissatisfaction and the experience of negative emotions and feelings (e.g., Berscheid, 1983/2002).

A compatible partner must possess both the *desire* and the *ability* to facilitate the individual's aims and activities. One without the other does not suffice. Some partners are like the pot and the kettle in Aesop's fable who wanted to be companions as they floated downstream but came to realize that the properties of the kettle, namely its hardness, could be injurious to the fragile pot if they became too close. Some partners, though they earnestly desire to travel together through life, possess attributes and properties that are injurious to the other person, or they lack the abilities and resources to facilitate the other's aims and activities and, thus, to enhance the other's well-being. In such cases, no amount of relationship counseling or relationship intervention is likely to transform the incompatible couple into a compatible one. Thus, incompatibility is not always a result of the individual being unmotivated to be facilitating; rather, the partner simply may not have the ability to do—or to be—what the individual wants. He may not have the intellect to play a decent game of chess, and she may not possess the hand-eye coordination to be an adequate tennis partner. Compatible partners, in contrast, are generally similar along many dimensions, including their values, goals, skills, and resources.

Most close relationships are compatible relationships because incompatibility and its usual accompaniment of negative emotion often cause the relationship to dissolve before closeness is achieved. However, not all compatible relationships are close relationships. One's relationship with one's bridge partner may be compatible, for example, but the relationship interaction is confined to the bridge table on Friday nights, and thus it is not a close relationship.

It is popularly believed that compatible relationships are *enduring* relationships. However, a relationship is likely to remain compatible and endure only if the individual's activities and goals do not change or if the partner is both able and willing to facilitate, or at least not interfere with, the individual's new activities and plans. People change over time. As old goals are achieved (often with the help of the partner), individuals develop new goals and interests that the partner may not share or may not have the desire or the resources to facilitate. They also acquire new skills and resources that make the partner's former facilitative activities no longer necessary or valued. Ironically, in many cases the individual has acquired independence from the relationship as a result of the relationship. Common examples are mentoring relationships and parent–child relationships. With respect to the latter, Berscheid (1985a) observes: "Parents who succeed in facilitating their children's mental and physical health, their education, skills, and resources—who succeed in developing an independent, self-sufficient human being—often find that their child has outgrown the relationship, a bittersweet outcome, at best, for some parents" (pp. 156–157).

Thus, people who are compatible at one point in time may not be compatible at another. When one person in the relationship is rapidly changing, for maturational reasons or because of outside influences such as schooling or the development of third-person relationships, and the other is not changing in concert, the chances of one or both partners "outgrowing" the original relationship—and becoming incompatible—are maximized. Long-distance relationships in which the partners are subject to very different external influences may be especially vulnerable to growing incompatibility.

Healthy Relationships

It also is popularly believed that compatible relationships are healthy relationships. In most cases, they probably are, if only because chronic negative emotion with its accompanying debilitating physiological effects is threatening to mental and physical health, as discussed in Chapter 2, "Relationships and Health." **Healthy relationships** have been defined as those which "maintain and/or promote both the individual's *immediate* survival and welfare and his or her *future* survival and welfare" (Berscheid, 1985a, p. 158). Given this definition of a healthy relationship, it is apparent that some compatible relationships are unhealthy. An example of a compatible but unhealthy relationship is that between two chemically dependent persons who support and enable each other's drug dependency. Such "days of wine and roses" relationships are destructive of the partners' immediate welfare and their future welfare and survival as well. Some compatible relationships are unhealthy not because they are currently destructive of the individual's welfare but because they threaten the individual's future survival and welfare. An example, which has become increasingly less common, is a traditional marriage in which the husband actively facilitates, through his economic and social support, virtually all of his wife's activities and goals and actively discourages the development of her own skills and resources through education, employment, or the creation of a personal social network. Such a relationship may be harmonious and happy, but because her life expectancy is significantly longer than his, the relationship places her future welfare in jeopardy.

Just as compatible relationships are often assumed to be healthy, incompatible relationships are believed to be unhealthy. However, incompatibility in a relationship isn't always destructive of the individual's welfare and in fact may enhance it. For example, considerations of the child's future welfare often induce parents to refuse to facilitate some of the child's aims and activities and to actively interfere with others, precipitating a great deal of negative emotion on the part of the child. Forcing the child to go to the dentist and to engage in other disliked but prospectively beneficial activities (or to refrain from engaging in desired but harmful activities) are frequent precipitators of turmoil and disruption in parent–child relationships. The often heard parental remark "You may hate me for this now, but you're going to thank me when you're older" reveals the survival-enhancing aim of the parent's behavior. Fortunately, some children *are* later grateful that they learned how to play the piano or were punished for not doing their homework. Nevertheless, at the time, the relationship between parent and child may have been stormy and "incompatible."

DIMENSIONS UNDERLYING RELATIONSHIPS

Descriptors of relationships are often viewed as discrete categories—an "intimate" relationship versus one that is "not intimate," for example—but like the descriptor "close," most are better viewed as anchoring continuous dimensions—for example, from "extremely close" to "superficial." Several relationship scholars have taken an empirical approach to identifying the dimensions that underlie relationships and thus are useful in differentiating one kind of relationship from another. One of the first studies to use factor analysis to identify the dimensions underlying the differentiations people make between one relationship and another was conducted by Wish, Deutsch, and Kaplan (1976). Four dimensions appeared to underlie their respondents' evaluations of relationships: (1) cooperative/friendly—competitive/hostile, (2) equal—unequal, (3) intense—superficial, and (4) socioemotional/informal—task-oriented/formal.

The socioemotional—task-oriented dimension appeared to incorporate two dimensions previously identified by Marwell and Hage (1970). The first of these, intimate—nonintimate, represents (1) relationship interactions characterized by many or few different activities, (2) interactions in many or few locations, and (3) the partners' degree of role overlap. (It will be noted that this usage of the term "intimate" is very different from Reis and Shaver's [e.g., 1988] usage, illustrating again the vast number of ways in which the term "intimate" has been used.) Marwell and Hage's second dimension, labeled "regulation," represents the extent to which the activities, times, and locations of the partners' interactions are at the discretion of the partners rather than dictated by outside forces such as an employer. Marwell and Hage's third dimension, "visibility," did not correspond to any of the dimensions identified by Wish and colleagues but seemed to refer to the extent to which the partners' interactions are private or public and thus vulnerable to intrusion by others.

Taking a theoretical rather than an empirical approach, sociologists Blumstein and Kollock (1988) theorize that five parameters define relationship space: (1) kin or nonkin, (2) sexual/ romantic—non-sexual/romantic, (3) cohabiting— noncohabiting, (4) hierarchical—egalitarian, and (5) cross-sex—same-sex. Of these, Scanzoni, Polonko, Teachman, and Thompson (1989), and many evolutionary psychologists, argue that the sexual/romantic versus non-sexual/romantic parameter is an especially useful classificatory construct.

Developmental psychologists Laursen and Bukowski (1997) offer a model of relationships based on structural dimensions that avoids constructs specific to a single type of relationship or developmental period. They argue that three global dimensions provide a "universal metric for comparing relationships that is independent of variation ascribed to setting or ontogeny" (p. 752): (1) *permanence*, which describes the degree to which the relationship is stable (e.g., obligatory relationships, such as those between kin, are viewed as closed-field relationships that are difficult to dissolve); (2) *power*, which may be hierarchical or egalitarian, vertical (e.g., parent–child) or horizontal (e.g., peer relationships; see Hartup & Laursen, 1999), or authoritative or mutual; and (3) *gender*, or the degree to which the organization of a relationship reflects sexual dimorphism and differences based on the partners' sex, gender roles, and sexual attraction. With respect to this last, many developmental psychologists believe that the sexual composition of a dyad sets the parameters of the relationship (e.g., Maccoby, 1990); men's relationships, for example, tend to be hierarchical and inclusive whereas women's relationships are often communal and exclusive. Each of these three dimensions, Laursen and Bukowski claim, applies to all relationships and is unique to none.

RELATIONSHIP TAXONOMIES

Many relationship taxonomies—classification schemes into which all varieties of relationship presumably can be fitted—also have played a role in scholars' efforts to describe relationships. For example, anthropologist A. P. Fiske (1992) argues that one of four basic relationship models directs an individual's behavior in all social interactions: (1) *communal sharing*, where both partners treat each other as equals and share a common identity; (2) *authority ranking*, where people attend to each other's status in a hierarchy; (3) *equality matching*, where the partners follow quid pro quo social exchange rules (i.e., attempt to reciprocate benefits); and (4) *market pricing*, where each partner rationally weighs the utility of his or her behavior in achieving desired outcomes in interaction with the other. Fiske, Haslam, and Fiske (1991) found support for this taxonomic scheme when they examined instances in which people confuse one person for another—for example, calling the other by the wrong name. They found that confusions are most likely to take place for partners who are *within* one of the four relationship types rather than across type. For example, a current lover is more likely to be called by a past lover's name (both are likely to represent a communal sharing relationship) than by an employer's name (an authority ranking relationship).

The communal sharing and equality matching distinctions were previously identified by Clark and Mills (1979, 1993, 2001; Mills & Clark, 1994), who proposed that whether the partners perceive their relationship to be a communal one or an exchange relationship makes an important and pervasive difference in the partners' behaviors. In a **communal relationship**, the norm that governs the giving and receipt of benefits in interaction is "each according to need"; thus, concern for the partner's happiness and welfare overrides considerations of deservingness. Marital relationships and parent–child relationships are usually communal relationships. As noted in Chapter 4, "The Concept of Relationship," partners in these types of relationships usually adopt communal rules of exchange. As opposed to communal relationships, **exchange relationships** are those in which benefits are given to the partner with the expectation of receiving in return a comparable benefit in the future or as a payment for a benefit previously received. Relationships between employers and employees are typically exchange relationships. Clark and her colleagues have found that whether people perceive their relationship to be a communal or an exchange relationship significantly influences their interaction behavior. For example, people in exchange relationships keep a close mental accounting of the benefits they give and receive, whereas people in communal relationships do not.

Bugental (2000) has taken a different approach to partitioning the relationship domain. She considers the basic problems people must solve within different social contexts and how children acquire the information they need to cope successfully with their social world. Unlike traditional socialization theorists, she argues that children do not learn one set of general rules of behavior that are then applied to all social situations. Rather, Bugental theorizes, children learn several sets of social rules. Each set is believed to be specific to one of five basic domains of social life, each of which is composed of a distinctive set of social situations that represent the kinds of reoccurring social problems humans encountered throughout their evolutionary history:

■ **Attachment.** The key problem to be solved within the attachment domain is the child's survival, as discussed in Chapter 1, "First Relationships." From the standpoint of the infant, attachment represents a safety maintenance system; from the standpoint of the parent, attachment involves an empathic protective or caregiving system that promotes the survival of the young and thus the reproductive success of the parent.

■ **Coalitional Group.** The problems to be solved within this domain involve the facili-

tation of mutual defense as well as the acquisition and protection of valuable resources through forming coalitions with others. In order to form coalitions, children need to be able to discriminate between groups of people, which means that they must be able to categorize others into groupings based on similarity and to learn and obey the rules of the groups to which they belong. As discussed in Chapter 1, human infants appear to be prepared to differentiate between individuals and between groups of others. Bugental theorizes that regulation of interaction within the group domain is organized around preference for similar others and hostility toward those outside the group.

■ **Hierarchical Power.** The hierarchical domain concerns the management of interests between individuals with unequal power and control over each other's outcomes. Bugental theorizes that interactions in this domain involve the provision of rewards and benefits, such as protection or resources, or limitation of punishments and costs, such as aggression, by the more powerful individual in return for the compliance or deference of the less powerful partner. Children appear to quickly learn how to strategically negotiate benefits and escape punishment from those in control of their resources and outcomes and also how to negotiate compliance from others when they themselves are in the more powerful position.

■ **Reciprocity.** Reciprocity is viewed as the provision of equivalent benefits over a period of time between functional equals. Reciprocal interactions require a long-term accounting of the relative costs and benefits that have been provided by both parties. It will be recalled from Chapter 1 that Cosmides and her associates (e.g., Cosmides & Tooby, 1992) found evidence that the human mind is adapted to keep track of the reciprocal provision of benefits within social interactions and to detect violations of social contracts. Many have noted that even very young children protest another's violation of a social contract, such as a failure to share toys or to help accomplish a task or goal. In short, rules in the reciprocity domain involve the management of costs and benefits between functional equals.

- ■ **Mating.** Bugental theorizes that the central problems to be solved within the mating domain are the optimal selection and retention of access to a sexual partner, as discussed in Chapter 12, "Mate Selection and Sex."

NEGLECTED TYPES OF CLOSE RELATIONSHIP

As previously discussed, most theory and research has been addressed to family relationships, particularly marital relationships, or to relationships that have the potential to end in marriage, often termed romantic, premarital, or courting relationships. Most people, however, establish and maintain nonfamily relationships that satisfy all closeness criteria and play an important role in their lives. In terms of theory and research, these types of relationship often have been slighted by relationship scholars.

Friend Relationships

Despite the importance of friendships to people's well-being, research on this type of relationship is fragmented and is not as rich in theory as that addressed to marital and other kinds of family relationships. The primary reason for the scarcity of theory directly addressed to friendship, as well as for many of the other difficulties friendship researchers encounter, concerns conceptual problems not unlike those that initially confronted researchers of close relationships.

People use the word "friend" in many ways (see Dickens & Perlman, 1981; Fehr, 1996). Some social commentators note that there has been "good friend" inflation in recent years, especially among politicians and celebrities who seem to count virtually everyone they know as a good friend, thereby "wrecking the meaning of the word friendship for the rest of us" (Hogan, 1994, p. 3E). In Western culture, there are no formal obligations or legal bases for friendship, and there also are few societal prescriptive norms for interaction within friendships. In contrast, some cultures take friendship seriously and prescribe certain rituals and behaviors for those who assume the role of friend (see Hays, 1988). Not only does the word "friend" lack cultural definition in Western society, but it also lacks structural definition: "An individual's friends are neither determined by blood ties, as relatives are, nor by residence, as neighbors are" (Adams, 1989, p. 19).

Although the development of a coherent body of knowledge about friendship has been hindered by the fact that people use the term "friend" loosely and idiosyncratically, Hays (1988) observes that the basis of friendship—interdependence—is no different from that of other relationships. However, the *nature* of the interdependence in friend relationships differs from that of many other types of relationship. First, friendships are almost always wholly voluntary. Second, the primary motivation for friendship interdependence usually is social-emotional (companionship, emotional support) rather than instrumental (the achievement of a specific goal not intrinsic to the interaction itself; see Wright, 1974). Hays concludes from his review of the friendship literature that when people are asked what the word "friend" means to them, the partners' enjoyment of each other's company consistently emerges as a central property of friendship. Argyle and Furnham (1982) compared the preferred activities of friends with those of kin and colleagues and found that friends' interactions were the least task-oriented and tended to revolve around leisure activities such as talking or eating. Similarly, a survey of adults conducted by Fischer (1982) found that sociability was the primary criterion for designating another as a friend. Children's friendships also primarily involve engagement in intense social activity (Newcomb & Bagwell, 1995).

Hays (1988) suggests that friendship be defined as "*voluntary interdependence between two persons over time, that is intended to facilitate social-emotional goals of the participants, and may involve varying types and degrees of companionship, intimacy, affection, and mutual assistance*" (p. 395, emphasis in original). This definition of friendship is as applicable to opposite-sex friends as it is to same-sex friends, but opposite-sex friends have been little studied. Like same-sex friends, cross-sex friends tend to be similar in age, education, and other characteristics. However, opposite-sex friendships appear to occur much less frequently than same-sex friendships. From early childhood (age 3), children are segregated by sex for recreational activities. Although social norms undoubtedly are partly responsible for the segregation, Maccoby (1990), who provides a developmental review of sex differences in relationships, cites evidence that children find same-sex play partners more compatible, and thus it is children themselves who are responsible for the segregation into groups within which distinctive sex-based interaction styles emerge. Children's preference for same- as opposed to opposite-sex partners is strong and is difficult to change until at least age 11. Maccoby also concludes that sex differences in children's behavior are minimal when the child is observed alone. Sex differences in behavior emerge in social situations, and the nature of these sex differences depends on the composition of the dyad or larger group. Research on childhood friendship has burgeoned as developmental psychologists have increasingly recognized the important role friendships play in a child's development (Berndt, 1999; Hartup, 1989; Newcomb, Bukowski, & Bagwell, 1999).

Cross-sex friendships also appear to be less stable than same-sex friendships. Again, social norms may play a role, but they also may be less stable because the partners' motivation for the two kinds of friendship is different. Bleske-Rechek and Buss (2001) found that, compared to women, men judge sexual attraction and a desire for sex as more important reasons for initiating an opposite-sex friendship and lack of sex as a more important reason for dissolving it; in contrast to men, women judge physical protection as a more important reason for initiating a cross-sex friendship and lack of protection as a more important reason for dissolving it.

Despite the paucity of theories directly addressed to friendship, the factors associated with the formation and development of friendships have been extensively studied empirically, particularly in terms of the factors that attract people to each other. Attraction and other factors associated with friendship formation and development are discussed in Chapter 6, "Birth of a Relationship," and Chapter 7, "Relationship Growth and Maintenance."

Relationships with Nonhumans

The conceptual definitions of the term "relationship" and many of its descriptors—including the descriptor "close"—do not preclude systematic study of the relationships many people have with infrahuman animals or with supernatural beings (e.g., God). Because such relationships are highly valued and play an important role in the lives of many people, they deserve much more study than they have yet received.

Relationships with Companion Animals

Americans own more than 500 million infrahuman pets, according to some estimates, and a nationally representative sample revealed that 58% of all U.S. households own one or more companion animals (Rowan, 1992). Many other countries show similar figures (Beck & Katcher, 1996). Americans spend more than $14 billion a year to feed and care for their animals, and they spend another $5 billion more for such accessories as leashes and collars, not to mention warm-up suits and galoshes (Beck & Katcher, 1996). The time and money and other resources many people devote to the maintenance of their relationships with companion animals reflect the importance these relationships assume in many people's lives, particularly in children's lives (Melson, 2001). Nevertheless, with the exception of researchers in the health sciences, who have begun to investigate the impact of human–animal companion relationships on physical and psychological well-being, this type of relationship has been neglected.

There is little question that many people believe their relationships with their animal companions are close (Figure 5.6). For example, *CNN Headline News* (August 21, 1999) presented the "factoid" that 83% of the pet owners surveyed said they would risk their life to save their pet. Stanley Coren (1998), a psychologist who has extensively studied people's relationships with their companion animals, relates the touching example of the poet Elizabeth Barrett Browning (author of "How do I love thee? Let me count the ways"), who was inordinately fond of her dog, Flush (pp. 12–13). When Flush was kidnapped by one of the several rings of dognappers operating in Victorian England and her father refused to pay yet another ransom (Flush had been kidnapped several times previously), Elizabeth refused to eat and couldn't sleep. Finally, she braved robbery and murder to search the rough neighborhoods of London for Flush. She found one of the thieves, a sympathetic woman, and Flush was returned to her.

Elizabeth's relationship with Flush met all criteria of closeness. It satisfied the criterion of strength of influence, for she was willing to endanger her own life to save her pet. It also met the criteria of frequency and diversity of influence, for the dog was her constant companion and participated in all her activities. For example, much of Elizabeth's time was devoted to educating

Flush because she was convinced that the spaniel's intelligence rivaled a human's. Her strenuous efforts to teach Flush to recognize letters of the alphabet did not go well, a failure which Elizabeth excused in her dog by concluding, "I am afraid that he has no very pronounced love for literature" (Coren, 1998, p. 14). Her subsequent efforts to teach Flush arithmetic also were futile, but again Elizabeth had an excuse: "His soul has the sensitivities of an artist, hence he finds the mechanics of arithmetic both tedious and inconvenient" (p. 14).

Another writer with a close relationship with his dog, Charley, was John Steinbeck, whose best-seller *Travels with Charley* could as well have been titled *Conversations with Charley*, as Coren notes. Steinbeck recounts a conversation with Charley as the latter was staring off in space:

"What's the matter Charley, aren't you well?"
His tail slowly waved his replies. "Oh, yes. Quite well, I guess."
"Why didn't you come when I whistled?"
"I didn't hear you whistle."
"What are you staring at?"
"I don't know. Nothing I guess."
"Well, don't you want your dinner?"
"I'm really not hungry, but I'll go through the motions." (pp. 99–100)

FIGURE 5.6 People value the relationships they develop with their animal companions. These relationships often meet all the criteria of closeness, and they have an important impact on people's physical and psychological well-being.

As these examples suggest, most of what is known about human–companion animal relationships comes from poets, novelists, and playwrights, many of whom have written about their close relationships with their pets. For example, when Eugene O'Neill's beloved dalmatian, Silverdeen Emblem O'Neill ("Blemie"), was aged and infirm, O'Neill (1940/1999) composed the dog's will, an eloquent document that rivals anything O'Neill ever wrote for the theater. In the will, Blemie expresses his affection for his master and mistress and his wish that they not grieve for him too long; he also bequeaths his overcoat, raincoat, collar, and leash—custom-tailored by Hermes of Paris—to his master's next companion:

> One last request I earnestly make. I have heard my Mistress say, "When Blemie dies we must never have another dog. I love him so much I could never love another one." Now I would ask her, for love of me, to have another. It would be a poor tribute to my memory never to have a dog again. . . .
>
> My successor can hardly be as well bred or as well mannered or as distinguished and handsome as I was in my prime. My Master and Mistress must not ask the impossible. But he will do his best, I am sure, and even his inevitable defects will help by comparison to keep my memory green. . . .
>
> One last work of farewell, dear Master and Mistress. Whenever you visit my grave, say to yourselves with regret but also with happiness in your hearts at the remembrance of my long, happy life with you: "Here lies one who loved us and whom we loved." No matter how deep my sleep, I shall hear you, and not all the power of death can keep my spirit from wagging a grateful tail. (pp. 23–24, 30, 36, 38, 42)

The grief felt upon the death of a companion animal is an example of disenfranchised grief, as discussed in Chapter 2, "Relationships and Health," but that situation may be changing. When another has caused the death of a companion animal, it has been usual for the courts to order compensation in the amount the pet initially cost its owner, but more and more pet owners are seeking redress for their emotional distress and for their loss of future com-

panionship. One who sued and won is former professional football player Stan Brock, whose two dogs were deliberately and cruelly killed by a man with a bow and arrow (Frank, 2000). The legal argument gaining attention and credence nationwide is that animal companions are not mere property—when the animal is harmed, the human who cares for the animal also is harmed.

Unfortunately, and like relationships between humans, human–animal relationships are not always happy. When poet Robert Browning married Elizabeth Barrett, he also married Flush. It was a miserable relationship, with Robert often complaining, according to Coren (1998), that "the dog was vociferous, arrogant, overbearing, and tyrannical with him. He also declared that Flush seemed to consider him 'to be created for the special purpose of doing him service'" (p. 14). Another unhappy human–animal relationship was between a wife of actor Rex Harrison and his aged basset hound Homer, whom the stage and screen star loved and spoiled shamefully. After the demise of the marriage, the wife recalled:

> Homer was ghastly. He hated women. He would stand in front of the door just as you were ready to go out and trip you up. . . . [Moreover, while we ate breakfast in bed] Homer would come right the way round and slobber all over my breakfast, leaving spittle all over it, and then he would wag his tail to Rex, who would pat him and say what a good dog he was. . . . Homer loathed me. (Coren, 1998, p. 9)

Harrison's former wife blamed Homer for the demise of her marriage. Her experience illustrates that just as spouses sometimes torment each other through their children, they also use their companion animals in this manner. (It seems doubtful that Harrison did not know that it infuriated his wife when he praised his dog for slobbering on her breakfast.) Her experience and that of Robert Browning also illustrate that no relationship exists in isolation from the partner's other relationships, including those with his or her companion animals.

Relationships with God

People have reported on their relationships with God at least since Moses was said to have come down the mountain carrying the tablets inscribed with the Ten Commandments (Figure 5.7). Random national surveys reveal that only a very small percentage (1% to 4%) of Americans do *not* believe in God (Weiss, 1988; "Divining the God Factor," 2000). Moreover, 83% of persons in the general population believe their relationship with God is a close one (Weiss, 1988). According to a 1997–1998 survey (Fetzer Institute, 1999), 61% say that they "desire to be closer to or in union with God," 57% "feel God's presence" most days or more frequently, 89% "believe in a God who watches over me," 51% engage in private prayer at least once a day (24% more than once), 64% "look to God for strength, support, and guidance," and 71% believe in an afterlife.

Although a majority of Americans believe they have a relationship with God and half communicate with God every day, religion has been neglected by psychologists ever since William James (1902/1999) wrote his classic *The Varieties of Religious Experience*. Baumeister (2002), in his attempt to account for the neglect, cites the fact that religiosity is negatively correlated with education; researchers are highly educated and tend not to be religious themselves, and, surrounded by other highly educated people, they may easily overlook the role that religion plays in most people's lives. Whatever the reason, people's relationships with God are rarely studied despite the fact that this relationship plays a central role in many people's lives; consumes much of their time, money, and other resources; and exerts a strong influence on many different aspects of human behavior (Hood, Spilka, Hunsberger, & Gorsuch, 1996; Schwartz & Huismans, 1995).

A formidable barrier to the study of relationships between humans and supernatural beings lies in the fact that the essence of a relationship is interaction; although the activities of the human partner in the relationship can be observed by outsiders, the response of the supernatural partner usually cannot. According to many religious writings, the response to human prayer occurs in many mediums and guises, including dreams and occurrences that have meaning to the human partner but little or none to outside observers. Nevertheless, a growing body of literature addresses the implications of this type of relationship for health outcomes. The evidence suggests that religiosity and spirituality are associated with better physical and mental health and longer life and that these effects are substantial in size (George, Ellison, & Larson, 2002). Religiosity/spirituality may affect health outcomes through several possible causal pathways: (1) It may protect against disease indirectly by association with healthy lifestyles. (2) It may provide social support through membership in

FIGURE 5.7 Many people have relationships with God, although the way they express their belief in this relationship varies.

religious communities. (3) Perceived support from God may have protective effects for the emotional and physical well-being of individuals in crisis. (4) It may elicit "relaxation responses" that oppose the physiological stress response syndrome (Fetzer Institute, 1999).

In addition to investigations of these possible causal routes whereby religiosity may promote health and longevity, "divine intervention" into an individual's health outcomes in response to intercessory prayer has been the subject of an increasing number of investigations. For example, of almost 400 patients admitted to a coronary care unit, Byrd (1988) randomly assigned approximately half to receive prayer from a Christian intercessory prayer group that met outside the hospital; the remaining half were not targets of prayer for their recovery. In this double-blind clinical trial, the investigator, the patients, and the health personnel involved were unaware of which patients had been assigned to the treatment (prayer) and control (no prayer) conditions. On admission to the hospital, all patients had been assessed on 26 health variables (patients in the treatment and control groups did not differ prior to the experimental treatment), and they were measured again on the same health variables on their release from the hospital. The two groups significantly differed in their health outcomes. Patients who were targets of prayer had fewer instances of congestive heart failure, cardiac arrest, and pneumonia, and fewer of them required medication and other aids at release. However, some observers have questioned whether the investigator and hospital personnel truly were "blind" to the participants' assignment to conditions. Most reviewers of studies of religion and health conclude that this literature is characterized by weak methodologies, with mixed and inconsistent findings, and that there is a great deal yet to be learned about how religion affects health (e.g., George et al., 2002; McCullough, 1995).

SUMMARY

Many varieties of relationship exist, each differing in the characteristics of the partners, the social norms that govern behavior in the relationship, the activities in which the partners engage, and so on. Of all the types and forms of relationship that occur, family relationships historically have received the most attention and systematic study. Much of the scholarly work on family relationships has focused on defining this type of relationship, an endeavor that remains difficult because of a plethora of changes (e.g., increases in divorce, cohabitation, and binuclear and single-parent households) that have occurred throughout the United States and other societies. Another type of relationship that has captured the interest of researchers is the close relationship. Like the term "family," the descriptor "close" has multiple meanings, ranging from subjective feelings of interconnectedness, to the experience of positive affect, to behavioral interdependence between the partners. Intimacy long has been considered a hallmark of close relationships; however, recent theoretical and empirical advancements now suggest that close relationships are not necessarily intimate ones and that the two constructs are not identical.

Other varieties of relationship that have begun to receive greater attention from relationship scholars include "compatible" and "healthy" relationships. The fragmented nature of much of the work on these and other types of relationship, coupled with the difficulty of adequately defining or conceptualizing terms like "close," "intimate," and "compatible," have led some researchers to attempt to identify the underlying dimensions that characterize relationships and that can be used to differentiate one type from another. Other scholars, recognizing that most people establish and maintain nonfamily relationships that satisfy all closeness criteria and that play an important role in their lives, have begun to examine previously neglected varieties of relationship, including friendship, human–companion animal relationships, and close relationships between humans and God. There is much still to be learned about these types of relationship.

PART 3
RELATIONSHIP INITIATION AND DEVELOPMENT

Chapter 6

Birth of a Relationship

INTRODUCTION

People often look at the relationships that other people form and wonder how or why the partners ever ended up together. Our curiosity is especially likely to be piqued when spouses seem to be badly mismatched—"odd fellows" whose pairing seems to defy the laws of nature and reason. "What can she possibly see in him?" we wonder. "What was he thinking? How did this relationship happen? It just doesn't make any sense." In such instances, we cannot imagine what the partners ever saw in each other that led them to form a relationship in the first place, never mind to institutionalize it with a marital contract.

To understand why others currently are in the relationships they are—and to understand why we ourselves developed the relationships we did—it is usually necessary to retrace the history of the relationship back to its very beginning and to identify the causal conditions that were in force at that time. It is especially important to identify the environmental conditions under which the relationship was established, because their influence is likely to be overlooked.

VOLUNTARY AND INVOLUNTARY INTERACTION: CLOSED VS. OPEN INTERACTION FIELDS

Each of us likes to think that our relationships are a matter of personal choice—that the causal conditions responsible for our initial interactions with another lie in ourselves and in the qualities of the other person. We like to believe that our own properties (P causal conditions)— our values, attitudes, personality, and preferences, for example—or the properties of other people (O causal conditions) that seemingly "attract" us are responsible for our being in the relationships we are. However, many of our initial interactions with others are *involuntary*; that is, certain features of our physical or social environment virtually compel us to interact with certain people because failure to interact with them will result in penalties of various kinds. For example, close physical proximity often combines with the social norms of courtesy most people internalize to require us to interact with the stranger a friend has brought to a study session; failure to interact is likely to alienate not only the stranger but our friend as well and, in addition, threaten our view of ourselves as polite persons. Similarly, assignment to the same project at work or school necessitates interaction with another; failure to interact may result in loss of a job or a failing grade. Most interactions can be placed on a **voluntariness of interaction** dimension that represents the extent to which two persons choose to interact because they believe the interaction itself will be intrinsically rewarding versus the extent to which they feel compelled to interact in order to avoid extrinsic penalties (those from external agents or circumstances).

The voluntariness-of-interaction dimension is often overlooked for at least two reasons: First, the causal conditions primarily responsible for involuntary interaction usually lie in the relationship's external environment, whose influence on relationships has been neglected by relationship scholars (Berscheid, 1999; Bradbury, Cohan, & Karney, 1998). Second, most people in Western culture believe that whether, and with whom, they initiate a relationship—especially a romantic relationship—is a matter of personal choice. As a consequence, the influence of environmental causal conditions on relationship initiation is often discounted and volitional personal factors, especially those associated with interpersonal attraction, are emphasized.

Some relationship theorists recognize that environmental forces often mandate that an individual initiate and maintain interaction with another for extrinsic reasons—that is, reasons apart from the positivity of sentiment felt for the other and apart from satisfaction with the quality of the interaction. For example, interdependence theory (e.g., Thibaut and Kelley, 1959) explicitly recognizes that some relationships are involuntary. Moreover, several of the theories interdependence theory has influenced assume, at least implicitly, that relationships may be initiated and maintained despite the personal prefer-

ences of the partners (e.g., Berscheid & Lopes, 1997; Johnson, 1991; Levinger, 1965).

Among the theorists who highlighted the importance of the voluntariness dimension was Murstein (1970), who distinguished between initial interactions that take place in **closed fields**, where individuals are virtually forced to interact, and those that take place in **open fields**, where people are free to interact or not without penalty (Figure 6.1). Murstein defined a closed interaction field as one

> in which both [persons] . . . are forced to interact by reason of the environmental setting in which they find themselves. Examples of such situations might be that of students in a small seminar in a college, members in a law firm, and workers in complementary professions such as doctor–nurse and "boss"–secretary. (p. 466)

An open interaction field, in contrast,

> refers to a situation in which the [persons] . . . do not as yet know each other. . . . Examples of such "open field" situations are "mixers," presence in a large school class at the beginning of a semester, and brief contacts in the office. The fact that the field is "open" indicates that either [individual] . . . is free to start the relationship or to abstain from initiating it, as they wish. (p. 466)

Identification of the causal conditions that generate the partners' first interaction, particularly those that determine whether the interaction takes place in an open or closed field, is important because the continuance and further development of the relationship depend on the nature of those initiating causal conditions. For example, if the first interaction is voluntary, continuance of the relationship depends on the partners' continued attraction to each other. If, however, the first interaction is involuntary—the environmental causal conditions in which the relationship is embedded are such that the partners feel compelled to interact—one can expect their interactions to continue only if (1) those environmental conditions do not change—for example, the partners continue to work in the same office or reside in the

FIGURE 6.1 People are virtually forced to interact in a closed interaction field (left). People are free to interact or not in an open interaction field (right).

same dorm room, or (2) those environmental conditions do change but the initial involuntary interactions produced sufficient attraction that the partners will want to maintain the relationship even in the absence of interaction-compelling conditions.

The distinction between involuntary and voluntary interactions is important for another reason: To the extent that the partners are consciously aware of the extrinsic forces compelling their interaction, certain psychological processes may be generated that will affect the relationship's quality and future. For example, Seligman, Fazio, and Zanna (1980) induced dating couples to adopt (1) an *intrinsic* cognitive set, in which they were encouraged to think about their enjoyment of each other as motivation to continue the relationship; (2) an *extrinsic* set, in which external reasons and pressures to continue the relationship were emphasized (e.g., the other provides a ride to work, continuing the relationship makes one's mother happy); or (3) no set, a *control* condition in which couples were not asked to think about their reasons for dating their partner. Seligman and colleagues found that individuals in the extrinsic condition, whose awareness of external pressures to continue the relationship had been heightened, subsequently viewed the probability of marrying their partners as significantly lower than did individuals in the

intrinsic or control conditions. Those in the extrinsic condition also reported less love for their partners. Other evidence, obtained from ongoing relationships, supports the association between people's perceptions that their motivation for continuing a relationship is intrinsic or extrinsic and such interpersonal outcomes as interaction quality (Fletcher, Fincham, Cramer, & Heron, 1987; also see Blais, Sabourin, Boucher, & Vallerand, 1990).

Why should thinking about extrinsic reasons for continuing a romantic relationship result in a diminution of love for the partner? Seligman and colleagues (1980) derived their hypothesis from Festinger's (1957) cognitive dissonance theory, but why should the cognition that one is receiving extrinsic benefits from a relationship be *dissonant* with loving or marrying the partner (and result in the dissonance reduction effects of a decrease in love for the partner and lowered probability of marriage)? The answer may lie in the popular belief that "true love" is not based on the external benefits another can provide but rather on the other's essential being. An anecdote told by Theodore Reik (1944/1972), a theorist of love, illustrates:

A man once asked his mistress whether she would love him if he were suddenly to become poor. "Of course," she answered. Then he asked whether she would love him if he became crippled by an accident. This question, too, was answered in the affirmative. But still the man was not satisfied. He tried again, asking whether her affection would be the same if, in addition to these handicaps, he were to become deaf, blind, and insane. The woman finally became impatient and said, "Why in the world should I love an impoverished, crippled, deaf and blind idiot?" (p. 156)

It is easy to sympathize with the man. Most of us wish to be loved unconditionally for the essence of ourselves and apart from those of our attributes that benefit our relationship partners. Few people wish to be loved for the resources they command, their appearance, their social status, their power, or their special skills. However, as Reik observes, the wish to be loved unconditionally by our relationship partners is both unreasonable and unrealizable. Similarly, our own aspirations to love another unconditionally—a kind of love Maslow (1954) called "B-love," or love for another's very being—are difficult to realize, as is testified to by the predictive success of the general theories of social interaction, all of which emphasize the rewards and costs people give and receive from each other in their interactions.

THE BEGINNING: ATTENTION TO ANOTHER PERSON

Several theorists identify the beginning of a relationship as the point at which one person pays attention to the other for the first time (see Chapter 4, "The Concept of Relationship"). For example, in their theory of relationship development, Levinger and Snoek (1972) state:

> The beginnings of a relationship appear when one person becomes aware of another. In defining this level, it is unimportant whether or not O in turn notices P. The only pertinent event is that P has information that forms a basis for his unilateral evaluation of O. (p. 6)

Thus, these theorists view the beginning of a relationship as the first time there is a causal linkage between the individual's behavior and another's behavior—another person has done something, perhaps walking into the individual's line of vision, that causes the individual to direct his or her attention to that other and away from where it was directed before. Redirection of attention to another is a necessary condition for beginning interaction, but it is not sufficient, of course, because interaction only rarely follows initial attention.

Selective Attention

Because paying attention to another for the first time is a necessary condition for interaction to proceed, Berscheid and Graziano (1979) argue that the question of who initiates a relationship with whom can be reframed as a question of social attention: "Who is likely to pay attention to whom?" Sometimes the answer to this question is simple: We pay attention to another *not* because he or she has "attracted" our attention but because a third party has instructed us to pay attention to that person. A friend says, "Look at that cute guy by the water fountain!" Or the researcher of social perception says, "Now I want you to become acquainted with the person seated on your left." Other times, we pay attention to others because the achievement of our personal aims and goals requires that we pay attention to them—as we buy our airline ticket or do our job at work. But what determines our attention to others in open-field situations? Who is likely to capture the attention of an individual standing at the threshold of a party surveying the guests, all of whom are strangers? The answer lies in the nature of the human's perceptual and cognitive faculties.

The evolutionary development of the human brain, most scholars agree, was directed toward *control of the environment* to protect and enhance the individual's welfare. In order to control our social environment, we must be able to *predict* other people's behavior—we cannot control events if we cannot predict their occurrence in advance. Unpredictability of the environment and its inevitable companion, lack of control, have been shown to be strongly associated with anxiety both in humans and in infrahuman animals (e.g., Lejuez, Zvolensky, Eifert, & Richards, 2000;

Thompson, 1981). Although we don't need to know everyone and everything, the more we know and the faster we know it, the better we can control our fate. As a consequence, the brain we humans have inherited appears to operate on the *principle of efficiency*—speed and economy. Selective attention is a manifestation of this principle.

Principles of Selective Attention

Attention is often identified with **consciousness**, our awareness of things and events. The human's conscious/attentional capacities are highly limited. We cannot pay attention to all of the information our five senses are receiving and passing on to the brain at any given moment. Were we to try, we would be overwhelmed. According to Berlyne (1960), "the human ear alone appears capable of receiving 10,000 or more bits per second while the eye, even with color differences disregarded, can receive over 4 million bits per second" (p. 14). To obtain those visual information "bits" (the smallest unit of information), roughly 10 million retinal measurements are sent to the brain each second, where they are processed by some billion cortical neurons (Barlow, 1981; Cherniak, 1990). Adding to these sums the information our other senses are receiving and sending on to the brain, the amount of sensory data potentially available to us at any given moment is staggering. Some scientists have estimated that our five senses are taking in over 11 million pieces of information every second. In contrast to the vast amount of information potentially available to us, it has been estimated that we are capable of consciously processing only about 40 bits of information a second, at best—more likely, only 1 to 16 bits (see Nørretranders, 1998, p. 127). This suggests that only about a millionth of what our senses are telling us about the world appears in consciousness. The remainder, received but not consciously perceived, also influences our behavior (see Wilson, 2002), as discussed in Chapter 8, "Cognitive Processes."

Because our conscious attention is a precious and limited resource, we must be selective in awarding it to people and events in our environment. The brain processes the information it receives from the senses and decides what bits are worthy of being passed on for our conscious attention. The criteria it appears to use—the two major principles of selective attention—have implications for understanding relationship dynamics, especially relationship initiation. The first principle is *novelty*: Unexpected events and unfamiliar people are likely to capture our attention in competition with more familiar stimuli. Returning to the individual standing at the threshold surveying the party guests, we can predict that the naked man wearing only a fig leaf and sunglasses will probably capture the individual's attention. We wouldn't necessarily predict that this stranger will be approached for interaction—attention is a necessary but not sufficient condition for the initiation of interaction—but we can confidently predict that the fig-leafed stranger will be noticed. It makes good evolutionary sense that a novel person should win the competition for our attention because unfamiliar people, events, and objects possess the potential to benefit us. They also have the potential to harm us. Or, they may be irrelevant to our welfare. To find out which of these alternatives is correct, we must allot them at least some of our valuable attention.

The second major principle of selective attention is *importance*. We almost instantly judge some persons, objects, and events to be more important than others. What is important to each of us is a *motivational* issue; it depends on our needs and goals at the moment. This is why the focus of our attention usually tells other people as much about us as it does about the person to whom we are paying attention. Given an array of people competing for our attention (and assuming they are equally novel), we are likely to award our attention to those persons whom we believe (1) possess the power to affect our welfare and (2) may be motivated to use that power for our good or ill. Such people are important. To protect our well-being, we must pay attention to them. In contrast, people who possess no power to affect our fortunes, or who do possess such power but are unlikely to use it (perhaps we are beneath their notice), seldom are the recipients of our limited attentional capacity for more than a few milliseconds. Indifference is our usual reaction to people who have no influence on our lives.

In accord with the theme of efficiency, the human mind in general, and attentional processes in particular, seem to operate on a "need to know" basis. The first question the mind seems to automatically and unconsciously ask of new and unfamiliar people and events is "What does this have to do with me?" If the answer is "Nothing," then our precious attention can be deployed elsewhere. If the answer is "He looks like a lecherous bore," that is all we need to know to take action—to avoid the buffet table where he is lurking. If the answer is "She looks like the answer to my prayers," then we can predict that not only will we continue to award the woman our attention but we probably have already stepped over the threshold of the party and are making our way across the room to initiate interaction with her.

Selective Attention in Open Interaction Fields

Social exchange theory (e.g., Homans, 1961, 1974) and interdependence theory (e.g., Thibaut & Kelley, 1959) have dominated the study of relationship initiation and development (Burgess & Huston, 1979). Both theories, it will be recalled, posit that people are sensitive to the goodness of outcomes they receive in interaction with another (see Chapter 4, "The Concept of Relationship"). The predictions these theories make about relationship initiation and maintenance are consistent with the principles of selective attention: Both theories predict that we are likely to pay attention to people on whom we are outcome-dependent—people who possess the power to benefit us or harm us.

The effect of outcome dependence on attentional processes was demonstrated by Berscheid, Graziano, Monson, and Dermer (1976), who recruited men and women college students to participate in a dating study that required them to sign a contract turning over their dating lives to the experimenters for a period of 5 weeks (agreeing to date whomever the experimenters designated, or no one, should they be randomly assigned to such a condition). Each participant

was initially asked to view a televised discussion said to be taking place down the hall among three other participants of the opposite sex. In actuality, the discussions had been videotaped in advance so that all men saw the same three women and all women saw the same three male discussants (strangers previously determined to be of equal dating desirability). The participants were told that because the experimenters had not been able to afford a wide-angle television lens, three cameras had been placed in the discussion room, each camera focused on one of the three discussants, and the discussion could be viewed by pressing one of the three buttons on the television monitor that would activate one of the three cameras. Participants were told that they were free to flick back and forth between cameras but that if no button were pressed, no audio or visual would be received. Each participant's viewing pattern of the three opposite-sex discussants over the 15-minute discussion period was recorded.

The results of Berscheid and her colleagues' study revealed that although the participants evenly distributed their attention among the three discussants for the first half of the discussion, at the midpoint—when the discussants introduced themselves to each other by name—viewing patterns began to diverge, and some participants began to focus on one of the discussants and neglect the other two. The principles of selective attention dictate that the discussant who was able to capture the participants' attention had to be either more novel or more important than the others. Because all of the discussants were strangers and thus equally novel, differential novelty could be eliminated as an explanation for differential attention to the discussants. Differential importance of the discussants to the participants had to be the explanation. It was.

All of the men and women who participated in the experiment had received the name of their partner ("Mary Smith" or "Joe Jones") and their first dating assignment just before they observed the discussion. Some had been informed they would be dating a different person each week over the 5-week period. When the discussants introduced themselves to each other, these participants (the *zero outcome dependence* condition) discovered that

Mary (or Joe), the person they were to date the first week, was *not* among the discussants they were viewing, and they continued to distribute their attention relatively equally among them. Men and women in the *low outcome dependence* condition also were told they would be dating a different person each week, but they discovered that their date for the first week (Mary or Joe) was one of the three discussants they were viewing. Although these participants were somewhat outcome-dependent on Mary (or Joe), their dependence was limited by the fact that they would date four other persons over the period. These participants paid somewhat more attention to Mary (or Joe) than they did to the other two discussants, but they did not exclusively attend to her (or him). In contrast, the men and women in the *high outcome dependence* condition riveted their attention on Mary (or Joe), whom, as they learned when the discussants introduced themselves to each other, they would be dating not only for the first week of the study but every week

thereafter. In sum, the amount of attention an individual paid to a discussant depended on the degree to which that individual was outcome-dependent on the discussant (Figure 6.2).

In addition to influencing attention, Berscheid and her colleagues found that men and women in the high outcome dependence condition, relative to the other conditions, tended to remember more about the person on whom they were dependent and to evaluate that person's attributes more confidently and with extreme trait ratings. Moreover, the more outcome-dependent the participant was on the other, the more attractive he or she thought the other was, as measured by the favorability of the traits attributed to the other and reports of liking for each of the three discussants. Thus, the greater the outcome dependence, the more attention paid to the other, the more confident people were that they knew what their prospective partner was like, and the more they liked him or her.

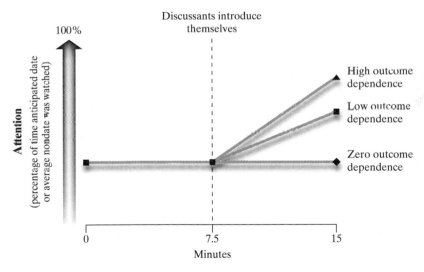

FIGURE 6.2 Outcome dependence and attentional patterns. People pay attention to those upon whom they are outcome-dependent. Participants in the Berscheid et al. (1976) experiment who discovered that their dating partner was not among the discussants (zero outcome dependence) distributed their viewing equally among the three individuals. Participants who discovered that their dating partner for the first week was among the discussants, but who knew that they would be dating different people for the remaining 4 weeks of the study (low outcome dependence) awarded somewhat more attention to that individual. Participants who discovered that their dating partner was present at the discussion and who expected to date only that individual for 5 weeks (high outcome dependence) allocated a great deal of their attention to that person. *Data are from Berscheid, Graziano, Monson, & Dermer (1976).*

Subsequent experiments replicated and extended these findings. For example, Erber and Fiske (1984) found that people who anticipate being outcome-dependent on another pay more attention to inconsistent information about the other and think more about that information than do those who are not outcome-dependent on that person. (Consistent information about the partner produced no attentional differences as a function of outcome dependence in this study.) These investigators conclude that people want to construct accurate impressions of those on whom their welfare depends and thus are sensitive to inconsistent information (which signals that an accurate impression is yet to be achieved), a conclusion supported by the results of other investigations (e.g., Darley, Fleming, Hilton, and Swann, 1988; Neuberg & Fiske, 1987; Stevens & Fiske, 2000, Experiment 1).

In asymmetrical power relationships, the more outcome-dependent partner is likely to engage in careful and effortful processing of information about the more powerful partner in order to construct an accurate impression, but the less outcome-dependent partner is not as likely to do so (Fiske, 1993). Powerful people do not need to form detailed and accurate impressions of their subordinate relationship partners in order to maximize their benefits and minimize their costs in interactions with the partner. A mouse interacting with an elephant must keep a careful eye on the elephant and predict the elephant's next moves to avoid getting crushed, accidentally or intentionally. Elephants, gorillas, and powerful people can sit anywhere they want.

In sum, if the first milliseconds of attention paid to another person reveal that the other is neither novel nor important, chances are no further attention will be awarded to that person unless social courtesy or other external environmental forces demand it—in other words, that is that, in terms of relationship development.

Attention and Attraction

Some scholars have drawn a connection between attention and attraction. Sociologist Erving Goffman (1963) observed that eye contact plays a spe-cial role in social interaction because it is a mutually understood signal that the communication channel between two people is open. Avoidance of eye contact is a signal that one doesn't wish to interact; for example, strangers in elevators and other confined spaces usually studiously avoid looking at the others sharing the space (Figure 6.3). Folk wisdom, too, often implies that attention and attraction are positively associated. It is popularly believed, for example, that couples who are in love spend a great deal of time simply looking at each other (Figure 6.4). That belief was examined by Rubin (1973) as part of his effort to document the validity of his Love Scale. He measured eye gaze and eye contact between dating partners who were seated across from each other at a table while waiting for an experiment to begin. Rubin found that "strong lovers" (those who had scored above the median on the Love Scale) did not differ from "weak lovers" (who had scored below the median) in the sheer amount of time they spent looking at their partners. They did significantly differ, however, in the amount of time they engaged in *mutual* eye contact; strong lovers were more likely to look at one another simultaneously than weak lovers.

The folk assumption that attention and attraction are associated implies that the *amount* of attention another person pays to us is a good indicant of the degree to which he or she is attracted to us. For example, people sometimes complain to their partner, "You no longer pay attention to me; I guess you don't love me anymore." That conclusion fails to consider that the importance of the other engages only one principle of selective attention and that novelty may override importance, resulting in the attentional neglect of people who are important to us. Novelty is the wild card that often renders attention a misleading index of attraction.

Partners gradually lose their novelty value and become increasingly familiar to each other as the relationship develops. Becoming more familiar means that the partner is no longer a perceptual mystery. We no longer must spend time talking to them and observing them to accurately predict their behavior and control our outcomes

FIGURE 6.3 Avoidance of eye contact is a potent signal that one does not wish to interact.

FIGURE 6.4 It is popularly believed that people who are deeply in love spend a great deal of time simply looking at each other.

in interaction with them. We have them "figured out." We can accurately predict their behavior in a variety of situations, particularly those situations in which we typically interact with them. Thus, it is not unusual for partners in long-term relationships to complain that they are being "taken for granted." They are. That's not all bad because it means their partners can devote their precious attention to other perceptual mysteries and problems—for example, figuring out a new boss. If we are the ones being taken for granted by a long-term relationship partner to whom we have become familiar, the situation is likely to continue until we change the contingencies that guide our behavior and become, once again, unpredictable to our partner. If he or she is still outcome-dependent on us, our partner's attention is likely to revert back to us. In sum, there is no direct association between attraction and attention.

The Gain–Loss Theory of Attraction

The fact that attention and attraction are not always positively correlated is illustrated by a number of experiments carried out under the aegis of Aronson's gain–loss theory of attraction (e.g., 1969), which predicts that *changes* in rewarding or punishing behavior from another have more impact than consistent rewards or punishments from another. Thus, *gains* in reward from a partner are hypothesized to have a stronger positive impact than invariant positive behavior, and *losses* in reward are proposed to have a more negative impact than consistently punitive behavior. To test this hypothesis, Aronson and Linder (1965) constructed a "get acquainted" situation in which an individual conversed with another over several occasions and, after each occasion, inadvertently overheard the other's evaluation of him or her. Participants in the *consistently positive* condition overheard the other say exclusively positive things about them each time; those in the *consistently negative* condition overheard only negative evaluations; those in the *gain* condition overheard the other say negative things at first but then grow more positive after each interaction; and those as-

signed to the *loss* condition overheard the other initially evaluate them positively but gradually become negative. As predicted, the gain partner was liked the most, more than the consistently positive evaluator; and the loss evaluator was liked the least—even less than the consistently negative evaluator. Aronson and Linder interpreted their results as illustrating a "law of infidelity"; that is, doting and faithfully positive partners may lose out to a stranger whose esteem represents a gain in reward.

Infidelity in romantic relationships, however, usually involves receiving evaluative comments simultaneously from two persons, the current partner (whose evaluations may be positive but not novel) and a new partner (whose increasingly positive evaluations represent a gain). Berscheid, Brothen, and Graziano (1976) gave their participants the opportunity to overhear *two* persons who were simultaneously evaluating them. Each evaluator, as in the Aronson and Linder (1965) study, interacted with the individual intermittently and provided a fresh evaluation of the individual after each interaction. One evaluator provided consistently positive evaluations, whereas the other provided a gain in positivity (providing negative evaluations at first but becoming more positive toward the individual over time). Because the evaluators were speaking simultaneously, the individual could listen to only one evaluator at a time. To whom did the individuals award their attention? Just as Aronson's theory and the principles of selective attention predict, they tended to "tune out" the consistently positive evaluator in favor of the gain evaluator, whose evaluations were changing and who thus was the more unpredictable of the two. But whom did they like best in the end? The consistently positive evaluator. When there is competition for the individual's attention—as there almost always is in naturalistic situations—unpredictable people may capture the individual's attention (and consistently "doting" partners may be neglected), but they may not capture the individual's heart. Again, there appears to be no direct association between attention and attraction.

AFFILIATION

The question of who will choose to interact with whom was the first to be addressed by investigators of interpersonal attraction because they believed the answer to the question "Who likes whom?" was the same as "Who interacts with whom?" In other words, it was assumed that people interact only with people they like and avoid interaction with those they dislike. Thus, questions of **affiliation**—who interacts with whom—were confounded with questions of attraction, or who likes whom. The "sociometric literature," which measured desire to interact, and the "interpersonal attraction literature" were simply two different labels for the same body of theory and research (Berscheid, 1985b). Gradually, however, it became apparent to investigators that they were confusing three conceptually distinct factors: (1) *desire to interact* with another, which the sociometric technique measures; (2) *de facto affiliation* (or actual interaction), which social network researchers typically measure; and (3) *attraction*, or positive sentiment felt for another.

Voluntary Affiliation and Attraction

Although attraction is a frequent reason people interact with another in an open field, we do not always approach people to whom we are attracted. Huston (1973), for example, demonstrated that an individual may not attempt to interact with another if he or she believes that person will reject the interaction attempt. Men were given an opportunity to select a date from an array of women who differed in physical attractiveness. Whereas some of the men were told that each of the women in the array would welcome an opportunity to date them, for others it was left unclear whether any one of the women would agree to a date even if they chose her. Those men who had been assured of acceptance tended to choose the most physically attractive woman in the array, but those who were unsure the women would reciprocate their choice chose less attractive women. Similarly, Kiesler and Baral (1970) found that men whose self-esteem had been lowered displayed more romantic approach behaviors toward a moderately physically attractive woman than toward a very attractive one, whereas men whose self-esteem had been raised showed the reverse pattern.

Vorauer and Ratner (1996) found that when people are contemplating making the "first move" in initiating a relationship with another, they often explain their inaction in terms of their fear of being rejected, but they tend to attribute their potential partner's inaction to a lack of interest in developing a relationship with them. Moreover, in a series of studies, Vorauer, Cameron, Holmes, and Pearce (2003) found that fears of rejection often cause people to exhibit what the investigators call a *signal amplification bias* whereby they believe that their overtures to a potential romantic partner communicate more romantic interest than the potential partner actually perceives. It appears that people with strong fears of rejection incorrectly assume that the potential partner will take their inhibitions into account when interpreting how much interest their behavior conveys.

The anticipation of rejection by the target of an interaction attempt is presumed to be frequently responsible for the "disconnect" between people's attraction to another and their attempts to affiliate with that person. Accordingly, Huston and Levinger (1978) propose a "two-factor" model of affiliation:

> The person contemplating initiating an encounter must consider at least two factors: (a) the degree to which he [or she] finds the attributes of the potential partners attractive; and (b) the degree to which he [or she] anticipates they would find his [or her] attributes attractive and hence respond favorably to the initiative. (pp. 126–127)

As in other endeavors, it makes sense that people will not attempt to reach even a highly desirable goal if they believe that they have little chance of attaining it. To predict the goals an individual will try to achieve, "level of aspiration" theories often *multiply* (rather than add) the desirability of the goal by the individual's subjective probability of achieving the goal should he or she try to obtain it (e.g., Lewin, Dembo, Festinger, & Sears, 1944). Thus, if the individual's subjective probability of achieving a goal is zero, it doesn't matter how desirable the goal is because zero times even a very large number is still zero. It appears that attraction is not a sufficient condition for a person to attempt to interact with another.

Other Determinants of Voluntary Affiliation

Attraction also is not a necessary condition for an interaction attempt because there are a multitude of reasons why a person may attempt to interact with a specific other apart from attraction. Researchers have focused primarily on two motives for making interaction attempts in the absence of attraction: ingratiation and information uncertainty.

Ingratiation

Ingratiation involves feigning attraction to another in order to induce that person to like us and thereby provide us with the rewards and benefits he or she commands or restrain from administering the costs and punishments he or she might otherwise mete out. As viewed by Jones and his associates (e.g., Jones, 1964; Jones & Pittman, 1982; Jones & Wortman, 1973), people are likely to make ingratiation attempts when (1) it is important that the other be attracted to them—for example, because they are outcome-dependent on the other; (2) they believe that an ingratiation attempt will be successful (perhaps the other is known to be a "sucker for flattery"); and (3) they believe an ingratiation attempt would be morally legitimate (it would not severely violate their personal moral code).

People who contemplate inducing another to like them in the absence of genuine regard for

that person commonly face what Jones terms the **ingratiator's dilemma**: To the extent that the individual's welfare is dependent on the other, the incentive value of ingratiation *increases* but the probability that the ingratiation attempt will be successful *decreases*. Its probability of success decreases because the target of the ingratiation attempt—typically a more powerful person who can influence the potential ingratiator's outcomes for good or for ill—usually is aware of the power differential and thus is likely to carefully scrutinize the authenticity of the individual's behavior, such as an expression of admiration. An early test of this hypothesis found that indeed, attraction to another increased as the favorability of the other's evaluation increased *only* when there was no possibility that the evaluator could have an ulterior motive for making the positive evaluation (see Jones, 1964, pp. 169–180).

Consistent with the original hypotheses of Jones and his colleagues, Leary and Kowalski's (1990) review of the ingratiation literature led them to theorize that (1) *impression motivation*, the extent to which an individual will want to control how another perceives him or her, is strongly influenced by the individual's dependence on the other; and (2) as status differences between the individual and the target increase, the individual becomes more likely to choose an oblique and less transparent ingratiation tactic because ingratiation becomes risky. If the ingratiation target concludes that an ulterior motive underlies the ingratiator's expressions of esteem and admiration, the ingratiator is likely to end up worse off than before because the ingratiation attempt may have created hostility, as suggested by the results of a study conducted by Anderson (1968). Anderson obtained "likeableness" ratings of over 500 personality trait adjectives commonly used to describe people. At the top of the list of highly valued attributes are adjectives having to do with honesty, such as "genuine," "sincere," "honest," and "straightforward"; and at the very bottom are adjectives having to do with dishonesty, such as "liar," "deceptive," "insincere," and "phony," all traits likely to be applied to a person whose ingratiation attempt has failed. It makes good sense that people value honesty in others because it is difficult to protect one's own welfare in interaction with a dishonest person.

Sometimes ingratiation is effective. Gordon (1996) concluded from his review and meta-analysis of ingratiation studies that there is a small positive effect of ingratiation on performance evaluations and a significantly stronger positive effect for liking the ingratiator. These effects are modified, however, by such factors as the transparency of the ingratiation attempt and the status differential between the ingratiator and his or her target, as we have discussed. Vonk (2002) finds evidence that ingratiation often works because people who are flattered are more likely to find the ingratiator credible than observers are; this is the case whether the target has high or low self-esteem.

Information Uncertainty

In 1950, Leon Festinger (Figure 6.5) formulated a theory of informal social communication to address the forces that motivate people to interact with each other. The theory hypothesizes that three conditions are especially conducive to affiliation (and communication) attempts:

1. **Emotional states.** Because people are often uncertain that their emotional reactions to an event are appropriate, they may seek out others to help them make this determination ("Do you think I have reason to be upset?" "Wouldn't you be angry?").
2. **Desire to change one's position or status.** People often wish to change the power structure of a dyadic relationship (or their status within a larger group). In asymmetrical power relationships, it usually is the low-power partner who wishes to interact and communicate with the high-power partner, often to negotiate a more equal power distribution. The high-power partner typically

has nothing to gain (but something to lose) by communicating with the low-power person (Kelley, 1951).

3. **Pressures toward uniformity of opinion.** Couples, as well as members of larger groups, often have to take joint action that will influence their future welfare, but the partners cannot act until they agree on which action would be most beneficial. Thus, partners often seek each other out to discuss possible courses of action and to reduce their mutual uncertainty about which would be best.

Most research derived from the theory of informal social communication focused on the effect of pressures toward uniformity of opinion in generating interaction with others. A substantial

FIGURE 6.5 Leon Festinger.

body of findings confirmed Festinger's hypotheses that relationship partners are likely to attempt to interact when (1) they perceive that their opinions are highly discrepant, (2) the issue on which the discrepancy of opinion occurs is relevant to the functioning of the relationship, and (3) the partners are highly **cohesive** (they are highly attracted to each other and to the relationship). Thus, the more the partners like each other, the more they are motivated to interact to reduce perceived discrepancies of opinion, especially if the discrepancy is large and relevant to the functioning of the relationship; for example, a discrepancy of opinion between spouses on which house to buy is more relevant to their relationship than a discrepancy of opinion on what political candidate they should vote for. The theory also predicts that when a discrepancy of opinion on an important issue cannot be resolved, the partner will be disliked and the relationship may be dissolved. "Irreconcilable differences," of course, are often cited by separating partners as their reason for terminating their relationship.

Festinger's theory of social comparison processes (1954) subsequently extended and elaborated the theory of informal social communication. The basic assumption, that people need and want to hold correct beliefs and attitudes, remained the same, and again, the theory predicts that when an individual is uncertain about the validity of his or her beliefs and attitudes or wishes to assess his or her standing along some dimension, he or she will seek out information to reduce the uncertainty. Two sources of information may be used to make validity assessments, according to social comparison theory. Sometimes the individual can assess the validity of his or her beliefs and attitudes by using the standard of *physical reality* as represented by sensory data (touching the heat register can confirm or disconfirm the belief that the furnace is working). In some instances, however, using physical reality to evaluate the correctness of a belief is dangerous (putting one's hand on a downed power line is a bad way to find out whether it is "hot"). In yet other instances, a physical reality standard is not available; there is no physical test for the belief that one's partner may be dishonest or that

Bob would be a better mate than George. In such instances, social comparison theory predicts that the individual will evaluate the correctness of his or her beliefs and attitudes against *social reality*, the standard provided by the beliefs and attitudes held by others. Assessment of social reality often requires interaction, or affiliation, with others.

The first to investigate Festinger's hypothesis that people often want to affiliate with others in order to assess the appropriateness of an emotion they are experiencing was his student Stanley Schachter, who published a report of his classic experiments in *The Psychology of Affiliation* (1959). In the best-known experiment, women college students were greeted at the laboratory door by a man wearing a white lab coat with a stethoscope dribbling out of the pocket. Introducing himself as "Dr. Gregor Zilstein of the Medical School's Department of Neurology and Psychiatry," Zilstein (a.k.a. Schachter) told the women they had been selected for an experiment on electric shock. He told *high fear* condition participants that if he was to learn anything helpful to humanity, it would be necessary for him to administer intense high-voltage shocks, adding "No need to worry—they'll do no permanent damage." In contrast, he reassured the *low fear* participants that the shocks would resemble a tickle or tingle. The women then were asked if, during a slight delay to set up the equipment, they wanted to wait "together" with others, "alone," or "didn't care." In the high fear condition, 63% of the women chose to wait with others, whereas in the low fear condition, only 33% wanted to wait with others.

Schachter would have liked to conclude that the women in the high fear condition wanted to wait with others in order to evaluate the correctness of their appraisal of the situation and whether the emotion they were experiencing (fear) was appropriate. But there are many reasons why people might want to affiliate with others when fearful— for example, people are distracting and take our minds off our problems. As a consequence, Schachter conducted a second experiment, much the same as the first, but this time half of the women (the *same* condition) could choose between waiting alone or waiting with another woman who was participating in the same experiment and thus could provide social comparison information about the appropriate degree of emotional arousal in that situation. The other half (the *different* condition) could choose between waiting alone or with a woman who was waiting for a different experiment to begin and thus could *not* provide social comparison information. Sixty percent of women in the same condition chose to wait with the other, in contrast to none in the different condition. Schachter (1959) concluded, "Misery doesn't love just any kind of company, it loves only miserable company" (p. 24).

People do not always seek out others when they are in an emotional state, however, as noted in Chapter 2, "Relationships and Health." For example, Latané and Wheeler (1966), who studied the reactions of men who participated in a body search following an airplane crash, found that those who were highly emotional about what they saw indicated little desire to talk to others, whereas nonemotional men wrote more letters home and had a greater desire to communicate. According to a review by Wheeler (1974), the association between heightened emotion and the desire to affiliate may be reduced by (1) the absence of a need to decrease uncertainty, (2) the desire to avoid embarrassment or a depressive reaction, and (3) a desire to avoid having the emotional response heightened by others.

The social comparison literature, now voluminous, details the sometimes complex associations between the individual's social comparison needs and affiliation (see Suls & Wheeler, 2000). On the whole, however, this body of research confirms Festinger's prediction that when people feel uncertain about the correctness of their beliefs and attitudes, they are likely to attempt to interact with others for social comparison purposes.

Interaction Accessibility

When we think about an individual in an open field selecting someone with whom to interact, it is important to remember that life rarely presents anyone with a smorgasbord of interaction possibilities. As sociologist Kerckhoff (1974) put it,

people always make their interaction selections from a **field of availables**—people who are available and accessible for interaction. Thus, who initiates an interaction with whom for the first time critically depends on the composition of the individual's field of availables.

Physical Proximity

Persons available and easily accessible for interaction are usually within close physical proximity of the individual. However, an early study of the association between proximity and relationship development revealed that it is *interaction accessibility*, and not physical distance itself, that is important (Festinger, Schachter, & Back, 1950). Moreover, although proximity is often named as a "principle" of attraction, it is more accurately viewed as an environmental condition that facilitates interaction because attraction does not always develop within the interaction.

The potency of physical proximity for relationship development, and the interaction accessibility that usually accompanies it, has been documented by many studies showing that people who live very close to one another are more likely to become friends than those who live even a bit farther away. A frequently cited study by Nahemow and Lawton (1975) examined friendship choices in a housing project in Manhattan and found that of all first-chosen friends, 88% lived in the same building and nearly half lived on the respondent's own floor. Similarly, Segal (1974) examined Maryland state police trainees' friendship choices after their training period (for which they had been grouped alphabetically) and found that the closer together in the alphabet the first letters of the surnames of any two trainees were, the more likely they were to name each other as their closest friend on the force. Proximity in the alphabet was a better predictor of friendship among the trainees than similarity of religion, age, marital status, ethnic background, and several other characteristics often associated with attraction and friendship choice.

The association between attraction and physical proximity, at least when it represents interaction accessibility, is consistent with Homans's (e.g., 1961, 1974) social exchange theory, which hypothesizes that interactions with people who are physically close are less expensive in time, money, and energy than interactions with more physically distant people. Less costly interactions yield more profit, other things being equal, than do more expensive interactions with less accessible people and thus are more likely to be maintained.

High costs of relationship maintenance often are blamed for the instability of long-distance relationships. Such relationships do seem to be less stable than others. Rindfuss and Stephen (1990), who examined a national longitudinal sample, found that noncohabitation between marital partners was surprisingly common for a variety of reasons, including dual careers, military service, incarceration, or marital discord. Eliminating from their sample those couples who were separated because of marital discord, these investigators found that spouses who were living apart at the beginning of the study were twice as likely to have experienced marital dissolution by the end of the study 3 years later. Not only does the cost of maintaining a long-distance relationship often reduce its profitability, but separated partners also are exposed to different physical and social environments and may grow in incompatible ways. Partners who live together can gradually accommodate each other's changes on a daily basis, and they also can influence each other's personal development in ways that increase, rather than decrease, compatibility. The longer partners are apart, the greater the likelihood that one or both will change in ways that make readjustment upon reunion difficult.

Although interaction accessibility comes close to being a necessary condition for relationship formation and attraction, it is not a sufficient condition—we do not always like those with whom we must interact. Ebbesen, Kjos, and Konecni (1976) examined choices of friends and enemies in a Southern California complex of three "village" clusters of townhouses. About 62% of the residents' "like most" choices lived in the same cluster as the individual, but the association between physical proximity and people's

"dislike most" choices was even stronger. The average straight-line physical distance between a person and his or her disliked choices was significantly shorter than the distance between the person and his or her liked choices. Reasons given for disliking the physically proximal other often cited that person behaving in ways that spoiled the individual's living environment. The authors conclude that "environmental spoiling" is a frequent reason for enmity among physically close persons.

Influence of the Social Environment

That it is interaction accessibility that is important to relationship initiation and development—not mere physical proximity—has been underscored by recent advances in telecommunication. Parks and Eggert's (1991) social contextual model of relationship initiation emphasizes the importance of *communicative distance*, or the number of people in each potential partner's communication network the two persons must "go through" to reach each other for the first time. Confirming their hypothesis that increases in communicative distance are associated with decreases in first interaction probability, these investigators found that two-thirds of the participants in one of their studies had met at least one member of their partner's network of close associates prior to meeting their partner.

In addition to interaction accessibility, the probability of initial interaction also is a function of social norms that prescribe who are appropriate and desirable partners for particular individuals and for certain kinds of relationships. With respect to mate selection, Winch (1958) coined the phrase **field of eligibles** to describe those persons whom society dictates are appropriate marriage partners for certain people. Social norms influence an individual's interaction attempts in a number of ways. First, social norms are usually internalized into the individual's beliefs about who is an appropriate partner, and thus they influence with whom the individual will attempt to interact. Second, social norms influence the individual's field of availables: Members of the individual's social network may actively facilitate initial encounters with desirable partners (as matchmakers often do) and hinder or prevent encounters with persons they deem undesirable (as parents often do). For example, Clark, Shaver, and Abrahams (1999) examined men's and women's accounts of the initiation of their romantic relationships and found that friends and family members often were highly instrumental in promoting the relationship—for example, by discovering whether a potential partner was available and interested in dating, by encouraging the choice of a particular partner, and by introducing the partners to each other.

People in the partners' social network not only influence relationship initiation; they also influence whether the relationship continues. Originally, some researchers hypothesized that as a relationship became close, the partners withdrew from their social network and, as a consequence, the influence of others on further development of the relationship diminished (see Parks & Eggert, 1991; Reis & Wheeler, 1991; Surra, 1990). Direct evidence relevant to the **social withdrawal hypothesis** is inconsistent. Some researchers have found that the size of each partner's network decreases as the couple advances in courtship (Johnson & Leslie, 1982), but in a longitudinal diary study, Milardo, Johnson, and Huston (1983) found that as courtship progressed, the partners not only tended to maintain contact with about the same number of people as before but also interacted with kin and best friends as frequently (they did, however, interact somewhat less with less close friends and acquaintances).

If the social withdrawal hypothesis were correct, the effect of the network's approval or disapproval on the further development of the relationship should diminish over time. It does not. Romantic partners' perceptions that people in their social network approve of the relationship are significantly associated with further relationship development (e.g., Johnson & Milardo, 1984; Parks, Stan, & Eggert, 1983; Sprecher & Felmlee, 1992; Surra, 1990). Although studies have shown this to be true for both men and women, Sprecher and Felmlee (2000) find suggestive evidence that women may be particularly sensitive to the disapproval of people in their social network. Thus, the social environment in which a relationship is embedded is an important determinant of who initiates interaction with whom, and it also influences whether an initiated relationship will develop further.

ATTRACTION IN FIRST ENCOUNTERS

As we have noted, attraction to another—whether manifested in liking, love, esteem, respect, or admiration—is believed to be the most usual motivation for voluntary attempts to initiate interaction in open fields. In closed-field situations such as the classroom or the workplace, interaction is not dependent on attraction between the partners; however, attraction may develop between them and sustain their relationship even after the environmental mandates for interaction change (for example, the class in which both individuals were enrolled ends, or one partner changes jobs). It is not surprising that closed-field situations often generate attraction—they frequently require that the partners talk and spend a good deal of time together, and these intimacy-promoting behaviors are the very ones that people report using to initiate and intensify open-field romantic relationships (Clark et al., 1999).

Positive or negative sentiment for others long has been regarded as the fundamental theme of all interpersonal relationships (e.g., Heider, 1958). Because issues of interpersonal attraction permeate human life, throughout recorded time people have been eager to discover the principles that govern whether others will be attracted to them. *How to Win Friends and Influence People*, published by Dale Carnegie in 1936, made history by remaining on the best-seller list for a record-breaking 10 years, and it remains popular today along with the Bible and other classics. Like Homans (e.g., 1961), Carnegie believed that people crave the esteem of others. His advice was simple: To win a person's esteem, be "hearty" in one's praise and "lavish" in one's approbation of that person. The finding that flattery often is successful supports Carnegie's advice, although the ingratiator's dilemma suggests that the situation is not always quite so simple.

Positive and negative affect not only is the theme of our relationships with other people; it also is the theme of our transactions with the physical environment. Studies examining the dimensions that underlie our symbolic representations of people and objects find that the evaluative (good–bad) dimension underlies human language (e.g., Osgood, Suci, & Tannenbaum, 1957). Osgood, May, and Miron (1975) interpret the pervasiveness of the affective dimension in language in evolutionary terms:

> We humans are still animals at base. What is important to us now, as it was back in the age of Neanderthal man, about the sign of a thing, is, first, does it refer to something *good* for me or *bad* for me (is it an antelope or a saber-toothed tiger)? . . . Survival, then and now, depends on the answers. (p. 395)

An individual's ability to evaluate whether another person is "good for me or bad for me" is critical to well-being and survival, and thus it is not surprising that a person's judgment of whether another is likely to enhance or harm his or her welfare is the underlying theme of the well-established principles of attraction. Our judgments of another's potential to help or harm are made automatically and immediately. Much research has shown that people, usually without conscious awareness, evaluate a stimulus as good or bad within a fraction of second (250 milliseconds or less) after it is perceived (e.g., Bargh, Chaiken, Raymond, & Hymes, 1996).

The Attraction Construct

Most systematic investigations of interpersonal attraction have been conducted by social psychologists. Because **attitude** is the social psychologist's "construct of choice," it perhaps was

inevitable that attraction has been defined as a positive *or* negative attitude toward another person—a relatively stable predisposition to respond to another in a favorable or unfavorable manner (Berscheid & Walster [Hatfield], 1969). As a consequence, attraction typically has been measured just as attitudes usually are measured, through self-report questionnaires that present the respondent with a bipolar scale anchored at one end with "like very much" and at the other with "dislike very much." Because such scales ask respondents to indicate either liking *or* disliking for another, affective ambivalence in relationships has been infrequently studied. This is unfortunate because ambivalence is not unusual in people's ongoing close relationships, as opposed to brief encounters with strangers in the laboratory (the setting in which attraction has been most frequently investigated). In close relationships, for example:

> What we see is people who love each other (or at least they say so, on their bipolar affective appraisals) literally beating each other about the head and shoulders, as those who investigate family violence are documenting. . . . We see people experiencing the most intense positive emotion in association with persons whom they indicate, on the ubiquitous "kind" and "industrious" adjective checklist, to be neither "kind" nor "industrious," but rather thoroughly unreliable scoundrels, and, conversely, we see persons giving the most glowing appraisals to a person they have just decided to dump in the divorce court—"a prince of a fellow," she says, "but I no longer wish to associate with him." (Berscheid, 1982, p. 42)

Gable and Reis (2001) have persuasively argued that the traditional bipolar view of affective processes is inadequate to account for many phenomena in close relationships. They and others believe that a two-dimensional model is more appropriate—one dimension ranging from neutral to positive and another ranging from neutral to negative, as discussed further in Chapter 9, "Affective Processes." Despite the fact that bipolar, unidimensional attraction scales cannot capture ambivalent affective feelings, appraisals, emotions, evaluations, and other behaviors of relationship partners, many investigators continue to measure attraction to the partner and to the relationship using unidimensional scales. An exception is marital and family researchers, who, almost from the beginning, assessed positive and negative feelings and behaviors in relationships separately, as Wills, Weiss, and Patterson's (1974) study illustrates (see Chapter 4, "The Concept of Relationship").

Learning Theory Approaches to Attraction

It will be recalled that virtually all of the general theories of social interaction reflect psychological learning theory principles. The learning theories also strongly influenced theories of attraction. Illustrative is Lott and Lott's (e.g., 1974) theory of attraction, which assumes that

> liking for a person will result under those conditions in which an individual experiences *reward in the presence of that person*, regardless of the relationship between the other person and the rewarding event or state of affairs. (p. 172; emphasis in original)

People may receive rewards in the presence of another because (1) the other possesses personal characteristics that are rewarding, such as an aesthetically pleasing appearance; (2) the other directly provides rewards such as money to the individual; (3) the other is instrumental in mediating rewards for the individual (perhaps the person's expertise assures the success of a group project); or (4) the other is simply *associated* with circumstances that are rewarding for the individual. Thus, in addition to instrumental conditioning processes, Lott and Lott correctly predicted that attraction could result from classical conditioning. For example, Griffitt and his colleagues (1970; Griffitt & Veitch, 1971) found that people in physically uncomfortable environments such as hot and crowded rooms were more likely to express negative attitudes toward a stranger than those who interacted in more pleasant surroundings.

General Principles of Attraction

An individual's attraction to another is influenced by many variables, all of which may interact, in ways both known and unknown, to influence attraction in first encounters and as the relationship develops. Attraction researchers have focused on four of these variables, each of which has been extensively documented to produce attraction, particularly in first encounters.

Familiarity

The **familiarity principle** of attraction is perhaps the most basic of the four. As opposed to the unfamiliar, familiar people usually are judged to be safe and unlikely to cause harm. The familiarity effect was experimentally demonstrated long ago by Hartley (1946), who asked people to give their impressions of various national groups, including such fictitious groups as "Danerians." Although there was no consensus about just exactly what attributes unfamiliar peoples such as the Danerians possessed (no doubt because they didn't exist), there was strong agreement that they possessed undesirable attributes and everyone disliked them.

The human is not the only creature in the animal kingdom who fears the unfamiliar. Comparative psychologists, who study the behavior of infrahuman animals in order to gain insights into human behavior, have found that most animals react with fear—and often with aggression—toward strangers in their midst. For example, in a field experiment in India, Southwick, Siddiqi, Farooqui, and Pal (1974; cited by Rajecki, 1985) introduced captive rhesus monkeys into natural troops. All were almost immediately recognized to be strangers, and all except a few infant monkeys were quickly killed or driven off. It is assumed that the infants survived because unlike the larger and stronger adults, they presented little threat to the group.

A stranger may be strange in two ways, both of which are likely to increase xenophobic reactions to him or her. First, the animal may *look* unfamiliar in appearance, and second, the animal may *behave* in unfamiliar ways. Rajecki (1985) recounts van Lawick-Goodall's (1968) description of the fate of some members of a chimpanzee society whose behavior suddenly became strange during an epidemic that paralyzed their limbs:

> Three mature males displayed violently at the old male who had lost the use of both legs. One of them actually attacked him, stamping on his back and half rolling him over as he cowered on the ground. A second, when the sick male was in a nest high in a tree, shook the branches violently, hitting the victim on many occasions, until the latter was shaken out of his nest. Two young mature males, who both lost the use of one arm, were repeatedly subjected to quite violent attacks by other adolescent and mature males for the first few weeks after their affliction. (p. 279, quoted in Rajecki, 1985, p. 25)

A similar incident was observed by Fossey (1983), Rajecki notes, when a young female gorilla contracted malaria. As she grew weakened and exhibited unusual behavior, she increasingly became the target of aggression from the other gorillas as they tried, but failed, to elicit from the dying gorilla the familiar behaviors they expected of her.

Humans also display fear and aggression toward those who, because they are strange, represent potential sources of harm. In 1867, a group of shipwreck survivors made their way to North Sentinel Island in the Indian Ocean, only to be driven off by naked men firing arrows ("The Tribe Has Spoken," 2000). Years later, in 1896, an escapee from a penal colony landed on the beach. His body later was found full of arrows. After this, the island, not surprisingly, was left alone for nearly a century. In 1974, however, a group of documentary filmmakers attempted to land on the island. When their friendly gestures were greeted with a hail of arrows, the intruders beat a hasty retreat. Not giving up, they landed their dinghy out of arrow range, dropped some trinkets on the beach, and quickly moved out to sea to observe the natives' reaction to their gifts. More arrows. No documentary has yet been made of the inhabitants of North Sentinel Island. "Civilized" peoples, of course, often express their fear and aggression toward strangers in more subtle ways.

Just as humans appear to have an innate dislike of the unfamiliar, we also seem to have a fondness for the familiar. Familiarity is no doubt partly responsible for the finding that people are more likely to initiate relationships with others in close physical proximity than they are with people even a short distance away. Not only does physical proximity usually facilitate the ease of initiating interaction and reduce interaction costs, as previously discussed, but it increases familiarity with the other person prior to the interaction attempt. Brockner and Swap (1976), for example, found that the more individuals had seen (but not interacted with) another, the more likely they were to voluntarily choose to interact with that person. Many investigations of what has been called the **mere exposure hypothesis** (Zajonc, 1968) have confirmed that repeated exposure to almost any stimulus enhances attraction to it under a wide range of conditions (e.g., see R. F. Bornstein, 1989, and Harrison, 1977, for reviews). In one unusual test of the hypothesis, Mita, Dermer, and Knight (1977) reasoned that each of us is exposed more frequently to our mirror facial image, whereas our friends and lovers are exposed more frequently to our true image. These investigators found that, as hypothesized, people prefer photos of themselves that are reversed to depict their mirror image over photos depicting their true image, but their close friends and lovers tend to prefer the true image.

The effect of increasing familiarity in long-term relationships is not as clear, however, and may not be as sanguine. Not only do familiar persons often lose their ability to capture the individual's attention over time, as previously discussed, but familiarity may diminish sexual attraction under some conditions. Wolf's (1995) research relevant to the Westermarck hypothesis (see Chapter 3, "The Development of Relationship Science") confirms that humans raised together in childhood may have diminished sexual attraction to each other in adulthood. Some researchers have hypothesized that even when partners first meet as adults, increasing familiarity diminishes their sexual attraction to each other. The supposition that sexual attraction decreases with familiarity is called the **Coolidge effect**, which got its name from an incident alleged to have taken place when President Calvin Coolidge and Mrs. Coolidge toured a chicken farm. Walking ahead of the President with a group of newspaper reporters, Mrs. Coolidge noticed that although there were many hens on the chicken farm, there was only one rooster. She asked the farmer where all the other roosters were. "There are no other roosters," he replied. "One rooster's sexual appetite is sufficient for all the hens." Mrs. Coolidge quipped to the reporters, "Be sure to tell that to Mr. Coolidge!" When the reporters obliged, President Coolidge thought for a moment before asking the farmer, "Does the rooster mate with the same hen every day?" "Oh no," the farmer replied, "it's a different hen every time." "Be sure to tell that to Mrs. Coolidge," President Coolidge told the reporters. Dewsbury (1981) concludes from his review of evidence pertinent to the Coolidge effect that infrahuman animals do seem to exhibit such an effect. For example, a sexually sated and exhausted male rat will revive his sexual interest if a new female is introduced to his cage. Human sexual attraction is discussed further in Chapter 12, "Mate Selection and Sex."

Similarity

The **similarity principle** of attraction (Figure 6.6) can be viewed as a corollary of the familiarity principle because people similar to oneself also are familiar people (for who is more familiar than oneself?). There is overwhelming evidence that a person's mate (e.g., Burgess & Wallin, 1943), friends, and associates are more likely to be similar to that person on virtually every dimension examined, both positive and negative. With respect to the latter, for example, there is strong evidence that antisocial people marry others who also possess antisocial tendencies (Krueger, Moffitt, Caspi, Bleske, & Silva, 1998).

Evidence that people tend to form and maintain relationships with similar others was sometimes interpreted as evidence that people *prefer* to interact with similar others. However, **de facto similarity** between relationship partners is not necessarily the result of personal preference for similar over dissimilar others. As a consequence of the fact that Mother Nature sorts people in time and space according to the principle of similarity, an individual's field of availables is largely composed of people similar to the individual. Thus, if we are to interact with anyone at all, it probably

FIGURE 6.6 People tend to form and maintain relationships with similar others.

will be with someone who is similar to us. In addition to being exposed more frequently to similar than to dissimilar others, however, there is evidence that when people do have a choice, they do prefer to interact with similar people. Two independent forces—the nature of the field of availables and personal preference—virtually guarantee that most people, most of the time, are surrounded by familiar and similar people.

One of the first studies to show that similarity produces attraction was conducted by Theodore Newcomb (1961), who also was the first to develop a theoretical model exclusively addressed to interpersonal attraction (Newcomb, 1956). Like other attraction theories, Newcomb's theory reflected learning theory principles. He proposed that an individual's attraction to another is a function of the frequency with which the individual receives rewards from the other and, further, that the likelihood that an individual will receive rewards from another varies with the frequency with which the individual gives rewards to the other. Like Festinger (1954), Newcomb assumed that people need to correctly perceive the world and that they often use other people's beliefs, opinions, and attitudes to satisfy that need. Newcomb thus hypothesized that an important reward people frequently give each other is **belief validation**, or agreement with another's attitudes and beliefs, and thus we should be attracted to those who hold similar beliefs, values, attitudes, and opinions.

In the first longitudinal study of attraction, Newcomb tested his similarity hypothesis by offering men transferring to the University of Michigan free room and board in return for participation in his project. Strangers to each other, each man's attitudes and values were assessed before he met the others in the residential house, and these, as well as the men's feelings of attraction for others in the group, were assessed periodically over the academic year. In his classic book detailing the results of his study, *The Acquaintance Process* (1961), Newcomb reported that whereas there was little association between actual attitude similarity and attraction at the beginning of the academic year, by the end of the year there was a significant and positive corre-lation between the degree to which the men shared similar attitudes with a housemate and the extent to which they liked each other.

Donn Byrne (e.g., 1971) and his associates later collected a great deal of evidence in support of Byrne's central hypothesis that an individual's attraction to another is a linear function of the proportion (not the number) of the other's attitudes that are similar to the individual's own. Most of the evidence that increasing proportions of similar to dissimilar attitudes lead to increases in attraction was derived from Byrne's "bogus stranger" experimental paradigm in which a stranger's responses to an attitude questionnaire were systematically varied to represent different degrees of similarity to the individual's own attitudes. After the respondent examined the nonexistent stranger's attitudes, his or her attraction to the stranger was assessed. In hundreds of studies, sampling many different populations of respondents, Byrne and his associates found overwhelming evidence that attitude similarity generates attraction.

Rosenbaum (1986), however, noted that Byrne's experimental procedure did not include a control group of individuals who possessed no attitudinal information about the stranger, and thus Bryne could not determine whether (1) similarity produced attraction, (2) dissimilarity produced "repulsion," or (3) both effects occurred. In an experiment that included such a control group, Rosenbaum found that whereas attitude dissimilarity produced repulsion (or dislike of the stranger), attitude similarity did not generate attraction beyond that felt for the control stranger. Byrne, Clore, and Smeaton (1986) quickly pointed out, however, that the stranger in Rosenbaum's control group, obviously another student participating in the study, was probably *assumed* by the participants to be similar to themselves and thus did not generate attraction beyond that observed for the stranger in the similarity condition.

The similarity–attraction effect has been elaborated by evidence that the *kind* of similarity shared may interact with the individual's personal characteristics to influence attraction. For example, Jamieson, Lydon, and Zanna (1987) demonstrated that the similarity effect is moderated by the personality variable of **self-monitoring.** High self-monitors are attentive to their social environment and use cues from other people to guide their behavior in social situations, whereas low self-monitors tend to behave more consistently across situations and display their private attitudes and opinions regardless of their social environment (see Snyder, 1979). Jamieson and his colleagues found that for low self-monitors, *attitudinal similarity* influenced attraction more than *activity preference similarity*, but the reverse was true for high self-monitors. This and other evidence (e.g., Snyder, Berscheid, & Glick, 1985) suggests that different personality dispositions may be associated with differential attention to the kinds of information first encounters yield, resulting in their differential influence on attraction.

Several researchers have hypothesized that the similarity–attraction association in first encounters may be mediated by people's assumptions that similar others will like them and dissimilar others will dislike them. Thus, they reason, it is not similarity itself that produces attraction but rather the perception that the similar person will like them. Condon and Crano (1988) experimentally manipulated both attitudinal similarity and the positivity of another's evaluation and found that although both variables influenced attraction, the similarity–attraction association indeed was strongly mediated by people's inferences that the similar stranger would like them. These investigators conclude that the similarity–attraction effect is best explained by an expectation of mutual need gratification based on reciprocal liking.

In naturalistic interactions, similarity and attraction undoubtedly feed back on each other: An individual's perception that another is similar produces liking, and that positive sentiment is likely to produce avoidance of disagreement and conflict, which then increases the perception of similarity—more similarity than actually exists (Levinger & Breedlove, 1966; see Sillars, 1985). Perception of increased similarity, in turn, enhances attraction. Whether two people perceive they are similar, however, often depends on the environment in which they meet and interact. Heider (1958), applying Gestalt principles of perception, noted that two Kansans meeting in China are more likely to perceive each other as similar and to be attracted to each other than if they meet in Kansas, surrounded by other Kansans (as discussed further in Chapter 8, "Cognitive Processes").

The only rival to the similarity hypothesis has been the **personality complementarity hypothesis**, derived from Winch's (1958) theory of complementary needs. Winch hypothesized that people who possess different but compatible personality traits—for example, a dominant person paired with a submissive partner—will interact harmoniously and will be attracted to each other. Winch's original study, which seemed to confirm the hypothesis, was almost immediately attacked on a number of methodological grounds (see Berscheid, 1985b), and subsequent supporting evidence has not been forthcoming.

Although it is not clear that the complementarity hypothesis has ever been adequately tested, there is evidence that dissimilarity is antithetical to harmonious interaction. For example, using the dyadic interaction experimental paradigm, Ickes and colleagues (1990) found that dissimilarity in partners' sex-role orientation was associated with interaction incompatibility; that is, dyads composed of masculine men and feminine women (a dissimilar and seemingly "complementary" combination of sex-role orientations) typically exhibit *less* involvement in interaction and *less* liking for each other than do partners with similar sex-role orientations (both masculine or both feminine). Moreover, even on personality and other psychological traits, the evidence indicates that people select as mates those similar to themselves (e.g., Catell & Nesselroade, 1967; Keller, Thiessen, & Young, 1996). There is virtually no evidence that "opposites attract."

Reciprocity of Attraction

Like Homans, all attraction theorists view another's expression of esteem as a valuable reward and predict that the individual will reciprocate in kind. In this way, "attraction breeds attraction," as

Newcomb put it. Backman and Secord (1959) experimentally demonstrated the **principle of liking reciprocity**. More recently, Kenny and his associates demonstrated the principle using the SRM method, finding that although some people tend to be more liked by others than other people are, and some people are more likely to like others than other people, these actor and partner effects (individual-level effects) are relatively small compared to attraction reciprocity (relationship effects) (Kenny & La Voie, 1984; Kenny & Nasby, 1980). Kenny (1994b) examined dyadic reciprocity correlations from 10 studies and concluded that attraction reciprocity becomes more substantial in longer-term relationships, just as one might expect as people gradually learn of their partners' sentiments.

An old proposition in the attraction literature is that people who dislike themselves ought to constitute an exception to the liking reciprocity principle. Relative to people who possess high self-esteem, people who dislike themselves should be more comfortable with others who also dislike them and thus validate their poor opinion of themselves. Deutsch and Solomon (1959) found some support for the hypothesis, but they also found a strong "positivity effect" such that even people who have a negative opinion of themselves are likely to reciprocate another's expression of esteem—a finding consistent with Vonk's (2002) more recent findings that flattery is as successful with persons who have low self-esteem as it is with people who think highly of themselves. Swann (1990) and his associates reexamined the hypothesis in the context of self-verification theory, which posits that people gravitate toward relationship partners who see them as they see themselves. Although it is clear that people seem to overwhelmingly prefer positivity in first encounters, Swann, Hixon, and De La Ronde (1992) found some evidence that among spouses who possessed negative self-concepts, those whose partners negatively evaluated them expressed more commitment to continuing the marriage than did those who had positively evaluating partners. These researchers speculate that people with negative self-concepts may seek positive evaluations in some contexts and unfavorable but self-verifying appraisals in long-term close relationships.

Physical Attractiveness

Today, it is widely recognized that an individual's physical attractiveness makes a difference in how people respond to him or her in interaction. Not so very long ago, however, most people believed that a person's appearance made little difference in their lives—books couldn't be judged by their covers, beauty was only skin deep, and if physical attractiveness made any difference at all, it was dispelled after the first few moments of interaction when the person's "inner" character and other qualities were revealed.

The Matching Hypothesis

The first unequivocal demonstration of the influence of physical attractiveness on attraction was conducted by Walster [Hatfield], Aronson, Abrahams, and Rottman (1966), who designed a college "computer" dance. A student's purchase of a ticket not only allowed the student to attend the dance but also provided him or her with a date chosen by a computer program (pairing actually was random). Those students who, by chance, were paired with dates whose "social desirability" matched their own—whether both were high or both low—were predicted to like each other more than mismatched persons. Intelligence, social skills, and personality, all of which had been assessed prior to the dance when the students entered the university, were believed to be the most important components of social desirability. Only as an afterthought were the ticket-takers at the dance asked to jot down their rough opinion of each student's physical attractiveness. The investigators found no evidence that similarity in social desirability (at least desirability as defined by the experimenters) influenced attraction. Nor did the date's intelligence, social skills, or personality influence how much he or she was liked. Only physical attractiveness, as quickly estimated by the harried ticket-takers, was associated with how much the date was liked: The more physically attractive the date, the more he or she was liked.

Although the computer dance study did not support the social desirability matching hypothesis, a subsequent study by Berscheid, Dion,

Walster [Hatfield], and Walster (1971) demonstrated matching in dating choice along the physical attractiveness dimension, and subsequent studies corroborated the finding. White (1980), for example, measured the relative physical attractiveness of dating partners in various stages of courtship (from casual dating through engagement and marriage) and found, in a follow-up 9 months later of those who had initially been casually or seriously dating, that similarity of physical attractiveness was predictive of courtship progress. White also found that the more attractive member of the pair enjoyed greater availability of opposite-sex friends and worried less about the partner's involvement with others than did the less attractive member.

Feingold (1988) performed a meta-analysis of the many physical attractiveness "matching" studies that had been conducted by the 1980s and found a significant positive correlation between the physical attractiveness levels of romantic partners. He also found a significant positive correlation between the attractiveness levels of male same-sex friends; no such association for women and their same-sex friends was observed. One possible explanation for the sex difference is that men's social interactions, from childhood onward, appear to reflect status hierarchies more than women's social interactions do (see Maccoby, 1990). If attractive men enjoy higher social status, then the matching effect on the attractiveness dimension may be an indirect effect of males pairing off in friendship according to social status.

Kalick and Hamilton (1986) reanalyzed the matching data of Berscheid and her colleagues and found that although a significant matching effect existed, it was small in comparison to a large effect that had been overlooked: People tended to choose to date the most attractive person available to them. If everyone prefers the most physically attractive person he or she can obtain in the dating and mating arena, the question arises of how de facto physical attractiveness matching occurs. Burley (1983) explains that the fact that romantic partners are matched in physical attractiveness need not imply that the matching occurred because the partners *wanted* to pair with a person of their own attractiveness level:

For any phenotypic gradient along which individuals can be ranked in terms of their quality/desirability as mates, high quality individuals will tend to pair assortatively [like with like]. In a finite population, this will leave lower quality individuals to mate among themselves, not because they prefer to mate assortatively, but because their own desirability precludes them access to better mates. (p. 192)

The Physical Attractiveness Stereotype

The computer dance findings were an unpleasant surprise to many, not the least because they challenged deeply held beliefs that beauty is only skin deep and that a person's appearance is irrelevant to important outcomes in life. Many investigators subsequently tried to reconcile their belief that appearance is unimportant with the emerging findings on the effects of physical attractiveness by seeking benign explanations and limitations. For example, Dion, Berscheid, and Walster [Hatfield] (1972) hypothesized that when the computer dance students responded favorably to an attractive face, they actually were responding to the favorable interior qualities they assumed their attractive date possessed. To investigate whether there is a constellation of positive personal qualities believed to be characteristic of physically attractive people, male and female college students were asked to evaluate photos of men and women of varying attractiveness levels and to correctly estimate their personalities and other characteristics. In contrast to those of lesser attractiveness, physically attractive men and women were believed by almost everyone to be more sensitive, kind, interesting, strong, poised, modest, sociable, outgoing, exciting, and sexually warm and responsive. Attractive people also were believed to be more likely to capture better jobs, to have more successful marriages, and to experience happier and more fulfilling lives than their less attractive counterparts. These findings were reflected in the report's title: "What Is Beautiful Is Good."

The results of the study by Dion and colleagues were replicated throughout the world, partly because investigators in other states and other countries hoped the effect was confined to Minnesota or, if not to that state, then to the

United States. (One Italian TV announcer reporting the findings wondered whether the coldness of the Minnesota climate was responsible for the students' differential attributions of traits to attractive and unattractive people—Italian men and women, it was opined, would never be so "superficial" in their judgments of others.) Eagly, Ashmore, Makhijani, and Longo (1991) conducted a meta-analysis of the many studies of the physical attractiveness stereotype available by the early 1990s and concluded that people do ascribe more favorable personality traits and more successful life outcomes to attractive people. Differential inferences appear to be largest on social competence dimensions, intermediate on personal adjustment and intellectual competence dimensions, and nonexistent on indices having to do with integrity and concern for others.

The content of the physical attractiveness stereotype may differ across cultures, however. Wheeler and Kim (1997) found that what is "good" in collectivist cultures, which stress harmony in relationships, is different from what is regarded as good in individualistic cultures, and that whatever is good in a culture tends to be viewed as characteristic of physically attractive people. North Americans, for example, perceive attractive persons to be high in potency, whereas Koreans do not. Koreans perceive attractive people to be higher in integrity and concern for others, but North Americans do not (as the results of the Eagly meta-analysis, which mostly included studies conducted in North America, reflect).

Although the computer dance results suggested that physical attractiveness played a larger role in dating choice than anyone wanted to believe, many people took refuge in the belief that the effect was confined to the adolescent dating-and-mating marketplace. The first clue that the impact of physical attractiveness was not so limited emerged from a study by Dion and Berscheid (1974), who obtained adult ratings of the attractiveness of nursery school children. (These ratings were obtained only with difficulty because most people said they could not make discriminations among children along the attractiveness dimension because "all children are beautiful.") When adults' attractiveness ratings were compared to the sociometric rankings the children had received from their nursery school peers, the results were clear. First, despite the protestations that children do not differ in physical attractiveness, adults showed good agreement as to which children were attractive and which were unattractive. Moreover, the adults' attractiveness ratings were significantly, and positively, correlated with the children's popularity in the nursery school and with their peers' attributions of the child's other characteristics; for example, unattractive little boys were regarded as "scary" by the other children.

Today the physical attractiveness literature is massive, and book-length surveys are now available (e.g., Bull & Rumsey, 1988; Hatfield & Sprecher, 1986b; Patzer, 1985). Over the years, many people have tried to dismiss the findings that a person's physical attractiveness matters. As Judith Langlois and her associates (2000) detail, critics have charged that (1) physical attractiveness effects are largely trivial in magnitude; (2) they occur primarily in laboratory and artificially contrived situations and do not generalize to "ecologically valid" (naturalistic) situations; (3) at best, they occur only in first encounters and dissipate rapidly with increasing acquaintance; and (4) physical attractiveness is more important for women than for men. To examine the validity of these charges, Langlois and her colleagues examined almost 2,000 studies of physical attractiveness, discarding all those conducted in "ecologically invalid" settings such as laboratory studies, and then conducted meta-analyses on the approximately 900 studies remaining. From these analyses, the investigators concluded:

- Attractiveness effects are robust and pandemic—not trivial.
- Attractive children and adults are judged and treated more favorably than the unattractive in significant and meaningful life contexts such as educational and occupational settings.
- Attractiveness is as important for boys and men as it is for girls and women.
- There is more than a kernel of truth to the physical attractiveness stereotype. Attractive and unattractive people possess different traits

and behave differently, although the nature of the mechanisms that produce these differences is not yet clear.

■ Judgments of an individual's facial attractiveness are more similar than different, even across ethnic groups and cultures.

Langlois and her associates also found substantial evidence that attractiveness may become more—not less—important as familiarity with the individual increases. For example, teachers and parents familiar with the children they evaluate are as strongly (sometimes more strongly) affected by the child's physical attractiveness as those unfamiliar with the child. Moreover, longitudinal studies of the effects of attractiveness over the school year show stronger differential effects of others' treatment of the individual by the end of the year than early in the year. Even mothers show differential effects in their treatment of their own infants—mothers of attractive infants pay more attention to their infants, and hold and fondle their infants more, than do mothers of unattractive infants (Langlois, Ritter, Casey, & Sawin, 1995).

The weight of the evidence is that the physically attractive are preferred over the physically unattractive in a wide variety of settings and thus receive preferential social treatment in many ways. Moreover, the preference for physically attractive people appears to cut across all ages, both sexes, and all socioeconomic stations and life situations.

Characteristics of the Physically Attractive

To determine whether the attractiveness stereotype has some truth to it, Feingold (1992b) conducted a meta-analysis of studies examining the actual characteristics of attractive and unattractive people. Attractive men and women were found to be less lonely and more popular than unattractive people, as well as more socially skilled and sexually experienced. Associations with personality measures and mental ability were trivial. In a subsequent and methodologically rigorous study, Diener, Wolsic, and Fugita (1995) found only small associations between attractiveness and subjective well-being. However, as previously noted, Langlois and her associates (2000), in their large-scale meta-analyses, found substantial behavioral and trait differences as

a function of attractiveness. Attractiveness was most strongly related to "popularity," "dating/sexual experience," and "intelligence/performance." (The last probably differs from Feingold's results because Langlois and her colleagues included a greater number of studies and only those possessing ecological validity.)

Most studies examining the characteristics of attractive and unattractive people have focused on the college student population, whose variability and range on such dimensions as mental ability and adjustment are considerably more restricted than they are in the general population. Restricted range may decrease the size of the correlations between these variables and attractiveness, for studies of broader populations reveal significant effects. For example, Burns and Farina (1992) examined the influence of attractiveness on adjustment across the life span in several nonstudent samples and concluded that attractiveness accounts for 6% to 16% of the variance in subjective, sociometric, and behavioral measures of adjustment from age 4 through 75. Economists Hamermesh and Biddle (1994), examining data from large-scale quality-of-life surveys in the United States and Canada that included an interviewer's rating of the respondent's physical appearance, found that plain people earn less than people of average looks, who earn less than attractive people; the monetary "penalty" for plainness is estimated to be about 5% to 10% and the "premium" for beauty only slightly less, a 10% to 20% range in earnings. They also found that the earning effects of physical attractiveness were mostly independent of occupation and those for men were at least as great as those for women.

Thus, as Langlois and her associates (2000) conclude, there appears to be some truth to the physical attractiveness stereotype—a truth at least partially caused by the stereotype itself, of course, and by the preferential treatment physically attractive people receive. For at least two reasons, it is not surprising that the effects of preferential treatment are substantial: First, because there is consensus on who is attractive and unattractive, the differential treatment an individual receives from others is likely to be in one consistent direction. Second, an individual's physical attractiveness level appears to remain relatively stable, at least as compared to his or her peers. Zebrowitz, Olson, and Hoffman (1993) found evidence of the "differential stability" of physical attractiveness over the life span; that is, relative to their age-group peers, the attractive remain attractive, although the *absolute* level of attractiveness decreases with age for both men and women.

Physical Attractiveness and Interaction

To investigate the association between physical attractiveness and the nature of the individual's social interactions, Reis and his associates (e.g., Reis, Nezlek, & Wheeler, 1980; Reis et al., 1982) asked men and women of varying attractiveness levels to complete the Rochester Interaction Record. (As previously noted, the RIR requires respondents to record in a structured diary each social encounter lasting 10 minutes or longer and to rate the interaction along such dimensions as intimacy.) A male college student's physical attractiveness was associated with the number, percentage, and average length of his opposite-sex interactions per day, as well as the number of different women with whom he interacted. No such associations were found for female students. Both physically attractive men and women, however, rated their interactions as more pleasant than unattractive men and women did.

Other evidence of the impact of physical attractiveness on interaction comes from research using Ickes's dyadic interaction procedural paradigm. Garcia, Stinson, Ickes, Bissonnette, and Briggs (1991) found that people's physical attractiveness is strongly associated with both their own and their randomly selected partner's interaction behavior. For example, men's physical attractiveness is positively associated with the percentage of positive thoughts and feelings both partners report and also with the amount of time the partners smile at each other. A woman's attractiveness is strongly associated with the partners' frequency and duration of talking during the interaction, involvement in the interaction, liking for each other, and ratings of interaction quality.

Determinants of the Perception of Attractiveness

Researchers are trying to identify the physical features that lead others to judge a person as attractive. Whatever those criteria are, it is clear that they are widely shared and that they result in agreement about who is or is not physically attractive, even across cultural groups. To take just one example, Cunningham, Roberts, Barbee, Druen, and Wu (1995) found that the mean correlations between the attractiveness judgments of photos of Asian, Hispanic, and black and white American women made by recently arrived native Asian and Hispanic students and white Americans were extraordinarily high, with correlation coefficients in the .90s.

Initially, it was assumed that the culture transmitted standards of physical attractiveness that children absorbed only gradually. As a consequence, it also was believed that physical attractiveness standards did not begin to influence social preferences until young childhood (about ages 3 or 4). The first study to cast doubt on this assumption was conducted by Langlois and her associates (1987), who found that 3-month-old infants spent significantly more time looking at attractive faces (as judged by adults) than unattractive faces. In a subsequent experiment, Langlois, Roggman, and Rieser-Danner (1990) found that babies 12 months of age interacted differently with a female stranger depending on whether the lifelike professional theater mask she wore was (unknown to her) attractive or unattractive, even though the stranger's behavior was standardized. The infants' approach, withdrawal, and other behaviors (such as smiles) in interaction clearly indicated that they preferred the attractive stranger over the unattractive one; for example, they became more involved in play with the attractive stranger.

Because the preference for facially attractive people is evident early in human life—just hours after birth (Slater et al., 1998)—the preference may be innate (see Chapter 1, "First Relationships"). It is not known why facial attractiveness is so important to the human that preferences in accord with adults' judgments of facial attractiveness appear to be present shortly after birth and are clearly present and expressed by 3 months of age. Some (e.g., Berscheid & Walster [Hatfield], 1974b) have speculated that physical attractiveness may convey good physical health and, implicitly, "good genes." Evidence pertinent to this hypothesis, as well as others associated with physical attractiveness and mating, is discussed in Chapter 12, "Mate Selection and Sex."

Determinants of the perception of facial attractiveness have been studied in two ways. The traditional approach has been to try to identify configurations of facial features associated with attractiveness judgments. Perhaps the first systematic application of this approach was reported by Sir Henry Finck (1887), who, in *Romantic Love and Personal Beauty*, not only considered each and every facial feature but also the aesthetic qualities of the big toe and every anatomical feature in between the toes and the face. Michael Cunningham and his associates have examined features empirically found to be associated with attractiveness judgements. For example, Cunningham (1986) found that men seemed to judge women as more attractive if they had large eyes (but see Grammer & Thornhill, 1994, who find small eyes preferred), a small nose, prominent cheekbones, and a large smile. Studies of features associated with women's judgments of men's attractiveness often find that such attributes as a broad jaw are attractive (e.g., Cunningham, Barbee, & Pike, 1990).

In contrast to the *empirically inductive* approach taken by Cunningham and others, Langlois and her associates have taken a *theoretically deductive* approach to the question (e.g., Langlois & Roggman, 1990; Langlois, Roggman, & Musselman, 1994). They began by noting that any theory about the determinants of attractiveness must take into account two sets of empirical findings: First, the preference for facially attractive people is apparent very early in life, and second, judgments of facial attractiveness are more similar than different across cultures (e.g., Jones & Hill, 1993; McArthur & Berry, 1987; Perrett, May, & Yoshikawa, 1994).

Drawing on evolutionary theory, Langlois and her colleagues observed that evolutionary pressures favor human attributes, including morphological (physical) features, close to the population mean because they are less likely to carry harmful genetic mutations than extreme attributes; thus, they should be preferred. Drawing on cognitive theory

as well, Langlois and her associates observed that human cognitive processes appear to favor members of a category of persons ("men," "children"), objects, or events closest to the **category prototype**, which represents the average value of each attribute possessed by all the members of the category. After seeing several members of a category, people respond to an averaged representation of the attributes of these members as though it were familiar even though they have never seen the prototype before. Even young infants recognize facial prototypes composed of the averaged values of previously viewed facial features; that is, they respond to the prototype, or averaged, face as familiar even though they have never seen that face before (e.g., Strauss, 1979). Their deductive analysis led Langlois and her associates to hypothesize that people should find others whose physical attributes best represent the mean, or average, for the human population more attractive than those whose physical attributes significantly deviate from the average.

To test this hypothesis, Langlois and her colleagues (e.g., 1990) formed computer-generated composite images of many faces to produce an "average" face and found that the more faces they put into the composite face, the more attractive it was judged to be. Moreover, composite faces were judged as more attractive than any of the individual faces entered into the composite. Thus, these investigators conclude that what is physically attractive is what is *average* for the population (Figure 6.7).

The attractive-is-average conclusion has been controversial. First, the attractive-is-average findings must be reconciled with findings that certain configurations of facial features are preferred (such as large eyes in female faces). However, Langlois contends that when many faces are entered into the composite, these tend to be the facial configurations displayed by the composite. Second, some investigators have found that although averaged faces are attractive, the faces judged to be the *most* attractive are not average (e.g., Alley & Cunningham, 1991; Perrett et al., 1994). Third, some have argued that the averaging procedure produces *symmetrical* faces and that it is their feature of symmetry—not their averageness—that is associated with attractiveness (see Grammer & Thornhill, 1994). The evidence

Number of faces in composite

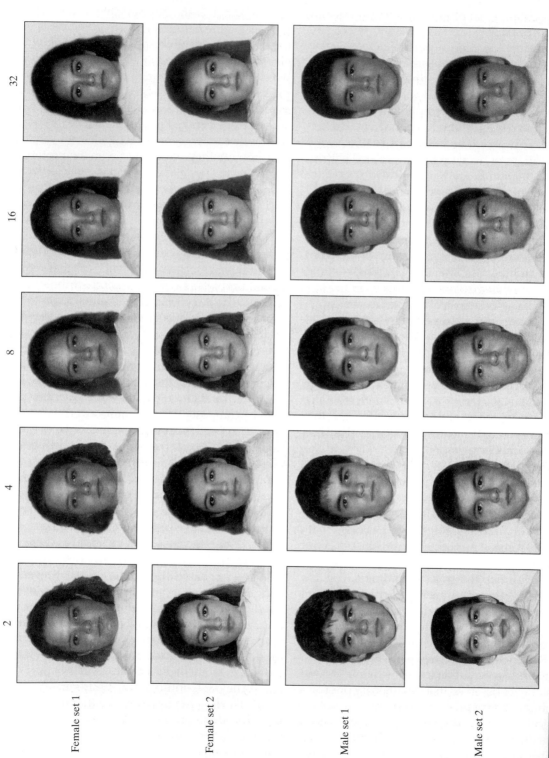

FIGURE 6.7 What is attractive is average. Using computer-generated composites of faces similar to those pictured here, Langlois and her associates found that the more faces they put into the composite, the more attractive the composite was judged to be. This provides support for the hypothesis that what is physically attractive is what is average for the population.

on this latter issue is conflicting. Langlois and her associates (e.g., 1994), who have reversed the left side of a face and superimposed it on the right to produce a perfectly symmetrical face, have found that increased symmetry does not necessarily produce an increase in attractiveness. Finally, some have proposed that average faces are more familiar and familiarity is itself associated with attractiveness. Familiarity, however, is precisely the mechanism through which Langlois hypothesizes that averaged faces are regarded as attractive. In fact, Langlois and her colleagues (1994) report that the association between perceived attractiveness and perceived familiarity in randomly selected samples of male and female individual faces is strong and positive; moreover, an averaged face is perceived as more familiar than the individual faces contributing to the composite. Thus, familiarity may underlie the physical attractiveness principle of interpersonal attraction, just as it appears to underlie the principles of similarity and attraction reciprocity.

Those seeking the determinants of physical attractiveness have focused almost exclusively on *facial* attractiveness. The contribution of other morphological characteristics to an individual's judgment of another's attractiveness has received relatively little attention. One exception has been examinations of **waist-to-hip ratio (WHR)**, an index of body fat distribution. Before puberty, both sexes exhibit a similar WHR; after puberty, women deposit more fat in their buttocks and thighs and men deposit more fat in the central and upper body regions, including the shoulders and abdomen. Typically, the WHR ranges from 0.67 to 0.80 in healthy premenopausal women (an hourglass shape) and from 0.80 to 0.90 in healthy men (a straighter, more tubular shape). Research on preferences for targets with varying WHRs reveals that men and women from different ages, races, and cultural backgrounds prefer as romantic partners, and find most attractive, individuals who possess a typical or normal WHR (e.g., Furnham, Tan, & McManus, 1997; Singh, 1993, 1995; Singh & Luis, 1995).

Bodily attractiveness also may interact with facial attractiveness to influence overall judgments of an individual's physical attractiveness. Alicke, Smith, and Klotz (1986) assessed the relative and combined influence of faces and bodies of varying attractiveness and found strong effects for both face and body as well as a strong face–body interaction, which reflected significantly decreased attractiveness judgments when a highly attractive face was paired with an unattractive body.

Height, especially in males, has been another exception to the focus on facial attractiveness. Many studies have found a positive association between a man's height and his likelihood of success in occupational positions. For example, Feldman (1975) found that males 6 feet, 2 inches tall and over were more likely to be hired and had higher starting salaries than males under 6 feet tall. It is not as evident that taller males have an advantage in dating situations. Graziano, Brothen, and Berscheid (1978) found that males of medium height (5'9" to 5'11") were rated by women as more attractive and more desirable as a date than males described as short (5'5" to 5'7") or tall (6'2" to 6'4"); this curvilinear relationship held regardless of the height of the female rater (4'10" to 6'1"). Shepperd and Strathman (1989) found that women expressed a general preference for dating men taller than themselves, but although they reported dating taller men more frequently, they did *not* rate their tall dates as more attractive than their shorter dates. Moreover, no relationship was found between a man's height and his self-reported frequency of dating. Men, regardless of their own height, rated shorter women as more attractive than taller women and preferred shorter women as dates. Shorter females did date more frequently.

Finally, it should be noted that despite the massive quantity of the physical attractiveness literature, some important questions about physical attractiveness remain unanswered. First, most studies examine people of two levels of attractiveness—high or low (or, in studies that split the sample in half, at the median, "higher" or "lower"). Even after meta-analyzing the results of hundreds of studies, Langlois and her associates (2000) could conclude only that attractive and unattractive individuals are judged and treated differently. Because they could not determine whether either group was significantly different from individuals of average attractiveness, they could not establish whether the differences observed between attractive and unattractive individuals occur because attractiveness is an advantage, unattractiveness is a disadvantage, or both attractiveness and unattractiveness contribute to the effects observed.

Second, it is not known how physical attractiveness is distributed in the population. It is possible that most people are attractive, that most are unattractive, or that attractiveness is normally distributed (and thus most people are "average" relative to others). Arguments can be made for each of these possibilities. For example, few would question the statement that the media propagates very high standards of physical attractiveness—standards that even the airbrushed, filtered, and otherwise modified models and actors portrayed cannot themselves meet in their daily lives. In an interview with *W* magazine, actress Jennifer Aniston remarked:

> I was always reading those beauty magazines and wanting to become this unattainable thing. Then one day, you're in it—you're the girl in the pictures, and suddenly you realize it's all smoke and mirrors, airbrushing, lighting, stretching. No wonder people are killing themselves. Starving themselves. Popping pills. They're all trying to achieve something impossible. (Cutter, 2003)

The images portrayed by the media make a difference. Kenrick and Gutierres (1980) found that men who viewed pictures of attractive nude women subsequently rated the sexual attractiveness of their current romantic partner lower than did men who viewed pictures of artworks, and they also expressed less love for their partners (a "contrast" effect). Women were not similarly influenced by pictures of nude men. Thus, compared to the high standards many people have absorbed, it seems possible that many people regard themselves and others as average in attractiveness or even somewhat unattractive.

Third, it is not known how an individual's physical attractiveness, which is heavily genetically determined, interacts with other genetically influenced attributes. Although many lament that physical attractiveness is not evenly distributed in the human population (just one more example of Mother Nature's unfairness), few seem to be as distressed that intelligence also is unevenly distributed and may

be the greater gift. It is not known how intelligence (or any other attribute) interacts with physical attractiveness to affect an individual's life. For example, would the life of Charles Steinmetz, the great genius of electricity who constructed the first electrical generators in the United States, have been different had he not been extremely short and unattractive by conventional standards? Would he have been as likely to devote himself to his solitary scholarly work had he been as handsome as Rudolph Valentino? Would we still be lighting our houses with candles?

SUMMARY

The question "Who likes whom?" has long captivated relationship scholars. Historically, it was assumed that attraction toward another individual would manifest itself in interaction; thus, it was believed that people interact with those they like and avoid interaction with those they do not like. However, it is now recognized that environmental and other forces sometimes mandate that a person initiate and maintain interaction with another for reasons apart from his or her degree of liking for that individual. For example, in closed fields such as work and school settings, people are forced to interact by reason of the environmental situation in which they find themselves; it is only in open fields that people have the choice of selecting an interaction partner. It is important to recognize, however, that even in open fields interaction does not necessarily reflect attraction, nor does lack of interaction reflect repulsion. For instance, we may not interact with another simply because we do not notice—and not because we dislike—him or her. In addition, we may elect not to interact with others, even when strongly attracted to them, if we believe they will reject our interaction attempts. Similarly, we may interact with others in an attempt to ingratiate ourselves with them or to obtain information from them. Our choice of partner in open-field settings also is strongly influenced by physical proximity (the availability of the partner for interaction) as well as by social norms that dictate whether the individual would make an "acceptable" or "unacceptable" interaction and/or relationship partner. In sum, interaction is only one of the hallmarks of attraction. Subsequent research has succeeded in identifying and elaborating four general principles of attraction. Specifically, we tend to prefer others who are familiar, who are similar to us, who reciprocate our liking, and who are physically attractive.

Chapter 7

Relationship Growth and Maintenance

INTRODUCTION

The time, energy, and other resources required to develop and maintain a relationship ensure that our first interaction with another is usually our last. Of those few encounters that are followed by subsequent interactions, most come to represent a superficial relationship that is minimally maintained. Some relationships, however, continue to grow and become close and enduring. Virtually all relationship development theorists assume that development entails increasing frequency of interaction and increasing levels of interdependence.

The question of why, and how, some interactions progress into a close relationship whereas others either fall by the wayside or are maintained at low levels of interdependence has long been of interest. Relationship development theorists have attempted to identify the factors likely to influence whether a relationship will grow, the progression it will take toward closeness, and the processes by which it does so. Closely related to questions of relationship development are those concerning factors that determine whether, and how, a relationship is maintained or dissolved. Whereas **relationship development** generally refers to the relationship's progression toward closeness, **relationship maintenance** refers to the processes by which people continue their relationship at a given level of interdependence, and **relationship stability** refers to questions concerning when, why, and how a relationship is likely to be dissolved. These three terms are sometimes used interchangeably because the questions associated with each are intertwined—for example, a developing relationship obviously is not being dissolved—and because many of the interaction processes and outcomes important to relationship development are also involved in relationship maintenance and stability.

Researchers usually study relationship development in romantic relationships, and occasionally in friendships, because many of these types of relationship are young and still progressing toward closeness. Moreover, romantic relationships either tend to develop further or are dissolved; rarely are they maintained for a long period of time at a low level of interdependence.

It should be noted that the term **romantic relationship** often is used loosely by most researchers. The term may refer to any opposite-sex relationship that has the *potential* for romantic feelings such as strong positive sentiments and sexual attraction, although such feelings may not presently characterize the relationship (as in a casual dating relationship). It also may refer to exclusive dating relationships, to couples engaged to marry, or to cohabiting relationships. These are often called **premarital relationships**, not because they necessarily end in marriage but because the potential for marriage is reasonably high. Marital relationships also usually are romantic relationships, of course, but the term "marital" usually takes precedence over "romantic" in referring to relationships in which a legal marital contract is in force. The romantic relationship domain also includes same-sex partners who experience romantic feelings for each other and consider themselves to be a couple, as well as those who cohabit, have formed a domestic partnership, or have married in states and countries permitting same-sex marriage.

Whereas relationship development is usually studied in romantic relationships, relationship maintenance is usually studied in longer-term, established relationships, such as marital relationships, many of which have ceased their development toward closeness but are maintained at some level (usually a high level) of interdependence. The factors associated with the maintenance and stability of marital relationships have been of special concern to relationship scholars because of the importance of the marital relationship to the partners, to their children, and to society. Indeed, much of the impetus for studying premarital relationships has been the expectation of gaining insight into the marital relationship. The voluminous research on issues concerning marital relationships is discussed in Part 6, "Relationships Over Time." This chapter primarily focuses on the development and maintenance of romantic relationships and friendships; however, most of the theories and constructs addressed to these types of relationship are also used to understand and predict marital satisfaction and stability.

CAUSAL CONDITIONS AFFECTING RELATIONSHIP DEVELOPMENT AND STABILITY

The causal conditions in force at the time of an initial interaction between two people influence whether the pair's interactions will continue and whether their relationship is likely to grow. Among the most important of these causal conditions for predicting the future of the relationship are those associated with closed- and open-field settings (see Chapter 6, "Birth of a Relationship"). If the initial interaction takes place in a closed field where the two persons would suffer penalties for failing to interact, it is likely the relationship will be maintained as long as those initial causal conditions remain stable, although the relationship may never progress beyond a low level of interdependence. A relationship with a co-worker, for example, may be maintained over many years, but the partners' mutual influence often is limited to work activities.

If the causal conditions that originally compelled interaction in the closed field disappear, the relationship may weaken or dissolve. Co-workers who change jobs, neighbors who move to a different locale, and students who transfer to a different school often promise to maintain their relationships—to call or write or get together periodically—but often, after a few such attempts, many of these relationships wither. Among the reasons for the demise of relationships that began in a closed-field setting are, as previously discussed, the higher cost of maintaining a relationship with a person some distance away (closed initial interaction fields almost always put the interactants in close physical proximity) and reduced attraction to a person who no longer is as similar as he or she once was when, for example, work, neighborhood, or school concerns were shared. If, however, strong attraction developed between the individuals in their interactions in the closed field in which they began the relationship, their association may survive these vicissitudes even when the causal forces that initially compelled interaction weaken or disappear. Attraction to another, with all the factors associated with the generation of attraction (see Chapter 6), is assumed to be the preeminent force promoting relationship development.

GENERAL THEORIES OF RELATIONSHIP DEVELOPMENT

Most relationship development theories focus on the microevents and outcomes of the partners' interactions and their implications for relationship growth. As this suggests, most theories assume that the initial interaction takes place in an open field, where the partners are free to interact or not. Another shared assumption, often not explicitly stated, is that it takes time for a relationship to grow. Moreover, as previously noted, most theories of relationship development are addressed, either explicitly or implicitly, to the development of adult romantic relationships, but some are applicable to other varieties of relationship.

The Fundamental Assumption

All theories of relationship development have been derived from, or heavily influenced by, the general theories of social interaction (see Chapter 4, "The Concept of Relationship"). Thus, the fundamental assumption underlying relationship development theories is that in open fields, profitable relationships will be maintained and grow toward closeness, whereas unprofitable relationships will be dissolved. This principle was expressed by Irv Altman and Dalmas Taylor and by George Levinger, among the first relationship development theorists, and endorsed by virtually all who followed. Altman and Taylor (1973) state in their social penetration theory:

> Following initial contact, persons *evaluate immediate rewards and costs* from the exchange and make forecasts, or projections, for potential rewards from future exchange. If evaluations and forecasts are favorable, the relationship should continue to grow; if they are negative, the bond should terminate or

proceed slowly. . . . To the extent that newly obtained rewards outweigh costs, outcomes confirm forecasts, and the cumulative level of positive outcomes in central memory outweighs cumulative costs, the relationship should continue at the same and at more intimate levels of exchange. (p. 128; emphasis in the original)

As Levinger (1980) explains in a later elaboration of his theory:

> Thus a progressing relationship is one in which expected rewards become increasingly probable relative to expected costs; in contrast, a deteriorating relationship is one in which expected rewards become less and less probable, and the costs more and more probable. (p. 525)

Huston and Burgess (1979) state the principle even more succinctly in their overview of relationship development theories: "People join together only insofar as they believe and subsequently find it in their mutual interest to do so" (p. 4).

Although all relationship development theories assume that received and anticipated profitability is a central determinant of relationship development and maintenance, other factors have been shown to be important as well, as we shall discuss.

Interdependence Theory

The fundamental assumption of most theoretical approaches to relationship development is clearly expressed in interdependence theory, which introduced two important constructs addressed to relationship development (e.g., Thibaut & Kelley, 1959): comparison level and comparison level for alternatives.

Comparison level (CL) is theorized to be the standard against which people judge the goodness of the outcomes they are currently receiving in the present relationship and thus their *satisfaction* with the relationship. CL is defined as the average value of all the outcomes known to the person (in relationships of a specific type) weighted by their salience—for example, the likelihood that these outcomes will be brought to mind when evaluating the relationship. People learn of the outcomes typical of a relationship through their own experiences, by observing their friends' and acquaintances' relationships, and also by reading or hearing about the relationships of people they do not personally know. In the salience weighting process, the individual's recently experienced past outcomes, or the outcomes he or she sees currently being received by a close friend in that type of relationship, presumably will be more salient, and thus more heavily weighted, than the outcomes received in distant past relationships or strangers' relationships.

An individual's CL for a given relationship thus represents the individual's *expectations of profit* from the relationship. If current outcomes in the relationship are above CL, the individual should be satisfied with the relationship; if current outcomes are below CL, he or she should be unhappy with it. The prediction that relationship satisfaction will be greater to the extent that partners' actual outcomes exceed their CL expectations was supported by Dainton (2000), who gave people currently involved in a romantic relationship a list of everyday behaviors encompassing five general dimensions: positivity (e.g., behaving in a cheerful and optimistic manner), openness (e.g., self-disclosure), assurance (e.g., of commitment), social networks (e.g., relying on common friends), and sharing tasks. For each activity, participants evaluated the extent to which their partner's behavior compared, either favorably or unfavorably, to the participant's expectation level for that activity. They also completed a relationship satisfaction measure. Dainton found that the more people perceived their partner behaving in ways congruent with expectations, the more satisfied they were with the relationship.

Thus, interdependence theory predicts that the absolute goodness of outcomes a person receives from the relationship does not determine whether the individual will be satisfied with it; rather, *it is the positive or negative discrepancy of current outcomes from CL that determines satisfaction.* As a consequence, which relationships the individual uses as comparison will influence his or her satisfaction. For example, Buunk, Oldersma, and de Dreu (2001) asked some of their participants to list features of their current romantic

relationship that were better than other people's relationships (the *downward comparison* condition) and asked others to simply list their relationship's good features (*no comparison* condition). Those who had thought about the ways in which their relationship was better than others expressed significantly more satisfaction with their relationship.

The second construct important to relationship development introduced by interdependence theory was **comparison level for alternatives (CLalt)**, defined as the goodness of outcomes available in the individual's best currently available alternative to the present relationship (including having no relationship of that type). CLalt is theorized to be the standard by which the individual decides whether to remain in the relationship or terminate it. If the level of outcomes the individual is currently receiving in the relationship is higher than the level of outcomes perceived to be available in the best available alternative relationship, then the individual is *dependent* on the relationship and should maintain it; if current outcomes fall below CLalt, then the relationship is theorized to be vulnerable to dissolution.

Thus, interdependence theory distinguishes between relationship satisfaction (determined by CL) and relationship continuance and stability (determined by CLalt). The theory underscores that although relationship satisfaction is an important determinant of relationship stability, it is not the only determinant. An individual may be satisfied with the relationship, for example, but not dependent on it. According to the theory, if presented with a better alternative, people may dissolve even happy relationships. Thus, it is not necessarily true that only unhappy relationships dissolve. Conversely, it is not necessarily true that if a relationship dissolves, it must have been an unhappy one—which casts doubt on the old saw "No one can break up a happy relationship," an excuse often heard from interlopers who maintain that if the relationship had been happy, their intrusion could not have made a difference. In addition, interdependence theory draws attention to the plight of entrapped individuals who are dissatisfied with their relationship but are unable to leave it because even worse out-

FIGURE 7.1 Different combinations of outcomes, CL, and CLalt from interdependence theory. Interdependence theory predicts that relationship satisfaction and stability are a function of three factors: (1) the level of outcomes a person receives from the relationship, (2) the outcomes a person expects to receive from a relationship (CL), and (3) the outcomes a person believes are available from alternatives to the present relationship. The positive or negative discrepancy of current outcomes from CL determines satisfaction, whereas the discrepancy of current outcomes from CLalt determines stability. For example:

(a) A *satisfying and stable* relationship—in this example, the individual's current outcomes exceed his or her expectations of profit from the relationship and also the outcomes he or she believes are available from alternatives to the relationship.

(c) An *unsatisfying and unstable* relationship—the individual's level of current outcomes is below his or her expectations of profit from the relationship and also below the outcomes he or she anticipates receiving from alternatives to the relationship.

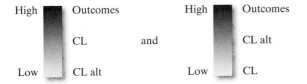

(b) A *satisfying but unstable* relationship—here, the individual's current outcomes exceed his or her expectations but do not exceed the outcomes he or she anticipates receiving from an alternative relationship.

(d) An *unsatisfying but stable* relationship—in this example, the outcomes the individual is currently receiving from the relationship are below his or her expectations of profit from the relationship. However, the individual does not anticipate receiving greater outcomes from alternatives to the relationship.

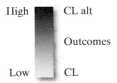

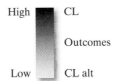

comes lie elsewhere. In other words, it is not necessarily true that if an individual were truly unhappy in the relationship, he or she would leave it (Figure 7.1).

Despite the fact that interdependence theory posits that CLalt, not relationship satisfaction itself, determines relationship stability, satisfaction no doubt figures *indirectly* into stability because the higher the individual's goodness of outcomes in the current relationship, the less likely it is that an alternative relationship will exceed those outcomes. Nevertheless, the usefulness of separating questions of relationship satisfaction from questions of relationship stability has been demonstrated in many studies. For example, sociologists Booth and White (1980) examined interview data from more than 1,000 married persons and compared those who indicated that they were thinking about divorce with those who were not. These investigators concluded that

"there are powerful factors which operate to keep some unhappy husbands and wives from even thinking about divorce and other factors which encourage some happily married people to consider dissolving their marriages" (p. 605). For example, the fact that a wife was employed and less dependent on the marital relationship did not have a strong influence on her marital satisfaction, but it was an important factor in the likelihood that she had thought about divorce.

The Intersection Model

Levinger and Snoek's (1972) intersection model provides a bird's-eye view of stages of relationship development. The model proposes that two people progress from a state of unrelatedness, or *zero contact* (Level 0), to *unilateral awareness* (Level 1), in which one person becomes aware of the other but interaction has not yet occurred. If

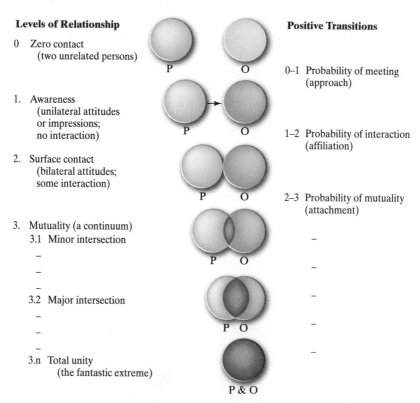

Levels of Relationship

0 Zero contact
   (two unrelated persons)

1. Awareness
   (unilateral attitudes
   or impressions;
   no interaction)

2. Surface contact
   (bilateral attitudes;
   some interaction)

3. Mutuality (a continuum)
   3.1 Minor intersection

   –

   –

   –

   3.2 Major intersection

   –

   –

   –

   3.n Total unity
        (the fantastic extreme)

Positive Transitions

0–1 Probability of meeting
     (approach)

1–2 Probability of interaction
     (affiliation)

2–3 Probability of mutuality
     (attachment)

–

–

–

–

–

–

FIGURE 7.2 An intersection model of pair relatedness. Levinger's model suggests that relationships develop as the partners move to increasingly greater levels of involvement, commitment, and symmetry. Conceived graphically, involvement is the size and shading of the intersection between partners, commitment is the strength or solidarity of the pair's boundary, and symmetry is the relative size of the circles. *From Levinger, "Figure Versus Ground: Micro- and Macroperspectives on the Social Psychology of Personal Relationships" (1994), Fig. 1.2, p. 10.*

interaction occurs, the model proposes that the partners are likely to share limited information about themselves, which is characterized as progression to *surface contact* (Level 2). If the partners disclose unique or interesting information, their superficial exchange may lead to a deeper involvement, or *mutuality* (Level 3). A relationship is theorized to be mutual to the extent that the partners "possess shared knowledge of each other, care emotionally for each other, assume responsibility for promoting the other's outcomes, and have developed private norms for regulating their association" (Levinger, 1977, p. 6). As depicted in Figure 7.2, relationships in the mutuality stage may vary from shallow ("minor intersection") to deep ("total unity").

Levinger (1994) theorizes that as a relationship moves from the initial interaction toward interdependence, at least four important changes occur: (1) communication shifts from superficial to highly personal disclosure, (2) shared knowledge expands from the public to the private spheres, (3) interaction moves from stereotypic role-taking to the mutually expected (as a result of past interactions), and (4) pair maintenance changes from passive to active mutual concern.

The Cohesiveness Model

Whereas the intersection model provides a general view of relationship development, Levinger's cohesiveness model (e.g., 1965, 1979,

1994) addresses whether an established relationship is likely to be maintained or dissolved. The term "cohesiveness" was intended to represent the fact that the model attempts to predict relationship stability—the degree to which the partners are likely to "stick together." The cohesiveness model originally was addressed to marital relationships, but it is applicable to many varieties of relationship.

Incorporating concepts from interdependence theory (e.g., Thibaut & Kelley, 1959) and field theory (Lewin, 1936/1951), Levinger assumes that people who are deciding whether to continue or end their relationship exist in a field of both internally based and externally based forces: (1) attraction forces, which either attract the partners to the relationship or repel them from it; and (2) barrier forces, which block exit from a relationship if ending the relationship is contemplated. A partner's relationship $\text{Cohesiveness}_p = (\text{Sum} [\text{Attractions}_{p\text{-rel}} + \text{Barriers}_{p\text{-rel}}]$ of the present relationship $minus$ $\text{Sum} [\text{Attractions}_{p\text{-alt}} + \text{Barriers}_{p\text{-alt}}]$ of the best alternative relationship).

Relationship continuity is theorized to be the sum of each partner's cohesiveness: $\text{Continuity} = (\text{Cohesiveness}_p + \text{Cohesiveness}_o)$. As Levinger (1991) notes, there is a flaw in his cohesiveness equation that limits its applicability to situations in which both partners' cohesiveness sums are positive; that is, a pair's cohesiveness cannot be the simple sum of the two partners' net scores because "no matter how positive the pair's total score, either individual member's negative score could sink the relationship" (p. 147). Again, in order for a relationship to grow or be maintained, *both* partners must want interaction to continue. If either partner does not wish to continue the relationship, it is likely to be dissolved. In other words, most relationship theorists subscribe to the "weak link hypothesis" (Attridge, Berscheid, & Simpson, 1995; see Chapter 4, "The Concept of Relationship"). The fact that it takes two people to develop or maintain a relationship but only one to dissolve it has at least two implications: First, a developing relationship has less chance to grow than it does to dissolve. Second, it is impossible to predict the future of the relationship by considering the attractions and barriers of only one partner.

ROMANTIC RELATIONSHIP DEVELOPMENT

Whereas general models of relationship development and maintenance address virtually all varieties of relationship, other theorists have exclusively focused on the developmental route romantic relationships are likely to travel.

Romantic Relationship Development: Theory

Most theories of romantic relationship development are *stage theories*, or "successive hurdles" theories, because they posit that once initiated, relationships must satisfy successive sets of criteria to be continued. If the relationship hurdles the first set of criteria, it passes on to a second stage in which it confronts a second set of criteria, and only if those additional criteria are satisfied will the relationship continue on to the succeeding stage, in which it will confront the criteria associated with that stage. Each relationship development stage is believed to revolve around particular issues and problems, and it is their successful resolution that is theorized to propel the couple to the next stage. Stage theories of romantic relationship development usually posit marriage to be the outcome of successful transit through the stages, and marriage also is assumed to be a marker of a close relationship. Although most stage theories expressly address the progression of romantic relationships, several are applicable to the development of other kinds of relationships such as friendship.

Kerckhoff and Davis's Filter Theory

Kerckhoff and Davis (1962) conducted a longitudinal study of college students' courtships and found suggestive evidence that relationship development seemed to involve three sequential "filtering" factors. Filter theory, which was subsequently developed on the basis of these data, posits that potential partners first are evaluated in terms of their *similarity of social attributes* such as religion, education, and social class. After potential partners have been successfully screened on the basis of these attributes, their attitude and value similarity are then assessed; *value consensus* thus is theorized to be the second stage of romantic relationship development. Finally, in a third stage, prospective partners are theorized to be evaluated with respect to *need complementarity*.

Other researchers failed to replicate Kerckhoff and Davis's original findings. Levinger, Senn, and Jorgensen (1970) conducted a large-scale extension of the original Kerckhoff and Davis study at two other colleges and found that neither value similarity nor need complementarity was associated with courtship progress. Levinger (1994) notes that between the time the original study was conducted and the time he and his colleagues attempted a replication, the need scores of college students had changed dramatically in tandem with general cultural shifts in the United States. National surveys showed that most Americans' need for individualism, self-fulfillment, personal freedom, and intimacy rose significantly between 1957 and 1976 (e.g., Veroff, Douvan, & Kulka, 1981). Although it is not clear that this change was responsible for failures to replicate Kerckhoff and Davis's results, changes in macroenvironmental factors may influence relationships in ways few theorists can anticipate.

Reiss's "Wheel of Love" Theory

Another early model of romantic relationship development was proposed by sociologist Ira Reiss (e.g., 1960, 1980). According to his wheel theory of love, the development of a romantic relationship involves four sequential but interrelated phases. In the initial stage, *rapport*, potential partners assess the extent to which they feel at ease with and understand each other. Feelings of rapport, facilitated by social and cultural similarity, increase the likelihood that the partners will begin a process of mutual *self-revelation* in which they disclose varying degrees of information about their values and belief systems. Acts of self-disclosure, in turn, are theorized to contribute to *mutual dependency*, such that each partner becomes dependent on the other's cooperation in enacting certain behaviors—for example, one

needs the other as a confidant or sexual partner. In the fourth and final phase, *intimacy need fulfillment*, the partners evaluate whether their interactions satisfy basic intimacy needs for love, sympathy, and support. Although Reiss theorizes that these processes arise in clear sequence, he also views them as highly interdependent and ongoing throughout the relationship.

Murstein's Stimulus-Value-Role Theory

Yet another early relationship development theory that postulated distinct developmental stages was stimulus-value-role theory (Murstein, 1970, 1987), which posits that romantic relationships systematically move through three stages: (1) a *stimulus* stage in which people perceive the other's physical, social, mental, or reputational attributes (perhaps from their physical appearance) and evaluate the potential profitability of association with the other as well as the extent to which their own qualities might prove attractive to the other; (2) a *value* stage in which actual interaction occurs and the potential partners appraise their value compatibility, such as their attitudes toward politics and religion, which, in turn, helps them assess the potential rewards of continued association; and (3) a *role* stage in which the two partners evaluate themselves and each other concerning their suitability for the role of spouse (or friend, or parent, or presumably any other role perceived to be relevant to the relationship).

Each of the three stages is theorized to be relatively distinct. Murstein (1987) asserts, in fact, that during the first encounter stimulus information is gathered; during the second to seventh interactions, value information is collected; and after the eighth interaction, role assessments are made. Nevertheless, he notes that individuals make stimulus, value, and role assessments of each other throughout the entire courtship process—each factor simply becomes more prominent at a particular time in the developing relationship.

Lewis's Model of Premarital Dyadic Formation

According to the premarital dyadic formation model (Lewis, 1972, 1973), romantic relationships pass through six sequential phases on the road to marriage: (1) perception of similarities in demographic background, values and interests, and personality through observation and interaction; (2) achievement of pair rapport through the perception of similarity, which induces positive emotional and behavior responses to the partner, promotes effective communication, and engenders feelings of self-validation and satisfaction with the other and the relationship; (3) inducement of self-disclosure of intimate personal events and experiences through rapport; (4) role-taking, or empathy with the other's role and taking on the other's perspective, which is facilitated by self-disclosure; (5) achievement of interpersonal role-fit, in which the partners assess their degree of similarity and complementarity in personality, needs, and roles; and (6) achievement of dyadic crystallization, in which the partners become increasingly involved and committed to the relationship and form an identity as a committed couple. All six processes are presumed to be completed prior to marriage.

Scanzoni's Three-Stage Model

Sociologist Scanzoni's (1979) three-stage model of relationship development is addressed to all types of relationships, not only romantic relationships. The first stage of relationship development is posited to be *exploration* (excepting, of course, family relationships and arranged marriages). The exploration stage encompasses the initial interactions between individuals and their efforts to discover relevant information about each other. In their initial interactions, the partners attempt to discover whether further contact with each other is likely to be worthwhile. Scanzoni believes that relationships are extremely fragile in the exploration phase because the partners lack investment in the relationship, their mutual dependence is low or nonexistent, and they can easily choose to terminate their association (again, it is assumed that the initial interactions are taking place in an open field where there is no external penalty for discontinuing interaction). Scanzoni theorizes that if the partners continue to experience attraction and a desire to affiliate with one another, they will communicate their interests and begin to negotiate their roles,

their distribution of resources, and rules to govern the relationship. Communications and negotiations that result in the partners' belief that the relationship will promote their mutual (as opposed to individual) interests is believed to foster the partners' trust of each other.

Mutual trust is theorized to propel the relationship into the second stage, *expansion*, which is marked by higher levels of attraction on an increasing variety of dimensions, enhanced feelings of obligation or concern for mutual well-being, and increasingly complex bargaining and negotiation processes. Evidence of what Scanzoni calls meshed "interest spheres" is often found; for example, the partners may choose to share economic resources or cohabit. The shift from expansion to *commitment*, the third stage, is believed to be so gradual that it often goes unnoticed. Commitment is characterized by strong feelings of solidarity and cohesion. Conflict and conflict resolution, including the renegotiation of obligations and rules, are believed to arise during this phase. Scanzoni posits that willingness to engage in conflict reflects commitment; that is, by the time the partners reach this stage, they realize that some of their goals conflict, but they have enough confidence in the durability of their union to be willing to express negative emotions and work out their differences.

A Composite View of Romantic Relationship Development

Although there is some disagreement in the number, sequence, and features of the phases relationships are theorized to pass through on their way to closeness (see Levinger, 1983/2002), there also is a good deal of overlap. Huston and Burgess (1979, p. 8) provide a composite view of the changes that romantic relationship development theorists believe take place as a romantic relationship grows closer. As the relationship progresses, the partners

- interact more often, for longer periods of time, and in a widening array of settings
- attempt to restore proximity when separated, and feel comforted when proximity is regained

- "open up" to each other (e.g., disclose secrets and share physical intimacies)
- become less inhibited (e.g., more willing to share positive and negative feelings and praise and criticize each other)
- develop their own communication system and become more efficient in using it
- increase their ability to map and anticipate each other's views of social reality
- begin to synchronize their goals and behavior and develop stable interaction patterns
- increase their investment in the relationship, thus enhancing its importance in their lives
- increasingly believe that their separate interests are inextricably tied to the well-being of their relationship
- increase their liking, trust, and love for each other
- see the relationship as irreplaceable or at least unique
- more and more relate to others as a couple rather than as two separate individuals

Romantic Relationship Progression: Research

Empirical research has shown that all the factors associated with attraction (see Chapter 6, "Birth of a Relationship") are associated with romantic relationship progression and maintenance. For example, the Boston Couples Study, a major longitudinal study of romantic relationship continuation and breakup, found that the factors associated with breakups of dating relationships over a 2-year period included unequal involvement in the relationship and dissimilarity of age, educational aspirations, intelligence, and physical attractiveness (e.g., Hill & Peplau, 1998; Hill, Rubin, & Peplau, 1976). Breakups were seldom mutual; women were more likely than men to perceive problems in the relationship and somewhat more likely to precipitate the breakup (which is also true of marital relationships). In addition, men seemed to fall in love more readily than women, and there was some evidence that they took the breakups harder emotionally.

In a more recent longitudinal study, Felmlee, Sprecher, and Bassin (1990) administered a romantic relationship questionnaire to students early and then again late in the semester and found that the rate at which relationships dissolved was a function of CLalt, amount of time spent together, racial dissimilarity, support from the partner's social network, and duration of the relationship (i.e., relationships that had endured longer before the semester began were more likely to survive over the semester). Many other studies have found similar results (e.g., Drigotas & Rusbult, 1992).

Other evidence of the progression of romantic dating relationships was provided by King and Christensen (1983), who constructed a self-report measure of the events likely to occur as a romantic relationship progresses, the Relationship Events Scale (Figure 7.3). The items in this measure of courtship progress form a **Guttman scale**, in which a partner's endorsement of certain events as having occurred in the relationship at a later level of progress signifies that the respondent probably also has endorsed event items representative of earlier progress levels. For example, an individual who has endorsed a Level 3 item ("My partner has said 'I love you' to me") probably also has endorsed items in Level 1 ("My partner has called me an affectionate name (sweetheart, darling, etc.)") and Level 2 ("My partner has referred to me as his/her boyfriend/girlfriend").

King and Christensen summarize the stages they found to be characteristic of developing romantic relationships: First, the partners express mutual attraction and the amount and variety of interactions between them increase. Second, both the partners and the people in their social network come to regard them as a couple. Third, emotional investment in the relationship increases as the participants identify their feelings as love and as they terminate or avoid rival romantic involvements. Fourth, the partners begin to project their relationship into the future and consider pursuing maximum levels of interdependence and commitment. Fifth, the time, money, and activities of the individuals are coordinated for the benefit of joint interests. Sixth, a commitment to the permanence and exclusiveness of the relationship is made in a conventional and relatively irrevocable form, such as

Level 1 Respondent must "pass," or endorse, 2 items in order to have achieved this level of progress.

My partner has called me an affectionate name (sweetheart, darling, etc.).

I have called my partner an affectionate name (sweetheart, darling, etc.).

We have spent a whole day with just each other.

We have arranged to spend time together without planning any activity.

We have felt comfortable enough with each other so that we could be together without talking or doing an activity together.

Level 2 Respondent must pass 1 item.

We have received an invitation for the two of us as a couple.

My partner has referred to me as his/her girlfriend/boyfriend.

I have referred to my partner as my girlfriend/boyfriend.

Level 3 Respondent must pass 2 items.

My partner has said "I love you" to me.

I have said "I love you" to my partner.

My partner does not date anyone other than myself.

I do not date anyone other than my partner.

Level 4 Respondent must pass 1 item.

We have discussed the possibility of getting married.

We have discussed living together.

Level 5 Respondent must pass 2 items.

I have lent my partner more than $20 for more than a week.

My partner has lent me more than $20 for more than a week.

We have spent a vacation together that lasted longer than three days.

Level 6 Respondent must pass 1 item.

We are or have been engaged to be married.

We have lived together or we live together now.

FIGURE 7.3 The Relationship Events Scale. *From C.E. King and Christiansen, "The Relationship Events Scale: A Guttman Scaling of Progress in Courtship," in Journal of Marriage and the Family, 45, pp. 671–678. Reprinted by permission.*

engagement, cohabitation, or marriage. These empirically identified steps in the growth of a courting relationship qualify as stages because it appears that people rarely arrive at a later step in the progression without having experienced the preceding relationship phases.

A growing body of evidence reveals that although certain stages may occur in a relatively invariant order, the amount of time a couple takes to complete any one phase may vary considerably. For example, some investigators have interviewed couples at the point at which they have made a relatively irrevocable commitment such as marriage and asked them to retrospect on the path they took to that commitment (e.g., Huston, Surra, Fitzgerald, & Cate, 1981). Catherine Surra (1985) extensively interviewed newlyweds and asked them to graph their recollected levels of commitment (defined as "the chance of marrying" the spouse during each period of their courtship). The graph presented to respondents was anchored at "0% or greater" on the date the relationship began and 100% on the wedding day. As illustrated in Figure 7.4, Surra found four distinct relationship commitment trajectories to marriage: (1) an ac-

celerated path, in which the partners moved smoothly and rapidly to certainty of marriage, showing steady increases in interdependence and commitment and increasingly withdrawing from social network activities as their relationship progressed; (2) an accelerated–arrested route, in which the couple experienced high levels of interdependence and moved rapidly to a high chance of marriage and then stalled at a plateau before moving on to reach high commitment; (3) an intermediate path, in which the couple progressed in a more moderate fashion toward commitment—not as rapidly as the two accelerated types, and not as slowly as the prolonged type—and tended to be relatively less interdependent, not withdrawing as much from their individual and social network activities as other couples did; and (4) a prolonged trajectory to marital commitment, in which the couple spent a large portion of their courtship time seriously dating and proportionately less time engaged, continuing to interact with their separate and joint social networks more than other couples did. Cate, Huston, and Nesselroade (1986) identified similar courtship patterns.

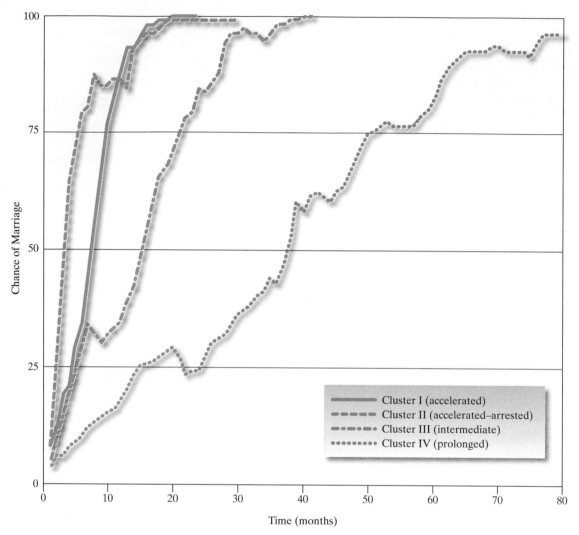

FIGURE 7.4 Trajectories to marriage. Surra (1985) identified four distinct relationship commitment trajectories to marriage. Couples on the *accelerated* path experience a smooth rise in commitment during courtship. Couples on the *accelerated-arrested* route commit early but undergo a plateau or decrease in commitment during engagement, followed by a second rapid rise in commitment. The *intermediate* trajectory is marked by less interdependence and commitment than the accelerated paths. The *prolonged* trajectory is characterized by an extended courtship with gradual increases in commitment. *From Surra, "Courtship Types: Variations in Interdependence between Partners and Social Networks" (1985), Fig. 2, p. 365.*

Surra (1987) later examined the reasons partners gave for their levels of commitment during courtship; however, the couples' accounts provided few insights. For example, the accelerated group tended to refer the fact that it was the appropriate time for marriage for them and the other was the right partner, whereas the prolonged couples often mentioned adverse external circumstances, such as being hired or fired from a job, leaving or entering school, or changing residence, as the reason for their lengthy courtship.

FRIENDSHIP DEVELOPMENT

Compared to romantic and marital relationships, adult friendships have received little attention (see Blieszner, 1994), and as a consequence, theories of adult friendship development are not as numerous or as highly articulated as theories of romantic relationship development. Nevertheless, friendships are important for many reasons. For example, people with many friends are more likely to survive (see Chapter 2, "Relationships and Health"), and at least one study has found that adults more often named a "close friend" as an attachment figure (someone they used as a "safe haven" and "secure base") than persons in any other social category, including romantic partners, mother, father, and other family members (Mikulincer, Gillath, & Shaver, 2002). Children's and adolescents' friendships have received more attention because they are an important context for human development (see Hartup & Laursen, 1991), especially for the development of social competence and other skills, including those involved in school achievement (see Berndt, 1999; Berndt & Ladd, 1989; Hartup, 1989). Many developmental psychologists now believe that same-sex childhood relationships constitute the developmental foundations of adolescent romantic relationships (Furman, Brown, & Feiring, 1999; Hartup, 1999). It would be surprising if early friendships did not influence later romantic relationships, because feelings of friendship, liking, and attachment appear to be an essential component of most contemporary adult romantic relationships (Hendrick & Hendrick, 1993; Meyers & Berscheid, 1997), as discussed in Chapter 11, "Love." The developmental significance of adolescent romantic relationships has recently become of great interest to psychologists as evidence has accumulated that these relationships are neither trivial nor transitory (see Collins, 2002) and that they play an important role in further social and emotional development (Shulman & Collins, 1997; Sippola, 1999).

Most friendship development theorists posit that progress toward a close friendship—one marked by high interdependence—is similar to that of other close relationships, including close romantic relationships, and that the processes involved in that progression also are similar. For example, reviews of the friendship literature (e.g., Blieszner & Adams, 1992; Fehr, 2000; Hays, 1988) suggest that friendships progress from a formation stage to a maintenance stage and, sometimes, a deterioration and dissolution phase, the length of each phase varying from relationship to relationship. The friendship formation phase is believed to involve (1) the identification of another as a potential friend; (2) attraction to the other; (3) increasing interaction, especially daily contact; and (4) the exchange of information through self-disclosure and other means.

During this initial formation stage, partners in open fields are believed to be forecasting the profitability of continuing the relationship (as in other types of relationship). All of the factors associated with attraction are presumed to influence whether the friendship will be continued. For example, college students who evaluated the importance of factors leading to the formation of a close same-sex friendship named attitude similarity as highly desirable (Knapp & Harwood, 1977), and in his longitudinal study of initially unacquainted roommates over the academic year, Berg (1984) found that those who decided not to room together the next year perceived themselves as dissimilar to their roommate. Proximity, to take another example, is an important factor in the selection of friends at all ages, and it is especially critical in children's selection of friends, as is the approval of parents and caretakers, who often take an active role in facilitating or inhibiting friendships among young children (Epstein, 1989).

If the relationship survives the formation stage, it may be maintained across an individual's entire life span, waxing and waning in its level of interdependence. The maintenance phase is viewed as highly variable because friends sustain their relationships in many ways, including sharing activities, spending time together, engaging in rewarding and effective communication, and providing support to each other. Adding a dimension to their view of friendship development that seldom appears in other theories, Blieszner and Adams (1992) posit that the friendship formation stage also "involves the emergence of new networks and the integration of individuals and dyads into existing networks" (p. 16). Network integration may promote friendship maintenance. For example, there is some evidence that dense social networks promote friendship stability by facilitating communication among network members (Adams, 1989). Salzinger (1982) found that members of dense network clusters reported fewer changes in friendships over a period of 3 months than did those who did not belong to such clusters; moreover, reported friendship changes tended to be additional friendships with other members of the cluster and the termination of friendships with noncluster members.

From his own review of the friendship literature, Hays (1988) concludes that friendships may develop more slowly than romantic relationships. In his longitudinal studies of friendship development among college students, Hays found that the first 3 weeks of acquaintance showed Guttman scale progression from superficial interaction such as watching television together to increasing self-disclosure (e.g., discussing personal problems; Hays, 1984, 1985). In his longitudinal study of roommates, Berg (1984), too, found that self-disclosure was higher in the spring than in the fall semester, suggesting a gradual progression toward closeness. Another mark of friendship progression has been hypothesized to be increasingly personalized, synchronized, and efficient communication patterns between the partners (Knapp, 1978; see Baxter & Wilmot, 1986).

The longitudinal studies of friendship conducted by Hays, as well as by others, confirm the fundamental assumption made by virtually all relationship development theorists: Ratings of the benefits received in the relationship are highly correlated with ratings of closeness and satisfaction at all periods in the friendship. However, the association between satisfaction and the individual's progressive levels of relationship involvement—that is, the proportion of time spent with the other—may not be perfectly linear. Eidelson (1980) conducted two separate longitudinal studies in which first-year college students evaluated their satisfaction with their newly developing friend relationships at 2-week intervals over the first semester. Eidelson predicted that satisfaction would rise at low levels of involvement in the beginning of the relationship, but as restrictions on the individual's independence grew at intermediate levels of involvement, acceleration of satisfaction would halt and even decline. Eidelson hypothesized that increasing constraints on independence would cause the individual to pause and carefully evaluate whether current and anticipated rewards and costs from the relationship warranted further increases or a reduction in involvement. Indeed, Eidelson found that satisfaction increased with increasing involvement but decreased slightly (and significantly) at intermediate levels of involvement before rising again with greater involvement (Figure 7.5).

Some friendships dissolve because the partners experience life span changes such that the friendship no long provides the benefits and satisfactions it once did. Rose (1984) asked students to describe why one of their close same-sex friendships had ended and found that most named physical separation, new relationships that crowded out the old (especially new dating relationships or a marital relationship), and a growing dislike of the friend's behavior or personality. Thus, the factors that lead to the dissolution of friendships appear to be little different from those that lead to the dissolution of other kinds of relationship.

The few longitudinal studies of friendship that have been conducted rarely span more than a year. Most studies of friendship across the life span have been cross-sectional examinations of the friendships of people in different age cohorts. Reaching conclusions about the developmental course of relationships from cross-sectional studies is difficult under any circumstances, but it is especially difficult in the domain of friendships because, as Blieszner and Adams (1992) observe, friendship researchers tend to focus on different topics depending on the age cohort sampled, use different measures of the same construct, and include only males or only females and only one age cohort in a single study.

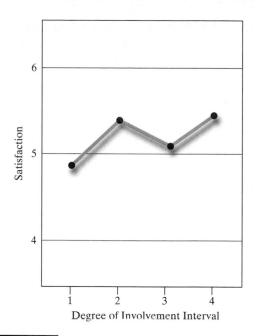

FIGURE 7.5 Degree of involvement. In a longitudinal investigation of friendship formation, Eidelson (1980) found that relationship satisfaction increased as the two people became increasingly involved and spent more time together, then decreased slightly (but significantly) at intermediate levels of involvement (as restrictions on each individual's independence grew), and then finally increased again with greater involvement. *From Eidelson, "Interpersonal Satisfaction and Level of Involvement: A Curvilinear Relationship" (1980), Fig. 5, p. 464.*

The propensity to use only males or only females of one age in studies of friendship makes generalizations of sex differences hazardous. However, at least two sex effects in children's and adolescents' friendship seem to be well established: First, children and adolescents tend to have friends of the same sex, and second, girls' friendships tend to be more intimate than boys' friendships (Maccoby, 1990). For example, girls' relationships generally include more self-disclosure. The sex difference in intimacy of friendships has been found in fifth graders (Buhrmester & Furman, 1987), in high school students, and in college students and other adults. Moreover, whether the individual is male or female, his or her interactions

with women (whether friend or acquaintance) tend to be more intimate (e.g., Reis & Wheeler, 1991; see Chapter 6, "Birth of a Relationship"). Thus, females' same-sex friendships and men's cross-sex friendships are likely to be more intimate than men's same-sex friendships. The greater intimacy of friendships involving women is supported by evidence that men seem to differentiate between their same- and opposite-sex friends to a greater extent than women do; men are more likely to emphasize the affective aspects (emotional support) of their friendships with women and the instrumental aspects (shared activities) of their friendships with men.

Same-sex friendships, at least the amount of time spent in social interaction with same-sex friends, appears to decrease in adulthood, according to a longitudinal study conducted by Reis, Lin, Bennett, and Nezlek (1993). Men and women completed the Rochester Interaction Record for 2 weeks, reporting their social interactions and evaluating them along several dimensions, at three separate times: during their first year of college, again in their senior year, and yet again about 6 years later (when the participant was about 30 years of age). From college onward, same-sex interactions decreased (including interactions with same-sex best friends), as did mixed-sex (more than 2-person) interactions and group (more than 3-person) interactions. Opposite-sex interactions increased, however, including interaction with opposite-sex best friends. Moreover, the reported intimacy of the interactions increased after college (although satisfaction with those interactions did not).

Although the quantity of time spent in interaction with same-sex friends may decrease in adulthood, cross-sex friendships appear to be less stable than same-sex friendships, as previously discussed (see Chapter 5, "Varieties of Relationship"). Differences in the partners' motivations for establishing and continuing the friendship may be partly responsible (Bleske & Buss, 2000) but other factors undoubtedly contribute, including the operation of gender stereotypes involving women's sociability and men's instrumentality, which influence each partner's interpretation of the other's behavior and erode feelings of solidarity (McWilliams & Howard, 1993). In addition, romantic relationship commitments may interfere with the maintenance of cross-sex friendships.

Cross-sectional studies suggest that the number of friendships a person has does not vary a great deal across the life span. For example, Nahemow and Lawton (1975), who studied the effects of similarity on friendship, found that young people, middle-aged adults, and older adults did not differ in their number of friends (2 to 2.5). Whereas the number of friends or other close relationship partners may be relatively stable, their identity may not be—hence, the often heard sarcastic description of some relationship partners as the individual's "new best friend." The scarcity of longitudinal studies of friendship over substantial time periods leaves unanswered the question of the frequency of friend "turnover." Lang and Carstensen (1994) found that the number of close relationships of "very old" people and "younger old" people did not differ, although social network size and social contact do shrink with age (see Chapter 2, "Relationships and Health"). Lang, Staudinger, and Carstensen (1998) found, however, that the identity of elderly persons' close relationship partners may change depending on whether nuclear family members are available. When family members are available, nonrelatives are rarely reported as being close, but when relatives are not available, nonkin may be incorporated into the individual's circle of close relationships.

Other systematic changes in the composition of adults' friendships over time have yet to be identified. With respect to children's and adolescents' relationships, Laursen and Bukowski's (1997) review of the literature suggests that fewer than half qualify as close relationships, and those that are close usually are some combination of friendships and parent–child, sibling, and romantic relationships. Consistent with Surra and Milardo's (1991) findings with young adults (see Chapter 2, "Relationships and Health"), Laursen and Bukowski also conclude that the size and diversity of the total relationship network correspond little to the composition of the close relationship network of children and adolescents.

PROCESSES ASSOCIATED WITH RELATIONSHIP DEVELOPMENT AND MAINTENANCE

In addition to overlap in theorists' views of the nature of the sequential stages that developing relationships pass through, there also is a good deal of overlap in the processes that stage theorists identify as important to relationship development. Other theorists also believe these processes are important, but unlike stage theorists, they do not specify a certain order or time in which they occur in the life of the relationship.

Self-Disclosure: Altman and Taylor's Social Penetration Theory

Of all the processes that have been theorized to be essential to relationship development, none has been viewed as more important than the interactants' willingness to disclose information about themselves to each other (Harvey & Omarzu, 1997). Communication of self-relevant information appears in almost all relationship development theories, and it plays a central role in one of the first and most influential theories exclusively addressed to relationship development, social penetration theory.

Altman and Taylor (1973) proposed that relationships progress toward greater closeness and commitment as a function of the reciprocal exchange of information. Initially, relationships are believed to be characterized by superficial, shallow disclosures in which the partners reveal relatively impersonal information about themselves along a limited number of dimensions. If the initial interaction is rewarding, and if each partner expects that future interactions will continue to be rewarding, the theory predicts that the partners will continue to interact and will increase the *depth* of their self-disclosures by revealing increasingly intimate, emotional, and detailed personal information about themselves. The partners' self-disclosures are theorized to also increase in *breath* by providing information along a greater variety of dimensions. In sum, the principle mechanism by which relationships are believed to become progressively closer is self-disclosure.

Researchers initially believed that it was self-disclosure itself that produced feelings of intimacy and propelled the relationship forward on its path toward closeness. Today, in accord with Reis and Shaver's (1988) theory of intimacy (see Chapter 1, "First Relationships"), it is recognized that it is the *responsiveness* of the partner to the individual's disclosures—not self-disclosure per se—that produces intimacy and promotes further relationship development. Relationship growth is furthered by responses to self-disclosures that leave the partner feeling validated, understood, cared for, accepted, and nurtured. Assuming that the partner is responsive, Reis and Shaver hypothesize that, as opposed to the disclosure of factual information, it is the self-disclosure of feelings and emotions that is important to further relationship development, a hypothesis that has received some support (Lin, 1992).

Psychologists long had an interest in self-disclosure (e.g., Jourard, 1964, 1971), but it was social penetration theory that generated hundreds of experimental studies of the antecedents and consequences of self-disclosure. Collins and Miller's (1994) review of the voluminous literature concludes that (1) people who disclose personal information tend to be liked more than people who disclose less, (2) people disclose more to those they initially like, and (3) people like others who disclose to them. Collins and Miller observe, "Disclosing to another communicates that we trust that person to respond appropriately, that we value his or her opinions and responses, that we are interested in knowing them and having them know us" (p. 471). In naturalistic situations, attraction and self-disclosure probably operate in a reciprocal causation feedback loop: Attraction increases disclosure, disclosure further enhances attraction, and attraction generates more disclosure. This reciprocal process may be responsible for the fact that some researchers find that self-disclosure *precedes* the development of romantic feelings (e.g., Berg & McQuinn, 1986; see Huston & Levinger, 1978) whereas others report that it *follows* positive feelings for the other (e.g., Adams & Shea, 1981).

In addition to the association between self-disclosure and attraction, the **principle of self-disclosure reciprocity** has been documented by many researchers. Some individuals disclose more to others and some individuals are disclosed to more than others. For example, Bradford, Feeney, and Campbell (2002) have found adult attachment style differences in this regard. However, studies using the social relations model find that these individual-level effects are small compared to relationship effects, or dyadic reciprocity in self-disclosure (see Kenny, 1994a). For instance, Miller and Kenny (1986) found that relationship factors were responsible for most of the variance (over 80%) in self-disclosure of highly personal topics in a group of sorority women. Although one partner's disclosure is likely to be reciprocated—usually by a disclosure matched in content and depth—there are exceptions to the rule. When the disclosure is perceived to be manipulative in intent, symptomatic of psychopathology, or situationally inappropriate, it is not likely to be reciprocated (see Berscheid & Reis, 1998). In addition, the failure to reciprocate another's disclosure is sometimes used to signal that the recipient of the disclosure does not wish to develop the relationship further (see Miell & Duck, 1986).

Both self-disclosure and intimacy are hallmarks of close, as opposed to casual, relationships. For example, when Parks and Floyd (1996) asked a group of college students to list the elements of a close friendship, both men and women overwhelmingly made references to aspects of self-disclosure (talking, disclosing, "telling each other everything," and sharing information) and intimacy (experiencing trust, acceptance, respect, and understanding). Children, particularly those in middle childhood (11 to 13 years old), appear to possess a similar view of friendship, for they differentiate friends from acquaintances by willingness to self-disclose, attempts to understand each other, and also perceived similarity (Bigelow, 1977; for a review see Rubin, Coplan, Nelson, Cheah, & Lagace-Seguin, 1999).

Planalp and Benson (1992) provide further evidence of the perceived association among disclosure, intimacy, and relationship status. Naive observers listened to taped conversations between two individuals and then judged whether the conversation was between friends or acquaintances and listed the reasons for their decision. When the conversants showed mutual and shared knowledge about each other, engaged in greater self-disclosure, and made more intimate, emotional, and detailed exchanges, they were judged to be friends rather than acquaintances. In a follow-up study, Planalp (1993) analyzed the content of the conversations judged in the previous study and found that friends' conversations contained evidence of a great deal of prior reciprocal disclosure. Friends truly did possess more mutual knowledge, including shared information about other people the friends knew and awareness of each other's past and present life, including relationships, activities, and beliefs. In contrast, the conversations of acquaintances revealed little knowledge of each other's present life. Acquaintances' disclosures tended to be more superficial, ranging from people they might know in common to introductory revelation of basic biographical information. Reciprocal disclosure and intimacy also appear to be features of the close relationships of children. A meta-analysis of studies examining aspects of friendship in middle childhood and early adolescence revealed that in their interactions with friends, children and young adolescents demonstrate greater reciprocity of affect and emotional intensity, and higher levels of emotional understanding, than they do in their interactions with nonfriends (Newcomb & Bagwell, 1995).

Consistent with the predictions of many relationship development theories, self-disclosure and intimacy appear to be integrally associated with relationship satisfaction and stability. Research on dating and marital relationships reveals that individuals who self-disclose, who perceive their partners as self-disclosing, and who believe their disclosures and confidences are understood by their partners experience greater need fulfillment, satisfaction, and love than individuals whose relationships contain lower levels of intimacy and disclosure (e.g., Prager & Buhrmester, 1998; Rosenfeld & Bowen,

1991; Weigel & Ballard-Reisch, 1999). Indeed, people often deliberately use self-disclosure and expressions of intimacy as a means of furthering or solidifying their romantic relationships. When Haas and Stafford (1998) asked men and women involved in committed homosexual romantic relationships to report on the behaviors they used to maintain their relationships, about half reported that open and honest self-disclosure and communication about thoughts and feelings are effective maintenance strategies. Research conducted with heterosexual samples yields similar results (see Dindia, 2000). People also rely on self-disclosure as a means of facilitating their friendships (Afifi, Guerrero, & Egland, 1994; Canary, Stafford, Hause, & Wallace, 1993) and they view intimate and supportive friendships as more satisfying and enjoyable than those that are not (Bank & Hansford, 2000).

Although women generally self-disclose more than men do, especially in same-sex interactions (as discussed in Chapter 10, "Dispositional Influences"), the process of revealing oneself to another plays a critical role in relationship development for both sexes. It is assumed, as previously noted, to play an especially important role in the beginning of romantic relationships. Romantic relationship stage theorists generally posit that other processes become more important as the relationship progresses. There is some evidence to support this view. For example, the longitudinal Boston Couples Study of developing courtship relationships found that dating couples had little additional factual information to disclose to each other after a relatively short period of time (Rubin, Hill, Peplau, & Dunkel-Schetter, 1980). Friendship development studies also find that self-disclosure may be high early in the relationship, but later conversations focus more on mundane matters (e.g., Hays, 1985).

Trust

Growth in trust of the partner figures into virtually all theories of relationship development. The construct of **trust**, usually defined as belief in the responsiveness and beneficence of another in time of need, has had a long history in psychology (Holmes, 1991). It often has been viewed as a personality trait—a chronic personal predisposition to trust or distrust others in general (e.g., Rotter, 1980). More recently, trust has been viewed as an important component of another trait—adult attachment style orientation. However, most relationship development theorists prefer to view trust as a relationship variable—that is, as specific to a particular relationship partner.

Trust is important in relationship development because, as theorists Holmes and Rempel (1989) explain, "the desire for increased closeness raises the specter of giving more to the relationship and becoming more dependent on the partner" (p. 187). Growing dependence, in turn, places the individual in a position of risk. Without an accompanying growth of trust in the partner, it is unlikely that the relationship will proceed to high levels of interdependence. The close association between dependency and trust is reflected in Attridge, Berscheid, and Sprecher's (1998) development of two reliable "companion" scales that assess dependence and insecurity in a relationship.

Larzelere and Huston (1980) were among the first to develop an instrument to assess an adult's trust of a specific relationship partner. Like most other trust theorists, these investigators posit that "trust exists to the extent that a person believes another . . . to be benevolent and honest" (p. 596), where benevolence refers to whether the partner is selfishly motivated as opposed to genuinely concerned with the individual's welfare. They administered their 8-item Dyadic Trust Scale, as well as a number of other scales measuring feelings such as love, to a large sample of dating persons and married couples. The latter included newlywed couples, longer-married couples, and also separated or divorced partners, who completed the Trust Scale with reference to their former spouses. As predicted, divorced partners and former dating partners had the least trust for their (ex-) partners than did other groups, followed in order by casual dating partners, exclusively dat-

ing partners, engaged and/or cohabiting couples, and finally longer-married couples and newlyweds, both of whom displayed the most trust. Casual daters trusted their partners significantly less than did engaged, cohabiting, or newlywed couples, and exclusive daters trusted their partners significantly less than newlyweds.

Larzelere and Huston found that trust of the partner was strongly, and positively, associated with love for the partner in all groups and for both males and females. Trust was also significantly associated with depth of self-disclosure to the partner, and moreover, the strength of the association increased as commitment to the relationship increased. Partners displayed reciprocity of trust; in fact, trust reciprocity was even stronger than the partners' reciprocity of love. Importantly, Lazelere and Huston found that their relationship-specific measure of trust always corresponded more to love and self-disclosure in the relationship than a measure of trust of "people in general."

Rempel, Holmes, and Zanna's (1985) Trust Scale assesses three dimensions of trust these investigators believe correspond to relationship progression: (1) predictability of the partner's behavior; (2) dependability, which goes beyond predictions of the partner's behavior to judgments of the partner's character in terms of honesty, reliability, and so on; and (3) faith, or emotional security that enables individuals "to go beyond the available evidence and feel, with assurance, that their partner will be responsive and caring despite the vicissitudes of an uncertain future" (p. 97).

From their consideration of apparent differences in trust between Americans and Japanese, Yamagishi and Yamagishi (1994) have developed a potentially useful theory that distinguishes between *trust*, which is based on the expectation that the partner will behave with good will and benign intent, and *assurance*, which is based on the incentive structure within which the relationship is embedded and that helps ensure that the partner will behave in trustworthy ways. Yamagishi and Yamagishi illustrate the difference:

Suppose I have a tie with the Mafia, and my trading partner knows this. I am certain he will not cheat on me; he knows that if he does he will be quickly sent to a mortuary. My expectation of the partner's "honesty" is based on the fact that acting "honestly" is in his own interest, not on the belief that he is a benevolent person. Here, assurance exists but not trust. (p. 132)

Both trust and assurance are theorized to increase the predictability of the partner's interaction behavior. Where there is no strong incentive structure to promote assurance, then trust of the partner becomes extremely important. If, however, the social structure provides assurance, as it does for business relationships in Japan, trust in the good will of the partner becomes less important. Similarly, in societies in which the social structure provides assurance for marital relationships, trust that the partner will not behave in harmful ways is, again, less important. Yamagishi and Yamagishi provide survey evidence that challenges the popular impression that partners in Japanese social and business relationships are more trusting than Americans are in their relationships. Americans were found to be significantly more trustful of others in general than the Japanese, who, at least in business, prefer to interact with others who are embedded in a dense network of committed relationships that provides assurance.

Commitment

Virtually all theories of relationship development single out the point when the partners commit themselves to the relationship as a special one, for a variety of reasons. When the partners make an explicit commitment to maintaining their relationship, psychological commitment itself constitutes a new causal condition that promotes continuance of the relationship through several cognitive processes. In addition, the act of commitment often generates changes in other causal conditions that are themselves associated with relationship stability, such as moving to the same residence (a physical environmental condition) or being viewed by parents and friends as a cou-

ple (a social environmental condition). Commitment is believed to be an especially important factor in the development of romantic relationships. Commitment to marry, it will be recalled, is the final stage in King and Christensen's (1983) Relationship Events Scale, and marriage itself signals a major commitment to the relationship for most people.

In an early article outlining the need for research on commitment in marriage, Rosenblatt (1977) defined **commitment** as *"an avowed or inferred intent of a person to maintain a relationship"* (p. 73, emphasis in original). This global conceptualization of commitment refers to the individual's subjective state of mind, and it is the definition that most theorists and researchers of commitment subsequently adopted. When commitment is viewed as a property of the individual, certain dispositional variables become important in predicting commitment. For example, a secure attachment style has been found to be associated with a willingness to commit, whereas an avoidant attachment style is associated with reluctance (Davis, 1999).

Some relationship development theorists believe commitment is better viewed as a property of the relationship as opposed to a property of the individual (e.g., Rusbult, Wieselquist, Foster, & Witcher, 1999); knowledge of *both* partners' commitment to the relationship and the influence of each partner's commitment on the other's commitment is thus necessary to forecast relationship development. When commitment is viewed as a property of the relationship, asymmetry of commitment between the partners becomes a consideration because the less committed person represents the relationship's weak link insofar as the continuance of the relationship, and its further development, is concerned.

Theorists also have differed with respect to whether commitment should be viewed as a discrete variable or one that varies in degree, and whether commitment is a stable state or subject to continuous reconsideration. After reviewing the evidence relevant to these two issues, Adams and Spain (1999) argue persuasively that it is most useful to view commitment as a dynamic process rather than a static construct and that the most appropriate index of commitment is not its level at a given point in time but rather its variability over time. And finally, theorists differ with respect to whether commitment is most usefully viewed as a unidimensional, global intention to continue the relationship or as a multidimensional construct.

Johnson's Theory of Commitment

The multidimensional view is reflected in the work of sociologist M. P. Johnson (1991, 1999), who has provided a comprehensive theoretical analysis of commitment. Johnson (1991) views commitment as a personal, subjective decision to maintain a relationship through "lines of action that will prevent the elimination of interdependence" (p. 120). However, Johnson theorizes that an individual's decision to continue a relationship is a function of three different, subjectively felt, types of commitment: *personal* commitment, or the individual's feeling that he or she wants to continue the relationship; *moral* commitment, or the feeling that it ought to be continued; and *structural* commitment, or the feeling that he or she must continue it. Personal and moral commitment, Johnson theorizes, is experienced as having originated internally, whereas structural commitment is experienced as having external sources.

Personal commitment, or the *desire* to continue the relationship, is itself believed to be a function of three components: attitude toward the relationship, attitude toward the partner, and relational identity, or the extent to which the individual's involvement in the relationship as wife, husband, sister, and so on has been incorporated into his or her self-concept. Johnson notes that the distinction between an individual's commitment to the partner as opposed to the relationship often is not recognized in commitment theory and research. Although the two doubtless are highly correlated in most instances, it is nonetheless an important distinction because an individual's commitment to the partner and his or her welfare may require that the relationship be relinquished, as in cases of "tough love," imposed when the relationship is enabling the partner to continue along destructive paths.

However, as Johnson (1991) discusses, the fact that relationships are dynamic systems that change over time raises the question of *what* relationship the individual is committed to continuing, even when it is clear that the individual is committing to the relationship:

> Suppose that Year 1 of a relationship between two particular people is that of a seriously dating couple, while Year 3 of the relationship is that of a married couple with a child. Has this couple "maintained" their relationship, or are they now involved in a "new" relationship? (p. 119)

Or, if a couple has moved from a romantic courtship relationship to a marital relationship, have the partners maintained their courtship relationship, or did they dissolve that relationship in order to establish a different type of relationship that involves either a renewal or a change in level of commitment? Some contemporary brides and grooms revise the traditional marriage vows to specify more exactly the kind of relationship they are committing themselves to—that is, they commit themselves to the partner and the relationship not "so long as we both shall live" but rather "so long as we both shall love," foreseeing the possibility that the present relationship may change into one to which they do not wish to commit themselves to continuing.

Moral commitment, the subjective feeling that the relationship ought to be continued, often has its source in the individual's religious beliefs and may be responsible for the fact that religiosity has consistently been found to be associated with marital stability. Religiosity is likely to be associated with behaviors that preserve the relationship. For example, most religions prohibit adultery. Extramarital sex, in turn, is named worldwide as the most frequent cause of divorce (see Chapter 12, "Mate Selection and Sex"). In their longitudinal study of marital problems and subsequent divorce, Amato and Rogers (1997) found, as others have, that extramarital sex was a precursor of divorce but that religiosity (measured by frequency of church attendance) was strongly, and negatively, correlated with infidelity.

Structural commitment, an individual's feeling that the relationship *must* be continued, is theorized to be a function of (1) irretrievable investments in the relationship in terms of time and other resources; (2) social reaction, usually from members of the individual's social network; (3) difficulty of termination procedures (breaking up a marriage is almost always time-consuming and costly); and (4) availability of acceptable alternatives.

Adams and Jones (1997) empirically analyzed the many questionnaire items investigators have used to measure commitment and concluded that there are three dimensions of marital commitment: (1) commitment to the spouse, based on love and personal dedication; (2) commitment to marriage, perhaps as a sacred institution; and (3) feelings of entrapment based on an appraisal of factors that make dissolving the marriage difficult, such as financial hardship. These three dimensions map closely onto Johnson's (e.g., 1991) concepts of personal, moral, and structural commitment, and the entrapment dimension captures Levinger's (1965) concept of "barrier forces" in his cohesiveness model. From their investigation, Adams and Jones also concluded that each of the three dimensions may contribute to the stability of a relationship in different ways at different times and may be more or less potent in affecting stability under different circumstances. With respect to the latter, for example, when people are satisfied with their relationship, barriers to its termination are not likely to be salient, nor is the availability of relationship alternatives; these aspects of commitment are likely to become relevant only when the individual becomes dissatisfied with the relationship.

Kelley's Theory of Commitment

Kelley (1983/2002b) observes that the construct of commitment has been used primarily to predict whether a relationship will endure. As a consequence, Kelley believes that forecasters need to identify the causal conditions that act to keep a person in a relationship as well as those that push or draw the person out of the relationship. Thus, unlike most commitment theorists, who view commitment as the individual's subjective intention to maintain a relationship, Kelley views commitment as a set of causal conditions and processes that contribute to relationship stability. Causal conditions that keep the person in the relationship, such as satisfaction with the relationship and the costs that would be incurred on leaving the relationship, are called the pros of the relationship. Conditions that push or draw the person out of the relationship, such as the attractiveness of an alternative relationship, represent the cons of the relationship.

Kelley (1983/2002b) theorizes that the key feature of the causal conditions associated with relationship continuance is the "consistency with which, over time and situations, the pros outweigh the cons" (p. 289) for each person in the relationship. Moreover, *"If membership is to be stable, the average degree to which the pros outweigh the cons must be large relative to the variability in this difference"* (p. 290, emphasis in the original). If there is a large difference in favor of the pros for each partner, then there can be a high degree of fluctuation in the level of the pros and cons without affecting the stability of the relationship because the pros will continue to outweigh the cons, even though they may come close to converging at times. If the average degree to which the pros outweigh the cons is small, however, it is important that each remain relatively constant because, if they fluctuate, the cons are likely to outweigh the pros at some point for at least one of the partners, putting the relationship at risk for dissolution. Thus, Kelley views commitment as continuously in flux, with the pro and con causal conditions fluctuating over time.

Like most commitment theorists, Kelley sees causal conditions associated with relationship satisfaction as pros for the relationship. Fluctuation in satisfaction was investigated in two longitudinal studies conducted by Arriaga (2001). Satisfaction and commitment were assessed in recently formed romantic relationships (averaging 8 weeks' duration) and each of these variables was reassessed each week for 9 weeks. Relationship status (intact vs. dissolved) was then assessed 4 months later. In accord with past findings, partners in intact relationships as opposed to partners in dissolved relationships were likely to have been more satisfied initially, to have become more satisfied over time, and to have a higher overall satisfaction level during the period investigated. However, even after controlling for overall satisfaction level, the degree of *fluctuation in satisfaction* was found to influence the stability of the relationship: Greater fluctuation was associated with greater chance of breakup, and this was particularly true of individuals whose satisfaction levels were either increasing or high overall. Those who exhibited relatively stable satisfaction levels reported higher levels of commitment to the relationship than did those whose satisfaction levels fluctuated. Arriaga thus found that even happy relationships were likely to end if the partners were not *consistently* happy and that even less happy relationships persisted so long as the partners' satisfaction levels remained stable.

Rusbult's Investment Model

Despite its name, Caryl Rusbult's (e.g., 1983) investment model is a theory of relationship commitment, and as such, it has been responsible for the lion's share of empirical research on relationship commitment and related phenomena. Like Levinger's (e.g., 1999) cohesiveness model, the investment model was deeply influenced by interdependence theory propositions and constructs. Although most tests of the model have involved romantic relationships, it has been empirically shown to be applicable to many other types of relationships, including friendships.

The investment model posits that Commitment = f (Satisfaction − Alternatives + Investments) (Figure 7.6). In accord with interdependence theory, Satisfaction = f([Rewards − Costs] − Comparison Level) (Rusbult, 1983). Perception of alternatives also is as defined by interdependence theory. Investments, which play only a minor role in Johnson's view of commitment and none in interdependence theory, play a central role in this model. Rusbult views **investments** as anything of value to the individual that has become attached to the relationship, including time, money, energy, and reputation. Investments usually increase the costs of dissolving the relationship because many, if not most, relationship investments are not transferable out of the relationship; if the relationship is

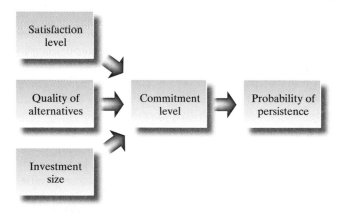

FIGURE 7.6 Rusbult's investment model. Like interdependence theory, the investment model recognizes that the outcomes an individual obtains from his or her relationship, as well as the perceived quality of alternatives to that relationship, are important contributors to relationship stability. Specifically, this model proposes that people will feel committed to their relationships to the extent that they feel satisfied, believe that they have few good alternatives to the relationship, and have invested important resources in the relationship. This feeling of commitment, in turn, influences whether or not a relationship will endure. *From Rusbult, Martz, & Agnew, "The Investment Model Scale: Measuring Commitment Level, Satisfaction Level, Quality of Alternatives, and Investment Size" (1998), Fig. 1, p. 360.*

dissolved, those investments either are lost altogether or decline in value.

The investment model predicts that an individual's decision to maintain the relationship is a direct function of the individual's commitment to the relationship—*not* of his or her satisfaction with it. Satisfaction is theorized to play a role in relationship stability only through its contribution to commitment level. Thus, the investment model implies that satisfaction and commitment need not be strongly associated. For example, strong commitment may be maintained in the face of dissatisfaction as a result of poor alternatives and large investments. Many studies conducted in the United States and other countries have supported the basic tenets of the investment model (see Le & Agnew, 2003; Rusbult, Martz, & Agnew, 1998).

In an initial test of the model (Rusbult, 1983), partners in ongoing romantic relationships answered questions about their rewards, costs, alternatives, investments, satisfaction, and commitment every 17 days over 7 months. Before the study ended, 29% of the relationships had dissolved. Relationship commitment increased with increases in satisfaction, declines in the quality of alternatives, and increases in investment size. Although increases in rewards led to corresponding increases in satisfaction, variations in costs did not affect satisfaction until later stages of involvement (3 to 7 months), at which time increases in costs were associated with decreases in satisfaction. Similarly, increasing rewards were associated with increases in commitment, but changes in costs had no impact on commitment until later in the relationship. In sum, for those men and women whose relationships were maintained over the 7 months of the study, rewards increased, costs rose slightly, satisfaction grew, quality of alternatives declined, investment size increased, and commitment to the relationship rose. The reverse was true for those whose relationships dissolved.

Interestingly, Rusbult (1983) found that a small subgroup of people did not dissolve the relationship despite the fact that they experienced relatively low increases in satisfaction; moreover, they continued to invest heavily in the relationship. Their behavior perhaps is explained by the fact that their alternatives had declined in quality. The economic concept of "sunk costs" also may be relevant. Sunk costs often prompt people to try to retrieve profits from their past poor financial investments by "throwing good money after bad" (continuing to invest) instead of admitting they made a bad investment decision and cutting their losses short. Prior investments in a relationship may become sunk costs that keep a person in the relationship, desperately trying to retrieve some profit.

Findings from Kurdek's (2000) 5-year longitudinal study of heterosexual spouses and cohabiting gay and lesbian couples supports basic interdependence theory propositions as well as several of its cohesiveness model and investment model variations. Over the period, the couples evaluated their relationships along four dimensions: (1) attraction to the relationship (current relationship reward and cost outcomes and their discrepancy with CL and CLalt); (2) constraints against leaving the relationship (level of investment and termination barriers); (3) commitment; and (4) relationship satisfaction. Kurdek found that all partners, hetero- or homosexual, who reported high levels of attraction to the relationship and high levels of constraint against leaving it tended to report correspondingly high levels of commitment. Both spouses and homosexual partners who showed declines in attraction during the 5-year period showed reductions in their commitment level. Declines in constraints against leaving the relationship also were associated with reductions in commitment for spouses but not for same-sex partners.

Kurdek also found that changes in an individual's attraction to the relationship and constraints against dissolution forecast later changes in his or her partner's commitment level. Although relationship commitment was positively correlated with satisfaction for both heterosexual and homosexual couples, satisfaction was *not* the most significant predictor of commitment: Both attraction to the relationship (which included the perception of alternatives) and constraints (barriers and investments) were uniquely and significantly associated with commitment to the relationship. Similarly, Rusbult and her colleagues (1998) found that satisfaction, attraction, and investment size accounted for unique variance in commitment level, which was associated with romantic relationship stability 2 to 5 months later.

Rusbult and her associates (1999) have theorized that commitment and trust are integrally connected: "Trust develops when the partner observes that the individual possesses feelings of commitment sufficient to motivate costly and effortful maintenance behaviors such as sacrifice, accommodation, or derogation of alternatives" (p. 444). As people observe their partner's trust and commitment growing, they become more willing to increase their dependence on the relationship, to increase their investments, and, in short, to increase their commitment to the relationship. As the partner perceives that the individual's trust and commitment have increased, the partner, in turn, should be even more willing to invest in the relationship and, in this and other ways, increase commitment to the relationship. Trust and commitment, in other words, are theorized to exhibit what Rusbult and colleagues term "mutual cyclical growth." Thus, the investment model highlights that commitment is associated with relationship-maintaining behaviors, including self-sacrifice, accommodation and facilitation of the partner's interests and welfare, and other behaviors that require the individual to forgo immediate self-gratification and self-interest. These behaviors, which are conducive to relationship development and maintenance, are discussed in Chapter 13, "Satisfaction and Stability."

Commitment-Preserving Processes

Commitment appears to be associated with several psychological processes, some of which produce what have been called positive illusions about the relationship, that act to preserve the commitment and to promote relationship stability.

Positive Illusions and Relationship Threat

Just as positive illusions in other personal realms appear to be protective of mental and physical health (see Taylor, Kemeny, Reed, Bower, & Grue-

newald, 2000), positive illusions that reduce the individual's doubts and anxiety about the partner and the relationship may be beneficial to the relationship's stability. As Holmes (2000) explains, most people

> need to quell feelings of emotional vulnerability that result from the perceived risks of depending on a less than perfect partner. With serious stakes attached to the situation of interdependence, they need to possess a sense of conviction that the partner really is the "right" person. (p. 464)

The stakes are indeed serious, especially in marriage. Norval Glenn (1991), sociological scholar of marriage and the family, comments that "when the probability of marital success is as low as it is in the United States today, to make a strong unqualified commitment to marriage . . . is so hazardous that no totally rational person would do it" (p. 269).

Many romantic partners aren't "totally rational," as John Holmes, Sandra Murray, and their associates have demonstrated in a series of studies. People in the thrall of a romantic relationship are notorious for developing rosy and idealistic images of their partner—images that seem to be relatively impervious to the reality everyone around them sees. Murray and Holmes (1993) wondered how people cope with threats to their positive illusions about their partners and the relationship and somehow manage to maintain their cherished visions even when those visions are under attack. To find out, people in ongoing dating relationships were asked to complete a scale measuring the extent to which their partner "initiated conflicts" in the relationship. The experimenters assumed that most people believe that a partner who frequently initiates conflict is an undesirable partner and detrimental to relationship quality. After completing the scale, Murray and Holmes then exposed half of the participants (those in the *threat* condition) to bogus *Psychology Today* articles by "relationship experts" that claimed "conflict engagement" actually was a symptom of a strong, intimate relationship (those in the control condition performed an unrelated task and read the article later). All participants were then asked to complete another scale that asked them to describe their partners' willingness to engage in conflict and also to write open-ended narratives describing the ways in which their partners inhibited or facilitated the development of intimacy in the relationship. The investigators found that those who experienced the greatest threat to their feelings for their partner and belief in the strength of their relationship—those who had indicated that their partner rarely initiated conflict in the relationship but who then were exposed to information that conflict engagement was a hallmark of intimacy—subsequently showed a dramatic rise in the amount of conflict they perceived in their relationship; moreover, their narratives revealed a remarkable ability to see the virtues in their partners' ostensible faults. Those who were not threatened did not show such a bolstering effect. It appears that a threat to a strongly held positive view of the partner and of the relationship not only may not weaken that view but may actually strengthen it.

In their extensive program of research investigating the cognitive processes that enhance maintenance of ongoing relationships, these investigators have also found that people's images of their ideal partner also color their perceptions of their actual partner's traits (Murray & Holmes, 1999; Murray, Holmes, & Griffin, 1996).

Derogation of Alternative Partners

People who are satisfied and committed to their relationship tend not to look at or think about attractive alternative partners (Miller, 1997). However, if circumstances do compel attention to attractive alternative partners, those who are highly committed to their relationship may derogate the attractiveness of the alternatives (Johnson & Rusbult, 1989). For example, Simpson, Gangestad, and Lerma (1990) asked heterosexual male and female college students, ostensibly participating in a study of magazine advertisements, to view and rate 16 advertisements, 6 of which featured people of the opposite sex. Those participants who were in ongoing dating relationships rated the opposite-sex persons as sig-

nificantly less physically and sexually attractive than did individuals not currently involved in a dating relationship. Because sexual deprivation has been shown to increase the attractiveness of the opposite sex (e.g., Stephan, Berscheid, & Walster, 1971), and because those who were not in a romantic relationship were more likely to be sexually deprived than those who were, Simpson and colleagues examined whether differential sexual deprivation could have been responsible for the fact that those not in a romantic relationship perceived the opposite-sex persons to be more sexually attractive than those who were in a romantic relationship. When each participant's self-reported degree of sexual activity was statistically controlled, the difference between the two groups remained.

Nevertheless, because statistical control of a variable is always less satisfactory than experimental control, these researchers conducted a second experiment to more rigorously examine the sexual deprivation alternative explanation of their finding and to explore other possible explanations as well. Participants evaluated 15 new slides; 5 depicted young, opposite-sex persons; 5 depicted older, opposite-sex persons; and 5 depicted young, same-sex persons. Those participants who were romantically involved did not differ from those who were not romantically involved in their evaluations of the attractiveness of young, same-sex persons or in their evaluations of the attractiveness of older, opposite-sex persons. Once again, however, they did differ in their attractiveness judgments of same-age, opposite-sex persons—the very people who presumably represented the greatest threat to their ongoing romantic relationship. The fact that the attractiveness ratings of the romantically involved were lower than those of the noninvolved only when they were rating same-age, opposite-sex persons suggests that in the service of preserving commitment to an ongoing relationship, the attractiveness of alternative partners may be derogated. Because the opposite-sex persons in the advertisements were unavailable to the respondents, derogation of attractive opposite-sex others by those in a current romantic relationship appears not to be confined to possible alternative partners.

The Relationship Superiority Bias

A great deal of research has demonstrated that most people evaluate their relationships positively—perhaps more positively than is objectively warranted (e.g., Buunk & Van Yperen, 1991; Van Lange & Rusbult, 1995). The **relationship superiority bias**—the tendency to view one's own relationships as better than other people's relationships—also serves to maintain commitment to ongoing relationships. A study by Endo, Heine, and Lehman (2000) suggests that this bias may be universal. Japanese, Asian Canadians, and European Canadians all rated their own relationships (with their best friend, their closest family member, and their romantic partner) significantly more positively than the relationships of their peers. Perceiving one's own relationships as better than other people's relationships was not associated with an individual's self-esteem. Thus, these investigators conclude that the relationship superiority bias does not grow out of a need for self-enhancement but rather may serve the need for belongingness and the preservation of existing relationships.

Like Murray and Holmes (1993), Rusbult, Van Lange, Wildschut, Yovetich, and Verette (2000) reasoned that the relationship superiority bias may help people cope with relationship challenges and doubts and sustain commitment to the relationship. They asked people to freely list the positive and negative qualities that came to mind when they thought about their own and others' relationships. Those in the *control* condition were told, "We're interested in how your dating relationship may be similar to versus different from other people's dating relationships." *Accuracy* condition participants were instructed, "In describing your own and others' relationships we would like you to be as honest and accurate as you possibly can." Finally, *threat* condition participants were told, "We are especially interested in college students' dating relationships because previous research has demonstrated that in comparison to other types of relationships, college students' relationships are less likely to persist over time and tend to exhibit lower levels of overall adjustment." Relative to accuracy and control participants, the men and women in the threat condition not only saw their relationships as better than others' relationships (possessing more positive qualities) but also as not as bad (possessing fewer negative qualities). Moreover, as predicted, the more committed the individual was to the relationship, the stronger the relationship superiority bias he or she displayed, especially in the threat condition. (The instruction to be "accurate," however, weakened the commitment–superiority bias association.) In a follow-up study of these participants' relationships, the investigators found that perceived relationship superiority was associated with relationship continuance and with increasing relationship satisfaction. Furthermore, and consistent with the results of Endo and associates (2000), Rusbult and her colleagues found that even when individuals' self-esteem was controlled, commitment to the relationship still accounted for a unique portion of the variance in perceived superiority.

Unrealistic Optimism

People also display unrealistic optimism concerning the durability of their romantic relationships. Fowers, Lyons, Montel, and Shaked (2001) found that married partners consistently, and dramatically, underestimate their probability of divorce. Whereas estimates of divorce for the general population run from a conservative 43% to as high as 64% for those marrying since the late 1980s (Cherlin, 1992; Martin & Bumpass, 1989), 45% of their married respondents estimated their personal chance of divorce at 0% and 89% estimated their divorce chance as 25% or less.

Fowers and associates experimentally demonstrated that positive illusions about marriage are so strong that they are virtually impervious to threatening information. Single men and women (89% of whom had never been married) were asked to indicate how likely it was that they would marry in the future, that their marriage would end in divorce if they did marry, and that they would have an above-average marriage if they married. Respondents were divided into three groups that received different information: (1) A *control* group was only told that the study was about relationships; (2) an *informational* group was given the divorce statistics for the general population; and (3) an *information highlight* group received information emphasizing the likelihood of divorce ("[The statistic] means that when couples marry, it is like flipping a coin—heads they'll stay married, tails they'll divorce" [2001, p. 104]). The results revealed no sex differences, and no differences were found among the groups in (1) likelihood estimates of marrying in the future (the majority thought their chance of marrying was 100%); (2) likelihood of their own marriage ending in divorce (55% gave a 0% likelihood of divorce and only 12% gave a 50% or greater probability); or (3) likelihood estimates of having a better-than-average quality marriage (the most common estimate was 100%). Never-married and previously married men and women did not differ in their estimates of their own likelihood of future divorce or of having a superior-quality marriage. Because the unmarried respondents significantly underestimated their divorce likelihood, and because they did so even when the divorce statistic was emphasized, Fowers and colleagues concluded that positive illusions about marriage predate satisfaction with any particular relationship.

In a subsequent study, Fowers, Veingrad, and Dominicis (2002) asked engaged people to explain their responses to such items on the Idealistic Distortion Scale as "Every new thing I have learned about my partner has pleased me." The most frequent response given was some variant on "It's the truth." The investigators conclude that respondents see their illusions as matters of fact and thus show no tentativeness in asserting them as such, and like other researchers they reason that positive illusions spring from a paradox: Although marriage is enormously important and

beneficial to people, marriages are fragile and illusions may help shore up a marriage by promoting the sense that the relationship is satisfying and worth maintaining. The investigators additionally note, however, that positive illusions are a reflection of the excessive expectations people have about marriage. They suggest that it would be wise for social scientists and policymakers "to seek alternative conceptions of marriage that are less likely to lead to divorce and do not require positive illusions for their maintenance" (p. 108).

Identifying Positive Illusions

Identifying what constitutes a positive illusion—as opposed to an accurate perception about a partner or a relationship—is difficult. The problem created by the absence of an objective and reliable standard against which to judge the accuracy of an individual's judgments of another person, object, event, or relationship has plagued psychology for years (e.g., see Gage & Cronbach, 1955; Kenny, 1994b). There is no simple solution to the well-known accuracy problem. As Kruglanski (1989) discusses, "the most prevalent definition of accuracy has been that of a correspondence between judgment and criterion" (p. 401). Usually, however, the criterion represents someone else's judgment, whose accuracy itself may be suspect.

With respect to the perception of partners and relationships, an individual's positive illusions have been identified in three ways. First, the positivity of the evaluations people make of their own partners and relationships has been compared to the positivity of their evaluations of other people's partners and relationships (e.g., Endo et al., 2000). Because it logically cannot be the case that every person's relationships are better than every other person's relationships (only in Lake Wobegon can everyone be above average), higher ratings given to one's own relationship are regarded as positive illusions (although some of these relationships actually may be better than most other people's relationships).

Second, positive illusions have been identified by comparing the positivity of an individual's evaluation of the partner with the partner's evaluation of him- or herself. If the individual's evaluation of the partner is more positive than the partner's self-evaluation, it is viewed as a positive illusion. In other words, this method assumes the partner's self-evaluation is accurate and the individual's more positive evaluation is an illusion. Such an assumption may be unwarranted. In an unknown number of these cases, it may be that the individual's positive evaluation is accurate and the partner's less positive self-evaluation is inaccurate. Murray (1999) argues that because many studies of self-perception suggest that people's self-concepts are themselves often positively colored, "self-perceptions may prove a very conservative benchmark for indexing a partner's illusions" (p. 25, footnote 2).

Third, some researchers have used the general method employed by Murray and Holmes (1993): They experimentally construct a situation they believe will motivate the individual to revise upward his or her evaluation of the partner and the relationship—for example, by arousing doubts about the partner or relationship—and they also predict the dimension on which the revision is likely to take place (usually the dimension on which doubt was raised). Because an individual's before-doubt and after-doubt evaluations cannot be equally accurate, and because the hypothesis that led to the experiment specified the timing, direction, and content of the after-doubt evaluations, the experimenter is justified in labeling the after-doubt evaluation a positive illusion.

Conflict

Relationships do not continue to move toward closeness indefinitely. Most relationships reach a plateau in their level of interdependence. The point at which interdependence ceases to increase is thought to be marked by the appearance of conflict in the relationship, which impedes further growth of interdependence. In fact, it is growth of interdependence that has set the stage for conflict. For example, Braiker and Kelley (1979) ex-

amined newlyweds' retrospective accounts of the history of their relationship through the first 6 months of their marriage. As the partners' interdependence increased, conflict began to appear in their relationship. Although the types and intensity of conflict varied for different couples, conflict was evident in *all* relationships. On the basis of their experiences with couples in marital therapy, Goldstine, Larner, Zuckerman, and Goldstine (1977) proposed that the harmony and mutual delight of what they called Stage 1 of marital relationships is followed, "with the relentlessness of death and taxes," by Stage II: "The bright illusion *We are one* fades into the bleak conviction *We are hopelessly different*" (p. 1, emphasis in original). The "hopelessly different" conclusion often follows conflictful interaction. Conflict in premarital and marital relationships is discussed further in Part 6, "Relationships Over Time."

Virtually all stage theorists posit that conflict occurs in a developing relationship. Moreover, relationship scholars believe that conflict, in varying degrees, is characteristic of all close relationships. Interestingly, however, there is evidence that some people believe that a defining feature of a close relationship is an *absence* of conflict. (This and other dysfunctional adult relationship beliefs are discussed in Chapter 13, "Satisfaction and Stability.") The belief that the absence of conflict is a defining feature of a close relationship also seems to be held in middle childhood, when children report few conflicts and arguments with those they nominate as their best friends (Berndt & Perry, 1986). However, by later childhood and early adolescence, most children recognize that friendship and other types of relationship often involve conflict as well as support.

Sources of conflict differ among various types of relationship. For example, conflict in adult friendships and romantic relationships often arises over rebuff or rejection, personal criticism or mockery, betrayal of trust, breach of confidence, and cumulative irritations and annoyances (e.g., Davis & Todd, 1985; Fehr, Baldwin, Collins, Patterson, & Benditt, 1999). According to interview data collected by Joshi, Melson, and Ferris (2001), important sources of conflict in the friendships of children are relationship violations and trust issues—for example, breaking a promise or choosing someone else to be on a team. Conflicts also arose frequently over general standards of behavior (whether or not tattling is acceptable), courses of action, factual matters (How much is 24 multiplied by 3?), and aggressive behavior such as teasing, insulting, hitting, and destroying toys. Parent–child relationships are particularly vulnerable to conflict, usually involving parental demands and expectations in opposition to the impulses and desires of the child or adolescent (Mills & Grusec, 1988).

Collins and Laursen (2000) conclude from their review of parent–adolescent and adolescent peer relationships that "conflicts are neither inimical to closeness nor inevitably harmful to either the relationship or the partners in it" (p. 65). Whether a conflict is helpful to the continued growth of the relationship or contributes to its demise depends, of course, on how the partners manage their conflicts. Research conducted with married couples reveals that the use of positive conflict resolution strategies (such as acknowledging the other partner's views, actively listening or questioning, expressing clear support for the partner, and making compromises) is associated with satisfaction (Noller, Feeney, Bonnell, & Callan, 1994). Similarly, when conflict arises in children's friendships, friends—more than nonfriends or acquaintances—seem to be concerned with reaching equitable resolutions rather than with win–lose outcomes. Friends also tend to rely more on negotiation and disengagement when resolving disagreements (e.g., Hartup, 1996; Hartup, Laursen, Stewart, & Eastenson, 1988; Newcomb & Bagwell, 1995). By increasing the likelihood that the conflict will be resolved, these strategies enhance satisfaction and promote the continuity of the relationship. Additional research on conflict, including the course of a conflict episode, the causal attributions made during conflict, and the effects of conflict, is discussed in Chapter 13, "Satisfaction and Stability."

ENVIRONMENTAL FACTORS INFLUENCING RELATIONSHIP GROWTH AND MAINTENANCE

Most theories of relationship development and maintenance focus on the "interior" of the relationship—the dynamics and outcomes of the partners' interactions. The voluminous literature associated with the determinants of attraction and other positive sentiments reflects this emphasis. Less is known about the influence of the relationship's "exterior"—the social and physical environments in which the relationship is embedded, including the relationship's sociocultural context. Levinger (1994) and others (e.g., Karney & Bradbury, 1995b) have discussed the tendency of relationship researchers to neglect the influence of macroenvironmental forces on relationships and to focus almost exclusively on interaction microevents in order to understand and predict most relationship phenomena, including initiation, development, and dissolution. Family sociologist Willard Waller (1930/1967) long ago observed that the stability of a marriage is not necessarily related to the sweetness of its contents. He was referring to the fact that many unsatisfying marriages were maintained because of societal barriers to dissolving them.

Inspired by Levinger's (e.g., 1965) cohesiveness model and his concept of barrier forces, Berscheid and Campbell (1981) attempted to account for the changing longevity of romantic relationships observed over the latter half of the twentieth century. They reasoned that divorce became less difficult for many marital couples as a result of social changes, including reductions in the following: (1) economic barriers (women—half the partners of romantic relationships—became more economically independent); (2) legal barriers (including the establishment of "no-fault" divorce laws); (3) religious barriers (for example, the ease of obtaining annulments); (4) barriers associated with children (control over fertility provided by the 1959 invention of a contraceptive pill and a subsequent drop in the fertility rate); and (5) social barriers (less stigma associated with divorce). There is evidence that as barriers to the continuance of marital relationships weakened, personal satisfaction and emotional gratification became the primary rationale for establishing and maintaining marital relationships (see Attridge & Berscheid, 1994).

Not only did weakened barriers have a direct effect on the incidence of marital breakup, but, Berscheid and Campbell (1981) argue, they also had the indirect effect of decreasing the partners' satisfaction with the relationship. When there are few barriers to dissolution, the partners are in the position of freely choosing whether to remain in a relationship. Like other freedoms, the freedom to choose to maintain or dissolve the relationship has a cost: Having perpetual choice means that the individual must choose over and over again, expending time and energy to reevaluate the wisdom of the current choice. As a consequence, partners must continually "take the pulse" of the relationship to determine their satisfaction with it as compared to available alternatives. Not only must the partners continually reassess their own satisfaction and alternatives, but they also must assess those of their partner because the partner's continuation of the relationship is not assured by the presence of barriers against leaving it. Berscheid and Campbell argue that the cost of perpetually evaluating the relationship, both from one's own perspective and that of the partner, along with the insecurity that is both the cause and effect of such assessments, can sour the "sweetness of the contents" of the relationship and make its dissolution more likely. In addition, as more marital relationships broke apart as a result of both direct and indirect effects of social changes, the pool of available alternative partners to current spouses increased, raising the probability that current relationship outcomes would fall below CLalt.

Extending Berscheid and Campbell's analysis, Berscheid and Lopes's (1997) temporal model of relationship stability departs from the custom of predicting relationship stability from the partners' subjective commitment to continue the relationship (and the factors that contribute to commitment, such as attraction and other factors that "sweeten" the relationship's contents). As in Kelley's (1983/2002b) model of commitment, these theorists assume that predicting relationship stability is equivalent to predicting the continuance of interaction. To predict interaction continuance, it is necessary to identify not only the relatively stable personal and environmental causal conditions that *currently* compel (or repel) interaction but to forecast how these conditions are likely to *change* over time. Thus, the model emphasizes the need to identify how the environmental context of a relationship—its "ecological niche" (Karney & Bradbury, 1995b)—may change in systematic ways over time. The model distinguishes between changes in environmental conditions that emerge from the interaction and are made by the partners themselves (such as romantic partners who change their place of residence to be in closer physical proximity) and environmental conditions that originate outside the relationship but influence the outcomes of the partners' interaction (such as an economic recession that places stresses on the partners and thus increases likelihood of conflict, dissatisfaction, and dissolution). The model assumes, then, that the partners' satisfaction with the relationship and the relationship's environmental context interact with each other to determine the fate of the relationship.

Social Environmental Factors

Several features of the social environment in which the relationship is embedded are likely to influence relationship development and maintenance. Two of these have been well documented to affect relationship maintenance.

Approval of Persons in the Social Network

As we have discussed, a number of studies have demonstrated that the approval or disapproval of people in the partners' social networks may facilitate or inhibit relationship development (e.g., Sprecher & Felmlee, 1992). This is as true for gay and lesbian couples as it is for heterosexual couples (Smith & Brown, 1997). More information on this point is still needed, however, particularly regarding the identity of persons whose approval or disapproval is especially likely to have an impact. For example, Leslie, Huston, and Johnson (1986) found that parental support of a dating relationship over a 4-month period was *not* associated with a change in relationship involvement.

Availability of Alternatives

The attractiveness of alternatives to the present relationship plays a role in many theories of relationship development and maintenance, as we have discussed. There now is a host of evidence that the availability of attractive alternatives to the present relationship does decrease the probability that the present relationship will be maintained. The power of alternatives to influence the stability of the marital relationship was demonstrated by Udry's (1981) examination of longitudinal data from a panel of married, white, urban couples that asked spouses how easily they could replace their spouse with one of comparable quality. Udry found that the perception of alternatives was a better predictor of marital stability than was marital satisfaction. However, as Miller (1997) demonstrated in his study of premarital relationship stability, high relationship satisfaction may provide some protection against the presence of desirable alternatives; men and women who are satisfied with, invested in, and committed to their relationships are less likely to monitor their alternatives than those who are dissatisfied with the relationship. In fact, Miller found that a good predictor of relationship failure was high attentiveness to alternatives. Similarly, and in accord with Levinger's (e.g., 1965) cohesiveness theory, White and Booth (1991) found that marital instability in a national panel of spouses was associated with the perception of alternatives to the relationship, and also with relationship dissatisfaction and few barriers to dissolving the relationship.

The potency of alternatives in the social environment also was documented by South and Lloyd (1995), who found that the risk of marital dissolution in the United States is highest in geographical areas where there is an abundance of potential alternatives to the present spouse. The number of potential alternatives may be large for both spouses or it may be greater for one than the other. For example, *Time* magazine reported in 1999 ("Numbers") that single women outnumbered single men in New York City by 537,311, whereas there were 5,372 more single men than single women age 45 and younger in Santa Clara Country, California, the heart of Silicon Valley.

The finding that risk of divorce is highest in geographic areas where either husbands or wives are likely to encounter numerous alternatives to their current partner was replicated by South, Trent, and Shen (2001), who also found that couples are more likely to divorce when the wife's occupation has relatively many men and few women (husbands' occupational sex ratio had no effect on dissolution risk). These relationship-destabilizing effects were as strong among couples who possessed few other risk factors for divorce as it was for those who possessed many.

Physical Environmental Factors

Most studies of relationship development only hint at the role of physical environmental factors. For example, the Boston Couples Study (Hill, Rubin, & Peplau, 1976) found that the timing of breakups of romantic relationships was related to the school calendar. Most breakups occurred in May–June, September, and December–January. Thus, either past physical separation or anticipated future separation appears to have been a factor in the breakups, confirming other findings suggesting that any environmental factor resulting in the physical separation of the partners increases likelihood of dissolution (just as environmental changes that *increase* physical proximity should promote relationship continuity).

In addition to physical proximity or distance, other features of the physical environment are likely to play a role in relationship development and maintenance. For example, people who interact in physically uncomfortable settings are less likely to like each other than people who interact in pleasant physical environments (see Chapter 6, "Birth of a Relationship"). Moreover, unhealthy physical environments also undoubtedly affect relationship development and maintenance. People who are ill, in physical pain, or tired are not as likely to enjoy their interactions with each other as much as healthy people are, and they are less likely to have the energy to devote to developing new relationships or to maintaining established ones. Demographic variables such as socioeconomic status that indicate the likelihood that the partners interact in pleasant versus unpleasant physical circumstances are rarely examined in studies of relationship development and maintenance, perhaps because most studies are conducted with college students.

Reasons for the Neglect of Environmental Factors

Several factors seem responsible for the lack of information on the influence of the physical and social environment in which the relationship is embedded on relationship development and maintenance. First, as noted above, most studies have been conducted with college students, who are relatively homogeneous with respect to socioeconomic status (which often is a good index of the individual's physical and social environments). Second, in most investigations of the relationships of people who are not college students, such as married couples, the samples are too small to adequately represent different socioeconomic groups. Third, it is often difficult to predict changes in the relationship's environmental conditions so that the influence of the change can be assessed. To predict the continuance of a newly formed relationship, for example, it might be useful to know whether an economic downturn is in the offing; financially distressed partners may be forced to work overtime or relocate, cutting short their budding relationship. In contrast, an economic upturn may reduce many of the partners' current sources of conflict and increase their leisure time, permitting their relationship to develop faster than otherwise. Even economists, however, have difficulty forecasting economic conditions.

At least one other factor is likely responsible for the absence of information on how environmental conditions influence relationship development and maintenance. As previously discussed, people in Western cultures believe that relationships are formed and maintained by personal choice. A corollary to that belief appears to be that the quality of a relationship is entirely dependent on the partners themselves—that is, independent of the environmental conditions under which they are attempting to develop or maintain their relationship. Most people seem to be unaware of the extent to which the relationship's exterior may affect its interior quality. For example, when Berscheid, Lopes, Ammazzalorso, and Langenfeld (2001) asked college students to tell what was responsible for the high quality of their ongoing romantic relationships, the respondents overwhelmingly named relational causal conditions; that is, they attributed their satisfying relationships almost entirely to the felicitous combination of their own and their partner's personal characteristics or to the positive manifestations of those characteristics in their interaction ("We communicate well"). Virtually no one mentioned the contributions of the physical or social environments in which their relationships were embedded. When respondents were asked to account for the quality of their *past* romantic relationships or a friend's current romantic relationship, however, they were significantly more likely to name environmental conditions as influential. The investigators suggest that psychological distance was responsible for the effect. Just as physical distance allows an individual to see the entire forest in which a particular tree is located, psychological distance from a particular relationship may allow a person to appreciate how the relationship's environment is (or was) affecting it.

Similarly, Lamm, Wiesmann, and Keller (1998), who asked women college students how they would come to like, love, or be in love with another and what factors were likely to cause those feelings to end, found that environmental causes were rarely mentioned as responsible either for the rise or decline of these positive sentiments. A 1999 letter to one of the authors from a former relationship course student who became a Peace Corps volunteer provides a concrete example:

> It was interesting to me that although everyone in the training group was acutely aware that we were in a physical and social environment drastically different from home, few members of the group seemed to be cognizant of how that change might affect their attraction toward others inside or outside of the social group. Many folks began training with S.O.'s [significant others] back home and finished it dating another volunteer or [local citizen], but most people were reluctant to attribute any of their attraction to factors other than [the] personal factors of the one they were dating, or [the] negative personal factors of the one with whom they broke up. I think few people noticed that loneliness and severe restriction of the pool of availables had any effect on whom they were attracted to. Have you ever considered using a Peace Corps training group as a subject group in a study . . . ?

SUMMARY

Recognizing that only a very few relationships survive beyond initial interactions, relationship scholars have attempted to identify the factors that influence whether a relationship will continue to develop toward closeness and how that relationship will be maintained over time. Most theories of relationship development and maintenance focus on microevents and outcomes (as opposed to external structural or environmental forces) and assume that in open fields, profit and reward provide the impetus for relationship progression. Interdependence theory, which is applicable to the development and maintenance of all types of relationships, represents an early and clear expression of this fundamental assumption.

Not surprisingly, romantic relationship development has received a great deal of attention, with many theorists adopting an approach that assumes that all relationships progress through a series of stages in which various hurdles must be negotiated or passed on the path toward closeness (typically defined as marriage). Although these theories differ in the number, sequence, and features of the developmental phases they propose, they all suggest that increased interaction, disclosure, communication, behavioral and goal synchrony, investment, and positive affect (love, liking, trust) are associated with progression of romantic relationships. Less attention has been paid to friendship development; however, reviews of the friendship literature suggest that this type of relationship progresses through many of the same phases as do romantic relationships, although friendships may develop at a slower pace.

Other theorists have focused not on the stages of relationship development but on the processes that occur between partners and that fuel progression toward closeness. A growing body of evidence reveals that changes in self-disclosure, intimacy, commitment, investment, trust, and conflict are integrally associated with both the growth and maintenance of relationships. In addition to forces associated with the "interior" of the relationship, such as the dynamics and outcomes of the partners' interactions, environmental factors influence relationship development and maintenance. Although environmental and other macro-level variables continue to be understudied, we now know that the economic, social, and physical context in which a relationship is embedded influences its quality and stability.

PART 4

RELATIONSHIP PROCESSES

Chapter 8

Cognitive
Processes

INTRODUCTION

All relationships begin with two people who are strangers to each other. Even the relationship between a mother and her infant begins with two strangers. The process by which people form impressions of strangers thus is of great consequence for understanding relationships. Fortunately, impression formation is one of the most studied and understood topics in social psychology. Researchers have learned that the instant a stranger has captured our attention, we begin to form an impression of that person. With extraordinary speed and efficiency, our mind begins processing clues to the stranger's nature, particularly his or her likely behavior in interaction with us and the implications of that behavior for our personal welfare. Many of these clues are immediately provided by the person's appearance, which usually contains information about his or her sex, age, race, physical attractiveness, and a wealth of other characteristics. The situation in which we encounter the stranger often provides more clues—about the person's occupation and interests, for example. As a re-

sult of our mind's activity, we often feel we know a great deal about the stranger, or at least enough to guide our behavior in our initial interactions. Over time and many interactions, we may come to know the person well—sometimes better than we know ourselves. In this chapter, we discuss how the human mind processes information about the strangers we encounter and about the people who over time have become our closest relationship partners.

KNOWING ANOTHER PERSON

How we come to know another person can be viewed as the process by which we learn to accurately predict how that person will behave—particularly in interaction with us. Those who know Kevin can predict that in a restaurant, he will always select steak over chicken and chicken over fish, except on Mondays, when he will choose a vegetarian casserole; that he is always at least 30 minutes late for a date; and that he will sneeze and break out in hives in the vicinity of a cat. Knowing a person very well means that we can accurately predict how he or she will behave under a wide variety of conditions, even in situations in which we never before have seen that person behave. Partners who have been in a close relationship for many years may be able to accurately predict what each other will say or do in response to virtually every event likely to occur in the settings in which they customarily interact. Each partner's ability to accurately predict the other's behavior is, of course, essential for the partners to coordinate their behaviors and to move from the awkwardness that often characterizes initial interactions to the smooth and effortless flow of interaction in most established relationships.

Over time we may come to know some people better than they know themselves; that is, we can predict their behavior more accurately than they can. When our best friend enthusiastically reports she has signed up for a rugged wilderness trip, for example, we know that disaster is lurking just around the corner—because we know that she is terrified of "creepy-crawlies" and last climbed a flight of stairs a year ago when the elevator broke down. Our partners frequently acknowledge that we may know them better than they know themselves. They ask, "Do you think I could be happy living with a workaholic like Susan?" or other questions that usually begin "Do you think I'm the sort of person who . . .?" This is one reason our close relationship partners carry special weight in shaping our self-concepts. They also have special impact on our self-esteem, which is why it is so disturbing to hear our partner say, "Everyone else may think you're a prince (or princess), but I know the *real* you." It's disturbing because most of us believe our close relationship partners *do* know the real us, and thus their opinion matters.

In reality it is relatively rare that we ever come to know anyone extremely well. We usually see the majority of our relationship partners in circumscribed circumstances, and even in those restricted circumstances, much of their behavior, as well as our own, is prescribed by social norms and conventions that govern behavior in those settings—not by personal preferences, beliefs, values, personality traits, and other dispositions that guide social interaction and relationship be-

havior in other settings (see Chapter 10, "Dispositional Influences"). Because we often are not aware that the range of settings in which we interact with a specific partner is relatively small and that much of our partner's behavior and our own is governed by situation-specific norms and conventions, we often think we know other people better than we actually do. When our neighbor is reported in the newspapers to have embezzled pension funds, we exclaim, "I can't believe it! He was such a honest man." He *was* an honest man when he confessed he oversprayed his weed killer and inadvertently killed our tulips, but what he was outside the restricted neighborhood setting in which we customarily interacted with him, we obviously didn't know. The point is, we didn't have to know. Not only do we not have to know everyone, but we don't have to know everything even about the few people who are important to us (Swann, 1984). We just have to know enough about them to protect and enhance our personal welfare.

Expectancies

Expectancies are the beliefs we hold about the probable behavior of other people and the probable occurrence of other future events. The cognitive construct of expectancy was introduced to psychology in the early 1930s by Edward Tolman (1932), who emphasized the purposive, goal-directed quality of human behavior that is so evident in most social interactions (see Chapter 4, "The Concept of Relationship"; Hilton & Darley, 1991). At the time, however, most psychologists were busily studying *molecular* behaviors—for example, a single stimulus–response unit like the knee-jerk reflex—on which most learning theories focused. They were not receptive to examining *molar* behaviors (getting up in the morning and going to school) from which the purposive quality of human behavior is most easily seen, and they were even less receptive to examining the mind and such cognitive constructs as expectancy.

Psychologists' aversion to studying the mind from the 1930s through the 1950s was ironic given that Wilhelm Wundt, generally viewed as the founder of psychology, had conceptualized the discipline as the science of conscious experience. Wundt believed that psychology's principal method would be *introspection*—the examination and analysis of a person's *self-report* of his or her mental state (see Boring, 1950; Schultz & Schultz, 2000). Unfortunately, people's self-reports of such phenomena as their "stream of consciousness" had yielded little of value. The method of introspection was subsequently discredited by the behaviorists, who insisted that the observational base of psychology consists only of objectively verifiable behavior—*not* of mental events that could be observed and reported by just one person. With no useful way to study it, most psychologists conceded that the mind was a padlocked "black box," inaccessible to scientific observation and analysis. As a consequence, the role that expectancies play in human behavior was neglected by psychologists for several decades, as were all other constructs essential to understanding the mind's activities (see Bargh & Ferguson, 2000).

Although relationship scholars heavily depend on self-report—on a person's report of his or her satisfaction with a relationship, for example, or degree of love for another—traces of skepticism about the value of self-report and cognitive constructs remain among some relationship scholars, as discussed further in Chapter 14, "Intervention and Dissolution." Commenting on Fincham, Bradbury, and Scott's (1990) review of research on the cognitive attributions spouses make about the causes of each other's behavior, for example, influential relationship researcher Neil Jacobson (1990) stated warily, "I would assert that cognitive theorists assume a certain burden of proof by virtue of their decision to examine variables to which we will never have direct access" (p. 268).

It was not until the mid-1950s that the mind once again became a proper object of psychological study. Jerome Bruner (1957), one of the seminal figures in what has become known as psychology's cognitive revolution, revived the construct of expectancy in his classic essay titled "On Perceptual Readiness." Today, expectancy ranks among the most important constructs in

psychology (Kirsch, 1999). Tolman (1932) had theorized that expectancies represent the means by which people use the knowledge they have accumulated from their past experiences to predict future events. Many psychologists now endorse cognitive neuroscientist Dennett's often quoted claim, "The fundamental purpose of brains is to produce future" (1991, p. 177).

Although expectancies influence most human behavior, the construct of expectancy is particularly important to those who hope to understand relationships because *social interactions flow forward on a river of the partners' expectancies about each other's behavior*. This point of view is elaborated by Holmes (2002), who argues that expectancies play an "imperial" role in social cognition (p. 2). Of particular importance for social behavior are expectations about the features of situations and expectations about other people's goals and motivations, which together comprise the individual's *social situation*. Unfortunately, as Baucom, Epstein, Sayers, and Sher (1989) state in their review of the role of cognition in marital relationships, "there is scant research on the role of expectancies in intimate relationships" (pp. 33–34). That state of affairs is changing, however.

Olson, Roese, and Zanna (1996) theorize that social expectancies vary along four dimensions. *Certainty* is the subjective level of probability associated with the occurrence of the future event. For example, expectancies associated with a 100% estimated probability are termed factual expectancies because the individual holding the expectancy views the statement as objectively certain and true. *Accessibility* is the ease and speed with which the expectancy comes to mind. *Explicitness* refers to whether or not the individual is consciously aware of holding the expectancy. *Importance* refers to the extent to which the expectancy is relevant to the individual's needs, motives, or values. For example, the expectancy that Jim will be receptive to an interaction attempt is more important to an individual looking for a date than it is to someone who already has plans with a friend.

People's beliefs about the probable occurrence of future events presumably develop from the same sources as their other beliefs: (1) their own experiences; (2) other people's beliefs (via social interaction and the media, for example); and (3) logical derivations from other beliefs and expectancies ("Sara and Bob are inseparable; Bob is moving to California; therefore, I expect Sara probably will move to California"; see Olson et al., 1996). Understanding precisely how expectancies develop, how they are maintained or changed, and how they influence behavior is a central task of cognitive psychology.

Consciousness and the Mind's Activities

The principal mission of cognitive psychology is to understand the psychological *structure* of the human mind and the *processes* by which it operates. Perhaps the most important contribution that contemporary cognitive psychology has made to our understanding of the human mind is that most mental activities not only are not accessible to other people—they are not accessible to the very person whose mind it is. We usually are not aware of the processes by which our mind attends to, interprets, stores, and accesses information about our physical and social environments and our internal states and how that information is then used to guide our behavior. Typically, we are aware of only a few of the *products* of the mind's work when they appear in consciousness.

William James (1890) characterized consciousness as the "ultimate mystery" for psychologists to solve. Although consciousness itself remains a mystery, many cognitive psychologists now associate it not with the entirety of the mind, as Wundt did, but with focal attention (e.g., Mandler, 1975). The human's attentional capacity is limited, and thus our window of conscious awareness is small compared to the extraordinary amount of information our minds process, as discussed in Chapter 6, "Birth of a Relationship." Freud is given credit for bringing the unconscious to the attention of psychologists, but some cognitive psychologists believe he may

have led the field astray by suggesting that behavior influenced by unconscious knowledge is unusual, even pathological (Goldman, 1999). It is now clear that behavior performed without the individual's full awareness is at least as usual, and perhaps more usual, than behavior under our conscious awareness and control.

Because many of our mental activities are not subjectively accessible to us, psychologists cannot study the mind by using the method of introspection—asking us to report on its workings. If someone asks us how we knew almost instantly that we'd like Joe, we usually don't really know. We might respond that we just had an "intuition" that Joe was a good guy, or we had a "gut feeling" we'd like Joe, or that the "chemistry" between us was right, or that Joe's "vibes" were good. Cognitive psychologists now know that intuition, gut feelings, chemistry, and vibes are manifestations of the workings of the extraordinarily efficient and powerful human mind—a mind that has processed the information available to it and reached a preliminary verdict about Joe, namely, that he is a "good guy." That tentative verdict will guide our initial interaction with Joe.

Social Cognitive Psychology

As opposed to knowledge of the physical environment, social cognitive psychologists focus exclusively on knowledge of the social environment—on how we *process* information about people, how we *structure* and organize that information in memory, and how we *access* the store of information we have accumulated from our past experiences with people to make predictions about their behavior in order to protect and enhance our welfare.

The perception of people differs in a number of ways from the perception of the physical environment. First, as Kenny (1994a) and others have discussed, person perception is *reciprocal*, whereas the perception of physical objects is one-sided; two people in interaction are simultaneously forming or revising their mental impressions of each other, but the car we are thinking of buying is not forming an impression of us as we form an impression of it sitting in the dealer's showroom. Second, we are *aware of the reciprocality* of person perception; not only are we usually aware that the other person is forming an impression of us, but we often wonder what that impression is because we know that it will guide his or her behavior in our interactions. Third, as Kenny notes, our perception of other people is often *influenced by our perception of ourselves*; we often assume, for example, that others are similar to ourselves, and we behave accordingly ("I would probably lie under those circumstances, so he may be lying"), but we rarely believe that the nature of a physical object is similar to our own nature. Finally, perhaps the most important difference between the perception of objects and the perception of people is that the attributes of people usually are *more difficult to determine* than the attributes of objects.

The attributes of objects not only tend to be less ambiguous than the attributes of people, but once determined, they remain relatively stable. For example, a red and round object seldom changes its color or shape. The attributes of a person undergo many changes over his or her lifespan. Even within a relatively short time, a person's behavior may alter as the situational context in which he or she is behaving changes. A man may be rude when interacting with his employee in the afternoon but courteous with his spouse in the evening. Another reason it is often difficult to determine another's nature is that people, unlike objects, have the capability of deliberately deceiving us about their attributes. Like ourselves, other people hope to maximize the goodness of their outcomes in social interaction and thus often engage in deceptive self-presentational strategies such as ingratiation to further their goals. As a consequence, we cannot always take a person's behavior at face value.

Social cognitive psychologists have identified many of the principles that govern how our minds process, structure, and access information about people (see Fiske & Taylor, 1991; Kunda, 1999). Unless we have taken a course in social cognition, however, we are unlikely to be aware of the rules by which our mind operates. Whether we are aware of them or not, these rules have profound implications for all aspects of our relationships with others. The principles of social cognition, for example, help us understand the truth of the old saw "You never get a second chance to make a first impression." They also help explain why it is difficult to change interaction patterns within an established relationship even when both partners are highly motivated to do so.

Social cognitive psychologists initially followed the lead of experimental cognitive psychologists, who were almost exclusively concerned with object perception. As a consequence, for many years social cognitive processes were studied in the laboratory under highly structured conditions; typically, participants were given minimal information about a stranger and were instructed to form an impression of him or her. Thus, much research in the field of social cognition is more applicable to first encounters with strangers and first impressions than it is to people's cognitive activities in naturalistically formed and ongoing relationships (e.g., see Berscheid, 1994; Wyer & Gruenfeld, 1995). Fiske and Taylor (1991) comment, "Social perception concerning important life events and intimate relationships may differ considerably from social perception in the lab experiment in important ways from the picture of these processes as it has emerged from the laboratory" (p. 557). Fortunately, it has become increasingly recognized that social cognition operates in the service of people's life goals.

As a consequence of increased recognition that people's social interactions usually have implications for the achievement or frustration of their goals and, moreover, that people's goals often directly concern their relationships (Cantor & Malley, 1991), many psychologists have concluded that social cognition is best investigated in the relationship context (S. T. Fiske, 1992). Knowledge is growing rapidly about **relationship cognition**, or how people process, store, and access information about their relationships (Berscheid, 1994; Berscheid & Reis, 1998; Fletcher & Fincham, 1991; Fletcher & Fitness, 1996; Reis & Downey, 1999). The importance of understanding relationship cognition has been underscored by the growing influence of the evolutionary approach to cognition. Because relationships with others were of critical importance to the survival of our ancestors, it is now believed that the evolutionary development of the human brain, and thus of the mind, was strongly influenced by our ancestors' need to cope effectively with other members of the species (as discussed in Chapter 1, "First Relationships"). As evolutionary psychologists Cosmides and Tooby (1992) explain, our ancestors needed to construct an accurate cognitive "social map of the persons, relationships, motives, interactions, emotions, and intentions that made up their social world" (p. 163). Such a social map is as necessary to our survival today as it was back in evolutionary time.

The field of social cognition, however, is very much a work in progress and on the cusp of dramatic change as a result of advances in the field of cognitive neuroscience, which focuses on the brain's neurological activities as people perceive and think about their internal and external environments. Although almost all of the empirical findings in social cognition are based on older, traditional models of cognition, there is every indication that the growing dominance of new models, which are more plausible in terms of what is now known about brain activity, not only will account for established findings but will be especially well suited for further investigations of relationship cognition (Smith, 1996, 1998).

PROCESSING SOCIAL INFORMATION

Most contemporary theories of how we process, store, and access information about other people have been termed **dual process theories** of social cognition because they posit that people use two different methods to process information about others. Although different theorists give these two modes of social information processing different names, there is good agreement about their respective natures (see Figure 8.1).

Automatic/Associative Information Processing

Automatic/associative processing has been characterized as the "quick and dirty" approach we take to knowing another. Bargh (1994, 1996) describes **automatic information processing** as possessing four features: (1) unintentionality (we do not have to consciously direct our mind to search our memory for people we have known in the past who resemble the stranger—it does so "automatically"); (2) uncontrollability (we cannot stop ourselves from searching our memory for similar people and events—the mind does so involuntarily); (3) inaccessibility (we are not consciously aware of our mind processing the information); and (4) efficiency (because it occurs outside conscious awareness, automatic processing consumes little, if any, of our precious attentional capacity).

Automatic information processing also has been called **associative information processing**. When

Automatic /Associative Mode		Controlled/Rule-based Mode
• Unintentional		• Intentional
• Uncontrollable		• Controllable
• Inaccessible to awareness	*versus*	• Accessible to awareness
• Efficient (requires little attention)		• Effortful (requires attention)
• Accesses long-term memory system		• Accesses long-term and short-term memory systems

FIGURE 8.1 Features of the Two Modes of Processing Social Information

we encounter an unfamiliar person, our mind often associates his or her features (female, red hair) with people we have known in the past, or have heard or read about, who possess those same features (Smith & DeCoster, 2000). On the basis of our accumulated knowledge of people who seem to be like the stranger, we make predictions about him or her. In automatic/associative processing, then, the *similarity* of the new, unknown person to other persons about whom we have information stored in memory is the fundamental principle by which previously acquired information is accessed to produce expectancies about the stranger.

Because automatic/associative information processing is not subjectively accessible, it usually is not reportable. If our past experiences with people similar to the stranger were unpleasant (our third-grade teacher was a red-haired woman who frequently rapped our hand with a ruler), we may immediately "intuit" that the red-haired woman in the physician's waiting room is not someone we want to sit next to even though the only available seat is next to her. If our friend asks why we are standing, we may not really know. "I just didn't feel like sitting," we might say. Or, if the affect associated with our former teacher is strongly negative, we might whisper, "I didn't want to sit by that scary old lady"—a response that might puzzle our friend, for his mind's eye sees only an elderly woman.

The Associative Memory System and Regularities in the Social Environment

Although debate and investigation continue, most cognitive psychologists believe that humans have three memory systems (each of which may subsume other systems; see Baddeley, 1999). The first of these, the *sensory memory system(s)*, serves to register and briefly retain incoming information from the senses. It is the brief retention of sensory images that allows objects in a succession of static film snapshots to be seen as moving (hence, the "movies"). Sensory memory is so brief that it generally is regarded as part of the per-

ceptual process. A second memory system has been called *short-term memory* or sometimes *working memory* because we can hold objects in that system long enough to "work" on them— to figure out what they mean, to add or divide the numbers we hold there, to compare images, and so forth. When most of us think of memory, we think of the third system, *long-term memory*, which holds information we have stored for long periods of time.

The characteristics of the long-term memory system, like all the other memory systems posited by psychologists, are subject to debate and continuing investigation. However, Smith and DeCoster (2000), along with many other cognitive psychologists, believe that this system records information slowly and incrementally, incorporating an experience only when it has been frequently repeated in the past and is thus likely to be repeated in the future. Because they believe the automatic/associative mode of information processing accesses *only* this system, Smith and DeCoster call the long-term system the **associative memory system**, thereby connecting the labels of the structure and the process characteristic of the structure. The associative memory system is believed to be large, and the expectancies it generates are believed to be stable because they are based on tried-and-true regularities in the physical and social environments. The slowness of the associative memory system to incorporate new experiences is posited to be in the service of keeping unusual and rare events, which are unlikely to be repeated in the future, from disrupting its organization. Smith and DeCoster theorize that if our long-term knowledge structures were vulnerable to rapid change, seldom encountered experiences could overwhelm more trustworthy social information and thus imperil the accuracy of our social expectancies.

The associative memory system may possess another important feature that has many implications for relationship phenomena: If an experience has been repeated frequently in the past, it may be incorporated into the associative memory system even though the individual was not consciously aware of those experiences when they occurred. There is a great deal of evidence that people can learn general regularities in the environment without awareness of the experiences that form the regularity. Thus, not only may we behave in accord with an expectancy we are not consciously aware of holding, but we may *never* have been aware of the experiences that formed the regularity and produced the expectancy. If this type of expectancy is the source of our dysfunctional relationship behavior, we are unlikely to know why we are behaving in a particular way (which does not, of course, prevent us from coming up with plausible, but inaccurate, ideas when asked for reasons).

The human brain appears to be especially attuned to detecting *regularities*, or "invariances," in the social and physical environments that are then stored in the associative memory system. Although the task of extracting regularities from our complex and sometimes chaotic environ-

ments sounds as though it would demand a powerful brain and conscious attention, even a chicken brain can do it, as the Gestalt psychologist Kohler (1929) demonstrated in a classic experiment (see Figure 8.2). From the time baby chicks popped out of their shells, Kohler put their corn on a medium gray platter which he placed alongside a light gray platter. After a time, the chickens ignored the light gray platter and directly headed to the medium gray platter to eat. Kohler then removed the light gray platter and put a dark gray platter alongside the medium gray platter. The experimental question was, which platter would the chickens approach—the medium gray platter on which they had found food every single day of their lives or the new dark gray platter, which they had never seen before but which presented the same light–dark relationship to the other platter? When the chickens

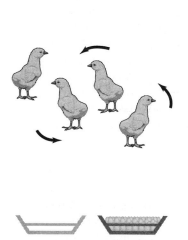  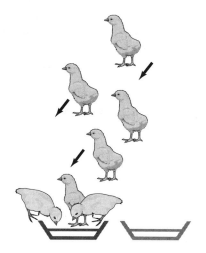

Phase 1
From the time they hatched, baby chicks were fed corn on a medium gray platter placed next to a light gray platter.

Phase 2
After a short while, the chicks ignored the light gray platter and quickly headed toward the medium gray one at feeding time.

Phase 3
The experimenter removed the light gray platter and replaced it with a dark gray one. The hungry chicks approached the dark gray platter over the one that had always held their dinner.

FIGURE 8.2 Kohler's (1929) Experiment
This experiment clearly demonstrated that the chicks had focused not on the individual properties of each platter (its color), but on the *relationship* between the two platters in the environment. Their food had always been presented in the darker of two platters, and so they continued to select the darker object in Phase 3.

strutted out for their dinner, they headed directly for the new dark gray platter and ignored the medium gray platter—the dish that since their birth had held their food. Kohler thus demonstrated that the chickens were *not* responding to the *absolute properties* of each platter (its shade of gray); rather, the chickens' behavior was governed by the *invariant relationship* between these two objects in their physical environment.

Kohler's experiment demonstrated the *principle of perceptual constancy*. The fact that the chickens could reliably distinguish kernels of corn from pebbles and other inedible objects not only when the kernels glittered in bright sunlight (and thus were as white as snow) but were shaded (and were as dark as coal) also illustrates this principle and the chickens' ability to detect and respond to the relationships between objects in the environment rather than to the absolute properties of each object in isolation from its context. The human's ability to extract regularities from the environment allows us to recognize the tune of "Three Blind Mice" whether it is played on the cello, the kazoo, or even a musical instrument we have never heard before. Because it is the relationship between the notes we respond to—not the properties of each individual sound—we can predict the next note in the series even though we may have never heard that particular instrument play that sound before. It is the *context* in which the sound is heard that influences how it is perceived and the expectancies it generates—not the sound alone.

The work of the Gestalt psychologists on the perception of physical objects strongly influenced Fritz Heider, whose book *The Psychology of Interpersonal Relations* (1958) is regarded as the seminal work in social cognition and person perception. Heider observed that the human mind is as attuned to extracting regularities from the social environment as from the physical environment. Many of the regularities we extract from the social environment, sometimes without intention and awareness, are a person's stable and enduring attributes, which Heider referred to as **person dispositions** to behave in certain ways across many different situations. Some of these person dispositions are *personality traits*: "any personality trait refers to something that characterizes the person, that is, holds over time in spite of irregularities of circumstance and behavior" (p. 30). Another class of dispositions is *attitudes*, which, once determined, also often allow us to predict a person's behavior across many different situations. Heider's theorizing about how we extract regularities from the social environment—that is, person dispositions—spawned the **causal attribution theories** (e.g., Jones & Davis, 1965; Kelley, 1967) whose implications for relationships are discussed later in this chapter. (Many person dispositions that have been shown to have potent implications for relationships are discussed in Chapter 10, "Dispositional Influences.")

The characteristics of the associative memory system and its store of information about the regularities in our environment reveal at least one important inadequacy of the computer–mind analogy so often used in discussions of human information processing. Although the slow-learning associative memory system is sometimes likened to the storage system in a computer, there is an important difference: The information stored in a computer is easily erasable, but information stored in the associative memory system is not. Perhaps with the help of a relationship therapist we may come to realize that that the information stored in our associative memory system about romantic relationships is inaccurate and dysfunctional and is interfering with our present relationship. We might have become aware that every time we look at our new lover or spouse—who probably resembles our ex-lover or spouse in a number of ways, including sex, age, and, often, appearance—negative thoughts of our previous romantic partner come to mind and exert inappropriate influence on our current behavior. Under these circumstances, it would be nice if we could press the "delete" key and start over afresh, freed from the ghosts of our past. However, much as we might wish to banish all memories of our past relationship and its harmful effects on our behavior in our new relationship, we cannot do so easily. Our past relationship will continue to exert its influence, for good or for ill, on our new relationship until time, and repeated new relationship experiences, take precedence over the past experiences stored in the associative memory system or until we exert a great deal of conscious and deliberate effort to prevent those unbidden and unwelcome memories from influencing our present behavior. Such conscious and deliberate effort will require us to use the second way we process information.

Controlled/Rule-Based Information Processing

In addition to the fast automatic/associative mode of processing, dual process theories posit a slower mode, which is usually called **controlled information processing**. Controlled processing is theorized to be the mirror image of automatic processing: intentional, controllable, accessible to consciousness, demanding of the individual's attention, and usually slower than automatic processing (Bargh, 1996). Smith and DeCoster (2000) call this type of processing **rule-based** because it is associated with conscious decision-making and problem-solving and because when we make decisions and solve problems we often apply rules and strategies we have learned or are trying to learn. Learning to play golf, for example, requires conscious attention to the rule "Keep your head down and your eye on the ball" while simultaneously trying to remember other rules concerning the proper grip on the club and configuration of the feet. Such processing is effortful and demanding of our attention; our concentration is easily broken by the people behind us who are impatiently waiting for us to tee off. Learning new behaviors and changing old behaviors that have become automatic—habits—demand our attention.

Smith and DeCoster theorize that controlled/rule-based processing accesses not only the slow-learning, long-term, associative memory system but also the short-term memory system, which they term the **fast-learning memory system**. The fast-learning memory system allows us to re-member a single occurrence of an event, such as the advice (often in the form of rules) given us by an instructor, our friends, or a therapist. This memory system allows us to take immediate advantage of others' experiences and knowledge; we don't have to be stung by a yellow insect many times, or even once, to learn to avoid it. In controlled/rule-based processing, both the rules and the process usually are subjectively accessible and therefore reportable—for example, we can tell others to avoid yellow insects.

The upside to the fast-learning memory system is that we can remember important experiences, advice, rules, and strategies even though they have not been repeated often enough to become regularities. The downside is that the experiences represented in the fast-learning memory system are vulnerable to being quickly forgotten (hence, "short-term" memory) if not repeated and consolidated over time into the slow-learning memory system. (As any student can testify, the forgetting curve over time for new rules and information is steep.) In sum, and unlike the automatic/associative information processing mode that exclusively uses the associative memory system, the slower, rule-based processing mode is believed to access *both* memory systems—both our stored knowledge of regularities and new and recently acquired knowledge.

Dual process theorists of social cognition believe that we use the more demanding and effortful controlled/rule-based processing mode primarily under two conditions: when we are highly motivated to make accurate predictions about another's behavior, and when we have time to engage in effortful processing. Research has shown that when another person is not important to us, or when we are busy performing other cognitive tasks and are therefore under high **cognitive load** and have little extra cognitive capacity, we are likely to process information about another quickly and automatically by using automatic/associative processing (e.g., Gilbert, 1989).

Assuming that we are not operating under high cognitive load and that we have the time, we are likely to use the more effortful mode of processing information about another person when we are outcome-dependent on him or her. Because such people are important to us, we are likely to be motivated to spend the time, effort, and conscious thought necessary to generate accurate predictions about their nature. Moreover, because we award them more of our attention (as discussed in Chapter 6, "Birth of a Relationship"), we are more likely to notice clues to their nature, and we may spend a good deal of time thinking about the implications of their **individuating characteristics**, features that set them apart from other people. (For this reason, controlled/rule-based processing is sometimes called individuated processing.)

People in close relationships are outcome-dependent on their partners and thus are usually motivated to process information accurately about those individuals. However, they also are often busy, distracted, and tired—in other words, they often are operating under high cognitive load. Moreover, as discussed in Chapter 6, the fact that a person is important to us does not necessarily mean we will award that person our attention and process his or her behavior in a careful and controlled fashion. In long-term established relationships, we generally know the partner well and are likely to process his or her behavior automatically. Fincham, Bradbury, and Scott (1990) state, "As any marital therapist can testify, behavior in marital interactions is often overlearned, unfolds at astonishing speed, and appears to proceed without much thought" (p. 139). They are among many marital researchers who have commented on this fact.

But because unexpected events tend to capture attention, if our close relationship partners violate our expectancies about their behavior, it is likely that controlled/rule-based processing will be used to solve the puzzle their behavior represents. Relatedly, we are likely to be motivated to use controlled/rule-based processing when we encounter information about a stranger that is inconsistent with our expectancies (see Fiske & Neuberg, 1990). Violated expectancies about someone we thought we knew and inconsistent information about a stranger both signal that we do not have an accurate impression of either person. Before we can interact confidently with each, we need to do some controlled, deliberate puzzle-solving—and that takes time and effort.

Although all dual process theorists incorporate the automatic/associative and controlled/rule-based modes of social information processing, they differ in the details. One unresolved question concerns whether the two kinds of processing typically occur sequentially or simultaneously (in parallel). Some theorize that in first-impression situations, the fast, automatic/associative mode is used first and then, assuming the individual has the motivation and the time, the slower, controlled/rule-based mode is used (Brewer, 1988; Fiske & Neuberg, 1990). Others contend that the two forms of processing usually occur simultaneously (Smith & DeCoster, 2000). Recent evidence supports the view that automatic/associative processing and controlled/rule-based processing do often occur simultaneously.

The two forms of social information processing were originally believed to be mutually exclusive, but it now is recognized that "pure" forms of each rarely occur (Bargh, 1996). Because automatic/associative processing demands little of our attentional or other cognitive capacities, we are free to perform other tasks that demand our conscious attention, and thus controlled/rule-based processing often occurs in parallel with automatic/associative processing. For example, some people will drive a car, processing changing road conditions and responding to them (usually an automatic process for experienced drivers), while carrying on an attention-demanding discussion on a cell phone. This practice is dangerous, however, because automatic/associative processing almost always places at least some demand on cognitive capacity. If the conversation partner announces out of the blue that he or she has just filed for divorce, the car may end up in a ditch—the driver's cognitive capacity will be fully captured by the unexpected news and the capacity needed to drive the car will not be available.

Bargh (1996) emphasizes that automatic processing often requires a conscious and deliberate act of will to begin; for example, the individual consciously decides to drive to his girlfriend's house, but the driving itself is largely an automatic process once started. Moreover, with conscious effort, the individual can often short-circuit an automatic process, as we try to do when we are trying to change any entrenched and automatically performed behavior. However, people cannot even attempt to control and change an automatic process unless they are aware that it is affecting their behavior. For example, a person may not realize that negative experiences with a former partner are influencing his or her behavior in a new relationship. Unfortunately, people usually are not aware of the effects of automatic/associative processing. In sum, the automatic/associative and controlled/rule-based processing modes are best viewed as opposing anchors of a single dimension, with most social information processing located somewhere between the two extremes.

FIRST IMPRESSIONS

The impressions people form in their first encounters with each other are critical to the future of their relationship for at least two reasons. First, in an open field, the first impression will determine whether there will be subsequent interactions. If one or both persons form an unfavorable first impression, interaction is likely to be terminated and future interactions avoided. Second, if the interaction continues, whether in an open or closed field, the partners' first impressions of each other will influence the nature of their future interactions because the expectancies an individual forms about another in the first interaction not only will guide that individual's own future interaction behavior but also will influence the individual's attention to, and interpretation of, the other's behavior.

The first thing we need to determine in an initial encounter is whether the stranger is a friend, a foe, or irrelevant to our well-being. In a dimly lit parking garage, we must quickly determine whether the man walking toward us with a shiny object in his hand is a security guard with a walkie-talkie, a mugger with a gun, a tired shopper with a cell phone, or a good Samaritan bringing us the keys we dropped as we got off the elevator. Precisely how the human mind routinely accomplishes this remarkable feat with lightning speed has been the subject of a great deal of theory and research.

Social Categorization

As previously noted, it is the *similarity* between a newly encountered stranger and people we have known in the past that is the "open sesame" to our personal warehouse of social knowledge stored in the associative memory system. The *process* by which we associate the features of the newly encountered person to people we have known in the past who possess similar features is called **social categorization**, a term that derives from Bruner's (1957) classic essay on perceptual readiness:

> Perception involves an act of categorization. . . . we stimulate an organism with some appropriate input and he responds by referring the input to some class of things or events. "That is an orange," he states. (p. 123)

Bruner's example illustrates the speed of the automatic/associative processing system. We are not conscious of perceiving a small, round, yellowish-red object and then effortfully searching for similar objects in memory to **encode** it, or interpret its meaning. Rather, we instantly see an orange, and almost as quickly, we access our knowledge about oranges and expect the orange to be edible, to be a source of vitamin C, and so forth. The categorization, and the resultant encoding, often seems to take place almost as fast as our senses detect the object. The entire process occurs so quickly, in fact, that the categorization and encoding of the object's meaning seems to be part of the act of perception itself. If we are hungry, for example, we may be reaching for the orange almost as soon as we see it on the table. Whether we also immediately and spontaneously encode another's behavior into personality trait terms—for example, whether a person helping an old woman cross the street immediately is encoded as "kind"—is still a question. Some investigators have found that we do (e.g., Uleman, Newman,

& Moskowitz, 1996), but others conclude that this occurs only when we are explicitly asked to form an impression of another from his or her behavior (e.g., Gilbert & Hixon, 1991).

As the concept of categorization suggests, all cognitive psychologists believe that information stored in memory is *organized* in some way—the human's memory systems do not store knowledge in higgledy-piggledy fashion. Exactly how that information is organized, and how that organizational structure may influence the processing of new information and the retrieval of old information, remains the subject of investigation and debate. In general, however, most theorists agree that the contents of our memory systems seem to be internally organized into categories of like objects, persons, and events. Memories of people organized according to their similarity are called **social categories**. Each social category has been viewed as containing abstract information centered around a person ("Aunt Betty," "myself") or around a group of people ("women," "diplomats") or social events ("weddings") that possess similar features. The term **social schema** is often used synonymously with "social category." Like categories, schemas have been defined as "mental structures that include beliefs and other information about a concept or a class of objects" (Olson et al., 1996, p. 212). The term "schema" has slightly different nuances, including loos-

er, fuzzier, and less rigid boundaries than the word "category" conveys.

Both "category" and "schema" are **hypothetical constructs**; that is, they are convenient fictions that allow scholars to talk about how the mind seems to work (no one ever opened up a brain and saw a warehouse of categories and schemas labeled "men," "frogs," and "Mondays," all neatly organized according to the principle of similarity). Both terms are intended to represent cognitive units of general knowledge. Although most theorists agree that similarity is the major principle by which units of knowledge seem to be organized, different theorists believe that different *types* of similarity are important—for example, functional similarity, appearance similarity, similarity of the time at which the experience occurred, similarity of the pattern of the neuronal brain structures activated by sensing the person or object.

Social categories and schemas are themselves believed to be organized *internally*. Many theorists believe they are organized hierarchically, according to their inclusiveness and level of abstraction. For example, "female" is a larger, higher-level, and more inclusive category than "mother," which in turn is a larger category than "my mother," which has a membership of one (see Figure 8.3). Not all category members are exactly similar, of course, and thus each member can be graded for its *typicality* or degree of similarity to

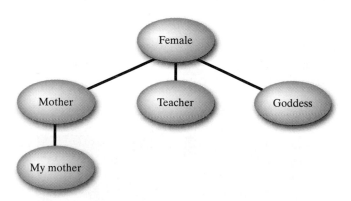

FIGURE 8.3 The Organization of Social Categories
Theorists believe that social categories are organized in a hierarchical fashion according to their inclusiveness and degree of abstraction.

the other category members. The member of a category that best represents the features of all members of the category is called the **prototype** (see Figure 8.4). Both categories and schemas are believed to be *activated*—brought to mind upon an encounter with a relevant person or object or shown to be "active" in influencing behavior—in an all-or-none fashion; that is, categories and schemas are believed to possess internal integrity such that they are accessed whole rather than in fragments. Despite continued debate about how social categories and schemas are organized and how the information they represent is retrieved, virtually all cognitive psychologists agree that it is by accessing these mental structures held in memory that we are able to make predictions about another person's behavior in interaction with us. Social cognitive psychologists Fiske and Taylor (1991) state, "Categories and schemas are ways of talking about *expectations* and their effects" (p. 97, emphasis added).

When the content of a social category is shared by many people, it often is called a **stereotype**. The knowledge we and many other people share about a group of people may or may not be accurate. Little is known about the accuracy of social stereotypes (Judd & Park, 1993). In addition to being shared with others, stereotypes have

another characteristic that distinguishes them from other social categories: The features that people in the social category share with the other category members usually are quickly and easily discernible in just a fraction of a second of interaction. Often they are features of the person's physical appearance. For example, there are gender stereotypes, age stereotypes, physical attractiveness stereotypes, racial stereotypes, and ethnic stereotypes, among many others.

It is rare that we can't categorize strangers in the first seconds of interaction and access a great deal of stored information about them—or at least about people who seem to be similar to them. There is evidence, for example, that people can reliably evaluate someone's physical attractiveness in less time than it takes to blink an eye. Goldstein and Papageorge (1980) found that 150-millisecond exposures of faces varying in physical attractiveness produced highly reliable attractiveness ratings; that is, those ratings significantly correlated with the ratings of people who had been given an unlimited time to look at the faces. The exposure time of the faces was so brief that not only was no eye movement possible, but participants later could not even recognize the faces they saw. Similar findings have been reported by Simpson and Crandall (1972),

FIGURE 8.4 Category Prototypes
A prototype is a "typical" member of a category, one that best represents the features of all the category members. For example, golden retrievers are more prototypical of the category "pet" than are horses or birds. For the concept "dad," the television character Heathcliff Huxtable (*The Cosby Show*) probably is more prototypical than Al Bundy (*Married with Children*) or Ozzy Osbourne (*The Osbournes*).

who found that judgments of the magnitude of a person's smile could be made reliably within 20 milliseconds, although later recognition of the faces was little better than chance. Once we have categorized the person as physically attractive, we know that he or she is "warm" and has all the other traits contained in the physical attractiveness stereotype, and once we have determined that the stranger is smiling—the universal signal of friendliness—we can predict that the person is unlikely to do us harm.

Social categorization, like other efficiencies in information processing, has a price: error. The expectancies about strangers produced by quick and dirty automatic/associative information processing are always in error to some degree because no individual is precisely the same as any other, and thus the stranger is always somewhat different from people we have known in the past. Moreover, we may make a wrong categorization of the person and retrieve misleading information, which may be either our mistake or the result of the other's deliberate deception. The inaccurate categorization of a young, handsome, nicely dressed man with a cast on his arm as a harmless college student cost many women their lives—they became the victims of serial killer Ted Bundy.

If an error in social categorization leads to a negative expectancy, the interaction probably will be terminated and the error never discovered. To discover that our first, and negative, impression of another is inaccurate, it usually is necessary for us to continue interaction—something we are not likely to do. Only if we believe that the other person is likely to enhance our welfare are we likely to continue to voluntarily interact with that person in an open field. This is one reason negative but inaccurate first impressions and the stereotypes that often underlie them are difficult to change. They often are corrected only when persons holding the inaccurate impression find themselves in a closed field with the other. Even then it may be difficult to change a mistaken first impression, as we shall shortly discuss.

On rare occasions, our mind comes up blank because we have never in the past known anyone even remotely like the stranger. In such cases, we may have the uneasy feeling that the person might be harmful to us. If we are in a closed field, we probably will be wary and cautious and especially attentive to the person's behavior, engaging in controlled/rule-based processing of information to try to determine that person's nature. If we are in an open field, the default option is to terminate the interaction. Wholly unfamiliar people may be harmful or they may not be, but "better safe than sorry" generally seems to describe most people's reactions to them.

Principles of Social Categorization

Two principles determine whether, and how, we use our stored social knowledge to cope with newly encountered people. Again, the first and most important principle is the degree of similarity between the stranger and people we have known in the past: The more features a person shares with other people in a social category, the more likely that category or schema, and the expectancies it represents, will be accessed. The second principle is *category accessibility*.

Category Accessibility

Some social categories seem to be in the attic of our minds and hard to retrieve, whereas others are highly accessible. The more frequently and recently a category has been used, or the more often it is expected to be used, the more accessible it is likely to be and the more likely it is to be used to categorize a stranger. For example, if we have been interrupted repeatedly by door-to-door solicitors, the category "solicitor" is likely to be highly accessible. The more accessible the category, the fewer features the stranger needs to share with other members of that category to be categorized in that way. For example, any stranger who subsequently rings the doorbell is likely to be categorized as a solicitor, and we may be embarrassed to later discover that we slammed the door in our new neighbor's face. Moreover, the more ambiguous the features of a person, the more likely he or she is to be placed in an accessible category. We are particularly likely to mistake our neighbor as a solicitor if the porch light is out and we cannot see her features clearly.

Over time, if a category has been repeatedly used, it may become **chronically accessible** to the individual and any stranger encountered is likely to be categorized in that way. For some people, certain person traits—"untrustworthy," for example—have become highly accessible and the mere hint of dishonest behavior may cause a stranger to be categorized as an untrustworthy person. Chronically accessible social categories, schemas, and person constructs are presumed to be unique to the individual, developing from frequent and consistent experiences within his or her history of social interaction. For example, Andersen and her colleagues have demonstrated that the schemas of significant others tend to be chronically accessible and that the positive or negative affect associated with the schema of a significant other can be transferred to an unfamiliar person who resembles the significant other (e.g., Andersen & Baum, 1994). Moreover, transference of affect (positive or negative) toward the stranger who resembles a significant other may cause the other to feel similarly in return, thus recreating in some respects the previous relationship (Berk & Andersen, 2000).

To study the effects of categorization in general, and category accessibility in particular, cognitive psychologists often **prime** a category; that is, they increase the accessibility of a particular social category (or person construct), often by presenting the category or construct subliminally, below the individual's threshold of awareness. In *semantic priming*, for example, the name of the category (say, "lecher") or words associated with the category ("womanizer," "philanderer") are presented on a computer or a slide for such short exposures that the individual is not aware that a word has been presented. Carver, Ganellen, Froming, and Chambers (1983) asked their experimental participants to play the role of "teacher" in a learning task in which they were to administer electric shocks to a "learner" when an incorrect response was made. Some of the participants were subliminally primed with words associated with the person trait of "hostility" before they performed the task, whereas other participants were primed with neutral words. The *hostility*-primed teachers administered longer shocks to the learner (a confederate of the experimenters who did not actually receive the shocks) than did *neutral* teachers. Because the hostility prime had been subliminal, participants in the hostility group were unaware of their bias and the true cause of their behavior. It should be noted that the effects of category priming are the same whether or not the individual is consciously aware of the priming stimulus. The important difference between the two situations, as Bargh (1996) discusses, is whether we are aware of the effects of increased category accessibility on our behavior.

To take another example of the power of priming on the activation of cognitive constructs, Mikulincer, Gillath, and Shaver (2002) hypothesized and found that people showed evidence of heightened accessibility of representations of persons they had previously named as attachment figures after threat-related words like "failure" had been primed by rapid subliminal presentation; that is, on a lexical decision task, which required participants to identify whether a string of letters on a computer screen formed a word, reaction times after a threat prime were significantly faster for the names of their attachment figures than they were for the names of persons with whom they were in a close relationship (but who were not attachment figures), names of known persons, and names of unknown persons. When the prime was a neutral word like "hat," this effect was not found, providing evidence for the central hypothesis of attachment theory that threat activates the attachment system in adults. Although individuals' attachment style did not modify these overall findings, it did make a difference: Attachment anxiety was significantly associated with faster reaction times to the names of attachment figures regardless of the primed context (threat or neutral), suggesting that for these people, attachment figures are chronically accessible. Attachment avoidance seemed to inhibit the accessibility of attachment figures when the threat-related word "separation" was primed, suggesting that avoidant persons have learned not to appeal to attachment figures when those figures threaten to leave. A previous study conducted by Mikulincer, Birnbaum, Woddis, and Nachmias (2000) found that subliminally primed threats also heightened the accessibility of proximity-related constructs such as "love" and "closeness."

In tests of their accessibility model, Higgins (e.g., 1989) and his associates have found that another's behavior is more likely to be encoded in terms of a recently primed construct after a very short delay following the priming event (as is the case in most laboratory studies), but it will be encoded in terms of a more frequently primed construct after a longer delay (Bargh, Lombardi, & Higgins, 1988). In naturalistic situations, many different competing categories and constructs may be primed (as opposed to laboratory situations in which only a single construct is primed). Given the competition for dominance of primes in most naturalistic situations, the shortness of recency effects, and evidence that the priming effect is easily erased by the intrusion of a single intervening item (see Smith, 1998, p. 423), people can be expected to quickly revert to their uniquely personal chronically accessible constructs in most situations.

Frequency and recency of use are the two most commonly investigated determinants of category accessibility. However, accessibility also may be influenced by the person's *motivational state*—goals, needs, and desires—at the time he or she categorizes another person. For example, Stephan, Berscheid, and Walster (1971) asked men to form an impression of a woman who was *available* or *unavailable* for a date while they were either sexually *aroused* (from reading an erotic love story) or *unaroused* (from reading about the sex life of the herring gull). The aroused men found the available woman to be more attractive than did the unaroused men, and they also formed a very different impression of her. In contrast to the impression formed by the unaroused men, those in the aroused–available condition believed the woman to be more "promiscuous" and "liberal"—person traits congruent with wish fulfillment and satisfaction of their sexual desires. Another example of the effect of motivational

state on the perception of others is provided by Mongrain, Vettese, Shuster, and Kendal (1998), who found that women with a strong need for harmony saw their partners as more loving than their partners actually felt or than external observers perceived their partners to be.

Finally, and in addition to frequency and recency of use of a social category and our motivational state, perhaps the most usual determinant of category accessibility in social interaction is our *expectancies* at the time we make the categorization. Our initial expectancies about how a person is likely to behave and about other events likely to occur in an interaction situation often prime the social categories, schemas, and person constructs relevant to these expectancies.

Expectancies and Category Accessibility

The efficiency with which our minds operate is reflected in the fact that our expectancies prime categories and schemas relevant to the events we believe are likely to unfold in the course of interaction. Having the appropriate categories accessible and "at the ready" increases the speed with which we can recognize the expected persons, objects, or events even when they are ambiguous, and it also facilitates access to the information we need to interact with them. For example, we confidently recognize the dim outlines of a familiar person at a moonlight beach party because the person said he or she would be there, and so we expect to see that individual. If the same person should appear in an unusual environment, one in which we have no expectation of seeing him or her, we may overlook that person's presence or inaccurately identify him or her. People commonly give lack of expectancy as a reason for delayed or inaccurate recognition ("Oh, I didn't recognize you! I didn't expect to see you here").

Although expectancies facilitate speedy control of the environment by increasing category accessibility, once again we sometimes pay the price of error because expectancies not only influence the *speed* with which events are perceived, but they also often influence *what* events capture our attention and how those events are interpreted. The influence of a categorization-produced expectancy on attention was illustrated by Zadny and Gerard (1974), who asked college men and women to observe a live skit in which a male college student attempted to enroll for classes at a computer station operated by a person playing the role of registrar. Before they saw the skit, some observers were told that the student they were about to see was a chemistry major, others were told he was a music major, and the remainder were told he was a psychology major. The skit began when the actor/student entered the room with his arms full of books and other materials associated with student life, stumbled, and dropped at the feet of his audience three items related to chemistry (such as a slide rule), three to music (Beethoven sheet music), and three to psychology (a copy of *Psychology Today*). He then tried to enroll in six different classes, two in each of the three areas of specialization. Immediately after the skit, participants were asked to list the objects the actor/student had dropped and the classes mentioned, taking as much time as they wished. Observers in the chemistry condition recalled a significantly higher percentage of chemistry items and classes than did the observers in the music and psychology conditions; parallel findings were obtained for the observers in the latter conditions.

In a follow-up experiment, Zadny and Gerard demonstrated that the expectancies generated by the initial categorization influenced whether the observers even saw the object dropped or heard the class mentioned; that is, people failed to report events in the incongruent social categories not because their memories failed them but because they simply hadn't seen the objects incongruent with their expectancies in the first place. Thus, Zadny and Gerard demonstrated that categorization produces expectancies that often direct our attention to events congruent with those expectancies, causing us to overlook events that would disconfirm them. In this experiment, as in others that have shown that expectancies direct attention, the participants' expectancies were strong.

Other research indicates that when the individual does not have a well-established ex-pectancy, as is sometimes the case in first encounters, people attend to and recall not expectancy consistent information but information inconsistent with their initial, preliminary expectancy (Hastie & Kumar, 1979; Higgins & Bargh, 1987). Again, in initial encounters people often are trying to form an accurate impression of the other's nature and may be sensitive to any inconsistencies, for they suggest that a reliable impression has yet to be formed.

Strongly held but inaccurate expectancies may be confirmed in social interaction not only because they direct attention to behavior consistent with the expectancy and away from inconsistent behavior but also because our own interaction behavior may *elicit* from our partners the very behavior we expected them to exhibit (e.g., Kelley & Stahelski, 1970). The self-fulfilling nature of expectancies produced by social categorization was illustrated by Snyder, Tanke, and Berscheid (1977), who led men who had been recruited to participate in a "getting acquainted" study to think that they were conversing on the telephone with either a physically attractive or an unattractive woman. In actuality, the men were conversing with a randomly selected woman participating in the study. The man's and woman's contributions to the telephone conversation were recorded separately and his or her side of the conversation was evaluated by judges, who did not know the circumstances of the conversation but were asked to form an impression of the person they heard speaking. The judges' evaluations revealed that women whom the men believed to be physically attractive (but who were of a variety of physical attractiveness levels) came to behave in a more likable and sociable manner than women who, unbeknownst to them, were interacting with a man who believed them to be unattractive. Outside observers who listened to the men's side of the conversation judged those men who believed they were interacting with an attractive women to be significantly more sociable, sexually warm, interesting, independent, sexually permissive, bold, outgoing, humorous, and socially adept than their counterparts. These men also impressed the judges as being significantly more attractive, confident, and animated in their conversations. Thus, the men's categorization of the woman affected their *own* behavior in interaction, which, in turn, influenced the women's behavior in ways congruent with the men's initial expectancies.

The influence of our expectancies on what we subsequently perceive and how we interpret what we perceive can be insidiously powerful and difficult to guard against (Snyder & Stukas, 1999). Although this is true in the perception of physical objects, it is especially true in the perception of people because the properties of people, and the meaning of their behaviors, tend to be more ambiguous, as we have noted, thus permitting greater opportunity to interpret behavior in line with the expectancy. All of the mechanisms that result in a person's expectancies being confirmed in interaction form yet another reason it is difficult to change a person's initial impression of another. Each confirmation of the individual's initial expectancies about his or her partner's nature further strengthens the initial categorization, which in turn results in the individual entering subsequent interactions laden with even more compelling expectancies.

Expectancies generated in the first encounter, then, are the primary reason why people "never get a second chance to make a first impression" and why the initiating conditions of the first encounter cast a shadow over the entire relationship. Once an interaction starts along one track rather than another, it becomes very difficult for the individual to cognitively "break set" on the partner and change the trajectory of the relationship.

New Models of Cognition

The hypothetical constructs of social categories and schemas, as well as other metaphors used in traditional models of social cognition, view units of knowledge stored in memory as "things" (Smith, 1998). Advances in cognitive neuroscience are generating new models of cognition that picture the mind not as a warehouse of thing-like units of knowledge that are retrieved whole but rather as being more like a television set: Detection of a person or object by our senses generates a particular pattern of electrical impulses in the brain, each pattern unique to each experience of the person, object, or event. Just as any pixel on a television screen can play a part in projecting an image of an orange or an apple or a great many other objects, depending on the pattern of the pixels that are activated, any neuron in the human brain can contribute to many different images projected to consciousness and to the many different patterns of brain activity that influence our behavior. These new models of the human mind—sometimes called *connectionist* models or *parallel distributing processing* models of cognition—view cognitive units of information not as hypothetical fixed and static things like categories and schemas that are "retrieved" but rather as unique *patterns of brain activity* generated by a person or an object.

These new models of cognition, yet to be fully developed and applied to social cognition, will be especially useful to relationship scholars, for they have several nuances and implications that traditional models of cognition lack. Moreover, they are more in accord not only with what is now known about the brain but also with what is known about relationships. For example, and as we have discussed, traditional models of social cognition suggest that information about "Aunt Betty" is stored in a fixed category somewhere in the brain that contains all beliefs, expectations, and other information about Aunt Betty, and that it is this stable repository of information that is accessed when one thinks about or interacts with Aunt Betty. The new models of cognition paint a different picture. To paraphrase cognitive neuroscientist Damasio (1994), Aunt Betty does not exist at one single site in the brain in an "Aunt Betty" category; rather, Aunt Betty is distributed all over the brain in certain neurons that are activated when we see her (see pp. 102–103).

Thus, it is useful to think of Aunt Betty as a distributed representation of knowledge that is recreated or *reconstructed* in a context-sensitive way when next we think about Aunt Betty or interact with her. "Context-sensitive" means that it is not Aunt Betty alone who determines what neurons will be activated when we think about her; other elements in the context in which we are thinking about Aunt Betty or interacting with her, including our own motivational and internal states, help determine what image of Aunt Betty will be activated and brought to consciousness. Very different visions of Aunt Betty may come to mind when we walk through a grove of willow trees (she used willow switches to paddle our behinds) than when we pass a bakery and smell muffins just like the ones she used to make. In the latter instance, we may remember a much kinder and gentler Aunt Betty, particularly if we are hungry. Thus, the new models suggest that we do not access a fixed, thing-like category that contains information about Aunt Betty. Rather, these models suggest that we have many mental representations of our partners, and the one likely to be activated in any given situation depends on the *context*—the environmental situation and our internal state—in which we are remembering, or encountering, that person. These new models of cognition regard units of knowledge as brain states, not things organized in category pigeonholes.

Like traditional models of cognition, the new models incorporate the rule of similarity. For example, a large orange is presumed to produce a pattern of brain activity somewhat similar to that produced by a tangerine, which may somewhat overlap the pattern produced by the sun setting over the horizon. Again, knowledge is presumed to be accessed on the basis of similarity between the presently encountered person or object and past experiences with that person or object. Smith (1996) has outlined some of the implications of connectionist models of cognition for our understanding of social cognition, but their development and application are ongoing. In the meantime, it is important to recognize that virtually all that is currently known about social cognition derives from thing-like metaphors of the mind and that this knowledge ultimately will be subsumed and integrated within new models of cognition.

RELATIONSHIP SCHEMAS

Although social categories and schemas have been viewed as organized around individual persons or groups of persons, much social informa-

tion concerns social relationships, including our own relationships with others. The term "relationship schema" was introduced by Sally Planalp (1987) to describe knowledge structures that represent a person's relationship with another. Mark Baldwin (1992) subsequently reviewed classic and current contributions to the concept of **relationship schema**, which he defined as "cognitive structures representing regularities in patterns of interpersonal relatedness" (p. 461). Baldwin theorizes that relationship schemas contain three elements: a *self schema* that represents in memory how the self is experienced in a specific relationship, a *person schema* for the relationship partner, and an *interaction script* that represents the expected interaction pattern formed from repeated interaction experiences. All three components are theorized to be linked in a single knowledge structure. Thus, activation of one component of the relationship schema is theorized to activate the other two components as well.

Evidence supporting the view that social information may be organized around relationships was provided by Aron, Aron, Tudor, and Nelson (1991). These investigators primed a close relationship partner for some participants and a celebrity for others and then asked each participant to decide whether a series of person traits were descriptive of themselves. In contrast to participants in the celebrity condition, decision times were longer for those in the close relationship condition on traits on which they and their partner differed; the longer response latencies were believed to be the result of participants' integration of the mental representations of themselves and their partner and the resulting difficulty of separating their own traits from those of their partners. Indeed, a subsequent study found that people are more likely to confuse traits rated as characteristic of the self with traits rated as characteristic of close others than they are with traits of nonclose others (Mashek, Aron, & Boncimino, 2003). Prentice (1990) found that representations of the self differ less from familiar people than from unfamiliar others. Moreover, when two people are described as close relationship partners, information about each person appears to be mentally linked when it is encoded and also when it is recalled (Sedikides, Olsen, & Reis, 1993). Thus, evidence is accumulating that the perception of a relationship between two people may influence how social knowledge is organized in memory.

The concept of relationship schema has many implications. For example, although it traditionally has been assumed that people have one unitary self-concept, the relationship schema construct implies that we may have several, each tied to a specific relationship (Ogilvie & Ashmore, 1991). Each view of the self within a particular relationship schema may become highly accessible and activated when the relationship schema is activated. In one early study of this phenomenon, Baldwin, Carrell, and Lopez (1990) demonstrated that graduate students evaluated themselves more negatively when the frowning face of their mentor was primed through subliminal presentation. Others have since presented corroborating evidence that when a specific relationship schema is activated, the person's self-evaluation changes as a function of his or her view of the self in that relationship (e.g., Hinkley & Andersen, 1996; Leary, Tambor, Terdal, & Downs, 1995); in other words, we may value some relationships more than others not necessarily because we like our partners more but because we like ourselves more in that relationship.

Relatedly, in recent years several personality theorists have advocated conceptualizing personality structure and coherence in terms of *Person × Situation* interactions, as opposed to the traditional view of personality as being independent of situation. Mendoza-Denton, Ayduk, Mischel, Shoda, and Testa (2001) elaborate: "There is now compelling evidence that individuals' distinctive, highly contextualized, but stable *if . . . then . . .* patterns of situation–behavior relationships (e.g., if Situation X, then person does A, but if Situation Y, then person does B) are a locus of behavioral stability and an expression of the underlying process dynamics of the individual" (p. 533). Kelley and colleagues (2003) go further, taking the view that "situations and person factors are inextricably linked such that each cannot be understood in isolation from the other" (p. 9); these theorists offer an "atlas" of generic social situations, each of which affords the expression of certain dispositions in social interaction and inhibits the expression of others.

Connectionist or state-like (as opposed to thing-like) models of social cognition can be expected to advance the new theoretical views of the association between personality and situation and of the multiple-selves phenomenon (such as that displayed by Dr. Jekyll and Mr. Hyde); such models posit that representations of the self (or anything else) are always reconstructed somewhat differently, depending on the situational context and the individual's internal states, such as emotions, at the time the relevant information is accessed. State-like models of cognition also are likely to facilitate further investigation of preliminary evidence that we have more than one schema for our relationship partner, depending on the different situations in which we interact with him or her. In addition, these models suggest that different remembrances of another may have different affective tones, as we have discussed. Srull and Wyer's (1989) model posits that the phenomenon of affective ambivalence toward our relationship partner is especially likely in long-term close relationships in which we have interacted with the partner in many different settings ("Jim is a great lover but a lousy accountant"). These theorists speculate that "when the behaviors of a person in one situation (or role) tend to differ evaluatively from those performed in another situation (or role), people may not attempt to reconcile the differences and may not even see them as inconsistent" (p. 80). In other words, cognitive consistency processes may not come into play.

In sum, many recent models of social cognition suggest that people may have multiple schemas for a single relationship, each representing different interaction patterns and different partner- and self-schemas, depending on the situation ("my relationship with Mom on Saturdays at the playground" and "my relationship with Mom on weekdays when she comes home tired from her job"). Although our current knowledge of how relationship information is represented in memory is scant (Collins & Read, 1994; Holmes, 2000), there now is little doubt that much social information *is* organized around relationships and that relationship schemas operate like other social categories and schemas; that is, the expectancies associated with relationship schemas direct attention and guide behavior, sometimes in ways that promote confirmation of the expectancies generated by the schema. Moreover, many specific kinds of relationship schemas have been shown to be chronically accessible to certain people. The most prominent example is an adult's attachment style. Baldwin, Fehr, Keedian, Seidel, and Thomson (1993) found that people who have a secure adult attachment style recognize words representing positive interpersonal themes faster than people with an insecure style, who recognize negative interpersonal words more quickly.

An example of the insidious effects some chronically accessible relationship schemas can have is the "threat-oriented" parent–child relationship schema held by some parents. Seeking to understand the dynamics of interaction within families at risk for violence, Bugental and her associates (e.g., Bugental, 1992; Bugental et al., 1993) observed that physically abusive parents and their children appear to engage in "role-reversed" relationships in which the parents attribute higher levels of power to their children than to themselves. Accordingly, these parents believe that their negative interactions with children are caused by factors controllable by the child but uncontrollable by themselves. When their threat-oriented schema is activated within an interaction situation, it triggers a chain of events that support and perpetuate the parent's schema.

Using computer simulations, Bugental and her colleagues (1993) examined the interaction patterns of adults, preselected to be threat-oriented or not (the Control group), who were instructed to teach a child a maze-learning game. The child's behavior, depicted on a computer screen, was programmed to be responsive or unresponsive to the adult's directions. Activation of the threat-oriented adults' schema by anticipation of the task was apparent when they saw (through a one-way mirror) the child they believed they would be teaching; some made negative remarks such as "He looks like he'd be developmentally slow." After the teaching task, the threat-oriented adults, in contrast to controls, rated the unresponsive children more negatively and the responsive children more positively. Moreover, over the course of their interactions with the child, threat-oriented adults, in contrast to controls, exhibited increasing negative thoughts, increasing physiological arousal, and increasing use of sanctions (awarding fewer "happy faces" to the child for his or her performance).

Bugental and her associates (2002) subsequently examined an intervention program designed to prevent the maltreatment of infants at risk for abuse. The program included a procedure intended to alter mothers' causal appraisals of their caregiving difficulties (the *causal appraisal/home visitation* intervention condition), which lowered the prevalence of abuse to 4% in contrast to a control condition (26%), in which the mothers were simply given information, and also in contrast to a home visitation only condition (23%). The randomly assigned mothers in the causal appraisal condition were assisted in evaluating a reported caregiving problem in a way that directed attribution of cause away from both themselves and the child. For example, these women were steered away from causes that suggested the infant was challenging parental power or otherwise intentionally behaving badly. Instead, they were encouraged to think of actions that could be taken to deal with the problem (change the baby's formula, sing to soothe the infant), thereby increasing their feelings of efficacy and power to deal with the situation. It should be emphasized that chronically accessible relationship schemas facilitate automatic/associative processing of information in relationships, and it is unlikely that these schemas can easily be changed without intervention (e.g., see Fletcher, Rosanowski, & Fitness, 1994).

Interaction Scripts

The concept of interaction script, believed to be an element of a relationship schema, is especially important because it is the partners' interaction pattern that most relationship researchers, and the partners themselves, wish to understand, to predict, and, in the case of therapeutic intervention, to change. An **interaction script** is viewed as the partners' expectancies about the temporal ordering of their own and each other's behavior and other events in a particular setting. As Ginsberg (1988) discusses, interaction scripts "facilitate the coordination of action, reduce the effort of interaction, reduce the necessity of attention to small details and allow joint action to be organized in large rather than minute chunks" (p. 30). Although not a great deal is known about interaction scripts in relationships, largely because most social cognition research has been restricted to first impressions of strangers, they, like other schemas, have been shown to guide the interpretation and memory of another's interaction behaviors.

Just as other schemas do, relationship interaction scripts develop gradually. At the beginning of a relationship, interaction with the partner usually requires effortful and controlled information processing as the partners try to coordinate their actions and reduce the awkwardness of their exchanges. Over time, as the partners learn to coordinate their actions, the same temporal sequence of behavioral events may begin to occur

So you want a sprinkling of dirt on these eggs?

FIGURE 8.5 Over time, interaction sequences between relationship partners demand less and less conscious attention. Consequently, partners become able to perform demanding tasks (like reading the newspaper, cooking breakfast, or doing the crossword puzzle) while interacting with each other — a situation that can produce comical results.

repeatedly. With repetition, those interaction sequences are likely to become smoother and less variable in content. They also will demand less and less conscious attention for their performance and may recede from conscious awareness. Cartoonists frequently capitalize on the fact that long-term spouses can perform demanding tasks while interacting with each other—the husband does a *Times* crossword puzzle at breakfast while conversing absent-mindedly with his wife, nodding in assent when she asks him whether he would like a sprinkle of dirt on his eggs.

The partner's mind is, indeed, "absent" during the performance of many interactions in long-term relationships. Berscheid (1983/2002) called attention to the fact that over time, the partners may develop even long and complex interaction sequences that are performed automatically and without conscious awareness. As we discussed in Chapter 4, "The Concept of Relationship," many such complex interactions are meshed; that is, each person's behavior in the action sequence is triggered by the partner's immediately previous act, and that behavior serves as the stimulus for the partner's next act. As with other organized action sequences that are at first performed with effort and conscious thought—for example, learning to drive a car—over time and with frequent and consistent repetition, these action sequences become automatically performed. Unlike automatically performed individual chained-action sequences, however, meshed interaction sequences depend on *both* partners performing the appropriate action at the appropriate time in the sequence, as discussed previously. Such interaction sequences allow the partners to devote their conscious attention to other tasks. Over time, an increasing portion of the partners' interactions may be characterized by automatic/associative processing (see Scott, Fuhrman, & Wyer, 1991; Surra & Bohman, 1991).

Chronically accessible relationship schemas, including the expectancies and interaction scripts associated with them, constitute one reason intervention into a distressed relationship is most likely to be successful if it is undertaken early in the relationship and before a dysfunctional schema becomes entrenched (Olson, 1990). After the partners' schema-associated expectancies have become strongly established and inaccessible to conscious awareness, the partners often must exert superhuman effort to change an unhappy relationship, as discussed in Chapter 14, "Intervention and Dissolution." Negative partner behaviors consistent with negative expectancies are likely to be noticed, even under the cognitive overload conditions in which much close relationship interaction takes place, whereas the partner's attempts to perform "new leaf" behaviors may be overlooked because they are incongruent with the expectancies. Moreover, even when people are busy and distracted by other tasks, it appears that they are particularly likely to notice negative social stimuli, such as the partner's undesirable behaviors (Bargh, 1994).

MEMORY FOR RELATIONSHIP EVENTS

Because of their heavy reliance on the self-report method, usually retrospective self-report of relationship events, knowledge of the factors that affect memory of personal experiences is of special interest to relationship scholars. Unfortunately, cognitive psychologists have primarily focused on abstract knowledge structures such as categories and schemas, which are theorized to contain information that has been distilled from specific event experiences. Neglect of memory for particular events was commented on by Ulric Neisser (1982) in the early 1980s: "If X is an interesting or socially significant aspect of memory, then psychologists have hardly ever studied X" (p. 4). A notable exception was Brown and Kulik's (1977) classic paper on "flashbulb memories," which focused on the vivid memories many adults possessed of momentous and shocking events such as President John F. Kennedy's assassination. A subsequent study of people's vivid autobiographical memories revealed that most were of high personal importance (not national importance) and that they tended to be surprising, consequential, and emotional, although some were not (Rubin & Kozin, 1984). Nevertheless, there is "no comprehensive theo-ry of particular instances: how they are remembered and how they influence the life course" (Pillemer, 1998, p. 24). Thus, there is little understanding of the role particular experiences play in schema development (Smith, 1998).

Cognitive psychologists' neglect of people's memory of their personal experiences is ironic because the first scholars to study memory—Galton, Ebbinghaus, and Freud—were particularly interested in memory for autobiographical events. An important subset is **autobiographical relationship events**—events that the individual has personally experienced within the context of a relationship. One of the principles found to govern the content and quantity of autobiographical memories and other kinds of information is the steep forgetting curve over time. Between one-third and two-thirds of all autobiographical memories people spontaneously recall are for events within the past year (Cohen, 1989; Rubin, 1986). However, the autobiographical forgetting curve shows two irregularities: *childhood amnesia*, in which there appears to be an "extra" forgetting of events that occurred during the first 5 years of life, just as Freud supposed (Wetzler & Sweeney, 1986); and *reminiscence*, beginning by age 50, which reveals an increase (beyond what one would expect from the forgetting curve) in memory for events that occurred when the individual was 10 to 30 years old (Rubin, Wetzler, & Nebes, 1986). In addition, autobiographical events that are unique and unexpected and have important consequences tend to be well remembered (Stangor & McMillan, 1992). Interest in memory for autobiographical events, including relationship events, has increased. For example, some social cognitive psychologists have attempted to incorporate individual experiences into their schema theories (e.g., Fiske & Neuberg, 1990), and others have developed theories centered on what they call *exemplars*, mental representations of specific experiences, including their details and context (e.g., Smith & Zarate, 1992).

Researchers' investigations have established that one partner's memory of a relationship event often does not agree with the other partner's memory, even for "factual" events and even when the report is made a short time after the occurrence of the event (see Metts, Sprecher, & Cupach, 1991). In one early study, Christensen, Sullaway, and King (1983) found low agreement between partners on a highly structured event checklist that simply asked married couples just 24 hours later, and dating couples a few days later, whether an event had or had not occurred.

One systematic feature of memory of relationship events has been termed the **egocentric memory bias**. Ross and Sicoly (1979) found that when married couples were asked to report how they apportioned responsibility for performing various household chores, both husbands and wives tended to overestimate their own contributions and underestimate their partner's. Christensen and associates (1983) also found evidence that spouses tended to ascribe more responsibility for relationship events to themselves than to their partners, with the exception of couples in older relationships, who tended to attribute responsibility for negative events to their partners. Subsequent research has confirmed that whether people claim themselves to be responsible for a relationship event depends on whether the event is positive or negative and whether the individual is satisfied or dissatisfied with the relationship. Dissatisfied couples are more likely to attribute responsibility for negative events to their partner than satisfied couples are; the latter show an egocentric bias for negative events but tend to assign responsibility for positive events to their partner (Bradbury & Fincham, 1990).

Emotion-provoking relationship events, which are often unexpected and consequential to the individual's well-being, tend to be remembered (e.g., Harvey, Flanary, & Morgan, 1986), although the time that has elapsed from the event's occurrence needs to be taken into consideration. Taylor's (1991) review of the literature, and her **mobilization–minimization hypothesis** of memory, suggests that negative personal events may initially be remembered better than positive events (in the service of helping the individual mobilize resources to cope with the negative event), but over time, negative events seem to be minimized and to fade in memory such that positive events are better remembered. (This phe-

nomenon is sometimes referred to as the Pollyanna principle; see Matlin & Stang, 1978.) In one longitudinal study, for example, Field (1981) examined interviews made when the participants were at ages 30, 47, and 70 and found that the number of individuals reporting a happy childhood significantly increased with each successive interview. A single-subject longitudinal diary study by Wagenaar (1986) showed a similar effect. Several studies by Skowronski and Thompson and others have corroborated that the affective tone of the event makes a difference in its likelihood of remembrance. For example, using a diary technique, Skowronski, Betz, Thompson, and Shannon (1991) showed a memory preference for positive over negative daily events that happened to the self, but no such preference for events that happened to a close relationship partner. Strongly positive or negative events were recalled better than neutral events for both the self and the partner.

The positivity or negativity of the individual's mood at the time of recall may enhance the recall of mood-congruent information (Bower, 1981a; Forgas, 1991, 2000). Some evidence suggests that there is a more reliable effect for the recall of mood-congruent material in positive mood states than in negative (Clark & Williamson 1989; Singer & Salovey, 1988), but Erber (1991) found both positive and negative mood effects, with negative moods increasing the accessibility of negative person-trait categories. Mood may also direct attention to certain partner behaviors and away from others. For example, Forgas and Bower (1987) demonstrated that people asked to form an impression of another spent more time reading and thinking about information about the other that matched their mood state.

Another kind of systematic bias for the memory of relationship events is the disproportionate influence recent relationship events may have on memory of past events. Miell (1987) asked people to graphically depict the "strength" of one of their four ongoing relationships each week for 10 weeks and found that recall of the strength of a relationship at a time past was based at least as much on the individual's estimation of the *current* strength of the relationship as it was on the estimation that had actually been made at the previous point in time. Although people displayed poor recall of the absolute levels of strength characteristic of their relationship at different times in its development, they did accurately remember the general developmental pattern. McFarland and Ross (1987) also found that the favorability of people's recalled impressions of their dating partners tended to be more consistent with their current impressions than actually had been the case at the previous time.

On the basis of these and other studies, Ross (1989) theorizes that recall of relationship events is an active, constructive, schema-guided process that depends importantly upon individuals' implicit theories concerning the stability of their own and another's attributes as well as their current estimations of these attributes. The theory predicts, for example, that people who believe a person trait such as "happiness" generally stays stable over time will exaggerate the similarity between what is currently true and what was true in the past even when there has been a change along that attribute dimension from past to present.

The accuracy of relationship memories may also depend on the sex of the partner doing the remembering. Ross and Holmberg (1990) found that women recall relationship events—a first date, for example—more vividly and in greater detail than their male partners do. They speculate that this gender effect may stem partly from the greater importance of relationships to women and their greater tendency to reminisce about relationship events. Supporting this view, Acitelli (1992; Acitelli & Holmberg, 1993) found that women demonstrate more awareness of factors such as interaction patterns than men do when talking about the relationship. Good memory has been shown to depend on relating inputs to well-differentiated knowledge structures (e.g., Bower & Gilligan, 1979), and thus one possible explanation of women's better memory for relationship events is that women may possess more highly developed relationship schemas than men do; that is, a more elaborated relationship schema

may facilitate the encoding and representation of relationship information.

Finally, memory for events in the relationship also may be a function of what kind of event is being remembered. Wegner, Giuliano, and Hertel (1985) observed that couples often develop a communal memory bank, which they call **transactive memory**, defined as the organized store of knowledge contained in the individual memory systems of *both* partners and the set of transactive communication processes that the partners use to access each other's memory stores. Some portions of the joint, or transactive, memory structure may become highly differentiated—the wife knows all the family birthdays and the husband knows when the car needs oil—whereas others may become highly integrated. Through communication about an event, both partners may modify their memory of it and arrive at the same representation. Surra and Bohman (1991) also discuss how, through lengthy discussion, an event may become "reified" in each partner's mind. Wegner and colleagues predict that dysfunctional transactive memory in a relationship forecasts relationship breakdown and that some of the difficulties that accompany relationship dissolution are the result of the absence of transactive memory and the consequent loss of access to important personal information.

Account Narratives

Instead of focusing on the accuracy of autobiographical and relationship memories, an increasing number of researchers are investigating the reconstructive quality of such memories to learn how people make sense out of their past, particularly past relationship events, and how these reconstructions influence their current behavior (e.g., Gergen & Gergen, 1988). The term **account narrative** refers to the stories people construct of events that span a considerable period of time and that are presented in relatively unstructured formats such as diaries.

John Harvey, Ann Weber, and their associates (e.g., Harvey, Agostinelli, & Weber, 1989) have been the leaders in the use of account narratives in relationship research. Influenced by Weiss's (1975) finding that the accounts constructed by separated spouses concerning the dissolution of their relationship were important in helping them adjust to its loss, theory and research developed by Harvey and his colleagues focus on when people are likely to be motivated to construct cohesive account narratives. Their research suggests that people may be especially motivated to construct accounts after major negative life events, such as the loss of a relationship through death or divorce, in order to better understand the meaning of the event and its future implications for their lives. There also is evidence that the construction of a coherent account of the troubling event may promote physical and mental health, perhaps through self-esteem enhancement or improved sense of control (Harvey, Weber, & Orbuch, 1990).

Although there is strong evidence of an association between account-making and adaptation to negative life events, the direction of causation and the mediating mechanisms remain the subject of study (Berscheid & Reis, 1998). Accounts that incorporate the meaning of the event to the individual take time to construct. The sheer passage of time alone may promote adaptation to the negative event—as Shakespeare observed, "Time heals all wounds." That time alone may promote emotional distancing from unpleasant events is suggested by a study conducted by Nigro and Neisser (1983), who found that recent memories tend to be "copy-type" memories reflecting the individual's point of view at the time the event took place, whereas older memories show evidence not only of reconstruction but of the use of an outside observer's viewpoint as well. Ginsberg (1991) has discussed how the effects of time alone, and the psychological distance from the event it affords, usually are confounded with the effects of an account constructed over that time period. In other words, it is difficult to separate the beneficial effect of the passage of time and the adaptive effects of account construction.

In addition to the question of the adaptive effects of account construction apart from the sheer passage of time, another question concerns the effect of rendering the account publicly. Pennebaker (1989, 1990) and his associates have shown that adjustment to traumatic events is associated with confiding to others about the event. The extent to which the increase in adjustment is the result of simply constructing an account or of confiding a constructed account is not yet clear.

Account narratives are believed to reflect and maintain current relationship orientations. In a study of couples in first marriages during their first 4 years, Veroff and his collaborators (e.g., Veroff, Douvan, & Hatchett, 1993) asked each couple in their first year to record on tape, together and in their own words, the "story of their relationship" from the time they first met, up until the present, and on into the future. In their third year of marriage, participants were asked to tell their story again. Comparing the affective content of memory changes of couples who had shown a decline in their marital well-being with those whose well-being had remained stable, Holmes and Veroff (reported in Holmberg & Holmes, 1993) found that husbands whose marital well-being had declined currently reported significantly unhappier memories of the same relationship events—for example, the wedding—than they had reported in their first year; similarly, the memories of husbands whose well-being had improved were currently less negative. Wives did not show the effect. Revising history to put in a negative light relationship events that once were viewed as positive may be predictive of divorce (Buehlman, Gottman, & Katz, 1992).

MAJOR THEORIES OF SOCIAL COGNITION: IMPLICATIONS FOR RELATIONSHIP PHENOMENA

As the study of cognition dominated psychology in the latter half of the twentieth century and theory and research on social cognition burgeoned, the implications of the major theories of social cognition for relationship phenomena began to be explored. The major theories of social cognition appeared in two waves. The cognitive consistency theories arrived first, followed by the attribution theories.

Theories of Cognitive Consistency

An important principle by which information is internally organized is consistency. Asch (1946) was the first to demonstrate the principle of cognitive consistency in the realm of person perception. When Asch asked people to form an impression of another from a listing of that person's traits, the insertion into identical lists of either the adjective "warm" or the adjective "cold" significantly changed the meaning of the other traits on the list—for example, "intelligent" in the "cold" list was seen as a calculating kind of intelligence—such that a coherent, internally consistent view of the person was achieved.

All theories of cognitive consistency assume that people try to keep their thoughts, sentiments, and behaviors toward another person logically consistent. Inconsistency is assumed to be psychologically uncomfortable, at least in part because inconsistency makes it difficult to know what actions are appropriate in interaction with that other. In a variation on the Asch experiment, Kelley (1950) included the phrase "rather cold" in his introduction of a lecturer to one group students and the phrase "very warm" in his introduction to another student group. This one alteration in the description resulted in the two groups forming very different impressions of the lecturer. The association between the students' perception of the lecturer and their subsequent behavior was demonstrated by evidence that the "warm" group interacted more frequently with the lecturer than the "cold" group did.

Balance Theory

The grandfather of the consistency theories was Heider's (1958) balance theory, which posited that people try to keep their *sentiment relationship* (positive or negative) toward another or an object consistent with their perceived *unit relationship* with it, a unit relationship being the perception

that they and the other "belong" together or are united in some way. People who find themselves in a closed field with another often perceive that they are in a unit relationship with the other, as do people who are married or "tied together" in other ways. Heider predicted that we tend to like those with whom we perceive we are in a unit relationship, for this constitutes a cognitively "balanced" state; thus, he predicted that if fate puts us in a unit relationship with another, we will *induce* positive sentiment toward the other to achieve cognitive balance.

In one of the few experimental tests of balance theory, Darley and Berscheid (1967) recruited women to participate in a study in which they anticipated they would be discussing intimate matters over many weeks with an assigned partner. Participants were told they would be allowed to read some background information about their future partner and about another woman participating in the study with someone else. The information about the two women, although voluminous, was vague. Half of the women were told that Person A would be their partner, the other half that they had been assigned to Person B. After examining the information, participants were asked to give their impressions of the two women and tell how much they liked each. Just as Heider predicted, the mere prospect of future interaction generated attraction toward the partner before any interaction occurred. The women liked the person whom fate had assigned to them significantly more than they liked the nonpartner and were prepared to go into interaction with a positive orientation toward her. Many studies have since corroborated the **prospect of future interaction effect**—that we tend to try to like others with whom we must interact in closed fields. Devine, Sedikides, and Fuhrman (1989) have shown that we also are likely to exert greater cognitive effort in processing information about people with whom we expect to interact than those with whom we expect little contact.

The prospect of future interaction effect is sometimes strong and difficult to eradicate, as was demonstrated by Berscheid, Boye, and Darley (1968), who conducted a similar experiment, with two exceptions. First, in contrast to the nonpartner, the person with whom the participant was paired was presented as objectively less desirable (one fictional woman was described as somewhat "unclean," and in pretests, not a single person voluntarily selected her as a partner). Second, after having been assigned to the partner and after making their evaluations both of her and the more desirable nonpartner, the participants were told the experimenters had made a mistake in making the assignment: Each could now freely choose which of the two persons she wanted as her partner. Again, the women achieved cognitive consistency by coming to see their partner as significantly more likable than did those not paired with her. Moreover, when told they could have their choice between the two women—in other words, the unit relationship was dissolved—a significant number of participants who had initially been paired with the undesirable woman freely chose her again; that is, when the door to the closed field with the undesirable partner was opened, their cognitive machinations to achieve cognitive balance led them back to the objectively undesirable partner.

Whether we will perceive ourselves in a unit relationship with another depends on several factors, including the social environment. As discussed in Chapter 6, "Birth of a Relationship," two Americans who meet in the United States are unlikely to feel a sense of belongingness, but two Americans who meet in Africa, surrounded by Africans, are likely to perceive that they are in a unit relationship and liking for each other will probably result.

Despite the wealth of evidence that people prefer cognitively balanced to imbalanced states, Newcomb (1968) demonstrated that people strongly prefer positive sentiment relationships with others even if some such relationships may be cognitively imbalanced in Heider's view. For example, liking another person who holds dissimilar opinions is an imbalanced state, one that should tend toward balance by disliking the person or changing one's own opinions. Newcomb found that people prefer not to change a positive sentiment relationship into a negative relationship in order to achieve balance (in this case,

rather than disliking the other, they would prefer to change their own attitudes or attempt to persuade the other to change his or her attitudes). Similarly, people seem eager to change a negative sentiment relationship toward another to a positive one. In short, although people like cognitive balance, people also like to like people.

Cognitive Dissonance Theory

Heider's balance theory spawned many other consistency theories, the most influential of which was Festinger's (1957) theory of cognitive dissonance. Perhaps the most important contribution dissonance theory research made to our understanding of relationships is that although we commonly believe that whether we like or dislike another is a function of the other's behavior toward us, the true cause sometimes is our *own* behavior, which may be under the control of forces that have nothing to do with the partner or the relationship; that is, in order to reduce the dissonance our behavior has aroused, we may alter our liking of our partner. In one of the first studies derived from dissonance theory, for example, Aronson and Mills (1959) found that women who had undergone a severe initiation experience to be admitted into what they later discovered to be a boring discussion group reduced their cognitive dissonance (aroused by the realization that they had suffered in order to interact with uninteresting people) by coming to perceive the other women in the group to be more attractive than did those women who experienced either a mild initiation or no initiation at all.

The power of cognitive consistency has been demonstrated in many programs of relationship research. To take just one example, it will be recalled from Chapter 7, "Relationship Growth and Maintenance," that Murray and Holmes (e.g., 1993) found that threats to a romantic relationship not only may not destroy the individual's positive illusions about the relationship but actually may succeed in strengthening them. Other kinds of processes that preserve commitment to a relationship, such as overly optimistic views of the durability of the relationship and relationship superiority illusions, also may be construed as having their roots in cognitive dissonance aroused by uncertainty about the outcomes of one's own behavior, including getting married.

Many other experiments derived from cognitive dissonance theory subsequently demonstrated that changes in our sentiment for another sometimes are the result not of changes in our partner's behavior but of our need to reduce the dissonance aroused by our own behavior. In their seminal experiment, Davis and Jones (1960) coerced some participants to deliver a harsh personality evaluation to their partner (the no choice group). Other participants believed they had some choice about doing so, although all agreed to perform the act. Half of the participants in each group were told they could interact later with their partner (and, presumably, tell him or her that they really didn't mean their unkind words), whereas the other half were told no interaction with their partner would be possible (and thus they would have no opportunity to undo the harm they had done). Davis and Jones reasoned that because most of us think of ourselves as kind persons who do not inflict harm on innocent others, those who chose to hurt their partner and who could not undo the harm would experience dissonance which they could reduce by convincing themselves that their negative evaluation of their partner was justified. The hypothesis was confirmed: The "choice–no interaction" participants, relative to the other groups, derogated their partner's personality attributes and disliked their partner.

Equity Theory

Much subsequent research on the effects of inadvertently hurting another—a commonplace event in most close relationships—was carried out under the aegis of equity theory, which incorporated cognitive consistency principles. Equity theory predicts that people who unjustly harm their partners, and thus create inequity in the relationship, may reduce their self-concept distress (aroused by the inconsistency between their belief that they are good persons and their harmful behavior) by coming to believe their harmful behavior was justified, thereby restor-

ing *psychological equity* to the relationship, or by compensating their partner for the harm done, thereby restoring *actual equity* to the relationship (see Chapter 4, "The Concept of Relationship"). Although the self-concept distress of the perpetrator is reduced in both instances, the two equity restoration methods have different implications for the partner and for the future of the relationship.

Berscheid and Walster (1967) found that people who possessed the resources to *adequately* compensate the person they had hurt did make compensation and did not derogate their partner. When their available resources were such that they could provide only *partial* compensation to their partner for the harm, however, they tended to not compensate their partner at all; rather, they restored psychological equity by derogating their partner. Partial compensation, the investigators reasoned, does not entirely restore equity to the relationship. It also blocks the usual modes of dissonance reduction when we have hurt another: "I didn't do it" (something or someone else was responsible); "I did it, but my partner wasn't actually hurt;" and "I did it and my partner was hurt; but he or she deserved the harm". Compensation is an admission of personal responsibility for a harmful act, and it also is an admission that another was hurt and did not deserve it.

Thus, it is sometimes the case that people who have been hurt by their partners not only suffer the consequences of the injury itself but also risk the added insult of derogation ("This person deserved to be hurt"). Derogation and other routes to restoring psychological (rather than actual) equity increase the likelihood that the partner will perform the harmful act again—a dangerous situation for the person who has already been hurt and who continues to be in a relationship with that person. To prevent insult on top of an injury, Berscheid, Boye, and Walster (1968) wondered whether victims could prevent derogation when compensation was not possible if they threatened retaliation, thereby producing the anticipation that equity would be restored to the relationship. Accordingly, these investigators led participants to believe they had chosen to administer a series of strong electric shocks to their partner in conjunction with the performance of a learning task. Half subsequently were led to expect their partner to retaliate (to deliver strong shocks to the participant in return) and half to expect that their partner would have no retaliation opportunity. The investigators found that those perpetrators who thought their partners would have no retaliation opportunity derogated their victims (as expected), but those who anticipated retaliation did not. In the latter condition, perpetrators expected that their victim would shortly restore actual equity to the relationship, thus making it unnecessary for them to restore equity through the psychological justification pathway.

Lerner (1980) and his associates subsequently conducted an extensive program of research based on the assumption that most people believe in a "just world"—a world in which everyone gets exactly what he or she deserves. He and his colleagues demonstrated that people who simply observe others unjustly suffer (whether due to fate, chance, or the actions of others) will derogate them and decrease their liking for them, presumably in an effort to reduce the discomfort caused by two inconsistent cognitions: the world is just, and an innocent person is suffering. Derogation of the suffering person ("He brought it on himself," "She isn't really hurt," "He's a bad person who deserves to be hurt") allows people to maintain their belief that the world is just.

As a whole, this body of research contradicts what many people in close relationships seem to believe—that the more they exaggerate the harm their partner has unintentionally done them, the more likely they are to receive compensation. Such a strategy is likely to be effective only if the partner has the resources to fully compensate for the harm. As the magnitude of the harm escalates ("You have ruined my life, and there is nothing you can do to make up for it"), the likelihood that the partner will be able to fully compensate decreases and the likelihood that derogation or other psychological equity restoration steps will be taken increases. Many of us also seem to believe that if we convince our partners that they have hurt us gravely—so much so that no compensation is possible—they at least will feel

guilty. They may feel guilty, but not for long. Guilt (and dissonance) may be reduced by their coming to see us as deserving of the harm they did us or by efforts to achieve equity in other ways (perhaps by minimizing the amount of harm they did or by denying responsibility for their harmful behavior), all of which is likely to increase the probability that the harmful action will be repeated.

Unfortunately, as discussed in Chapter 14, "Satisfaction and Stability," it is difficult to know when it is wise to turn one's cheek to the partner's harmful acts for the good of the relationship and when it is wiser to immediately retaliate. A great deal of research suggests that "accommodation" to the partner's destructive behavior is associated with relationship satisfaction (e.g., Yovetich & Rusbult, 1994) and reciprocity of negative behavior is a hallmark of distressed marriages (see Weiss & Heyman, 1990).

The Attribution Theories

Like the cognitive consistency theories, the attribution theories had their origin in Heider's (1958) theorizing about the need for people to make sense of their complex and sometimes chaotic social environment. Predicting someone else's behavior requires an understanding of that person's personality traits, attitudes, and other stable dispositions to behave in consistent ways across many different situations. The question addressed by the attribution theories is "How do people get from the observation of another's behavior to knowledge of that person's stable, underlying dispositions?" The answer, according to Heider, was that people consider the situation in which the behavior occurred, and in general, if the cause of the behavior is deemed to lie in situational forces—the law, social norms—then the individual's behavior is *not* informative of his or her personal dispositions; everyone in that particular situation would behave that way. If, however, situational forces cannot explain the behavior, then its cause must lie within the individual's stable dispositions. The details of this answer were fleshed out by attribution theorists Kelley (e.g., 1967) and Jones and Davis (1965) and a multitude of researchers who usually asked people to read about a stranger's or a hypothetical person's behavior in a particular situation and to indicate whether that behavior was caused by the "situation" or by his or her "disposition," usually an attitude or personality trait.

The first study to examine attribution processes in ongoing relationships was conducted by Kelley, Cunningham, and Braiker-Stambul (1973; cited in Braiker & Kelley, 1979), who investigated the kinds of conflicts experienced by young married and cohabiting couples and found that partners defined their problems with differing levels of generality—from concrete conflicts over specific behaviors (failure to take out the garbage) to conflicts over the rules and norms that should govern their relationship (who was going to be responsible for what household chores) as well as highly generalized problems reflecting arguments about the correct attribution of the cause of each other's behavior. Kelley and colleagues observed that partners tend to escalate conflict from the specific and momentary act to stable and global dispositions affecting many marital behaviors and facets—that is, from the partner's failure to take out the garbage yesterday to an attribution of congenital laziness today. This tendency undoubtedly contributes to the spiraling of negativity observed in some marital relationships.

Orvis, Kelley, and Butler (1976) subsequently asked romantic couples who had been together for some time to list behaviors, performed by themselves or their partner, for which they and their partner had "a different explanation"—that is, they had made different causal attributions for the behavior. The investigators found that the couples listed mostly *negative* behaviors. Moreover, it was apparent that participants tended to justify and excuse their own negative behaviors and blame the partners for theirs. Thus, perhaps the most important finding of this work was that when we make attributions of the cause of our own and our partner's behavior in an ongoing relationship, we are *not* proceeding as "objective scientists searching for cause" (as the formal attribution theories and the many attribution laboratory studies conducted with strangers and hypothetical others depict us). Rather, in addition to making *accurate* attributions of cause, we appear to have a stake in making attributions that put ourselves in a favorable light and preserve a positive self-concept (e.g., Sedikides, Campbell, Reeder, & Elliot, 2002). We often can satisfy the latter aim without jeopardizing the former; Orvis and colleagues (1976) observe: "The true causes for behavior are usually quite complex. They encompass numerous factors present at the time of the behavior, each further traceable among a tangled skein of causality to prior factors. Given this complexity, any single causal explanation is bound to be selective" (p. 363). It is this feature of causal ambiguity that gives us latitude in the selection of cause and that produces the differing attributions partners sometimes make for the same behavior.

Differences in the causes to which partners attribute each other's behavior are especially apparent when couples discuss their problems. For example, Sillars, Roberts, Leonard, and Dun (2000) videotaped married couples while they discussed a current issue of conflict. Each spouse later viewed the videotape while simultaneously reporting the thoughts and feelings he or she remembered experiencing during the discussion. The spouses tended to treat their own inferences as objective observations ("She's lying"), showed little evidence of taking the partner's perspective, and seemed mostly unaware of the ways in which their behavior influenced the spouse and vice versa. Both spouses attributed positive communicative acts—such as collaboration and cooperation, disclosure and openness, solicitation of information and attention to the partner—more often to themselves than to the partner; they also attributed negative acts and intentions—including avoidance and withdrawal, topic shifting, stonewalling, lying, and insincerity—more often to the partner than to themselves.

Bradbury and Fincham's (1988, 1989) "contextual" model of marriage drew attention to the fact that when spouses interact, each person's overt behavior elicits rapid affective and cognitive processing from the other, and it is on the basis of the outcome of this processing that each partner acts. They hypothesized that an important component of the cognitive processing that is characteristic of distressed spouses' conflict interactions is the kinds of attributions each partner makes for the other's behavior. The question of how sentiment toward the partner and the relationship is associated with the kinds of attributions spouses make for each other's positive or negative behaviors has been the subject of much research (for reviews, see Bradbury & Fincham, 1990; Fincham, 2001). It has been firmly established that spouses who are highly satisfied with their relationship are likely to attribute their partner's positive behavior to positive, stable, and global internal dispositions and negative partner behavior to external circumstance or a temporary, specific state of the partner ("He had a toothache"). Distressed spouses show the opposite tendencies; they attribute positive behavior to situational, unstable, and restricted causes and negative behavior to negative, stable, and global dispositions. In sum, as Fincham, Harold, and Gano-Phillips (2000) explain, "attributions that accentuate the impact of negative relationship events and minimize the impact of positive relationship events are associated with lower relationship satisfaction" (p. 268).

Many attribution researchers have tried to determine which came first—the negative attributions or the dissatisfaction —or whether both are caused by such third variables as depression or other forms of negative affectivity (e.g., Karney, Bradbury, Fincham, & Sullivan, 1994). On the whole, satisfaction and causal attributions of partner behavior and relationship problems, like so many other variables in the relationship realm, appear to be reciprocally causal. Longitudinal studies suggest that positive (or negative) attributions for the partner's behavior appear to be associated with later satisfaction (or dissatisfaction) and that satisfaction (or dissatisfaction) is associated with later positive (or negative) attributions for the partner's behavior (see Fincham, 2001; Fincham, Harold, & Gano-Phillips, 2000).

Most relationship attribution research has been conducted using highly structured self-report questionnaires in which the experimenter, but not the partner, is privy to the causal attributions being made of the partner's behavior. However, a few investigators have observed the kind of attributions spouses make when they discuss a problem in their marriage. Holtzworth-Munroe and Jacobson (1988), for example, corroborated the finding of Orvis and associates (1976) that partners tend to make self-serving justifications for their own negative behaviors. Rempel, Ross, and Holmes (2001) also observed couples discussing a marital problem, but in addition to coding the interaction for the kinds of attributions the spouses were communicating to each other, they asked participants to privately evaluate their partners' motives for behaving as they had. The investigators predicted and found that trust of the partner has a critical influence on the kinds of attributions people communicate to their partners (as opposed to keep to themselves). Partners who highly trusted each other emphasized the positive aspects of the relationship both publicly and privately; the attributions of medium-trust partners' were more negative, both publicly and privately; and although low-trust partners' private attributions were the most negative, their communicated attributions were almost as positive as those of the high-trust partners, confirming the prediction that low-trust partners would moderate their true opinions to decrease the risk of hostile reactions and more conflict. It is of interest that the partners' satisfaction with the relationship could not account for the results in this study.

Investigators have wondered *when* partners tend to make causal attributions for each other's behavior. Holtzworth-Munroe and Jacobson (1985) found evidence that couples are most likely to do so when they are experiencing conflicts. Weiner (1985) and Bradbury and Fincham (1990) hypothesize that people are most likely to search for a causal explanation when expectancies about the partner have been violated, which is consistent with much other psychological theorizing (e.g., Mandler, 1975). However, a good deal of research now suggests that people spontaneously and automatically (unintentionally and without awareness) infer cause for various events, at least impersonal events that occur in laboratory situations. Moreover, as Heider (1958) and many others have theorized and found, people have a predilection for making trait as opposed to situational causal inferences, at least for other people's behavior. Virtually all attribution studies have been conducted with people in Western individualist cultures, however. Morris and Peng (1994) have presented evidence that in contrast to American students, Chinese students are more likely to attribute social behavior to situational causes. There also is mounting evidence that Americans, at least, tend to make trait attributions at the encoding, as opposed to the retrieval, stage of perceiving another's behavior (see Hassin, Bargh, & Uleman, 2002; Uleman, Newman, & Moskowitz, 1996).

Again, however, sentiment toward the partner and toward the relationship influences the *kind* of attributions people make for their partner's behavior. A study of spouses' recollections of the process that led to their disaffection with the relationship and progress toward divorce conducted by Kayser (1993) found that whereas the attributions spouses initially made for their marital problems were complex, attributions became simpler as disenchantment with the partner and the relationship grew: There was a significant decrease in attributions of the cause of marital problems to the self and to extra-dyadic sources (events and people outside the relationship), and attributions to the partner became more frequent. Moreover, these attributions of problems to the partner became rigid.

SUMMARY

Although all relationships begin between two strangers (as we noted earlier, even a mother and a newborn infant are unfamiliar to each other when they first meet), over time and repeated interactions those two individuals may come to know each other very well—or at least feel as if they do. The process by which we come to know someone well enough to be able to predict his or her behavior in interaction with us is strongly influenced by our expectancies about the situation and the other individual's goals and motivations and by basic principles of social perception—for example, most people have a tendency to assume that others possess attributes similar to their own. In addition, social cognitive psychologists have identified many of the principles that govern how our minds process, structure, and access information about other people. For example, people use two modes to process social information: an automatic/associative processing mode that quickly, efficiently, and without conscious awareness detects regularities in the social environment (including another's stable and enduring attributes); and a slower controlled processing mode which requires effort and which usually is engaged when people are outcome-dependent on another individual (and thus motivated to generate accurate predictions about his or her nature). In close relationships, people are often outcome-dependent on their partners, but at the same time, their preexisting knowledge of their partners, coupled with heavy cognitive load, may increase the likelihood that they will rely on automatic processing.

Recognizing that first impressions often determine whether subsequent interactions between two people will occur, some researchers have become interested in the ways in which previously stored information influences the process of impression formation. It is believed that social information stored in memory is organized into categories of like objects, called social schemas or social categories, that are themselves internally organized. These stored social categories are accessed automatically and used to guide our impressions of another individual, particularly if they are highly accessible. Relationship schemas—knowledge structures that represent a person's relationships with others—are also stored in memory and seem to operate like other social categories; for example, the expectancies associated with them direct attention and guide behavior. Chronically accessible relationship schemas explain why it is difficult to change distressed relationships: Once schema-associated negative expectancies have become strongly established and inaccessible to conscious awareness, partners must exert supreme effort to become aware of and to alter them.

Other scholars have explored memories for relationship events. A number of systematic biases have been identified, including the tendency for people to attribute more responsibility for positive relationship events to themselves than to their partners. Memory for relationship events also appears to be a function of the nature of the communal or transactive memory bank that each couple develops, and there is growing evidence that relationship memory is often reconstructed in the service of helping individuals make sense of various relationship events, such as dissolution.

Chapter 9

Affective Processes

INTRODUCTION

Many questions people ask about their relationships concern the emotions they experience—or fail to experience—in them. For examples: Why does a person we know to be a scoundrel sometimes inspire our passion and pursuit? Why, conversely, do we sometimes find it impossible to fall in love with, or even like, a potential partner who is kind, generous, trustworthy, and head over heels in love with us? Why do we often experience the most intense negative emotions and feelings in association with partners we love, admire, and respect? And why do we fail to experience positive emotion—or any emotion at all—in relationships we thought would bring us joy and happiness? Such questions often are asked about romantic relationships because, as we have noted, more than ever before people believe that romantic relationships should be a major source of their positive emotional experiences (Attridge & Berscheid, 1994).

Relationship scholars have been forced to confront the mysteries of human emotion because an understanding of a person's emotional experiences in his or her relationship with another is crucial to understanding the relationship itself. Many have turned to psychological theory and research on emotion for help with their questions but have been disappointed in the quality of psychology's answers. The study of emotion has a tortured history in psychology, one fraught with frustration and controversy. As a consequence, answers to questions about emotional experience in the context of interpersonal relationships remain few in number and tentative in nature.

THE SOCIAL CONTEXT OF HUMAN EMOTION

Most of what is known about emotion as it occurs in the context of relationships with others has been learned relatively recently despite the fact that relationships are an especially fertile breeding ground for emotional experience. Close relationships, in fact, are the setting in which humans most frequently experience intense emotion, both positive and negative. For example, an early diary study of the experience of anger conducted by Fitz and Gerstenzang (1978) found that when people experienced intense anger in their daily lives, it most likely was directed toward their close relationship partners—usually blood relatives and romantic partners, including spouses. More recently, Barrett, Robin, Pietromonaco, and Eyssell (1998) asked people to record in a diary for 7 days a variety of emotions they experienced and expressed, such as happiness, in the context of any social interaction lasting 10 minutes or longer. The frequency and intensity of people's emotional experiences, as well as the extent to which they expressed their emotions in interaction, were strongly and positively associated with their ratings of the closeness of their relationship with the interaction partner.

The tendency for an experienced emotion to be expressed to others has been well documented. For example, Rimé and his associates investigated emotion-sharing after traffic, domestic, or work accidents; childbirth; bereavement; academic examinations; and (for medical students) the dissection of a human corpse (Rimé, Finkenauer, Luminet, Zech, & Philippot, 1998; Rimé, Philippot, Boca, & Mesquita, 1992). Most emotional experiences were shared with others shortly after the event. More than half of accident victims had shared the emotion-arousing episode with others the first day (60%), and some (35%) shared it almost every day for 6 weeks. Anxiety-arousing exams prompted social sharing by all (100%) within the first week, decreasing only to 94% during the second week; attending the dissection of a corpse garnered 100% sharing during both the first and the second week after the experience.

The urge to share one's emotional experiences may stem from several sources. It will be recalled from Chapter 6, "Birth of a Relationship," that Festinger (1950), in his theory of informal social communication, was the first to hypothesize that the experience of emotion was a potent force for communication, and that Schachter (1959) found considerable evidence that people seek out others to evaluate the appropriateness of their emotional state. Rimé and colleagues (1998) outline a number of other reasons people may share their emotional experiences, including the need for social support and assistance in coping. These investigators also provide evidence that the tendency to share an emotional experience is a widespread phenomenon, present in all of the several cultures studied.

As the diary study by Barrett and colleagues (1998) suggests, however, there is evidence that people do not share their emotional experiences indiscriminately; rather, they share more readily with close others than with less close others. The strong association between close relationships and emotional experience and expression has been further documented by Margaret Clark and her associates (e.g., Clark & Brissette, 2000; Clark, Fitness, & Brissette, 2001; Clark, Pataki, & Carver, 1996). Recall that Clark and Mills (e.g., 1979) argue that most close relationships are *communal* relationships, in which the partners are concerned with each other's welfare and are responsive to each other's needs, as contrasted to *exchange* relationships, in which partners typically feel little responsibility for each other's welfare and provide benefits in accord with quid pro quo rules (see Chapter 5, "Varieties of Relationship"). Clark and her colleagues theorize that an individual's feeling of responsibility for another's welfare is an important variable in understanding and predicting that individual's emotional life, for at least two reasons. First, a person's expression of emotion carries information about his or her needs. When we experience an emotion, we often communicate our needs to ourselves and also to others in the social environment who observe our emotional experience. Second, the experience of emotion often communicates both to ourselves and to others the extent to which we care about the needs of another person or group of persons. We weep at the misfortunes of those we love but remain unmoved by the trials and travails of those for whom we care little or not at all. As a consequence, people should express more emotion and react more positively to their partners' expressions of emotion in communal relationships, where they expect their needs to be met, than in exchange relationships, where such expectations are absent.

The linkage between communal relationships and the experience of emotion is supported by the results of several studies. For example, Clark and Taraban (1991) found that people far preferred to talk about emotional topics with friends rather than strangers. Brissette and Clark (1999; cited in Clark et al., 2001) asked people to rate their willingness to express a variety of emotions such as hurt in each of a number of their ongoing relationships and found a strong positive correlation between willingness to express positive and negative emotion and the extent to which the person viewed the relationship as communal. There was one exception: People were not especially willing to express anger and disappointment in a communal relationship when these emotions were caused by their partner.

Not only are expressions of emotion more common in communal than in noncommunal relationships, but the partner is more likely to react positively to the revelation—with more liking and more responsiveness. In addition, those people who chronically feel responsible for others' needs react more positively to any person's emotional expressions than do people who score low on a measure of "communal orientation" (Clark, Ouellette, Powell, & Milberg, 1987). Differences in adult attachment style also seem to reflect individual differences in the belief that others will be responsive to one's needs: Feeney (1995) found that members of dating couples who scored high in comfort (analogous to a secure classification) were less likely than others to report that they suppressed expressions of negative feelings to their partners, a finding subsequently corroborated in a sample of spouses (Feeney, 1999).

The abundance of evidence that people are most likely to experience and express emotions in the context of their relationships with others is in contrast to the scarcity of knowledge about emotional experience in relationships. Psychologists traditionally have adopted an individualistic approach to the study of emotion and have neglected the influence of the context in which

humans usually experience emotion. In recent years, however, more emotion theorists have formally recognized the emotion–relationship association. Zajonc (1998), for example, states:

> Emotions, even though their hallmark is the internal state of the individual—the viscera, the gut—are above all social phenomena. They are the basis of social interaction, they are the products of social interaction, their origins, and their currency. (pp. 619–620)

FACIAL EXPRESSIONS OF EMOTION

The long neglect of the social context of emotional experience is surprising not only because emotions are most likely to be experienced and expressed in the relationship context but also because the association was emphasized by Darwin, who first brought the subject of emotion into the scientific arena in his classic treatise *The Expression of the Emotions in Man and Animals* (1872/1899). In his concluding remarks, Darwin stated:

> The movements of expression in the face and body, whatever their origin may have been, are in themselves of much importance for our welfare. They serve as the first means of communication between the mother and her infant; she smiles approval, and thus encourages her child on the right path, or frowns disapproval. We readily perceive sympathy in others by their expression; our sufferings are thus mitigated and our pleasures increased; and mutual good feeling is thus strengthened. The movements of expression give vividness and energy to our spoken words. They reveal the thoughts and intentions of others more truly than do words, which may be falsified. (p. 364)

Darwin's interest in the facial expression of emotion grew out of his primary objective, which was to substantiate his theory of evolution and the thesis that "man is derived from some lower animal form" (p. 365). Darwin realized that evidence of similarity of the facial expression of

FIGURE 9.1 According to Darwin, the fact that dogs and many other domestic animals display many of the same emotional expressions that humans do suggests a commonality of evolutionary history.

emotions across all human groups would support his belief in the common origin of *Homo sapiens*. His correspondence with missionaries working with aboriginal and tribal peoples led him to conclude that all humans do display similar emotional expressions. Additional supporting evidence that humans and nonhuman animals share commonalties in their evolutionary histories was obtained from observations of his retriever, Bob; his fox terrier, Polly; and other domestic animals, who, Darwin contended, display many of the same emotional expressions humans do—for example, baring of teeth in expressions of anger (Figure 9.1).

The Universality of Emotional Expression Hypothesis

Psychologists did not confront Darwin's hypothesis in earnest until the early 1960s, when they more than compensated for their long neglect of emotion with a blizzard of activity. Few questions have been the subject of so much empirical effort by psychologists, nor has so much passion been invested in the several theoretical positions taken. According to Fridlund

(1994), who dissects the sometimes confusing **universality of emotional expression hypothesis**, controversies have arisen around four related propositions: (1) Specific patterns of facial muscle movement occur in all humans so that there is universality of facial movement patterns. (2) Each facial movement pattern is a manifestation of the same emotion in all humans. (3) People everywhere attribute the same emotional meaning to a specific pattern of facial movement (Figure 9.2). (4) Attributions of emotional meanings to the different facial patterns are accurate, and the person displaying the facial expression actually is experiencing the emotion attributed.

Many logical, methodological, and analytical problems have plagued studies examining the universality hypothesis. However, after reviewing the massive literature now available, Russell and his colleagues (1994; Russell & Fernández-Dols, 1997) concluded that when people across many cultures are given photographs of facial expressions putatively tied to a specific emotion such as anger, even people in relatively isolated cultures are fairly accurate in identifying the emotion displayed. Smiles top the list for consistency of identification with a "happy" emotional

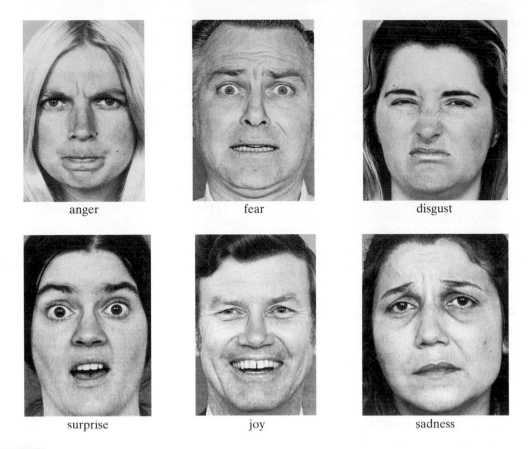

anger   fear   disgust

surprise   joy   sadness

FIGURE 9.2 Studies of facial expression recognition typically ask participants to indicate which emotional states are depicted in photos such as these. People from a variety of cultures demonstrate high levels of agreement on this task.

state. However, ease of recognition is not the same for all emotion expressions. In addition, a person's accuracy is somewhat dependent on the extent to which that person has been exposed to Western culture. Most cross-cultural studies of facial expression have been conducted by Westerners, and the actors depicting emotions also have been Westerners. Evidence that their depictions of emotions may be more intelligible to Westerners than to non-Westerners vitiates claims of the pan-human nature of facial expression.

The methodology initiated by Darwin—having actors portray a facial expression of a specific emotion and asking people to identify the emotion displayed—continues to be used to test the universality of emotional expression hy-

pothesis. This methodology, however, presents problems of interpretation. For example, when the heroine of Victorian melodramas wished to convey despair and grief (as when she learned that the mustachioed villain was foreclosing on the farm), she would fling the back of her hand to her forehead and slump her knees forward. The audience immediately recognized the emotion the actress was trying to convey. It is doubtful, however, that people who are actually experiencing despair and grief behave in that way; more likely, they look like the person sitting next to us—or even ourselves as we go about the business of life despite our emotional aches and pains. The same appears to be true of happiness. Fernández-Dols and Ruiz-Belda (1995) studied gold medalists at the Olympic Games during the awards ceremony. Although almost all of the athletes said they were extraordinarily happy, they rarely smiled as they received the medal and listened to their national anthem. Similarly, Kraut and Johnston (1979) observed facial behavior in natural settings in which people were presumably happy, such as bowlers rolling a strike, and found that people smiled mostly during social interaction—not when they saw all 10 pins fall, but when they turned to face their fellow bowlers.

Strangely enough, the facial expressions people spontaneously make when experiencing a particular emotion in naturalistic social situations had yet to receive systematic investigation by the end of the twentieth century (see Russell, 1994). Almost all studies of the universality issue have stripped the expression and decoding of emotional meaning from its usual relationship context. People typically have been presented with photos or videotapes of strangers attempting to express an emotion they may or may not have been actually experiencing. Evidence from the interactions of distressed marital couples, however, clearly reveals that associations between an individual's emotional experience, his or her emotional expression, and his or her partner's decoding of the meaning of that expression are not always straightforward, nor do they mirror those found between strangers in decontextualized laboratory situations, as discussed further in Part 6, "Relationships Over Time."

The thesis that the experience of a particular emotion is inevitably accompanied by a particular facial expression also has been challenged by accumulating evidence of **cultural emotion display rules** that prescribe appropriate contexts for the display of an emotion. These rules are taught during the socialization process and enforced by social sanctions. As the studies conducted by Clark and her associates (e.g., 2001) suggest, one of these display rules in Western culture is that it is inappropriate to express emotion, especially negative emotion, in noncommunal relationships. Little is yet known about the display rules for different types of relationships and for the situations in which the partners customarily interact within Western culture, but there now is a great deal of evidence that there are significant differences (as well as some commonalities) between cultures in display rules and also in the likelihood of the experience of certain emotions (Mesquita & Frijda, 1992; Russell, 1991). Moreover, from his review of available evidence, Russell (1991) concludes that

> people of different cultures and speaking different languages categorize emotions somewhat differently. . . . Thus, neither the word *emotion* nor words for even alleged basic emotions, such as *anger* and *sadness*, are universal. (p. 444)

On the other hand, Russell tentatively concludes that there is great similarity in emotion *categories* across different cultures and languages.

Of particular interest have been emotion differences between individualist and collectivist cultures (see Chapter 3, "The Development of Relationship Science"). Mesquita (2001) found that in contrast to individualist cultures, in collectivist cultures emotions tend to have their source in assessments of social worth, are taken to reflect reality to a large extent (as opposed to the subjective world of the individual), and, not surprisingly, are associated with the self–other relationship (e.g., tend to reflect the connections between individuals), whereas emotions in individualist cultures underline the disparity between the self and others. Mesquita concludes that "emotional experience differs fundamentally between individualist and collectivist cultures" (p. 72). Eid and Diener (2001) found both within- and between-nation differences in two individualist cultures (the United States and Australia) and two collectivist cultures (China and Taiwan) in terms of norms for emotional experience. Individualist and collectivist nations differed most in norms for self-reflective emotions such as pride and guilt. Even when norms were held constant, Eid and Diener found strong national differences in the kinds of emotional experiences people reported. For example, people in China had the lowest frequency and intensity scores of both positive and negative affects, possibly because many Chinese believe that emotions are dangerous and can cause illness.

Theories of Basic Emotions

Although Darwin recognized, at least implicitly, that there were differences within and between cultures in emotion displays, he stated, "Whenever the same movements of the features or body express the same emotions in several distinct races of man, we may infer with much probability, that such expressions are true ones—that is, are innate or distinctive" (1872/1899, p. 15). Cultural conventions, he believed, resulted in people learning to make facial expressions that *falsely* implied emotional experience. Darwin's distinction between innate, or "true," expressions of emotion as opposed to false expressions of emotion led to the idea that some emotions are "basic" or "fundamental" whereas others are not.

The several modern "basic emotion" theories, and the studies of the facial expression of emotion derived from them, were generated by Tomkins's (1962, 1963) theory of basic emotions, which asserted that facial behavior is paramount in the experience of affect. Theorists who posit the existence of certain basic emotions generally believe that each **basic emotion,** such as fear or anger (both of which appear in all theories), is automatically expressed in a characteristic facial pattern as well as in characteristic physiological, neurological, behavioral, and experiential patterns that together comprise that particular emotion's *affect program*. Each basic emotion's affect program is believed (1) to be innate and adaptive, (2) to occur automatically given certain triggering stimuli, and (3) to be most clearly seen in infants because it is often later modified by experience or learned to be suppressed (Figure 9.3).

When a basic emotion is *not* modified or suppressed, its facial expression is believed to be a "readout" of the individual's emotional state. Even when modified or suppressed, however, the innate and automatic expression of a basic emotion is believed to "leak" into facial expression in detectable ways, such as those provided by rigorously developed facial coding systems of emotion (e.g., Ekman & Friesen, 1978).

Despite, or perhaps because of, the plethora of theories and research subsequently devoted to the basic emotion thesis, there appears to be little consensus about the criteria an emotion must meet to be termed "basic." Some have theorized that if an emotion can be linked to a specific facial expression, it is basic. Others maintain that what makes an emotion basic is that it has its own unique neural circuitry. Despite advances in affective neuroscience, however, the neural circuitry involved in emotional states is not yet clear (fear being a possible exception; see Le Doux, 1995). Still others believe that what makes an emotion basic is that it cannot be reduced to a combination, or *blending*, of other emotions. The idea that two or more basic emotions may be blended is important to basic emotion theorists because it helps them account for the richness and complexity of emotional experience. For example, Izard's (e.g., 1991) basic emotion theory lists fear and anger as basic emotions but asserts that jealousy is a combination of the two and thus a "secondary," blended, emotion.

The failure to agree on criteria for identifying a basic emotion and on which emotions are basic has severely undermined the persuasiveness of the basic emotion argument (see Fridlund, 1994).

joy   fear   anger   surprise   sadness   disgust

FIGURE 9.3 According to Izard (e.g., 1991), the basic emotions are present at birth and produce the characteristic facial expressions depicted by these young infants.

Ortony and Turner (1990) point out that some accounts list only 2 basic emotions (pain and pleasure), while others list between 8 and 18. Moreover, Mandler (1997) observes that lust fails to appear on any list of basic emotions, a disconcerting omission considering the likely role this emotion has played in the continuation of the species (see Fisher, 1998).

One of several offshoots of the proposition that there is a crucial link between the facial expression of an emotion and emotional experience is the **facial feedback hypothesis**. This thesis holds that particular configurations of the facial musculature not only express a specific emotion but may *produce* it. To investigate the role of facial feedback in generating emotion, investigators have asked people to maintain a certain facial expression, such as a smile or a frown, while performing a task and later report the affect they experienced while doing the task. The evidence for this hypothesis remains sparse and conflicting (see Cacioppo, Klein, Berntson, & Hatfield, 1993) as well as controversial (see Fridlund, 1994).

Observing Emotion in Social Interaction

Like other emotion research, research on basic emotions tends to be "context-free." Apart from some attention to the triggering stimuli likely to activate the affect program theorized to be associated with a specific basic emotion, the context in which the emotion is experienced and displayed is relatively ignored. This is unfortunate for relationship scholars because a relationship cannot be understood without understanding the feelings and emotions partners spontaneously experience and display in their interactions. Indeed, Soskin and John (1963), who gave a vacationing husband and wife a backpack containing an audio transmitter and antenna and continuously recorded their conversations, found that most of the couple's communications were affectional—not informational, as is often supposed.

Systems that code marital and other relationship interactions always include affect codes. For example, affect codes were included in one of the earliest systems, the Marital Interaction Coding System (MICS; Hops, Wills, Patterson, & Weiss, 1972). Although the MICS had several affect codes, for analytical purposes most observations were simply classified into two affect categories, positive and negative—a practice that most marital interaction researchers have continued (see Chapter 14, "Intervention and Dissolution"). Hoping to progress beyond the simple positive–negative affect categories commonly in use and to code the partners' experience of specific emotions, Gottman and his associates valiantly attempted to apply Ekman and Friesen's (1978) Facial Action Coding System (FACS) to couples' interactions (see Gottman, 1993b). Encountering insurmountable problems, they concluded that observational systems for coding emotional expression have not been designed for studying emotion in social interaction. For example, the FACS produces sets of specific "action units," but there is no dictionary that allows those to be translated into emotion words such as "anger" to describe the data—for example, the number of times a spouse expresses anger. In addition, of course, interacting couples express their emotions and feelings not only through facial expression but also in other nonverbal ways such as voice pitch. These interact with each other and with verbal expressions.

Gottman and his associates (see Gottman, McCoy, Coan, & Collier, 1996) subsequently developed the Specific Affect Coding System in which a team of observers considers an emotion "Gestalt"—consisting of a partner's facial expression, verbal content, voice tone, gestures, body movement, and context—and codes it into specific positive and negative affect categories. The positive category includes "interest," "affection," "humor," "validation," and "excitement/joy," whereas the negative category includes "anger," "belligerence," "domineering," "contempt," "disgust," "tension/fear/worry," "sadness," "whining," and "defensiveness." (Several of these codes, it should be noted, do not map onto traditional emotion categories.) The coding scheme also includes partner "listener codes": "neutral," "positive," "negative," and "stonewalling" (listener withdrawal from interaction). As discussed in Chapter 14, certain emotions, such as contempt, expressed in marital interaction are particularly diagnostic of the relationship's future.

The Social Interactional View of Facial Expression

As opposed to viewing facial expressions as reflections of emotional states, some psychologists and many ethologists who study infrahuman animals highlight the social interactional and communicative nature of facial displays. The **behavioral ecology view of facial displays** emphasizes the interaction between the person displaying the facial expression and the person who is viewing it, decoding its meaning, and adjusting his or her behavior in accord with that meaning. As Fridlund (1994) describes:

> displays are declarations that signify our trajectory in a given social interaction, that is, what we will do in the current situation, or what we would like the other to do. And this "context" depends considerably not only on the structural features of the situation, but on the succession of interactants' displays and their responses to them. (p. 130)

The behavioral ecology view suggests that rather than one prototypical facial expression of anger, there may be dozens of expressions of "about to attack"; which expression is displayed depends on the identities of the interactants, their relationship with one another, and the situational context in which the current interaction is occurring (including culturally learned display rules and conventions pertinent to that situation). The behavioral ecology view can accommodate the fact that a facial display may be interpreted as "contempt" in one situation, "exasperation" in another, or even "constipation" in yet another (p. 129).

In the behavioral ecology view, then, facial displays are *not* readouts of emotional experience. In fact, no reference need be made to emotions or to emotion terms because social motives alone are theorized to determine displays. Frid-

lund (1994) notes, "We may be courteous, loving, amusing, or reassuring, and smile accordingly, if we are so moved—regardless of whether we feel happy, sad, angry or fearful" (p. 135). Similarly, "threat displays" may or may not reflect anger. Hinde (1985) observes that threat displays usually occur in situations in which the individual's actual aggression is dependent on the recipient's next actions ("If you do that one more time. . ."). In fact, if it is the individual's intention to attack at the time of the display, it is more advantageous to attack immediately, without expressive forewarning. Thus, rather than as evidence of the emotional experience of anger, it may be more accurate to view threat displays and other signal systems that involve facial expression as social tools that benefit both the displayer and the target of the display by furthering both persons' welfare and survival—for example, the viewer of an "about to attack" display can flee or prepare to fight. But in order for an emotion display to promote survival, the individual must have *control* over the display. The individual must not facially display emotion or otherwise signal to others automatically, because in some instances that would lead to death (as when a scream of fear would be more likely to reveal the individual's position to a predator than to attract help). Displayers of emotion must signal only when it is beneficial for them to do so.

Given their survival value, some facial displays and other expressive behaviors may be innate or selected for over evolutionary time. Distress signals in humans and nonhumans may be an example. Fridlund (1994) reasons that evolution should have equipped human infants with displays that are "intense attention grabbers" (loud, piercing cries; flashbulb smiles) because infants who could not attract the attention of their caregivers were more likely to be neglected and die; as a consequence, "natural selection should directly shape the production of exaggerated, plangent, canonical infant displays" (p. 133)—a fact worth remembering if one intends to spend much time in the vicinity of infants. For a display to have been selected, both the display itself *and* vigilance for the display (for noticing and correctly interpreting it) must have evolved together.

In sum, the behavioral ecology model and contemporary evolutionary theories have revised, elaborated, and extended many of Darwin's original ideas about the role of the expression of emotions in the survival of the species. Russell, Bachorowski, and Fernández-Dols (2003) succinctly explain after reviewing recent studies of the facial and vocal expressions of emotion: "Emotion expressions . . . may not be related to emotions in any simple way" (p. 342). Consideration of the naturalistic context in which emotional displays are seen makes it obvious that the individual's display of emotion may or may not be accompanied by the actual experience of emotion, and in any case the display is often directed toward a specific receiver for a specific purpose—a purpose often discerned by the receiver, who may or may not infer that the sender is actually experiencing an emotion.

PHYSIOLOGICAL AROUSAL AND EMOTION

Darwin noticed that there seemed to be an association between what he called "nervous excitation" and the experience of emotion. What the nature of the association was, he did not know. Hence, in the very last sentence of his treatise on emotion, Darwin (1872/1899) stated that emotion "deserves still further attention, especially from any able physiologist" (p. 366).

The James–Lange Theory

The first to respond to Darwin's call was not a physiologist but rather the American psychologist William James (1884, 1890). James expressed his dismay that psychologists seemed content to merely catalogue and classify the different emotions:

> The trouble with emotions in psychology is that they are regarded too much as absolutely individual things. So long as they are set down as so many eternal and sacred psychic entities, like the old immutable species in natural history, all that *can* be done with them is reverently to catalog their separate characters, points, and effects. But if we regard them as products of more general causes . . . the mere distinguishing and cataloguing becomes of subsidiary importance. Having the goose which lays the golden eggs, the description of each egg already laid is a minor matter. (1890, Vol. 2, p. 449)

James proceeded to describe the possible nature of the "golden goose" producing all emotions. He theorized that an individual's perception of an "exciting fact" (perhaps an angry partner) caused bodily changes and that it was the perception of these internal, bodily changes as they occurred that constituted the emotional experience—at least the emotional experiences James (1884) believed it was important for psychologists to understand. To experience an emotion, according to James, was to sense a specific pattern of bodily changes and to recognize that pattern as fear or joy or some other emotion. Especially important to emotional experience, James believed, were changes in the state of the viscera (the large organs in the cavities of the body, such as the heart and stomach). Carl Lange (1885/1922) advanced a similar theory, but he believed that changes in the circulatory system—for example, in blood pressure—were especially important. Because both theories emphasized that changes in the peripheral nervous system are important to emotional experience, the two theories became referred to as the James–Lange theory (Figure 9.4).

The James–Lange theory inspired a great deal of emotion research, but this activity came to an

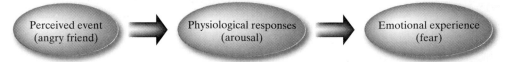

FIGURE 9.4 The James–Lange theory of emotion.

268 CHAPTER 9

FIGURE 9.5 Stanley Schachter.

abrupt halt when finally an "able physiologist," the redoubtable Walter Cannon, responded to Darwin's call to examine the association between nervous excitation and emotion. After reviewing the volumes of research the James–Lange theory had produced, Cannon (1927, 1929) wrote a devastating critique of the theory. He concluded that the richness and variety of the subjective experience of emotion were not matched by a comparable richness and variety in patterns of bodily visceral changes. For one thing, it had become clear that the viscera were relatively insensitive structures, and for another, the same bodily changes seemed to occur in very different emotional states and in nonemotional states as well. As a result of Cannon's critique, the study of emotion went dormant in psychology, not to be revived until after midcentury when some psychologists began to pursue Darwin's ideas about facial expression, as previously discussed, and other psychologists—most notably Stanley Schachter (e.g., 1964; see Figure 9.5)—revisited Darwin's observation of the association between nervous excitation and the experience of emotion.

Schachter's Two-Component Theory

A great deal of evidence had accumulated in support of Darwin's original proposition: Excitement of the sympathetic portion of the autonomic nervous system (ANS) did appear to be associated with emotional states. Physiological symptoms of arousal of the **sympathetic nervous system (SNS)** portion of the ANS (as opposed to the other component of the ANS, the parasympathetic nervous system) include increased heart rate, decreased cutaneous blood flow, increased muscle and cerebral blood flow, and increased blood sugar level. Subjectively, SNS arousal is often felt as palpitation, accelerated breathing, flushing, tremor, and sweaty hands. These symptoms (Figure 9.6) are part of Selye's general alarm system (discussed in Chapter 2, "Relationships and Health") as well as what Cannon called the "fight or flight" response to threat.

In accord with Cannon's critique, Schachter (e.g., 1964) acknowledged that a visceral formulation of emotion, such as that proposed by James, could not completely account for the complexity and richness of people's emotional experiences. However, Schachter (1959) had experimentally demonstrated that people wanted to interact with others when fearful (see Chapter 6, "Birth of a Relationship"), which suggested that people often sought an explanation for their internal state of physiological arousal. Schachter (1964) began to think about the role that the situation in which arousal is experienced might play in providing explanations for the arousal, thus influencing the subjective experience of emotion:

> Cognitions arising from the immediate situation [in which arousal is perceived to occur] as interpreted by past experience provide the framework within which one understands and labels his [or her] feelings [of arousal]. (p. 51)

Schachter also observed that in most naturalistic situations the situation not only produces the *feeling* of internal arousal but simultaneously provides an external *explanation* for the arousal:

> In most emotion inducing situations, of course, the two factors are completely interrelated. Imagine a man walking alone down a dark alley when a figure

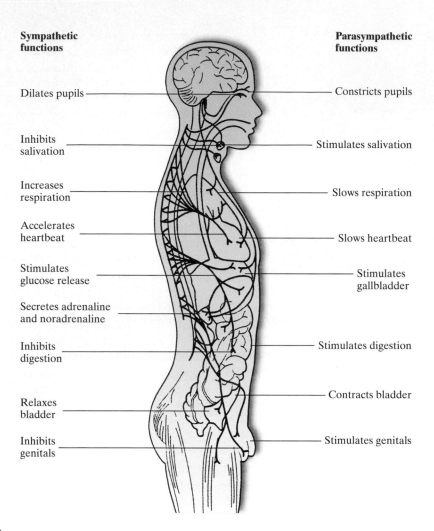

Sympathetic functions

Dilates pupils

Inhibits salivation

Increases respiration

Accelerates heartbeat

Stimulates glucose release

Secretes adrenaline and noradrenaline

Inhibits digestion

Relaxes bladder

Inhibits genitals

Parasympathetic functions

Constricts pupils

Stimulates salivation

Slows respiration

Slows heartbeat

Stimulates gallbladder

Stimulates digestion

Contracts bladder

Stimulates genitals

FIGURE 9.6 The autonomic nervous system is divided into two components. The sympathetic system controls the involuntary activities of various glands and organs and mobilizes the body for "fight or flight." The parasympathetic system calms the body and conserves energy. *From Kassin, Psychology (2001), Fig. 9.5, p. 333.*

with a gun suddenly appears. The perception–cognition "figure with a gun" in some fashion initiates a state of physiological arousal; this state of arousal is interpreted in terms of knowledge about dark alleys and guns, and the state of arousal is labeled "fear." Similarly, a student who unexpectedly learns that he [or she] has made Phi Beta Kappa may experience a state of arousal which he [or she] will label "joy." (p. 51)

Because the perception of the internal event of arousal and the cognitive explanation for the arousal tend to be confounded in naturalistic sit-uations, it was necessary for Schachter to experimentally separate them in order to demonstrate that neither one alone is sufficient for people to report that they are experiencing an emotion. To do so, Schachter and Singer (1962) told volunteers they would be injected with a vitamin compound, "Suproxin," to study its effects on vision. In actuality, some volunteers were injected with a placebo (saline solution) and others with epinephrine (or adrenalin) to mimic discharge of the SNS. Some of those in the latter group, the *aroused–informed* group, were informed of the side effects they would experience, including pounding heart, warm and flushed face, and tremulous hands (all supposedly due to Suproxin). Because these volunteers had an explanation (nonemotional) for their arousal (the Suproxin), they were not expected to search for an explanation in their immediate situation or to report the experience of emotion. The *aroused–ignorant* group, however, was told that Suproxin had *no* side effects; because people in this group had no explanation for their internal arousal, they were expected to search for one in their environment. Finally, yet another group, the *aroused–misinformed* group, was told that side effects of the Suproxin injection would include numb feet, itching, and a slight headache; because these volunteers had an inappropriate explanation of their actual symptoms of arousal, they, too, were expected to seek an explanation for their internal state. The *unaroused–placebo* group was told Suproxin had no side effects, and because people in this group were not experiencing any physiological effects, they were not expected to report emotion.

Thus, some participants would be experiencing physiological arousal while others would not, and some who experienced arousal would have a ready-made, nonemotional explanation for their arousal while others would not. It remained for Schachter and Singer to manipulate the situation in such a way that those participants who were seeking an explanation for their arousal—those in the aroused–ignorant and the aroused–misinformed groups—would find it. After their injection, the volunteers waited with a confederate of the experimenter, who was posing as another volunteer. The confederate acted in a happy, euphoric manner—for example, shooting paper basketballs and playing with a hula hoop. The prediction that participants in the aroused–ignorant and aroused–misinformed conditions (who were aroused and who did not have a ready-made explanation for their arousal) would behave in a more euphoric fashion (as coded by an observer) and would be more likely to report they felt "good or happy" than those in the aroused–informed condition (who were aroused but who already had a nonemotional explanation for their arousal) was confirmed (placebo volunteers were

in between). [Some volunteers in the placebo, aroused–informed, and aroused–ignorant conditions were exposed to an angry confederate rather than to the euphoric confederate; as hypothesized, aroused–ignorant volunteers were significantly more angry than those in the aroused–informed and placebo conditions.]

Schachter and Wheeler (1962) subsequently extended the range of sympathetic activation by injecting more volunteers, who believed they were participating in a experiment on the effects of "Suproxin" on vision, with a *placebo*, *epinephrine*, or *chlorpromazine* (an ANS depressant, popularly termed a tranquilizer) before all watched a film comedy. The degree to which each volunteer responded emotionally to the film was assessed by two independent observers, blind to each volunteer's condition, who recorded every time the volunteer showed mild amusement, smiled, grinned or smiled with teeth showing, laughed, or "belly laughed." As the investigators had predicted, degree of overt amusement was positively associated with degree of manipulated SNS arousal.

On the basis of these studies, Schachter (e.g., 1964) concluded that people are unlikely to report that they are experiencing an emotion unless (1) they perceive that they are experiencing the internal event of physiological arousal (a pounding heart, sweaty palms, and other physiological events usually associated with discharge of the sympathetic portion of the ANS) and (2) they have cognitively interpreted both the internal event of arousal and the external context in which it has occurred to mean that they are experiencing an emotion. Figure 9.7 illustrates Schachter's theory.

Misattribution of the Source of Arousal

In naturalistic situations, as Schachter observed, the same event that produces physiological arousal also often provides an explanation for the arousal (and usually a ready emotional label for the experience, such as "fear"). Schachter speculated that in some cases, however, people in naturalistic situations mistakenly identify the source of their arousal (just as participants in the

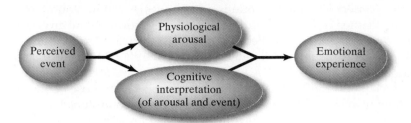

FIGURE 9.7 Schachter's two-component theory of emotion.

aroused–ignorant condition did), which then influences the nature of the emotion they experience. Many of the first experiments to test this speculation were conducted by Valins (e.g., 1970), who noted that both the James–Lange theory and Schachter's theory address bodily changes that not only actually occur but that also are *perceived* to occur. (Cannon's critique of the James–Lange theory, it should be noted, was addressed to the actual occurrence of bodily changes—not to the individual's perception of bodily change.) Because previous research had suggested that not all bodily changes are perceived, and that even those perceived by most people are not perceived by some, Valins argued that not only did actual bodily change and perceived bodily change need to be distinguished but, if Schachter was correct, *perceived change alone* could influence emotional experience.

To test this hypothesis, Valins (1966) showed slides of female nudes to male participants whose heart rates ostensibly were assessed by a device that audibly represented the individual's heartbeat. One group heard an *increase in their heart rates* in apparent reaction to five of the slides and no change in reaction to the other five slides; a second group heard a *decrease in their heart rates* to five slides and no change to the others; and, finally, two control groups heard the same recordings as those in the two experimental groups but were told that the heart sounds had been recorded in advance and were not their own. Valins found that nudes to which the men perceived that their heart rates had *changed*, whether by increasing or decreasing, were liked significantly more than nudes not associated with the perception of heart rate change.

Like Schachter, Valins (1970) concluded that people need to evaluate and understand their internal bodily changes and that to do so, they often seek an explanation from the environment in which they are experiencing the changes. Indeed, Valins (1966) found evidence that the men attended closely to the nudes being shown at the time their heart rate ostensibly changed, seemingly to try to account for what their heart rate change was telling them. Because all of the nudes were attractive, a reasonable explanation for the change in heart rate was that the nude associated with the change was exceptionally attractive. Interviews one month later showed that the men's preferences were enduring, and another experiment revealed that not even disclosing to the men that their prior heart rate feedback was false succeeded in changing their patterns of liking for the nudes.

The difference between actual change and perceived change in bodily state is important for a number of reasons. One of these reasons engages an enduring controversy spawned by Schachter's two-component theory of emotion: The theory assumes that peripheral physiological arousal is relatively *undifferentiated*—that people do not ordinarily perceive differences among instances of arousal, irrespective of whether or not such differences actually occur and can be assessed by devices that measure autonomic functions such as heart rate. In contrast, and as we have discussed, the James–Lange theory and several theories of basic emotion assume that there is a distinctive "affect program" associated with each basic emotion, including a distinctive physiological pattern. As a consequence, much research effort has been devoted to trying to identify those physiological patterns. From their review of this research, Cacioppo and associates (1993) conclude, "The research on the autonomic differentiation of emotions is provocative, but the cumulative evidence for emotion-specific autonomic patterns remains inconclusive" (p. 132).

Cacioppo, Klein, Berntson, and Hatfield (1993) offer a somatovisceral model of emotion which outlines the many ways in which either the actual experience of somatovisceral activity or the perception of such activity, such as changes in facial musculature or heart rate, may contribute to emotional experience. This model does not preclude the possibility that distinctive patterns of activity may yet be found to be associated with at least some emotions. However, the success of experiments on the misattribution of the source of arousal, such as those conducted by Schachter, Valins, and many others (see Reisenzein, 1983), suggests that either ANS arousal is undifferentiated or that the differentiations that exist are too slight for most people to notice.

In suggesting that misattribution of the source of arousal sometimes occurs, Schachter (1964) briefly speculated that such misattribution might account for some instances of romantic love. Berscheid and Walster [Hatfield] (1974a) expanded on his conjecture in their two-component theory of romantic love. In accord with Schachter, they theorized that in order to label an emotion as romantic love, the individual needed to experience physiological arousal in association with the partner and also to label those feelings as love. It followed from this formulation that arousal from another source could be misattributed to the partner and heighten the individual's romantic feelings. In support of their theory, they cited a study by Brehm, Gatz, Goethals, McCrommon, and Ward (unpublished, 1970) in which one group of men, the threat group, were led to believe they would soon receive three "pretty stiff" electric shocks; men in another group, the threat relief group, were initially told they would receive shock but then were informed that a mistake had been made and they would not receive shock; and men in a control group were told nothing about any electric shocks. Each man was then introduced to a woman and later asked how much he liked her. Men in both the threat group and the threat relief group (who, although relieved of the threat, were believed to be experiencing residual arousal from the threat) liked the woman more than did men in the control group, who were not experiencing arousal from a frightening event.

The misattribution of arousal effect also was found by Dutton and Aron (1974), who arranged for an attractive woman interviewer to ask men to fill out a questionnaire for her class project just after they had crossed a narrow and rickety 450-foot suspension bridge that hung a terrifying 230 feet over a rocky riverbed. After they filled out her questionnaire, she gave the men her name and phone number and invited them to call if they wanted to hear more about her project. In contrast to men who had been approached by the interviewer just after they had traversed a low, well-constructed bridge, significantly more of the men who crossed the rickety bridge later called her. Dutton and Aron interpreted their results as demonstrating that an increase in physiological arousal, whose source in this instance was crossing a rickety bridge, was misattributed and contributed to greater attraction to the female interviewer. The general misattribution effect of arousal on attraction has since been documented by other researchers (e.g., White & Kight, 1984).

The two-component love theory sometimes has been misinterpreted to mean that romantic love *always* is a result of misattribution of arousal to the partner. In actuality, it is likely that most of the time the source of the arousal *is* the partner and is *correctly* attributed to him or her. The theory simply predicts that increases in arousal, whether correctly or incorrectly attributed to the partner, should increase feelings of romantic love for the partner if situational factors lead the individual to interpret the increase in arousal as evidence of romantic love (as they often do, given the popular belief that people who are in love feel their hearts pound and faces flush in association with the partner).

Allen, Kenrick, Linder, and McCall (1989) demonstrated that even arousal experienced in association with an attractive partner, but which has its source elsewhere and is *correctly* attributed to the extraneous source, can enhance attraction. Their hypothesis that arousal would strengthen the dominant response (attraction) in their experimental situation was derived from learning and motivation theories suggesting that arousal "energizes" the performance of responses made to any environmental stimulus. As Hebb (1955) originally explained, arousal "is an energizer but not a guide; an engine but not a steering gear" (p. 249). The role of arousal in enhancing attraction when it is the dominant response in a situation also was demonstrated in several studies conducted by Aron, Norman, Aron, McKenna, and Heyman (2000). Couples who were experimentally assigned to participate together in novel, arousing, and pleasant activities subsequently showed significant increases in their evaluations of the quality of their relationship in terms of such feelings as satisfaction and passionate love as contrasted to couples who had not.

Transfer of Excitation

The "steering gear" of arousal, according to Schachter, is cognition, particularly cognitions about the environment in which the arousal is being experienced. Because decay of sympathetic activation is relatively slow, activation may linger for some time after the individual has exited the situation that produced arousal. Dolf Zillmann and his colleagues hypothesized that excitation from an arousal-producing situation may "transfer" to a subsequent situation and produce a more intense emotional experience in the latter situation than otherwise would have occurred (see Zillman, 1983; Zillman, Katcher, & Milavsky, 1972; Zillman & Zillman, 1996). In one of several tests of the **transfer of excitation** hypothesis, Cantor, Zillmann, and Bryant (1975) asked men to engage in strenuous physical exercise, which produces sympathetic activation, and then view an erotic film during one of three time periods after exercise: *immediately after* exercise, when the excitation from the exercise was high but also likely to be attributed to the exercise; a *short time later*, when residual arousal from the exercise was still present but unlikely to be at-

tributed to the exercise; and after a *long delay*, when the arousal had completely decayed. The men's self-reports of their sexual excitement while watching the film confirmed the investigators' prediction: Men who watched the film while residual arousal was still present but attribution of arousal to the exercise was unlikely (the short time later group) reported significantly more sexual excitement than did men in the immediate and the long delay groups.

Zillman and his colleagues could make the prediction that residual sympathetic arousal would enhance sexual excitement because virtually all accounts of the sequence of physiological activities associated with sexual behavior indicate that although genital vasocongestion itself is mostly mediated by the parasympathetic portion of the ANS, sexual arousal is accompanied by strong sympathetic discharge in almost all nongenital structures (Masters & Johnson, 1966). This fact has been used to better understand the association between sex and aggression (Zillmann, 1984). It also has been used by Palace to better understand women's sexual dysfunction in romantic relationships.

Palace (e.g., 1995, 1999) noted that there is a high degree of similarity between men's penile response and their report of how aroused they feel, but women's reports of arousal are more likely to be independent of their actual physical response; for example, women may be "feeling" aroused cognitively without an accompanying physical response, or they may experience vasocongestion and lubrication but not "feel" sexually aroused. Because of their less easily perceived physiological feedback system, some women may experience difficulty in attending to or labeling arousal cues. (It should be noted that this sex difference may extend beyond sexual arousal cues; Roberts and Pennebaker [1995] found that men seem to be more accurate in perceiving their internal states than women, who appear to be more dependent on external cues.) From a series of experimental studies, Palace (1999) concludes, "Sexual dysfunction may be explained as the interaction between a physiological tendency for low autonomic response and negative cognitive expectancy, which produce a negative feedback loop of dysfunctional sexual responses" (p. 187).

Palace (e.g., 1999) has shown that transfer of autonomic arousal—for example, through physical exercise—is highly effective in enhancing women's subsequent physiological sexual response and also in increasing expectations of sexual arousal. Her model of sexual process is *additive*, not compensatory, which suggests that cognitive intervention cannot replace simultaneous physiological intervention in programs that treat female sexual dysfunction. In light of Palace's findings, it is ironic that anxiety-reducing and relaxation techniques are almost exclusively used in the treatment of female sexual dysfunction (Masters & Johnson, 1970) because many sex researchers believe that anxiety and other emotions characterized by high sympathetic activation contribute to sexual dysfunction by disrupting parasympathetic functioning (which, as previously noted, is associated with genital vasocongestion). Although it appears that the appropriate treatment for sexual dysfunction in women has yet to be established, Palace's research provides additional evidence for the important role played by autonomic arousal in the experience of emotion.

Physiological Arousal in Social Interaction

One of the earliest studies to examine partners' physiological responses during interaction was conducted by Kaplan, Burch, and Bloom (1964), who found that pairs of students who disliked each other were more likely to display physiological covariation during interaction than pairs who either liked each other or felt neutral toward each other. Most studies that followed were of client–therapist pairs. From their review of these studies, Notarius and Herrick (1989) concluded that "the receipt of criticism, conflict, or confrontations expressed in client–therapist dyads has been found to be associated with greater autonomic reactivity, whereas the sending of these messages has been found to be associated with both increases and decreases of autonomic activation" (p. 396).

One of the first studies of physiological response during marital interaction was conducted by Notarius and Johnson (1982), who recorded one measure of autonomic activity (skin potential) as spouses engaged in a problem-solving discussion. They found that wives were more overtly expressive and had fewer skin potential responses (indicative of less emotion) than husbands and that husbands exhibited more autonomic activity when receiving their wives' negative messages than did wives in the same situation. From their findings, Notarius and Johnson speculated:

> As a husband receives an emotionally provocative message from his wife, he appears to be more likely to experience greater physiological reactivity and more likely to inhibit emotional display. A wife is likely to read her husband's lack of overt emotional response as disinterest, nonattending, unresponsiveness, or all of these and is likely to escalate her affective display to solicit a response from him. Nonresponsiveness from an intimate appears to be an evocative interpersonal stimulus. As she escalates her emotional display, the husband's somatic response is likely to be enhanced and, in a nice illustration of a positive feedback loop, husband and wife systematically produce in each other the behaviors that they would most like to avoid. (p. 405)

The first study to sample a relatively broad range of indicants of ANS arousal during interaction was conducted by Levenson and Gottman (1983; see Chapter 4). Reminiscent of the findings of Kaplan and colleagues (1964) with student pairs who disliked each other, it will be recalled that these investigators found that distressed couples showed more covariation in their physiological responses during a problem-solving discussion than did satisfied couples. Unfortunately, studies of partners' physiological behaviors known to be associated with affect and emotional experience during interaction are still relatively rare despite the fact that, as Cacioppo, Berntson, Sheridan, and McClintock (2000) discuss, a great deal of evidence has accumulated that multilevel integrative research that spans molar and molecular levels of analysis is needed to advance knowledge of the mechanisms that link social and biological events and processes.

COGNITION AND EMOTION

For centuries, scholars maintained a firewall between cognition and affect, believing that reason and passion were opposing forces and each could be understood independent of the other. The idea that human behavior could be divided into three distinct faculties—feeling (affect), knowing (cognition), and action (conation)—first emerged in the eighteenth century and became entrenched when the influential philosopher Immanuel Kant adopted this tripartite classification of behavior (see Forgas, 2000). Psychologists' belief that each of the three types of behavior were separate and distinct, and thus could be studied in isolation from the others, was partially responsible for their long neglect of emotion. It was not that emotion was not of interest to psychologists—James's attempt to find the theoretical golden goose of emotion and the flurry of empirical work his theory inspired testify otherwise—but when the mysteries of emotion were not easily solved, psychologists felt free to abandon emotion and study the seemingly more tractable components of the behavioral trio, confident that each could be understood independent of an understanding of emotion. As a consequence, conation and cognition—not emotion—became the focus of the two theoretical and research paradigms that dominated twentieth-century psychology.

The first paradigm, behaviorism, was concerned with observable and goal-oriented actions. Along with other behaviorists, B. F. Skinner (e.g., 1953) explicitly removed the study of cognition from the arena of psychological inquiry because he believed that little could be learned about the workings of the "black box" of the mind (see Chapter 8, "Cognitive Processes"). Emotion fared no better in the behaviorist paradigm (beyond Skinner's cursory notation that when pigeons in the Skinner box failed to receive the pellet they had earned by pecking the bar, they often displayed "emotional behavior"). The "cognitive revolution" in psychology overthrew the dominance

of behaviorism and brought the second paradigm into ascendance, but it too reflected the belief that matters of affect could be neglected with impunity. Cognitive theory and research focused almost entirely on "cold," or affectless, cognition. Cognition was, and continues to be, studied primarily in highly structured, minimal stimulus situations devoid of the motivational considerations that permeate daily life and produce the feelings and emotions that usually accompany cognition. Not only did the cognitive paradigm reflect the belief that cognition could be understood apart from affect, but it also reinforced the long-standing, and still popularly held, belief that emotions are, at best, frivolous behavioral effluvia and, at worst, antithetical to sound reason.

The absence of emotion from psychology, particularly love and other emotions of great consequence to people in their daily lives, was commented on by Abraham Maslow (1954):

> It is amazing how little the empirical sciences have to offer on the subject of love. Particularly strange is the silence of the psychologists, for one might think this to be their particular obligation. Probably this is just another example of the besetting sin of the academicians, that they prefer to do what they are easily able than what they ought, like the not-so-bright kitchen helper I knew who opened every can in the hotel one day because he was so *very* good at opening cans. (p. 235)

Psychologists at midcentury did not have the theoretical means to open up the study of emotion, but they were proving very good at prying cognitive phenomena out from under behaviorist dogma. Cognition became reunited with affect a decade later in Schachter's (e.g., 1964) two-component theory, and the wealth of research it generated dealt a mortal blow to the traditional tripartite sectioning of human behavior.

Any lingering remnants of the belief that human mental life can be neatly partitioned into three independent domains have been buried by findings in cognitive neuroscience and in the rapidly developing field of affective neuroscience (e.g., Le Doux, 1995; Panksepp, 1998). Affect, cognition, and action have been shown to be highly integrated in the neural circuitry of the brain and in the operations of the mind. Illustrative is the work of Damasio (1994), a neurologist who became fascinated with records of a nineteenth-century construction worker, Phineas Gage, who suffered a terrible accident in which the premature detonation of an explosive caused a iron rod to pass through his left eye and emerge from the top of his skull (Figure 9.8). Miraculously, Gage not only survived but was speaking and thinking rationally almost immediately after the accident. His powers of attention, perception, memory, language, and intelligence

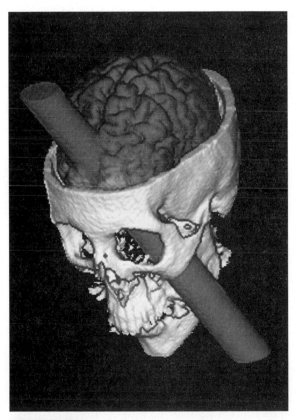

FIGURE 9.8 Phineas Gage's skull.

seemed to be unaffected, both then and later. However, Gage's personality underwent a catastrophic change. His social behavior become rude and destructive to himself and others, and his life ended in ruin.

Damasio subsequently discovered "Elliot," a modern counterpart to Gage. As the result of surgery to remove a tumor, Elliot suffered a lesion in the frontal lobe region of his brain. His cognitive faculties appeared to be unaffected, but his ability to act in his own best interests was impaired. Although he had been a successful businessman and a good husband and father prior to surgery, afterward he showed extremely poor judgment in personal, financial, and business matters. To try to understand the change, Damasio first focused on Elliot's intelligence and powers of reasoning. Rigorous and extensive testing revealed that Elliot was of superior intelligence and his powers of memory, new learning, language, and reasoning remained exceptional. Only belatedly did Damasio recognize that he had overlooked Elliot's capacity to experience emotion. Perhaps he overlooked Elliot's emotional life because, on close scrutiny, it appeared that Elliot didn't have one:

> Elliot was able to recount the tragedy of his life with a detachment that was out of step with the magnitude of the events. He was always controlled, always describing scenes as a dispassionate, uninvolved spectator. . . . Topics that once had evoked strong emotion no longer caused any reaction, positive or negative. (pp. 44–45)

As Damasio puts it, "We might summarize Elliot's predicament as *to know but not to feel*" (p. 45), which impairs an individual's ability to plan and to act wisely in his or her self-interest. Making decisions that protect and enhance our welfare is difficult if no alternative is ever more or less desirable than any other alternative. The very word "goal" implies that the associated outcome is positively valued. If an individual is incapable of feeling positively or negatively about an outcome, or about the actions that would lead to that outcome, deciding between several courses of action becomes impossible. Damasio concludes that not only is emotion *not* in opposition to reason, but affect operates in concert with cognition to promote survival. Discovering how affect interacts with cognition in terms of brain anatomy and neural processes is high on the agenda of many affective neuroscientists. How affect and cognition interact in terms of their effect on the mind has been of great interest to psychologists and the source of many controversies.

The Concept of Emotion

James's (1884) initial paper on the subject of emotion was titled "What Is an Emotion?" Psychologists have yet to definitively answer the question. Emotion theorist and reviewer Le Doux (1995) states:

> Controversy abounds over the definition of emotion, the number of emotions that exist, whether some emotions are more basic than others, the commonality of certain emotional response patterns across cultures and across species, whether different emotions have different physiological signatures, the extent to which emotional responses contribute to emotional experiences, the role of nature and nurture in emotion, the influence of emotion on cognitive processes, the dependence of emotion on cognition, and on and on. (pp. 209–210)

As a consequence, the emotion literature is difficult to understand. Emotion theorists seem to speak different dialects (Berscheid, 1990), and few agree on the answers to even the most fundamental questions about emotion (Ekman & Davidson, 1994b), including what an emotion is.

Most definitions of emotion can be arrayed along a dimension representing the *inclusiveness* of the events the theorist is willing to regard as an instance of emotional experience. At the highly inclusive end of the dimension are those theorists who regard an emotion to be any experienced state that carries **positive or negative valence**, including preferences (say, for vanilla over chocolate) and values (perhaps liberal vs. conservative) as well as attitudes, appraisals,

evaluations, feelings, and moods. Because any state that has positive or negative valence is viewed as an emotional state, even boredom, lassitude, or ennui—because they are usually regarded as negative states by the individual experiencing them—are regarded as emotional states by some theorists.

At the more restricted end of the spectrum are theorists who argue that by defining emotional events so broadly, virtually all of human experience becomes defined as emotional experience, a far too large and heterogeneous array to provide special insight into the kinds of emotional events in which most people are interested (e.g., Mandler, 1997). Supporting their argument are the results of the factor analytic studies of human language, which, as we have noted previously, consistently reveal that positive and negative valence is the primary dimension underlying people's symbolic representations of the external world, including our representations of animate and inanimate objects, events, and experiences (Osgood, Suci, & Tannenbaum, 1957). For this reason, these emotion theorists have followed Schachter's (e.g., 1964) lead and restrict the kinds of events they are willing to call an emotion to valenced experiences that *also* are accompanied by ANS arousal. They recognize that other physiological systems are involved in emotional experience, but they believe that the experience of autonomic arousal comes very close to being a necessary (though not sufficient) condition for people to perceive that they are experiencing an emotion.

Theorists who take a restricted view of emotion argue that the antecedents and consequences of events associated with arousal are different from those associated only with valence, so these two types of experiences demand different theoretical approaches. In support of this view, Mandler (1975) argues that ANS arousal is in itself, and apart from its contribution to emotional experience, an important event for the human, as evidenced by findings suggesting that the brain is wired such that the experience of the internal event of arousal has high-priority status for representation in the human's limited capacity of consciousness. In other words, if ANS arousal occurs, the individual is likely to notice it. Recent neuroscientific evidence also supports the contention that arousal is an important event for the human and that arousal states differ from nonarousal states in their consequences (e.g., Arnsten, 1998). For example, it long has been observed that affective events accompanied by arousal are better remembered than those that are not. A possible explanation is provided by evidence that the arousal that accompanies many affective states influences the neuroendocrine processes that regulate memory storage (e.g., Gold, 1992).

Affect

Despite differences in their definitions of the term "emotion," most theorists agree that the term **affect** refers to *all* states, including emotional states, that carry *positive or negative valence*—that is, states that are evaluated positively or negatively by the person experiencing them, as evidenced by that person's self-report or by his or her approach or avoidance behavior. Thus, the term "affect" is a large umbrella under which gather many different kinds of behaviors—feelings, preferences, moods, values, attitudes, and emotions.

Many psychologists have attempted to identify the principal dimensions that underlie the large assortment of experiences the term "affect" encompasses. Perhaps the oldest model of affective space is Russell's (1980; Russell & Carroll, 1999) **circumplex model of affect**, which proposes that "emotion" and other affect terms can be arranged in a circle that is bisected by two independent bipolar dimensions—horizontally by an *pleasant–unpleasant dimension* such as happy–sad and vertically by an *activation–deactivation dimension* such as alert–lethargic (Figure 9.9). The bipolarity of these two dimensions reflects evidence that people who report they are "happy" are unlikely to report that they are "sad" or to report that they are simultaneously experiencing any other sets of emotions located at opposite poles.

Tellegen and his associates (e.g., Watson, Clark, & Tellegen, 1988; Watson & Tellegen, 1999) proposed a somewhat similar model of affective space featuring a circular ordering of emotion terms, again characterized by two underlying dimensions, *positive activation* and *negative activation*—but these refer only to *highly activated* positive and negative emotions such as excitement or distress. These investigators generally assess the extent to which the individual is

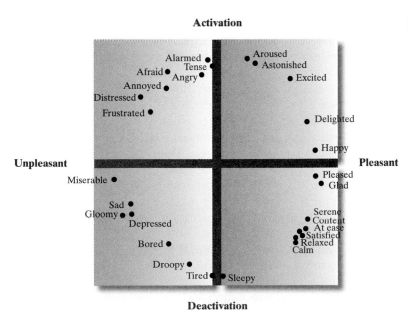

FIGURE 9.9 Russell's circumplex model of affect proposes that emotion and other affect terms can be arranged in a circle that is bisected by two independent and bipolar dimensions: pleasant–unpleasant and activation–deactivation. In this figure, a variety of affect terms fall on a circle in a two-dimensional space in a manner analogous to points on a compass. *Adapted from Russell, "Measures of Emotion" (1989), Fig. 4.1, p. 86.*

experiencing an emotion by using two *unipolar scales*, one ranging from "not at all happy" to "extremely happy" and the other ranging from "not at all sad" to "extremely sad," for example (as opposed to one *bipolar scale* ranging from "extremely happy" to "extremely sad") (see Figure 9.11). They believe that the positive and negative dimensions of affect are not bipolar opposites but instead are relatively independent of each other. Like the circumplex model, however, this model generally predicts that the people who report experiencing strong positive affect are unlikely to report experiencing strong negative affect.

Whereas other models of affective space focus on the individual's *self-report* of the experience of affect, Cacioppo and Berntson's (1994) **evaluative space model** (**ESM**) addresses the *underlying processes* that produce the conscious and reportable affective experience. These theorists note that throughout evolution, humans have been exposed to complex environments in which the opportunity for reward and the experience of positive affect often exists side by side with the possibility of punishment and the experience of negative affect. For example, the sighting of a wild boar by a hungry human provides the opportunity for a tasty dinner, but it also presents the possibility of an untimely death for the human if the boar has anything to say about it. Larsen, McGraw, and Cacioppo (2001) reason, "The organism that can process such appetitive and aversive cues in parallel is better able to swiftly approach or withdraw from environmental stimuli than is an organism that can only process such conflicting cues in serial [order]" (p. 694).

Consistent with this argument, several emotion theorists have posited two functionally separate affect systems, one for rewarding, or *appetitive*, stimuli and one for punishing, or *aversive*, stimuli. For example, Gray's theory of emotion (e.g., 1987, 1994) includes a **behavioral approach system** (**BAS**)—theorized to be sensitive to signals of reward, nonpunishment, and escape from punishment—that activates responses to rewarding stimuli. It also includes a **behavioral inhibition system** (**BIS**)—sensitive to signals of punishment, nonreward, and novelty or unfamiliarity—that inhibits behavior that may lead to negative outcomes. Carver and White's (1994) development of self-report scales to assess dispositional BAS and BIS sensitivities has facilitated research on individual differences in the strength of these systems. Gable, Reis, and Elliot (2000), for example, found that people with higher BAS sensitivity tend to experience more positive affect on a daily basis, whereas people with higher BIS sensitivity report more negative affective experiences. Other investigators have found that factor analyses of measures of temperament in infants and children, which include scales for such specific emotions as sadness, anger, and fear, tend to form a trait-like "negative emotionality" factor (see Izard, 2002). As discussed in Chapter 10, "Dispositional Influences," models of temperament (e.g., introversion), models of personality (e.g., neuroticism), and models of emotionality (negative affectivity, BIS) overlap considerably and have many implications for relationship phenomena.

Carver (2001) has offered a functional analysis of affect that posits two separate affect self-regulatory systems theorized to convey information about whether goal-directed behavior is going well or poorly. One system is theorized to manage *approach and incentive-related affects*—both positive affects such as elation and eagerness when things are going well and negative affects such as sadness and depression when things are going poorly. The second system is theorized to manage *avoidance and threat-related affects*—both positive affects such as relief when things are going well in avoiding the threat and negative affects such as fear and anxiety when things are going poorly. Thus, Carver argues for two bipolar (not unipolar) affect dimensions. The plausibility that humans have more than one affect system has been strengthened by evidence from affective neuroscience that the neural processes and structures involved in processing negative affect only partially overlap those involved in processing positive affect (Davidson, 1998; Sutton & Davidson, 1997).

However, the view that humans possess two affect systems—one for approach to positive, appetitive stimuli and another for avoidance of negative, aversive stimuli—raises the disconcerting possibility that both systems could be activated at once and, theoretically at least, a person could feel both positive affect (and be attracted) and negative affect (and be repelled) at the very same time. In strong opposition to this theoretical derivation, however, is massive empirical evidence that people almost always say they are experiencing *either* positive affect *or* negative affect; as most models of affective space reflect, people rarely report positive and negative affect coexisting together. That people should report they feel either positive affect (associated with approach behavior) or negative affect (associated with withdrawal) makes sense from a survival perspective. Ambivalence ("affective dissonance," it might be called) should, like cognitive dissonance, tend toward resolution one way or the other because an approach action requires a unidirectional affect orientation, as does an avoidance action. The hungry hunter who is dithering between approaching or avoiding the wild boar is paralyzed for action, which threatens his or her survival; while the hunter is vascillating between the two opposing actions, the boar may either slip away into the forest and deprive the hunter of a meal or decide that the hunter looks appetizing and act accordingly.

Cacioppo, Gardner, and Berntson (1999) have attempted to resolve the inconsistency between these two eminently reasonable but opposing points of view. They theorize that the experience and subsequent report of positive or negative valence represents the *product* of an integration at the neural processing level of two separable and partially distinct affect systems, one for positivity (sensitive to appetitive stimuli) and another for negativity (sensitive to threat and aversive stimuli). Like other models, the ESM posits that positivity fosters approach and that negativity fosters avoidance, but because they are partially separate at the level at which the brain processes information, these two affect systems may be *coactivated* at the neural processing level (a change in one system institutes a parallel change in the other), *coinhibited* (a change in one system may be associated with the opposite change in the other), or *uncoupled* (the activation of one has no influence on the other). Although the model predicts

that affective processes gravitate toward bipolarity and a single action orientation over time, it also implies that on rare occasions, the effects of the two affect systems can be simultaneously present in consciousness.

To test the hypothesis that people can sometimes be happy and sad at the same time, Larsen, McGraw, and Cacioppo (2001) asked people to report their current affective state on several unipolar scales (each measuring either positive or negative affect) *before* they saw the film *Life Is Beautiful* (a drama-comedy set in a World War II concentration camp) and then again *after* they saw the film. Only 10% of the participants felt both happy and sad before the film; after the film, however, 44% reported that they felt both happy and sad. In a second study, it was hypothesized that undergraduates would be more likely to feel both happy and sad on the day they moved out of their dormitories for summer vacation than they would on a typical day, and in a third study, it was hypothesized that college students would be more likely to feel both happy and sad on their graduation day than on a typical day. These predictions were confirmed. The investigators note that although their studies show that coactivation of both positivity and negativity is possible, such ambivalence provides a poor guide for behavior; thus, it is likely to be unpleasant, unstable, and short-lived. In sum, the ESM model of affective space assumes that the common metric governing an individual's approach toward, or withdrawal from, a person or object is a bipolar (positive–negative) dimension at the *response stage*, but underlying the response dimension at the *initial information processing stage* are two partially independent systems and metrics—one for positivity and one for negativity.

Cacioppo and Gardner (1999) warn that assuming "the affect system consists only of a single bipolar evaluative channel can . . . be costly in terms of the fertile avenues of research it precludes" (p. 203). This is especially true in the study of relationships. As Gable and Reis (2001) elaborate, a two-system affect model has very different implications for understanding relationships than a single bipolar (positive to

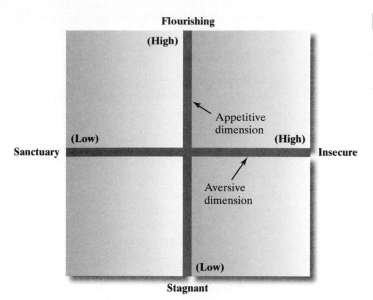

FIGURE 9.10 Gable and Reis's model of appetitive and aversive dimensions in close relationships. *From Gable and Reis, "Appetitive and Aversive Social Interaction" (2001), Fig. 9.1, p. 182.*

negative) model does. Their own model of appetitive and aversive dimensions in close relationships (Figure 9.10) grew out of this question: "Why has relationship research emphasized the causal antecedents and consequences of negative processes such as conflict, criticism, betrayal, stress, divorce, bereavement, rejection, social isolation, jealousy, violence, loneliness, hostility, and intrusiveness to the exclusion of more positive processes?" (p. 189). Among the several cogent answers to this question is that bipolar affect scales, such as relationship satisfaction scales that range from "very satisfied" to "very dissatisfied," easily lead to the conclusion that dissatisfaction is caused by negative relationship events alone—as opposed to the *absence* of positive relationship experiences. As discussed further in Part 6, "Relationships Over Time," the view that negative and positive affect should be measured separately is gaining hold in relationship research and providing insights not possible when bipolar affect scales are used (Figure 9.11). Here, we merely note that relationships located in different parts of the Gable and Reis grid are very different and that their differences would be masked by one bipolar scale ranging from positive to negative.

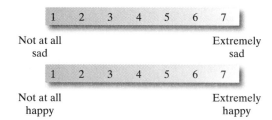

FIGURE 9.11 The measurement of affect. Bipolar scales presuppose that positive and negative affect cannot be simultaneously experienced. A very different, and more complete, view is offered by unipolar scales. For example, it is possible for an individual to feel high amounts of both positive emotion (happiness, contentment) and negative emotion (sadness, frustration) within a specific relationship and for a particular partner. A single bipolar scale which forces the individual to locate his or her affective experience somewhere in between "happy" and "sad," for example, will mask this important emotional fact.

Preferences

Widespread agreement among emotion theorists and researchers about what the term "affect" means is the exception to the rule of definitional chaos in the emotion domain. Differences and misunderstandings about the meaning of most emotion terms have contributed to many of the controversies that have preoccupied emotion theorists and researchers. An example is the heated debate that followed Zajonc's (1980) famous declaration that "preferences need no inferences." Reminiscent of earlier tripartite reasoning, Zajonc was asserting that affect and cognition are distinct and conceptually separable processes and, moreover, that affective reactions are "primary" and can take place *without cognitive input*. Zajonc reached the conclusion that affect is distinct from cognition from research that had documented a highly reliable association between increases in exposure to a stimulus and attraction to that stimulus (the "mere exposure effect"; see Chapter 6) and also from demonstrations that attraction to a stimulus may occur as a result of exposure even if the individual is unaware of the exposure. Kunst-Wilson and Zajonc (1980), for example, exposed a stimulus subliminally, below their participants' level of awareness, and a later presented both the subliminal stimulus and a novel stimulus. Participants could not report which of the two stimuli they had seen before—but when asked which one they liked best, they significantly preferred the stimulus to which they had been subliminally exposed.

Thus, in this and other experiments, Zajonc and his associates demonstrated that preferences can develop without an individual's awareness of the source of the preference and also that the individual's subjective impression of the familiarity of a stimulus does not mediate the effect. Moreover, Monahan, Murphy, and Zajonc (described in Zajonc, 2000) showed that repeated subliminal exposure of a stimulus increases the positivity of the viewer's mood and that increased positive mood, in turn, increases preference for stimuli presented while the individual is in that positive mood state. Zajonc concludes that "repetition of experience, even when not accessible to awareness, constitutes a positive hedonic event" (p. 54).

Zajonc was puzzled that his contention that preferences [affect] need no inferences [cognition] "invited such agitated opposition" (p. 31). At least part of the controversy hinged on differences between his construals of the terms "affect" and "cognition" and the meaning of the terms to others. Zajonc believes that the "prototype" of affective responses is an individual's *preference* for one stimulus over another and that the "prototype" of cognitive responses is *conscious recognition* of a stimulus as familiar (because recognition requires mentally comparing the present stimulus to one retained in memory, a cognitive processing operation). He argues that because preferences can develop without conscious recognition, it follows that "preferences need no [cognitive] inferences." However, not everyone agrees that preference is the prototype of affective responses or that conscious recognition of a stimulus is the prototype of cognitive responses. More important, almost no one agrees that nonconscious recognition of a stimulus does not require cognitive processing. Research associated with semantic priming (see Chapter 8) demonstrates that responses to stimuli can be generated with lightning speed through automatic processing, which is nonconscious and nondeliberative yet is cognitive processing nonetheless.

Whether or not affect is "primary" in the sense of Zajonc's (1980) argument, a great deal of research shows that exposure to a subliminal stimulus influences the individual's affective response. This fact supports the philosopher Pascal's contention "The heart has its reasons of which reason knows nothing" (1643/1995, p. 127)—or, at the least, reasons of which we are not conscious and thus which we cannot report. This finding has implications for relationship partners and therapists who often dismiss as "irrational" an individual's preferences when he or she cannot present a lawyer's brief of reasons to support liking or disliking someone or something; the preference may be perfectly rational, but its rationale may be inaccessible to consciousness.

Mood

As the heated debate inspired by Zajonc's declaration that preferences need no inferences illustrates, one of the most active theoretical and research areas in recent years has focused on gaining a better understanding of the interaction between affect and cognition and, in particular, the interaction between mood and cognition. Distinguishing **mood** from an emotion and other forms of affect, Forgas (2000) states that moods

> can be defined as relatively low-intensity, diffuse, and enduring affective states that have no salient antecedent cause and therefore little cognitive content (such as feeling good or feeling bad, being in a good or bad mood). In contrast distinct emotions are more short-lived, intense phenomena and usually have a highly accessible and salient cause, as well as clear, prototypical cognitive content (e.g., disgust, anger, or fear). (p. 6)

Evidence that a person's mood may affect an individual's evaluations of another was provided by attraction researchers, who found that attraction can be classically conditioned (see Chapter 6). For example, Gouaux (1971) found that people who had watched a happy film evaluated another person more positively than did people who had watched a sad film. Apart from studies that applied the classical conditioning paradigm to attitude change and interpersonal attraction, however, theory and research on how moods affect people's evaluations and memories of other people and relationship events did not begin in earnest until the late 1970s when Isen, Shalker, Clark, and Karp (1978) demonstrated that simply finding a dime in a phone booth sufficiently elevated people's moods to produce evaluations that were more positive than those made by people who were not so lucky—a **mood-congruent evaluation effect**.

Isen (1987) and her associates subsequently showed that people's moods influence not only their evaluations of other individuals and events (*what* people think, a content effect), but also the kind of information processing they use (*how* people think). The experience of positive affect appears to be associated with automatic/associative information processing; that is, it appears to be less systematic, more creative, and less effortful than the more controlled and deliberate information processing people seem to do when they are in a negative affective state (see Clark & Isen, 1982, for a review). Fiedler (2001) maintains that positive moods enhance generative, assimilative, and "top-down" productive thinking that produces the creative use of existing information; negative moods, on the other hand, seem to be associated with attention to external, situational information and with inductive, "bottom-up" thinking.

How mood affects cognitive processing is important for understanding many relationship phenomena, including the outcome of couples' attempts to solve problems in their relationship. Knapp and Clark (1991) induced either a happy, sad, angry, or neutral (control) mood in their experimental participants and subsequently asked couples to solve a resource dilemma problem— the kind of problem common among couples. Those who were sad or angry were less successful (they were more likely to deplete their resources) than were those in a happy or neutral mood, the latter two groups not differing in their problem-solving performance. In naturalistic situations, the trigger for a problem-solving interaction is often a conflict between the partners. Bolger, DeLongis, Kessler, and Schilling (1989) found that interpersonal conflicts were the best predictor of day-to-day variations in mood. Thus, a relationship conflict may produce a bad mood at the same time as it arouses a need for a solution, the former reducing the likelihood that the latter will be achieved.

At about the same time that Isen and her associates were demonstrating mood-congruent evaluation effects, Bower and his colleagues (1981b) were finding that people in positive and negative moods (which could be induced through hypnosis) tended to recall information that was affectively congruent with their mood at the time of recall; that is, people in good moods tended to recall positive information and people in bad moods tended to recall negative information—a **mood-congruent recall effect**. Other researchers were soon to show that good moods also increased an individual's estimates of the frequency and likelihood of the occurrence of positive events, whereas bad moods decreased those estimates (e.g., DeSteno, Petty, Wegener, & Rucker, 2000; Johnson & Tversky, 1983).

What is retrieved from memory, however, seems to depend not only on the individual's affective state *at the time of recall* but also on its congruency with the individual's affective state *at the time the information was encoded*—a **mood state–dependent memory** effect. State-dependent memory effects, which long have been of interest to learning researchers, are often illustrated with anecdotes about the effects of mood-altering drugs on memory. For example, a person may hide money while inebriated, forget where it is when sober, but remember its hiding place during the next drinking episode; that is, recall seems to be facilitated by congruency between the individual's state at recall and his or her state at encoding. However, mood state–dependent memory effects, like other interactions between mood and cognition, appear to be highly context-sensitive. For example, they appear to depend on factors such as the kind of information recalled (see Eich & Macaulay, 2000). Experiments that ask people in a bad or good mood to recall a list of unrelated words learned when the person was in a bad or good mood often fail to show the effect, but studies in which the individual is asked to recall autobiographical events (as relationship events always are) reveal robust and reliable mood state–dependent memory effects. People in a bad mood tend to remember autobiographical events (both good and bad) that happened and were encoded when they were in a bad mood better than they do events that were encoded when they were in a good mood (Eich, Macaulay, & Ryan, 1994).

Given the dependence of relationship scholars and therapists on people's self-report of their relationship history and their present satisfaction with their relationship, mood effects on recall assume considerable importance. Forgas, Levinger, and Moylan (1994) stopped moviegoers after they had seen a predominantly happy or sad film (a successful mood induction procedure) and asked them, "How do you currently feel about your relationship with your partner?" Compared to people in a control condition (who were interviewed immediately before, rather than after, they saw a film), those who had seen a happy film and were in a good mood judged their relationship significantly more positively, and those in a sad mood judged their relationship significantly more negatively. Additional controlled laboratory experiments replicated the effect.

Several theoretical models have been proposed to account for mood effects on cognitive processing. One is the *affect-as-information* model, generated from a seminal experiment conducted by Schwarz and Clore (1983), who found that their participants' sad moods influenced judgments of their life satisfaction (a mood-congruent evaluation effect). Schwarz and Clore reasoned that when asked to evaluate their lives, people in a sad mood asked themselves, "Well, how *do* I feel about my life?" and answered using their preexisting mood state (sad) as information about how they felt; in other words, they made an inferential error. The investigators found they could easily erase the sad participants' negative judgments by inducing them to attribute their sad mood (either correctly or incorrectly) to an external source such as the rainy weather. In general, mood-as-information effects appear to be most prevalent when people lack the motivation or time to think deeply about the answer to the judgment question posed; that is, "off-the-cuff" responses to affective questions are most likely to reflect the "How do I feel about it?" heuristic (see Clore et al., 2001; Forgas, 2002; Schwarz, 2001).

Another model used to account for mood-congruent effects is the *affect priming* model originally posited by Bower (e.g., 1981b). Positive (or negative) mood is believed to "prime" the recall of positive (or negative) memories and ideas. For example, when asked how satisfied they are with their relationship, people in a good mood may recall pleasant relationship events; as a consequence, they are more likely to state they are satisfied than if they had been asked the question when in a bad mood. Like other mood effects, affect priming effects have been shown to be "context-sensitive," meaning that they are sometimes found and sometimes not, and the investigator frequently does not know why.

To attempt to account for the many inconsistencies in research on how mood affects behavior and judgments, Forgas (e.g., 1995, 2001, 2002) proposed the *affect infusion model* (AIM). The AIM predicts that the person's current affect will be "infused" into (and thus influence) his or her judgments and other behaviors *only* when the individual faces complex situations that require the use of *constructive* information-processing strategies. Constructive information processing is more effortful than the mere retrieval and reproduction of existing cognitive representations, such as retrieving from memory a detailed and previously constructed impression of a longtime friend. Constructive information processing is likely if the task is complex, demanding, or novel and the individual is motivated to perform the task well. Such tasks require the individual to go beyond the information provided to reach a judgment (that is, to draw on memory stores of knowledge to interpret new information). Forming an impression of a stranger who controls the individual's future outcomes is an example of a task that likely requires constructive information processing and thus will be affected by the individual's mood at the time he or she is trying to form an accurate impression.

A great deal of evidence supports the AIM and has confirmed some of its less obvious predictions. For example, the AIM predicts that when people are asked to explain interpersonal conflicts in their close relationships, their current affect should exert more influence on their explanations for *serious* conflicts (explanations that are assumed to demand more elaborate thought and information processing) than for *simple* conflicts. Indeed, in a series of experiments in which participants were randomly assigned to positive and negative mood induction procedures such as viewing a happy or sad film or hearing a happy or sad story, people in a sad mood were more likely to blame themselves for their relationship conflicts than were people in a happier mood (Forgas et al., 1994). Moreover, people in a sad mood were more likely to attribute their relationship conflicts to internal, stable, and global causes than people in a happy mood were, and they did so more often for serious conflicts than

for simple ones, the former being shown to require more processing time to produce judgments than simple conflicts. The AIM model, which specifies many other contextual factors that may affect how mood influences information processing, posits that affect may "infuse" judgments *indirectly* by priming affect-related categories, or it may do so *directly* through the "How do I feel about it?" heuristic; in other words, the AIM attempts to specify not only when affect will influence the products of cognitive processing but also when each of the two principal affect infusion mechanisms is likely to occur.

Cognitive Theories of Emotion

Although virtually all theories of emotion incorporate cognition in some way, some theories are more cognitive than others. Richard Lazarus (e.g., 1984) for example, was among the emotion theorists who vigorously opposed Zajonc's contention that cognition is not always involved in emotion. Lazarus argues that not only is cognition primary in emotional experience (emotion being defined as a valenced state) but cognitive mediation is a necessary and sufficient condition for the experience of emotion (1991, 1994). Lazarus (1994) also believes that the social environment is the source of most emotional experiences:

> An emotion is always about certain substantive features of the relationship between a person and an environment. Although this relationship can occur with the physical world, most emotions involve two people who are experiencing either a transient or stable interpersonal relationship of significance. What makes the relationship personally significant, and hence worthy of an emotion, is that what happens is relevant to the well-being of one or both parties; in effect, each has personal goals at stake. (pp. 209–210)

Thus, according to Lazarus, for people to experience emotion in social interaction, they must perceive that achievement of a *personal goal is at stake*: "If there is no goal at stake, and none emerges from the encounter, there is no possibility of an emotion taking place" (p. 211).

Whether the emotion experienced will be positive or negative is theorized to depend on whether the events in the interaction are cognitively appraised as favorable or unfavorable. It is the perceived aspects of those events that determine the nature of the emotion experienced; Lazarus believes that different negative emotions result from different types of harm and different positive emotions from different types of benefit. Anger, for example, is theorized to involve the protection and enhancement of self-esteem and is aroused by "a demeaning offense against me and mine" (p. 212). Thus, like many emotion theorists before him, Lazarus emphasizes the role of a *cognitive appraisal process* in emotional experience, in which the meaning of events for the achievement of the individual's goals is evaluated.

Analysis of the meaning of events also plays a central role in cognitive "constructionist" views of emotion. As opposed to basic emotion theorists, who believe that certain innately given basic emotions are experienced in similar form from one occasion to the next, cognitive constructionists believe that each emotional experience is cognitively formed afresh at the time of its experience from the elements present in the immediate situation. Because no situation is ever likely to repeat itself in all its particulars, constructionists take the position that there are innumerable emotional states, some of which bear similarities to each other but are never precisely the same from one occasion to the next. For several of these theorists, cognitive expectancies play a critical role in emotion.

Cognitive Expectancies and Emotion

Cognitive expectancies have played a role in at least some theories of emotion ever since Hebb (1946) published his influential theoretical analysis of fear. Prior to Hebb's experiments, many psychologists believed that an understanding of fear could be obtained by cataloguing all the objects associated with fear—snakes, earthquakes, and so forth—and distilling their common properties. As a consequence of his experiments with monkeys, however, Hebb declared that "no amount of analysis of the stimulating conditions alone [e.g., the properties of a grizzly bear or a snake that make them feared] can be expected to elucidate the nature of fear, or lead to any useful generalization concerning its causes" (p. 274). Rather, Hebb proposed that "fear originates in the disruption of temporally and spatially organized cerebral activities" (p. 274). A large and important subset of events that disrupt "organized cerebral activities" includes violations of expectancies.

Cognitive expectancies play a central role in one of the first theories of emotion to extensively incorporate findings from cognitive psychology. George Mandler's (e.g., 1975, 1997) **discrepancy detection theory** of emotion is based on the observation that our ability to detect whether the state of the world around us is the *same* as before or *different* from before is perhaps our most important evolutionary inheritance because detecting a change in our environment is essential to survival. If the world has changed—if it is unfamiliar and different from the world we expected and have adapted to—it is potentially dangerous, and action to protect our well-being may be required. Our changed environment, however, may also present us with new opportunities to enhance our well-being; if so, action also may be required to take advantage of the opportunity. In either case, the detection of a discrepancy between the world as it currently is and the world as we have known it in the past signals that new ways of living, adapting, and behaving may be required to protect or enhance our welfare.

Mandler thus believes that humans have evolved to be cognitively sensitive to the discrepancies between the world as we expected it to be and the world as we currently perceive it. He also theorizes that we automatically undergo bodily changes to help us take actions that will promote our survival when a discrepancy is detected. There is extensive evidence that humans do react quickly and automatically to unexpected changes in their environment (e.g., MacDowell & Mandler, 1989; Meyer, Reisenzein, & Schutzwohl, 1997; Stiensmeier-Pelster, Martini, & Reisenzein, 1995). Any unexpected disruption or interruption in the individual's customary behavioral routines, progress toward current goals and plans, and beliefs about people and events appears to produce ANS arousal.

Mandler theorizes that activation of the sympathetic nervous system prepares the individual to *physically* respond to the changed environment (by fight or flight) and also that perception of the internal event of SNS arousal may act as a *cognitive backup warning*, alerting the individual that his or her environment has changed and that action may be required to protect or enhance well-being. Because the internal symptoms of arousal have priority status for representation in consciousness, Mandler believes that people will be aware of their arousal even if they are unaware of what caused it. This view assumes that environmental changes may be processed by the mind and result in SNS activation and the perception of internal SNS symptoms *before* the perception of environmental change reaches conscious awareness. Indeed, as we have discussed, people have been shown to react autonomically—for example, with increased heart rate—to stimuli they have not consciously perceived and cannot report (e.g., Kunst-Wilson & Zajonc, 1980; Ohman & Soares, 1994). Also supporting Mandler's view that arousal may act as a backup for alerting the individual that the world has changed in some way are Schachter's (e.g., 1964) demonstrations that awareness of unexplained arousal is likely to precipitate a scanning of the environment to locate its cause. Finally, the view that the human may need an arousal backup for detecting environmental changes is supported by studies of the visual detection of change. A striking "blindness" to change can be induced under a variety of conditions, supporting the view that focused attention is needed to see change (Rensink, 2002, p. 259). As we have discussed, however, human attentional capacities are limited, and thus the perception of the internal event of arousal may ensure that environmental changes will be noticed.

Mandler theorizes that the longer the discrepancy exists without successful adaptation to the new environment, the more intense the arousal and thus the more intense the emotion should be. Successful adaptation is often marked by the individual's resumption of previously disrupted behavioral routines and progress toward his or her plans and goals *or* by cognitive resolution of

the violated expectations (e.g., by determining that the consequences are not as threatening as first believed and require no action). When adaptation is achieved, emotional experience is theorized to end. Violated expectancies—that is, sudden and unexpected disruptions, often of goal-oriented behaviors—are cited by many other theorists as the occasion for cognitive analysis of the situation and mental rumination about the events (e.g., Martin & Tesser, 1989), and for emotional experience (e.g., Rimé et al., 1992).

In sum, Mandler believes that violation of an expectancy provides the occasion for arousal, which then combines with a positive or negative valenced cognitive evaluation of the situation—as one that presents a threat to well-being or an opportunity to enhance well-being—to produce emotional experience: "The construction of emotion consists of the concatenation in consciousness of some cognitive evaluative schema together with the perception of visceral arousal" (1997, p. 71). Discrepancy detection, in other words, is believed to fulfill a necessary (but not sufficient) condition for emotional experience.

Expectancy violation plays a role in many other theories of emotion, including Gray's (e.g., 1994) theoretical analysis. As previously noted, Gray postulates the BAS and the BIS (as well as a fight-or-flight system, which his theory relatively neglects in favor of elaboration of the other two). Gray believes that each of these affect systems can be described on the behavioral, neural, and cognitive levels. His analysis of the cognitive level, which has focused primarily on the BIS, includes a hypothetical construct he calls "the comparator." The comparator function is theorized to be a continuous monitoring of whether the current state of the world is the same as, or different from, the expected state of the world.

Expectancies and Emotion in Relationships

Most people are Schachterians, if the questions they ask about the emotions they experience in relationships are any indication. When most people talk about their "emotions," they usually are referring to experiences in which their knees tremble, their faces flush, and their hearts pound, or to what is often referred to as "hot" emotion;

they usually are *not* referring to states of boredom, mildly favorable or unfavorable appraisals of their partner, or their own or their partner's preferences. In other words, they usually are referring to states in which they experience the symptoms of SNS activation. To understand why "hot" emotions (accompanied by arousal) are more often experienced in close relationships than superficial relationships, and to better understand *when* a relationship event is likely to generate intense emotion, Berscheid extended and elaborated Mandler's theoretical view of emotion in her **emotion-in-relationship model (ERM)** (1983/2002, 1986, 1991; Berscheid, Gangestad, & Kulakowski, 1984; Berscheid & Ammazzalorso, 2001).

Berscheid reasons that the infrastructure of a close relationship satisfies many of the necessary conditions for intense emotional experience for two reasons. First, by definition, partners in close relationships are highly dependent on each other's behavior for the performance of many daily activities, and these in turn are essential to the achievement of their plans and goals. Thus, violations of expectancies in close relationships usually have more potent consequences for the individual's welfare than do violations of expectancies about people on whom we are less outcome-dependent. Second, individuals in close relationships hold many more expectations about their partners' behavior than do individuals in superficial relationships. As a consequence, the potential for expectancy violation is greater in close than in superficial relationships.

ERM predicts that the violation of a relationship expectancy will produce positive emotion when the consequences are perceived to enhance the individual's welfare (as when the partner unexpectedly *facilitates* the achievement of an ongoing goal) and negative emotion when they are perceived to threaten welfare (as when the partner unexpectedly *interferes* with the achievement of plans and goals). Facilitation, and the resultant enhancement of our welfare, is the raison d'être of most close relationships, especially romantic and marital relationships. Strong positive emotions at the beginning of a new relationship often reflect the unexpected nature

of events and the element of surprise that accompanies expectancy violation. People who have fallen in love, for example, often express wonder that their world has dramatically changed in a felicitous way ("I can't believe this is happening to me!" "Can it be that someone so wonderful could care for me?").

The ERM maintains that an important class of expectancies in close relationships involves the individual's daily behavioral routines, which are often performed in the service of achieving larger goals. Plans and goals generally have a hierarchical structure—for example, going to class in order to obtain credits, in order to obtain a college degree, in order to get a better job, in order to have the resources to get married and raise children. Interference with a behavioral activity that is part of a nested series of higher-order plans can be expected to result in more emotion than interruption of a behavioral activity that is not. Over time, if the relationship is to survive, each individual will learn to coordinate his or her daily activities with the partner's so as to reduce interference with the partner's achievement of personal goals and to increase their facilitation. The partners' efforts to facilitate their achievement of mutual goals is likely to result in the development of highly meshed interaction sequences of behavior—that is, organized, and often automatically performed, interaction routines in which each partner's behavior facilitates the other partner's subsequent behavior in the sequence (see Chapter 4). If many of the individual's daily and routinely performed behavioral sequences are meshed to the partner's but the partner fails to perform as expected, then the individual's expectancies are violated, his or her customary performance of the sequence is disrupted, arousal should occur (unless some substitute for the partner's failed actions is quickly found), a negative cognitive valence should be attached to the failure, and a negative emotional experience should result. In close relationships, where many of the individual's daily activities are meshed with the partner's activities in the service of achieving important goals, unexpected loss of the relationship should be the occasion for the experience of intense negative emotion.

Thus, the expectancies an individual holds about the partner and the relationship are theorized to represent the individual's degree of **emotional investment** in the relationship because each expectancy has the potential for violation and, subsequently, the experience of emotion. The greater the number of expectancies and the more strongly they are held, the greater the potential for emotion to be experienced "in" the relationship—that is, emotion caused by the partner or a relationship event. The individual's potential for emotional experience may never be realized during the life of a relationship, however, because the expectancies may never be disconfirmed. When the relationship is dissolved, the individual's emotional reaction is predicted to be a function of two variables: (1) the degree of interdependence characteristic of the relationship (the closer the relationship, the more the disruption because the more likely it is that many behavioral routines and plans have been affected) and (2) the speed with which the individual is able to find the means to resume disrupted behavioral activities and make progress toward plans and goals and thus restore his or her well-being. The latter suggests that the intensity and duration of an individual's emotional reaction to relationship dissolution often depends on the speed with which a "substitute" partner can be found—one who can step into the role the absent partner once played in the individual's life and who can facilitate the individual's goals as well as the former partner did.

ERM predictions about emotional reactions to separation and dissolution were supported by Simpson (1987), who found that both relationship closeness and fewer alternative partners were associated with the experience of greater distress following the dissolution of a romantic relationship. The results of a natural field experiment conducted by Attridge (1995) also confirms ERM predictions. Women separated from their romantic relationship partners because of participation in a "study abroad" program, in contrast to those not separated, reported experiencing intense emotions more frequently during the separation as a function of the closeness of

their relationship and their scores on a "disruption potential" measure (which included assessment of the availability of alternative partners). As predicted, closeness and disruption potential did not *by themselves* lead to emotional experience; rather, they interacted with the event of separation to produce the experience of emotion. Neither the length of the relationship nor the individual's satisfaction with it was associated with emotional experience for either separated or nonseparated partners.

Expectancies also are at the center of Burgoon's (e.g., 1993) emotional communication theory, which she suggests might be dubbed "expectancy violations theory." The theory proposes that in order to understand people's emotional experiences and expressions in their relationships, it is necessary to know (1) what experiences and expressions they expect in interpersonal relationships; (2) the extent to which enacted expressions deviate, positively or negatively, from expectancies; (3) the degree to which other types of expectancy violations generate emotional expressions; and (4) the effects of deviating from entrenched patterns of emotional expression.

Development of Relationship Expectancies

As a relationship develops, the partners come to know each other increasingly well and develop expectancies about each other's habits, attitudes, personality, character, and other behavioral dispositions that allow them to predict how the other will behave in many different situations (see Chapter 8). Although some expectancies are derived from observing the partner's behavior and thus are "custom-tailored" to him or her, many of our expectancies about our partners and the relationship are of the ready-made, "one size fits all" variety that we bring to the relationship regardless of who our partner happens to be. Many of the preformed expectancies we drape over our unsuspecting partner are embedded in our stable dispositions, such as our personality and attitudes, as discussed in Chapter 10, "Dispositional Influences." Other expectancies about our partner derive from information about other people's relationships or have their source in cultural norms, customs, and understandings about relationships.

Our partners may be aware of some of the contents of the extensive baggage of expectancies we bring to our relationships with them. In particular, they are likely to be aware of the relationship expectancies the culture instills, for if they have been raised in the same culture, they share those expectations. But it is unlikely that our partners are aware of *all* of our expectancies, especially those that are idiosyncratic to us and to our past relationship experiences. Moreover, they are likely to remain unaware of our idiosyncratic expectancies until they inadvertently violate one of them. When they fail to do something we we expected them to do or do something we did not expect them to do, they usually become the target of an emotional outburst. People may not be aware of all of their expectancies about the partner and the relationship, and for this reason, emotional episodes in relationships are often a learning experience for the person feeling the emotion (as well as for the partner). An emotional experience generally is an opportunity to become better acquainted with the assumptions and expectations we hold about our partner and the relationship.

In sum, beneath the surface of every relationship is a web of expectancies the partners hold for each other's behavior. These expectancies allow the partners to coordinate their actions and plans to maximize their own and the other's welfare. When repeatedly confirmed, these expectancies allow interactions to run smoothly (see Snyder & Stukas, 1999). The closer and more enduring the relationship, the more likely it is that these expectancies are not only numerous but also strongly held because they have been repeatedly confirmed. The violation of those expectancies is likely to be the occasion for emotional experience.

SUMMARY

Many of the most significant questions people ask themselves (and others, including therapists) concern the emotions they experience (or do not experience) in their relationships. Despite the fact that relationships are an important source of intense positive and negative emotional experience, little is known about emotion as it is experienced and expressed within the context of close relationships. This theoretical and empirical state of affairs is somewhat surprising given Darwin's well-publicized hypothesis about the universality of the facial expression of emotion and his contention that such expressions served to facilitate interpersonal communication and therefore human welfare. However, most tests of Darwin's hypotheses about emotional expression have been conducted in decontextualized and impersonal experimental situations. Current theory and research are revealing that the experience, expression, and decoding of the meaning of emotion between relationship partners not necessarily resemble what transpires in context-free laboratory situations.

Early theoretical work on emotion focused on exploring the association between physiological arousal and the experience of emotion, a connection first noted by Darwin. Although a number of theories specifying the exact nature of the association have been proposed, Schachter's two-component theory appears to provide the most complete account. In accordance with this theory, people are most likely to report that they are experiencing an emotion when they perceive that they are experiencing physiological arousal and they have cognitively interpreted the internal event of arousal and the context in which it has occurred as meaning that they are experiencing an emotion. This finding has implications for relationship phenomena. For example, although the relationship partner is often the source of arousal (and therefore provides a ready emotional label for the experience), additional research indicates that people sometimes mistakenly identify the source of their arousal, which in turn influences the nature of the emotions they experience. There is much still to be learned, however, about the connection between partners' physiological responses and emotional experiences during interaction.

Schachter's theory brought affective behavior and cognitive behavior together after centuries of belief that affect and cognition were independent spheres of human behavior and thus could be studied and understood separate from one another. Cognition and affect now are known to be highly integrated in the neural circuitry of the brain and in the operations of the mind. Virtually all theories of emotion incorporate cognition in some way, and a growing body of evidence reveals not only that affect influences cognition (e.g., affective states influence the evaluations people make of others and how people process social information) but also that cognition influences affect (e.g., cognitive appraisals of an interaction event as positive or negative influence affective experience). Of increasing scientific interest is the role that cognitive expectancies play in emotional experience. Expectancy violations are believed to produce arousal, which combines with a cognitive evaluation of the situation to produce an emotional response. Insofar as partners in close relationships are highly dependent on one another for the achievement of goals and plans and hold many expectations about each other's behavior, the potential for expectancy violation (and, consequently, for emotion) is great. Close relationships, then, constitute a potent source of emotional experience.

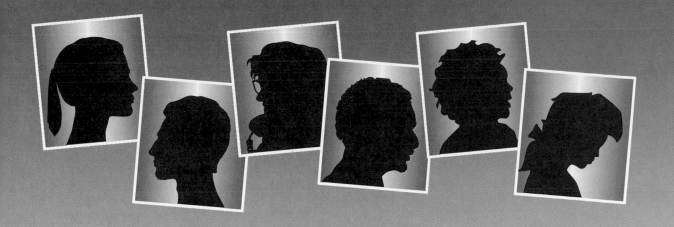

Chapter 10

Dispositional Influences

INTRODUCTION

To each of our social interactions, we bring ourselves—a unique collection of numerous personal properties that will influence the relationship that develops. These relatively stable personal causal conditions include such properties as would appear in our partner's description of us—our demographic properties, for example, including our age, sex, education, socioeconomic status, and occupation. Several of these easily discerned properties are likely to be associated with less visible dispositions to respond to others in certain ways; for example, age goes hand in hand with age-related beliefs, and socioeconomic status may be linked with political affiliation. Our visible attributes are just the tip of the personal property iceberg, which includes our temperament, personality traits, attitudes, expectations, beliefs, motivations, goals, and an array of relationship schemas. All of these may influence how we respond to others and how other people respond to us in interaction.

Many psychologists have tried to determine how certain dispositional properties influence the relationships a person is likely to develop. Most investigators adopt an *individualistic approach* (sometimes called the individualistic–psychometric approach). Typically, the researcher measures one or more of the person's properties (neuroticism, depression, attachment style, and so on) and one or more relationship behaviors or outcomes (such as satisfaction) to determine whether there is a significant association between the two. The assumption is that the individual will display and express his or her properties in interaction with most partners and in most interaction situations and that the effects of those properties will be similar across partners and across situations.

Although the individualistic approach has been the usual research route, many psychologists have concluded that the insights it has yielded have not been commensurate with the effort. One reason for its limited success is that each individual's interaction partner is no mere passive and inert figure. The partner also brings his or her personal properties to the interaction, and these, depending on how they combine with the individual's properties, will actually determine

293

the nature of the interaction that develops. In other words, the nature of the interaction that develops is a function of *both* partners' properties. Chapter 1, "First Relationships," noted that developmental psychologists have found that the quality of the social interaction between pairs of children depends not simply on one child's attachment history but on the attachment histories of both children (e.g., Sroufe & Fleeson, 1986).

Not only do both partners' properties interact with each other, but each individual's properties and dispositions are likely to interact with the *situation* in which the interaction takes place to determine the interaction pattern that develops. Some situations do not allow an individual to *express* certain of his or her personal dispositions. For example, two avoidant children paired for play alone may develop an aggressive interaction pattern—but when a large, authoritative adult is standing nearby supervising their play, they may interact nearly as harmoniously as two secure children do (see Berscheid & Kelley, 2002). As Rusbult and Van Lange (2003) explain: Interaction = f (Situation, Properties of A, Properties of B), or, in other words, the interaction that develops between persons A and B is a function of the interaction between the properties of A, the properties of B, and the properties of the situation in which they interact. Although this is a complex equation, it is one that relationship researchers cannot avoid and are beginning to confront. In the meantime, however, there exists a large body of research that attempts to draw associations between an individual's characteristics and the relationships he or she is likely to develop.

MALENESS AND FEMALENESS

The most fundamental dimension along which we classify and categorize ourselves and other people is that of maleness–femaleness. **Biological sex** refers to whether a person possesses the chromosomes, external genitalia, and internal reproductive organs of a male or a female. **Psychological gender** or **sex-role orientation** refers to whether a person possesses traits or

characteristics that are believed to be associated with, and considered socially appropriate for, each biological sex, such as assertiveness and competitiveness in men or nurturance and cooperation in women. Maleness–femaleness is a powerful individual difference variable, coloring many aspects of a person's relational world.

Biological Sex

Although popular culture promotes the notion that the sexes are so different as to come from separate worlds (e.g., Gray, 1992), both men and women are members of the same species, exist on the same planet, and must adapt to the same physical environment. That said, sex differences remain an undeniable and ubiquitous element of relationship research. For example, as discussed in Chapters 11, "Love," and 12, "Mate Selection and Sex," men and women tend to adopt different approaches to love and also endorse different sexual standards. In addition, as considered below, sex differences have been observed in a number of other domains, including friendship patterns, interaction styles, social support, loneliness, communication, and responses to conflict (see Beall & Sternberg, 1993; Canary & Dindia, 1998; C. Hendrick, 1988; Maccoby & Jacklin, 1974; Peplau, 1983/2002). In some of these areas, a sufficient number of studies now exist for researchers to conduct qualitative literature reviews and quantitative meta-analyses to determine the pervasiveness and strength of the purported sex differences. As discussed elsewhere in this text, meta-analysis is a powerful statistical tool that allows researchers to combine the results from different studies that examine the same empirical question (for additional information on the application of meta-analytic techniques to the examination of sex differences, see Hyde, 1996).

Empathic Accuracy

Empathic accuracy is usually defined as the ability to decode the meaning of another's behavior (see Chapter 1). Research on attitudes about men and women reveals a widespread belief that women possess greater empathic accuracy than men. Specifically, women are believed to have more emotional insight, greater sensitivity to the feelings of others, and higher levels of interpersonal empathy (e.g., Broverman, Vogel, Broverman, Clarkson, & Rosenkrantz, 1994; Manstead, 1992). These beliefs imply that the purported sex difference in interpersonal sensitivity is due to differential ability, with women possessing greater empathic ability than men. However, when Graham and Ickes (1997) reviewed the existing literature, they concluded that reliable differences favoring female perceivers occurred in only 3 of the 10 available studies of empathic accuracy. These reviewers also concluded that when sex differences occur, they reflect differential motivation rather than differential ability, a conclusion also reached by Klein and Hodges (2001; see Chapter 1) and by other researchers (see Berman, 1980; Eisenberg & Lennon, 1983).

More recently, Ickes, Gesn, and Graham (2000) conducted a quantitative meta-analysis of 15 studies for which sex-of-perceiver differences in empathic accuracy could be tested (these included the 10 studies that were evaluated in Graham and Ickes's [1997] qualitative review and 5 more recent studies). Their results provided clear evidence that the presence or absence of significant sex-of-perceiver effects was moderated by the methodological differences in the various studies. In 5 out of 6 studies in which the methodology required perceivers to estimate the accuracy of each of their inferences about the target (and thus made them aware that they were being evaluated along the dimension of empathic accuracy), women demonstrated higher empathic accuracy scores than men. However, in all 9 studies in which the methodology did not require perceivers to make such self-inferences, no sex differences were found. Thus, it does not appear to be the case that women possess greater empathic ability than men; rather, women appear more motivated to present themselves as empathic when situational cues indicate that empathy-relevant behavior is being assessed (and when, presumably, sex-role stereotypes have been activated).

Coping Behavior

Men and women also have been thought to differ with respect to coping styles. **Coping** is typically defined as cognitive or behavioral responses made to counter a real or perceived threat. Most researchers follow the classification scheme proposed by Lazarus and Folkman (1984), who distinguished between problem-focused and emotion-focused coping. **Problem-focused coping** encompasses cognitive and behavioral responses designed to overcome or alter the stressor or threat, including confronting the situation directly and engaging in problem-solving and planning activities. **Emotion-focused coping** involves behaviors designed to manage the emotional response to the threat. Examples include accepting the situation or reappraising it in a positive light, venting emotions, ruminating, and blaming the self for the situation. The results of a number of early studies on coping were interpreted as indicating that men engage in problem-focused coping, whereas women utilize emotion-focused coping; some researchers concluded that the problem-oriented, "male" coping style was more adaptive than the emotion-oriented, "female" coping style (e.g., Billings & Moos, 1981; Pearlin & Schooler, 1978; Veroff, Kulka, & Douvan, 1981). As noted by Tamres, Janicki, and Helgeson (2002), these conclusions are not warranted, for several reasons. First, the constructs of emotion- and problem-focused coping, although useful in conceptualizing coping, may not be helpful when examining sex differences because a wide array of discrete behaviors are included in each coping category and sex differences may be confined to only some of the behaviors within a category (and thus not characteristic of the overall category). If men are more likely to engage in one behavior and women are more likely to display another behavior, these differences "cancel" each other if the behaviors are grouped into the same category. Second, the authors argue that it may not be the case, as previous researchers have suggested, that one general coping strategy is "better" or more adaptive than the other; instead, some of the specific behaviors within each larger coping category may be more adaptive than others. And third,

Tamres and colleagues posit that the adaptiveness of a coping strategy is heavily dependent on the nature of the stressor. They hypothesize, for example, that problem-focused coping behaviors might be more successful when the stressor is controllable, whereas emotion-focused coping behaviors might be more useful when the stressor is not controllable.

To examine their hypotheses, Tamres and associates performed a meta-analysis of 50 coping studies conducted between 1990 and 2000. Their first goal was to examine sex differences in 17 specific behaviors, each of which was evaluated by at least 6 studies. Some behaviors were classified as problem-focused, including *active coping* (efforts to change or remove the stressor), *planning* (gathering information and reviewing possible solutions), and *seeking instrumental social support* (seeking specific, concrete help from friends and family that is directed toward problem-solving). Other behaviors were considered emotion-focused, such as *venting* (the active and sometimes public acting out or expressing of emotions, as in crying, yelling, and swearing), *wishful thinking* (wishing that the stressor were not there or imagining that the stressor might simply disappear on its own), *seeking emotional social support* (seeking comfort from others), *avoidance* (behavioral and mental efforts to distract oneself from or to avoid the stressor), and *positive self-talk* (making self-statements that encourage oneself to feel better). Two additional behaviors were identified that were not readily classifiable as problem-focused or emotion-focused (seeking nonspecific social support and religion).

The authors first explored whether there were sex differences in coping. The meta-analysis revealed that women generally report greater use of coping behaviors than men. Specifically, women engaged in a significantly greater amount of 3 of the 4 problem-focused coping behaviors, 6 of the 11 emotion-focused coping behaviors, and both of the "other" coping behaviors. For no specific behavior did men display higher amounts than women. These sex differences, however, tended to be small and heterogenous (variable) across the individual studies. Tamres and colleagues conclude that "the

one sex difference that should be taken seriously is seeking social support for emotional reasons because these data are homogeneous across studies" (p. 16).

The second question examined by the authors concerned whether any of the observed sex differences were moderated by the nature of the stressor. Four types of stressor were examined: personal health (injury or illness), relationship (family conflicts, marital problems), achievement (work or school stress), and others' health (injury, illness, or death). Many of the coping strategies showed variable sex differences across the different stressors. For example, the sex difference favoring women that was found for the emotion-focused strategies of venting and wishful thinking was significant only for stressors that reflected personal health problems and the health problems of others; that is, women displayed greater amounts of venting and wishful thinking than did men only when the stressor concerned their own or another's health problems. Men were significantly more likely than women to use venting as a way of coping with achievement and relationship stressors. The results for the emotion-focused strategy of avoidance were similar. Women were more likely than men to use avoidance as a way of coping with own and others' health stressors, and men were more likely than women to use avoidance when attempting to cope with relationship and achievement stressors. As before, the authors found that the sex difference in emotional social support seeking remained consistent when the nature of the stressor was examined. Women were more likely than men to seek social support for emotional reasons for all four types of stressors. Interestingly, women were also more likely than men to seek instrumental social support for all but relationship stressors.

The authors also explored the *pattern* of sex differences across the coping strategies for each of the four stressors separately. They found, for example, that women were more likely than men to report engaging in 13 of the 17 individual coping strategies when facing a personal health stressor. There was no coping strategy that men used more than women in the domain of personal health, a finding that the authors speculate may reflect women's greater concern about health issues. The same pattern was found when the stressor domain of others' health was examined; women reported using 9 strategies more than did men when coping with the illness, injury, or death of another. The fewest sex differences in coping were found for relationship stressors. Specifically, when attempting to deal with relationship stressors, women displayed greater amounts of only 6 strategies (among them active coping, seeking emotional support, isolation, and rumination). Men were more likely to cope with relationship stress through avoidance and venting.

From their meta-analysis, Tamres and associates conclude first, that the conventional wisdom that men engage in more problem-focused coping than women and that women engage in more emotion-focused coping than men is incorrect. Women report using more coping strategies in general than men across both behavioral domains. Second, most of the observed sex differences are small and/or inconsistent across studies. Third, several of the differences are moderated by the type of stressor; for example, women report more rumination and active coping, and men report more venting and avoidance, when coping with relationship stressors. And fourth, there is only one robust effect consistent across studies and stressor domains—women report seeking emotional social support more than men.

Self-Disclosure and Intimacy

Men and women also differ in their degree of self-disclosure and intimacy (see Chapter 7, "Relationship Growth and Maintenance," for a general overview of the self-disclosure and intimacy literatures). For example, men expect to experience more negative consequences for disclosing personal or private information than women do (Petronio & Martin, 1986). These differing expectations about the impact of revealing self-relevant information may reduce men's willingness to engage in the process of disclosure. Whatever the reason, qualitative reviews and quantitative meta-analyses reveal that women, on average, self-disclose more to others than men do (Dindia & Allen, 1992; Petronio & Sargent, 2003). Women also report higher levels of self-disclosure and aspects of intimacy, such as affection, understanding, and reliance on each other, in their closest same-sex friendships (Hussong, 2000). Similarly, in contrast to men and boys, who prefer engaging in activities with their friends, women and girls prefer talking with friends, which is essential to self-disclosure and the communication of intimacy (see Fehr, 1996; Rose & Asher, 2000). The topics men and women choose to talk about with their friends also are qualitatively different. Men are more likely than women to discuss nonpersonal issues such as work, sports, computers, or cars, whereas women are more likely than men to talk about personal and relationship issues such as problems with roommates or partners, needs, and feelings (see Fehr, 2000).

These sex differences, however, are attenuated in heterosexual romantic relationships. For example, men and women attach similar importance to achieving openness and self-disclosure—comfort with disclosure of personal information, willingness to express emotions and feelings, and willingness to talk about needs, wants, and bothers—in their own long-term romantic relationships (Vangelisti & Daly, 1997). In addition, men and women demonstrate similar patterns of self-disclosure in marital relationships (Prager, 2003). Disclosure also appears to be associated with similar relational experiences for men and women. It will be recalled from Chapter 6, "Birth of a Relationship," that (appropriate) self-disclosure is associated with attraction for both sexes. Specifically, both men and women disclose more to those they like than to those they dislike; men and women who self-disclose generally are liked better than those who do not self-disclose; and both men and women tend to like other individuals as a result of having disclosed to them (Collins & Miller, 1994).

Aggression

Researchers and theorists traditionally have distinguished between **physical aggression** (hitting, kicking, slapping, using a weapon) and **verbal**

aggression (yelling, making threats, name-calling, using insults). Both of these forms of aggression may be **direct**, in which no attempt is made to hide the harmful intent (as in punching or name-calling) or **indirect**, in which the intent to cause harm is hidden (as in destruction of property, gossiping, or spreading rumors). Aggressive behavior also may be of a sexual nature or used in the service of obtaining sexual goals; this form of interpersonal aggression is discussed in Chapter 12.

Early reviews suggested that boys and men generally engage in more physically and verbally aggressive behavior than girls and women in a variety of contexts and across cultures (e.g., Eagly & Steffen, 1986; Maccoby & Jacklin, 1974; Whiting & Edwards, 1973). For example, Omark, Omark, and Edelman (1973; cited in Maccoby & Jacklin, 1974) observed the school playground behavior of children in the United States, Switzerland, and Ethiopia and reported that in all three countries boys displayed more physical aggression (defined as pushing or hitting without smiling) than did girls. Similarly, on the basis of a review of observational, experimental, and survey (questionnaire) research, Maccoby and Jacklin (1974) concluded that (1) boys engage in higher levels of physical aggression during free play with peers than girls do; (2) boys exhibit more physical aggression following exposure to an aggressive model than girls do; (3) when presented with an opportunity to "shock" an experimental confederate, boys and men administer shocks of higher intensity and longer duration than girls and women do; and (4) boys and men are rated as more aggressive than girls and women are by peers, parents, and teachers (and rate themselves as more aggressive than girls and women rate themselves).

Additional research indicates that this sex difference in physical aggression is moderated by relational context and/or type of partner. For example, questionnaire studies (e.g., Gergen, 1990; Harris, 1992; for a review see Archer, 2000b) of self-reported physical aggression toward same-sex opponents (strangers, acquaintances, friends) reveal that men are much more likely than women to engage in a variety of actions, including kicking, punching, pushing or shoving, threatening with a weapon, or hitting with an object. However, as discussed in Chapter 2, "Relationships and Health," women report engaging in an equal or even greater amount of aggressive behavior than men do with an opposite-sex romantic partner. Moreover, it will be recalled that in a nationally representative sample of married couples, Straus, Gelles, and Steinmetz (1980) found that equal percentages of husbands and wives (about 12%) said that they had engaged in physically aggressive acts against their spouses in the previous 12 months. Archer (2000a) concluded from his meta-analysis that men and women display similar levels of physical aggression toward their partners.

The similarity between men and women in levels of physically aggressive behavior toward romantic partners should not be interpreted as indicating that aggression poses an equal problem for the sexes within their dating and mating relationships. As noted by O'Leary (2000) and others (e.g., Christopher & Lloyd, 2000; Crowell & Burgess, 1996), men's physical aggression is far more likely than women's to inflict hurt or injury, and the injuries sustained by women are more severe than those sustained by male victims in studies of dating couples (e.g., Foshee, 1996; Langley, Martin, & Nada-Rada, 1997). Consequently, although men and women may experience fairly equal amounts of direct physical aggression at the hands of their mates, the emotional and physical consequences of that aggression for them are likely to be vastly different.

Theoretical Explanations for Sex Differences

Theoretical efforts to explain sex differences in coping, aggression, and other behaviors generally fall into two general categories. The first category focuses on *social factors* that create and sustain enduring differences between the sexes. Some theorists believe that sex differences reflect social learning and are produced by socialization processes that, for example, emphasize the expression of emotion as a female rather than a male characteristic, view aggression as an appropriate interpersonal response for males but not females, teach girls and women to value interdependence and to establish intimacy through self-disclosure and affective communication, and teach boys and men to value independence and competition and to maintain power and autonomy in intimate relationships (see Jacklin & Reynolds, 1993; Maccoby, 1990; Tannen, 1990; Wood, 1994). This may be particularly true in the United States and other Western cultures. In their review of the literatures on the self-concept and sex differences, Cross and Madson (1997) propose that the social, institutional, and cultural environment of the United States promotes the construction and maintenance of radically different self-construals by men and women. In particular, men are socialized to develop an independent self-construal, whereas women are socialized to develop an interdependent or relational self-construal. These different self-construals, in turn, are posited to influence men's and women's interpersonal behavior.

It is likely that the differential responses that boys and girls receive during childhood from parents, teachers, peers, and other agents of socialization contribute to differences observed later in thinking, feeling, and behaving. For example, parents respond more positively to girls who ask for help or assistance during play than they do to boys (Lott & Maluso, 1993), which may explain women's greater tendency, relative to men, to engage in support-seeking behavior when faced with a stressor. Similarly, boys receive more attention for physically aggressive behavior, and more encouragement for rough physical play, from teachers and parents than do girls (Lott & Maluso, 1993; Maccoby & Jacklin, 1974), a social "fact" which may serve to encourage aggressive proclivities in men but to diminish them in women (Figure 10.1). Furthermore, research on sex-role stereotypes, attitudes toward men and women, and parents' conceptions of male and female children reveals that dominance, assertion, competitiveness, physical roughness, and independence are considered normative elements of masculinity and the male sex role, whereas traits involving nurturance, emotional expressiveness, and interpersonal warmth and sensitivity are commonly ascribed to women and girls and viewed as part of the female sex role (Beall, 1993; Maccoby & Jacklin, 1974). These normative beliefs may account for the differences in self-disclosure, use of emotional support to cope with stressors, physical aggression, and other behaviors observed between men and women.

FIGURE 10.1 Boys are often encouraged to engage in rough, physical play, whereas girls are often socialized to engage in quiet, cooperative play.

The second explanatory framework that has been used to account for sex differences in social behavior focuses on *biological or genetic influences*. Differential male and female biology, including neurotransmitter activity and sex hormone levels, is believed to produce the characteristic behavioral differences displayed by men and women. For example, in humans and other mammalian species, postpubertal males typically exhibit substantially higher levels of the androgenic sex hormone testosterone than do postpubertal females (Regan & Berscheid, 1999). The relationship between testosterone levels and physical aggression in animals is well established (e.g., Breuer, McGinnis, Lumia, & Possidente, 2001; McGinnis, Lumia, Breuer, & Possidente, 2002). Among humans, the evidence is less clear, in part due to the ethical and methodological difficulties of experimentally manipulating levels of circulating hormones and the corresponding paucity of experimental data. However, literature reviews and quantitative meta-analyses suggest that a weak to moderate correlation exists between testosterone levels and physically aggressive behavior (Book, Starzyk, & Quinsey, 2001; Harris, 1999), and at least one study has demonstrated that the administration of testosterone produces an increase in self-reported hostility among men

and women (Dabbs, Karpas, Dyomina, Juechter, & Roberts, 2002). Thus, it is possible that differences in levels of circulating androgenic hormones may account, at least partly, for the higher levels of physical aggression displayed by boys and men relative to girls and women.

Other sex differences also may be linked to differential biology. For example, Taylor, Klein, and colleagues (2000) note that women are far more likely than men to respond to stressors with a "tend-and-befriend" orientation or a propensity to nurture and affiliate. They also note that men and women experience a similar array of hormonal reactions in response to stress but that women exhibit higher levels of the pituitary hormone oxytocin, which is associated with downregulation of the sympathetic nervous system and facilitation of the parasympathetic nervous system. These theorists hypothesize that the greater tendency among females to nurture and affiliate under times of stress may be partly due to the action of oxytocin. Several animal studies support their proposition. The administration of oxytocin stimulates maternal behavior toward offspring, such as grooming and touching, in female sheep and rats, and enhances affiliative behavior, such as social contact and grooming, in female rats and prairie voles (Figure 10.2). Additional research is needed to

FIGURE 10.2 Some researchers hypothesize that maternal behavior toward offspring, such as grooming and touching, is partly due to the action of the hormone oxytocin.

establish an association between oxytocin levels and tend-and-befriend responses in humans.

It is next to impossible to disentangle biological and socialization sources of sex differences in coping, aggression, and other behaviors. For example, men possess more testosterone than women, and this may account for their higher levels of aggression; but men also are encouraged to be more competitive and assertive than women, and physical displays of rough-and-tumble behavior are more tolerated in males than females. Similarly, although the higher level of oxytocin found in women may account for their tendency to affiliate and nurture when stressed, women are also encouraged to disclose feelings and to seek help and support from others more than are men. In sum, the relative contribution of biology or socialization in creating observed sex differences is difficult to determine.

Psychological Gender or Sex-Role Orientation

In addition to whether they are biologically male or female, people differ in the extent to which they possess or endorse attributes that stereotypically are associated with each sex and that are considered socially desirable for each sex to possess. Measures of psychological gender include the Bem Sex Role Inventory (BSRI; Bem, 1974), the Personal Attributes Questionnaire (PAQ; Spence & Helmreich, 1978), and the masculinity and femininity subscales of the California Personality Inventory (Gough, 1987). A person's gender is determined by his or her self-ratings on various attribute dimensions. Men and women who describe themselves as having traits stereotypically associated with maleness and socially valued for males to possess ("independent," "assertive," "forceful") are considered **masculine**; those who present themselves as possessing stereotypically (and socially valued) female traits ("yielding," "compassionate," "warm") are considered **feminine**; those who endorse both male and female attributes are classified as **androgynous**; and those who feel that they possess neither male nor female traits are

considered **undifferentiated**. Men who endorse masculine attributes, and women who endorse feminine attributes, often are identified as **sex-typed** or **traditional** in their gender or sex-role orientation.

Some researchers believe that the combination of instrumental and expressive attributes characteristic of people with an androgynous sex-role orientation may contribute positively to self-disclosure, which, in turn, enhances relationship development and maintenance (e.g., Ickes, 1981). For example, androgynous men and women express greater willingness to disclose information on a variety of topics (ranging from attitudes, opinions, and interests to personal shortcomings, feelings, and sexual behavior) to their family, friends, and lovers—and report higher levels of actual disclosure—than sex-typed or undifferentiated individuals (e.g., Lavine & Lombardo, 1984; Sollie & Fischer, 1985). In addition, the friendships of androgynous people are characterized by higher levels of satisfaction. People find their friendships with androgynous partners to be more rewarding than those they have with masculine, feminine, or undifferentiated partners (Wright & Scanlon, 1991), and androgynous individuals themselves evaluate their friends more positively, and are more satisfied with their relationships, than nonandrogynous individuals (Jones, Bloys, & Wood, 1990).

There is some evidence that androgyny also is associated with positive experiences in romantic relationships. Peterson, Baucom, Elliott, and Farr (1989) assessed sex-role orientation and marital adjustment (using a self-report scale of global marital satisfaction) among a large sample of married couples. Half of the couples were recruited from a psychology clinic and were seeking marital therapy; the other half were recruited from the community at large. When the researchers examined the frequency of each possible husband–wife sex-role pairing (for example, androgynous husband—feminine wife, androgynous husband—androgynous wife), they discovered a striking difference between the clinic and nonclinic samples. Of the 16 possible husband–wife sex-role pairings, androgynous husband—androgynous wife was the most frequent pairing among the nonclinic couples and the least frequent pairing among the clinic couples. The opposite pattern was found when the undifferentiated husband—undifferentiated wife pairing was considered. This was the most frequent pairing among the clinic couples and the least frequent pairing among the nonclinic couples. In addition, each of the 6 sex-role pairings that involved only one androgynous spouse occurred with greater frequency among nonclinic couples than among clinic couples. Thus, androgyny—of one or both spouses—characterized married couples who were not seeking therapy, and undifferentiation (and lack of androgyny) was common among distressed married couples.

When the researchers examined the association between sex-role orientation and marital adjustment, they found that adjustment scores were higher for both men and women when the spouses were both androgynous than when they demonstrated any other pattern of sex-role pairing. Femininity also was associated with marital adjustment; above-average adjustment scores were seen among couples with two feminine partners and among those with one feminine partner. Other researchers have found evidence that a feminine sex-role orientation (often called "expressivity") is associated with marital satisfaction (e.g., Juni & Grimm, 1993; Lamke, Sollie, Durbin, & Fitzpatrick, 1994; Livingston, Burley, & Springer, 1996). This research is examined in greater detail in Chapter 13, "Satisfaction and Stability." The only sex-role orientation found by Peterson and her colleagues to be consistently associated with lack of marital well-being was undifferentiation. Men and women married to undifferentiated partners (partners who do not feel that they possess traits that society believes are appropriate and valuable for either men or women to possess) generally scored below average in terms of their self-reported levels of marital satisfaction, and the lowest levels of adjustment and satisfaction occurred in pairings involving two undifferentiated individuals or an undifferentiated person married to a masculine one.

Considered as a whole, then, research on sex-role orientation and relationship experiences indicates that people who report possessing at-tributes that are socially valued in men and women, and who thus presumably have access to a wide array of potential responses, may be better equipped to satisfy both themselves and their partners. Men and women with an undifferentiated sex-role orientation, who bring neither expressive nor instrumental qualities to their interactions (and who believe they lack socially valued male and female attributes), may be particularly unlikely to fulfill the demands of their relational roles and to satisfy their partners.

PERSONALITY

In addition to being male or female, each person possesses a distinct pattern of behaviors, thoughts, and emotions referred to as **personality**. Personality is assumed to be relatively stable over time and across situations. However, in the years since Mischel (1968) published his seminal critique of personality trait theories, the "interactionist" view of personality has gained ascendance (see Chapter 8, "Cognitive Processes") This view acknowledges that the association between an individual's personality traits and his or her behavior is mediated by the situational context in which the behavior occurs. In social situations, of course, one of the most important and salient components of the situational context in which the individual is behaving is the partner. Unfortunately, as mentioned in the introduction to this chapter, this more complex view of personality is not yet well reflected in relationship research, most of which continues to seek "simple and sovereign" effects of personality traits across interaction partners and situational contexts (see Berscheid & Kelley, 2002).

Supertraits

Most personality theorists and researchers agree that the best representation of personality trait structure is provided by the **five-factor model** (Digman, 1990; Goldberg, 1993; Hampson, 1999). According to this model, most personality traits can be described in terms of five basic dimensions or **supertraits**: extraversion or surgency, neuroticism, openness to experience (also called intellect, imagination, or culture), agreeableness, and conscientiousness or will to achieve (McCrae & Costa, 1997). Each of these dimensions represents the common variance among a larger set of more specific traits or facets of personality. For example, people who are competent tend also to be orderly, dutiful, achievement-oriented, and self-disciplined, and together these specific traits define the dimension or supertrait called conscientiousness. Research indicates that the five supertraits are heritable, stable across the life span, and culturally universal, and they adequately capture much of the variance in human temperament. Two in particular—extraversion and neuroticism—have received the lion's share of attention from relationship scholars.

Extraversion

As discussed in Chapter 1, **extraversion** reflects the degree to which an individual is oriented positively to the social environment and enjoys being the center of social attention. People high on this personality dimension (called extraverts) have an active orientation toward the social environment and find being the center of social attention highly rewarding. They seek out others, enjoy social interaction, behave in an outgoing and sociable manner, and tend to be characterized by themselves and others as warm, gregarious, assertive, energetic, self-confident, and cheerful. People low on this dimension (usually called introverts) are wary of social interaction; do not find social attention to be rewarding; prefer solitary activities; direct their attention inward to their own thoughts and feelings; are described as withdrawn, quiet, and reserved; and report lower levels of energy and self-confidence.

Scores on measures of extraversion are associated with several relationship experiences. For example, highly extraverted people engage in more frequent social contact, derive greater enjoyment from their social encounters, and possess larger friendship networks than their less outgoing counterparts (e.g., Berry & Hansen, 1996, 2000). Von Dras and Siegler (1997) measured levels of extraversion in a sample of 3,318

college students. Twenty years later, the researchers reassessed the (now middle-aged) participants' extraversion levels and also collected data about various aspects of their current social lives. Responses to the individual questions about social life—for example, number of visits with friends and family members each month; number of club, society, or association meetings attended each month; number of friends who visited or phoned each day—were summed to create an overall index of social activity. The results revealed that college and midlife extraversion levels were significantly positively correlated: Participants with low extraversion levels at college entry continued to demonstrate low levels of extraversion two decades later, providing additional evidence that personality structure is relatively stable. The researchers also found that college extraversion scores were positively correlated with midlife social activity levels; that is, men and women with higher levels of extraversion at college entry engaged in more social activity in middle adulthood (and, similarly, midlife extraversion levels were positively associated with midlife social activity levels). Thus, the disposition of extraversion appears to be an important predictor of social involvement or interpersonal activities.

The connection between extraversion and marital outcomes has been extensively investigated, with inconclusive results. Some researchers find that relatively high levels of extraversion in one or both partners are associated with positive marital adjustment (e.g., Nemechek & Olson, 1996), whereas other researchers find that high levels of extraversion are correlated with lower levels of marital well-being (e.g., Bouchard, Lussier, & Sabourin, 1999; Lester, Haig, & Monello, 1989). The evidence is also mixed with respect to the association between extraversion and marital stability. Cross-sectional surveys often reveal a positive correlation between extraversion and marital dissolution (e.g., Eysenck, 1980). For example, Jockin, McGue, and Lykken (1996) assessed levels of extraversion (using a standard personality inventory) in a large sample of men and women who had been married at least once. Participants also provided information about their marital histories, including whether or not they had ever divorced. Divorce status could be reliably predicted from participants' scores on the extraversion measure; that is, the higher that men and women scored on extraversion, the more likely it was that they had experienced marital dissolution. However, other studies—including prospective longitudinal studies that are better able to assess whether extraversion levels predict *later* relational outcomes—do not find evidence that this personality dimension is associated with marital stability (e.g., Kurdek, 1993c).

Researchers also have begun to explore whether partners' extraversion levels are implicated in the interpersonal dynamics of their relationship. Cutrona, Hessling, and Suhr (1997) assessed the personality traits of a large sample of married couples prior to observing each couple in a 10-minute interaction. The interactions occurred in a laboratory room furnished to resemble a living room. One partner was randomly assigned to play the role of "support recipient," which involved describing a recent personally stressful situation to the spouse. The other member of the couple was given the role of "support provider" and was instructed to listen and react naturally and spontaneously to the partner's description. The two partners then switched roles and the process was repeated. These interactions were videotaped and the researchers examined the support providers' verbal behavior for the presence of four types of positive communication: *emotional support* (expressions of love and concern), *esteem support* (expressions of respect), *informational support* (provision of helpful advice and information), and *tangible aid* (offers to provide goods or services). The frequencies with which these four types of positive communication occurred during the interaction were summed to create an overall index of support behavior provided by each spouse.

The results revealed that support behavior was positively correlated with extraversion levels. Specifically, husbands and wives higher in extraversion made more positive, supportive statements in general to their spouses than less did extraverted individuals. They did not, however,

receive more support themselves from their spouses. In discussing this finding that extraverts gave but did not receive more support, the authors conclude:

> The results that emerged for extraversion highlight the importance of considering the personal characteristics of both the individual and his or her primary source of social support. Contrary to prediction, the extraversion of support *recipients* did not directly predict the amount of support they received from the spouse. Rather, the extraversion of support *providers* proved to be most important. Thus, a shy introvert who married a gregarious extravert might be amply supplied with a lifetime of social support, by virtue of his or her partner's interpersonally oriented nature. (p. 390, emphasis in original)

Additional analyses revealed that reciprocity of support was evident in the couples' behavior; that is, the higher the amount of support a husband or wife *provided* during the first interaction, the more support he or she subsequently *received*. This suggests that extraverted people may indirectly affect their own relational outcomes via the support they provide their partners. Specifically, individuals who are high in extraversion are likely to provide high levels of social support; these positive behaviors, in turn, seem to evoke corresponding reactions from their partners. For the extravert, then, the adage "what goes around, comes around" seems accurate.

Neuroticism

Neuroticism, also called *emotional instability* or *negative affectivity*, refers to a person's sensitivity to negative stimuli, propensity to experience negative emotions, and stability of behavior over time. Individuals high on neuroticism are emotionally volatile and moody, are characterized as high-strung and touchy, and are prone to frequent and intense negative emotions (including anxiety, anger, hostility, and depression). People low on this personality dimension are characterized by emotional stability and are generally calm, even-tempered, relaxed, and secure. The association between neuroticism and relationship outcomes has been investigated primarily in the context of marital relationships, and research suggests that neuroticism is correlated both with dissolution (e.g., Cramer, 1993; Eysenck, 1980; Jockin et al., 1996; Kurdek, 1993c; Tucker, Kressin, Spiro, & Ruscio, 1998) and satisfaction, adjustment, or well-being (e.g., Bouchard et al., 1999; Karney & Bradbury, 1997; Newton & Kiecolt-Glaser, 1995; see Chapter 13, "Satisfaction and Stability").

In one classic longitudinal investigation, Kelly and Conley (1987) followed a sample of 249 married couples from the time of their engagement during the 1930s to 1980. The first data collection occurred between 1935 and 1941. During this time, and prior to their marriage, the members of each couple were rated by several of their acquaintances on various personality traits, including neuroticism. Also during this time, but after their marriage, the spouses provided annual reports about their current level of marital happiness; these reports were averaged to create a measure of marital happiness in early marriage. The second data collection took place in 1954–1955, and the third and final data collection occurred in 1980–1981. During these two periods, spouses were asked how satisfied they were with their marriage, whether they would still marry their partner if they had their life to live over, whether they had ever regretted their marriage, and whether they had ever considered divorce or separation from their partner. Responses to these four items were summed to create an overall index of marital satisfaction. Finally, at each data collection period, the researchers noted whether the couples had divorced or were still married.

Both marital outcomes—satisfaction and dissolution—were predicted by premarriage levels of neuroticism. For example, the men and women who divorced early (1935–1954) or late (1955–1980) had higher premarriage levels of neuroticism than their still-married counterparts. In addition, their neuroticism seemed to play a role in the dissolution of their marriages. When asked by the researchers to explain their reasons for ending the marriage, over one-third (36%) cited various manifestations of their own or their partner's neuroticism, including "emotional

instability," "emotional overreactions," "irritability," and "emotional immaturity."

Kelly and Conley also examined whether initial neuroticism was associated with marital satisfaction among stably married couples (couples who were still married at the time of any given assessment). For men, premarriage neuroticism levels were negatively correlated with marital satisfaction at the first and second data collection times: Men who were higher in neuroticism at the beginning of the study subsequently reported lower marital happiness (first data collection) and satisfaction (second data collection) than did men with lower levels of this trait. Women's neuroticism levels were negatively associated with their marital satisfaction at the second and third data collection times; that is, women with higher levels of premarriage neuroticism were less satisfied and more regretful about their marriages later on than were women with lower premarriage neuroticism levels.

In recent years, relationship scientists have sought to understand why this particular personality trait is negatively associated with marital happiness and stability. One hypothesis that has been explored is whether neuroticism contributes to dysfunctional exchanges between romantic partners, which, in turn, may affect relational satisfaction and stability. Using a procedure similar to the one utilized by Cutrona and colleagues (1997) and described earlier, Pasch, Bradbury, and Davila (1997) examined the relationship between neuroticism and supportive behavior in a sample of newlywed couples. Couples completed measures of marital satisfaction and neuroticism and then were audiotaped during two interactions. In the first interaction, one spouse was randomly selected to serve as the "helpee." Helpees were instructed to talk about an important personal characteristic, problem, or issue they would like to change about themselves (and that did not constitute or reflect an existing source of tension in the marriage). The other spouse served as the "helper." The helper was instructed to be involved in the discussion and to respond in whatever way he or she wished. The spouses then switched roles so that both had the opportunity to function as helper and helpee.

The investigators then examined the participants' verbal behaviors for the presence of various positive and negative features. For example, *positive helpee behaviors* included offering a specific and clear analysis of the problem, expressing feelings related to the problem, and asking for help or stating needs in a clear and useful way. *Positive helper behaviors* included such instrumental acts as making specific suggestions and giving helpful advice as well as emotional acts ranging from providing reassurance, to giving encouragement, to conveying love and esteem for the helpee. *Negative helpee behaviors* included making demands for help, criticizing the helper and his or her suggestions, whining about the problem, and complaining about the situation. *Negative helper behaviors* consisted of criticizing or blaming the spouse or offering inconsiderate advice.

The analyses revealed that, for husbands, neuroticism was negatively correlated with providing positive instrumental communications to the helpee. In other words, the higher a husband scored on neuroticism, the less often he made specific suggestions and provided helpful advice to his wife. A similar pattern was found for wives. The higher a wife scored on neuroticism, the less often she displayed positive helper behavior—and the more often she displayed negative helper behavior—to the helpee (her husband). Thus, men and women who were high in neuroticism seemed to provide support in a largely negative and unhelpful manner.

The researchers also examined the audiotaped conversations for evidence of *negative reciprocity* of social support behavior, or exchanges characterized by reciprocal displays of negative communications (for example, the helpee whines about the situation and the helper then criticizes; the helper blames the helpee and the helpee then demands help). Results indicated that husbands who scored high on neuroticism were more likely to reciprocate their wives' negative behavior when they (the husbands) were in the role of helper; they were also more likely to have their negative helper behavior reciprocated by their wives. The wives' level of neuroticism, however, was not related to reciprocity of negative behavior. In discussing the entire set of results, the authors conclude that

> although support provision is associated with negative affectivity [neuroticism] for husbands and wives, it is the husband's negative affectivity that may have the most detrimental effect on actual interactions between husbands and wives. When husbands were in the role of providing support to their wives and when they were high in negative affectivity, social support interactions were characterized by extended sequences involving negative reciprocity . . . and it is plausible to assume that negative reciprocity occurring in the context of soliciting and providing social support may have negative consequences for the marriage and the individual. (p. 376)

The evidence is clear with respect to neuroticism. High levels of this personality trait are associated with marital disruption and dissatisfaction. In addition, neuroticism appears to manifest itself in maladaptive behaviors—including a failure to provide positive support and the reciprocation of negative behavior and communication—that are not conducive to relational well-being.

Personal Motives

Like traits, **personal motives** are conceptualized as relatively enduring, stable dispositions that operate relatively unconsciously and that energize, direct, and select behavior in particular situations (McClelland, 1971). Of the variety of basic human needs or motives that have been proposed, two in particular have relevance to the formation and maintenance of close relationships: the need for intimacy and the need for power. Individual differences in the strength of these motives often are measured via content analysis of narratives written in response to the ambiguous pictures (e.g., two figures sitting on a park bench) in the Thematic Apperception Test (TAT) developed by personality theorist Henry Murray (1943); see Figure 10.3. The scoring systems

FIGURE 10.3 Sample pictures from the Thematic Apperception Test (TAT).

for the intimacy and power motives are provided by McAdams (1980) and Winter (1973), respectively (also see Smith, 1992).

The Need for Intimacy

Chapter 1 extensively considered the hypothesis that over evolutionary time, the human species developed a fundamental motivation to form interpersonal attachments—a "need to belong." Although the **intimacy motive** is similar to the need to belong, it reflects not only a general affiliative tendency (which all individuals possess) but also a specific need to *feel close* to others (which some individuals possess to a greater or lesser degree than others). People high in intimacy motivation habitually prefer, are ready to experience, and actively seek out warm, communal, and intimate interpersonal interactions (McAdams, 1985, 1999).

Intimacy motivation has primarily been investigated in the context of friendship and peer relations. Research indicates that a person's degree of intimacy motivation is significantly related to the evaluative responses he or she receives from other individuals. For example,

men and women high in intimacy motivation are evaluated by their peers (strangers, acquaintances, and friends) as significantly more warm, loving, sincere, and appreciative than men and women who score lower on this dimension (McAdams, 1980; McAdams & Powers, 1981). Similarly, children high in intimacy motivation are viewed by their teachers as more friendly, affectionate, sincere, and popular—and are nominated less often as a "disliked" person by other children—than boys and girls lower in the intimacy motive (McAdams & Losoff, 1984).

In addition, intimacy motivation is associated with patterns of friendship. McAdams, Healy, and Krause (1984) asked a sample of undergraduate men and women to recall and describe 10 "friendship episodes"—defined as interactions with friends that lasted at least 15 to 20 minutes—that had occurred during the previous 2 weeks. Participants high in intimacy motivation (measured with the TAT) reported a greater number of dyadic (as opposed to group) friendship episodes, more self-disclosure within those episodes (particularly involving personal topics such as feelings, emotions, fantasies, and fears), more listening to the disclosures of their friends, and greater concern for the well-being of their friends than did participants low in intimacy motivation.

Some researchers have examined whether individual differences in intimacy motivation are associated with dimensions of social interaction. In an early investigation using an experience sampling method, McAdams and Constantian (1983) provided college students with electronic pagers that beeped on different occasions during each of 7 consecutive days. Upon being paged, the students immediately recorded their current thoughts, feelings, and behaviors. An analysis of these daily experience records indicated that participants high in intimacy motivation spent a greater proportion of their time thinking about specific other people or relationships, talking with or writing to people, and feeling good ("happy," "carefree") about their interactions with people than did their less intimacy-oriented counterparts.

More recently, Craig, Koestner, and Zuroff (1994) explored the relation between intimacy motivation and social interaction using the Rochester Interaction Record (RIR; see Chapter 4, "The Concept of Relationship"). During the first phase of this study, the researchers administered the TAT to a sample of college student participants and scored their responses for intimacy motivation. The second phase of the study consisted of a 7-day period during which participants completed the RIR each day for every interaction that lasted 10 minutes or longer. The outcome variables of interest included the percentage of dyadic (as opposed to group) interactions that occurred, the valence of the interactions (a composite measure consisting of ratings of quality of the interaction, satisfaction with the interaction, and feelings about the self in the interaction), and the correlation between an individual's self-disclosure and the closeness of the relationship. Intimacy motivation was significantly associated with the three outcome measures. Participants high in intimacy motivation reported a significantly greater percentage of dyadic interactions, were more likely to describe their interactions as positive, and were signifi-

cantly more likely to vary their level of self-disclosure based on the closeness of their relationship with the interaction partner than were participants low in intimacy motivation; that is, with a close friend, high- as opposed to low-intimacy participants were more likely to self-disclose a great deal, whereas with a casual acquaintance they were more likely to self-disclose a little. In discussing this pattern of results, the researchers suggest the following:

> The present findings indicate that *n* Int [intimacy motivation] is associated with a very differentiated and sophisticated pattern of social behavior. It appears as if *n* Int leads people to become intuitive relationship experts who understand exactly what a thorough review of relationship literature would suggest: to ensure close, warm and communicative exchanges with others, one's strategy should involve spending a greater percentage of one's time in dyads rather than groups . . . and carefully matching one's level of self-disclosure to the closeness of the relationship with one's interaction partner. (p. 503)

Additional evidence that individual differences in intimacy motivation are associated with differences in interpersonal behavior is provided by McAdams, Jackson, and Kirshnit (1984). These researchers focused on nonverbal behavior and utilized an experimental paradigm. Men and women college students who had previously been assessed for intimacy motivation via the TAT and divided into high-intimacy (upper quartile) or low-intimacy (lower quartile) groups were randomly assigned to participate in one of two experimental conditions: a *one-way interview* in which they answered questions posed to them by a same-sex interviewer (confederate) who did not relate any personal information about him- or herself, or a *reciprocal interview* in which participants answered questions posed by a same-sex interviewer who disclosed corresponding self-relevant information. The interviews were videotaped and then examined for three types of participant nonverbal behavior (these constituted the dependent measures): smiling (percentage of time spent smiling while speaking to the interviewer), eye contact (percentage of time direct eye contact was made while speaking to the interviewer), and laughter (number of outbursts of laugher or chuckling expressed while speaking to the interviewer). The analysis revealed a strong main effect for intimacy motivation; in both interpersonal contexts, high-intimacy men and women spent significantly more time engaging in all three forms of behavior than did low-intimacy men and women. The researchers concluded that individuals high in intimacy motivation manifest a recurrent preference or readiness for "experiences of warm, close, and communicative interpersonal interaction" (p. 269) and therefore display high levels of nonverbal behavior associated with positive interpersonal regard, such as smiling and eye contact.

In sum, people who are highly intimacy-oriented seek out situations that provide the opportunity for positive interpersonal contact, engage in behavior that is perceived by others as warm and disclosing, consider their close relationships with others to be a source of positive affect, and vary their behavior in ways that appropriately match the interpersonal or dyadic context.

The Need for Power

The **power motive**, or the need to have impact on others, also has implications for interpersonal behavior and close relationships. Individuals high in power motivation may express their need in a variety of ways, ranging from direct efforts to forcefully control other people to indirect attempts to influence, charm, persuade, and even help others (Winter, 1973, 1988). For both men and women, the need for power is related to leadership behavior in groups and organizations—for example, holding office in volunteer groups or participating in student governance in college (Winter, 1988). The power motive is also related to friendship experiences, with high-power men and women adopting an agentic orientation in this relationship domain. For example, McAdams and colleagues (1984) collected accounts of naturally occurring "friendship episodes" in the lives of college students. Men and women high in power motivation tended to recount interactions with friends in which they themselves took an assertive, agentic role; for example, they assumed responsibility, made a point in an argument, or helped or gave advice to the friend. Indeed, when asked to recall a single episode that strengthened their relationship with a "best friend," people with high levels of power motivation provided narratives that reflected themes of helping and providing assistance (McAdams, 1984).

In addition, some evidence indicates that the power motive is also associated with relational difficulties, including physical aggression—at least for men. For example, Mason and Blankenship (1987) reported that high need for power was significantly correlated with the infliction of physical abuse on dating partners by men but not by women. For men, high need for power also is related to interpersonal dissatisfaction. Stewart and Rubin (1976) surveyed a sample of dating couples as part of a longitudinal study on romantic relationships. During the initial assessment phase, all of the couples reported being very satisfied with their relationships. However, men's level of power motivation was negatively related to their amount of relationship satisfaction and to their estimates of their partners' satisfaction level (and the girlfriends of these power-oriented men did, in fact, report lower levels of satisfaction than the partners of less power-motivated men). Furthermore, men high in the need for power felt less love for their partners and were particularly likely to anticipate problems in their relationships in the upcoming year. These same associations did not hold for women. A follow-up of the couples 2 years later revealed a similar sex difference. Women's scores on power motivation were unrelated to the stability of their relationships. However, 50% of the couples with a male partner high in power motivation had ended the relationship, compared to only 15% of the couples with a male partner low in the need for power. Similarly, marriage was a much more common outcome of relationships involving a low-power male partner (52%) than of pairings involving a high-power male partner (9%).

Self-Monitoring

In addition to underlying personality traits and needs, individuals also differ in the domain of self-presentation and expressive behavior. As discussed in Chapter 6, "Birth of a Relationship," self-monitoring refers to the dispositional tendency to monitor or regulate the images that one presents to others (Snyder, 1987). High self-monitors essentially treat their social interactions as dramatic performances that can be used to gain attention, entertain, and make impressions. These social chameleons are strongly motivated to modify their self-presentations, are able to present themselves in a variety of ways to different audiences, and are attentive to social cues and the impressions they make on others. Low self-monitors, in contrast, are motivated to convey their authentic feelings, attitudes, and dispositions to others; are more attentive to their own internal states than to the social climate; and behave consistently across situations and audiences. Although some disagreement exists about how to best conceptualize and measure this construct (e.g., Lennox & Wolfe, 1984), the 25-item scale originally developed by Snyder (1974) appears to be a reliable instrument (see John, Cheek, & Klohnen, 1996).

Self-monitoring is associated with a number of interpersonal phenomena, including friendship formation during childhood (with high self-monitors reporting larger friendship networks than low self-monitors; Musser & Browne, 1991) and adulthood (e.g., Snyder, Gangestad, & Simpson, 1983). Researchers generally find that high self-monitors adopt an activity-based orientation toward friendship, selecting friends on the basis of activity-relevant skills and attributes, and choosing different people for particular activities—Tom for tennis, Elizabeth for theater, Rebecca for parties. Low self-monitors possess an affect-based orientation to friendship, selecting their friends on the basis of general characteristics, similarity, and feelings of liking. As a result, they tend to engage in multiple activities with the same well-liked individual—Chris for tennis, theater, and parties.

Nowhere is the potential impact of self-monitoring more evident than in the domain of romantic relationships. For example, high self-monitors pay considerably more attention to the external appearance of their romantic partners than to internal, dispositional characteristics; low self-monitors do the opposite (e.g., Jones, 1993; Snyder, 1987). In fact, experiments reveal that when forced to choose between two prospective dates—one with a desirable personality and an unattractive appearance, the other with an undesirable personality and an attractive appearance—high self-monitors willingly sacrifice personality for looks, whereas low self-monitors trade looks for personality (Snyder, Berscheid, & Glick, 1985).

High and low self-monitors also display different behaviors during romantic relationship initiation. Simpson, Gangestad, and Biek (1993) videotaped men and women who were classified as high or low self-monitors during a question-and-answer session with an attractive opposite-sex individual. Participants believed that the attractive interviewer was evaluating them, along with a number of other people, prior to selecting one for a "lunch date." During the interview sessions, men and women who scored high on self-monitoring smiled and glanced flirtatiously at the interviewer more often than did those scoring low on self-monitoring.

Similarly, a series of studies conducted by Rowatt, Cunningham, and Druen (1998) revealed that high self-monitoring individuals are more willing to strategically and deceptively alter their self-presentation to attract a potential date than are low self-monitoring individuals. For example, if a desirable prospective partner said that he or she valued attributes related to expressiveness, such as kindness, emotionality, or gentleness, high self-monitors described themselves as possessing those particular attributes. If the prospective date said that he or she valued instrumentality (independence, assertiveness, self-confidence), high self-monitors changed their self-descriptions to reflect those characteristics. Low self-monitors did not alter their self-descriptions (also see Leck & Simpson, 1999).

Given these attitudinal and behavioral differences, it is not surprising that high and low self-monitors often have very different dating histories. High self-monitors report lower levels of commitment to their romantic relationships, express greater willingness to exchange a current partner for a "better" alternative, possess a larger network of current dating partners, and have less stable relationships (e.g., Goodwin & Soon, 1994). In one study, Snyder and Simpson (1984) surveyed undergraduates (previously classified as high or low self-monitors) about their dating experiences. High self-monitors had dated about twice as many different partners in the previous year as had low self-monitors. In addition, among those participants who were currently involved in an exclusive dating relationship, high self-monitors reported having been involved in that relationship only half as long as low self-monitors.

Similar results were reported by Norris and Zweigenhaft (1999), who found a strong tendency for heterosexual dating partners to have similar self-monitoring scores; within each couple, the self-monitoring scores for the partners were significantly correlated, and in the majority of couples the partners could be classified as either both high or both low in self-monitoring. In addition, individuals in low self-monitoring unions (both partners scoring low in self-monitoring) scored higher than individuals in high self-monitoring unions on interpersonal trust. For example, they believed in each other's honesty, reliability, and commitment to the relationship more than did individuals in unions consisting of two high self-monitors. Low self-monitoring also was associated with a higher estimated likelihood of marriage. Men and women in low self-monitoring partnerships believed that it was more likely they would eventually marry their partner (75%) than men and women in high self-monitoring relationships (51%). The authors noted that these perceptions may be very accurate: High self-monitors do not think it likely that they will make a formal, long-term commitment to their partner (marriage), and when asked to evaluate the commitment level of their partner

(who is typically another high self-monitor and presumably just as commitment-shy as they are themselves), they provide similarly low estimates.

Locus of Control

Locus of control is a personality dimension that concerns beliefs about one's efficacy as a causal agent and responsibility for one's own life outcomes (Rotter, 1966). People with an *internal* locus of control see themselves as captains of their fate; they believe that events are under their personal control, and they accept responsibility for the things that happen to them. Conversely, individuals with an *external* locus of control believe that the events that befall them are beyond their personal control; their outcomes are attributed to luck, chance, powerful others, and similar external agents.

There is little evidence that locus of control is strongly associated with long-term relationship outcomes such as divorce (Constantine & Bahr, 1980; Doherty, 1983). However, internality, or the belief that one is in control of one's fate, may enable people to cope more effectively with stressful interpersonal events or difficult relationship transitions. For example, Terry (1991) interviewed couples both before and after the transition from childlessness to new parenthood. First-time parents with an internal locus of control (as assessed at the initial, prenatal interview) were more psychologically adjusted and reported higher levels of happiness 4 months after the birth of their child than parents with an external locus of control. Although it is unclear exactly how an internal orientation enables people to successfully cope with difficult relational transitions, some researchers have noted an association between internality and perceived social support, as well as help-seeking in times of duress (Klein, Tatone, & Lindsay, 1989; Schonert-Reichl & Muller, 1996). Perhaps the conviction that they are responsible for their fate prompts people to take action and to effectively utilize their social support networks when they feel overwhelmed by life events.

This personality dimension does appear to be associated with love experiences and attitudes.

Men and women with an internal locus of control are less likely to report having experienced passionate love, and they also tend to view love in pragmatic, nonidealistic terms. Those with an external orientation, however, tend to see love as a mysterious and volatile experience (Dion & Dion, 1973; Munro & Adams, 1978). Whether one is "swept away" by passion, then, may partly be a function of one's locus of control.

Sociosexual Orientation

Sociosexual orientation (also called **sociosexuality**) reflects the extent to which people require emotional intimacy and commitment before becoming sexually involved with a romantic partner (Gangestad & Simpson, 1990). Men and women who possess a *restricted* sociosexual orientation generally are unwilling to engage in sex outside of a committed relationship, and they require greater emotional closeness and commitment before engaging in sexual activity with a romantic partner. Men and women with an *unrestricted* or permissive orientation require substantially less affection or commitment before having sex with a romantic partner. This personality construct is assessed with the 7-item Sociosexual Orientation Inventory (SOI) developed by Jeffry Simpson and Steven Gangestad (1991). Items on the SOI measure aspects of sexual behavior, cognition, and attitudes.

Scores on the SOI are correlated with a number of romantic and sexual experiences. For example, restricted and unrestricted men and women prefer different sets of attributes in their dating partners. Unrestricted individuals tend to emphasize characteristics related to sexuality, such as sex appeal and sexual experience, and to external physical and social appearance, such as attractiveness and social status. Restricted individuals pay greater attention to internal, dispositional features (like kindness, sense of humor, and loyalty) and to attitudinal similarity (e.g., Jones, 1998; Sprecher, Regan, McKinney, Maxwell, & Wazienski, 1997). For example, Simpson and Gangestad (1992) asked a group of men and women to complete the SOI and to rate how important each of 15 attributes would be in

influencing their selection of a romantic partner. Correlational analyses revealed a strong association between SOI scores and attribute ratings. The more unrestricted (permissive) that men and women were, the more importance they attached to a romantic partner's physical attractiveness and sex appeal, and the less importance they placed on dispositional attributes (such as kindness and understanding or faithfulness and loyalty), similarity, and parenting qualities (for example, desire for children).

In addition, compared to their less permissive counterparts, men and women with an unrestricted orientation have sex at an earlier point in their dating relationships; are involved in relationships characterized by less love, commitment, and investment; express greater willingness to pursue alternative romantic and sexual relationships; and are more likely to have been sexually unfaithful to their current dating partners (e.g., Seal, Agostinelli, & Hannett, 1994; Simpson & Gangestad, 1991). In addition, they are more likely to display nonverbal cues that signal sexual or romantic interest, including smiling and flirtatious glances, during initial encounters with potential partners (e.g., Simpson et al., 1993).

There is some evidence that sociosexuality is related to the quantity and quality of people's everyday social interactions. Hebl and Kashy (1995) measured SOI levels in a group of men and women college students. They then asked their participants to complete daily interaction records for a 1-week period. These records required participants to report the number of interactions in which they engaged as well as their responses to each interaction. The results revealed that sociosexuality was significantly related to opposite-sex network size and frequency of opposite-sex social encounters—for women. Women higher in sociosexuality—that is, who were more unrestricted or permissive—had larger male social networks, and interacted more frequently with men, than did women lower in sociosexuality. Follow-up interviews conducted by the authors revealed that women higher in SOI also were more likely to have ended their romantic relationships than their less permissive counterparts.

DISPOSITIONAL AFFECT

Chronic mood states can color how people feel about themselves and how they feel about and behave in their relationships with others. The *Diagnostic and Statistical Manual of Mental Disorders*, fourth edition (DSM-IV), published in 1994 by the American Psychiatric Association, provides diagnostic and treatment information about a number of mood disorders, including bipolar I disorder (mania with or without major depression), bipolar II disorder (hypomania with major depression), cyclothymic disorder (numerous brief episodes of hypomania and minor depression), dysthymic disorder (prolonged minor depression without mania/hypomania), and major depressive disorder (major depression without mania). Of these disorders, **major depressive disorder** is the most common. Depression affects over 20 million people in the United States at any given time (Tolman, 2001), and between 15% and 20% of the population will experience an episode of major depressive disorder at some point during their life span (Gotlib & Kasch, 2003). The primary diagnostic criterion for major depression is a marked and abnormal mood disturbance (depressed mood in adults and depressed or irritable mood in children and adolescents) that lasts at least 2 weeks, that causes impaired physical and/or psychological functioning, and that is not due to normal bereavement, physical illness, alcohol, drugs, or medication. *Physical symptoms* of depression include abnormal appetite (either loss of appetite and weight loss or excessive appetite and weight gain); sleep disturbances such as difficulty falling asleep, frequent awakenings once asleep, or excessive sleeping; fatigue and loss of energy; and psychomotor agitation or retardation (for example, observable pacing and restlessness or physical slowing of speech, movement, and thinking). *Cognitive symptoms* include inappropriate self-reproach or guilt (e.g., marked lowering of self-esteem and self-confidence, thoughts of pessimism, hopelessness, and helplessness), poor concentration or indecisiveness (e.g., mental fatigue and forgetfulness), and thoughts of death or suicide.

In recent reviews of the literature on depression, Gotlib and Kasch (2003) and Dubas and Petersen (2003) discuss the biological, psychological, and social (interpersonal) factors implicated in this mental disorder. For example, although no specific gene or genes for depression have been identified, studies conducted with twins and biological relatives suggest that vulnerability to depression is heritable. Among monozygotic (identical) twins, an individual with a depressed sibling has an approximately 67% likelihood of also being depressed. Similarly, children and adults whose biological relatives have been diagnosed with depression have an increased risk of developing depression; for example, a child with two depressed parents has a 40% chance of developing the disorder him- or herself. Brain and hormonal processes are also implicated in the etiology of depression. Researchers have found abnormal patterns of cortisol and dehydroepiandrosterone, prolactin, and growth hormone in depressed children and adolescents, and abnormal cortisol levels and thyroid activity in depressed adults.

In addition to biological factors, psychological factors appear to be associated with major depression. Depressed individuals often hold negative and dysfunctional beliefs about failure and loss (that other people never fail, that personal failure is inexcusable), attend to negative events and stimuli more readily than positive events and stimuli, and exhibit an attributional pattern in which negative events are attributed to stable, global, and internal factors but positive events are attributed to unstable, specific, and external factors. In addition, depressed children, adolescents, and adults tend to rely on ineffective coping strategies when faced with stressors, including *rumination* (the tendency to focus repetitively on one's depressed mood without taking any steps to alleviate the negative feelings) and *avoidance* (the tendency to withdraw from stressors and/or deny their existence). These psychological factors may have a negative impact on the afflicted individual's relationship experiences, as well as on the interpersonal outcomes of those in his or her relational network.

Depression also is associated with social factors, and it appears to be linked with negative experiences in a variety of relationship contexts. Adults with chronic depression, for example, often report feeling lonely and socially isolated, believe that they lack social opportunities, view themselves as socially unappealing and unskilled, and are evaluated by outside observers as possessing fewer social skills than nondepressed individuals (e.g., Anderson, 1999; Gable & Shean, 2000; Hagerty & Williams, 1999; Segrin, 2000; Tucker & Mitchell-Kernan, 1998). In addition, although depressed men and women do not necessarily have lower levels of everyday social interaction than nondepressed people, they seem to derive less enjoyment and intimacy from their interactions with others (e.g., Nezlek, Imbrie, & Shean, 1994). Similarly, depressed individuals report experiencing—and actually do experience—a host of negative responses from others, including rejection and avoidance (e.g., Joiner, Alfano, & Metalsky, 1992; Thompson, Whiffen, & Blain, 1995). Segrin and Dillard (1992) conducted a meta-analysis of literature examining reactions to depressed and nondepressed targets following real or imagined interaction. Their results revealed a significant relationship between depression and interpersonal rejection; depressed individuals are not liked by others and are frequently rejected by them.

The friendships and romantic relationships of depressed adults appear similarly at risk. Men and women with depression report less overall satisfaction with their friendships and romantic relationships, and their relationships are characterized by low levels of intimacy and poor communication (e.g., Schmitt & Kurdek, 1985; Segrin, Powell, Givertz, & Brackin, 2003). Among married couples, depression (of one or both spouses) is strongly correlated with marital instability, global dissatisfaction and distress, difficulties in specific areas of the marital relationship such as sexual function, and the use of dysfunctional patterns of communication (Gotlib & Kasch, 2003; Schreiner-Engel & Schiavi, 1986; Wade & Cairney, 2000).

Depression is associated with a number of problematic outcomes for the parent–child relationship as well. In their review, Dubas and Petersen (2003) noted that compared with nondepressed mothers, clinically depressed mothers are more likely to use maladaptive coping strategies such as withdrawal and avoidance when attempting to deal with child noncompliance. In addition, depressed parents (both fathers and mothers) tend to display more hostility and irritability when interacting with their children than do nondepressed parents. Similarly, the families of depressed children and adolescents are characterized by greater levels of parent–child conflict and lower levels of family cohesion and social support than are the families of nondepressed youth.

Because most research conducted in this area is correlational, it is difficult to determine the precise nature of the connection between depression and relationship experiences. Do depressed people behave in a manner that impedes social interaction and pushes others away? Or does a pattern of social rejection and a repeated failure to develop positive relationships produce negative affect? Some theorists argue in favor of the former. Lykken and Tellegen (1996) assert that individuals are born with genetic predispositions to positive or negative mood which cause them to engage in behaviors that are either conducive or disruptive to close relationship formation. As we have noted, there is evidence that depressed people display behaviors that may result in an increased likelihood of social rejection. A literature review by Segrin (1998) revealed that depressed individuals typically speak in a slow, monotonous style that is peppered with hesitancies and silences; make negative self-statements; self-disclose negative information at inappropriate times; refrain from direct eye contact; and utilize few gestures when interacting with others. In addition, researchers who have observed couples during laboratory interactions find that depressed men and women make fewer supportive statements to their dating partners when discussing an area of conflict in the relationship (e.g., Gurung, Sarason, & Sarason, 1997). This overall pattern of verbal and nonverbal communication is unlikely to evoke positive responses from a relational partner.

Alternately, it is possible that individuals who repeatedly experience rejection from others or negative outcomes in their close relationships become depressed. One of the most pervasive themes in theories of human development and motivation is that humans are social beings possessing an inherent need or drive to establish meaningful connections with others, and that failure to satisfy this need results in emotional maladjustment (e.g., Deci & Ryan, 1991; Epstein, 1994; Fairbairn, 1954; Mahler, Pine, & Bergman, 1975; Maslow, 1954; also see Baumeister & Leary, 1995). Because human nature is inherently social, a paucity of intimate relationships or satisfying, supportive interactions has the potential to powerfully influence a person's mood, sense of well-being, and self-concept. Both processes probably shape the relational context of individuals with chronic negative affects and their partners in a reciprocally causal manner. That is, dispositional negativity predisposes people to perceive and respond to others in ways that do not promote positive interpersonal outcomes, and this failure to achieve satisfying interactions and relationships then reinforces negative affect and a sense of lowered self-worth.

A growing body of research highlights the importance of interpersonal factors in the successful treatment of major depressive disorder. Depression is highly amenable to treatment, and several different forms of intervention are available. Individual-level treatments, which focus on the depressed individual alone, include drug therapy, cognitive-behavioral therapy, and social skills training. Couple- or family-level interventions include marital therapy (in which both spouses participate), behavioral family therapy (in which the individual and his or her family are educated about depression and are taught communication and problem-solving skills), and cognitive-behavioral family therapy (which includes training in communication and problem-solving, along with cognitive restructuring to alter maladaptive attributions and irrational beliefs held by the depressed individual and family members). Therapies that involve both the individual and his or her relational partner(s) appear to be most effective. After reviewing the clinical literature, Gotlib and Kasch (2003) conclude that

> marital therapy is as effective as individual cognitive-behavioral therapy in alleviating depressive symptoms of spouses in distressed marriages. Moreover, patients receiving marital therapy have been found to report higher marital satisfaction than do patients receiving cognitive-behavior therapy. (p. 404)

Depression is a complex disorder with a diversity of causes and consequences, and with a clear and pernicious influence on an individual's social and relational well-being.

INTERPERSONAL BELIEF SYSTEMS

People bring to relationships not only their own enduring personality traits and affective tendencies but also a variety of stable, relationship-relevant beliefs and expectations. Known as relational schemata (Baldwin, 1992, 1995), implicit or lay relationship theories (Fletcher & Thomas, 1996; Knee, 1998), or general relationship beliefs (Bradbury & Fincham, 1988; Fletcher & Kininmonth, 1992), these mental representations consist of a rich web of beliefs, attitudes, values, and expectations and are presumed to develop over time and to influence interpersonal behavior (see Chapter 8). Two relational schemata or interpersonal belief systems that researchers have found to be useful in predicting relationship behavior and outcomes are attachment styles and rejection sensitivity.

Adult Attachment Style

Building on the theoretical foundation laid by John Bowlby's (e.g., 1969) attachment theory and the typology of attachment patterns created by Mary Ainsworth and her colleagues (e.g., Ainsworth, Blehar, Waters, & Wall, 1978; see Chapter 1), relationship scholars have proposed the concept of **adult attachment style**, which refers to a person's characteristic beliefs, attitudes, and expectations about the self (worthy of love and support vs. not worthy of love and support), others (available and supportive vs. unavailable and rejecting), and relationships (rewarding vs. punishing). Hazan and Shaver (1987) created a typology of attachment styles in adults that matched the attachment behavior patterns in children described earlier by Ainsworth. In addition, these researchers constructed the first measure of adult attachment style; this single-item self-report measure consisted of paragraph descriptions of how the typical secure, avoidant, and anxious–ambivalent adult might feel, think, and behave with respect to romantic relationships and partners. In the years since Hazan and Shaver's seminal paper was published, two important conceptual and methodological advancements occurred. First, Bartholomew (e.g., 1990; Bartholomew & Horowitz, 1991) proposed a four-category typology of adult attachment style (Figure 10.4) that included the three categories described by Hazan and Shaver and an additional dismissive–avoidant category. Second, the original single-item categorical scale proposed by Hazan and Shaver was replaced by multi-item continuous scales (e.g., Brennan, Clark, & Shaver, 1998; Collins & Read, 1990).

Attachment theorists and researchers now generally agree that four adult attachment styles exist, each derived from two underlying dimensions. The first dimension, anxiety, refers to the degree to which an individual worries or is concerned about being rejected or unloved; the second dimension, avoidance, refers to the degree to which an individual actively avoids or approaches intimacy, connection, and interdependence with others. These dimensions combine to create the following prototypic adult attachment styles. Individuals who possess a *secure* attachment style have low levels of attachment-related anxiety and attachment-related avoidance, and as a result they are comfortable with intimacy, able and willing to

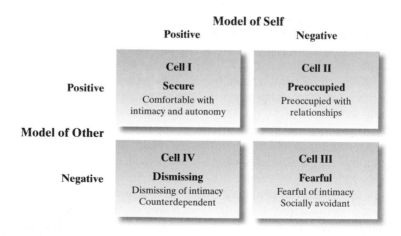

FIGURE 10.4 Bartholomew's four-category typology of adult attachment style. Bartholomew and colleagues propose that people's abstract image of the self and their abstracted image of the other can be dichotomized as positive or negative, thus combining to produce four adult attachment patterns. Each cell represents a theoretical ideal or prototype that different people might approximate to different degrees. *Adapted from Bartholomew and Horowitz, "Attachment Styles Among Young Adults: A Test of a Four-Category Model" (1991), Fig. 1, p. 227.*

rely on others for support, and confident that they are worthy of being loved and valued by others. People with a *preoccupied* (anxious–ambivalent) attachment style have a high level of attachment-related anxiety coupled with a low level of attachment-related avoidance. These individuals possess an extreme and exaggerated need for closeness with, and dependence on, others, yet paradoxically also have an intense fear of being rejected by others. *Dismissing avoidant* individuals demonstrate the opposite pattern; these people have a low level of attachment-related anxiety and a high level of attachment-related avoidance. Viewing closeness and intimacy as relatively unimportant, they value independence and self-reliance more than they do the formation and maintenance of close bonds with others. Finally, adults with a *fearful avoidant* attachment style are high in both attachment-related anxiety and avoidance; they truly desire close, intimate connections with others but are fearful of being rejected and so carefully avoid intimacy.

Several general conclusions can be drawn from the vast literature on adult attachment style. First, like extraversion and other dispositional characteristics, attachment style seems relatively stable over time among adults, with reports of stability over intervals ranging from 1 week to 4 years (e.g., Feeney, Noller, & Callan, 1994; Hammond & Fletcher, 1991; Keelan, Dion, & Dion, 1994; Levy & Davis, 1988; Shaver & Brennan, 1992). For example, Scharfe and Bartholomew (1994) assessed attachment style in a sample of young adults using three different methods—self-report ratings made by the participants themselves, expert ratings based on semistructured interviews, and reports made by the participants' romantic partners. Assessments were made during two sessions 8 months apart, and the results of correlational analyses indicated moderate stability of classifications over this period of time. For example, the majority of participants were placed in the same attachment category at both times by the expert interviewers (77%), by their own partners (70%), and by themselves on self-report measures (59%). Thus, attachment style appears to possess moderate continuity and to resemble other dispositional variables.

Second, despite the fact that attachment style shows moderate stability over time, there is growing evidence that the nature of a person's attachment style may vary across specific relationships and partners (e.g., Baldwin, Keelan, Fehr, Enns, & Koh-Rangarajoo, 1996; Cook, 2000). In other words, a person is not necessarily securely attached to everyone in his or her social world but rather may be more or less securely attached to particular others. A study conducted by La Guardia, Ryan, Couchman, and Deci (2000) demonstrates this phenomenon. These researchers asked a group of young adults to rate how well different attachment styles reflected their own relationships with various targets, including their mother, father, romantic partner, and best friend. The results revealed significant amounts of within-person variability in attachment, with both men and women experiencing varying degrees of attachment security across their relationships. Thus, although attachment style is moderately stable (Phil is securely attached at Time 1 and Time 2, and he rates himself and is rated by others as securely attached), there also is a substantial amount of variability in the nature of a person's attachments across relational partners (Phil experiences more attachment security with Nancy than he does with Pat). This finding has important implications for researchers interested in attachment style and other dispositional variables insofar as it suggests that person-level constructs influence and are influenced by qualities of the relational partner and do not simply exist at a given and unchanging level.

A third, and related, conclusion concerns the level of specificity of attachment-related beliefs. Current theorizing suggests not only that an individual's attachment-relevant beliefs and expectations may differ across relational partners but also that these beliefs and expectations may differ in their level of specificity. Cozzarelli, Hoekstra, and Bylsma (2000), for example, argue that people possess both attachment-related beliefs about a particular partner and relationship (partner-specific mental models) and attachment-related beliefs about people and relationships in general (general mental models). The fact that the two types of attachment-related belief systems differ in the way they relate to psychological adjustment and relationship outcomes provides support for the researchers' argument. Using a sample of undergraduates, Cozzarelli and associates (2000) found that scores on measures of general attachment style were more strongly correlated with life satisfaction and well-being scores than were scores on measures of specific attachment; conversely, specific attachment scores were more strongly correlated with current relationship satisfaction levels than were general attachment scores.

A fourth conclusion that can be drawn from the available (and primarily correlational) literature is that individual differences in adult attachment style are associated with qualitative differences in relationship experience. Although some work has been conducted on adult friendship (e.g., Grabill & Kerns, 2000), most researchers have focused on romantic relationship experiences. Recent reviews by B. Feeney and Collins (2003) and J. Feeney, Noller, and Roberts (1998, 2000) provide several general conclusions about relationship quality and attachment style. First, the dating and marital relationships of securely attached men and women contain higher levels of commitment, satisfaction, trust, and positive affect than those of less securely attached (for example, avoidant or anxious/preoccupied) men and women. Second, the romantic relationships of securely attached men and women are characterized by lower levels of conflict, interpersonal difficulty, jealousy, and negative affect than those of less securely attached men and women. Third, securely attached men and women engage in more intimate and personal self-disclosure with their romantic partners than do insecurely attached individuals, and they report experiencing a greater level of comfort when making such disclosures.

Romantic relationship quality is clearly linked with attachment orientation. However, the evidence with respect to relationship stability is mixed. Early research suggested that secure individuals enjoyed the greatest relationship stability (e.g., Hazan & Shaver, 1987). As noted by Feeney and Collins (2003), prospective studies have revealed a more complex set of findings, with some indicating high relationship stability among anxious/ambivalent (preoccupied) respondents and others demonstrating higher levels of stability among insecurely attached respondents than among securely attached respondents.

Most of the adult attachment literature is correlational in nature; that is, researchers interested in this dispositional variable typically ask men and women to complete a self-report measure of attachment style and at the same point in time to complete some other self-report measure of relationship outcome such as satisfaction or adjustment. This reliance on participant self-report and correlational methodology does not address the issue of whether differences in attachment style actually manifest themselves in behavioral differences in ongoing interaction and, if so, whether these behavioral differences have any subsequent relational impact. Some investigators, however, have begun to explore this issue, with preliminary evidence suggesting that attachment style may exert some influence on people's ongoing social interactions. For example, Simpson, Rholes, and Nelligan (1992) examined the behavior of dating couples during a laboratory interaction. In this study, members of the couples first completed a self-report measure of attachment style. Next, the female member of each couple was informed that she soon would be exposed to a set of experimental procedures that "arouse considerable anxiety and distress in most people" (p. 437). She was not, however, told the specific nature of these procedures. Immediately following this anxiety-provoking manipulation, each woman was allowed to interact with her partner during a 5-minute "waiting" period. The couple's interactions were videotaped without their awareness, and raters then viewed the videotapes and evaluated the behavior of both members of the couple during the 5-minute period.

The results revealed that for women, scores on the self-report attachment style measure were associated with support-seeking behavior. Specifically, among more secure women, increases in observer-rated anxiety were positively correlated with increased levels of observer-rated support seeking: women with higher levels of self-reported security sought comfort and support from their partners as their anxiety increased, according to the behavioral observations of the raters. The reverse pattern was observed among more avoidant women: those with higher levels of self-reported avoidance demonstrated less support-seeking as their anxiety levels increased. Men's support-giving behavior also was predicted by their own attachment style. As their partners' levels of anxiety increased, more secure men offered more, and more avoidant men offered less, support. Similarly, as women discussed their feelings of anxiety more, secure men made more supportive remarks and avoidant men made fewer. These results demonstrate that differences in attachment style manifest themselves in behavioral differences during interaction between relational partners. In addition, these results highlight the fact that any interaction or relationship between two individuals will be influenced by the properties of both. As noted by the authors:

> More avoidant men, for example, cannot be characterized as cold, distant, or aloof *in general*. Although they do behave in this manner when their partner experiences higher levels of distress, their behavior is not the same when their partner's distress is lower. (p. 442, emphasis in original)

Thus, a person's attachment style, like other dispositional attributes, cannot be considered in isolation; rather, an individual's attachment style interacts with the relational context, and with the disposition of the other partner, to produce particular interaction behavior and relational outcomes.

Rejection Sensitivity

Another class of beliefs and expectations, those having to do specifically with rejection, can shape the course of adult intimate relationships. Drawing on attachment theory, Downey and her colleagues (e.g., Downey, Bonica, & Rincon, 1999) have proposed that **rejection sensitivity**—the tendency to anxiously anticipate, readily perceive, and emotionally and behaviorally overreact to rejection from significant others—develops as a self-protective response to parental rejection, rebuff, or punitiveness. People who are high in rejection sensitivity expect to be rejected by their partners in situations where rejection is possible (for example, during times of conflict). As a result, they perceive rejection even when none is intended and then often overreact in response to the (often imagined) slight. Conversely, individuals who are low in rejection sensitivity enter their encounters and relationships calmly expecting acceptance and support, and they respond to conflict or rejection with equanimity.

Rejection sensitivity, like attachment style, typically is assessed with a multi-item self-report measure. People are asked to imagine being in various situations that involve requesting assistance from others, including acquaintances, romantic partners, and family members—asking a classmate to borrow his or her notes, asking a boyfriend or girlfriend to cohabit, or asking parents for help with college applications. For each situation, participants are instructed to indicate the extent to which they would be concerned or anxious about the other person's response to their request, and the extent to which they would expect their request to be met by the other individual. People who report feeling concern or anxiety about the outcome of their request, and who expect rejection, are considered high in rejection sensitivity, whereas those who report less anxiety and concern and a greater expectation of assistance are considered low in rejection sensitivity.

Several lines of evidence provide support for the notion that people who are high in rejection sensitivity perceive rejection in the behavior of others. For example, in one experiment Downey and Feldman (1996) invited college students to participate in two brief "get acquainted" sessions with another student (actually a confederate working with the experimenters). After an initial, friendly conversation with the confederate, participants were told that he or she had opted not to meet with them a second time. Men and women who were high in rejection sensitivity reported feeling more rejected by the confederate's decision than those who were lower in rejection sensitivity. The researchers found similar results with a sample of people who had recently begun a new romantic relationship. In this study, participants were asked to imagine that their new partner had committed a variety of insensitive actions—for example, had acted cool and distant, had been intolerant of something the participant had done, or had begun to spend less time with the participant. Participants then indicated the extent to which they believed each action reflected the partner's intentional desire to hurt them. As before, the results revealed a positive correlation between rejection sensitivity and perceived hurtful intent. The more sensitive a participant was to rejection, the greater the amount of hurtful intent he or she perceived in a variety of potential partner behaviors. Thus, it seems that men and women who anxiously anticipate rejection do actually "see" rejection in the actions of others.

Much of the early work on rejection sensitivity, like that on attachment style, was correlational in nature and typically involved participants completing two self-report measures (rejection sensitivity and relationship satisfaction, for example) at the same point in time. This research revealed that rejection sensitivity (like attachment style) is associated with a number of relationship experiences. For example, compared to less rejection-sensitive individuals, men and women who are high in rejection sensitivity typically report feeling less satisfied with their romantic relationships, are more likely to endorse negative beliefs about their relationships ("My partner feels trapped in our relationship"), and magnify the extent of their partner's dissatisfaction—for example, they believe that their dating partners are less satisfied than is actually the case (Downey & Feldman, 1996).

Rejection sensitivity also is correlated with relationship stability. In one of the few longitudinal studies conducted to date, Downey, Freitas, Michaelis, and Khouri (1998) asked dating couples to complete a self-report measure of rejection sensitivity and then contacted the couples a year later and asked them about the current status of their relationship. The results revealed that rejection-sensitive individuals were more likely than non-rejection-sensitive people to be involved in unstable relationships. Relationship termination was far more common among couples with at least one rejection-sensitive partner (43%) than among those with non-rejection-sensitive partners (15%).

An important question is whether sensitivity to rejection actually manifests itself in maladaptive behavior and produces negative interpersonal outcomes. Downey and colleagues argue that it does. They suggest that rejection sensitivity, when activated by an appropriate situational cue or interpersonal context such as a conflict episode, may set in motion a self-fulfilling relational prophecy whereby individuals who anxiously anticipate rejection—that is, who possess higher levels of rejection sensitivity—behave in ways that actually elicit rejection from their partners, thereby confirming their initial rejection expectancy. In order to examine this hypothesis, the researchers collected three pieces of information from 39 heterosexual dating couples. First, they asked each partner to complete preinteraction self-report measures of rejection sensitivity, relationship satisfaction, relationship commitment, and mood (depression, anxiety about the relationship, and anger at the partner). Next, they observed the partners' behavior during a 20-minute laboratory interaction that took place 1 to 2 weeks after the preinteraction measures were collected. Couples were instructed to discuss an area of ongoing conflict in their relationship (conflict was presumed to be a situation that would activate anxious expectations of rejection). Each partner's behavior during the conflict discussion then was examined for negative verbal and nonverbal elements such as hostile tone of voice, verbal put-downs, and gestures that communicate disgust or disagreement. These verbal and nonverbal elements were combined to form a negative behavior composite. Finally, each participant completed a post-interaction self-report measure of anger toward the partner (used as an index of rejection).

The results supported what the researchers termed their "behavioral mediation hypothesis"— for women but not for men. Specifically, women's preinteraction levels of rejection sensitivity significantly predicted both the amount of negative behavior they displayed during the interaction and their partners' level of postinteraction anger. That is, women with higher levels of rejection sensitivity engaged in greater amounts of negative behavior during a conflict discussion, and their partners reported more anger about the relationship following the discussion, than women with lower levels of rejection sensitivity. In addition, women's negative interaction behavior significantly predicted their male partners' level of postinteraction anger; the greater the amount of negative behavior that women displayed during the conflict discussion, the greater the amount of anger reported by their partners. Most important for establishing mediation (see Baron & Kenny, 1986), the women's rejection sensitivity did not significantly predict their partners' postdiscussion anger when the women's negative interaction behavior was statistically controlled; this statistical finding demonstrates that the relationship between women's rejection sensitivity and partners' subsequent anger is accounted for, or mediated by, women's negative interaction behaviors. In other words, men paired with rejection-sensitive women were angrier (more rejecting) following a conflict discussion than men paired with non-rejection-sensitive women because of the negative verbal and nonverbal behavior displayed by their partners. These results held irrespective of the preinteraction mood, relationship satisfaction, and commitment of either the women or their partners. In discussing their findings, the researchers conclude:

> Our results confirm that women's expectancies help create their own reality in romantic relationships. During conflicts, women's expectations of rejection led them to behave in ways that elicited confirmatory reactions from their romantic partners. More-over, even when controlling for a partner's relationship satisfaction and commitment, rejection sensitivity proved a potent predictor of relationship breakup. Eventually, then, as conflicts accumulate, the realities of HRS [high rejection-sensitive] women's relationships may merge more closely with their expectations. (pp. 558–559)

It may be the way in which rejection sensitivity manifests itself in behavior during actual interaction that is significant and that influences both partners' subsequent relational experiences.

SUMMARY

Each person possesses a host of enduring dispositional attributes that can influence both the quantity and the quality of his or her interpersonal interactions and the relationships he or she forms with others. As we have seen, one of the most significant of these attributes is maleness or femaleness—both biological sex and psychological gender are associated with a variety of relational experiences and outcomes. Personality traits, chronic affective states, needs or motives, and interpersonal belief systems also seem to play a role in relationship initiation and maintenance. Of course, it is important to keep in mind that no single disposition, need, feeling state, or set of beliefs inevitably determines what happens between partners or the fate of their association. Rather, it is the particular constellation of personal attributes that one individual possesses, and how well those attributes mesh with the enduring characteristics of his or her partner, that ultimately will have the largest impact on any given relationship. Thus, an extraverted, securely attached person with high self-esteem may experience interpersonal dissatisfaction and conflict, and an emotionally unstable, chronically depressed person with an insecure attachment style and extreme rejection sensitivity may find lasting friendship and love.

PART 5
MATING RELATIONSHIPS

Chapter *11*

Love

INTRODUCTION

Like all great dramatic works, the story of each individual human life can, in many instances, be whittled down to one fundamental leitmotif: the question of who loves us (and who does not) and when and where and how love occurs. As noted in Chapter 1, "First Relationships," each of us owes the fact of our existence to the attraction (whether it be affectionate or lustful, long-standing or fleeting) that once existed between two individuals, and our extreme fragility during infancy—the evolutionary inheritance of our species—as well as the continued impact that others have upon both the quality and quantity of our lives ensures that most, if not all, of us will devote considerable effort to finding an answer to that very question.

In doing so, many of us might turn to the scores of poets, playwrights, novelists, and artists who have, over the centuries, sought to capture love's essence in the pages and on the canvases of their works. From Shakespeare alone we would learn that love is experienced by and between many types of individuals (friends, lovers, relatives, spouses, children, and adults) and that

it has a diversity of features and produces a variety of consequences. For example, in *Romeo and Juliet*, the love between Romeo Montague and Juliet Capulet is sudden, idealistic, intensely passionate and joyful, and ultimately destructive, bringing grief to both their families and resulting in the lovers' joint suicide. Beatrice and Benedick from *Much Ado About Nothing* also love each other, but their love is calmer and tempered with a healthy dose of reality about themselves and about each other. It produces a much happier result—marriage, not death, is the outcome. The love in *Othello*—that felt by Iago for his friend and commander Othello and by Othello for his wife Desdemona—is possessive and jealous, leading to lies, betrayal, murder, and suicide. Durability, warmth, and deep affection characterize the love between Cecilia and Rosalind in *As You Like It* and Horatio and Hamlet in *Hamlet*; Cecilia and Horatio willingly share in the adversity faced by their respective friends and remain true and loyal when others do not.

For Shakespeare and his literary successors, the depiction of love in all its many forms provided an opportunity to entertain and, in some instances, to educate the public. Scientists have had a different goal. In order to understand love and the role that love plays in human lives, scientists have recognized that it is necessary to identify whether different types of love exist and what features distinguish them from each other. Existential psychologist Erich Fromm stated the issue clearly in his classic book *The Art of Loving* (1956):

> This desire for interpersonal union is the most powerful striving in man. It is the most fundamental passion, it is the force which keeps the human race together, the clan, the family, society. The failure to achieve it means insanity or destruction—self-destruction or destruction of others. Without love, humanity could not exist for a day. Yet, if we call the achievement of interpersonal union "love," we find ourselves in a serious difficulty. Fusion can be achieved in different ways—and the differences are not less significant than what is common to the various forms of love. Should they all be called love? Or should we reserve the word "love" only for a specific kind of union . . .? As with all semantic difficulties, the answer can only be arbitrary. What matters is that we know what kind of union we are talking about when we speak of love. (p. 18)

The search to determine what is common across all love types and what is unique to each variety has consumed thinkers from a variety of disciplines for many years. Early theorists developed their taxonomies from personal observation and inductive reasoning, from literature, and from previous philosophical, theological, and scientific discourse; contemporary theorists increasingly have relied on empirically based methods to develop their classification systems. But love is a complex and multifaceted phenomenon, and the science of love is still in its infancy. For example, investigators have yet to develop a common conceptual vocabulary, and most have developed their taxonomies with little regard to the work of other researchers and theorists.

TAXONOMIES OF LOVE

An approach often taken by investigators interested in the nature of love is to identify and catalogue different proposed varieties. One of the earliest known treatises on the nature of love, a work titled *The Art of Courtly Love*, appeared in France during the late twelfth century. Written by Andreas Capellanus (André le Chapelain), supposedly at royal behest, the three-part treatise considers the nature of love—its origins, manifestations, and effects; who can feel love; how love may be acquired, increased, decreased, and terminated; and what a lover should do if the beloved is unfaithful. Capellanus posits, for example, that love is experienced as a "certain inborn suffering derived from the sight of and excessive meditation upon the beauty of the opposite sex" (1184/1960, p. 28) and that love consists of two varieties. "Pure" love is less sexual, more cerebral, and more durable than "mixed" or "common" love:

> One kind of love is pure, and one is called mixed. It is the pure love which binds together the hearts of two lovers with every feeling of delight. This kind consists in the contemplation of the mind and the affection of the heart; it goes as far as the kiss and the embrace and the modest contact with the nude lover, omitting the final solace, for that is not permitted to those who wish to love purely. This is the kind that anyone who is intent upon love ought to embrace with all his might, for this love goes on increasing without end, and we know that no one ever regretted practicing it, and the more of it one has the more one wants. . . . But that is called mixed love which gets its effect from every delight of the flesh and culminates in the final act of Venus. What sort of love this is you may clearly see from what I have already said, for this kind quickly fails, and lasts but a short time, and one often regrets having practiced it. . . . But I do not say this as though I meant to condemn mixed love, I merely wish to show which of the two is preferable. But mixed love, too, is real love, and it is praiseworthy, and we say that it is the source of all good things, although from it grave dangers threaten, too. Therefore I approve of both pure love and mixed love, but I prefer to practice pure love. (pp. 122–123)

According to Capellanus, both pure and mixed love arise from the act of seeing and meeting another individual who possesses certain attractive qualities (in particular an excellent character, ready speech, and a beautiful figure) and obsessively and passionately meditating upon those qualities. Because love is dependent on vision, mental reflection, and passion, only those persons capable of these experiences are able to acquire love; Capellanus therefore excludes the blind, who cannot see anything upon which their minds can immoderately reflect; the excessively lustful, who can see but who are unable to concentrate their attention on one love object; and the very young and old, who lack the requisite passion. For example:

> We must now see what persons are fit to bear the arms of love. You should know that everyone of sound mind who is capable of doing the work of Venus may be wounded by one of Love's arrows unless prevented by age, or blindness, or excess of passion. Age is a bar, because after the sixtieth year in a man and the fiftieth in a woman, although one may have intercourse his passion cannot develop into love; because at that age the natural heat begins to lose its force, and the natural moisture is greatly increased, which leads a man into various difficulties and troubles him with various ailments, and there are no consolations in the world for him except food and drink. Similarly, a girl under the age of twelve and a boy before the fourteenth year do not serve in love's army. (p. 32)[1]

Once acquired, the effects of love (on the lover) are believed to be overwhelmingly positive and to include increased nobility of character, humility, a desire to perform services for others, gratitude, and fidelity. Some contemporary literary critics have questioned Capellanus' motives in creating his treatise on love and whether he truly believed what he wrote; nonetheless, this work remains one of our earliest examples of discourse on the nature of love.

Other early scholars also proposed that multiple varieties of love exist, each containing specific features (although none of these theorists devoted as much attention as Capellanus to discussing the origins and consequences of the various love types). As illustrated in Figure 11.1, William James (1890/1950), the founder of American psychology, distinguished between maternal love and a form of (unnamed) love that was characterized by sexuality and exclusivity—that is, it was directed toward one particular individual to the exclusion of all others. At around the same

time, the German physician Krafft-Ebing (1886/1945) suggested that true love (a hardy mixture of altruism, closeness, and sexuality) differed from sensual love (a fleeting love based on sexual desire and "romantic idealising" [p. 11]), platonic love (characterized by compatibility), and sentimental love (about which Krafft-Ebing had little more to say than that it was "nauseating" [p. 12]). Psychotherapist Albert Ellis (1954) proposed an even greater variety of possible love types, ranging from romantic love, sexual love, and conjugal love to parental love and familial love to religious love and self-love. Fromm (1956) agreed with Ellis that a diversity of loves existed and could be experienced by individuals over the life span. According to his typology, love can be divided into two basic categories: real (or mature) love and pseudo-love. Varieties of real love include brotherly love, motherly love, fatherly love, erotic love, self-love, and love of God. Each of these love types contains four basic elements—care, responsibility, respect, and knowledge—along with particular unique features. For example, motherly love is unconditional and altruistic, whereas erotic love is fragile and sexual. The pseudolove types share some of the features of real love but are experienced by people with various personality disorders, who lack a strong sense of identity and are incapable of engaging in "love between equals."

Unlike his contemporaries Ellis and Fromm, religious theoretician C. S. Lewis contented himself with just four types of love, each based on earlier discourse by Greek philosophers. In his engaging and aptly titled book *The Four Loves* (1960/1988), Lewis describes affection (called *storge* by the Greeks) as "the humblest and most widely diffused of loves" (p. 31). Affectionate love, which resembles the strong attachment seen between parents and offspring, is often experienced for and by a diversity of love objects (family members, pets, acquaintances, and lovers). It is based on proximity and familiarity and is characterized by feelings of warmth, interpersonal comfort, and satisfaction in being together. The second variety of love depicted by Lewis is friendship (*philias*), a version of love based on common interests, insights, or tastes, coupled

Theorist/Researcher	Proposed Nature of Love		
	Number of Varieties	**Type(s)**	**Features**
Capellanus (1184)	2	Pure Common (mixed)	Durability, affection Fragility, sexuality
Krafft-Ebing (1886)	3+	Sensual love True love Platonic love Sentimental love	Fragility, idealization of beloved, sexuality Durability, closeness (interdependence), altruism, sexuality Compatibility Selfindulgent sentimentality
James (1890)	2	Love Parental (maternal) love	Exclusivity, sexual appetite, intensity "Passionate devotion," altruism

A. Ellis (1954)	11+	Conjugal love, parental love, familial
		  love, religious love, self-love, sexual love, etc.
		Romantic love
			Unspecified
			
			Exclusivity, idealization of beloved,
			  emotional intensity, sexuality

Fromm (1956)	6+	Real love(s):
		  Brotherly love ⎫
		  Motherly love ⎪ care, respect,
		  Fatherly love ⎬ responsibility,
		  Erotic love ⎪ knowledge
		  Self-love ⎪
		  Love of God ⎭
		Pseudo-love(s):
		  Idolatrous love
		
		  Sentimental love
		  Etc.
			
			Universal
			Universal, unconditional, altruistic
			Universal, conditional
			Exclusive, fragile, sexual
			Self-focused
			Universal, oneness with God
			
			Idealization/worship of beloved, intensity,
			  sudden onset, fragility
			Idealization of (empty) relationship

Lewis (1960)	4	Affection
		
		Friendship
		Eros
		
		Charity
			Slow onset/growth, warmth,
			  comfortableness
			Similarity, durability, respect, admiration
			Exclusivity, sexuality, fragility, idealization
			  of beloved, cognitive preoccupation
			Tolerance, altruism

Berscheid (1985)	4	Altruistic love Attachment Philias or friendship Eros or romantic love	Promotion of other's welfare Proximity-seeking, separation distress Positive evaluation (anticipation of reward) Sexual desire, emotional intensity

Sternberg (1986, 1988)	8	Nonlove
		
		Liking
		Infatuation
		
		Empty love
		Romantic love
		
		Companionate love
		Fatuous love
		Consummate love
			(Absence of intimacy, passion, decision/
			  commitment)
			Intimacy (closeness, bondedness, warmth)
			Passion, idealization of beloved, cognitive
			  preoccupation, physical arousal
			Commitment
			Physical attraction, liking (closeness
			  bondedness, warmth)
			Intimacy, commitment
			Passion, commitment, sudden onset
			Passion, intimacy, commitment

FIGURE 11.1 A sample of love classification systems, including the number of distinct love types proposed to exist, the varieties of love specified by each theorist, and the hypothesized characteristic features of the different love varieties.

with cooperation, mutual respect, and understanding. More than mere companionship, Lewis argued that friendship develops when "two people . . . discover that they are on the same secret road" (p. 67) and become kindred souls. Eros, or "that state which we call 'being in love'" (p. 91), is a love type characterized by sexuality, idealization of the beloved, preoccupation with thoughts of him or her, and a short life span. The final love type is charity, a selfless love based on tolerance, forbearance, and forgiveness; it involves no expectation of reward and desires only what is "simply best for the beloved" (p. 128). Charity allows us to love those who are not lovable (a state that Lewis believed was experienced by everyone at some time).

All these theorists agree that love is multifaceted—that is, that more than one variety of love exists—and all made progress in specifying at least some of what they believed to be the characteristic manifestations of the various love types. Yet they disagreed about the number of love varieties that exist, and moreover, none of these theoretical classification systems was developed sufficiently to provide an adequate guide for research (for example, by clearly specifying the causal antecedents and consequences of the individual love types). An exception is the classification system proposed by Berscheid (1985b), who reviewed clinical and anecdotal literature, examined existing scientific conceptualizations of love, and considered empirical evidence about the causes and effects of certain attraction phenomena in an effort to identify the varieties of love that theorists and researchers might find useful to distinguish. Her review led her to propose four distinct varieties of love—altruistic love, attachment, philias or friendship, and eros or romantic love. Importantly, each of these love types has different causal antecedents. For example, Berscheid notes that the primary antecedent of attachment appears to be sheer familiarity rather than positive evaluations or the anticipation of rewards (which are the principal determinants of philias or friendship) or sexual attraction (which is a distinguishing feature of eros or romantic love). (For additional discussion of the attachment construct, see Chapter 1.) Similarly, the determinants of altruistic love do not reside in sexual attraction, positive evaluations, the anticipation of reward, or familiarity. As discussed by Berscheid, people often care about and act to promote the welfare of others they may not know, like, respect, or wish to associate with for any length of time, and the determinants of altruistic behavior thus differ importantly from the determinants of other varieties of love (and have, in fact, been extensively documented by social psychologists; see Batson, 1998).

PSYCHOMETRIC APPROACHES TO LOVE

As we have discussed, theorists interested in developing love classification systems often rely heavily on earlier discourse and literature dealing with the topic. Recognizing the limitations of this approach, however, several researchers also have adopted a **psychometric approach**, attempting to identify the dimensions that underlie the reported experiences of individuals involved in love relationships (usually through cluster analysis, factor analysis, or other statistical techniques). The assumption of this approach is that identification of the common elements in the actual love experiences of persons in ongoing relationships provides an effective way of distinguishing between love types.

Sternberg's Triangular Theory of Love

On the basis of previous social psychological theory and research on love as well as factor analysis of the self-reported experiences of men and women in dating relationships, psychologist Robert Sternberg (e.g., 1986, 1998; Sternberg & Beall, 1991; Sternberg & Grajek, 1984) suggests that love can be understood in terms of three basic components that can be viewed as a triangle: intimacy, passion, and decision/commitment (see Figure 11.2). The **intimacy component** is primarily emotional or affective in nature and involves feelings of warmth, closeness, connection,

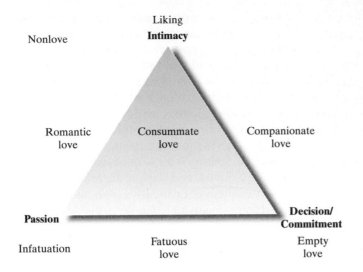

Liking
Intimacy

Nonlove

Romantic
love

Consummate
love

Companionate
love

Passion

**Decision/
Commitment**

Infatuation

Fatuous
love

Empty
love

FIGURE 11.2 Sternberg's triangular model of love. The three components of love are located at each of the vertices of the triangle. Various types of love are produced by different combinations of the three components. *Adapted from Sternberg, "Triangulating Love" (1988), Fig. 6.2, p. 122.*

and bondedness in the love relationship. Signs of intimacy include desiring to promote the welfare of the loved one; experiencing happiness, mutual understanding, and intimate communication with the loved one; having high regard for the loved one; giving and receiving emotional support; being able to count on the loved one in times of need; sharing oneself and one's possessions with the loved one; and valuing the loved one in one's life (Sternberg & Grajek, 1984). The **passion component** is motivational and consists of the drives that are involved in romantic and physical attraction, sexual consummation, and related phenomena. Although Sternberg posited that passion takes the form of sexuality in many relationships, he also suggested that other needs (including the need for affiliation, for dominance over others, and for self-esteem) may contribute to the experience of passion. The **decision/ commitment component** is largely cognitive and consists of both the short-term decision that one individual loves another and the longer-term commitment to maintain that love.

These three components of love are hypothesized to differ with respect to various properties, including stability, conscious controllability, and experiential salience. For example, once present, the emotional intimacy component and the cognitive decision/commitment component are posited to be relatively stable within a close rela-

tionship, whereas the motivational passion component is presumed to be less stable and predictable. Similarly, although most individuals possess some degree of conscious control over the level of commitment they make to a relationship, they generally do not possess much conscious control over the amount of passion they feel.

Sternberg hypothesizes that these three components combine to produce eight different love experiences or love types. *Nonlove* encompasses casual interactions that are characterized by the absence or very low levels of intimacy, passion, and decision/commitment. The majority of our transient, casual relationships can be defined as nonlove. *Liking* refers to friendships that contain intimacy and emotional closeness but no passion or decision/commitment; one might care for another individual without feeling intense passion or a sustained commitment to the relationship. *Infatuation* is described by Sternberg as a "love at first sight" experience that is characterized by high degrees of passion (attraction and psychophysiological arousal) in the absence of any real emotional intimacy and decision/commitment. *Empty love* consists of decision/commitment alone; it is often seen at the end of long-term relationships (or at the beginning of arranged marriages). Here, the partners are committed to each other and to the relationship, but they lack emotional involvement and passionate attraction. *Romantic love* involves high levels of emotional intimacy (feelings of closeness and connection) coupled with physical attraction and related experiences. *Companionate love* is essentially a long-term, stable, and committed friendship that is characterized by a high degree of emotional intimacy, the decision to love the partner, and the commitment to remain in the relationship. Sternberg suggests that this type of love is often seen in long-term marriages in which sexual attraction has faded. Couples who experience *fatuous love* base their commitment to each other on passion in the absence of deep emotional intimacy. These "whirlwind" relationships are typically unstable and at risk for termination. Finally, *consummate love* or "complete" love results from the combination of all three components. According to Sternberg, this is the type of love many individuals strive to attain, particularly those in romantic (dating or marital) relationships. The majority of love relationships will "fit" into one or more categories, or will reflect some amalgamation of categories, because the three basic components of love (that is, intimacy, passion, and decision/commitment) occur in varying degrees.

Lee's Colors of Love Taxonomy

Sociologist John Lee (e.g., 1973, 1977, 1988) used the metaphor of color as the basis for his typology of love, likening each variety of love (or love style) to a primary or secondary color. Like earlier theorists, he drew heavily on literature and early discourse on the nature of love in developing his classification system, and like Sternberg, he employed psychometric techniques (in this case, cluster analysis of love "symptoms" derived from literature and factor analysis of the results of a task in which men and women sorted 1,500 cards containing brief descriptions of love-related events, behaviors, ideas, or emotions to describe their own individual "love stories"). The results of Lee's analysis eventually produced a typology containing six styles or colors of love, each with characteristic features (Figure 11.3).

Lee posits the existence of three primary love styles. The first, *eros*, is an intensely emotional experience whose most typical symptom is an immediate and powerful attraction to the beloved individual. The erotic lover is "turned on" by a particular physical type, is prone to fall instantly and completely in love with a stranger (experiences "love at first sight"), rapidly becomes preoccupied with pleasant thoughts about that individual, feels an intense need for daily contact with the beloved, and wishes the relationship to remain exclusive. Erotic love also has a strong sexual component; for example, not only does the erotic style of loving always begin with a strong physical attraction, but the erotic lover usually seeks some form of sexual involvement early in the relationship. *Storge* is the second primary love color. Described by Lee (1977) as "love without fever or folly" (p. 77), storge resembles Lewis's concept of affection and Fromm's notion of brotherly love in that it is stable and is based on a solid foundation of trust, respect, and friendship. Indeed, the typical storgic lover views and treats

Love Style	Characteristic Features
Primary	
Eros	Exclusivity, sexuality, sudden onset, cognitive preoccupation
Storge	Exclusivity, durability, affection, commitment, slow onset/growth
Ludus	Nonexclusive (pluralistic), absence of commitment, emotional control
Secondary	
Pragma	Compatibility, emotional control
Mania	Sudden onset, cognitive preoccupation, jealousy, possessiveness, physical distress
Agape	Universal, caring, altruism

Additional combinations are possible.

FIGURE 11.3 Lee's colors of love typology. Lee (e.g., 1973, 1988) based his love taxonomy on an analogy to the color wheel. He suggested that three primary love styles or colors existed, each of which could be combined to form three secondary varieties of love. *From J.A. Lee, The Psichology of Love (New Haven, CT: Yale University Press, 1988). Reprinted by permission of Yale University Press.*

the partner as an "old friend," does not experience the intense emotions or physical attraction to the partner associated with erotic love, prefers to talk about and engage in shared interests with the partner rather than to express direct feelings, is shy about sex, and tends to demonstrate his or her affection in nonsexual ways. The third primary color of love is *ludus*. The ludic lover views love as a game, to be played with skill and often with several partners simultaneously. Commitment is antithetical to ludus. Ludic lovers enjoy a variety of physical types, avoid seeing the partner too often, believe that lies and deception are justified, expect the partner to remain in control of his or her emotions, and view sexual activity as an opportunity for pleasure rather than for intense emotional bonding.

Like the primary colors, the primary love styles can be combined to form secondary colors or styles of love. The three secondary styles identified by Lee (1973) contain features of the primaries, but they also possess their own unique characteristics. *Pragma*, a combination of storge and ludus, is "the love that goes shopping for a suitable mate" (p. 124). The pragmatic lover has a practical outlook to love and seeks a compatible lover. He or she creates a shopping list of features or attributes desired in the partner and will select a mate based on how well that individual fulfills the requirements. Pragmatic love is essentially a faster-acting version of storge that has been quickened by the addition of ludus. *Mania*, the combination of eros and ludus, is another secondary love style. Manic lovers lack the self-confidence associated with eros and the emotional self-control associated with ludus; rather, this obsessive, jealous love style is characterized by self-defeating emotions, desperate attempts to force affection from the beloved, and the inability to trust in and to enjoy any mutuality of feeling the beloved does display. The manic lover is eager, even anxious, to fall in love. He or she begins immediately to imagine a future with the partner, wants to see the partner daily, tries to force the partner to show love and commitment, distrusts the partner's sincerity, and is extremely possessive. The last secondary color of love is *agape*, a combination of eros and storge. Agape is similar to Lewis's concept of charity; it represents an all-giving, selfless love style that implies an obligation to love and care for others without any expectation of reciprocity or reward. This love style is universal in the sense that the typical agapic lover feels that everyone is worthy of love and that loving others is a duty of the mature person. With respect to personal love relationships, agapic lovers will unselfishly devote themselves to the partner, even stepping aside in favor of a rival who seems more likely to meet the partner's needs. Interestingly, although Lee felt that many lovers respected the agapic ideal, he also believed that it did not exist in practice. That is, the give-and-take that characterizes most adult romantic relationships precludes the occurrence of purely altruistic love. Near agapic experiences do, however, characterize some relationships, labeled by Lee as storgic eros.

The Measurement of Love

Not surprisingly, given their psychometric basis, both Sternberg's and Lee's classification systems inspired the development of multi-item scales designed to measure each of the proposed love types or components. Lee's typology has received the most sustained attention in terms of scale development. For example, the Lasswells created a 50-item true–false instrument designed to measure each of the six love styles (Hatkoff & Lasswell, 1977; Lasswell & Lasswell, 1976). This original scale subsequently was revised by Clyde and Susan Hendrick and their colleagues (Hendrick & Hendrick, 1986; Hendrick, Hendrick, Foote, & Slapion-Foote, 1984), who created new items and incorporated a Likert-type response format. A second major revision of the Love Attitudes Scale (LAS) was undertaken several years later, when Hendrick and Hendrick (1990) recrafted the LAS so that all of the items refer to a specific love relationship (as opposed to more general attitudes about love). In addition, they created a shorter, 28-item version of the scale (Hendrick, Hendrick, & Dicke, 1998). Extensive psychometric testing of the original and revised scales with various samples of adult respondents has revealed that each of the six subscales (which presumably assess the six love styles) is systematically distinguishable from the others. For example, six distinct, nonoverlapping dimensions emerge from analyses; the items in each subscale are highly correlated; and the subscales have low intercorrelations with each other. This finding has led researchers to conclude not only that the scales reliably capture the actual love experiences of persons in ongoing relationships but that the theory itself is fundamentally correct and six distinct varieties of love exist.

This conclusion—and the psychometric approach in general—is problematic for several reasons. Certainly the availability of a reliable measurement instrument is essential for the scientist interested in understanding love and identifying its antecedents, correlates, and consequences. However, the use of such instruments also may contribute to a misleading view of love. Lee (1988) did not believe that the existing love style scales could adequately illuminate people's ideological conceptions of love:

> The need to avoid ethnocentrism and ahistoricism in studying love is best resolved by approaching love as a problem of competing ideologies about the optimum arrangement of intimate adult partnering. It is not met, I argue, by limiting one's research to a checklist of attitudinal statements. I have described elsewhere (Lee, 1973, p. 232) my own early experiences in attempting to use Likert scales to measure respondents' experiences in love. Yet much contemporary love research is done this way—including, ironically, some of the validation tests on my typology. Only a very few contemporary students of love (for example, Snead, 1980; Sandor, 1982) have noticed the contradiction in testing an ideological typology of love by an attitude scale. (p. 59)

More important, there is an inherent logical flaw in the process of arguing, for instance, that six distinct love styles exist, developing items to reflect these distinctions, employing statistical techniques designed to produce a pattern of nonoverlapping factors which are then labeled love styles, and finally using this empirical finding to support the original argument that six distinct love styles exist. This procedure is tantamount to arguing that all fish are silver, throwing out one's net and hauling in a catch, systematically discarding the nonsilver ones, and then triumphantly pointing to the remaining fish as evidence that indeed, all fish are silver.

In addition, because the theories themselves are based on self-report data rather than tied to existing theories of psychological functioning, they tend to have a "thrown together" quality and are deficient with regard to specification of the development and mechanisms of love—that is, the origins and consequences of various love types. And finally, these theories arose out of the self-reported experiences of adult men and women involved in romantic relationships (dating, cohabiting, or married), and their associated measurement instruments are designed to focus on these relationships. (For example, respondents are instructed to answer with respect to a current or previous romantic relationship partner.) Thus, these theories are more aptly considered taxonomies of adult (heterosexual) romantic love; they may have little to say about other varieties of love experience.

THE PROTOTYPE APPROACH TO LOVE

Like psychometric theorists, researchers who adopt the **prototype approach** to love rely on empirical methodologies and collect data directly from men and women about their love experiences. Unlike psychometric theorists, however, these researchers typically do not confine their investigations to romantic varieties, and they focus more specifically on people's knowledge and beliefs—their mental representations—of the concept of love.

Eleanor Rosch (e.g., 1973, 1975, 1978), an early pioneer in the use of prototype analysis, argued that natural language concepts could be viewed as having both a vertical and horizontal dimension. The **vertical dimension** reflects the hierarchical organization of concepts, or relations among different levels of concepts. Concepts at one level may be included within or subsumed by those at another, higher level. For example, the set of concepts "mammal" "dog," and "collie" illustrates an abstract-to-concrete hierarchy with superordinate, basic, and subordinate levels. Using the methods originally developed by Rosch, some researchers have investigated the hierarchical structure (vertical organization) of the concept of love. Shaver, Fischer, and their colleagues (e.g., Fischer, Shaver, & Carnochan, 1990; Shaver, Schwartz, Kirson, & O'Connor, 1987) provided evidence that "love" is a basic-level concept contained within the superordinate category of "emotion" and subsuming a variety of subordinate concepts that reflect types or varieties of love such as passion, infatuation, and liking. That is, the majority of individuals consider passion, infatuation, and liking to be types of love, which, in turn, is viewed as a type of (positive) emotion (Figure 11.4).

Natural language concepts also may be examined along a **horizontal dimension**. According to Rosch, this dimension concerns the differentiation of concepts at the same level of inclusiveness (e.g., the dimension on which such subordinate-level concepts as "collie," "German shepherd," and "golden retriever" vary). Rosch suggested that many natural language concepts

or categories have an internal structure whereby individual members are ordered in terms of the degree to which they resemble a prototype. As discussed in Chapter 8, "Cognitive Processes," a prototype is the best, clearest example of the concept (the "doggiest" dog—say, a golden retriever). Individuals presumably decide whether a new item belongs within a particular concept by comparing the item with the concept's prototype. For example, in determining whether or not she is in love with her partner, a woman might compare the feelings, thoughts, and behaviors she has experienced during their time together with her prototype or mental model of "being in love." If what she is experiencing sufficiently matches her prototype, she will be likely to conclude that she is, in fact, in love with her partner.

The prototype approach has been used extensively to explore the horizontal structure of a variety of interpersonal concepts, including love. Fehr and Russell (1991), for example, asked men and women to generate as many types of love as they could in a specified time; then they asked another sample of individuals to rate these love varieties in terms of prototypicality or

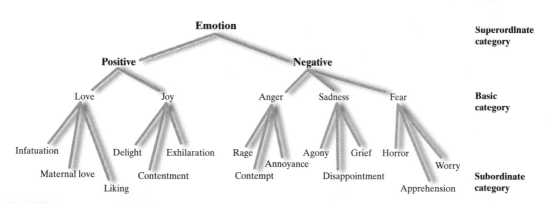

FIGURE 11.4 The hierarchy of love and other emotions. Research conducted by Shaver, Fehr, and their colleagues (e.g., Fehr & Russell, 1991; Shaver, Schwartz, Kirson, & O'Connor, 1987) suggests that love is a basic-level natural language concept contained within the superordinate category "emotion" and subsuming a variety of subordinate concepts that reflect types or varieties of love. Of these varieties, maternal love appears to be viewed as the most prototypical. *Adapted from Shaver, Schwartz, Kirson, and O'Connor, "Emotion Knowledge: Further Exploration of a Prototype Approach" (1987), Fig. 1, p. 1067, and from Fischer, Shaver, and Carnochan, "How Emotions Develop and How They Organize Development" (1990), Fig. 2, p. 90.*

"goodness-of-example." Of the 93 subtypes generated, maternal love was rated as the best or most prototypical example of love, followed by parental love, friendship, sisterly love, romantic love, brotherly love, and familial love (infatuation was considered one of the least prototypical examples of love). The prototypic features (as opposed to types) of love have also been investigated. Fehr (1988) asked one group of participants to list the characteristics of the concept "love" and a second group to rate how central or important each feature was to the concept. Her results, illustrated in Figure 11.5, revealed that love is believed to contain such central features as trust, caring, honesty, friendship, respect, and loyalty. Features considered peripheral or unimportant to the concept of love include "see only the other's good qualities," "butterflies in stomach," "uncertainty," "dependency," and "scary."

Prototype researchers are interested in exploring what people think of when they are asked about love and how they differentiate love from related concepts. Unfortunately, their efforts have met with mixed success. After examining their participants' responses, for example, Fehr and Russell (1991) concluded that "the folk definition of love is complex and provides no sharp boundary between love and other, related experiences" (p. 435). In addition, this approach has not been able to identify how people form their conceptualizations of love, and how these conceptualizations or mental representations influence subsequent interpersonal behavior and outcomes.

Many people who have searched for answers to the mysteries of love have been disappointed by the underdeveloped state and contradictory nature of existing scientific knowledge. Regardless of the method used, and despite literally hundreds of years of more or less disciplined inquiry, scholars disagree over the number of love types that purportedly exist; they disagree about what to call the varieties of love they identify as being "real"; and they have not yet sufficiently specified the origins, characteristic features or observable manifestations, and personal and interpersonal consequences of the various love types (see Kelley, 1983/2002b).

Despite their disagreements, an examination of scholarly discourse and empirically derived classification schemes reveals a few converging themes about the nature of love. First, there is agreement that love is intricately and importantly connected with the quality of individual human life and, consequently, there is agreement that the study of love has merit. Second, most love scholars agree that there are many different kinds of love, which dovetails nicely with people's commonsense or implicit theories of love and their reports of actual love experiences. In other words, love probably is best conceptualized as being composed of some number of subtypes or varieties rather than as one monolithic experience. Third, typologies of love and people's reports of their experiences in romantic relationships seem to suggest that love (or more specifically, adult romantic love) is composed at a minimum of two

---

FIGURE 11.5 The prototype of love. Fehr (1988) surveyed a group of men and women about the features of love. *Copyright © 1988 by the American Psychological Association. Adapted with permission.*

Most Prototypical Features of Love	Least Prototypical Features of Love
Trust	Scary
Caring	Dependency
Honesty	Uncertainty
Friendship	Butterflies in stomach
Respect	Seeing only the other's good qualities
Concern for the other's well-being	Gazing at the other
Loyalty	Euphoria
Commitment	Heart rate increases
Accept the other the way he or she is	Energy
Supportiveness	Thinking about the other all the time

distinct varieties—a version that is intense, emotional, fleeting, and sexually charged, and a version that is durable, slow to develop, and infused with warmth and intimacy. These two types of love (variously called passionate, romantic, or erotic love and companionate, friendship-based, or affectionate love) have assumed special importance in contemporary relationship research, in part because their unique correlates or manifestations have been more clearly specified than have those of other varieties of love, and in part because of their presumed association with personal and species survival (as noted by Lewis [1960]: "Without Eros none of us would have been begotten and without Affection none of us would have been reared" [p. 58]). We turn now to a consideration of these two types of love.

PASSIONATE (ROMANTIC) LOVE

The letters of famous people to their loved ones testify to the importance of passionate love in their lives:

> I hope to hold you in my arms before long, when I shall lavish upon you a million kisses, burning as the equatorial sun.
> —Napoleon Bonaparte to Josephine (Spring 1797)[2]

> Even when I am in bed my thoughts rush to you, my eternally beloved . . . no other woman can ever possess my heart—never—never— . . . Your love has made me both the happiest and the unhappiest of mortals.
> —Ludwig van Beethoven to the "Immortal Beloved" (c. 1811–12)[3]

> Marie! Marie! Oh let me repeat that name a hundred times, a thousand times over; for three days now it has lived within me, oppressed me, set me afire. I am not writing to you, no, I am close beside you. I see you, I hear you. . . . Eternity in your arms. . . . Heaven, hell, all is within you and even more than all. . . . This is to be! To be!!
> —Franz Liszt to Marie d'Agoult (December 1834)[4]

Of all the varieties of love that have been identified, **passionate love** has received the lion's share of attention from theorists and researchers. The focus on this type of love (and the corre-

sponding lack of attention allocated to others) is somewhat justified by the fact that the experience of passionate love appears to be a cross-cultural universal (Jankowiak & Fischer, 1992; Sprecher, Aron, et al., 1994) and has become the sine qua non of the marriage contract in many cultures (e.g., Levine, Sato, Hashimoto, & Verma, 1995; Simpson, Campbell, & Berscheid, 1986). More important, this type of love appears to have several features that differentiate it from other varieties and that appear amenable to empirical investigation.

Early Theoretical Discourse on Passionate Love

A consideration of early theoretical discourse on passionate love suggests that this experience consists of a number of basic features, some characteristic of but not unique to passionate love, and some which may in fact differentiate passionate love from other love varieties. These features include a swift onset, relatively short duration, idealization of and cognitive preoccupation with the beloved and/or the romantic relationship, intense (and often fluctuating) emotions, sexual attraction, and physiological arousal or its concomitants (Figure 11.6). For example, Capellanus (1184/1960) considered emotional distress, mental preoccupation, affectionate feelings, and lust to be characteristic features of both kinds of adult heterosexual love included in his typology. The occurrence of sexual intercourse and a short life span (largely attributed to the satiation of lust via sexual intercourse) were distinguishing attributes of the love type he labeled common love.

Similarly, Krafft-Ebing (1886/1945) argued that sensual love involved idealization of the loved one, a short duration, and an intense sexual attraction that differentiated this type of love from other varieties. He wrote, for example, "Since love implies the presence of sexual desire it can only exist between persons of different sex capable of sexual intercourse. When these conditions are wanting or destroyed it is replaced by friendship" (p. 13). This view is antiquated—it is now

Theorist	Label	Features	Distinguishing Feature?
Capellanus (1184)	Common love	Emotional distress: "suffering"	No
		Cognitive preoccupation: "thinks about [beloved] continually"	No
		Sexual attraction: "desires of the flesh"	No
		Sexual intercourse: "the final act of Venus"	Yes
		Short duration: "quickly fails"	Yes
		Exclusivity: "they keep themselves for each other"; "no one can love two people at the same time"	No
		Affection: "affection of the heart"	No
Krafft-Ebing (1886)	Sensual love	Idealization of beloved: "romantic idealising"	Yes
		Short duration: "never true and lasting"	Yes
		Sexual desire	Yes
James (1890)	Love	Sexual desire: "sexual appetite"	Yes
		Exclusivity: "the direction of the sexual instinct towards one individual tends to inhibit its application to other individuals"	Yes
H. Ellis (1897–1928, 1933)	Sexual love	Sexual desire: "lust"	Yes
		Affection: "friendship"	No
Freud (1908)	Love-impulse	Sexual desire: "intensity of sensual passion"	Yes
		Affection: "tenderness"	No
A. Ellis (1954)	Romantic love	Sexual desire (thwarted): "sexual teasing and blocking"	Yes
		Exclusivity: "one paramount love object"	Yes
		Idealization of beloved: "over-evaluates and fictionalizes his beloved"	Yes
		Emotional intensity: "goes from one violent passion to another"	Yes
		Short duration: "not sustained by the realities of either living or loving"	Yes
Reik (1944, 1945)	Love	Sexual desire: "sex-urge"	Yes
		Short life span	Yes
		Idealization of beloved	Yes
		Affection	No
Fromm (1960)	Erotic love	Care: "active concern"	No
		Responsibility: "response to the [psychic] needs of another"	No
		Respect: awareness of other's "unique individuality"	No
		Knowledge: empathy, seeing other "in his [her] own terms"	No
		Exclusivity: "restricted to one person"	Yes
		Sexual desire: "desire for physical union"	Yes
Lewis (1960)	Erotic love (Eros)	Exclusivity	Yes
		Sexual desire: "sexual appetite"	Yes
		Cognitive preoccupation: "delighted pre-occupation with the Beloved"	Yes
		(False) idealization of beloved: "delusion"	Yes
		Affection	No
		Short life span: "the most mortal of our loves"	Yes

FIGURE 11.6 Early theoretical statements about passionate love. The labels used by various theorists are noted, along with the characteristic features of this experience and whether each feature is considered unique to the passionate love experience.

acknowledged that passionate love and sexual desire can and do occur within same-sex relationships—but the assertion that sexual desire is one of the primary features of passionate love has been made by many other theorists throughout the past century.

A substantial portion of English physician Havelock Ellis's many-volumed *Studies in the Psychology of Sex* is devoted to an examination of the relationship between love, sex, and marriage. Although his purpose was neither to develop a typology of love nor to discuss passionate love, Ellis nonetheless concluded that the love that frequently occurs between men and women is best viewed as a mixture of lust, or the physiological sexual impulse, and friendship, which includes other impulses of a more tender, affectionate nature (see, for example, 1933/1963, p. 234).

Sigmund Freud, one of Ellis's contemporaries and the founder of psychoanalytic theory, also associated passionate love or what he termed the "love-impulse" (1908/1963, p. 34) with sexual desire. According to psychoanalytic theory, passionate love is produced when the sexual instinct inherent within all individuals manifests itself as a psychical attachment to the current love-object. In other words, passionate love stems from a primitive sexual urge and represents the suppression or sublimation of this sexual instinct. Viewed in this manner, passionate love becomes essentially the same as sexual attraction or desire, reflected or interpreted psychically. Interestingly, Freud later modified his view of this type of love to include an affiliative or affectionate component, ultimately concluding that "to ensure a fully normal attitude in love, two currents of feeling have to unite—we may describe them as the tender, affectionate feelings and the sensual feelings" (1912/1963, p. 59).

The view that sexual desire is a characteristic and distinguishing feature of passionate love is echoed by psychotherapist Albert Ellis in his classic (1954) work, *The American Sexual Tragedy*. Following a thorough examination of the popular mass media of the time as well as a diverting excursion through the personal experiences of colleagues and friends and the free associations and dreams of his clients, he concluded:

All love is not, of course, romantic love. Love itself consists of any kind of more of less intense emotional attraction to or involvement with another. It includes many different types and degrees of affection, such as conjugal love, parental love, familial love, religious love, love of humanity, love of animals, love of things, self-love, sexual love, obsessive-compulsive love, etc. Although *romantic* has become, in our day, virtually a synonym for *loving*, romantic love is actually a special type of love, and has several distinguishing features. (p. 101)

According to Ellis, these distinguishing features include idealization of the beloved, intense and changeable emotions, fragility, exclusivity, and sexual desire. The latter was believed to be the most powerful antecedent of passionate love:

Romantic love, again, is largely based on the sexual teasing and blocking of modern courtship. Its very intensity, to a large part, grows out of the generous promises combined with the niggardly actualities of sex fulfillment which exist during the courtship stages. (p. 113)

Ellis believed that the heady, emotionally volatile, idealized experience of passionate love was far more fleeting than the calm, steady, enduring, domestic love that characterized well-adjusted marital relationships. Indeed, the former was posited to survive only as long as sexual desire was permitted no outlet. Once the urgent pangs of desire were sated via intercourse, Ellis posited that passionate love would perish—"sexual and marital consummation indubitably, in the vast majority of instances, maims, bloodies, and finally kills romanticism until it is deader than—well, yesterday's romance" (p. 116).

Noted love theorist and psychotherapist Theodor Reik would have agreed that passionate love is short-lived and idealistic, but he would have taken issue with the amount of notice given to sexual desire in traditional psychoanalytic discourse. According to Reik (1944, 1945), we fall out of love *not* when we no longer sexually desire our beloved but when the pedestal upon which we have placed that individual inevitably cracks and tumbles to the ground as the result of the numerous disappointments that eventually taint any romantic relationship. Reik theorized that passionate love is much more than the "sex in disguise" (1944, p. 15) or "washed-out sexual urge" (1945, p. 18) so dear to Freudian theory or the thwarted sexual desire posited by Albert Ellis:

That love between men and women is in most cases accompanied by sexual desire has nothing to do with the nature of love itself. A chemist who examines the fusion of two materials will not assert that they are the same or have the same properties. Their affinity does not mean that they are identical or that their formulas are the same. (1945, pp. 101–102)

However, the fact that love and sexual desire are fundamentally different phenomena does not mean that the presence of sexual desire is antithetical to that of passionate love. Although Reik (1944) theorized that the two are not one and the same, he conceded that they frequently coexist and thus may be experienced as one emotion. In fact, he wrote that love stems from the fusion of three distinct drives—sexual desire or the sex-urge, the will to conquer, and affection. It is not clear whether this love of which Reik wrote in 1944 is in fact passionate love or rather some more global construct, but he argued in his 1945 work *Psychology of Sex Relations* that romantic or passionate love was born at a time in our ancestral past when love finally advanced into the realm of sexual expression and that it can therefore be understood as a combination of sexual and tender feelings. Thus, although sexual desire does not constitute passionate love, it nonetheless is intricately linked to, and appears to be a distinguishing feature of, that phenomenon.

Similarly, although existentialist Fromm (1956) also took issue with the original Freudian notion that passionate love is exclusively the expression (or, more accurately, the suppression) of the sexual instinct, sexual desire remains firmly associated with this type of love in his theoretical musings. According to Fromm's typology, erotic love—"the craving for complete fusion, for union with one other person" (pp. 52–53)—shares four common features with all other forms of love; these are care, responsibility, respect, and knowledge. In addition, however, this love type pos-

sesses several distinguishing characteristics, including exclusivity ("completely individual attraction, unique between two specific persons," p. 57) and sexual desire. Because sexual desire is so closely associated with erotic love, Fromm cautioned that many individuals are easily misled to conclude that they are in love with each other when in fact they simply feel sexual desire. We are in love with the objects of our sexual desire only when they are also the objects of our affection.

This theme is echoed by Lewis (1960) in *The Four Loves*. Like other love types, erotic love or the "state which we call 'being in love'" (p. 91) was posited to contain affection. Lewis also concluded, as did Fromm, that passionate love is marked by exclusivity (even possessiveness):

When the two people who thus discover that they are on the same secret road are of different sexes, the friendship which arises between them will very easily pass—may pass in the first half-hour—into erotic love. Indeed, unless they are physically repulsive to each other or unless one or both already loves elsewhere, it is almost certain to do so sooner or later. And conversely, erotic love may lead to Friendship between the lovers. But this, so far from obliterating the distinction between the two loves, puts it in a clearer light. If one who was first, in the deep and full sense, your Friend, is then gradually or suddenly revealed as also your lover you will certainly not want to share the Beloved's erotic love with any third. But you will have no jealousy at all about sharing the Friendship. (p. 67)

Also like Fromm and other early theorists, Lewis believed that erotic love contains a "carnal or animally sexual element" (p. 92) that essentially is an individualized sexual desire directed toward the beloved (as opposed to a more general appetite for sex). And finally, he, too, noted the short-lived or transitory nature of this variety of love:

And all the time the grim joke is that this Eros whose voice seems to speak from the eternal realm is not himself necessarily even permanent. He is notoriously the most mortal of our loves. The world rings with complaints of his fickleness. (p. 113)

It is the transitory nature of desire and passion, coupled with lovers' (unrealistic) beliefs in permanence, that Lewis felt gave erotic love its unique blend of "strength, sweetness, terror and high port" (p. 115).

In sum, the majority of early love theorists conceived of passionate love as a short-lived or fleeting state that is characterized by idealization of the loved one (and often the relationship), preoccupation or obsessive thinking, and intense emotions. In addition, passionate love is viewed as an exclusive rather than an inclusive or generalized experience. That is, unlike lust or brotherly love or charity, which can be experienced as general states without clearly specified objects, passionate love is assumed to be directed at one particular individual and, furthermore, the passionate lover is presumed to be incapable of being in love with more than one individual at any given time. And finally, most theoretical statements include the idea that passionate love contains or is caused by sexual desire (which is often accompanied by other nonsexual, affectionate feelings). Of these attributes, sexual desire, idealization of the beloved and/or the relationship, a short life span, and exclusivity seem to be considered the most distinguishing features of passionate love.

Social Psychological Theories of Passionate Love

As discussed in Chapter 6, social psychologists long had been interested in discovering the determinants of interpersonal attraction. Most believed that if they could identify the causal conditions that produced attraction, they also would have identified the determinants of love. That is, it was assumed that liking another and loving another had the same causes and that these causes simply were more strongly present in the case of love than in the case of liking. That state of affairs changed in the early 1970s, when Berscheid and Hatfield (then Walster; 1974a; Walster & Berscheid, 1971) argued that liking and romantic (passionate) love were different animals altogether, with different antecedents and consequences. They hypothesized that greater amounts of the presumed causes of liking would probably result in a lot of liking—and not necessarily in romantic love. Their classification scheme differentiated companionate love, which *was* believed to be subject to the laws of interpersonal attraction, from romantic love, which seemed to possess different characteristics. Romantic love, for example, appeared to be fragile and short-lived whereas companionate love (and liking) seemed to be more durable.

Of these two varieties of love (and the others that have been proposed), social psychologists have devoted most of their attention to passionate love. Many have attempted to define passionate love and to identify the qualities that distinguish it from other varieties of love (see Hendrick & Hendrick, 1992, 2000; Sternberg & Barnes, 1988). The majority emphasize the intense, idealistic, emotional, sexual, and fleeting nature of this type of love. For example, Dion and Dion (1973) argue that passionate love is an "intense, mysterious, and volatile" (p. 51) experience characterized by such symptoms as daydreaming, sleep difficulties, feelings of euphoria and depression, agitation and restlessness, and decreased ability to concentrate. Similarly, as discussed earlier, Lee (e.g., 1973, 1977) concluded that passionate (or what he termed erotic) love always begins with a strong physical attraction and is associated with cognitive preoccupation and emotional intensity—the erotic lover is "eager to get to know the beloved quickly, intensely—and undressed" (1988, p. 50).

In their original articles, Berscheid and Walster, inspired by Schachter's two-component theory of emotion, offered a two-component theory of love (see Chapter 9, "Affective Processes"). They proposed that passionate love blossoms when an individual is extremely aroused physiologically and when situational or contextual cues indicate that "passionate love" is the appropriate label for that arousal. These theorists suggested that a variety of emotional experiences that are associated with physiological arousal (including fear, rejection, frustration, hatred, excitement, and sexual gratification) are instrumental in producing and enhancing passionate feelings. In addition, like Albert Ellis (1954), Berscheid and Walster posit that sexuality is intricately linked with the experience of passionate love, and that thwarted sexual desire—for example, the sexual challenge provided by "hard to get" individuals—often increases feelings of passionate attraction. More recent conceptualizations provided by these authors and their colleagues (e.g., Berscheid, 1988; Hatfield, 1988; Hatfield & Rapson, 1993; Regan & Berscheid, 1999) continue to emphasize the transitory nature of passionate love and more clearly target sexual desire (as opposed to other sexual phenomena) as an important, and perhaps even necessary, feature of the passionate love experience.

Dorothy Tennov (e.g., 1979, 1998) characterizes "limerence" or the state of being in love as a subjective experience marked by persistent, intrusive thought about the object of passionate desire (called the limerent object or 'LO'), acute longing for reciprocation, mood fluctuations, intense awareness of the LO's actions, fear of rejection, shyness, physical reactions (for example, "heartache"), emotional highs and lows depending on the LO's perceived reciprocity, and idealization of the LO's positive qualities. A particularly important hallmark of limerence is exclusivity. Tennov (1998), like many of the earlier theorists, argues that there can be only one LO at a time, and that once an LO is selected, "limerence cements the reaction and locks the emotional gates against competitors" (p. 86). Although limerence is not the same as sexual attraction, and sexual activity is not enough to satisfy the limerent need, Tennov (1979) strongly believed that sexual feelings are a necessary part of the limerent experience. She wrote:

> I am inclined toward the generalization that sexual attraction is an essential component of limerence. This sexual feeling may be combined with shyness, impotence or some form of sexual dysfunction or disinclination, or with some social unsuitability. But LO, in order to become LO, must stand in relation to the limerent as one for whom the limerent is a potential sex partner. Sexual attraction is not "enough," to be sure. Selection standards for limerence are, according to informants, not identical to those by which "mere" sexual partners are evaluated, and sex is seldom the main focus of limerence. Either the potential for sexual mating is felt to be there, however, or the state described is not limerence. (pp. 24–25)

Tennov (e.g., 1998) suggests that limerence may have a biological basis and may have served an adaptive purpose such as the promotion of pair-bonding during the ancestral past of our species.

Other theorists have also emphasized the biological and/or evolutionary nature of passionate love. For example, Shaver, Hazan, and their colleagues conceptualize passionate love as a biological process that has been designed by evolution to facilitate the attachment between adult sexual partners (e.g., Hazan & Shaver, 1987; Shaver & Hazan, 1988; Shaver, Hazan, & Bradshaw, 1988). These researchers note that the key features of infant–caregiver attachment are remarkably similar to those of adult romantic love. For example, both infants and lovers tend to idealize the other. Infants in early states of development experience the attachment object as powerful, beneficent, and all-knowing, and adults in the throes of passionate love ignore or deny the love object's negative qualities and perceive the love object as powerful, special, all-good, miraculous, and so forth. Both experiences are also exclusive. That is, although an infant can be attached to more than one person at a time, there usually is one key attachment relationship. Similarly, although many adults may experience love toward more than one other person, passionate love tends to occur with only one partner at a time. A third commonality between infant–caregiver attachment and passionate love concerns physical expression; both infants and lovers are focused on maintaining proximity and contact with the desired other, and both engage in behaviors designed to achieve that goal (holding, touching, kissing, clinging, caressing, smiling, and so on). A number of other similarities can be observed between the two experiences. However, the authors also note that passionate love differs from infant–caregiver attachment in two important ways: Not only do adult romantic partners engage in reciprocal caregiving and enjoy a more balanced distribution of power and status, but sexual attraction and sexual behavior are an important part of their experience. Thus, Shaver and colleagues argue that adult romantic love involves the integration of three independent, biologically based behavioral systems:

attachment, caregiving, and sexuality (described as an innate system consisting of a cycle of desire and arousal followed by sexual behavior and orgasm). Although different romantic love relationships involve different mixtures of these components (as in one-sided "crushes" and nonsexual romantic relationships), these researchers contend that prototypical adult passionate love contains all three elements.

Buss (e.g., 1988) also takes an evolutionary approach to passionate love, arguing that the key consequences of this experience center around reproduction. Specifically, he hypothesizes that the acts or behaviors associated with passionate love evolved to serve functions, accomplish tasks, or achieve goals that are linked with reproductive success. These proximate goals or tasks include mate attraction and retention, sexual intimacy, reproduction, resource sharing, and parental investment. In fact, Buss proposes that sexual intimacy is the sine qua non of "heterosexual love," described as the state of being in love. Love acts of sexual intimacy—which include engaging in sexual intercourse, losing one's virginity to the loved one, and being "sexually open" with one's partner—serve to seal the bond between lovers and may result in the conception of offspring.

The Measurement of Passionate Love

Researchers interested in assessing the experience of passionate love and/or investigating the correlates of this experience typically employ single-item self-report measures (for example, asking participants whether they are currently in love with their partner or asking them to rate the quantity or intensity of passionate love they currently feel for their partner) or multi-item scales that have been developed specifically to measure the theoretically important dimensions of passionate love. Several multi-item scales have been created over the years, including measures by Swensen and colleagues (e.g., Swensen, 1961; Swensen & Gilner, 1963); Pam, Plutchik, and Conte (1975); Critelli, Myers, and Loos (1986); Hendrick and Hendrick (1986); and Hatfield and

Sprecher (1986a). Of these various measures, the erotic subscale of the Love Attitudes Scale developed by Hendrick and Hendrick (1986) and the Passionate Love Scale developed by Elaine Hatfield and Susan Sprecher (1986a) are the most commonly utilized and most closely tied to theoretical discourse.

The Passionate Love Scale represents perhaps the most reliable and valid measure of passionate love currently available. Drawing on past theoretical conceptualizations, previously developed measures, and in-depth personal interviews, Hatfield and Sprecher crafted a series of items designed to assess the cognitive, emotional, and behavioral components of the passionate love experience. Subsequent administration and revision of this original set of items resulted in a 30-item scale that reliably discriminates between feelings of passionate love versus other types of love—for example, companionate love. This scale is reproduced in Figure 11.7.

Research on the Nature of Passionate Love

Some of the theoretical suppositions we considered earlier have received empirical support. Passionate love does appear to be relatively fragile, or at least to be less durable than other varieties of love. For example, with a sample of 197 couples, Sprecher and Regan (1998) examined whether the number of months that each couple had been dating was related to the amount of passionate love the partners reportedly felt for each other (assessed with a single-item measure and with a modified version of the Passionate Love Scale). The results provided evidence that passionate love is indeed related to relationship duration; the longer partners had been together, the lower their passionate love scores (also see Hatfield, Traupmann, & Sprecher, 1984). In addition, research conducted with dating couples reveals that idealization plays a role in the experience of passionate love. As discussed in Chapter 7, "Relationship Growth and Maintenance," men and women often perceive their romantic partners and their relationships in an excessively positive and idealistic light, and this

Instructions

We would like to know how you feel when you are *passionately* in love with someone. Please think of the person whom you love most passionately right now. If you are not in love *right now*, please think of the last person with whom you were in love. If you have never been in love, think of the person you came closest to caring for in that way. Try to tell us how you felt at the time when your feelings were the most intense.

Response scale

1	2	3	4	5	6	7	8	9
Not at all true				Moderately true				Definitely true

Items

1. Since I've been involved with _____, my emotions have been on a roller coaster.
2. I would feel deep despair if _____ left me.
3. Sometimes my body trembles with excitement at the sight of _____.
4. I take delight in studying the movements and angles of _____'s body.
5. Sometimes I can't control my thoughts; they are obsessively on _____.
6. I feel happy when I am doing something to make _____ happy.
7. I would rather be with _____ than with anyone else.
8. I'd get jealous if I thought _____ were falling in love with someone else.
9. No one else could love _____ like I do.
10. I yearn to know all about _____.
11. I want _____ —physically, emotionally, mentally.
12. I will love _____ forever.
13. I melt when looking deeply into _____'s eyes.
14. I have an endless appetite for affection from _____.
15. For me, _____ is the perfect romantic partner.
16. _____ is the person who can make me feel the happiest.
17. I sense my body responding when _____ touches me.
18. I feel tender toward _____.
19. _____ always seems to be on my mind.
20. If I were separated from _____ for a long time, I would feel intensely lonely.
21. I sometimes find it difficult to concentrate on work because thoughts of _____ occupy my mind.
22. I want _____ to know me—my thoughts, my fears, and my hopes.
23. Knowing that _____ cares about me makes me feel complete.
24. I eagerly look for signs indicating _____'s desire for me.
25. If _____ were going through a difficult time, I would put away my own concerns to help him/her out.
26. _____ can make me feel effervescent and bubbly.
27. In the presence of _____, I yearn to touch and be touched.
28. An existence without _____ would be dark and dismal.
29. I possess a powerful attraction for _____.
30. I get extremely depressed when things don't go right in my relationship with _____.

FIGURE 11.7 The Passionate Love Scale. *Reprinted from Hatfield, E. & and Sprecher, S., "Measuring Passionate Love in Intimate Relationships," The Journal of Adolescence, 9, pp. 383–410, Copyright 1986, with permission from Elsevier.*

tendency is associated with—and, more important, predicts subsequent—relationship satisfaction (Fletcher & Simpson, 2000; Murray & Holmes, 1997; Murray, Holmes, & Griffin, 1996; also see Knee, Nanayakkara, Vietor, Neighbors, & Patrick, 2001).

The notion that sexual desire is associated with, and may be a distinguishing feature of, passionate love has garnered the most empirical support. Certainly people *believe* that sexual attraction is an essential component of the state of being in love. When Ridge and Berscheid

(1989) asked a sample of undergraduates whether they thought that there was a difference between the experience of being in love with and that of loving another person, almost all (87%) emphatically claimed that there indeed was a difference between the two experiences. In addition, when asked to specify the nature of that difference, sexual attraction was listed as a key distinguishing feature: Participants were much more likely to cite sexual desire as descriptive of the "in love" than of the "loving" experience.

Similar results were reported by Regan, Kocan, and Whitlock (1998), who conducted a prototype analysis of the concept of passionate love (further defined for participants as the state of being in love with another person). Participants in that study were asked to list in a free response format all of the features they considered to be characteristic or prototypical of the state of "being in love." Out of 119 spontaneously generated features, sexual desire received the second-highest frequency rating (65.8%; trust was first, cited by 80% of respondents). In other words, when thinking of passionate love, two-thirds of the participants automatically thought of sexual desire. In addition, this feature was viewed as more important to the passionate love concept than behavioral sexual events, including caresses (cited by only 1.7% of participants), kissing (cited by 10%), and sexual activity (cited by 25%). A second study confirmed these results; men and women who received the list of features generated by participants in the first study rated sexual desire as a highly central (important) feature of passionate love.

Two person perception experiments provide additional support for these prototype study results. In the first experiment, Regan (1998a) provided a sample of 60 undergraduate men and women with two self-report questionnaires ostensibly completed by "Rob" and "Nancy," a student couple enrolled at the same university. The members of this couple reported experiencing either no sexual desire or a high amount of sexual desire for each other, and that they were currently engaging in sexual intercourse with each other or were not sexually active. Participants

then estimated the likelihood that the partners experienced passionate love as well as a variety of other relationship phenomena. The results revealed that both men and women believed that dating partners who desire each other sexually are more likely to be in love with one another (and to experience a host of other relationship events) than dating partners who do not desire each other sexually, regardless of their current level of sexual activity.

A second experiment, a conceptual replication of the first, confirmed these results. Here, men and women received information about the members of a heterosexual, dating "student couple" who ostensibly reported that they were currently passionately in love with each other, that they loved each other, or that they liked each other. Participants then estimated the likelihood that the members of the couple experienced sexual desire for each other and the amount of desire that they feel for each other. Analyses revealed that participants perceived partners who were characterized as being passionately in love as more *likely* to experience sexual desire than partners who loved each other or who liked each other. Similarly, partners who were passionately in love were believed to experience a greater *amount* of sexual desire for each other than partners who loved each other or who liked each other. Interestingly, sexual desire was believed to be no more likely in a "loving" relationship than in a "liking" relationship, and greater amounts of sexual desire were not believed to occur in loving relationships than liking relationships. Again, it seems that sexual desire is viewed as an important feature of passionate love relationships—and not of relationships characterized by feelings of love and/or liking.

Research conducted with individuals involved in ongoing romantic relationships, although scarce, also supports the association between sexual desire and passionate love. For example, Berscheid and Meyers (1996) asked a large sample of undergraduate men and women to list the initials of all the people they currently loved, the initials of all those with whom they were currently in love, and the initials of all those toward whom they currently felt sexual attraction or desire. As illustrated in Figure 11.8, 87% of the persons in the "in love" category also were listed in the "sexually desire" category, whereas only 2% of those in the "love" category (and not cross-listed in the "in love" category) were listed in the "sexually desire" category. Thus, the objects of respondents' feelings of passionate love (but not their feelings of love) also tended to be the objects of their desire. In addition, passionate love was a much more exclusive experience than was sexual desire or love; in accord with the theoretical predictions we reviewed earlier, participants generally listed one individual in the "in love" social category and many more in the other two categories. In sum, passionate love was experi-

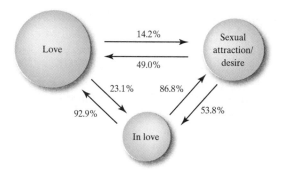

FIGURE 11.8 The social categories of lust, love, and "in love." Meyers and Berscheid (1996) asked a sample of undergraduates to list all the members of three social categories: those people with whom they were in love, those for whom they felt sexual attraction, and those whom they loved. The membership size of each category is approximated by the size of its circle. Respondents named more people in the "love" category than in the others. The arrows represent the probability that a member of one category (tail end of the arrow) is also a member of the second category (head of the arrow). For example, only 14.2% of the people listed in the "love" category were also listed in the "sexual attraction" category. However, 86.8% of the people listed in the "in love" category were also listed in the "sexual attraction" category. *From Meyers and Berscheid, "The Language of Love: The Difference a Preposition Makes" (1996), Fig. 1, p. 355.*

enced for one and only one person, and that person was also an object of sexual desire.

More recently, Regan (2000) asked a sample of heterosexual dating couples to indicate the amount of sexual desire, passionate love (further defined as the state of being "in love with" the partner), liking, and love they currently experienced in their relationships (assessed via single-item measures). She found that sexual desire and passionate love were positively correlated; the more the participants desired their dating partners sexually, the more they were in love with those partners. Similar associations were not found between sexual desire and liking or between sexual desire and loving.

As a whole, these results suggest that passionate love is a qualitatively different experience from other love varieties and that exclusiveness, fragility, idealization of the beloved and, in particular, sexual desire are among its distinguishing features.

The Biochemistry of Passion

Recently, scientists have begun to investigate whether passion, desire, and other phenomena implicated in the experience of being in love have a particular biochemical basis. In particular, they have focused on three possible unique precursors to, or correlates of, this variety of love: pheromones, sex hormones, and neural activity.

Pheromones

Pheromones are chemical secretions that elicit unlearned behavioral or developmental responses from others (Karlson & Lüscher, 1959). Interest in these substances has been fueled by four lines of evidence that provide support for the speculation that a person's scent or odor may stimulate feelings of passion. First, research indicates that pheromones regulate sexual behavior in many nonhuman mammalian species (Azar, 1998; Berliner, Jennings-White, & Lavker, 1991; Cohn, 1994). Second, compounds that have pheromonal properties in pigs (androstenol and androstenone) are found in the urine and sweat of men and, to a lesser extent, women (see Gower &

Ruparelia, 1993). Third, human infants, children, and adults are able to discriminate between other individuals on the basis of olfactory cues (e.g., Cernoch & Porter, 1985; Macfarlane, 1975; Wallace, 1977). Fourth, the human nasal cavity may contain a functional or nonvestigial vomeronasal organ—a structure that, in nonhuman animals, contains pheromone receptors (e.g., Garcia-Velasco & Mondragon, 1991; Kouros-Mehr et al., 2001; Monti-Bloch & Grosser, 1991; Stensaas, Lavker, Monti-Bloch, Grosser, & Berliner, 1991).

Certainly the perfume industry subscribes to the notion that scent is capable of stimulating romantic attraction. A recent search of a retail Internet Web site made by the authors of this book revealed a proliferation of men's and women's fragrances whose names implicitly or explicitly conjure images of passionate love: Amore Eterno, I Love You, Aimez Moi, Desire, Passion, True Love, Allure, Sex Appeal, Fire, Obsession, Romance, and Head Over Heels, to name but a few. Many of these fragrances do, in fact, contain pheromonal substances, albeit derived from nonhuman sources. One group of researchers identified 400 fragrances for women and 350 fragrances for men that contained pheromones (or their synthetic equivalents) from a variety of mammals, including the musk deer, civet cat, beaver, and pig (Berliner et al., 1991). There is little evidence, however, that these substances actually influence human behavior or cause individuals to become passionately attracted to another. For example, an early study revealed that exposure to the pig pheromone androstenol over a 1-month period did not significantly influence women's self-reported feelings of "sexiness" (Benton, 1982; also see Benton & Wastell, 1986), and another study found that men and women who interacted with an opposite-sex person wearing androstenol did not find that person to be more attractive than one wearing a synthetic musk fragrance or no applied odor (Black & Biron, 1982). In addition, at least one research team has found that women report feeling *less* sexual or passionate after exposure to androstenone than when exposed to no odor, a pleasant fruity odor, or an unpleasant fecal odor (Filsinger, Braun, Monte, & Linder, 1984).

Pheromones are species-specific. Thus, it is hardly surprising that exposure to nonhuman pheromones does not directly influence attraction in humans. However, it is possible that these substances have an indirect effect on passionate feelings; that is, a scent or an odor may elicit a pleasant emotional response which, in turn, may increase the likelihood or intensity of attraction to the individual associated with the scent. In addition, it is likely that a particular scent or odor—for example, a specific brand of cologne or perfume—that has been paired repeatedly with an object of passionate love may come to produce a *learned* attraction response. Of course, these types of elicited or learned responses do not constitute a true pheromone reaction.

Some research suggests that a human pheromone in fact may exist. For example, both men and women have odor-producing apocrine glands in the underarm, nipple, and genital areas (Cohn, 1994). These glands become active at puberty, and their secretions may influence some aspects of reproductive physiology. For instance, the menstrual cycles of women who engage in heterosexual sexual activity on a regular basis are more regular than the menstrual cycles of women who do not engage in regular sexual activity, perhaps due to their more frequent exposure to male apocrine gland secretions (e.g., Cutler, Preti, Huggins, Erickson, & Garcia, 1985). Whether the apocrine glands influence other reproductive or sexual responses has yet to be determined.

Other researchers posit that dead skin cells (desquamating horny cells) and the sebum (secretions) from the mouth and lips also may possess pheromonal properties (e.g., Berliner et al., 1991; Nicholson, 1984). For example, Berliner and colleagues (1991) argue that skin cells may produce pheromones and/or process pheromone precursors supplied by the blood. They suggest that these pheromones or pheromone precursors subsequently are stored within the cells, incorporated into cellular structures, or secreted into intercellular material and then are released when the skin cells or the intercellular material is sloughed off into the environment.

As this discussion indicates, researchers are making concerted efforts to identify the chemical and biochemical structure of potential pheromones, the mechanism of pheromone communication between individuals, and the possible impact of pheromones on human emotional responses and social behavior. To date, however, the evidence for a human pheromone that influences romantic attraction remains speculative.

Sex Hormones

The sex hormones (androgens, estrogens, progesterone, and prolactin) constitute a second category of substances targeted by researchers as a possible cause or correlate of desire, passion, and other elements of human attraction. These hormones are produced by several of the various glands that comprise the endocrine system, including the adrenal glands, the pituitary gland, the ovaries in women, and the testes in men. Of the sex hormones, the androgens (masculinizing hormones) seem to be the most strongly implicated in the experience of attraction (for a review, see Regan, 1999). The primary naturally occurring androgens are testosterone, androstenedione, and dehydroepiandrosterone; under normal circumstances, a man's bloodstream contains a much greater concentration of these hormones than does a woman's bloodstream (Naik & Pennington, 1981).

Researchers interested in the relation between the androgens and attraction have concentrated primarily on testosterone, the most potent androgen, and its impact on *sexual* attraction or desire. Testosterone is present in unbound and bound forms in both the blood (serum or plasma) and urine. Nearly all of this hormone is bound to protein and therefore is not available to enter target cells and exert biological effects. The remaining portion, called free, unbound, or bioavailable testosterone, is the fraction available to target tissues. Free testosterone, then, is the hormonal component most useful for assessing androgenic influences on or correlates of human behavior. However, because the portion of testosterone bound to albumin can dissociate to free, active testosterone, it is often difficult for researchers to obtain reliable measurements of free testosterone and consequently to come to reli-

able conclusions about its association with human behavior.

These measurement issues notwithstanding, a growing body of evidence indicates that the experience of sexual attraction is to some extent androgen-dependent in both men and women (for additional discussion, see Davis, 1998). For example, a literature review conducted by Regan and Berscheid (1999) revealed the following conclusions:

■ Levels of free testosterone are significantly correlated with self-reported levels of sexual desire and frequency of sexual thoughts in both men and women. Similarly, decreased feelings of desire have been observed in women who have undergone surgical procedures such as adrenalectomy (removal of the adrenal glands) that result in a sudden and uniform decrease in circulating levels of plasma testosterone.

■ Treatment with synthetic steroids that suppress the synthesis of testosterone and interfere with the activity of the adrenal androgens is associated with diminished sexual desire. For example, men treated with the antiandrogenic substances cyproterone acetate or medroxyprogesterone usually report a reduction in their erotic urges, fantasies, and desires. Marked decreases in desire also have been noted in prostate cancer patients who receive antiandrogenic treatment in combination with medical or surgical castration as a means of completely depriving cancerous cells of the stimulation provided by the adrenal sex steroids. Similarly, although the use of androgen antagonists is generally viewed as a viable form of treatment for androgen-dependent hair and skin problems such as acne, alopecia, hirsutism, and seborrhea, some researchers have noted a loss of passion and desire as one of the substances' various side effects.

■ Not only does a decrease in the level of circulating androgens (whether brought about by surgical procedures or the administration of antiandrogenic steroids) reliably diminish desire in both men and women, but an increase in androgen level yields an associated increase in sexual desire. The administration of exogenous androgens (usually testosterone) has been noted to increase the strength and/or frequency of sexual desire, lust, libido, or passion of (1) men and women complaining of diminished sexual interest; (2) men with hypogonadism or eugonadism, which are conditions caused by various disorders of the endocrine system that result in abnormally low levels of testosterone; and (3) women with androgen deficiency caused by chemotherapy, hysterectomy, or oophorectomy.

These research findings suggest that some specified level of androgens may be necessary (though by no means sufficient) for the experience of sexual attraction. Obviously a great many factors other than circulating levels of sex hormones influence whether one individual will experience lust or attraction for another. Additionally, it is important to remember that sexual desire is merely one element of the passionate love experience. Consequently, the relationship between the sex hormones and passionate love is, at best, an indirect one that is possibly mediated by sexual desire. That is, androgen levels (in particular, testosterone) clearly are associated with the experience of sexual desire, which, in turn, is implicated in the experience of passionate love. In sum, although a series of testosterone injections given to someone with a low level of desire may enhance that person's ability to experience sexual attraction, the impact will be temporary, general (that is, it may not produce attraction to a specific other), and certainly not sufficient to produce the syndrome we call "being in love."

The Brain

Other researchers believe that specific neurotransmitters (electrochemical messages released by neurons or the cells of the nervous system) are associated with the experience of passionate love (e.g., Fisher, 1998, 2000; Hawkes, 1992). Although a number of different types of neurotransmitter exist, the monoamines—in particular, the indoleamine serotonin and the catecholamines dopamine and norepinephrine—have received the most attention due to their demonstrated association with mood and generalized arousal. For example, high levels of serotonin and low levels of norepinephrine and dopamine are commonly seen in individuals diagnosed with clinical depression (Lambert, Johansson, Agren, & Friberg, 2000), and drugs that block serotonin transport and reduce the concentration of synaptic serotonin have been successfully used to treat depression and elevate mood (Schloss & Williams, 1998).

Struck by the similarity between the primary properties of the monoamines and the purported psychophysiological characteristics of passionate love, Helen Fisher (e.g., 1998, 2000) has argued that romantic attraction constitutes a discrete emotion system that is common to all birds and mammals and that is related to a specific constellation of neural correlates:

> The attraction system (termed *passionate love, obsessive love,* or *infatuation* in humans) is characterized by increased energy and focused attention on a preferred mating partner. In humans, attraction is also characterized by feelings of exhilaration, intrusive thinking about the love object, and a craving for emotional union with this partner or potential partner. Attraction is associated primarily with high levels of the catecholamines, dopamine and norepinephrine, and low levels of the indoleamine, serotonin, in the brain. (2000, p. 96)

Fisher's hypothesis about the neurochemistry of romantic attraction was based on surveys of the social science literature on passionate love and the neuroscience literature on monoamines, as well as the implementation of original empirical research on the properties of romantic love (e.g., Mashek, Aron, & Fisher, 2000). Examples of her findings include the following:

■ People who are in love report focusing on specific events or objects associated with the beloved and remembering and musing over things that the beloved said or did. Increased levels of dopamine are associated with heightened attention, and increased levels of norepinephrine are associated with enhanced memory for novel stimuli.
■ People in the throes of intense passion report thinking about the loved one obsessively, and

low levels of serotonin are implicated in the intrusive thinking associated with obsessive–compulsive disorder.

■ Passionate lovers often report feelings of euphoria and exhilaration coupled with heightened energy, loss of appetite, and sleeplessness. These same psychophysical experiences are associated with increased concentrations of dopamine in the brain.

The commonalities observed between the experience of being in love and the psychophysiological effects of the monoamines may, of course, be coincidental. However, a study conducted by Marazziti, Akiskal, Rossi, and Cassano (1999) demonstrated that the serotonin levels in healthy individuals in the early phases of "falling in love" were not different from those of individuals diagnosed with obsessive–compulsive disorder, and, moreover, that the serotonin levels of both of these sets of participants were significantly lower than those of a control group of healthy, not-in-love participants. Although additional research is needed, these findings suggest that the experience of passionate love may be associated with a particular neurochemical milieu.

COMPANIONATE LOVE

The following letters clearly illustrate the importance and enduring nature of companionate love:

> I hope and pray I shall be able to make you happy and secure during my remaining years, and cherish you my darling one as you deserve, and leave you in comfort when my race is run. What it has been to me to live all these years in yr heart and companionship no phrases can convey. Time passes swiftly, but is it not joyous to see how great and growing is the treasure we have gathered together . . .?
> —*Winston Churchill to his wife, Clementine (January 23, 1935)[5]*

> You have been with me constantly, sweetheart. At Kangerdlooksoah I looked repeatedly at Ptarmigan Island and thought of the time we camped there. At Nuuatoksoah I landed where we were. And on the 11th we passed the mouth of Bowdoin Bay in brilliant weather, and as long as I could I kept my eyes on Anniversary Lodge. We have been great chums

> dear. . . . In fancy I kiss your dear eyes and lips and cheeks sweetheart; and dream of you and my children, and my home till I come again. Kiss my babies for me.
> —*Arctic explorer Robert Peary to his wife, Josephine (August 17, 1908)[6]*

Although they have devoted most of their attention to passionate love, social psychologists and other love theorists also have attempted to further elaborate the nature of **companionate love**. Variously described as affectionate love, friendship love, attachment, storge, and conjugal love, companionate love reflects "the affection and tenderness we feel for those with whom our lives are deeply entwined" (Hatfield & Rapson, 1993, p. 9). Krafft-Ebing (1886/1945) called this type of love "true love" and stated that it "is rooted in the recognition of the moral and mental qualities of the beloved person, and is equally ready to share pleasures and sorrows and even to make sacrifices" (p. 12), a conceptualization that resembles Lewis's (1960) definition of affection and the definitions provided by other contemporary theorists (e.g., Brehm, 1985; Sternberg, 1988). Berscheid (1985b) notes that some love theorists conceptualize companionate love as a combination of altruistic love, attachment, and friendship. Companionate love is hypothesized to be characterized by several basic features, including a relatively slow onset, durability, interdependence, and feelings of affection, intimacy, and commitment.

Like passionate love, companionate love is commonly assessed via self-report on single items or multi-item scales. For example, Sternberg (1986) defines companionate love as the combination of high levels of intimacy with high levels of decision/commitment; thus, the items on his scale that ostensibly reflect those components provide one measure of companionate love. The Storge subscale on the LAS also may assess this type of love. Perhaps the most commonly utilized measure of companionate love, however, is the 13-item Love Scale created by Rubin in 1970 (e.g., Fehr, 1994; Hatfield & Rapson, 1990). Other researchers (e.g., Sprecher & Regan, 1998) subsequently have revised the scale by removing several items that reflected a more passionate experience and adding items that assess interpersonal trust.

Research substantiates the notion that companionate love is characterized by the experience of positive affect. Fehr's (1988) participants identified feelings of trust, caring, respect, and friendship as prototypical features of this kind of love. Lamm and Wiesmann (1997) reported similar results when they asked students to identify the difference between loving another person and liking or being in love with that individual. The most common indicator of companionate love (loving) generated by the participants was positive mood (listed by 53%). Distinctive indicators—that is, elements that were listed significantly more frequently for loving than for liking or being in love—included such positive affective experiences as trust (41%), tolerance (21%), and relaxedness or calmness (12%). In a study conducted with dating couples, Sprecher and Regan (1998) found that positive affective experiences such as trust, liking, contentment, satisfaction, and respect were positively correlated with, and that negative affective experiences such as anger, hatred, depression, anxiety, and loneliness were negatively correlated with, the amount of companionate love reported by participants. In addition, not only did companionate lovers feel high degrees of *emotional* intimacy and warmth, but they also reported relatively more feelings of *sexual* intimacy (the ability to communicate openly with the partner about sexuality) than did passionate lovers. Thus, feelings of intimacy—emotional and, perhaps, sexual—are a hallmark of the companionate love experience.

Companionate love also seems to be relatively durable. Although the dating couples in Sprecher and Regan's study reported lower levels of passionate love over time, their companionate love scores did not change as a function of the length of their relationship. Some theorists speculate that companionate love may even grow stronger over time because it is grounded in intimacy processes that require time to develop fully (e.g., Hatfield & Rapson, 1993); others propose that romantic relationships may progress in a linear fashion from passionate love to companionate love (e.g., Coleman, 1977; Safilios-

Rothschild, 1977; Sternberg, 1988). Longitudinal data, however, are needed to adequately address this supposition.

The Biochemistry of Affection

As with passionate love, scientists have begun to explore the biochemical correlates of affection and attachment. Two peptide hormones in particular have come under scrutiny—oxytocin and vasopressin. These substances are released as neurotransmitters in the central nervous system and as hormones from the posterior portion of the pituitary gland, and they have multiple biological functions involving the kidneys and the cardiovascular and reproductive systems. For example, vasopressin increases blood pressure and facilitates the flow of blood through the kidneys, and oxytocin acts on smooth muscle cells and stimulates uterine contractions during childbirth as well as the release of milk during lactation.

A large body of research demonstrates that these hormones are associated with a variety of reproductive and parental caregiving behaviors among nonhuman mammals, including pair-bond formation (see Insel, 1997, 2000; Leckman & Herman, 2002; for additional discussion of the pair-bonding and nurturance functions of oxytocin, see Chapter 10, "Dispositional Influences"). In addition, decreased levels of plasma oxytocin and other alterations in the endocrine oxytocin and vasopressin systems have been observed in children diagnosed with autism, a developmental disorder characterized by severe social impairment and the inability to form interpersonal connections and enduring emotional attachments (Green et al., 2001). Based on these two lines of research, some social scientists have hypothesized that oxytocin and vasopressin may be involved in the ability to form attachments and to experience feelings of companionate love:

> The attachment system (usually termed *companionate love* in humans) is characterized in birds and mammals by mutual territory defense and/or nest building, mutual feeding and grooming, the maintenance of close proximity, separation anxiety, shared parental chores, and other affiliative behaviors. In

humans, attachment is also characterized by feelings of calm, security, social comfort, and emotional union. Attachment is associated primarily with the neuropeptides, oxytocin and vasopressin. This emotion system evolved to motivate individuals to engage in positive social behaviors and/or sustain their affiliative connections long enough to complete species-specific parental duties. (Fisher, 2000, p. 96)

As of yet, however, researchers have not specifically explored whether hormone levels or activity are associated with the social and emotional experiences of healthy adult humans.

PROBLEMATIC ASPECTS OF LOVE

The passionate and companionate love relationships that people form during the course of their lives often are associated with a variety of positive outcomes. However, the experience of love for another individual, particularly if it is unrequited or obsessive, can also prove destructive and problematic. Some of the potentially destructive aspects of love relationships (including sexual jealousy and loss of passion) are discussed in Chapter 12, "Mate Selection and Sex." Here we consider unrequited passionate love, obsession and relational stalking, and mismatched love styles.

Unrequited Passionate Love

Earlier in this chapter we alluded to the possibility that negative emotions are associated more with unrequited passionate love (love that is felt for another who does not return one's affections) than with requited passionate love. As we discussed, requited passionate love for most people appears to be an intense—and overwhelmingly positive—experience, frequently characterized by joy, sharing, intimacy, fulfillment, desire, and other positively valenced feelings and behaviors. Although researchers only recently have begun to explore the dynamics and correlates of unrequited passionate love, their findings suggest that unrequited love is just as strongly associated

as is requited love with emotion—but in this case, the emotional experiences are primarily negative, particularly for the object of unrequited passion.

In one of the first studies to attempt to explore the dynamics of unrequited love, Baumeister, Wotman, and Stillwell (1993) asked 71 unrequited lovers to write autobiographical accounts of their experiences as would-be suitors and rejectors. Their results indicated that unrequited love is a negative experience for both the rejector and the rejected lover (although more for the former than the latter). For example, the majority of the rejectors reported feeling annoyed by the suitor's unwanted advances (51%), feeling uncomfortable and guilty about delivering a rejection message (61%), and experiencing a range of negative emotions, including frustration, anger, and resentment (70%). Baumeister and Wotman (1992) concluded:

> It was hard for the rejector to feel that his or her life had been enriched by this experience. . . . [Rejectors] were forced to respond to a situation they never wanted, and these responses were difficult for them, bringing uncertainty, guilt, aggravation, all of which went for naught. . . . Thus they had plenty to resent and regret. (p. 62)

Unrequited love also proved to be an unpleasant experience for the would-be suitors. Many (44%) reported that the situation caused them to feel intense pain, suffering, and disappointment, jealousy and anger (usually directed at the loved one's romantic partner), and frustration. However, they also reported experiencing a panoply of positive emotional outcomes, including happiness, excitement, and elation at the state of being in love. Unlike the rejectors, over half (53%) of the would-be suitors also looked back upon the entire episode with some degree of positive feeling. By and large, however, unrequited love was a negative experience for both of the individuals involved.

Unfortunately, unrequited love is also a relatively common experience for adolescents and young adults, particularly among men (Hill, Blakemore, & Drumm, 1997). In addition, there is no easy panacea for recovering from romantic rejection. Individuals who find their passionate overtures rebuffed by the ones they love may need to restore and bolster their self-esteem by focusing on their good qualities and/or other positive relationships they currently have or that they have had in the past. Those who reject the romantic advances of another may need to engage in self-justification as a way of coming to terms with their feelings of guilt about causing pain to another individual.

Obsession

A 32-year-old woman interviewed by one of the authors described the effects of a romantic obsession:

> At first I thought it was sort of cute and romantic that he wanted to be with me all the time. He would ask me to give him a detailed account of my day, all the places I went, the people I talked with, the things I did. When I would go to a friend's house or to visit my mom, he would call several times just to see if I was there. I felt flattered that I had a boyfriend who loved me so much. But then it got out of hand. I mean, he wouldn't even let me drive to the store by myself! Sometimes he would even stand really close to me and listen when I was on the phone. After we broke up, he began calling me at home, usually several times a night. He also started calling me at work, which made things difficult for me with my boss. So I stopped taking his calls at work and I changed to an unlisted number at home. I think what really made me realize that I needed to take some action and tell people what was going on was when he started spying on me. One morning, I was standing by the window looking outside and I noticed his car. He was just sitting there, watching me. I have no idea how long he had been there, but it really scared me. I felt trapped and violated.

Many individuals experience unreciprocated passionate or romantic attachment to another person. Although these unrequited love occurrences are for the most part unpleasant, the majority of people manage to successfully negotiate them. In some cases, however, these experiences produce or are associated with obsessive thinking,

psychopathology, and even violent behavior (Meloy, 1989; Mintz, 1980). *Obsessive relational intrusion* (ORI) is defined as "repeated and unwanted pursuit and invasion of one's sense of physical or symbolic privacy by another person, either stranger or acquaintance, who desires and/or presumes an intimate relationship" (Cupach & Spitzberg, 1998, pp. 234–235). Also referred to in the literature as "relational stalking" (Emerson, Ferris, & Gardner, 1998), "domestic stalking" (Dunn, 1999), and "intimate partner stalking" (Tjaden & Thoennes, 2000), ORI involves one person (the pursuer) desiring and actively seeking an intimate relationship with another individual (the target) who does not want this type of relationship or who simply wants no relationship at all.

Survey data reveal that relational stalking is far more common than has been supposed. Among college student samples, for example, rates range from 20% to 30%, with men and women equally at risk for this type of victimization (e.g., Coleman, 1997; Fremouw, Westrup, & Pennypacker, 1997; Spitzberg & Cupach, 1996). As discussed by Spitzberg and Cupach (2002), ORI can be viewed as a warped version of the normal courtship process. For example, the development of most romantic relationships is marked by reciprocal and progressively deeper levels of self-disclosure, intimacy, closeness, and familiarity (see Chapter 7, "Relationship Growth and Maintenance"). In an ORI relationship, however, the self-disclosure that occurs is one-sided, premature, and excessive. Additionally, hyperactive possessiveness takes the place of closeness, and familiarity is created through violations of privacy rather than through the mutual exchanges that characterize normal relationships. In sum:

> ORI relationships are characterized by forms of intimacy that are distorted, exaggerated, accelerated, more intense, and more desperate, compared to the normal prototype for developing intimacy. Although the same dimensions of intimacy that characterize normal relations apply to ORI relations, their manifestations are more forced, fabricated, prematurely escalated, and disinhibited in ORI relations. (p. 206)

The unwanted attention that pursuers inflict on their targets takes a variety of forms. For example, approximately 22% of the individuals who rejected the advances of others in the study of unrequited love by Baumeister and colleagues (1993) reported that their would-be suitors engaged in such unscrupulous behaviors as lying about the nature of the relationship to other people and promising to go out as platonic friends but subsequently using the occasion for romantic overtures. Other individuals report receiving unwanted letters, notes, phone calls, visits, or gifts or being followed or watched by a pursuer (e.g., Herold, Mantle, & Zemitis, 1979; Jason, Reichler, Easton, Neal, & Wilson, 1984; Roscoe, Strouse, & Goodwin, 1994).

To date, the most exhaustive list of ORI behaviors has been developed by Cupach and Spitzberg (1997; Spitzberg & Cupach, 1996, 1998). These researchers argue that ORI behaviors run the gamut from mildly intrusive, invasive, and threatening (receiving unwanted gifts, notes, or messages; being repeatedly asked for a date) to moderately intrusive, invasive, and threatening (reputational sabotage; watching or spying) to extremely intrusive, invasive, and threatening (home invasion; verbal threats; physical and/or sexual assault; property damage). Not surprisingly, the milder forms of ORI behavior are the most frequently experienced. For example, the majority of participants in their studies reported that their pursuer repeatedly called and argued with them (73%), asked them if they were seeing someone romantically (72%), called and hung up without speaking (70%), begged them for another chance (64%), watched or stared at them from a distance (62%), refused to take hints that he or she was not welcome (61%), made exaggerated claims about his or her affection (61%), gossiped or bragged about the relationship (61%), checked up on them via mutual acquaintances (58%), and constantly apologized for past transgressions or wrongs (57%). Less common but significantly more invasive and threatening behaviors included threatening physical harm (30%), following the target from place to place (27%), damaging the

target's property or possessions (26%), exposing himself or herself to the target (26%), forcing the target to engage in sexual behavior (16%), taking photos without the target's knowledge or consent (11%), sending a multitude of email messages (11%), recording conversations without the target's consent (8%), breaking into the target's home or apartment (8%), and sending offensive photographs (5%).

Obsessive relational intrusion can have a variety of consequences for the targeted individual. As illustrated by the work of Spitzberg, Cupach, and others (e.g., Meloy, 1996, Mullen & Pathé, 1994), violent behavior can occur. In addition, victims of ORI often experience a panoply of psychological and emotional reactions, including fear, anxiety, hopelessness, paranoia, depression, self-blame, and hostility (e.g., Herold et al., 1979; Mullen & Pathé, 1994; Spitzberg, Nicastro, & Cousins, 1998; Wallace & Silverman, 1996). Interpersonally, ORI targets may lose the ability to trust other people, and they may avoid and/or otherwise curtail social and work-related activities.

One fundamental question for researchers in this area concerns coping responses to victimization. What responses, for example, are most effective at minimizing or eliminating stalking or intrusive behavior? What strategies can victims use to reduce their risk of negative outcomes in these situations? Unfortunately, there is little systematic empirical work in this area. Some researchers have attempted to identify the constellation of responses typically made by individuals who have been harassed, stalked, or pursued by obsessive relational intruders. The results of these studies suggest that many targets simply ignore the situation or make no response at all. For example, on the basis of their data, Baumeister and his colleagues (1993) concluded that most people lack a clear script for responding to unwanted romantic attention. This "scriptlessness" produces feelings of confusion and self-blame on the part of the target and contributes to a passive avoidance of the would-be lover or the situation. In addition, the researchers reported that those targets who actively rejected the lover often did so in ways that failed to effectively convey the rejection message. More recently, Spitzberg and Cupach (1998) surveyed a group of young adults and identified five general coping categories: (1) direct interaction (have a serious talk with the person, yell at the person); (2) protection or formal coping (obtain a restraining order, call the police); (3) avoidance (ignore the pursuer, avoid eye contact with the person); (4) retaliation (hit the pursuer, ridicule the person); and (5) informal coping (obtain caller ID on the telephone, ask others for advice).

Although the effectiveness of these types of responses is unknown to date, some professionals who work with individuals who have been targeted by stalkers believe that statements and actions that directly and unequivocally convey rejection and/or disinterest are most effective at managing unwanted attention (e.g., De Becker, 1998).

Mismatched Love Styles

Unrequited passion and obsession are not the only potentially problematic outcomes or occurrences associated with loving another individual. There are several other ways in which love relationships can go awry. In particular, it is possible that an individual's general style of loving may influence the quality and even the quantity (i.e., duration or length) of his or her romantic relationships. For example, after interviewing a large sample of men and women, Lee (1973) concluded that some erotic lovers are prone to jealousy and possessiveness; that some ludic lovers may experience guilt at violating social and relational norms about love (e.g., romantic relationships should be monogamous, committed, and long-term); and that some storgic lovers may be perceived as unexciting and passionless by partners who do not share their friendship-based approach to love:

> When a lover whose preferred type of loving is storge becomes involved with a partner whose understanding of true love is some other type, difficulties naturally occur. (p. 80)

Perhaps the most potentially destructive love style, however, is mania—the combination of eros and ludus. Called "demonic love" by Lee, mania is characterized by extreme jealousy, helpless obsession, and unhappiness. Although manic attachments may develop into a more mature and lasting love, this is unusual. It is no wonder, then, that men and women who adopt this approach to love often demonstrate lowered levels of self-esteem (Hendrick & Hendrick, 1986).

In addition, some love styles are related to relationship satisfaction and longevity. For example, Hendrick, Hendrick, and Adler (1988) surveyed 57 dating couples on a variety of interpersonal measures. Their results indicated that an erotic love style predicted overall dyadic adjustment; that is, the more passionately that men and women loved, the greater the level of satisfaction they reported feeling in their relationships. Additional analyses revealed that women's scores on eros, agape, and ludus were related to their partners' self-reported satisfaction. Specifically, women who loved passionately or selflessly tended to have highly satisfied partners, whereas women who adopted a game-playing approach to love had less satisfied partners. Finally, the researchers recontacted a subsample of couples two months after the time of their initial participation and asked them about the status of their relationship. They found that couples who had terminated their relationship originally scored higher on ludus and lower on eros than couples who were still together.

As illustrated in the quotation cited above, Lee (1973) believed that the *pattern* of a couple's love style—that is, whether the partners endorsed the same style of loving—was an important determinant of their interpersonal dynamics and romantic outcomes. However, only a few researchers have actually assessed the love styles of both members of a given sample of couples, and they find a general tendency for individuals to pair with others who share the same love style (e.g., Davis & Latty-Mann, 1987; S. Hendrick et al., 1988; Morrow, Clark, & Brock, 1995). We still know little about the impact of a couple's love style pattern on relationship adjustment.

SUMMARY

In an effort to understand the nature of love, social and behavioral scientists have proposed various typologies or classification schemes that specify types of love. Although there is disagreement about the number and the nature of the different love types, there are several points of rapprochement. Virtually all early and contemporary love theorists agree that love is intricately associated with the quality of human life, that different varieties of love exist, and that at a minimum there are two commonly experienced types of (adult romantic) love—a passionate variety that is intense, emotional, fleeting, and sexually charged and a companionate variety that is durable, intimacy-infused, and stable. These theoretical suppositions are largely supported by empirical research on people's implicit conceptions of love and their reports of their ongoing experiences in love relationships.

It is important to recognize that other types of love undoubtedly exist and are experienced by most people over the course of their lifetimes. For example, Chapter 6 discussed the concept of liking, a variety of interpersonal attraction that is strongly rooted in reciprocity, similarity, and physical attractiveness. Some theorists argue that altruistic love (sometimes called agapic, brotherly, charitable, or communal love) is another distinct variety of love (see Berscheid, 1985b; Kelley, 1983/2002b). However, the unique antecedents and consequences of the many purported love types have yet to be determined or to receive as much empirical attention as have passionate and companionate love.

One of the most important questions that has yet to be answered by love scholars is the temporal course of love. For example, although all forms of love may be experienced in different proportions at one time in the same relationship, certain types may be more characteristic of some stages of relationship development than others (particularly, as noted by Berscheid [1985b], if their determinants are more likely to be in force at some stages than at others). Investigation of this hypothesis requires the collection of longitudinal data and/or recruitment of a broader range of couple types (who differ in length of relationship) than is typical in most love research.

Chapter 12

Mate Selection and Sex

INTRODUCTION

The fact that mating relationships are often referred to by a variety of names—including romantic or love relationships, dating or courtship relationships, cohabiting relationships, reproductive relationships, and spousal or marital relationships—poses problems for researchers. For example, some mating relationships are not characterized by romantic or passionate love, and not all mating relationships result in cohabitation, marriage, or reproduction. To alleviate this conceptual confusion and to classify types of relationships in a way that facilitates insight into their commonalities and differences, sociologists Scanzoni, Polonko, Teachman, and Thompson (1989) argue that **sexually based primary relationships** constitute an exceedingly important—and separate—relationship category whose various forms are united by the fact that *sexual exchanges and activities are viewed by the partners as a legitimate expectation for their relationship* regardless of whether or not they are currently engaging in sexual activity. This definition avoids the com-

plication posed by using such terms as "romantic" or "marital" or "reproductive" to describe mating relationships, and it also allows for the possibility that some mating relationships may not be characterized by high amounts of (or by any) ongoing sexual activity. Some partners do not engage in sexual activity (couples in early stages of dating relationships) or have ceased to engage in sexual activity (spouses in longer-term marriages); although sexual activity is not occurring, the partners and others would view such activity as legitimate and socially acceptable if it were to occur. This chapter explores a number of aspects of human mating, including theories of mating dynamics, empirical research on mate preferences, and three seeming "universals" associated with mate selection (marriage, monogamy, and divorce). We also consider attitudes about the role of sex in mating relationships, the factors that influence sexual attraction between partners, sexual satisfaction and communication in beginning and established mating relationships, and sexual problems that some partners experience.

THEORETICAL APPROACHES TO MATING RELATIONSHIPS

Two broad theoretical frameworks have been used to explain the dynamics of human mating relationships: social context theories and evolutionary theories.

Social Context Theories

Social context theories of mating focus on proximal mechanisms—forces located in the contemporary social, cultural, and historical milieu—that are implicated in mate preference, sex, and other aspects of mating relationships. **Exchange or equity models** of social interaction and relationship development represent one such framework (e.g., Homans, 1961; Murstein, 1970, 1976). These theories, which assume that people are sensitive to the rewards they gain and the costs they incur in social interaction, propose that people will actively attempt to maximize their profits (rewards minus costs) in social interaction by seeking out those persons with whom social interaction will be profitable and avoiding those from whom less profit is anticipated (see Chapter 4, "The Concept of Relationship"). Applied to human mate selection, these theories predict that most men and women will be attracted to, and attempt to pair with, individuals who possess socially desirable characteristics. Insofar as physical attractiveness is highly socially desirable (see Chapter 6, "Birth of a Relationship"), this perspective predicts that physical appearance will be an important determinant of sexual attraction and mate preference. Exchange principles also predict that a person's own assets will determine the extent to which he or she is actually able to obtain his or her mating goals. People who possess a great many desirable characteristics will have a correspondingly greater number of romantic and sexual opportunities and will presumably seek—and be sought after by—equally desirable others. Those who possess fewer desirable (or more undesirable) attributes may wish to establish mating relationships with highly desirable others, but they will be con-strained by their own level of desirability and, as a result, will form liaisons with less desirable persons. As discussed in Chapter 6, the exchange process is presumed to result in matching, or the pairing of individuals of roughly equal social value. There is strong evidence that men and women do, in fact, marry spouses who resemble them on a number of dimensions. Called **assortative mating**, **assortment**, or **homogamy**, the tendency for similar individuals to pairbond has been documented extensively. For example, researchers have found positive correlations between married partners on personality traits, cognitive abilities, physical attractiveness, and demographic attributes (including education, socioeconomic status, race, and ethnicity; Buss, 1985; Murstein, 1980; Vandenburg, 1972).

Other social context theories focus on sex differences in (heterosexual) mating relationships. For example, **social role theory** (e.g., Eagly, 1987; Eagly & Karau, 1991) posits that people develop expectations for their own and others' behavior based on their beliefs about sex-appropriate behavior and attributes. These beliefs and expectations are assumed to arise from the distribution of men and women into different social roles in natural settings; specifically, the sexes are believed to possess attributes suited for the roles each typically occupies. In Western cultures, the male role traditionally has centered on occupational and economic tasks, whereas the female role traditionally has focused on domestic tasks. Consequently, sex differences in social behavior are believed to be caused in part by the tendency of people to behave in a manner consistent with their sex roles. Applied to mating behavior, this principle suggests that, to the extent that people prefer others to behave in accordance with existing sex-role stereotypes, "male" characteristics, attributes, and concerns such as a high-paying job and assertiveness will be valued more by women than by men when considering and selecting a potential mate, and "female" characteristics, attributes, and concerns, such as nurturance and presenting an attractive appearance, will be valued more by men than by women.

Other social forces also act to shape mating behavior, including social learning processes (e.g.,

Hogben & Byrne, 1998; Mischel, 1966) and social and cultural scripts (e.g., Reiss, 1967, 1981, 1986; Simon & Gagnon, 1986). **Sociocultural scripts**, which define and organize social experience and are used to guide and assess behavior in social situations, are developed through social interaction and observational or social learning (Gagnon & Simon, 1973). Like social role theory, social learning and script theories have been used to account for sex differences in mate preference and choice. For example, the different patterns of reinforcement and punishment that men and women receive for their mating behavior, coupled with the existence of normative beliefs about male and female sexuality—for example, that men actively seek sexual activity, or that women associate sex with love and restrict sexual activities to love relationships—may encourage men to hold more positive attitudes than women do toward premarital and extramarital sexual activity.

Media depictions of sex, love, courtship, and marriage constitute a potent source of information for theorists interested in identifying social norms and scripts regarding mating relationships. In an effort to uncover the prevailing sociocultural "rules" of mating that existed in what was then modern-day America, psychotherapist Albert Ellis (1954) conducted an in-depth analysis of a large sample of popular mass media available on January 1, 1950 (for example, all newspapers, plays, songs, radio and television shows that were published, broadcast, or available that day in New York City). Ellis's analysis led him to conclude that social forces teach men and women, and boys and girls, the "folklore" of sex, love, and marriage, including, among other things, the role that physical appearance should play in attraction and mate selection:

> The one thing most consistently emphasized and embellished in today's most popular publications and productions is not, as you might think, sex, nor love, nor marriage. It is, rather, the great American prerequisite to sex, love, and marriage—feminine pulchritude. In innumerable ways, female beauty is thrown in the faces of our readers, viewers, and listeners, and is made to seem a debateless desideratum not only for men to view and women to possess, but for women to ogle as well as to flaunt.

> Indeed, although the implication behind the modern emphasis on feminine loveliness is that it is largely for the attraction and distraction of males, beauty in its own right, beauty for the sake of female appraisal and approval, has become as much the rule as the exception today. (pp. 16–17)

Ellis argued that although there undoubtedly is an innate human predisposition to find certain features or individuals to be more attractive than others, present-day concepts of beauty, along with the pervasive focus on female physical appearance, are strongly rooted in "a consensus of (socially learned) opinion" (p. 27).

In sum, social context theories explain the dynamics of human mating by focusing on processes of exchange that occur between partners, on social learning and the patterns of reinforcement and punishment that individuals receive with respect to mating behavior, and on the scripts and normative expectations about mating that characterize a particular society or culture.

Evolutionary Theories

A second category of theoretical approaches to mating relationships focuses on distal rather than contemporary, proximal mechanisms. **Evolutionary models of human mating** are grounded in the theoretical principles of evolutionary psychology, expressed by Cosmides and Tooby (1997) in this statement:

> The mind is a set of information-processing machines that were designed by natural selection to solve adaptive problems faced by our hunter-gatherer ancestors. (p. 1)

Evolutionary psychologists believe that the human mind evolved through the processes of natural and sexual selection originally articulated by Charles Darwin (1859, 1871) and was designed to solve adaptive problems (the recurrent problems in human evolutionary history that had implications for reproduction and survival). Focusing on the design of the human mind (the neural circuitry we possess that processes information), evolutionary psychologists conceptualize the mind as composed of many specialized processing systems (see Tooby & Cosmides, 1992). One of those specialized processing systems, they believe, is devoted to the problems of mate selection. The neural circuitry specialized for mate selection is theorized to be different from the circuitry we possess for language acquisition or food choice.

Models of human mating based on evolutionary principles thus are oriented toward our species' very distant past and toward the problems that affected the daily existence of our hunter-gatherer forebears. These models consider the ways in which contemporary mating behavior is influenced by psychological mechanisms that were selected for in the human ancestral past because they overcame obstacles to reproduction and enabled our ancestors to make "appropriate" mating decisions. An appropriate mating decision, from an evolutionary perspective, is one that results in a high(er) probability of gene replication and the production of offspring who survive to reach reproductive maturity; an "inappropriate" mating decision is one that produces a low(er) chance of reproductive success for the individual. Thus, an appropriate partner is one who possesses attributes that enhance, and/or who lacks attributes that hinder, the individual's reproductive success (for additional discussion of this point, see Regan, 2002).

A consideration of evolutionary principles suggests that four major types of partner attribute have implications for reproductive success: (1) the potential partner's *physical or genetic fitness*; (2) his or her *emotional fitness*, or willingness to invest in the reproductive partner, the reproductive relationship, and resulting offspring; (3) his or her *relational fitness*, or ability to become exclusively attached to one particular individual and to confine reproductively relevant behaviors to the primary relationship; and (4) his or her *social fitness*, or ability to negotiate the social hierarchy and provide tangible resources to the relational partner and offspring (e.g., Buss & Kenrick, 1998; Cunningham, Druen, & Barbee, 1997; Gangestad & Simpson, 1990; Regan, 2002). Ancestral humans who selected as mates individuals who possessed these features presum-

ably would have enjoyed greater reproductive success than those who selected mates on the basis of other characteristics.

Some evolutionary models highlight certain characteristics more than others. Grounded in principles originally proposed by Bowlby (1969, 1973b), attachment-based evolutionary models (e.g., Cunningham et al., 1997; Miller & Fishkin, 1997; Zeifman & Hazan, 1997) theorize that the human biological design favors the formation of enduring mating relationships. Because the child's period of dependency extends well beyond infancy, these models argue that for both sexes, successful pair-bonding and child rearing depend on the ability to select an ideal attachment figure—a mate who can and will provide sustained social and emotional support. Consequently, both men and women are presumed to be particularly desirous of partners who possess prosocial personality characteristics and interpersonal attributes. (For additional discussion of the pair-bond maintenance function of the attachment system, see Kirkpatrick [1998].)

Other models focus on sex differences in mating behavior. Founded on Trivers's (1972) theory of parental investment, parental investment–based evolutionary models (e.g., Buss & Schmitt, 1993; Kenrick, Sadalla, Groth, & Trost, 1990) posit that women, who invest more direct physiological resources in their offspring than men (by contributing body nutrients during pregnancy and lactation), will be more sensitive to resource limitations and thus particularly attentive to a reproductive partner's social status, which, over evolutionary time, presumably was related to the ability to provide resources in the form of food, material possessions, and physical protection. Men's reproductive success, on the other hand, is assumed to have been more dependent on access to mates who could produce viable offspring; thus, these models propose that men should be relatively more sensitive than women to partner characteristics that reflect reproductive capacity (health and fertility and their presumed observable indices, physical attractiveness and youth). These models also propose that the differential reproductive investment of the sexes will result in differences in selectivity. Because women's parental investment is greater than men's, mating mistakes are theorized to be (or to have been, in the ancestral past) more costly to women than to men: Men stand to lose little more than time and a small amount of easily replenished sperm, but women stand to lose much more time and significant physiological resources. These models consequently posit that women will be less permissive than men with respect to sexual behavior outside a primary mating relationship.

MATE PREFERENCES

Mate preferences are commonly investigated with self-report methodologies, including ranking procedures in which participants order features in terms of their importance or desirability (e.g., Hill, 1945; Regan & Berscheid, 1997), rating procedures in which participants evaluate the importance or desirability of features with Likert-type scales (e.g., Wiederman & Allgeier, 1992), and percentile ranking procedures in which participants indicate how much of a particular characteristic they would like a potential partner to possess relative to other same-sex peers (e.g., Kenrick, Groth, Trost, & Sadalla, 1993). Only a very few researchers have used experimental methods to examine mate preference (e.g., Graziano, Jensen-Campbell, Todd, & Finch, 1997; Townsend & Levy, 1990).

None of these methods is directly tied to the observational base of relationship science (see Chapter 4), and therefore none allows for an exploration of the actual mating choices that occur during ongoing interaction between potential partners. Indeed, some critics of mate preference research contend that because "wanting and getting ain't the same" (van den Berghe, 1992, p. 116; also see Bayer, 1992), self-report methodologies provide little insight into the real world of human mating. In addition, some methods may provide a more accurate picture of mating dynamics than others. Sprecher (1989) conducted an experimental study in which men and women received information about an opposite-

sex target who was presented as highly attractive or unattractive, high or low in earning potential, and high or low in expressiveness. After evaluating the target's desirability as a dating partner, participants then were asked to indicate which of these factors—the target's attractiveness, earning potential, or expressiveness—they believed had influenced their evaluations. Men reported being more influenced than women said they were by the target's physical appearance, but the experimental data revealed that men and women were equally affected by the manipulation: Both men and women overwhelmingly preferred the physically attractive target. Similarly, women reported being more influenced than men said they were by the target's earning potential, but there was no actual sex difference in the impact of that variable on perceptions of the target's dating desirability. These results suggest that the sexes are differentially aware of (or perhaps differentially willing to reveal) the factors that influence their evaluations of potential mates. As a result, studies that rely on self-report data and descriptive paradigms may yield less insight into mating dynamics than studies that utilize data garnered from experimental paradigms or from behavioral observation of mate choice.

Despite the interpretive difficulties associated with self-report measures, most researchers interested in mate preference rely on them. The self-reported mate preference literature is vast and reveals a robust and universal pattern. Both men and women report preferring intelligent, honest, and emotionally stable long-term partners who are attractive and who possess a good sense of humor and an exciting personality (e.g., Buss & Barnes, 1986; Howard, Blumstein, & Schwartz, 1987; Regan, Levin, Sprecher, Christopher, & Cate, 2000). For example, in one of the earliest documented examinations of mate preference, Hill (1945) asked a sample of college students to rank order a list of 18 characteristics in terms of their importance in a dating partner. The most important attributes, according to his participants, were dependable character, emotional stability, a pleasing disposition, and mutual attraction. As illustrated in Figure 12.1, other researchers have since replicated these results using the same or similar lists of features (e.g., Hudson & Henze, 1969; McGinnis, 1958; also see Regan & Berscheid, 1997).

Men and women not only tend to prefer the same set of features when considering a potential mate, but they appear to have similar aversions. Research on undesirable partner attributes by Michael Cunningham, Anita Barbee, and their colleagues (e.g., Cunningham, Barbee, & Druen, 1996; also see Rowatt et al., 1997) indicates that men and women are equally repulsed by individuals who consistently violate social norms such as overimbibing alcohol, gambling often, smoking, and gossiping about others. In addition, they seek to avoid partners who display bad habits such as poor table manners, a loud speaking voice, and a shrill laugh or who appear to be highly oversexed (for example, they look longingly at members of the opposite sex, brag about sexual prowess, or talk often about past relational partners). A more complete list of these undesirable attributes, deemed "social allergens" by the researchers, is provided in Figure 12.2.

In addition to preferring—and disliking—similar features when considering potential long-term partners, men and women appear to be equally discriminating. Kenrick and colleagues

(1993) asked a sample of young adults to use a percentile ranking procedure to indicate their minimum mate selection standards—the lowest amount of various characteristics that they would consider acceptable when selecting a marriage partner. As shown in Figure 12.3, neither men nor women would consider marrying someone unless he or she was above average (the 50th percentile) on almost all attributes. In fact, summed across all characteristics, men's minimally acceptable marriage partner scored at the 56th percentile, and women's minimally acceptable partner scored at the 60th percentile. Similar results were reported by Regan (1998b). When it comes to preferences for a long-term mate, both sexes appear to be highly—and equally—selective.

There are only two attribute categories on which men and women demonstrate consistent differences, namely, physical appearance and social status. When considering a potential date or marriage partner, men tend to emphasize physical attractiveness more than women, and women tend to emphasize social or economic position more than men (for a review of the literature documenting this sex difference, see Feingold, 1992a). For example, Sprecher, Sullivan, and Hatfield (1994) asked a large national sample of men and women to indicate how willing they would be to marry someone who possessed a variety of characteristics. Men reported being less willing

FIGURE 12.1 The stability of mate preferences over time. Mate preferences among adult men and women living in the United States have remained fairly constant. Most people emphasize positive personality attributes and mutual attraction when considering someone for a long-term romantic or marital relationship. *Data from Hill, "Campus Values in Mate-Selection" (1945); Hudson & Henze, "Campus Values in Mate Selection: A Replication" (1969); and McGinnis, "Campus Values in Mate Selection: A Repeat Study" (1958).*

| | Rank Order | | | | | |
| | Men | | | Women | | |
Characteristic	1945	1958	1969	1945	1958	1969
Dependable character	1	1	1	2	1	2
Emotional stability	2	2	3	1	2	1
Pleasing disposition	3	4	4	4	5	4
Mutual attraction	4	3	2	5	6	3
Good health	5	6	9	6	9	10
Desire for home/children	6	5	5	7	3	5
Refinement/neatness	7	8	7	8	7	8
Good cook/housekeeper	8	7	6	16	16	16
Ambition/industriousness	9	9	8	3	4	6
Chastity	10	13	15	10	15	15
Education/intelligence	11	11	10	9	14	7
Sociability	12	12	12	11	11	13
Similar religious background	13	10	14	14	10	11
Good looks	14	15	11	17	18	17
Similar educational background	15	14	13	12	8	9
Favorable social status	16	16	16	15	13	14
Good financial prospect	17	17	18	13	12	12
Similar political background	18	18	17	18	17	18

Dimension 1: Someone who uses his or her appearance to get attention	Dimension 4: Someone who has bad habits

Dimension 1: Someone who uses his or her appearance to get attention
For example:
– dresses in a provocative, seductive manner
– uses a lot of cologne or perfume
– takes a long time to get ready to go out
– is overly concerned with the way he or she looks
– always wears "designer" clothing
– dyes his or her hair
– has had cosmetic surgery to change the way he or she looks
  (a nose job, breast implants, liposuction)

Dimension 2: Someone who is intrusive
For example:
– is competitive with you (at work, in leisure activities, etc.)
– demands that you serve him or her in front of others ("Get me some water")
– comments about your driving
– is a know-it-all
– has to pay your way all the time
– insists on helping you when you have not asked for assistance
– likes to speak in baby-talk to you
– tries to control how you act in public

Dimension 3: Someone who is insensitive
For example:
– puts his or her feet on the furniture
– asks embarrassing personal questions
– leaves his or her things everywhere
– asks for your advice but doesn't follow it
– complains constantly about personal problems
– honks the horn instead of coming to the door
– frequently asks for help or emotional support
– tries to get out of paying his or her own way

Dimension 4: Someone who has bad habits
For example:
– has poor table manners
– has a shrill laugh or talks in a loud voice
– has bad breath
– gets really upset over minor problems
– stands too close or stares inappropriately
– is careless with your things
– constantly plays on the computer

Dimension 5: Someone who is profane or "punk-like"
For example:
– uses a lot of profanity
– has a lot of body piercings (studs in eyebrows, nose, tongue, nipples, etc.)
– has two or more tattoos

Dimension 6: Someone who is oversexed
For example:
– looks longingly at other men or women while out with you
– brags about his or her sexual conquests or skills
– constantly talks about past relationship partners
– has had a lot of previous relationships
– acts "hard to get"

Dimension 7: Someone who violates social norms (rules of conduct)
For example:
– drinks too much alcohol
– gambles frequently
– is a risky or unsafe driver
– cheats at games
– arrives late all the time
– is often angry
– smokes
– gossips about other people
– never helps out around the house
– lies to people

FIGURE 12.2 Social allergens: what people seek to avoid in a long-term mate. Cunningham and his colleagues have identified a number of attributes that render someone undesirable as a romantic partner. *Data from Cunningham, Barbee, and Druen, "Social Allergens and the Reactions That They Produce: Escalation of Annoyance and Disgust in Love and Work" (1996); and Rowatt et al., "Men and Women Are from Earth: Life-span Strategy Dynamics in Mate Choices" (1997).*

than women to marry someone who was "not good looking," whereas women indicated being less willing than men to marry a partner who was "not likely to hold a steady job" and who "would earn less than you." It should be noted, however, that *neither* sex was eager to marry individuals with these attributes. Thus, attractiveness is not *un*important to women and social status is not *un*important to men when considering a potential mate. To the contrary, women as well as men prefer physically attractive partners (and are as affected by a target's attractiveness as men, according to the results of Sprecher's [1989] experiment), and men as well as women tend to prefer mates who are at least equal to

their own current or estimated social status (e.g., Regan, 1998b, 1998c; Kenrick et al., 1993). Appearance and status are important to both sexes, albeit differentially so.

Other variables appear to be more strongly associated with mate preferences than is biological sex. A team of researchers led by Buss (1989) surveyed over 10,000 men and women from a variety of countries and cultures (including Africa, Asia, Eastern Europe, North America, Western Europe, and South America) about their preferences in a spouse. Although men and women in all cultures emphasized positive dispositional attributes such as dependable character and emotional stability, there were robust

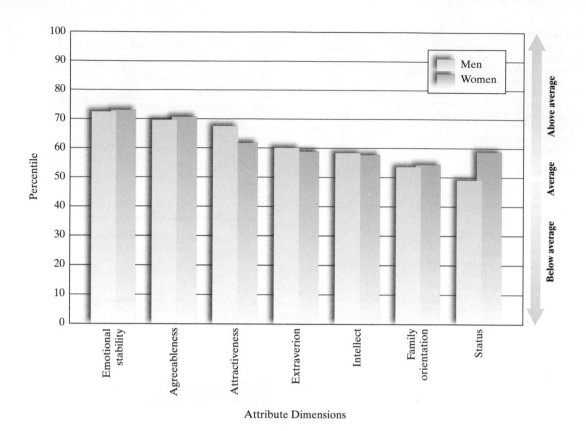

FIGURE 12.3 Minimum standards for a marriage partner. For each attribute dimension, participants were asked to identify the lowest amount they would consider acceptable in a potential marriage partner. Both men and women were quite selective. In general, neither sex was willing to consider a potential partner who was below average (the 50th percentile). In fact, on several attribute dimensions men and women demanded a partner who was significantly *above* average. For example, both sexes desired a marriage partner who was more emotionally stable than over 72% of the population. *Data from Kenrick, Groth, Trost, and Sadalla, "Integrating Evolutionary and Social Exchange Perspectives on Relationships: Effects of Gender, Self-Appraisal, and Involvement Level on Mate Selection Criteria" (1993).*

cross-cultural differences. For example, the characteristics "good housekeeper" and "desire for home and children" were highly desired among respondents from African and South American cultures but were considered unimportant by respondents from North America (the United States and Canada) and the majority of Western European countries. In addition to these cross-cultural differences, some researchers using multicultur-

al samples (ethnically diverse samples drawn from within one country) find that preferences differ as a function of ethnicity. In a study by Sprecher and colleagues (1994), Caucasian women reported significantly less willingness than African-American women to marry a man who lacked a steady job, whereas African-American women were less willing to marry a man who was not good-looking.

Self-Perception and Compromise

With rare exceptions, research on mate preferences has focused on what people *desire* to obtain from real and imagined romantic partners. Yet one of the unfortunate realities of human existence is that, to quote the Rolling Stones, "you can't always get what you want." Simply wanting a particular kind of partner, or one who possesses a particular set of attributes, is no guarantee that one actually will obtain the desired person or features. The ability to accurately perceive what one has to offer a potential mate, and to modify one's desires accordingly, is important, for without it, little actual mating can take place. Individuals who refuse to consider less-than-perfect partners will have fewer mating opportunities than their more flexible counterparts. Evolutionary theories focus almost exclusively on the individual's preferences for attributes that potential partners bring to the mating table, ignoring the person's own attributes. In addition, they consider unmoderated, ideal preferences that operate in the absence of real-life constraints. Social exchange theories, however, have devoted considerable attention to both self-perception and compromise (see Chapter 6). Murstein, for example, argued in his (1970) discussion of the early stages of mate selection that an accurate perception of one's own qualities and what one has to offer a relational partner is extremely important insofar as it prevents one from making costly mating mistakes—vainly seeking a partner who is substantially more desirable than oneself, or squandering one's assets on a much less desirable mate.

A small but growing body of research demonstrates that both self-perception and compromise do, in fact, characterize the process of mate selection. Regan (1998c) asked a sample of undergraduate men and women to identify how much of a set of attributes such as intelligence, attractiveness, and humor they desired in an ideal romantic partner, and then to estimate how much of each attribute they themselves possessed. She found a strong and positive correlation between preferences and self-perceptions. For example, women who thought that they possessed high amounts of attributes related to intellect, interpersonal skill and responsiveness, and social status demanded equally high amounts of these desirable features from a potential romantic partner, whereas women who felt that they possessed lower levels of the same attributes expected correspondingly lower levels from their potential partners. A similar pattern was found for men with respect to attributes related to social status and family orientation; men who perceived themselves as possessing a high amount of social status and a strong "hearth and home" orientation desired a partner who resembled themselves along those dimensions, whereas men who believed that they had less status and who were not as domesticity-minded sought partners with correspondingly lower levels of those attributes. The fact that people link their expectations to their self-evaluations provides support for the basic principles of social exchange and for matching (see Chapter 6).

Further evidence that people can and do alter their mating standards and make compromises and choices was provided by a creative field study conducted by Pennebaker and colleagues (1979). At three preselected times—9 P.M., 10:30 P.M., and midnight (30 minutes before closing)—these researchers entered various bars and taverns located near a college campus and asked a sample of the men and women in there to indicate how attractive they found the other bar patrons present at that time. Participants evaluated both same- and opposite-sex patrons. As closing time neared, the perceived attractiveness of opposite-sex, but not same-sex, bar patrons significantly increased. In other words, the men got handsomer (according to the women) and the women got prettier (according to the men) as closing time approached. Assuming, of course, that the bar patrons did not actually alter their appearance during the evening, and assuming that one goal of the participants was to select a potential mate from the existing array, these results indicate that mating standards are much more flexible and variable than one might be led to assume from the results of self-report preference surveys administered to participants at one point in time, and that mate preferences reflect not only individual desires but the operation of forces (e.g., time) external to the individual.

MATE ATTRACTION AND COURTSHIP

The majority of animal species perform courtship rituals designed to attract and secure the attention of a reproductive partner. Some of these displays are elaborate. For example, the male grouse positions himself on an assembly area (called a *lek*) with other males. Once a female or group of females approaches, he puffs out his chest, raises his white neck feathers, spreads his tail, and lifts his wings high against his body. As the final expression of his ardor, he makes a loud popping noise by suddenly expelling air from a specialized sac in his throat (Figures 12.4 and 12.5). While arguably less colorful, humans also perform various behaviors in the process of courting a potential mate.

FIGURE 12.4 Male black grouse perform courtship displays on a lek.

FIGURE 12.5 A typical male grouse display strut. Air is expelled noisily from the throat sac on the second-to-last step. *From Gould & Gould, Sexual Selection (1989), p. 198.*

Communicating Romantic Attraction in Initial Encounters

Researchers have identified a repertoire of facial expressions, gestures, and other nonverbal behaviors that communicate interest in and/or receptivity to a potential mate. Prolonged eye contact, the "eyebrow flash" (raising and then immediately lowering both eyebrows), smiling, and hand-to-face self-touch occur in flirtation and courtship contexts in a variety of Western and non-Western cultures (e.g., de Weerth & Kalma, 1995; Eibl-Eibesfeldt, 1975, 1989; Moore, 1985, 1995; Shotland & Craig, 1988). For example, McCormick and Jones (1989) observed 80 heterosexual, unmarried dyads interacting in bars, taverns, and cocktail lounges. Each dyad was observed for a period of 15 minutes, during which time their nonverbal behavior was recorded by trained confederates. The results revealed that men and women displayed a number of behaviors designed to increase intimacy or to attract another person. The most common behaviors exhibited by both sexes included moving closer to and gazing at the potential partner, displaying a positive facial expression (smiling or laughing), and grooming (smoothing hair, tightening abdomen, stretching).

Both men and women initiate and engage in flirtation (Perper, 1985), and both sexes make similar attributions about the behaviors that constitute flirting (Abrahams, 1994). However, there are robust sex differences in nonverbal flirtation behavior. For example, when interacting with potential romantic partners, women are more likely than men to smile and to engage in brief, nonintimate touching, whereas men are more likely than women to chin stroke and to engage in more intimate forms of touch (Kolaric & Galambos, 1995; McCormick & Jones, 1989).

Some researchers have investigated the effectiveness of these and other flirting behaviors in eliciting romantic responses from potential mates. Moore (1985) covertly observed a group of single women in four social settings—a local singles bar, a university snack bar, a university library, and a meeting at a university women's center—for a period of 1 hour. She recorded both the number and type of flirting behaviors (smiling, sustained gazing, hair flipping, head tossing) demonstrated by each woman. As illustrated in Figure 12.6, flirting behavior was context-specific; women in the singles bar (the most likely setting in which to meet a mate) engaged in a significantly greater amount of flirting behavior. Their rate of flirtatious display also increased over the hour, whereas it remained invariant in the other three contexts. In addition, these female courtship behaviors were effective at eliciting male romantic interest; regardless of the setting, the women who engaged in the most flirting behavior were also those who were approached most often by men.

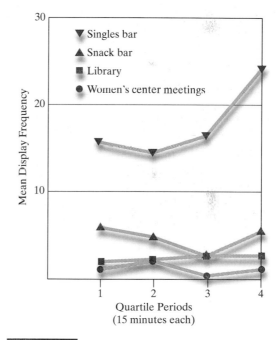

FIGURE 12.6 Nonverbal flirting behavior. Moore calculated the mean number of nonverbal flirting behaviors displayed over 1 hour by women observed in four social contexts. Women in the singles bar (the most likely setting in which to meet a potential partner) engaged in the highest number of flirting displays, and their flirting behavior increased over the observational period. *From Moore, "Nonverbal Courtship Patterns in Women: Context and Consequences" (1985), Fig. 1, p. 245.*

The First Date

After an initial encounter, two people may further their relationship by embarking on an "official" romantic interaction—the first date. Although dating does not occur in some cultures (Cate & Lloyd, 1992), in Western cultures the first date is an important event in the developmental trajectory of romantic relationships (Baxter & Bullis, 1986). Given the existence of social norms and sexual scripts that cast men in the role of initiator and women in the role of receiver, it is not surprising that men ask women out on first dates more than women ask men (McNamara & Grossman, 1991; Spreadbury, 1982) and that both sexes believe that it is more appropriate for a man than for a woman to initiate a date (Green & Sandos, 1983). However, men are likely to respond positively to a woman who initiates a first date (provided they like and want to date her; Muehlenhard & Miller, 1988), and women increasingly are engaging in this behavior (McNamara & Grossman, 1991).

Some researchers have investigated the reasons people elect *not* to pursue dates with others to whom they are attracted. As discussed in Chapter 6, Vorauer and Ratner (1996) identified one of those reasons—an attributional bias such that people attribute their *own* failure to make a romantic overture to fear of rejection but attribute the *other* person's inactivity to lack of interest. The researchers argue that this attributional pattern may prevent potentially rewarding romantic relationships from even starting.

Regardless of their own level of dating experience, by young adulthood most people have developed a general set of expectations about the events that typically take place during a first date (e.g., Rose & Frieze, 1989, 1993). Although men and women generally agree on the sequencing of events that commonly occur on a first date (Pryor & Merluzzi, 1985), heterosexual men often expect greater sexual involvement than do heterosexual women on a first date (Mongeau & Johnson, 1995), and, similarly, homosexual men are more likely than lesbians to view sexual activity as part of a first date (Klinkenberg & Rose, 1994).

The different expectations that the sexes bring to their initial romantic interactions may contribute to miscommunication and potentially negative relational outcomes. For example, a woman who wishes to communicate romantic interest may engage in behavior (smiling, eye contact) that her partner may (mis)perceive as indicative of sexual interest. Indeed, researchers have found that men are more likely than women to interpret a variety of interpersonal cues as signs of another's sexual attraction (e.g., Abbey, 1982; Abbey & Melby, 1986; Zellman & Goodchilds, 1983). Kowalski (1993), for instance, reported that in contrast to women, men imputed a higher desire for sexual intercourse to a woman who was described as having engaged in such common dating behaviors as accepting a man's invitation for a date, having dinner with a man, maintaining eye contact and smiling at him, allowing him to pay for dinner, and complimenting him. These perceptual differences may contribute to misunderstanding between partners in the very early stages of relationship formation.

Beyond the First Date

Once initial contact and interaction with a potential mate have occurred, some romantic relationships progress to more committed forms such as steady dating, cohabitation, and marriage. Qualitative data garnered from free response essays and narratives constitute a rich source of information about the early stages of romantic relationships. For example, Tolhuizen (1989) asked people who were currently (or who had been) involved in a serious dating relationship to describe how they had intensified the relationship and changed it from casual dating to serious and exclusive dating. Analysis of the free response data revealed that the most common strategies ranged from the nonverbal and indirect (over 39% reported simply increasing the frequency and duration of their contact with the partner) to the verbal and direct (29% indicated directly discussing their feelings and the relationship's future with the partner). Similar results were reported by Clark, Shaver, and Abrahams (1999), who asked undergraduates to describe the strategies they used when initiating romantic relationships. Most participants reported interacting with and disclosing to the other person (94% talked in person, 85% spent time, and 54% talked on the phone with the other) and taking direct and forward action (63% asked the other person directly to be their boyfriend/girlfriend). In both studies, men and women also made use of their social networks to promote the relationship. For example, 26% of the participants in Tolhuizen's study reported having sought advice, support, and assistance from friends and others in their social networks about ways to intensify the budding relationship, and about 86% of those in the study by Clark and colleagues similarly reported that third parties had helped them promote their relationships (usually by introducing them to the partner or by going out with the new couple as the relationship began to develop).

Assuming that a romantic relationship survives its initial phases and the two individuals become a "couple," theorists propose that their union will be characterized by increasing amounts of proximity, interaction, self-disclosure, investment, and positive affect. Each of the theories of relationship development discussed in Chapter 7, "Relationship Growth and Maintenance," is applicable to the establishment and progression of mating relationships.

MATE SELECTION

Marriage is a cross-cultural universal. Although not all preferences result in choices and not all courtships culminate in permanent unions, all known human societies endorse and practice some form of long-term mating arrangement between heterosexual partners (Betzig, 1989; Daly & Wilson, 1983) and marriage remains a common event in the life course of most men and women (see Chapter 5, "Varieties of Relationship").

Marriage typically involves economic, social, and reproductive cooperation between the partners, although the emphasis placed on these elements differs across cultures and historical time. The role of individual choice in selecting

the marriage partner also varies widely across societies. Collectivist societies (typically found in Asia, the Middle East, and South America) are group-oriented and limit the amount of freedom an individual has in selection of a marriage partner. As discussed in Chapter 3, "The Development of Relationship Science," these cultures emphasize the integration of individuals into cohesive groups; are characterized by explicit and firm group boundaries; focus on group loyalty, solidarity, and shared activities; and generally require individual members to subordinate their personal goals to those of the group. Marriage is viewed primarily as a vehicle for maintaining social order and for binding families together rather than as a means of fulfilling personal desires (Goodwin, 1999; Hatfield & Rapson, 1996). Given the emphasis placed on social integration and unity, it is not surprising that many collectivist cultures practice (or historically have practiced) arranged marriages in which the selection of a marital partner for an individual is made by family members or matchmakers (Feyisetan & Bankole, 1991; Ingoldsby, 1995). For example, the concept of ie ("stem family") is a core component of contemporary Japanese family life (Kumagai, 1995; Lebra, 1984, 1992). Under the traditional ie system, the primary function of marriage is to continue the family lineage, marriages are considered social contracts, and parents and other family members play a significant role in the selection of a marriage partner.

Individualist cultures (including the United States and Northern and Western Europe) typically allow the individual much greater freedom in the selection of a mate. In these societies, people are loosely connected and autonomous, group boundaries are flexible, and emphasis is placed on the fulfillment of personal goals in marriage and other life pursuits. Feelings of personal compatibility and mutual attraction between the partners, rather than an obligation to meet the needs of families or of society, serve as the primary motivation for marriage. In addition, individuals generally select their own partners rather than rely on their families or matchmakers to do so.

With increasing modernization and the blurring of formerly strong boundaries between cultures, marriage customs in many parts of the world have undergone at least some alteration. One of the most significant changes is a growing emphasis on love as a basis for marriage in collectivist and individualist cultures alike. For example, over 35 years ago in the United States, Kephart (1967) asked a sample of young men and women whether they would marry someone with whom they were not in love if that person possessed all the other qualities they desired in a spouse. Approximately one-third (35%) of the men, and three-fourths (76%) of the women, said yes. However, by the mid-1980s, these numbers had changed and love was seen as an essential prerequisite for marriage by *both* sexes: Simpson, Campbell, and Berscheid (1986) asked the same question of their participants and reported that 86% of the men and 80% of the women now considered love the primary basis for marriage (that is, they would *not* marry someone they did not love even if that person was "perfect" in every other respect).

Men and women living in collectivist cultures are also beginning to view love as an important consideration in marital choice. Levine, Sato, Hashimoto, and Verma (1995) asked a large sample of adults (most of them college students) from 11 countries to respond to the same question asked by Kephart (1967) and Simpson and associates (1986): "If a man/woman had all the qualities you desired, would you marry this person if you were not in love with him/her?" There were significant cultural differences, with adults living in collectivist countries such as India and Pakistan less likely than those in individualist countries such as the United States and England to view love as a necessary prerequisite to marriage. In no country, however, were participants unilaterally willing to marry in the absence of love. For example, the percentage of "no" responses to the question asked was as follows: United States 86%, Brazil 86%, England 84%, Mexico 81%, Australia 80%, Hong Kong 78%, Philippines 64%, Japan 62%, Pakistan 39%, Thailand 34%, and India 24%. Thus, significant numbers of men and women around the world report being unwilling to marry in the absence of love.

The growing importance placed on mutual love and emotional compatibility between partners has had a number of consequences within traditional collectivist cultures, including greater freedom of partner choice by individuals and a decrease in the number of arranged marriages. For example, according to Kumagai (1995), the ratio of arranged (*miai*) to love-based (*renai*) marriages in Japan has shifted dramatically in the past half-century. During World War II, the ratio was approximately 7 to 3: 70% of new marriages were arranged by parents and 30% were love or personal choice matches. By 1988, the ratio had reversed, with the percentage of love marriages at 75% and traditional arranged marriages at around 23% (the remainder reflected a mixture of the two). More recent data collected in the early 1990s showed an even greater decline in the proportion of marriages based on parental choice: In 1991, the proportion of all new marriages in Japan that could be considered arranged was down to 12.7%.

A second change in marriage customs that has occurred in collectivist cultures concerns the manner in which potential mates are found. In India, for example, many marriages continue to be arranged by the respective partners' families. Historically, potential spouses were identified through the recommendation of relatives and close friends, who considered such factors as religion, caste, education, economic background, and appearance when evaluating candidates (Gupta, 1976; Kapadia, 1954). In recent years, however, parents interested in finding a suitable match for their adult children have come to rely less on personal referrals and more on advertisements in matrimonial sections of newspapers or Internet sites. For example, the following advertisements were found on the Web site of *The India Tribune*, a newspaper published in the United States (May 25, 2003):

> Punjabi parents seek beautiful, professional match for their US citizen dentist son, 28, 5'8", very handsome, non-smoker, teetotaler.

> Alliance invited for Gujarati Brahmin boy, BE computer doing MCSE, Indian citizen, 26 years, 5'5" from qualified girl US citizen/green card holder. Caste no bar.

Hindu parents invite correspondence from highly accomplished professionals for their Australian born daughter. Vegetarian, physiotherapist, slim, smart, pretty, talented, 28, 5'2", visiting USA.

Muslim parents invite correspondence for their daughter, 25 years old, 5'5", MBA (hospital management). Green card holder. Looking for green card holder or citizen with equal or higher qualification.

Although the channel through which potential mates are solicited has changed, the family—in Indian culture, at least—is clearly still very much involved in the mate selection process.

Monogamy

Monogamy (a marriage system in which two individuals pair-bond) constitutes another universal aspect of human mating. However, other types of marriage structure have been identified. **Polygamy**, a mating system in which multiple individuals pair-bond, encompasses both polygyny and polyandry. In **polygyny** ("many females"), a man pairs with multiple women. In **polyandry** ("many males"), a woman pairs with multiple men. **Polygynandry** or **cenogamy** (group marriage) is a system in which husbands and wives form a household and share the same spouses (Fisher, 1989; Goodwin, 1999).

Much of the initial discourse on mate selection assumed that early human societies and aboriginal cultures followed none of the aforementioned arrangements but instead practiced a system of **promiscuous mating**. For example, Darwin's contemporaries—among them Morgan (1878), McLennan (1865), and Lubbock (1870)—proposed that in primeval times (and among present-day so-called primitive tribes), monogamy, polygamy, and other forms of male/female pair-bonding were nonexistent and every individual was free to engage in intercourse with whomever he or she chose. Darwin, however, disagreed. On the basis of records of primate behavior and of current customs among both "civilized" and "tribal" societies, Darwin (1871/1981) concluded that our early ancestors were not promiscuous but were either polygamous (that is, polygynous) or monogamous:

> Therefore, if we look far enough back in the stream of time, it is extremely improbable that primeval men and women lived promiscuously together. Judging from the social habits of man as he now exists, and from most savages being polygamists, the most probable view is that primeval man aboriginally lived in small communities, each with as many wives as he could support and obtain, whom he would have jealously guarded against all other men. (p. 362)

Ethnographic data suggest that Darwin was correct—at least partially. One of the most comprehensive sources of cross-cultural data on mating behavior is the *Ethnographic Atlas*, which contains information about aspects of family and social life in over 1,100 human societies. Information in Figure 12.7 on a subset of 862 of these societies compiled by Murdock (1967) reveals that, as Darwin suspected, both polygyny (practiced by roughly 83% of societies) and monogamy (occurring within 16%) are far more common than is polyandry (practiced by less than 1%; e.g., Daly & Wilson, 1983; van den Berghe, 1979; Regan, 2003).

Thus, in all but a small percentage of societies, the predominant form of mating arrangement practiced by women is monogamy; that is, most women marry one man (although that man may have multiple wives). Similarly, although the data appear to suggest that most men practice polygyny, a more accurate interpretation is that most societies *permit* men to marry multiple wives but few men are able to attract more than one partner and sustain more than one mating relationship. As a consequence, the majority of men, like women, ultimately enter into monogamous unions. As noted by Fisher (1992):

> Because of the genetic advantages of polygyny for men and because so many societies permit polygyny, many anthropologists think that harem building is a badge of the human animal. I cannot agree. Certainly it is a secondary *opportunistic* reproductive strategy. But in the vast majority of societies where polygyny is permitted, only about 5 to 10 percent of men actually have several wives simultaneously. Although polygyny is widely discussed, it is much less practiced. (p. 69; emphasis in original)

FIGURE 12.7 Prevalence of mating systems across 862 human societies. These frequencies were tabulated by Regan (2003) from raw data presented in the *Ethnographic Atlas* (Murdock, 1967, pp. 170–231). *From Regan, The Mating Game: A Primer on Love, Sex, and Marriage (2003), Table 13.1, p. 180.*

Mating System	Number and Percentage* of Practicing Societies
Polygyny	713 (82.7)
General, within extended families	202 (23.4)
General, within independent nuclear families	177 (20.5)
Occasional or limited, within independent nuclear families	174 (20.2)
Occasional or limited, within extended families	160 (18.6)
Monogamy	137 (15.9)
Within independent nuclear families	72 (8.4)
Within extended families	65 (7.5)
Polyandry	4 (0.5)
Within independent nuclear families	3 (0.3)
Within extended families	1 (0.1)
Unclassified	8 (0.9)

* Percentages are in parentheses.

Based on their own examination of the cross-cultural literature a decade earlier, Daly and Wilson (1983) drew the same conclusion, stating that "the tendency to keep most productive human matings within nuclear families that are most often monogamous means that our breeding system is effectively only mildly polygynous" (p. 321). Additional cross-cultural research on patterns of sexual and marital behavior confirms the fact that humans are not promiscuous—pair-bonding and cultural restraints on sexual activity are universal (Mackey & Immerman, 2001).

Divorce

The fact that all known cultures sanction marriage and that most men and women living within them enter monogamous unions does not imply that those who marry are sexually faithful or that their unions are permanent. If monogamous marriage is a mating universal, so too is divorce.

There are some cross-cultural commonalities in aspects of divorce. Fisher (1989) examined divorce records for 58 countries from the *Demographic Yearbook* of the United Nations for the years 1947 to 1982. She was interested in three primary questions, including the number of years marriages typically lasted prior to divorce, the average age of the partners when they divorced, and the number of children present at the time of divorce. Her analysis revealed a consistent cross-cultural pattern. The divorce peak, or year of marriage in which the greatest number of divorces occurred, varied across cultures. For example, Bulgarian couples in 1980 tended to divorce very early (after less than 1 year of marriage), Ecuadoran couples in 1974 tended to divorce after 2 years of marriage, and New Zealand couples in 1975 tended to divorce relatively late (after 7 years of marriage). Overall, however, it was clear that divorce tended to occur during the early years of marriage (peaking during the fourth year, the sample mode) and then decreased during subsequent years—a pattern that currently characterizes marriages in the United States, as discussed in Chapter 14, "Intervention and Dissolution."

Fisher also found that across cultures, the modal age category in which divorce occurred for both men and women was 25 to 29, with 57% of women and 50% of men ending their marriages during this period. Calculation of divorce risk (the percentage of men and women who divorced within each age category) revealed that over 75% of people who divorced did so during their 20s (ages 20 to 29). The number of children present at the time of divorce also appears to be pancultural. In 45 societies for which data were available, the modal number of children present when divorce occurred was 0. An examination of the percentage of divorces that occurred among couples with varying numbers of dependent children revealed that 40% of divorces involved couples with no children, 26% involved couples with one dependent child, 18% occurred among couples with two children, and very few divorces (7% or less) involved couples with more than two children. Finally, drawing on several data sources, Fisher identified yet another pancultural aspect of divorce—remarriage. In most societies, the majority of divorced individuals of reproductive age remarry.

Fisher concludes that human mating follows a general pattern of **serial monogamy** or **serial pair-bonding** such that most men and women marry (with the vast majority marrying one partner), divorce, and then remarry during their reproductive years. This pattern, coupled with the findings on cross-cultural aspects of divorce—for example, that divorce peaks after 4 years of marriage, the amount of time it would presumably have taken our ancestors to raise a single dependent child through infancy—suggests that

> serial pairbonding during the female's reproductive years evolved in the hominid lineage as an adaptation to rear highly dependent young through infancy and that this adaptation continues to contribute to the modern cross-cultural pattern of marriage/divorce/remarriage. (pp. 350–351)

We will never know whether the mating behaviors we see around us today represent evolved adaptations designed to overcome obstacles to reproductive success faced by our earliest hominid ancestors or whether they reflect the operation of contemporary social forces. We only know that people living in modern cultures exhibit a mating pattern of monogamous marriage, divorce, and then remarriage.

RELATIONAL SEX

We also know that most sexual activity necessary to an individual's reproductive success takes place in the context of a relationship with another person. The relational context of the act necessary for the survival of our species has been relatively ignored by researchers of human sexuality, who have focused almost exclusively on the sexuality of the individual. As a result, the pages of most sexuality textbooks are filled with precise depictions of human sexual anatomy, detailed lists of the genital and physiological events associated with the human sexual response cycle, statistics that reveal the prevalence of various sexual behaviors, and clinical discussions of sexual psychopathology. Given the history of contemporary sex research, its individualistic orientation is not surprising. Early sex researchers were particularly interested in aberrant sexual behaviors and based their conclusions about human sexuality on clinical case studies of prisoners, medical clients, and mental ward inmates (see, for example, Krafft-Ebing's [1886/1945] *Psychopathia Sexualis*). Their modern counterparts—most notably Kinsey (Kinsey, Pomeroy, & Martin, 1948; Kinsey, Pomeroy, Martin, & Gebhard, 1953) and Masters and Johnson (1966)—eschewed their forefathers' emphasis on deviant sexual behavior but continued to focus on the physiology of sexual response and the sexual practices of individuals isolated from their relational context. Due in large part to the work of these and other pioneering researchers, human sexuality gradually became a legitimate field of scientific inquiry—but one that was, and continues to be, relatively devoid of interpersonal considerations.

Just as sexuality researchers have neglected the relational context of much sexual behavior, relationship researchers have neglected sexuality, perhaps because only a very few of the relationships people form over their lifetimes involve sexuality, and because many sexual responses (including sexual arousal, sexual desire, and masturbatory sexual behaviors) do not necessarily require the presence of another person for their occurrence. Thus, like ships that pass in the night, the fields of human sexuality and close relationships historically have sailed different routes. In the last decade, however, relationship theorists and researchers have begun to recognize that a couple's sexual interactions are an exceedingly important component of their relationship, particularly in a marital relationship, and influence (and are influenced by) nonsexual interactions. As a consequence, there has been growing interest in **relational sex**—sexual responses that occur between partners in established relationships.

Relational sex differs in several ways from other forms of sexuality such as individual sexual responses·and casual sexual encounters between uninvolved persons. For example, although relational sex, individual sexual activity, and casual sex may stem from similar motives (a need for physical release), involve similar processes (physiological arousal), and produce similar outcomes (pleasure), relational sex has interpersonal meanings and consequences that other varieties of sexual experience do not. For example, with rare exceptions such as exhibitionism and voyeurism, the sexual activities in which an individual engages by him- or herself have little impact on others. Similarly, although sexual encounters between strangers or uncommitted individuals may have important consequences for the persons involved, they do not possess the same interpersonal implications as sexual encounters between partners with a relational past, present, and future. Unlike casual sex, sexual activity that occurs between relational partners may be generated by or enhance feelings of love, closeness, and intimacy; may serve to reaffirm the partners' commitment to the relationship and to each other; or may be used by partners to shift the balance of power or equity that exists within the relationship. In addition, some sexual experiences can only occur within an interpersonal context. For example, the occurrence of sexual infidelity and the experience of sexual jealousy presuppose the existence of a primary mating relationship. Sexual events that occur within an ongoing relationship thus have important nonsexual consequences for that relationship, and nonsexual events, in turn, may have an important impact on a couple's sex life.

SEXUAL ATTITUDES

Most people believe that sexuality is implicated in the experience of passionate love, as discussed in Chapter 11, "Love." This and other beliefs about the role of sexuality in mating relationships have been of considerable interest to researchers.

Beliefs About the Role of Sex in Dating Relationships

A large body of research on sexual standards and attitudes reveals that most people view intercourse and other sexual activities as most appropriate when they occur within the context of a committed relationship between partners who feel love for one another. For example, in one of the first empirical investigations of sexual standards, Reiss (1964) reported that men and women from a national probability sample of the U.S. population, as well as students from five high schools and colleges, were increasingly more accepting of premarital sexual intercourse between two people as their relationship became characterized by correspondingly greater amounts of love and commitment—for example, as the relationship progressed from relatively little affection to strong affection, and then to love and engagement. Similar results were reported two decades later by Sprecher, McKinney, Walsh, and Anderson (1988), who found that sexual intercourse between two people was viewed as increasingly acceptable as their relationship stage moved from the first date (28%) to casual dating (41%) to serious dating (72%) to preengagement (77%) and finally to engagement (82%).

Sexual expression in premarital relationships, including casual dating relationships, is becoming more acceptable in the United States and in many other countries. In particular, although men and women continue to view sex as most appropriate when it occurs between committed relational partners who love one another, there is a trend toward greater acceptance of sexual activity in casual dating relationships. Sherwin and Corbett (1985), for example, examined normative expectations about sexual activity in various types of dating relationships on a college campus. Three groups of students—the first surveyed in 1963, the second in 1971, and the third in 1978—were asked to indicate the extent to which various sexual activities generally were expected to play a part in the relationship between casually dating, steadily dating, and engaged couples. Increasingly liberal campus sexual norms among both men and women were evident over the 15-year period. For example, none of the men and women in the 1963 sample expected sexual intercourse to occur in a casual dating relationship; by 1978, however, 17% of the men and 9% of the women viewed intercourse as a normal part of casual dating. A more recent cross-sectional investigation conducted by Rubinson and de Rubertis (1991) yielded similar findings.

Various correlates of attitudes toward premarital sex have been identified. One of the most potent of these is biological sex. Women tend to associate sexual phenomena with love, commitment, and intimacy to a greater degree than do men (e.g., Oliver & Hyde, 1993). For example, Robinson, Balkwell, and Ward (1980) found that when college students were asked to write down their first five responses to the stimulus word "sex," more women (71%) than men (42%) responded with words indicative of love ("love," "loving," "being in love," "loving each other"), and more women (43%) than men (16%) responded with words associated with marriage or commitment ("being engaged," "husband," "wife"). Similarly, when Regan and Berscheid (1996) asked a sample of undergraduate men and women to provide a definition of "sexual desire," women's spontaneous responses contained significantly more references to love and emotional intimacy than did those of men. For example, women said:

Sexual desire is the longing to be emotionally intimate and to express love for another person.

I don't think we can limit sexual desire to only physical pleasures. Sexual desire can also include wanting to be in the company of the person of the opposite sex, desire to be able to build a relationship where the two can share feelings and thoughts, and perhaps simply wanting to be in close proximity of the person of the opposite sex.

Men said:

Wanting someone (opposite sex) in a physical manner. No strings attached. Just for uninhibited sexual intercourse. No relationship necessary.

Sexual desire is someone wanting to have sex with someone else because they find that person physically attractive, and the sex drive drives them to pursue that person.

Women, more than men, viewed sexual desire through an affective and relational lens.

More recently, Roche and Ramsbey (1993) asked a large sample of college students to indicate how appropriate they thought sexual intercourse would be between partners at five different stages of dating: dating with no particular affection (Stage 1), dating with affection but not love (Stage 2), dating and being in love (Stage 3), dating one person only and being in love (Stage 4), and engagement (Stage 5). Equally high numbers of men (76%) and women (67%) believed that sexual intercourse was appropriate between engaged partners, and equally low numbers (3% of the men, 0% of the women) felt that it was acceptable in the complete absence of commitment and affection (Stage 1). However, men and women diverged in their attitudes about the role of sex in relationships in the other stages of development. For example, 17% of the men, compared to only 1% of the women, believed that intercourse was appropriate when dating partners felt affection but not love (Stage 2). Similarly, many more men (44%) than women (15%) felt that sexual intercourse was acceptable when partners were dating and in love (Stage 3). Thus, both sexes viewed intercourse as increasingly acceptable as a dating relationship became characterized by greater amounts of commitment and affection. However, men felt that sex was appropriate at *earlier* relationship stages than did women (in fact, more men than women simply believed that sex was appropriate—regardless of relationship stage).

In addition, both sexes seem to know that women are more likely than men to associate sex with love and intimacy. In a second study, Regan and Berscheid (1995) asked undergraduates to specify the *causes* of male and female sexual desire. Over 40% of the participants stated that love caused women to experience a desire for sexual activity, but fewer than 10% believed that love caused men to want sex. Typical responses included the following:

From a male respondent: Thoughts of love and romance. Women tend to be more romantic. . . . Women do have sexual desires brought on by suggestive surroundings but not to the extent of men. Quiet, romantic surroundings and events seem to play a role in sexual desire.

From a male respondent: Sexual desire in a woman, on the average, is caused by love. . . . A woman tends to be in love when she feels desire or has sexual intercourse.

From a female respondent: Being in love. Sometimes women feel sexual desire for purely physical reasons, but I think that more often it has to do with being in love.

From a female respondent: Often the words "I love you" will cause sexual desire in a woman.

In contrast, participants depicted male sexual desire as much less connected with interpersonal events and affective experiences, and as much more the product of naturally occurring, internal forces (including hormones and "maleness"):

From a male respondent: Men have what I call a "defective gene" on their DNA ladder. This "defective gene" causes sexual desire in men. I label it as defective because it sometimes interferes with a man's way of thinking and decision making. It seems from my experience and listening to friends that guys constantly strive for their sexual desires. These same desires don't seem to be in women, thus, my conclusion that it has something to do with our DNA structure.

From a male respondent: Hormones play a big part, I think. . . . These things cause a wish, longing, or craving to seek out sexual objects.

From a female respondent: I'm not exactly sure what causes sexual desire in a man. I would say just about anything does. . . . In general, any man romantically involved or not tends to always have a sexual desire (or just about always). Anything seems to be able to set men off.

From a female respondent: Simply being male is an automatic cause for sexual desire.

These examples illustrate that both sexes believe that relationship factors—including love, affection, and intimacy—play a relatively more important role in female sexuality than they do in male sexuality.

Although it might be tempting to conclude that women simply do not experience as much sexual interest as do men for their dating partners, or that women desire less sexual involvement than men in general in their romantic relationships, that conclusion would be erroneous. Surveys of adolescents and young adults reveal that both boys *and* girls and men *and* women report thinking about sex often or fairly often (Juhasz, Kaufman, & Meyer, 1986) and experience sexual desire at least once a week (Useche, Villegas, & Alzate, 1990). Thus, it is not that women are less interested than men in becoming sexually involved with their dating partners, but rather that women generally prefer a greater amount of emotional commitment *prior* to sexual involvement. For example, McCabe and Collins (1984) asked men and women to indicate how much sexual activity they desired at three stages of a romantic relationship (first date, after several dates, and when going steady). Although men expressed a desire for a higher level of sexual activity at earlier relationship stages (for example, on the first date and after several dates) than their same-age female counterparts, there was no difference in the desired level of sexual activity between men and women at a later relationship stage (going steady). In other words, both sexes were willing for sexual activity to occur in a romantic relationship, but men wanted this activity to begin earlier in the developmental trajectory of the relationship than did women.

Beliefs About the Role of Sex in Marital Relationships

Attitudes about "normal" or socially sanctioned sexual experiences have garnered much less interest from sexuality researchers than have deviant sexual behavior and socially problematic sexual issues such as teenage pregnancy and sexually transmitted diseases. Thus, far more empirical attention has been devoted to delineating men's and women's beliefs about premarital sexuality than about marital sexuality. In part, this may reflect the pancultural assumption that sexual activity is a normal—even a necessary—

component of marital relationships. Marriage historically has been defined by secular and non-secular forces as a socially sanctioned sexual and reproductive relationship. In Western Europe, for example, medieval theological treatises specified *proles* (children) as one of the essential elements of marriage (Jeay, 1979), and seventeenth-century church doctrine identified sexual intercourse as a marital duty for both spouses (Leites, 1982). Noted sexologist Havelock Ellis (1933/1944) conceptualized marriage as "a sexual relationship entered into with the intention of making it permanent" (p. 256).

It continues to be expected that spouses will engage in sexual activities with each other and, in addition, will refrain from engaging in sexual activities with others. In other words, marital sex is assumed to be exclusive sex. Although sexual infidelity does occur (as we will shortly discuss), most people have strong expectations about marital sexual exclusivity (e.g., Wiederman & Allgeier, 1996) and disapprove of extramarital sexual relationships (e.g., Davis & Smith, 1991; Glenn & Weaver, 1979; Small, 1992). For example, 77% of the respondents in one national survey agreed with the statement "Extramarital sex is always wrong" (Michael, Gagnon, Laumann, & Kolata, 1994). Compared with women, however, men hold more permissive attitudes about extramarital sex (e.g., Oliver & Hyde, 1993; Thompson, 1984) and are more likely to express an interest in having an extramarital sexual relationship (e.g., Buunk & Bakker, 1995; Seal, Agostinelli, & Hannett, 1994).

Views about sexuality in marriage—in particular, the roles of, and relative power accorded to, husband and wife—differ as a function of historical and cultural context. For example, attitudes about the sexual roles of husband and wife have undergone extensive revision in the United States over the past 100 years. In 1896, a popular guide to marriage published in the United States stated:

Usually marriage is consummated within a day or two after the ceremony, but this is gross injustice to the bride. In most cases she is nervous, timid, and exhausted by the duties of preparation for the wedding, and in no way in a condition, either in body or mind, for the vital change which the married relation brings upon her. Many a young husband often lays the foundation of many diseases of the womb and of the nervous system in gratifying his unchecked passions without a proper regard for his wife's exhausted condition. . . . Young husband! Prove your manhood, not by yielding to unbridled lust and cruelty, but by the exhibition of true power in self-control and patience with the helpless being confided to your care! (Jefferis & Nichols, 1896, pp. 202–204)

The authors of this advice manual emphasize that marital sexual activity should be pleasurable for both husband and wife, but they also imply that sexual decisions are the province of the husband: He is the one who must guard against yielding to "unbridled lust"; he is the one who must determine the appropriate time for sexual initiation; and he is the one who must calmly and patiently guide the couple's first and subsequent physical interactions. The belief that the husband controls marital sexual activity has changed in recent years. Weinberg, Swensson, and Hammersmith (1983) analyzed 49 sex manuals published in the United States between 1950 and 1980. During the 1950s and 1960s, writers continued to emphasize differences between male and female sexuality and complementarity in sexual roles, with the husband as sexual teacher and the wife as sexual learner. By the late 1970s, however, both sexes were depicted as autonomous beings in control of their own sexuality, capable (and desirous) of sexual pleasure, and equally able to enact the parts of teacher and learner. In other parts of the world, such as Africa, Central America, and India, however, husbands rather than wives continue to be expected to make the major decisions about the sexual and reproductive aspects of married life (e.g., Bertrand, Makani, Edwards, & Baughman, 1996; Karra, Stark, & Wolf, 1997; Renne, 1997; Villasmil Prieto, 1997).

SEXUAL ATTRACTION

Sexual desire (also called sexual interest or sexual attraction) is associated with the experience of passionate love. As discussed in Chapter 11, descriptive and experimental research demonstrates that most men and women view sexual desire as an important and even essential element of the state of "being in love," and correlational research with dating couples substantiates the prediction that these two experiences (sexual desire and passionate love) are strongly associated with one another. Because of its association with passionate love and other positive interpersonal phenomena such as satisfaction, happiness, and adjustment (Regan, 2000), sexual desire may take on particular significance in initial encounters between potential partners and during very early relationship stages. For example, a person who experiences sexual desire for another individual may assume that he or she is becoming romantically interested in, or even is falling in love with, that other; these feelings, in turn, may prompt the active pursuit of a romantic relationship or propel an existing relationship into a deeper stage of development.

Although medical practitioners and mental health professionals traditionally have focused on intraindividual factors (P causal conditions) associated with sexual attraction, such as age, personality, mental and physical health, and sexual history (including trauma), theorists and researchers from other disciplines have begun to explore other variables that are implicated in this aspect of sexuality, particularly partner factors (O causal conditions). Two of these factors—a potential partner's sex appeal and his or her sexual history or level of prior sexual experience—have received the most attention.

Sex Appeal

The notion that an individual's sexual desirability, or sex appeal, plays an important role in attracting a mate and achieving interpersonal happiness abounds in contemporary Western culture. Indeed, a recent glance at magazine covers revealed the following gems of advice: A woman who wants to attract a man's interest should appear "bedable" (*Cosmopolitan*); boosting one's sex appeal is the only sure-fire way for women to "spark his desire" (*Redbook*); and a virile, sexually appealing man is "what women really want"

(*Men's Fitness*). Research on sex appeal has focused on delineating the specific features that conspire to create this aspect of sexuality. For example, Regan and Berscheid (1995, Study 2) asked a group of men and women to list all the characteristics that would make a man or a woman sexually appealing to others. As illustrated in Figure 12.8, a woman's sex appeal was believed to be primarily a function of appearance (90% of men and women specified this attribute), coupled with such dispositional dimensions as a good overall personality (23%), self-confidence (17%), and intelligence (15%). Male sex appeal was presumed to be a function of a similar constellation of features. Again, appearance was the most frequently mentioned characteristic (76%), demonstrating that the thesis of Ellis's (1954) *American Sexual Tragedy* is still valid. "Sensitivity" or a compassionate, kind disposition (35%), a good overall personality (24%), and a sense of humor (18%) followed appearance. These ancillary attributes are more likely to be attributed to physically attractive persons than to the unattractive, further magnifying the importance of physical attractiveness, as discussed in Chapter 6.

The belief that appearance plays an essential role in romantic attraction and mate choice is not new. For example, Darwin argued that "both sexes, if the females as well as the males were permitted to exert any choice, would have chosen their partners, not for mental charms, or property, or social position, but almost solely from external appearance" (1871/1981, p. 368). Although the effects of facial appearance have been most often investigated (see Chapter 6), other morphological features contribute to overall physical attractiveness and thus to an individual's sexual attractiveness. For example, as discussed in Chapter 6, men prefer and view as more attractive an "hourglass" female figure (e.g., Singh, 1993; Singh & Luis, 1995), whereas women prefer a tapering "V" physique in men (e.g., Lavrakas, 1975; Singh, 1995). General body size also may be an important determinant of sex appeal. Both men and women perceive thinner or normal-weight people of both sexes to be more physically attractive than extremely thin or very overweight individuals (e.g., Lamb, Jackson, Cas-

QUESTION: *What characteristics make a man sexually appealing?*

Men say:

I think a well-built, strong man would cause desire as opposed to a sloppy, overweight guy or a really skinny guy. I think women desire a guy who is open, honest, and is interested in pleasing them, instead of the opposite. I also think a woman desires men who appreciate her sexual appetites/preferences over ones who force their own wishes on her. Physical qualities would probably include muscles, and cleanliness or being well-groomed.

Women like men to be funny and caring. A major thing for women is that they want a man to be sensitive to their needs as women. Physical attractiveness is important to women, although they don't tend to show this as much as men do. I wish I knew more about this question myself—believe me!

Women say:

A great fit body, and nice clothes. This doesn't mean that's all I'm looking for, but to be sexually attracted—yes.

Based on physical characteristics I would say the way a person looks such as his face, eyes, lips, and a well-toned body. A man must be caring, kind, and gentle.

QUESTION: *What characteristics make a woman sexually appealing?*

Men say:

I think men want women to be willing, attractive, and interesting. It makes the desire stronger when he knows she wants the same thing, although not being able to get sex from her sometimes will do the same thing. Physically, I think a desirable woman would be soft, yet athletic, not fat, but not overly thin, with lots of curves and a nice face. A woman who is experienced and enjoys sex is more desirable than either an inexperienced, shy woman or else an overly experienced, "easy" woman.

Her appearance. Nothing else is needed. A man can be with any woman as long as he thinks she looks good. The easiest way to get a man interested in a woman is for his friends to say how good the girl looks. I truly feel that besides the body—no other characteristics are needed.

Women say:

Definitely an attitude that portrays that she wants "it." Flirtation seems to help men become more interested. A confident characteristic that would suggest that she is good at "it." Overall attractiveness (skinny, tall, nice smile).

Could be very thin with long, thin legs, long hair, white teeth. Could be voluptuous—I guess what I'm getting down to is physical attraction (very seldom is it intellectual!).

FIGURE 12.8 Sexually appealing characteristics. Participants were asked to indicate in a free response format all the attributes and characteristics that would make a man or a woman particularly sexually appealing. These samples are typical responses. *From Regan and Berscheid, "Gender Differences in Beliefs About the Causes of Male and Female Sexual Desire" (1995).*

siday, & Priest, 1993; Singh, 1993; Wiggins, Wiggins, & Conger, 1968). Obese persons are perceived to be less sexually appealing than normal-weight individuals, as well as less capable of experiencing sexual desire, attracting a sexual partner, and developing a satisfying sexual relationship (see Regan, 1996).

Sexual History

Virginity or chastity—complete premarital sexual inexperience—long has been lauded as a desirable sexual attribute in Western European cultures, particularly for women. British literary history, for example, is replete with tales of sexually innocent young women struggling to preserve their premarital virginity from brutish men. The chaste heroine in Samuel Richardson's *Pamela or, Virtue Rewarded* (1740/1971) spends much of the novel guarding her "maiden and bridal purity" (p. 412) from the fumbling attacks of the lascivious Mr. B., while the virtuous Sophia, the female protagonist in Henry Fielding's *The History of Tom Jones, a Foundling* (1749/1979) similarly struggles to maintain "the highest degree of innocence and modesty" (p. 139) in the face of attempted rape and arranged marriage. Both women successfully defend their chastity, and both ultimately are rewarded for their efforts by marriage to wealthy men. In the fictional world of the early English romance novel, virginity is a prized female attribute.

Whether premarital chastity continues to enjoy exalted status in contemporary Western societies is debatable, although research suggests that little premarital sexual experience is considered more desirable than extensive experience. When Regan and Berscheid (1997) asked a group of men and women to rank order a list of characteristics in terms of their desirability in a potential romantic partner, "being sexually available or 'easy'" was ranked as the *least* desirable attribute. Male participants in two studies conducted by Buss and Schmitt (1993) also viewed such sexual attributes as "promiscuous" and "sexually experienced" as undesirable in a potential mate, and other studies continue to confirm this general effect (e.g., Bettor, Hendrick, & Hendrick, 1995; O'Sullivan, 1995; Sprecher, Regan, McKinney, Maxwell, & Wazienski, 1997). Similar findings are provided by researchers who examined the influence of a target person's sexual *attitudes*— as opposed to his or her sexual behavior—on romantic attraction. Both men and women judge persons who hold sexually permissive attitudes lower in marriage desirability than those who hold nonpermissive attitudes (Oliver & Sedikides, 1992).

Although most people prefer their potential dates and mates to possess lower rather than higher levels of past sexual activity, this does not mean that people necessarily value partners who possess no sexual experience. Chastity, or complete sexual inexperience, has become increasingly unimportant to both men and women. In one of the earliest mate preference studies (Hill, 1945), men and women ranked chastity, defined as "no previous sexual experience," 10th in importance out of 18 attributes. A replication two decades later by Hudson and Henze (1969) found that chastity had fallen to 15th in importance as a partner attribute. Ten years after that, Hoyt and Hudson's (1981) replication revealed that women ranked chastity second to last (17th) and men ranked it last (18th) in importance. Participants in yet another even more recent replication

(Sprecher et al., 1997) continued to place little value on chastity. Thus, although a high level of sexual experience is not considered extremely desirable in a potential mate in the United States, neither is complete sexual inexperience. Men and women from Western European countries (Belgium, West Germany, Great Britain, Sweden, Italy, Greece, and Norway) also consider chastity to be irrelevant or even undesirable in a marriage partner, according to a study conducted by Buss (1989). However, Buss also reports that people in many Asian countries (Taiwan, Japan, China, Indonesia, and India) view "no previous sexual experience" as an extremely important attribute in a potential marriage partner. Adults living in African and South American countries were in between these two extremes.

SEXUALITY IN BEGINNING RELATIONSHIPS

Insofar as most teenagers and college-age adults believe that sex is an appropriate element of committed romantic relationships (Reiss, 1964; Sprecher et al., 1988) and can bring a couple closer together (Muram, Rosenthal, Tolley, Peeler, & Dorko, 1991), it is not surprising that many young people have engaged in some form of sexual activity, including intercourse, by the age of 16 (e.g., Brook, Balka, Abernathy, & Hamburg, 1994; Leitenberg & Saltzman, 2000; Zelnik & Kantner, 1980). The factors that influence the decision to have sex for the first time with a particular partner, the different pathways to sexual involvement that a couple may follow, and the ways in which men and women attempt to influence their sexual interactions with their dating partners have been the subject of considerable research.

The First Sexual Encounter

The first sexual encounter is usually a highly significant event in developing relationships, and most people remember their first sexual episode in vivid detail (Harvey, Flanary, & Morgan, 1986). Romantic partners often have sex in order to express closeness or love (Jessor, Costa, Jessor, &

Donovan, 1983; Leigh, 1989) and report feeling increased commitment to the relationship after becoming sexually intimate (Baxter & Bullis, 1986; Cate, Long, Angera, & Draper, 1993).

The Decision to Have Sex for the First Time in a Relationship

Couples appear to weigh a number of factors when deciding whether to become sexually active. Emotional intimacy and closeness with the partner appears to matter the most. For example, Christopher and Cate (1984) asked a group of sexually experienced men and women to rate how important various considerations were in their decision to have sex for the first time in a premarital relationship and found four factors to be influential: (1) *positive affection and communication* (how much love they felt for the partner, the possibility that the relationship would result in marriage, and level of commitment or involvement); (2) *arousal and receptivity*, including their own or their partner's level of sexual arousal immediately prior to intercourse and their receptivity to the partner's sexual advances; (3) *obligation and pressure* (feelings of obligation to have sex with the partner, as well as the partner's pressure or insistence on having sex); and (4) *circumstance*, such as the amount of drugs or alcohol they or the partner had consumed or the "specialness" of that particular date. Two sex differences were found. Positive affect and communication were more important in women's decision to have sex for the first time with a partner, whereas obligation and pressure played a greater role in men's sexual decision-making.

Research on why people *refrain* from having sex with a particular partner also highlights the impact of the relationship's emotional tenor. In an analysis of college students' reasons for feeling ambivalent about engaging in sexual activity despite having the opportunity to do so, O'Sullivan and Gaines (1998) found that the most common reason given by men (35%) and women (49%) concerned relationship and intimacy issues, including an insufficient level of commitment and uncertainty about their feelings for the partner. Unlike Christopher and Cate (1984) and other researchers (e.g., Carroll, Volk, & Hyde, 1985) who have found

that emotional intimacy, commitment, and other interpersonal factors play a greater role in women's than in men's sexual decision making (consistent with research on sex differences in sexual attitudes reviewed earlier in this chapter), O'Sullivan and Gaines found no such difference.

Pathways to Sexual Involvement

Some couples become sexually active relatively early in their relationship—for example, after the first date or a few dates—whereas others decide to wait until they reach much later relationship stages, such as after engagement or marriage. In the longitudinal Boston Couples Study, Peplau and colleagues (1977) surveyed dating couples periodically over a 2-year period about their sexual (and other) experiences. Like Christopher and Cate (1985), who conducted a retrospective study in which they asked a sample of dating couples to think back over their relationship and report about various events and experiences, they found that some couples chose to limit their sexual interactions to nonintercourse activities (for example, kissing and light petting). These couples generally believed that love alone did not serve to justify sexual intercourse, that intercourse should be saved for marriage, and that abstinence from intercourse was a sign of their love and respect for each other. These couples also tended to hold conservative sexual attitudes and to have lower overall levels of sexual experience than other couples. Both research teams found evidence of the other extreme—couples who engaged in intercourse very early in their relationship (sometimes on the first date or after a few dates). These couples viewed sex without love as acceptable and did not require commitment in order to have and enjoy intercourse. Their decision to have intercourse stemmed primarily from physical pleasure and arousal motives rather than from any emotional concern or relationship factor. Both studies also found that still other couples were located between these low and rapid involvement extremes. For example, the most common couple type identified by Christopher and Cate (1985) engaged in extremely low levels of sexual activity until they made a commitment to each other and the relationship.

Sexual Influence

Individuals involved in dating and other forms of romantic relationship often attempt to influence their partners' decisions about sexual activity, including whether or not to engage in intercourse for the first time and on subsequent occasions. Although direct requests are sometimes made, it appears that most individuals utilize *indirect* techniques, including sitting closer to the partner and touching, snuggling, kissing, or holding hands with him or her (Jesser, 1978; McCormick, 1979). For example, Perper and Weis (1987) asked women college students to describe in an essay the strategies they would use to influence a sexual interaction. Three primary tactics were identified from the respondents' essays: (1) Environmental and situational strategies ranged from dressing in a sexually suggestive or seductive manner to offering to get the partner a drink to creating a romantic setting. (2) Verbal strategies included paying the partner compliments and engaging in romantic or sexually suggestive talk. (3) Nonverbal strategies included such behaviors as using eye glances, moving close, cuddling, touching, and kissing the partner as a way to initiate a sexual interlude.

Christopher and Frandsen (1990) asked a group of men and women to think about any sexual encounter that had occurred during their last date and report about the extent to which they had used a variety of different tactics (identified by the researchers) to influence that encounter. Four general sexual influence strategies were apparent: (1) antisocial acts that involved imposing sexual wishes on a dating partner in socially unacceptable ways—for example, threatening to use or using force against the partner, ridiculing and insulting the partner, and getting angry, or sulking, pleading, and making the partner feel guilty; (2) emotional and physical closeness behaviors such as expressing affection or love or paying compliments; (3) logic and reason strategies, including presenting a list of reasons why the couple should become sexually intimate or claiming to be knowledgeable about how sexual the relationship ought to be; and (4) pressure and manipulation tactics such as using drugs or

alcohol to influence the partner. For both men and women, the use of emotional and physical closeness behaviors was most often reported. Men, however, were more likely than women to report having used pressure and manipulation tactics to influence their sexual outcomes. More important than sex or gender in the use of influence strategies was the individual's desired level of sexual involvement: Men and women who desired a greater level of sexual involvement were more likely to employ antisocial influence strategies and to pressure and manipulate the partner than were those who were satisfied with the current level of sex or who desired less sexual involvement, and those who desired lower levels of sexual intimacy from their partner were more likely to use logic and reasoning strategies.

SEXUALITY IN ESTABLISHED RELATIONSHIPS

Because individuals involved in established or long-term committed relationships presumably have access to a sex partner, they make ideal participants for researchers interested in aspects of relational sex. Of the several types of established relationship, such as marital, cohabiting heterosexual, and cohabiting homosexual relationships, marital relationships have received the most attention.

Sexual Frequency and Its Decline Over Time

The frequency with which spouses engage in sexual intercourse has been the subject of much research. In the late 1940s and early 1950s, Kinsey and his colleagues (1948, 1953) surveyed over 11,000 men and women in the United States about a variety of sexual issues and found that young married couples tended to have sex approximately 2 to 3 times per week. Twenty years later, Hunt (1974) reported slightly higher frequencies—on average, young married men and women (ranging in age from 18 to 24) had sex 3.25 times a week. A more recent national study conducted by Michael and colleagues (1994) found that most married couples have sex an average of 7 times a month (or slightly less than twice a week), suggesting that the amount of sexual activity between spouses has not continued to rise. Other national surveys of married couples in the 1990s yielded similar results (e.g., Call, Sprecher, & Schwartz, 1995; Donnelly, 1993). However, there is tremendous variability in the frequency of sexual intercourse in marital relationships. Some couples are celibate or have sex very infrequently, whereas others engage in intercourse on a daily basis. For example, Greenblat (1983) interviewed 80 people who had been married 5 years or less. The number of times spouses recalled having had sexual intercourse each month during their first year of marriage ranged from 1 (or an average of 12 times that year) to 45 (or 540 times that first year).

Surveys reveal that cohabiting heterosexual couples and homosexual male couples have sexual intercourse (defined as genital contact) more frequently than do married couples (e.g., Blumstein & Schwartz, 1983; Call et al., 1995; Rao & DeMaris, 1995). Homosexual female (lesbian) couples, on the other hand, have sex less frequently than other couple types, although they engage in more nongenital physical contact such as cuddling and hugging. Despite these differences, *all* forms of long-term, committed partnerships—married or cohabiting, heterosexual or homosexual—are associated with greater sexual frequency than is singlehood. For example, Michael and associates (1994) examined the yearly frequency of sexual intercourse in three groups: single men and women, married men and women, and (primarily heterosexual) cohabiting men and women. Their results revealed that paired individuals have sex more often than their single counterparts. About 40% of married people engaged in sexual intercourse with their spouse 2 or more times a week, and well over half of the unmarried cohabitors had sex at least that often. However, fewer than 25% of the single respondents engaged in intercourse with the same frequency. In fact, almost one-fourth of the single men and one-third of the single women reported having had no sex at all during the past 12 months. Few individuals in established relationships reported such low fre-

quencies of sexual activity. Thus, contrary to popular views of the "swinging single," it is the married and cohabiting people among us—those who have ready access to an available sex partner—who have the most frequent sex.

The frequency with which couples engage in sex is affected both by the age of the partners and by the age of their relationship. In general, older couples have sex less frequently than younger couples (e.g., Rao & DeMaris, 1995). Call and associates (1995) found that sexual activity was highest among the youngest respondents in their national survey (those ranging in age from 19 to 29) and became progressively lower in older age groups, reaching its nadir among respondents in their 70s. In addition, the longer couples have been married or have cohabited, the less often they have sex (e.g., Lever, 1995; Rao & DeMaris, 1995; Samson, Levy, Dupras, & Tessier, 1991). For example, James (1981) analyzed diaries kept by newlywed couples over the course of their first year of marriage. Couples reported having sex on 17 or more occasions during their first month of married life, but by the end of the year, their rate of intercourse had declined to approximately 8 times a month.

Because these two age-related factors are linked—as a relationship ages, so do the partners—it is difficult to know whether it is chronological age that causes the decline in sexual frequency or if the critical factor is habituation from having the same sex partner year after year. Both factors probably play a role. As men and women age, changes in their physical abilities, increased incidence of illness, and negative attitudes about sex in the elderly may contribute to a less active sex life. At the same time, the loss of novelty that results from having sexual intercourse with the same partner over and over again may reduce levels of activity (see the discussion of the "Coolidge effect" in Chapter 6). A desire for sexual novelty is a frequent reason men and women give for having engaged in a casual sexual encounter (Regan & Dreyer, 1999) or for having been sexually unfaithful to their spouse (Buunk, 1984).

A decline in sexual frequency is associated with other events that occur during the course of a couple's relationship. Greenblat (1983) found that when married men and women explained why their rate of sexual activity had declined after the first year of marriage, they cited (1) birth control and pregnancy reasons, such as a lack of interest during pregnancy and/or after having given birth; (2) reasons related to children and child care, such as fatigue caused by child-rearing activities or a lack of privacy; and (3) work reasons such as heavy work schedules or fatigue caused by work. All of these factors may limit a couple's desire and opportunity for sex.

Sexual Satisfaction

Most partners—whether cohabiting or married, heterosexual or homosexual—report that they are satisfied with the sexual aspects of their relationship (e.g., Blumstein & Schwartz, 1983; Kurdek, 1991b; Lawrance & Byers, 1995). In a national survey of over 650 married couples, approximately one-third of the husbands and wives reported a "very great deal" of sexual satisfaction, and an additional one-third reported experiencing a "great deal" of satisfaction (Greeley, 1991). Similarly, over 80% of the married or cohabiting respondents in a study by Michael and colleagues (1994) stated that they were "extremely" or "very" physically and emotionally satisfied by sexual activity with their partner. Homosexual men and women appear equally satisfied sexually; over 40% of the gay men (most of whom were partnered) in Lever's (1994, 1995) reports rated their current sex life as "great" or "good," and over 30% of the partnered lesbians felt that their sex life was "great."

According to the interpersonal exchange model of sexual satisfaction (Lawrance & Byers, 1995), sexual satisfaction is strongly influenced by the interpersonal context in which sexual activity occurs—that is, by the costs and rewards that a couple exchanges over time in their relationship. This model is based on principles expressed in Homans's (e.g., 1961) social exchange theory (see Chapter 4) and proposes that sexual satisfaction will be highest when sexual rewards (aspects of the sexual relationship that are pleasing or gratifying) are high, sexual costs (aspects of the sexual relationship that require effort or that cause pain, anxiety, or embarrassment) are low, sexual rewards exceed sexual costs, the obtained sexual rewards and costs in the relationship compare favorably to the expected sexual rewards and costs, and one partner's sexual rewards and costs do not greatly exceed those of the other partner. Research with married, cohabiting, and dating couples generally supports these predictions (e.g., Byers, Demmons, & Lawrance, 1998). This model predicts that a couple's degree of sexual satisfaction should not be adversely or permanently affected by one or a small number of unrewarding sexual episodes. If both partners have a history of high reward, low cost sexual interactions, a single unequal, unsatisfying, or even averse sexual encounter should not affect their general level of sexual satisfaction.

Researchers have tended to focus on the association between sexual satisfaction and such "objective" sexual variables as frequency of intercourse and number of orgasms. Not surprisingly, one of these variables, frequency of sexual intercourse, is strongly correlated with sexual satisfaction in both hetero- and homosexual relationships (e.g., Lever, 1995; Young, Denny, Luquis, & Young, 1998).

Sexual satisfaction also is related to nonsexual relational factors, including closeness or behavioral interdependence. Hurlbert, Apt, and Rabehl [Meyers] (1993) administered measures of objective sexual variables (such as frequency of activity, number of orgasms, and sexual excitability), personality dimensions (such as sexual assertiveness), and relationship factors (such as communication and closeness [behavioral interdependence] as assessed by the Relationship Closeness Inventory) to a sample of women. The women's scores on a sexual satisfaction scale were significantly correlated with virtually all of the measures included in the study, but only three variables—the two personality dimensions of sexual assertiveness and erotophilia/erotophobia and the relationship factor of closeness—added to the prediction of sexual satisfaction over and above the sexual variables. In fact, these three variables alone accounted for well over half of the variance in women's sexual satisfaction.

Both heterosexual and homosexual couples who are satisfied with the nonsexual areas of their relationship tend also to be satisfied with the sexual aspects of their partnership (for reviews, see Christopher & Sprecher, 2000; Kurdek, 1991b). For example, Lawrance and Byers (1995) asked a large sample of heterosexual men and women who were currently involved in long-term (mostly marital) relationships to rate their sexual relationship and their overall relationship on five bipolar scales: good–bad, pleasant–unpleasant, positive–negative, satisfying–unsatisfying, and valuable–worthless. Ratings on these individual scales were summed to create a global index of satisfaction. They found a strong association between the two global satisfaction measures. Specifically, the more satisfied participants were with their sexual relationship (the more they rated it as "good," "pleasant," "positive," and so on), the more satisfied they were with their relationship in general. Henderson-King and Veroff (1994) found the same association in their sample of newly married African-American and Caucasian couples. Regardless of one's sex or racial identity, then, sexual happiness is associated with feeling good about one's relationship.

Unfortunately, the type of correlational data that characterizes research in this area (which generally consists of self-reported feelings and experiences, made at one point in time, and usually by only one partner) does not allow inferences about the *direction* of the association between sexuality (frequency and satisfaction, for example) and interpersonal adjustment or relationship satisfaction. Moreover, as discussed in Chapter 13, "Satisfaction and Stability," many of the variables known to be associated with relationship satisfaction have a reciprocally causal linkage with satisfaction. For example, an unsatisfying relationship is likely to promote sexual dissatisfaction, and sexual dissatisfaction is likely to contribute to an unsatisfying relationship. Individuals who are unhappy, stressed, or conflicted about nonsexual aspects of the relationship probably will have difficulty becoming sexually interested in and aroused by their partners, particularly when the partner is viewed as a source of the conflict or unhappiness. And a person who is not satisfied with either the quantity or the quality of sex with the current partner is likely to become dissatisfied with other aspects of the relationship.

Sexual Communication

As in other areas of the relationship, effective communication about sexual needs, preferences, expectations, and attitudes is necessary if the partners are to successfully negotiate their level of sexual involvement and maintain the quality of their sexual relationship over time. Reviews of the scholarly literature on sexual communication in developing relationships (e.g., Cupach & Metts, 1991; Edgar & Fitzpatrick, 1990; Metts & Spitzberg, 1996; Metts, Sprecher, & Regan, 1998) suggest a number of general conclusions: (1) Sexual initiation tactics are often indirect and nonverbal. (2) Men are more likely than women to engage in overt behaviors that initiate sexual interactions. (3) Women are more likely than men to use indirect strategies for sexual initiation. (4) Any initiation tactics utilized by women are perceived as effective, given men's proclivities to pursue sexual activity. (5) Both sexes are aware of and endorse interpersonal sexual scripts that cast men as active initiators and pursuers of sex and women as reactive regulators and sexual gatekeepers. (6) Unlike sexual initiation attempts, which are often nonverbal and indirect, sexual refusals tend to be verbal and relatively direct.

Research on sexual communication within established heterosexual relationships yields similar conclusions: (1) Men continue to function as the sexual initiators and women continue to serve as the sexual regulators (Blumstein & Schwartz, 1983). (2) Most sexual initiation attempts are successful—most individuals respond positively to their partner's sexual invitations (Byers & Heinlein, 1989). (3) Sexual initiations, and positive responses to initiation attempts, generally are communicated nonverbally and indirectly (Brown & Auerback, 1981; Byers & Heinlein, 1989). (4) Sexual refusals tend to be communicated verbally and directly (Cupach & Metts, 1991).

PROBLEMATIC ASPECTS OF RELATIONAL SEX

Partners who engage in frequent and satisfying sexual experiences generally experience a panoply of positive outcomes, including happiness, feelings of equity, and satisfaction with each other and with the relationship. Sometimes, however, sex is implicated in negative relationship outcomes.

Sexual Disinterest

Over time, partners often experience decreased sexual attraction for each other. Because many people routinely experience fluctuations in their general level of sexual desire, and because sexual desire is associated with age, physical health, drug use, mood, hormonal variations, and other intraindividual causes, a lessening of one's sexual attraction to the partner does not necessarily indicate relationship conflict or dissatisfaction (Kaplan, 1979; Regan & Berscheid, 1999). Sometimes, however, a reduction in desire (particularly if it occurs suddenly and/or is sustained for a long period of time) may signal a relationship problem. Clinicians and health professionals believe that sexual desire is strongly influenced by interpersonal causal conditions, including the emotions experienced within a relationship and/or directed toward a partner (e.g., Pietropinto, 1986). Indeed, many case studies illustrate the corrosive impact of anger, hostility, anxiety, stress, and other emotions on sexual desire. For example, on the basis of case studies of men and women with sexual desire disorders, Kaplan (e.g., 1979, 1996) concluded that inhibited sexual desire may result from anger and anxiety and that the partner is often the primary source of these emotions. Fears of rejection by and envy of the partner, poor communication, and power conflicts produce anxiety and anger, which appear to rapidly, and usually automatically, activate an emotional "turnoff" mechanism that suppresses sexual desire. Trudel (1991) and Arnett, Prosen, and Toews (1986) similarly suggest that negative affect stemming from interpersonal conflict may elicit a stress response that causes diminished sexual desire.

Empirical research supports the prediction that diminished sexual desire signals the existence of problems or difficulties in a couple's relationship. Stuart, Hammond, and Pett (1987) administered the Dyadic Adjustment Scale (DAS) to a sample of married women who were diagnosed with inhibited sexual desire (ISD), married women who reported normal sexual desire, and the spouses of women in both groups. The women in the ISD group scored significantly lower in marital adjustment on all four subscales of the DAS (Consensus, Satisfaction, Cohesion, and Affection) and on the total scale than did women in the non-ISD group. The spouses of women in the ISD group also reported significantly lower overall adjustment in their marriages than did the spouses of women in the non-ISD group.

Studies conducted with nonclinical samples confirm that relationship quality affects sexual desire for the partner. On two occasions 6 years apart, Hallstrom and Samuelsson (1990) asked a large sample of married or cohabiting women to indicate their present degree of sexual desire (whether they perceived it as strong, moderate, weak, or absent) and to report whether they received sufficient emotional support from their partner and had a "confiding" relationship with him. Although causality cannot be determined from this correlational (albeit longitudinal) design, a decrease in self-reported sexual desire over time was predicted by a perceived lack of a confiding relationship with, and insufficient support from, the partner at the first interview. Similar results were reported by Regan (2000), who surveyed a sample of dating couples and found that the amount of sexual desire that men and women experienced for their partners was strongly and positively correlated with relationship satisfaction and negatively correlated with emotional frustration felt toward the partner, thoughts of terminating the current relationship, and thoughts of starting a new relationship.

Overall, clinical case studies and empirical research suggest that sexual desire may function as a "thermometer" to relationship quality. The fact that therapeutic interventions for sexual desire disorders have traditionally targeted the individual—usually through the use of drug therapy (e.g., androgen replacement therapy; Mathews, Whitehead, & Kellet, 1983; Rabkin, Rabkin, & Wagner, 1995) or sexual behavior training (e.g., directed masturbation; Hurlbert, 1993)—while ignoring the individual's interpersonal situation may partially explain why these disorders are notoriously difficult to treat. Recent clinical outcome studies reveal that the most successful therapies conceptualize sexual desire disorders as a couple issue rather than as an individual problem, and incorporate techniques that involve both partners (see Ullery, Millner, & Willingham, 2002, for a review). An example is provided by Trudel and colleagues (2001), who randomly assigned couples in which the female partner was diagnosed with ISD to a treatment group or a control group. The 12-week treatment program combined traditional cognitive-behavioral interventions that target the individual, such as sexual fantasy exercises and cognitive restructuring training, with techniques that target the interpersonal dynamics between the partners—training in verbal communication skills, emotional communication, and sexual intimacy. At the end of the 12-week program, 74% of the women in the treatment group were diagnosed as improved or cured, and 64% continued to experience alleviated symptoms at a 3-month and 1-year follow-up (interpretation is muddied by the fact that comparable percentages were not given for the control group). Although the treatment and control groups showed no mean difference in relationship satisfaction at the onset of the study, women who completed the treatment program—and their spouses—showed significant increases in satisfaction at the end of the study. This suggests that a sexual therapy program that focuses on interpersonal skills training—in particular, communicative competence—not only is effective in alleviating sexual problems but enhances other areas of the relationship as well. Although additional outcome studies using appropriate methodologies such as treatment and control groups and longitudinal designs are necessary to evaluate the efficacy of the type of multipronged program created by Trudel and associates, the results are encouraging and further underscore the important role played by the relational context in creating and sustaining sexual attraction between partners.

Sexual Aggression

Two broad categories of sexual aggression sometimes occur within romantic relationships: sexual coercion and sexual assault (see Christopher, 2001; Muehlenhard, Goggins, Jones, & Satterfield, 1991; Sprecher & McKinney, 1993). **Sexual coercion** involves the use of nonphysical—that is, verbal or psychological—tactics to manipulate, pressure, or coerce the partner to comply with sexual demands. **Sexual assault** (also called **sexual violence**) involves the threatened or actual use of physical force to obtain sexual contact; sexual assault also may involve engaging in sexual activity with another while the other was unable to consent (perhaps due to intoxication or lack of consciousness).

Sexual aggression (typically male-to-female) between dating partners is distressingly common. In an early survey conducted by Kanin (1967), over one-fourth (26%) of college men reported having made a forceful attempt at intercourse while on a date that had prompted a fighting, crying, or screaming response from their partners. Similar results were presented 20 years later by Koss, Gidycz, and Wisniewski (1987), who reported that 25% of the men who participated in their national college student survey had used some form of sexual coercion or aggression on a dating partner (an additional 3.3% admitted to having attempted rape, and 4.5% admitted to rape). More recently, Finley and Corty (1993) reported that approximately one-third of college women have experienced nonconsensual sex as a result of a partner's force, threat of force, or verbal coercion.

The recognition that sexual aggression occurs with some frequency between dating partners and with the context of romantic relationships has contributed to an increased interest in identifying the factors that may be implicated in coercion and assault. Some researchers have focused on individual-level variables. One of the most significant of these is biological sex: Most victims of sexual force are female and most perpetrators are male. A survey by Michael and colleagues (1994) revealed that many more women (22%) than men (2%) reported having experienced forced sexual activity at some time in their lives. Nearly all of the women and one-third of the men who were forced into sexual activity reported that their assailant was male. Men and women also have very different reactions to depictions of date rape. When evaluating a date rape scenario, men tend to attribute more responsibility for the sexual assault to the female target, believe the male target's behavior is more justified, and think the female target is more sexually willing than do women evaluating the same scenario (e.g., Feltey, Ainslie, & Geib, 1991; Kowalski, 1992; Proite, Dannells, & Benton, 1993).

Certain interpersonal and sociocultural factors may create an environment conducive to sexual aggression within close relationships: (1) sex-role scripts associated with heterosexual dating situations (see Christopher, 2001); (2) socialization processes that foster the acquisition and acceptance of rape myths (see Burt, 1980); (3) peer group norms that promote exploitative attitudes toward women and the use of forceful or coercive sexual strategies (see Kanin, 1984, 1985; Martin & Hummer, 1989); and (4) the **sexual double standard**, which encompasses the normative beliefs that sexuality is an inherent aspect of masculinity, that the male sex drive is an uncontrollable and powerful force, and that women's expressions of resistance to sex are merely token and not reflective of their true feelings (see Muehlenhard et al., 1991). These factors not only may contribute to sexually coercive behavior but also may make it difficult for partners to acknowledge, report, or seek appropriate physical or psychological treatment when necessary.

The effects of sexual aggression on the victim are diverse. Victims of **acquaintance assault**—also called date rape—report decreased feelings of confidence, well-being, and safety; increased feelings of powerlessness; difficulties with interpersonal trust; and a host of additional psychological and physical consequences (see Frazier, Conlon, & Glaser, 2001). In addition, they are much more likely than the victims of assault by a stranger to blame themselves for the incident (see Calhoun & Wilson, 2000). The fact that sexual coercion, assault, and violence are not uncommon and have serious personal and interpersonal consequences for the victim attests to the need for additional research on this dark side of relational sex.

Sexual Infidelity

As we have discussed, one of the most fundamental beliefs that people hold about marital and other long-term, committed relationships is that the partners should be *sexually exclusive*. Once an individual is romantically committed to another, the general presumption is that he or she will confine all sexual activities to that relationship (or, in polygamous mating systems, to those relationships). Although other types of betrayal occur between relational partners (see Baxter et al., 1997), **sexual infidelity** (also called **extrarelational sex**, **extramarital sex**, or **adultery**)—the act of engaging in sexual activities with someone other than the primary romantic partner (and typically without the knowledge or consent of the primary partner)—has received the most attention from researchers.

Early surveys conducted with married individuals suggested that extramarital sex was relatively common, with prevalence rates ranging from 18% to 50% (Kinsey et al., 1948, 1953; Hunt, 1974; for a review see Thompson, 1983). More recent research, however, reveals lower incidence rates. Michael and colleagues (1994) asked married, cohabiting, and single participants in their large national survey to indicate how many sex partners they had had during the previous 12 months. According to the researchers, the responses demonstrated "how likely people are to remain faithful to their sexual partners" (p. 101). Specifically, 95% of the married men and women, 75% of the never-married but cohabiting men and women, and 82% of the divorced and now cohabiting men and women had engaged in intercourse with one person (their partner) over the past year. Those who reported having more than one sex partner during the previous

12 months tended to be single, but only 36% of single people reported having more than one sexual partner. The researchers concluded:

About 90 percent of Americans have married by the time they are thirty and a large majority spends much of their adulthood as part of a wedded couple. And marriage, we find, regulates sexual behavior with remarkable precision. No matter what they did before they wed, no matter how many partners they had, the sexual lives of married people are similar. Despite the popular myth that there is a great deal of adultery in marriage, our data and other reliable studies do not find it. Instead, a vast majority are faithful while the marriage is intact. (pp. 88–89)

Similar results were reported by Wiederman (1997), who analyzed data collected from a nationally representative sample of men and women (General Social Survey, Davis & Smith, 1994). The majority of married men (78%) and women (88%) consistently reported no participation in extramarital sex at all—not during the past year, and not during their lifetime. In fact, in the total sample, which included divorced or separated respondents as well as married respondents, fewer than 5% of the men, and fewer than 2% of the women, reported having engaged in extramarital sex during the previous 12 months. Other national surveys reveal similar low percentages (e.g., 2% to 3% of married men and women; Choi & Catania, 1996).

Given the array of punishments meted out to those who indulge in extrarelational sex—ranging from public reprimand and monetary fines in some cultures to divorce, imprisonment, torture, and even death in others (Frayser, 1989)—even the low incidence of infidelity has created interest in identifying its causes. In their quest to delineate the origins of infidelity, researchers have taken three approaches (see Drigotas & Barta, 2001): descriptive, normative (social context), and evolutionary.

Researchers who adopt the relatively atheoretical *descriptive approach* attempt to identify the demographic and attitudinal correlates of infidelity and the reasons people give for their extrarelational sexual behavior. In the United States,

researchers generally find that extramarital sex is related to ethnicity, with African-American and Latino men and women reporting higher rates relative to Caucasian men and women (Choi, Catania, & Dolcini, 1994; Forste & Tanfer, 1996; Wiederman, 1997). In addition, adults living in urban environments express more positive attitudes toward, and a higher lifetime incidence of, extramarital sex than those living in rural areas (Kinsey et al., 1948; Weis & Jurich, 1985). One of the most potent correlates of extramarital sexual attitudes and behavior is biological sex: Compared with women, men express more positive attitudes toward sexual infidelity and are more likely to report having engaged in an extramarital sexual encounter (Choi et al., 1994; Oliver & Hyde, 1993). However, this sex difference is most commonly found among older cohorts of respondents. For example, although Wiederman's (1997) survey revealed a significant sex difference in lifetime incidence of extramarital sex (with 22.7% of the men and 11.6% of the women indicating having engaged in sex with someone other than their spouse during the time of their marriage), no sex difference was found among younger respondents (those less than 40 years of age). Thus, the double standard with regard to involvement in extramarital sex appears to have faded in younger generations—both younger men and women disapprove of extramarital sex and seem to act in accordance with their beliefs.

Researchers who take the *normative approach* also tend to rely on self-report data and retrospective accounts, but they emphasize the sociocultural context in which infidelity occurs and derive their hypotheses from social context theories (several of which were reviewed earlier in this chapter). Thus, these researchers attribute the occurrence of extrarelational sex to the existence of pervasive social and cultural norms that govern male and female sexual behavior and sex roles. Many of the sociocultural norms that exist today emerged in the twelfth century in Western Europe and can be traced to a code of sexual conduct that arose among the nobility and upper social classes. This code expressed the belief that sexual experience was a core component of masculinity and that the male sex drive was sometimes uncontrollable. Hence, it also prescribed that sexual infidelity (if not excessive) was to be tolerated in a man:

> But what if the man should be unfaithful to his beloved—not with the idea of finding a new love, but because he has been driven to it by an irresistible passion for another woman? What, for instance, if chance should present to him an unknown woman in a convenient place or what if at a time when Venus is urging him on to that which I am talking about he should meet with a little strumpet or somebody's servant girl? Should he, just because he played with her in the grass, lose the love of his beloved? We can say without fear of contradiction that just for this a lover is not considered unworthy of the love of his beloved unless he indulges in so many excesses with a number of women that we may conclude that he is overpassionate. (Capellanus, 1184/1960, p. 161)

Sexual infidelity was *not*, however, to be tolerated in a woman:

> The old opinion, held by some, is that when the woman is at fault the same rule should be followed as in the case of the man just mentioned. But this rule, although old, should not be respected on that account, since it would lead us into great error. God forbid that we should ever declare that a woman who is not ashamed to wanton with two men should go unpunished. Although in the case of men such a thing is tolerated because it is so common and because the sex has a privilege by which all things in this world which are by their nature immodest are more readily allowed to men, in the case of a woman they are, because of the decency of the modest sex, considered so disgraceful that after a woman has indulged the passions of several men everybody looks upon her as an unclean strumpet unfit to associate with other ladies. (Capellanus, 1184/1960, p. 162)[1]

This constellation of social attitudes and normative expectations, apparent over the following eight centuries, contributed to a sociocultural climate that encouraged men to actively seek sexual opportunities, while prohibiting women from doing the same, and condoned men's participation in sexual encounters with extrarelational partners. Recent failures to find sex differences in the incidence of infidelity among young men and women illustrate that social mores change. In

their review of the literature on infidelity, Drigotas and Barta (2001) suggest that the "decline in male participation in extradyadic sex observed over the course of the 20th century may reflect changing attitudes toward male sexual entitlement and conquest" (p. 178).

Researchers who adopt the *evolutionary approach* to sexual behavior believe that sexual infidelity may have served a biologically adaptive purpose in the ancestral environment. Recall that by Darwinian standards, reproductive success for both sexes is measured by the production of offspring who survive to reach reproductive maturity and who themselves then mate and perpetuate the individual's genetic makeup. Over evolutionary time, men who sought out multiple sexual partners and who engaged in extrarelational sex presumably would have enhanced their reproductive success; that is, they would have experienced an increased chance, relative to other men, of producing offspring and perpetuating their genetic lineage (see Buss, 2003; Symons, 1979). The adaptive significance of infidelity for women is not as readily apparent, in part because women are limited in the number of children they can produce and raise over their lifetimes; that is, a woman who mates with many men does not necessarily produce any more offspring than a woman who mates with one man, because both are limited in the lifetime number of offspring they can produce. However, after reviewing the cross-cultural and ethnographic literatures, Fisher (1992) suggests that infidelity may have enhanced the reproductive success of ancestral women as well as that of ancestral men. Fisher contends that women who formed sexual associations with multiple partners would have had access to additional goods and services that, in turn, would have ensured greater health and protection for themselves and their offspring. In addition to supplementary subsistence, infidelity might have provided a woman with a suitable replacement mate should her primary partner have died or disappeared. Third, infidelity might have allowed a woman pair-bonded with a poor male specimen to increase her reproductive success by having children with a different, and presumably better, mate (a point also made by Drigotas & Barta, 2001). And finally, Fisher (1992) theorizes that the children of women who engaged in intercourse with an array of men would have displayed genetic diversity, which would have increased the likelihood that at least some of them would survive and reach reproductive maturity in the face of a changing environment. In sum, the evolutionary theoretical approach to infidelity views extrarelational sexual behavior among contemporary men and women as a reflection of an evolved mating psychology that originated early in the development of our species and that served to promote the genetic fitness of our forebears. Fisher concludes that "it is the millennia of sneaking off with lovers—and the genetic payoffs these dalliances accrued—that have produced the propensity for adultery around the world today" (p. 97).

Whether human sexual infidelity reflects the operation of contemporary sociocultural forces or causes located in the ancestral environment of humans, it is associated with a number of outcomes. Some scholars have argued, based primarily on clinical anecdotes and interviews, that extrarelational sex can produce positive outcomes for the participants, including physical pleasure, a feeling of personal growth, a sense of adventure and excitement, and the formation of an intense physical and/or emotional connection with the extrarelational partner (e.g., Bringle & Buunk, 1991; O'Neill & O'Neill, 1972; Weil, 1975). Most survey and clinical research, however, finds that infidelity is far more likely to be associated with negative outcomes, both for the relationship and for the partners. Infidelity is one of the leading causes of relationship dissolution, in the United States and throughout the world (e.g., Amato & Rogers, 1997; Atkins, Baucom, & Jacobson, 2001; Betzig, 1989). People who engage in extrarelational sex frequently report experiencing guilt about betraying their partners, conflict about violating moral standards about exclusivity and fidelity, and anxiety about disease, pregnancy, and getting caught (Bringle & Buunk, 1991; Spanier & Margolis, 1983). Betrayed partners often experience feelings of abandonment and violation, self-doubt and lowered self-esteem, and anger and intense jealousy (Buunk, 1995; Charny & Parnass, 1995).

Sexual Jealousy

Sexual jealousy (also called **romantic jealousy**) usually is defined as a psychological state aroused by a perceived threat to a valued mating relationship that motivates behavior designed to counter the threat (Daly & Wilson, 1983). Researchers who investigate jealousy and other responses to infidelity often ask participants to imagine their romantic partner engaging in *emotional infidelity* (falling in love with someone else) or *sexual infidelity* (having intercourse with someone else) and then to indicate which type of infidelity would be the most upsetting. Women usually say their partner's emotional infidelity would be more upsetting than his sexual infidelity (Buss, Larsen, Westen, & Semmelroth, 1992; Buss et al., 1999; Buunk, Angleitner, Oubaid, & Buss, 1996; Harris, 2002; Harris & Christenfeld, 1996; Wiederman & Allgeier, 1993; Wiederman & Kendall, 1999). Men's responses are not as clear-cut; some studies find that men also select emotional infidelity as more upsetting than sexual infidelity (e.g., Buss et al., 1999, Study 1; Harris, 2002; Harris & Christenfeld, 1996), but other studies find the reverse (e.g., Buss et al., 1992; Buss et al., 1999, Study 2). This frequently found interaction between type of infidelity and sex of respondent is illustrated by a replication of Buss and colleagues (1992) conducted by Harris and Christenfeld (1996), who asked college students to imagine their romantic partner engaging in sexual infidelity ("trying different sexual positions" with another person) and emotional infidelity ("falling in love" with another person). When asked which of the two types of infidelity would be most upsetting, the majority of women (78%) selected the emotional infidelity scenario, and men were fairly evenly split (with 53% choosing emotional infidelity and 47% selecting sexual infidelity as most upsetting).

The origin of the difference between men and women in their reactions to sexual versus emotional infidelity has been the source of debate. Evolutionary psychologists believe that sex differences in jealousy reflect the evolved mating psychologies of men and women, which are posited to differ as a function of the different obstacles to reproductive success faced by ancestral men and women. As Daly and Wilson (1983) describe:

> The threat to a man's fitness resides in the risk of alien insemination of his adulterous wife, whereas the threat to a woman's fitness lies not so much in her adulterous husband's sexual contacts as in the risk that he will divert resources away from the wife and family. It follows that male jealousy should have evolved to be more specifically focused upon the sexual act, and female jealousy upon the loss of male attention and resources. (p. 294)

According to the evolutionary perspective, men are more likely than women to be sensitive to and distressed by cues to sexual infidelity because that form of infidelity jeopardizes a man's certainty of paternity and increases his risk of investing resources in another man's offspring. Women's jealousy is more likely than men's to be triggered by cues to emotional infidelity because that type of infidelity jeopardizes a woman's continued procurement of resources and increases the risk that her partner will divert important resources to the rival and any resultant offspring.

The evolutionary framework does not imply that infidelity per se is less upsetting to one sex than to the other. On the contrary, as we discussed earlier in this chapter, the relative frailty and extended infancy characteristic of human offspring favors the formation of a committed, enduring, and exclusive pair-bond between parents; consequently, behavior of any kind that threatens this bond should be distressing to both sexes. Rather, the evolutionary framework suggests that to the extent that the sexes faced different obstacles to reproductive success over the expanse of human evolutionary history, they developed different psychological sensitivities to different types of infidelity.

Methodological Problems in Jealousy Research

In contrast to the evolutionary explanation for the sex difference commonly observed in responses to sexual versus emotional infidelity, some researchers believe that the interaction may be the result of methodological artifact. This criticism of studies that rely on self-reported forced-choice responses to imagined infidelity is valid. A number of methodological problems plague studies of sex differences in response to types of infidelity.

First, self-report paradigms tend to magnify sex differences. Feingold (1990), who conducted a meta-analysis of mate preference studies, found that sex differences were greater in self-report paradigms than in behavioral research paradigms. It will be recalled, for example, that Sprecher (1989) found sex differences when men and women were asked to indicate what factors influenced their dating decisions but no sex differences when the same factors were experimentally manipulated and their actual behavioral impact was assessed. In other words, what men and women *say* influences their decisions is not always what actually *does* influence their decisions. Thus, it is important to keep in mind that most research conducted on infidelity and other aspects of human mating relies on self-reports—often self-reports in situations in which people are asked to *imagine* their reactions to an event they have not actually experienced.

In addition to the problem that people cannot always accurately report *why* they do what they do or what they *will* actually do, forced-choice response options tend to magnify sex differences. Some researchers employ forced-choice methods precisely because they are unable to find sex differences with response options that allow participants to indicate how upsetting they find each type of infidelity rather than forcing them to select one type over the other. For example, Buss and colleagues (1999) state:

> We continue to use the forced-choice methodology for an important methodological reason: Likert-type rating scales are subject to ceiling effects when they are used to rate the magnitude of upset one would experience in response to a partner's infidelity. . . . The forced-choice method—an analogue to Sophie's Choice—is one strategy for circumventing these ceiling effects and revealing patterns of preference and emotion for which Likert-type rating scales are insensitive. (p. 130)

The reference to the dilemma in *Sophie's Choice* is appropriate. No one doubts (or should doubt) that men and women are extremely distressed by both types of infidelity (or that Sophie deeply loved both her children). By forcing men and women to make a choice, researchers may uncover differences that are obscured by other self-report methods. Nevertheless, if ceiling effects are common—if men and women consistently report being highly distressed by *both* types of infidelity—and if sex differences can only be found by severely constraining participants' response options, it is questionable that the obtained sex difference allows us to better understand or predict their behavior.

The use of hypothetical scenarios to examine men's and women's responses to infidelity also has been criticized. The question is whether the type of infidelity that men and women *imagine* would be most upsetting *actually* would be most upsetting if they were confronted with the situation in their relationships. Harris (2002) addressed this question. As usual, she asked a sample of men and women to indicate which type of infidelity would upset them more: imagining their romantic partner "trying different sexual positions" with another person, or imagining their romantic partner "falling in love" with someone else (taken from Buss et al., 1992). However, she *also* asked participants to report whether they had ever *actually* experienced a romantic partner's infidelity. Those who said "yes" were instructed to recall their most recent experience and to indicate the extent to which they focused on the emotional and sexual aspects of the infidelity. The results for the forced-choice, hypothetical infidelity question were in accord with previous research; a higher percentage of men (26%) than women (approximately 11%) selected sexual infidelity as more upsetting than emotional infidelity, and a higher percentage of women (approximately 89%) than men (74%) chose emotional infidelity as more upsetting than sexual infidelity. For those who had actually experienced infidelity, however, no sex difference was observed in the degree to which they reported having focused on the sexual versus the emotional aspects of their partner's infidelity: *Both* sexes said they had focused more on the emotional than on the sexual aspects of their partner's infidelity.

Finally, an alternative explanation for the usually obtained Sex × Type of infidelity interaction has been proposed by several researchers, among them DeSteno and Salovey (1996) and Harris and Christenfeld (1996), who note that men and women possess different beliefs about the likelihood that the occurrence of one type of infidelity implies the occurrence of the other type for each sex. As we have reviewed, men possess more positive attitudes about sex in the absence of love and commitment than do women, and women, more than men, prefer to engage in intercourse only after the relationship is characterized by commitment and love. Because most people are aware of sex differences in these and related beliefs and preferences, it makes sense that men would be relatively more upset by sexual infidelity than by emotional infidelity and that women would demonstrate the reverse pattern. A woman's sexual infidelity (which implies the presence of *both* sexual and emotional involvement) should be more disturbing to men than emotional infidelity (which implies emotional involvement alone). For women, the situation is reversed. Women may assume that a sexually unfaithful man is not necessarily emotionally involved with his partner but that an emotionally unfaithful man probably is sexually involved. Thus, a man's emotional infidelity (which implies both emotional and sexual involvement) is more upsetting to women than sexual infidelity (which implies only sexual involvement). Essentially, then, the argument is that each sex selects as most upsetting the type of infidelity that implies their mate's greatest degree of extrarelational involvement and, thus, that poses the greatest overall threat to the relationship. Harris and Christenfeld found strong support for the hypothesis that the sexes differ in the extent to which they believe each form of infidelity implies the other. Men believed much more strongly than did women that a woman's sexual infidelity implied love, whereas women were somewhat more certain than men that a man's emotional infidelity implied sexual involvement.

Amid the controversies associated with sex differences in reactions to infidelity, it is important to recognize, first, that sexual jealousy is a pervasive human response to real, imagined, or implied infidelity. *Both* men and women report experiencing considerable emotional distress when asked to imagine or to recall a romantic partner's infidelity. Second, jealousy is produced by *both* types of infidelity (and probably by other types yet to be empirically examined). Neither sex remains emotionally unmoved when faced with their partner's real or imagined sexual infidelity, and neither sex remains unmoved by their partner's emotional infidelity.

Several levels of explanation ultimately will be needed to fully understand men's and women's reactions to infidelity. Conspicuous in its absence is a consideration of the influence of contemporary social and cultural forces on whether sexual jealousy occurs at all and, if it does, how it is experienced (a notable exception is Harris's [2003] social-cognitive theory of jealousy). Not all people in all societies exhibit sexual jealousy when their partners engage in extrarelational sex. As Ellis (1954) recounts, sexual jealousy is unknown among certain Eskimo tribes, Australian aborigines, Zuni Indians, and other societies. In contrast, after a systematic examination of the messages portrayed in American mass media, Ellis observed:

> In our particular culture, our romantic–monogamic ideals of sex, love, and marriage produce widespread and deeprooted anxieties and insecurities which, in turn, result in intense and almost all-pervading feelings of sexual jealousy. (p. 130)

Some of these media-fostered beliefs include the idea that each person has only one true mate, that infidelity poses a continual danger, that "cuckolds" are to be despised and "deserted wives" to be pitied, and that infidelity occurs when the deserted partner is not sufficiently adequate to "hold" his or her mate. All of these beliefs feed feelings of personal insecurity and possessiveness and create a climate conducive to the experience of jealousy and, also, to taking action to dissolve the relationship when a mate has been unfaithful.

SUMMARY

Human mating has important consequences for the individual, the partner, the society and/or culture, and the species. Current theorizing about the nature of mating relationships suggests that the preferences we have and the choices we make when selecting a mate reflect a unique blend of the sociocontextual factors that exist in the world today and the reproductive and survival obstacles faced by our hunter-gatherer ancestors. Irrespective of race, ethnicity, country of origin, historical era, biological sex, or sexual orientation, most people seek to form mating relationships with partners who possess a constellation of positive dispositional, physical, and social characteristics. Sexuality is an important part of mating relationships, and research indicates that the attitudes that partners hold about relational sex, the timing and manner of their sexual initiations, the amount of sex that they have, and how they communicate with each other about their needs and desires can have an enormous impact on their level of sexual satisfaction and on their happiness with the relationship in general. Although there is no "right" amount or type of sex that characterizes healthy relationships, partners generally are most satisfied when sexual activity is used to express feelings of love, commitment, and intimacy; when they agree about and communicate openly and honestly with each other about the role that sex plays in their relationship; and when they confine their sexual activities to the primary relationship.

PART 6
RELATIONSHIPS OVER TIME

Chapter *13*

Satisfaction and Stability

INTRODUCTION

People devote much of their lives to achieving and maintaining satisfying relationships with others. Unfortunately, that goal proves to be distressingly, sometimes tragically, elusive for some. The recipe for satisfying and enduring relationships has been the grail for which relationship scholars long have been searching, as documented by the frequency with which relationship satisfaction and stability have been the outcomes of interest in theory and research discussed in previous chapters.

The search for the ingredients of a satisfying relationship continues unabated, fueled in part by the high premium people place on relationship satisfaction, especially satisfaction in marriage (Attridge & Berscheid, 1994). The current preoccupation with relationship quality, Levinger (1997) speculates, stems from several converging historical trends, including increasing emphasis on individuality and personal choice, a greater range of possible relationship partners, and a lowering of barriers to relationship dissolution, especially divorce. When most people

were born, lived, and died in the same community, the individual's choice of relationship partners was confined to a small and stable field of availables. Although many no doubt wished their relationships were happier or dreamed of extricating themselves from a noxious relationship web, there were few opportunities for people to "reinvent" themselves in new environments with different spouses, friends, employers, and co-workers. Having little choice in partners and little opportunity to terminate unsatisfying relationships, it is unlikely that people in the past spent as much time as people currently do monitoring their own and their partners' satisfaction with their relationships.

The search for the ingredients of success also is fueled by the belief that satisfaction is the prime determinant of a relationship's stability and thus that discovery of the formula for satisfaction would reduce the historically high divorce rates in the United States and throughout the world. In 2002, for example, the U.S. Census Bureau forecast that 9 out of 10 citizens will marry sometime in their lifetime, yet at least half of those marriages will dissolve (Westphal, 2002), many within the first 7 years (Cherlin, 1992). The instability of marital and other family relationships is costly to society, as discussed in Chapter 3, "The Development of Relationship Science," and continues to alarm both federal and state governments. The Bush administration, like so many before it, announced that shoring up the institution of marriage would be a top priority in constructing domestic legislation. Tired of waiting for federal initiatives, some states such as Louisiana are trying to promote marital stability by instituting "covenant" marriage, which usually involves premarital counseling and makes legal dissolution of the marriage difficult. Other states have begun divorce prevention programs. The Oklahoma Marriage Initiative, intended to reduce the second-highest divorce rate in the nation, involves marriage "ambassadors" who conduct "relationship rallies" and train counselors and educators in techniques to increase spouses' satisfaction with each other and their relationship (Schaffer, 2002; Tyre, 2002).

In their attempt to identify the causal conditions associated with relationship satisfaction and stability, researchers have faced the usual conceptual, methodological, and analytical obstacles. It might be surprising to some that they also continue to encounter beliefs that made relationships difficult to study before the mid-twentieth century. In an article titled "The Science of a Good Marriage," *Newsweek* reported the progress John Gottman and other relationship researchers have made in identifying the determinants of a satisfying marriage (Kantrowitz & Wingert, 1999). As is customary, the magazine published a summation of responses to the article ("For Better, for Worse"):

> Most readers we heard from on our April 19 article "The Science of a Good Marriage" weren't sold on . . . [the] view that the ingredients of connubial contentment can be quantified and mapped. The idea that any set of guidelines can determine whether a couple should stay married is "ridiculous and insulting," said one reader. (p. 20)

The public's belief that relationships are too complex to be "quantified and mapped" coexists with society's ravenous appetite for relationship information, as is illustrated by booksellers' shelves sagging under the weight of countless "relationship improvement" books. It also coexists with mounting evidence that threats to the institution of marriage are not likely to decrease soon. Two months after the *Newsweek* article was published, the National Marriage Project at Rutgers University (Levy, 1999) issued a press release reporting that young people are increasingly pessimistic about achieving a satisfying marriage. The percentage of high school girls who expect to stay married for life dropped from 68% in 1976 to 64% in 1995; moreover, 53% said it was worthwhile to have a child out of wedlock compared with 33% in 1976. Project investigators speculated that children of divorce, particularly women, have grown wary of marriage.

MEASURING RELATIONSHIP SATISFACTION AND STABILITY

Because the marital relationship plays a central role in most people's lives, and because society has a heavy stake in the stability of marriage, studies of relationship satisfaction and stability have focused heavily on premarital and marital relationships. The former have the potential to end in marriage, and thus, in addition to being interesting and important in themselves, the study of premarital relationships is believed to have the added benefit of providing insight into the marital relationship. With relatively few exceptions, relationship satisfaction and stability have been examined in North American, white, middle-class marriages and in the premarital relationships of North American college students. Other types of relationship, which usually are dissolved more easily and with less consequence, have been of lesser interest. Finally, because satisfaction lies at the core of questions about relationship development and maintenance, virtually all of the theories discussed in Chapter 7, "Relationship Growth and Maintenance," are relevant to questions of marital satisfaction and stability, as further discussed in this chapter.

Marital Stability

Like the concept of relationship itself, stability is a temporal concept, referring to whether an entity stays the same or changes over time. As used by researchers, the term **marital stability** refers to the continuation or dissolution of the marriage; in other words, it is the marital contract that is either stable (the contract continues) or unstable (the contract has been terminated through permanent separation or divorce). The stability of a relationship usually is assessed by the individual's self-report that the relationship is intact. Although such self-reports may not agree with those of outside observers, as discussed in Chapter 4, "The Concept of Relationship," they usually are taken at face value; corroborating information, including that from public divorce records, rarely is obtained.

The accepted definition of marital stability does not imply that other features of the relationship, including the partners' satisfaction with it, are stable. Even if the marriage continues, the partners' satisfaction may be unstable—fluctuating in various ways at different times over the course of the relationship. Thus, marital stability does not necessarily reflect stability of marital satisfaction (see Karney, Bradbury, & Johnson, 1999). Relationships may take different paths to the same end—for example, dissolution. This phenomenon is termed **relationship equifinality**, which means that knowing a relationship's destination is not informative of the route it took to its fate.

Marital Satisfaction

Most measures used in the field have been designed to assess marital satisfaction as opposed to satisfaction in other types of relationships. An exception is the Relationship Assessment Scale, a short generic scale permitting comparison across different types of relationship (S.S. Hendrick, 1988; Hendrick, Dicke, & Hendrick, 1998). In contrast to the scarcity of instruments used to assess satisfaction across and within other kinds of relationship, measures of marital satisfaction abound. The proliferation is a result of re-searchers' chronic dissatisfaction with marital satisfaction measures.

The earliest measure of marital satisfaction, developed by Hamilton (1929), was followed by numerous others over the next few decades. Surveying the array that had accumulated, Locke and Wallace (1959) culled 15 items they personally judged to be "basic" to form the Locke–Wallace Marital Adjustment Test (MAT), which quickly became popular and remains in use today. The first item on the MAT, which is more heavily weighted in the total score than other items, assesses **global marital satisfaction** (positive or negative sentiment toward the relationship). The respondent is asked to check a dot on a line labeled "very unhappy" at one end (and said to be appropriate for "those few who are very unhappy in marriage") to "happy" at midpoint (said to represent "the degree of happiness most people get from marriage") to "perfectly happy" (to be endorsed by "those few who experience extreme joy or felicity in marriage"). The remaining items ask the respondent to report on various activities and behaviors such as agreements or disagreements in the handling of several matters, including family finances.

Like the MAT, virtually all marital satisfaction scales contain at least one item that asks the respondent to report his or her global satisfaction with the relationship on a unidimensional scale ranging from negative to positive. Evidence that affective space is best viewed as two-dimensional, and thus that positive and negative affect toward a person or relationship are relatively independent and should be measured separately (as discussed in Chapter 9, "Affective Processes"), has yet to influence many satisfaction measures, although persuasive arguments for such a change have been presented. Fincham, Beach, and Kemp-Fincham (1997), for example, observe that although unidimensional scales can differentiate between highly satisfied and highly distressed spouses, they cannot discriminate between these two groups and spouses who are ambivalent toward the relationship (very possibly many long-term spouses) and also spouses who have become indifferent (Figure 13.1).

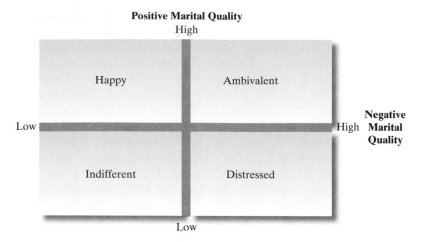

Positive Marital Quality
High

Happy	Ambivalent

Low ————————————————— High **Negative Marital Quality**

Indifferent	Distressed

Low

FIGURE 13.1 Fincham and colleagues (1997) propose a two-dimensional conceptualization of marital quality. Positive and negative marital quality are crossed to produce a typology of couples who can be distinguished in terms of important characteristics of their marriages. Those high on positive marital quality and low on negative marital quality fit the traditional definition of "happy" or "satisfied" couples, and those who show the reverse pattern (low positive, high negative) of marital quality fit the usual understanding of "distressed" or "dissatisfied" couples. Unidimensional scales of marital satisfaction can differentiate between these two couple types. However, they cannot differentiate between the two other couple types (ambivalent and indifferent). *Adapted from Fincham, Beach, and Kemp-Fincham, "Marital Quality: A New Theoretical Perspective" (1997), Fig. 11.1, p. 284.*

The MAT failed to satisfy some researchers, most notably Spanier (1972), who subsequently devised the Dyadic Adjustment Scale (DAS; 1976). The DAS contains 12 of the 15 MAT items and, not surprisingly, correlates highly with the MAT. Although the DAS currently appears to be the most frequently used marital satisfaction measure, conceptualization and articulation of the construct the DAS was intended to measure (marital satisfaction) are vague, a feature shared by the MAT and many other scales. Because they have been developed without theoretical guidance (see Fincham et al., 1997; Heyman, Sayers, & Bellack, 1994), few marital satisfaction measures are accompanied by information attesting to **construct validity**—information documenting that the instrument actually measures the construct it claims to measure (Cronbach & Meehl, 1955).

Construct validity is one of the most important concepts in psychology. As Westen and Rosenthal (2003) explain, construct validity "is at the heart of any study in which researchers use a measure as an index of a variable that is not itself directly observable" (p. 608). Relationship satisfaction is such a variable. Validity cannot be determined if the construct is not embedded within a theoretical framework that clearly defines it and specifies its presumed associations (positive, negative, or neutral) with other constructs. Validity is established by demonstrations that the measure possesses *discriminant validity* (it is *not* associated with valid measures of other constructs with which the theory specifies it should be unrelated) and *convergent validity* (it is positively or negatively associated with valid measures of constructs with which the theory states it should be associated). Westen and Rosenthal have developed simple procedures for estimating construct validity. Unfortunately, relationship satisfaction measures often possess only *face validity*—the items "look like" they measure the construct named in the scale's label.

Moreover, despite the fact that instruments claiming to assess marital satisfaction are variously labeled as measures of marital *satisfaction*, marital *adjustment*, marital *quality*, and marital *happiness*, these labels neither reflect different conceptualizations of the satisfaction construct nor are diagnostic of a measure's content. As a consequence, comparisons across studies can be hazardous (e.g., Sabatelli, 1988), and calculations of algorithms that permit across-scale score comparisons have constituted a cottage industry for marital researchers.

Problems in Identifying the Determinants of Satisfaction

Researchers frequently ask people to complete measures of both satisfaction and the variable hypothesized to be a determinant of satisfaction, such as love. These nonexperimental data typically are subjected to a type of regression analysis to determine whether a person's satisfaction score is associated with, and thus can be predicted from, his or her score on the measure of the hypothesized determinant (see Chapter 4). Frequently, several other suspected or known determinants are measured on the same occasion, and the data are subjected to multiple regression analysis (MRA) to estimate how well each variable predicts satisfaction (when statistically isolated from the other variables) or how well the data fit the investigator's idea of how the variables should be associated with each other as well as with satisfaction. These MRA statistics, representing the degree of association between satisfaction and its hypothesized determinant(s) and the associations between each determinant and the other determinants, are often inflated; that is, the *true* associations are often weaker than the coefficients indicate.

Shared Content Between Measures

One reason the true association between the measure of satisfaction and the measure of its suspected determinant is usually less than the regression statistic represents is that the two measures often share the same content—they are assessing the same thing. Several marital satisfaction scales—including the MAT and the DAS—have been characterized as omnibus mea-sures because they ask respondents to report their subjective, global satisfaction with the marriage—that is, their positive or negative sentiment toward the marriage—*and* to describe various marital activities and processes believed to be determinants of satisfaction, such as degree of agreement or disagreement on important issues. For example, less than 25% of the total variance in the DAS can be attributed to satisfaction alone (Eddy, Heyman, & Weiss, 1991). In other words, a respondent's score on an omnibus satisfaction measure not only represents the satisfaction *outcome* but it also represents some of the *processes* believed to cause satisfaction. As a consequence, if the researcher is testing the hypothesis that the degree to which partners experience conflict influences marital satisfaction, the respondents' conflict scores necessarily will be positively correlated with their MAT scores because the MAT contains 8 items assessing the degree to which the spouses agree or disagree on important matters. There is a *confound* between the measure of the predictor variable and the measure of the outcome variable—both are partially measuring the same thing (see Kelley, 1992; McNulty and Karney, 2001).

The problem of shared content has led to a distinction between omnibus marital satisfaction measures and **global marital satisfaction measures**, which measure *only* sentiment toward the relationship (e.g., the Quality Marriage Index; Norton, 1983). It should be noted that the problem with omnibus measures is *not* that their components do not cohere; for example, scores on the Satisfaction subscale of the DAS correlate highly with scores on its three other subscales (Sabourin, Lussier, Laplante, & Wright, 1991). Moreover, the problem is *not* that omnibus scales do not correlate highly with global measures; Heyman and colleagues (1994), who contrasted the performance of two global measures of marital satisfaction with the omnibus DAS, found that all the scales correlated highly with each other. Similarly, Karney and Bradbury (1997) found no noteworthy differences in performance between the omnibus MAT and three global satisfaction scales. Some investigators define the satisfaction construct as multidimensional and have developed scales to measure each dimension theorized to constitute a facet of the construct (e.g., Hassebrauck & Fehr, 2002). In short, the problem is not that omnibus scales are not valuable measures of marital satisfaction. In fact, use of the MAT and DAS facilitates across-study comparisons of results because so many past studies have used these measures. The problem is that *when* there is content overlap between an outcome measure such as satisfaction and the measure of its hypothesized predictor, the association statistic used is likely to be spuriously high.

Measures of suspected determinants of satisfaction tend to be highly correlated not only with satisfaction but also with each other. For example, Attridge, Berscheid, and Simpson (1995) administered a measure of satisfaction as well as measures of many variables believed to be associated with satisfaction, including investment, self-disclosure, commitment, goodness of alternatives, love, trust, dependency, subjective closeness, and behavioral closeness. All were highly correlated with satisfaction and with each other. Like satisfaction, the construct validity of many measures of the suspected determinants of satisfaction is not known; also like satisfaction, their labels do not always reflect their contents. For example, Ponzetti and Cate (1987) administered several measures of constructs believed to be associated with satisfaction and stability, but unlike some investigators, they were careful to describe the contents of each scale they used ("Love was assessed by ten items that measured feelings of closeness, belonging and commitment" [p. 7]). If other investigators were to use that particular Love scale on the basis of its label and without examining its content, a spuriously high correlation likely would be found between it and a closeness measure and also between it and a commitment measure because these pairs of measures are partially assessing the same thing.

Shared Method Between Measures

In addition to content, the satisfaction measure and the measure of its suspected determinant often share the same method. For example, relationship satisfaction is measured by an indi-

vidual's self-report on a pencil-and-paper questionnaire, as we have discussed, and the variables hypothesized to be determinants of satisfaction, such as love, also are usually measured by questionnaire self-report. Moreover, they are often measured at the same time and in the same setting, as they were in the 1995 study by Attridge and colleagues. When measures share the same method— for example, self-report—any response biases associated with the method (such as the tendency for people to present themselves in socially desirable ways) or with the time and setting (for example, mood) are likely to influence all measures in the same way and contribute to inflated statistical indices of association.

When relationship satisfaction is the variable of interest, another type of response bias contributes to shared method variance: sentiment override, which is the tendency for an individual's global sentiment toward the partner and the relationship to color his or her reports of the partner's behavior, attitudes, and activities (see Chapter 9). Attridge and colleagues discovered that a single factor—representing positive or negative sentiment toward the partner and the relationship—appeared to underlie people's evaluations of their partners on the satisfaction measure and on the many measures of putative satisfaction determinants.

Another example of sentiment override is provided by Lorenz, Conger, Simon, Whitbeck, and Elder (1991), who asked wives and husbands to report on the degree of hostility and warmth their spouses displayed in their interactions with them. The investigators found that "wives' reports of their husbands' hostility and warmth, and vice versa, say more about their own marital quality than they do about the concepts supposedly measured" (p. 383). Lorenz and colleagues conclude, "The phenomenon of method variance, witnessed by the inflation of correlations between concepts measured by a single informant, constitutes a major threat to theory testing efforts." It should be noted, however, that sentiment override, which helps assure that responses to affectively saturated variables such as relationship satisfaction and most of its presumed determinants will be highly correlated with each other, is a genuine psychological phenomenon; that is, people's reports of their spouses' behaviors undoubtedly reflect their true perceptions. Those perceptions constitute "error" and "method variance" only when the investigator takes them to be objective reports of behavior.

Fortunately, Lorenz and associates did not rely exclusively on the self-report method; they also obtained outside observers' reports of each partner's behavior, which allowed them to estimate the presence of method variance due to sentiment override and to control for its effects. The high correlations frequently found among variables when only one method has been used to measure them has been termed "glop" (Bank, Dishion, Skinner, & Patterson, 1990; see Gottman, 1998). Glop is a severe problem in relationship satisfaction research. Problems created by shared method variance are the principal reason methodologists and psychometricians advise using more than one method to measure constructs (see Campbell & Fiske, 1959).

Reciprocal Causality

Although shared content and shared method often contribute to the spuriously high correlations found between satisfaction and its presumed determinants, it is important to note that these variables—and many other relationship variables—truly *are* highly associated with each other. One reason for their close association is **reciprocal causation feedback loops**. Not only are trust and satisfaction likely to be causally reciprocal (see Chapter 7) but reciprocal causation feedback loops are likely to be found between satisfaction and most of its determinants and between each of those determinants and the others. For example, not only may an increase in trust raise satisfaction and the increase in satisfaction then raise trust, but an increase in satisfaction may increase commitment, which may enhance trust, which may increase investment in the relationship, which may increase love, all of which, separately or collectively, may feed back to further raise satisfaction, which may then feed back to increase positive feelings on other dimensions. Conversely, of course, distrust may produce dissatisfac-

tion, which may then reverberate through the relationship to influence all relationship dimensions associated with satisfaction. Such negative reciprocal causation processes undoubtedly contribute to "negative spiraling," the accelerating downhill slide observed in some marital relationships (Waller, 1930/1967).

The fact that measures of the known and suspected determinants of satisfaction tend to produce a highly glutinous mass in nonexperimental data—a situation statisticians call **multicollinearity of predictors** in regression analyses—presents a problem for researchers who wish to statistically disentangle the effect on satisfaction of just one variable in the mass from the effects of the other variables. The results of such analyses tend to be unstable. They often do not replicate, even when the samples of respondents in the studies are nearly identical (see Gordon, 1968; Maruyama, 1998; Shively, 1998). Cate, Levin, and Richmond's (2002) review of the premarital satisfaction and stability literature cites several replication failures involving MRA; high multicollinearity of the predictors of satisfaction is the likely culprit.

In sum, in the natural world, good things (and bad things) tend to be found together. One reason they often are found together is that positive (or negative) events frequently cause other positive (or negative) events to happen and prevent negative (or positive) events from happening. It is difficult to separate in nonexperimental data what Mother Nature has joined together in the natural world. The severe limitations of nonexperimental studies that measure satisfaction and its suspected determinants at a single point in time have increased appreciation of the value of longitudinal studies, which sometimes provide insight into temporal processes, as we shall shortly discuss. However, when surveying the legions of studies that have attempted to identify the determinants of relationship satisfaction, it is useful to remember that nonexperimental data—even longitudinal data—are a poor substitute for experimental data, where randomization is possible and the temporal occurrence of the variables of interest is known (see McKim & Turner, 1997; Rutter, Pickles, Murray, & Eaves, 2001).

MARITAL SATISFACTION OVER TIME

National surveys indicate that at any given time, most Americans say they are highly satisfied with their marriages. In Veroff, Douvan, and Kulka's (1981) nationally representative survey, 80% said their marriages were either very happy or above average in happiness, consistent with the results of an earlier survey in which 90% reported they were above average in happiness (Campbell, Converse, & Rodgers, 1976). These survey data agree with evidence that married people are happier than persons who are unmarried, separated, divorced, or widowed (see Chapter 2, "Relationships and Health"), and they also are consistent with smaller-scale studies. For example, most of the 354 married persons who responded to Kayser's (1993) mail questionnaire reported that they loved their partners; only a minority (19%) exhibited even some degree of emotional withdrawal from their marriages, although women were more likely to be disaffected than men. Levels of satisfaction and happiness in gay and lesbian unions appear to be comparable to those of heterosexual couples (see Peplau & Spalding, 2000). Moreover, the processes associated with satisfaction and stability in established homosexual partnerships appear to be no different than those in heterosexual marriages (e.g., see Kurdek, 2000).

Some evidence suggests, however, that the quality and character of intact marriages may be changing. Glenn and Weaver (1988) found a steady decline from 1972 through 1986 in the association between reported happiness and marriage (primarily because of an increase in the self-reported happiness of never-married men and a decrease in the happiness of married women). Indeed, Glenn (1991) concluded from his review of studies of marital success in the United States that self-reports of marital happiness declined slightly from the early 1970s to the late 1980s and that measures of **marital success** (defined as self-reports from persons in intact marriages who describe their marriage as "very happy") declined substantially. Rogers and Amato (1997) examined marital quality in a national probability sample representing people married between 1969 and 1980 and between 1981 and 1992 and found that both men and women in the latter group reported higher levels of marital conflict and problems.

A more recent comparison of 1980 national survey data with 2000 data led Amato, Johnson, Booth, and Rogers (2003) to conclude that marital satisfaction and likelihood of divorce changed little over the period, but the degree to which spouses shared activities had declined significantly. Moreover, although marital quality did not appear to change overall, the factors contributing to and detracting from the marriage's quality had changed (but balanced out each other's effects). Dissimilarity of spouses' race, ethnicity, religion, education, and age increased, as did premarital cohabitation and wives' job demands and increased hours of employment; all of these changes were associated with *declines* in marital quality. Associated with *increases* in quality were increases in economic resources, more egalitarian marital relations such as equality of decision-making, and increased belief in lifelong marriage.

Survey data thus continue to present a relatively sanguine portrait of marital satisfaction. It is only when the grim reality of divorce statistics—which suggest that at least one-half, perhaps as many as two-thirds, of all marriages will end in divorce or permanent separation (e.g., Cherlin, 1992)—are placed against that backdrop that the picture changes. The discrepancy between the percentage of spouses who say they currently are happy with their marriage and the percentage projected to divorce invites many explanations: (1) Because it takes two people to continue a relationship and only one to dissolve it, some satisfied respondents may be married to dissatisfied spouses who dissolve the marriage. (2) Measures of marital satisfaction are invalid and unreliable and possibly subject to the social desirability response bias. A 1989 Gallup poll, for example, found that when first asked, 84% of married people said they were "very satisfied" with their marriages, but further questioning revealed that 40% had considered leaving their partners and 20% said they had bad marriages half the time (see Olson, 1990). (3) While marital satisfaction has stayed the same, barriers to divorce have fallen and alternatives have increased, so the threshold of marital satisfaction prompting divorce appears to be lower than it used to be (see White & Booth, 1991). (4) Relatedly, people who are satisfied with their marriage at one point in time—or even most of the time—but find themselves dissatisfied at any point quickly dissolve the relationship.

Cross-Sectional Studies of Satisfaction

Until recently, most studies of marital satisfaction were cross-sectional; that is, the happiness of different groups of couples married for different lengths of time was measured at a single point in time. Principally from such studies, but also from at least one longitudinal study (e.g., Pineo, 1961), Glenn (1989) estimated that marital satisfaction decreases with age of the marriage for the first 10 years and perhaps for as long as 25 years but shows a slight upswing in long-term marriages. The so-called U-curve of marital satisfaction (actually a reverse J-curve) became a familiar feature in many marriage texts.

Cross-sectional studies of the association between marital satisfaction and marital duration suffer from several problems (see Glenn & Weaver, 1978). Most important is the fact that the people in each cross-sectional group are different from the people in the other groups in a multitude of unknown ways. There is no random assignment to marital duration groups; rather, "the deed has been done" not by the researcher but by the participants, who have selected themselves into different marital duration groups for reasons unknown. The slightly higher levels of satisfaction observed in cross-sectional studies for couples married 20 years or longer (compared to their younger counterparts) sometimes has been attributed to those couples' improved financial status and to their children having left home (and with their departure, a reduction in stress). However, it is equally if not more likely that these cross-sectional data reflect the fact that

dissatisfied couples who married at the same time as those in the long duration groups divorced and are now absent from this cohort. In other words, the couples who remain in the longer-duration cohort may *always* have been more satisfied with their marriages than the other couples. If so, the longer-duration couples experienced no upswing in satisfaction—from the very beginning, they were happier than other couples who married at the same time they did. Cross-sectional studies may be suggestive, but only longitudinal studies, which follow the same people through time, can trace the temporal course of satisfaction.

Longitudinal Studies of Satisfaction and Stability

A 40-year longitudinal study of men's health reported by Vaillant and Vaillant (1993) cast suspicion on the so-called U-curve of marital satisfaction found in cross-sectional studies. Marital satisfaction had been periodically assessed for the men (and some of their wives) over the course of the study, and these data revealed that the participants' satisfaction had declined continuously over the four decades. When they were asked to *retrospectively* recall how satisfied they had been at different points over the marital course, however, the U-curve was found.

Longitudinal studies of premarital and marital satisfaction and stability were scarce for many years. After a 1938 study by Terman and associates, which principally tried to identify the personality correlates of satisfaction, the next major longitudinal study was conducted by sociologists Burgess and Wallin (1953), who interviewed engaged couples in the late 1930s. The couples were interviewed again in the early 1940s after they had been married for at least 3 years (see Pineo, 1961) and then again approximately 10 years later, after they had been married up to 20 years (see Dizard, 1968). An early drop in marital satisfaction was observed. Supplementary evidence suggested that erosion of the romanticism and idealization of the partner present during courtship was responsible.

Longitudinal studies have increased exponentially in recent years because of the recognition that such studies are essential to answer many questions about relationships, including questions of satisfaction and stability (see Karney & Bradbury, 1995b; Bradbury, 1998). However, most have been two-wave studies, with second-wave data collected shortly after the initial data collection (see Karney, Bradbury, & Johnson, 1999). Although more informative than cross-sectional studies, two-wave prospective studies usually can provide only minimal information about the dynamics of satisfaction over time. Over long marriages, some couples may experience rises, declines, or plateaus in satisfaction, and some—perhaps most—may experience all three types of change; moreover, they may experience these changes in different sequences, for different durations, and at different times. By allowing only for an examination of the association between Time 1 and Time 2 satisfaction measurements, two-wave studies permit only one of three inferences: satisfaction stayed the same, declined, or rose over time.

Long-term multiple-wave studies are still relatively rare because of the enormous costs they impose on researchers, who, not infrequently, must devote their entire professional lives to following a single group of people over many years. Nevertheless, studies in which satisfaction and stability are measured at several points in time over a long period are crucial to an understanding of satisfaction dynamics. Not only can such studies map the flow of satisfaction over time, but they sometimes are able to draw inferences between the occurrence of certain events and subsequent satisfaction changes. Only a handful of multiple-wave longitudinal studies of marital satisfaction and stability have yet been conducted, but their findings generally have been consistent and of great value.

The PAIR Project

The Processes of Adaptation in Intimate Relationships (PAIR) project conducted by Ted Huston and his colleagues studied 168 newly-wed couples, who had married for the first time and had been identified from marriage licenses. Most were white and from working-class backgrounds. The first intensive phase of data collection took place 2 months after the couples' wedding, and assessments continued periodically over the first year; the second phase took place 1 year later and the third phase 1 year after that; a fourth phase of data collection took place 10 years after the third phase, or 13 years after the couples had married. By this last phase, 56 couples had divorced, 4 spouses had been widowed, and 104 were still married (the status of 4 couples could not be determined).

Huston, McHale, and Crouter (1986) report that by the first anniversary, spouses' marital satisfaction had significantly declined on all indicants of satisfaction. The decline occurred whether the partners had or had not cohabited before marriage, and it also occurred whether or not they became parents. Wives reported more dissatisfaction than husbands both initially and 1 year later.

Declines in satisfaction over the first few years of marriage have been attributed to at least three different processes, characterized by Huston and his colleagues (e.g., Huston, Caughlin, Houts, Smith, & George, 2001) as the **enduring dynamics model** (sometimes called the perpetual problems model), which posits that problems that arise in courtship simply continue on into marriage; the **emergent distress model**, which states that marriage increases the couple's interdependence, in turn precipitating *new* problems and conflicts; and the **disillusionment model**, which posits that as couples become more interdependent and interact more frequently in a wider array of situations, rosy illusions about the partner and the relationship that developed in the premarital relationship—through the concealment of weaknesses, avoidance of disagreements, and cognitive processes that reduce doubts—are destroyed. Citing the epigram "Marriage is the remedy for the disease of love—a remedy which operates by destroying the love," the first dean of marriage theorists, sociologist Willard Waller (1938), believed that reality begins to intrude on the fantasy and illusion that fueled the romance "when the honeymoon's over" (p. 309).

The title of the 1986 report by Huston and colleagues on the PAIR project spouses' decline in satisfaction by their first anniversary—"When the Honeymoon's Over"—reflected the fact that accompanying the newlyweds' self-reports of satisfaction decrease was a striking change in the *affective tone* of the couples' interactions—thus providing support for the disillusionment model. There was a dramatic reduction (about 40%) in the extent to which the newlyweds said and did things pleasurable to their spouses and also in the extent to which they displayed affection through hugging, kissing, or sexual intercourse. The rate at which the spouses reported specific displeasing behaviors by their partner was low in the beginning and did not increase over the first year, but global reports of negativity and conflict in their marriage did increase significantly.

Despite the decrease in positive affective tone and increase in overall negativity and conflict, the investigators noted that the typical husband and wife felt far from neutral toward each other on their first anniversary, "the differences among the couples being more a matter of degree of satisfaction (or love) than a matter of some couples being satisfied (or in love) and others being distressed (or hostile)" (p. 125). Thus, even though the affective tone of marital interaction became less positive over the year, it remained highly positive overall for most couples (excepting the 12 who separated). Importantly, the degree of negativity present in the marriage at the beginning of the first year was not associated with the newlyweds' initial marital satisfaction, but it did forecast the partners' degree of negativity and marital satisfaction by the end of the year.

The three popular explanations for early satisfaction decline are not mutually exclusive; all three processes may operate in concert in varying degrees in most marriages. Although the increasingly strong inverse correlations between love and both negativity and conflict provide support for the disillusionment model of marital distress, the investigators also found support for the perpetual problems model. Couples who reported having trouble getting along while they were courting were more likely to experience greater levels of conflict at each successive year of their marriage; in other words, premarital conflict and ambivalence foretold how satisfied and how much in love spouses would be two years into marriage (Huston, 1994; Huston & Houts, 1998).

Huston and colleagues (2001) were able to contact 156 of the original 168 PAIR couples 13 or 14 years after they had wed and found that 100 couples remained married. Of these 100 still-married couples, 68 scored above "neutral" on a marital satisfaction scale and were classified as *happily married*, and 32 scored below "neutral" and were classified as *unhappily married*. Of the 56 couples who had divorced (a divorce rate similar to the national divorce rate of couples who married at the same time as those in the sample), 10 had *quickly divorced* (before their second anniversary), 21 had *divorced early* (after 2 to 7 years of marriage), and 25 had *divorced later* (after 7 years). Couples who were happily married a decade later initially had been more deeply in love, had seen each other as possessing more "responsive" personalities, and had reported less ambivalence about their relationship than those in the unhappily married and the divorced early groups. They also had expressed less negativity toward each other initially than had those in the unhappily married group. Strangely enough, the divorced later couples had behaved more affectionately with each other than any other group of couples during their early years and had been comparable to the happily married couples in their degree of love. Couples who quickly divorced, however, were less in love at the beginning and displayed more negativity than any of the other four groups of couples.

Within the divorced group as a whole, *initial levels* of love and responsiveness were associated with whether the couple divorced quickly, early, or late. However, a comparison of the entire divorced group with the entire still married group revealed that *changes* over the first 2 years in the couple's love, ambivalence, and perceptions of the spouse's responsiveness and "contrariness" were associated with later marital stability even after differences in the initial levels of these variables were controlled. The researchers conclude that the strength of the partners' romantic bond initially and its decline in strength over time, as opposed to increases in negativity, presage divorce.

Satisfaction Trajectories

Multiple-wave longitudinal studies permit the investigator to use **growth curve analysis** to describe two parameters of the trajectory each partner's relationship satisfaction has taken over time: the partner's initial satisfaction level (that is, the *intercept*), and the *slope* of subsequent changes in satisfaction (e.g., see Karney et al., 1999; Raudenbush, Brennan, & Barrett, 1995). This analytical technique was used by Karney and Bradbury (1997), who asked a sample of 60 newlywed couples to rate their marital satisfaction at several points over a 4-year period. The course of satisfaction experienced over the 4 years by two husbands is illustrated in Figure 13.2. Husband A starts out higher in satisfaction than Husband B (has a higher intercept) and remains higher at all points, despite a significant decline in satisfaction over the period. Although Husband B starts the marriage with lower satisfaction than Husband A, his satisfaction fluctuates but does not decline. Karney and Bradbury point out that knowing only one of these dimensions presents an incomplete, and possibly misleading, picture of how these marriages differ.

Karney and Bradbury found that both husbands and wives reported relatively high marital satisfaction as newlyweds, corroborating the findings of Huston and colleagues (1986). Although substantial differences were found among couples in their initial satisfaction levels, these differences were *not* predictive of the marital dissolution of the 32% who divorced or permanently separated within the first 4 years; in other words, those who dissolved their marriages began at approximately the same satisfaction levels as those whose marriages remained intact. Overall, satisfaction of both husbands and wives declined linearly over time. Moreover, Karney and Bradbury's several early data points allowed them to determine that a significantly greater decline in satisfaction occurred during the first year than in the subsequent 3 years. Marital satisfaction declined more steeply in marriages that dissolved than in stable marriages, although the decline in the latter was still significantly negative (declining about 3% of the total range of each satisfaction measure each year). A few spouses (10%) beat the odds and showed a rise—not a decline—in satisfaction over the period.

Karney and Bradbury found that absolute levels of satisfaction did not appear to play an important role in decisions to divorce. Low levels of satisfaction appeared to lead to dissolution only to the extent that such marriages experienced relatively steep declines. This result suggests that the rate of *change* in satisfaction over time is important in predicting dissolution, a finding

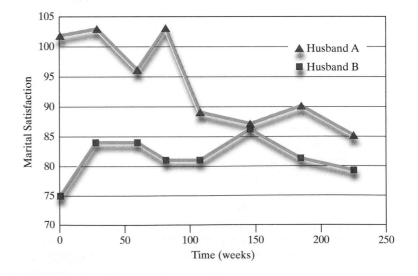

FIGURE 13.2 Four years of marital satisfaction for two husbands. *From Karney and Bradbury, "Neuroticism, Marital Interaction, and the Trajectory of Marital Satisfaction" (1997), Fig. 1, p. 1076.*

consistent with basic research findings. Hsee and Abelson (1991) found that current satisfaction with an outcome depends not only on whether the outcome currently is better or worse than it was previously but also on the speed with which the change in outcome quality occurs. Their model suggests that the faster a good outcome declines, the more dissatisfied the person will be; conversely, the quicker a poor outcome improves, the happier the person will be (see also Hsee, Salovey, & Abelson, 1994).

Like the PAIR project couples, where the husband and wife within each couple showed a similar decline in satisfaction and love over the first 2.5 years of marriage (MacDermid, Huston, & McHale, 1990), Karney and Bradbury found that a wife and her husband showed equivalent declines; the satisfaction trajectories of wives and husbands within pairs did not differ. Thus, wives overall were no more or less likely to experience a reduction in satisfaction than husbands. Taken as a group, most of

Karney and Bradbury's couples were highly content after 4 years. Although their satisfaction scores had gradually decreased, they remained well above average, just as Huston and colleagues (1986) had found with PAIR project couples.

At least two longitudinal studies have followed marriages for a decade. One of these was conducted by Kurdek (e.g., 1998a, 1998b, 1999, 2002b), who followed 522 couples (not all of whom were in first marriages) for 10 years beginning from the time they were newlyweds (93 couples remained at the end of the period). Again, as newlyweds, the couples started their marriages with high levels of satisfaction, and again, these initial high satisfaction levels were followed by an accelerated decline over the next 4 years. Satisfaction subsequently stabilized for a time before showing an accelerated decline at about the eighth year of marriage (Figure 13.3). Once again, husbands' and wives' trajectories of change in satisfaction were very similar to each

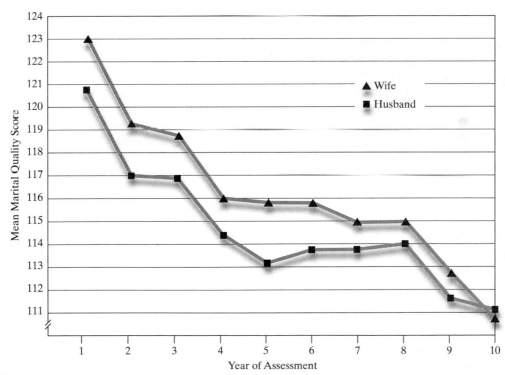

FIGURE 13.3 A longitudinal study of satisfaction in marriage. *Adapted from Kurdek, "The Nature and Predictors of the Trajectory of Change in Marital Quality for Husbands and Wives Over the First 10 years of Marriage" (1999), Fig. 1, p. 1290.*

other, with the exception that wives showed a steeper rate of change. Couples who separated or divorced during the period, in contrast to the 93 couples who remained married at the 10-year point, were less satisfied initially and the wives showed steeper decreases in satisfaction.

Stabilization of marital satisfaction following early decline also was found by the 10-year Denver Family Development Project (e.g., Lindahl, Clements, & Markman, 1998). Satisfaction declined for about 3 years after marriage but then stabilized, with most couples remaining in the nondistressed range of satisfaction. Unlike Kurdek's (2002b) couples, however, no further significant declines were observed.

Most studies of satisfaction stability—whether cross-sectional, two-wave longitudinal, or multiple-wave longitudinal—are consistent in indicating that (1) most newlyweds, whether married for the first time or previously married, start out on the marital road highly satisfied; (2) virtually all couples show significant declines in satisfaction by the end of the first year, although most are still very satisfied with their marriages; (3) husband and wife pairs show similar satisfaction declines; (4) satisfaction after marriage continues to decline for at least 3 years, possibly 4, according to three multiple-wave longitudinal studies, and then, according to the longest longitudinal study available, stabilizes for a period, possibly starting to decline again around the eighth year of marriage; and (5) people who are initially less satisfied than others show steeper satisfaction declines than those who start their marriages at higher satisfaction levels.

In general, most marital scholars agree with Blood's (1967) conclusion, reached on the basis of his early cross-sectional investigation of marriages in the United States and Japan, that there is a

nearly inevitable deterioration of husband–wife relationships under normal conditions. The only way of insulating marriage against attrition is to end it abortively—before children arrive and especially before the honeymoon glow fades. This is one motive for the serial polygamy practiced by movie stars and other romantics in pursuit of eternally youthful relationships. Or one can end relationships even sooner, heeding the warning that "marriage is the death of love"—and pursue lover after lover, only to abandon each once he [or she] surrenders and thereby falls in danger of being taken for granted. (p. 179)

Serial marriage, of course, is no longer practiced only by movie stars and incorrigible romantics—it has become an "emerging family form" (see Brody, Neubaum, & Forehand, 1988), as evidenced by the fact that almost half of all marriages contracted today involve at least one previously divorced person (Cherlin, 1992).

FACTORS ASSOCIATED WITH SATISFACTION

The multitude of factors that someone at some time has hypothesized to influence relationship satisfaction fall into the three general classes of causal conditions (discussed in Chapter 4): personal, environmental, and relational.

Person Conditions

Many researchers have tried to identify the properties and dispositions an individual brings to the relationship that predispose him or her to be satisfied or dissatisfied with it. The early attempt of Terman and associates (1938) to find the personality profile of people who enjoy satisfying marital relationships is an example. Chapter 10, "Dispositional Influences," examined the association between a variety of person conditions and relationship quality. This chapter highlights only a few of these.

Personality Characteristics

An individual's personality may affect only his or her own marital satisfaction, only the partner's satisfaction, or both partners' satisfaction. At least three personality dimensions are reliably associated with marital satisfaction and stability: emotional instability, expressivity, and adult attachment style.

Emotional Instability

Emotional instability—sometimes called neuroticism, negative affectivity, negative emotionality, or psychological distress—is generally viewed as the tendency to experience and express negative thoughts and feelings (see Chapter 10). In addition to correlational studies that show significant associations between an individual's score on a neuroticism scale and his or her score on a marital satisfaction scale at a single point in time (e.g., Russell & Wells, 1994), longitudinal studies also find the association. It will be recalled from Chapter 10 that Kelly and Conley (1987) found that neuroticism, as assessed in the 1930s, was positively correlated with later marital dissolution. Neuroticism also was prospectively associated with later instability in Kurdek's (1993c, 1999) multiple-wave longitudinal study. Karney and Bradbury's (1997) multiple-wave 4-year study of newlyweds' satisfaction trajectories found neuroticism to be associated with lower initial levels of satisfaction, but it had no effect on rate of satisfaction change.

Shackelford and Buss (1997) concluded from their review of research on the associations between marital satisfaction and "Big Five" personality characteristics that emotional stability—as well as agreeableness, conscientiousness, and openness—is associated with marital satisfaction. It is not surprising that positive personality characteristics should be associated with positive outcomes, including marital satisfaction, and that negative personality characteristics—such as depression and other forms of negative affectivity—are associated with dissatisfaction. Negative affectivity and marital dissatisfaction are likely to be causally reciprocal; that is, relationship dissatisfaction often is a cause of negative affectivity as well as the reverse (see Gottman, 1998). Negative affectivity is likely to manifest itself in numerous deleterious ways in marital interaction. One of those ways, Karney and associates (1994) have shown, is through maladaptive attributions of the causes of the spouse's behavior (for example, to malignant as opposed to benign motives), which are likely to increase dissatisfaction and, in turn, negative af-

fectivity. Also illustrating that bad things tend to travel together, at least as far as marriage is concerned, Gotlib, Lewinsohn, and Seeley (1998) found that adolescents with a history of negative affectivity (depression) are more likely than others to marry early; teen marriages, as we shall shortly discuss, are particularly vulnerable to dissolution for a host of reasons.

Robins, Caspi, and Moffitt (2000) examined the association between relationship quality and satisfaction and partners' negative and positive emotionality (the latter included a measure of the individual's ability to provide comfort and express warmth to others). One member in each of 360 dating and married couples had been measured on these variables 3 years earlier as part of a longitudinal health study; the other partner was measured when both partners were interviewed to assess each person's perception of the relationship's quality and his or her satisfaction with it. Both men and women who *themselves* were high in negative emotionality reported lower levels of relationship quality and satisfaction. Moreover, both men and women whose *partners* were high in negative emotionality reported less quality and satisfaction (thus reflecting an additive effect of the partners' negative emotionality on the relationship).

Overall, Robins and colleagues found that low negative emotionality seemed to be a stronger predictor of relationship quality and satisfaction than positive emotionality. However, women were more likely to be satisfied in relationships in which the man was high in positive emotionality, whereas men's happiness was associated only with their female partner's low negative emotionality. Similarity between the partners in these two traits was only weakly associated with relationship quality and satisfaction.

Expressivity

Although several scales are available to measure **expressivity** (see Trierweiler, Eid, & Lischetzke, 2002), generally viewed as a predisposition to express experienced emotion (whether positive or negative), most studies of its association with marital satisfaction index expressivity by using an individual's femininity score on a sex-role inventory (e.g., Bem, 1974). A high femininity score results when the individual endorses as characteristic of him- or herself those items popularly believed to be especially desirable for women—for example, items reflecting sensitivity and concern for others and the tendency to express affection. Men's and women's expressivity has been found to be positively associated with both their own and their partner's satisfaction in heterosexual married couples (e.g., Bradbury & Fincham, 1988; Huston & Geis, 1993; King, 1993; Lamke, 1989; Lamke, Sollie, Durbin, & Fitzpatrick, 1994) and in cohabiting heterosexual, gay, and lesbian couples (Kurdek, 2002a; Kurdek & Schmitt, 1986). Couples in which both partners are high in femininity tend to be happier than couples in which one partner is low on this dimension (Antill, 1983; Zammichieli, Gilroy, & Sherman, 1988).

Houts, Robins, and Huston (1996) report that for couples in the longitudinal PAIR project, problems in courtship were positively associated with both men and women's negative affectivity and inversely associated with their expressivity. The impact of these two personality dispositions on marital satisfaction was as strongly evident 2 years into the marriage as when the couples were newlyweds; both husbands and wives with expressive personalities were more affectionate and more in love with their partners, and they reported less relationship conflict. Moreover, the couples' level of affectional expression appeared to "buffer" the customary inverse association between negativity and satisfaction (Huston & Chorost, 1994). No such buffering effect was found after 13 years of marriage, however, although the partner's affectional expression was positively associated with both husbands' and wives' satisfaction (Caughlin & Huston, 2002).

Attachment Style

Adult attachment style is the most recent predisposition whose association with relationship satisfaction has attracted attention. In one of the earliest studies of the association, Shaver and Brennan (1992) found that attachment style accounted for variability in relationship satisfaction even when Big Five personality traits

(including neuroticism) were controlled. Since then, many investigators have found that attachment style is associated with marital satisfaction in theoretically predictable ways; that is, individuals classified as secure are more likely to be satisfied than insecure individuals (e.g., Feeney, 2002; Kirkpatrick & Davis, 1994; Lussier, Sabourin, & Turgeon, 1997).

Attachment style usually is measured either by Collins and Read's (1990) Adult Attachment Survey (AAS), which classifies individuals as secure, avoidant, or anxious–ambivalent, or Griffin and Bartholomew's (1994) Relationship Scales Questionnaire (RSQ), which assesses a larger variety of attachment styles. Noting that the psychometric properties of neither scale had been well established, Kurdek (2002a) undertook to compare their performance (controlling for the Big Five personality factors) in a study of married, gay, and lesbian couples drawn from an ongoing longitudinal investigation. Kurdek concluded that the RSQ, but not the AAS, yielded psychometrically sound attachment style scores, and that relationship-specific anxiety (as distinguished from depression and also from generalized anxiety, which is a facet of neuroticism) accounts for unique variability in relationship outcomes. In contrast to many previous investigations, the couples were older and in established relationships as opposed to college students in dating relationships.

Ideals, Standards, Beliefs, and Expectations

People tend to use their personal standards and their ideas about the ideal partner and ideal relationship to evaluate the goodness of their romantic relationships (Burgess & Wallin, 1953; Wayment & Campbell, 2000). Today, according to Fletcher, Simpson, Thomas, and Giles (1999), the qualities of an ideal romantic partner are represented by three factors—warmth–trustworthiness, vitality–attractiveness, and status–resources—whereas the ideal romantic relationship seems to be represented by the factors of intimacy–loyalty and passion. The ideal standards model, articulated by Simpson, Fletcher, and Campbell (2001), posits that partner and relationship ideals serve three functions: to estimate and *evaluate* the quality of partners and relationships, to *explain* events in the relationship (thus influencing, for example, the causal attributions individuals make for their partner's behavior), and to *regulate* the individual's behavior, in order to control or adjust to the partner's behavior. The model also proposes that different ideals are held with different degrees of rigidity and that situational factors influence whether those ideals are strictly applied. For example, some researchers have found that people apply their ideals and standards more flexibly to heterosexual short-term relationships than to such long-term relationships as marriage (e.g., Regan, 1998c).

Fletcher, Simpson, and Thomas (2000) assessed the ideal standards of people in newly formed dating relationships (about 3 weeks old) as well as their perceptions of the quality of their relationship once a month for 3 months and again 9 months later for those couples whose relationships were still intact. Congruency between the individual's ideals and perceptions of relationship quality was associated with relationship satisfaction, as others have also found (e.g., Fletcher et al., 1999; Murray, Holmes, & Griffin, 1996). Satisfaction, in turn, was associated with lower dissolution probability. Consistent with an early study by Strauss (1946), however, people who remained in the relationship over the first 3 months appeared to change their ideal standards to fit their perceptions of their current partners and relationships rather than the reverse. The investigators speculate that because perceptions of the current partner and relationship are moored in reality, they are more resistant to change than ideals are.

People's expectations about how they themselves and their partner will act and should act have potent implications for relationship satisfaction and stability. As discussed in Chapter 9, there is a close association between the disconfirmation of an expectancy and the experience of negative emotion. Psychotherapists generally, and marital therapists particularly, long have been aware of the association. For example, Ellis's (1976) rational-emotive therapy seeks to ameliorate the negative emotions of distressed individuals by uncovering their unrealistic beliefs and expectations. Unrealistic expectations about a partner or the relationship are doomed to be disconfirmed. If the expectation is rigidly held even in the face of repeated disconfirmation, the individual is likely to chronically experience negative emotion in the relationship and become dissatisfied (see Berscheid & Ammazzalorso, 2001).

Eidelson and Epstein (1982) developed the Relationship Belief Inventory to assess the degree to which relationship partners hold unrealistic beliefs and expectations about their relationship. The inventory, based on beliefs named by marital therapists as frequent causes of relationship dissatisfaction and those frequently mentioned in the clinical literature, assesses the extent to which the individual believes (1) disagreement is destructive; (2) mind reading is expected—for example, people who care about each other should be able to sense each other's needs without overt communication; (3) partners cannot change; (4) one should be a perfect sexual partner; and (5) men and women differ dramatically in their personalities and relationship needs. Scores on all five subscales were negatively associated with marital satisfaction, and scores on the Partners Cannot Change subscale most highly differentiated distressed couples from nondistressed couples.

Others, too, have found that spouses' realistic expectations are associated with marital satisfaction (e.g., Fincham & Bradbury, 1993; Olson & Larsen, 1989). Kurdek (1992) found that both unrealistic beliefs and unrealistic standards were associated with lower relationship satisfaction in nonclinical samples of heterosexual and homosexual couples. In contrast to spouses, Sabatelli (1988) found that unmarried people hold significantly higher and more idealistic expectations about their prospective spouse and the relationship; he concludes that unrealistic expectations may help account for the reliable and significant drop in marital satisfaction during the first year of marriage.

Baucom, Epstein, Rankin, and Burnett (1996) argue that assessments of relationship schemas should differentiate clearly between beliefs about the ways relationships *actually* operate and those about how they *should* operate. To measure the latter, their Inventory of Specific Relationship Standards assesses *boundaries* the spouses consider appropriate, such as the amount of time spent together and the extent of shared interests and activities; *power–control*, such as the degree to which decisions should reflect compromise as opposed to one partner's wishes; and *investment* in the relationship, or how much the partners should give to the marriages, both instrumentally and expressively. The investigators found that the standards people held, as well as the extent to which they perceived that their standards were being met, were associated with marital satisfaction. Partners with more extreme standards, who required more of the marriage, had higher levels of marital satisfaction, a result reminiscent of Sanderson and Evans' (2001) finding that female college students with higher intimacy goals experience more—not less— relationship satisfaction.

Fletcher and Kininmonth (1992) developed the Relationship Beliefs Scale to assess people's relationship beliefs in 18 categories, including communication ("It is essential for partners to express all their feelings in relationships"), love ("Close relationships cannot work without love"), and trust ("There must be complete honesty between partners"). These investigators found that relationship beliefs moderated the association between an individual's self-reported behavior and relationship satisfaction.

College students' standards for a high-quality romantic relationship were identified by Hassebrauck (1997) using a prototype approach. Twelve clusters of features appear to define the concept of romantic relationship quality—for example, sexuality, similarities, equality, and autonomy. By a wide margin, the most frequently listed single feature of relationship quality was trust—consistent with Acitelli, Kenny, and Weiner's (2001) finding that trust in the partner was the most strongly and widely endorsed item in their study of marital values. In addition to trust, Hassebrauck found that love and honesty had high prototype centrality to the concept of relationship quality. Having similar interests was more peripheral to the concept of relationship quality,

again consistent with the findings of Acitelli and colleagues.

According to Hassebrauck, men judged features associated with harmony and lack of conflict as more central to relationship quality than women did; women judged features related to openness, equality, and dialogue as more central than men did. The latter finding is consistent with several studies that find that women emphasize the importance of communication more than men do (e.g., Feeney, Noller, and Ward, 1997). Indeed, Acitelli (1992) found that wives were more satisfied with their marriages the more they perceived that their husbands talked about the relationship. Tannen (1986), who discusses differences in men's and women's communication styles, argues that women tend to see communication about the relationship as important to closeness, whereas men tend to be anxious about such interactions—perhaps with good reason, for, as discussed further in Chapter 14, "Intervention and Dissolution," women generally have more complaints about the relationship than men do. Regardless of an individual's sex, however, there is evidence that the closer a specific relationship is to his or her prototype of a high-quality relationship, the more satisfied he or she will be (Hassebrauck & Aron, 2001).

Hassebrauck (1997) also examined the extent to which the DAS represents relationship quality and concluded that although the subscales of this widely used omnibus marital satisfaction measure do tap central features of relationship quality, several groups of features named by his research participants are not represented, including some concerned with reciprocity, openness, empathy, and independence-equality.

Environmental Conditions

In contrast to the influence of person conditions on relationship satisfaction and stability, the impact of features of the relationship's physical and social environments has been less frequently studied, particularly by psychologists (Berscheid & Lopes, 1997; Karney & Bradbury, 1995b). As Waller (1930/1967) commented long ago, when a marriage collapses, the inference usually is that it did so because of its inherent weaknesses, which is like saying that a house "just falls to pieces of itself, wind and weather being left out of the demonstration" (p. 107). Sociologists, who tend to view marital and other family relationships as nested in larger social systems whose perturbations are likely to influence the systems they encapsulate, have been more sensitive than psychologists to the effect of wind, weather, and other contextual factors on relationships. Chapter 7 discussed two social environmental factors that psychologists theorize may affect relationship development and stability and whose influence has been supported empirically by sociologists as well as psychologists: the approval of persons in the partners' social network, and the availability of attractive alternatives to the present partner and relationship. This chapter discusses the influence on marital partners' satisfaction and divorce risk of the sociocultural environment in which their relationship is embedded. The importance of the sociocultural context in understanding marital stability is reflected in sociologist Lynn White's (1990) comment, "A shift in the lifetime divorce probability from 10% to well over 50% cannot be explained at the micro level" (p. 904).

Demographic Factors

Sociologists frequently examine the influence of macroeconomic and other social changes on marital satisfaction and stability by searching for significant correlations between these outcomes and identifiable subgroupings within the general population. In large-scale, often atheoretical surveys, the associations between marital satisfaction and stability and several demographic factors (sometimes called structural factors) have been investigated. These factors include age, race, gender, religion, and components of socioeconomic status such as education, income, and occupation. Although demographic factors are sometimes viewed as person conditions because they are located in the individual, Larson and Holman (1994) argue persuasively that they are better viewed as "proxies" for the sociocultural context in which the relationship is embedded; that is,

demographic variables often serve as rough indicators of the relationship's social and physical environments. Race is an example.

Black couples have a higher divorce rate than white couples (Cherlin, 1992). In a longitudinal study of urban couples, Orbuch, Veroff, Hassan, and Horrocks (2002) found that whereas 29% of the white couples had separated or divorced by the 14-year point, 50% of the black couples had (a difference comparable to that seen in national statistics). Higher levels of education were associated with decreases in separation or divorce for white husbands and white and black wives but not for black husbands. These two variables, race and education, accounted for significant variance in separation and divorce, independent of the couple's descriptions of their interaction dynamics (for example, having a destructive conflict style).

Although race is a property of the individual, it is highly unlikely that race *per se* is associated with relationship satisfaction and stability; rather, it is the sociocultural context in which black and white marriages in the United States are embedded that undoubtedly accounts for the association between race and divorce. Black couples are overrepresented in several disadvantaged demographic groups, including low education, low income, and low occupational status, all of which represent low socioeconomic status and a harsh sociocultural environment for the relationship—one that is likely to have an adverse effect on marital satisfaction and stability. Low socioeconomic status, for example, is consistently associated with poor health (Gallo & Matthews, 2003). Regardless of their race, people in poor health—who may be in pain, have impaired mobility, and suffer from low energy—are less likely to be able to maintain satisfying relationships than people who enjoy good health. To take another example, because black men and women have experienced high divorce rates for generations, the present black generation is more likely than white men and women to have had divorced parents. Parental divorce, regardless of the individual's race, is associated with divorce risk (see Chapter 5, "Varieties of Relationship"). Finally, those at the low end of the socioeconomic distribution are disproportionately represented in social and physical environments that expose them to violence, conflict, abuse, and other stressors (Leventhal & Brooks-Gunn, 2000; Taylor, Repetti, & Seeman, 1997; see Chapter 2).

Age at marriage is another demographic factor consistently and strongly related to marital quality and stability (Amato & Rogers, 1997; Heaton, 1991; Holman & Linford, 2001; Karney & Bradbury, 1995b). Teenage marriages are significantly less stable than marriages contracted when the partners are in their mid-20s or older. Somewhat relatedly, several studies have found that the longer partners have dated or known each other prior to marriage, the less likely they are to divorce (e.g., Kurdek, 1991a). Religiosity, often measured by church attendance, is associated with marital stability (e.g., Amato & Rogers, 1997), and parental divorce and remarriage are, as previously discussed, significantly associated with instability.

Employment also is associated with marital satisfaction and stability. The husband's employment has been shown to be positively correlated with satisfaction for both spouses, and the wife's employment is negatively correlated with satisfaction for both spouses (see Karney & Bradbury, 1995b). The wife's income, but not the husband's income, is positively associated with divorce (Amato & Rogers, 1997); indeed, some studies have shown that women's employment and income is positively associated with their thinking about divorce (Booth, Johnson, White, & Edwards, 1984). Evidence relating to the influence of education is inconsistent, but most investigators find that the less educated have an increased likelihood of divorce (e.g., Amato & Rogers, 1997; Kurdek, 1991a). Generally, positive variables are associated with positive marital outcomes and negative variables with negative marital outcomes (see Karney & Bradbury, 1995b).

Socioeconomic status is not often included as a variable in longitudinal studies of marital satisfaction and stability, usually because samples are too small to allow representation along this dimension. Several researchers whose longitudinal samples have been large enough and varied enough to investigate these factors have remarked on the potency of socioeconomic variables in predicting satisfaction and stability (see

Kurdek, 1999; Leonard & Roberts, 1998; Orbuch, et al., 2002). Again, most studies have been conducted with white, middle-class couples, a notable exception being the longitudinal study of black and white marriages conducted by Veroff and his associates (see Veroff, Douvan, Orbuch, & Acitelli, 1998) and the studies noted above (see Bradbury, 1998).

Family Crisis Theories

Structural explanations of divorce maintain that spouses who occupy lower socioeconomic positions experience significantly more stress from sources outside the marital relationship than higher-status partners do, and consequently they have fewer resources to develop satisfying and stable marriages. Several theories of marital satisfaction and stability incorporate the concept of environmental stressors.

Sociologist Reuben Hill's study of the effect of partner separations and reunions in wartime led to his ABCX family crisis theory (1949). The stressor (A)—for example, separation—is theorized to interact with the partners' resources (B), which interact with how the partners interpret the meaning (C) of the stressful situation, which produces the crisis (X). Hill defined crises as stressful situations for which the partners are unprepared and that require the partners to develop new ways of behaving and adapting. Such situations are likely to generate a variety of negative emotions (see Chapter 9).

Hill's ABCX model underscores the fact that an environmental event may be stressful for some families but not for others who have more resources to cope with the stressors they encounter. Some couples have adequate financial resources, a supportive social network, knowledge of helping agencies, and confidence in their ability to surmount the stressor. Other families may have few resources. Having a sick child, for example, is a crisis for families who have no health insurance, no day care, no support network, dual jobs, and few financial resources. The *meaning* the partners make of their situation plays a central role in Hill's theory because some partners may interpret a stressor—say, failure to receive an invitation to a charity ball—as relatively benign, whereas others may construe the same event as a catastrophic one that threatens their friendships, their career, and their children's future.

To recognize that crises sometimes "pile up" and decrease partners' ability to cope with a newly encountered stressor, McCubbin and Patterson (1982) proposed the double ABCX model. The first ABCX refers to the single most recent stressor, and the second ABCX refers to the accumulated stressful events the family was trying to cope with when the most recent stressor occurred. To assess a family's burdens, McCubbin, Patterson, and Wilson (1980) developed the Family Inventory of Life Events and Changes, modeled after Holmes and Rahe's (1967) Social Readjustment Rating Scale. Relationship stressor events typically include situational stressors such as war, illness, natural disasters, and occupational demands; developmental stressors such as parenthood and retirement; and transitional stressors such as death or a change of residence.

Patterson's (e.g., 2002) family adjustment and adaptation response model goes even further in emphasizing that a couple's success in coping with any one stressor depends on what else the partners are dealing with at the time. Crises occur when demands exceed capabilities. Family demands include events of change, ongoing family strains, and daily hassles. It can be seen that the family demand concept is similar to that of an individual's allostatic load (see Chapter 2). Family capabilities include what the family has in terms of tangible and psychosocial resources, such as a support network, and what the family does in terms of efficient coping behaviors. Families attempt "to balance *family demands* with *family capabilities* as these interact with *family meanings* to arrive at a level of *family adjustment* or *adaptation*" (p. 350, emphasis in the original). Adaptation is viewed as a process of restoring balance between the family's capabilities and the demands pressing on it.

The Iowa Youth and Families Project

In 1989, as many families in rural Iowa were coping with farm foreclosures and a severe downturn in the rural economy, Rand Conger and his associates began a longitudinal study of 451 families in which the spouses were biological parents of a seventh grade child and another child within 4 years of the seventh grader's age (see Conger & Conger, 2002). This study provides a classic illustration of how adverse macroeconomic conditions may affect partners' interactions and sour the relationship. The several reports that have emerged from this study document that harsh economic conditions put pressure on the couple, producing emotional distress (depression, anxiety); that emotional distress often leads to conflict in marital interaction; and that marital conflict leads to increasingly negative evaluations of the relationship—and, in some cases, consideration of divorce or separation. Economic pressure on the Iowa couples not only promoted hostility in their marital interactions but also tended to reduce the frequency of supportive behaviors in the relationship—at the very time, of course, that husbands and wives needed supportive behaviors from each other (Conger et al., 1990).

A subgroup of wives and husbands, however, showed little or no increase in emotional distress despite the fact that they, too, were coping with economic adversity. According to Conger and his colleagues (1990), these spouses did not engage in high levels of conflict, did not withdraw from each other, and gave each other support. They also continued to be nurturant toward their children and involved in parenting, which decreased the harmful effects of the economic downturn on their children; nurturant and involved parenting, in fact, subsequently was found to be associated with the quality of the children's romantic relationships in young adulthood (Conger, Cui, Bryant, & Elder, 2001). Conger and his associates conclude that couples' *resilience* to economic hardship is associated with husbands' and wives' provision of emotional support to each other, effective problem-solving skills, and a sense of mastery and self-confidence that helps couples persevere in trying to surmount their economic difficulties (Figure 13.4).

Support from other people in the Iowa families' social network helped them cope with adversity (Figure 13.5). Bryant and Conger (1999) found that the support specifically provided for

FIGURE 13.4 Families living in rural areas of the United States often face severe environmental and economic pressures.

FIGURE 13.5 Social support can help families cope with adversity.

the couple's *relationship* (as opposed to personal support) was associated with a positive change in marital success over a 4-year period. Because the couples had been married for an average of 20 years, the investigators conclude that the influence of the social environment on relationship satisfaction and stability—evident in premarital relationships (see Chapter 7)—remains significant even in long-term marital relationships.

Many other studies of the effects of economic hardship have shown that this environmental factor is likely to increase hostility in the couple's interactions and decrease supportive behavior. In Vinokur, Price, and Caplan's (1996) longitudinal study of 815 recently unemployed job seekers and their spouses (or partners), financial strain increased depressive symptoms in both partners, which, in turn, increased the negativity of their interactions, causing increases in conflict, withdrawal of support, and undermining behaviors. These effects not only reduce marital satisfaction but also are likely to reduce parenting quality, sowing the seeds of future crises involving parents and children.

Although studies of financial strain on marital interaction are more numerous than studies of other kinds of environmental stressors such as natural disasters, these are no less likely to have a negative impact on marital happiness. Among other common environmental stressors are demanding jobs that generate emotional distress which then "spills over" into marital interaction. How spouses react to their partners' job stress is important. Repetti (1989) examined the association between male air traffic controllers' daily workload—for example, high or low air traffic volume—and their family interactions that evening and found that wives' social support in terms of comfort and sympathy was associated with husbands' withdrawal from family interaction (which may have helped the men recover from a stressful day) and fewer expressions of anger. As the number of husbands and wives who both work outside the home increases, the likelihood that job stress will affect their rela-

tionship rises. Bolger, DeLongis, Kessler, and Wethington (1989) found that stress contagion from work to home was evident for both husbands and wives but that husbands were more likely than their wives to bring their work stresses home. That, too, may change as wives ascend to higher-paying and more demanding positions.

The Vulnerability-Stress-Adaptation Model

Karney and Bradbury's (1995b) vulnerability-stress-adaptation model incorporates several concepts from family crisis theory, but it focuses directly on the spouses (as opposed to the larger family unit) and on marital satisfaction and stability (Figure 13.6). The model predicts that

> couples with effective adaptive processes who encounter relatively few stressful events and have few enduring vulnerabilities will experience a satisfying and stable marriage, whereas couples with ineffective adaptive processes who must cope with many stressful events and have many enduring vulnerabilities will experience declining marital quality, separation, or divorce. Couples at other points along these three dimensions are expected to fall between these two extreme outcomes. (p. 25)

Among the couple's enduring vulnerabilities may be the negative person conditions previously discussed. For example, emotional instability of one or both partners—the propensity to experience and express negative emotion—may

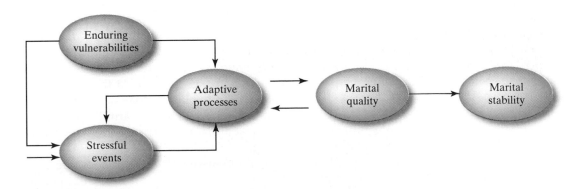

FIGURE 13.6 Karney and Bradbury's vulnerability-stress-adaptation model of marriage. *From Karney and Bradbury, "The Longitudinal Course of Marital Quality and Stability: A Review of Theory, Method, and Research" (1995), Fig. 3, p. 23.*

make a bad situation worse in a crisis. Both chronic vulnerabilities and the absence of adaptation skills (many of which are developed through education and experience, and thus often absent in people with low socioeconomic status and in teenage spouses) may increase the likelihood that stresses will eventually overwhelm the relationship. If coping with the crisis is successful, however, most theorists predict that the partners' bond may be strengthened and their feelings of confidence about coping with future crises increased (see Bradbury, Fincham, & Beach, 2000).

No relationship is free of environmental stressors. However, the number of demands the environment places on a relationship—and their severity—is likely to change over time. Wallerstein and Blakeslee (1995), who have attempted to identify the characteristics of a "good" marriage, observe that solid marriages are like the house made of bricks in the story of "The Three Little Pigs"—so strong that when the Big Bad Wolf came to the door, he could not blow the house down. The wolf comes to virtually every door:

> Because crises are inevitable, a marriage is never out of danger. Threats from without include such unpredictable events as the loss of a job, a forced move to a new area, a natural disaster. The stresses on a marriage inside its walls include maturational changes associated with parenthood, midlife, retirement, and aging, and tragedies such as illness and death. The threat of divorce lurks both outside and inside the house. All major changes—accidental or developmental—have the potential for either weakening the walls of the marriage or leading to their reinforcement. . . . Many of the divorcing couples that I have observed failed to construct a marriage strong enough to withstand the inevitable, acute, and ongoing stresses of life. (p. 27)

Some couples encounter a greater number of stresses, and more severe stresses, than others do, however. Thus, as Karney and Bradbury (1995b) and Berscheid and Lopes (1997) emphasize, predicting the future of a relationship depends not only on identifying a couple's vulnerabilities but also on predicting the environmental changes the relationship is likely to

undergo through time. Many environmental changes will be generated by factors over which the couple has little or no control (job loss, aging), and others will result from decisions the couples themselves make (to raise a child). It will be recalled from Chapter 7 that few people seem to be aware of the extent to which a relationship's environment influences its quality and the partners' sentiment for one another. It thus seems likely that many couples fail to steer their relationship away from environments whose adverse effects it is not strong enough to withstand.

Parenthood

One frequent and far-reaching decision couples make that extensively changes their environment and exposes their relationship to a host of new stressors is their decision to raise a child. A great deal of research has been addressed to how the introduction of an infant affects the marital relationship. Folklore presents conflicting views of that effect. As Belsky (1990) discusses, one view is that children are a reflection of the couple's love and happiness and their presence brings even greater satisfaction and pleasure to the marriage. The opposing view is that children are demanding, expensive, and stressful and erode marital satisfaction. Although family crisis theories predict that both views may be true—depending on the extent of the couple's vulnerabilities and coping resources—the evidence consistently favors the negative view (for reviews, see Belsky, 1990; Sanders, Nicholson, & Floyd, 1997). Although significant, the magnitude of the effect has been estimated to be relatively small on average (about an 8% to 9% reduction in satisfaction). At the same time as children reduce marital satisfaction, they also seem to slightly increase marital stability, an effect most apparent when the children are very young.

As previously noted, the appearance of children early in marriage and their disappearance from the home later has been presumed to be responsible for the U-curve of marital satisfaction found in a multitude of cross-sectional studies. That is, there is a decrease in satisfaction in the early years when children appear; the nadir of satisfaction occurs when the children are adolescents; and a slight upswing in satisfaction appears at the stage when children leave home. Studies that have directly compared the happiness of couples with children to the happiness of those without children who have been married for comparable lengths of time support this interpretation of the satisfaction U-curve. For example, Glenn and McLanahan (1982) found in a large national sample that the presence of children was negatively correlated with a single-item measure of marital satisfaction for both husbands and wives and regardless of race, religion, education, age, socioeconomic status, and marital duration. However, as Belsky (1990) observes, such data are not necessarily the consequence of a negative effect of children on the marital relationship—they may simply reflect the fact that people who are happy with their marriage may decide not to have children. In these ex post facto correlational studies, the different couples have selected themselves into the parental and childless groups for reasons largely unknown to the investigators, and these selection biases may be responsible for the association between satisfaction and childlessness.

Data from longitudinal PAIR project, which followed couples through their transition to parenthood, showed no marital satisfaction differences between the first-time parents and nonparents during the first year of marriage (McHale & Huston, 1985). Nevertheless, most studies—both short-term longitudinal studies that cover the transition to parenthood and cross-sectional studies—show an erosion effect (see Lindahl, Malik, & Bradbury, 1997). Moreover, the changes that have been found to take place in the spouses' interaction patterns are consistent with satisfaction erosion. For example, MacDermid, Huston, and McHale (1990) and others (e.g., Kurdek, 1993b) find that the introduction of a child significantly decreases the amount of time couples spend in companionate interactions and increases the extent to which couples divide household labor in traditional ways. Moreover, Belsky and his colleagues (see Belsky, 1990) have found that expressions of affection, as reported by both the husband and the wife and confirmed by observational data, declined from the first trimester of pregnancy through 9 months postpartum while, at the same time, conflict interactions increased in frequency. As for other environmental events that place strong demands on the marital relationship, it seems likely that successful coping may increase the strength of the marital bond, whereas unsuccessful coping and a continuation of stresses will weaken it.

Relational Characteristics

Relational causal conditions represent how the properties of the partners interact with each other. Of the many relational conditions whose association with satisfaction and stability has been investigated, we focus on two in this chapter: similarity and conflict. Chapter 14 discusses how properties of the partners' interaction pattern, a relational characteristic that emerges from the properties of both partners, influence satisfaction and stability.

Similarity

It will be recalled that when people are asked to rank the importance of various marital values, they tend to put similarity at the bottom of their list. Hattie Andrews, who on July 24, 1976, at age 93, celebrated the 75th anniversary of her wedding to William Andrews, aged 98, disagreed. When asked for her recipe for a long marriage, Mrs. Andrews replied, "Just hang on, trust in the Lord, and don't marry opposites."

Partner similarity is strongly associated with relationship formation and development (see Chapter 6, "Birth of a Relationship"), and, like partners in other kinds of relationships, marriage partners are far more similar to each other than chance would predict. For example, Burgess and Wallin's (1953) longitudinal study of engaged couples found, as have subsequent studies, that spouses are similar to each other on an extraordinarily wide range of social, physical, and psychological characteristics. High **actual similarity**—as measured by objective outside observers and instruments—of spouses' attitudes, beliefs, and values is associated with high marital quality (e.g., Fowers & Olson, 1986).

As many studies have demonstrated, a great deal of similarity undoubtedly exists at the beginning of the relationship. Several general theories of social interaction predict that the partners will become even more similar as the relationship progresses (e.g., Festinger's [1950] theory of informal communication; see Chapter 6). Davis and Rusbult (2001) have found experimental evidence of a process they term *attitude alignment* between relationship partners. Couples completed attitude questionnaires, rated the centrality of each attitude issue to their personal identity, and completed the DAS. Each couple then discussed four of eight issues on which the experimenters had determined the partners disagreed (the *salient* discrepancy of opinion condition); they did not discuss the other four issues (the *nonsalient* condition). Two of the issues in each condition were those on which the man said the issue was central to his personal identity but the woman said the issue was peripheral to her identity, and two were the reverse. Davis and Rusbult found that tendencies toward attitude alignment—reduction of the partners' discrepancy postdiscussion—were greater in the salient condition (where issues were discussed) than in the nonsalient condition. Moreover, an individual's alignment tendencies were greater to the extent the issue was central to the partner (and peripheral to the self) and greater in satisfied than unsatisfied couples.

Other processes may increase a couple's attitude similarity over time. Acitelli, Kenny, and Weiner (2001) hypothesized that partners are likely to share the same marital values as a result of their similar exposure to media portrayals of relationships, including television sitcoms, talk shows, and advice columns. Members of unmarried and married couples living in the same household were asked to rank the importance of their own and their partners' marriage values, as well as to complete relationship satisfaction measures. The investigators found a strong *cultural stereotype of marital values* shared by both men and women; that is, there was little vari-

ability in the values ranked by everyone in the sample as important to a good marriage. As previously noted, the value that received the strongest endorsement by everyone was trust in the partner, and the lowest was having similar beliefs. The couples' actual value similarity was significantly, although modestly, associated with relationship satisfaction and duration. When the cultural stereotype portion of their similarity was removed, however, their "unique similarity" (the degree to which they shared values different from the values other couples shared) was very low and was not associated with either satisfaction or duration. Sharing culturally endorsed marital values apparently contributes to marital satisfaction and duration.

Acitelli and colleagues (2001) also examined **understanding**, usually defined as the extent to which an individual accurately perceives the partner's true beliefs, attitudes, and, in this case, values. Whereas men and women's actual value rankings were highly similar, their rankings of what they *thought* their partner most highly valued were somewhat different: Men thought their partners highly valued doing things together more than they actually did, while women thought their partners valued being sexually satisfied more than they did. After stereotypical responding was removed, unique understanding was not associated with satisfaction or duration.

Many studies have found that marital partners' **perceived similarity** often is significantly higher than their actual similarity (e.g., Byrne & Blaylock, 1963; Levinger & Breedlove, 1966) and that perceived similarity is more strongly associated with marital satisfaction than is actual similarity (e.g., Acitelli, Douvan, & Veroff, 1993). A number of explanations have been offered for the effect: (1) Happy couples are likely to emphasize their similarities and minimize their dissimilarities, particularly differences of opinion, in order to avoid conflict. (2) Attraction breeds the perception of similarity in the absence of information about actual similarity (see Chapter 6). (3) Dissimilarity of attitude with a loved one is uncomfortable, as the cognitive consistency theories predict, and thus, in the service of consistency, people may achieve a degree of perceptual consistency not reflected in reality. Indeed, Murray, Holmes, Bellavia, Griffin, and Dolderman (2002) found that people in satisfying and stable relationships tended to "assimilate" their partner's attitudes to their own, perceiving similarities that do not exist.

The evidence on the association between similarity and satisfaction and stability supports Hattie Andrews's recipe for a long marriage. Most relationship scholars believe that similarity is associated with satisfaction primarily because it increases correspondence of outcomes (the same outcomes are rewarding to both partners) and thus reduces the likelihood of conflict. Irreconcilable differences, of course, are the most frequent reason couples give for why their relationship dissolved.

Conflict

Psychologists have been interested in marital conflict—how to predict it and how to reduce it—for a very long time (see Holmes & Murray, 1996, for a review). One of the first theoretical treatments of the subject was published by Kurt Lewin (1940/1948) in an article titled "The Background of Conflict in Marriage." Not only has marital conflict been viewed as the major cause of marital unhappiness and divorce, but it has deleterious effects on the health of the spouses as well, especially wives (Kiecolt-Glaser, Malarkey, Cacioppo, & Glaser, 1994).

Conflict, of course, is by no means confined to premarital and marital relationships. Most theories of relationship growth and maintenance posit that all relationships encounter conflict as they move toward interdependence (see Chapter 7). Canary and Messman (2000), who review the prevalence of conflict in several types of close relationship, note that even toddlers only 18 months old engage in conflict. Conflict has most frequently been studied, however, in the context of marital and premarital relationships.

Two theoretical approaches to conflict have been dominant: social learning theory and interdependence theory. The social learning theory approach to conflict, which has been taken mostly by marital and family therapy researchers who seek strategies for intervention into conflict-ridden distressed relationships, is discussed in Chapter 14. The interdependence theory approach posits that conflict principally arises from noncorrespondence of the partners' outcomes; for example, one partner would find it more rewarding to vacation at the ocean, but the other would enjoy the mountains. This theory also posits that it is increasing interdependence that sets the stage for conflict, and thus conflict is inevitable in close relationships.

A mountain of evidence documents the ubiquity of conflict in virtually all marital relationships—happy or unhappy—no matter whether the partners are similar or dissimilar (although dissimilar couples are more vulnerable to conflict). Nearly all married couples have unpleasant disagreements at least some of the time, with most couples reporting one to three disagreements per month, according to wide-scale surveys (McGonagle, Kessler, & Schilling, 1992). Moreover, as many relationship development theorists predict, conflict begins before marriage. Burgess and Wallin (1953) concluded from their longitudinal study of engaged couples, "Evidently disagreements in one or more areas of the relationship are the rule and 'always' or 'almost always' agreeing [is] the exception" (p. 247). Kelley, Cunningham, and Braiker-Stambul's (1973) survey of young married and cohabiting couples found that no relationship was problem-free, and most couples reported themselves to be wrestling with a great diversity of problems (see Braiker & Kelley, 1979).

The effect of conflict, and the negative feelings that accompany it, on marital relationship satisfaction appears to depend on the age of the relationship. Braiker and Kelley asked young married couples to provide retrospective accounts of their relationship from their initial acquaintance through their first 6 months of marriage. Several themes were evident in the couples' descriptions of their courtships. One prevalent theme was conflict and negative affect (at the serious dating stage), and another was love (at the serious dating and engagement stages). What was striking to the investigators was that the couples often spoke of their feelings of love while, at the same time, recounting their fights, hassles, and unhappiness, a finding consistent with that reported earlier by Orden and Bradburn (1968). Because the couples had moved on to marriage, Braiker and Kelley concluded that conflict is not necessarily destructive or disruptive of relationship growth and maintenance (a view taken by most relationship development theorists) and that love and conflict/negativity are independent dimensions of relationship growth, at least for couples who eventually marry. They also concluded, "There appears to be no relation between the amount of interdependence and love in a relationship, on the one hand, and the amount of negative affect and open conflict, on the other hand" (p. 152).

Braiker and Kelley's conclusion has been illuminated by more recent findings. First, given the divorce statistics for couples who married in the mid- to late 1970s, it is likely that at least half of the newlyweds who participated in Braiker and Kelley's study subsequently divorced. Second, it is probable that the conflict and negativity Braiker and Kelley observed co-existing quietly alongside the young couple's love and positivity soon reared its ugly head and played its usual destructive role in the demise of at least some of those marriages. It will be recalled that Huston, McHale, and Crouter (1986) found that although there initially was a positive association between their PAIR project newlyweds' affectional behaviors and the extent to which they felt positively toward each other and the relationship, just a year later positive affectional behavior showed little association with either the husbands' or wives' attitudes toward their marriage. Moreover, although initially there was little association between the newlyweds' propensity to behave negatively toward their spouse and their attitudes toward the marriage, just a year later the spouses' negative behaviors were associated with their evaluation of the marriage. In other words, the "couples' negativity at the end of the first year of marriage could be predicted by their negativity shortly after marriage" (p. 131), but

their positivity at the end of their first year could not be predicted by their positivity shortly after marriage.

Huston and associates concluded that negativity has a corrosive effect over time on marital satisfaction and that "premarital counselors and family life educators, would be well advised to be attentive to early signs of negativity and to be less concerned about outward manifestations of love and affection" (p. 131). Negativity of feelings, emotions, and behavior in relationships is usually the by-product of conflict. Why conflict erodes and eventually destroys some relationships while others not only survive but emerge stronger than before has been a central issue in much satisfaction and stability research.

Several possible explanations have been offered for the differential effects of conflict. First, some couples may experience a *greater number of conflicts* than other couples. Although almost all couples experience conflict, an early study in which couples kept diaries of their conflicts found that maritally distressed couples experienced conflict at a substantially higher rate over a 5-day period than nondistressed couples (3.4 conflicts vs. 1.0; Birchler, Weiss, & Vincent, 1975). Second, some couples may experience *more severe and intractable* conflicts. When relationship therapists were asked to list the marital problems they have found most difficult to treat successfully, alcoholism ranked first, and value conflicts also were in their top 10 (Geiss & O'Leary, 1981). Third, it is likely that some couples deal with their conflicts more effectively, and with less harm to the relationship, than other couples. It is this last explanation—that *effective conflict management skills* can attenuate the deleterious effects of conflict on the relationship—that has received the most attention, probably because conflict resolution skills can be taught, as discussed further in Chapter 14.

The Course of a Conflict

Many of the factors we have discussed—certain personality dispositions, partners' dissimilarity of attitudes and values, unrealistic relationship beliefs and expectations, and vulnerability to external stressors on the relationship, for example—

constitute *predisposing conditions* for open conflict between partners. For example, Bolger and Zuckerman (1995) report that people high in neuroticism indicate having more conflictful interactions than others, are more likely to be absorbed by the conflict they experience, and use a variety of coping responses that seem only to increase—not decrease—their anger and depression.

According to Peterson's (1983/2002) model of the course of conflict (Figure 13.7), when the couple's predisposing conditions for conflict (for example, value dissimilarities) are brought to the surface by an initiating event (usually criticism, a rebuff, an illegitimate demand, or cumulative annoyance), couples have a choice of engaging in conflict avoidance (withdrawing from each other or minimizing and denying the conflict) or conflict engagement. If conflict engagement is chosen, partners' interactions may differ in two ways: Some couples will proceed to direct negotiation and resolution, using positive conflict resolution strategies such as reason, assertion (direct expression of opinions and desires), and partner support (acknowledging the partner's view; see Noller & Feeney, 1998). The interaction of other couples, however, will quickly degrade into angry personal attacks, coercion, threats, and perhaps even physical violence, leading to escalation and intensification of the conflict.

Peterson observes that if the conflict interaction results in escalation, the partners typically move in one of two directions: (1) They may engage in acts and expressions of *conciliation* designed to reduce the intensity of the negative emotion produced during the escalation phase and to signal their willingness to further negotiate. (2) They may *separate* temporarily, which may later lead to a process of *reconciliation* in which each partner takes personal responsibility for the problem, expresses an interest in negotiation, and engages in unusual or extreme expressions of affection and relationship commitment. Reconciliation, however, is less likely when the separation is characterized by hurtful "parting shots."

Peterson's model outlines several ways the conflict may finally end. First, some conflict interactions not only resolve the specific conflict but also result in structural improvement of the relationship. The partners may have learned more about their own and the other's needs, goals, expectations, and values. Moreover, in the process of resolving their conflict, they may have reached an integrative agreement reconciling their divergent interests. That agreement, which will govern the partners' future interactions, helps ensure that similar conflicts are avoided in the future. These new agreements often represent compromises of both partners' original aspirations and expectations and are a healthy outcome of the conflict interaction.

Not infrequently, however, conflict interactions end in ways that are unhealthy for one or both of the partners or for the relationship itself. First, of course, the conflict may be terminated, without resolution, by permanent separation and dissolution of the relationship. There is another unhealthy way a conflict may be terminated. As Peterson discusses, conflict interactions sometimes end in conquest or domination; that is, one partner capitulates while the other partner continues to pursue his or her own personal goals. Kayser (1993) found that when highly dissatisfied couples were asked what contributed most to their unhappiness with their marital relationship, most frequently cited were the partner's control and a lack of intimate behaviors. In fact, when these spouses were asked to name the "critical turning point for the worse" in their marriages, over half named their partner's attempt to control them—for example, by making important decisions unilaterally. Domination is likely to occur in relationships in which power asymmetry is high—the partner with the most resources and the least commitment to the relationship "wins." In interdependence theory terms, power asymmetry is associated with one partner having high behavior control, or even fate control, over the other (see Chapter 4). If the relationship is involuntary, or if the outcomes available in the low-power partner's best alternative relationship are poor, the relationship is likely to be maintained despite domination. Gray-Little and Burks (1983) conclude from their review of studies that have examined the association between spouses' power disparities and marital satisfaction that marriages in which

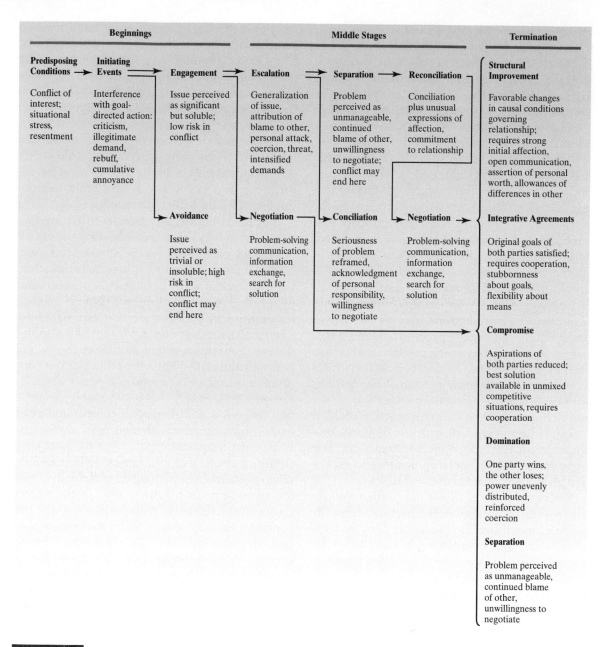

FIGURE 13.7 The course of a conflict. According to Peterson, a conflict may take many possible courses from its beginnings, through its middle stages, to its termination. Arrows indicate the likely sequences, ending with avoidance or any of five possible terminations. *From Peterson, "Conflict" (1983/2002), Fig. 9.2, p. 383.*

the wife appears to be dominant are most likely to be unhappy and partners in egalitarian marriages are most likely to be happy.

Building on Peterson's model, Christensen and Pasch (1993) elaborate the first four stages of conflict and expand it to include other stages. They assert that the precipitating event bringing an underlying conflict of interest to the surface most likely will pertain to one of the central dimensions of relationships, such as closeness or power, and that the conflict will be exacerbated if the partners are currently living under stressful circumstances—for example, after the birth of an infant, or in cases in which one partner has a demanding job. Like Peterson, they believe that some couples will proceed to positive mutual engagement, others will proceed to negative mutual engagement involving behaviors such as attack and blame, and in still other couples one partner will attempt to discuss the problem while the other attempts to avoid the conflict and withdraws (the demand–withdraw pattern is discussed further in Chapter 14). At this point, Christensen and Pasch depart from Peterson's model and posit two other phases: *immediate outcome*, the period immediately after the conflict in which the partners have time to analyze why the conflict occurred and to sort out their feelings; and *return to normal*, which refers to the supposition that sometime later, the partners will resume their usual way of relating to each other. Christensen and Pasch note that little is known about this phase, although anecdotally it is clear that some couples behave as though nothing untoward occurred, some apologize and reconcile, and others go on but bearing scars and resentment.

The ELVN Model

The ELVN (exit, loyalty, voice, neglect) model developed by Rusbult (e.g., 1987; Rusbult, Zembrodt, & Gunn, 1982) is addressed to the behavior a person may elect to perform in response to what he or she views as the partner's "destructive" behavior or in response to general dissatisfaction with the relationship. The array of possible responses is defined by two dimensions, active–passive and destructive–constructive, which yield four abstract categories of response. *Exit* (active–destructive responses) may include walking out of conflictful interactions, threatening to dissolve the relationship, and physical and emotional abuse. *Loyalty* (passive–constructive responses) generally involves waiting for conditions to improve, making benign attributions for the partner's bad behavior (such as attributing it to temporary job stress), and continuing to support the partner in other ways. *Voice* (active–constructive responses) includes constructive conflict engagement and negotiation or other behaviors designed to improve the situation, such as changing one's own behavior or seeking therapeutic advice. *Neglect* (passive–destructive responses) allows conditions to deteriorate by ignoring the partner and refusing to confront problems.

Several tests of the ELVN model suggest that greater problem severity tends to produce the active responses of voice and exit. The constructive responses of voice and loyalty, which tend to be chosen by partners who are satisfied with their relationship or have high investment in it, appear to result in more favorable outcomes than exit and neglect (e.g., Rusbult, Johnson, and Morrow, 1986).

Accommodation

The ELVN model led Rusbult and her colleagues to the concept of **accommodation**, defined as an individual's tendency to inhibit the impulse to behave destructively (with neglect or exit) and instead to behave constructively (with voice or loyalty) in response to a partner who has behaved destructively. Constructive responses to conflict or dissatisfaction are theorized to be the result of a *transformation of motivation* that leads the individual to look beyond his or her immediate self-interest and consider long-term goals such as continuance of the relationship, furtherance of the partner's well-being, and observance of social and religious norms important to self-concept. Accommodation requires the individual to "turn the other cheek" in the face of the partner's destructive behavior. As we have discussed (and will discuss further in Chapter 14), the more prevalent impulse is to return hurt with hurt; asking partners to accommodate after they have been harmed is, psychologically at least, "swimming upstream."

Longitudinal tests of the hypothesis that accommodation behavior is associated with relationship satisfaction have revealed that although the destructive responses of exit and neglect are harmful to the couple's happiness, the constructive responses of voice and loyalty do not produce a commensurate satisfaction uplift (see Rusbult, Bissonnette, Arriaga, & Cox, 1998). Once again, the disproportionate impact of positive and negative relationship behavior is apparent (see Chapter 9, "Affective Processes"); positive behavior is expected and taken for granted, whereas negative behavior usually is unexpected, noticed, and elicits response.

Although an accommodation response usually is viewed as being in the individual's *own* best interest and necessary to the achievement of long-term goals, accommodation is sometimes referred to as a "self-sacrificial" act (e.g., Rusbult et al., 1998). Van Lange and his colleagues (e.g., Van Lange, Agnew, Harinck, & Steemers, 1997; Van Lange, Rusbult, Drigotas, Arriaga, Witcher, & Cox, 1997) have investigated the willingness to sacrifice in dating and marital relationships by asking people to rank order the most important activities in their life (other than their relationship with their partner), to imagine that they could not engage in the first-ranked activity and maintain their relationship, and then indicate the extent to which they would consider ending the relationship. Willingness to sacrifice was found to be associated with high relationship satisfaction, poor alternatives, high investment, and strong relationship commitment (with willingness to sacrifice accounting for significant variance in satisfaction beyond commitment). Sacrifices reduce overt conflict, but the possibility that they may have harmful "sleeper effects" on the relationship—for example, resentment on the part of sacrificers and guilt on the part of their partners—has not been investigated. Indeed, studies of sacrifice usually ask people to *imagine* what they would do in a sacrifice situation. What people *actually* do is not known, but the prevalence of relationship conflict perhaps provides a clue.

With few exceptions (e.g., Gonzales, Haugen, & Manning, 1994), the same "imagine" methodology is usually used to examine the individual's willingness to forgive the partner's destructive behavior. In one of the few studies that have used spouse participants, Fincham, Paleari, and Regalia (2002) asked Italian husbands and wives, who completed a marital satisfaction scale, to vividly imagine their spouse performing a transgression and then to answer questions about the causes of the spouse's behavior, their likely emotional reactions to the transgression, and their likelihood of forgiving the spouse. Maritally satisfied spouses were more likely to explain their partner's negative behaviors with benign causal attributions, such as external causes ("The devil made her do it") or unstable causes ("a bad hair day"), which seem to promote benign responsibility attributions (the act was neither intentional nor selfishly motivated) and to reduce negative affect, both of which appear to promote forgiveness. The investigators concluded that marital satisfaction is not *directly* linked to forgiveness; rather, satisfaction produces benign responsibility attributions which, in turn, promote—and perhaps are even critical to—forgiveness. Again, however, how people actually would react if their spouse engaged in the harmful behaviors named in this study is not known. The investigators caution that because transgression severity is known to influence the probability of forgiveness of a stranger, it would be unwise to generalize their findings to severe transgressions by close relationship partners. They note, in fact, that deciding whether a single-process model can account for forgiveness of both minor and severe transgressions is a challenge for future research.

THE CONTRIBUTION OF SATISFACTION TO STABILITY

Although relationship satisfaction is important, it is not the sole determinant of relationship *stability*. Moreover, in many instances, satisfaction is not the primary determinant. Different types of relationship are likely to show different satisfaction/dissatisfaction thresholds for triggering dissolution. For example, dissatisfying friendships should be more quickly dissolved than dissatisfying marital relationships because enjoyment of interaction with the partner is the raison d'être of friendships and because there usually are few barriers to dissolving the relationship if satisfaction declines. Although barriers to dissolving a marriage have been considerably reduced in the past few decades, they still are greater than those associated with abandoning most other types of relationships, which may help explain the paradoxes that as marriages age, satisfaction decreases but stability increases and that when the couple become parents, satisfaction decreases but stability increases. Comparative data on the association between satisfaction and stability in different types of close relationship are not available.

Partly as a result of interdependence theory, which severed the theoretical connection between satisfaction and stability by positing CL as the determinant of satisfaction and CLalt as the determinant of stability, the belief that satisfaction is the primary determinant of marital stability has weakened in recent years. Karney and Bradbury (1995b), who reviewed the findings of over 100 longitudinal studies of marriage (representing over 45,000 marriages), conclude that although marital satisfaction has a larger effect on stability than most other variables that have been investigated and remains the most reliable proximal predictor of divorce, the effect is "not particularly large" (p. 20). The success of Rusbult's (e.g., 1983) investment model in predicting stability also testifies that although satisfaction contributes to stability (through commitment), size of investment and goodness of alternatives are also important contributors to stability. From his own longitudinal study of marriage, Huston (2000), too, questions the heavy focus on marital satisfaction as the primary cause of marital stability. He contends that satisfaction "provides only a pale representation of the total constellation of psychological forces that draw spouses toward one another" (p. 315). One of these forces, Huston notes, is love. Although love has been often investigated as a force for the initiation of marriage (see Chapter 12, "Mate Selection and

Sex"), it has been less frequently examined as a force that keeps spouses together. There is no reason why love for the partner and dissatisfaction with the relationship cannot and do not sometimes coexist, at least for a time (and, in people for whom hope springs eternal, perhaps for a very long time). Indeed, love has often been thought of as the anesthetic that dulls the pain of early conflict and keeps people contained in the relationship as they work out their problems and conflicts.

Dissatisfied Stable Marriages

Recognition that factors other than satisfaction contribute to marital stability has led to greater interest in marriages that remain stable despite the couples' dissatisfaction. The existence of such couples has been anecdotally noted for years. For example, Cuber and Haroff (1965) identified "conflict-habituated" marriages as a distinct type—quarreling, arguments, and bickering were a way of life for these stably married couples.

Heaton and Albrecht (1991) examined the factors associated with unhappy–stable marriages, estimated to constitute about 11% of married couples, and found that many of these couples held attitudes that reflected commitment to the institution of marriage—for example, "Marriage is for life." They also tended to be older. White and Booth (1991) found that barriers and alternatives vary systematically with age and marital duration; older spouses and spouses in longer-duration marriages (who also tend to be older) are likely to have higher barriers to dissolution (more investments, for example) and fewer alternatives.

An individual's fears of abandonment and feelings of being unworthy of love, as measured by the Collins and Read (1990) Revised Adult Attachment Scale, were found by Davila and Bradbury (2001) to put that person at risk for staying in an unhappy marriage. Consistent with the results of an earlier longitudinal study of dating couples conducted by Kirkpatrick and Davis (1994), attachment insecurity strongly distinguished unhappy couples in stable marriages from unhappy couples who divorce and also from happy couples. Compared to the couples who divorced over the 4 years of their longitudinal study, Davila and Bradbury found that the unhappy–stable couples had lower MAT satisfaction scores, both initially and over time, and they also displayed the highest levels of depressive symptoms, both initially and over the course of the study. Although most of those who divorced were childless and most of those who stayed married had children (as is consistently found), attachment insecurity was a better predictor of marital outcome than was the presence of children. The investigators also concluded that this variable was a better predictor of divorce than neuroticism, attitudes toward divorce, or self-esteem.

SUMMARY

Scholars long have sought to identify the ingredients of relationship satisfaction, in part because of the high premium placed by most men and women on relationship quality (particularly in marriage) and in part because of the widespread belief that satisfaction with a relationship is the prime determinant of its stability. In their attempt to discover the causal conditions associated with satisfaction and stability, researchers have faced an array of conceptual, methodological, and analytic obstacles. For example, they typically ask individuals to complete a satisfaction measure as well as measures of a variety of presumed determinants of satisfaction such as love, usually on the same occasion; correlational or regression analyses then are conducted to estimate the degree of association between satisfaction and the hypothesized determinants. Unfortunately, this association is often inflated (and therefore not an accurate estimate) because of shared item content between the two measures and the use of a shared methodology (for example, self-report). In addition, reciprocal causal feedback loops exist between

satisfaction and trust, commitment, and other hypothesized determinants of satisfaction. This situation has created a problem for researchers who wish to disentangle the impact of any one presumed causal variable on satisfaction. Consequently, the importance of longitudinal studies, which may sometimes provide insight into temporal processes, and experimental studies, which allow randomization and control over the temporal occurrence of variables, cannot be overemphasized.

Many researchers have sought to track the trajectory of satisfaction over time in married and cohabiting couples. Until recently, most studies of marital satisfaction were cross-sectional and suffered from cohort effects and other problems that muddied interpretation of their results. However, a growing number of two-wave and multiple-wave longitudinal investigations of premarital and marital satisfaction and stability have been conducted. Both cross-sectional and longitudinal studies are consistent in indicating that satisfaction levels are relatively high in the early years of marriage, tend to decrease over time, are similar for husbands and wives, and do not appear to play an important role in dissolution (rather, it is the rate of change in satisfaction that predicts subsequent dissolution). Other researchers have explored various personal, relational, and environmental factors associated with relationship satisfaction. For example, numerous studies indicate that emotional instability, unrealistic beliefs and standards about romantic relationships, demographic and socioeconomic variables such as education and race, and relationship processes such as conflict are strongly associated with relationship quality and satisfaction. The recognition that factors other than satisfaction contribute to relationship stability has led to an increased interest in investigating other positive forces—for example, love and goodness of alternatives—that keep couples together, as well as an interest in marriages that remain stable despite high levels of dissatisfaction.

Chapter 14

Intervention and Dissolution

INTRODUCTION

The size and quality of the relationship web in which we live out our lives are continuously in flux. Although a few relationships endure for a lifetime, most die. When we look in our relational rear-view mirrors, most of us see stretching back over the road of time a series of dead or moribund relationships with co-workers, teachers and mentors, neighbors, friends, and lovers—and, for some, spouses and children. Sometimes fate ended the relationship—taking away our beloved partner through death, an illness such as Alzheimer's disease, or involuntary and insurmountable geographical separation. Other times the relationship simply withered away without either ourselves or our partners caring or even noticing its demise. Sometimes the relationship was dissolved by mutual consent, other times we ended it, and still other times it was our partner who decided to do so. If the relationship was an important one, it is likely that neither we nor our partner let the relationship die without putting up a fight, one that may have included the services of a relationship therapist.

Of most interest to researchers have been relationships whose death certificates read "homicide" (or, perhaps more accurately, "relaticide," a word that is not in the dictionary but should be). These are relationships that one or both of the partners decided to terminate because they saw that the relationship was dying or they realized that it had become hazardous to their physical or mental health. Sick and dying marriages have captured the most attention—and for good reason. Few people ever make a decision more consequential to the quality of the remainder of their life than the decision to marry—or even the decision to spend what many later describe as "the best years of my life" in cohabitation with another. In addition to the partners themselves, such decisions affect the happiness and welfare of their children—past or future—and the partners' families, friends, and associates.

The odds of success of a decision to enter into a marital relationship are tantamount to a roll of the dice—even less than 50–50 if marital satisfaction as well as stability is the outcome hoped for. As a consequence, people who value their

425

life, liberty, and happiness will not make such a decision lightly. Most people don't. However, many do make the decision to marry another in a rosy fog of ignorance—a fog that characteristically starts to lift only too late, after the contract has been finalized. When doubts about the wisdom of the decision arise beforehand, they often are quickly banished by that extraordinary cognitive agility even the dullest human mind is capable of displaying when it is guarding what it regards as treasure (see Chapter 7, "Relationship Growth and Maintenance"). The decision is made even more hazardous by the several "disconnects" between factors associated with happiness early in the relationship and those that assume importance later. As we've discussed, conflicts lurk in the shadows early in the relationship while love and its associated pleasures frolic on center stage. Communication skills appear to contribute little to happiness early in a relationship—it is only later that their importance surfaces (Markman & Hahlweg, 1993). Similarly, those characteristics of the partner that are so attractive in the beginning often seem to undergo an unpleasant metamorphosis—his endearing protectiveness becomes suffocating possessiveness and her confidence becomes insufferable arrogance—later in the relationship (Felmlee, 1995, 1998; Whitehouse, 1981). Perhaps it is not surprising, then, that most prospective spouses believe their personal chances for marital success are somewhere around 100%.

Because the cards seem stacked for success, only a few couples will engage in premarital counseling, perhaps because their church requires it, or because their family or friends have talked them into it, or because they have already learned the hard way just how consequential the decision to marry is. More likely, a relationship counselor will enter the picture only later—when things inexplicably have gone wrong and it is not clear how they can ever be put right.

As we discussed in Chapter 4, "The Concept of Relationship," the therapist who is asked to intervene into a distressed relationship has a tripartite task: to *observe and describe* the regularities in the couple's interaction pattern that have led to distress; to *identify the stable causal conditions* responsible for those regularities; and to help the couple *modify those causal conditions* when feasible. This chapter discusses the progress relationship researchers and therapists have made in identifying the causal conditions underlying distressed relationships and the methods they have developed to help people repair their relationships. It should be noted, however, that it is the distressed marital relationships of white, middle-class partners in the United States who can afford the services of a relationship therapist and whose education and cultural background facilitate intervention that have been studied almost exclusively.

HAPPY AND UNHAPPY MARRIAGES

Researchers usually sort marriages into two groups: satisfied and dissatisfied. Somewhere within the satisfied group there presumably are some very happy marriages. Outside of the gothic romance novel, however, not much is known about very happy marriages. In contrast, a great deal is known about unsatisfying marriages, particularly those that are highly distressed and on the verge of dissolution. With an eye to prevention and intervention into distressed marriages, unhappy marriages have been the primary focus of most marital research. As a consequence, and as Weiss and Heyman (1997) observe:

> The literature often suggests an illogical conclusion: marital health is the absence of marital distress. This seems to suggest that in order to be well adjusted couples should *not* say and do what distressed couples say and do. Since aspirin cures headaches, we cannot conclude that the lack of aspirin causes headaches. *Marital harmony is not just the absence of whatever it is that dissatisfied couples do.* (p. 17; emphasis in the original)

In other words, a happy marriage is unlikely to be the film negative of a photo of an unhappy marriage.

Happy Marriages

At present, the only portrait available of a very happy marriage is a two-dimensional jigsaw picture cobbled together from shards of knowledge about the personal, relational, and environmental conditions associated with marital satisfaction (see Chapter 13, "Satisfaction and Stability"). Noting the vacuum on the positive side of the marital ledger, some marital and family therapists recently have undertaken to provide at least a conceptual definition of a good marriage. Halford, Kelly, and Markman (1997) define a "healthy long-term couple relationship" as follows:

> A developing set of interactions between partners which promotes the individual well-being of each partner and their offspring, assists each partner to adapt to life stresses, engenders a conjoint sense of emotional and sexual intimacy between the partners, and which promotes the long-term sustainment of the relationship within the cultural context in which the partners live. (p. 8)

These investigators recognize that the "long-term sustainment" portion of their definition is a value judgment. Nevertheless, the existing evidence justifies the conclusion that people who sustain long-term relationships generally are better off, mentally and physically, than those who do not (see Chapter 2, "Relationships and Health"). Although "healthy" relationships aren't always "happy" relationships (see Chapter 5, "Varieties of Relationship"), unhealthy relationships are most certainly doomed to eventual distress, and consequently, a healthy relationship is likely to be a necessary, if not sufficient, condition, for a happy marriage.

Family psychologist and therapist Judith Wallerstein (Wallerstein & Blakeslee, 1995) has sketched the outlines of a happy marriage by means of a qualitative study of 50 predominantly white, middle-class, and well-educated couples in stable, happy marriages of varying durations. From her extensive interviews, Wallerstein concludes that to have a "good" marriage the spouses must successfully achieve nine tasks, including emotionally separating from the family of origin and redefining one's connections with it, creating togetherness while preserving individual autonomy, absorbing the impact of a child and protecting privacy, confronting and mastering the inevitable crises of life, providing nurturance and comfort to each other, and providing and keeping alive the "early romantic, idealized images of falling in love while facing the sober realities of the changes wrought by time" (p. 28). All easier said than done.

Wallerstein and Blakeslee report that good marriages naturally sort into four types: *romantic*, based on a lasting, passionate sexual relationship; *rescue*, where the partners' early experiences have been traumatic and the central theme is the healing that takes place over the course of the marriage; *traditional*, where roles and responsibilities are clearly divided; and *companionate*, which has friendship and equality at its core. This last form of marriage is believed to reflect social changes over the last several decades and to be the most common type of marriage among younger couples. A major task companionate partners seem to confront is balancing their emotional investment in their jobs with their emotional investment in their relationship and their children; degeneration into a brother-and-sister relationship appears to be the primary danger of such marriages.

Typologies of intact marriages (not necessarily especially good marriages) have been offered by other researchers. For example, communication studies researcher Mary Anne Fitzpatrick (e.g., 1988) took the more familiar quantitative approach. Large numbers of couples were measured on the three dimensions Fitzpatrick theorized to underlie marriage: *interdependence*, signified, for example, by the amount of time the partners spend together and their level of companionship; *ideology*, or the beliefs, standards, and values that individuals hold concerning relationships; and *conflict*, which is measured by the partners' general level of assertiveness and their willingness to engage in conflict.

Although it was logically possible for marriages to cluster into eight types (defined by high and low levels of each of the three dimensions), Fitzpatrick found that most marriages fall into three types: *traditional*, in which the partners display high interdependence, conventional relationship values, and a nonassertive communication style (but also a willingness to engage in conflict on serious issues); *independent*, in which each spouse maintains a separate physical space and controls his or her accessibility but also exhibits a high level of sharing and companionship, an ideological orientation opposite from the traditional type (for example, a belief that marriage should not constrain individual freedom), and assertiveness and willingness to engage in conflict; and *separate*, in which the partners are less interdependent than the other two types, are not highly companionable, and avoid open conflict with each other. No significant differences were found among the couple types with respect to marital duration, previous marriages, number of children, religion, education, employment, or income.

About 60% of the couples Fitzpatrick has examined are "pure" types in which both partners share the same view of their marriage; the remainder are "mixed"—for example, the husband is separate and the wife traditional. Some of Fitzpatrick's distinctions appear in other marriage typologies but with somewhat different labels. For example, Fitzpatrick's separate pattern is similar to Peplau's (1983/2002) *egalitarian* pattern, in which the couple rejects male dominance and role specialization by gender. In Peplau's *traditional* marriage, the husband dominates the wife and there is considerable role specialization. Fitzpatrick identifies this type as mixed (husband separate, wife traditional).

Unhappy Marriages

In the opinion of marital therapist Frank Pittman (1997): "The concept of unhappy marriage implies that marriage is supposed to make one happy, which is a helluva lot to expect. Marriage is actually supposed to make you married, and whatever else it does, it keeps you from having to date and waste time searching for romantic love" (p. 311). Using data from a longitudinal study of over 24,000 people to examine the effects of marital transitions (marriage or widowhood) on happiness, Lucas, Clark, Georgellis, and Diener (2003) found that on average, people reacted to the transition and then reverted back to their previous happiness levels. This average trend masked, however, strong individual differences in tendency to revert to baseline happiness. For example, some people who initially reacted strongly sustained that reaction for years while others exhibited no reaction to the event at all. Although people more than ever before look to marriage for happiness, this study as well as other evidence indicates that some people find it, others do not, and still others find it and lose it.

As opposed to what little is known of the joys of happy couples, a great deal is known about the complaints of unhappy couples. One of the earliest studies of divorce was conducted by Goode (1956), who asked a quasi-representative sample of over 400 urban women shortly after they divorced, "What was the cause of the divorce?" Their responses fell into several categories, including the husband's personality, values, dominance, cruelty, lack of affection, desertion and nonsupport, extramarital affairs, his consumption of money and other resources, drinking, and a "complex" described as "drinking, gambling, and helling around" (p. 117).

Levinger (1966), who subsequently examined both husbands' and wives' complaints in a large sample of couples who had applied for divorce, found that wives had almost twice as many complaints about the marriage as husbands did (their complaints being similar to those detailed by Goode, including the husband's drinking, physical and verbal abuse, neglect, and lack of love). In only two categories did husbands have more complaints than wives—sexual incompatibility and in-law troubles. Using the Goode coding system, Kitson and Sussman (1982) examined the marital complaints of couples who filed for divorce in the mid-1970s and found, again, that women had more complaints than men; women were more likely to mention their spouse's personality, dominance, drinking, nonsupport, sexual problems, and infidelity than men were.

Bloom, Niles, and Tatcher (1985) noted, however, that in contrast to earlier studies, the complaints of Kitson and Sussman's couples seemed to show an increasing concern for the emotional and sexual aspects of the marriage. In their study of newly separated but not yet divorced persons, Bloom and colleagues found that dissatisfaction tended to be rooted in the failure of the marriage to serve as a source of interpersonal nurturance and individual gratification and growth. Consistent with that finding, Albrecht, Bahr, and Goodman (1983; see Meredith & Holman, 2001) found that infidelity and loss of love were the top two reasons cited by 500 "ever divorced" persons for the failure of their marriage. Similarly, Gigy and Kelly (1992) found that 80% of the men and women participating in a divorce mediation project said their major reason for divorcing was that they had gradually grown apart and felt unloved and unappreciated by their spouse.

It is not always clear in retrospective self-report studies of the causes of divorce whether the problems the spouses cite preceded or followed (as justification) the decision to separate and divorce. Another approach was taken by Geiss and O'Leary (1981), who asked a sample of relationship therapists to estimate the percentage of couples they had seen in the past year who had mentioned a specific problem in their marriage, to rank the problems they had most difficulty in treating, and to rank the problems they believed were most damaging to the relationship. Fifteen years later, Whisman, Dixon, and Johnson (1997) replicated Geiss and O'Leary's study with another sample of practicing relationship therapists. Overall, despite many changes in the structure and function of marital relationships over the period, few changes were found in the kinds of marital problems encountered by therapists. Communication and power struggles were seen most frequently. Most difficult to treat were "lack of loving feelings" and alcoholism. Most damaging to the relationship, the therapists believed, were abuse and extramarital affairs. Considering the therapists' responses to all three questions combined, five problems ranked highest in importance: lack of loving feelings, power struggles, communication, extramarital affairs, and unrealistic expectations.

Whisman and colleagues note that compared to research attention given to the other problems, extramarital affairs and lack of love have received relatively little systematic investigation. This situation prevails despite the fact that extramarital affairs are the most commonly cited cause of marital dissolution in the United States and throughout the world (e.g., Betzig, 1989; Kitson, Babri, & Roach, 1985; see Chapter 12, "Mate Selection and Sex"). Indeed, South and Lloyd (1995) report that in at least one-third of U.S. divorce cases, one or both spouses have been involved with another person prior to marital dissolution. Many therapists believe that lack of love and extramarital affairs are highly associated—that extramarital affairs are usually not about sex but rather about the search for love, understanding, and friendship (e.g., Gottman, 1999). Love, and the lack of it in a relationship expected to provide it, has been a "forgotten variable" in marital therapy even though, as Roberts (1992) discusses, most couples marry because they have "fallen in love" and tend to divorce when they "fall out of love." Many marital researchers are calling for more research on love and other factors that keep people together as opposed to the heavy emphasis on factors that pull them apart (e.g., Conger & Conger, 2002; Huston, 2000; Pasch & Bradbury, 1998). Love, of course, has been recognized as a legitimate topic for scientific inquiry only in recent years.

Evidence that couples' reports of their current problems truly are harbingers of divorce and not post hoc rationalizations comes from Amato and Rogers's (1997) examination of the extent to which a spouse's report of marital problems in 1980 predicted later divorce (between 1980 and 1992). In this nationally representative sample, husbands and wives reported similar numbers of marital problems caused by husbands, but husbands reported significantly fewer marital problems caused by wives than did the wives themselves. Overall, both husbands' and wives' reports of problems caused both by themselves and by their spouse were positively associated with future divorce. The most consistent predictors of later divorce were reports by either spouse of infidelity (associated with an especially large increase in the odds of divorce), jealousy, spending money foolishly, and drinking or using drugs. These predictors, along with two others (irritating habits and moodiness), made independent contributions to divorce prediction. Information beyond reports of these six problems did not increase prediction.

THE CLINICAL RESEARCH APPROACH TO DISTRESSED RELATIONSHIPS

Mental health professionals have been dealing with people's relationship problems for a very long time. People seeking psychotherapy usually report interpersonal problems (for example, with intimacy) as well as psychiatric symptoms such as depression and anxiety in their first interview, according to Horowitz and Vitkus (1986). These theorists note that although psychological disorders are classified in terms of an individual's symptoms, the actual work of treatment usually focuses on interpersonal events, conflicts, and goals—in other words, on the individual's troubled relationship(s).

Growth of the Field of Relationship Therapy

Therapy in which the *relationship*, not the individual "identified patient," is the focus of the therapeutic effort achieved legitimacy only in the latter half of the twentieth century. According to Broderick and Schrader (1991), relationship therapy arose from four mostly independent movements: (1) the marriage counseling movement, which grew from attempts by many in the helping professions—psychology, medicine, education, social work, the ministry—to address an increase in marital and sexual problems following World War I; (2) the sex therapy movement, which involved many of those in the marriage counseling movement and achieved prominence

when Masters and Johnson published *Human Sexual Inadequacy* (1970); (3) marital therapy and (4) family therapy, both of which originated in the development of social psychiatry in America after World War II.

The history of relationship therapy is in many respects the story of how mental health practitioners gradually transcended the one-on-one, therapist–patient method of treatment practiced by Freud and his disciples and moved to **conjoint relationship therapy**, in which both partners (or in the case of a family, all members) receive treatment, usually at the same time, in the same room, by the same therapist. Although Freud himself tried it, he didn't like it. He also recognized, however, that individual treatment of each partner in a troubled relationship was unlikely to be successful: "When it comes to the treatment of relationships I must confess myself utterly at a loss and I have altogether little faith in any individual therapy of them" (Freud, 1912, cited in Broderick & Schrader, 1991, p. 19). Among several concerns, he and later therapists thought that neither relationship partner would be willing to express his or her true beliefs and feelings in the presence of the other and also that the therapist would devolve into a referee and ultimately lose the confidence of one or both of the partners.

Gradually, however, conjoint therapy came to be seen as efficacious for relationship problems. Among the many practitioners who were instrumental in gaining acceptance of this approach was John Bowlby, who was trained in psychoanalysis (see Chapter 1, "First Relationships"). In his work at the Tavistock Child Guidance Clinic, Bowlby (1949) became frustrated with his lack of progress in treating a teenager and began using conjoint family interviews to supplement individual interviews. John Bell, a professor of psychology in the United States who is often regarded as the "father" of family therapy, heard of Bowlby's approach and determined to try it himself with a troubled teenager he was treating. His request to the boy's family for their participation met with a reaction that is familiar to relationship therapists even today: The boy's father, a bank official, protested that it was all a lot of nonsense—it was Billy who had the trouble, the rest of the family was fine! As Bell suspected, however, the boy's family was not "fine." The boy's mother was a rigid perfectionist and hostile to her adopted son; the father, unable to cope with his wife, had taken to alcohol; and when the family began to disintegrate, the boy's behavior problems began.

It perhaps is no accident that it was in the treatment of troubled children that these and other practitioners began to discover that the participation of family members in therapy—treatment of the entire family system—was essential to progress. Today, in fact, it seems strange that psychotherapists ever thought that a child could somehow be restored to mental health without intervention into the involuntary relationship web in which the child is ensnared.

The term "conjoint therapy" was coined some years later by Don Jackson (1959), a psychiatrist who met Bell in 1957 and who became part of the "Palo Alto group" founded by anthropologist and philosopher Gregory Bateson. Bateson had obtained a research grant that allowed him to hire Jackson as well as Jay Haly, a communications scholar and the first editor of *Family Process* (a journal Jackson was instrumental in founding), and John Weakland, an anthropologist. Their famous, controversial, and now discredited paper "Toward a Theory of Schizophrenia" proposed that the mother's "double-bind" communications—messages that she did not love the child while punishing the child for accurately decoding those messages—were a crucial familial determinant of childhood schizophrenia (Bateson, Jackson, Haley, & Weakland, 1956). Jackson later formed a clinic focused on family therapy and hired Virgina Satir, whose background was in social work and who helped popularize conjoint therapy. The Palo Alto group's work was presented in a highly influential book, *Pragmatics of Human Communication* (Watzlawick, Beavin, & Jackson, 1967), which was followed by a popular "how to improve your marriage" book, *The Mirages of Marriage*, by Lederer and Jackson (1968).

Broderick and Schrader (1991) comment that, given its long and active gestation period, one might suppose that by the 1960s the field of marriage and family therapy would have established a clear identity and approach to the treatment of distressed relationships. However, just as the probability of divorce in the United States was about to escalate dramatically and families were to experience disruption at an unprecedented rate, only about 15% of marriage and family practitioners were using conjoint couple interviews—the usual approach still being one-on-one interviews with an individual whose relationship problems had driven him or her to seek help. Even by 1965, the vast majority (75%) of the members of the American Association of Marriage Counselors identified themselves as being primarily something other than a "marriage counselor"; marriage counseling was simply a sideline to their primary activities in the ministry, medicine, or psychology.

The public's demand for marriage and family therapy caught the field flat-footed on at least two other counts. First, there was no coherent theoretical approach to the treatment of relationships. Given its source in many locations and in different professions with different aims, the field was highly fragmented by many different (but firmly held) approaches to couple therapy, a situation that continued to characterize the field well into the 1980s. Second and worse, there was no systematic body of knowledge to support practitioners' rapidly growing activities. Several journals had been established before midcentury to report research on marriage and family counseling—for example, the *Journal of Marriage and the Family* had been established in 1939 under a different name—but Goodman's (1973) analysis of a sample of marriage counseling articles that actually presented research findings revealed that almost one-third of these contained no references. Most writings on therapeutic techniques simply presented nuggets of personal wisdom the author had extracted from clinical experience. Moreover, Broderick and Schrader (1991) note that in the new multidisciplinary field of marriage and family therapy, "each practitioner played to his or her home discipline, for the most part untouched by the work of marriage counselors from different disciplines who published in journals he or she never read" (p. 14)—a situation not unfamiliar today to scholars in the developing multidisciplinary relationship field.

In their "coming of age" review on the cusp of the twenty-first century, Johnson and Lebow (2000) observe that couple therapy has become firmly established as the accepted treatment of choice for couple problems, the science of relationships is blossoming, and the American Association of Marriage and Family Therapy now counts more than 20,000 members. One dark cloud remains, however. Pinsof and Wynne (2000) allege that research has had little impact on the practice of most couple and family therapists, and Gottman, Ryan, Carrère, and Erley (2002) comment, "Generally speaking, current marital therapies are not based on empirical research findings" (p. 152).

The Research Paradigm

As the practice of marital and family therapy escalated dramatically in the 1960s, the cry that practice had outstripped research was frequently heard. In the late 1960s, some clinical psychologists began to apply to distressed relationships the dominant psychological theories of the day—namely, the learning theories (the cognitive revolution in psychology not yet having come to a boil; see Chapter 4). Stuart (e.g., 1969) advocated using the principles of operant conditioning to treat marital discord. The "Oregon group," arguably the most influential of the early research venues, also took the behavioral approach as their "framework for conceptualizing marital conflict" (Weiss, Hops, & Patterson, 1973) and for developing their intervention technique, behavioral marital therapy (BMT), now often referred to as behavioral couple therapy (BCT) in recognition of the fact that many distressed couples who seek therapy are not married.

Robert Weiss and his colleagues began by distilling behavior in marital relationships into three essential types: the exchange of affectional behaviors; problem-solving behaviors (for example, for the appropriate distribution of resources); and behaviors intended to change the partner's behavior. With respect to this last, these theorists believed that people attempt to change their partners mostly through aversive or coercive control—a process based on the principles of negative reinforcement, which are guaranteed to perpetuate, if not also escalate, conflict. For example: (1) One partner may nag the other to behave (or not to behave) in a certain way; (2) to stop the aversive nagging, the other may eventually, often grudgingly, behave as requested; (3) this reinforces the nagging partner and increases the probability that he or she will use nagging (aversive control) again in the future to control the other's behavior. Weiss and colleagues (1973) state that one of their intervention aims was to change distressed spouses' "faulty behavior-change operations" and give them "appropriate training in behavioral principles" (p. 310).

The behavioral principles used by Weiss and his associates were discovered by such learning theorists as B. F. Skinner, whose principal research activity was observing and recording changes in a rat's rate of a behavior as a function of the application or removal of positive and negative reinforcements. Learning researchers placed a high premium on the *observation* of behavior as opposed to *self-reports* of behavior (which not only were not available from the non-English-speaking Norway laboratory rats whose behavior they mostly studied but, in the case of humans, emerged from the mysterious "black box" of the mind and were considered unverifiable and untrustworthy). Like many other researchers who take the learning theory approach to understanding relationship behavior today, Weiss and his colleagues were wary of self-reports and relied on behavioral observation.

Behavioral observation, however, was not without its problems. Weiss and his associates knew, for example, that *context* influences behavior. (Even rats had been shown to be highly sensitive to slight changes in context; they could be conditioned, for example, to work hard pressing the Skinner bar for pellets when a red light was on but could be found loafing around the cage when the light was off.) Because it was important to observe couples behave in their natural habitat, Weiss and his colleagues sometimes made their behavior observations in the couples' homes. This was not an entirely satisfactory solution, however, not only because of observation reactivity (see Chapter 4) but because many people object to having a stranger with a clipboard stationed in their living room, never mind more private rooms, and refuse to participate in the research. Some early investigators tried other solutions. Soskin and John (1963) gave a vacationing husband and wife a backpack containing an audio transmitter and antenna and continuously recorded the couple's conversations except when the couple turned the transmitter off for privacy (see Chapter 9, "Affective Processes"). This procedure produced monstrous volumes of data to be transcribed and coded, and despite many technological advancements in audio recording, it was never used again.

The problem for Weiss and his colleagues was that they needed to construct a method that would provide reliable observations, in the couples' natural habitat, of the spouses' provision of rewards and punishments to each other in their interactions. In the end, the researchers compromised: Observations would be made in the home but by the partners themselves; to increase accuracy, however, they would report on their spouse's behavior, not their own, and they would do so using the structured Spouse Observation Checklist (SOC). To learn whether the spouse's behavior was rewarding or punishing, Wills, Weiss, and Patterson (1974) also asked the partners to record whether the partner's behavior was "pleasing" or "displeasing" and, in addition, to keep a frequency count of the spouse's affectional behaviors on a wrist counter (see Chapter 4 for more details about this experiment). This was the first study to demonstrate that the tendency to reciprocate displeasing behaviors (negative reciprocity) was stronger than the tendency to reciprocate pleasing behaviors, which spouses often quickly forgot—a tendency noted earlier by Wills and colleagues which led to their use of wrist counters for spouses to immediately record the occurrence of an affectional behavior. In addition, this was the first study to document that the spouse's negative behaviors had more of an impact on global marital satisfaction than positive behaviors did.

At about the same time the Oregon group was developing their learning approach to the study of distressed marital relationships, Harold Raush and his associates—also following a general learning theory approach and also highly distrustful of people's self-reports of behavior—were bringing newlywed couples into their laboratory and observing their interactions (Raush, Barry, Hertel, & Swain, 1974). The Oregon group also had begun to investigate whether a couple's laboratory interactions accurately reflected their behavior in their natural context. Birchler, Weiss, and Vincent (1975) found that the laboratory interactions of both distressed and nondistressed couples mirrored their home interactions; distressed couples engaged in fewer positives and more negatives than did nondistressed couples during both a casual conversation and a problem-solving conversation in the laboratory. Birchler and colleagues also observed each spouse interact with two opposite-sex strangers (one from a distressed dyad and one from a nondistressed dyad). Marital partners—whether distressed or nondistressed—were less positive and more negative to one another than they were to perfect strangers, confirming folk wisdom that one can tell whether two people are married by how badly they treat each other.

These early studies set the basic theoretical and procedural approach to the study of distressed relationships that, with numerous variants, was to be followed by hundreds of other investigators and is followed today: The spouses identify problems in their marriage; they are instructed to discuss one of the problems for a short period of time (10 or 15 minutes) and try to reach a resolution; the interaction is videotaped; and the behavior is coded, with special attention to the affective (positive and negative) behaviors the spouses display in their interaction.

Although it might appear that this laboratory procedure would induce reactivity to observation as well as socially desirable behavior, couples seem to quickly habituate and revert to their usual interaction patterns (see Weiss & Heyman, 1997). Even when couples are instructed to "look good" or "look bad," observers can reliably discriminate happy from unhappy couples. For example, unhappy couples "leak" negative affect, often nonverbally (Vincent, Friedman, Nugent,

& Messerly, 1979). However, Heavey, Christensen, and Malamuth (1995) observe that because most spontaneous conflicts are stimulated by an upsetting event in the course of daily interactions, it is possible that conflicts discussed in the home differ from those formally listed and subsequently discussed in the laboratory. Gottman (1999) contends that conflict discussions in the laboratory *are* somewhat different from those at home—couples tend to be less negative in the laboratory, and thus laboratory observations may *underestimate* the communication differences between happy and unhappy couples.

Communication Patterns of Distressed Couples

The aim of identifying the microinteraction patterns that distinguish unhappy from happy partners when they communicate with one another has been twofold: to predict the future stability of the relationship more accurately than self-report measures do (see Chapter 13, "Satisfaction and Stability"), and to identify the interaction patterns that sustain the unhappiness of distressed couples and that thus constitute prime targets for intervention.

Affect Patterns

Using the basic observational research paradigm, researchers have unearthed what Heyman (2001) calls "stubborn facts" about marriage (see also Weiss & Heyman, 1997). Most of these facts concern the positive and negative affect couples display in their interactions as they attempt to resolve a marital problem. Not surprisingly, distressed partners behave more negatively toward each other than nondistressed partners do; they begin their problem-solving discussions with hostility and maintain negativity throughout the discussion.

Some investigators have found that certain negative behaviors are more associated with marital distress than others. According to Gottman (1999), where the future of a marriage is concerned; the "Four Horsemen of the Apocalypse" are criticism, defensiveness, stonewalling, and contempt. Of these, Gottman believes that con-tempt, defined as "any statement of nonverbal behavior that puts oneself on a higher plane than one's partner" (p. 45), is most corrosive of a relationship. Gottman finds virtually no expressions of contempt in happy, stable marriages—evidence in support of the aged French aphorism "Love is possible only between equals." Partners in Gottman's marital therapy sessions who express contempt toward their partner (for example, mockery and ridicule) are immediately told that such behavior will not be permitted.

Reciprocity

It appears to be human nature to respond in kind to another's behavior—negative for negative and positive for positive, with the former being a significantly more reliable effect than the latter. Although negative reciprocity sometimes can be seen in nondistressed as well as distressed couples, it is a hallmark of distressed couples—more so, in fact, than a high base rate of negative behavior. Some investigators have found that distressed partners also are more likely to reciprocate each other's positive behaviors. For example, Filsinger and Thoma (1988) found that positive reciprocity in interaction predicted dissolution 1.5, 2.5, and 5 years later. Although positive affect reciprocity generally is a less reliable discriminator of distressed and nondistressed couples than negative reciprocity, its sporadic appearance supports the general view that distressed couples are more sensitive to each other's affective behavior than nondistressed couples are (Jacobson, Follette, & McDonald, 1982).

The difference in the reliability of negative and positive reciprocity to discriminate between distressed and nondistressed couples is reflected in the results of a study conducted by Ebling and Levenson (2003), who examined people's ability to predict marital satisfaction and stability from viewing short interaction videotapes of married couples. Among their several findings was that participants who reported paying attention to spouses' expressions of disgust, contempt, or criticism made more accurate predictions of the couple's satisfaction than did those who paid attention to expressions of positive affect, personality, or sadness.

FIGURE 14.1 In the demand–withdraw pattern, one partner (typically the wife) pressures the other (typically the husband) for change and the other then retreats.

Intervention into an interaction regularity requires knowledge of the causal conditions responsible, as we have discussed. Christensen and his associates suspected that in many couples, the roots of the demand–withdraw pattern lie in a **balance of closeness dilemma**. Many partners fail to agree on the balance between interdependence and independence; one partner wishes to be closer to the other, spending more time together, sharing more activities, and disclosing more, but the other partner not only does *not* wish to increase relationship closeness but, on the contrary, desires more independence, separateness, and privacy. The person who wants greater closeness can achieve that goal only with the cooperation of the partner. However, the person who wants more independence usually can achieve that goal unilaterally, resisting the partner's protests and influence attempts by withdrawing from interactions in which the problem is raised.

Christensen and his colleagues began their research program by demonstrating the following: (1) Marital distress is significantly associated with asymmetry between the partners' answers to two questions—one concerning a desire to spend more or less time with their partner and the other concerning a desire for more partner self-disclosure

or for more "privacy" for themselves. (2) Partners who experience the balance of closeness dilemma can report, on the Communication Patterns Questionnaire (see Christensen, 1988), whether the demand–withdraw pattern characterizes their relationship and, if so, which partner typically plays what role. (3) Their reports are accurate, as measured by observation of the couple's interaction in the laboratory. This preliminary research also confirmed clinicians' reports that the wife usually is the demander and the husband the withdrawer. Although Christensen and his colleagues had not yet shown any causal connections between the closeness dilemma, the demand–withdraw interaction pattern, and marital distress, they had demonstrated that all three were correlated, thus leaving open the possibility of causal associations.

Two causal conjectures about the pattern previously had been advanced. The first pointed to a *relational* causal condition, namely, that the combination of dispositions characteristic of many women and those characteristic of many men is toxic. This explanation focuses on differential socialization processes, positing that (1) most women are socialized to be affiliative and value relationships, to be emotionally expressive, and to be dependent on men; (2) most men are socialized to be independent, unemotional, and self-reliant; and, therefore, (3) this combination (not either set of characteristics alone) inevitably leads to a balance of closeness dilemma in most marital relationships: The wife wants more interdependence whereas the husband wants more independence.

The second popular conjecture was that the demand–withdraw pattern has its roots not in dispositional differences between men and women but rather in a *social environmental causal condition*—namely, the asymmetrical power positions of husbands and wives in most marriages. This "social structural" explanation of the demand–withdraw pattern points to the greater benefits and lower costs of marriage for husbands, who should be satisfied with the status quo and should want to avoid confrontations that might reduce their advantaged status. Wives, on the other hand, are more likely to regard the marital situation as unfair and unpleasant (and, indeed, women have more complaints about their marriages than men do; see Jacobson, 1990) and are motivated to demand change. Supporting the social structural explanation, previous experimental research had established that people in higher-power positions in relationships shun communication with those in lower-power positions, whereas lower-power persons try hard to communicate with those of higher power, often to discuss changing their status in the relationship (Kelley, 1951).

The first experimental question Christensen and his associates asked was "When it is the husband who wants change, does *he* become the demander and the wife the withdrawer?" If so, the pattern is associated with a power imbalance in the relationship (and a social structure that favors husbands over wives)—not a toxic combination of dispositions. Christensen and Heavey (1990) observed couples discussing two of their child-rearing conflicts, one of which was an issue on which the wife wanted her husband to change his behavior and the other an issue on which the husband wanted the wife to change. Overall, women did more demanding regardless of who wanted change, but there also was a significant interaction between the sex of the demander and whether it was the husband or the wife who wanted the partner to change. Christensen and Heavey concluded that although gender is associated with the roles taken by spouses in the demand–withdraw interaction pattern, the structure of the conflict (which partner wants change) also plays a powerful role in determining the nature of the interaction.

To examine the alternative explanation that the results of the first study could be explained by the wives wanting a higher level of change from their husbands than husbands wanted from them, Heavey, Layne, and Christensen (1993) allowed spouses to request changes in a wide range of their partner's behaviors and were careful to match the level of change each spouse requested. The results were the same as those of Christensen and Heavey (1990): During discussions of husbands' issues, wives and husbands did not differ in their demand–withdraw behavior, but when discussing

wives' issues, wives were more demanding and husbands were more withdrawing.

Many investigators have found that the "wife demand, husband withdraw" pattern generally is associated with marital unhappiness (e.g., Heavey, Christensen, & Malamuth, 1995; Noller, Feeney, Bonnell, & Callan, 1994; Sagrestano, Christensen, & Heavey, 1998). However, Caughlin and Huston (2002) found that regardless of which spouse reported the pattern and which spouse demanded while the other withdrew, the presence of the pattern was inversely associated with both wives' and husbands' marital satisfaction. Moreover, these investigators provide evidence that the presence of the demand–withdraw pattern accounts for variation in marital satisfaction over and above the partners' sheer base rates of negativity, a finding that supports many therapists' belief that this interaction pattern is more deadly in a marriage than garden-variety negativity.

In addition, the demand–withdraw pattern has been shown to be associated with physical violence in couples (Berns, Jacobson, & Gottman, 1999; Sagrestano, Heavey, & Christensen, 1999) and with divorce (e.g., Gottman & Levenson, 2000). Finally, although certain personality variables, such as neuroticism, appear to contribute to the frequency with which the demand–withdraw pattern is likely to be observed (Caughlin & Vangelisti, 2000), the social structural explanation for the pattern has received the most support (e.g., Vogel & Karney, 2002).

Limitations of the Observational Research Paradigm

Observational research of couples' conflict interactions has produced many insights into relationship dynamics. However, this research protocol is not without limitations—some inherent in the procedure and some associated with how the protocol has been used. With respect to the latter, observational couple interaction research suffers from restricted sampling. Because such observational research is laborious and expensive, small "convenience" samples, usually of young couples, often newlyweds, are usual.

Another set of problems derives from the manner in which the interactions are coded. What investigators see depends on what they are looking for, and the behaviors they are looking for are reflected in the behavioral coding scheme they select and in the ways in which those codes subsequently are collapsed to form an operationalization of the theoretical construct(s) of interest (say, behavioral negativity). Many microanalytic couples observation coding systems are available. One of the oldest and most frequently used is the Marital Interaction Coding System (MICS; e.g., Weiss & Summers, 1983), which has over 30 codes. Noting that the construct of behavioral negativity has been operationalized with the MICS in at least 15 different ways, making across-study comparisons difficult, Heyman, Eddy, Weiss, and Vivian (1995) factor analyzed the products of a large number of couples' conflict interactions that had been coded with the MICS. Four factors emerged: humor, hostility, constructive problem discussion, and responsibility discussion (denying or accepting responsibility for an event).

Other coding schemes employ other codes and offer other suggestions for classifying codes into categories. For example, the Couple Interaction Scoring System (CISS; Gottman, 1979; Notarius & Markman, 1981) gives each unit of a couple's interaction (a unit is defined as a grammatical clause) one of 36 verbal content codes and one of 3 nonverbal affect codes, yielding 4 categories, or summary codes: problem-solving facilitation, problem-solving inhibition, emotional validation, and emotional invalidation.

Perhaps because coding systems and code category systems for couples' interaction behavior have proliferated as rapidly as marital satisfaction scales, they suffer from many of the same problems. For example, Heyman (2001) concludes his review of the reliability and validity of microinteraction coding systems with a plea for the field to "develop constructs in a psychometrically and theoretically sound manner" (p. 5). Similarly, Snyder, Cozzi, and Mangrum (2002) believe the "core deficit" of the discipline of marital and family therapy is "the proliferation of measures without adequate attention to issues of reliability and

validity" (p. 69). Establishment of the validity of a construct requires that it be adequately conceptualized in theory and its hypothesized associations with other constructs be clearly specified. In their review of couple therapy, Johnson and Lebow (2000) warn that if practitioners do not "adopt some unifying frameworks to describe, predict, and explain relationship problems and guide intervention, the field may be in danger of fragmentation and marginalization" (p. 33). Theories provide "unifying frameworks" and are indispensable to progress in any field of inquiry.

Another problem stems from the fact that investigators typically pay scant attention to the difficulty of the problems that distressed and nondistressed couples list and discuss in the laboratory. Researchers have widely assumed that it doesn't matter *what* conflict is discussed—it only matters *how* it is discussed. In other words, all conflicts are assumed to be created equal, and little is known about the relative severity of the problems discussed by distressed and nondistressed couples (see Berscheid, 1998). In an early two-wave longitudinal study of newlyweds over their first 4 years of marriage, Bentler and Newcomb (1978) found that the problems of couples who later divorced were qualitatively different from those of couples who remained married. For example, divorced couples had rated finances as a more severe problem in their marriage. However, Rogge and Bradbury (1999) asked couples themselves to rate the severity of the problem topics they discussed and found no differences among satisfied, distressed, and separated couples. This somewhat curious result deserves further explanation, given evidence that the problems of distressed couples generally are more severe and difficult to resolve than those of satisfied couples (see Chapter 13).

Some information on how the difficulty of a problem may influence the manner in which it is discussed has been provided by Sanford (2003). In this study, couples named and discussed sequentially four marital problems. In addition, a group of licensed psychologists rated the difficulty of the four problems listed and discussed by each couple. Couples did *not* change their communication patterns across the four problem-solving conversations depending on problem difficulty. Rather, a couple's communication pattern was a function of the most serious problem they discussed; that is, couples who were experiencing a difficult problem in their marriage used negative forms of communication in all of their problem-solving conversations regardless of the difficulty of the specific problem they were discussing.

Sanford's results may reflect the operation of several processes: (1) Severe problems may lead to marital distress, which then leads to negative communication patterns. (2) Negative communication patterns may exacerbate the severity of any problem encountered and increase marital distress. (3) Third variables, such as neuroticism, may be responsible for both severe problems and negative communication patterns. (4) All of these processes together may be responsible for the association between the existence of a severe problem in the marriage and habitual use of a negative communication style. It seems likely that reciprocal causal relationships will be found among these variables. At the least, the association between distress, problem severity, and communication pattern deserves more investigation than it has yet received, especially because outcome studies indicate that marital therapy is less effective with highly distressed couples (see Bray & Jouriles, 1995). Degree of distress is likely associated with the severity of the problem as well as the manner of discussing the problem; although the therapist may not be able to alleviate the problem—only the manner in which the problem is discussed—neglect of the role of problem severity in producing marital distress leaves a peculiar gap in understanding marital dynamics.

Finally, the observational research paradigm is limited in another way: The kind of task the couple performs influences the nature of the interaction the researcher sees (Melby, Ge, Conger, & Warner, 1995). Heyman (2001) notes that it is relatively easy to get couples to argue on command but not so easy to find tasks that allow laboratory observation of behaviors associated with love and caring. Some researchers are branching out to develop tasks on which the spouses are given opportunities to display positive behaviors in their interaction. For example,

Griffin (1993) asks couples to remember a pleasant relationship event as well as to talk about a problem in their marriage, and some researchers have developed tasks that allow the partners to provide each other with social support (e.g., Pasch & Bradbury, 1998; Pasch, Bradbury, & Davila, 1997).

THERAPEUTIC INTERVENTIONS FOR DISTRESSED RELATIONSHIPS

Most distressed couples who knock on a therapist's door and ask for help will get "potluck." They are unlikely to inquire about the approach the therapist will take to their relationship problems. Many will not even inquire whether that individual has been trained as a relationship therapist or simply uses an idiosyncratic potpourri of individualistic therapies. Here, we discuss only those approaches to relationship therapy that focus exclusively on couples (married, cohabiting, heterosexual, or homosexual partners in distressed relationships), that have achieved an identity beyond their different labels, and that are research-oriented—meaning that empirical research has guided their development and evaluations of their effectiveness.

Contraindications for Therapy

Not every couple who requests a relationship therapist's help will receive it. Just as wise clients have standards for selecting the therapist to whom they will entrust their relationship, many relationship therapists exercise standards in the selection of clients. These standards differ from therapist to therapist and approach to approach and are usually derived from the therapist's beliefs about the kind of client who can be helped by the particular therapeutic approach he or she practices.

Sometimes clients whose primary presenting problems are sexual in nature are referred to a sex therapist. (Reflecting the unfortunate separation of relationship therapy and research from sex therapy and research [see Chapter 12], sex therapists often return the favor by sending their clients to a marital therapist.) Other marital therapists proceed on the assumption that the couple's sexual problems will disappear along with their other marital problems. They don't. According to research by Jacobson and his colleagues (see Jacobson & Holtzworth-Munroe, 1986), improvement in the sexual area following marital therapy is rare. This fact suggests that sexual problems need specific attention either before, during, or after marital therapy. "During" would be optimal but would require a better integration of sex therapy and marital therapy than has been achieved so far.

Other factors may lead to a couple's rejection by the potential therapist. Gottman (1994), as previously noted, believes that expressions of contempt in a relationship are so lethal that he forbids them in therapy sessions; presumably, an incorrigible client is told to find another therapist. Clients whose relationships are characterized by physical violence or alcoholism and other drug abuse also are rejected by many marital therapists (e.g., Christensen & Jacobson, 2000). These very serious problems need concerted, specialized, and immediate treatment. Many therapists also will not take a client currently involved in an ongoing extramarital relationship if he or she is unwilling to dissolve that relationship.

Finally, most therapists try to ascertain each partner's commitment to improving the relationship. Sometimes both partners seek marital therapy only to convince themselves and others that they have done all humanly possible to salvage the relationship. Other times one of the partners wants to end the relationship and is present only to mollify the partner who wishes to continue the relationship; these are sometimes called "polarized couples" (see Crosby, 1989). When it is clear that one or both partners are simply "going through the motions," the marital therapist may practice "divorce therapy," helping the couple to achieve a constructive separation that wreaks as little damage as possible on the partners themselves as well as their children and other family members (e.g., see Kressel & Deutsch, 1977). Most marital therapists now believe that helping couples with unresolvable and irreconcilable differences to divorce and achieve healthy postdivorce adjustment may be a legitimate goal of marital therapy (see Bray & Jouriles, 1995) and thus they also practice divorce therapy (e.g., Kaslow & Schwartz, 1987; Kressel, 1985).

Therapeutic Approaches

Certain commonalties exist across approaches to marital or couples therapy. Most couple therapies share the aim of changing the partners' affective responses to each other by "accentuating the positive and eliminating the negative"—increasing the frequency and strength of positive affective responses in the partners' interactions and reducing negative affect. Another commonality is communication training, which usually is a component of the therapeutic technique used to achieve that goal (see Jacobson & Holtzworth-Munroe, 1986).

Communication Training

In contrast to nondistressed couples, distressed couples reliably show a number of dysfunctional communication patterns, as we have discussed; moreover, there is suggestive evidence that communication deficiencies present early in the relationship may be associated with later distress. Different therapeutic approaches emphasize different aspects of communication, but the partners' communication during their problem-solving interactions is the focus of most. Historically, most marital therapists have taken the view that conflict engagement—confronting and attempting to resolve problems—is more constructive than conflict avoidance. Indeed, several researchers have found that couples who report that they avoid discussing conflicts are more likely to be distressed than other couples (e.g., Christensen & Shenk, 1991; Noller & White, 1990), and in a prospective study, Smith, Vivian, and O'Leary (1990) found that premarital disengagement in conflict was negatively associated with satisfaction after 18 and 30 months of marriage.

Whether the benefits of conflict engagement always exceed those of conflict avoidance has been called into question by Fitzpatrick's (1988) and Gottman's (1993a) identification of certain types of relatively happy and stable married couples who assiduously avoid conflict. Even Raush and his associates (1974) retreated somewhat from their initial belief that confrontation was always desirable when they observed in their early studies that some of their happy couples displayed an aversion to conflict that, to the investigators, seemed to verge on pathological avoidance. At the least, more information is needed about when, and for whom, confrontation is efficacious. Christensen and Pasch (1993) note that the typical problem-solving methodology used to observe interaction in the laboratory is not conducive to studying conflict avoidance.

Communication training often involves teaching partners expressive skills (to voice their thoughts and feelings) and listening skills, both of which are believed to be essential to conflict resolution (see Jacobson & Holtzworth-Munroe, 1986). Expressive skills training usually includes teaching partners to make constructive requests for change that do *not* include overgeneralizations ("You always forget . . .," "You never . . ."), character assassination ("You are a congenitally lazy and inconsiderate bum"), and irrelevancies ("And, besides, . . ."). Partners also are taught to make their requests specific ("It would make me happy if you would take out the garbage when the can is overflowing"). Listening skills include paraphrasing what the partner is saying (to ascertain that the partner's communication is understood), reflecting on the communication ("I guess that means that you . . ."), and validation ("I can understand why you feel as you do").

Gottman (1994) asserts that the **active listening model** is the most influential theory of marital therapy and forms the basis of most marital treatments: "The hypothesis is that stable, happy marriages are characterized by active, empathic listening during conflict resolution, and that ailing marriages are characterized by the absence of this quality" (p. 8). However, Gottman states that in the interactions he has observed, active listening exchanges hardly ever occur, which he does not find particularly surprising: "When people feel attacked, they tend to respond negatively; usually in stable happy marriages, they respond in kind [e.g., to anger with anger] while in un-

stable and unhappy marriages, they escalate the negativity" (p. 8). Indeed, Christensen and Pasch (1993) believe that trying to change how couples behave in the midst of conflict is futile: "The action is too fast, the emotions too hot, the thinking too automatic" (p. 13). They suggest that therapy focus on the beginnings of conflict—for example, on how stress from external sources may exacerbate negativity in conflict discussions—and on the postconflict recovery period, when the partners return to "normal" and can assess the conflict rationally.

In an attempt to provide some insight into whether destructive communication patterns are present before marriage or whether they develop over the course of marriage, Noller and Feeney (1998) conducted a four-wave longitudinal study that examined change in specific communication behaviors from before marriage through the first 2 years of marriage. The investigators assumed that relationship satisfaction depends on adequacy in three areas: communications dealing with conflicts; daily communication habits, such as frequency of talk and self-disclosure; and partners' ability to understand each other's communications. The usual differences were found between happy and unhappy couples (happy couples reported more positivity, less disengagement, and less conflict), but neither the satisfied nor the dissatisfied couples showed much change over time on any of the communication measures. Noller and Feeney conclude, "Although the literature has tended to emphasize the effect of communication on later relationship satisfaction, we found at least as much support for the proposition that relationship satisfaction affects later communication" (p. 40).

An earlier study conducted by Noller (1981) agrees with Noller and Feeney's conclusion. Noller found that in contrast to satisfied spouses, dissatisfied spouses performed poorly when decoding the meaning of their *partner's* communication, but no differences between satisfied and dissatisfied spouses were found when they were asked to decode the communications of *strangers*. This result suggests that many dissatisfied spouses possess adequate communication skills but simply do not use them when communicating with their partner. In sum, it may be the case that relationship satisfaction and communication patterns are reciprocally causal, as so many other relationship variables are. It also may be the case that *both* relationship satisfaction and communication patterns are directly and simultaneously influenced by the frequency and severity of the conflicts couples experience. Thus, communication training itself may not produce the desired therapeutic outcome.

Behavioral Couple Therapy

Also known as behavioral marital therapy, behavioral couple therapy (BCT) originally was aimed at modifying partners' behavior through the application of learning principles, as illustrated in the 1974 study by Wills and colleagues discussed previously. Typically, spouses were asked to identify the behaviors of their partner they found desirable or offensive, to track their own and their partners' positive and negative behaviors, and to increase their sensitivity to the consequences of their own behavior. As practiced, BCT generally contained a communication training component to help couples discuss and solve their problems. The learning theory foundation of BCT led to the use of contingency contracting.

Contingency Contracting

In behavioral **contingency contracting,** couples make explicit, often written, contracts in which each partner promises to stop behaving in ways the other finds objectionable and to start behaving in ways the other finds pleasurable in return for the other doing the same. The Palo Alto group, with its underlying systems perspective (see Segraves, 1990), popularized contingency contracting. Lederer and Jackson (1968), in fact, devoted several chapters of their well-known book *The Mirages of Marriage* to instructing couples on the establishment of quid pro quo contracts that were believed to achieve and maintain homeostasis in the marital system. Without such contracting, the authors asserted, the number and variety of differences that ordinarily exist between spouses tend to run amok and create chaos in the marital system. The book gave detailed instructions for holding "quid pro quo meetings," which were billed as an important ritual (rivaling the marriage ceremony), to work out contracts. The authors gave numerous examples of quid pro quo contracting successes—and failures. With respect to the latter, readers were told, "If, after a reasonable trial the spouses are convinced they cannot bargain, their alternatives, as has been mentioned, are to seek outside help, to separate, or to permit one spouse to dominate entirely" (p. 287). Ominously, the chapters on quid pro quo contracting were immediately followed by a chapter titled "How to Select a Spouse."

Although contingency contracting was congruent with learning theory principles and seemed reasonable on the surface, not only did it fail to make unhappy marriages happier, but it often seemed to increase the couple's dissolution risk. Murstein, Cerreto, and MacDonald (1977) found that an "exchange" orientation was more characteristic of unhappy marriages than of happy ones. In retrospect, the failure of contingency contracting likely was a result of the now established finding that although people regard quid pro quo exchange rules as appropriate for business and other nonclose relationships, for close relationships in general, and marital relationships in particular, most people believe a communal orientation, in which benefits are given according to need and without thought of immediate return, is appropriate (Clark & Mills, 1979, 2001).

Cognitive-Behavioral Couple Therapy

Following the cognitive revolution in psychology, cognitive-behavioral couple therapy (CBCT) evolved on the premise that in human relationships, it is not just the surface aspects of behavior that are important but also how the partners interpret the *meaning* of the behavior (e.g., see Baucom & Epstein, 1990; Baucom, Epstein, & Rankin, 1995; Epstein, Baucom, & Daiuto, 1997). It became recognized that to understand marital distress, the therapist must consider the individual's *attributions* for the cause of the partner's behavior (see Chapter 8, "Cognitive Processes") as well as the individual's *expectations* about the partner's behavior (see Chapter 13). The affective consequences of the partners' interpretations of each other's behavior remained at the forefront; that is, malignant attributions for the partner's behavior and unrealistic expectations were seen to require "cognitive restructuring" in order to achieve behavioral change. Cognitive restructuring is accomplished through various means, including logical analysis.

Integrative Behavioral Couple Therapy

The most recent evolution of BCT is integrative behavioral couple therapy (IBCT), which was developed by Jacobson and Christensen (1996; Christensen & Jacobson, 2000; Jacobson, Christensen, Prince, Cordova, & Eldridge, 2000) after they observed that many couples experience incompatibilities that cannot be resolved by compromise or accommodation. To ameliorate the negative affect associated with these intractable "perpetual" problems, IBCT integrates the fundamental premises and techniques of BCT and CBCT with strategies that promote the partners' acceptance and tolerance of each other's unpleasant behaviors through coming to see those behaviors in the "larger context of the other and of their relationship together" (Christensen & Walczynski, 1997, p. 266). IBCT is often referred to as "acceptance therapy" because one of its aims is acceptance of the partner as a whole, integrated person. Partners are reminded:

> The good qualities you like in your partner may be part of a natural constellation that includes some qualities that you don't like. Your partner's personality is inevitably a "package deal," and you have no "line-item veto" whereby you can cancel some qualities but keep others. (Christensen & Jacobson, 2000, p. 74)

The purpose of the therapy is not to promote resignation to an unsatisfactory relationship; rather, partners are encouraged to change their own expectancies and demands, as well as to change their own behavior to better meet their partner's expectations. It is assumed that a combination of changing one's own behavior and accepting the

partner's behavior will be more powerful than either alone because individuals who receive acceptance of their behaviors may be more motivated to try to change their actions to accommodate the partner. Acceptance of the partner, of course, reduces the negative tone of the relationship, which in itself is facilitative of change.

Emotion-Focused Couple Therapy

Emotion-focused couple therapy (ECT; Greenberg & Johnson, 1988; Johnson & Greenberg, 1995) is based on several tenets of Bowlby's attachment theory (see Chapter 1), including the premise that distress results when an attachment relationship fails to provide a secure base for one or both partners. Essential to secure attachment is trust—specifically, a belief that the partner will be available and willing to help in time of need. It will be recalled that trust, the single most frequently named feature of a high-quality relationship, is central to most people's concept of relationship quality (see Chapter 13). Moreover, attachment insecurity has been shown to be associated with relationship distress and with an individual's tendency to remain in an unsatisfying marriage (see Chapters 10, "Dispositional Influences," and 13).

The principal aim of ECT is to reestablish bonds to satisfy the partners' attachment needs. In therapeutic sessions, the distressed partners are encouraged to express their emotions and fears. It is assumed that anger in the relationship often stems from fear of the partner's abandonment. ECT also recognizes the importance of caregiving, the other side of the attachment coin. Among others, Pasch and Bradbury (1998) observe that caregiving has been neglected by marital researchers; that is, in their heavy focus on the role of conflict in reducing relationship satisfaction, researchers have failed to recognize the importance of the emotional and instrumental support spouses give each other when each is under stress emanating from sources outside the relationship (such as job stress). Failure to provide the partner with support when he or she is in need of it is believed to be especially detrimental to the relationship. Johnson, Makinen, and Millikin (2001) term a violation of the individual's expectation that his or her partner will offer comfort and caring in times of danger or distress an **attachment injury**. Most therapists recognize attachment injuries as serious threats to the relationship. Attachment injuries, particularly infidelity, are extremely difficult to treat (Glass & Wright, 1995).

Sound Marital House Therapy

On the basis of his own research and that of others, Gottman (1994) and his colleagues have developed what he calls sound marital house theory, on which he and his associates base their approach to relationship therapy. As in other therapeutic approaches, the aim of this intervention is to increase the partners' positive affective experiences in the relationship and reduce negative experiences. Unlike other approaches, Gottman emphasizes the role of positive affect. The foundation of the "sound marital house" is assumed to be *friendship*, which, in turn, is believed to create positive affect in mundane, everyday nonconflict interactions with the partner.

The assumption that friendship is the foundation of a sound marriage has a number of implications for the prevention of marital distress and for intervention into distressed relationships. For example, it suggests that a "bank account" filled with positive affective experiences in nonconflict interactions creates *positive sentiment override*, which plays an important role in Gottman's theory. He believes that only positive sentiment override allows partners to exit negative cycles within the conflict interactions that are inevitable in all close relationships and allows a partner's *repair attempts* (to reduce the negativity of an interaction when it reaches high levels) to be effective. Positive sentiment override also promotes benign attributions of the cause of a partner's negative behavior in conflict interactions as well as in other circumstances.

Gottman, Ryan, Carrère, and Erley (2002) identify another implication of the assumption that friendship is the foundation of a satisfying marriage: "Unlike many of the current marital therapies, the theory suggests that intervention not be based solely or primarily on how couples resolve conflict" (p. 162). Particularly important to relieving "conflict gridlock," Gottman believes, is helping the partners construct shared meanings, which means spouses must learn to respect each other's life dreams and aspirations. Exploring the symbolic meaning of the partners' positions on issues, and establishing the perception that the marriage is effective in facilitating each partner's objectives, is posited to be essential to a successful intervention.

Congruent with his belief that intervention need not be based primarily on conflict resolution, Gottman (1994) believes that only about a third of the conflicts couples discuss are resolvable and that the role of problem-solving has been exaggerated. He states that

> even in the best marriages, while some minor fraction of marital problems does get solved, over time most marital problems do *not* get solved at all; instead, they become what we call "perpetual" issues. . . . *What matters is the affect with which people don't solve their perpetual problems.* (p. 16, emphasis in original)

Despite the importance of positive affect to a "sound marital house," Gottman notes that it is extremely difficult to create positive affective experiences in a distressed marriage. Because almost all marriages begin with a high degree of positivity, it may be as true of marital illness as it is of physical illness that an ounce of prevention against losing health (or, in this case, positivity) is worth a pound of cure. Indeed, therapy appears to be most likely to be successful with younger couples and with couples who are less distressed, still emotionally engaged with each other, and not depressed or showing other symptoms of individual psychopathology (see Bray & Jouriles, 1995).

Intervention Effectiveness

On the basis of a *Consumer Reports* survey of customer satisfaction with different kinds of psychotherapy (see Seligman, 1995), it is frequently asserted that relationship therapy is less effective than other types (see Berscheid & Reis, 1998). However, the flaws of that survey are so numerous and serious that the results have been dismissed by almost all informed observers (see Nathan, Stuart, & Dolan, 2000). The results of outcome studies are more sanguine, if not as positive as many have hoped.

Clinical researchers distinguish between outcome studies of psychotherapy's efficacy and its effectiveness. Studies of **psychotherapy efficacy** measure the effects of specific interventions administered to a random sample of participants as contrasted to the outcomes shown by a control group (for example, couples placed on a waiting list) or a comparison treatment group. Studies of **psychotherapy effectiveness** assess whether treatments, often administered by clinicians who are not trained in that treatment protocol, have broadly defined beneficial effects such as a change in quality of life across broad populations of persons (often self-selected into groups). Both types of study are useful, but studies of psychotherapy effectiveness better reflect the outcomes of a therapeutic treatment as it is likely to be administered in naturalistic settings. From their consideration of previous literature reviews of studies of the efficacy of marital therapy, Bray and Jouriles (1995) conclude that there is general agreement that, compared to no-treatment controls, marital therapy is effective in reducing marital conflict and promoting short-term marital satisfaction.

In their review of empirical investigations of the benefits of couple interventions, Christensen and Heavey (1999) also conclude that couple therapy generally reduces relationship distress in comparison to no-treatment groups. They also observe, however, that a statistically significant difference between a treatment group and a no-treatment group may be achieved even if treatment couples score only a few points higher than their no-treatment counterparts. As opposed to a statistically significant difference alone, it is important for researchers to assess the **clinical effectiveness** of a therapeutic treatment by calculating the percentage of couples who not only show an increase in satisfaction but, against the benchmark provided by

normative data, have moved from the distressed range into the nondistressed range following therapy. The evidence that marital therapies are clinically effective is thin. A meta-analysis of marital therapy outcome studies conducted by Shadish and colleagues (1993) found that there is a 60% chance that a couple receiving therapy will have improved following treatment in comparison to a couple who did not receive therapy (and thus 40% of those who received marital therapy did *not* improve). At the same time, only 41% of treated couples will have moved from the distressed to the nondistressed range following treatment (see Nathan et al., 2000). As previously noted, negative therapeutic outcomes are associated with severe relational problems, increasing age, emotional disengagement, and high gender-role preference polarization (Jacobson & Addis, 1993). With respect to the question of which type of marital therapy has been found to be most efficacious, only three types have more than one published study supporting their effectiveness (see Christensen & Heavey, 1999) and overall, there is little evidence that one form of therapy is better than another. BCT, however, has been the subject of most research, and its positive effects have been the most thoroughly documented.

Almost all investigations of marital therapy outcomes have been efficacy studies; that is, they have been conducted under controlled conditions, with carefully selected samples and extensive therapist training in the treatment protocol (and often with ongoing supervision to prevent "therapist drift"). Only one study of the effectiveness of relationship intervention under naturalistic conditions—in which the couples are more heterogeneous, the treatment is loosely defined, and the therapist may never have received specialized relationship training—has been conducted (Shadish, Ragsdale, Glaser, & Montgomery, 1995; see Christensen & Heavy, 1999). This study found no differences between treatment and no-treatment groups.

Few studies have examined the *durability* of improvement following therapy. Reviews of such data as exist, however, suggest that many couples relapse quickly. Opinion is growing that for distressed couples, periodic "booster shots" of therapy may be helpful (see Jacobson & Addis, 1993). Considering the time and money people spend in an effort to keep their teeth in healthy condition, such a regimen for a valued relationship does not seem excessive and may be an important component of "minding the relationship" (Harvey & Omarzu, 1997). Booster therapy may be especially advantageous at times of transition (such as parenthood) or in other periods of disruption and stress that threaten the health of the relationship and the partners.

Finally, it should be noted that participants in outcome studies generally are white, middle-class, and in their first marriages. Difference in treatment effectiveness with people from different ethnic, racial, cultural, and socioeconomic backgrounds is not known, nor is the effectiveness of marital therapy with remarried partners.

Preventive Intervention

Programs devised to prevent later marital distress and dissolution are highly diverse. Participants in prevention programs tend to be couples who are experiencing little or no distress, and who are usually contemplating marriage (see Silliman, Stanley, Coffin, Markman, & Jordan, 2002). Prevention programs often involve assessment of the individual couple's divorce risk. *Dynamic risk* factors that are believed to be amenable to change, such as dysfunctional communication patterns, are targeted for intervention (as opposed to *static risk* factors such as parental divorce and age). Thus, most prevention programs begin by assessing the couple's standing on dimensions associated with marital satisfaction and stability—such as communication, conflict resolution, parenting attitudes, religious beliefs, and self-confidence—via such instruments as the PRE-PARE questionnaire (e.g., Olson, Fournier, & Druckman, 1989). Many programs also try to strengthen factors believed to *protect* the couple against divorce, such as religiosity.

Prevention programs usually contain at least one of three elements: *education* (an instructor, or written materials, may provide relevant information about healthy relationships); *discussion* *groups* (usually semistructured to focus on critical issues); and *skills training* (for example, in listening or communication skills). The Prevention and Relationship Enhancement Program (PREP) devised by Howard Markman and his associates (e.g., Markman, Stanley, & Blumberg, 1994) includes all three—lecture, partner interaction, and skill practice.

Again, outcome data suggest that several of these programs produce at least short-term improvements in communication skills and relationship satisfaction. Long-term benefits, provided by two 5-year follow-ups, have been reported for the PREP program. Markman, Renick, Floyd, Stanley, and Clements (1993) matched over 100 couples on whether or not they were engaged or planning marriage, confidence that they would actually marry, relationship satisfaction, and ratings of communication impact. Of these, 25 couples participated in the *intervention* condition, 47 couples composed the *control* group, and 42 couples who had *declined* to participate in the intervention made up a second control group. Prior to marriage, 4% of the intervention couples ended their relationship, in contrast to approximately 25% of the control couples and 26% of the couples who had declined intervention. Although a similar pattern emerged for relationship dissolution at the postmarriage follow-up, differences among the groups were not significant.

An outcome study of a PREP project in Germany (Thurmaier, Engl, & Hahlweg, 1999, described in Silliman et al., 2002) found that couples who had received the PREP treatment 5 years earlier had a divorce rate of 3%, whereas those who had not (the control couples) had a 16% divorce rate. It should be underscored that the outcome research associated with the PREP prevention technique is an exception—little is known of the presumed benefits of other distress prevention and relationship enrichment programs. Moreover, it is not clear that premarital prevention programs—including the PREP—are reaching those most at risk for dysfunction and divorce. Sullivan and Bradbury (1997) found that couples who participated in premarital programs were not at greater risk for marital problems than those who did not.

PATHS TO DIVORCE AND SEPARATION

On their way to divorce or separation, most couples do not stop at the relationship therapist's office for help, and even if they do, the intervention attempt may not be successful. Despite the fact that the path couples tread to dissolution is seldom short or straightforward, researchers historically have viewed relationship dissolution as an event rather than an extended process (see Duck, 1982). In part, this may be attributed to researchers' predilection for studying dissolution in premarital romantic relationships, many of which tend to be volatile and of short duration. Most researchers now recognize that dissolution, even in many premarital romantic relationships, is a process that occurs over time, sometimes a substantial length of time, and some investigators have tried to identify common patterns in this process.

Duck's model of the disengagement process specifies four stages: an *intrapsychic* phase in which the individual thinks about his or her dissatisfactions with the partner and the relationship; a *dyadic* phase in which the individual negotiates dissolution with the partner; a *social* phase in which the dissolution, impending or accomplished, is revealed to persons in the couple's social network; and a *grave-dressing* phase in which the individual engages in retrospection about the relationship and begins to recover. Empirical evidence relevant to these posited phases is lacking.

With respect to marital dissolution, Gottman (e.g., 1994; see Figure 14.2) has proposed the distance and isolation cascade model. The first element in the cascade of events toward dissolution is hypothesized to be *flooding of negative emotion*, in which the spouse becomes overwhelmed—even shell-shocked—by the ferocity of the partner's expressions of negative emotion. Helpless to stop the partner's outbursts, and believing that discussing marital problems with the partner is an exercise in futility, the individual becomes hypervigilant to cues of an impending outburst by the partner and takes evasive action, "turning away" from the partner and the marriage—for example, minimizing interaction with the spouse. A "parallel" marriage develops, which leads to loneliness, in turn increasing vulnerability to extradyadic relationships and ultimately to divorce.

The Distance and Isolation Questionnaire (see Gottman, 1994, pp. 357–359), which attempts to locate the place of the spouse in the cascade, consists of four subscales: Flooding ("When my partner gets negative, stopping it is like trying to stop an oncoming truck"); How Lonely Is Your Marriage ("I feel restless and sad even when we're together"); Can You Work Things Out? ("Talking things over with my partner only seems to make them worse"); and Do You Lead Parallel Lives? ("We don't spend very much time together anymore").

A bird's-eye view of the marital dissolution process has been provided by sociologist Diane Vaughn (1986), who interviewed 103 separated or divorced persons (identified through a snowball sampling strategy in which current participants suggested additional participants). All were asked to talk about their relationship "beginning with the moment when they first sensed something was wrong" (p. 199). Few breakups, Vaughn found, were mutual; one person clearly was the "initiator" while some of their partners were unaware, even at the point of separation, that the relationship was in jeopardy.

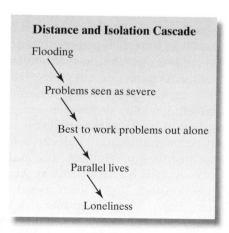

FIGURE 14.2 The distance and isolation cascade model. *From Gottman, What Predicts Divorce? The Relationship Between Marital Processes and Marital Outcomes (1994), Fig. 2.8, p. 73.*

The behavior of breakup initiators seemed to follow a chronological order, beginning with attempts—often veiled and indirect—to communicate their dissatisfaction with the relationship to the partner. Vaughn believes that in close relationships, people "routinely resort to indirect strategies to discontinue interaction rather than use direct confrontation" (p. 192). As a consequence of the ambiguity of the initiator's initial messages of dissatisfaction, partners are unlikely to correctly interpret their seriousness and may view them as temporary or normal. If so, initiators tend to escalate, using various strategies: (1) waiting until the partner responds to the initiator's discontent by behaving badly, whereupon the initiator seizes on the partner's "fatal mistake" as evidence of the relationship's failure; (2) decreasing interaction with the partner and increasing interaction with others; and (3) violating previously agreed-upon relationship rules such as sexual fidelity, sometimes in public ways that threaten the partner's dignity. At this point, Vaughn concludes, reconciliation is almost impossible because the initiator has been progressing toward dissolution for some time.

Vaughn concludes that before the partner is fully aware of the extent to which the relationship is in trouble, initiators are likely to have (1) reconstructed their view of the relationship, the partner, and themselves; (2) planned an exit strategy; (3) developed other relationships to support the exit, possibly including a "transitional partner" who will substitute for many of the original partner's beneficial activities; and (4) begun to construct an account of the demise of the relationship. Initiators have a great advantage over their partners because they are unlikely to directly and forcefully bring up separation and divorce until they themselves have made many of the adjustments that will ease the inevitable separation. Whereas the initiator is prepared for separation, the partner, often in a state of shock and feeling the pain of rejection, is not. According to Vaughn, at this point "initiators may stay, but for all practical purposes, they are gone" (p. 113). They may agree to marital therapy only to convince themselves and others that they did everything possible to "save" the relationship.

Like many other couple therapists, Karen Kayser (1993) wondered how spouses' feelings of love for each other could turn so quickly to apathy and indifference. Kayser distinguishes marital *disaffection*, "the gradual loss of an emotional attachment, including a decline in caring about the partner, an emotional estrangement and an increasing sense of apathy and indifference toward one's spouse" (p. 6), from marital *dissatisfaction*, in which the individual may be dissatisfied with the relationship but still feel love for the spouse. Marital disaffection—the absence of loving feelings—generally occurs, she believes, after an accumulation of dissatisfactions with the marriage and may or may not result in divorce. Like Vaughn, she believes that partners rarely experience the same level of disaffection, and this situation presents a challenge to relationship therapists.

To learn more about the disaffection process, Kayser interviewed 50 highly disaffected spouses (71% female, mostly college graduates) who were still married although some had filed for divorce. Kayser had postulated a priori a five-phase model of the disaffection process, but she found only three phases: (1) an initial *disappointment* phase, in which there is awareness that the relationship is not going as well as expected, doubts arise about the partner and the marriage decision, and attempts are made to please the partner and change oneself; (2) a *middle* phase, in which intense feelings of anger and hurt are experienced, the partner's negative behaviors are seen as a stable pattern, the partner is confronted about problems, the rewards and costs of the marriage are evaluated, dissolution is contemplated, and physical and emotional withdrawal from the marriage is begun; and (3) a *disaffection* phase characterized by feelings of anger, apathy, and hopelessness, in which problems are attributed to the partner and plans are made, and actions taken, to dissolve the marriage.

The process of relationship disengagement in premarital romantic relationships (of an average duration of 6 months) was examined by Baxter (1984), who found that the dissolution process seemed to vary with respect to a number of critical features: gradual versus sudden onset of relationship problems, unilateral versus mutual desire to terminate the relationship, use of direct versus indirect actions to accomplish the dissolution, presence versus absence of relationship repair attempts, and the final outcome of termination versus relationship continuation. As for Vaughn's spouses, and as other investigators of premarital romantic relationships have found (e.g., Hill, Rubin, & Peplau, 1976), most relationships were dissolved unilaterally (68%). Because they varied with respect to each of the features of the dissolution process, Baxter concludes that a single set of steps does not characterize all, or even most, premarital relationship dissolutions.

BEREAVEMENT

Bereavement has been defined as the totality of an individual's responses to a major relationship loss, and **grief** has been viewed as the individual's *emotional* responses to such loss. Both bereavement and grief are viewed as processes occurring over time, ideally culminating in adaptation to the loss. Harvey and Hansen (2000) believe adaptation has occurred when there is evidence that "the person has confronted the loss experience and many of its personal meanings and is functioning in society" (p. 361).

Harvey and Hansen note that little research has been conducted comparing bereavement and grief resulting from the death of the partner as opposed to the dissolution of the relationship by one or both partners. An exception is a study conducted by Farnsworth, Lund, and Pett (1989), who compared the bereavement experiences of persons who had lost their spouse through death within the past 2 years with persons who had been divorced during the same period. Widowed and divorced persons reported similar feelings of shock, helplessness, avoidance, and grief, and both also were similar in overall life satisfaction and felt relatively positive about their ability to cope. However, widowed persons were significantly more depressed than divorced persons, whereas the divorced reported more difficulty than the widowed with anger, guilt, and confusion.

Harvey and his associates (e.g., Harvey, Weber, & Orbuch, 1990), who have extensively studied the processes of adaptation to bereavement, believe there is a great deal of overlap in grief and coping responses to bereavement from different causes. There clearly is overlap between the loss of a partner through death and loss through divorce in the kinds of stressors that often follow the event, including change of residence, sometimes a change of job, changes in financial and social status, changes in the social network—the list is long and explains the presence of death of spouse and divorce at the top of Holmes and Rahe's (1967) list of life events associated with illness (see Chapter 2).

People who lose a spouse through death often lose an important attachment figure—their "safe haven." Divorced persons may suffer a similar loss. Weiss (1975) noticed that despite the fact that the recently separated and divorced men and women in his Parents Without Partners groups had little love and trust for their partners by the time separation occurred, attachment—a sense of connection and being emotionally bound to the other—often persisted:

> They may still thrill at the sight of the other; they may still feel comfortable only when with the other. . . . Yet how perplexing: Why, after all that happened, with all the bitterness they feel, with so much of their love entirely gone, should a feeling of connection remain? (p. 37)

Feelings of comfort and ease, or, as Weiss puts it, "at-homeness" when the former partner is present or accessible and, conversely, feelings of *dis*ease, strangeness, and disorientation when the partner is absent or inaccessible, must be puzzling indeed to those who have striven to free themselves from an unhappy relationship. Weiss believes that "once a certain other has been accepted as an attachment figure, that person can again elicit attachment feelings, at least until he or she is understood as having become intrinsically different" (p. 46). The persistence of attachment despite intense dissatisfaction with the partner and the relationship may be responsible for the vacillations—sequences of separations and reunions—that often accompany progress toward divorce. It also may be the source of the old saying "You can't live with them and you can't live without them!"

There are few systematic studies of adjustment to dissolution of a romantic relationship by one or both of the partners. The event is generally assumed to be painful, as suggested by the abundance of popular advice about how to "get over" the loss of a romantic relationship (for example, by engaging in aerobic exercise). However, the frequency and rapidity with which people enter new romantic relationships, including remarriage, suggests that recovery is usual. As discussed in Chapter 8, development of an account of the event has been found to be associated with recovery. In addition, how well and how quickly the individual adapts to the loss of a romantic relationship presumably depends on other factors known to be associated with adaptation to other major life events, such as social support (see Chapter 2).

Studying the course of recovery is difficult in the case of divorce and the dissolution of other romantic relationships because it is often hard to determine precisely when an individual experienced the loss. As we have discussed, the loss occurs much earlier for initiators than for their partners, and they are likely to have begun—and perhaps even concluded—adaptation processes long before the relationship has been "officially" dissolved. Some studies have found that, at least in premarital romantic relationships, women report more positive outcomes from dissolution than men do. However, women appear to be more sensitive to the weakening viability of the relationship (Hill, Rubin, & Peplau, 1976; Rands, 1988), and thus they may be further along in recovery by the time the relationship dissolves and the relationship researcher assesses adjustment to the loss.

Gray and Silver (1990), who compared the perceptions of both members of divorced couples whose marriages had lasted an average of 13 years, found that the more the individual attributed control for the breakup to the spouse, the lower the individual's level of adjustment and resolution of the breakup. (Overall, both partners agreed that the female partner had had more control over the breakup than the male partner, but still the male partner was seen as having a fair amount of control.) Those who desired to reconcile with their ex-spouse also showed lower levels of adjustment. Adjustment levels of each member of the pair were mostly independent, but not surprisingly, ex-spouses saw themselves in a positive light and had a negative view of their former spouse.

The "positive psychology movement" (Aspinwall & Staudinger, 2003; Seligman & Csikszentmihalyi, 2000) has raised the possibility that the breakup of a romantic relationship may stimulate personal growth. Buehler (1987), for example, found that those individuals who initiated their divorce were more likely to report (retrospectively) positive growth outcomes than noninitiators were. Tashiro and Frazier (2003) asked 92 college students (75% women and mostly Caucasian) who had experienced a relationship breakup in the past 9 months (average relationship length 9 months) to "describe what positive changes, if any, have happened as a result of your breakup that might serve to improve your future romantic relationships" (p. 118). Participants named an average of five positive changes. Personal changes were most frequent (for example, more self-confidence, more independence), followed by positive environmental changes such as better friendships as a result of the breakup. No differences were found between initiators and noninitiators in degree of distress or degree of growth, and no differences were found between men and women in level of breakup distress. Women, however, reported more growth than men. People who attributed the decline and dissolution of the relationship to factors associated with the partner (Other conditions) and to environmental conditions experienced more distress. Neuroticism, as expected, was associated with distress and the personality factor agreeableness was associated with more growth.

A great deal of research has been addressed to questions associated with adjustment to the death of a spouse. The typical length of the recovery period has been of particular interest, with some researchers suggesting that people can move through the grief occasioned by a major relationship loss within 18 to 24 months (see Harvey & Hansen, 2000). However, some bereavement scholars have lengthened the expected time course of recovery in recent years (Shuchter & Zisook, 1993). Others have increased their appreciation of individual differences in length of bereavement; Hansson, Stroebe, and Stroebe (1988), for example, conclude that "grief is by no means a straightforward, universal process, with a progression of fixed stages or phases, each with its typical symptoms" (p. 211).

Many investigators have tried to identify the risk factors for particularly severe and debilitating reactions to the death of a spouse. Some, for example, have hypothesized that people who enjoyed a satisfying relationship suffer the greater loss and thus should feel more bereaved than those whose marriages were unhappy. Others have hypothesized the opposite, suspecting that ambivalence during marriage is likely to lead to feelings of guilt—for example, feelings that one was unjust to the partner—and discomfort arising from the inability to make amends. Reviewing these studies, Stroebe and Stroebe (1987) suggest that at least two characteristics of a marital relationship may be related to poor bereavement outcome: dependency and ambivalence. Those spouses who were devoted to the marriage and highly dependent on it psychologically, socially, and financially

appear to have more trouble adjusting to their spouse's death than those who were less dependent. Moreover, those who enjoyed satisfying, loving relationships with their spouses seem to fare better in bereavement than those who were affectively ambivalent about their spouse and who experienced marital conflict and doubts. (Ambivalence, however, is different from detachment; Parkes and Weiss [1983] found that when attachment no longer existed between the partners and they were no longer invested in the marriage, grieving was brief and recovery was rapid.)

Many of these frequently asked questions about bereavement were addressed by Bonanno and associates (2002) in an unusual longitudinal study in which prospective data on over 200 elderly widowed persons (180 women and 25 men; mean age 72) were gathered as part of a study of older couples. Information on the deaths of study participants was gathered from the obituary sections of newspapers, and widowed participants were interviewed 6 and 18 months after their spouse's death. The availability of preloss data allowed the investigators to distinguish chronic grief reactions from preexisting chronic depression and also to investigate the possibility that,

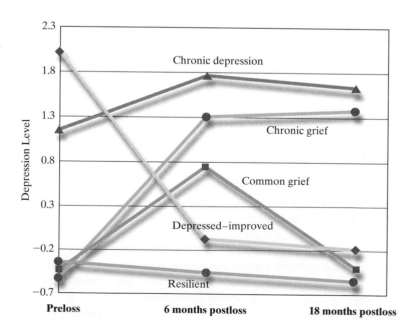

FIGURE 14.3 Patterns of bereavement following death of a spouse. *From Bonanno et al., "Resilience to Loss and Chronic Grief: A Prospective Study from Preloss to 18 Months Postloss" (2002), Fig. 1, p. 1157.*

for some individuals, well-being might *improve* following the death of their spouse.

Bonanno and colleagues found five clear bereavement patterns (Figure 14.3): *resilient* (46% of the sample), where little grief was experienced; *chronic grief* (16%), where preloss dependency on the spouse was higher than in the resilient group; *common grief* (11%); *chronic depression* (8%); and *depressed–improved* (10%), where death of the spouse resulted in a reduction of depression from preloss to postloss. Individuals in this last group, the depressed–improved, were significantly less positive, more negative, and more ambivalent about their spouse and their marriage than were those in the resilient, chronic grief, and common grief groups. Depressed–improved spouses also had the lowest levels of instrumental support, and they appeared to be highly introspective and emotionally unstable.

Perhaps the most startling finding, however, was that almost half of the widowers, the resilient group, showed little grief at any time following their loss. Many bereavement theorists have speculated that mild or absent grief reactions are unhealthy, but Bonanno and colleagues found evidence that widowers in the resilient group were relatively well-adjusted people with adequate coping resources. Moreover, no evidence was found that these individuals were superficially attached to their spouse or avoidant and emotionally distant. There was evidence, however, that resilient individuals were more accepting of death and held the "just world" view. Whether a sample of younger persons would show as high a frequency of resiliency following death of a spouse is not known. It also is not known, as Bonanno and associates note, whether the same type of outcome trajectories would be found following divorce. These investigators conclude that the wide range of grief patterns they found "suggests a need to reevaluate common notions about what constitutes a normal response to a major loss" (p. 1162). They note that because people in the social network who are potential sources of support are often unaware of the wide variability in response to loss, they often are unjustly critical of bereaved individuals who show "too much" or "too little" grief.

One type of loss that may result in a particularly debilitating bereavement is **ambiguous loss**, created when it is not known with certainty that the person is irrevocably gone, as in persons missing in action in military service, children or others who have been abducted, and, now increasingly, persons with Alzheimer's disease who are physically present but psychologically absent. Boss (1999), a researcher and family therapist who has worked with over 4,000 families who have suffered such a loss (including families with members who died in the bombing of the World Trade Center towers in 2001 and whose bodies were never recovered), believes that ambiguous loss is the most devastating of all relationship losses. She describes such survivors as "frozen in grief." Survivors cannot problem-solve because they do not know whether the loss is permanent or temporary; they cannot reorganize their roles and relationships with the loved one; and they are often denied the supportive societal rituals that accompany definite loss.

In addition to many other unknowns about loss and bereavement, cultural differences in beliefs about how adaptation is best achieved following loss have been neglected. Some of these differences are likely to be reflected in the evolution of historical beliefs about how people can best deal with a major loss. Stroebe, Gergen, Gergen, and Stroebe (1992) observe that traditionally, many societies have believed that people must move beyond the loss relatively quickly by breaking their bond with the deceased partner. "Moving on" involves an avoidance of thinking about the other, which, in turn, often involves eliminating "reminders"— getting rid of the painting the partner liked so much, redecorating the house, avoiding the old, familiar places. According to Stroebe and colleagues, a more contemporary view involves maintaining bonds to the deceased with long-term grieving. Hansson, Berry, and Berry (1999) review studies in which children, for example, actively maintain an emotional and symbolic bond with their deceased parents. Many Asian cultures encourage such bonds with formal rituals of "worship" of ancestors, even those whom one did not personally know. More needs to be learned about whether "moving on" or "maintaining bonds" is likely to be adaptive.

Findings from the longitudinal study of Bonanno and associates (2002), combined with other evidence (e.g., Bonanno & Kaltman, 2001), suggest that the death of a spouse may be less devastating for some individuals than for others; those persons may find it more adaptive (and easier) to move on rather than to maintain bonds.

SUMMARY

The decision to form a long-term partnership with another through cohabitation or marriage is one of the most consequential decisions any individual will make in his or her lifetime. For this reason, distressed marital relationships have received the most attention from therapists, whose tripartite task includes not only observing and describing the regularities in a couple's interaction pattern that have produced distress but also identifying and modifying the causal conditions responsible for that distress-inducing pattern. Although much more is known about unhappy marriages than about happy ones, researchers have identified several characteristics of both general types. For example, spouses in happy marriages tend to serve as positive sources of nurturance and comfort for each other, whereas those embroiled in unhappy marriages often do not.

Clinical intervention programs, which originally were characterized by an individualistic, one-on-one approach, gradually have moved to conjoint relationship therapy in which both partners engage in treatment at the same time—an important development since the root of many marital problems lies not in the behavior of the individual partners but in the unique interaction pattern that arises between them. In an effort to more thoroughly identify the maladaptive interactions that occur between spouses, clinical researchers have adopted numerous naturalistic and laboratory methods, including self-report and behavioral observation, each of which possesses various limitations. Despite these limitations, investigators have unearthed certain "facts"

about the communication patterns of distressed couples. These include the presence of negative communicative behavior such as expressions of contempt, negative affect reciprocity, and the demand–withdraw behavior pattern. These particular behaviors and interaction patterns appear to sustain the unhappiness of spouses in distressed relationships and thus constitute prime targets for intervention. Although a number of specific types of marital therapy exist, such as behavioral couple therapy, cognitive behavioral marital therapy, and emotion-focused couple therapy, most approaches focus on changing each partner's affective responses to the other, reducing negative affect, and replacing dysfunctional communication patterns with more effective ones. Reviews of the clinical literature generally suggest that these forms of couple therapy do work—at least temporarily. Research also demonstrates that many couples relapse quickly into their former maladaptive patterns. Consequently, periodic "booster shots" of therapy may be helpful. Less is known about the efficacy of preventive intervention, or programs that are designed to prevent later unhappiness in couples currently characterized by little or no distress.

Despite the couple's or the therapist's best efforts, many marital relationships eventually end. Several scholars have attempted to identify common patterns in the process of dissolution. Their work reveals that the dissolution process occurs over time (sometimes over a substantial length of time), often involves several phases, and varies between relationships as a function of several factors (gradual vs. sudden onset of problems, unilateral vs. mutual desire to end the relationship, and so on). Regardless of how a relationship ends, many people experience both bereavement and grief at the loss of a valued partnership. Bereavement and grief are processes which, like relationship dissolution itself, occur gradually over time. Although individuals deal with relationship loss in different ways, many people experience depression, loneliness, a change in their social networks, and stress. Fortunately, given enough time, most bereaved individuals will eventually adapt to their loss.

Glossary

accommodation   inhibition of the impulse to behave destructively in response to a partner's destructive behavior; essentially requires the individual to "turn the other cheek"

account narratives   stories people construct of autobiographical events that span a considerable period of time (e.g., relationship dissolution) that are presented in relatively unstructured formats (e.g., diaries); hypothesized to help individuals understand the meaning of the events and their implications for the future

acquaintance assault   "date rape"; sexual aggression (assault or coercion) that occurs within an ongoing relationship

active listening model   a model of marital therapy which assumes that stable, happy marriages are characterized by active, empathic listening during conflict resolution and that distressed marriages are characterized by the absence of this quality; this assumption is incorporated into many marital therapies

actual similarity   the extent to which spouses are similar to each other (e.g., on social, physical, and psychological characteristics) as measured by objective outside observers and instruments

adult attachment style   an individual difference variable paralleling attachment classifications derived from the strange situation administered to children; a person's characteristic beliefs, attitudes, and expectations about the self (worthy of love and support vs. not worthy of love and support), others (available and supportive vs. unavailable and rejecting), and relationships (rewarding vs. punishing)

adultery   *see sexual infidelity*

affect   all states, including emotional states, that carry positive or negative valence (i.e., that are evaluated positively or negatively by the person experiencing them, as evidenced by that person's self-report or by his or her approach or avoidance behavior); this term refers to many different kinds of valenced behaviors—feelings, preferences, moods, values, attitudes, and emotions

affiliation   actual interaction with another

allostasis   a term meaning "stability through change" that refers to the body's ability to increase or decrease the level of bodily functions to a new steady state in response to environmental challenges

allostatic load   the strain on the body produced by repeated increases or decreases in physiological response in an attempt to adapt to prolonged environmental demands

ambiguous loss   a type of loss in which it is not known with certainty that the person is irrevocably gone; believed to result in an especially debilitating bereavement

androgynous sex-role orientation   a sex-role orientation in which the individual describes him- or herself as possessing traits stereotypically associated with both maleness and femaleness and socially valued for both males and females

associative information processing   *see automatic information processing*

associative memory system   also called the long-term memory system; believed to record information slowly and incrementally, admitting an experience to the system only when it has been frequently repeated in the past and thus is likely to be repeated in the future

assortative mating   also called assortment or homogamy, this is the tendency for similar individuals to marry or pair-bond

attachment behavior   behavior that results in the achievement or maintenance of proximity between one individual and another

attachment injury   a violation of the individual's expectation that his or her partner will offer comfort and caring in times of danger or distress; considered by most relationship therapists to constitute a serious threat to the relationship's well-being

attachment theory   theory proposed by John Bowlby which posits that humans are born with an innate proximity-promoting mechanism that leads them to stay physically close to others who can protect and nurture them

attitude   a relatively stable predisposition to respond to another in a favorable or unfavorable manner; typically assessed via self-report

autobiographical relationship events   events the individual has personally experienced within the context of a relationship

automatic/associative information processing   a mode of information processing that is unintentional, uncontrollable, inaccessible to consciousness, and efficient (i.e., not demanding of conscious attention);

hypothesized to access only the associative or long-term memory system

autonomic nervous system (ANS) the portion of the human nervous system that includes the sympathetic and the parasympathetic nervous systems; controls arousal (fight or flight) and relaxation (rest and repair) responses; believed to be activated in strong emotional experiences

balance of closeness dilemma partners' disagreement about the appropriate balance between their interdependence and independence; one partner wishes to be closer to the other partner, whereas the other partner desires more independence, separateness, and privacy; may contribute to the demand–withdraw pattern seen in distressed couples

basic emotion an emotion believed to be innate and adaptive, to be associated with a characteristic "affect program" (facial, physiological, neurological, behavioral, and experiential patterns), to occur automatically in response to certain triggering stimuli, and to be most clearly seen in infants; sometimes called a "true" or "fundamental" emotion

behavior base rate the rate at which a behavior occurs over a specified unit of time

behavior control an interdependence theory concept that refers to an interpersonal situation in which one partner, by varying his or her own behavior, can make it desirable for the other partner to elect to perform one behavior rather than another

behavioral approach system (BAS) one of two functionally separate affect systems posited in Gray's (e.g., 1990, 1994) theory of emotion and hypothesized to be sensitive to signals of reward, nonpunishment, and escape from punishment; activates responses to rewarding stimuli

behavioral ecology view of facial displays perspective that highlights the social interactional and communicative nature of facial displays of emotion; emphasizes the interaction between the person displaying the facial expression and the person who is viewing it, decoding its meaning, and adjusting his or her behavior in accord with that meaning

behavioral inhibition system (BIS) one of two functionally separate affect systems posited by Gray's theory of emotion (e.g., 1990, 1994); sensitive to signals of punishment, nonreward, and novelty or unfamiliarity; inhibits behavior that may lead to negative outcomes

belief validation agreement with another's attitudes and beliefs; believed to be an important reward that helps explain why similarity produces attraction

bereavement the totality of an individual's responses to a major relationship loss

binuclear family a family configuration consisting of groupings of stepparents and half-siblings; usually composed of the remnants of previous nuclear families; sometimes called a reconstituted family, stepfamily, or blended family

biological sex biological or genetic maleness or femaleness; possessing male or female chromosomes, external genitalia, and internal reproductive organs; the most fundamental individual difference dimension along which we categorize ourselves and others

caregiving system posited by Bowlby's attachment theory to be the adult complement to the infant attachment behavioral system

category prototype *see also prototype* an object that represents the average value of each attribute possessed by all the members of the category

causal attribution theories cognitive theories about the processes by which people determine the causes of others' behavior or events in their attempt to extract regularities from the social environment (i.e., person dispositions)

causal condition a relatively stable force that influences a relationship interaction pattern

causal linkages the invisible causal interconnections between two persons' behaviors; deduced from observing the effects of one partner's behavior on the other partner's behavior

causally reciprocal (variables) variables that operate as both causes and effects of each other in the natural world

chronic stressors prolonged stressors; threatening stimuli (ones the individual can neither escape nor destroy) which persist over time and which contribute to general adaptation syndrome

chronically accessible category a social category, schema, or person construct that has been repeatedly used by the individual and thus comes easily to mind and is likely to be used in categorizing newly encountered objects or events; presumed to be unique to the individual and to develop from frequent and consistent experiences within his or her history of social interaction

circumplex model of affect Russell's (e.g., 1980) model of affective space that proposes that emotion and other affect terms can be arranged in a circle that is bisected by two independent bipolar dimensions—horizontally by an pleasant–unpleasant dimension (e.g., happy–sad) and vertically by an activation–deactivation dimension (e.g., alert–lethargic)

classic experimental design Mills's "method of difference," which rests on the assumption that causes always precede their effects; the experimental method hinges on knowing the temporal occurrence of X (independent variable) and Y (dependent variable)

clinical effectiveness a measure of whether a clinical treatment "works" in terms of the percentage of couples who show an increase in satisfaction following a therapeutic intervention and who, against the benchmark provided by normative data, have moved from the distressed range into the nondistressed range

closed field a situation in which individuals are compelled to interact with each other by reason of the environmental setting in which they find themselves (e.g., two co-workers who share an office)

cognitive load the level of demand on an individual's cognitive processing systems; high cognitive load resulting from other tasks increases the likelihood that information about another person will be processed quickly and automatically by using automatic/associative processing

cohesiveness the extent to which partners are highly attracted to each other and to the relationship

collectivist cultures socially interdependent cultures in which people view themselves as highly connected to others and often subordinate personal goals to those of the group

commitment a person's avowed or inferred intent to maintain a relationship; sometimes also conceptualized as a relationship property

communal relationships relationships in which the partners adopt a norm of "each according to need" that governs the giving and receipt of benefits in interaction; relationships in which concerns about the partner's happiness and welfare override considerations of deservingness

communal rule of exchange an exchange rule prescribing that each partner's goodness of outcomes will be proportionate to his or her needs even if this means that one partner's goodness of outcomes exceeds that of the other partner

communion a personality trait associated with support-giving and generally conceptualized as a focus on connection with others; often assessed with instruments that measure emotional expressivity and psychological femininity

companionate love a type of love described as affectionate love, friendship love, attachment, storge, and conjugal love; reflects the tenderness and affection we feel for those with whom our lives are deeply connected; believed to be characterized by a relatively slow onset, durability, interdependence, and feelings of affection, intimacy, and commitment

comparison level (CL) an interdependence theory concept that refers to an individual's expectations of profit from a given relationship; the standard against which people judge the goodness of the outcomes they are currently receiving from the present relationship and, thus, their satisfaction with it; defined as the average value of all the outcomes known to the person (in a specific type of relationship) weighted by their salience

comparison level for alternatives (CLalt) an interdependence theory concept that refers to the goodness of outcomes available in the individual's best currently available alternative to the present relationship (including having no relationship of that type); the standard by which the individual decides whether to remain in the relationship or terminate it

competence hypothesis a hypothesis derived from attachment theory, stating that securely attached children become more socially and emotionally competent than do insecurely attached children

conjoint relationship therapy a type of therapy in which both partners (or in the case of a family, all members) receive treatment, usually at the same time, in the same room, by the same therapist

consciousness our awareness of things and events; often associated with focal attention

conspecific a member of the individual's own species

construct validity refers to whether an instrument actually measures the construct it claims to measure; can only be determined if the construct (e.g., relationship satisfaction) is embedded within a theoretical framework that clearly defines it and specifies its presumed associations (positive, negative, or neutral) with other constructs; established by demonstrations that the measure possesses discriminant and convergent validity

contingency contracting a procedure sometimes used by behavioral couple (marital) therapists in which the couple makes an explicit, often written, contract in which each partner promises to stop behaving in ways the other finds objectionable and to start behaving in ways the other finds pleasurable in return for the other partner doing the same

continuous causal feedback loop a condition in which reciprocally causal variables influence each other over time (e.g., A influences B, which then influences A)

controlled (rule-based) information processing a mode of information processing that is intentional, controllable, accessible to consciousness, and demanding of the individual's attention; used primarily when people are highly motivated to make accurate predictions about another's behavior and when they have time to engage in effortful processing; believed to access both the long-term and short-term memory systems

Coolidge effect the supposition that sexual attraction decreases with familiarity

coping cognitive or behavioral responses made to counter a real or perceived threat

correlational data nonexperimental data in which the degree of association between two or more variables is observed

correlational studies studies that examine the degree and type of association between two or more variables

cross-sectional studies studies in which variables are measured at a single point in time in several groups of people who differ from each other along some dimension (e.g., age)

cross-validation the process of determining whether a predictive formula (say, for divorce risk) developed from one sample of participants accurately predicts across other samples of participants

cultural emotion display rules culture-specific rules and norms that prescribe appropriate contexts for the display of an emotion; taught during the socialization process and enforced by social sanctions

decision/commitment component (of love) one of the three components in Sternberg's triangular theory of love; primarily cognitive in nature; consists of both the short-term decision that one individual loves another and the longer-term commitment to maintain that love

de facto similarity the fact that relationship partners tend to be similar to each other in many ways (e.g., demographically, attitudinally)

dependency the degree to which an individual's behavior is influenced by another's behavior

dependent variable in an experiment, the variable whose appearance is presumed to be dependent on the appearance of the manipulated independent (causal) variable

developmental neuroscience a field that examines the neurobiological structures and processes underlying behavioral development; uses the techniques of cognitive and affective neuroscience (e.g., functional magnetic resonance imaging, or fMRI) to study human brain activity in response to controlled stimuli

direct aggression forms of physical or verbal aggression in which no attempt is made to hide the harmful intent (e.g., hitting, name-calling)

direct effects hypothesis of social support a hypothesis positing that a direct relationship exists between support and well-being such that the greater the support, the higher the well-being

discrepancy detection theory a theory of emotion proposed by George Mandler (e.g., 1975, 1997); proposes that humans have evolved to be cognitively sensitive to discrepancies between the world as we expected it to be and the world as we currently perceive it and that we automatically undergo bodily changes (e.g., internal symptoms of arousal) to help us respond effectively when a discrepancy is detected

disenfranchised grief grief that is not commonly recognized by society (e.g., grief at the loss of a close relationship with a companion animal)

disillusionment model a perspective used to explain the well-documented decline in satisfaction couples experience over their first years of marriage; suggests that as couples become more interdependent and interact more frequently in a wider array of situations, rosy illusions about the partner and the relationship that developed in the premarital relationship—through the concealment of weaknesses, avoidance of disagreements, and cognitive processes that reduce doubts—are destroyed

dual process theories (of social cognition) models of cognition that propose that people use two different methods to process information about others—an automatic or associative method that is efficient, unintentional, unconscious, and uncontrollable, and a controlled or rule-based method that is effortful, deliberative, and conscious

dyadic interaction procedure a technique commonly used to study empathic accuracy, in which (1) participants view a videotape of their spontaneous interaction with another person and stop the tape when they recall having had a specific thought or feeling, (2) the tape is replayed for the interaction partner and stopped at each point at which the participants reported having had their specific thoughts or feelings, and (3) the interaction partner then reports what he or she believes the participant was thinking or feeling at that point

dyadic reciprocity the relationship partners are responding to each other; can be determined by using the social relations model technique or sequential analysis

dyads two-person groups

editing   a precise sequence of interaction in which a spouse responds positively (or even neutrally) immediately after accurately perceiving his or her partner's behavior to be negative; suggests that at least one of the partners is monitoring the interaction and taking action to prevent it from descending even further into negativity; similar to the process of accommodation

effective outcome matrix   an interdependence theory concept that refers to the transformation of the given relationship outcome matrix by the partners (e.g., by adoption of a rule that the partners' outcomes shall be equal even though the given matrix would allow one partner better outcomes than the other); the effective outcome matrix guides the partners' actual behavior in the relationship

egalitarian marriage   a type of marriage in which the spouses share roles and responsibility in all spheres of married life, including emotional caregiving and expression and the economic welfare of the family; also called peer or equal-status marriage

egocentric memory bias   a systematic bias in memory of relationship events; refers to the tendency for individuals to overestimate their own contributions to a relationship (particularly with respect to positive events) and to underestimate those of their partner

emergent distress model   a perspective used to explain the well-documented decline in satisfaction couples experience over their first years of marriage; proposes that marriage increases the couple's interdependence, which, in turn, precipitates new problems and conflicts

emotional investment   the potential for emotional experience in a relationship; represented by the expectancies an individual holds about the partner and the relationship (i.e., the greater the number of expectancies and the more strongly they are held, the greater the potential for emotion to be experienced in the relationship)

emotion-focused coping   cognitive or behavioral responses that are designed to manage one's emotional response to a real or perceived threat

emotion-in-relationship model (ERM)   Berscheid's (e.g., 1983) model that posits that the infrastructure of a close relationship satisfies many of the necessary conditions for intense emotional experience; predicts that violation of relationship expectancies will produce positive emotion when the consequences of the violation are perceived to enhance the individual's welfare and negative emotion when the conse-

quences of the violation are perceived to threaten the individual's welfare

empathic accuracy   the ability to accurately decode the meaning of another's behavior

enacted support   support a person believes he or she has provided or support that outside observers believe the person has given

encode (encoding)   a process whereby the individual interprets the meaning of an event or object

enduring dynamics model   a perspective used to explain the well-documented decline in satisfaction couples experience over their first years of marriage; proposes that problems that arise in courtship simply continue on into marriage; sometimes called the perpetual problems model

environmental causal conditions   factors in a relationship's physical and social environments that influence the relationship interaction pattern

equality rule of exchange   an exchange rule which prescribes that both partners' goodness of outcomes are to be equal

equitable relationship   a relationship in which the ratio of one partner's outcomes (rewards or benefits) to inputs (costs and investments) is equal to the other partner's ratio of outcomes to inputs

evaluative space model (ESM)   a model of affective space proposed by Cacioppo and Berntson (1994); proposes that humans possess two separable and partially distinct affect systems (one for positivity and one for negativity) which may be coactivated, coinhibited, or uncoupled at the neural processing level; predicts that affective processes gravitate toward bipolarity and a single action orientation over time but allows for the possibility that the two affect systems can, on rare occasions, be present together in consciousness

evolutionary models of human mating   frameworks that are grounded in the theoretical principles of evolutionary psychology and explain contemporary humans' mate preferences and mating behavior by focusing on partner attributes that may have had implications for reproductive success in the ancestral environment

exchange models   theories of social interaction and relationship development that assume people are sensitive to the rewards they gain and the costs they incur in social interaction and will actively attempt to maximize their social interaction profits; Homans's (e.g., 1961) social exchange theory is a prime example, but many other general theories of social interaction incorporate this assumption (e.g., the equity theories, social learning theory, and interdependence theory)

exchange relationships   relationships in which the rule of exchange is that for a benefit given, a comparable benefit will be received in return

expectancies   the beliefs we hold about the probable behavior of other people and the probable occurrence of other future events that guide and direct social behavior

expressivity   a predisposition to express experienced emotion (whether positive or negative); often assessed with measures of psychological femininity from sex-role inventories

extramarital sex   *see sexual infidelity*

extrarelational sex   *see sexual infidelity*

extraversion   a personality characteristic reflecting the degree to which an individual is oriented positively to the social environment and enjoys being the center of social attention

extraversion–introversion   a personality dimension characterized by a positive vs. negative orientation toward the social environment and toward being the object of social attention; one of the "Big Five" personality factors believed to principally underlie individual differences in personality

facial feedback hypothesis   the hypothesis that particular configurations of the facial musculature not only express a specific emotion but also may produce it

facilitative interaction sequence   an interaction sequence in which the partner's behavior helps the individual execute established action sequences, personal plans, and goals

familiarity principle (of attraction)   a basic principle of attraction which states that familiar others are usually judged to be safe and unlikely to cause harm and thus tend to be preferred over unfamiliar others

fast-learning memory system   also called the short-term memory system; believed to record information quickly even if it has not been repeated often enough to become a regularity, thereby allowing us to remember a single occurrence of an event and to take immediate advantage of others' experiences and knowledge; loses encoded information quickly unless that information is repeated and consolidated over time into the associative (long-term) memory system

fate control   an interdependence theory concept that refers to a situation in which one partner can influence the other's outcomes regardless of what the other does

feminine sex-role orientation   a sex-role orientation in which the individual describes him- or herself as having traits stereotypically associated with femaleness and socially valued for females to possess (e.g., nurturance, compassion, warmth)

field of availables   people who are available and accessible for interaction to a specific individual

field of eligibles   those persons whom society dictates are appropriate mates (e.g., marriage partners) for a specific individual

fight-or-flight reaction   a syndrome of physiological responses to an environmental threat, originally identified by physiologist Walter Cannon; emergency reaction that mobilizes the body's energy resources to help the individual defend against the threat by attacking it or fleeing

five-factor model of personality   a representation of personality trait structure which asserts that most personality traits can be described in terms of five basic dimensions (extraversion, neuroticism, openness to experience, agreeableness, and conscientiousness)

functional social support   the fulfillment of people's psychological needs and goals within the relationships that compose the social network

general adaptation syndrome   a general pattern of physiological reactions produced by prolonged stressors identified by Selye (e.g., 1936); consists of alarm, adaptation, and exhaustion phases

generative theories of causation   theories that identify the precise mechanism (often called the mediator variable) by which a cause produces its effect

given outcome matrix   an interdependence theory concept that refers to the relationship partners' set of behavioral options within a given time frame and the goodness of outcomes, determined by external reward and incentive systems, associated with each option

global marital satisfaction   a person's overall positive or negative sentiment toward his or her marital relationship

global marital satisfaction measures   marital satisfaction measures that assess a person's overall positive or negative sentiment toward the relationship

goodness of outcomes   an interdependence theory concept that refers to the individual's rewards minus costs in a relationship

grief   the individual's emotional responses to relationship loss

growth curve analysis   an analytic technique which permits the investigator to describe various parameters of the trajectory that relationship experiences (e.g., satisfaction) take over time

Guttman scale   a type of self-report measurement scale in which an individual's endorsement of certain items representative of later levels (of behavior, progress, etc.) signifies that he or she probably also has endorsed items representative of earlier levels

healthy relationships   relationships that maintain and/or promote the partners' immediate and future survival and welfare

homeostasis   the maintenance of equilibrium in bodily processes

horizontal dimension (of natural language concepts)   a dimension that concerns the differentiation of concepts at the same level of inclusiveness (e.g., the dimension on which such subordinate-level concepts as "maternal love," "friendship," and "romantic love" differ)

hypothetical constructs   convenient fictions that allow scholars to talk about how the mind seems to work; examples of hypothetical constructs intended to represent cognitive units of general knowledge include "social category" and "social schema"

independent variable   the manipulated variable in an experiment; the presumed causal variable that appears at Time 1 in the experimental or treatment group but does not appear at Time 1 in the control group

indirect aggression   forms of physical or verbal aggression in which the intent to cause harm to the target is hidden (e.g., destruction of property, gossiping, spreading rumors)

individualistic cultures   cultures in which individuals view themselves as autonomous and oriented toward independent success and achievement

individuating characteristics   features that set a person apart from other people; typically noticed and encoded via controlled or rule-based information processing

informed consent   an important aspect of the process of collecting data from human research participants; refers to the ethical rule that researchers must inform potential participants about the nature of their participation and its possible negative consequences

ingratiator's dilemma   as the incentive value of ingratiation increases, the probability that the ingratiation attempt will be successful decreases

innate behavioral response systems   human behavioral systems that are present at birth and unlearned

instincts   complicated, concatenated behaviors that unfold serially in response to appropriate stimulation

interaction   the "living tissue" of a relationship; an influence episode in which one partner's behavior affects how the other partner subsequently behaves and vice versa

interaction episode   a limited span of time in which interactions between partners occur

interaction pattern   the repeated occurrence of interaction sequences

interaction script   an element of a relationship schema that consists of the partners' expectancies about the temporal ordering of their own and the other's behavior and other events in a particular setting; develops gradually and is believed to facilitate the coordination of action, reduce the effort of interaction, reduce the necessity of attention to small details, and allow joint action to be organized in large rather than minute chunks

interdependence   the extent to which two people are in a relationship with each other; reflects their degree of mutual influence

interfering action sequence   an interaction sequence involving two relationship partners, in which the behavior of one partner hinders the execution of the other partner's established action sequences, personal plans, and goals

intimacy   an interactive process in which the individual, as a result of the partner's response to the individual's behavior, comes to feel understood, validated in terms of personal worth, and cared for by the partner

intimacy component (of love)   one of the three love components in Sternberg's triangular theory of love; constitutes the emotional or affective part of love; involves feelings of warmth, closeness, connection, and bondedness in the love relationship

intimacy motive   a personal motive reflecting the degree to which an individual habitually prefers, is ready to experience, and actively seeks out warm, communal, and intimate interpersonal interactions; involves both a general affiliative tendency (which all individuals possess) and a specific need to feel close to others (which some individuals possess to a greater or lesser degree than others)

investments   a relationship concept introduced by Homans (e.g., 1961) which refers to the individual's positively or negatively valued past activities and personal characteristics for which commensurate relationship profits are expected; investments also refer to resources and other things of value that an individual puts into the relationship, including time, money, energy, and reputation; this concept plays a role in the equity theories and in Rusbult's (e.g., 1983) investment model

invisible social support   support that occurs outside of the recipient's awareness (e.g., supportive advice given in an indirect way to preclude the recipient from coding it as support)

kin   persons joined by blood or legal contract

locus of control   a personality dimension that concerns beliefs about one's efficacy as a causal agent and responsibility for one's own life outcomes

loneliness   typically defined as a perceived discrepancy between a desired and an achieved pattern of social relationships; occurs when a person's existing social relationships are discrepant from his or her desired or expected relationships

longitudinal studies   studies in which the same people are measured at successive times on the same variable

major depressive disorder   a mood disorder whose primary diagnostic criterion is a marked and abnormal mood disturbance that lasts at least 2 weeks, that causes impaired physical and/or psychological functioning, and that is not due to normal bereavement, physical illness, alcohol, drugs, or medication; associated with physical (e.g., abnormal appetite, sleep disturbances) and cognitive (e.g., inappropriate self-reproach, poor concentration) symptoms

marital stability   the continuation or dissolution of the marriage; the marital contract is either "stable" (i.e., the contract continues) or "unstable" (i.e., the contract has been terminated through permanent separation or divorce); typically assessed with the individual's self-report that the marriage is "intact"

marital success   a term used to describe the state experienced by persons in intact marriages who report their marriage to be "very happy"

masculine sex-role orientation   a sex-role orientation in which the individual describes him- or herself as having traits stereotypically associated with maleness and socially valued for males to possess (e.g., independence, assertiveness)

mediating (mediator) variable   a variable that produces the association between two other variables

mere exposure hypothesis   an empirically supported proposition that repeated exposure to almost any stimulus enhances attraction to it under a wide range of conditions

meshed interaction sequences   interaction sequences in which both partners are simultaneously performing organized action sequences; each individual's action is both a response to the partner's action and a stimulus not only for the individual's own next action but also for the partner's next action

meta-analysis   a quantitative procedure whereby the findings of many studies testing the same hypothesis are synthesized in order to reach a more reliable conclusion about the truth of the hypothesis than is afforded by any one study

mobilization–minimization hypothesis   a hypothesis about human memory which suggests that negative personal events may be initially remembered better than positive events (in the service of helping the individual mobilize resources to cope with the negative event) but that, over time, negative events are minimized and fade in memory such that positive events are better remembered; also called the Pollyanna principle

moderator variable   a variable that increases or decreases the rate at which a behavior is performed

monogamy   a marriage system in which two individuals pair-bond; a universal aspect of human mating

mood   relatively low-intensity, diffuse, and enduring affective states that have no salient antecedent cause and little cognitive content

mood-congruent evaluation effect   a phenomenon which occurs when people's moods influence their evaluations of other people and events

mood-congruent recall effect   a phenomenon in which people tend to recall information that is affectively congruent with their mood at the time of recall (i.e., people in good moods recall positive information and people in bad moods recall negative information)

mood state–dependent memory effect   refers to the finding that what is retrieved from memory depends on the congruency between the individual's affective state at the time of recall and his or her affective state at the time the information was encoded (e.g., people in bad moods remember positive and negative autobiographical events that happened and were encoded when they were in a bad mood better than they do events that were encoded when they were in a good mood)

morbidity   disease

mortality   likelihood of death

multicollinearity of predictors   in regression analyses, a statistical situation produced when measures of a variable's known and suspected determinants (i.e., predictor variables) are highly correlated

multiple regression analysis (MRA)   any one of several related statistical methods for evaluating the effects of more than one "independent" variable on one or more "dependent" variables; a statistical method intended to extract causal information from nonexperimental data

multiple-wave study   a type of longitudinal or prospective study in which measurements are made at several points in time (often over a period of years)

mutual behavior control   an interdependence theory concept that refers to interpersonal situations in which both partners have the power to influence each other's outcomes

natural experiment   a research situation that is created when some naturally occurring event acts as an independent variable by randomly affecting some people (the experimental group) and not others (the control group)

need to belong   believed to be a fundamental human motivation for interpersonal attachment that is manifested in a drive to form and maintain a minimum number of lasting, positive, and significant relationships

negative affect reciprocity   an interaction pattern reliably displayed by couples in unhappy relationships; occurs when one partner's negative emotional behavior at an earlier point in time predicts the other partner's later negative emotional behavior (and vice versa)

neural plasticity   the ability of the brain to alter its functional organization

neuroticism   a personality dimension reflecting a person's sensitivity to negative stimuli, propensity to experience negative emotions, and stability of behavior over time; also called emotional instability or negative affectivity

nonexperimental data   data consisting of responses to levels of variables which are not manipulated and not randomly assigned or controlled in other ways

nonexperimental studies   studies in which levels of variables are not manipulated and are not randomly assigned or controlled in other ways; examples include surveys, longitudinal studies, and cross-sectional studies

nuclear family   a type of family form in which any children are born after the two parents were married and in which both biological parents are present

nurture   environmental factors that influence human development and behavior (i.e., an individual's experience with the environment)

observation reactivity   a problem associated with direct observation of interaction; occurs when people behave differently when they know they are being observed than when they believe they are not

observational base (of relationship science)   consists of the behaviors of two persons (usually denoted by "Person" and "Other," or simply "P" and "O") observed over the same real timeline; refers to the fact that theories about human behavior must make contact with observable behavior in order to be experimentally tested

open fields   situations in which people are free to interact or not to interact with each other without penalty

open systems   systems that exchange information, energy, and material with the other systems in which they are nested and also with the systems they encapsulate

organized action sequences   habits or sequences of actions that are emitted as a single unit; when the first action in the sequence occurs, the remainder almost always follow because each action in the sequence is both a response to the previous action and the stimulus for the next action

outcome matrix   an interdependence theory concept referring to a matrix that represents the behavioral options available to each partner at a given point in time and the goodness of outcomes likely to result for each person should the partners jointly perform a particular combination of behaviors in that time frame

passion component (of love)   one of the three components in Sternberg's triangular theory of love; primarily motivational in nature; consists of the drives that are involved in romantic and physical attraction, sexual consummation, and related phenomena

passionate love   the variety of love most strongly associated with marriage in many cultures; believed to possess such features as a swift onset, relatively short duration, idealization of and cognitive preoccupation with the beloved and/or the romantic relationship, intense (and often fluctuating) emotions, sexual attraction, and physiological arousal or its concomitants

perceived similarity   the extent to which an individual believes he or she is similar to the partner (e.g., on social, personality, psychological, attitudinal, or behavioral dimensions)

perceived support   support an individual believes he or she has received

perceived support availability   support an individual believes is available in the future should it be needed

person dispositions   regularities that perceivers extract from the social environment, consisting of an individual's stable and enduring attributes (i.e., his or her tendency to behave in certain ways across many different situations); examples include personality traits and attitudes

personal causal conditions the stable factors associated primarily with an individual partner (P or O) that affect the relationship interaction pattern

personal motives enduring, stable dispositions that operate relatively unconsciously and that energize, direct, and select behavior in particular situations

personality a person's distinct pattern of behaviors, thoughts, and emotions; assumed to be relatively stable over time and across situations

personality complementarity hypothesis the hypothesis that people who possess different but compatible personality traits (e.g., a dominant person paired with a submissive partner) will interact harmoniously and be attracted to each other; derived from Winch's (1958) theory of complementary needs

pheromones species-specific chemical secretions that elicit unlearned behavioral or developmental responses from others

physical aggression physical responses directed toward a target that are intended to cause harm (e.g., hitting, kicking, slapping, using a weapon, destruction of property)

physiological arousal the greater or lesser increase in activity—or "activation"—of the physiological systems involved in the fight-or-flight reaction; usually assessed by instruments measuring galvanic skin response, heart rate, and blood pressure

polyandry "many males"; a polygamous mating system in which a woman pairs with multiple men

polygamy a mating system in which multiple individuals pair-bond; encompasses both polygyny and polyandry

polygynandry (cenogamy) group marriage; a mating system in which husbands and wives form a household and share the same spouses

polygyny "many females"; a polygamous mating system in which a man pairs with multiple women

positive (or negative) valence refers to whether an event, object, or state is subjectively experienced as positive (good or beneficial or enjoyable) or negative (bad or harmful or unpleasant)

power motive a personal motive that reflects the need to have impact on others; may be expressed in a number of ways, including direct efforts to forcefully control others and indirect attempts to influence, charm, persuade, or even help others

predictive validity used to evaluate the usefulness of any measurement scale, device, or instrument; refers to whether an instrument reliably predicts the behaviors that it is intended to predict

premarital relationships *see also romantic relationship* relationships in which the potential for marriage is reasonably high; often refers to exclusive dating relationships, couples engaged to marry, or cohabiting relationships

prime (priming) a technique used by cognitive psychologists to increase the accessibility of a particular social category (or person construct); often involves surreptitiously presenting the category or construct below the individual's threshold of awareness (i.e., subliminally)

principle of distributive justice Homans's (e.g., 1961) hypothesis that a person in an exchange relation with another will expect that the rewards of each partner be proportional to his or her costs (i.e., the greater the rewards, the greater the costs) and that the net rewards, or profits, of each person be proportional to his or her investments (i.e., the greater the investments, the greater the profit); generated the equity theories

principle of fatigue a social exchange principle: the more often the individual recently has performed a costly activity, the more costly it is for him or her to perform additional units of that activity

principle of least interest the partner who is least dependent on the relationship is able to dictate the conditions for its continuance (and is the partner most likely to leave should those conditions be violated); originally proposed by sociologist Willard Waller

principle of liking reciprocity refers to the tendency for people to like those who like them; derived from the supposition that a person's expression of esteem to another is a valuable reward and predicts that the recipient will respond in kind (in this way, "attraction breeds attraction")

principle of satiation a social exchange principle: the more of a specific rewarding activity a person has recently received from an interaction partner, the less valuable to the individual are further units of that activity; proposed by Homans (e.g., 1961) in his social exchange theory

principle of scarcity a social exchange principle: the scarcer the reward the partner provides, the higher the price the partner can demand for it and the more costs the individual is likely to have to endure to obtain it; proposed by Homans (e.g., 1961) in his social exchange theory

principle of self-disclosure reciprocity one partner's disclosure tends to be reciprocated, both in content and in depth, by the other partner's disclosure

problem-focused coping cognitive and behavioral responses that are designed to overcome or alter a real or perceived threat

profits rewards minus costs in social interaction

promiscuous mating a mating system in which pair-bonding is nonexistent and each individual is free to engage in intercourse with whomever he or she chooses; believed (erroneously) to characterize early human societies

prospect of future interaction effect a well-documented phenomenon that people tend to try to like others with whom they must interact (e.g., as in a closed field)

prototype the member of a category that best represents the features of all members of the category

prototype approach (to love) an approach to understanding love which relies on empirical methodologies and the collection of data from men and women about their love experiences; seeks to understand people's knowledge and beliefs (their mental representations) of the concept of love

psychological gender *see also* **sex-role orientation** the psychological state of maleness or femaleness; possessing traits or characteristics that are believed to be associated with, and that are considered socially appropriate for, each biological sex

psychological stress a negative emotional experience accompanied by predictable biochemical, physiological, and behavioral changes that are directed toward adaptation either by manipulating the situation to alter the stressor or by accommodating its effects

psychometric approach (to love) an approach used to create love classification systems by identifying the dimensions that underlie the reported experiences of individuals involved in love relationships (usually through cluster analysis, factor analysis, or other statistical techniques); assumes that identification of the common elements in people's actual love experiences provides an effective way of distinguishing among love types

psychoneuroimmunology the scientific discipline that studies the influence of the mind on bodily processes

psychosomatic medicine the study of how the mind ("psycho") and body ("soma") interact to affect health

psychotherapy effectiveness (studies of) examine whether treatments have broadly defined beneficial effects (e.g., change in quality of life) across broad populations of persons (often self-selected into groups)

psychotherapy efficacy (studies of) examine the effects of specific interventions administered to a random sample of participants as contrasted to the outcomes shown by a control group or a comparison treatment group

random assignment an important component of experimental design; refers to the random placement of participants to the experimental and control groups; such placement helps to "control" for causes of Y (dependent variable) other than X (independent variable) by assuring that the unknown causes of Y are equally represented in both the experimental and control groups

reciprocal causation feedback loops *see also continuous causal feedback loop* a situation created when variables are both causes and effects of each other in the natural world (e.g., increases in trust produce increases in satisfaction, and increases in satisfaction feed back to produce increases in trust and also to increase commitment, which in turn increases trust); loops create difficulty for researchers hoping to disentangle the effect of one variable from those of the others with which it is associated

reductionism methodological mainstay of Western science which often breaks apart the whole of a dynamic, functioning system in order to closely examine its individual parts

regression methods of causal inference statistical methods that are intended to extract causal information from nonexperimental data and that assume that statistical control can replace experimental manipulation of an independent variable and control of other possible causes of the dependent variable

regularity theories of causation theories that focus on covariation (which can be determined by correlational studies in which both responses are made at a single point in time) and on regularity of succession (which can be determined by longitudinal studies showing that Y consistently follows X)

rejection sensitivity an individual difference variable or relationship schema that reflects the tendency to anxiously anticipate, readily perceive, and emotionally and behaviorally overreact to rejection from significant others; believed to develop as a self-protective response to parental rejection, rebuff, or punitiveness

relational (P × O) causal conditions stable factors that result from the joint configuration of each partner's characteristics (e.g., similarity) or that emerge from the partners' previous interactions (e.g., behavioral norms) and that affect the relationship interaction pattern

relational sex sexual responses that occur between partners in established relationships

relationship the association between two individuals that resides in the interaction that occurs between them; interactions that demonstrate mutual influence, that are not role-based, and that are present in each person's mental representations provide evidence for a relationship's existence

relationship cognition the processes by which people process, store, and access information about their relationships

relationship compatibility refers to the ratio of facilitating to interfering events in the partners' interaction; obtained when the partners facilitate the satisfaction of each other's needs and the achievement of each other's goals

relationship development a relationship's progression toward closeness

relationship equifinality a term used to describe the fact that because relationships may take different paths to the same end (e.g., dissolution), knowing a relationship's destination is not informative of the route it took to its fate

relationship infrastructure the pattern of causal linkages between the partners' behaviors

relationship maintenance the processes by which people continue their relationship at a given level of interdependence

relationship reinforcement erosion an effect predicted by the social exchange principles of satiation and fatigue; occurs in long-term relationships when the value of repeated rewards decreases and the value of repeated costs increases; associated with increasing relationship dissatisfaction

relationship schema a cognitive knowledge structure representing regularities in patterns of interpersonal relatedness; hypothesized to contain three elements, including a self schema that represents in memory how the self is experienced in a specific relationship, a person schema for the relationship partner, and an interaction script that represents the expected interaction pattern formed from repeated interaction experiences

relationship stability a relationship's likelihood of continuance versus dissolution; refers to questions concerning when, why, and how a relationship is likely to be dissolved

relationship superiority bias the tendency to view one's own relationships as better than other people's relationships; maintains commitment to ongoing relationships

Rochester Interaction Record a diary method in which participants note, describe, and evaluate each of their daily social interactions that last ten minutes or longer

role-based interactions interactions in which each person's behavior is influenced not by the partner's behavior but by societal norms and prescriptions that govern the behavior of all people who assume that particular role

romantic relationship *see also **sexually based primary relationship*** a term used loosely by most researchers to refer to any (usually opposite-sex) relationship that is characterized by, or has the potential for, the experience of romantic feelings (e.g., strong positive sentiments and sexual attraction); also may refer to dating, engaged, cohabiting, or married couples

rule-based information processing *see **controlled information processing***

secure base hypothesis derived from attachment theory; the hypothesis that children are more likely to explore the environment when they feel protected by their caregiver's presence

self-esteem perseverance phenomenon refers to the well-documented empirical finding that self-esteem manipulations in research experiments are difficult to erase and tend to persevere over time

self-monitoring an individual difference variable; the dispositional tendency to monitor and regulate the images that one presents to others; people high in self-monitoring are attentive to the social environment and use cues from others to guide their behavior in social situations, whereas people low in self-monitoring are attentive to their internal states and tend to behave consistently across situations and audiences

sensitivity hypothesis derived from attachment theory; the proposition that sensitive care results in secure attachment

sentiment a person's positive or negative regard for another

serial marriage a remarriage pattern in which the individual has experienced at least three marriages

serial monogamy or **serial pair-bonding** a well-documented human mating pattern in which most men and women marry (with the vast majority marrying one partner), divorce, and then remarry during their reproductive years

sex ratio   the number of males per 100 females in a given society or culture

sex-role orientation   an individual difference variable reflecting psychological maleness or femaleness; the possession of traits or characteristics that are believed to be associated with, and that are considered socially appropriate for, each biological sex

sex-typed (traditional) sex-role orientation   a term used to describe individuals whose biological sex "matches" their sex-role orientation (i.e., men who endorse masculine attributes and women who endorse feminine attributes)

sexual assault (also called **sexual violence**)   a type of sexual aggression; involves the threatened or actual use of physical force to obtain sexual contact; may involve engaging in sexual activity with another while the other was unable to consent (e.g., due to intoxication or lack of consciousness)

sexual coercion   a type of sexual aggression; involves the use of nonphysical (i.e., verbal or psychological) tactics to manipulate, pressure, or coerce the partner to comply with sexual demands

sexual double standard   encompasses the normative beliefs that sexuality is an inherent aspect of masculinity, that the male sex drive is an uncontrollable and powerful force, and that women's expressions of resistance to sex are merely token and not reflective of their true feelings; may be implicated in sexual aggression

sexual infidelity (also called **extrarelational sex**, **extramarital sex**, or **adultery**)   the act of engaging in sexual activities with someone other than the primary romantic partner (and typically without the knowledge or consent of the primary partner)

sexual jealousy (also called **romantic jealousy**)   a psychological state aroused by a perceived threat to a valued mating relationship that motivates behavior designed to counter the threat

sexually based primary relationships   a relationship category whose various forms are united by the fact that sexual exchanges and activities are viewed by the partners as a legitimate expectation for their relationship regardless of whether or not they are currently engaging in sexual activity

similarity principle (of attraction)   a corollary of the familiarity principle of attraction (because people similar to oneself also are familiar people); refers to the well-documented tendency for people to prefer and to select similar others as partners

social categories   memories of people organized according to their similarity; contain abstract information centered around a person ("Alice"), a group of people ("students"), or social events ("weddings") that possess similar features; hypothetical constructs intended to represent cognitive units of general knowledge; also called social schemas

social categorization   the process by which the features of a newly encountered person are associated with people known in the past who possess similar features; generally occurs quickly, effortlessly, and automatically via automatic/associative information processing

social context theories of mating   theories which explain the dynamics of human mating relationships by focusing on proximal mechanisms or forces located in the contemporary social, cultural, and historical milieu (e.g., exchange theories, social role theory)

social integration   the extent to which an individual possesses ties to others; often measured by combining assessments of marital status, degree of contact with friends and relatives, participation in formal and informal organizations, and church membership

social network   a group composed of persons with whom the individual regularly interacts; usually includes friends and kin

social neuroscience   a scientific field that integrates the biological and social approaches to human health and behavior

social role theory   a social context theory that focuses on sex differences in mating relationships and social behavior; proposes that people develop expectations for their own and others' behavior based on their beliefs about sex-appropriate behavior and attributes, and that sex differences in social behavior are caused in part by people's tendencies to behave in a manner consistent with their sex roles

social schema   often used synonymously with the term "social category"; a mental structure that includes beliefs and other information about a concept or a class of objects; has looser, fuzzier, and less rigid boundaries than a social category; a hypothetical construct intended to represent a cognitive unit of general knowledge

social undermining   behaviors toward another that display negative affect (e.g., anger); that demonstrate negative evaluation of the person in terms of his or her attributes, actions, and efforts (e.g., criticism); and/or that interfere with the attainment of the other's goals

social withdrawal hypothesis   the hypothesis that as a relationship becomes close, the partners withdraw from their social network and, as a consequence, the influence of others on further development of the relationship diminishes

sociocultural scripts schemas or rules that define and organize social experience, are used to guide and assess behavior in social situations, and are developed through social interaction and observational or social learning

sociometry a technique used to examine affective relational patterns within a group

sociosexual orientation (also called **sociosexuality**) an individual difference variable that reflects the extent to which people require emotional intimacy and commitment before becoming sexually involved with a romantic partner

state loneliness loneliness that is time-limited and strongly associated with an individual's social situations, such as those in which the individual feels rejected, misunderstood, and estranged from others or those in which desired activities must be forgone for lack of a partner

stereotype a social category or social schema whose content is shared by many people

strange situation procedure a situation that activates an infant's attachment behavioral system by exposing the infant to persons who, and settings that, are "strange" to him or her; how the infant responds to the situation is used to assess the quality of his or her attachment to the caregiver

stress the process by which people perceive and respond to events that threaten their welfare

stress-buffering effect hypothesis of social support a hypothesis that predicts that perceived social support protects and enhances well-being if stress is experienced but has no effect when stress is absent

stressor a physical or psychological event that triggers the process of coping and adjusting to the threat

structural social support the relatively objective features of social ties and activities, such as those social network analysts typically examine

subjective well-being a combination of happiness and life satisfaction, typically assessed via self-report

supertraits extraversion, neuroticism, openness to experience, agreeableness, and conscientiousness; the "Big 5" personality dimensions believed to capture most of the variance in differences in personality

symmetry (of influence) an important relationship property that represents the degree to which the partners' influence on each other's behavior is equal

sympathetic nervous system (SNS) the part of the autonomic nervous system involved in arousal (fight or flight) responses; activation produces such physiological symptoms as increased heart rate, decreased cutaneous blood flow, increased muscle and cerebral blood flow, and increased blood sugar level

system a dynamic, interrelated collection of parts, components, or constructs; evidenced in a relationship by the fact that a change in one part of the system (e.g., the wife in the marital relationship) is likely to produce a change in another part of the system (e.g., the husband)

temperament any moderately stable, differentiating emotional or behavioral quality whose appearance in childhood is influenced by inherited biological factors, including differences in brain neurochemistry

theory a network of constructs connected by causal statements; conjectures about the nature of the world which propose that a certain effect is produced by certain causal conditions

traditional sex-role orientation *see sex-typed sex-role orientation*

traditional marriage a type of marriage in which roles and responsibilities are allocated on the basis of biological sex

trait loneliness loneliness that is enduring and cross-situational and that is linked to personality function and mental health

transactional model of stress a model proposing that the interaction between the properties of an event and the properties of the person determines whether an event will be perceived as threatening and subsequently invoke coping responses

transactional perspective of social support the view of social support as a process that involves transactions between the individual and the support network; requires attention to the interaction between the person and his or her social environment as well as attention to the different kinds of relationships that may or may not compose the individual's support network

transactive memory a communal memory bank that couples develop; consists of the organized store of knowledge contained in the individual memory systems of both partners and the set of transactive communication processes that the partners use to access each other's memory stores

transfer of excitation refers to the transfer of arousal from an initial arousal-producing situation to a subsequent situation, which may produce a more intense emotional experience in that situation than otherwise would have occurred

transformation of disposition a process in which partners undergo changes in their personal preferences and thereby change their relationship's outcome matrix by increasing (or decreasing) their correspondence of outcomes

transformation of motivation a process in which partners undergo changes in their personal motivations and thereby change the relationship's outcome matrix by increasing (or decreasing) their correspondence of outcomes and reducing (or enhancing) their likelihood of conflict

trust belief in the responsiveness and beneficence of another in time of need; has been conceptualized as a personality trait (a chronic personal predisposition to trust or distrust others in general) but increasingly is viewed as a relationship variable (i.e., as specific to a particular partner)

two-wave study a type of longitudinal or prospective study in which respondents are measured at two points in time; usually, the time interval between measurements is relatively short (months rather than years)

understanding the extent to which an individual accurately perceives the partner's true beliefs, attitudes, and values

undifferentiated sex-role orientation a sex-role orientation in which the individual describes him- or herself as having neither stereotypically and socially valued male nor stereotypically and socially valued female traits

unit of analysis the type of response observed and analyzed; in relationship research the unit of analysis is individualistic (the responses of single individuals whose behaviors are independent of each other) or dyadic (the responses of individuals whose behaviors are interdependent)

universality of emotional expression hypothesis a set of four related and controversial propositions concerning the Darwinian idea that all humans display similar emotional expressions and therefore all share a common evolutionary origin: (1) specific patterns of facial muscle movement occur in all humans (i.e., there is universality of facial movement patterns); (2) each facial movement pattern is a manifestation of the same emotion in all humans; (3) people everywhere attribute the same emotional meaning to a specific pattern of facial movement; (4) attributions of emotional meanings to the different facial patterns are accurate (i.e., the person displaying the facial expression actually is experiencing the emotion attributed)

unmitigated communion a personality trait associated with support-giving; generally viewed as an excessive focus on the needs of others coupled with a neglect of one's own needs

verbal aggression verbal responses directed toward a target that are intended to cause harm (e.g., yelling, making threats, name-calling, gossiping, spreading rumors)

vertical dimension (of natural language concepts) reflects the hierarchical organization of concepts, or relations among different levels of concepts (e.g., the set of concepts "emotion," "love," and "maternal love" illustrates an abstract-to-concrete hierarchy with superordinate, basic, and subordinate levels)

voluntariness of interaction an important feature of interactions; represents the extent to which two persons choose to interact because they believe the interaction itself will be intrinsically rewarding versus the extent to which they feel compelled to interact with each other in order to avoid extrinsic penalties (i.e., from external agents or circumstances)

waist-to-hip ratio (WHR) an index of body fat distribution calculated by dividing the circumference of the waist by the circumference of the hips

Westermarck hypothesis the hypothesis that there is a natural human aversion to sexual relations with familiar persons, particularly among persons living closely together from childhood

References

Abbey, A. (1982). Sex differences in attributions for friendly behavior: Do males misperceive females' friendliness? *Journal of Personality and Social Psychology, 42,* 830–838.

Abbey, A., Abramis, D. J., & Caplan, R. D. (1985). Effects of different sources of social support and social conflict on emotional well-being. *Basic and Applied Social Psychology, 6,* 111–129.

Abbey, A., & Melby, C. (1986). The effects of nonverbal cues on gender differences in perceptions of sexual intent. *Sex Roles, 15,* 283–298.

Abrahams, M. F. (1994). Perceiving flirtatious communication: An exploration of the perceptual dimensions underlying judgments of flirtatiousness. *The Journal of Sex Research, 31,* 283–292.

Acitelli, L. K. (1992). Gender differences in relationship awareness and marital satisfaction among young married couples. *Personality and Social Psychology Bulletin, 18,* 102–110.

Acitelli, L. K., Douvan, E., & Veroff, J. (1993). Perceptions of conflict in the first year of marriage: How important are similarity and understanding? *Journal of Social and Personal Relationships, 10,* 5–19.

Acitelli, L. K., & Duck, S. (1987). Intimacy as the proverbial elephant. In D. Perlman & S. Duck (Eds.), *Intimate relationships: Development, dynamics, and deterioration* (pp. 297–308). Newbury Park, CA: Sage.

Acitelli, L. K., & Holmberg, D. (1993). Reflecting on relationships: The role of thoughts and memories. In W. H. Jones & D. Perlman (Eds.), *Advances in personal relationships* (Vol. 4, pp. 71–100). London: Jessica Kingsley.

Acitelli, L. K., Kenny, D. A., & Weiner, D. (2001). The importance of similarity and understanding of partners' marital ideals to relationship satisfaction. *Personal Relationships, 8,* 167–185.

Adams, C. R. (1946). The prediction of adjustment in marriage. *Educational and Psychological Measurement, 6,* 185–193.

Adams, G. R., & Shea, J. A. (1981). Talking and loving: A cross-lagged panel investigation. *Basic and Applied Social Psychology, 2,* 81–88.

Adams, J. M., & Jones, W. H. (1997). The conceptualization of marital commitment: An integrative analysis. *Journal of Personality and Social Psychology, 72,* 1177–1196.

Adams, J. M., & Spain, J. S. (1999). The dynamics of interpersonal commitment and the issue of salience. In J. M. Adams & W. H. Jones (Eds.), *Handbook of interpersonal commitment and relationship stability* (pp. 165–179). New York: Kluwer Academic/Plenum.

Adams, J. S. (1965). Inequity in social exchange. In L. Berkowitz (Ed.), *Advances in experimental social psychology* (Vol. 2, pp. 266–300). New York: Academic Press.

Adams, R. G. (1989). Conceptual and methodological issues in studying friendships of older adults. In R. G. Adams & R. Blieszner (Eds.), *Older adult friendship: Structure and process* (pp. 17–41). Newbury Park, CA: Sage.

Afifi, W. A., Guerrero, L. K., & Egland, K. L. (1994, May). *Maintenance behaviors in same- and opposite-sex friendships: Connections to gender, relational closeness, and equity issues.* Paper presented at the conference of the International Network on Personal Relationships, Iowa City, IA.

Aharon, I., Etcoff, N., Ariely, D., Chabris, C. F., O'Connor, E., & Breiter, H. C. (2001). Beautiful faces have variable reward value: fMRI and behavioral evidence. *Neuron, 32,* 537–551.

Ainsworth, M. D. S., Blehar, M. C., Waters, E., & Wall, S. (1978). *Patterns of attachment: A psychological study of the strange situation.* Hillsdale, NJ: Erlbaum.

Ainsworth, M. S. (1989). Attachments beyond infancy. *American Psychologist, 44,* 709–716.

Albrecht, S. L., Bahr, H. M., & Goodman, K. L. (1983). *Divorce and remarriage: Problems, adaptations, and adjustments.* Westport, CT: Greenwood Press.

Alexander, J. F., Sexton, T. L., & Robbins, M. S. (2001). The developmental status of family therapy in family psychology intervention science. In H. A. Liddle, D. A. Santisteban, R. A. Levant, & J. H. Bray (Eds.), *Family psychology: Science-based interventions* (pp. 17–40). Washington, DC: American Psychological Association.

Alicke, M. D., Smith, R. H., & Klotz, M. L. (1986). Judgments of physical attractiveness: The role of faces and bodies. *Personality and Social Psychology Bulletin, 12,* 381–389.

Allen, J. B., Kenrick, D. T., Linder, D. E., & McCall, M. A. (1989). Arousal and attraction: A response-facilitation alternative to misattribution and negative-reinforcement models. *Journal of Personality and Social Psychology, 57,* 261–270.

Allen, K., Blascovich, J., & Mendes, W. B. (2002). Cardiovascular reactivity and the presence of pets, friends, and spouses: The truth about cats and dogs. *Psychosomatic Medicine, 64,* 727–739.

Allen, K. M., Blascovich, J., Tomaka, J., & Kelsey, R. M. (1991). Presence of human friends and pet dogs as moderators of autonomic responses to stress in women. *Journal of Personality and Social Psychology, 61,* 582–589.

Allen, K. R., & Walker, A. J. (2000). Qualitative research. In C. Hendrick & S. S. Hendrick (Eds.), *Close relationships: A sourcebook* (pp. 19–30). Thousand Oaks, CA: Sage.

Alley, T. R., & Cunningham, M. R. (1991). Averaged faces are attractive, but very attractive faces are not average. *Psychological Science, 2,* 123–125.

Allport, F. H. (1924). *Social psychology.* Boston: Houghton Mifflin.

Altman, I., & Taylor, D. A. (1973). *Social penetration: The development of interpersonal relationships.* New York: Holt, Rinehart, & Winston.

Amato, P. R. (2001). Children of divorce in the 1990s: An update of the Amato and Keith (1991) meta-analysis. *Journal of Family Psychology, 15*, 355–370.

Amato, P. R., & Booth, A. (1997). *A generation at risk: Growing up in an era of family upheaval.* Cambridge, MA: Harvard University Press.

Amato, P. R., Johnson, D. R., Booth, A., & Rogers, S. J. (2003). Continuity and change in marital quality between 1980 and 2000. *Journal of Marriage and Family, 65*, 1–22.

Amato, P. R., & Keith, B. (1991). Parental divorce and the well-being of children: A meta-analysis. *Psychological Bulletin, 110*, 26–46.

Amato, P. R., & Rogers, S. J. (1997). A longitudinal study of marital problems and subsequent divorce. *Journal of Marriage and the Family, 59*, 612–624.

American Council of Life Insurance (1978). (Study reported in *Parade* magazine, September 24, 1978)

American Psychiatric Association. (1994). *Diagnostic and statistical manual of mental disorders* (4th ed.). Washington, DC: Author.

Americans marrying later, survey finds. (2001, June 29). *Minneapolis Star Tribune*, p. A16.

Andersen, S. M., & Baum, A. (1994). Transference in interpersonal relations: Inferences and affect based on significant-other representations. *Journal of Personality, 62*, 459–498.

Anderson, C. A. (1999). Attributional style, depression, and loneliness: A cross-cultural comparison of American and Chinese students. *Personality and Social Psychology Bulletin, 25*, 482–499.

Anderson, E. (1961). *The letters of Beethoven.* London: Macmillan.

Anderson, N. H. (1968). Likableness ratings of 555 personality-trait words. *Journal of Personality and Social Psychology, 9*, 272–279.

Antill, J. K. (1983). Sex role complementarity versus similarity in married couples. *Journal of Personality and Social Psychology, 45*, 145–155.

Archer, J. (2000a). Sex differences in aggression between heterosexual partners: A meta-analytic review. *Psychological Bulletin, 126*, 651–680.

Archer, J. (2000b). Sex differences in physical aggression to partners: A reply to Frieze (2000), O'Leary (2000), and White, Smith, Koss, and Figueredo (2000). *Psychological Bulletin, 126*, 697–702.

Argyle, M. (1986). *The psychology of happiness.* London: Methuen.

Argyle, M., & Furnham, A. (1982). The ecology of relationships: Choice of situations as a function of relationship. *British Journal of Social Psychology, 21*, 259–262.

Arnett, J. L., Prosen, H., & Toews, J. A. (1986). Loss of libido due to stress. *Medical Aspects of Human Sexuality, 20*, 140–148.

Arnsten, A. F. T. (1998). The biology of being frazzled. *Science, 280*, 1711–1712.

Aron, A., & Aron, E. N. (1996). Self and self-expansion in relationships. In G. J. O. Fletcher & J. Fitness (Eds.), *Knowledge structures in close relationships: A social psychological approach* (pp. 325–344). Mahwah, NJ: Erlbaum.

Aron, A., Aron, E. N., & Smollan, D. (1992). Inclusion of Other in the Self Scale and the structure of interpersonal closeness. *Journal of Personality and Social Psychology, 63*, 596–612.

Aron, A., Aron, E. N., Tudor, M., & Nelson, G. (1991). Close relationships as including other in the self. *Journal of Personality and Social Psychology, 60*, 241–253.

Aron, A., Melinat, E., Aron, E. N., Vallone, R. D., & Bator, R. J. (1997). The experimental generation of interpersonal closeness: A procedure and some preliminary findings. *Personality and Social Psychology Bulletin, 23*, 363–377.

Aron, A., Norman, C. C., Aron, E. N., McKenna, C., & Heyman, R. (2000). Couples' shared participation in novel and arousing activities and experienced relationship quality. *Journal of Personality and Social Psychology, 78*, 273–283.

Aronson, E. (1969). Some antecedents of interpersonal attraction. In W. J. Arnold & D. Levine (Eds.), *Nebraska Symposium on Motivation* (Vol. 17, pp. 143–173). Lincoln: University of Nebraska Press.

Aronson, E., & Linder, D. (1965). Gain and loss of esteem as determinants of interpersonal attractiveness. *Journal of Experimental Social Psychology, 1*, 156–172.

Aronson, E., & Mills, J. (1959). The effect of severity of initiation on liking for a group. *Journal of Abnormal and Social Psychology, 59*, 177–181.

Arriaga, X. B. (2001). The ups and downs of dating: Fluctuations in satisfaction in newly formed romantic relationships. *Journal of Personality and Social Psychology, 80*, 754–765.

Asch, S. E. (1946). Forming impressions of personality. *Journal of Abnormal and Social Psychology, 41*, 258–290.

Ashton, M. C., Lee, K., & Paunonen, S. V. (2002). What is the central feature of extraversion? Social attention versus reward sensitivity. *Journal of Personality and Social Psychology, 83*, 245–252.

Aspinwall, L. G., & Staudinger, U. M. (Eds.). (2003). *A psychology of human strengths: Fundamental questions and future directions for a positive psychology.* Washington, DC: American Psychological Association.

Atkins, C. J., Kaplan, R. M., & Toshima, M. T. (1991). Close relationships in the epidemiology of cardiovascular disease. In W. H. Jones & D. Perlman (Eds.), *Advances in personal relationships* (Vol. 2, pp. 207–231). London: Jessica Kingsley.

Atkins, D. C., Baucom, D. H., & Jacobson, N. S. (2001). Understanding infidelity: Correlates in a national random sample. *Journal of Family Psychology, 15*, 735–749.

Attridge, M. (1995). *Reactions of romantic partners to geographic separation: A natural experiment.* Unpublished doctoral dissertation, University of Minnesota, Minneapolis.

Attridge, M., & Berscheid, E. (1994). Entitlement in romantic relationships in the United States: A social exchange perspective. In M. J. Lerner & G. Mikula (Eds.), *Entitlement and the affectional bond: Justice in close relationships* (pp. 117–147). New York: Plenum Press.

Attridge, M., Berscheid, E., & Simpson, J. A. (1995). Predicting relationship stability from both partners versus one. *Journal of Personality and Social Psychology, 69*, 254–268.

Attridge, M., Berscheid, E., & Sprecher, S. (1998). Dependency and insecurity in romantic relationships: Development and validation of two companion scales. *Personal Relationships, 5*, 31–58.

AuWerter, S. (2001, August 26). Smart money. *Minneapolis Star Tribune*, p. D7.

Axinn, W., & Thornton, A. (1992). The relationship between cohabitation and divorce: Selectivity or causal influence? *Demography, 29*, 357–374.

Azar, B. (1998, January). Communicating through pheromones. *APA Monitor, 29*, 1, 12.

Bach, G. R., & Wyden, P. (1969). *The intimate enemy: How to fight fair in love and marriage*. New York: Morrow.

Backman, C. W., & Secord, P. F. (1959). The effect of perceived liking on interpersonal attraction. *Human Relations, 12*, 379–384.

Baddeley, A. D. (1999). *Essentials of human memory*. East Sussex, UK: Psychology Press.

Badr, H., Acitelli, L., Duck, S., & Carl, W. J. (2001). Weaving social support and relationships together. In B. R. Sarason & S. Duck (Eds.), *Personal relationships: Implications for clinical and community psychology* (pp. 1–14). Chichester, UK: Wiley.

Bakermans-Kranenburg, M. J., van IJzendoorn, M. H., & Juffer, F. (2003). Less is more: Meta-analyses of sensitivity and attachment interventions in early childhood. *Psychological Bulletin, 129*, 195–215.

Baldwin, J. M. (1897). *Social and ethical interpretations in mental development*. New York: Macmillan.

Baldwin, M. W. (1992). Relational schemas and the processing of social information. *Psychological Bulletin, 112*, 461–484.

Baldwin, M. W. (1995). Relational schemas and cognition in close relationships. *Journal of Social and Personal Relationships, 12*, 547–552.

Baldwin, M. W., Carrell, S., & Lopez, D. (1990). Priming relationship schemas: My advisor and the Pope are watching me from the back of my mind. *Journal of Experimental Social Psychology, 26*, 435–454.

Baldwin, M. W., Fehr, B., Keedian, E., Seidel, M., & Thomson, D. W. (1993). An exploration of the relational schemata underlying attachment styles: Self-report and lexical decision approaches. *Personality and Social Psychology Bulletin, 19*, 746–754.

Baldwin, M. W., Keelan, J. P. R., Fehr, B., Enns, V., & Koh-Rangarajoo, E. (1996). Social-cognitive conceptualization of attachment working models: Availability and accessibility effects. *Journal of Personality and Social Psychology, 71*, 94–109.

Bandura, A. (1973). *Aggression: Social learning analysis*. Englewood Cliffs, NJ: Prentice-Hall.

Bandura, A. (1997). *Self-efficacy: The exercise of control*. New York: Freeman.

Bandura, A., Ross, D., & Ross, S. A. (1961). Transmission of aggression through imitation of aggressive models. *Journal of Abnormal and Social Psychology, 63*, 575–582.

Bank, B. J., & Hansford, S. L. (2000). Gender and friendship: Why are men's best same-sex friendships less intimate and supportive? *Personal Relationships, 7*, 63–78.

Bank, L., Dishion, T., Skinner, M., & Patterson, G. R. (1990). Method variance in structural equation modeling: Living with "glop." In G. R. Patterson (Ed.), *Depression and aggression in family interaction* (pp. 247–279). Hillsdale, NJ: Erlbaum.

Bargh, J. A. (1994). The four horsemen of automaticity: Awareness, intention, efficiency, and control in social cognition. In R. S. Wyer & T. K. Srull (Eds.), *Handbook of social cognition* (2nd ed., Vol. 1, pp. 1–40). Hillsdale, NJ: Erlbaum.

Bargh, J. A. (1996). Automaticity in social psychology. In E. T. Higgins & A. W. Kruglanski (Eds.), *Social psychology: Handbook of basic principles* (pp. 169–183). New York: Guilford Press.

Bargh, J. A., Chaiken, S., Raymond, P., & Hymes, C. (1996). The automatic evaluation effect: Unconditionally automatic attitude activation with a pronunciation task. *Journal of Experimental Social Psychology, 32*, 185–210.

Bargh, J. A., & Ferguson, M. J. (2000). Beyond behaviorism: On the automaticity of higher mental processes. *Psychological Bulletin, 126*, 925–945.

Bargh, J. A., Lombardi, W. J., & Higgins, E. T. (1988). Automaticity of Person X Situation effects on impression formation: It's just a matter of time. *Journal of Personality and Social Psychology, 55*, 599–605.

Barlow, H. B. (1981). Critical limiting factors in the design of the eye and visual cortex. *Proceedings of the Royal Society of London, 212*, 1–34.

Barnett, R. C., & Gareis, K. C. (2000). Reduced-hours employment: The relationship between difficulty of trade-offs and quality of life. *Work and Occupations, 27*, 168–187.

Baron, R. A., & Richardson, D. R. (1994). *Human aggression* (2nd ed.). New York: Plenum Press.

Baron, R. M., & Kenny, D. A. (1986). The moderator-mediator variable distinction in social psychological research: Conceptual, strategic and statistical considerations. *Journal of Personality and Social Psychology, 51*, 1173–1182.

Baron-Cohen, S. (1995). *Mindblindness: An essay on autism and theory of mind*. Cambridge, MA: MIT Press.

Barrett, L. F., Robin, L., Pietromonaco, P. R., & Eyssell, K. M. (1998). Are women the "more emotional" sex? Evidence from emotional experiences in social context. *Cognition and Emotion, 12*, 555–578.

Bartholomew, K. (1990). Avoidance of intimacy: An attachment perspective. *Journal of Social and Personal Relationships, 7*, 147–178.

Bartholomew, K., & Horowitz, L. M. (1991). Attachment styles among young adults: A test of a four-category model. *Journal of Personality and Social Psychology, 61*, 226–244.

Bateson, G., Jackson, D. D., Haley, J., & Weakland, J. H. (1956). Toward a theory of schizophrenia. *Behavioral Science, 1*, 251–264.

Batson, C. D. (1998). Altruism and prosocial behavior. In D. T. Gilbert, S. T. Fiske, & G. Lindzey (Eds.), *The handbook of social psychology* (4th ed., Vol. 2, pp. 282–316). Boston: McGraw-Hill.

Baucom, D. H., & Epstein, N. (1990). *Cognitive-behavioral marital therapy*. New York: Brunner/Mazel.

Baucom, D. H., Epstein, N., & Rankin, L. A. (1995). Cognitive aspects of cognitive-behavioral marital therapy. In N.

S. Jacobson & A. S. Gurman (Eds.), *Clinical handbook of couple therapy* (pp. 65–90). New York: Guilford Press.

Baucom, D. H., Epstein, N., Rankin, L. A., & Burnett, C. K. (1996). Assessing relationship standards: The Inventory of Specific Relationship Standards. *Journal of Marriage and the Family, 10,* 72–88.

Baucom, D. H., Epstein, N., Sayers, S., & Sher, T. G. (1989). The role of cognitions in marital relationships: Definitional, methodological, and conceptual issues. *Journal of Consulting and Clinical Psychology, 57,* 31–38.

Baucom, D. H., & Sayers, S. (1989). The behavioral observation of couples: Where have we lagged and what is the next step in the sequence? *Behavioral Assessment, 11,* 149–159.

Baum, A. (1990). Stress, intrusive imagery, and chronic distress. *Health Psychology, 9,* 653–675.

Baumeister, R. F. (2002). Religion and psychology: Introduction to the special issue. *Psychological Inquiry, 13,* 165–167.

Baumeister, R. F., Bratslavsky, E., Finkenauer, C., & Vohs, K. D. (2001). Bad is stronger than good. *Review of General Psychology, 5,* 323–370.

Baumeister, R. F., & Leary, M. R. (1995). The need to belong: Desire for interpersonal attachments as a fundamental human motivation. *Psychological Bulletin, 117,* 497–529.

Baumeister, R. F., & Wotman, S. R. (1992). *Breaking hearts: The two sides of unrequited love.* New York: Guilford Press.

Baumeister, R. F., Wotman, S. R., & Stillwell, A. M. (1993). Unrequited love: On heartbreak, anger, guilt, scriptlessness, and humiliation. *Journal of Personality and Social Psychology, 64,* 377–394.

Baumrind, D. (1983). Specious causal attributions in the social sciences: The reformulated stepping-stone theory of heroin use as an exemplar. *Journal of Personality and Social Psychology, 45,* 1289–1298.

Baxter, L. A. (1984). Trajectories of relationship disengagement. *Journal of Social and Personal Relationships, 1,* 29–48.

Baxter, L. A., & Bullis, C. (1986). Turning points in developing romantic relationships. *Human Communication Research, 12,* 469–493.

Baxter, L. A., Mazanec, M., Nicholson, J., Pittman, G., Smith, K., & West, L. (1997). Everyday loyalties and betrayals in personal relationships. *Journal of Social and Personal Relationships, 14,* 655–678.

Baxter, L. A., & Wilmot, W. W. (1984). "Secret tests": Social strategies for acquiring information about the state of the relationship. *Human Communication Research, 11,* 171–201.

Baxter, L. A., & Wilmot, W. W. (1986). Interaction characteristics of disengaging, stable, and growing relationships. In R. Gilmour & S. Duck (Eds.), *The emerging field of personal relationships* (pp. 145–159). Hillsdale, NJ: Erlbaum.

Bayer, B. M. (1992). On the separation of reproduction from mating preferences. *Behavioral and Brain Sciences, 15,* 92–93.

Beall, A. E. (1993). A social constructionist view of gender. In A. E. Beall & R. J. Sternberg (Eds.), *The psychology of gender* (pp. 127–147). New York: Guilford Press.

Beall, A. E., & Sternberg, R. J. (Eds.). (1993). *The psychology of gender.* New York: Guilford Press.

Beck, A., & Katcher, A. (1996). *Between pets and people: The importance of animal companionship.* West Lafayette, IN: Purdue University Press.

Becker, G. S., & Murphy, K. M. (2000). *Social economics: Market behavior in a social environment.* Cambridge, MA: Harvard University Press.

Beech, H. (2001, August 6). China's lifestyle choice. *Time,* p. 32.

Beech, H. (2002, July 1). With women so scarce, what can men do? *Time,* p. 8.

Bell, D. C., & Richard, A. J. (2000). Caregiving: The forgotten element in attachment. *Psychological Inquiry, 11,* 69–83.

Bell, R. Q. (1968). A reinterpretation of the direction of effects in studies of socialization. *Psychological Review, 75,* 81–95.

Belsky, J. (1990). Children and marriage. In F. D. Fincham & T. N. Bradbury (Eds.), *The psychology of marriage: Basic issues and applications* (pp. 172–200). New York: Guilford Press.

Bem, S. L. (1974). The measurement of psychological androgyny. *Journal of Consulting and Clinical Psychology, 42,* 155–162.

Bennett, N. B., Bloom, D. E., & Craig, P. H. (1989). The divergence of Black and White marriage patterns. *American Journal of Sociology, 95,* 692–722.

Bennett, N. G., Blanc, A. K., & Bloom, D. E. (1988). Commitment and the modern union: Assessing the link between premarital cohabitation and subsequent marital stability. *American Sociological Review, 53,* 127–138.

Bentler, P. M., & Newcomb, M. D. (1978). Longitudinal study of marital success and failure. *Journal of Consulting and Clinical Psychology, 46,* 1053–1070.

Benton, D. (1982). The influence of androstenol—a putative human pheromone—on mood throughout the menstrual cycle. *Biological Psychology, 15,* 249–256.

Benton, D., & Wastell, V. (1986). Effects of androstenol on human sexual arousal. *Biological Psychology, 22,* 141–147.

Berg, J. H. (1984). Development of friendship between roommates. *Journal of Personality and Social Psychology, 46,* 346–356.

Berg, J. J., & McQuinn, R. D. (1986). Attraction and exchange in continuing and noncontinuing dating relationships. *Journal of Personality and Social Psychology, 50,* 942–952.

Berk, M. A., & Andersen, S. M. (2000). The impact of past relationships on interpersonal behavior: Behavioral confirmation in the social-cognitive process of transference. *Journal of Personality and Social Psychology, 79,* 546–562.

Berkman, L. F. (1995). The role of social relations in health promotion. *Psychosomatic Medicine, 57,* 245–254.

Berkman, L. F., & Syme, S. L. (1979). Social networks, host resistance, and mortality: A nine year follow-up study of Alameda County residents. *American Journal of Epidemiology, 100,* 186–204.

Berliner, D. L., Jennings-White, C., & Lavker, R. M. (1991). The human skin: Fragrances and pheromones. *Journal of Steroid Biochemistry and Molecular Biology, 39,* 671–679.

Berlyne, D. (1960). *Conflict, arousal, and curiosity.* New York: Academic Press.

Berman, P. W. (1980). Are women more responsive than men to the young? A review of developmental and situational variables. *Psychological Bulletin, 88,* 668–695.

Bernard, J. (1972/1973). *The future of marriage*. New York: World Publishing (Bantam, 1973).

Berndt, T. J. (1999). Friends' influence on children's adjustment to school. In W. A. Collins & B. Laursen (Eds.), *Minnesota Symposia on Child Psychology: Vol. 30. Relationships as developmental contexts* (pp. 85–108). Mahwah, NJ: Erlbaum.

Berndt, T. J., & Ladd, G. W. (Eds.). (1989). *Peer relationships in child development*. New York: Wiley.

Berndt, T. J., & Perry, T. B. (1986). Children's perceptions of friendships as supportive relationships. *Developmental Psychology, 22,* 640–648.

Berns, S. B., Jacobson, N. S., & Gottman, J. M. (1999). Demand–withdraw interaction in couples with a violent husband. *Journal of Consulting and Clinical Psychology, 67,* 666–674.

Berry, D. S., & Hansen, J. S. (1996). Positive affect, negative affect, and social interaction. *Journal of Personality and Social Psychology, 71,* 796–809.

Berry, D. S., & Hansen, J. S. (2000). Personality, nonverbal behavior, and interaction quality in female dyads. *Personality and Social Psychology Bulletin, 26,* 278–292.

Berscheid, E. (1982). Attraction and emotion in interpersonal relations. In M. S. Clark & S. T. Fiske (Eds.), *Affect and cognition: The Seventeenth Annual Carnegie Symposium on Cognition* (pp. 37–54). Hillsdale, NJ: Erlbaum.

Berscheid, E. (1985a). Compatibility, interdependence, and emotion. In W. Ickes (Ed.), *Compatible and incompatible relationships* (pp. 143–162). New York: Springer-Verlag.

Berscheid, E. (1985b). Interpersonal attraction. In G. Lindzey & E. Aronson (Eds.), *The handbook of social psychology* (3rd ed., Vol. 2, pp. 413–484). New York: Random House.

Berscheid, E. (1986). Mea culpas and lamentations: Sir Francis, Sir Isaac, and "The slow progress of soft psychology." In R. Gilmour & S. Duck (Eds.), *The emerging field of personal relationships* (pp. 267–286). Hillsdale, NJ: Erlbaum.

Berscheid, E. (1988). Some comments on love's anatomy: Or, whatever happened to old-fashioned lust? In R. J. Sternberg & M. L. Barnes (Eds.), *The psychology of love* (pp. 359–374). New Haven, CT: Yale University Press.

Berscheid, E. (1990). Contemporary vocabularies of emotion. In B. S. Moore & A. M. Isen (Eds.), *Affect and social behavior*. Cambridge, UK: Cambridge University Press.

Berscheid, E. (1991). The emotion-in-relationships model: Reflections and update. In W. Kessen & A. Ortony (Eds.), *Memories, thoughts, and emotions: Essays in honor of George Mandler*. Hillsdale, NJ: Erlbaum.

Berscheid, E. (1994). Interpersonal relationships. *Annual Review of Psychology, 45,* 79–129.

Berscheid, E. (1998). A social psychological view of marital dysfunction and stability. In T. N. Bradbury (Ed.), *The developmental course of marital dysfunction* (pp. 441–460). Cambridge, UK: Cambridge University Press.

Berscheid, E. (1999). The greening of relationship science. *American Psychologist, 54,* 260–266.

Berscheid, E. (2002). Emotion. In H. H. Kelley, E. Berscheid, A. Christensen, J. H. Harvey, T. L. Huston, G. Levinger, E. McClintock, L. A. Peplau, & D. R. Peterson (Eds.), *Close relationships* (pp. 110–168). Clinton Corners, NY: Percheron Press. (Original work published 1983)

Berscheid, E. (2002a). Lessons in "greatness" from Kurt Lewin's life and works. In R. J. Sternberg (Ed.), *The anatomy of impact: What has made the great works of psychology great?* Washington, DC: American Psychological Association.

Berscheid, E. (2002b). On stepping on land mines. In R. J. Sternberg (Ed.), *Psychologists defying the crowd: Stories of those who battled the establishment and won* (pp. 32–45). Washington, DC: American Psychological Association.

Berscheid, E., & Ammazzalorso, H. (2001). Emotional experience in close relationships. In G. J. O. Fletcher & M. S. Clark (Eds.), *Blackwell handbook of social psychology: Vol. 2. Interpersonal processes* (pp. 308–330). Malden, MA: Blackwell.

Berscheid, E., Boye, D., & Darley, J. (1968). Effect of forced association upon voluntary choice to associate. *Journal of Personality and Social Psychology, 8,* 13–19.

Berscheid, E., Boye, D., & Walster [Hatfield], E. (1968). Retaliation as a means of restoring equity. *Journal of Personality and Social Psychology, 10,* 370–376.

Berscheid, E., Brothen, T., & Graziano, W. (1976). Gain–loss theory and the "law of infidelity": Mr. Doting vs. the admiring stranger. *Journal of Personality and Social Psychology, 33,* 709–718.

Berscheid, E., & Campbell, B. (1981). The changing longevity of heterosexual close relationships. In M. J. Lerner & S. C. Lerner (Eds.), *The justice motive in social behavior* (pp. 209–234). New York: Plenum Press.

Berscheid, E., & Collins, W. A. (2000). Who cares? For whom and when, how, and why? *Psychological Inquiry, 11,* 107–109.

Berscheid, E., Dion, K. K., Walster [Hatfield], E., & Walster, G. W. (1971). Physical attractiveness and dating choice: A test of the matching hypothesis. *Journal of Experimental Social Psychology, 7,* 173–189.

Berscheid, E., Gangestad, S. W., & Kulakowski, D. (1984). Emotion in close relationships: Implications for relationship counseling. In S. D. Brown & R. W. Lent (Eds.), *Handbook of counseling psychology* (pp. 435–476). New York: Wiley.

Berscheid, E., & Graziano, W. (1979). The initiation of social relationships and interpersonal attraction. In R. L. Burgess & T. L. Huston (Eds.), *Social exchange in developing relationships* (pp. 31–60). New York: Academic Press.

Berscheid, E., Graziano, W., Monson, T., & Dermer, M. (1976). Outcome dependency: Attention, attribution and attraction. *Journal of Personality and Social Psychology, 34,* 978–989.

Berscheid, E., & Kelley, H. H. (2002). Introduction. In H. H. Kelley, E. Berscheid, A. Christensen, J. H. Harvey, T. L. Huston, G. Levinger, E. McClintock, L. A. Peplau, & D. R. Peterson (Eds.), *Close relationships* (pp. vii–xxvi). Clinton Corners, NY: Percheron Press.

Berscheid, E., & Lopes, J. (1997). A temporal model of relationship satisfaction and stability. In R. J. Sternberg & M. Hojjat (Eds.), *Satisfaction in close relationships* (pp. 129–159). New York: Guilford Press.

Berscheid, E., Lopes, J., Ammazzalorso, H., & Langenfeld, N. (2001). Causal attributions of relationship quality. In J. H. Harvey & V. Manusov (Eds.), *Attribution, communication behavior, and close relationships* (pp. 115–133). Cambridge, UK: Cambridge University Press.

Berscheid, E., & Meyers, S. A. (1996). A social categorical approach to a question about love. *Personal Relationships, 3,* 19–43.

Berscheid, E., & Peplau, L. A. (2002). The emerging science of relationships. In H. H. Kelley, E. Berscheid, A. Christensen, J. H. Harvey, T. L. Huston, G. Levinger, E. McClintock, L. A. Peplau, & D. R. Peterson (Eds.), *Close relationships* (pp. 1–19). Clinton Corners, NY: Percheron Press. (Original work published 1983)

Berscheid, E., & Reis, H. T. (1998). Attraction and close relationships. In D. T. Gilbert, S. T. Fiske, & G. Lindzey (Eds.), *The handbook of social psychology* (4th ed., Vol. 2, pp. 193–281). Boston: McGraw-Hill.

Berscheid, E., Snyder, M., & Omoto, A. M. (1989a). Issues in studying relationships: Conceptualizing and measuring closeness. In C. Hendrick (Ed.), *Close relationships: Vol. 10. Review of personality and social psychology* (pp. 63–91). Newbury Park, CA: Sage.

Berscheid, E., Snyder, M., & Omoto, A. M. (1989b). The Relationship Closeness Inventory: Assessing the closeness of interpersonal relationships. *Journal of Personality and Social Psychology, 57,* 792–807.

Berscheid, E., Snyder, M., & Omoto, A. M. (2004). Measuring closeness: The Relationship Closeness Inventory (RCI) revisited. In D. Mashek & A. Aron (Eds.), *The handbook of closeness and intimacy.* Mahwah, NJ: Erlbaum.

Berscheid, E., & Walster [Hatfield], E. (1967). When does a harm-doer compensate a victim? *Journal of Personality and Social Psychology, 6,* 435–441.

Berscheid, E., & Walster [Hatfield], E. (1969). *Interpersonal attraction.* Reading, MA: Addison-Wesley.

Berscheid, E., & Walster [Hatfield], E. (1974a). A little bit about love. In T. L. Huston (Ed.), *Foundations of interpersonal attraction* (pp. 355–381). New York: Academic Press.

Berscheid, E., & Walster [Hatfield], E. (1974b). Physical attractiveness. In L. Berkowitz (Ed.), *Advances in experimental social psychology* (Vol. 7, pp. 157–215). New York: Academic Press.

Bertrand, J. T., Makani, B., Edwards, M. P., & Baughman, N. C. (1996). The male versus the female perspective on family planning: Kinshasa, Zaire. *Journal of Biosocial Science, 28,* 37–55.

Bettor, L., Hendrick, S. S., & Hendrick, C. (1995). Gender and sexual standards in dating relationships. *Personal Relationships, 2,* 359–369.

Betzig, L. (1989). Causes of conjugal dissolution: A cross-cultural study. *Current Anthropology, 30,* 654–676.

Bianchi, S. M. (1995). The changing demographic and socioeconomic characteristics of single-parent families. *Marriage and Family Review, 20,* 71–97.

Bigelow, B. J. (1977). Children's friendship expectations: A cognitive-developmental study. *Child Development, 48,* 246–253.

Billings, A. G., & Moos, R. H. (1981). The role of coping responses and social resources in attenuating the stress of life events. *Journal of Behavioral Medicine, 4,* 139–157.

Birchler, G. R., Weiss, R. L., & Vincent, J. P. (1975). Multimethod analysis of social reinforcement exchange between maritally distressed and nondistressed spouse and stranger dyads. *Journal of Personality and Social Psychology, 31,* 349–360.

Black, J. E., Jones, T. A., Nelson, C. A., & Greenough, W. T. (1998). Neuronal plasticity and the developing brain. In N. E. Alessi, J. T. Coyle, S. I. Harrison, & S. Eth (Eds.), *Handbook of child and adolescent psychiatry: Vol. 6. Basic psychiatric science and treatment* (pp. 31–53). New York: Wiley.

Black, S. L., & Biron, C. (1982). Androstenol as a human pheromone: No effect on perceived physical attractiveness. *Behavioral and Neural Biology, 34,* 326–330.

Blair, S. L., & Johnson, M. P. (1992). Wives' perceptions of the fairness of the division of household labor: The intersection of housework and ideology. *Journal of Marriage and the Family, 54,* 570–581.

Blair, S. L., & Lichter, D. T. (1991). Measuring the division of household labor: Gender segregation of housework among American couples. *Journal of Family Issues, 12,* 91–113.

Blais, M. R., Sabourin, S., Boucher, C., & Vallerand, R. J. (1990). Toward a motivational model of couple happiness. *Journal of Personality and Social Psychology, 59,* 1021–1031.

Blakemore, C. (1998). How the environment helps to build the brain. In B. Cartledge (Ed.), *Mind, brain, and the environment* (pp. 28–56). Oxford, UK: Oxford University Press.

Blau, P. M. (1964). *Exchange and power in social life.* New York: Wiley.

Bleske, A. L., & Buss, D. M. (2000). Can men and women be just friends? *Personal Relationships, 7,* 131–151.

Bleske-Rechek, A. L., & Buss, D. M. (2001). Opposite-sex friendship: Sex differences and similarities in initiation, selection, and dissolution. *Personality and Social Psychology Bulletin, 27,* 1310–1323.

Blieszner, R. (1994). Close relationships over time. In A. L. Weber & J. H. Harvey (Eds.), *Perspectives on close relationships* (pp. 1–17). Needham Heights, MA: Allyn & Bacon.

Blieszner, R., & Adams, R. G. (1992). *Adult friendship.* Newbury Park, CA: Sage.

Blood, R. O., Jr. (1967). *Love match and arranged marriage: A Tokyo-Detroit comparison.* New York: Free Press.

Blood, R. O., Jr., & Wolfe, D. M. (1960). *Husbands and wives: The dynamics of married living.* Glencoe, IL: Free Press.

Bloom, B. L., Asher, S. J., & White, S. W. (1978). Marital disruption as a stressor: A review and analysis. *Psychological Bulletin, 85,* 867–894.

Bloom, B. L., Niles, R. L., & Tatcher, A. M. (1985). Sources of marital dissatisfaction among newly separated persons. *Journal of Family Issues, 6,* 359–373.

Blumstein, P., & Kollock, P. (1988). Personal relationships. *Annual Review of Sociology, 14,* 467–490.

Blumstein, P., & Schwartz, P. (1983). *American couples.* New York: William Morrow.

Bolger, N., DeLongis, A., Kessler, R. C., & Schilling, E. A. (1989). Effects of daily stress on negative mood. *Journal of Personality and Social Psychology, 57,* 808–818.

Bolger, N., DeLongis, A., Kessler, R. C., & Wethington, E. (1989). The contagion of stress across multiple roles. *Journal of Marriage and the Family, 51,* 175–183.

Bolger, N., Foster, M., Vinokur, A. D., & Ng, R. (1996). Close relationships and adjustment to a life crisis: The case of breast cancer. *Journal of Personality and Social Psychology, 70,* 283–294.

Bolger, N., & Zuckerman, A. (1995). A framework for studying personality in the stress process. *Journal of Personality and Social Psychology, 69,* 890–902.

Bolger, N., Zuckerman, A., & Kessler, R. C. (2000). Invisible support and adjustment to stress. *Journal of Personality and Social Psychology, 79,* 953–961.

Bonanno, G. A., & Kaltman, S. (2001). The varieties of grief experience. *Clinical Psychology Review, 20,* 1–30.

Bonanno, G. A., Wortman, C. B., Lehman, D. R., Tweed, R. G., Haring, M., Sonnega, J., Carr, D., & Nesse, R. M. (2002). Resilience to loss and chronic grief: A prospective study from preloss to 18 months postloss. *Journal of Personality and Social Psychology, 83,* 1150–1164.

Book, A. S., Starzyk, K. B., & Quinsey, V. L. (2001). The relationship between testosterone and aggression: A meta-analysis. *Aggression & Violent Behavior, 6,* 579–599.

Booth, A., & Johnson, D. R. (1994). Declining health and marital quality. *Journal of Marriage and the Family, 56,* 218–223.

Booth, A., Johnson, D. R., White, L., & Edwards, J. (1984). Women, outside employment, and marital instability. *American Journal of Sociology, 90,* 567–583.

Booth, A., & White, L. (1980). Thinking about divorce. *Journal of Marriage and the Family, 42,* pp. 605–616.

Borden, V. M. H., & Levinger, G. (1991). Interpersonal transformations in intimate relationships. In W. H. Jones & D. Perlman (Eds.), *Advances in personal relationships* (Vol. 2, pp. 35–56). London: Jessica Kingsley.

Boring, E. G. (1950). *A history of experimental psychology* (2nd ed.). New York: Appleton-Century-Crofts.

Bornstein, M. H. (1989). Sensitive periods in development: Structural characteristics and causal interpretations. *Psychological Bulletin, 105,* 179–197.

Bornstein, R. F. (1989). Exposure and affect: Overview and meta-analysis of research. 1968–1987. *Psychological Bulletin, 106,* 265–289.

Borys, S., & Perlman, D. (1985). Gender differences in loneliness. *Personality and Social Psychology Bulletin, 11,* 63–74.

Boss, P. (1999). *Ambiguous loss: Learning to live with unresolved grief.* Cambridge, MA: Harvard University Press.

Bouchard, G., Lussier, Y., & Sabourin, S. (1999). Personality and marital adjustment: Utility of the five-factor model of personality. *Journal of Marriage and the Family, 61,* 651–660.

Bower, G. H. (1981a). Emotional mood and memory. *American Psychologist, 36,* 129–148.

Bower, G. H. (1981b). Mood and memory. *American Psychologist, 36,* 129–148.

Bower, G. H., & Gilligan, S. G. (1979). Remembering information related to one's self. *Journal of Research in Personality, 13,* 404–419.

Bowlby, J. (1949). The study and reduction of group tension in the family. *Human Relations, 2,* 123–128.

Bowlby, J. (1953). Some pathological processes set in train by early mother–child separation. *Journal of Mental Science, 99,* 265–272.

Bowlby, J. (1958). The nature of the child's tie to his mother. *International Journal of Psychoanalysis, 39,* 350–373.

Bowlby, J. (1969). *Attachment and loss: Vol. 1. Attachment.* New York: Basic Books.

Bowlby, J. (1973a). Affectional bonds: Their nature and origin. In R. S. Weiss (Ed.), *Loneliness: The experience of emotional and social isolation.* Cambridge, MA: MIT Press.

Bowlby, J. (1973b). *Attachment and loss: Vol. 2. Separation: Anxiety and anger.* New York: Basic Books.

Bowlby, J. (1979). *The making and breaking of affectional bonds.* London: Tavistock.

Bowlby, J. (1980). *Attachment and loss: Vol. 3. Loss.* New York: Basic Books.

Bowlby, J. (1988). *A secure base.* New York: Basic Books.

Bradbury, T. N. (1994). Unintended effects of marital research on marital relationships. *Journal of Family Psychology, 8,* 187–201.

Bradbury, T. N. (Ed.). (1998). *The developmental course of marital dysfunction.* Cambridge, UK: Cambridge University Press.

Bradbury, T. N., Cohan, C. L., & Karney, B. R. (1998). Optimizing longitudinal research for understanding and preventing marital dysfunction. In T. N. Bradbury (Ed.), *The developmental course of marital dysfunction* (pp. 279–311). Cambridge, UK: Cambridge University Press.

Bradbury, T. N., & Fincham, F. D. (1988). Individual difference variables in close relationships: A contextual model of marriage as an integrative framework. *Journal of Personality and Social Psychology, 54,* 713–721.

Bradbury, T. N., & Fincham, F. D. (1989). Behavior and satisfaction in marriage: Prospective mediating processes. In C. Hendrick (Ed.), *Close relationships: Vol. 10. Review of Personality and Social Psychology* (pp. 119–143). Newbury Park, CA: Sage.

Bradbury, T. N., & Fincham, F. D. (1990). Attributions in marriage: Review and critique. *Psychological Bulletin, 112,* 461–484.

Bradbury, T. N., & Fincham, F. D. (1991). The analysis of sequence in social interaction. In D. G. Gilbert & J. J. Connolly (Eds.), *Personality, social skills, and psychopathology: An individual differences approach* (pp. 257–289). New York: Plenum Press.

Bradbury, T. N., Fincham, F. D., & Beach, S. R. H. (2000). Research on the nature and determinants of marital satisfaction: A decade in review. *Journal of Marriage and the Family, 62,* 964–980.

Bradford, S. A., Feeney, J. A., & Campbell, L. (2002). Links between attachment orientations and dispositional and diary-based measures of disclosure in dating couples: A study of actor and partner effects. *Personal Relationships, 9,* 491–506.

Braiker, H. B., & Kelley, H. H. (1979). Conflict in the development of close relationships. In R. L. Burgess & T. L. Huston (Eds.), *Social exchange in developing relationships* (pp. 135–168). New York: Academic Press.

Bray, J. H., & Jouriles, E. N. (1995). Treatment of marital conflict and prevention of divorce. *Journal of Marital and Family Therapy, 21,* 461–473.

Brehm, J. W., Gatz, M., Goethals, G., McCrommon, J., & Ward, L. (1970). *Psychological arousal and interpersonal attraction.* Unpublished manuscript.

Brehm, S. S. (1985). *Intimate relationships.* New York: Random House.

Brehm, S. S., & Kassin, S. M. (1996). *Social psychology* (3rd ed.). Boston, MA: Houghton Mifflin.

Brennan, K. A., Clark, C. L., & Shaver, P. R. (1998). Self-report measurement of adult attachment: An integrative overview. In J. A. Simpson & W. S. Rholes (Eds.), *Attachment theory and close relationships* (pp. 46–76). New York: Guilford Press.

Breuer, M. E., McGinnis, M. Y., Lumia, A. R., & Possidente, B. P. (2001). Aggression in male rats receiving anabolic androgenic steroids: Effects of social and environmental provocation. *Hormones & Behavior, 40,* 409–418.

Brewer, M. B. (1988). A dual process model of impression formation. In T. K. Srull & R. S. Wyer (Eds.), *Advances in social cognition* (Vol. 1, pp. 1–36). Hillsdale, NJ: Erlbaum.

Brewer, M. B., & Caporael, L. R. (1990). Selfish genes vs. selfish people: Sociobiology as origin myth. *Motivation and Emotion, 14,* 237–243.

Brines, J. (1994). Economic dependency, gender, and division of labor at home. *American Journal of Sociology, 100,* 652–660.

Bringle, R. G., & Buunk, B. P. (1991). Extradyadic relationships and sexual jealousy. In K. McKinney & S. Sprecher (Eds.), *Sexuality in close relationships* (pp. 135–153). Hillsdale, NJ: Erlbaum.

Brissette, I., & Clark, M. S. (1999). *Emotional expression in social relationships: The type of relationship matters.* Unpublished manuscript.

Brockner, J., & Swap, W. C. (1976). Effects of repeated exposure and attitudinal similarity on self-disclosure and interpersonal attraction. *Journal of Personality and Social Psychology, 33,* 531–540.

Broderick, C. B., & Schrader, S. (1991). The history of professional marriage and family therapy. In A. S. Gurman & D. P. Kniskern (Eds.), *Handbook of family therapy* (Vol. 2, pp. 3–40). New York: Brunner/Mazel.

Brody, G. H., Neubaum, E., & Forehand, R. (1988). Serial marriage: A heuristic analysis of an emerging family form. *Psychological Bulletin, 103,* 211–222.

Brook, J. S., Balka, E. B., Abernathy, T., & Hamburg, B. A. (1994). Sequence of sexual behavior and its relationship to other problem behaviors in African American and Puerto Rican adolescents. *Journal of Genetic Psychology, 155,* 107–114.

Broverman, I. K., Vogel, S. R., Broverman, D. M., Clarkson, F. E., & Rosenkrantz, P. (1994). Sex-role stereotypes: A current reappraisal. In B. Puka (Ed.), *Moral development: A compendium* (Vol. 6, pp. 191–210). New York: Garland.

Brown, M., & Auerback, A. (1981). Communication patterns in initiation of marital sex. *Medical Aspects of Human Sexuality, 15,* 105–117.

Brown, R., & Kulik, J. (1977). Flashbulb memories. *Cognition, 5,* 73–99.

Browne, A., & Bassuk, S. S. (1997). Intimate violence in the lives of homeless and poor house women: Prevalence and patterns in an ethnically diverse sample. *American Journal of Orthopsychiatry, 67,* 261–278.

Bruner, J. S. (1957). On perceptual readiness. *Psychological Review, 64,* 123–152.

Bryant, C. M., & Conger, R. D. (1999). Marital success and domains of social support in long-term relationships: Does the influence of network members ever end? *Journal of Marriage and the Family, 61,* 437–450.

Buck, R., & Ginsberg, B. (1997). Communicative genes and the evolution of empathy. In W. Ickes (Ed.), *Empathic accuracy* (pp. 17–43). New York: Guilford Press.

Buckley, J. T. (1996, August 21). This time, animal instincts saved the day. *USA Today,* p. 7A.

Buehler, C. (1987). Initiator status and the divorce transition. *Family Relations, 36,* 82–86.

Buehlman, K. T., Gottman, J. M., & Katz, L. F. (1992). How a couple views their past predicts their future: Predicting divorce from an oral history interview. *Journal of Family Psychology, 5,* 295–318.

Bugental, D. B. (1992). Affective and cognitive processes within threat-oriented family systems. In I. E. Siegel, A. V. McGillicudy-DeLisi, & J. J. Goodnow (Eds.), *Parental belief systems: The psychological consequences for children* (2nd ed., pp. 219–248). Hillsdale, NJ: Erlbaum.

Bugental, D. B. (2000). Acquisition of the algorithms of social life: A domain-based approach. *Psychological Bulletin, 126,* 187–219.

Bugental, D. B., Blue, J., Cortez, V., Fleck, K., Kopeikin, H., Lewis, J. C., & Lyon, J. (1993). Social cognitions as organizers of autonomic and affective responses to social challenge. *Journal of Personality and Social Psychology, 64,* 94–103.

Bugental, D. B., Ellerson, P. C., Lin, E. K., Rainey, B., Kokotovic, A., & O'Hara, N. (2002). A cognitive approach to child abuse prevention. *Journal of Family Psychology, 16,* 243–258.

Buhrmester, D., & Furman, W. (1987). The development of companionship and intimacy. *Child Development, 58,* 1101–1113.

Bull, R., & Rumsey, N. (1988). *The social psychology of facial appearance.* New York: Springer-Verlag.

Bumpass, L. L., & Sweet, J. A. (1989). National estimates of cohabitation. *Demography, 26,* 615–625.

Bumpass, L., Sweet, J., & Castro-Martin, T. (1990). Changing patterns of remarriage. *Journal of Marriage and the Family, 52,* 747–756.

Burgess, E. W. (1926). Topical summaries of current literature: The family. *American Journal of Sociology, 32,* 104–115.

Burgess, E. W., & Wallin, P. (1943). Homogamy in social characteristics. *American Journal of Sociology, 49,* 109–124.

Burgess, E. W., & Wallin, P. (1953). *Courtship, engagement and marriage*. Philadelphia: Lippincott.

Burgess, R. L., & Huston, T. L. (Eds.). (1979). *Social exchange in developing relationships*. New York: Academic Press.

Burgoon, J. K. (1993). Interpersonal expectations, expectancy violations, and emotional communication. *Journal of Language and Social Psychology, 12*, 30–48.

Burgoon, J. K., Steen, L. A., & Dillman, L. (1995). *Interpersonal adaptation: Dyadic interaction patterns*. Cambridge, UK: Cambridge University Press.

Burleson, B. R. (1994). Comforting messages: Significance, approaches, and effects. In B. R. Burleson, T. L. Albrecht, & I. G. Sarason (Eds.), *Communication of social support: Messages, interactions, relationships, and community* (pp. 3–28). Thousand Oaks, CA: Sage.

Burley, N. (1983). The meaning of assortative mating. *Ethology and Sociobiology, 4*, 191–203.

Burman, B., & Margolin, G. (1992). Analysis of the association between marital relationships and health problems: An interactional perspective. *Psychological Bulletin, 112*, 39–63.

Burns, G. L., & Farina, A. (1992). The role of physical attractiveness in adjustment. *Genetic, Social, and General Psychology Monographs, 118*, 157–194.

Burt, M. R. (1980). Cultural myths and supports for rape. *Journal of Personality and Social Psychology, 38*, 217–230.

Bushman, B. J. (2002). Does venting anger feed or extinguish the flame? Catharsis, rumination, distraction, anger, and aggressive responding. *Personality and Social Psychology Bulletin, 28*, 724–731.

Buss, D. M. (1985). Human mate selection. *American Scientist, 73*, 47–51.

Buss, D. M. (1988). Love acts: The evolutionary biology of love. In R. J. Sternberg & M. L. Barnes (Eds.), *The psychology of love* (pp. 100–118). New Haven, CT: Yale University Press.

Buss, D. M. (1989). Sex differences in human mate preferences: Evolutionary hypotheses tested in 37 cultures. *Behavioral and Brain Sciences, 12*, 1–49.

Buss, D. M. (2003). *The evolution of desire: Strategies of human mating* (Rev. ed.). New York: Basic Books.

Buss, D. M., & Barnes, M. (1986). Preferences in human mate selection. *Journal of Personality and Social Psychology, 50*, 559–570.

Buss, D. M., & Kenrick, D. T. (1998). Evolutionary social psychology. In D. T. Gilbert, S. T. Fiske, & G. Lindzey (Eds.), *The handbook of social psychology* (4th ed., Vol. 2, pp. 982–1026). Boston: McGraw-Hill.

Buss, D. M., Larsen, R. J., Westen, D., & Semmelroth, J. (1992). Sex differences in jealousy: Evolution, physiology, and psychology. *Psychological Science, 3*, 251–255.

Buss, D. M., & Schmitt, D. P. (1993). Sexual strategies theory: An evolutionary perspective on human mating. *Psychological Review, 100*, 204–232.

Buss, D. M., Shackelford, T. K., Kirkpatrick, L. A., Choe, J. C., Lim, H. K., Hasegawa, M., Hasegawa, T., & Bennett, K. (1999). Jealousy and the nature of beliefs about infidelity: Tests of competing hypotheses about sex differences in the United States, Korea, and Japan. *Personal Relationships, 6*, 125–150.

Buunk, B. (1984). Jealousy as related to attributions for the partners' behavior. *Social Psychology Quarterly, 47*, 107–112.

Buunk, B. P. (1995). Sex, self-esteem, dependency and extradyadic sexual experience as related to jealousy responses. *Journal of Social and Personal Relationships, 12*, 147–153.

Buunk, B. P., Angleitner, A., Oubaid, V., & Buss, D. M. (1996). Sex differences in jealousy in evolutionary and cultural perspective: Tests from the Netherlands, Germany, and the United States. *Psychological Science, 7*, 359–363.

Buunk, B. P., & Bakker, A. B. (1995). Extradyadic sex: The role of descriptive and injunctive norms. *The Journal of Sex Research, 32*, 313–318.

Buunk, B. P., Oldersma, F. L., & de Dreu, C. K. W. (2001). Enhancing satisfaction through downward comparison: The role of relational discontent and individual differences in social comparison orientation. *Journal of Experimental Social Psychology, 37*, 452–467.

Buunk, B. P., & Van Yperen, N. W. (1989). Social comparison, equality, and relationship satisfaction: Gender differences over a ten-year period. *Social Justice Research, 3*, 157–180.

Buunk, B. P., & Van Yperen, N. W. (1991). Referential comparisons, relational comparisons, and exchange orientation: Their relation to marital satisfaction. *Personality and Social Psychology Bulletin, 17*, 709–717.

Byers, E. S., Demmons, S., & Lawrance, K. (1998). Sexual satisfaction within dating relationships: A test of the interpersonal exchange model of sexual satisfaction. *Journal of Social and Personal Relationships, 15*, 257–267.

Byers, E. S., & Heinlein, L. (1989). Predicting initiations and refusals of sexual activities in married and cohabiting heterosexual couples. *The Journal of Sex Research, 26*, 210–231.

Byrd, R. C. (1988). The therapeutic effects of intercessory prayer in a coronary care unit. *Southern Medical Journal, 81*, 826–829.

Byrne, D. (1971). *The attraction paradigm*. New York: Academic Press.

Byrne, D., & Blaylock, B. (1963). Similarity and assumed similarity of attitudes between husbands and wives. *Journal of Abnormal and Social Psychology, 6*, 636–640.

Byrne, D., Clore, G. L., & Smeaton, G. (1986). The attraction hypothesis: Do similar attitudes affect anything? *Journal of Personality and Social Psychology, 51*, 1167–1170.

Cacioppo, J. T., & Berntson, G. G. (1992). Social psychological contributions to the decade of the brain: The doctrine of multilevel analysis. *American Psychologist, 47*, 1019–1028.

Cacioppo, J. T., & Berntson, G. G. (1994). Relationship between attitudes and evaluative space: A critical review with emphasis on the separability of positive and negative substrates. *Psychological Review, 115*, 401–423.

Cacioppo, J. T., Berntson, G. G., Sheridan, J. F., & McClintock, M. K. (2000). Multilevel integrative analyses of human behavior: Social neuroscience and the complementing nature of social and biological approaches. *Psychological Bulletin, 126*, 829–843.

Cacioppo, J. T., & Gardner, W. L. (1999). Emotion. *Annual Review of Psychology, 50,* 191–214.

Cacioppo, J. T., Gardner, W. L., & Berntson, G. G. (1999). The affect system has parallel and integrative processing components: Form follows function. *Journal of Personality and Social Psychology, 76,* 839–855.

Cacioppo, J. T., Klein, D. J., Berntson, G. G., & Hatfield, E. (1993). The psychophysiology of emotion. In M. Lewis & J. M. Haviland (Eds.), *Handbook of emotions* (pp. 119–142). New York: Guilford Press.

Calhoun, K. S., & Wilson, A. E. (2000). Rape and sexual aggression. In L. T. Szuchman & F. Muscarella (Eds.), *Psychological perspectives on human sexuality* (pp. 573–602). New York: John Wiley & Sons, Inc.

Call, V., Sprecher, S., & Schwartz, P. (1995). The incidence and frequency of marital sex in a national sample. *Journal of Marriage and the Family, 57,* 639–650.

Campbell, A., Converse, D. E., & Rodgers, W. L. (1976). *The quality of American life.* New York: Sage.

Campbell, D. T., & Fiske, D. W. (1959). Convergent and discriminant validation by the multitrait-multimethod matrix. *Psychological Bulletin, 56,* 81–105.

Canary, D. J., & Dindia, K. (Eds.). (1998). *Sex differences and similarities in communication: Critical essays and empirical investigations of sex and gender in interaction.* Mahwah, NJ: Erlbaum.

Canary, D. J., & Emmers-Sommer, T. M. (1997). *Sex and gender differences in personal relationships.* New York: Guilford Press.

Canary, D. J., & Messman, S. J. (2000). Relationship conflict. In C. Hendrick & S. S. Hendrick, *Close relationships: A sourcebook* (pp. 261–272). Thousand Oaks, CA: Sage.

Canary, D. J., Stafford, L., Hause, K. S., & Wallace, L. A. (1993). An inductive analysis of relational maintenance strategies: Comparisons among lovers, relatives, friends, and others. *Communication Research Reports, 10,* 5–14.

Cannon, W. B. (1927). The James–Lange theory of emotions: A critical examination and an alternative theory. *American Journal of Psychology, 39,* 106–124.

Cannon, W. B. (1929). *Bodily changes in pain, hunger, fear, and rage: An account of researches into the function of emotional excitement* (2nd ed.). New York: Appleton.

Cannon, W. B. (1932). *The wisdom of the body.* New York: Norton.

Cannon, W. B. (1942). "Voodoo" death. *American Anthropologist, 44,* 169–181.

Cantor, J. R., Zillmann, D., & Bryant, J. (1975). Enhancement of experienced sexual arousal in response to erotic stimuli through misattribution of unrelated residual excitation. *Journal of Personality and Social Psychology, 32,* 69–75.

Cantor, N., & Malley, J. (1991). Life tasks, personal needs, and close relationships. In G. J. O. Fletcher & F. D. Fincham (Eds.), *Cognition in close relationships* (pp. 101–126). Hillsdale, NJ: Erlbaum.

Capellanus, A. (1960). *The art of courtly love.* (J. J. Parry, Trans.). New York: Columbia University Press. (Original work created approximately 1184)

Caporael, L. R. (1997). The evolution of truly social cognition: The core configurations model. *Personality and Social Psychology Review, 1,* 276–298.

Capra, F. (1982). *The turning point: Science, society, and the rising culture.* New York: Simon and Schuster.

Capra, F. (1996). *The web of life: A new scientific understanding of living systems.* New York: Anchor Doubleday.

Carnegie, D. (1936). *How to win friends and influence people.* New York: Simon & Schuster.

Carroll, J. L., Volk, K. D., & Hyde, J. S. (1985). Differences between males and females in motives for engaging in sexual intercourse. *Archives of Sexual Behavior, 14,* 131–139.

Carstensen, L. L. (1991). Socioemotional selectivity theory: Social activity in life-span context. *Annual Review of Gerontology and Geriatrics, 11,* 195–217.

Carver, C. S. (2001). Affect and the functional bases of behavior: On the dimensional structure of affective experience. *Personality and Social Psychology Review, 5,* 345–356.

Carver, C. S., Ganellen, R. J., Froming, W. J., & Chambers, W. (1983). Modeling: An analysis in terms of category accessibility. *Journal of Experimental Social Psychology, 19,* 403–421.

Carver, C. S., & White, T. L. (1994). Behavioral inhibition, behavioral activation, and affective responses to impending reward and punishment: The BIS/BAS scales. *Journal of Personality and Social Psychology, 67,* 319–333.

Case, R., Moss, A., Case, N., McDermot, M., & Eberly, S. (1992). Living alone after myocardial infarction: Impact on prognosis. *Journal of the American Medical Association, 267,* 515–519.

Caspi, A., Bem, D. J., & Elder, G., Jr. (1989). Continuities and consequences of interactional styles across the life course. *Journal of Personality, 57,* 375–406.

Caspi, A., McClay, J., Moffitt, T. E., Mill, J., Martin, J., Craig, I. W., Taylor, A., & Poulton, R. (2002). Role of genotype in the cycle of violence in maltreated children. *Science, 297*(5582), 851–854.

Cassidy, J., & Shaver, P. R. (1999). *Handbook of attachment: Theory, research, and clinical applications.* New York: Guilford Press.

Castellan, N. J., Jr. (1979). The analysis of behavior sequences. In R. B. Cairns (Ed.), *The analysis of social interactions: Methods, issues, and illustrations* (pp. 81–116). Hillsdale, NJ: Erlbaum.

Castro-Martin, T., & Bumpass, L. L. (1989). Recent trends and differentials in marital disruption. *Demography, 25,* 37–51.

Cate, R. M., Huston, T. L., & Nesselroade, J. R. (1986). Premarital relationships: Toward the identification of alternative pathways to marriage. *Journal of Social and Clinical Psychology, 4,* 3–22.

Cate, R. M., Levin, L. A., & Richmond, L. S. (2002). Premarital relationship stability: A review of recent research. *Journal of Social and Personal Relationships, 19,* 261–284.

Cate, R. M., & Lloyd, S. A. (1992). *Courtship.* Newbury Park, CA: Sage.

Cate, R. M., Long, E., Angera, J. J., & Draper, K. K. (1993). Sexual intercourse and relationship development. *Family Relations, 42,* 158–164.

Catell, R. B., & Nesselroade, J. R. (1967). Likeness and completeness theories examined by sixteen personality factor measures on stably and unstably married couples. *Journal of Personality and Social Psychology, 7,* 351–361.

Caughlin, J. P., & Huston, T. L. (2002). A contextual analysis of the association between demand/withdraw and marital satisfaction. *Personal Relationships, 9,* 95–119.

Caughlin, J. P., & Vangelisti, A. L. (2000). An individual difference explanation of why married couples engage in the demand/withdraw pattern of conflict. *Journal of Social and Personal Relationships, 17,* 523–551.

Census Bureau says half of U.S. youngsters live in "nuclear families." (1994, August 30). *Minneapolis Star Tribune,* p. B1.

Cernoch, J. M., & Porter, R. H. (1985). Recognition of maternal axillary odors in infants. *Child Development, 56,* 1593–1598.

Charny, I. W., & Parnass, S. (1995). The impact of extramarital relationships on the continuation of marriages. *Journal of Sex & Marital Therapy, 21,* 100–115.

Chartrand, T. L., & Bargh, J. A. (1999). The chameleon effect: The perception–behavior link and social interaction. *Journal of Personality and Social Psychology, 76,* 893–910.

Cherlin, A. J. (1992). *Marriage, divorce, remarriage* (Rev. ed.). Cambridge, MA: Harvard University Press.

Cherniak, C. (1990). The bounded brain: Toward quantitative neuroanatomy. *Journal of Cognitive Neuroscience, 2,* 58–68.

China drafts measure declaring women are equal to men. (1992, March 28). *Saint Paul Pioneer Press,* p. 9A.

China's crackdown on births: A stunning, and harsh, success. (1993, April 25). *The New York Times,* p. 1.

Choi, K. H., & Catania, J. A. (1996). Changes in multiple sexual partnerships, HIV testing, and condom use among heterosexuals 18 to 49 years of age, 1990 and 1992. *American Journal of Public Health, 86,* 554–556.

Choi, K. H., Catania, J. A., & Dolcini, M. M. (1994). Extramarital sex and HIV risk behavior among U.S. adults: Results from the National AIDS Behavioral Survey. *American Journal of Public Health, 84,* 2003–2007.

Chomsky, N. (1965). *Aspects of the theory of syntax.* Cambridge, MA: MIT Press.

Christensen, A. (1988). Dysfunctional interaction patterns in couples. In P. Noller & M. A. Fitzpatrick (Eds.), *Perspectives on marital interaction* (pp. 31–52). Philadelphia: Multilingual Matters.

Christensen, A. (2002). Intervention. In H. H. Kelley, E. Berscheid, A. Christensen, J. H. Harvey, T. L. Huston, G. Levinger, E. McClintock, L. A. Peplau, & D. R. Peterson (Eds.), *Close relationships* (pp. 397–448). Clinton Corners, NY: Percheron Press. (Original work published 1983)

Christensen, A., & Hazzard, A. (1983). Reactive effects during naturalistic observation of families. *Behavioral Assessment, 5,* 349–354.

Christensen, A., & Heavey, C. L. (1990). Gender, power, and marital conflict. *Journal of Personality and Social Psychology, 59,* 73–81.

Christensen, A., & Heavey, C. L. (1999). Interventions for couples. *Annual Review of Psychology, 50,* 165–190.

Christensen, A., & Jacobson, N. S. (2000). *Reconcilable differences.* New York: Guilford Press.

Christensen, A., & Nies, D. C. (1980). The Spouse Observation Checklist: Empirical analysis and critique. *American Journal of Family Therapy, 8,* 69–79.

Christensen, A., & Pasch, L. (1993). The sequence of marital conflict: An analysis of seven phases of marital conflict in distressed and nondistressed couples. *Clinical Psychology Review, 13,* 3–14.

Christensen, A., & Shenk, J. L. (1991). Communication, conflict, and psychological distance in nondistressed, clinic, and divorcing couples. *Journal of Consulting and Clinical Psychology, 59,* 458–463.

Christensen, A., Sullaway, M., & King, C. (1983). Systematic error in behavioral reports of dyadic interaction: Egocentric bias and content effects. *Behavioral Assessment, 5,* 131–142.

Christensen, A., & Walczynski, P. T. (1997). Conflict and satisfaction in couples. In R. J. Sternberg & M. Hojjat (Eds.), *Satisfaction in close relationships* (pp. 249–274). New York: Guilford Press.

Christopher, F. S. (2001). *To dance the dance: A symbolic interactional exploration of premarital sexuality.* Mahwah, NJ: Erlbaum.

Christopher, F. S., & Cate, R. M. (1984). Factors involved in premarital sexual decision-making. *Journal of Sex Research, 20,* 363–376.

Christopher, F. S., & Cate, R. M. (1985). Premarital sexual pathways and relationship development. *Journal of Social and Personal Relationships, 2,* 271–288.

Christopher, F. S., & Frandsen, M. M. (1990). Strategies of influence in sex and dating. *Journal of Social and Personal Relationships, 7,* 89–105.

Christopher, F. S., & Lloyd, S. A. (2000). Physical and sexual aggression in relationships. In C. Hendrick & S. S. Hendrick (Eds.), *Close relationships: A sourcebook* (pp. 331–343). Thousand Oaks, CA: Sage.

Christopher, F. S., & Sprecher, S. (2000). Sexuality in marriage, family, and other relationships: A decade review. *Journal of Marriage and the Family, 62,* 999–1017.

Churchill, W. (1996). *From a native son: Selected essays on indigenism, 1985–1995.* Boston: South End Press.

Cizek, G. J. (1995). Crunchy granola and the hegemony of the narrative. *Educational Researcher, 24*(2), 26–28.

Clark, C. L., Shaver, P. R., & Abrahams, M. F. (1999). Strategic behaviors in romantic relationship initiation. *Personality and Social Psychology Bulletin, 25,* 707–720.

Clark, L. A., Kochanska, G., & Ready, R. (2000). Mothers' personality and its interaction with child temperament as predictors of parenting behavior. *Journal of Personality and Social Psychology, 79,* 274–285.

Clark, M. S., & Brissette, I. (2000). Relationship beliefs and emotion: Reciprocal effects. In N. H. Fridja, A. S. R. Manstead, & S. Bem (Eds.), *Emotions and beliefs: How feelings influence thoughts* (pp. 212–240). Cambridge, UK: Cambridge University Press.

Clark, M. S., & Chrisman, K. (1994). Resource allocation in intimate relationships: Trying to make sense of a confusing literature. In M. J. Lerner & G. Mikula (Eds.), *Entitlement and the affectional bond: Justice in close relationships* (pp. 65–88). New York: Plenum Press.

Clark, M. S., Fitness, J., & Brissette, I. (2001). Understanding people's perceptions of relationships is crucial to understanding their emotional lives. In G. J. O. Fletcher & M. S. Clark (Eds.), *Blackwell handbook of social psychology: Interpersonal processes* (pp. 253–279). Malden, MA: Blackwell.

Clark, M. S., & Isen, A. M. (1982). Towards understanding the relationship between feeling states and social behavior. In A. H. Hastorf & A. M. Isen (Eds.), *Cognitive social psychology* (pp. 73–108). New York: Elsevier.

Clark, M. S., & Mills, J. (1979). Interpersonal attraction in exchange and communal relationships. *Journal of Personality and Social Psychology, 37*, 12–24.

Clark, M. S., & Mills, J. (1993). The difference between communal and exchange relationships: What it is and is not. *Personality and Social Psychology Bulletin, 19*, 684–691.

Clark, M. S., & Mills, J. (2001). Viewing close romantic relationships as communal relationships: Implications for maintenance and enhancement. In J. Harvey & A. Wenzel (Eds.), *Close romantic relationships: Maintenance and enhancement* (pp. 13–26). Mahwah, NJ: Erlbaum.

Clark, M. S., Ouellette, R., Powell, M., & Milberg, S. (1987). Recipient's mood, relationship type, and helping. *Journal of Personality and Social Psychology, 53*, 94–103.

Clark, M. S., Pataki, S. P., & Carver, V. (1996). Some thoughts and findings on self-presentation of emotion in relationships. In G. J. O. Fletcher & J. Fitness (Eds.), *Knowledge structures in close relationships: A social psychological approach* (pp. 247–274). Mahwah, NJ: Erlbaum.

Clark, M. S., & Reis, H. T. (1988). Interpersonal processes in close relationships. *Annual Review of Psychology, 39*, 609–672.

Clark, M. S., & Taraban, C. B. (1991). Reactions to and willingness to express emotion in two types of relationships. *Journal of Experimental Social Psychology, 27*, 324–336.

Clark, M. S., & Williamson, G. M. (1989). Moods and social judgements. In H. Wagner & A. Manstead (Eds.), *Handbook of Social Psychophysiology* (pp. 347–370). New York: Wiley.

Clarkberg, M., Stolzenberg, R. M., & Waite, L. J. (1995). Attitudes, values, and entrance into cohabitational versus marital unions. *Social Forces, 74*, 609–632.

Clarke, S. C., & Wilson, B. F. (1994). The relative stability of remarriages: A cohort approach using vital statistics. *Family Relations, 43*, 305–310.

Clogg, C. C., & Haritou, A. (1997). The regression method of causal inference and a dilemma confronting this method. In V. R. McKim & S. P. Turner (Eds.), *Causality in crisis? Statistical methods and the search for causal knowledge in the social sciences* (pp. 83–112). Notre Dame, IN: University of Notre Dame Press.

Clore, G. L., Wyer, R. S., Jr., Dienes, B., Gasper, K. Gohm, C., & Isbell, L. (2001). Affective feelings as feedback: Some cognitive consequences. In L. L. Martin & G. L. Clore (Eds.), *Theories of mood and cognition* (pp. 27–62). Mahwah, NJ: Erlbaum.

Cobb, S. (1976). Social support as a moderator of life stress. *Psychosomatic Medicine, 38*, 300–314.

Coe, C. L., & Lubach, G. R. (2001). Social context and other psychological influences on the development of immunity. In C. D. Ryff & B. H. Singer (Eds.), *Emotion, social relationships, and health* (pp. 243–261). Oxford, UK: Oxford University Press.

Cohabitation remains illegal in N.D. (2003, April 4). *Minneapolis Star Tribune*, p. A12.

Cohan, C. L., & Kleinbaum, S. (2002). Toward a greater understanding of the cohabitation effect: Premarital cohabitation and marital communication. *Journal of Marriage and Family, 64*, 180–192.

Cohen, G. (1989). *Memory in the real world*. Hove, UK: Erlbaum.

Cohen, P. N., & Bianchi, S. M. (1999). Marriage, children, and women's employment: What do we know? *Monthly Labor Review, 122*(12), 22–31.

Cohen, S., Doyle, W. J., Skoner, D. P., Rabin, B. S., & Gwaltney, J. M., Jr. (1997). Social ties and susceptibility to the common cold. *Journal of the American Medical Association, 277*, 1940–1944.

Cohen, S., Frank, E., Doyle, W. J., Skoner, D. P., Rabin, B. S., & Gwaltney, J. M., Jr. (1998). Types of stressors that increase susceptibility to the common cold in healthy adults. *Health Psychology, 17*, 214–223.

Cohen, S., & Herbert, T. B. (1996). Health psychology: Psychological factors and physical disease from the perspective of human psychoimmunology. *Annual Review of Psychology, 47*, 113–142.

Cohen, S., Sherrod, D. R., & Clark, M. S. (1986). Social skills and the stress-protective role of social support. *Journal of Personality and Social Psychology, 50*, 963–973.

Cohen, S., & Wills, T. A. (1985). Stress, social support, and the buffering hypothesis. *Psychological Bulletin, 98*, 310–357.

Cohn, B. A. (1994). In search of human skin pheromones. *Archives of Dermatology, 130*, 1048–1051.

Coleman, F. L. (1997). Stalking behavior and the cycle of domestic violence. *Journal of Interpersonal Violence, 12*, 420–432.

Coleman, S. (1977). A developmental stage hypothesis for nonmarital dyadic relationships. *Journal of Marriage and Family Counseling, 3*, 71–76.

Collins, B. E. (2001). Two treks through the same trauma, with and without social support. *Journal of Social and Clinical Psychology, 20*, 341–353.

Collins, N. L., & Feeney, B. C. (2000). A safe haven: An attachment theory perspective on support seeking and caregiving in intimate relationships. *Journal of Personality and Social Psychology, 78*, 1053–1073.

Collins, N. L., & Miller, L. C. (1994). Self-disclosure and liking: A meta-analytical review. *Psychological Bulletin, 116*, 457–475.

Collins, N. L., & Read, S. J. (1990). Adult attachment, working models, and relationship quality in dating couples. *Journal of Personality and Social Psychology, 58*, 644–663.

Collins, N. L., & Read, S. J. (1994). Cognitive representations of attachment: The content and function of working models. In K. Bartholomew & D. Perlman (Eds.), *Advances in personal relationships: Vol. 5. Attachment processes in adulthood* (pp. 53–90). London: Jessica Kingsley.

Collins, W. A. (2002, April). *More than myth: The developmental significance of romantic relationships during adolescence.* Presidential address presented at the Biennial Meeting of the Society for Research on Adolescence, New Orleans, LA. (Available from author)

Collins, W. A., & Laursen, B. (2000). Adolescent relationships: The art of fugue. In C. Hendrick & S. S. Hendrick (Eds.), *Close relationships: A sourcebook* (pp. 59–69). Thousand Oaks, CA: Sage.

Collins, W. A., Maccoby, E. E., Steinberg, L., Hetherington, E. M., & Bornstein, M. H. (2000). Contemporary research on parenting: The case for nature *and* nurture. *American Psychologist, 55,* 218–232.

Condon, J. W., & Crano, W. D. (1988). Inferred evaluation and the relation between attitude similarity and interpersonal attraction. *Journal of Personality and Social Psychology, 54,* 789–797.

Conger, R. D., & Conger, K. J. (2002). Resilience in Midwestern families: Selected findings from the first decade of a prospective, longitudinal study. *Journal of Marriage and Family, 64,* 361–373.

Conger, R. D., Cui, M., Bryant, C. M., & Elder, G. H. (2001). Competence in early adult romantic relationships: A developmental perspective on family influences. *Prevention & Treatment, 4,* 1–24.

Conger, R. D., Elder, G. H., Jr., Lorenz, F. O., Conger, K. J., Simons, R. L., Whitbeck, L. B., Huck, S., & Melby, J. N. (1990). Linking economic hardship to marital quality and instability. *Journal of Marriage and the Family, 52,* 643–656.

Constantine, J. A., & Bahr, S. J. (1980). Locus of control and marital stability: A longitudinal study. *Journal of Divorce, 4,* 10–22.

Cook, W. L. (2000). Understanding attachment security in family context. *Journal of Personality and Social Psychology, 78,* 285–294.

Coontz, S. (1992). *The way we never were: American families and the nostalgia trap.* New York: Basic Books.

Coontz, S. (1997). *The way we really are: Coming to terms with America's changing families.* New York: Basic Books.

Coren, S. (1998). *Why we love the dogs we do.* New York: Free Press.

Coriell, M., & Cohen, S. (1995). Concordance in the face of a stressful event: When do members of a dyad agree that one person supported the other? *Journal of Personality and Social Psychology, 69,* 289–299.

Cosmides, L. (1989). The logic of social exchange: Has natural selection shaped how humans reason? Studies with the Wason selection task. *Cognition, 31,* 187–276.

Cosmides, L., & Tooby, J. (1989). Evolutionary psychology and the generation of culture, Part II. Case study: A computational theory of social exchange. *Ethology and Sociobiology, 10,* 51–97.

Cosmides, L., & Tooby, J. (1992). Cognitive adaptations for social exchange. In J. H. Barkow, L. Cosmides, and J. Tooby (Eds.), *The adapted mind: Evolutionary psychology and the generation of culture* (pp. 163–228). New York: Oxford University Press.

Cosmides, L., & Tooby, J. (1997). *Evolutionary psychology: A primer.* Retrieved September 1, 2003 from the University of California, Santa Barbara, Center for Evolutionary Psychology Web site: http://www.psych.ucsb.edu/research/cep/primer.html

Costa, P. T., & McCrae, R. R. (1980). Influence of extraversion and neuroticism on subjective well-being: Happy and unhappy people. *Journal of Personality and Social Psychology, 38,* 668–678.

Coyne, J. C., & Downey, G. (1991). Social factors and psychopathology: Stress, social support, and coping processes. *Annual Review of Psychology, 42,* 401–425.

Cozzarelli, C., Hoekstra, S. J., & Bylsma, W. H. (2000). General versus specific mental models of attachment: Are they associated with different outcomes? *Personality and Social Psychology Bulletin, 26,* 605–618.

Craig, J.-A., Koestner, R., & Zuroff, D. C. (1994). Implicit and self-attributed intimacy motivation. *Journal of Social and Personal Relationships, 11,* 491–507.

Cramer, D. (1993). Personality and marital dissolution. *Personality and Individual Differences, 14,* 605–607.

Critelli, J. W., Myers, E. J., & Loos, V. E. (1986). The components of love: Romantic attraction and sex role orientation. *Journal of Personality, 54,* 354–370.

Cronbach, L., & Meehl, P. (1955). Construct validity in psychological tests. *Psychological Bulletin, 52,* 281–302.

Crosby, J. F. (Ed.). (1989). *When one wants out and the other doesn't: Doing therapy with polarized couples.* New York: Brunner/Mazel.

Cross, S. E., & Madson, L. (1997). Models of the self: Self-construals and gender. *Psychological Bulletin, 122,* 5–37.

Crowell, N. A., & Burgess, A. (Eds.). (1996). *Understanding violence against women.* Washington, DC: National Academy Press.

Csikszentmihalyi, M., Larson, R., & Prescott, S. (1977). The ecology of adolescent activity and experience. *Journal of Youth and Adolescence, 6,* 281–294.

Cuber, J. F., & Harroff, P. B. (1965). *The significant Americans: A study of sexual behavior among the affluent.* New York: Appleton-Century.

Cunningham, J. D., & Antill, J. K. (1994). Cohabitation and marriage: Retrospective and predictive comparisons. *Journal of Social and Personal Relationships, 11,* 77–93.

Cunningham, M. R. (1986). Measuring the physical in physical attractiveness: Quasi-experiments on the sociobiology of female facial beauty. *Journal of Personality and Social Psychology, 50,* 925–935.

Cunningham, M. R., & Barbee, A. P. (2000). Social support. In C. Hendrick & S. S. Hendrick (Eds.), *Close relationships: A sourcebook* (pp. 273–285). Thousand Oaks, CA: Sage.

Cunningham, M. R., Barbee, A. P., & Druen, P. B. (1996). Social allergens and the reactions that they produce: Escalation of annoyance and disgust in love and work. In R. M. Kowalski (Ed.), *Aversive interpersonal behaviors* (pp. 189–214). New York: Plenum Press.

Cunningham, M. R., Barbee, A. P., & Pike, C. L. (1990). What do women want? Facialmetric assessment of multiple motives in the perception of male facial physical attractiveness. *Journal of Personality and Social Psychology, 59*, 61–72.

Cunningham, M. R., Druen, P. B., & Barbee, A. P. (1997). Angels, mentors, and friends: Trade-offs among evolutionary, social, and individual variables in physical appearance. In J. A. Simpson & D. T. Kenrick (Eds.), *Evolutionary social psychology* (pp. 109–140). Mahwah, NJ: Erlbaum.

Cunningham, M. R., Roberts, A. R., Barbee, A. P., Druen, P. B., & Wu, C. (1995). "Their ideas of beauty are, on the whole, the same as ours": Consistency and variability in the cross-cultural perception of female physical attractiveness. *Journal of Personality and Social Psychology, 68*, 261–279.

Cupach, W. R., & Metts, S. (1991). Sexuality and communication in close relationships. In K. McKinney & S. Sprecher (Eds.), *Sexuality in close relationships* (pp. 93–110). Hillsdale, NJ: Erlbaum.

Cupach, W. R., & Spitzberg, B. H. (1997, February). *The incidence and perceived severity of obsessive relational intrusion behaviors*. Paper presented at the Western States Communication Association convention, Monterey, CA.

Cupach, W. R., & Spitzberg, B. H. (1998). Obsessive relational intrusion and stalking. In B. H. Spitzberg & W. R. Cupach (Eds.), *The dark side of close relationships* (pp. 233–263). Mahwah, NJ: Erlbaum.

Cutler, W. B., Preti, G., Huggins, G. R., Erickson, B., & Garcia, C. R. (1985). Sexual behavior frequency and biphasic ovulatory type menstrual cycles. *Physiology and Behavior, 34*, 805–810.

Cutrona, C. E. (1990). Stress and social support: In search of optimal matching. *Journal of Social and Clinical Psychology, 9*, 3–14.

Cutrona, C. E. (1996). *Social support in couples: Marriage as a resource in times of stress*. Thousand Oaks, CA: Sage.

Cutrona, C. E., Hessling, R. M., & Suhr, J. A. (1997). The influence of husband and wife personality on marital social support interactions. *Personal Relationships, 4*, 379–393.

Cutrona, C. E., & Suhr, J. A. (1994). Social support communication in the context of marriage: An analysis of couples' supportive interactions. In B. R. Burleson, T. L. Albrecht, & I. G. Sarason (Eds.), *Communication of social support: Messages, interactions, relationships, and community* (pp. 113–135). Thousand Oaks, CA: Sage.

Cutter, K. (2003, February). The actress. *W, 120*, 123.

Dabbs, J. M., Jr., Karpas, A. E., Dyomina, N., Juechter, J., & Roberts, A. (2002). Experimental raising or lowering of testosterone level affects mood in normal men and women. *Social Behavior and Personality, 30*, 795–806.

Daigen, V., & Holmes, J. G. (2000). Don't interrupt! A good rule for marriage? *Personal Relationships, 7*, 185–201.

Dainton, M. (2000). Maintenance behaviors, expectations for maintenance, and satisfaction: Linking comparison levels to relational maintenance strategies. *Journal of Social and Personal Relationships, 17*, 827–842.

Daly, M., Salmon, C., & Wilson, M. (1997). Kinship: The conceptual hole in psychological studies of social cognition and close relationships. In J. Simpson & D. Kenrick (Eds.), *Evolutionary social psychology* (pp. 265–296). Mahwah, NJ: Erlbaum.

Daly, M., & Wilson, M. (1983). *Sex, evolution, and behavior* (2nd ed.). Belmont, CA: Wadsworth.

Damasio, A. R. (1994). *Descartes' error: Emotion, reason, and the human brain*. New York: Avon/Putnam Books.

Darley, J. M., & Batson, C. D. (1973). From Jerusalem to Jericho: A study of situational and dispositional variables in helping behavior. *Journal of Personality and Social Psychology, 27*, 100–108.

Darley, J. M., & Berscheid, E. (1967). Increased liking as a result of the anticipation of personal contact. *Human Relations, 20*, 29–40.

Darley, J. M., Fleming, J. H., Hilton, J. L., & Swann, W. B. (1988). Dispelling negative expectancies: The impact of interaction goals and target characteristics on the expectancy confirmation process. *Journal of Experimental Social Psychology, 24*, 19–36.

Darwin, C. (1859). *On the origin of the species by means of natural selection, or, preservation of favoured races in the struggle for life*. London: J. Murray.

Darwin, C. (1981). *The descent of man, and selection in relation to sex*. London: J. Murray (Original work published 1871)

Darwin, C. (1872/1899). *The expression of the emotions in man and animals*. London: Appleton. (Authorized 1899 edition, New York: Appleton)

Darwin, C. (1952). *The origin of the species by means of natural selection. The descent of man and selection in relation to sex*. In *Great Books of the Western World: Vol. 49. Darwin*. Chicago: Encyclopedia Britannica. (Original work published 1871)

Davidson, R. J. (1998). Anterior electrophysiological asymmetries, emotion and depression: Conceptual and methodological conundrums. *Psychophysiology, 35*, 607–614.

Davidson, R. J., Jackson, D. C., & Kalin, N. H. (2000). Emotion, plasticity, context, and regulation: Perspectives from affective neuroscience. *Psychological Bulletin, 126*, 890–909.

Davila, J., & Bradbury, T. N. (2001). Attachment insecurity and the distinction between unhappy spouses who do and do not divorce. *Journal of Family Psychology, 15*, 371–393.

Davis, D. (1982). Determinants of responsiveness in dyadic interaction. In W. Ickes & E. S. Knowles (Eds.), *Personality, roles, and social behavior* (pp. 85–139). New York: Springer-Verlag.

Davis, D., & Perkowitz, W. T. (1979). Consequences of responsiveness in dyadic interaction: Effects of probability of response and proportion of content-related responses on interpersonal attraction. *Journal of Personality and Social Psychology, 37*, 534–551.

Davis, J. A., & Smith, T. (1991). *General social surveys, 1972–1991*. Storrs, CT: University of Connecticut, Roper Center for Public Opinion Research.

Davis, J. A., & Smith, T. W. (1994). *General social surveys, 1972–1994: Cumulative codebook*. Chicago: National Opinion Research Center.

Davis, J. L., & Rusbult, C. E. (2001). Attitude alignment in close relationships. *Journal of Personality and Social Psychology, 81,* 65–84.

Davis, K. E. (1999). What attachment styles and love styles add to the understanding of commitment and relationship stability. In J. M. Adams & W. H. Jones (Eds.), *Handbook of interpersonal commitment and relationship stability* (pp. 221–238). New York: Kluwer Academic/Plenum.

Davis, K. E., & Jones, E. E. (1960). Changes in interpersonal perception as a means of reducing cognitive dissonance. *Journal of Abnormal and Social Psychology, 61,* 402–410.

Davis, K. E., & Latty-Mann, H. (1987). Love styles and relationship quality: A contribution to validation. *Journal of Social and Personal Relationships, 4,* 409–428.

Davis, K. E., & Todd, M. J. (1985). Assessing friendship: Prototypes, paradigm cases and relationship description. In S. Duck & D. Perlman (Eds.), *Understanding personal relationships: An interdisciplinary approach* (pp. 17–38). London: Sage.

Davis, M. H., & Kraus, L. A. (1997). Personality and empathic accuracy. In W. Ickes (Ed.), *Empathic accuracy* (pp. 144–168). New York: Guilford Press.

Davis, S. R. (1998). The clinical use of androgens in female sexual disorders. *Journal of Sex & Marital Therapy, 24,* 153–163.

De Becker, G. (1998). *The gift of fear: Survival signals that protect us from violence.* New York: Dell Publishing.

DeCasper, A. J., & Spence, M. J. (1986). Prenatal maternal speech influences newborns' perception of speech sounds. *Infant Behavior Development, 9,* 123–150.

Deci, E. L., & Ryan, R. M. (1991). A motivational approach to self: Integration in personality. In R. Dienstbier (Ed.), *Nebraska Symposium on Motivation: Vol. 38. Perspectives on motivation* (pp. 237–288). Lincoln: University of Nebraska Press.

Delespaul, P., Reis, H. T., & deVries, P. (1996). *Comparison of event-based and experience-sampling diaries.* Unpublished manuscript. Department of Social Psychiatry, Rijksuniversiteit Limburg, The Netherlands.

DeMaris, A., & Rao, K. V. (1992). Premarital cohabitation and subsequent marital stability in the United States: A reassessment. *Journal of Marriage and the Family, 54,* 178–190.

Dennett, D. C. (1991). *Consciousness explained.* Boston: Little, Brown.

Denzin, N. K., & Lincoln, Y. S. (2000). *Handbook of qualitative research* (2nd ed.). Thousand Oaks, CA: Sage.

DeSteno, D., Petty, R. E., Wegener, D. T., & Rucker, D. D. (2000). Beyond valence in the perception of likelihood: The role of emotion specificity. *Journal of Personality and Social Psychology, 78,* 397–416.

DeSteno, D. A., & Salovey, P. (1996). Evolutionary origins of sex differences in jealousy? Questioning the "fitness" of the model. *Psychological Science, 7,* 367–372.

Deutsch, M. (1954). Field theory in social psychology. In G. Lindzey (Ed.), *The handbook of social psychology: Vol. 1. Theory and method* (1st ed., pp. 181–222). Reading, MA: Addison-Wesley.

Deutsch, M., & Solomon, L. (1959). Reactions to evaluations by others as influenced by self evaluations. *Sociometry, 22,* 93–112.

de Vaus, D. (2002). Marriage and mental health: Does marriage improve the mental health of men at the expense of women? *Family Matters, 62,* 26–45.

Devine, P. G., Sedikides, C., & Fuhrman, R. W. (1989). Goals in social information processing: The case of anticipated interaction. *Journal of Personality and Social Psychology, 56,* 680–690.

de Weerth, C., & Kalma, A. (1995). Gender differences in awareness of courtship initiation tactics. *Sex Roles, 32,* 717–734.

Dewsbury, D. A. (1981). Effects of novelty on copulatory behavior: The Coolidge effect and related phenomena. *Psychological Bulletin, 89,* 464–482.

Diamond, R., & Carey, S. (1986). Why faces are and are not special: An effect of expertise. *Journal of Experimental Psychology: General, 115,* 107–117.

Dickens, W. J., & Perlman, D. (1981). Friendship across the life cycle. In S. Duck & R. Gilmour (Eds.), *Personal relationships: Vol. 2. Developing personal relationships* (pp. 91–122). London: Academic Press.

Dickson, L. (1993). The future of marriage and family in Black America. *Journal of Black Studies, 23,* 472–491.

Diener, E. (1984). Subjective well-being. *Psychological Bulletin, 95,* 542–575.

Diener, E., Gohm, C. L., Suh, E., & Oishi, S. (2000). Similarity of the relations between marital status and subjective well-being across cultures. *Journal of Cross-Cultural Psychology, 31,* 419–436.

Diener, E., Larson, R. J., & Emmons, R. A. (1984). Person × situation interactions: Choice of situations and congruence response models. *Journal of Personality and Social Psychology, 47,* 580–592.

Diener, E., & Lucas, R. E. (1999). Personality and subjective well-being. In D. Kahneman, E. Diener, & N. Schwarz (Eds.), *Well-being: The foundations of hedonic psychology* (pp. 214–229). New York: Russell Sage.

Diener, E., Wolsic, B., & Fugita, F. (1995). Physical attractiveness and subjective well-being. *Journal of Personality and Social Psychology, 69,* 120–129.

Digman, J. M. (1990). Personality structure: Emergence of the five-factor model. *Annual Review of Psychology, 41,* 417–440.

Dindia, K. (2000). Relational maintenance. In C. Hendrick & S. S. Hendrick (Eds.), *Close relationships: A sourcebook* (pp. 287–299). Thousand Oaks, CA: Sage.

Dindia, K., & Allen, M. (1992). Sex differences in self-disclosure: A meta-analysis. *Psychological Bulletin, 112,* 106–124.

Dion, K. K., & Berscheid, E. (1974). Physical attractiveness and peer perception among children. *Sociometry, 37,* 1–12.

Dion, K. K., Berscheid, E., & Walster [Hatfield], E. (1972). What is beautiful is good. *Journal of Personality and Social Psychology, 24,* 285–290.

Dion, K. L., & Dion, K. K. (1973). Correlates of romantic love. *Journal of Consulting and Clinical Psychology, 41,* 51–56.

DiTommaso, E., & Spinner, B. (1997). Social and emotional loneliness: A re-examination of Weiss' typology of loneliness. *Personality and Individual Difference, 22*, 417–427.

Divining the God factor: Are Americans really undergoing a spiritual revival? (2000, October 23). *U.S. News & World Report*, p. 22.

Dizard, J. (1968). *Social change in the family*. Chicago: Community of Family Study Center, University of Chicago.

Doherty, W. J. (1983). Impact of divorce on locus of control orientation in adult women: A longitudinal study. *Journal of Personality and Social Psychology, 44*, 834–840.

Doll, B. (1998, January 23). Ominous trend: Gender selection. *Minneapolis Star Tribune*, p. A21.

Dollard, J., Doob, L. W., Miller, N. E., Mowrer, O. H., & Sears, R. R. (1939). *Frustration and aggression*. New Haven, CT: Yale University Press.

Donnelly, D. A. (1993). Sexually inactive marriages. *Journal of Sex Research, 30*, 171–179.

Downey, G., Bonica, C., & Rincon, C. (1999). Rejection sensitivity and adolescent romantic relationships. In W. Furman, B. B. Brown, & C. Feiring (Eds.), *The development of romantic relationships in adolescence* (pp. 148–174). Cambridge, UK: Cambridge University Press.

Downey, G., & Feldman, S. I. (1996). Implications of rejection sensitivity for intimate relationships. *Journal of Personality and Social Psychology, 70*, 1327–1343.

Downey, G., Freitas, A. L., Michaelis, B., & Khouri, H. (1998). The self-fulfilling prophecy in close relationships: Rejection sensitivity and rejection by romantic partners. *Journal of Personality and Social Psychology, 75*, 545–560.

Downsized families. (1997, April 21). *Newsweek*, p. 13.

Drigotas, S. M., & Barta, W. (2001). The cheating heart: Scientific explorations of infidelity. *Current Directions in Psychological Science, 10*, 177–180.

Drigotas, S. M., & Rusbult, C. E. (1992). Should I stay or should I go? A dependence model of breakups. *Journal of Personality and Social Psychology, 62*, 62–87.

Dubas, J. S., & Petersen, A. C. (2003). Depression: Children and adolescents. In J. J. Ponzetti Jr. (Ed.), *International Encyclopedia of Marriage and Family* (2nd ed., Vol. 3, pp. 407–414). New York: Macmillan Reference USA.

Duck, S. (1982). A topography of relationship disengagement and dissolution. In S. Duck (Ed.), *Personal relationships: Vol. 4. Dissolving personal relationships* (pp. 1–29). London: Academic Press.

Duck, S., Pond, K., & Leatham, G. (1994). Loneliness and the evaluation of relational events. *Journal of Social and Personal Relationships, 11*, 253–276.

Dumas, J. E. (1986). Controlling for autocorrelation in social interaction analysis. *Psychological Bulletin, 100*, 125–127.

Dunham, P., Dunham, F., Tran, S., & Akhtar, N. (1991). The nonreciprocating robot: Effects on verbal discourse, social play, and social referencing at two years of age. *Child Development, 62*, 1489–1502.

Dunn, J. L. (1999). What love has to do with it: The cultural construction of emotion and sorority women's responses to forcible interaction. *Social Problems, 46*, 440–459.

Durkheim, E. (1963). *Suicide*. New York: Free Press. (Original work published 1897)

Dutton, D. G., & Aron, A. (1974). Some evidence for heightened sexual attraction under conditions of high anxiety. *Journal of Personality and Social Psychology, 30*, 510–517.

Eagly, A. H. (1987). *Sex differences in social behavior: A social-role interpretation*. Hillsdale, NJ: Erlbaum.

Eagly, A. H., Ashmore, R. D., Makhijani, M. G., & Longo, L. C. (1991). What is beautiful is good, but . . .: A meta-analytic review of research on the physical attractiveness stereotype. *Psychological Bulletin, 110*, 109–128.

Eagly, A. H., & Karau, S. J. (1991). Gender and the emergence of leaders: A meta-analysis. *Journal of Personality and Social Psychology, 60*, 685–710.

Eagly, A. H., & Steffen, V. J. (1986). Gender and aggressive behavior: A meta-analytic review of the social psychological literature. *Psychological Bulletin, 100*, 309–330.

Ebbesen, E. B., Kjos, G. L., & Konecni, V. J. (1976). Spatial ecology: Its effects on the choice of friends and enemies. *Journal of Experimental Social Psychology, 12*, 505–518.

Ebling, R., & Levenson, R. W. (2003). Who are the marital experts? *Journal of Marriage and the Family, 65*, 130–142.

Eddy, J. M., Heyman, R. E., & Weiss, R. L. (1991). An empirical evaluation of the Dyadic Adjustment Scale: Exploring the differences between marital "satisfaction" and "adjustment." *Behavioral Assessment, 13*, 199–220.

Edgar, T., & Fitzpatrick, M. A. (1990). Communicating sexual desire: Message tactics for having and avoiding intercourse. In J. P. Dillard (Ed.), *Seeking compliance: The production of interpersonal influence messages* (pp. 107–122). Scottsdale, AZ: Gorsuch Scarisbrick.

Eibl-Eibesfeldt, I. (1975). *Ethology: The biology of behavior* (2nd ed.). New York: Holt, Rinehart, & Winston.

Eibl-Eibesfeldt, I. (1989). *Human ethology*. New York: Aldine de Gruyter.

Eich, E., & Macaulay, D. (2000). Fundamental factors in mood-dependent memory. In J. P. Forgas (Ed.), *Feeling and thinking: The role of affect in social cognition* (pp. 109–130). Cambridge, UK: Cambridge University Press.

Eich, E., Macaulay, D., & Ryan, L. (1994). Mood dependent memory for events of the personal past. *Journal of Experimental Psychology: General, 123*, 201–215.

Eid, M., & Diener, E. (2001). Norms for experiencing emotions in difference cultures: Inter- and intranational differences. *Journal of Personality and Social Psychology, 81*, 869–885.

Eidelson, R. J. (1980). Interpersonal satisfaction and level of involvement: A curvilinear relationship. *Journal of Personality and Social Psychology, 39*, 460–470.

Eidelson, R. J., & Epstein, N. (1982). Cognition and relationship maladjustment: Development of a measure of dysfunctional relationship beliefs. *Journal of Consulting and Clinical Psychology, 50*, 715–720.

Eisenberg, N., & Lennon, R. (1983). Sex differences in empathy and related capacities. *Psychological Bulletin, 94*, 100–131.

Eisenberg, N., Murphy, B. C., & Shepard, S. (1997). The development of empathic accuracy. In W. Ickes (Ed.), *Empathic accuracy* (pp. 73–116). New York: Guilford Press.

Ekman, P., & Davidson, R. J. (1994a). Afterword: How is evidence of universals in antecedents of emotion explained? In P. Ekman & R. J. Davidson (Eds.), *The nature of emotion: Fundamental questions* (pp. 176–177). New York: Oxford University Press.

Ekman, P., & Davidson, R. J. (Eds.). (1994b). *The nature of emotion: Fundamental questions*. New York: Oxford University Press.

Ekman, P., & Friesen, W. V. (1978). *The Facial Action Coding System*. Palo Alto, CA: Consulting Psychologists Press.

Elbert, T., Heim, S., & Rockstroh, B. (2001). Neural plasticity and development. In C. A. Nelson & M. Luciana (Eds.), *Handbook of developmental cognitive neuroscience* (pp. 191–202). Cambridge, MA: MIT Press.

Ellis, A. (1954). *The American sexual tragedy*. New York: Twayne Publishers.

Ellis, A. (1976). Rational-emotive therapy. In V. Binder, A. Binder, & B. Rimland (Eds.), *Modern therapies* (pp. 21–34). Englewood Cliffs, NJ: Prentice-Hall.

Ellis, H. (1944). *Psychology of sex: A manual for students*. New York: Emerson Books. (Original work published 1933)

Ellis, H. (1963). *Psychology of sex: A manual for students*. New York: The New American Library of World Literature. (Original work published 1933)

Elman, J. L., Bates, E. A., Johnson, M. H., Karmiloff-Smith, A., Parisi, D., & Plunkett, K. (1999). *Rethinking innateness: A connectionist perspective on development*. Cambridge, MA: MIT Press.

Emerson, R. M., Ferris, K. O., & Gardner, C. B. (1998). On being stalked. *Social Problems, 45*, 289–314.

Endo, Y., Heine, S. J., & Lehman, D. R. (2000). Culture and positive illusions in close relationships: How my relationships are better than yours. *Personality and Social Psychology Bulletin, 26*, 1571–1586.

Engel, J. W. (1982). Marriage in the People's Republic of China. Analysis of a new law. *Journal of Marriage and the Family, 46*, 955–961.

Epstein, A. (1995, March 23). One house, one family, high court rules. *Saint Paul Pioneer Press*, p. 2A.

Epstein, J. L. (1989). The selection of friends: Changes across the grades and in different school environments. In T. J. Berndt & G. W. Ladd (Eds.), *Peer relationships in child development* (pp. 158–187). New York: Wiley.

Epstein, N. H., Baucom, D. H., & Daiuto, A. (1997). Cognitive-behavioural couples therapy. In W. K. Halford & H. J. Markman (Eds.), *Clinical handbook of marriage and couples intervention* (pp. 415–470). Chichester, UK: Wiley.

Epstein, S. (1994). Integration of the cognitive and the psychodynamic unconscious. *American Psychologist, 49*, 709–724.

Erber, R. (1991). Affective and semantic priming: Effects of mood on category accessibility and inference. *Journal of Experimental Social Psychology, 27*, 480–498.

Erber, R., & Fiske, S. T. (1984). Outcome dependency and attention to inconsistent information. *Journal of Personality and Social Psychology, 47*, 709–726.

Ernst, J. M., & Cacioppo, J. T. (1999). Lonely hearts: Psychological perspectives on loneliness. *Applied and Preventive Psychology, 8*, 1–22.

Ewart, C. K., Taylor, C. B., Kraemer, H. C., & Agras, W. S. (1991). High blood pressure and marital discord: Not being nasty matters more than being nice. *Health Psychology, 10*, 155–163.

Eysenck, H. J. (1980). Personality, marital satisfaction, and divorce. *Psychological Reports, 47*, 1235–1238.

Fairbairn, W. R. D. (1954). *An object-relations theory of the personality*. New York: Basic Books.

Family values strong, but outlook troubling. (1989, October 10). *Saint Paul Pioneer Press Dispatch*, p. 11A.

Farah, M. J. (2000). *The cognitive neuroscience of vision*. Malden, MA: Blackwell.

Farah, M. J., Wilson, K. D., Drain, M., & Tanaka, J. N. (1998). What is "special" about face perception. *Psychological Review, 105*, 482–498.

Farnsworth, J., Lund, D. A., & Pett, M. A. (1989). Management and outcomes of loss in later life: A comparison of bereavement and divorce. In D. A. Lund (Ed.), *Older bereaved spouses* (pp. 155–166). Washington, DC: Hemisphere.

Feeney, B. C., & Collins, N. L. (2003). Attachment: Couple relationships. In J. J. Ponzetti Jr. (Ed.), *International Encyclopedia of Marriage and Family* (2nd ed., Vol. 3, pp. 96–103). New York: Macmillan Reference USA.

Feeney, J., Peterson, C., & Noller, P. (1994). Equity and marital satisfaction over the family life cycle. *Personal Relationships, 1*, 83–99.

Feeney, J. A. (1995). Adult attachment and emotional control. *Personal Relationships, 2*, 143–159.

Feeney, J. A. (1999). Adult attachment, emotional control, and marital satisfaction. *Personal Relationships, 6*, 169–185.

Feeney, J. A. (2002). Attachment, marital satisfaction, and relationship satisfaction: A diary study. *Personal Relationships, 9*, 39–55.

Feeney, J. A., & Hohaus, L. (2001). Attachment and spousal caregiving. *Personal Relationships, 8*, 21–39.

Feeney, J. A., Noller, P., & Callan, V. J. (1994). Attachment style, communication and satisfaction in the early years of marriage. In K. Bartholomew & D. Perlman (Eds.), *Advances in personal relationships: Vol. 5. Attachment processes in adulthood* (pp. 269–308). London: Jessica Kingsley.

Feeney, J. A., Noller, P., & Roberts, N. (1998). Emotion, attachment, and satisfaction in close relationships. In P. A. Anderson & L. K. Guerrero (Eds.), *Handbook of communication and emotion: Research, theory, applications, and contexts* (pp. 473–505). San Diego, CA: Academic Press.

Feeney, J. A., Noller, P., & Roberts, N. (2000). Attachment and close relationships. In C. Hendrick & S. S. Hendrick (Eds.), *Close relationships: A sourcebook* (pp. 185–201). Thousand Oaks, CA: Sage.

Feeney, J. A., Noller, P., & Ward, C. (1997). Marital satisfaction and spousal interaction. In R. J. Sternberg & M. Hojjat (Eds.), *Satisfaction in close relationships* (pp. 160–189). New York: Guilford Press.

Fehr, B. (1988). Prototype analysis of the concepts of love and commitment. *Journal of Personality and Social Psychology, 55,* 557–579.

Fehr, B. (1994). Prototype-based assessment of laypeople's views of love. *Personal Relationships, 1,* 309–331.

Fehr, B. (1996). *Friendship processes.* Thousand Oaks, CA: Sage.

Fehr, B. (2000). The life cycle of friendship. In C. Hendrick & S. S. Hendrick (Eds.), *Close relationships: A sourcebook* (pp. 71–95). Thousand Oaks, CA: Sage.

Fehr, B., Baldwin, M., Collins, L., Patterson, S., & Benditt, R. (1999). Anger in close relationships: An interpersonal script analysis. *Personality and Social Psychology Bulletin, 25,* 299–312.

Fehr, B., & Russell, J. A. (1991). The concept of love viewed from a prototype perspective. *Journal of Personality and Social Psychology, 60,* 424–438.

Feingold, A. (1988). Matching for attractiveness in romantic partners and same-sex friends: A meta-analysis and theoretical critique. *Psychological Bulletin, 104,* 226–235.

Feingold, A. (1990). Gender differences in effects of physical attractiveness on romantic attraction: A comparison across five research paradigms. *Journal of Personality and Social Psychology, 59,* 981–93.

Feingold, A. (1992a). Gender differences in mate selection preferences: A test of the parental investment model. *Psychological Bulletin, 112,* 125–39.

Feingold, A. (1992b). Good-looking people are not what we think. *Psychological Bulletin, 111,* 304–341.

Feldman, P. J., Dunkel-Schetter, C., Sandman, C. A., & Wadhwa, P. D. (2000). Maternal social support predicts birth weight and fetal growth in human pregnancy. *Psychosomatic Medicine, 62,* 715–725.

Feldman, S. D. (1975). The presentation of shortness in everyday life—Height and heightism in American society: Toward a sociology of stature. In S. D. Feldman & G. W. Thielbar (Eds.), *Life styles: Diversity in American society.* Boston: Little, Brown.

Felmlee, D., Sprecher, S., & Bassin, E. (1990). The dissolution of intimate relationships: A hazard model. *Social Psychology Quarterly, 53,* 13–30.

Felmlee, D. H. (1995). Fatal attractions: Affection and disaffection in intimate relationships. *Journal of Social and Personal Relationships, 12,* 295–311.

Felmlee, D. H. (1998). Fatal attraction. In B. H. Spitzberg & W. R. Cupach (Eds.), *The dark side of close relationships* (pp. 3–31). Mahwah, NJ: Erlbaum.

Feltey, K. M., Ainslie, J. J., & Geib, A. (1991). Sexual coercion attitudes among high school students: The influence of gender and rape education. *Youth & Society, 23,* 229–250.

Fernandez-Dols, J. M., & Ruiz-Belda, M.-A. (1995). Are smiles a sign of happiness? Gold medal winners at the Olympic Games. *Journal of Personality and Social Psychology, 69,* 1113–1119.

Festinger, L. (1950). Informal social communication. *Psychological Review, 57,* 271–282.

Festinger, L. (1954). A theory of social comparison processes. *Human Relations, 7,* 117–140.

Festinger, L. (1957). *A theory of cognitive dissonance.* Stanford, CA: Stanford University Press.

Festinger, L., Schachter, S., & Back, K. (1950). *Social pressures in informal groups: A study of human factors in housing.* Stanford, CA: Stanford University Press.

Fetzer Institute/National Institute on Aging Working Group. (1999, October). *Multidimensional measurement of religiousness/spirituality for use in health research: A report of the Fetzer Institute/National Institute on Aging Working Group.* Kalamazoo, MI: Author.

Feyisetan, B., & Bankole, A. (1991). Mate selection and fertility in urban Nigeria. *Journal of Comparative Family Studies, 22,* 273–292.

Fiance hates dogs. (2000, September 14). *Star Tribune,* p. E3.

Fiedler, K. (2001). Affective influences on social information processing. In J. P. Forgas (Ed.), *The handbook of affect and social cognition* (pp. 163–185). Mahwah, NJ: Erlbaum.

Field, D. (1981). Retrospective reports by healthy intelligent elderly people of personal events of their adult lives. *International Journal of Behavior Development, 4,* 77–97.

Fielding, H. (1979). *The history of Tom Jones, a foundling* (3rd ed.). New York: The New American Library. (Original work published 1749)

Fiese, B. H., Tomcho, T. J., Douglas, M., Josephs, K., Poltrock, S., & Baker, T. (2002). A review of 50 years of research on naturally occurring family routines and rituals: Cause for celebration? *Journal of Family Psychology, 16,* 381–390.

Filsinger, E. E., Braun, J. J., Monte, W. C., & Linder, D. E. (1984). Human (*Homo sapiens*) responses to the pig (*Sus scrofa*) sex pheromone 5 alpha-androst-16-en-3-one. *Journal of Comparative Psychology, 98,* 219–222.

Filsinger, E. E., & Thoma, S. J. (1988). Behavioral antecedents of relationship stability and adjustment: A five-year longitudinal study. *Journal of Marriage and the Family, 50,* 785–795.

Fincham, F. D. (2001). Attributions in close relationships: From Balkanization to integration. In G. J. O. Fletcher & M. S. Clark (Eds.), *Blackwell handbook of social psychology: Interpersonal processes* (pp. 3–31). Malden, MA: Blackwell.

Fincham, F. D., Beach, S. R. H., & Kemp-Fincham, S. I. (1997). Marital quality: A new theoretical perspective. In R. J. Sternberg & M. Hojjat (Eds.), *Satisfaction in close relationships* (pp. 275–304). New York: Guilford Press.

Fincham, F. D., & Bradbury, T. N. (1990). Social support in marriage: The role of social cognition. *Journal of Social and Clinical Psychology, 9,* 31–42.

Fincham, F. D., & Bradbury, T. N. (1993). Marital satisfaction, depression, and attributions: A longitudinal analysis. *Journal of Personality and Social Psychology, 64,* 442–452.

Fincham, F. D., Bradbury, T. N., & Scott, C. K. (1990). Cognition in marriage. In F. D. Fincham & T. N. Bradbury (Eds.), *The psychology of marriage: Basic issues and applications* (pp. 118–149). New York: Guilford Press.

Fincham, F. D., Harold, G. T., & Gano-Phillips, S. (2000). The longitudinal association between attributions and marital satisfaction: Direction of effects and role of efficacy expectations. *Journal of Family Psychology, 14,* 267–285.

Fincham, F. D., Paleari, F. G., & Regalia, C. (2002). Forgiveness in marriage: The role of relationship quality, attributions, and empathy. *Personal Relationships, 9,* 27–37.

Finck, H. T. (1887). *Romantic love and personal beauty: Their development, causal relations, historic and national peculiarities.* New York: Macmillan.

Fine, M. A. (2000). Divorce and single parenting. In C. Hendrick & S. S. Hendrick (Eds.), *Close relationships: A sourcebook* (pp. 139–152). Thousand Oaks, CA: Sage.

Finley, C., & Corty, E. (1993). Rape on campus: The prevalence of sexual assault while enrolled in college. *Journal of College Student Development, 34,* 113–117.

Fischer, C. S. (1982). What do we mean by "friend"? An inductive study. *Social Network, 3,* 287–306.

Fischer, C. S., & Phillips, S. L. (1982). Who is alone? Social characteristics of people with small networks. In L. A. Peplau & D. Perlman (Eds.), *Loneliness: A source of current theory, research, and therapy* (pp. 21–39). New York: Wiley-Interscience.

Fischer, K. W., Shaver, P. R., & Carnochan, P. (1990). How emotions develop and how they organize development. *Cognition and Emotion, 4,* 81–127.

Fisher, H. E. (1989). Evolution of human serial pairbonding. *American Journal of Physical Anthropology, 78,* 331–354.

Fisher, H. E. (1992). *Anatomy of love: A natural history of mating, marriage, and why we stray.* New York: Fawcett Columbine.

Fisher, H. E. (1998). Lust, attraction, and attachment in mammalian reproduction. *Human Nature, 9,* 23–52.

Fisher, H. E. (2000). Lust, attraction, attachment: Biology and evolution of three primary emotion systems for mating, reproduction, and parenting. *Journal of Sex Education and Therapy, 25,* 96–104.

Fiske, A. P. (1992). The four elementary forms of sociality: Framework for a unified theory of social relations. *Psychological Review, 99,* 689–723.

Fiske, A. P., Haslam, N., & Fiske, S. T. (1991). Confusing one person with another: What errors reveal about the elementary forms of social relations. *Journal of Personality and Social Psychology, 60,* 656–674.

Fiske, A. P., Kitayama, S., Markus, H. R., & Nisbett, R. E. (1998). The cultural matrix of social psychology. In D. T. Gilbert, S. T. Fiske, & G. Lindzey (Eds.), *The handbook of social psychology* (4th ed., Vol. 2, pp. 915–981). Boston: McGraw-Hill.

Fiske, S. T. (1992). Thinking is for doing: Portraits of social cognition from Daguerreotype to laserphoto. *Journal of Personality and Social Psychology, 63,* 877–889.

Fiske, S. T. (1993). Controlling other people: The impact of power on stereotyping. *American Psychologist, 48,* 621–628.

Fiske, S. T., & Neuberg, S. L. (1990). A continuum of impression formation, from category-based to individuating processes: Influences of information and motivation on attention and interpretation. In M. P. Zanna (Ed.), *Advances in experimental social psychology* (Vol. 23, pp. 1–73). San Diego, CA: Academic Press.

Fiske, S. T., & Taylor, S. E. (1991). *Social cognition* (2nd ed.). New York: McGraw-Hill.

Fitz, D., & Gerstenzang, S. (1978). *Anger in everyday life: When, where, and with whom?* St. Louis: University of Missouri. (ERIC Document Reproduction Service No. ED160966)

Fitzpatrick, M. A. (1988). A typological approach to marital interaction. In P. Noller & M. A. Fitzpatrick (Eds.), *Perspectives on marital interaction* (pp. 98–120). Clevedon, UK: Multilingual Matters Ltd.

Fletcher, G. J. O., & Fincham, F. D. (Eds.). (1991). *Cognition in close relationships.* Hillsdale, NJ: Erlbaum.

Fletcher, G. J. O., Fincham, F. D., Cramer, L., & Heron, N. (1987). The role of attributions in the development of dating relationships. *Journal of Personality and Social Psychology, 53,* 481–489.

Fletcher, G. J. O., & Fitness, J. (Eds.). (1996). *Knowledge structures in close relationships: A social psychological approach.* Mahwah, NJ: Erlbaum.

Fletcher, G. J. O., & Kininmonth, L. A. (1992). Measuring relationship beliefs: An individual differences scale. *Journal of Research in Personality, 26,* 371–397.

Fletcher, G. J. O., Rosanowski, J., & Fitness, J. (1994). Automatic processing in intimate contexts: The role of close-relationship beliefs. *Journal of Personality and Social Psychology, 67,* 888–897.

Fletcher, G. J. O., & Simpson, J. A. (2000). Ideal standards in close relationships: Their structure and functions. *Current Directions in Psychological Science, 9,* 102–105.

Fletcher, G. J. O., Simpson, J. A., & Thomas, G. (2000). Ideals, perceptions, and evaluations in early relationship development. *Journal of Personality and Social Psychology, 79,* 933–940.

Fletcher, G. J. O., Simpson, J. A., Thomas, G., & Giles, L. (1999). Ideals in intimate relationships. *Journal of Personality and Social Psychology, 76,* 72–89.

Fletcher, G. J. O., & Thomas, G. (1996). Close relationship lay theories: Their structure and function. In G. J. O. Fletcher & J. Fitness (Eds.), *Knowledge structures in close relationships: A social psychological approach* (pp. 3–24). Mahwah, NJ: Erlbaum.

Florian, V., Mikulincer, M., & Bucholtz, I. (1995). Effects of adult attachment style on the perception and search for social support. *Journal of Psychology, 129,* 665–676.

For better, for worse. (1999, May 10). *Newsweek* (Letters, "Mail Call"), p. 20.

Forgas, J. P. (1991). Affect and cognition in close relationships. In G. J. O. Fletcher & F. D. Fincham (Eds.), *Cognition in close relationships* (pp. 151–174). Hillsdale, NJ: Erlbaum.

Forgas, J. P. (1995). Mood and judgment: The Affect Infusion Model (AIM). *Psychological Bulletin, 117,* 39–66.

Forgas, J. P. (2000). Introduction: The role of affect in social cognition. In J. P. Forgas (Ed.), *Feeling and thinking: The role of affect in social cognition* (pp. 1–28). Cambridge, UK: Cambridge University Press.

Forgas, J. P. (2001). The Affect Infusion Model (AIM): An integrative theory of mood effects on cognition and judgments. In L. L. Martin & G. L. Clore (Eds.), *Theories of mood and cognition* (pp. 99–134). Mahwah, NJ: Erlbaum.

Forgas, J. P. (2002). Feeling and doing: Affective influences on interpersonal behavior. *Psychological Inquiry, 13*, 1–28.

Forgas, J. P., & Bower, G. H. (1987). Mood effects on person perception judgments. *Journal of Personality and Social Psychology, 53*, 53–60.

Forgas, J. P., Levinger, G., & Moylan, S. J. (1994). Feeling good and feeling close: Affective influences on the perception of intimate relationships. *Personal Relationships, 1*, 165–184.

Forman, D. R., & Kochanska, G. (2001). Viewing imitation as child responsiveness: A link between teaching and discipline domains of socialization. *Developmental Psychology, 37*, 198–206.

Forste, R., & Tanfer, K. (1996). Sexual exclusivity among dating, cohabiting, and married women. *Journal of Marriage and the Family, 58*, 33–47.

Foshee, V. A. (1996). Gender differences in adolescent dating abuse: Prevalence, types, and injuries. *Health Education Research: Theory and Practice, 11*, 275–286.

Fossey, D. (1983). *Gorillas in the mist.* Boston: Houghton Mifflin.

Fowers, B. J., Lyons, E., Montel, K. H., & Shaked, N. (2001). Positive illusions about marriage among married and single individuals. *Journal of Family Psychology, 15*, 95–109.

Fowers, B. J., & Olson, D. H. (1986). Predicting marital success with PREPARE: A predictive validity study. *Journal of Marital and Family Therapy, 12*, 403–413.

Fowers, B. J., Veingrad, M. R., & Dominicis, C. (2002). The unbearable lightness of positive illusions: Engaged individuals' explanation of unrealistically positive relationship perceptions. *Journal of Marriage and Family, 64*, 450–460.

Frank, R. (2000, October 25). When pets are killed, some owners seek redress in courts. *Minneapolis Star Tribune*, p. E3.

Frayser, S. G. (1989). Sexual and reproductive relationships: Cross-cultural evidence and biosocial implications. *Medical Anthropology, 11*, 385–407.

Frazier, P., Arikian, N., Benson, S., Losoff, A., & Maurer, S. (1996). Desire for marriage and life satisfaction among unmarried heterosexual adults. *Journal of Social and Personal Relationships, 13*, 225–239.

Frazier, P., Conlon, A., & Glaser, T. (2001). Positive and negative life changes following sexual assault. *Journal of Consulting and Clinical Psychology, 69*, 1048–1055.

Fredrickson, B. L., & Carstensen, L. L. (1990). Choosing social partners: How old age and anticipated endings make people more selective. *Psychology and Aging, 5*, 335–347.

Freedman, D. A. (1997). From association to causation via regression. In V. R. McKim & S. P. Turner (Eds.), *Causality in crisis: Statistical methods and the search for causal knowledge in the social sciences* (pp. 113–161). Notre Dame, IN: University of Notre Dame Press.

Freedman, J. (1978). *Happy people: What happiness is, who has it, and why.* New York: Harcourt, Brace, Jovanovich.

Fremouw, W. J., Westrup, D., & Pennypacker, J. (1997). Stalking on campus: The prevalence and strategies for coping with stalking. *Journal of Forensic Sciences, 42*, 664–667.

Freud, S. (1912). [*Recommendations for physicians on the psychoanalytic method of treatment*] (J. Riviere, Trans.). Zentralblatt, Bd. II. Reprinted in Sammlung, Vierte Folge.

Freud, S. (1963). "Civilized" sexual morality and modern nervousness. In P. Rieff (Ed.), *Sexuality and the psychology of love* (pp. 20–40). New York: Collier Books. (Original work published 1908)

Freud, S. (1963). The most prevalent form of degradation in erotic life. In P. Rieff (Ed.), *Sexuality and the psychology of love* (pp. 58–70). New York: Collier Books. (Original work published 1912)

Fridlund, A. J. (1994). *Human facial expression: An evolutionary view.* San Diego, CA: Academic Press.

Friedmann, E., & Thomas, S. A. (1995). Pet ownership, social support, and one-year survival after acute myocardial infarction in the Cardiac Arrhythmia Suppression Trial (CAST). *American Journal of Cardiology, 76*, 1213–1217.

Fritz, H. L., & Helgeson, V. S. (1998). Distinctions of unmitigated communion from communion: Self-neglect and overinvolvement with others. *Journal of Personality and Social Psychology, 75*, 121–140.

Fromm, E. (1956). *The art of loving.* New York: Harper & Row.

Furman, W., Brown, B. B., & Feiring, C. (1999). *The development of romantic relationships in adolescence.* Cambridge, UK: Cambridge University Press.

Furman, W., & Buhrmester, D. (1992). Age and sex differences in perceptions of networks of personal relationships. *Child Development, 63*, 103–115.

Furnham, A., Tan, T., & McManus, C. (1997). Waist-to-hip ratio and preferences for body shape: A replication and extension. *Personality and Individual Differences, 22*, 539–549.

Gable, S. L., & Reis, H. T. (2001). Appetitive and aversive social interaction. In J. Harvey & A. Wenzel (Eds.), *Close romantic relationships: Maintenance and enhancement* (pp. 169–194). Mahwah, NJ: Erlbaum.

Gable, S. L., Reis, H. T., & Elliot, A. (2000). Behavioral activation and inhibition in everyday life. *Journal of Personality and Social Psychology, 78*, 1135–1149.

Gable, S. L., & Shean, G. D. (2000). Perceived social competence and depression. *Journal of Social and Personal Relationships, 17*, 139–150.

Gadlin, H. (1977). Private lives and public order: A critical view of the history of intimate relations in the United States. In G. Levinger & H. L. Raush (Eds.), *Close relationships: Perspectives on the meaning of intimacy* (pp. 33–72). Amherst: University of Massachusetts Press.

Gage, M. G., & Holcombe, R. (1991). Couples' perception of stressfulness of death of the family pet. *Family Relations, 40*, 103–105.

Gage, N. L., & Cronbach, L. J. (1955). Conceptual and methodological problems in interpersonal perception. *Psychological Review, 62*, 411–422.

Gagnon, J. H., & Simon, W. (1973). *Sexual conduct: The social sources of human sexuality.* Chicago: Aldine Publishing.

Gallo, L. C., & Matthews, K. A. (2003). Understanding the association between socioeconomic status and physical health:

Do negative emotions play a role? *Psychological Bulletin, 129*, 10–51.

Gander, M., & Lin, W. (1985, April 8). Peking's war on adultery. *Newsweek*, p. 46.

Gangestad, S. W., & Simpson, J. A. (1990). Toward an evolutionary history of female sociosexual variation. *Journal of Personality, 58*, 69–96.

Garcia, S., Stinson, L., Ickes, W., Bissonnette, V., & Briggs, S. (1991). Shyness and physical attractiveness in mixed sex dyads. *Journal of Personality and Social Psychology, 61*, 35–49.

Garcia-Velasco, J., & Mondragon, M. (1991). The incidence of the vomeronasal organ in 1,000 human subjects and its possible clinical significance. *Journal of Steroid Biochemistry and Molecular Biology, 39*, 561–563.

Gardner, W. L., Pickett, C. L., & Brewer, M. B. (2000). Social exclusion and selective memory: How the need to belong influences memory for social events. *Personality and Social Psychology Bulletin, 26*, 486–496.

Garmezy, N., & Masten, A. S. (1994). Chronic adversities. In M. Rutter, L. Herzov, & E. Taylor (Eds.), *Child and adolescent psychiatry* (pp. 191–208). Oxford, UK: Blackwell Scientific.

Gauthier, I., Skudlarski, P., Gore, J. C., & Anderson, A. (2000). Expertise for cars and birds recruit brain areas involved in face recognition. *Nature Neuroscience, 3*, 191–197.

Gazzaniga, M. S., Ivry, R. B., & Mangun, G. R. (1998). *Cognitive neuroscience: The biology of the mind.* New York: Norton.

Geis, F. L. (1993). Self-fulfilling prophecies: A social psychological view of gender. In A. E. Beall & R. J. Sternberg (Eds.), *The psychology of gender* (pp. 9–54). New York: Guilford Press.

Geiss, S. K., & O'Leary, D. (1981). Therapist ratings of frequency and severity of marital problems: Implications for research. *Journal of Marital and Family Therapy, 7*, 515–520.

George, C., & Solomon, J. (1999). Attachment and caregiving: The caregiving behavioral system. In J. Cassidy & P. R. Shaver (Eds.), *Handbook of attachment: Theory, research, and clinical applications* (pp. 649–670). New York: Guilford Press.

George, L. K., Ellison, C. G., & Larson, D. B. (2002). Explaining the relationships between religious involvement and health. *Psychological Inquiry, 13*, 190–200.

Georgesen, J. C., & Harris, M. J. (2000). The balance of power: Interpersonal consequences of differential power and expectancies. *Personality and Social Psychology Bulletin, 26*, 1239–1257.

Gergen, K. J., & Gergen, M. M. (1988). Narrative and self as relationship. In L. Berkowitz (Ed.), *Advances in experimental social psychology* (Vol. 21, pp. 17–56). San Diego, CA: Academic Press.

Gergen, M. (1990). Beyond the evil empire: Horseplay and aggression. *Aggressive Behavior, 16*, 381–398.

Gerin, W., Pieper, C., Levy, R., & Pickering, T. G. (1992). Social support in social interaction: A moderator of cardiovascular reactivity. *Psychosomatic Medicine, 54*, 324–336.

Gigy, L., & Kelly, J. B. (1992). Reasons for divorce: Perspectives of divorcing men and women. *Journal of Divorce and Remarriage, 18*, 169–187.

Gilbert, D. T. (1989). Thinking lightly about others: Automatic components of the social inference process. In J. S. Uleman & J. A. Bargh (Eds.), *Unintended thought* (pp. 189–211). New York: Guilford Press.

Gilbert, D. T., & Hixon, J. G. (1991). The trouble of thinking: Activation and application of stereotypic beliefs. *Journal of Personality and Social Psychology, 60*, 509–517.

Gilbert, L. (1993). *Two careers/one family.* Newbury Park, CA: Sage.

Gilligan, C. (1982). *In a different voice: Psychological theory and women's development.* Cambridge, MA: Harvard University Press.

Ginsberg, G. P. (1988). Rules, scripts, and prototypes in personal relationships. In S. Duck (Ed.), *Handbook of personal relationships: Theory, research and interventions* (pp. 23–39). Chichester, UK: Wiley.

Ginsberg, G. P. (1991). Accounting for accounts. *Contemporary Psychology, 36*, 1082–1083.

Glass, S. P., & Wright, T. L. (1995). Reconstructing marriages after the trauma of infidelity. In W. K. Halford & H. J. Markman (Eds.), *Clinical handbook of marriage and couples intervention* (pp. 471–508). New York: Wiley.

Glenn, N. D. (1989). Duration of marriage, family composition, and marital happiness. *National Journal of Sociology, 3*, 3–24.

Glenn, N. D. (1991). The recent trend in marital success in the United States. *Journal of Marriage and the Family, 53*, 261–270.

Glenn, N. D., & McLanahan, S. (1982). Children and marital happiness: A further specification of relationships. *Journal of Marriage and the Family, 44*, 63–72.

Glenn, N. D., & Weaver, C. N. (1978). A multivariate, multi-survey study of marital happiness. *Journal of Marriage and the Family, 40*, 269–282.

Glenn, N. D., & Weaver, C. N. (1979). Attitudes toward premarital, extramarital, and homosexual relations in the U.S. in the 1970's. *The Journal of Sex Research, 15*, 108–119.

Glenn, N. D., & Weaver, C. N. (1988). The changing relationship of marital status to reported happiness. *Journal of Marriage and the Family, 50*, 317–324.

Goffman, E. (1959). *The presentation of the self in everyday life.* Garden City, NY: Doubleday Anchor Books.

Goffman, E. (1963). *Behavior in public places.* New York: Free Press.

Gold, P. E. (1992). Modulation of memory processing: Enhancement of memory in rodents and humans. In L. R. Squire & N. Butters (Eds.), *Neuropsychology of memory* (pp. 402–412). New York: Guilford Press.

Goldberg, L. R. (1993). The structure of phenotypic personality traits. *American Psychologist, 48*, 26–34.

Goldman, M. S. (1999). Expectancy operation: Cognitive-neural models and architectures. In I. Kirsch (Ed.), *How expectancies shape experience* (pp. 41–63). Washington, DC: American Psychological Association.

Goldstein, A. G., & Papageorge, J. (1980). Judgments of facial attractiveness in the absence of eye movements. *Bulletin of the Psychonomic Society, 15*, 269–270.

Goldstine, O., Larner, K., Zuckerman, S., & Goldstine, H. (1977). *The dance-away lover.* New York: Ballantine.

Gonzales, M. H., Haugen, J. A., & Manning, D. J. (1994). Victims as "narrative critics": Factors influencing rejoinders and evaluative responses to offenders' accounts. *Personality and Social Psychology Bulletin, 20,* 691–704.

Gonzalez, R., & Griffin, D. (1997). On the statistics of interdependence: Treating dyadic data with respect. In S. Duck (Ed.), *Handbook of personal relationships: Theory, research and interventions* (2nd ed., pp. 271–302). Chichester, UK: Wiley.

Goode, W. J. (1956). *Women in divorce.* New York: Free Press.

Goodman, E. (1993, August 22). Social consensus seems to be that families are formed, not born. *Saint Paul Pioneer Press,* p. 6A.

Goodman, E. S. (1973). Marriage counseling a science: Some research considerations. *Family Coordinator, 22,* 111–116.

Goodwin, R. (1999). *Personal relationships across cultures.* London: Routledge.

Goodwin, R., & Soon, A. P. Y. (1994). Self-monitoring and relationship adjustment: A cross-cultural analysis. *The Journal of Social Psychology, 134,* 35–39.

Gordon, H. S., & Rosenthal, G. E. (1995). Impact of marital status on outcomes in hospitalized patients. *Archives of Internal Medicine, 155,* 2465–2471.

Gordon, R. A. (1968). Issues in multiple regression. *American Journal of Sociology, 73,* 592–616.

Gordon, R. A. (1996). Impact of ingratiation on judgments and evaluations: A meta-analytic investigation. *Journal of Personality and Social Psychology, 71,* 54–70.

Gotlib, I. H., & Kasch, K. L. (2003). Depression: Adults. In J. J. Ponzetti Jr. (Ed.), *International Encyclopedia of Marriage and Family* (2nd ed., Vol. 3, pp. 401–407). New York: Macmillan Reference USA.

Gotlib, I. H., Lewinsohn, P. M., & Seeley, J. R. (1998). Consequences of depression during adolescence: Marital status and marital functioning in early adulthood. *Journal of Abnormal Psychology, 107,* 686–690.

Gottman, J. M. (1979). *Marital interaction: Experimental investigations.* New York: Academic Press.

Gottman, J. M. (1993a). The roles of conflict engagement, escalation, and avoidance in marital interaction: A longitudinal view of five types of couples. *Journal of Consulting and Clinical Psychology, 61,* 6–15.

Gottman, J. M. (1993b). Studying emotion in social interaction. In M. Lewis & J. M. Haviland (Eds.), *Handbook of emotions* (pp. 475–487). New York: Guilford Press.

Gottman, J. M. (1994). *What predicts divorce? The relationship between marital processes and marital outcomes.* Hillsdale, NJ: Erlbaum.

Gottman, J. M. (1998). Psychology and the study of marital processes. *Annual Review of Psychology, 49,* 169–197.

Gottman, J. M. (1999). *The marriage clinic: A scientifically based marital therapy.* New York: Norton.

Gottman, J. M., Coan, J., Carrère, S., & Swanson, C. (1998). Predicting marital happiness and stability from newlywed interactions. *Journal of Marriage and the Family, 60,* 5–22.

Gottman, J. M., & Levenson, R. W. (1992). Marital processes predictive of later dissolution: Behavior, physiology, and health. *Journal of Personality and Social Psychology, 63,* 221–233.

Gottman, J. M., & Levenson, R. W. (2000). The timing of divorce: Predicting when a couple will divorce over a 14-year period. *Journal of Marriage and the Family, 62,* 737–745.

Gottman, J. M., McCoy, K., Coan, J., & Collier, H. (1996). The specific affect coding system (SPAFF). In J. M. Gottman (Ed.), *What predicts divorce: The measures.* Hillsdale, NJ: Erlbaum.

Gottman, J. M., Murray, J. D., Swanson, C. C., Tyson, R., & Swanson, K. R. (2002). *The mathematics of marriage: Dynamic nonlinear models.* Cambridge, MA: MIT Press.

Gottman, J. M., & Notarius, C. I. (2000). Decade review: Observing marital interaction. *Journal of Marriage and the Family, 62,* 927–947.

Gottman, J. M., & Roy, A. K. (1990). *Sequential analysis: A guide for behavioral researchers.* Cambridge, UK: Cambridge University Press.

Gottman, J. M., Ryan, K. D., Carrère, S., & Erley, A. M. (2002). Toward a scientifically based marital therapy. In H. A. Liddle, D. A. Santisteban, R. F. Levant, & J. H. Bray (Eds.), *Family psychology: Science-based interventions* (pp. 124–174). Washington, DC: American Psychological Association.

Gouaux, C. (1971). Induced affective states and interpersonal attraction. *Journal of Personality and Social Psychology, 20,* 37–43.

Gough, H. G. (1987). *CPI, California Psychological Inventory: Administrator's guide.* Palo Alto, CA: Consulting Psychologists Press.

Gould, J. L., & Gould, C. G. (1989). *Sexual selection.* New York: Scientific American Library.

Gove, W. R., Hughes, M., & Style, C. B. (1983). Does marriage have positive effects on the psychological well-being of the individual? *Journal of Health and Social Behavior, 24,* 122–131.

Gower, D. B., & Ruparelia, B. A. (1993). Olfaction in humans with special reference to odorous 16-androstenes: Their occurrence, perception and possible social, psychological and sexual impact. *Journal of Endocrinology, 137,* 167–187.

Grabill, C. M., & Kerns, K. A. (2000). Attachment style and intimacy in friendship. *Personal Relationships, 7,* 363–378.

Graham, T., & Ickes, W. (1997). When women's intuition isn't greater than men's. In W. Ickes (Ed.), *Empathic accuracy* (pp. 117–143). New York: Guilford Press.

Grammer, K., & Thornhill, R. (1994). Human (*Homo sapiens*) facial attractiveness and sexual selection: The role of symmetry and averageness. *Journal of Comparative Psychology, 108,* 233–242.

Gray, J. (1992). *Men are from Mars, women are from Venus: A practical guide for improving communication and getting what you want in your relationships.* New York: HarperCollins.

Gray, J. A. (1987). *The psychology of fear and stress* (2nd ed.). Cambridge, UK: Cambridge University Press.

Gray, J. A. (1994). Three fundamental emotion systems. In P. Ekman & R. J. Davidson (Eds.), *The nature of emotion: Fundamental questions* (pp. 243–247). New York: Oxford University Press.

Gray, J. D., & Silver, R. C. (1990). Opposite sides of the same coin: Former spouses' divergent perspectives in coping with their divorce. *Journal of Personality and Social Psychology, 59*, 1180–1191.

Gray-Little, B., & Burks, N. (1983). Power and satisfaction in marriage: A review and critique. *Psychological Bulletin, 93*, 513–538.

Grayson, D. K. (1990). Donner party deaths: A demographic assessment. *Journal of Anthropological Research, 46*, 223–242.

Graziano, W. G., Brothen, T., & Berscheid, E. (1978). Height and attraction: Do men and women see eye-to-eye? *Journal of Personality, 46*, 128–145.

Graziano, W. G., Jensen-Campbell, L. A., Todd, M., & Finch, J. F. (1997). Interpersonal attraction from an evolutionary psychology perspective: Women's reactions to dominant and prosocial men. In J. A. Simpson & D. T. Kenrick (Eds.), *Evolutionary social psychology* (pp. 141–167). Mahwah, NJ: Erlbaum.

Greeley, A. M. (1991). *Faithful attraction: Discovering intimacy, love, and fidelity in American marriage.* New York: St. Martin's Press.

Green, L., Fein, D., Modahl, C., Feinstein, C., Waterhouse, L., & Morris, M. (2001). Oxytocin and autistic disorder: Alterations in peptide forms. *Biological Psychiatry, 50*, 609–613.

Green, L. R., Richardson, D. S., Lago, T., & Schatten-Jones, E. C. (2001). Network correlates of social and emotional loneliness in young and older adults. *Personality and Social Psychology Bulletin, 27*, 281–288.

Green, S. K., & Sandos, P. (1983). Perceptions of male and female initiators of relationships. *Sex Roles, 9*, 849–852.

Greenberg, L. S., & Johnson, S. M. (1988). *Emotionally focused therapy for couples.* New York: Guilford Press.

Greenblat, C. S. (1983). The salience of sexuality in the early years of marriage. *Journal of Marriage and the Family, 45*, 289–299.

Greenhouse, L. (2000, January 5). What is a family? Grandparents' case has wide-ranging implications. *Minneapolis Star Tribune*, p. A3. (Reprinted from *The New York Times*)

Greenough, W. T., & Black, J. E. (1992). Induction of brain structure by experience: Substrates for cognitive development. In M. R. Gunnar & C. A. Nelson (Eds.), *Minnesota Symposia on Child Psychology: Vol. 24. Developmental behavioral neuroscience* (pp. 155–200). Hillsdale, NJ: Erlbaum.

Greenough, W. T., Black, J. E., & Wallace, C. S. (1987). Experience and brain development. *Child Development, 58*, 539–559.

Griffin, D., & Gonzalez, R. (1995). Correlational analysis of dyad-level data in the exchangeable case. *Psychological Bulletin, 118*, 430–439.

Griffin, D., Murray, S., & Gonzalez, R. (1999). Difference score correlations in relationship research: A conceptual primer. *Personal Relationships, 6*, 505–518.

Griffin, D. W., & Bartholomew, K. (1994). The metaphysics of measurement: The case of adult attachment. In K. Bartholomew & D. Perlman (Eds.), *Advances in personal relationships, Vol. 5: Attachment processes in adulthood* (pp. 17–52). London: Jessica Kingsley.

Griffin, W. A. (1993). Event history analysis of marital and family interaction: A practical introduction. *Journal of Family Psychology, 6*, 211–229.

Griffitt, W. (1970). Environmental effects on interpersonal affective behavior: Ambient effective temperature and attraction. *Journal of Personality and Social Psychology, 15*, 240–244.

Griffitt, W., & Veitch, R. (1971). Hot and crowded: Influences of population density and temperature on interpersonal affective behavior. *Journal of Personality and Social Psychology, 17*, 92–98.

Grote, N. K., & Clark, M. S. (2001). Perceiving unfairness in the family: Cause or consequence of marital distress. *Journal of Personality and Social Psychology, 80*, 281–293.

Groth, T., Fehm-Wolfsdorf, G., & Hahlweg, K. (2000). Basic research on the psychobiology of intimate relationships. In K. B. Schmaling & T. G. Sher (Eds.), *The psychology of couples and illness: Theory, research, and practice* (pp. 13–42). Washington, DC: American Psychological Association.

Gubrium, J. F., & Holstein, J. A. (1990). *What is family?* Mountain View, CA: Mayfield.

Gunnar, M. R. (2000). Early adversity and the development of stress reactivity and regulation. In C. A. Nelson (Ed.), *Minnesota Symposia on Child Psychology: Vol. 31. The effects of adversity on neurobehavioral development* (pp. 163–200). Mahwah, NJ: Erlbaum.

Gunnar, M. R. (2001). Effects of early deprivation: Findings from orphanage-reared infants and children. In C. A. Nelson & M. Luciana (Eds.), *Handbook of developmental cognitive neuroscience* (pp. 617–630). Cambridge, MA: MIT Press.

Gupta, G. R. (1976). Love, arranged marriage, and the Indian social structure. *Journal of Comparative Family Studies, 7*, 75–85.

Gurung, R. A. R., Sarason, B. R., & Sarason, I. G. (1997). Personal characteristics, relationship quality, and social support perceptions and behavior in young adult romantic relationships. *Personal Relationships, 4*, 319–339.

Guttentag, M., & Secord, P. F. (1983). *Too many women? The sex ratio question.* Beverly Hills, CA: Sage.

Haas, S. M., & Stafford, L. (1998). An initial examination of maintenance behaviors in gay and lesbian relationships. *Journal of Social and Personal Relationships, 15*, 846–855.

Hagerty, B. M., & Williams, R. A. (1999). The effects of sense of belonging, social support, conflict and loneliness on depression. *Nursing Research, 48*, 215–219.

Halford, W. K., Kelly, A., & Markman, H. J. (1997). The concept of a healthy marriage. In W. K. Halford & H. J. Markman (Eds.), *Clinical handbook of marriage and couples intervention* (pp. 3–12). New York: Wiley.

Hall, H. F. (1901). *Napoleon's letters to Josephine, 1796–1812.* London: J. M. Dent.

Hallstrom, T., & Samuelsson, S. (1990). Changes in women's sexual desire in middle life: The longitudinal study of women in Gothenburg. *Archives of Sexual Behavior, 19*, 259–268.

Halvorsen, R. (1998). The ambiguity of lesbian and gay marriages: Continuity and change in the symbolic order. *Journal of Homosexuality, 35,* 207–231.

Hamermesh, D. S., & Biddle, J. E. (1994). Beauty and the labor market. *American Economic Review, 84,* 1174–1195.

Hamilton, G. (1929). *A research in marriage.* New York: Boni.

Hammond, J. R., & Fletcher, G. J. O. (1991). Attachment styles and relationship satisfaction in the development of close relationships. *New Zealand Journal of Psychology, 20,* 56–62.

Hampson, S. (1999). State of the art: Personality. *Psychologist, 12,* 284–288.

Hannan, M. T., Tuma, N. B., & Groeneveld, L. P. (1977). Income and marital events: Evidence from an income-maintenance experiment. *American Journal of Sociology, 82,* 1186–1211.

Hansson, R. O., Berry, J. O., & Berry, M. E. (1999). The bereavement experience: Continuing commitment after the loss of a loved one. In J. M. Adams & W. H. Jones (Eds.), *Handbook of interpersonal commitment and relationship stability* (pp. 281–292). New York: Kluwer Academic/Plenum.

Hansson, R. O., Stroebe, M. S., & Stroebe, W. (1988). In conclusion: Current themes in bereavement and widowhood research. *Journal of Social Issues, 44,* 207–216.

Harlow, H. F. (1958). The nature of love. *American Psychologist, 13,* 673–685.

Harlow, H. F., & Mears, C. E. (1983). Emotional sequences and consequences. In R. Plutchik & H. Hellerman (Eds.), *Emotion: Theory, research, and experience: Vol. 2. Emotions in early development* (pp. 171–197). New York: Academic Press.

Harlow, H. F., & Suomi, S. J. (1970). The nature of love—simplified. *American Psychologist, 25,* 161–168.

Harris, C. R. (2002). Sexual and romantic jealousy in heterosexual and homosexual adults. *Psychological Science, 13,* 7–12.

Harris, C. R. (2003). A review of sex differences in sexual jealousy, including self-report data, psychophysiological responses, interpersonal violence, and morbid jealousy. *Personality and Social Psychology Review, 7,* 102–128.

Harris, C. R., & Christenfeld, N. (1996). Gender, jealousy, and reason. *Psychological Science, 7,* 364–366.

Harris, J. A. (1999). Review and methodological considerations in research on testosterone and aggression. *Aggression & Violent Behavior, 4,* 273–291.

Harris, M. B. (1992). Sex and ethnic differences in past aggressive behaviors. *Journal of Family Violence, 7,* 85–102.

Harrison, A. A. (1977). Mere exposure. In L. Berkowitz (Ed.), *Advances in experimental social psychology* (Vol. 10, pp. 40–83). New York: Academic Press.

Harter, S. (1999). *The construction of self: A developmental perspective.* New York: Guilford Press.

Hartley, E. L. (1946). *Problems in prejudice.* New York: King's Crown Press.

Hartup, W. W. (1989). Social relationships and their developmental significance. *American Psychologist, 44,* 120–126.

Hartup, W. W. (1996). The company they keep: Friendships and their developmental significance. *Child Development, 67,* 1–13.

Hartup, W. W. (1999). Foreword. In W. Furman, B. B. Brown, & C. Feiring (Eds.), *The development of romantic relationships in adolescence* (pp. xi–xv). Cambridge, UK: Cambridge University Press.

Hartup, W. W., & Laursen, B. (1991). Relationships as developmental contexts. In R. Cohen & A. W. Siegel (Eds.), *Context and development* (pp. 253–279). Hillsdale, NJ: Erlbaum.

Hartup, W. W., & Laursen, B. (1999). Relationships as developmental contexts: Retrospective themes and contemporary issues. In W. A. Collins & B. Laursen (Ed.), *Minnesota Symposia on Child Psychology: Vol. 30. Relationships as developmental contexts* (pp. 13–35). Mahwah, NJ: Erlbaum.

Hartup, W. W., Laursen, B., Stewart, M. A., & Eastenson, A. (1988). Conflicts and the friendship relations of young children. *Child Development, 59,* 1590–1600.

Harvey, J. H., Agostinelli, G. & Weber, A. L. (1989). Account-making and the formation of expectations about relationships. In C. Hendrick (Ed.), *Close relationships. Review of personality and social psychology* (Vol. 10, pp. 39–62). Newbury Park, CA: Sage.

Harvey, J. H., Christensen, A., & McClintock, E. (2002). Research methods. In H. H. Kelley, E. Berscheid, A. Christensen, J. H. Harvey, T. L. Huston, G. Levinger, E. McClintock, L. A. Peplau, & D. R. Peterson (Eds.), *Close relationships* (pp. 451–485). Clinton Corners, NY: Percheron Press. (Original work published 1983)

Harvey, J. H., Flanary, R., & Morgan, M. (1986). Vivid memories of vivid loves gone by. *Journal of Social and Personal Relationships, 3,* 359–373.

Harvey, J. H., & Hansen, A. M. (2000). Loss and bereavement in close romantic relationships. In C. Hendrick & S. S. Hendrick (Eds.), *Close relationships: A sourcebook* (pp. 359–370). Thousand Oaks, CA: Sage.

Harvey, J. H., & Omarzu, J. (1997). Minding the close relationship. *Personality and Social Psychology Review, 1,* 224–240.

Harvey, J. H., Weber, A. L., & Orbuch, T. L. (1990). *Interpersonal accounts: A social psychological perspective.* Cambridge, MA: Blackwell.

Hassebrauck, M. (1997). Cognitions of relationship quality: A prototype analysis of their structure and consequence. *Personal Relationships, 4,* 163–185.

Hassebrauck, M., & Aron, A. (2001). Prototype matching in close relationships. *Personality and Social Psychology Bulletin, 27,* 1111–1122.

Hassebrauck, M., & Fehr, B. (2002). Dimensions of relationship quality. *Personal Relationships, 9,* 253–270.

Hassin, R., & Trope, Y. (2000). Facing faces: Studies on the cognitive aspects of physiognomy. *Journal of Personality and Social Psychology, 78,* 837–852.

Hassin, R. R., Bargh, J. A., & Uleman, J. S. (2002). Spontaneous causal inferences. *Journal of Experimental Social Psychology, 38,* 515–523.

Hastie, R., & Kumar, P. A. (1979). Person memory: Personality traits as organizing principles in memory for behavior. *Journal of Personality and Social Psychology, 37,* 25–38.

Hatfield, E. (1988). Passionate and companionate love. In R. J. Sternberg & M. L. Barnes (Eds.), *The psychology of love* (pp. 191–217). New Haven, CT: Yale University Press.

Hatfield, E., Cacioppo, J. T., & Rapson, R. L. (1994). *Emotional contagion*. Cambridge, UK: Cambridge University Press.

Hatfield, E., & Rapson, R. L. (1987). Passionate love: New directions in research. In W. H. Jones & D. Perlman (Eds.), *Advances in personal relationships* (Vol. 1, pp. 109–139). London: Jessica Kingsley.

Hatfield, E., & Rapson, R. L. (1990). Passionate love in intimate relationships. In B. S. Moore & A. M. Isen (Eds.), *Affect and social behavior* (pp. 126–152). Cambridge, UK: Cambridge University Press.

Hatfield, E., & Rapson, R. L. (1993). *Love, sex, and intimacy: Their psychology, biology, and history*. New York: Harper-Collins.

Hatfield, E., & Rapson, R. L. (1996). *Love and sex: Cross-cultural perspectives*. Needham Heights, MA: Allyn & Bacon.

Hatfield, E., & Sprecher, S. (1986a). Measuring passionate love in intimate relationships. *Journal of Adolescence, 9*, 383–410.

Hatfield, E., & Sprecher, S. (1986b). *Mirror, mirror: The importance of looks in everyday life*. Albany: State University of New York Press.

Hatfield, E., Traupmann, J., & Sprecher, S. (1984). Older women's perceptions of their intimate relationships. *Journal of Social and Clinical Psychology, 2*, 108–124.

Hatfield, E., Traupmann, J., Sprecher, S., Utne, M., & Hay, J. (1985). Equity and intimate relations: Recent research. In W. Ickes (Ed.), *Compatible and incompatible relationships* (pp. 91–117). New York: Springer-Verlag.

Hatkoff, T. S., & Lasswell, T. E. (1977). Male–female similarities and differences in conceptualizing love. In M. Cook & G. Wilson (Eds.), *Love and attraction: An international conference* (pp. 221–227). Oxford, UK: Pergamon Press.

Hawkes, C. H. (1992). Endorphins: The basis of pleasure? *Journal of Neurology, Neurosurgery & Psychiatry, 55*, 247–250.

Hays, R. B. (1984). The development and maintenance of friendship. *Journal of Social and Personal Relationships, 1*, 75–98.

Hays, R. B. (1985). A longitudinal study of friendship development. *Journal of Personality and Social Psychology, 48*, 909–924.

Hays, R. B. (1988). Friendship. In S. Duck (Ed.), *Handbook of personal relationships: Theory, research, and interventions* (pp. 391–408). Chichester, UK: Wiley.

Hazan, C., & Shaver, P. R. (1987). Romantic love conceptualized as an attachment process. *Journal of Personality and Social Psychology, 52*, 511–524.

Hazan, C., & Shaver, P. R. (1994). Attachment as an organizational framework for research on close relationships. *Psychological Inquiry, 5*, 1–22.

Heaton, T. B. (1991). Time-related determinants of marital dissolution. *Journal of Marriage and the Family, 53*, 285–295.

Heaton, T. B., & Albrecht, S. L. (1991). Stable unhappy marriages. *Journal of Marriage and Family, 53*, 747–758.

Heavey, C. L., Christensen, A., & Malamuth, N. M. (1995). The longitudinal impact of demand and withdrawal during marital conflict. *Journal of Consulting and Clinical Psychology, 63*, 797–801.

Heavey, C. L., Layne, C., & Christensen, A. (1993). Gender and conflict structure in marital interaction: A replication and extension. *Journal of Consulting and Clinical Psychology, 61*, 16–27.

Hebb, D. O. (1946). On the nature of fear. *Psychological Review, 53*, 259–276.

Hebb, D. O. (1949). *The organization of behavior: A neuropsychological theory*. New York: Wiley.

Hebb, D. O. (1955). Drives and C. N. S. (conceptual nervous system). *Psychological Review, 62*, 243–254.

Hebb, D. O. (1958). *A textbook of psychology*. Philadelphia: W. B. Saunders.

Hebl, M. R., & Kashy, D. A. (1995). Sociosexuality and everyday social interaction. *Personal Relationships, 2*, 371–383.

Heider, F. (1958). *The psychology of interpersonal relations*. New York: Wiley.

Helgeson, V. S. (1994). Relation of agency and communion to well-being: Evidence and potential explanations. *Psychological Bulletin, 116*, 412–428.

Helgeson, V. S., & Cohen, S. (1996). Social support and adjustment to cancer: Reconciling descriptive, correlational, and intervention research. *Health Psychology, 15*, 135–148.

Helgeson, V. S., & Fritz, H. L. (1998). A theory of unmitigated communion. *Personality and Social Psychology Review, 2*, 173–183.

Henderson-King, D. H., & Veroff, J. (1994). Sexual satisfaction and marital well-being in the first years of marriage. *Journal of Social and Personal Relationships, 11*, 509–534.

Hendrick, C. (1988). Roles and gender in relationships. In S. Duck (Ed.), *Handbook of personal relationships: Theory, research, and interventions* (pp. 429–448). Chichester, UK: Wiley.

Hendrick, C., & Hendrick, S. S. (1986). A theory and method of love. *Journal of Personality and Social Psychology, 50*, 392–402.

Hendrick, C., & Hendrick, S. S. (1990). A relationship-specific version of the Love Attitudes Scale. *Journal of Social Behavior and Personality, 5*, 239–254.

Hendrick, C., Hendrick, S. S., & Dicke, A. (1998). The Love Attitudes Scale: Short form. *Journal of Social and Personal Relationships, 15*, 147–159.

Hendrick, C., Hendrick, S. S., Foote, F. H., & Slapion-Foote, M. J. (1984). Do men and women love differently? *Journal of Social and Personal Relationships, 1*, 177–195.

Hendrick, S. S. (1988). A generic measure of relationship satisfaction. *Journal of Marriage and the Family, 39*, 543–548.

Hendrick, S. S., Dicke, A., & Hendrick, C. (1998). The Relationship Assessment Scale. *Journal of Social and Personal Relationships, 15*, 137–142.

Hendrick, S. S., & Hendrick, C. (1992). *Liking, loving, & relating* (2nd ed.). Pacific Grove, CA: Brooks/Cole.

Hendrick, S. S., & Hendrick, C. (1993). Lovers as friends. *Journal of Social and Personal Relationships, 10*, 459–466.

Hendrick, S. S., & Hendrick, C. (2000). Romantic love. In C. Hendrick & S. S. Hendrick (Eds.), *Close relationships: A sourcebook* (pp. 203–215). Thousand Oaks, CA: Sage.

Hendrick, S. S., Hendrick, C., & Adler, N. L. (1988). Romantic relationships: Love, satisfaction, and staying together. *Journal of Personality and Social Psychology, 54*, 980–988.

Her illness makes him unwilling to have sex. (2001, September 24), *Minneapolis Star Tribune*, p. E3.

Herbert, T. B., & Cohen, S. (1993). Stress and immunity in humans: A meta-analytic review. *Psychosomatic Medicine, 55*, 364–379.

Herold, E. S., Mantle, D., & Zemitis, O. (1979). A study of sexual offenses against females. *Adolescence, 14*, 65–72.

Heyman, R. E. (2001). Observation of couple conflicts: Clinical assessment applications, stubborn truths, and shaky foundations. *Psychological Assessment, 13*, 5–35.

Heyman, R. E., Eddy, J. M., Weiss, R. L., & Vivian, D. (1995). Factor analysis of the Marital Interaction Coding System (MICS). *Journal of Family Psychology, 9*, 209–215.

Heyman, R. E., Sayers, S. L., & Bellack, A. S. (1994). Global marital satisfaction versus marital adjustment: An empirical comparison of three measures. *Journal of Family Psychology, 8*, 432–446.

Heyman, R. E., & Slep, A. M. S. (2001). The hazards of predicting divorce without crossvalidation. *Journal of Marriage and the Family, 63*, 473–479.

Higgins, E. T. (1989). Knowledge accessibility and activation: subjectivity and suffering from unconscious sources. In J. S. Uleman & J. A. Bargh (Eds.), *Unintended thought* (pp. 75–123). New York: Guilford Press.

Higgins, E. T., & Bargh, J. A. (1987). Social cognition and social perception. *Annual Review of Psychology, 38*, 369–426.

Hilditch, T. (1995, August 27). China's dying rooms: Cries finally heard 'round the world. *Minneapolis Star Tribune*, p. 16A.

Hilgard, E. R. (1948). *Theories of learning*. New York: Appleton-Century-Crofts.

Hill, C. A., Blakemore, J. E. O., & Drumm, P. (1997). Mutual and unrequited love in adolescence and young adulthood. *Personal Relationships, 4*, 15–23.

Hill, C. T., & Peplau, L. A. (1998). Premarital predictors of relationship outcomes: A 15-year follow-up of the Boston Couples Study. In T. N. Bradbury (Ed.), *The developmental course of marital dysfunction* (pp. 237–278). Cambridge, UK: Cambridge University Press.

Hill, C. T., Rubin, Z., & Peplau, L. A. (1976). Breakups before marriage: The end of 103 affairs. *Journal of Social Issues, 32*, 147–168.

Hill, R. (1945). Campus values in mate-selection. *Journal of Home Economics, 37*, 554–558.

Hill, R. (1949). *Families under stress*. New York: Harper.

Hilton, J. L., & Darley, J. M. (1991). The effects of interaction goals on person perception. *Advances in Experimental Social Psychology, 24*, 235–267.

Hinde, R. A. (1979). *Towards understanding relationships*. London: Academic Press.

Hinde, R. A. (1985). Expression and negotiation. In G. Zivin (Ed.), *The development of expressive behavior* (pp. 103–116). Orlando, FL: Academic Press.

Hinde, R. A. (1997). *Relationships: A dialectical perspective*. East Sussex, UK: Psychology Press.

Hinde, R. A. (1998). Humans and human habitats: Reciprocal influences. In B. Cartledge (Ed.), *Mind, brain, and the environment* (pp. 6–27). Oxford, UK: Oxford University Press.

Hinkley, K., & Andersen, S. M. (1996). The working self-concept in transference: Significant-other activation and self-change. *Journal of Personality and Social Psychology, 71*, 1279–1295.

Hobfoll, S. E. (1988). *The ecology of stress*. New York: Hemisphere.

Hobfoll, S. E., & London, P. (1986). The relationship of self-concept and social support to emotional distress among women during war. *Journal of Social and Clinical Psychology, 12*, 87–100.

Hobfoll, S. E., & Stokes, J. P. (1988). The process and mechanics of social support. In S. Duck (Ed.), *Handbook of personal relationships: Theory, research, and intervention* (pp. 497–517). Chichester, UK: Wiley.

Hogan, M. A. (1994, December 31). Power-vortex "friendship" skews meaning of word. *Minneapolis Star Tribune*, pp. 1E, 3E.

Hogben, M., & Byrne, D. (1998). Using social learning theory to explain individual differences in human sexuality. *The Journal of Sex Research, 35*, 58–71.

Holman, T. B., & Linford, S. T. (2001). Premarital factors and later marital quality and stability. In T. B. Holman (Ed.), *Premarital prediction of marital quality or breakup: Research, theory, and practice* (pp. 1–28). New York: Kluwer Academic/Plenum.

Holmberg, D., & Holmes, J. G. (1993). Reconstruction of relationship memories: A mental models approach. In N. Schwarz & S. Sudman (Eds.), *Autobiographical memory and the validity of retrospective reports* (pp. 267–288). New York: Springer-Verlag.

Holmberg, D., & Veroff, J. (1996). Rewriting relationship memories: The effects of courtship and wedding scripts. In G. J. O. Fletcher & J. Fitness (Eds.), *Knowledge structures in close relationships: A social psychological approach* (pp. 345–368). Mahwah, NJ: Erlbaum.

Holmes, J. G. (1991). Trust and the appraisal process in close relationships. In W. H. Jones & D. Perlman (Eds.), *Advances in personal relationships* (Vol. 2, pp. 57–104). London: Jessica Kingsley.

Holmes, J. G. (2000). Social relationships: The nature and function of relational schemas. *European Journal of Social Psychology, 30*, 447–495.

Holmes, J. G. (2002). Interpersonal expectations as the building blocks of social cognition: An interdependence theory perspective. *Personal Relationships, 9*, 1–26.

Holmes, J. G., & Levinger, G. (1994). Paradoxical effects of closeness in relationships on perceptions of justice: An interdependence-theory perspective. In M. J. Lerner & G.

Mikula (Eds.), *Entitlement and the affectional bond: Justice in close relationships* (pp. 149–174). New York: Plenum Press.

Holmes, J. G., & Murray, S. L. (1996). Conflict in close relationships. In E. T. Higgins & A. W. Kruglanski (Eds.), *Social psychology: Handbook of basic principles* (pp. 622–701). New York: Guilford Press.

Holmes, J. G., & Rempel, J. K. (1989). Trust in close relationships. In C. Hendrick (Ed.), *Close relationships: Vol. 10. Review of personality and social psychology* (pp. 187–220). Newbury Park, CA: Sage.

Holmes, M. E., & Poole, M. S. (1991). Longitudinal analysis. In B. M. Montgomery & S. Duck (Eds.), *Studying interpersonal interaction* (pp. 286–302). New York: Guilford Press.

Holmes, T. H., & Rahe, R. H. (1967). The social readjustment rating scale. *Journal of Psychosomatic Research, 11*, 213–218.

Holtzworth-Munroe, A., & Jacobson, N. S. (1985). Causal attributions of married couples: When do they search for causes? What do they conclude when they do? *Journal of Personality and Social Psychology, 48*, 1398–1412.

Holtzworth-Munroe, A., & Jacobson, N. S. (1988). Toward a methodology for coding spontaneous causal attributions: Preliminary results with married couples. *Journal of Social and Clinical Psychology, 7*, 101–112.

Homans, G. C. (1961). *Social behavior: Its elementary forms.* New York: Harcourt, Brace & World.

Homans, G. C. (1974). *Social behavior: Its elementary forms* (Rev. ed.). New York: Harcourt, Brace, Jovanovich.

Homans, G. C. (1979). Foreword. In R. L. Burgess & T. L. Huston (Eds.), *Social exchange in developing relationships* (pp. xv–xxii). New York: Academic Press.

Hood, R. W., Jr., Spilka, B., Hunsberger, B., & Gorsuch, R. (1996). *The psychology of religion: An empirical approach* (2nd ed.). New York: Guilford Press.

Hops, H., Wills, T. A., Patterson, G. R., & Weiss, R. L. (1972). *Marital interaction coding system.* Eugene: Oregon Research Institute.

Horowitz, L. M., Krasnoperova, E. N., Tatar, D. G., Hansen, M. B., Person, E. A., Galvin, K. L., & Nelson, K. L. (2001). The way to console may depend on the goal: Experimental studies of social support. *Journal of Experimental Social Psychology, 37*, 49–61.

Horowitz, L. M., & Vitkus, J. (1986). The interpersonal basis of psychiatric symptoms. *Clinical Psychology Review, 6*, 443–469.

House, J. S., & Kahn, R. L. (1985). Measures and concepts of social support. In S. Cohen & S. L. Syme (Eds.), *Social support and health* (pp. 83–108). Orlando, FL: Academic Press.

House, J. S., Landis, K. R., & Umberson, D. (1988). Social relationships and health. *Science, 241*, 540–545.

Houts, R. M., Robins, E., & Huston, T. L. (1996). Compatibility and the development of premarital relationships. *Journal of Marriage and the Family, 58*, 7–20.

Howard, J. A., Blumstein, P., & Schwartz, P. (1987). Social or evolutionary theories? Some observations on preferences in human mate selection. *Journal of Personality and Social Psychology, 53*, 194–200.

Hoyt, L. L., & Hudson, J. W. (1981). Personal characteristics important in mate preference among college students. *Social Behavior and Personality, 9*, 93–96.

Hsee, C. K., & Abelson, R. P. (1991). Velocity relation: Satisfaction as a function of the first derivative of outcome over time. *Journal of Personality and Social Psychology, 60*, 341–347.

Hsee, C. K., Salovey, P., & Abelson, R. P. (1994). The quasi-acceleration relation: Satisfaction as a function of the change in velocity of outcome over time. *Journal of Experimental Social Psychology, 30*, 96–111.

Hudson, J. W., & Henze, L. F. (1969). Campus values in mate selection: A replication. *Journal of Marriage and the Family, 31*, 772–775.

Hughes, C. W., & Lynch, J. J. (1978). A reconsideration of psychological precursors of sudden death in infrahuman animals. *American Psychologist, 33*, 419–429.

Hunt, M. (1974). *Sexual behavior in the 1970s.* Chicago: Playboy Press.

Hurlbert, D. F. (1993). A comparative study using orgasm consistency training in the treatment of women reporting hypoactive sexual desire. *Journal of Sex & Marital Therapy, 19*, 41–55.

Hurlbert, D. F., Apt, C., & Rabehl, S. M. (1993). Key variables to understanding female sexual satisfaction: An examination of women in nondistressed marriages. *Journal of Sex & Marital Therapy, 19*, 154–165.

Hussong, A. M. (2000). Distinguishing mean and structural sex differences in adolescent friendship quality. *Journal of Social and Personal Relationships, 17*, 223–243.

Huston, T. L. (1973). Ambiguity of acceptance, social desirability, and dating choice. *Journal of Experimental Social Psychology, 9*, 32–42.

Huston, T. L. (1994). Courtship antecedents of marital satisfaction and love. In R. Erber & R. Gilmour (Eds.), *Theoretical frameworks for personal relationships* (pp. 43–65). Hillsdale, NJ: Erlbaum.

Huston, T. L. (2000). The social ecology of marriage and other intimate unions. *Journal of Marriage and the Family, 62*, 298–320.

Huston, T. L., & Burgess, R. L. (1979). Social exchange in developing relationships: An overview. In R. L. Burgess & T. L. Huston (Eds.), *Social exchange in developing relationships* (pp. 3–28). New York: Academic Press.

Huston, T. L., Caughlin, J. P., Houts, R. M., Smith, S. E., & George, L. J. (2001). The connubial crucible: Newlywed years as predictors of marital delight, distress, and divorce. *Journal of Personality and Social Psychology, 80*, 237–252.

Huston, T. L., & Chorost, A. (1994). Behavioral buffers on the effect of negativity on marital satisfaction: A longitudinal study. *Personal Relationships, 1*, 223–239.

Huston, T. L., & Geis, G. (1993). In what ways do gender-related attributes and beliefs affect marriage? *Journal of Social Issues, 49*, 87–106.

Huston, T. L., & Houts, R. M. (1998). The psychological infrastructure of courtship and marriage: The role of personality and compatibility in romantic relationships. In T. N.

Bradbury (Ed.), *The developmental course of marital dysfunction* (pp. 114–151). Cambridge, UK: Cambridge University Press.

Huston, T. L., & Levinger, G. (1978). Interpersonal attraction and relationships. *Annual Review of Psychology, 29,* 115–156.

Huston, T. L., McHale, S. M., & Crouter, A. (1986). When the honeymoon's over: Changes in the marriage relationship over the first year. In R. Gilmour & S. Duck (Eds.), *Theoretical frameworks for personal relationships* (pp. 109–132). Hillsdale, NJ: Erlbaum.

Huston, T. L., & Robins, E. (1982). Conceptual and methodological issues in studying close relationships. *Journal of Marriage and the Family, 44,* 901–924.

Huston, T. L., Surra, C. A., Fitzgerald, N. M., & Cate, R. M. (1981). From courtship to marriage: Mate selection as an interpersonal process. In S. Duck & R. Gilmour (Eds.), *Personal relationships: Vol. 2. Developing personal relationships* (pp. 53–88). London: Academic Press.

Hyde, J. S. (1996). Where are the gender differences? Where are the gender similarities? In D. M. Buss & N. M. Malamuth (Eds.), *Sex, power, conflict: Evolutionary and feminist perspectives* (pp. 107–118). New York: Oxford University Press.

Ickes, W. (1981). Sex-role influences in dyadic interaction: A theoretical model. In C. Mayo & N. M. Henley (Eds.), *Gender and nonverbal behavior* (pp. 95–128). New York: Springer-Verlag.

Ickes, W. (1985). Introduction. In W. Ickes (Ed.), *Compatible and incompatible relationships* (pp. 1–10). New York: Springer-Verlag.

Ickes, W. (Ed.). (1997). *Empathic accuracy.* New York: Guilford Press.

Ickes, W., Bissonnette, V., Garcia, S., & Stinson, L. L. (1990). Implementing and using the dyadic interaction paradigm. In C. Hendrick & M. S. Clark (Eds.), *Research methods in personality and social psychology: Vol. 11. Review of personality and social psychology* (pp. 16–44). Newbury Park, CA: Sage.

Ickes, W., Buysse, A., Pham, H., Rivers, K., Erickson, J. R., Hancock, M., Kelleher, J., & Gesn, P. R. (2000). On the difficulty of distinguishing "good" and "poor" perceivers: A social relations analysis of empathic accuracy data. *Personal Relationships, 7,* 219–234.

Ickes, W., Gesn, P. R., & Graham, T. (2000). Gender differences in empathic accuracy: Differential ability or differential motivation? *Personal Relationships, 7,* 95–109.

Ingoldsby, B. B. (1995). Mate selection and marriage. In B. B. Ingoldsby & S. Smith (Eds.), *Families in multicultural perspective* (pp. 143–160). New York: Guilford Press.

Ingrassia, M., & Wingert, P. (1995, May 22). The new providers. *Newsweek,* pp. 36–38.

Insel, T. R. (1997). A neurobiological basis of social attachment. *American Journal of Psychiatry, 154,* 726–735.

Insel, T. R. (2000). Toward a neurobiology of attachment. *Review of General Psychology, 4,* 176–185.

Isen, A. M. (1987). Positive affect, cognitive processes and social behavior. In L. Berkowitz (Ed.), *Advances in experimental social psychology* (Vol. 20, pp. 203–253). New York: Academic Press.

Isen, A. M., Shalker, T. E., Clark, M., & Karp, L. (1978). Affect, accessibility of material in memory, and behavior: A cognitive loop? *Journal of Personality and Social Psychology, 36,* 1–12.

Ishii-Kuntz, M., & Coltrane, S. (1992). Remarriage, stepparenting, and household labor. *Journal of Family Issues, 13,* 215–233.

Isikoff, M., & Thomas, E. (2001, September 3). From bad to worse. *Newsweek,* pp. 20–23.

Ivins, M. (1999, May 7). "Equal pay for equal work" a distant goal. *Minneapolis Star Tribune,* p. A23.

Izard, C. E. (1991). *The psychology of emotions.* New York: Plenum Press.

Izard, C. E. (2002). Translating emotion theory and research into preventive interventions. *Psychological Bulletin, 128,* 796–824.

Jacklin, C. N., & Reynolds, C. (1993). Gender and childhood socialization. In A. E. Beall & R. J. Sternberg (Eds.), *The psychology of gender* (pp. 197–214). New York: Guilford Press.

Jackson, D. D. (1959). Family interaction, family homeostasis, and some implications for conjoint family therapy. In J. Masserman (Ed.), *Individual and family dynamics.* New York: Grune & Stratton.

Jackson, D. D., & Weakland, J. (1961). Conjoint family therapy: Some consideration on theory, technique, and results. *Psychiatry, 24,* 30–45.

Jacob, T., Tennenbaum, D., Seilhamer, R. A., Bargiel, K., and Sharon, T. (1994). Reactivity effects during naturalistic observation of distressed and nondistressed families. *Journal of Family Psychology, 8,* 354–363.

Jacobs, L., Berscheid, E., & Walster [Hatfield], E. (1971). Self-esteem and attraction. *Journal of Personality and Social Psychology, 17,* 84–91.

Jacobson, N. S. (1990). Commentary: Contributions from psychology to an understanding of marriage. In F. D. Fincham & T. N. Bradbury (Eds.), *The psychology of marriage: Basic issues and applications* (pp. 258–275). New York: Guilford Press.

Jacobson, N. S., & Addis, M. E. (1993). Research on couples and couple therapy: What do we know? Where are we going? *Journal of Consulting and Clinical Psychology, 61,* 85–93.

Jacobson, N. S., & Christensen, A. (1996). *Acceptance and change in couple therapy: A therapist's guide to transforming relationships.* New York: Norton.

Jacobson, N. S., Christensen, A., Prince, S. E., Cordova, J., & Eldridge, K. (2000). Integrative behavioral couple therapy: An acceptance-based, promising new treatment for couple discord. *Journal of Consulting and Clinical Psychology, 68,* 351–355.

Jacobson, N. S., Follette, W. C., McDonald, D. W. (1982). Reactivity to positive and negative behavior in distressed and nondistressed married couples. *Journal of Consulting and Clinical Psychology, 50,* 706–714.

Jacobson, N. S., & Holtzworth-Munroe, A. (1986). Marital therapy: A social learning–cognitive perspective. In N. S. Jacobson & A. S. Gurman (Eds.), *Clinical handbook of marital therapy* (pp. 29–70). New York: Guilford Press.

Jacobson, N. S., & Margolin, G. (1979). *Marital therapy: Strategies based on social learning and behavior exchange principles*. New York: Brunner/Mazel.

Jacobson, N. S., & Moore, D. (1981). Spouses as observers of events in their relationship. *Journal of Consulting and Clinical Psychology, 49*, 269–277.

James, W. (1884). What is an emotion? *Mind, 9*, 188–205.

James, W. (1890). *Principles of psychology*. New York: Henry Holt.

James, W. (1893). *Psychology*. New York: Henry Holt.

James, W. (1950). *The principles of psychology* (Vol. 1). New York: Dover. (Original work published 1890)

James, W. (1999). *The varieties of religious experience: A study in human nature*. New York: Modern Library (Random House). (Original work published 1902)

James, W. H. (1981). The honeymoon effect on marital coitus. *The Journal of Sex Research, 17*, 114–123.

Jamieson, D. W., Lydon, J. E., & Zanna, M. P. (1987). Attitude and activity preference similarity: Differential bases of interpersonal attraction for low and high self-monitors. *Journal of Personality and Social Psychology, 53*, 1052–1060.

Jankowiak, W. R., & Fischer, E. F. (1992). A cross-cultural perspective on romantic love. *Ethology, 31*, 149–155.

Jason, L. A., Reichler, A., Easton, J., Neal, A., & Wilson, M. (1984). Female harassment after ending a relationship: A preliminary study. *Alternative Lifestyles, 6*, 259–269.

Jeay, M. (1979). Sexuality and family in fifteenth-century France: Are literary sources a mask or a mirror? *Journal of Family History, 4*, 328–345.

Jefferis, B. G., & Nichols, J. L. (1896). *Search lights on health. Light on dark corners. A complete sexual science and a guide to purity and physical manhood. Advice to maiden, wife, and mother. Love, courtship and marriage*. (18th ed.). Naperville, IL: J. L. Nichols & Co.

Jemmott, J. B., III, & Magloire, K. (1988). Academic stress, social support, and secretory immunoglobulin A. *Journal of Personality and Social Psychology, 55*, 803–810.

Jesser, C. J. (1978). Male responses to direct verbal sexual initiatives of females. *Journal of Sex Research, 14*, 118–128.

Jessor, R., Costa, F., Jessor, L., & Donovan, J. E. (1983). Time of first intercourse: A prospective study. *Journal of Personality and Social Psychology, 44*, 608–626.

Jockin, V., McGue, M., & Lykken, D. T. (1996). Personality and divorce: A genetic analysis. *Journal of Personality and Social Psychology, 71*, 288–299.

John, O. P., Cheek, J. M., & Klohnen, E. C. (1996). On the nature of self-monitoring: Construct explication with Q-sort ratings. *Journal of Personality and Social Psychology, 71*, 763–776.

Johnson, D. J., & Rusbult, C. E. (1989). Resisting temptation: Devaluation of alternative partners as a means of maintaining commitment in close relationships. *Journal of Personality and Social Psychology, 57*, 967–980.

Johnson, E., & Tversky, A. (1983). Affect, generalization and the perception of risk. *Journal of Personality and Social Psychology, 45*, 20–31.

Johnson, M. H. (1999). Developmental neuroscience. In M. H. Bornstein & M. E. Lamb (Eds.), *Developmental psychology: An advanced textbook* (pp. 199–230). Mahwah, NJ: Erlbaum.

Johnson, M. H., Dziurawiec, S., Ellis, H., & Morton, J. (1991). Newborns' preferential tracking of face-like stimuli and its subsequent decline. *Cognition, 40*, 1–19.

Johnson, M. P. (1991). Commitment to personal relationships. In W. H. Jones & D. Perlman (Eds.), *Advances in personal relationships* (Vol. 2, pp. 117–143). London: Jessica Kingsley.

Johnson, M. P. (1995). Patriarchal terrorism and common couple violence: Two forms of violence against women. *Journal of Marriage and the Family, 57*, 283–294.

Johnson, M. P. (1999). Personal, moral, and structural commitment to relationships: Experiences of choice and constraint. In J. M. Adams & W. H. Jones (Eds.), *Handbook of interpersonal commitment and relationship stability* (pp. 73–87). New York: Kluwer Academic/Plenum.

Johnson, M. P., & Ferraro, K. J. (2000). Research on domestic violence in the 1990s: Making distinctions. *Journal of Marriage and the Family, 62*, 948–963.

Johnson, M. P., Huston, T. L., Gaines, S. O., Jr., & Levinger, G. (1992). Patterns of married life among young couples. *Journal of Social and Personal Relationships, 9*, 343–364.

Johnson, M. P., & Leslie, L. (1982). Couple involvement and network structure: A test of the dyadic withdrawal hypothesis. *Social Psychology Quarterly, 45*, 34–43.

Johnson, M. P., & Milardo, R. (1984). Network interference in pair relationships. *Journal of Marriage and the Family, 46*, 893–899.

Johnson, S., & Lebow, J. (2000). The "coming of age" of couple therapy: A decade review. *Journal of Marital and Family Therapy, 26*, 23–38.

Johnson, S. M., & Greenberg, L. S. (1995). The emotionally focused approach to problems in adult attachment. In N. S. Jacobson & A. S. Gurman (Eds.), *Clinical handbook of couple therapy* (pp. 121–141). New York: Guilford Press.

Johnson, S. M., Makinen, J. A., & Millikin, J. W. (2001). Attachment injuries in couple relationships: A new perspective on impasses in couples therapy. *Journal of Marital and Family Therapy, 27*, 145–155.

Joiner, T. E., Alfano, M. S., & Metalsky, G. I. (1992). When depression breeds contempt: Reassurance seeking, self-esteem, and rejection of depressed college students by their roommates. *Journal of Abnormal Psychology, 101*, 165–173.

Jones, D., & Hill, K. (1993). Criteria of facial attractiveness in five populations. *Human Nature, 4*, 271–296.

Jones, D. C., Bloys, N., & Wood, M. (1990). Sex roles and friendship patterns. *Sex Roles, 23*, 133–145.

Jones, E. E. (1964). *Ingratiation: A social psychological analysis*. New York: Appleton-Century-Crofts.

Jones, E. E., & Davis, K. E. (1965). From acts to dispositions: The attribution process in person perception. In L. Berkowitz (Ed.), *Advances in experimental social psychology* (Vol. 2, pp. 220–266). New York: Academic Press.

Jones, E. E., & Pittman, T. S. (1982). Toward a general theory of strategic self-presentation. In J. Suls (Ed.), *Psychological perspectives on the self* (Vol. 1, pp. 231–262). Hillsdale, NJ: Erlbaum.

Jones, E. E., & Wortman, C. (1973). *Ingratiation: An attributional approach.* Morristown, NJ: General Learning Press.

Jones, M. (1993). Influence of self-monitoring on dating motivations. *Journal of Research in Personality, 27*, 197–206.

Jones, M. (1998). Sociosexuality and motivations for romantic involvement. *Journal of Research in Personality, 32*, 173–182.

Jones, W. H. (1982). Loneliness and social behavior. In L. A. Peplau & D. Perlman (Eds.), *Loneliness: A sourcebook of theory, research, and therapy* (pp. 238–252). New York: Wiley.

Jones, W. H., Sansone, C., & Helm, B. (1983). Loneliness and interpersonal judgments. *Personality and Social Psychology Bulletin, 9*, 437–442.

Joshi, A., Melson, G. F., & Ferris, J. C. (2001, April). *Issues of conflicts with friends during middle childhood.* Paper presented at the meeting of the Society for Research in Child Development, Minneapolis, MN.

Jourard, S. M. (1964). *The transparent self.* New York: Van Nostrand.

Jourard, S. M. (1971). *Self-disclosure: An experimental analysis of the transparent self.* New York: Wiley.

Judd, C. M., & Park, B. (1993). Definition and assessment accuracy in social stereotypes. *Psychological Review, 100*, 109–128.

Juhasz, A. M., Kaufman, B., & Meyer, H. (1986). Adolescent attitudes and beliefs about sexual behavior. *Child and Adolescent Social Work, 3*, 177–193.

Juni, S., & Grimm, D. W. (1993). Marital satisfaction and sexroles in a New York metropolitan sample. *Psychological Reports, 73*, 307–314.

Jussim, L. (2002, Spring). Intellectual imperialism. *Dialogue* (Official Newsletter of the Society for Personality and Social Psychology), *17*, 18–20.

Just 20% of violent crime is committed by strangers. (2001, June 25). *Saint Paul Pioneer Press*, p. A2.

Kagan, J. (1982). The construct of difficult temperament: A reply to Thomas, Chess and Korn. *Merrill-Palmer Quarterly, 28*, 21–24.

Kagan, J. (1989). Temperamental contributions to social behavior. *American Psychologist, 44*, 668–674.

Kagan, J. (1994). *Galen's prophecy: Temperament in human nature.* New York: Basic Books.

Kalick, S. M., & Hamilton, T. E. (1986). The matching hypothesis re-examined. *Journal of Personality and Social Psychology, 51*, 673–682.

Kanin, E. J. (1967). An examination of sexual aggression as a response to sexual frustration. *Journal of Marriage and the Family, 29*, 428–433.

Kanin, E. J. (1984). Date rape: Unofficial criminals and victims. *Victimology: An International Journal, 9*, 95–108.

Kanin, E. J. (1985). Date rapists: Differential sexual socialization and relative deprivation. *Archives of Sexual Behavior, 14*, 219–231.

Kantrowitz, B., & Wingert, P. (1999, April 19). The science of a good marriage. *Newsweek*, pp. 52–57.

Kapadia, K. M. (1954). Changing patterns of Hindu marriage and family. *Sociological Bulletin (India), 3*, 131–157.

Kaplan, H., Burch, N. R., & Bloom, S. (1964). Physiological covariation and sociometric relationships in small peer groups. In P. H. Leiderman & D. Shapiro (Eds.), *Psychobiological Approaches to Social Behavior* (pp. 92–109). Stanford, CA: Stanford University Press.

Kaplan, H. S. (1979). *Disorders of sexual desire and other new concepts and techniques in sex therapy.* New York: Simon & Schuster.

Kaplan, H. S. (1996). Erotic obsession: Relationship to hypoactive sexual desire disorder and paraphilia. *American Journal of Psychiatry, 153*, 30–41.

Karlson, P., & Lüscher, M. (1959). "Pheromones:" A new term for a class of biologically active substances. *Nature, 183*, 55–56.

Karney, B. R., & Bradbury, T. N. (1995a). Assessing longitudinal change in marriage: An introduction to the analysis of growth curves. *Journal of Marriage and the Family, 57*, 1091–1092.

Karney, B. R., & Bradbury, T. N. (1995b). The longitudinal course of marital quality and stability: A review of theory, method, and research. *Psychological Bulletin, 118*, 3–34.

Karney, B. R., & Bradbury, T. N. (1997). Neuroticism, marital interaction, and the trajectory of marital satisfaction. *Journal of Personality and Social Psychology, 72*, 1075–1092.

Karney, B. R., Bradbury, T. N., Fincham, F. D., & Sullivan, K. T. (1994). The role of negative affectivity in the association between attributions and marital satisfaction. *Journal of Personality and Social Psychology, 66*, 413–424.

Karney, B. R., Bradbury, T. N., & Johnson, M. D. (1999). Deconstructing stability: The distinction between the course of a close relationship and its endpoint. In J. M. Adams & W. H. Jones (Eds.), *Handbook of interpersonal commitment and relationship stability* (pp. 481–499). New York: Kluwer Academic/Plenum.

Karney, B. R., & Coombs, R. H. (2000). Memory bias in long-term close relationships: Consistency or improvement? *Personality and Social Psychology Bulletin, 26*, 959–970.

Karney, B. R., Davila, J., Cohan, C. L., Sullivan, K. T., Johnson, M. D., & Bradbury, T. N. (1995). An empirical investigation of sampling strategies in marital research. *Journal of Marriage and the Family, 57*, 909–920.

Karra, M. V., Stark, N. N., & Wolf, J. (1997). Male involvement in family planning: A case study spanning five generations of a South Indian family. *Studies in Family Planning, 28*, 24–34.

Kaslow, F. W., & Schwartz, L. L. (1987). *The dynamics of divorce: A life cycle perspective.* New York: Brunner/Mazel.

Kassin, S. M. (2001). *Psychology* (3rd ed.). Upper Saddle River, NJ: Prentice-Hall.

Kayser, K. (1993). *When love dies: The process of marital disaffection.* New York: Guilford Press.

Keelan, J. P. R., Dion, K. L., & Dion, K. K. (1994). Attachment style and heterosexual relationships among young adults:

A short-term panel study. *Journal of Social and Personal Relationships, 11,* 201–214.

Keller, M. C., Thiessen, D., & Young, R. K. (1996). Mate assortment in dating and married couples. *Personality and Individual Differences, 21,* 217–221.

Kelley, H. H. (1950). The warm–cold variable in first impressions of persons. *Journal of Personality, 18,* 431–439.

Kelley, H. H. (1951). Communication in experimentally created hierarchies. *Human Relations, 4,* 39–56.

Kelley, H. H. (1967). Attribution theory in social psychology. In D. Levine (Ed.), *Nebraska Symposium on Motivation* (Vol. 15, pp. 192–240). Lincoln: University of Nebraska Press.

Kelley, H. H. (1979). *Personal relationships: Their structures and processes.* Hillsdale, NJ: Erlbaum.

Kelley, H. H. (1992). Common-sense psychology and scientific psychology. *Annual Review of Psychology, 43,* 1–23.

Kelley, H. H. (2002a). Epilogue: An essential science. In H. H. Kelley, E. Berscheid, A. Christensen, J. H. Harvey, T. L. Huston, G. Levinger, E. McClintock, L. A. Peplau, & D. R. Peterson (Eds.), *Close relationships* (pp. 486–504). Clinton Corners, NY: Percheron Press. (Original work published 1983)

Kelley, H. H. (2002b). Love and commitment. In H. H. Kelley, E. Berscheid, A. Christensen, J. H. Harvey, T. L. Huston, G. Levinger, E. McClintock, L. A. Peplau, & D. L. Peterson (Eds.), *Close relationships* (pp. 265–314). Clinton Corners, NY: Percheron Press. (Original work published 1983)

Kelley, H. H., Berscheid, E., Christensen, A., Harvey, J. H., Huston, T. L., Levinger, G., McClintock, E., Peplau, L. A., & Peterson, D. R. (2002). Analyzing close relationships. In H. H. Kelley, E. Berscheid, A. Christensen, J. H. Harvey, T. L. Huston, G. Levinger, E. McClintock, L. A. Peplau, & D. R. Peterson (Eds.), *Close relationships* (pp. 20–67). Clinton Corners, NY: Percheron Press. (Original work published 1983)

Kelley, H. H., Holmes, J. G., Kerr, N. L., Reis, H. T., Rusbult, C. E., & Van Lange, P. A. M. (2003). *An atlas of interpersonal situations.* Cambridge, UK: Cambridge University Press.

Kelley, H. H., & Stahelski, A. J. (1970). Social interaction basis of cooperators' and competitors' beliefs about others. *Journal of Personality and Social Psychology, 16,* 6–91.

Kelley, H. H., & Thibaut, J. W. (1978). *Interpersonal relations: A theory of interdependence.* New York: Wiley.

Kelly, E. L., & Conley, J. J. (1987). Personality and compatibility: A prospective analysis of marital stability and marital satisfaction. *Journal of Personality and Social Psychology, 52,* 27–40.

Kenny, D. A. (1990). Design issues in dyadic research. In C. Hendrick & M. S. Clark (Eds.), *Review of personality and social psychology: Research methods in personality and social psychology* (Vol. 11, pp. 164–184). Newbury Park, CA: Sage.

Kenny, D. A. (1994a). *Interpersonal perception: A social relations analysis.* New York: Guilford Press.

Kenny, D. A. (1994b). Using the social relations model to understand relationships. In R. Erber & R. Gilmour (Eds.), *Theoretical frameworks for personal relationships* (pp. 111–127). Hillsdale, NJ: Erlbaum.

Kenny, D. A., & Judd, C. M. (1986). Consequences of violating the independence assumption in analysis of variance. *Psychological Bulletin, 99,* 422–431.

Kenny, D. A., Kashy, D. A., & Bolger, N. (1998). Data analysis in social psychology. In D. T. Gilbert, S. T. Fiske, & G. Lindzey (Eds.), *The handbook of social psychology* (4th ed., Vol. 1, pp. 233–265). Boston: McGraw-Hill.

Kenny, D. A., & La Voie, L. (1984). The social relations model. *Advances in Experimental Social Psychology, 18,* 142–182.

Kenny, D. A., Mohr, C. D., & Levesque, M. J. (2000). A social relations variance partitioning of dyadic behavior. *Psychological Bulletin, 127,* 128–141.

Kenny, D. A., & Nasby, W. (1980). Splitting the reciprocity correlation. *Journal of Personality and Social Psychology, 38,* 249–256.

Kenrick, D. T., Groth, G. E., Trost, M. R., & Sadalla, E. K. (1993). Integrating evolutionary and social exchange perspectives on relationships: Effects of gender, self-appraisal, and involvement level on mate selection criteria. *Journal of Personality and Social Psychology, 64,* 951–969.

Kenrick, D. T., & Gutierres, S. E. (1980). Contrast effects and judgments of physical attractiveness: When beauty becomes a social problem. *Journal of Personality and Social Psychology, 38,* 131–140.

Kenrick, D. T., Sadalla, E. K., Groth, G., & Trost, M. R. (1990). Evolution, traits, and the stages of human courtship: Qualifying the parental investment model. *Journal of Personality, 58,* 97–116.

Kephart, W. M. (1967). Some correlates of romantic love. *Journal of Marriage and the Family, 29,* 470–474.

Kerckhoff, A. C. (1974). The social context of interpersonal attraction. In T. L. Huston (Ed.), *Foundations of interpersonal attraction* (pp. 61–76). New York: Academic Press.

Kerckhoff, A. C., & Davis, K. E. (1962). Value consensus and need complementarity in mate selection. *American Sociological Review, 27,* 295–303.

Kerig, P. K., & Lindahl, K. M. (2001). *Family observational coding systems: Resources for systemic research.* Mahwah, NJ: Erlbaum.

Kiecolt-Glaser, J. K., Garner, W., Speicher, C., Penn, G. M., Holliday, J., & Glaser, R. (1984). Psychosocial modifiers of immunocompetence in medical students. *Psychosomatic Medicine, 46,* 7–14.

Kiecolt-Glaser, J. K., Malarkey, W. B., Cacioppo, J. T., & Glaser, R. (1994). Stressful personal relationships: Immune and endocrine function. In R. Glaser & J. K. Kiecolt-Glaser (Eds.), *Handbook of human stress and immunity* (pp. 321–339). San Diego, CA: Academic Press.

Kiecolt-Glaser, J. K., McGuire, L., Robles, T. F., & Glaser, R. (2002). Emotions, morbidity, and mortality: New perspectives from psychoneuroimmunology. *Annual Review of Psychology, 53,* 83–107.

Kiecolt-Glaser, J. K., & Newton, T. L. (2001). Marriage and health: His and hers. *Psychological Bulletin, 127,* 472–503.

Kiernan, K. E. (1992). The impact of family disruption in childhood on transitions made in young adult life. *Population Studies, 46,* 213–224.

Kiesler, S., & Baral, R. (1970). The search for a romantic partner: The effects of self-esteem and physical attractiveness on romantic behavior. In K. Gergen & D. Marlowe (Eds.), *Personality and social behavior*. Reading, MA: Addison-Wesley.

King, C. E., & Christensen, A. (1983). The Relationship Events Scale: A Guttman scaling of progress in courtship. *Journal of Marriage and the Family, 45*, 671–678.

King, L. A. (1993). Emotional expression, ambivalence over expression, and marital satisfaction. *Journal of Social and Personal Relationships, 10*, 601–607.

Kinsey, A. C., Pomeroy, W. B., & Martin, C. E. (1948). *Sexual behavior in the human male*. Philadelphia: Saunders.

Kinsey, A. C., Pomeroy, W. B., Martin, C. E., & Gebhard, P. H. (1953). *Sexual behavior in the human female*. Philadelphia: Saunders.

Kirkpatrick, L. A. (1998). Evolution, pair-bonding, and reproductive strategies: A reconceptualization of adult attachment. In J. A. Simpson & W. S. Rholes (Eds.), *Attachment theory and close relationships* (pp. 353–393). New York: Guilford Press.

Kirkpatrick, L. A., & Davis, K. E. (1994). Attachment style, gender, and relationship stability: A longitudinal analysis. *Journal of Personality and Social Psychology, 66*, 502–512.

Kirn, W. (2000, September 25). Should you stay together for the kids? *Time*, pp. 75–88.

Kirsch, I. (1999). Response expectancy: An introduction. In I. Kirsch (Ed.), *How expectancies shape experience* (pp. 3–13). Washington, DC: American Psychological Association.

Kitson, G. C., Babri, K. B., & Roach, M. J. (1985). Who divorces and why: A review. *Journal of Family Issues, 6*, 255–293.

Kitson, G. C., & Sussman, M. B. (1982). Marital complaints, demographic characteristics, and symptoms of mental distress in divorce. *Journal of Marriage and the Family, 44*, 87–101.

Klein, H. A., Tatone, C. L., & Lindsay, N. B. (1989). Correlates of life satisfaction among military wives. *The Journal of Psychology, 123*, 465–475.

Klein, K. J. K., & Hodges, S. D. (2001). Gender differences, motivation, and empathic accuracy: When it pays to understand. *Personality and Social Psychology Bulletin, 27*, 720–730.

Klinetob, N. A., & Smith, D. A. (1996). Demand–withdraw communication in marital interaction: Tests of interspousal contingency and gender role hypotheses. *Journal of Marriage and the Family, 58*, 945–958.

Klinkenberg, D., & Rose, S. (1994). Dating scripts of gay men and lesbians. *Journal of Homosexuality, 26*, 23–35.

Klinnert, M. D. (1984). The regulation of infant behavior by maternal facial expression. *Infant Behavior and Development, 7*, 447–465.

Knapp, A., & Clark, M. S. (1991). Some detrimental effects of negative mood on individuals' ability to solve resource dilemmas. *Personality and Social Psychology Bulletin, 17*, 678–688.

Knapp, C. W., & Harwood, B. T. (1977). Factors in the determination of intimate same-sex friendship. *Journal of Genetic Psychology, 131*, 83–90.

Knapp, M. L. (1978). *Social intercourse: From greeting to goodbye*. Boston: Allyn & Bacon.

Knee, C. R. (1998). Implicit theories of relationships: Assessment and prediction of romantic relationship initiation, coping, and longevity. *Journal of Personality and Social Psychology, 74*, 360–370.

Knee, C. R., Nanayakkara, A., Vietor, N. A., Neighbors, C., & Patrick, H. (2001). Implicit theories of relationships: Who cares if romantic partners are less than ideal? *Personality and Social Psychology Bulletin, 27*, 808–819.

Kohler, W. (1929). *Gestalt psychology* (1st ed.). New York: Boni & Liveright.

Kolaric, G. C., & Galambos, N. L. (1995). Face-to-face interactions in unacquainted female–male adolescent dyads: How do girls and boys behave? *Journal of Early Adolescence, 15*, 363–382.

Koss, M. P., Gidycz, C. A., & Wisniewski, N. (1987). The scope of rape: Incidence and prevalence of sexual aggression and victimization in a national sample of higher education students. *Journal of Consulting and Clinical Psychology, 55*, 162–170.

Kosslyn, S. M., Cacioppo, J. T., Davidson, R. J., Hugdahl, K., Lovallo, W. R., Spiegel, D., & Rose, R. (2002). Bridging psychology and biology: The analysis of individuals in groups. *American Psychologist, 57*, 341–351.

Kouros-Mehr, H., Pintchovski, S., Melnyk, J., Chen, Y-J., Friedman, C., Trask, B., & Shizuya, H. (2001). Identification of non-functional human VNO receptor genes provides evidence for vestigiality of the human VNO. *Chemical Senses, 26*, 1167–1174.

Kowalski, R. M. (1992). Nonverbal behaviors and perceptions of sexual intentions: Effects of sexual connotativeness, verbal response, and rape outcome. *Basic and Applied Social Psychology, 13*, 427–445.

Kowalski, R. M. (1993). Inferring sexual interest from behavioral cues: Effects of gender and sexually relevant attitudes. *Sex Roles, 29*, 13–36.

Krafft-Ebing, R. von (1945). *Psychopathia sexualis* (12th ed.). New York: Pioneer Publications. (Original work published 1886)

Krantz, D. S., & McCeney, M. K. (2002). Effects of psychological and social factors on organic disease: A critical assessment of research on coronary heart disease. *Annual Review of Psychology, 53*, 341–369.

Kraut, R. E., & Johnston, R. E. (1979). Social and emotional messages of smiling: An ethological approach. *Journal of Personality and Social Psychology, 37*, 1539–1553.

Kressel, K. (1985). *The process of divorce: How professionals and couples negotiate settlements*. New York: Basic Books.

Kressel, K., & Deutsch, M. (1977). Divorce therapy: An in-depth survey of therapists' views. *Family Process, 16*, 413–443.

Krueger, R. F., Moffitt, T. E., Caspi, A., Bleske, A., & Silva, P. A. (1998). Assortative mating for antisocial behavior: Developmental and methodological implications. *Behavior Genetics, 28*, 173–186.

Kruglanski, A. W. (1989). On the psychology of being "right": The problem of accuracy in social perception and cognition. *Psychological Bulletin, 106,* 395–409.

Kumagai, F. (1995). Families in Japan: Beliefs and realities. *Journal of Comparative Family Studies, 26,* 135–163.

Kunce, L. J., & Shaver, P. R. (1994). An attachment-theoretical approach to caregiving in romantic relationships. In D. Perlman & K. Batholomew (Eds.), *Advances in personal relationships: Vol. 5. Attachment processes in adulthood* (pp. 205–237). London: Jessica Kingsley.

Kunda, Z. (1999). *Social cognition: Making sense of people.* Cambridge, MA: MIT Press.

Kunst-Wilson, W. R., & Zajonc, R. B. (1980). Affective discrimination of stimuli that cannot be recognized. *Science, 207,* 557–558.

Kurdek, L. A. (1991a). Predictors of increases in marital distress in newlywed couples: A 3-year prospective longitudinal study. *Developmental Psychology, 27,* 627–636.

Kurdek, L. A. (1991b). Sexuality in homosexual and heterosexual couples. In K. McKinney & S. Sprecher (Eds.), *Sexuality in close relationships* (pp. 177–191). Hillsdale, NJ: Erlbaum.

Kurdek, L. A. (1992). Assumptions versus standards: The validity of two relationship cognitions in heterosexual and homosexual couples. *Journal of Family Psychology, 6,* 164–170.

Kurdek, L. A. (1993a). The allocation of household labor in gay, lesbian, and heterosexual married couples. *Journal of Social Issues, 49,* 127–139.

Kurdek, L. A. (1993b). Nature and prediction of changes in marital quality for first-time parent and non-parent husbands and wives. *Journal of Family Psychology, 6,* 255–263.

Kurdek, L. A. (1993c). Predicting marital dissolution: A 5-year prospective longitudinal study of newlywed couples. *Journal of Personality and Social Psychology, 64,* 221–242.

Kurdek, L. A. (1998a). Developmental changes in marital satisfaction: A 13-year prospective longitudinal study of newlywed couples. In T. N. Bradbury (Ed.), *The developmental course of marital dysfunction* (pp. 180–204). Cambridge, UK: Cambridge University Press.

Kurdek, L. A. (1998b). The nature and predictors of the trajectory of change in marital quality over the first 4 years of marriage for first-married husbands and wives. *Journal of Family Psychology, 12,* 494–510.

Kurdek, L. A. (1999). The nature and predictors of the trajectory of change in marital quality for husbands and wives over the first 10 years of marriage. *Developmental Psychology, 35,* 1283–1296.

Kurdek, L. A. (2000). Attractions and constraints as determinants of relationship commitment: Longitudinal evidence from gay, lesbian, and heterosexual couples. *Personal Relationships, 7,* 245–262.

Kurdek, L. A. (2002a). On being insecure about the assessment of attachment styles. *Journal of Social and Personal Relationships, 19,* 811–834.

Kurdek, L. A. (2002b). Predicting the timing of separation and marital satisfaction: An eight-year prospective longitudinal study. *Journal of Marriage and Family, 64,* 163–179.

Kurdek, L. A., & Schmitt, J. (1986). Interaction of sex-role concept with relationship quality and relationship beliefs in married, heterosexual, cohabiting, gay, and lesbian couples. *Journal of Personality and Social Psychology, 51,* 367–372.

Kushner, T. (1993). *Angels in America: A gay fantasia on national themes.* New York: Theatre Communications Group.

LaGuardia, J. G., Ryan, R. M., Couchman, C. E., & Deci, E. L. (2000). Within-person variation in security of attachment: A self-determination theory perspective on attachment, need fulfillment, and well-being. *Journal of Personality and Social Psychology, 79,* 367–384.

Lakey, B., & Cassady, P. B. (1990). Cognitive processes in perceived social support. *Journal of Personality and Social Psychology, 59,* 337–343.

Lakey, B., & Cohen, S. (2000). Social support theory and measurement. In S. Cohen, L. G. Underwood, & B. H. Gottlieb (Eds.), *Social support measurement and intervention: A guide for health and social scientists* (pp. 29–52). New York: Oxford University Press.

Lakey, B., & Lutz, C. J. (2000). Social support and preventive and therapeutic interventions. In G. R. Pierce, B. R. Sarason, & I. G. Sarason (Eds.), *Handbook of social support and the family* (pp. 435–465). New York: Plenum Press.

Lamb, S. C., Jackson, L. A., Cassiday, P. B., & Priest, D. J. (1993). Body figure preferences of men and women: A comparison of two generations. *Sex Roles, 28,* 345–358.

Lambert, G., Johansson, M., Agren, H., & Friberg, P. (2000). Reduced brain norepinephrine and dopamine release in treatment-refractory depressive illness: Evidence in support of the catecholamine hypothesis of mood disorders. *Archives of General Psychiatry, 57,* 787–793.

Lamke, L. K. (1989). Marital adjustment among rural couples: The role of expressiveness. *Sex Roles, 21,* 579–590.

Lamke, L. K., Sollie, D. L., Durbin, R. G., & Fitzpatrick, J. A. (1994). Masculinity, femininity, and relationship satisfaction: The mediating role of interpersonal competence. *Journal of Social and Personal Relationships, 11,* 535–554.

Lamm, H., & Wiesmann, U. (1997). Subjective attributes of attraction: How people characterize their liking, their love, and their being in love. *Personal Relationships, 4,* 271–284.

Lamm, H., Wiesmann, U., & Keller, K. (1998). Subjective determinants of attraction: Self-perceived causes of the rise and decline of liking, love, and being in love. *Personal Relationships, 5,* 91–104.

Lang, F. R., & Carstensen, L. L. (1994). Close emotional relationships in late life: Further support for proactive aging in the social domain. *Psychology and Aging, 9,* 315–324.

Lang, F. R., Staudinger, U. M., & Carstensen, L. L. (1998). Perspectives on socioemotional selectivity in late life: How personality and social context do (and do not) make a difference. *Journal of Gerontology, 53B,* 21–30.

Lange, C. G. (1922). *The emotions.* Baltimore: Williams & Wilkins. (Original work published 1885)

Langley, J., Martin, J., & Nada-Raja, S. (1997). Physical assault among 21-year-olds by partners. *Journal of Interpersonal Violence, 12*, 675–684.

Langlois, J. H., Kalakanis, L., Rubenstein, A. J., Larson, A., Hallam, M., & Smoot, M. (2000). Maxims or myths of beauty? A meta-analytic and theoretical review. *Psychological Bulletin, 126*, 390–423.

Langlois, J. H., Ritter, J. M., Casey, R. C., & Sawin, D. B. (1995). Infant attractiveness predicts maternal behavior and attitudes. *Developmental Psychology, 31*, 462–472.

Langlois, J. H., & Roggman, L. A. (1990). Attractive faces are only average. *Psychological Science, 1*, 115–121.

Langlois, J. H., Roggman, L. A., Casey, R. J., Ritter, J. M., Rieser-Danner, L. A., & Jenkins, V. Y. (1987). Infant preferences for attractive faces: Rudiments of a stereotype? *Developmental Psychology, 23*, 363–369.

Langlois, J. H., Roggman, L. A., & Musselman, L. (1994). What is average and what is not average about attractive faces. *Psychological Science, 5*, 214–220.

Langlois, J. H., Roggman, L. A., & Rieser-Danner, L. A. (1990). Infants' differential social responses to attractive and unattractive faces. *Developmental Psychology, 26*, 153–159.

Larsen, J. T., McGraw, A. P., & Cacioppo, J. T. (2001). Can people feel happy and sad at the same time? *Journal of Personality and Social Psychology, 81*, 684–696.

Larson, J. H., & Holman, T. B. (1994). Premarital predictors of marital quality and stability: An applied literature review. *Family Relations, 43*, 228–237.

Larson, R., & Csikszentmihalyi, M. (1983). The experience sampling method. In H. T. Reis (Ed.), *Naturalistic approaches to studying social interaction* (pp. 41–56). San Francisco: Jossey-Bass.

Larzelere, R. E., & Huston, T. L. (1980). The Dyadic Trust Scale: Toward understanding interpersonal trust in close relationships. *Journal of Marriage and the Family, 42*, 595–604.

Lasswell, T. E., & Lasswell, M. E. (1976). I love you but I'm not in love with you. *Journal of Marriage and Family Counseling, 38*, 211–224.

Latané, B., & Glass, D. C. (1968). Social and nonsocial attraction in rats. *Journal of Personality and Social Psychology, 9*, 142–146.

Latané, B., & Wheeler, L. (1966). Emotionality and reactions to disaster. *Journal of Experimental Social Psychology, 1*, 95–102.

Laursen, B., & Bukowski, W. M. (1997). A developmental guide to the organisation of close relationships. *International Journal of Behavioral Development, 21*, 747–770.

Lavine, L. O., & Lombardo, J. P. (1984). Self-disclosure: Intimate and nonintimate disclosures to parents and best friends as a function of Bem sex-role category. *Sex Roles, 11*, 735–744.

Lavrakas, P. J. (1975). Female preferences for male physiques. *Journal of Research in Personality, 9*, 324–334.

Lawrance, K., & Byers, E. S. (1995). Sexual satisfaction in long-term heterosexual relationships: The interpersonal exchange model of sexual satisfaction. *Personal Relationships, 2*, 267–285.

Lazarus, R. S. (1984). On the primacy of cognition. *American Psychologist, 39*, 124–129.

Lazarus, R. S. (1991). Cognition and motivation in emotion. *American Psychologist, 46*, 352–367.

Lazarus, R. S. (1993). From psychological stress to the emotions: A history of changing outlooks. *Annual Review of Psychology, 44*, 1–21.

Lazarus, R. S. (1994). Appraisal: The long and short of it. In P. Ekman & R. J. Davidson (Eds.), *The nature of emotion: Fundamental questions* (pp. 208–215). New York: Oxford University Press.

Lazarus, R. S., & Folkman, S. (1984). *Stress, appraisal, and coping.* New York: Springer.

Le, B., & Agnew, C. R. (2003). Commitment and its theorized determinants: A meta-analysis of the investment model. *Personal Relationships, 10*, 37–57.

Leary, M. R., & Kowalski, R. M. (1990). Impression management: A literature review and two-component model. *Psychological Bulletin, 197*, 34–47.

Leary, M. R., Tambor, E. S., Terdal, S. K., & Downs, D. L. (1995). Self-esteem as an interpersonal monitor: The sociometer hypothesis. *Journal of Personality and Social Psychology, 68*, 518–530.

Lebra, T. S. (1984). *Japanese women: Constraint and fulfillment.* Honolulu: University of Hawaii Press.

Lebra, T. S. (Ed.). (1992). *Japanese social organization.* Honolulu: University of Hawaii Press.

Leck, K., & Simpson, J. (1999). Feigning romantic interest: The role of self-monitoring. *Journal of Research in Personality, 33*, 69–91.

Leckman, J. F., & Herman, A. E. (2002). Maternal behavior and developmental psychopathology. *Biological Psychiatry, 51*, 27–43.

Lederer, W. J., & Jackson, D. D. (1968). *The mirages of marriage.* New York: Norton.

Le Doux, J. E. (1995). Emotions: Clues from the brain. *Annual Review of Psychology, 46*, 209–235.

Lee, J. A. (1973). *Colours of love: An exploration of the ways of loving.* Toronto, Canada: New Press.

Lee, J. A. (1977). A typology of styles of loving. *Personality and Social Psychology Bulletin, 3*, 173–182.

Lee, J. A. (1988). Love-styles. In R. J. Sternberg & M. L. Barnes (Eds.), *The psychology of love* (pp. 38–67). New Haven, CT: Yale University Press.

Leigh, B. C. (1989). Reasons for having and avoiding sex: Gender, sexual orientation, and relationship to sexual behavior. *Journal of Sex Research, 26*, 199–209.

Leitenberg, H., & Saltzman, H. (2000). A statewide survey of age at first intercourse for adolescent females and age of their male partners: Relation to other risk behaviors and statutory rape implications. *Archives of Sexual Behavior, 29*, 203–215.

Leites, E. (1982). The duty to desire: Love, friendship, and sexuality in some puritan theories of marriage. *Journal of Social History, 15*, 383–408.

Lejuez, C. W., Eifert, G. H., Zvolensky, M. J., & Richards, J. B. (2000). Preference between onset predictable and unpredictable administrations of 20% carbon-dioxide-enriched air: Implications for better understanding the etiology and treatment of panic disorder. *Journal of Experimental Psychology: Applied, 6,* 349–358.

Lennox, R. D., & Wolfe, R. N. (1984). Revision of the self-monitoring scale. *Journal of Personality and Social Psychology, 46,* 1349–1364.

Leonard, K. E., & Roberts, L. J. (1998). Marital aggression, quality, and stability in the first year of marriage: Findings from the Buffalo Newlywed Study. In T. N. Bradbury (Ed.), *The developmental course of marital dysfunction* (pp. 44–73). Cambridge, UK: Cambridge University Press.

Lepper, M. R., Ross, L., & Lau, R. R. (1986). Persistence of inaccurate beliefs about the self: Perseverance effects in the classroom. *Journal of Personality and Social Psychology, 50,* 482–491.

Lerner, M. J. (1980). *The belief in a just world: A fundamental delusion.* New York: Plenum Press.

Leslie, L. A., Huston, T. L., & Johnson, M. P. (1986). Parental reactions to dating relationships: Do they make a difference? *Journal of Marriage and the Family, 48,* 57–66.

Lester, D. (1996). Trends in divorce and marriage around the world. *Journal of Divorce and Remarriage, 25,* 169–171.

Lester, D., Haig, C., & Monello, R. (1989). Spouses' personality and marital satisfaction. *Personality and Individual Differences, 10,* 253–254.

Levenson, R. W., & Gottman, J. M. (1983). Marital interaction: Physiological linkage and affective exchange. *Journal of Personality and Social Psychology, 45,* 587–597.

Levenson, R. W., & Gottman, J. M. (1985). Physiological and affective predictors of change in relationship satisfaction. *Journal of Personality and Social Psychology, 49,* 85–94.

Leventhal, T., & Brooks-Gunn, J. (2000). The neighborhoods they live in: The effects of neighborhood residence on child and adolescent outcomes. *Psychological Bulletin, 126,* 309–337.

Lever, J. (1994, August 23). The 1994 *Advocate* survey of sexuality and relationships: The men. *The Advocate: The National Gay & Lesbian Newsmagazine,* pp. 17–24.

Lever, J. (1995, August 22). The 1995 *Advocate* survey of sexuality and relationships: The women. *The Advocate: The National Gay & Lesbian Newsmagazine,* pp. 22–30.

Levine, R., Sato, S., Hashimoto, T., & Verma, J. (1995). Love and marriage in eleven cultures. *Journal of Cross-Cultural Psychology, 26,* 554–571.

Levine, S., & Wiener, S. G. (1988). Psychoendocrine aspects of mother–infant relationships in nonhuman primates. *Psychoneuroendocrinology, 13,* 143–154.

Levinger, G. (1965). Marital cohesiveness and dissolution: An integrative review. *Journal of Marriage and the Family, 27,* 19–28.

Levinger, G. (1966). Sources of marital dissatisfaction among applicants for divorce. *American Journal of Orthopsychiatry, 36,* 803–807.

Levinger, G. (1974). A three-level approach to attraction: Toward an understanding of pair relatedness. In T. L. Huston (Ed.), *Foundations of interpersonal attraction* (pp. 99–120). New York: Academic Press.

Levinger, G. (1977). The embrace of lives: Changing and unchanging. In G. Levinger & G. Raush (Eds.), *Close relationships: Perspectives on the meaning of intimacy* (pp. 1–16). Amherst: University of Massachusetts Press.

Levinger, G. (1979). A social exchange view on the dissolution of pair relationships. In R. L. Burgess & T. L. Huston (Eds.), *Social exchange in developing relationships* (pp. 169–193). New York: Academic Press.

Levinger, G. (1980). Toward the analysis of close relationships. *Journal of Experimental Social Psychology, 16,* 510–544.

Levinger, G. (1991). Commitment vs. cohesiveness: Two complementary perspectives. In W. H. Jones & D. Perlman (Eds.), *Advances in personal relationships* (Vol. 2, pp. 145–150). London: Jessica Kingsley.

Levinger, G. (1994). Figure versus ground: Micro- and macroperspectives on the social psychology of personal relationships. In R. Erber & R. Gilmour (Eds.), *Theoretical frameworks for personal relationships* (pp. 1–28). Hillsdale, NJ: Erlbaum.

Levinger, G. (1997). Prologue. In R. J. Sternberg & M. Hojjat (Eds.), *Satisfaction in close relationships* (pp. 1–6). New York: Guilford Press.

Levinger, G. (1999). Duty toward whom? Reconsidering attractions and barriers as determinants of commitment in a relationship. In J. M. Adams & W. H. Jones (Eds.), *Handbook of interpersonal commitment and relationship stability* (pp. 37–52). New York: Kluwer Academic/Plenum.

Levinger, G. (2002). Development and change. In H. H. Kelley, E. Berscheid, A. Christensen, J. H. Harvey, T. L. Huston, G. Levinger, E. McClintock, L. A. Peplau, & D. R. Peterson (Eds.), *Close relationships* (pp. 315–359). Clinton Corners, NY: Percheron Press. (Original work published 1983)

Levinger, G., & Breedlove, J. (1966). Interpersonal attraction and agreement: A study of marriage partners. *Journal of Personality and Social Psychology, 3,* 367–372.

Levinger, G., & Rands, M. (1985). Compatibility in marriage and other close relationships. In W. Ickes (Ed.), *Compatible and incompatible relationships* (pp. 309–331). New York: Springer-Verlag.

Levinger, G., Senn, D. J., & Jorgensen, B. W. (1970). Progress toward permanence in courtship: A test of the Kerckhoff–Davis hypotheses. *Sociometry, 33,* 427–433.

Levinger, G., & Snoek, J. D. (1972). *Attraction in relationship: A new look at interpersonal attraction.* Morristown, NJ: General Learning Press.

Levy, D. S. (1999, July 12). I don't. *Time,* p. 80.

Levy, M. B., & Davis, K. E. (1988). Lovestyles and attachment styles compared: Their relations to each other and to various relationship characteristics. *Journal of Social and Personal Relationships, 5,* 439–471.

Lewin, K. (1948). The background of conflict in marriage. In G. Lewin (Ed.), *Resolving social conflicts* (pp. 84–102). New York: Harper. (Original work published 1940)

Lewin, K. (1951). *Field theory in social science.* New York: Harper. (Original work published 1936)

Lewin, K., Dembo, T., Festinger, L., & Sears, P. (1944). Level of aspiration. In J. McV. Hunt (Ed.), *Personality and the behavior disorders* (pp. 333–378). New York: Ronald.

Lewin, T. (1995, May 30). Family structure changing worldwide, study says. *Minneapolis Star Tribune*, pp. 1A, 5A.

Lewis, C. S. (1988). *The four loves*. New York: Harcourt Brace. (Original work published 1960)

Lewis, R. A. (1972). A developmental framework for the analysis of premarital dyadic formation. *Family Process, 11*, 17–48.

Lewis, R. A. (1973). A longitudinal test of a developmental framework for premarital dyadic formation. *Journal of Marriage and the Family, 35*, 113–25.

Lieberson, S. (1997). Application of a probabilistic perspective. In V. R. McKim & S. P. Turner (Eds.), *Causality in crisis: Statistical methods and the search for causal knowledge in the social sciences* (pp. 359–385). Notre Dame, IN: University of Notre Dame Press.

Liddle, H. A., Santisteban, D. A., Levant, R. A., & Bray, J. H. (2001). *Family psychology: Science-based interventions*. Washington, DC: American Psychological Association.

Lin, Y. C. (1992). *The construction of the sense of intimacy from everyday social interaction*. Unpublished doctoral dissertation. University of Rochester, Rochester, NY.

Lindahl, K., Clements, M., & Markman, H. (1998). The development of marriage: A 9-year perspective. In T. N. Bradbury (Ed.), *The developmental course of marital dysfunction* (pp. 205–236). Cambridge, UK: Cambridge University Press.

Lindahl, K. M., Malik, N. M., & Bradbury, T. N. (1997). The developmental course of couples' relationships. In W. K. Halford & H. J. Markman (Eds.), *Clinical handbook of marriage and couples intervention* (pp. 203–223). Chichester, UK: Wiley.

Linton, R. (1936). *The study of man*. New York: Appleton-Century.

Lippert, T., & Prager, K. J. (2001). Daily experiences of intimacy: A study of couples. *Personal Relationships, 8*, 283–298.

Liu, D., Diorio, J., Tannenbaum, B., Caldji, C., Francis, E., Freedman, A., Sharma, S., Pearson, D., Meaney, M. J., & Plotsky, P. M. (1997). Maternal care, hippocampal glucocorticoid receptors, and hypothalamic-pituitary-adrenal responses to stress. *Science, 277* (5332), p. 1659.

Livingston, M. M., Burley, K., & Springer, T. P. (1996). The importance of being feminine: Gender, sex role, occupational and marital role commitment, and their relationship to anticipated work–family conflict. *Journal of Social Behavior and Personality, 11*, 179–192.

Locke, H., & Wallace, K. (1959). Short marital-adjustment and prediction tests: Their reliability and validity. *Marriage and Family Living, 21*, 251–255.

Lorenz, F. O., Conger, R. D., Simon, R. L., Whitbeck, L. B., & Elder, G. H., Jr. (1991). Economic pressure and marital quality: An illustration of the method variance problem in the causal modeling of family processes. *Journal of Marriage and the Family, 53*, 375–388.

Lorenz, K. (1952). *King Solomon's ring*. London: Methuen.

Lott, B., & Maluso, D. (1993). The social learning of gender. In A. E. Beall & R. J. Sternberg (Eds.), *The psychology of gender* (pp. 99–123). New York: Guilford Press.

Lott, B. E., & Lott, A. J. (1974). The role of reward in the formation of positive interpersonal attitudes. In T. L. Huston (Ed.), *Foundations of interpersonal attraction* (pp. 171–192). New York: Academic Press.

Lubbock, J. (1870). *The origin of civilisation and the primitive condition of man. Mental and social condition of savages*. New York: D. Appleton.

Lucas, R. E., Clark, A. E., Georgellis, Y., & Diener, E. (2003). Reexamining adaptation and the set point model of happiness: Reactions to changes in marital status. *Journal of Personality and Social Psychology, 84*, 527–539.

Lucas, R. E., & Diener, E. (2001). Understanding extraverts' enjoyment of social situations: The importance of pleasantness. *Journal of Personality and Social Psychology, 81*, 343–356.

Lucas, R. E., Diener, E., Grob, A., Suh, E., & Shao, L. (2000). Cross-cultural evidence for the fundamental features of extraversion. *Journal of Personality and Social Psychology, 79*, 452–468.

Lucas, R. E., & Fujita, F. (2000). Factors influencing the relation between extraversion and pleasant affect. *Journal of Personality and Social Psychology, 79*, 1039–1056.

Luepnitz, D. A. (1988). *The family interpreted*. New York: Basic Books.

Lussier, G., Deater-Deckard, K., Dunn, J., & Davies, L. (2002). Support across two generations: Children's closeness to grandparents following parental divorce and remarriage. *Journal of Family Psychology, 16*, 363–376.

Lussier, Y., Sabourin, S., & Turgeon, C. (1997). Coping strategies as moderators of the relationship between attachment and marital adjustment. *Journal of Social and Personal Relationships, 14*, 777–791.

Lykken, D. (1999). *Happiness: What studies on twins show us about nature, nurture, and the happiness set-point*. New York: Golden Books.

Lykken, D., & Tellegen, A. (1996). Happiness is a stochastic phenomenon. *Psychological Science, 7*, 186–189.

Lynch, J. J. (1977). *The broken heart: The medical consequences of loneliness*. New York: Basic Books.

Lynch, J. J., Thomas, S. A., Paskewitz, D. A., Katcher, A. H., & Weir, L. O. (1977). Human contact and cardiac arrhythmia in a coronary care unit. *Psychosomatic Medicine, 39*, 188–192.

Maccoby, E. E. (1990). Gender and relationships: A developmental account. *American Psychologist, 45*, 513–520.

Maccoby, E. E., & Jacklin, C. N. (1974). *The psychology of sex differences*. Stanford, CA: Stanford University Press.

MacDermid, S. M., Huston, T. L., & McHale, S. M. (1990). Changes in marriage associated with the transition to parenthood: Individual differences as a function of sex-role attitudes and changes in division of household labor. *Journal of Marriage and the Family, 52*, 475–486.

MacDowell, K., & Mandler, G. (1989). Constructions of emotion: Discrepancy, arousal, and mood. *Motivation and Emotion, 13*, 105–124.

Macfarlane, A. J. (1975). Olfaction in the development of social preferences in the human neonate. *Ciba Foundation Symposia, 33*, 103–117.

Mackey, W. C., & Immerman, R. S. (2001). Restriction of sexual activity as a partial function of disease avoidance: A cultural response to sexually transmitted diseases. *Cross-Cultural Research, 35*, 400–423.

Mackie, J. L. (1965). Causes and conditions. *American Philosophical Quarterly, 2*, 245–264.

Mahler, M. S., Pine, F., & Bergman, A. (1975). *The psychological birth of the human infant: Symbiosis and individuation.* New York: Basic Books.

Mandler, G. (1975). *Mind and emotion.* New York: Wiley.

Mandler, G. (1997). *Human nature explored: Psychology, evolution, society.* New York: Oxford University Press.

Manstead, A. (1992). Gender differences in emotion. In A. Gale & M. W. Eysenck (Eds.), *Handbook of individual differences: Biological perspectives* (pp. 355–387). Chichester, UK: Wiley.

Marangoni, C., & Ickes, W. (1989). Loneliness: A theoretical review with implications for measurement. *Journal of Social and Personal Relationships, 6*, 93–128.

Marazziti, D., Akiskal, H. S., Rossi, A., & Cassano, G. B. (1999). Alteration of the platelet serotonin transporter in romantic love. *Psychological Medicine, 239*, 741–745.

Margolin, L., & White, L. (1987). The continuing role of physical attractiveness in marriage. *Journal of Marriage and the Family, 49*, 21–27.

Markman, H. J., & Hahlweg, K. (1993). The prediction and prevention of marital distress: An international perspective. *Clinical Psychology Review, 13*, 29–43.

Markman, H. J., Renick, M. J., Floyd, F. J., Stanley, S. M., & Clements, M. (1993). Preventing marital distress through communication and conflict management training: A 4- and 5-year follow-up. *Journal of Consulting and Clinical Psychology, 61*, 70–77.

Markman, H. J., Stanley, S. M., & Blumberg, S. L. (1994). *Fighting for your marriage: Positive steps for preventing divorce and preserving a lasting love.* San Francisco: Jossey-Bass.

Markus, H. M., & Kitayama, S. (1991). Culture and the self: Implications for cognition, emotion, and motivation. *Psychological Review, 98*, 224–253.

Married-couple families wane. (2001, May 15). *Minneapolis Star Tribune,* pp. A1, A3.

Marsolek, C. J. (1999). Dissociable neural subsystems underlie abstract and specific object recognition. *Psychological Science, 10*, 111–118.

Martin, L. L., & Tesser, A. (1989). Toward a motivational and structural theory of ruminative thought. In J. S. Uleman & J. A. Bargh (Eds.), *Unintended thought* (pp. 306–325). New York: Guilford Press.

Martin, L. R., Friedman, H. S., Tucker, J. S., Schwartz, J. E., Criqui, M. H., Wingard, D. L., & Tomlinson-Keasey, C. (1995). An archival prospective study of mental health and longevity. *Health Psychology, 14*, 381–387.

Martin, P. V., & Hummer, R. A. (1989). Fraternities and rape on campus. *Gender and Society, 3*, 457–473.

Martin, T. C., & Bumpass, L. (1989). Recent trends in marital disruption. *Demography, 26*, 37–52.

Maruyama, G. M. (1998). *Basics of structural equation modeling.* Thousand Oaks, CA: Sage.

Marwell, G., & Hage, J. (1970). The organization of role relationships: A systematic description. *American Sociological Review, 35*, 884–900.

Mashek, D., & Aron, A. (Eds.). (2004). *The handbook of closeness and intimacy.* Mahwah, NJ: Erlbaum.

Mashek, D. J., Aron, A., & Boncimino, M. (2003). Confusions of self with close others. *Personality and Social Psychology Bulletin, 29*, 382–392.

Mashek, D., Aron, A., & Fisher, H. (2000). Identifying, evoking, and measuring intense feelings of romantic love. *Representative Research in Social Psychology, 24*, 48–55.

Maslow, A. H. (1954). *Motivation and personality.* New York: Harper.

Mason, A., & Blankenship, Y. (1987). Power and affiliation motivation, stress, and abuse in intimate relationships. *Journal of Personality and Social Psychology, 52*, 203–210.

Masten, A. S., & Coatsworth, J. D. (1998). The development of competence in favorable and unfavorable environments: Lessons from research on successful children. *American Psychologist, 53*, 205–220.

Masters, W. H., & Johnson, V. E. (1966). *Human sexual response.* Boston: Little, Brown.

Masters, W. H., & Johnson, V. E. (1970). *Human sexual inadequacy.* Boston: Little, Brown.

Mathews, A., Whitehead, A., & Kellet, J. (1983). Psychological and hormonal factors in the treatment of female sexual dysfunction. *Psychological Medicine, 13*, 83–92.

Mathis, J. L. (1964). A sophisticated version of voodoo death. *Psychosomatic Medicine, 26*, 104–107.

Matlin, M. W., & Stang, D. J. (1978). *The Pollyanna principle: Selectivity in language, memory, and thought.* Cambridge, MA: Schenkman.

McAdams, D. P. (1980). A thematic coding system for the intimacy motive. *Journal of Research in Personality, 14*, 413–432.

McAdams, D. P. (1984). Human motives and personal relationships. In V. J. Derlega (Ed.), *Communication, intimacy, and close relationships* (pp. 41–70). New York: Academic Press.

McAdams, D. P. (1985). *Power, intimacy, and the life story: Personological inquiries into identity.* Homewood, IL: Dorsey Press.

McAdams, D. P. (1989). *Intimacy: The need to be close.* New York: Doubleday.

McAdams, D. P. (1999). Motives. In V. J. Derlega, B. A. Winstead, & W. H. Jones (Eds.), *Personality: Contemporary theory and research* (2nd ed., pp. 162–194). Chicago: Nelson-Hall.

McAdams, D. P., & Constantian, C. A. (1983). Intimacy and affiliation motives in daily living: An experience sampling analysis. *Journal of Personality and Social Psychology, 45,* 851–861.

McAdams, D. P., Healy, S., & Krause, S. (1984). Social motives and patterns of friendship. *Journal of Personality and Social Psychology, 47,* 828–838.

McAdams, D. P., Jackson, R. J., & Kirshnit, C. (1984). *Journal of Personality, 52,* 261–273.

McAdams, D. P., & Losoff, M. (1984). Friendship motivation in fourth and sixth graders: A thematic analysis. *Journal of Social and Personal Relationships, 1,* 10–27.

McAdams, D. P., & Powers, J. (1981). Themes of intimacy in behavior and thought. *Journal of Personality and Social Psychology, 40,* 573–587.

McArthur, L. Z., & Berry, D. S. (1987). Cross-cultural agreement in perceptions of baby-faced adults. *Journal of Cross-Cultural Psychology, 18,* 165–192.

McCabe, M. P., & Collins, J. K. (1984). Measurement of depth of desired and experienced sexual involvement at different stages of dating. *The Journal of Sex Research, 20,* 377–390.

McCaskill, J. W., & Lakey, B. (2000). Perceived support, social undermining, and emotion: Idiosyncratic and shared perspectives of adolescents and their families. *Personality and Social Psychology Bulletin, 7,* 820–832.

McClelland, D. C. (1971). *Assessing human motivation.* Morristown, NJ: General Learning Press.

McClintock, E. (2002). Interaction. In H. H. Kelley, E. Berscheid, A. Christensen, J. H. Harvey, T. L. Huston, G. Levinger, E. McClintock, L. A. Peplau, & D. R. Peterson (Eds.), *Close relationships* (pp. 68–109). Clinton Corners, NY: Percheron Press. (Original work published 1983)

McClure, E. B. (2000). A meta-analytic review of sex differences in facial expression processing and their development in infants, children, and adolescents. *Psychological Bulletin, 126,* 424–453.

McCormick, N. B. (1979). Come-ons and put-offs: Unmarried students' strategies for having and avoiding sexual intercourse. *Psychology of Women Quarterly, 4,* 194–211.

McCormick, N. B., & Jones, A. J. (1989). Gender differences in nonverbal flirtation. *Journal of Sex Education & Therapy, 15,* 271–282.

McCrae, R. R., & Costa, P. T., Jr. (1997). Personality trait structure as a human universal. *American Psychologist, 52,* 509–516.

McCrae, R. R., Costa, P. T., Jr., Ostendorf, F., Angleitner, A., Hrebícková, M., Avia, M. D., Sanz, J., & Sánchez-Bernardos, M. L. (2000). Nature over nurture: Temperament, personality, and life span development. *Journal of Personality and Social Psychology, 78,* 173–186.

McCubbin, H. I., & Patterson, J. M. (1982). Family adaptation to crises. In H. I. McCubbin, A. E. Cauble, & J. M. Patterson (Eds.), *Family stress, coping, and social support.* Springfield, IL: Thomas.

McCubbin, H. I., Patterson, J. M., & Wilson, L. (1980). *Family Inventory of Life Events and Changes (FILE).* St. Paul: University of Minnesota, Department of Family Social Science.

McCullough, J. M., & Barton, E. Y. (1991). Relatedness and mortality risk during a crisis year: Plymouth Colony, 1620–1621. *Ethology and Sociobiology, 12,* 195–209.

McCullough, M. E. (1995). Prayer and health: Conceptual issues, research review, and research agenda. *Journal of Psychology and Theology, 23,* 15–29.

McDonald, H. E., & Hirt, E. R. (1997). When expectancy meets desire: Motivational effects in reconstructive memory. *Journal of Personality and Social Psychology, 72,* 5–23.

McEwen, B. S., & Stellar, E. (1993). Stress and the individual: Mechanisms leading to disease. *Archives of Internal Medicine, 153,* 2093–2101.

McFarland, C., & Ross, M. (1987). The relation between current impressions and memories of self and dating partners. *Personality and Social Psychology Bulletin, 13,* 228–238.

McGinnis, M. Y., Lumia, A., Breuer, M. E., & Possidente, B. (2002). Physical provocation potentiates aggression in male rats receiving anabolic androgenic steroids. *Hormones & Behavior, 41,* 101–110.

McGinnis, R. (1958). Campus values in mate selection: A repeat study. *Social Forces, 35,* 368–373.

McGonagle, K. A., Kessler, R. C., & Schilling, E. A. (1992). The frequency and determinants of marital disagreements in a community sample. *Journal of Social and Personal Relationships, 9,* 507–524.

McHale, S., & Huston, T. L. (1985). The effect of the transition to parenthood on the marriage relationship. *Journal of Family Issues, 6,* 409–434.

McKim, V. R., & Turner, S. P. (Eds.). (1997). *Causality in crisis? Statistical methods and the search for causal knowledge in the social sciences.* Notre Dame, IN: University of Notre Dame Press.

McLennan, J. F. (1865). *Primitive marriage.* Edinburgh, UK: A. & C. Black.

McLoyd, V. C. (1998). Socioeconomic disadvantage and child development. *American Psychologist, 53,* 185–204.

McNamara, J. R., & Grossman, K. (1991). Initiation of dates and anxiety among college men and women. *Psychological Reports, 69,* 252–254.

McNulty, J. K., & Karney, B. R. (2001). Attributions in marriage: Integrating specific and global evaluations of a relationship. *Personality and Social Psychology Bulletin, 27,* 943–955.

McWilliams, S., & Howard, J. A. (1993). Solidarity and hierarchy in cross-sex friendships. *Journal of Social Issues, 49,* 191–202.

Mead, G. H. (1934). *Mind, self, and society.* Chicago: University of Chicago Press.

Meaney, M. J., Aitken, D. H., Bodnoff, S. R., Iny, L. J., Tararewicz, J. E., & Sapolsky, R. M. (1985). Early postnatal handling alters glucocorticoid receptor concentrations in selected brain regions. *Behavioral Neuroscience, 99,* 765–770.

Median-wise, American are 35.3 years old. (2001, May 15). *Minneapolis Star Tribune,* p. 2A.

Melby, J. N., Ge, X., Conger, R. D., & Warner, T. D. (1995). The importance of task in evaluating positive marital interactions. *Journal of Marriage and the Family, 57,* 981–994.

Meloy, J. R. (1989). Unrequited love and the wish to kill: Diagnosis and treatment of borderline erotomania. *Bulletin of the Menninger Clinic, 53*, 477–492.

Meloy, J. R. (1996). Stalking (obsessional following): A review of some preliminary studies. *Aggression and Violent Behavior, 1*, 147–162.

Melson, G. F. (1998). The role of companion animals in human development. In C. C. Wilson & D. C. Turner (Eds.), *Companion animals in human health* (pp. 219–237). Thousand Oaks, CA: Sage.

Melson, G. F. (2001). *Why the wild things are: Animals in the lives of children.* Cambridge, MA: Harvard University Press.

Mendelsohn, R. (1975, December 8). Can the American family survive? *Saint Paul Pioneer Press,* p. 9.

Mendoza-Denton, R., Ayduk, O., Mischel, W., Shoda, Y., & Testa, A. (2001). Person × situation interactionism in self-encoding (*I am . . . When . . .*): Implications for affect regulation and social information processing. *Journal of Personality and Social Psychology, 80*, 533–544.

Meredith, D. B., & Holman, T. B. (2001). Breaking up before and after marriage. In T. B. Holman, *Premarital prediction of marital quality or breakup* (pp. 47–77). New York: Kluwer Academic/Plenum.

A mere 26% are married with children in household. (1999, November 24). *Minneapolis Star Tribune,* p. A4.

Mesquita, B. (2001). Emotions in collectivist and individualist contexts. *Journal of Personality and Social Psychology, 80*, 68–74.

Mesquita, B., & Frijda, N. H. (1992). Cultural variations in emotions: A review. *Psychological Bulletin, 112*, 179–204.

Metts, S., & Spitzberg, B. H. (1996). Sexual communication in interpersonal contexts: A script based approach. In B. R. Burleson (Ed.), *Communication yearbook 19* (pp. 49–92). Thousand Oaks, CA: Sage.

Metts, S., Sprecher, S., & Cupach, W. R. (1991). Retrospective self-reports. In B. M. Montgomery & S. Duck (Eds.), *Studying interpersonal interaction* (pp. 162–178). New York: Guilford Press.

Metts, S., Sprecher, S., & Regan, P. C. (1998). Communication and sexual desire. In P. A. Andersen & L. K. Guerrero (Eds.), *Handbook of communication and emotion: Research, theory, applications, and contexts* (pp. 353–377). Orlando, FL: Academic Press.

Meyer, T. J., & Mark, M. M. (1995). Effects of psychosocial interventions with adult cancer patients: A meta-analysis of randomized experiments. *Health Psychology, 14*, 101–108.

Meyer, W., Reisenzein, R., & Schutzwohl, A. (1997). Toward a process analysis of emotions: The case of surprise. *Motivation and Emotion, 21*, 251–274.

Meyers, S. A., & Berscheid, E. (1997). The language of love: The difference a preposition makes. *Personality and Social Psychology Bulletin, 23*, 347–362.

Michael, R. T., Gagnon, J. H., Laumann, E. O., & Kolata, G. (1994). *Sex in America: A definitive survey.* Boston: Little, Brown.

Miell, D. (1987). Remembering relationship development: Constructing a context for interactions. In R. Burnett, P.

McGhee, & D. D. Clarke (Eds.), *Accounting for relationships: Explanation, representation, and knowledge* (pp. 60–73). London: Metheun.

Miell, D. E., & Duck, S. W. (1986). Strategies in developing friendships. In V. J. Derlega & B. A. Winstead (Eds.), *Friendship and social interaction* (pp. 129–143). New York: Springer.

Mikulincer, M., Birnbaum, G., Woddis, D., & Nachmias, O. (2000). Stress and accessibility of proximity-related thoughts: Exploring the normative and intraindividual components of attachment theory. *Journal of Personality and Social Psychology, 78*, 509–523.

Mikulincer, M., Gillath, O., & Shaver, P. R. (2002). Activation of the attachment system in adulthood: Threat-related primes increase the accessibility of mental representations of attachment figures. *Journal of Personality and Social Psychology, 83*, 881–895.

Milardo, R. M. (1987). Changes in social networks of women and men following divorce: A review. *Journal of Family Issues, 8*, 78–96.

Milardo, R. M. (1988). Families and social networks: An overview of theory and methodology. In R. M. Milardo (Ed.), *Families and social networks* (pp. 13–47). Newbury Park, CA: Sage.

Milardo, R. M., & Helms-Erikson, H. (2000). Network overlap and third-party influence in close relationships. In C. Hendrick & S. S. Hendrick (Eds.), *Close relationships: A sourcebook* (pp. 33–46). Thousand Oaks, CA: Sage.

Milardo, R. M., Johnson, M. P., & Huston, T. L. (1983). Developing close relationships: Changing patterns of interaction between pair members and social networks. *Journal of Personality and Social Psychology, 44*, 964–976.

Mill, J. S. (1965). *A system of logic* (8th ed.). London: Longmans Green. (Original work published 1872)

Miller, L. C., & Fishkin, S. A. (1997). On the dynamics of human bonding and reproductive success: Seeking windows on the adapted-for-human-environmental interface. In J. A. Simpson & D. T. Kenrick (Eds.), *Evolutionary social psychology* (pp. 197–235). Mahwah, NJ: Erlbaum.

Miller, L. C., & Kenny, D. A. (1986). Reciprocity of self-disclosure at the individual and dyadic levels: A social relations analysis. *Journal of Personality and Social Psychology, 50*, 713–719.

Miller, N. E., & Dollard, J. (1941). *Social learning and imitation.* New Haven, CT: Yale University Press.

Miller, R. S. (1997). Inattentive and contented: Relationship commitment and attention to alternatives. *Journal of Personality and Social Psychology, 73*, 758–766.

Mills, J., & Clark, M. S. (1994). Communal and exchange relationships: Controversies and research. In R. Erber & R. Gilmour (Eds.), *Theoretical frameworks for personal relationships* (pp. 29–42). Hillsdale, NJ: Erlbaum.

Mills, R. S. L., & Grusec, J. E. (1988). Socialization from the perspective of the parent–child relationship. In S. Duck (Ed.), *Handbook of personal relationships: Theory, research, and interventions* (pp. 177–191). Chichester, UK: Wiley.

Mineka, S. (1987). A primate model of phobic fears. In H. Eysenck & I. Martin (Eds.), *Theoretical foundations of behaviour therapy*. New York: Plenum Press.

Mintz, E. E. (1980). Obsession with the rejecting beloved. *The Psychoanalytic Review, 67*, 479–492.

Mischel, W. (1966). A social-learning view of sex differences in behavior. In E. E. Maccoby (Ed.), *The development of sex differences* (pp. 56–81). Stanford, CA: Stanford University Press.

Mischel, W. (1968). *Personality and assessment*. New York: Wiley.

Mita, T. H., Dermer, M., & Knight, J. (1977). Reversed facial images and the mere-exposure hypothesis. *Journal of Personality and Social Psychology, 35*, 597–601.

Mongeau, P. A., & Johnson, K. L. (1995). Predicting cross-sex first-date sexual expectations and involvement: Contextual and individual difference factors. *Personal Relationships, 2*, 301–312.

Mongrain, M., Vettese, L., Shuster, B., & Kendal, N. (1998). Perceptual biases, affect, and behavior in the relationships of dependents and self-critics. *Journal of Personality and Social Psychology, 75*, 230–241.

Montgomery, B. M., & Duck, S. (Eds.). (1991). *Studying interpersonal interaction*. New York: Guilford Press.

Monti-Bloch, L., & Grosser, B. I. (1991). Effect of putative pheromones on the electrical activity of the human vomeronasal organ and olfactory epithelium. *Journal of Steroid Biochemistry and Molecular Biology, 39*, 573–582.

Moore, M. M. (1985). Nonverbal courtship patterns in women: Context and consequences. *Ethology and Sociobiology, 6*, 237–247.

Moore, M. M. (1995). Courtship signaling and adolescents: "Girls just wanna have fun"? *The Journal of Sex Research, 32*, 319–328.

More boys favor 1950s family life. (1994, July 11). *Saint Paul Pioneer Press*, p. A1.

Moreno, J. L. (1947). Organization of the social atom. *Sociometry, 10*, 80–84.

Moreno, J. L. (1953). *Who shall survive?* (2nd ed.). Beacon, NY: Beacon House. (First edition published 1934)

Morgan, L. H. (1878). *Ancient society; or, Researches in the lines of human progress from savagery through barbarism to civilization*. New York: H. Holt.

Morgan, S., Lye, D., & Condran, G. (1988). Sons, daughters, and the risk of marital disruption. *American Journal of Sociology, 94*, 110–129.

Mornell, P. (1979). *Passive men, wild women*. New York: Ballentine Books.

Moroney, R. M. (1979). The issue of family policy: Do we know enough to take action? [Special Issue: *Family Policy*]. *Journal of Marriage and the Family, 41*, 461–464.

Morris, M. W., & Peng, K. (1994). Culture and cause: American and Chinese attributions for social and physical events. *Journal of Personality and Social Psychology, 67*, 949–971.

Morrow, G. D., Clark, E. M., & Brock, K. F. (1995). Individual and partner love styles: Implications for the quality of romantic involvements. *Journal of Social and Personal Relationships, 12*, 363–387.

Morton, J., & Johnson, M. H. (1991). CONSPEC and CONLERN: A two-process theory of infant face recognition. *Psychological Review, 98*, 164–181.

Most families now two-income. (2000, October 24). *Minneapolis Star Tribune*, pp. A1, A8.

Muehlenhard, C. L., Goggins, M. F., Jones, J. M., & Satterfield, A. T. (1991). Sexual violence and coercion in close relationships. In K. McKinney & S. Sprecher (Eds.), *Sexuality in close relationships* (pp. 155–175). Hillsdale, NJ: Erlbaum.

Muehlenhard, C. L., & Kimes, L. A. (1999). The social construction of violence: The case of sexual and domestic violence. *Personality and Social Psychology Review, 3*, 234–245.

Muehlenhard, C. L., & Miller, E. N. (1988). Traditional and nontraditional men's responses to women's dating initiation. *Behavior Modification, 12*, 385–403.

Mullen, P. E., & Pathé, M. (1994). Stalking and the pathologies of love. *Australian and New Zealand Journal of Psychiatry, 28*, 469–477.

Munro, B. E., & Adams, G. R. (1978). Correlates of romantic love revisited. *The Journal of Psychology, 98*, 210–214.

Muram, D., Rosenthal, T. L., Tolley, E. A., Peeler, M. M., & Dorko, B. (1991). Race and personality traits affect high school senior girls' sexual reports. *Journal of Sex Education and Therapy, 17*, 231–243.

Murdock, G. P. (1967). Ethnographic atlas: A summary. *Ethnology, 6*, 109–236.

Murray, H. A. (1943). *Thematic apperception test*. Cambridge, MA: Harvard University Press.

Murray, S. L. (1999). The quest for conviction: Motivated cognition in romantic relationships. *Psychological Inquiry, 10*, 23–34.

Murray, S. L., & Holmes, J. G. (1993). Seeing virtues in faults: Negativity and the transformation of interpersonal narratives in close relationships. *Journal of Personality and Social Psychology, 65*, 707–722.

Murray, S. L., & Holmes, J. G. (1996). The construction of relationship realities. In G. J. O. Fletcher & J. Fitness (Eds.), *Knowledge structures in close relationships: A social psychological approach* (pp. 91–120). Mahwah, NJ: Erlbaum.

Murray, S. L., & Holmes, J. G. (1997). A leap of faith: Positive illusions in romantic relationships. *Personality and Social Psychology Bulletin, 23*, 586–604.

Murray, S. L., & Holmes, J. G. (1999). The ties that bind: The structure of conviction in romantic relationships. *Journal of Personality and Social Psychology, 77*, 1228–1244.

Murray, S. L., Holmes, J. G., Bellavia, G., Griffin, D. W., & Dolderman, D. (2002). Kindred spirits? The benefits of egocentrism in close relationships. *Journal of Personality and Social Psychology, 82*, 563–581.

Murray, S. L., Holmes, J. G., & Griffin, D. W. (1996). The benefits of positive illusions: Idealization and the construction of satisfaction in close relationships. *Journal of Personality and Social Psychology, 70*, 79–98.

Murray, S. L., Holmes, J. G., Griffin, D. W., Bellavia, G., & Rose, P. (2001). The mismeasure of love: How self-doubt contaminates relationship beliefs. *Personality and Social Psychology Bulletin, 27*, 423–436.

Murstein, B. I. (1970). Stimulus-value-role: A theory of marital choice. *Journal of Marriage and the Family, 32,* 465–481.

Murstein, B. I. (1976). *Who will marry whom? Theories and research in marital choice.* New York: Springer.

Murstein, B. I. (1980). Mate selection in the 1970s. *Journal of Marriage and the Family, 42,* 777–792.

Murstein, B. I. (1987). A clarification and extension of the SVR theory of dyadic pairing. *Journal of Marriage and the Family, 49,* 929–947.

Murstein, B. I., Cerreto, M., & MacDonald, M. G. (1977). A theory and investigation of the effect of exchange-orientation on marriage and friendships. *Journal of Marriage and the Family, 39,* 543–548.

Musser, L. M., & Browne, B. A. (1991). Self-monitoring in middle childhood: Personality and social correlates. *Developmental Psychology, 27,* 994–999.

Myers, D. G. (1993). *The pursuit of happiness.* New York: Avon.

Myers, D. G. (1999). Close relationships and the quality of life. In D. Kahneman, E. Diener, & N. Schwarz (Eds.), *Well-being: The foundations of hedonic psychology* (pp. 376–393). New York: Russell Sage Foundation.

Myers, D. G. (2000). The funds, friends, and faith of happy people. *American Psychologist, 55,* 56–67.

Myers, D. G., & Diener, E. (1995). Who is happy? *Psychological Science, 6,* 10–19.

Nachmias, M., Gunnar, M., Mangelsdorf, S., Parritz, R., & Buss, K. (1996). Behavioral inhibition and stress reactivity: Moderating role of attachment security. *Child Development, 67,* 508–522.

Nahemow, L., & Lawton, M. P. (1975). Similarity and propinquity in friendship formation. *Journal of Personality and Social Psychology, 32,* 205–213.

Naik, S., & Pennington, G. W. (1981). Female gonadal function: The ovary. In G. W. Pennington & S. Naik (Eds.), *Hormone analysis: Methodology and clinical interpretation* (Vol. 2, pp. 27–61). Boca Raton, FL: CRC Press.

Nathan, P. E., Stuart, S. P., & Dolan, S. L. (2000). Research on psychotherapy efficacy and effectiveness: Between Scylla and Charybdis? *Psychological Bulletin, 126,* 964–981.

Nathanielsz, P. (1999). *Life in the womb: The origin of health and disease.* Ithaca, NY: Promethean Press.

Neisser, U. (1982). *Memory observed: Remembering in natural contexts.* San Francisco: Freeman.

Nelson, C. A., & Luciana, M. (Eds.). (2001). *Handbook of developmental cognitive neuroscience.* Cambridge, MA: MIT Press.

Nemechek, S., & Olson, K. R. (1996). Personality and marital adjustment. *Psychological Reports, 78,* 26.

Neubeck, G., & Schletzer, V. M. (1962). A study of extramarital relationships. *Journal of Marriage and the Family, 24,* 279–281.

Neuberg, S. L., & Fiske, S. T. (1987). Motivational influences on impression formation: Outcome dependency, accuracy-driven attention and individuating processes. *Journal of Personality and Social Psychology, 53,* 431–444.

Newcomb, A. F., & Bagwell, C. L. (1995). Children's friendship relations: A meta-analytic review. *Psychological Bulletin, 117,* 306–347.

Newcomb, A. F., Bukowski, W. M., & Bagwell, C. L. (1999). Knowing the sounds: Friendship as a developmental context. In W. A. Collins & B. Laursen (Eds.), *Minnesota Symposia on Child Psychology: Vol. 30. Relationships as developmental contexts* (pp. 63–84). Mahwah, NJ: Erlbaum.

Newcomb, T. M. (1956). The prediction of interpersonal attraction. *American Psychologist, 11,* 575–586.

Newcomb, T. M. (1961). *The acquaintance process.* New York: Holt, Rinehart, and Winston.

Newcomb, T. M. (1968). Interpersonal balance. In R. P. Abelson, E. Aronson, W. J. McGuire, T. M. Newcomb, M. J. Rosenberg, and P. H. Tannenbaum (Eds.), *Theories of cognitive consistency: A sourcebook* (pp. 28–51). Chicago: Rand McNally.

Newton, T. L., & Kiecolt-Glaser, J. K. (1995). Hostility and erosion of marital quality during early marriage. *Journal of Behavioral Medicine, 18,* 601–619.

Nezlek, J. B., Imbrie, M., & Shean, G. D. (1994). Depression and everyday social interaction. *Journal of Personality and Social Psychology, 67,* 1101–1111.

Nicholson, B. (1984). Does kissing aid human bonding by semiochemical addiction? *British Journal of Dermatology, 111,* 623–627.

Nigro, G., & Neisser, W. (1983). Point of views in personal memories. *Cognitive Psychology, 15,* 467–482.

Noller, P. (1981). Gender and marital adjustment differences in decoding messages from spouses and strangers. *Journal of Personality and Social Psychology, 41,* 272–278.

Noller, P., & Feeney, J. A. (1998). Communication in early marriage: Responses to conflict, nonverbal accuracy, and conversational patterns. In T. N. Bradbury (Ed.), *The developmental course of marital dysfunction* (pp. 11–43). Cambridge, UK: Cambridge University Press.

Noller, P., Feeney, J. A., Bonnell, D., & Callan, V. J. (1994). A longitudinal study of conflict in early marriage. *Journal of Social and Personal Relationships, 11,* 233–252.

Noller, P., & Ruzzene, M. (1991). Communication in marriage: The influence of affect and cognition. In G. J. O. Fletcher & F. D. Fincham (Eds.), *Cognition in close relationships* (pp. 203–234). Hillsdale, NJ: Erlbaum.

Noller, P., & White, A. (1990). The validity of the Communication Patterns Questionnaire. *Psychological Assessment: A Journal of Consulting and Clinical Psychology, 2,* 478–482.

Nørretranders, T. (1998). *The user illusion* (J. Sydenham, Trans.). New York: Viking.

Norris, S. L., & Zweigenhaft, R. L. (1999). Self-monitoring, trust, and commitment in romantic relationships. *The Journal of Social Psychology, 139,* 215–220.

Norton, R. (1983). Measuring marital quality: A critical look at the dependent variable. *Journal of Marriage and the Family, 45,* 141–151.

Notarius, C. I., & Herrick, L. R. (1989). The psychophysiology of dyadic interactions. In H. Wagner & A. Manstead

(Eds.), *Handbook of social psychophysiology* (pp. 393–419). New York: Wiley.

Notarius, C. I., & Johnson, J. (1982). Emotional expression in husbands and wives. *Journal of Marriage and the Family, 44,* 483–489.

Notarius, C. I., & Markman, H. J. (1981). The Couples' Interaction Scoring System. In E. Filsinger & R. Lewis (Eds.), *Assessing marriage: New behavioral approaches* (pp. 117–136). Beverly Hills, CA: Sage.

Numbers. (1999, July 19). *Time,* p. 25.

Nye, F. I., & McDonald, G. (1979). Introduction to the special issue [Special Issue: *Family Policy*]. *Journal of Marriage and the Family, 41,* 447–448.

Ochsner, K. N., & Lieberman, M. D. (2001). The emergence of social cognitive neuroscience. *American Psychologist, 56,* 717–734.

Ogilvie, D. M., & Ashmore, R. (1991). Self-with-other representation as a unit of analysis in self-concept research. In R. C. Curtis (Ed.), *The relational self* (pp. 282–314). New York: Guilford Press.

Ohman, A., & Soares, J. J. F. (1994). "Unconscious anxiety": Phobic responses to masked stimuli. *Journal of Abnormal Psychology, 103,* 231–240.

Olausson, H., Lamarre, Y., Backlund, H., Morin, C., Wallin, B. G., Starck, G., Ekholm, S., Srigo, I., Worsley, K., Vallbo, A. B., & Bushnell, M. C. (2002, July 29). Unmyelinated tactile afferents signal touch and project to insular cortex. *Nature Neuroscience.* (Published online, www.nature.com/natureneuroscience)

O'Leary, A. (1990). Stress, emotion, and human immune function. *Psychological Bulletin, 108,* 363–382.

O'Leary, K. D. (2000). Are women really more aggressive than men in intimate relationships? Comment on Archer (2000). *Psychological Bulletin, 126,* 685–689.

O'Leary, K. D., & Cascardi, M. (1998). Physical aggression in marriage: A developmental analysis. In T. N. Bradbury (Ed.), *The developmental course of marital dysfunction* (pp. 343–374). Cambridge, UK: Cambridge University Press.

Oliver, M. B., & Hyde, J. S. (1993). Gender differences in sexuality: A meta-analysis. *Psychological Bulletin, 114,* 29–51.

Oliver, M. B., & Sedikides, C. (1992). Effects of sexual permissiveness on desirability of partner as a function of low and high commitment to relationship. *Social Psychology Quarterly, 55,* 321–333.

Olson, D. H. (1977). Insiders' and outsiders' view of relationships: Research studies. In G. Levinger & H. Raush (Eds.), *Close relationships* (pp. 115–135). Amherst: University of Massachusetts Press.

Olson, D. H. (1990). Marriage in perspective. In F. D. Fincham & T. N. Bradbury (Eds.), *The psychology of marriage: Basic issues and applications* (pp. 402–419). New York: Guilford Press.

Olson, D. H., Fournier, D. G., & Druckman, J. M. (1989). *PREPARE, PREPARE-MC, ENRICH inventories* (3rd ed.). Minneapolis, MN: PREPARE/ENRICH.

Olson, D. H., & Larsen, A. S. (1989). Predicting marital satisfaction using PREPARE: A replication study. *Journal of Marital and Family Therapy, 15,* 311–322.

Olson, J. M., Roese, N. J., & Zanna, M. P. (1996). Expectancies. In E. T. Higgins & A. W. Kruglanski (Eds.), *Social psychology: Handbook of basic principles* (pp. 211–238). New York: Guilford Press.

O'Neill, E. (1999). *The last will and testament of an extremely distinguished dog.* New York: Henry Holt. (Original work published 1940)

O'Neill, N., & O'Neill, G. (1972). *Open marriage; a new life style for couples.* New York: M. Evans.

Orbuch, T. L., & Eyster, S. L. (1997). The division of household labor among black couples and white couples. *Social Forces, 76,* 301–332.

Orbuch, T. L., & Timmer, S. G. (2001). Differences in his marriage and her marriage. In D. Vannoy (Ed.), *Gender mosaics: Social perspectives* (pp. 155–164). Los Angeles: Roxbury Press.

Orbuch, T. L., Veroff, J., Hassan, H., & Horrocks, J. (2002). Who will divorce: A 14-year longitudinal study of black couples and white couples. *Journal of Social and Personal Relationships, 19,* 179–202.

Orden, S. R., & Bradburn, N. M. (1968). Dimensions of marriage happiness. *American Journal of Sociology, 73,* 715–731.

Ortony, A., & Turner, T. J. (1990). What's basic about basic emotions? *Psychological Review, 97,* 315–331.

Orvis, B. R., Kelley, H. H., & Butler, D. (1976). Attributional conflict in young couples. In J. H. Harvey, W. J. Ickes, & R. E. Kidd (Eds.), *New directions in attribution research* (Vol. 1, pp. 353–386). Hillsdale, NJ: Erlbaum.

Osgood, C. E., May, W. H., & Miron, M. S. (1975). *Cross-cultural universals of affective meaning.* Urbana: University of Illinois Press.

Osgood, C. E., Suci, G. J., & Tannenbaum, P. H. (1957). *The measurement of meaning.* Urbana: University of Illinois Press.

Oster, H., Daily, L., & Goldenthal, P. (1989). Processing facial affect. In A. W. Young & H. D. Ellis (Eds.), *Handbook of research on face processing* (pp. 107–161). Amsterdam: Elsevier.

O'Sullivan, L. F. (1995). Less is more: The effects of sexual experience on judgments of men's and women's personality characteristics and relationship desirability. *Sex Roles, 33,* 159–181.

O'Sullivan, L. F., & Gaines, M. E. (1998). Decision-making in college students' heterosexual dating relationships: Ambivalence about engaging in sexual activity. *Journal of Social and Personal Relationships, 15,* 347–363.

Ouellette, J. A., & Wood, W. (1998). Habit and intention in everyday life: The multiple processes by which past behavior predicts future behavior. *Psychological Bulletin, 124,* 54–74.

Oyserman, D., Coon, H. M., & Kemmelmeier, M. (2002). Rethinking individualism and collectivism: Evaluations of theoretical assumptions and meta-analyses. *Psychological Bulletin, 128,* 3–72.

Palace, E. M. (1995). Modification of dysfunctional patterns of sexual response through autonomic arousal and false physiological feedback. *Journal of Consulting and Clinical Psychology, 63,* 604–615.

Palace, E. M. (1999). Response expectancy and sexual dysfunction in women. In I. Kirsch (Ed.), *How expectancies shape experience* (pp. 173–196). Washington, DC: American Psychological Association.

Pam, A., Plutchik, R., & Conte, H. R. (1975). Love: A psychometric approach. *Psychological Reports, 37*, 83–88.

Panksepp, J. (1998). *Affective neuroscience: The foundations of human and animal emotions.* New York: Oxford University Press.

Parke, R. D. (2000). Beyond white and middle class: Cultural variations in families—assessments, processes, and policies. *Journal of Family Psychology, 14*, 331–333.

Parkes, C. M., & Weiss, R. S. (1983). *Recovery from bereavement.* New York: Basic Books.

Parks, M. R., & Eggert, L. L. (1991). The role of social context in the dynamics of personal relationships. In W. H. Jones & D. Perlman (Eds.), *Advances in personal relationships* (Vol. 2, pp. 1–34). London: Jessica Kingsley.

Parks, M. R., & Floyd, K. (1996). Meanings for closeness and intimacy in friendship. *Journal of Social and Personal Relationships, 13*, 85–107.

Parks, M. R., Stan, C. M., & Eggert, L. L. (1983). Romantic involvement and social network involvement. *Social Psychology Quarterly, 46*, 116–131.

Pascal, B. (1995). *Pensées* (A. J. Krailsheimer, Trans.). (Rev. ed.). London: Penguin Books. (Original work published 1643)

Pascalis, O., de Haan, M., & Nelson, C. A. (2002). Is face processing species-specific during the first year of life? *Science, 296*, 1321–1323.

Pasch, L. A., & Bradbury, T. N. (1998). Social support, conflict, and the development of marital dysfunction. *Journal of Consulting and Clinical Psychology, 66*, 219–230.

Pasch, L. A., Bradbury, T. N., & Davila, J. (1997). Gender, negative affectivity, and observed social support in marital interaction. *Personal Relationships, 4*, 361–378.

Pastor, D. L. (1981). The quality of mother–infant attachment and its relationship to toddler' initial sociability with peers. *Developmental Psychology, 17*, 326–335.

Patterson, G. R. (1979). A performance theory for coercive family interaction. In R. B. Cairns (Ed.), *The analysis of social interactions: Methods, issues, and illustrations.* Hillsdale, NJ: Erlbaum.

Patterson, J. M. (2002). Integrating family resilience and family stress theory. *Journal of Marriage and Family, 64*, 349–360.

Patzer, G. L. (1985). *The physical attractiveness phenomenon.* New York: Plenum Press.

Pearlin, L. I., & Schooler, C. (1978). The structure of coping. *Journal of Health and Social Behavior, 19*, 2–21.

Pennebaker, J. W. (1989). Confession, inhibition, and disease. In L. Berkowitz (Ed.), *Advances in experimental social psychology* (Vol. 22, pp. 211–244). San Diego, CA: Academic Press.

Pennebaker, J. W. (1990). *Opening up: The healing power of confiding in others.* New York: Morrow.

Pennebaker, J. W., & Beall, S. K. (1986). Confronting a traumatic event: Toward an understanding of inhibition and disease. *Journal of Abnormal Psychology, 95*, 274–281.

Pennebaker, J. W., Dyer, M. A., Caulkins, R. S., Litowitz, D. L., Ackreman, P. L., Anderson, D. B., & McGraw, K. M. (1979). Don't the girls get prettier at closing time: A country and western application to psychology. *Personality and Social Psychology Bulletin, 5*, 122–125.

Peplau, L. A. (2002). Roles and gender. In H. H. Kelley, E. Berscheid, A. Christensen, J. H. Harvey, T. L. Huston, G. Levinger, E. McClintock, L. A. Peplau, & D. R. Peterson (Eds.), *Close relationships* (pp. 220–264). Clinton Corners, NY: Percheron Press. (Original work published 1983)

Peplau, L. A., & Gordon, S. L. (1985). Women and men in love: Gender differences in close heterosexual relationships. In V. E. O'Leary, R. K. Unger, & B. S. Wallston (Eds.), *Women, gender, and social psychology* (pp. 257–291). Hillsdale, NJ: Erlbaum.

Peplau, L. A., & Perlman, D. (Eds.). (1982). *Loneliness: A sourcebook of current theory, research, and therapy.* New York: Wiley.

Peplau, L. A., Rubin, Z., & Hill, C. T. (1977). Sexual intimacy in dating relationships. *Journal of Social Issues, 33*, 86–109.

Peplau, L. A., Russell, D., & Heim, M. (1979). The experience of loneliness. In I. H. Frieze, D. Bar-Tal, & J. S. Carroll (Eds.), *New approaches to social problems: Applications of attribution theory.* San Francisco: Jossey-Bass.

Peplau, L. A., & Spalding, L. R. (2000). The close relationships of lesbians, gay men and bisexuals. In C. Hendrick & S. S. Hendrick (Eds.), *Close relationships: A sourcebook* (pp. 111–123). Thousand Oaks, CA: Sage.

Perper, T. (1985). *Sexual signals: The biology of love.* Philadelphia: ISI Press.

Perper, T., & Weis, D. L. (1987). Proceptive and rejective strategies of U.S. and Canadian college women. *The Journal of Sex Research, 23*, 455–480.

Perrett, D. I., May, K. A., & Yoshikawa, S. (1994). Facial shape and judgments of female attractiveness. *Nature, 368*, 239–242.

Peterson, C. D., Baucom, D. H., Elliott, M. J., & Farr, P. A. (1989). The relationship between sex role identity and marital adjustment. *Sex Roles, 21*, 775–787.

Peterson, D. R. (2002). Conflict. In H. H. Kelley, E. Berscheid, A. Christensen, J. H. Harvey, T. L. Huston, G. Levinger, E. McClintock, L. A. Peplau, & D. R. Peterson, (Eds.), *Close relationships* (pp. 360–396). Clinton Corners, NY: Percheron Press. (Original work published 1983)

Petronio, S., & Martin, J. (1986). Ramifications of revealing private information: A gender gap. *Journal of Clinical Psychology, 42*, 499–506.

Petronio, S., & Sargent, J. (2003). Self-disclosure. In J. J. Ponzetti Jr. (Ed.), *International encyclopedia of marriage and family* (2nd ed., Vol. 3, pp. 1414–1418). New York: Macmillan Reference USA.

Pickering, M. (1993). *August Comte: An intellectual biography, Volume 1.* Cambridge, UK: Cambridge University Press.

Pierce, G. R., Sarason, B. R., & Sarason, I. G. (1992). General and specific support expectations and stress as predictors of perceived supportiveness: An experimental study. *Journal of Personality and Social Psychology, 63*, 297–307.

Pierce, G. R., Sarason, I. G., & Sarason, B. R. (1991). General and relationship-based perceptions of social support: Are two constructs better than one? *Journal of Personality and Social Psychology, 61,* 1028–1039.

Pierce, G. R., Sarason, I. G., & Sarason, B. R. (Eds.). (1996). *Handbook of social support and the family.* New York: Plenum Press.

Pietropinto, A. (1986). Inhibited sexual desire. *Medical Aspects of Human Sexuality, 20*(10), 46–49.

Pillemer, D. B. (1998). *Momentous events, vivid memories.* Cambridge, MA: Harvard University Press.

Pineo, P. C. (1961). Disenchantment in the later years of marriage. *Marriage and Family Living, 23,* 3–11.

Pinker, S. (1994). *The language instinct: How the mind creates language.* New York: Morrow.

Pinsker, H., Nepps, P., Redfield, J., & Winston, A. (1985). Applicants for short-term dynamic psychotherapy. In A. Winston (Ed.), *Clinical and research issues in short-term dynamic psychotherapy* (pp. 104–116). Washington, DC: American Psychiatric Association.

Pinsof, W. M., & Wynne, L. C. (2000). Toward progress research: Closing the gap between family therapy practice and research. *Journal of Marital and Family Therapy, 26,* 1–8.

Pittman, F. (1997). Just in love. *Journal of Marital and Family Therapy, 23,* 309–312.

Planalp, S. (1987). Interplay between relationship knowledge and events. In R. Burnett, P. McGhee, & D. Clarke (Eds.), *Accounting for relationships: Explanation, representation, and knowledge* (pp. 175–191). London: Methuen.

Planalp, S. (1993). Friends' and acquaintances' conversations II: Coded differences. *Journal of Social and Personal Relationships, 10,* 339–354.

Planalp, S., & Benson, A. (1992). Friends' and acquaintances' conversations I: Perceived differences. *Journal of Social and Personal Relationships, 9,* 483–506.

Plutchik, R. (1980). A general psychoevolutionary theory of emotion. In R. Plutchik & H. Kellerman (Eds.), *Emotion: Theory, research, and experience* (Vol. 1, pp. 3–33). London: Academic Press.

Ponzetti, J. J., Jr., & Cate, R. M. (1987). The developmental course of conflict in the marital dissolution process. In C. A. Everett (Ed.), *The divorce process: A handbook for clinicians* (pp. 1–15). New York: Haworth Press.

Popper, K. (1964). *The poverty of historicism.* New York: Harper.

Prager, K. J. (1995). *The psychology of intimacy.* New York: Guilford Press.

Prager, K. J. (2003). Intimacy. In J. J. Ponzetti Jr. (Ed.), *International encyclopedia of marriage and family* (2nd ed., Vol. 3, pp. 941–948). New York: Macmillan Reference USA.

Prager, K. J., & Buhrmester, D. (1998). Intimacy and need fulfillment in couple relationships. *Journal of Social and Personal Relationships, 15,* 435–469.

Prentice, D. (1990). Familiarity and differences in self- and other-representations. *Journal of Personality and Social Psychology, 59,* 369–383.

Press, J. E., & Townsley, E. (1998). Wives' and husbands' housework reporting: Gender, class, and social desirability. *Gender and Society, 12,* 188–218.

Priming the body's natural defenses. (2000, October 2). *U.S. News & World Report,* p. 50.

Proite, R., Dannells, M., & Benton, S. L. (1993). Gender, sex-role stereotypes, and the attribution of responsibility for date and acquaintance rape. *Journal of College Student Development, 34,* 411–417.

Pryor, J. B., & Merluzzi, T. V. (1985). The role of expertise in processing social interaction scripts. *Journal of Experimental Social Psychology, 21,* 362–379.

Quality not quantity. (1994, November 28). *Newsweek,* pp. 36–37.

Rabkin, J. G., Rabkin, R., & Wagner, G. (1995). Testosterone replacement therapy in HIV illness. *General Hospital Psychiatry, 17,* 37–42.

Rajecki, D. W. (1985). Predictability and control in relationships: A perspective from animal behavior. In W. Ickes (Ed.), *Compatible and incompatible relationships* (pp. 11–32). New York: Springer-Verlag.

Rands, M. (1988). Changes in social networks following marital separation and divorce. In R. M. Milardo (Ed.), *Families and social networks* (pp. 127–146). Newbury Park, CA: Sage.

Rao, K. V., & DeMaris, A. (1995). Coital frequency among married and cohabiting couples in the United States. *Journal of Biosocial Science, 27,* 135–150.

Raudenbush, S. W., Brennan, R. T., & Barnett, R. C. (1995). A multivariate hierarchical model for studying psychological change within married couples. *Journal of Family Psychology, 9,* 161–174.

Raush, H. L., Barry, W. A., Hertel, R. K., & Swain, M. E. (1974). *Communication, conflict, and marriage.* San Francisco: Jossey-Bass.

Regan, P. (2003). *The mating game: A primer on love, sex, and marriage.* Thousand Oaks, CA: Sage.

Regan, P. C. (1996). Sexual outcasts: The perceived impact of body weight on sexuality. *Journal of Applied Social Psychology, 26,* 1803–1815.

Regan, P. C. (1998a). Of lust and love: Beliefs about the role of sexual desire in romantic relationships. *Personal Relationships, 5,* 139–157.

Regan, P. C. (1998b). Minimum mate selection standards as a function of perceived mate value, relationship context, and gender. *Journal of Psychology and Human Sexuality, 10,* 53–73.

Regan, P. C. (1998c). What if you can't get what you want? Willingness to compromise ideal mate selection standards as a function of sex, mate value, and relationship context. *Personality and Social Psychology Bulletin, 24,* 1294–1303.

Regan, P. C. (1999). Hormonal correlates and causes of sexual desire: A review. *The Canadian Journal of Human Sexuality, 8,* 1–16.

Regan, P. C. (2000). The role of sexual desire and sexual activity in dating relationships. *Social Behavior and Personality, 28,* 51–60.

Regan, P. C. (2002). Functional features: An evolutionary perspective on inappropriate relationships. In R. Goodwin & D. Cramer (Eds.), *Inappropriate relationships: The unconventional, the disapproved, and the forbidden* (pp. 25–42). Mahwah, NJ: Erlbaum.

Regan, P. C., & Berscheid, E. (1995). Gender differences in beliefs about the causes of male and female sexual desire. *Personal Relationships, 2,* 345–358.

Regan, P. C., & Berscheid, E. (1996). Beliefs about the state, goals, and objects of sexual desire. *Journal of Sex & Marital Therapy, 22,* 110–120.

Regan, P. C., & Berscheid, E. (1997). Gender differences in characteristics desired in a potential sexual and marriage partner. *Journal of Psychology and Human Sexuality, 9,* 25–37.

Regan, P. C., & Berscheid, E. (1999). *Lust: What we know about human sexual desire.* Thousand Oaks, CA: Sage.

Regan, P. C., & Dreyer, C. S. (1999). Lust? Love? Status? Young adults' motives for engaging in casual sex. *Journal of Psychology & Human Sexuality, 11,* 1–24.

Regan, P. C., Kocan, E. R., & Whitlock, T. (1998). Ain't love grand! A prototype analysis of romantic love. *Journal of Social and Personal Relationships, 15,* 411–420.

Regan, P. C., Levin, L., Sprecher, S., Christopher, F. S., & Cate, R. (2000). Partner preferences: What characteristics do men and women desire in their short-term sexual and long-term romantic partners? *Journal of Psychology & Human Sexuality, 12,* 1–21.

Reik, T. (1944). *A psychologist looks at love.* New York: Farrar & Rinehart.

Reik, T. (1945). *Psychology of sex relations.* New York: Grove Press.

Reik, T. (1972). *A psychologist looks at love.* New York: Lancer Books. (Original work published 1944 by Farrar & Rinehart)

Reis, H. T. (1994). Domains of experience: Investigating relationship processes from three perspectives. In R. Erber & R. Gilmour (Eds.), *Theoretical frameworks for personal relationships* (pp. 87–110). Hillsdale, NJ: Erlbaum.

Reis, H. T. (2001). Relationship experiences and emotional well-being. In C. D. Ryff & B. H. Singer (Eds.), *Emotion, social relationships, and health* (pp. 57–86). Oxford, UK: Oxford University Press.

Reis, H. T., Collins, W. A., & Berscheid, E. (2000). The relationship context of human behavior and development. *Psychological Bulletin, 126,* 844–872.

Reis, H. T., & Downey, G. (1999). Social cognition in relationships: Building essential bridges between two literatures. *Social Cognition, 17,* 97–117.

Reis, H. T., & Franks, P. (1994). The role of intimacy and social support in health outcomes: Two processes or one? *Personal Relationships, 1,* 185–197.

Reis, H. T., & Gable, S. L. (2000). Event-sampling and other methods for studying daily experience. In H. T. Reis & C. Judd (Eds.), *Handbook of research methods in social and personality psychology* (pp. 190–222). Cambridge, UK: Cambridge University Press.

Reis, H. T., Lin, Y., Bennett, M. E., & Nezlek, J. B. (1993). Change and consistency in social participation during early adulthood. *Developmental Psychology, 29,* 633–645.

Reis, H. T., Nezlek, J., & Wheeler, L. (1980). Physical attractiveness in social interaction. *Journal of Personality and Social Psychology, 38,* 604–617.

Reis, H. T., & Patrick, B. C. (1997). Attachment and intimacy: Component processes. In E. T. Higgins & A. Kruglanski (Eds.), *Social psychology: Handbook of basic principles* (pp. 367–389). New York: Guilford Press.

Reis, H. T., & Shaver, P. (1988). Intimacy as an interpersonal process. In S. Duck (Ed.), *Handbook of personal relationships: Theory, research, and interventions* (pp. 367–389). Chichester, UK: Wiley.

Reis, H. T., Sheldon, K. M., Gable, S. L., Roscoe, J., & Ryan, R. M. (2000). Daily well-being: The role of autonomy, competence and relatedness. *Personality and Social Psychology Bulletin, 26,* 419–435.

Reis, H. T., & Wheeler, L. (1991). Studying social interaction with the Rochester Interaction Record. In M. P. Zanna (Ed.), *Advances in experimental social psychology* (Vol. 24, pp. 269–318). San Diego, CA: Academic Press.

Reis, H. T., Wheeler, L., Spiegel, N., Kernis, M., Nezlek, J., & Perri, M. (1982). Physical attractiveness in social interaction: II. Why does appearance affect social experience? *Journal of Personality and Social Psychology, 43,* 979–996.

Reisenzein, R. (1983). The Schachter theory of emotion: Two decades later. *Psychological Bulletin, 94,* 239–264.

Reiss, I. L. (1960). Toward a sociology of the heterosexual love relationship. *Marriage and Family Living, 22,* 139–145.

Reiss, I. L. (1964). The scaling of premarital sexual permissiveness. *Journal of Marriage and the Family, 26,* 188–198.

Reiss, I. L. (1967). *The social context of premarital sexual permissiveness.* New York: Holt, Rinehart, and Winston.

Reiss, I. L. (1980). *Family systems in America* (3rd ed.). New York: Holt, Rinehart & Winston.

Reiss, I. L. (1981). Some observations on ideology and sexuality in America. *Journal of Marriage and the Family, 43,* 271–283.

Reiss, I. L. (1986). *Journey into sexuality: An exploratory voyage.* Englewood Cliffs, NJ: Prentice-Hall.

Rempel, J. K., Holmes, J. G., & Zanna, M. P. (1985). Trust in close relationships. *Journal of Personality and Social Psychology, 49,* 95–112.

Rempel, J. K., Ross, M., & Holmes, J. G. (2001). Trust and communicated attributions in close relationships. *Journal of Personality and Social Psychology, 81,* 57–64.

Renne, E. P. (1997). The meaning of contraceptive choice and constraint for Hausa women in a northern Nigerian town. *Anthropology & Medicine, 4,* 159–175.

Rensink, R. A. (2002). Change detection. *Annual Review of Psychology, 53,* 245–277.

Repetti, R. L. (1989). Effects of daily workload on subsequent behavior during marital interaction: The roles of social withdrawal and spouse support. *Journal of Personality and Social Psychology, 57,* 651–659.

Repetti, R. L., Taylor, S. E., & Seeman, T. E. (2002). Risky families: Family social environments and the mental and physical health of offspring. *Psychological Bulletin, 128,* 330–366.

Richardson, S. (1971). *Pamela; or, virtue rewarded.* Boston: Houghton Mifflin. (Original work published 1740)

Richter, C. P. (1955). Phenomenon of sudden death in man and animals. *Science, 121,* 624.

Ridge, R. D., & Berscheid, E. (1989, May). *On loving and being in love: A necessary distinction.* Paper presented at the annual convention of the Midwestern Psychological Association, Chicago, IL.

Rimé, B., Finkenauer, C., Luminet, O., Zech, E., & Philippot, P. (1998). Social sharing of emotion: New evidence and new questions. *European Review of Social Psychology, 9,* 145–189.

Rimé, B., Philippot, P., Boca, S., & Mesquita, B. (1992). Long-lasting cognitive and social consequences of emotion: Social sharing and rumination. *European Review of Social Psychology, 3,* 225–258.

Rindfuss, R. R., & Stephen, E. H. (1990). Marital noncohabitation: Separation does not make the heart grow fonder. *Journal of Marriage and the Family, 52,* 95–105.

Ritchie, W. C., & Bhatia, T. K. (Eds.). (1999). *Handbook of child language acquisition.* San Diego, CA: Academic Press.

Roach, M. (1996, May 19). Cruising attitude. *USA Weekend,* pp. 4–6.

Roberts, T.-A., & Pennebaker, J. W. (1995). Gender differences in perceiving internal state: Toward a his-and-hers model of perceptual cue use. In M. P. Zanna (Ed.), *Advances in experimental social psychology* (Vol. 27, pp. 143–176). San Diego, CA: Academic Press.

Roberts, T. W. (1992). Sexual attraction and romantic love: Forgotten variables in marital therapy. *Journal of Marital and Family Therapy, 18,* 357–364.

Robins, R. W., Caspi, A., & Moffitt, T. E. (2000). Two personalities, one relationship: Both partners' personality traits shape the quality of their relationship. *Journal of Personality and Social Psychology, 79,* 251–259.

Robinson, E. A., & Price, M. G. (1980). Pleasurable behavior in marital interaction: An observational study. *Journal of Consulting and Clinical Psychology, 48,* 117–118.

Robinson, I. E., Balkwell, J. W., & Ward, D. M. (1980). Meaning and behavior: An empirical study in sociolinguistics. *Social Psychology Quarterly, 43,* 253–258.

Robinson, J. P., Yerby, J., Fieweger, M., & Somerick, N. (1977). Sex-role differences in time use. *Sex Roles, 3,* 443–458.

Roche, J. P., & Ramsbey, T. W. (1993). Premarital sexuality: A five-year follow-up study of attitudes and behavior by dating stage. *Adolescence, 28,* 67–80.

Rogers, S. J., & Amato, P. R. (1997). Is marital quality declining? The evidence from two generations. *Social Forces, 75,* 1089–1100.

Rogge, R. D., & Bradbury, T. N. (1999). Till violence does us part: The differing roles of communication and aggression in predicting adverse marital outcomes. *Journal of Consulting and Clinical Psychology, 67,* 340–351.

Rook, K. S. (1984). The negative side of social interaction: Impact on psychological well-being. *Journal of Personality and Social Psychology, 46,* 1097–1108.

Rook, K. S. (1987). Social support versus companionship: Effects on life stress, loneliness, and evaluation by others. *Journal of Personality and Social Psychology, 52,* 1132–1147.

Rook, K. S. (1988). Towards a more differentiated view of loneliness. In S. Duck (Ed.), *Handbook of personal relationships: Theory, research, and interventions* (pp. 571–590). Chichester, UK: Wiley.

Rook, K. S. (1998). Investigating the positive and negative sides of personal relationships: Through a lens darkly? In B. H. Spitzberg & W. R. Cupach (Eds.), *The dark side of close relationships* (pp. 369–393). Mahwah, NJ: Erlbaum.

Rook, K. S., & Pietromonaco, P. (1987). Close relationships: Ties that heal or ties that bind? *Advances in Personal Relationships, 1,* 1–35.

Rosch, E. H. (1973). On the internal structure of perceptual and semantic categories. In T. E. Moore (Ed.), *Cognitive development and the acquisition of language* (pp. 111–144). New York: Academic Press.

Rosch, E. H. (1975). Cognitive representations of semantic categories. *Journal of Experimental Psychology, 104,* 192–233.

Rosch, E. H. (1978). Principles of categorization. In E. Rosch & B. B. Lloyd (Eds.), *Cognition and categorization* (pp. 27–48). Hillsdale, NJ: Erlbaum.

Roscoe, B., Strouse, J. S., & Goodwin, M. P. (1994). Sexual harassment: Early adolescent self-reports of experiences and acceptance. *Adolescence, 29,* 515–523.

Rose, A. J., & Asher, S. R. (2000). Children's friendships. In C. Hendrick & S. S. Hendrick (Eds.), *Close relationships: A sourcebook* (pp. 47–57). Thousand Oaks, CA: Sage.

Rose, S., & Frieze, I. H. (1989). Young singles' scripts for a first date. *Gender and Society, 3,* 258–268.

Rose, S., & Frieze, I. H. (1993). Young singles' contemporary dating scripts. *Sex Roles, 28,* 499–509.

Rose, S. M. (1984). How friendships end: Patterns among young adults. *Journal of Personal and Social Relationships, 1,* 267–277.

Rosenbaum, M. E. (1986). The repulsion hypothesis: On the nondevelopment of relationships. *Journal of Personality and Social Psychology, 51,* 1156–1166.

Rosenblatt, P. C. (1977). Needed research on commitment in marriage. In G. Levinger & H. L. Rausch (Eds.), *Close relationships: Perspectives on the meaning of intimacy.* Amherst: University of Massachusetts Press.

Rosenblatt, P. C. (1983). *Bitter, bitter tears: Nineteenth-century diarists and twentieth-century grief theories.* Minneapolis: University of Minnesota Press.

Rosenfeld, L. B., & Bowen, G. L. (1991). Marital disclosure and marital satisfaction: Direct-effect versus interaction-effect models. *Western Journal of Speech Communication, 55,* 69–84.

Rosenthal, R. (1991). *Meta-analytic procedures for social research* (2nd ed.). Beverly Hills, CA: Sage.

Rosenthal, R., & DiMatteo, M. R. (2001). Meta-analysis: Recent developments in quantitative methods for literature reviews. *Annual Review of Psychology, 52,* 59–82.

Rosenthal, R., & Rosnow, R. L. (1975). *The volunteer subject.* New York: Wiley.

Rosenzweig, M. R. (1996). Aspects of the search for neural mechanism of memory. *Annual Review of Psychology, 47,* 1–32.

Ross, C. E., Mirowsky, J., & Goldsteen, K. (1990). The impact of the family on health: The decade in review. *Journal of Marriage and the Family, 52,* 1059–1078.

Ross, M., & Holmberg, D. (1990). Recounting the past: Gender differences in the recall of events in the history of a close relationship. In J. M. Olson & M. P. Zanna (Eds.), *Ontario Symposium: Vol. 6. Self-inference processes* (pp. 135–152). Hillsdale, NJ: Erlbaum.

Ross, M., & Sicoly, F. (1979). Egocentric biases in availability and attribution. *Journal of Personality and Social Psychology, 37,* 322–336.

Ross, M. A. (1989). The relation of implicit theories to the construction of personal history. *Psychological Review, 96,* 341–357.

Ross, W. D. (1966). *The works of Aristotle translated into English: Vol. IX. Ethica nicomachea; Magna moralia; Ethica Eudemia.* London: Oxford University Press. (First edition published 1915)

Rothbart, M. K., Ahadi, S. A., & Evans, D. E. (2000). Temperament and personality: Origins and outcomes. *Journal of Personality and Social Psychology, 78,* 122–135.

Rothbart, M. K., & Bates, J. E. (1998). Temperament. In W. Damon & N. Eisenberg (Eds.), *Handbook of child psychology: Vol. 3. Social, emotional, and personality development* (5th ed., pp. 105–176). New York: Wiley.

Rothbaum, F., Weisz, J., Pott, M., Miyake, K., & Morelli, G. (2000). Attachment and culture: Security in the United States and Japan. *American Psychologist, 55,* 1093–1104.

Rotter, J. B. (1966). Generalized expectancies for internal versus external control of reinforcement. *Psychological Monographs, 80* (1, Whole No. 609).

Rotter, J. B. (1980). Interpersonal trust, trustworthiness, and gullibility. *American Psychologist, 35,* 1–7.

Rowan, A. (1992). Companion animals demographics and unwanted animals in the United States. *Anthrozoos, 5,* 222–225.

Rowatt, T. J., Cunningham, M. R., Rowatt, W. C., Miles, S. S., Ault-Gauthier, L. K., Georgianna, J., & Shamblin, S. (1997, July). *Men and women are from Earth: Life-span strategy dynamics in mate choices.* Paper presented at the meeting of the International Network on Personal Relationships, Oxford, OH.

Rowatt, W. C., Cunningham, M. R., & Druen, P. B. (1998). Deception to get a date. *Personality and Social Psychology Bulletin, 24,* 1228–1242.

Rubenstein, C. M., & Shaver, P. (1982). The experience of loneliness. In L. A. Peplau & D. Perlman (Eds.), *Loneliness: A sourcebook of current theory, research, and therapy* (pp. 206–223). New York: Wiley.

Rubin, D. C. (Ed.). (1986). *Autobiographical memory.* Cambridge, UK: Cambridge University Press.

Rubin, D. C., & Kozin, M. (1984). Vivid memories. *Cognition, 16,* 81–95.

Rubin, D. C., Wetzler, S. E., & Nebes, R. D. (1986). Autobiographical memory across the lifespan. In D. C. Rubin (Ed.), *Autobiographical memory* (pp. 202–221). Cambridge, UK: Cambridge University Press.

Rubin, K. H., Coplan, R. J., Nelson, L. J., Cheah, C. S. L., & Lagace-Seguin, D. G. (1999). Peer relationships in childhood. In M. H. Bornstein & M. E. Lamb (Eds.), *Developmental psychology: An advanced textbook* (4th ed., pp. 451–501). Mahwah, NJ: Erlbaum.

Rubin, L. (1976). *Worlds of pain: Life in the working class family.* New York: Basic Books.

Rubin, Z. (1970). Measurement of romantic love. *Journal of Personality and Social Psychology, 16,* 265–273.

Rubin, Z. (1973). *Liking and loving: An invitation to social psychology.* New York: Holt, Rinehart, & Winston.

Rubin, Z., Hill, C. T., Peplau, L. A., & Dunkel-Schetter, C. (1980). Self-disclosure in dating couples: Sex roles and the ethic of openness. *Journal of Marriage and the Family, 42,* 305–317.

Rubin, Z., & Mitchell, C. (1976). Couples research as couples counseling: Some unintended effects of studying close relationships. *American Psychologist, 31,* 17–25.

Rubinson, L., & de Rubertis, L. (1991). Trends in sexual attitudes and behaviors of a college population over a 15-year period. *Journal of Sex Education and Therapy, 17,* 32–41.

Rusbult, C. E. (1983). A longitudinal test of the investment model: The development (and deterioration) of satisfaction and commitment in heterosexual involvements. *Journal of Personality and Social Psychology, 45,* 101–117.

Rusbult, C. E. (1987). Responses to dissatisfaction in close relationships: The exit-voice-loyalty-neglect model. In D. Perlman & S. Duck (Eds.), *Intimate relationships: Development, dynamics, and deterioration* (pp. 209–237). Newbury Park, CA: Sage.

Rusbult, C. E., Bissonnette, V. L., Arriaga, X. B., & Cox, C. L. (1998). Accommodation processes during the early years of marriage. In T. N. Bradbury (Ed.), *The developmental course of marital dysfunction* (pp. 74–113). Cambridge, UK: Cambridge University Press.

Rusbult, C. E., Johnson, D. J., & Morrow, G. D. (1986). Determinants and consequences of exit, voice, loyalty, and neglect: Responses to dissatisfaction in adult romantic involvements. *Human Relations, 39,* 45–63.

Rusbult, C. E., Martz, J. M., & Agnew, C. R. (1998). The Investment Model Scale: Measuring commitment level, satisfaction level, quality of alternatives, and investment size. *Personal Relationships, 5,* 357–391.

Rusbult, C. E., & Van Lange, P. A. M. (1996). Interdependence processes. In E. T. Higgins & A. W. Kruglanski (Eds.), *Social psychology: Handbook of basic principles* (pp. 133–168). New York: Guilford Press.

Rusbult, C. E., & Van Lange, P. A. M. (2003). Interdependence, interaction, and relationships. *Annual Review of Psychology, 54*, 351–375.

Rusbult, C. E., Van Lange, P. A. M., Wildschut, T., Yovetich, N. A., & Verette, J. (2000). Perceived superiority in close relationships: Why it exists and persists. *Journal of Personality and Social Psychology, 79*, 521–545.

Rusbult, C. E., Wieselquist, J., Foster, C. A., & Witcher, B. S. (1999). Commitment and trust in close relationships: An interdependence analysis. In J. M. Adams & W. H. Jones (Eds.), *Handbook of interpersonal commitment and relationship stability* (pp. 427–449). New York: Kluwer Academic/ Plenum.

Rusbult, C. E., Yovetich, N. A., & Verette, J. (1996). An interdependence analysis of accommodation processes. In G. J. O. Fletcher & J. Fitness (Eds.), *Knowledge structures in close relationships: A social psychological approach* (pp. 63–90). Mahwah, NJ: Erlbaum.

Rusbult, C. E., Zembrodt, I. M., & Gunn, L. K. (1982). Exit, voice, loyalty, and neglect: Responses to dissatisfaction in romantic involvements. *Journal of Personality and Social Psychology, 43*, 1230–1242.

Russell, D., Peplau, L. A., & Cutrona, C. E. (1980). The revised UCLA Loneliness Scale: Concurrent and discriminant validity evidence. *Journal of Personality and Social Psychology, 39*, 472–480.

Russell, J. A. (1980). A circumplex model of affect. *Journal of Personality and Social Psychology, 39*, 1161–1178.

Russell, J. A. (1989). Measures of emotion. In R. Plutchik & H. Kellerman (Eds.), *Emotion: Theory, research, and experience: Vol. 4. The measurement of emotions* (pp. 83–111). San Diego, CA: Academic Press.

Russell, J. A. (1991). Culture and the categorization of emotions. *Psychological Bulletin, 110*, 426–450.

Russell, J. A. (1994). Is there universal recognition of emotion from facial expressions? A review of the cross-cultural studies. *Psychological Bulletin, 115*, 102–141.

Russell, J. A., Bachorowski, J., & Fernández-Dols, J. M. (2003). Facial and vocal expressions of emotion. *Annual Review of Psychology, 54*, 329–349.

Russell, J. A., & Carroll, J. M. (1999). On the bipolarity of positive and negative affect. *Psychological Bulletin, 125*, 3–30.

Russell, J. A., & Fernández-Dols, J-M. (Eds.). (1997). *The psychology of facial expression*. New York: Cambridge University Press.

Russell, R. J. H., & Wells, P. A. (1994). Predictors of happiness in married couples. *Personality and Individual Differences, 17*, 313–321.

Rutter, M., Pickles, A., Murray, R., & Eaves, L. (2001). Testing hypotheses on specific environmental causal effects on behavior. *Psychological Bulletin, 127*, 291–324.

Rutter, M., & Silberg, J. (2002). Gene–environment interplay in relation to emotional and behavioral disturbance. *Annual Review of Psychology, 53*, 463–490.

Ryan, R. M., & Deci, E. L. (2001). On happiness and human potentials: A review of research on hedonic and eudaimonic well-being. *Annual Review of Psychology, 52*, 141–166.

Ryff, C. D., & Singer, B. H. (2001). Introduction: Integrating emotion into the study of social relationships and health. In C. D. Ryff & B. H. Singer (Eds.), *Emotion, social relationships, and health* (pp. 3–22). Oxford, UK: Oxford University Press.

Ryff, C. D., Singer, B. H., Wing, E., & Love, G. D. (2001). Elective affinities and uninvited agonies: Mapping emotion with significant others onto health. In C. D. Ryff & B. H. Singer (Eds.), *Emotion, social relationships, and health* (pp. 133–175). Oxford, UK: Oxford University Press.

Sabatelli, R. M. (1988). Measurement issues in marital research: A review and critique of contemporary survey instruments. *Journal of Marriage and the Family, 50*, 891–915.

Sabourin, S., Lussier, Y., Laplante, B., & Wright, J. (1991). Unidimensional and multidimensional models of dyadic adjustment: A hierarchical integration. *Psychological Assessment, 2*, 219–230.

Safilios-Rothschild, C. (1977). *Love, sex, and sex roles*. Englewood Cliffs, NJ: Prentice-Hall.

Sagrestano, L. M., Christensen, A., & Heavey, C. L. (1998). Social influence techniques during marital conflict. *Personal Relationships, 5*, 75–89.

Sagrestano, L. M., Heavey, C. L., & Christensen, A. (1999). Perceived power and physical violence in marital conflict. *Journal of Social Issues, 55*, 65–79.

Salovey, P., Rothman, A. J., Detweiler, J. B., & Steward, W. T. (2000). Emotional states and physical health. *American Psychologist, 55*, 110–121.

Salzinger, L. L. (1982). The ties that bind: The effect of clustering on dyadic relationships. *Social Networks, 4*, 117–145.

Samson, J. M., Levy, J. J., Dupras, A., & Tessier, D. (1991). Coitus frequency among married or cohabiting heterosexual adults: A survey in French-Canada. *Australian Journal of Marriage & Family, 12*, 103–109.

Sanders, M. R., Nicholson, J. M., & Floyd, F. J. (1997). Couples' relationships and children. In W. K. Halford & H. J. Markman (Eds.), *Clinical handbook of marriage and couples interventions* (pp. 225–253). Chichester, UK: Wiley.

Sanderson, C. A., & Evans, S. M. (2001). Seeing one's partner through intimacy-colored glasses: An examination of the processes underlying the intimacy goals–relationship satisfaction link. *Personality and Social Psychology Bulletin, 27*, 463–473.

Sanford, K. (2003). Problem-solving conversations in marriage: Does it matter what topics couples discuss? *Personal Relationships, 10*, 97–112.

Sarason, B. R., Sarason, I. G., & Gurung, R. A. R. (2001). Close personal relationships and health outcomes: A key to the role of social support. In B. R. Sarason & S. Duck (Eds.), *Personal relationships: Implications for clinical and community psychology* (pp. 15–42). New York: Wiley.

Sarason, B. R., Sarason, I. G., Hacker, T. A., & Basham, R. B. (1985). Concomitants of social support: Social skills, physical attractiveness, and gender. *Journal of Personality and Social Psychology, 49*, 469–480.

Sarason, B. R., Sarason, I. G., & Pierce, G. R. (Eds.). (1990a). *Social support: An interactional view*. New York: Wiley.

Sarason, I. G., Sarason, B. R., & Pierce, G. R. (1990b). Social support: The search for theory. *Journal of Social and Clinical Psychology, 9*, 133–147.

Sarason, I. G., Sarason, B. R., & Pierce, G. R. (1995). Social and personal relationships: Current issues, future directions. *Journal of Social and Personal Relationships, 12*, 613–619.

Scanlon-Jones, S., Collins, K., & Hong, H. (1991). An audience effect on smile production in 10-month-old infants. *Psychological Science, 2*, 45–48.

Scanzoni, J. (1979). Social exchange and behavioral interdependence. In R. L. Burgess & T. L. Huston (Eds.), *Social exchange in developing relationships* (pp. 61–98). New York: Academic Press.

Scanzoni, J., Polonko, K., Teachman, J., & Thompson, L. (1989). *The sexual bond: Rethinking families and close relationships.* Newbury Park, CA: Sage.

Schachter, S. (1959). *The psychology of affiliation: Experimental studies of the sources of gregariousness.* Stanford, CA: Stanford University Press.

Schachter, S. (1964). The interaction of cognitive and physiological determinants of emotional state. In L. Berkowitz (Ed.), *Advances in experimental social psychology* (Vol. 1, pp. 49–80). New York: Academic Press.

Schachter, S., & Singer, J. E. (1962). Cognitive, social, and physiological determinants of emotional state. *Psychological Review, 69*, 379–399.

Schachter, S., & Wheeler, L. (1962). Epinephrine, chlorpromazine, and amusement. *Journal of Abnormal and Social Psychology, 65*, 121–128.

Schaffer, M. (2002, March 11). Marriage proposal: Should the government spend your tax dollars to encourage holy vows? *U.S. News & World Report*, p. 26.

Scharfe, E., & Bartholomew, K. (1994). Reliability and stability of adult attachment patterns. *Personal Relationships, 1*, 23–43.

Schloss, P., & Williams, D. C. (1998). The serotonin transporter: A primary target for antidepressant drugs. *Journal of Psychopharmacology, 12*, 115–121.

Schmaling, K. B., & Sher, T. G. (Eds.). (2000). *The psychology of couples and illness: Theory, research, and practice.* Washington, DC: American Psychological Association.

Schmitt, J. P., & Kurdek, L. A. (1985). Age and gender differences in and personality correlates of loneliness in different relationships. *Journal of Personality Assessment, 49*, 485–496.

Schonert-Reichl, K. A., & Muller, J. R. (1996). Correlates of help-seeking in adolescence. *Journal of Youth and Adolescence, 25*, 705–731.

Schreiner-Engel, P., & Schiavi, R. C. (1986). Lifetime psychopathology in individuals with low sexual desire. *Journal of Nervous and Mental Disease, 174*, 646–651.

Schultz, D. P., & Schultz, S. E. (2000). *A history of modern psychology* (7th ed.). New York: Harcourt Brace.

Schultz, S., & Kulman, L. (1999, August 9). Racing for the cure: How cyclist Lance Armstrong beat cancer and the competition. *U.S. News & World Report*, pp. 60–61.

Schwartz, P. (1994). *Peer marriage: How love between equals really works.* New York: Free Press.

Schwartz, P., & Rutter, V. (1998). *The gender of sexuality.* Thousand Oaks, CA: Pine Forge Press.

Schwartz, S. H., & Huismans, S. (1995). Value priorities and religiosity in four western religions. *Social Psychology Quarterly, 58*, 88–107.

Schwarz, N. (2001). Feelings as information: Implications for affective influences on information processing. In L. L. Martin & G. L. Clore (Eds.), *Theories of mood and cognition* (pp. 159–176). Mahwah, NJ: Erlbaum.

Schwarz, N., & Clore, G. L. (1983). Mood, misattribution, and judgments of well-being: Informative and directive functions of affective states. *Journal of Personality and Social Psychology, 45*, 513–523.

Scott, C. K., Fuhrman, R. W., & Wyer, R. S., Jr. (1991). Information processing in close relationships. In G. J. O. Fletcher & F. D. Fincham (Eds.), *Cognition in close relationships* (pp. 37–68). Hillsdale, NJ: Erlbaum.

Scott, J. P. (1967). Genetic analysis of social behavior. In N. L. Segal, G. E. Weisfeld, & C. C. Weisfeld (Eds.), *Uniting psychology and biology: Integrating perspectives on human development* (pp. 131–144). Washington, DC: American Psychological Association.

Seal, D. W., Agostinelli, G., & Hannett, C. A. (1994). Extradyadic romantic involvement: Moderating effects of sociosexuality and gender. *Sex Roles, 31*, 1–22.

Sears, R. R. (1951). A theoretical framework for personality and social behavior. *American Psychologist, 6*, 476–482.

Secord, P. F. (1983). Imbalanced sex ratios: The social consequences. *Personality and Social Psychology Bulletin, 9*, 525–543.

Sedikides, C., Campbell, W. K., Reeder, G. D., & Elliott, A. J. (2002). The self in relationships: Whether, how, and when close others put the self "in its place." *European Review of Social Psychology, 12*, 237–265.

Sedikides, C., Olsen, N., & Reis, H. T. (1993). Relationships as natural categories. *Journal of Personality and Social Psychology, 64*, 71–82.

Seeman, T. E. (1996). Social ties and health: The benefits of social integration. *Annals of Epidemiology, 6*, 442–451.

Seeman, T. E. (2001). How do others get under our skin? Social relationships and health. In C. D. Ryff & B. H. Singer (Eds.), *Emotion, social relationships, and health* (pp. 189–210). Oxford, UK: Oxford University Press.

Seeman, T. E., Singer, B. H., Rowe, J. W., Horwitz, R. I., & McEwen, B. S. (1997). The price of adaptation: Allostatic load and its health consequences: MacArthur studies of successful aging. *Archives of Internal Medicine, 157*, 2259–2268.

Segal, M. W. (1974). Alphabet and attraction: An unobtrusive measure of propinquity in a field setting. *Journal of Personality and Social Psychology, 30*, 654–657.

Segraves, R. T. (1990). Theoretical orientations in the treatment of marital discord. In F. D. Fincham & T. N. Bradbury (Eds.), *The psychology of marriage: Basic issues and applications* (pp. 281–298). New York: Guilford Press.

Segrin, C. (1998). Interpersonal communication problems associated with depression and loneliness. In P. A. Andersen & L. K. Guerrero (Eds.), *Handbook of communication and* emotion: Research, theory, applications, and contexts (pp. 215–242). San Diego, CA: Academic Press.

Segrin, C. (2000). Social skills deficits associated with depression. *Clinical Psychology Review, 20*, 379–403.

Segrin, C., & Dillard, J. P. (1992). The interactional theory of depression: A meta-analysis of the research literature. *Journal of Social and Clinical Psychology, 11*, 43–70.

Segrin, C., Powell, H. L., Givertz, M., & Brackin, A. (2003). Symptoms of depression, relational quality, and loneliness in dating relationships. *Personal Relationships, 10*, 25–36.

Seligman, C., Fazio, R. H., & Zanna, M. P. (1980). Effects of salience of extrinsic rewards on liking and loving. *Journal of Personality and Social Psychology, 38*, 453–460.

Seligman, M. E. P. (1971). Phobias and preparedness. *Behavior Therapy, 2*, 307–320.

Seligman, M. E. P. (1975). *Helplessness: On depression, development, and death.* San Francisco: Freeman.

Seligman, M. E. P. (1995). The effectiveness of psychotherapy: The *Consumer Reports* study. *American Psychologist, 50*, 965–974.

Seligman, M. E. P., & Csikszentmihalyi, M. (2000). Positive psychology: An introduction. *American Psychologist, 55*, 5–14.

Selye, H. (1936, July 4). A syndrome produced by diverse nocuous agents. *Nature, 138*, 32.

Selye, H. (1956/1976/1978). *The stress of life.* New York: McGraw-Hill.

Serpell, J. (1991). Beneficial effects of pet ownership on some aspects of human health and behaviour. *Journal of the Royal Society of Medicine, 84*, 717–720.

Shackelford, T. K., & Buss, D. M. (1997). Marital satisfaction in evolutionary psychological perspective. In R. J. Sternberg & M. Hojjat (Eds.), *Satisfaction in close relationships* (pp. 7–25). New York: Guilford Press.

Shadish, W. R., Cook, T. D., & Campbell, D. T. (2001). *Experimental and quasi-experimental designs for generalized causal inference.* Boston: Houghton Mifflin.

Shadish, W. R., Montgomery, L. M., Wilson, P., Wilson, M. R., Bright, I., & Okwumabua, T. (1993). Effects of family and marital psychotherapies: A meta-analysis. *Journal of Consulting and Clinical Psychology, 61*, 992–1002.

Shadish, W. R., Ragsdale, K., Glaser, R. R., & Montgomery, L. M. (1995). The efficacy and effectiveness of marital and family therapy: A perspective from meta-analysis. *Journal of Marital and Family Therapy, 21*, 345–360.

Shatz, C. J. (1992). The developing brain. *Scientific American, 267*(3), 61–67.

Shaver, P., Furman, W., & Buhrmester, D. (1985). Aspects of a life transition: Network changes, social skills and loneliness. In S. Duck & D. Perlman (Eds.), *Understanding personal relationships: An interdisciplinary approach* (pp. 193–219). London: Sage.

Shaver, P., Hazan, C., & Bradshaw, D. (1988). Love as attachment: The integration of three behavioral systems. In R. J. Sternberg & M. L. Barnes (Eds.), *The psychology of love* (pp. 68–99). New Haven, CT: Yale University Press.

Shaver, P., Schwartz, J., Kirson, D., & O'Connor, C. (1987). Emotion knowledge: Further exploration of a prototype ap-

proach. *Journal of Personality and Social Psychology, 52*, 1061–1086.

Shaver, P. R., & Brennan, K. A. (1992). Attachment styles and the "big five" personality traits: Their connections with each other and with romantic relationship outcomes. *Personality and Social Psychology Bulletin, 18*, 536–545.

Shaver, P. R., & Hazan, C. (1988). A biased overview of the study of love. *Journal of Social and Personal Relationships, 5*, 473–501.

Shelton, B. A., & John, D. (1993). Does marital status make a difference? Housework among married and cohabiting men and women. *Journal of Family Issues, 14*, 401–420.

Shepperd, J. A., & Strathman, A. J. (1989). Attractiveness and height: The role of stature in dating preferences, frequency of dating, and perceptions of attractiveness. *Personality and Social Psychology Bulletin, 15*, 617–627.

Sher, K. (1991). *Children of alcoholics: A critical appraisal of theory and research.* Chicago: University of Chicago Press.

Sherwin, R., & Corbett, S. (1985). Campus sexual norms and dating relationships: A trend analysis. *The Journal of Sex Research, 21*, 258–274.

Shively, W. P. (1998). *The craft of political research* (4th ed.). Upper Saddle River, NJ: Prentice Hall.

Shotland, R. L., & Craig, J. M. (1988). Can men and women differentiate between friendly and sexually interested behavior? *Social Psychology Quarterly, 51*, 613–73.

Shuchter, S. R., & Zisook, S. (1993). The course of normal grief. In M. S. Stroebe, W. Stroebe, & R. O. Hansson (Eds.), *Handbook of bereavement: Theory, research, and intervention* (pp. 23–43). Cambridge, UK: Cambridge University Press.

Shulman, S., & Collins, W. A. (Eds.). (1997). *Romantic relationships in adolescence: Developmental perspectives.* In W. Damon (Series Ed.), *New directions in child development* (No. 78, Winter). San Francisco: Jossey-Bass.

Shultz, T. R. (1982). Rules of causal attribution. *Monographs of the Society for Research in Child Development, 47*(1, Serial No. 194), 1–51.

Shye, D., Mullooly, J. P., Freeborn, D. K., & Pope, C. R. (1995). Gender differences in the relationship between social network support and mortality: A longitudinal study of an elderly cohort. *Social Science and Medicine, 41*, 915–947.

Siegel, D. J. (1999). *The developing mind: Toward a neurobiology of interpersonal experience.* New York: Guilford Press.

Sillars, A., Roberts, L. J., Leonard, K. E., & Dun, T. (2000). Cognition during marital conflict: The relationship of thought and talk. *Journal of Social and Personal Relationships, 17*, 479–502.

Sillars, A. L. (1985). Interpersonal perception in relationships. In W. Ickes (Ed.), *Compatible and incompatible relationships* (pp. 277–305). New York: Springer-Verlag.

Sillars, A. L. (1991). Behavioral observation. In B. M. Montgomery & S. Duck (Eds.), *Studying interpersonal interaction* (pp. 197–218). New York: Guilford Press.

Silliman, B., Stanley, S. M., Coffin, W., Markman, H. J., & Jordan, P. L. (2002). Preventive intervention for couples. In H. A. Liddle, D. A. Santisteban, R. F. Levant, & J. H. Bray (Eds.),

Family psychology: Science-based interventions (pp. 123–146). Washington, DC: American Psychological Association.

Simon, R., & Cannon, A. (2001, August 6). An amazing journey: The mirror of the census reveals the character of a nation. *U.S. News & World Report*, pp. 10–18.

Simon, W., & Gagnon, J. H. (1986). Sexual scripts: Permanence and change. *Archives of Sexual Behavior, 15*, 97–120.

Simpson, J. A. (1987). The dissolution of romantic relationships: Factors involved in relationship stability and emotional distress. *Journal of Personality and Social Psychology, 53*, 683–692.

Simpson, J. A., Campbell, B., & Berscheid, E. (1986). The association between romantic love and marriage: Kephart (1967) twice revisited. *Personality and Social Psychology Bulletin, 12*, 363–372.

Simpson, J., A., Fletcher, G. J. O., & Campbell, L. (2001). The structure and ideal function of ideal standards in close relationships. In G. J. O. Fletcher & M. S. Clark (Eds.), *Blackwell handbook of social psychology: Interpersonal processes* (pp. 86–106). Malden, MA: Blackwell.

Simpson, J. A., & Gangestad, S. W. (1991). Individual differences in sociosexuality: Evidence for convergent and discriminant validity. *Journal of Personality and Social Psychology, 60*, 870–883.

Simpson, J. A., & Gangestad, S. W. (1992). Sociosexuality and romantic partner choice. *Journal of Personality, 60*, 31–51.

Simpson, J. A., Gangestad, S. W., & Biek, M. (1993). Personality and nonverbal social behavior: An ethological perspective of relationship initiation. *Journal of Experimental Social Psychology, 29*, 434–461.

Simpson, J. A., Gangestad, S. W., & Lerma, M. (1990). Perception of physical attractiveness: Mechanism involved in the maintenance of romantic relationships. *Journal of Personality and Social Psychology, 59*, 1192–1201.

Simpson, J. A., & Rholes, W. S. (Eds.). (1998). *Attachment theory and close relationships*. New York: Guilford Press.

Simpson, J. A., Rholes, W. S., & Nelligan, J. S. (1992). Support-seeking and support-giving within couple members in an anxiety-provoking situation: The role of attachment styles. *Journal of Personality and Social Psychology, 62*, 434–446.

Simpson, W. E., & Crandall, S. J. (1972). The perception of smiles. *Psychonomic Science, 29*, 197–200.

Singer, J. A., & Salovey, P. (1988). Mood and memory: Evaluating the network theory of affect. *Clinical Psychology Review, 8*, 211–251.

Singh, D. (1993). Adaptive significance of female physical attractiveness: Role of waist-to-hip ratio. *Journal of Personality and Social Psychology, 65*, 293–307.

Singh, D. (1995). Female judgment of male attractiveness and desirability for relationships: Role of waist-to-hip ratio and financial status. *Journal of Personality and Social Psychology, 69*, 1089–1101.

Singh, D., & Luis, S. (1995). Ethnic and gender consensus for the effect of waist-to-hip ratio on judgment of women's attractiveness. *Human Nature, 6*, 51–65.

Sippola, L. K. (1999). Getting to know the "other": The characteristics and developmental significance of other-sex relationships in adolescence. *Journal of Youth and Adolescence, 28*, 407–418.

Skinner, B. F. (1953). *Science and human behavior*. New York: Macmillan.

Skowronski, J. J., Betz, A. L., Thompson, C. P., & Shannon, L. (1991). Social memory in everyday life: Recall of self-events and other-events. *Journal of Personality and Social Psychology, 60*, 831–843.

Slater, A., Von der Schulenburg, C., Brown, E., Badenoch, M., Butterworth, G., Parsons, S., & Samuels, C. (1998). Newborn infants prefer attractive faces. *Infant Behavior and Development, 21*, 345–354.

Small, M. F. (1992). The evolution of female sexuality and mate selection in humans. *Human Nature, 3*, 133–156.

Smith, C. P. (Ed.). (1992). *Motivation and personality: Handbook of thematic content analysis*. Cambridge, UK: Cambridge University Press.

Smith, D. A., Vivian, D., & O'Leary, K. D. (1990). Longitudinal prediction of marital discord from premarital expressions of affect. *Journal of Consulting and Clinical Psychology, 58*, 790–797.

Smith, E. R. (1996). What do connectionism and social psychology offer each other? *Journal of Personality and Social Psychology, 70*, 893–912.

Smith, E. R. (1998). Mental representation and memory. In D. T. Gilbert, S. T. Fiske, & G. Lindzey (Eds.), *The handbook of social psychology* (4th ed., Vol. 1, pp. 391–445). Boston: McGraw-Hill.

Smith, E. R., & DeCoster, J. (2000). Dual-process models in social and cognitive psychology: Conceptual integration and links to underlying memory systems. *Personality and Social Psychology Review, 4*, 108–131.

Smith, E. R., & Zarate, M. A. (1992). Exemplar-based model of social judgment. *Psychological Review, 99*, 3–21.

Smith, R. B., & Brown, R. A. (1997). The impact of social support on gay male couples. *Journal of Homosexuality, 33*, 39–61.

Smock, P. J. (2000). Cohabitation in the United States: An appraisal of research themes, findings, and implications. *Annual Review of Sociology, 26*, 1–20.

Snyder, D. K., Cozzi, J. J., & Mangrum, L. F. (2002). Conceptual issues in assessing couples and families. In H. A. Liddle, D. A. Santisteban, R. F. Levant, & J. H. Bray (Eds.), *Family psychology: Science-based interventions* (pp. 69–87). Washington, DC: American Psychological Association.

Snyder, M. (1974). The self-monitoring of expressive behavior. *Journal of Personality and Social Psychology, 30*, 526–537.

Snyder, M. (1979). Self-monitoring processes. *Advances in Experimental Social Psychology, 12*, 85–128.

Snyder, M. (1987). *Public appearances/private realities: The psychology of self-monitoring*. New York: Freeman.

Snyder, M., Berscheid, E., & Glick, P. (1985). Focusing on the exterior and the interior: Two investigations of the initiation of personal relationships. *Journal of Personality and Social Psychology, 48*, 1427–1439.

Snyder, M., Gangestad, S., & Simpson, J. A. (1983). Choosing friends as activity partners: The role of self-monitoring. *Journal of Personality and Social Psychology, 45*, 1061–1072.

Snyder, M., & Simpson, J. A. (1984). Self-monitoring and dating relationships. *Journal of Personality and Social Psychology, 47*, 1281–1291.

Snyder, M., & Stukas, A. A. (1999). Interpersonal processes: The interplay of cognitive, motivational, and behavioral activities in social interaction. *Annual Review of Psychology, 50*, 273–303.

Snyder, M., Tanke, E. D., & Berscheid, E. (1977). Social perception and interpersonal behavior: On the self-fulfilling nature of social stereotypes. *Journal of Personality and Social Psychology, 35*, 656–666.

Soames, M. (1979). *Clementine Churchill.* London: Cassell.

Sollie, D. L., & Fischer, J. L. (1985). Sex-role orientation, intimacy of topic, and target person differences in self-disclosure among women. *Sex Roles, 12*, 917–929.

Soskin, W. F., & John, V. P. (1963). The study of spontaneous talk. In R. G. Baker (Ed.), *The stream of behavior* (pp. 228–287). New York: Appleton-Century-Crofts.

South, S. J., & Lloyd, K. M. (1995). Spousal alternatives and marital dissolution. *American Sociological Review, 60*, 21–35.

South, S. J., & Spitze, G. (1994). Housework in marital and nonmarital households. *American Sociological Review, 59*, 327–347.

South, S. J., Trent, K., & Shen, Y. (2001). Changing partners: Toward a macrostructural-opportunity theory of marital dissolution. *Journal of Marriage and Family, 63*, 743–754.

Southwick, C. H., Siddiqi, M. F., Farooqui, M. Y., & Pal, B. C. (1974). Xenophobia among free-ranging rhesus groups in India. In R. L. Holloway (Ed.), *Primate aggression, territoriality, and xenophobia: A comparative perspective* (pp. 185–209). New York: Academic Press.

Spanier, G. B. (1972). Further evidence on methodological weaknesses in the Locke–Wallace Marital Adjustment Scale and other measures of adjustment. *Journal of Marriage and the Family, 34*, 403–404.

Spanier, G. B. (1976). Measuring dyadic adjustment: New scales for assessing the quality of marriage and similar dyads. *Journal of Marriage and the Family, 38*, 15–28.

Spanier, G. B., & Margolis, R. L. (1983). Marital separation and extramarital sexual behavior. *Journal of Sex Research, 19*, 23–48.

Spanier, G. B., & Thompson, L. (1984). *Parting: The aftermath of separation and divorce.* Newbury Park, CA: Sage.

Spence, J. T. (1984). Masculinity, femininity, and gender-related traits: A conceptual analysis and critique of current research. In B. A. Maher & W. B. Maher (Eds.), *Progress in experimental personality research* (Vol. 13, pp. 1–97). San Diego, CA: Academic Press.

Spence, J. T., & Helmreich, R. L. (1978). *Masculinity and femininity: Their psychological dimensions, correlates, and antecedents.* Austin: University of Texas Press.

Spence, J. T., Helmreich, R. L., & Stapp, J. (1974). The Personal Attributes Questionnaire: A measure of sex-role stereotypes and masculinity–femininity. *JSAS Catalog of Selected Documents in Psychology, 4*, 127.

Spiegel, D., Bloom, J. R., Kraemer, H. C., & Gotthel, E. (1989, October 14). Effect of psychosocial treatment on survival of patients with metastatic breast cancer. *The Lancet, 2*, 888–891.

Spitzberg, B. H., & Cupach, W. R. (1996, July). *Obsessive relational intrusion: Victimization and coping.* Paper presented at the conference of the International Society for the Study of Personal Relationships, Banff, Alberta, Canada.

Spitzberg, B. H., & Cupach, W. R. (Eds.). (1998). *The dark side of close relationships.* Mahwah, NJ: Erlbaum.

Spitzberg, B. H., & Cupach, W. R. (2002). The inappropriateness of relational intrusion. In R. Goodwin & D. Cramer (Eds.), *Inappropriate relationships: The unconventional, the disapproved, and the forbidden* (pp. 191–219). Mahwah, NJ: Erlbaum.

Spitzberg, B. H., Nicastro, A. M., & Cousins, A. V. (1998). Exploring the interactional phenomenon of stalking and obsessive relational intrusion. *Communication Reports, 11*, 33–47.

Spreadbury, C. L. (1982). First date. *Journal of Early Adolescence, 2*, 83–89.

Sprecher, S. (1989). Importance to males and females of physical attractiveness, earning potential, and expressiveness in initial attraction. *Sex Roles, 21*, 591–607.

Sprecher, S., Aron, A., Hatfield, E., Cortese, A., Potapova, E., & Levitskaya, A. (1994). Love: American style, Russian style, and Japanese style. *Personal Relationships, 1*, 349–369.

Sprecher, S., & Felmlee, D. (1992). The influence of parents and friends on the quality and stability of romantic relationships: A three-wave longitudinal investigation. *Journal of Marriage and the Family, 54*, 888–900.

Sprecher, S., & Felmlee, D. (2000). Romantic partners' perceptions of social network attributes with the passage of time and relationship transitions. *Personal Relationships, 7*, 325–340.

Sprecher, S., & McKinney, K. (1993). *Sexuality.* Newbury Park, CA: Sage.

Sprecher, S., McKinney, K., Walsh, R., & Anderson, C. (1988). A revision of the Reiss premarital sexual permissiveness scale. *Journal of Marriage and the Family, 50*, 821–828.

Sprecher, S., & Regan, P. C. (1998). Passionate and companionate love in courting and young married couples. *Sociological Inquiry, 68*, 163–185.

Sprecher, S., Regan, P. C., McKinney, K., Maxwell, K., & Wazienski, R. (1997). Preferred level of sexual experience in a date or mate: The merger of two methodologies. *Journal of Sex Research, 34*, 327–337.

Sprecher, S., & Schwartz, P. (1994). Equity and balance in the exchange of contributions in close relationships. In M. J. Lerner & G. Mikula (Eds.), *Entitlement and the affectional bond: Justice in close relationships* (pp. 11–42). New York: Plenum Press.

Sprecher, S., Sullivan, Q., & Hatfield, E. (1994). Mate selection preferences: Gender differences examined in a national sample. *Journal of Personality and Social Psychology, 66*, 1074–1080.

Sroufe, L. A. (1985). Attachment classification from the perspective of infant–caregiver relationships and infant temperament. *Child Development, 56*, 1–14.

Sroufe, L. A., Egeland, B., & Kreutzer, T. (1990). The fate of early experience in developmental change: Longitudinal approaches to individual adaptation in child development. *Child Development, 61,* 1363–1373.

Sroufe, L. A., & Fleeson, J. (1986). Attachment and the construction of relationships. In W. Hartup & Z. Rubin (Eds.), *Relationships and development* (pp. 51–71). Hillsdale, NJ: Erlbaum.

Sroufe, L. A., & Fleeson, J. (1988). The coherence of family relationships. In R. A. Hinde & J. Stevenson (Eds.), *Relationships within families: Mutual influences* (pp. 27–47). Oxford, UK: Oxford University Press.

Srull, T. K., & Wyer, R. S. (1989). Person memory and judgment. *Psychological Review, 96,* 58–83.

Stack, S., & Eshleman, J. R. (1998). Marital status and happiness: A 17-nation study. *Journal of Marriage and the Family, 60,* 527–536.

Stangor, C., & McMillan, D. (1992). Memory for expectancy-congruent and expectancy-incongruent information: A review of the social and social developmental literatures. *Psychological Bulletin, 111,* 42–61.

Steil, J. M. (2000). Contemporary marriage: Still an unequal partnership. In C. Hendrick & S. S. Hendrick (Eds.), *Close relationships: A sourcebook* (pp. 125–136). Thousand Oaks, CA: Sage.

Steiner, I. D. (1974). Whatever happened to the group in social psychology? *Journal of Experimental Social Psychology, 10,* 93–108.

Stensaas, L. J., Lavker, R. M., Monti-Bloch, L., Grosser, B. I., & Berliner, D. L. (1991). Ultrastructure of the human vomeronasal organ. *Journal of Steroid Biochemistry and Molecular Biology, 39,* 553–560.

Stephan, W., Berscheid, E., & Walster [Hatfield], E. (1971). Sexual arousal and heterosexual perception. *Journal of Personality and Social Psychology, 20,* 93–101.

Sterling, P., & Eyer, J. (1988). Allostasis: A new paradigm to explain arousal pathology. In J. Fisher & J. Reason (Eds.), *Handbook of life stress, cognition, and health* (pp. 629–649). New York: Wiley.

Sternberg, R. J. (1986). A triangular theory of love. *Psychological Review, 93,* 119–135.

Sternberg, R. J. (1988). Triangulating love. In R. J. Sternberg & M. L. Barnes (Eds.), *The psychology of love* (pp. 119–138). New Haven, CT: Yale University Press.

Sternberg, R. J. (1998). *Cupid's arrow: The course of love through time.* Cambridge, UK: Cambridge University Press.

Sternberg, R. J., & Barnes, M. L. (Eds.). (1988). *The psychology of love.* New Haven, CT: Yale University Press.

Sternberg, R. J., & Beall, A. E. (1991). How can we know what love is? An epistemological analysis. In G. J. O. Fletcher & F. D. Fincham (Eds.), *Cognition in close relationships* (pp. 257–278). Hillsdale, NJ: Erlbaum.

Sternberg, R. J., & Grajek, S. (1984). The nature of love. *Journal of Personality and Social Psychology, 47,* 312–329.

Stevens, L. E., & Fiske, S. T. (2000). Motivated impressions of a powerholder: Accuracy under task dependency and mis-perception under evaluation dependence. *Personality and Social Psychology Bulletin, 26,* 907–922.

Stewart, A. J., & Rubin, Z. (1976). The power motive in the dating couple. *Journal of Personality and Social Psychology, 34,* 305–309.

Stiensmeier-Pelster, J., Martini, A., & Reisenzein, R. (1995). The role of surprise in the attribution process. *Cognition and Emotion, 9,* 5–31.

Straub, R. O. (2001). *Health psychology.* New York: Worth.

Straus, M. A. (1980). Measuring intrafamily conflict and violence: The Conflict Tactics (CT) scales. *Journal of Marriage and the Family, 41,* 75–88.

Straus, M. A., Gelles, R. J., & Steinmetz, S. (1980). *Behind closed doors: Violence in the American family.* New York: Doubleday.

Strauss, A. (1946). The ideal and chosen mate. *American Journal of Sociology, 52,* 204–208.

Strauss, M. S. (1979). Abstraction of prototypical information by adults and 10-month-old infants. *Journal of Experimental Psychology: Human Learning and Memory, 5,* 618–632.

Strelau, J. (1994). The concepts of arousal and arousability as used in temperament studies. In J. E. Bates & T. D. Wachs (Eds.), *Temperament: Individual differences at the interface of biology and behavior* (pp. 117–141). Washington, DC: American Psychological Association.

Stroebe, M. S., Gergen, M. M., Gergen, K. J., & Stroebe, W. (1992). Broken hearts or broken bonds: Love and death in historical perspective. *American Psychologist, 47,* 1205–1212.

Stroebe, W., & Stroebe, M. S. (1987). *Bereavement and health: The psychological and physical consequences of partner loss.* Cambridge, UK: Cambridge University Press.

Stroebe, W., & Stroebe, M. S. (1996). The social psychology of social support. In E. T. Higgins & A. Kruglanski (Eds.), *Social psychology: Handbook of basic principles* (pp. 597–621). New York: Guilford Press.

Strube, M. J., & Davis, L. E. (1998). Race, gender, and romantic commitment. In V. C. de Munck (Ed.), *Romantic love and sexual behavior: Perspectives from the social sciences* (pp. 155–169). Westport, CT: Praeger Publishers.

Stryker, S. (1980). *Symbolic interactionism.* Menlo Park, CA: Benjamin/Cummings.

Stuart, F. M., Hammond, D. C., & Pett, M. A. (1987). Inhibited sexual desire in women. *Archives of Sexual Behavior, 16,* 91–106.

Stuart, R. B. (1969). Operant interpersonal treatment for marital discord. *Journal of Consulting and Clinical Psychology, 33,* 675–682.

Sullivan, K. T., & Bradbury, T. N. (1997). Are premarital prevention programs reaching couples at risk for marital dysfunction? *Journal of Consulting and Clinical Psychology, 65,* 24–30.

Suls, J., & Wheeler, L. (Eds.). (2000). *Handbook of social comparison theory and research.* New York: Kluwer Academic/Plenum.

Sumbadze, N. (1999). *The social web: Friendships of adult men and women.* Leiden, The Netherlands: DSWO Press, Leiden University.

Suomi, S. (1987). Genetic and maternal contributions to individual differences in Rhesus monkeys' biobehavioral development. In N. A. Krasnagor, E. M. Blass, M. A. Hofer, & W. P. Smotherman (Eds.), *Perinatal development: A psychobiological perspective* (pp. 397–420). New York: Academic Press.

Suomi, S. (1999). Attachment in Rhesus monkeys. In J. Cassidy & P. R. Shaver (Eds.), *Handbook of attachment* (pp. 181–197). New York: Guilford Press.

Surra, C. A. (1985). Courtship types: Variations in interdependence between partners and social networks. *Journal of Personality and Social Psychology, 49*, 357–375.

Surra, C. A. (1987). Reasons for changes in commitment: Variations by courtship type. *Journal of Social and Personal Relationships, 4*, 17–33.

Surra, C. A. (1990). Research and theory on mate selection and premarital relationships in the 1980s. *Journal of Marriage and the Family, 52*, 844–865.

Surra, C. A. (1991). What is family? No answer yet. [Review of the book *What is family?*]. *Contemporary Psychology, 36*, 897.

Surra, C. A., & Bohman, T. (1991). The development of close relationships: A cognitive perspective. In G. J. O. Fletcher & F. D. Fincham (Eds.), *Cognition in close relationships* (pp. 281–305). Hillsdale, NJ: Erlbaum.

Surra, C. A., & Milardo, R. M. (1991). The social psychological context of developing relationships: Interactive and psychological networks. In W. H. Jones & D. Perlman (Eds.), *Advances in personal relationships* (Vol. 2, pp. 1–36). London: Jessica Kingsley.

Surra, C. A., & Ridley, C. A. (1991). Multiple perspectives on interaction: Participants, peers, and observers. In B. M. Montgomery & S. Duck (Eds.), *Studying interpersonal interaction* (pp. 35–55). New York: Guilford Press.

Survey by the Roper Organization (Roper Reports 92–3), February 1992.

Sutton, S. K., & Davidson, R. J. (1997). Prefrontal brain symmetry: A biological substrate of the behavioral approach and inhibition systems. *Psychological Science, 8*, 204–210.

Swann, W. B., Jr. (1984). Quest for accuracy in person perception: A matter of pragmatics. *Psychological Review, 91*, 457–477.

Swann, W. B., Jr. (1990). To be adored or to be known: The interplay of self-enhancement and self-verification. In R. M. Sorentino & E. T. Higgins (Eds.), *Motivation and cognition* (Vol. 2, pp. 408–488). New York: Guilford Press.

Swann, W. B., Jr., Hixon, J. G., & De La Ronde, C. (1992). Embracing the bitter "truth": Negative self concepts and marital commitment. *Psychological Science, 3*, 118–121.

Swensen, C. H. (1961). Love: A self-report analysis with college students. *Journal of Individual Psychology, 17*, 167–171.

Swensen, C. H., & Gilner, F. (1963). Factor analysis of self-report statements of love relationships. *Journal of Individual Psychology, 19*, 186–188.

Symons, D. (1979). *The evolution of human sexuality*. New York: Oxford University Press.

Talmon, Y. (1964). Mate selection in collective settlements. *American Sociological Review, 29*, 491–508.

Tamplin, R. (Ed.). (1995). *Famous love letters: Messages of intimacy and passion.* Pleasantville, NY: Reader's Digest Association.

Tamres, L. K., Janicki, D., & Helgeson, V. S. (2002). Sex differences in coping behavior: A meta-analytic review and an examination of relative coping. *Personality and Social Psychology Review, 6*, 2–30.

Tanaka, J. W., & Farah, M. J. (1993). Parts and wholes in face recognition. *Quarterly Journal of Experimental Psychology, 46*, 225–245.

Tannen, D. (1986). *That's not what I meant: How conversational styles make or break relationships.* New York: Ballentine Books.

Tannen, D. (1990). *You just don't understand: Women and men in conversation.* New York: William Morrow.

Tashiro, T., & Frazier, P. (2003). "I'll never be in a relationship like that again": Personal growth following romantic relationship breakups. *Personal Relationships, 10*, 113–128.

Taylor, S. E. (1991). Asymmetrical effects of positive and negative events: The mobilization–minimization hypothesis. *Psychological Bulletin, 110*, 67–85.

Taylor, S. E., Kemeny, M. E., Reed, G. M., Bower, J. E., & Gruenewald, T. L. (2000). Psychological resources, positive illusions, and health. *American Psychologist, 55*, 99–109.

Taylor, S. E., Klein, L. C., Lewis, B. P., Gruenewald, T. L., Gurung, R. A. R., & Updegraff, J. A. (2000). Biobehavioral responses to stress in females: Tend-and-befriend, not fight-or-flight. *Psychological Review, 107*, 411–429.

Taylor, S. E., Repetti, R. L., & Seeman, T. (1997). Health psychology: What is an unhealthy environment and how does it get under the skin? *Annual Review of Psychology, 48*, 411–447.

Teachman, J. D., & Polonko, K. A. (1990). Cohabitation and marital stability in the United States. *Social Forces, 69*, 207–220.

Tennov, D. (1979). *Love and limerence.* New York: Stein and Day.

Tennov, D. (1998). Love madness. In V. C. de Munck (Ed.), *Romantic love and sexual behavior: Perspectives from the social sciences* (pp. 77–88). Westport, CT: Praeger.

Terman, L. M. (1938). *Psychological studies in marital happiness.* New York: McGraw-Hill.

Terman, L. M., Buttenweiser, P., Ferguson, L. W., Johnson, W. B., & Wilson, D. P. (1938). *Psychological factors in marital happiness.* New York: McGraw-Hill.

Terry, D. J. (1991). Stress, coping and adaptation to new parenthood. *Journal of Social and Personal Relationships, 8*, 527–547.

Thibaut, J. W., & Kelley, H. H. (1959). *The social psychology of groups.* New York: Wiley.

Thomas, A., & Chess, S. (1977). *Temperament and development.* New York: Brunner/Mazel.

Thompson, A. P. (1983). Extramarital sex: A review of the research literature. *Journal of Sex Research, 19*, 1–22.

Thompson, A. P. (1984). Emotional and sexual components of extramarital relations. *Journal of Marriage and the Family, 46*, 35–42.

Thompson, J. M., Whiffen, V. E., & Blain, M. D. (1995). Depressive symptoms, sex and perceptions of intimate relationships. *Journal of Social and Personal Relationships, 12,* 49–66.

Thompson, L., & Walker, A. (1982). The dyad as the unit of analysis: Conceptual and methodological issues. *Journal of Marriage and the Family, 44,* 889–900.

Thompson, R. A., & Nelson, C. A. (2001). Developmental science and the media: Early brain development. *American Psychologist, 56,* 5–15.

Thompson, S. C. (1981). Will it hurt less if I can control it? A complex answer to a simple question. *Psychological Bulletin, 90,* 89–101.

Thurmaier, F., Engl, J., & Hahlweg, K. (1999). Eheglüek auf Dauer? Methodik, Inhalte und Effektivität eines präventiven Paarkommunikationstrainings—Ergebnisse nach fünf Jahren. *Zeitschrift für Klinische Psychologies, 28,* 54–62.

Tjaden, P., & Thoennes, N. (2000). Prevalence and consequences of male-to-female and female-to-male intimate partner violence as measured by the National Violence Against Women Survey. *Violence Against Women, 6,* 142–161.

Tolhuizen, J. H. (1989). Communication strategies for intensifying dating relationships: Identification, use and structure. *Journal of Social and Personal Relationships, 6,* 413–434.

Tolman, A. O. (2001). *Depression in adults: Assessment and treatment strategies.* Kansas City, MO: Compact Clinicals.

Tolman, E. C. (1932). *Purposive behavior in animals and man.* New York: Appleton-Century-Crofts.

Tolson, J. (2000, March 13). No wedding? No ring? No problem. *U.S. News & World Report,* p. 48.

Tomkins, C. (1998). *Living well is the best revenge.* New York: Random House (Modern Library edition). (Original work published 1971, Viking Press)

Tomkins, S. S. (1962). *Affect, imagery, consciousness: Vol. 1. The positive affects.* New York: Springer.

Tomkins, S. S. (1963). *Affect, imagery, consciousness: Vol. 2. The negative affects.* New York: Springer.

Tooby, J., & Cosmides, L. (1992). The psychological foundations of culture. In J. H. Barrow, L. Cosmides, & J. Tooby (Eds.), *The adapted mind: Evolutionary psychology and the generation of culture* (pp. 19–136). Oxford, UK: Oxford University Press.

Townsend, J. M., & Levy, G. D. (1990). Effects of potential partners' costume and physical attractiveness on sexuality and partner selection. *Journal of Psychology, 124,* 371–389.

Triandis, H. C. (1995). *Individualism and collectivism.* Boulder, CO: Westview Press.

The tribe has spoken. (2000, November 25). *Minneapolis Star Tribune,* p. E3.

Trierweiler, L. I., Eid, M., & Lischetzke, T. (2002). The structure of emotional expressivity: Each emotion counts. *Journal of Personality and Social Psychology, 82,* 1023–1040.

Trivers, R. L. (1972). Parental investment and sexual selection. In B. Campbell (Ed.), *Sexual selection and the descent of man* (pp. 136–179). Chicago: Aldine.

Trobst, K. K. (2000). An interpersonal conceptualization and quantification of social support transactions. *Personality and Social Psychology Bulletin, 26,* 971–986.

Tronick, E., Als, H., Adamson, L., Wise, S., & Brazelton, T. B. (1978, Spring). The infant's response to entrapment between contradictory messages in face-to-face interaction. *Journal of the American Academy of Child Psychiatry,* 1–13.

Trudel, G. (1991). Review of psychological factors in low sexual desire. *Sexual and Marital Therapy, 6,* 261–272.

Trudel, G., Marchand, A., Ravart, M., Aubin, S., Turgeon, L., & Fortier, P. (2001). The effect of a cognitive-behavioral group treatment program on hypoactive sexual desire in women. *Sexual and Relationship Therapy, 16,* 145–164.

Tucker, J. S., Kressin, N. R., Spiro, A., III, & Ruscio, J. (1998). Intrapersonal characteristics and the timing of divorce: A prospective investigation. *Journal of Social and Personal Relationships, 15,* 210 225.

Tucker, M. B., & Mitchell-Kernan, C. (Eds.). (1995). *The decline in marriage among African Americans: Causes, consequences, and policy implications.* New York: Russell Sage Foundation.

Tucker, M. B., & Mitchell-Kernan, C. (1998). Psychological well-being and perceived marital opportunity among single African American, Latina, and White women. *Journal of Comparative Family Studies, 29,* 57–72.

Turk, D. C. (2000). Foreword. In K. B. Schmaling & T. G. Sher (Eds.), *The psychology of couples and illness: Theory, research, and practice* (pp. xi–xiv). Washington, DC: American Psychological Association.

Turner, R. H. (1970). *Family interaction.* New York: Wiley.

Tyre, P. (2002, February 18). Giving lessons in love. *Newsweek,* p. 64.

Tzeng, M. (1992). The effects of socioeconomic heterogamy and changes on marital dissolution for first marriages. *Journal of Marriage and the Family, 54,* 609–619.

Uchino, B. N., Cacioppo, J. T., & Kiecolt-Glaser, J. K. (1996). The relationship between social support and physiological processes: A review with emphasis on underlying mechanisms and implications for health. *Psychological Bulletin, 119,* 488–531.

Udry, J. (1981). Marital alternatives and marital disruption. *Journal of Marriage and the Family, 43,* 889–897.

Uleman, J. S., Newman, L. S., & Moskowitz, G. B. (1996). People as flexible interpreters: Evidence and issues from spontaneous trait inference. In M. P. Zanna (Ed.), *Advances in experimental social psychology* (Vol. 28, pp. 211–279). San Diego, CA: Academic Press.

Ullery, E. K., Millner, V. S., & Willingham, H. A. (2002). The emergent care and treatment of women with hypoactive sexual desire disorder. *The Family Journal: Counseling and Therapy for Couples and Families, 10,* 346–350.

U.S. Census Bureau. (1994). *Statistical abstract of the United States.* Washington, DC: U.S. Government Printing Office.

U.S. Census Bureau. (1998, March). Marital status and living arrangements. (Update). *Current population reports: Population characteristics.* (Series P20–514). Washington, DC: U.S. Government Printing Office.

U.S. Census Bureau. (1999, September). Poverty in the United States. *Current population reports: Consumer income.* (Series P60–210). Washington, DC: U.S. Government Printing Office.

Useche, B., Villegas, M., & Alzate, H. (1990). Sexual behavior of Colombian high school students. *Adolescence, 25,* 291–304.

Vaillant, C. O., & Vaillant, G. E. (1993). Is the U-curve of marital satisfaction an illusion? A 40-year study of marriage. *Journal of Marriage and the Family, 55,* 230–239.

Valins, S. (1966). Cognitive effects of false heart-rate feedback. *Journal of Personality and Social Psychology, 4,* 400–408.

Valins, S. (1970). The perception and labeling of bodily changes as determinants of emotional behavior. In P. Black (Ed.), *Physiological correlates of emotion* (pp. 229–243). New York: Academic Press.

van den Berghe, P. L. (1979). *Human family systems: An evolutionary view.* New York: Elsevier.

van den Berghe, P. L. (1992). Wanting and getting ain't the same. *Behavioral and Brain Sciences, 15,* 1113–117.

van den Boom, D. C. (1994). The influence of temperament and mothers on attachment and exploration: An experimental manipulation of sensitive responsiveness among lower-class mothers with irritable infants. *Child Development, 65,* 1457–1477.

Vandenburg, S. G. (1972). Assortative mating, or who marries whom? *Behavioral Genetics, 2,* 127–157.

Vangelisti, A. L., & Daly, J. A. (1997). Gender differences in standards for romantic relationships: Different cultures or different experiences? *Personal Relationships, 4,* 203–219.

van IJzendoorn, M. H., & Sagi, A. (1999). Cross-cultural patterns of attachment: Universal and contextual dimensions. In J. Cassidy & P. R. Shaver (Eds.), *Handbook of attachment: Theory, research, and clinical applications* (pp. 713–734). New York: Guilford Press.

Van Lange, P. A. M., Agnew, C. R., Harinck, F., & Steemers, G. E. M. (1997). From game theory to real life: How social value orientation affects willingness to sacrifice in ongoing close relationships. *Journal of Personality and Social Psychology, 73,* 1330–1344.

Van Lange, P. A. M., & Rusbult, C. E. (1995). My relationship is better than—and not as bad as—yours is: The perception of superiority in close relationships. *Personality and Social Psychology Bulletin, 21,* 32–44.

Van Lange, P. A. M., Rusbult, C. E., Drigotas, S. M., Arriaga, X. B., Witcher, B. S., & Cox, C. L. (1997). Willingness to sacrifice in close relationships. *Journal of Personality and Social Psychology, 72,* 1373–1395.

van Lawick-Goodall, J. (1968). The behaviour of free-living chimpanzees in the Gombe Stream Reserve. *Animal Behavior Monographs, 1,* 161–311.

Van Yperen, N. W., & Buunk, B. P. (1994). Social comparison and social exchange in marital relationships. In M. J. Lerner & G. Mikula (Eds.), *Entitlement and the affectional bond: Justice in close relationships* (pp. 89–116). New York: Plenum Press.

Vaughn, D. (1986). *Uncoupling: Turning points in intimate relationships.* New York: Vintage Books.

Vaux, A. (1988). *Social support: Theory, research, and intervention.* New York: Praeger.

Veroff, J., Douvan, E., & Hatchett, S. (1993). Marital interaction and marital quality in the first year of marriage. In D. Perlman & W. H. Jones (Eds.), *Advances in personal relationships* (Vol. 4, pp. 103–137). London: Jessica Kingsley.

Veroff, J., Douvan, E., & Kulka, R. A. (1981). *The inner American: A self-portrait from 1957 to 1976.* New York: Basic Books.

Veroff, J., Douvan, E., Orbuch, T. L., & Acitelli, L. K. (1998). Happiness in stable marriages: The early years. In T. N. Bradbury (Ed.), *The developmental course of marital dysfunction* (pp. 152–179). Cambridge, UK: Cambridge University Press.

Veroff, J., Kulka, R. A., & Douvan, E. (1981). *Mental health in America: Patterns of help-seeking from 1957 to 1976.* New York: Basic Books.

Villasmil Prieto, M. C. (1997). Social representation of feminine sexuality: An interpretation from a gender perspective. *Sociologica, 12,* 159–182.

Vincent, J. P., Friedman, L. C., Nugent, J., & Messerly, L. (1979). Demand characteristics in observations of marital interaction. *Journal of Consulting and Clinical Psychology, 47,* 557–566.

Vincenzi, H., & Grabosky, F. (1989). Measuring the emotional/social aspects of loneliness and isolation. In M. Hojjat & R. Crandall (Eds.), *Loneliness: Theory, research, and applications* (pp. 257–270). Newbury Park, CA: Sage.

Vinokur, A. D., Price, R. H., & Caplan, R. D. (1996). Hard times and hurtful partners: How financial strain affects depression and relationship satisfaction of unemployed persons and their spouses. *Journal of Personality and Social Psychology, 71,* 166–179.

Vinokur, A. D., & van Ryn, M. (1993). Social support and undermining in close relationships: Their independent effects on the mental health of unemployed persons. *Journal of Personality and Social Psychology, 65,* 350–359.

Vital statistics. (2001, February 26). *U.S. News & World Report,* p. 10.

Vogel, D. L., & Karney, B. R. (2002). Demands and withdrawal in newlyweds: Elaborating on the social structure hypothesis. *Journal of Social and Personal Relationships, 19,* 685–701.

Von Dras, D. D., & Siegler, I. C. (1997). Stability in extraversion and aspects of social support at midlife. *Journal of Personality and Social Psychology, 72,* 233–241.

Vonk, R. (2002). Self-serving interpretations of flattery: Why ingratiation works. *Journal of Personality and Social Psychology, 82,* 515–526.

Vorauer, J. D., Cameron, J. J., Holmes, J. G., & Pearce, D. G. (2003). Invisible overtures: Fears of rejection and the signal amplification bias. *Journal of Personality and Social Psychology, 84,* 793–812.

Vorauer, J. D., & Ratner, R. K. (1996). Who's going to make the first move? Pluralistic ignorance as an impediment to relationship formation. *Journal of Social and Personal Relationships, 13,* 483–506.

Wade, T. J., & Cairney, J. (2000). Major depressive disorder and marital transition among mothers: Results from a national panel study. *Journal of Nervous and Mental Disease, 188,* 741–750.

Wagenaar, W. (1986). My memory: A study of autobiographical memory over six years. *Cognitive Psychology, 18,* 225–252.

Wallace, H., & Silverman, J. (1996). Stalking and post traumatic stress syndrome. *Police Journal, 69,* 203–206.

Wallace, P. (1977). Individual discrimination of humans by odor. *Physiology and Behavior, 19,* 577–579.

Waller, W. (1937). The rating and dating complex. *American Sociological Review, 2,* 727–734.

Waller, W. (1938). *The family: A dynamic interpretation.*

Waller, W. (1967). *The old love and the new: Divorce and readjustment.* Carbondale: Southern Illinois University Press. (Original work published 1930)

Waller, W., & Hill, R. (1951). *The family, a dynamic interpretation.* New York: Dryden Press.

Wallerstein, J. Lewis, J., & Blakeslee, S. (2000). *The unexpected legacy of divorce: A 25 year landmark study.* New York: Hyperion.

Wallerstein, J. S. (1991). The long-term effects of divorce on children: A review. *Journal of the American Academy of Child and Adolescent Psychiatry, 30,* 349–360.

Wallerstein, J. S., & Blakeslee, S. (1995). *The good marriage: How and why love lasts.* New York: Warner Books.

Walster [Hatfield], E., Aronson, V., Abrahams, D., & Rottman, L. (1966). Importance of physical attractiveness in dating behavior. *Journal of Personality and Social Psychology, 4,* 508–516.

Walster [Hatfield], E., & Berscheid, E. (1971). Adrenaline makes the heart grow fonder. *Psychology Today, 5,* 47–62.

Walster [Hatfield], E., & Walster, G. W., & Berscheid, E. (1978). *Equity: Theory and research.* Boston: Allyn & Bacon.

Watson, D., Clark, L. A., & Tellegen, A. (1988). Development and validation of brief measures of positive and negative affect: The PANAS scales. *Journal of Personality and Social Psychology, 54,* 1063–1070.

Watson, D., & Pennebaker, J. W. (1989). Health complaints, stress, and distress: Exploring the central role of negative affectivity. *Psychological Review, 96,* 234–254.

Watson, D., & Tellegen, A. (1999). Issues in the dimensional structure of affect—effects of descriptors, measurement error, and response formats: Comment on Russell and Carroll (1999). *Psychological Bulletin, 125,* 601–610.

Watson, J. B. (1914). *An introduction to comparative psychology.* New York: Holt.

Watzlawick, P., Beavin, J. H., & Jackson, D. D. (1967). *Pragmatics of human communication.* New York: Norton.

Watzlawick, P., & Jackson, J. H. (Eds.). (1977). *The interactional view.* New York: Norton.

Wayment, H. A., & Campbell, S. (2000). How are we doing? The impact of motives and information use on the evaluation of romantic relationships. *Journal of Social and Personal Relationships, 17,* 31–52.

Weber, A. L. (1998). Losing, leaving, and letting go: Coping with nonmarital breakups. In B. H. Spitzberg & W. R. Cupach (Eds.), *The dark side of close relationships* (pp. 267–306). Mahwah, NJ: Erlbaum.

Wegner, D. M., Giuliano, T., & Hertel, P. T. (1985). Cognitive interdependence in close relationships. In W. Ickes (Ed.), *Compatible and incompatible relationships* (pp. 253–276). New York: Springer-Verlag.

Weigel, D. J., & Ballard-Reisch, D. S. (1999). Using paired data to test models of relational maintenance and marital quality. *Journal of Social and Personal Relationships, 16,* 175–191.

Weil, M. W. (1975). Extramarital relationships: A reappraisal. *Journal of Clinical Psychology, 31,* 723–725.

Weinberg, M. S., Swensson, R. G., & Hammersmith, S. K. (1983). Sexual autonomy and the status of women: Models of female sexuality in U.S. sex manuals from 1950 to 1980. *Social Problems, 30,* 312–324.

Weiner, B. (1985). Spontaneous causal search. *Psychological Bulletin, 97,* 74–84.

Weinfield, N. S., Sroufe, A. L., Egeland, B., & Carlson, E. A. (1999). The nature of individual differences in infant–caregiver attachment. In J. Cassidy & P. R. Shaver (Eds.), *Handbook of attachment: Theory, research, and clinical applications* (pp. 68–88). New York: Guilford Press.

Weis, D. L., & Jurich, J. (1985). Size of community of residence as a predictor of attitudes toward extramarital sex. *Journal of Marriage and the Family, 47,* 173–178.

Weiss, D. E. (1988). *100% American.* New York: Poseidon Press.

Weiss, R. L., & Heyman, R. E. (1990). Observation of marital interaction. In F. D. Fincham & T. N. Bradbury (Eds.), *The psychology of marriage: Basic issues and applications* (pp. 87–117). New York: Guilford Press.

Weiss, R. L., & Heyman, R. E. (1997). A clinical-research overview of couples interactions. In W. K. Halford & H. J. Markman (Eds.), *Clinical handbook of marriage and couples intervention* (pp. 13–42). Chichester, UK: Wiley.

Weiss, R. L., Hops, W., & Patterson, G. R. (1973). A framework for conceptualizing marital conflict, a technology for altering it, some data for evaluating it. In L. A. Hamerlynck, L. C. Handy, & E. Mash (Eds.), *Behavior change: Methodology, concepts, and practice* (pp. 309–342). Champaign, IL: Research Press.

Weiss, R. L., & Margolin, G. (1975). Assessment of marital conflict and accord. In A. R. Ciminero, K. S. Calhoun, & H. E. Adams (Eds.), *Handbook of behavioral assessment* (pp. 555–602). New York: Wiley.

Weiss, R. L., & Summers, K. J. (1983). Marital Interaction Coding System—III. In E. E. Filsinger (Ed.), *A sourcebook of marriage and family assessment* (pp. 85–115). Beverly Hills, CA: Sage.

Weiss, R. S. (Ed.). (1973). *Loneliness: The experience of emotional and social isolation.* Cambridge, MA: MIT Press.

Weiss, R. S. (1975). *Marital separation.* New York: Basic Books.

Weisse, C. S. (1992). Depression and immunocompetence: A review of the literature. *Psychological Bulletin, 111,* 475–489.

Weissman, M. M. (1987). Advances in psychiatric epidemiology: Rates and risks for major depression. *American Journal of Public Health, 77,* 445–471.

Werner, G., & Latané, B. (1974). Interaction motivates attraction: Rats are fond of fondling. *Journal of Personality and Social Psychology, 29,* 328–334.

Westen, D., & Rosenthal, R. (2003). Quantifying construct validity: Two simple measures. *Journal of Personality and Social Psychology, 84*, 608–618.

Westermarck, E. (1922). *The history of human marriage* (5th ed., Vol 2). New York: Allerton.

Westmaas, J. L., & Silver, R. C. (2001). The role of attachment in responses to victims of life crises. *Journal of Personality and Social Psychology, 80*, 425–438.

Westphal, D. (2002, February 8). Census forecast: 9 in 10 marry, but half may divorce. *Minneapolis Star Tribune*, p. A20.

Wethington, E., & Kessler, R. C. (1986). Perceived support, received support, and adjustment to stressful life events. *Journal of Health and Social Behavior, 27*, 78–89.

Wetzler, S. E., & Sweeney, J. A. (1986). Childhood amnesia: An empirical demonstration. In D. C. Rubin (Ed.), *Autobiographical memory* (pp. 191–201). Cambridge, UK: Cambridge University Press.

Wheeler, L. (1974). Social comparison and selective affiliation. In T. L. Huston (Ed.), *Foundations of interpersonal attraction* (pp. 309–329). New York: Academic Press.

Wheeler, L., & Kim, Y. (1997). What is beautiful is culturally good: The physical attractiveness stereotype has different content in collectivist cultures. *Personality and Social Psychology Bulletin, 23*, 795–800.

Wheeler, L., Reis, H. T., & Nezlek, J. (1983). Loneliness, social interaction, and sex roles. *Journal of Personality and Social Psychology, 45*, 943–953.

Whisman, M. A., Dixon, A. E., & Johnson, B. (1997). Therapists' perspectives of couple problems and treatment issues in couple therapy. *Journal of Family Psychology, 11*, 361–366.

White, G. L. (1980). Physical attractiveness and courtship progress. *Journal of Personality and Social Psychology, 39*, 660–668.

White, G. L., & Kight, T. D. (1984). Misattribution of arousal and attraction: Effects of salience of explanations for arousal. *Journal of Experimental Social Psychology, 20*, 55–64.

White, L. K. (1983). Determinants of spousal interaction: Marital structure of marital happiness? *Journal of Marriage and the Family, 45*, 511–520.

White, L. K. (1990). Determinants of divorce: A review of research in the eighties. *Journal of Marriage and the Family, 52*, 904–912.

White, L. K., & Booth, A. (1991). Divorce over the life course. *Journal of Family Issues, 12*, 5–21.

Whitehouse, J. (1981). The role of the initial attracting quality in marriage: Virtues and vices. *Journal of Marital and Family Therapy, 7*, 61–67.

Whiting, B., & Edwards, C. P. (1973). A cross-cultural analysis of sex differences in the behavior of children aged three through 11. *Journal of Social Psychology, 91*, 171–188.

Wickrama, K. A. S., Lorenz, F. O., Conger, R. D., & Elder, G. H., Jr. (1997). Marital quality and physical illness: A latent growth curve analysis. *Journal of Marriage and the Family, 59*, 143–155.

Wiederman, M. W. (1997). Extramarital sex: Prevalence and correlates in a national survey. *Journal of Sex Research, 34*, 167–174.

Wiederman, M. W., & Allgeier, E. R. (1992). Gender differences in mate selection criteria: Sociobiological or socioeconomic explanation? *Ethology and Sociobiology, 13*, 115–124.

Wiederman, M. W., & Allgeier, E. R. (1993). Gender differences in sexual jealousy: Adaptionist or social learning explanation? *Ethology and Sociobiology, 14*, 115–140.

Wiederman, M. W., & Allgeier, E. R. (1996). Expectations and attributions regarding extramarital sex among young married individuals. *Journal of Psychology and Human Sexuality, 8*, 21–35.

Wiederman, M. W., & Kendall, E. (1999). Evolution, sex, and jealousy: Investigation with a sample from Sweden. *Evolution and Human Behavior, 20*, 121–128.

Wiggins, J. S., Wiggins, N., & Conger, J. C. (1968). Correlates of heterosexual somatic preference. *Journal of Personality and Social Psychology, 10*, 82–90.

Wile, D. B. (1981). *Couples therapy: A nontraditional approach*. New York: Wiley.

Will, G. (1999, March 29). Lies, damned lies and . . . Statistics, such as the "74 cents" factoid used to prove pervasive sex discrimination. *Newsweek*, p. 84.

Williams, R. B., Barefoot, J. C., Califf, R. M., Haney, T. L., Saunders, W. B., Pryor, D. B., Hlatky, M. A., Siegler, I. C., & Mark, D. B. (1992). Prognostic importance of social and economic resources among medically treated patients with angiographically documented coronary artery disease. *Journal of the American Medical Association, 267*, 520–524.

Wills, T. A., Weiss, R. L., & Patterson, G. R. (1974). A behavioral analysis of the determinants of marital satisfaction. *Journal of Consulting and Clinical Psychology, 42*, 802–811.

Wilson, C. C., & Turner, D. C. (Eds.). (1998). *Companion animals in human health*. Thousand Oaks, CA: Sage.

Wilson, E. O. (1998). *Consilience: The unity of knowledge*. New York: Knopf.

Wilson, M. I., & Daly, M. (1992). Who kills whom in spouse killings? On the exceptional sex ratio of spousal homicides in the United States. *Criminology, 30*, 189–215.

Wilson, T. D. (1994). The proper protocol: Validity and completeness of verbal reports. *Psychological Science, 5*, 249–252.

Wilson, T. D. (2002). *Strangers to ourselves: Discovering the adaptive unconscious*. Cambridge, MA: Harvard University Press.

Winch, R. F. (1958). *Mate selection: A study of complementary needs*. New York: Harper.

Winstead, B. A., & Derlega, V. J. (1991). An experimental approach to studying social interaction and coping with stress among friends. In W. H. Jones & D. Perlman (Eds.), *Advances in personal relationships* (Vol. 2, pp. 107–132). London: Jessica Kingsley.

Winstead, B. A., Derlega, V. J., & Rose, S. (1997). *Gender and close relationships*. Thousand Oaks, CA: Sage.

Winter, D. G. (1973). *The power motive*. New York: Free Press.

Winter, D. G. (1988). The power motive in women—and men. *Journal of Personality and Social Psychology, 54*, 510–519.

Wish, M., Deutsch, M., & Kaplan, S. J. (1976). Perceived dimensions of interpersonal relations. *Journal of Personality and Social Psychology, 33*, 409–420.

Wittenberg, M. T., & Reis, H. T. (1986). Loneliness, social skills, and social perception. *Personality and Social Psychology Bulletin, 12,* 121–130.

Witwer, M. (1993). U.S. men and women now have highest mean age at marriage in this century, Census Bureau finds. *Family Planning Perspectives, 25,* 190–191.

Wolf, A. P. (1995). *Sexual attraction and childhood association: A Chinese brief for Edward Westermarck.* Stanford, CA: Stanford University Press.

Wood, J. T. (1994). *Gendered lives: Communication, gender, and culture.* Belmont, CA: Wadsworth.

Wood, W., Quinn, J. M., & Kashy, D. A. (2002). Habits in everyday life: Thought, emotion, and action. *Journal of Personality and Social Psychology, 83,* 1281–1297.

Wood, W., Rhodes, N., & Whelan, M. (1989). Sex differences in positive well-being: A consideration of emotional style and marital status. *Psychological Bulletin, 106,* 249–264.

Wright, P. H. (1974). The delineation and measurement of some variables in the study of friendship. *Representative Research in Social Psychology, 5,* 93–96.

Wright, P. H., & Scanlon, M. B. (1991). Gender role orientations and friendship: Some attenuation, but gender differences abound. *Sex Roles, 24,* 551–566.

Wyer, R. S., Jr., & Gruenfeld, D. H. (1995). Information processing in social contexts: Implications for social memory and judgment. In M. P. Zanna (Ed.), *Advances in experimental social psychology* (Vol. 27, pp. 52–93). San Diego, CA: Academic Press.

Yamagishi, T., & Yamagishi, M. (1994). Trust and commitment in the United States and Japan. *Motivation and Emotion, 18,* 129–166.

Young, M., Denny, G., Luquis, R., & Young, T. (1998). Correlates of sexual satisfaction in marriage. *Canadian Journal of Human Sexuality, 7,* 115–127.

Yovetich, N. A., & Rusbult, C. E. (1994). Accommodative behavior in close relationships: Exploring transformation of motivation. *Journal of Experimental Social Psychology, 30,* 138–164.

Zadny, J., & Gerard, H. B. (1974). Attributed intentions and informational selectivity. *Journal of Experimental Social Psychology, 10,* 34–52.

Zajonc, R. B. (1968). The attitudinal effects of mere exposure. *Journal of Personality and Social Psychology Monograph Supplement, 9*(2, Pt. 2), 1–27.

Zajonc, R. B. (1980). Feeling and thinking: Preferences need no inferences. *American Psychologist, 35,* 151–175.

Zajonc, R. B. (1998). Emotions. In D. T. Gilbert, S. T. Fiske, & G. Lindzey (Eds.), *The handbook of social psychology* (4th ed., Vol. 1, pp. 591–632). Boston: McGraw-Hill.

Zajonc, R. B. (2000). Feeling and thinking: Closing the debate over the independence of affect. In J. P. Forgas (Ed.), *Feeling and thinking* (pp. 31–58). Cambridge, UK: Cambridge University Press.

Zaldivar, R. A. (1992, June 14). Number of single-father families rising. *Saint Paul Pioneer Press,* p. 3A.

Zammichieli, M. E., Gilroy, F. D., & Sherman, M. F. (1988). Relation between sex-role orientation and marital satisfaction. *Personality and Social Psychology Bulletin, 14,* 747–754.

Zebrowitz, L. A. (1997). *Reading faces: Window to the soul?* Boulder, CO: Westview Press/HarperCollins.

Zebrowitz, L. A., Olson, K., & Hoffman, K. (1993). The stability of babyfaceness and attractiveness across the lifespan. *Journal of Personality and Social Psychology, 64,* 453–466.

Zeifman, D., & Hazan, C. (1997). A process model of adult attachment formation. In S. Duck (Ed.), *Handbook of personal relationships: Theory, research, and interventions* (2nd ed., pp. 179–195). Chichester, UK: Wiley.

Zellman, G. L., & Goodchilds, J. D. (1983). Becoming sexual in adolescence. In E. A. Allgeier & N. B. McCormick (Eds.), *Changing boundaries: Gender roles and sexual behavior* (pp. 49–63). Palo Alto, CA: Mayfield.

Zelnik, M., & Kantner, J. F. (1980). Sexual activity, contraceptive use and pregnancy among metropolitan-area teenagers: 1971–1979. *Family Planning Perspectives, 12,* 230–237.

Zillmann, D. (1983). Transfer of excitation in emotional behavior. In J. T. Cacioppo & R. E. Petty (Eds.), *Social psychophysiology: A sourcebook* (pp. 215–240). New York: Guilford Press.

Zillmann, D. (1984). *Connections between sex and aggression.* Hillsdale, NJ: Erlbaum.

Zillmann, D. (1989). Aggression and sex: Independent and joint operations. In H. Wagner & A. Manstead (Eds.), *Handbook of social psychophysiology* (pp. 229–259). New York: Wiley.

Zillmann, D., Katcher, A. H., & Milavsky, B. (1972). Excitation transfer from physical exercise to subsequent aggressive behavior. *Journal of Experimental Social Psychology, 8,* 247–259.

Credits

Text Credits

Chapter 1 *Page 28:* [1]From E. Tronick, H. Als, L. Adamson, S. Wise, & T. B. Brazelton, "The Infant's Response to Entrapment Between Contradictory Messages in Face-to-Face Interaction," from *Journal of American Academy of Child Psychiatry*, Spring 1978, pp. 1–13. Reprinted with permission. **Chapter 3** *Page 75:* [1]Reprinted with permission from Prof. Ladd Wheeler. **Chapter 11** *Page 324:* [1]From A. Capellanus, *The Art of Courtly Love*, trans by J. J. Parry (Columbia University Press, 1960); *p. 333:* [2]Hall (1901), [3]Anderson (1961), [4]Tamplin (1995); *p. 346:* [5]Reprinted with permission from Curtis Brown, Ltd.; *p. 346:* [6]Reprinted with permission from Reader's Digest. **Chapter 12** *Page 386:* [1]From A. Capellanus, *The Art of Courtly Love*, trans by J. J. Parry (Columbia University Press, 1960).

Photo Credits

Page abbreviation are as follows: (T) top, (C) center, (B) bottom, (L) left, (R) right.
Chapter 1 *Page 1:* Bettmann Archive/Corbis Digital Stock; *p. 7:* Harlow Primate Laboratory/University of Wisconsin; *p. 8:* Harry F. Harlow/Harlow Primate Laboratory/University of Wisconsin; *p. 9:* (TL) © Roger De La Harpe/Animals Animals, (BL) Photo Researchers, Inc., (TR) © Alissa Crandall/CORBIS, (BR) Pearson Education/PH College; *p. 10:* Getty Images Inc. - Hulton Archive Photos; *p. 11:* (L) Art Wolfe/Getty Images Inc. - Stone Allstock, (R) Life Magazine © 1955 TimePix; *p. 12:* (L) © G. Kochaniec/R.M.N./CORBIS SYGMA, (R) AP/Wide World Photos; *p. 13:* Mary Ainsworth, University of Virginia. Photo by Daniel Grogan; *p. 18:* Robert Allison/Contact Press Images Inc.
Chapter 2 *Page 33:* (T) Bob Daemmrich/Stock Boston, (B) Jeff Greenberg/PhotoEdit; *p. 35:* AP/Wide World Photos; *p. 38:* © Reuters NewMedia Inc./CORBIS; *p. 46:* © Bettmann/CORBIS; *p. 47:* (T) AP/Wide World Photos; *p. 57:* Pamela C. Regan.
Chapter 3 *Page 64:* © Topham/The Image Works; *p. 89:* Archives of the History of American Psychology-The University of Akron.
Chapter 4 *Page 98:* UPI/Corbis/Bettmann; *p. 109:* Sharon Fentiman/Relationship Research Institute; *p. 119:* Paul C. Rosenblatt; *p. 125:* Courtesy UCLA Sociology Department.

Chapter 5 *Page 132:* (TL) © Paul Barton/CORBIS, (TR) © Russell Underwood/CORBIS, (BL) © Peter Hvizdak/The Image Works, (BR) © Bill Lai/The Image Works; *p. 155:* (L) Amy Wagner, (R) Judy Carlson; *p. 157:* (T) Joe Roedle/Getty Images, Inc. - Liaison, (B) © Mike Greenlar/The Image Works.
Chapter 6 *Page 161:* (L) Frank Siteman/PhotoEdit, (R) Jeff Greenberg/PhotoEdit; *p. 167:* (T) Andrew Yates Productions/Getty Images Inc. - Image Bank, (B) Bokelberg, Werner/Getty Images Inc. - Image Bank; *p. 171:* Francis Bello/Photo Researchers, Inc.; *p. 179:* © Barbera Stitzer/PhotoEdit Inc.; *p. 188:* University of Texas at Austin, Department of Psychology, Austin, TX.
Chapter 8 *Page 238:* (TL) Pamela C. Regan, (TC) Pamela C. Regan, (TR) Pamela C. Regan, (BL) NBC–TV/Picture Desk, Inc./Kobal Collection, (BC) Columbia Pictures/Embassy Pictures/The Kobal Collection, (BR) REUTERS/Landov.
Chapter 9 *Page 262:* (L) © Ralph A. Clevenger/CORBIS, (R) Jeff Greenberg/PhotoEdit; *p. 263:* From Ekman & Friesen, 1975. © Paul Ekman Ph.D. 1975; *p. 265:* Izard, C.E., Fantauzzo, C.A., Castle, J.M., Haynes, O.M., Rayias, M.F., and Putnam, P.H. (1995). The ontogeny and significance of infants' facial expressions in the first nine months of life. "Developmental Psychology" 31, 997–1013; *p. 269:* Columbia University Archives - Columbia Library; *p. 277:* From Damasio H, Grabowski T, Frank R, Galaburda AM, Damasio AR: "The Return of Phineas Gage: Clues about the brain from a famous patient." "Science," 264: 1102–1105, 1994. Department of Neurology and Image Analysis Facility, University of Iowa.
Chapter 10 *Page 299:* (L) Tony Freeman/PhotoEdit, (R) © Roy Morsch/CORBIS; *p. 300:* (L) © Martin Rugner/AGE Fotostock America, Inc., (R) J. Dennis/Photo Researchers, Inc.; *p. 307:* (L) Harvard University Press, (R) © Spencer Grant/Photoedit Inc.
Chapter 12 *Page 362:* (T) Hermansen/Photo Researchers, Inc.
Chapter 13 *Page 412:* (T) © Philip Wallick/CORBIS, (B) Taro Yamasaki/Time Life Pictures/Getty Images, Inc.
Chapter 14 *Page 437:* Pamela C. Regan.

Index

Dyadic interaction, 22, 23, 308
Dyadic reciprocity, 107–8
Dyads, 4

Eastern culture, 92–3
Ecological niche, 114
Ecological validity, 116
Economic hardships, 411–3
Economics, 91–2
Editing, 435
Education, 409, 410
Effective outcome matrix, 128
Egalitarian marriage, 102, 428
Egocentric memory bias, 249
ELVN Model, 421–2
Emergent distress model, 400
Emotion. *See* Human emotion
Emotional infidelity, 387
Emotional instability, 405
Emotional investment, 290
Emotional loneliness, 59–60
Emotional support, 40, 42
Emotional Tone Index, 143, 144
Emotion-focused coping, 295
Emotion-focused couple therapy, 444–5
Emotion-in-relationship model (ERM), 289
Empathic accuracy, 21–3, 294–5
Empty love, 327–8
Enacted support, 40, 41
Encode, 236
Endocrine system, 31
Enduring dynamics model, 400
Environmental causal conditions, 114
Environmental conditions. *See also*
    Physical environment; Social environment
  marital satisfaction influenced by, 408–15
physiological changes in, 287–8
Equality rule of exchange, 128
Equitable relationship, 123–4
Equity models of social exchange, 354
Equity theory, 123–4, 254–5
Eros, 328
Erotic love, 336–7. *See also* Passionate love
Evaluative space model (ESM), 280, 281
Event-contingent sampling method, 116
Evolutionary models of human mating, 355–7
Evolutionary psychology
  on biological inheritance, 3–4
  brain development and, 25
  cognition and, 230
  on mate selection, 355–7
  on sexual infidelity, 386–7
  on sexual jealousy, 388
Exchange models of social interaction, 354
Exchange relationships, 260
Expansion, 199
Expansion of self theory, 141
Expectancies
  category accessibility and, 241–3
  defined, 226
  development of relationship and, 290–1
  emotion and, 287–90
  memory and, 232
  sources of, 227–8

studying, 226–7
  violated, 235
Experimental studies, 73–7
Explicitness, 227
Exploration, 199
Ex posto facto correlational studies, 78–9
Expressivity, 405–6
Extramarital sex, 384. *See also* Infidelity
Extrarelational sex, 384
Extraversion–introversion, 16–7, 303–4
Extraverts, 16–7, 303
Extrinsic cognitive set, 161
Eye contact, 166

Face perceptual system, 19–21
Facial Action Coding System (FACS), 266
Facial expressions
  basic emotion and, 264–5
  effect on emotions, 265–6
  false expression of emotion and, 264
  social interactional view of, 266–7
  theory of evolution and, 261–2
  universality of, 262–4
Facial feedback hypothesis, 265–6
Facial prototypes, 187
Facilitate, 111
Familiarity principle of attraction, 177–9
Family crisis theories, 410–1
Family emotional loneliness, 59
Family Inventory of Life Events and Changes, 411
Family relationships *See also* Marital relationships
  binuclear, 136
  in colonial times, 133–4
  defining, 131–3
  economic adversity and, 411–3
  evolving notions of, 139–40
  observation of interaction in, 117–8
  physical aggression and violence in, 52–4
  psychological aggression in, 54–8
  single parent, 136–7
  stress and, 50–2
  stressors for, 410–1
  traditional, 133
  worldwide changes in, 136
Family therapy, 89–90, 430–1
Fast-learning memory systems, 234
Fate control, 127
Fatuous love, 328
Fearful avoidant attachment style, 317
Fears of rejection, 169
Females. *See* Sex differences
Feminine sex–role orientation, 301, 302
Festinger, Leon, 171–2, 253
Field of availables, 173
Field of eligibles, 174
Fight-or-flight reaction, 45
Filter theory, 197–8
Financial strains, 411–3
First dates, 364
First impressions, 229, 236–44
First sexual encounter, 376–7
Five-factor model, 302–3
Flirting behaviors, 363
Frequency of sexual activity, 378–80

Friendship
  of androgynous people, 301
  conflicts in, 219–20
  cross-sex, 153, 154
  defining, 153–4
  depression and, 314
  development of, 203–6
  disclosure and, 208
  intimacy motivation and, 307–8
  love and, 324, 326
  same-sex, 153–4
  self-monitoring and, 310
Functional social support, 39–40

Gain condition, 168
Gain–loss theory of attraction, 168
Gender-based abortions, 2–3
Gender differences. *See* Sex differences
Gender-role attitudes, 126, 354, 373. *See also*
    Sex differences
General adaptation system, 47
Generative theories of causation, 81
Genetic influences on sex differences, 300–1
Gestalt psychologists, 232–3
Gestational life, 2
Given outcome matrix, 128
Global marital satisfaction, 393, 395–6
God, relationships with, 157–8
Goodness of outcome, 125
Grandparents, 132–3
Grief, 156, 450
Growth curve analysis, 402
Guttman scale, 200–1

Happiness
  facial expressions and, 263
  marriage and, 426–8
  relationships and, 58–60
Harlow, Harry, 6–9, 15, 65
Harrison, Rex, 156, 389
Health. *See also* Social support
  adverse effects of relationships on, 52–8
  biological and social approaches to, 31–2
  marital relationships and, 50–1
  religiosity/spirituality and, 157–8
  social integration and, 33–6
  stress and, 45–8
Healthy relationships, 149–50
Heart disease, 34
Hierarchical power, 152
High outcome dependence, 165
Homeostasis, 47–8
Homogamy, 354
Horizontal dimension of language, 331
Human emotion. *See also* Affect; Love
  absent from research, 276
  behaviorism and, 276
  cognitive theories of, 286–91
  cultural differences and, 264
  defining, 278–9
  display rules for expressing, 264
  expectancies and, 287–90
  expression of, 259–61
  facial expressions and, 261–7

  mysteries of, 259
  observed in social interaction, 266
  physiological arousal and, 268–75
  theories of basic, 264–6
Human evolution, 4
Hypotheses, 73
Hypothetical constructs, 237

Idealistic Distortion Scale, 218
Ideals, relationship, 406–7
Ideology, 427
Immune system, 31
Immunity. *See also* Health
  caregiving and, 51–2
  marital relationships and, 51
  mother–infant relationship and, 49
  social support and, 50
Importance, 227
Impression formation, 225
Inclusion of Other in the Self Scale (IOS), 141, 144–5
Incompatible relationships, 150
Independent variable, 74, 79–80
India, 366–7
Indirect aggression, 298
Individualistic approach, 293
Individualistic cultures, 92–3, 264
Individualistic–psychometric approach
    to human behavior, 87
Individual-level effect, 107
Individuating characteristics, 235
Infants. *See also* Attachment behavior; Innate behavioral
      response systems; Innate social response systems
  biological inheritance of, 3–4
  immune response in, 49
  relationship initiation/maintenance and, 27–8
  relationship with mother, 2
  significance of early relationships of, 28–9
  social inheritance of, 3
Infatuation, 327
Infidelity
  causes of, 385–7
  commitment and, 211
  distressed relationships and, 429
  emotional vs. sexual, 387–9
  gain–loss theory of attraction and, 168
  prevalence of, 384–5
  sex differences and, 386
Informal social communication, 260
Informal social communication theory, 171–2
Information processing, 230–6
Information uncertainty, 171–3
Informed consent, 67–8
Ingratiation, 170–1
Ingratiator's dilemma, 170
Inhibited sexual desire (ISD), 382
In-home observation, 117–8
Innate behavioral response systems, 6.
      See also Attachment behavior
  empathic accuracy, 21–3
  instinctive behavior and, 6
  love system, 6–9
Innate social response systems
  caregiving system, 18–9
  face perceptual system, 19–21

Name Index

Baumeister, R.F., 5, 46, 51, 315, 348
Baumrind, Diana, 81
Baxter, L.A., 101, 204, 364, 377, 384, 449–50
Bayer, B.M., 357
Beach, S.R.H., 393, 414
Beall, A.E., 294, 299
Beavin, J.H., 431
Becker, Gary, 91, 154
Beech, H., 2, 91, 92
Bell, D.C., 18
Bell, John, 430–1
Bell, Richard, 88
Bellack, A.S., 394
Bellavia, G., 14, 417
Belsky, J., 92, 102, 414, 415
Bem, S.L., 113, 301, 406
Benditt, R., 219–20
Bennett, M.E., 205
Bennett, N.G., 135
Bennett, N.B., 134
Benson, S., 134, 207
Bentler, P.M., 439
Benton, D., 343, 384
Berg, J.H., 203, 204
Berg, J.J., 207
Bergman, A., 315
Berkman, L.F., 33, 37
Berliner, D.L., 342, 343
Berlyne, D., 163
Bernard, J., 102
Berndt, T.J., 154, 203, 219
Berns, S.B., 438
Berntson, G.G., 32, 266, 275, 280, 281
Berry, D.S, 187, 303
Berry, J.O. 100, 453
Berry, M.E. 100, 453
Berscheid, Ellen, 18, 22, 29, 39–40, 64, 68, 73, 76, 88, 89, 95,
    97, 102, 113, 114, 115, 120, 140, 141, 142, 143, 144, 146,
    149, 150, 160, 162, 164–5, 168, 176, 181, 182–3, 184, 187,
    189, 197, 203, 207, 209, 216, 220, 221, 223, 229, 230, 241,
    242, 247, 251, 252–3, 254, 259, 273, 278, 289, 294, 300,
    310, 325, 326, 333, 337–8, 340–2, 344–5, 357, 358, 366,
    371–2, 374, 376, 382, 391, 396, 407, 408–9, 414, 439, 446
Bertrand, J.T., 373
Bettor, L., 376
Betzig, L., 365, 387, 429
Bhatia, T.K., 23
Bianchi, S.M., 136, 137
Biddle, J.E., 185
Biek, M., 310
Bigelow, B.J., 207
Billings, A.G., 295
Birchler, G.R., 433
Birnbaum, G., 241
Biron, C., 343
Bissonnette, V., 23, 186, 422
Black, S.L., 343
Black, J.E., 24
Blain, M.D., 314
Blair, S.L., 103
Blais, M.R., 161
Blakemore, Colin, 2, 24, 25, 27, 348
Blakeslee, S., 139, 414, 427
Blanc, A.K., 135
Blascovich, J., 57, 58

Blaylock, B., 416
Blehar, M.C., 1978, 12
Bleske, A.L., 179, 205
Bleske-Rechek, A.L., 154
Blieszner, R., 203–4
Blood, R.O., 102, 404
Bloom, B.L., 33, 44, 134, 135, 275, 429
Bloys, N., 301
Blumberg, S.L., 447
Blumstein, P., 151, 357, 379, 380, 381
Boca, S., 260
Bohman, T., 247, 250
Bolger, N., 41, 70, 284, 413, 419
Bonanno, G.A., 452–3, 454
Boncimino, M., 244
Bonica, C., 319
Bonnell, 220, 438
Book, A.S., 300
Booth, A., 37, 137, 138–9, 194, 222, 398, 399, 410, 423
Borden, V.M.H., 129
Boring, E.G., 74, 227
Bornstein, M.H., 24, 25
Bornstein, R.F., 178
Borys, S., 61
Boss, P., 453
Bouchard, G., 303, 305
Boucher, C., 161
Bowen, G.H., 208
Bower, G.H., 215, 249, 250, 284, 285
Bowlby, John, 9–11, 12, 14, 15, 18, 356, 430
Boye, D., 252–3, 254
Brackin, A., 314
Bradburn, N.H., 418
Bradbury, T.N., 40, 66–7, 70, 79, 97, 109, 136, 160, 220, 221,
    227, 235, 249, 256, 256–7, 305–6, 315, 393, 395, 400, 402,
    402–3, 405, 406, 407, 408–9, 410, 413, 414, 415, 423,
    423–4, 429, 435, 439, 440, 444, 447
Bradford, S.A., 207
Broverman, I.K., 295
Brown, A., 222
Brown, B.B., 203
Brown, M., 381
Brown, R., 248
Browne, A., 3, 310
Bruner, Jerome, 227, 236
Bryant, C.M., 411–2
Bryant, J., 274
Buck, R., 22–3
Buehler, C., 451
Buehlman, K.T., 71, 251
Bugental, D.B., 152, 246
Buhrmester, D., 60, 205, 208
Bukowski, W.M., 151, 154, 206
Bull, R, 184
Bullis, C., 364, 377
Bumpass, L., 134, 135, 217
Burch, N.R., 275
Burgess, A., 298
Burgess, E.W., 65, 64–5, 66, 71, 179, 399, 406, 417
Burgess, R.L., 164, 193, 199–200
Burgoon, J.K., 4, 290
Burks, N., 419
Burley, N., 183, 302
Burman, B., 50
Burnett, P., 407–8

Burns, G.L., 185
Bushman, B.J., 44
Buss, D.M., 5–6, 27, 154, 205, 339, 354, 356, 357, 376, 386, 387, 405
Butler, D., 256
Buunk, B.P., 124, 194, 217, 373, 379, 387
Byers, E.S., 380, 381
Bylsma, W.H., 317
Byrne, Donn, 180, 354–5, 416

Cacioppo, J.T., 32, 40, 44, 51, 59, 60, 266, 275, 280, 281, 417
Cairney, J., 314
Calhoun, K.S., 384
Call, V., 379
Callan, V.J., 220, 317, 438
Cameron, J.J., 169
Campbell, D.T., 397
Campbell, A.M., 58, 398
Campbell, B., 220, 221, 333, 366
Campbell, D.T., 82–3
Campbell, L., 207, 406–7
Campbell, S., 406
Campbell, W.K., 256
Canary, D.K., 66, 208, 294, 417
Cannon, A., 134, 137
Cannon, Walter B., 45, 46, 47–8, 55, 269
Cantor, J.R., 274
Cantor, N., 229
Capellanus, Andreas, 323–4, 325, 333, 334, 386
Caplan, R.D., 55, 412–3
Caporael, L.R., 4
Capra, Fritjof, 72, 104
Carer, 260
Carey, S., 20
Carlson, E.A., 13, 40
Carnegie, Dale, 175–6
Carnochan, P., 331
Carrell, S., 245
Carrére, S., 71, 432, 435, 445
Carroll, J.L., 377
Carstensen, L.L., 62, 206
Carver, C.S., 240, 260, 280
Cascardi, M., 52, 54
Case, R., 34
Casey, R.C., 185
Caspi, A., 26, 113, 179, 405
Cassady, P.B., 42
Cassano, G.B., 346
Cassiday, P.B., 374–5
Cassidy, J., 15, 18
Castellan, N.J., Jr., 109
Castro-Martin, T., 134
Catania, J.A., 385
Cate, R.M., 201, 363, 377, 396, 397
Catell, R.B., 181, 201, 357
Caughlin, J.P., 400, 406, 438
Cernoch, J.M., 343
Cerreto, M., 124, 443
Chaiken, S., 176
Chambers, W., 240
Charny, I.W., 387
Chartrand, T.L., 4
Cheah, C.S.L., 207
Cheek, J.M., 310

Cherlin, A.L., 134, 217, 392, 398, 404, 409
Cherniak, C., 163
Chess, S., 16
Choi, K.H., 385
Chomsky, Noam, 23
Chorost, A., 406, 435
Christenfeld, N., 387, 389
Christensen, Andrew, 90, 103, 115, 117, 120, 122, 127, 200, 210, 249, 421, 434, 436–7438, 441, 442, 444, 446
Christopher, F.S., 52, 298, 357, 377, 378, 381, 383, 384
Churchill, W., 93
Cizek, G.J., 83
Clark, 17, 175, 365, 443
Clark, Margaret S., 42, 103, 124, 140, 151, 249, 260, 264, 79, 284, 316, 351, 428
Clark, C.L., 175, 364–5
Clarkberg, M., 135
Clarke, S.C., 134
Clarkson, F.E., 295
Clements, M., 118, 404, 447
Clogg, C.C., 80
Clore, G.L., 180, 285
Coan, J., 71, 266, 435
Coatsworth, J.D., 25
Cobb, S., 38
Coe, C.L., 49
Coffin, W., 447
Cohan, C.L., 66–7, 135
Cohen, S., 34, 35, 39, 44, 45, 48, 49, 50 1, 136
Cohen, G., 248
Cohn, B.A., 342, 343
Coleman, F.L., 349
Collier, H., 266
Collins, Barry, 42
Collins, J.K., 372
Collins, L., 219–20, 318
Collins, N.L., 207, 245, 297, 316, 406, 423
Collins, W.A., 18, 25, 29, 42, 73, 203, 220
Coltrane, S., 103
Comte, August, 100
Condon, J.W., 181
Condran, G., 92
Conger, R.D., 51, 117, 374–5, 396, 411–2, 429, 440
Conger, K.F., 2002, 429
Conley, J.J., 87, 305, 405
Conlon, A., 384
Constantian, C.A., 308
Constantine, J.A., 311
Conte, H.R., 339
Converse, D.E., 58, 398
Cook, T.D., 82–3
Cook, W.L., 15, 317
Coombs, R.H., 115, 116
Coontz, Stephanie, 133, 134
Coplan, R.J., 207
Cordova, J., 444
Coren, Stanley, 154, 154–6
Coriell, M., 40
Corty, E., 383
Cosmides, L., 5, 152, 230, 355, 355–6
Costa, 17, 376
Costa, P.T., 303
Couchman, C.E., 15, 317
Cousins, A.V., 350
Cox, C.L., 422

Coyne, J.C., 52
Cozzarelli, C., 317, 318
Cozzi, J.J., 439
Craig, J., 134, 308, 363
Cramer, D., 161, 305
Crandall, S.J., 238
Crano, W.D., 181
Critelli, J.W., 339
Cronbach, L.J., 218, 394
Crosby, J.F., 441
Cross, S.E., 299
Crouter, A., 400, 418
Crowell, N.A., 298
Csikszentmihalyi, M., 59, 451
Cuber, J.F., 423
Cui, M., 411
Cunningham, J.D., 135
Cunningham, M.R., 43, 186, 187, 188, 256, 310, 356, 358, 417
Cupach, W.R., 52, 115, 249, 349, 350–1, 381
Cutrona, C.E., 39, 40, 50, 60, 117, 304, 305

Dabbs, J.M., 300
Daigen, V., 82
Daily, L., 22
Dainton, M., 194
Daiuto, A., 443
Daly, M., 54, 140, 297, 365, 367, 368, 387, 388
Damasio, Antonio R., 20, 242, 276–7
Dannells, M., 384
Darley, J.M., 42, 166, 252, 252–3
Darwin, Charles, 1–2, 63–4, 261–2, 264, 268, 367
Davidson, R.J., 21, 32, 278, 280
Davies, D., 133
Davila, J., 66–7, 305–6, 423–4, 440
Davis, D., 148
Davis, J.A., 373, 385, 406, 423
Davis, J.L., 416
Davis K.E., 197, 210, 219–20, 233, 254, 255–6, 317, 351
Davis, M.H., 23
Davis, S.R., 134, 344
Deater-Deckard, K., 133
DeBecker, G., 351
DeCasper, A.J., 23
Deci, E.L., 15, 58, 315, 317
DeCoster, J., 231, 234, 235
de Dreu, C.K.W., 194
de Haan, M., 21
De La Ronde, C., 182
Delespaul, P., 59
DeLongis, A., 284, 413
DeMaris, A., 135, 136, 379
Dembo, T., 170
Demmons, S., 380
Dennett, D.C., 227
Denny, G., 380
Denzin, N.K., 83
Derlega, V.J., 44, 66
Dermer, M., 164–5, 178
DeSteno, D.A., 285, 389
Detweiler, J.B., 41
Deutsch, M., 88, 150, 182, 441
De Vaus, D., 102
DeVries, P., 59
De Weerth, C., 363
Dewsbury, D.A., 179

Diamond, R., 20
Dicke, A., 329, 393
Dickens, W.J., 96, 153
Diener, E., 17, 58, 59, 185, 264, 428
Digman, J.M., 302
Dillard, J.P., 314
Dillman, L., 4
Dindia, K., 208, 294, 297
Dion, K.K., 182–3, 184, 312, 317, 337
Dion K.L., 337
Dishion, T., 397
DiTommaso, E., 59
Dixon, A.E., 429
Dizard, J., 399
Doherty, W.J., 311
Dolan, S.L., 446
Dolcina, M.M., 385
Dolderman, D., 417
Doll, B., 92
Dollard, John, 120
Dominicis, C., 218
Donnelly, D.A., 379
Donovan, J.E., 376
Doob, L., 120
Dorko, 376
Douvan, E., 52, 198, 251, 295, 398, 410, 416
Downey, G., 52, 89, 230, 319, 319–20, 320
Downs, D.L., 245
Doyle, W.J., 34
Drain, M., 20
Draper, K.K., 377
Dreyer, C.S., 379
Drigotas, S.M., 102, 200, 385, 386, 422
Druckman, J.M., 447
Druen, P.B., 186, 356, 358
Drumm, P., 348
Dubas, J.S., 312, 314
Duck, S., 40, 60, 115, 146, 207, 448
Dumas, J.E., 110
Dunham, P., 148
Dunham, F., 148
Dunkel-Schetter, C., 2, 208, 256
Dunn, J.L., 133, 349
Dupras, A., 379
Durbin, R.G., 302, 406
Durkheim, Emile, 33, 56, 59, 64, 90
Dutton, D.G., 273
Dyomina, N., 300
Dziurawiec, S., 21

Eagly, A.H., 298, 354
Eastenson, A., 220
Easton, J., 350
Eaves, L., 397
Ebbesen, E.B., 174
Eberly, S., 34
Eddy, J.M., 395, 439
Edelman, 298
Edgar, T., 381
Edwards, C.P., 298, 373, 410
Egeland, B., 13, 14–5
Eggert, L.L., 174, 175
Egland, K.L., 208
Eibl-Eibesfeldt, L., 10–1, 363
Eich, E., 285

Eid, M., 264, 405
Eidelson, R.J., 204, 407
Eifert, G.H., 162
Eisenberg, N., 22, 295
Ekman, P., 21, 265, 266, 278
Elbert, Tr., 23, 24
Elder, G.H., 51, 113, 396, 411
Eldridge, K., 444
Elliot, A., 51, 280
Elliot, A., 256
Elliott, M.J., 301
Ellis, Albert, 324, 325, 334, 335, 336, 337, 355, 374,
   390, 407
Ellis, Havelock, 334, 335, 373
Ellis, S., 21
Ellison, C.G., 157
Elman, J.L., 6
Emerson, R.M., 349
Emmers-Sommer, T.M., 66
Emmons, R.A., 59
Endo, Y., 217, 218
Engel, J.W., 92
Engl, J., 447
Enns, V., 317
Epstein, A., 139
Epstein, J.L., 203, 227
Epstein, N., 407–8, 443
Epstein, S., 315
Erber, R., 166, 249
Erley, A.M., 432, 445
Ernst, J.M., 59, 60
Eshleman, J.R., 58
Evans, D.E., 16
Evans, S.M., 408
Ewart, C.K., 51
Eyer, J., 48
Eysenck, H.J., 303, 305
Eyssell, K.M., 260
Eyster, S.L., 103

Fairbairn, W.R.D., 315
Farah, M.J., 20
Farina, A., 185
Farnsworth, J., 450
Farooqui, M.Y., 177
Farr, P.A., 301
Fazio, R.H., 161
Feeney, B., 318
Feeney, J., 318
Feeney, J.A., 19, 42, 58, 90, 102, 207, 220, 260, 317, 406, 408,
   419, 438, 442
Fehm-Wolfsdorf, G., 51
Fehr, B., 2, 42, 219–20, 246, 297, 317, 332, 346, 347, 396
Feingold, A., 183, 185, 358, 388
Feiring, C., 203
Feldman, P.J., 2
Feldman, S.D., 189
Feldman, S.I., 319–20
Felmlee, D.H., 175, 200, 222, 426
Feltey, K.M., 384
Ferguson, L.W., 227
Fernández-Dols, J.M., 20, 262, 263, 267
Ferraro, K.J., 53
Ferris, K.O., 219–20, 349
Festinger, Leon, 161, 170, 171, 171–2, 173, 180, 253

Fetzer Institute, 157
Feyisetan, B., 365
Fiedler, K., 284
Field, D., 249
Fiese, B.H., 112
Fieweger, M., 103
Filsinger, E.E., 81, 82, 343, 434
Fincham, F.D., 40, 97, 109, 161, 227, 230, 235, 249, 256–7,
   315, 357, 393, 406, 407, 414, 422
Finck, Sir Henry, 187
Fine, M.A., 137
Finkenauer, C., 51, 260
Finley, C., 383
Fischer, C.S., 61, 153
Fischer, J.L., 301
Fischer E.F., 1, 333
Fisher, H.E., 265, 345, 347–8, 367, 368, 386–7
Fisher, Helen, 345
Fishkin, S.A., 356
Fiske, A.P., 151, 229, 235, 238, 397
Fiske, S.T., 89, 92, 93, 166, 229, 248
Fitz, D., 259–60
Fitzgerald, N.M., 201
Fitzpatrick, Mary Anne, 381, 406, 427–8, 436, 441–2
Fitzpatrick, J.A., 302
Flanary, R., 249, 376
Fleeson, J., 14, 294
Fleming, J.H., 166
Fletcher, G.J.O., 161, 230, 315, 317, 340, 406–7, 408
Floyd, F.J., 414, 447
Floyd, K., 207,
Folkman, S., 295
Follette, W.C., 434
Foote, F.H., 329
Forehand, R., 134, 404
Forgas, J.P., 249, 276, 284, 285, 286
Forman, D.R., 120
Forste, R., 385
Foshee, V.A, 298
Fossey, D., 178
Foster, C.A., 41, 128, 210
Fournier, D.G., 447
Fowers, B.J., 71, 217, 218, 416
Frandsen, M.M., 378
Frank, R., 156
Frazier, P., 134, 384, 451
Frederickson,
Freeborn, D.K., 36
Freedman, D.A., 80
Freitas, A.L., 320
Fremouw, W.J., 349
Freud, Sigmund, 64, 84–5, 228, 248, 334, 335, 430
Friberg, P., 345
Fridlund, A.J., 265, 266–7
Friedman, L.C., 1979, 433–4
Friedmann, E., 57, 117
Friesen, W.V., 265, 266
Frieze, D., 364
Frijda, N.H., 264
Fritz, H.L., 42, 43–44
Froming, W.J., 240
Fromm, Erich, 323, 325, 334, 336
Fugita, F., 185
Fuhrman, R.W., 247
Fujita, F., 17
Furman, W., 60, 203, 205

Gable, S.L., 51, 59, 116, 176, 280, 281, 314
Gadlin, H., 133–4
Gage, N.L., 1955, 218
Gage, M.G. 1991, 57
Gage, Phineas, 277
Gagnon, J.H., 355, 373
Gaines, M.E., 377
Gaines, S.O., 102
Galambos, N.I., 363
Gale, Harlow, 65
Galen of Perganon, 16
Gallo, L.C., 409
Galton, 248
Gander, M., 136
Ganellen, R.J., 240
Gangestad, S.W., 216, 289, 310, 312, 356
Gano-Phillips, S., 257
Garcia, S., 23, 186
Garcia-Velasco, J., 343
Gardner, W.L., 5, 281, 349
Gareis, K.C., 136
Garmezy, N., 25
Gatz, M., 273
Gauthier, I., 20
Gazzaniga, M.S., 20
Ge, X., 440
Gebhard, P., 369
Geib, A., 384
Geis, F.L., 406
Geiss, S.K., 418, 429
Gelles, R.J., 52, 53, 298
George, C., 19, 117
George, L.J., 400
George, L.K., 157, 158
Georgellis, Y., 428
Georgesen, J.C., 127
Gergen K.J., 250, 453
Gergen, M., 298
Gergen, M.M., 250, 453
Gerin, W., 49, 50
Gerstenzang, S., 259–60
Gesn, P.R., 295
Gidycz, C.A., 383
Gigy, L., 429
Gilath, 240
Gilbert, D.T., 234, 237
Gilbert, L., 102
Giles, L., 406
Gillath, O., 15, 203, 240
Gilligan, C., 103, 250
Gilner, F., 339
Gilroy, F.D., 406
Ginsberg, G.P., 22–3, 247, 251
Giuliano, T., 250
Givertz, M., 314
Glaser T., 50, 51, 384, 417, 446
Glass, D.C., 48–9, 147–8
Glass, S.P., 445
Glenn, Norval D., 59, 138, 215, 373, 398, 399, 415
Glick, P., 181, 310
Goethals, G., 273
Goffman, Erving, 83, 91, 166
Goggins, M.F., 383
Gohm, C., 58
Gold, P.E., 279

Goldberg, L.R., 16, 302
Goldenthal, P., 22
Goldman, M.S., 228
Goldsteen, K., 50, 132
Goldstein, A.G., 238
Goldstine, O., 219
Goldstine H., 219
Gonzales, M.H., 422
Gonzalez, R., 69, 70
Goodchilds, J.D., 364
Goode, W.J., 428
Goodman, Ellen, 139
Goodman, E.S., 431
Goodman, K.L., 429
Goodwin, R., 311, 350, 365, 367
Gordon, H.S., 50
Gordon, R.A., 171, 397
Gordon, S.L., 96
Gore, J.C., 20
Gorsuch, R., 157
Gotlib, I.H., 312, 314, 315, 405
Gotthel, E., 44
Gottman, John, 71, 98, 109–11, 120, 127, 251, 266, 275, 392, 405, 429, 432, 434, 435, 436, 438, 439, 441, 441–2, 442, 445, 448
Gouaux, C., 284
Gough, H.G., 301
Gove, W.R., 58
Gower, D.B., 342–3
Grabill, C.M., 318
Grabosky, F., 59
Graham, T., 295
Grammer, K., 188
Gray, J., 294
Gray, J.A., 280, 288
Gray, J.D., 451
Gray-Little, B., 419
Grayson, Donald, 35–6, 91, 114–5
Graziano, W.B., 97, 162, 164–5, 168, 189, 357
Greeley, A.M., 380
Green, S.K., 364
Green, L.R., 60, 347
Greenberg, L.S., 444
Greenblat, C.S., 379–80
Greenhouse, L., 132
Greenough, W.T., 24, 62
Griffin, D.W., 14, 340, 407, 417
Griffin, D., 69, 70
Griffin, W.A., 440
Griffitt, W., 177
Grimm, D.W., 302
Grob, A., 17
Groeneveld, L.P., 68
Grosser, B.I., 343
Grossman, K., 364
Grote, N.K., 103, 124
Groth, T., 51, 356, 357
Gruenewald, T.L., 215
Gruenfeld, D.H., 229
Grusec, J.E., 220
Gubrium, J.F., 132
Guerrero, L.K., 208
Gunn, L.K., 421
Gunnar, M.R., 24, 27
Gupta, G.R., 366

Gurung, R.A.R., 40, 41, 315
Gutierres, S.E., 189
Guttentag, M., 91–2
Gwaltney, J.M., 34

Haas, S.M., 208
Hacker, T.A., 42
Hage, J., 150–1
Hagerty, B.M., 314
Hahlweg, K., 51, 426, 447
Haig, C., 303
Haley, J., 431
Halford, W.K., 427
Hallstrom, T., 382
Haluska, Frank, 47
Halvorsen, R., 135
Haly, Jay, 431
Hamburg, B.A., 376
Hamermesh, D.S., 185
Hamilton, G., 183, 393
Hammersmith, S.K., 373
Hammond, J.R., 317, 382
Hampson, S., 302
Hannan, N.T., 68
Hannett, C.A., 312, 373
Hansen, A.M., 450, 451
Hansen, J.S., 303
Hansford, S.L., 42
Hansson, R.O., 100, 452
Harinck, F., 422
Haritou, A., 80
Harlow, Harry, 6–9, 15, 18, 19, 21, 65
Haroff, 423
Harold, 257
Harris, C.R., 387, 389
Harris, J.A., 300
Harris, M.B., 298
Harris, M.J., 127
Harrison, A.A., 178
Harter, S., 52
Hartley, E.L., 177
Hartup, W.W., 28, 151, 154, 203, 220
Harvey, John, 115, 206, 249, 250–251, 376, 447, 450, 451
Harwood, B.T., 203
Hashimoto, T., 333, 366
Haslam, N., 151
Hassan, H., 409
Hassebrauck, M., 396, 408
Hassin, R., 20, 258
Hastie, R., 242
Hatchett, S., 251
Hatfield, 337, 338
Hatfield, E. *See also* Walster (Hatfield), E., 1, 44, 124, 176, 182–3, 184, 187, 266, 337, 338, 339, 346, 347, 358–9, 365
Hatkoff, T.S., 329
Haugen, J.A., 422
Hause, K.S., 208
Hawkes, C.H., 345
Hay, J., 124
Hays, R.B., 153, 203, 204
Hazan, C., 15, 16, 19, 316, 318, 338, 356
Hazzard, A., 117
Healy, S., 307
Heaton, T.B., 410, 423
Heavey, C.L., 434, 436, 438, 446

Heavey, C.L., 446
Hebb, Donald, 6, 27, 274, 287
Hebl, M.R., 312
Heider, Fritz, 175, 181, 233, 252, 255, 257
Heim, M., 61
Heim, S., 23
Heine, S.J., 217
Heinlein, L., 381
Helgeson, V.S., 43–4, 44, 50, 295–7
Helm, B., 60
Helmreich, R.L., 43, 301
Helms-Erikson, H., 36
Henderson-King, D.H., 381
Hendrick, Clyde, 203, 294, 329, 337, 339, 351, 376, 393
Hendrick, Susan S., 203, 329, 337, 339, 351, 376, 393
Henze, L.F., 358, 376
Herbert, T.B., 48, 50–1
Herman, A.E., 347
Herold, E.S., 350
Heron, 161
Herrick, L.R., 275
Hertel, R.K., 250, 433
Hessling, R.M., 304
Hetherington, E.M., 25
Heyman, R., 274
Heyman, R.E., 71, 116, 121, 274, 394, 395, 426, 434, 439
Higgins, E.T., 241, 242
Hilditch, T., 2–3
Hill, C.A., 348
Hill, C.T., 67, 71, 102, 200, 208, 222, 450, 451
Hill, R., 101, 357
Hill, Reuben, 410–1
Hilton, J.L., 166
Hinde, Robert, 25, 64, 65, 84, 87, 95, 96, 97, 267
Hinkley, K., 245
Hirt, E.R., 116
Hixon, J. G., 182, 237
Hobfoll, S.E., 39, 44
Hodges, S.D., 22, 295
Hoekstra, S.J., 317
Hoffman, K., 186
Hogan, M.A., 153
Hogben, M., 354–5
Hohaus, I., 19
Holcombe, R., 57
Holman, T.B., 71, 409, 410, 429
Holmberg, D., 116, 250, 251
Holmes, J.G., 82, 215–6, 227, 245, 251, 253, 340, 407, 411, 417, 450
Holmes, M.E., 79, 209
Holmes, T.H., 38, 56
Holstein, J.A., 132
Holtzworth-Munroe, A., 257, 441, 442
Homans, George, 97, 121–2, 164, 173–4, 354, 380
Hood, R.W., Jr., 157
Hops, H., 117, 266, 432
Horowitz, L.M., 39, 316, 430
Horrocks, J., 409
Horwitz, R.I., 48
House, J.S., 34, 36
Houts, R.M., 400, 401
Howard, J.A., 206, 357
Hoyt, L.L., 376
Hsee, C.K., 403

Makani, R., 373
Makhijani, M.G., 184
Makinen, J.A., 444–5
Malamuth, N.M., 434, 438
Malarkey, W.B., 51, 417
Malik, N.M., 415, 435
Malley, J., 229
Maluso, D., 299
Mandler, George, 257, 265, 278–9, 287, 288
Mangelsdorf, S., 27
Mangrum, L.F., 439
Mangun, G.R., 20
Manning, D.J., 422
Mantle, D., 350
Marangoni, C., 59, 60
Marazziti, D., 346
Margolin, G., 122
Margolin, G., 50
Margolin, L., 80
Margolis, R.L., 387
Mark, D.B., 44
Markman, Howard, 118, 404, 426, 427, 439, 447
Markus, H.R., 92, 96
Marsolek, C.J., 20
Martin, C.E., 65, 369
Martin, J., 297, 298
Martin, L.L., 288
Martin, L.R., 37
Martin, P.V., 384
Martin, T.C., 217
Martini, A., 287
Martz, J.M., 214
Maruyama, G.M., 79, 397
Marwell, G., 150–1
Mashek, D., 146, 244, 345
Maslow, Abraham, 276, 315
Masten, A.S., 25
Masters, W.H., 275
Mathews, A., 382, 383
Mathis, J.L., 54
Matlin, M.W., 249
Matthews, K.A., 409
Maurer, S., 134
Maxwell, K., 312, 376
May, W.H., 176, 187
Mead, G.H., 91
Meaney, M.J., 27
Meany, George, 73
Mears, C.E., 6, 21
Meehl, P., 394
Melby, C., 364
Melby, J.N., 117, 440
Melinat, E., 145
Meloy, J.R., 349, 350
Melson, G.F., 57, 154, 219–0
Mendelsohn, Robert, 93
Mendes, W.B., 58
Mendoza-Denton, R., 245
Meredith, D.B., 429
Merluzzi, T.V., 364
Mesquita, B., 260, 264
Messerly, L., 117, 433–4
Messman, S.J., 417
Metalsky, G.I., 314
Metts, S., 115, 249, 381

Meyer, H., 372
Meyer, T.J., 44
Meyer, W., 287
Meyers, S.A., 203, 341–2
Michael, R.T., 378–9, 380, 384
Michaelis, B., 320, 373
Miell, D., 116, 207, 249
Mikulincer, M., 15, 16, 203, 240, 241
Milardo, R.M., 36, 38, 61, 62, 140, 175
Milavsky, B., 274
Milberg, S., 260
Mill, John Stuart, 74, 75
Miller, E.N., 364
Miller, L.C., 207, 216, 222, 297, 356
Miller, Neal, 120
Millikin, J.W., 444–5
Millner, V.S., 383
Mills, J., 151, 260
Mills, R.S.L., 220
Mineka, S., 25
Mintz, E.E., 349
Mirkowsky, 50
Miron, 176
Mirowsky, J., 132
Mischel, W., 245, 302, 354–5
Mita, T.H., 178
Mitchell, C., 67
Mitchell-Kernan, C., 134, 314
Miyake, K., 15
Moffitt, T.E., 179, 405
Mohr, C.D., 107, 113
Monahan, 283
Mondragon, M., 343
Monello, R., 303
Mongeau, P.A., 364
Mongrain, M., 241
Monson, T., 164–5
Monte, W.C., 343
Montel, K.H., 217, 343
Montgomery, B.M, 115, 446
Monti-Bloch, L., 343
Moore, D., 103
Moore, M.M., 363
Morelli, G., 15
Moreno, Jacob, 36, 62
Morgan, L.H., 367
Morgan, M., 249, 397
Morgan, S., 92
Mornell, P., 436
Moroney, R.M., 132
Morris, M.W., 258
Morrow, G.D., 351
Moskowitz, G.B., 236–7, 258
Moss, A., 34, 295
Mowrer, O.H., 120
Moylan, S.J., 285
Muehlenhard, C.L., 52, 364, 383, 384
Mullen, P.E., 350
Muller, J.R., 311
Mullooly, J.P., 36
Munro, B.E., 312
Munroe, A., 441
Muram, D., 376
Murdock, G.P., 367
Murphy, 283

Murphy, B.C., 22
Murphy, K.M., 91
Murray, Sandra, 215–6
Murray, S.L., 14, 70, 253, 340, 397, 407, 417
Murray, J.D., 435
Murstein, B.I., 124, 160, 198, 354, 361, 443
Musselman, L., 187, 188
Musser, L.M., 310
Myers, D.G., 58, 59
Myers, E.J., 339

Nachmias, M., 27, 241
Nada-Raja, S., 298
Nahemow, L., 173, 206
Naik, S., 344
Nanayakkara, A., 340
Nasby, W., 182
Nathan, P.E., 446
Nathanielsz, P., 2
Neal, A., 350
Nebes, R.D., 248
Neighbors, C., 340
Neisser, Ulric, 248, 251
Nelligan, J.S., 19, 318
Nelson, C.A., 2, 21, 24
Nelson, G., 244
Nelson, L.J., 207
Nemechek, S., 303
Nepps, P., 52
Nesselroade, J.R., 181, 201
Neubaum, E., 134, 404
Neubeck, Gerhard, 100
Neuberg, S.L., 166, 235, 248
Newcomb, A.F., 153, 154, 208, 220, 439
Newcomb, Theodore, 180
Newcomb, T.M., 253
Newman, L.S., 236–7
Newton, T.B., 305
Newton, T.L., 50, 51, 102
Nezlek, J.B., 60, 186, 205, 314
Ng, R., 41
Nicastro, A.M., 350
Nicholson, B., 343
Nicholson, J.M., 414
Nies, D.C., 103
Nigro, G., 251
Niles, R.L., 429
Nisbett, R.E., 92
Noller, P., 58, 90, 102, 220, 317, 318, 408, 419, 438, 441, 442
Norman, C.C., 274
Norretranders, T., 163
Norris, S.L., 311
Norton, R., 395
Notarius, C.I., 275, 435, 439
Nugent, J., 117, 433–4
Nye, F.I., 132

Ochsner, K.N., 32
O'Connor, C., 331
Ogilvie, D.M., 245
Oishi, S., 58
Olausson, H., 9
Oldersma, F.L., 194
O'Leary, A., 48
O'Leary, D., 418, 429

O'Leary, K.D., 52, 54, 298, 441
Oliver, M.B., 371, 373, 376, 385
Olsen, N., 245
Olson, D.H., 71, 101, 247, 407, 416, 447
Olson, J.M., 227, 228, 237, 303
Olson, K., 186
Omark, 298
Omarzu, J., 206, 447
Omoto, A.M., 141, 143
O'Neill, Eugene, 156
O'Neill, G., 387
O'Neill, N., 387
Orbuch, T.L., 103, 251, 409, 410, 450
Orden, S.R., 418
Ortony, A., 265
Orvis, B.R., 256
Osgood, C.E., 176, 278
Oster, H., 22
O'Sullivan, L.F., 376, 377
Oubaid, V., 387
Ouelette, J.A., 112, 260
Oyserman, D., 93, 94

Pal, B.C., 177
Palace, E.M., 274–5
Paleari, F.G., 422
Pam, A., 339
Panskepp, J., 276
Papageorge, J., 238
Park, B., 238
Parke, R.D., 92
Parks, M.R., 174, 175, 207
Parnass, S., 387
Parritz, R., 27
Pascalis, O., 21
Pasch, L.A., 305–6, 421, 429, 440, 442, 444
Paskewitz, D.A., 34
Pastor, D.L., 15
Pataki, S.P., 260
Pathé, M., 350
Patrick, B.C., 146
Patrick, H., 340
Patterson, Gerald, 120
Patterson, G.R., 117, 120–1, 141, 266, 397, 432, 433
Patterson, J.M., 411
Patterson, S., 219–20
Patzer, G.L., 184
Paunonen, S.V., 17
Pearce, D.G., 169
Pearlin, L.I., 295
Peeler, M.M., 376
Peng, K., 258
Pennebaker, J.W., 42, 251, 274, 361
Pennington, G.W., 344
Pennypacker, J., 349
Peplau, L.A., 60, 61, 64, 67, 71, 95, 96, 102, 135, 140, 200, 208, 222, 294, 377, 398, 428, 450, 451
Perkowitz, W.T., 148
Perlman, D., 60, 61, 96, 153
Perper, T., 363, 378
Perrett, D.I., 187, 188
Perry, T.B., 219
Petersen, A.C., 312, 314
Peterson, C., 58
Peterson, C.D., 301

Rosenkrantz, P., 295
Rosenthal, G.E., 50
Rosenthal, T.L., 376
Rosenthal, W., 394
Rosenzweig, M.R., 28–9
Ross, C.E., 50
Ross, D., 120
Ross, L., 68
Ross, M., 116, 124, 249, 250, 257
Ross, M.A., 250
Ross, S.A., 120
Rossi, A., 346
Rothbart, M.K., 16, 17
Rothbaum, F., 15
Rothman, A.J., 41
Rotter, J.B., 209, 311
Rottman, L., 182
Rowan, A., 154
Rowatt, T.J., 358
Rowatt, W.C., 310
Rowe, J.W., 48
Rubenstein, A.J., 61
Rubertis, L., 371
Rubin, D.C., 248
Rubin, K.H., 207
Rubin, L., 102
Rubin, Z., 67, 166, 200, 208, 222, 309, 450, 451
Rubinson, L., 371
Rucker, D.D., 285
Ruiz-Belda, M.A., 263
Rumsey, N., 184
Ruparelia, B.A., 343
Rusbult, C.E., 102, 124, 128, 200, 210, 214, 216, 217, 255, 294, 416, 421, 422, 423
Rusbult, Caryl, 128, 213
Ruscio, J., 305
Russell, J.A., 2
Russell, D., 60, 61
Russell, J.A., 20, 262, 263, 264, 267, 279, 331
Russell, R.J.H., 59, 405
Rutter, M., 26, 397
Rutter, V., 134
Ruzzene, M., 90
Ryan, K.D., 445
Ryan, L., 285
Ryan, R.M., 15, 58, 59, 317, 432
Ryff, C.D., 33, 48, 49

Sabatelli, R.M., 395, 407
Sabourin, S., 161, 303, 395, 406
Sadalla, E.K., 356, 357
Safilios-Rothschild, C., 347
Sagi, A., 13
Sagrestano, L.M., 438
Salmon, C., 140
Salovey, 45, 50, 389, 403
Salovey, P., 249
Saltzman, H., 376
Salzinger, L.L., 204
Samson, J.M., 379
Samuelsson, S., 382
Sanders, M.R., 414
Sanderson, C.A., 408
Sandman,C.A., 2
Sandos, P., 364

Sanford, K., 439–40
Sansone, C., 60
Santisteban, D.A., 90
Sarason, B.R., 39, 40, 41, 42, 50, 87, 315
Sarason, I.G., 39, 40, 41, 42, 50, 87, 315
Sargent, J., 297
Satir, Virginia, 431
Sato, S., 333, 366
Satterfield, A.T., 383
Sawin, D.B., 185
Sayers, S., 117, 227, 394
Sayers 1989, 227
Scanlon, M.B., 301
Scanzoni, J., 90, 102, 151, 199, 353
Schachter, Stanley, 67, 172–3, 260, 269–72, 276
Schaffer, M., 392
Scharfe, E., 317
Schatten-Jones, E., 60
Schiavi, R.C., 314
Schilling, E.A., 284, 417
Schloss, P., 345
Schmaling, K.B., 51–2
Schmitt, D.P., 356, 376
Schmitt, J., 406
Schmitt, J.P., 314
Schonert-Reichl, K., 311
Schooler, C., 295
Schrader, S., 430, 431
Schreiner-Engel, P., 314
Schultz, D.P., 227
Schultz, S., 38
Schultz, S.E., 227
Schutzwohl, A., 287
Schwartz, J., 331
Schwartz, L.L., 441
Schwartz, P., 102, 134, 357, 379, 380
Schwartz, S.H., 157
Schwarz, N., 285
Scott, C.K., 227, 235, 247
Seal, D.W., 312, 373
Sears, Robert, 88, 120, 170
Secord, P.F., 91–2, 182
Sedikides, C., 245, 256, 376
Seeley, J.R., 405
Seeman, T.E., 29, 48, 49, 50, 410
Segal, M.W., 173
Segraves, R.T., 443
Segrin, C., 314
Seidel, M., 246
Seilhamer, R.A., 117
Seligman, C., 161
Seligman, M.E.P., 26, 54, 445, 451
Selye, Hans, 46–7
Semmelroth, J., 387
Senn, D.J., 198
Serpell, J., 57
Sexton, T.L., 90
Shackelford, T.K., 405
Shadish, W.R., 82–3, 446
Shaked, N., 217
Shalker, T.E., 284
Shannon, L., 249
Shao, L., 17
Sharon, T., 117
Shatz, C.J., 24

Shaver, P.R., 7, 15–6, 18, 19, 60–1, 146–7, 150, 175, 203, 207, 240, 316–7, 318, 331, 338, 364–5
Shea, J.A., 207
Shean, G.D., 14
Sheldon, K.M., 59
Shelton, B.A., 135
Shen, Y., 222
Shenk, J.L., 441
Shepard, S., 22
Shepperd, J.A., 189
Sher, K., 76
Sheridan, J.F., 32, 51–2, 227, 275
Sherman, M.F., 406
Sherrod, D.R., 42
Shively, W.P., 397
Shoda, Y., 245
Shotland, R.L., 363
Shuchter, S.R., 452
Shulman, S., 203
Shultz, T.R., 81
Shuster, B., 241
Shye, D., 36
Sicoly, F., 124, 249
Siddiqi, M.F., 177
Siegel, D.J., 27
Siegler, I.C., 303
Silberg, J., 26
Sillars, A., 117, 181, 256
Silliman, B., 447
Silva, P.A., 179
Silver, R.C., 451
Silverman, J., 350
Simon, A., 134, 137
Simon, R.L., 396
Simon, W., 355
Simpson, J.A., 15, 19, 102, 197, 216, 290, 310, 311, 312, 318, 333, 340, 356, 366, 396, 406–7
Simpson, Jeffry, 312
Simpson, W.E., 238
Singer, B.H., 33
Singer, J.E., 67, 270
Singer, J.A., 249
Singh, D., 374–5
Sippola, L.K., 203
Skinner, B.F., 276, 397, 432
Skoner, D.P. 34
Skowronski, J.J., 249
Skudlarski, P., 20
Slapion-Foote, M.J., 329
Slater, A., 186
Slep 2001, 71
Small, M.F., 373
Smeaton, G., 180
Smith, D.A., 436, 441
Smith, E.R., 230, 231, 234, 235, 241, 248
Smith, R.B., 222
Smith, R.H., 189
Smith, S.E., 400
Smith, T., 385
Smock, P.J., 135
Smollan, D., 141, 144–145
Snoek, J.D., 162, 195
Snyder, D.K., 439
Snyder, M., 141, 143, 144, 181, 242, 291, 310, 311
Sollie, S.L., 301, 302, 406

Solomon, J., 19, 182
Somerick, N., 103
Soon, A.P.Y., 311
Soskin, W.F., 266, 433
South, S.J., 103, 135, 429
Southwick, C.H., 177
Spain, J.S., 210–1
Spalding, L.R., 135, 398
Spanier, G.B., 38, 387
Spence, J.T., 23, 43, 301
Spiegel, D., 44
Spilka, B., 157
Spinner, B., 59
Spiro, A., 305
Spitzberg, B.H., 52, 349, 350–1, 381
Spitze, G., 103, 135
Spreadbury, C.L., 364
Sprecher, S., 115, 124, 142, 175, 200, 209, 222, 249, 312, 333, 339, 357, 358, 358–359, 370, 376, 379, 381, 383, 388
Springer, T.P., 302
Sroufe, L.A., 13, 14–15, 17, 294
Srull, T.K., 245
Stack, S., 58
Stafford, L., 208
Stahelski, A.J., 242
Stangor, C., 248, 249
Stanley, S.M., 83, 175, 447
Stapp, J., 43
Stark, N.N., 373
Starzyk, K.B., 300
Staudinger, U.M., 206, 451
Steemers, G.E.M., 422
Steen, L.A., 4
Steffen, V.J., 298
Steil, J.M., 103
Steinberg, L., 25
Steiner, I.D., 89
Steinmetz, S., 52, 53, 298
Stellar, E., 48
Stensaas, L.J., 343
Stephan, W., 216, 241
Stephen, E.H., 174
Sterling, P., 48
Sternberg, R.J., 294, 325, 327, 347
Sternberg, Robert, 326, 328
Stevens, L.E., 166
Steward, W.T., 41
Stewart, A.J., 309
Stewart, M.A., 220
Stiensmeier-Pelster, J., 287
Stillwell, A.M., 348
Stinson, L., 23, 186
Stolzenberg, R.M., 135
Strathman, A.J., 189
Straub, R.O., 31
Strauss, A., 407
Strauss, M.S., 187
Straus, M.A., 52, 53, 298
Strelau, J., 17
Stroebe, M.S., 39, 50, 56, 452, 453
Stroebe, W., 39, 50, 56, 452, 453
Strouse, J.S., 350
Strube, M.J., 134
Stuart, F.M., 382
Stuart, S.P., 446